The Encyclopedia of
Police Science

The Encyclopedia of

Police Science

THIRD EDITION

Volume 1
A–I
INDEX

Jack R. Greene

Editor

Routledge
Taylor & Francis Group
New York   London

Routledge is an imprint of the
Taylor & Francis Group, an informa business

Routledge
Taylor & Francis Group
270 Madison Avenue
New York, NY 10016

Routledge
Taylor & Francis Group
2 Park Square
Milton Park, Abingdon
Oxon OX14 4RN

© 2007 by Taylor & Francis Group, LLC
Routledge is an imprint of Taylor & Francis Group, an Informa business

Printed in the United States of America on acid-free paper
10 9 8 7 6 5 4 3 2 1

International Standard Book Number-10: 0-415-97000-8 (Hardcover)
International Standard Book Number-13: 978-0-415-97000-6 (Hardcover)

Library of Congress Cataloging-in-Publication Data

The encyclopedia of police science / edited by Jack R. Greene. -- 3rd ed.
      p. cm.
   Previous ed. edited by William G. Bailey.
   Includes bibliographical references and index.
   ISBN 0-415-97000-8 (978-0-415-97000-6 : alk. paper)
   1. Police--United States--Encyclopedias. 2. Justice, Administration of--United States--Encyclopedias. I. Greene, Jack R.

HV7901.E53 2007
363.203--dc22
                                                                                                    2006026827

Visit the Taylor & Francis Web site at
http://www.taylorandfrancis.com

and the Routledge Web site at
http://www.routledge-ny.com

CONTENTS

ASSOCIATE
EDITORS

Gary W. Cordner
College of Justice and Safety
Eastern Kentucky University, Richmond, Kentucky

Edward R. Maguire
Administration of Justice Program
George Mason University, Manassas, Virginia

Peter K. Manning
College of Criminal Justice
Northeastern University, Boston, Massachusetts

CONTRIBUTORS

Julie C. Abril
University of California, Irvine

Geoffrey Alpert
University of South Carolina, Columbia

Karen L. Amendola
Police Foundation, Washington, DC

Malcolm Anderson
University of Edinburgh, Scotland

W. Carsten Andresen
Northeastern University

Edward J. Appel
Joint Council on Information Age Crime
Bethesda, Maryland

Richard M. Ayers
Fredericksburg, Virginia

Ryan Baggett
Eastern Kentucky University

William G. Bailey
Sam Houston State University

Thomas E. Baker
University of Scranton

Clifford Barcliff
Police Futurists International

Emmanuel P. Barthe
University of Nevada–Reno

Margaret E. Beare
Nathanson Centre for the Study of
Organized Crime and Corruption
York University, Toronto, Canada

Joanne Belknap
University of Cincinnati

Eric Bellone
University of Massachusetts–Lowell

Trevor Bennett
University of Glamorgan
Pontypridd, Wales

Julie Berg
Institute of Criminology, University of
Cape Town, South Africa

Elizabeth P. Biebel
Eastern Kentucky University

Pia Biswas
Rutgers University

William P. Bloss
The Citadel

John M. Boal
The University of Akron

Heidi S. Bonner
State University of New York at Albany

Jeb A. Booth
Northeastern University

Anthony V. Bouza
Minneapolis Police Department

Lorenzo M. Boyd
University of North Texas

Rebecca J. Boyd
Indiana University of Pennsylvania

CONTRIBUTORS

Anthony A. Braga
Harvard University

Jean-Paul Brodeur
Université de Montreal, Québec, Canada

Michael F. Brown
Southeast Missouri State University

Michael E. Buerger
Bowling Green State University

Richard Butler
New Jersey State Parole Board

Donald A. Cabana
University of Southern Mississippi

Dawn M. Caldwell
Isle of Palms Police Department

Jack E. Call
Radford University

Liqun Cao
Eastern Michigan University

Philip E. Carlan
University of Southern Mississippi

David L. Carter
Michigan State University

Derral Cheatwood
University of Texas at San Antonio

Steven Chermak
Indiana University, Bloomington

Alice H. Choi
California State University, Sacramento

Stephen E. Clark
University of California, Riverside

Janice E. Clifford
Auburn University

Peter A. Collins
Boise State University

John A. Conley
University of Wisconsin–Milwaukee

Ed Connors
Institute for Law and Justice
Alexandria, Virginia

Gary Cordner
Eastern Kentucky University

Elizabeth Corzine McMullan
University of Southern Mississippi

Tom Cowper
Police Futurists International

Stephen M. Cox
Central Connecticut State University

Charles Crawford
Western Michigan University

Shea W. Cronin
American University

G. David Curry
University of Missouri–St. Louis

Douglas Davenport
Truman State University

Phillip A. Davidson
Tennessee Law Enforcement
Training Academy

Andrew Davies
State University of New York at Albany

Michael Davis
Illinois Institute of Technology

Robert C. Davis
Police Foundation, Washington, DC

Scott H. Decker
University of Missouri–St. Louis

Mathieu Deflem
University of South Carolina, Columbia

Rolando V. del Carmen
Sam Houston State University

Ronald G. DeLord
Combined Law Enforcement Association
of Texas

Stephen Demuth
Bowling Green State University

Ramesh Deosaran
The University of the West Indies
St. Augustine, Trinidad

Sara Buck Doude
University of Southern Mississippi

Jerry L. Dowling
Sam Houston State University

Roger G. Dunham
University of Miami

Terence Dunworth
Justice Policy Center, The Urban
Institute, Washington, DC

Mary Ann Eastep
University of Central Florida

Max Edelbacher
Federal Police of Austria

Steven A. Egger
Sangamon State University

Katherine W. Ellison
Montclair State University

Preston Elrod
Eastern Kentucky University

Ayn Embar-Seddon
Capella University

Edna Erez
Kent State University

Richard V. Ericson
University of Toronto

Michael Erp
Washington State University

Finn-Aage Esbensen
University of Missouri–St. Louis

Stephanie Fahy
Northeastern University

David N. Falcone
Illinois State University

Amy Farrell
Northeastern University

Graham Farrell
Loughborough University
Leicestershire, United Kingdom

Gilles Favarel-Garrigues
Centre d'Etudes et de Recherches
Internationales, Paris, France

Mora L. Fiedler
Denver, Colorado Police Department

Nigel G. Fielding
University of Surrey, United Kingdom

Janet E. Fine
Massachusetts Office for Victim
Assistance, Boston, Massachusetts

Vern L. Folley
Independent Scholar

David R. Forde
University of Memphis

Brian Forst
American University

J. Price Foster
University of Louisville

James Alan Fox
Northeastern University

Lorie A. Fridell
Police Executive Research Forum
Washington, DC

CONTRIBUTORS

Larry K. Gaines
California State University,
San Bernardino

Catherine A. Gallagher
George Mason University

Venessa Garcia
Kean University

Jennifer F. Gardner
University of Alabama

Shirley Garick
Texas A&M University

Gilbert Geis
University of California, Irvine

Martin Gill
Perpetuity Research & Consultancy
International Ltd
Leicester, United Kingdom

Lauren Giordano
Northeastern University

Ronald W. Glensor
City of Reno, Nevada, Police Department

Barry Goetz
Western Michigan University

Zenta Gomez-Smith
University of Florida, Gainesville

Lindsey Green
University of Missouri–St. Louis

Jack R. Greene
Northeastern University

Roberta Griffith
Northeastern University

M. R. Haberfeld
City University of New York

Douglas R. Haegi
Georgia State University

Kevin D. Haggerty
University of Alberta, Edmonton,
Alberta, Canada

Bernard E. Harcourt
University of Chicago

Erin Harrell
Eastern Kentucky University

Craig Hemmens
Boise State University

Nicole J. Henderson
Vera Institute of Justice, New York

Vincent E. Henry
Homeland Security Management Institute
of Long Island University

Matthew J. Hickman
U.S. Department of Justice
Washington, DC

Dennis E. Hoffman
University of Nebraska–Omaha

Larry T. Hoover
Sam Houston State University

Frank Horvath
Michigan State University

Martin Innes
University of Surrey
Guildford, Surrey, United Kingdom

Silvina Ituarte
California State University, East Bay

Jenephyr James
Indiana University of Pennsylvania

John P. Jarvis
Federal Bureau of Investigation

Charles L. Johnson
Washington State University

Richard Johnson
University of Cincinnati

Greg Jones
Police Foundation
Washington, DC

Tom Jordan
Texas A&M University

Josephine A. Kahler
Texas A&M University

Robert J. Kane
Northeastern University

Victor E. Kappeler
Eastern Kentucky University

Sinead Keegan
City University of New York

Todd D. Keister
Bureau of Criminal Investigation
Binghamton, New York

Roger L. Kemp
City Manager
Vallejo, California

Michael Kempa
University of Ottawa, Ontario, Canada

Dennis Jay Kenney
City University of New York

Raymond G. Kessler
Sul Ross State University

Denise Kindschi Gosselin
Western New England College

William R. King
Bowling Green State University

Brian F. Kingshott
Grand Valley State University

Paul M. Klenowski
Indiana University of Pennsylvania

David Klinger
University of Missouri–St. Louis

Peter B. Kraska
Eastern Kentucky University

Tyler S. Krueger
University of Georgia

Kristen J. Kuehnle
Salem State College

Joseph B. Kuhns, III
University of North Carolina at Charlotte

Henry C. Lee
University of New Haven

Tina L. Lee
The University of Tennessee at Martin

David Lester
Stockton State College

John Liederbach
University of North Texas

Edith Linn
Kean University

Elizabeth Loftus
University of California, Irvine

Kamala London
University of Toledo

Vivian B. Lord
University of North Carolina, Charlotte

Roy Lotz
City University of New York

Nicholas P. Lovrich
Washington State University

Cynthia M. Lum
George Mason University

Arthur J. Lurigio
Loyola University Chicago

M. Kimberly MacLin
University of Northern Iowa

CONTRIBUTORS

Donal E. J. MacNamara
City University of New York

Sean Maddan
University of Nebraska at Omaha

Edward R. Maguire
George Mason University

Peter K. Manning
Northeastern University

Catherine M. D. Marcum
Indiana University of Pennsylvania

Otwin Marenin
Washington State University

Chris E. Marshall
University of Nebraska at Omaha

Ineke Haen Marshall
Northeastern University

Mark Marsolais
Northern Kentucky University

Gary T. Marx
Massachusetts Institute of Technology

Bill Maxwell
Royal Canadian Mounted Police

David C. May
Eastern Kentucky University

Linda Mayberry
Eastern Kentucky University

Lorraine Mazerolle
Griffith University
Brisbane, Queensland, Australia

Paul Mazerolle
University of Queensland, Brisbane,
Queensland, Australia

Kimberly A. McCabe
Lynchburg College

Timothy E. McClure
Eastern Kentucky University

Jack McDevitt
Northeastern University

David McDowall
State University of New York at Albany

J. Thomas McEwen
Institute for Law and Justice,
Alexandria, Virginia

Paul McKenna
University of Toronto

E. Roland Menzel
Texas Tech University

Greg Meyer
Los Angeles Police Academy

J. Mitchell Miller
University of South Carolina,
Columbia

Gilbert Moore
U.S. Department of Justice
Washington, DC

Andrew Morabito
International Association of Chiefs of
Police, Alexandria, Virginia

Stephen J. Morewitz
The Society for the Study of Social
Problems, San Francisco, California

Laura J. Moriarty
Virginia Commonwealth University

Frank Morn
Illinois State University

Nancy Morris
University of Maryland

Gregory B. Morrison
Ball State University

Melissa Motschall
Eastern Michigan University

Jerry Needle
International Association of Chiefs of
Police, Alexandria, Virginia

Elaine Niederhoffer
New York City Public School System

Robert S. Newsom
San Diego County Sheriff's Department

Lisa S. Nored
University of Southern Mississippi

Carla M. Noziglia
Las Vegas Metropolitan Police

Martin L. O'Connor
Long Island University

Timothy N. Oettmeier
Houston Police Department

Godpower O. Okereke
Texas A&M University

Lacey N. Ore
Lynchburg College

Timothy M. Palmbach
University of New Haven

George Parangimalil
Texas A&M University

Joseph E. Pascarella
University of Maryland

Nikos Passas
Northeastern University

Allan D. Pass
National Behavioral Science Consultants

Antony M. Pate
Development Services Group
Washington, DC

April Pattavina
University of Massachusetts–Lowell

Derek Paulsen
Eastern Kentucky University

Brian K. Payne
Old Dominion University

Kenneth J. Peak
University of Nevada–Reno

William V. Pelfrey, Jr.
University of Wisconsin–Milwaukee

Wendy Perkins
University of Cincinnati

Glenn L. Pierce
Northeastern University

Alex R. Piquero
University of Florida, Gainesville

Mark R. Pogrebin
University of Colorado, Denver

Eric D. Poole
University of Colorado, Denver

Gary W. Potter
Eastern Kentucky University

Tony G. Poveda
State University of New York at
Plattsburgh

Tim Prenzler
Griffith University
Brisbane, Queensland, Australia

Daniel Price
Providence College

Faiza Qureshi
Loughborough University
Leicestershire, United Kingdom

Michael L. Radelet
University of Colorado–Boulder

CONTRIBUTORS

R. K. Raghavan
Tata Consultancy Services Limited

Raymond R. Rainville
St. Peter's College

Melissa M. Reuland
Police Executive Research Forum
Washington, DC

Malcolm Richards
Gloucestershire Constabulary
United Kingdom

James F. Richardson
University of Akron

Albert R. Roberts
Rutgers University

Jennifer B. Robinson
Northeastern University

Marcus K. Rogers
Purdue University

Jeff Rojek
University of South Carolina

Kevin Roland
Urban Institute, Washington, DC

Michael R. Ronczkowski
Miami-Dade Police Department

Danielle Rousseau
Northeastern University

Lorie Rubenser
Sul Ross State University

Gregory Saville
University of New Haven

Kathryn E. Scarborough
Eastern Kentucky University

Joseph A. Schafer
Southern Illinois University,
Carbondale

Christopher J. Schmidt
Pennsylvania Supreme Court

Jennifer Schwartz
The Pennsylvania State University

Forrest R. Scogin
University of Alabama

Ellen Scrivner
Bureau of Administrative Services, City of
Chicago Police Department

Thomas M. Seamon
Hallcrest Systems, Inc.
North Wales, Pennsylvania

Thomas D. Shahady
Lynchburg College

Clifford Shearing
The Australian National University
Canberra, Australia

Lawrence W. Sherman
University of Pennsylvania

Stan Shernock
Norwich University

Wallace W. Sherwood
Northeastern University

Eli Silverman
City University of New York

David R. Simon
University of North Florida

Simon I. Singer
Northeastern University

Wesley G. Skogan
Northwestern University

John J. Sloan, III
University of Alabama–Birmingham

Beverly A. Smith
Illinois State University

Loretta J. Stalans
Loyola University, Chicago

Darrell Steffensmeier
The Pennsylvania State University

Dennis J. Stevens
University of Southern Mississippi

James K. Stewart
Center for Naval Analysis
Alexandria, Virginia

Victor G. Strecher
Sam Houston State University

Kathleen M. Sweet
Purdue University

Gary W. Sykes
Mercyhurst College

Morris A. Taylor
Southern Illinois University

Robert W. Taylor
University of North Texas

R. Alan Thompson
Old Dominion University

Jeremy Travis
City University of New York

Craig D. Uchida
Justice and Security Strategies
Silver Spring, Maryland

Jason S. Ulsperger
Arkansas Tech University

Sean P. Varano
Northeastern University

Tracy A. Varano
Criminal History Systems Board
Chelsea, Massachusetts

William J. Vizzard
California State University,
Sacramento

Robert B. Voas
Pacific Institute for Research and
Evaluation, Calverton, Maryland

Maria R. Volpe
City University of New York

Donald B. Walker
Kent State University

Jeffery T. Walker
University of Arkansas, Little Rock

Samuel Walker
University of Nebraska at Omaha

Harvey Wallace
California State University, Fresno

Patrick D. Walsh
Loyola University, New Orleans

John Wang
California State University, Long Beach

Richard H. Ward
Sam Houston State University

Vincent J. Webb
Southern Illinois University, Carbondale

Barbara Webster
Institute for Law and Justice
Alexandria, Virginia

Ralph A. Weisheit
Illinois State University

L. Edward Wells
Illinois State University

William Wells
Southern Illinois University, Carbondale

Chuck Wexler
Police Executive Research Forum
Washington, DC

Carrie Morgan Whitcomb
National Center for Forensic Science
Orlando, Florida

CONTRIBUTORS

Michael D. White
City University of New York

Brian N. Williams
University of Georgia

Frank Williams
University of Houston–Downtown

Donald C. Witham
FBI Academy

Russell Wolff
Northeastern University

Robert E. Worden
State University of New York at Albany

Shiho Yamamoto
California State University, Fresno

Olivia Yu
University of Texas–San Antonio

Jihong Zhao
University of Nebraska at Omaha

Israt T. Zohra
University of Arkansas, Little Rock

INTRODUCTION

The Encyclopedia of Police Science, Third Edition, elaborates and extends the discussion of its previous two volumes by deepening and broadening scientific knowledge about policing. The study of police science has undergone considerable change in the decade since the last publication of this *Encyclopedia* and the nearly two decades since the first edition. This advancement in knowledge about the police is linked to, yet separate from, the conceptual and methodological underpinnings of criminology and the administration of justice. These linkages and differences are important to highlight to better understand their contribution to "explaining" policing.

Criminology is focused on explanations of crime and society's reaction to crime. As a social science that attempts to explain criminal behavior first, and then how justice and other systems react to crime, criminology has often been separated from the study of the police. For many years criminology rarely informed policing, except perhaps in macro level discussions about deterrence.

Since the early 1980s and continuing to the present, however, the overlap in criminological study with that of the police has substantially increased, making criminology more relevant to the study of the police, and policing more acceptable as a target of criminological research. This is particularly the case when considering recent emphases in criminology and policing on communities as major places for crime and partners in crime prevention, deterrence, or mitigation.

Similarly, study of the administration of justice has often focused on the serial ordering of offenders as they pass through criminal justice institutions, as well as how these same institutions react to victims and the public at large. And, while policing was included within the general purview of the administration of justice, much of that literature was at best distant from the range of decisions and actions police undertook to make cities and towns safer.

In recent years, police science has incorporated the best from both the criminological and administration of justice perspectives. From criminology, police science adopted a broader array of theory—theory about individuals, groups, communities, and institutions—that better informs our understanding of the question "why policing," while also incorporating the advantage of a methodological revolution in criminology. From the administration of justice perspective police science has integrated a broader policy research viewpoint, as well as greater emphasis on evidence of what works through better and more systematic (and scientific) evaluation research.

By incorporating the best from the perspectives of criminology and the administration of justice, police science has greatly accelerated scientific knowledge about what constitutes policing, how it is made operational in a variety of social settings, how its institutions reflect or diverge from broader social and political values, what theoretical frameworks guide policing, and how police perform and their effect. So, today police science integrates the social theories of criminology with the institutional and systems perspectives of the administration of justice. In this respect police science has become more theory driven and evidence-led. *The Encyclopedia of Police Science, Third Edition*, reflects these important developments.

Even with the inclusion of criminological and administration of justice perspectives, police science still remains different in focus and in the use of other conceptual frameworks that inform our understanding about the police. Police science is concerned with policing in its broadest sense ranging from policing as an individual set of behaviors through the interconnections of policing across the world. It rests at the intersection of law, the physical sciences (in the case of forensics), psychology, social psychology, sociology, public policy, history, economics, and evaluation methods and statistical analysis, as well as criminology and the administration of justice. Variety is considerable in the domains of knowledge that informs our understanding of policing. The breadth of entries in this volume attests to the complexity of studying the police, and the multiplicity of perspectives used and indeed needed for such understanding.

The Evolution of Study on the Police

The social, formal, and institutional nature of policing and police science has changed profoundly in the last half of the twentieth century, continuing into the twenty-first century. While yesterday's police were largely concerned with fighting crime and maintaining order in public places, today's police are confronted by the globalization and internationalization of crime and terrorism, their manifest connection with new and complicated technologies, the newly emerging networked and organized varieties of criminal enterprise, the shift toward new forms of crime and deviance, and the confounding effects these changes have on effectively providing public safety and security. At the same time, modern-day police agencies must continue to address and cope with their historical functions, including social regulation and the prevention and response to "ordinary crime." In most respects the police remain the foremost organization people call when they are confronted by life's crimes as well as its annoyances.

Policing in this modern era has changed its language, symbols, technology, and analytics, while also broadening its range of interventions, clients, and outcomes. Yet in some ways the police remarkably resemble their nineteenth-century predecessors, presenting themselves in symbolic and substantive ways as singularly responsible for public safety in its broadest sense, while often replicating bygone service delivery patterns. As much as the police are thought to have changed, they continue to present themselves in very consistent ways over time. To the general public the police continue to represent a visible, uniformed force charged with responding to citizens' crime, order, and safety concerns.

Perhaps the most strident changes that have occurred in policing over the past half century are: (1) the broader role the police play in providing public safety and in the reassurance of safety to the public through programs focused on community quality-of-life, the coproduction of safety with community and other institutional partners, and community policing; (2) the change in data-driven and intelligence-led models of policing, including such issues as problem solving, crime analysis, crime mapping, COMPSTAT, and other more empirical and technological approaches to understanding and then addressing crime and social disorder problems; (3) the reemergence of concerns with police ethics and accountability, including the need for assuring police legality and judicial oversight of police actions, the legitimacy they derive from their communities, and the all-too-often revelations about police misconduct, abuse of authority, and public trust; (4) the internationalization of policing to include issues of addressing terrorism (domestic and international), police intelligence gathering and its legal consequences, and the cross-jurisdictional and trans-national interactions of police agencies throughout the world; (5) the changing nature of police work itself and those who undertake it, including shifts in the demographics of the police in terms of diversity, increased concerns with stress and its implications for those who do policing, and the professional expectations and outcomes that policing sets for itself; and, (6) the application of scientific methods, including the growth of the forensic sciences in police investigation and legal practice, and the emergence of a broad social science research literature on the police, their functioning, and impacts. These major trends are continuing to shape the structure and function of policing and they portend greater changes for law enforcement agencies and police officers in the coming years. Some brief consideration of these trends is warranted by way of introduction to *The Encyclopedia of Police Science, Third Edition.*

Broadening the Police Role

Beginning in the early twentieth century, policing has continued to evolve and change in light of broad and substantial social, economic, and political changes that have occurred in society. Entering the twentieth century the police in the U.S. were closely connected to local political sponsorship, but over the past century they have taken on more professional administrative practice and symbolism, have gotten closer to the communities they serve, have built extra-institutional alliances to prevent and respond to crime, have broadened their role from crime fighting to providing community quality of life and reducing fear of crime, and have taken on a more expansive public safety role through problem solving. Importantly, the police are now struggling with their appropriate role in matters of national security and terrorism.

Throughout these changes the police institution, albeit at times begrudgingly, has changed, opening itself more toward externals—particularly the community and other institutional partners. The movement in community policing, actually begun in the 1940s and 1950s over matters of race relations, and carried into the 1980s and 1990s as a means of improving police effectiveness particularly in disadvantaged communities, has helped to shape the police internally on matters of police training and socialization, and externally in matters of their interactions and cooperation with a wide array of others. All of these changes have import for how we see the role of the police in a democratic society. How the police will continue to evolve in light of their new challenges with terrorism is yet unknown. Nonetheless, it is anticipated that what the police have learned in their former transformations may help them grapple with an increasingly complex world.

Policing in an Information Age

In the nineteenth-century, police technology involved a good pair of shoes, a truncheon, and perhaps a firearm. Police collected and acted on information, but as individuals, not as a police system. Beginning in the early twentieth century with the advent of auto and radio technology, policing got greater mobility, but not much more information. While radios were a lifeline to the police headquarters, they were used more for "managing" police officers at a distance, rather than as conduits of information about crime and crime problems within neighborhoods or business districts. The widespread adoption of

911 computer-assisted dispatch systems has indeed altered the ways in which the police first understand and then manage their workload.

With the further development of information technology in the 1950s to the present, policing has often followed trends in government that emphasize greater information collection, storage, retrieval, and analysis. In the 1990s, information technology began to more clearly permeate the boundaries of police organizations, and practices and the language of "accountability" began to fuel the use of such technology as more sophisticated records management systems, calls for service technology, and crime analysis in its many varieties came on line. Whereas in the history of policing information was private and built on the knowledge of individuals, toward the end of the twentieth century information took on a more strategic posture and its character shifted from an individual perspective to that of the organization, or at least larger parts of the organization.

Managing patrol operations, detective caseloads, crime responses targeted to particular communities or crime types, and adopting the language and symbolism of efficient information use, captured the imagination and some of the practice of policing. And, while struggles remain in information sharing both within and outside police agencies, their characterization by Bittner paraphrased as "police agencies being bureaucracies or hierarchies built on the premise of systematic information denial," has indeed changed over the past fifty years. The police now collect, process, and use much more information than they have in the past, and in this sense, have truly joined the information age.

Police and Legitimacy: A Return to Roots

Progress in policing attributable to changes in their modes of operation (shifting from reactive to proactive), their problem focus, and the aggressive crime attack model of policing that has been part of the fabric of policing from its onset, more recently revived as zero-tolerance, has also resurfaced problems in public acceptance of police methods. Concerns with abuse of those in disadvantaged communities, or members of various racial and ethnic groups have fueled a discussion about how the police derive and sustain the legitimacy they need to work in community settings.

Here concerns with racial profiling, zero tolerance, and other aggressive police practices that appear to have differential application and impact have once again raised the specter of an equity divide between the police and those policed, most especially if those policed are from minority, multiethnic, or socially and economically disadvantaged communities. Revelations of police abuse of power found in several of America's largest cities continue to reinforce the idea of different forms of justice aimed at different types of people. Such practices and the beliefs that they sustain call into question the legitimacy given to the police by the body politic, or at least subsets of it.

While policing in the late nineteenth and early twentieth centuries was perhaps seen as more communal (although highly political and disproportionately adverse to minority communities), shifts in police focus and institutional arrangements seem to reinforce a drift of the police away from their roots—the community. At times it has been clear that the police have lost their community context. This loss of community context appears throughout the history of U.S. policing, and continues to be a problem, most particularly in large urban cities.

Recent research on how the legitimacy of the police either supports or deflects their efforts, particularly in marginalized communities, reminds us that the police derive their authority (not their power) from the larger community, and that their actions and behavior can reinforce or detract from the authority the community actually gives to the police. Linking police effectiveness to community acceptance of the police and their actions reinforces the notion that legitimate authority, not institutional power, is a fundamental requirement in democratic policing.

The Scope of Policing: From Street Corner to World Stage

Policing in the US and elsewhere began as a localized public place issue, providing some level of oversight to public places so that people could use them without fear of victimization. And, in earlier societies the police were also the "watch and ward" focused on sounding the alarm for fires, toppled buildings, wayward livestock or other public hazards that might occur.

The watching role of the police continues to this date, albeit in a more sophisticated way with the use of technologies of all sorts. But the premise, that crime and other forms of deviance will be dissuaded when there is someone watching (now called a capable guardian) remains fundamental in the crime prevention literature.

With the advent of modern terrorism, the local watching role of the police has been made more complicated. Now the police must watch for suspicious behaviors that may lead to crime or terrorism. Moreover, transposing a political idea that "all terrorism is local" in its effects and consequences, has raised the bar for the local police, coupled with state, federal, and international policing to assess risk and vulnerability, and design programs and actions that prevent, mitigate, or respond to the consequences of such acts.

Policing on the world stage includes concern for extra-jurisdictional crimes that have local consequences. This includes Internet child pornography and fraud, the trafficking of women and children for the sex industry, and any number of international criminal organizations focused on the sale of drugs, people, identities, or other fungible commodities that, while having a market, are illegal. Moreover, new cyber-crimes challenge old assumptions about the relationship between offenders and victims and the distances over which crime and victimization can occur. Indeed, whether such criminal organizations are local or not, their local impact is indisputable. So policing worldwide has been challenged to share information and participate in what might be called a "collective policing" effort. This, of course, is new territory for the police, as such arrangements are emergent, their practices and consequences remain uncertain, yet the need for their rapid evolution is equally compelling. This is indeed the new frontier for policing in the twenty-first century.

Policing as Practice

Just as policing institutions have been reshaped over the past century, and most especially in the second half of the twentieth century, so too have the practices, orientations, and behaviors of individual police officers. Moreover, those who "do policing" are different from their historical referents—they include more persons of color and women for example. The demographic changes within policing have been substantial, often reflecting greater diversity among the people who take up policing as an occupation. This has resulted in a rather subtle reshaping of policing, in that as new people come to this occupation, so too do their values, expectations, and ideas.

In addition to the demographic changes in policing we have witnessed, policing as a set of occupational practices and cultures has changed as well. With the advent of information and dispatch technology, community and problem-oriented policing concepts and practices, and focuses such as preventing crime and improving quality-of-life, police officers have acquired a wide range of techniques and orientations their predecessors generally lacked.

Today's police are generally better educated, trained, equipped, supervised, and disciplined in comparison to police of the late nineteenth and early twentieth centuries. They are also tasked with a wider array of responses and interventions that require broad-based knowledge in topics like conflict resolution, consensus building, public speaking as well as understanding an ever more complex set of local ordinances, and state and federal laws. Whereas police at the mid-point of the twentieth century needed to be philosophers, friends, and guides, today's police need to add to that set of qualities such skills as first medical responder, community advocate and problem solver, and legal practitioner operating with a complex set of powers and responsibilities. Indeed, as we move into the twenty-first century, changes in police practice and those who "do policing" are likely to continue, perhaps more rapidly than over the past fifty years or so. Fast changing technologies, social problems, and world events seem to be accelerating change and are likely to continue to do so in the near and long-term.

Scientific Policing

At its onset policing was rather a-scientific, that is, not well connected to scientific knowledge. Rapid advancements in science throughout the twentieth century have altered the need for police scientific proficiency. This is not to mean that all police officers need to be scientists; rather, it suggests that the actions and practices of the police condition and influence the use of science in the detection and amplification of crime, and in the identification of offenders.

In the late twentieth century the forensic sciences finally took their rightful place in the crime detection business. Indeed the police early on quickly embraced finger printing and blood typing as investigative tools to address serious crime. But acceptance and adoption of other scientific practices has been uneven. While forensic sciences have been on the back stage of policing for many years, a few notorious trials involving the use of physical evidence moved forensics to the front stage of the criminal justice process, including policing. Moreover, the use of forensics investigation technologies and techniques, particularly DNA technology, has resulted in a number of offender convictions being overturned or reviewed, and, in at least one state, the mass commutation of death sentences was tied to concerns about the adequacy of physical evidence used to convict these people. Such scientific concerns now place greater burdens on the police in the identification, collection, preservation, and analysis of physical evidence.

As we crossed into the Millennium, the role of scientific investigation and inquiry expanded and is likely to continue to expand with advances in the forensic sciences. Moreover, from about the early 1970s to the present there has been a heightened level of research and scientific inquiry into what the police actually do, and the impacts and unintended consequences of police actions. Federal funding for these efforts, coupled with an expanded police research community, has resulted in better knowledge about policing. And, while the application of science to policing has many unresolved issues, it is clear that the body of research on the police continues to shape the research community's and the practitioners' understanding of the police, their role and function in society, and their interventions and public acceptance of those interventions. In many ways this edition of *The Encyclopedia of Police Science* benefits immensely from such advances in knowledge about the police.

On the Third Edition

The vast changes to policing occurring in the last two decades of the twentieth century are well reflected in this third edition of *The Encyclopedia of Police Science*. They include a revolution in thinking about the police and their clientele (community and business inter-actions), community and problem-oriented policing, crime prevention, placed-based theories of crime, police accountability, "quality of life" policing, zero-tolerance, and the like. Moreover, police interventions with youth, family violence, and other forms of interpersonal problem solving are included in this volume as well. And, the emerging role of the police in providing responses for terrorism and domestic security, which have emerged in the past five years, also broadens the role of policing in democratic society, and is considered here as is the growing emphasis on the internationalization of crime and hence, of policing.

This volume of *The Encyclopedia of Police Science* expands on the work of its predecessors (the first and second editions) by incorporating these changes and many others that confront modern-day police agencies. This edition is a robust collection of entries that review and expand our knowledge on topics that have shaped and continue to shape policing. Entries included in the third edition of *The Encyclopedia of Police Science* were written and selected emphasizing three important criteria:

First, we designed this collection and selected entries on their ability to inform readers about recent trends in policing. Of the 354 topics covered in this work, 196 are new to this edition and an additional 127 entries have been updated from the previous edition. Our editorial group sought to expand the range of topics previously presented, in part reflecting the changes that policing has confronted over about a decade since the last edition, but also to provide readers with a broad, contextual understanding of the police as they are imbedded in larger social, economic, and political changes that have occurred in rapid succession. Viewing the police in this context, we believe, helps readers make the connection between policing, government, and social change.

Second, we emphasize a connection in these trends to the underlying research on policing that addresses such trends. As previously indicated, the second half of the twentieth century witnessed an explosion in research on the police. Prior to the 1970s there were a handful of well-crafted, often observational studies, of the police. Since then the research community, fueled by federal research investments and a growing acceptance of police and criminal justice studies at major universities, has produced a voluminous body of research on policing, especially in the U.S., Canada, western Europe, and Australia.

Police studies have continued to migrate throughout the world and today the range of interest and scholarship on the police is remarkable. This edition of *The Encyclopedia of Police Science* sought to capture the state of research on policing over a myriad of topics. Our intent was to help codify extant policing research and literature into a usable volume as a premier source for information about policing. Research-led inquiry, then, was an important aspect of commissioning the entries contained in this volume.

Third, our focus spans all levels of discussion about police, from concerns for and with police officers, their subcultures, their organizations and institutions, and the web of interactions they have with the public and other institutional actors. The idea of taking on a project that had the ambition of accurately describing policing of necessity requires that the units of analysis vary. That is to say, policing can be variously understood as the behaviors, attitudes, and orientations of individual police officers; police work cultures and the informal or social organization of policing; police organizations themselves including their various structural and functional subdivisions; and, the larger "institution" of policing, spanning many police agencies and largely defining the occupational trends, practices, beliefs, and symbols that shape police organizations and the public's understanding of them. As the reader will see, all these levels of policing are discussed in this volume, and through the use of cross references contained within each entry, the connection of these units of analysis is made possible throughout the edition.

How to Use This Book

Just as important as the coverage itself, each entry provides a substantial reference base for the reader to further explore any particular topic under consideration. Authors have provided detailed **References and Further Readings** for this purpose within each entry. Moreover, the collective reference library that emerges from all of the entries contained in this edition, should be a substantial aid to the serious scholar as well. Cross references with other entries, noted in the **See also** section of each entry, suggest the close relationships among many topics covered herein; both beginning and more advanced students will benefit from using the **See alsos** to guide them from entry to entry. With 354 entries, each with its own references, and cross listings with other entries, *The Encyclopedia of Police Science, Third Edition*, represents one of the most up-to-date references libraries on policing. Two hundred and ninety-two serious scholars have provided materials contained in this volume; their collective effort represents a major contribution to the codification of scientific knowledge on the police.

Volumes like this third edition of *The Encyclopedia of Police Science* are indeed long-term projects. Like the epic movies of the past, editions like the current volume take years to stage and complete, while combining the orchestrated (and sometimes random) efforts of hundreds of people. And, like those epic movies, volumes such as these have a broad and detailed story to tell; they span large time frames, while capturing the moments in time of individuals and events. They draw attention to the macro, meso, and micro level interactions that shape events, and they arrive at destinations built on analysis of these interactions. I hope this edition of *The Encyclopedia of Police Science*, like an epic movie, provides a broad and sweeping context to the many individuals, organizations, and events that have shaped policing we have come to know. It is a deep and rich story, certainly one worth telling, and I hope the price of admission.

Throughout the development of this third edition of *The Encyclopedia of Police Science*, I have been mindful of the work that has gone before, most especially the work of William G. Bailey, editor of the first two editions. Professor Bailey's sharp eye on matters of policing shaped and filled in the contours of the first two editions, setting the stage for the present work. I hope that Professor Bailey would have approved this expansion of his original work, and I hope he would be pleased with the outcome—building on his legacy was an opportunity and burden, an opportunity to carry on an important line of work, and a burden to make sure this work advances on each and every level, just as the previous volumes under Bailey's direction. I leave it to the reader to determine whether the opportunity was maximized and the burden overcome.

I would also like to thank all of the contributors to this volume, 292 in all. In e-mails and telephone conversations with many of them, as well as reading their entries, I have come to know the vibrancy of this field and the passion of those who contribute to our understanding of police and policing. Reading the range of entries contained in this edition of *The Encyclopedia of Police Science* was to me an affirmation of scholarship on the police, and the ways in which that scholarship is defined and presented. There is no single method advocated here; just the consistent admonition to be clear and direct.

To my associate editors who served as the editorial board to this project, Drs. Gary W. Cordner of Eastern Kentucky University, Edward Maguire of George Mason University, and Peter K. Manning of Northeastern University, I offer my deepest appreciation, in helping to shape and recruit for the entries, and as the reader will see, making important contributions to the third edition. The collegiality, patience, and good humor of Cordner, Maguire, and Manning, as well as their scholarship and intellect are especially admired—I hope I have represented them well in this enterprise.

I am also indebted to Routledge, the publisher of this edition. Recommissioning a third edition some ten years after the last edition demonstrated to me a commitment to advancing scholarship on the police and a willingness to broaden that discussion with, perhaps a newer generation of scholars. Marie-Claire Antoine, acquisitions editor for Routledge, was a kind philosopher, friend, and guide throughout this process, supportive of innovation, yet clearly focused on the final product. She was instrumental in drawing my colleagues and me to this project, and then holding us accountable for the work that needed to be done.

Special appreciation is also extended to Susan Cronin, assistant development editor, at Routledge who was "task mistress" for this project. Susan praised, coaxed, cajoled, at times demanded adherence to time lines and work product. While we may have set the time, Susan ran the clock with precision, and while academics are want to drift off into some contemplation of future states, Susan kept me at least in the here and now. I thank her for her perseverance, tact and drive; conditions without which this edition may have faltered. And, to the editorial staff at Routledge I am also deeply appreciative of your focus on the detail and copyediting of this volume. This entire effort was greatly enhanced in the team spirit that shaped and completed this third edition of *The Encyclopedia of Police Science*.

Lastly, I would like to acknowledge the work of my departed mentor Robert S. Sheehan, the founding dean of the College of Criminal Justice at Northeastern University. Bob was a stickler for detail, and a visionary for police science; I sincerely hope he is pleased with the results of this work.

Jack R. Greene
Boston

LIST OF ENTRIES
A–Z

xxix

ABATEMENT OF NUISANCE PROPERTY SEIZURE

In the late 1980s, a promising tool was developed for deterring drug sales from indoor locations that are difficult to attack using regular police enforcement tactics. This tool applies nuisance abatement ordinances to pressure property owners to take action to stop drug sales on their premises under threat of closure or confiscation. This article discusses the types of abatement programs, evidence about their effectiveness, and concerns about their use or misuse.

Variety of Abatement Programs

Drug abatement laws vary in content and form (Finn and Hylton 1994). They can involve both civil remedies and criminal sanctions. Some drug abatement laws require only that neighborhood residents report drug activity, whereas others require the intervention of the police or district attorney. The laws are significant because they compel property owners to prevent drug sales on their premises. They also provide property owners, who might otherwise be to reluctant to evict dealers on their own, with the legal authority and mechanisms to rid their residences of drug-dealing tenants.

By 1992, an American Bar Association (ABA) study found that twenty-four states had passed statutes specifically designed to control drug activities on private properties (Smith et al. 1992). A number of these statutes updated old "bawdy house" laws designed to curb prostitution. With the filing of civil actions, most states authorize temporary injunctions requiring that the premises be immediately vacated. Judges issue permanent injunctions after civil hearings. The most common sanction is closing properties for up to one year. In practice, such orders are frequently stayed if owners post cash or property bonds. A few states allow buildings to be sold at auction with the proceeds going to state or local governments.

There are a wide range of abatement programs. Most are run by district or city attorneys and police departments and operate without any special funding. Most programs initiate abatement efforts with letters to property owners, which describe drug nuisances and the consequences of allowing them to continue. This first warning is typically enough leverage to compel owners to take actions. Programs that issue warning letters seldom have to file civil suits to induce compliance. Studies have found that civil suits are filed in less than 5% of abatement actions in cities that initiate actions with warning letters to property owners (Davis and Lurigio 1998).

Other abatement programs follow a different strategy. Instead of warning property owners, they immediately file civil suits against them. Temporary injunctions are obtained (in some states without giving property owners opportunities to participate in court hearings) and the problem buildings are ordered closed. These orders are usually stayed if property owners post cash bonds and agree to permanent injunctions.

In a few cases, cities have sent in SWAT teams with battering rams to vacate and padlock properties on the same day that temporary restraining orders are issued and before owners have been notified of the court order (Smith et al. 1992). Needless to say, such extreme measures are not well received by property owners. Moreover, padlocking of buildings in marginal areas creates a substantial risk that these properties will be vandalized or abandoned and kept out of the rental housing market.

Effectiveness of Abatement Programs

Abatement programs that rely primarily on warning letters have adopted a low-cost, and potentially effective, approach to controlling illegal drugs. Two comprehensive studies on drug abatement programs were conducted in the early 1990s by the ABA (Smith et al. 1992) and Loyola University of Chicago (Lurigio et al. 1998). The ABA study involved abatement programs in five cities (Milwaukee, Houston, Toledo, San Francisco, and Alexandria), whereas the Loyola University study focused on a single program in Cook County (Chicago). Both studies examined whether the programs actually had abated drug nuisances and assessed the impact of abatement actions on the quality of neighborhood life as judged through local residents' eyes.

Across all six cities included in the ABA and Loyola studies, program records showed that most property owners complied with directives and that no further problems were experienced on the premises in at least 85% of the targeted properties. In the vast majority of cases, compliance was achieved through evictions of problem tenants.

The ABA and Loyola studies also investigated program impact on the quality of life in neighborhoods. The ABA study reported that abatement actions were highly visible and well received. Approximately half of residents surveyed in the five cities studied by the ABA were aware of the abatement actions, and more than 90% endorsed the local abatement programs. Community awareness was highest in cities in which the abatement programs padlocked properties and publicized their efforts through the media. Awareness was lowest in cities in which abatement actions usually consisted of letters followed by the quiet evictions of problem tenants.

There is evidence from the ABA study that abatement efforts reduced signs of neighborhood disorder. One in three residents believed that the actions had reduced drug sales on their blocks, and one in four believed that the actions had reduced crime in general. Similarly, one-quarter believed that the problems of public drinking and adolescents hanging out on the blocks had been reduced as a result of the abatement actions.

The positive changes in residents' perceptions of crime and disorder observed in the ABA study are difficult to interpret because researchers did not include a comparison group of unabated properties. That is, they did not assess residents' perceptions before the abatement actions occurred, and they failed to compare the perceptions of residents in areas in which abatements occurred to those of residents in other, similar neighborhoods in which no abatements had taken place. Loyola University's investigation of Cook County's abatement program addressed these shortcomings.

Findings from the Loyola study, which included surveys with residents on control blocks that had not experienced abatement efforts, were less favorable than the ABA study's findings. Residents on targeted blocks were no more likely than residents on untargeted blocks to perceive reductions in drug activity and other signs of disorder, and improvements in safety on the block. These results might be explained by the fact that only one in five residents living on blocks with targeted properties was aware of the abatement actions.

In contrast, the majority of community leaders and police personnel surveyed in the Loyola study believed that the program's initiatives resulted in visible neighborhood changes and that the program was an important component of community efforts to reduce drug activity. An ethnographic study also determined that blocks targeted by the abatement program evidenced fewer signs of physical disorder than did comparison blocks.

An evaluation of another abatement program in Chicago reinforced the finding that abatement programs are effective in reducing drug crimes. The program, designed to attack problem properties with code violations and abatement actions, was reported to reduce narcotics offenses (but not other violent or property crimes) dramatically (Higgins 2000).

Two recent studies of abatement programs employed more rigorous methodologies in which sites were randomly assigned either to be targeted by an abatement action or not. These designs are important because they increase confidence that any observed differences between targeted and untargeted locations are the result of abatement actions and not attributable to other causes.

Eck and Wartell (1998) conducted a randomized experiment on the effects of abatement actions in San Diego. A total of 121 rental buildings in which the police had evidence of drug sales as the result of enforcement actions were assigned to one of three experimental conditions. In the first condition, property owners were sent letters informing them of drug activities and warning them of fines or closures of their buildings if the problems were not abated. In the second condition, owners received similar letters, which also requested that they attend meetings with the police. In the third condition, properties received no abatement notices. Follow-up during the next thirty months showed significantly fewer reported crimes in the two abatement conditions when compared with the control condition. Furthermore, letters alone were as effective in reducing crime as letters and meetings.

Green-Mazerolle, Roehl, and Kadleck (1998) conducted a randomized experiment in which one hundred drug hot spots were assigned to traditional police enforcement (surveillance, arrests, and field interrogations) or to traditional police enforcement plus civil enforcement (abatement actions and code enforcement). The civil enforcement properties showed more decreases in drug sales and disorder compared with the properties assigned to traditional enforcement only.

Concerns about Abatement Programs

Reviewing the literature on crime prevention, Welsh and colleagues (2002) conclude that abatement programs are effective in ridding buildings of drug nuisances. The cost of the programs is minimal. Most abatements are achieved just through mailings of warning letters. In fact, many cities engage in drug nuisance abatement activities with funds from existing municipal budgets.

Despite many successes, serious concerns have been raised about drug abatement programs (for a thorough discussion, see Cheh 1991, 1998). Because abatement strategies hold property owners accountable for tenants' behavior, nuisance statutes might be infringing on owners' rights to use and enjoy their properties (Smith and Davis 1998). Moreover, as alleged in legal suits filed in Milwaukee, statutes that permit authorities to close properties without notifying owners may infringe on due process rights.

As abatement programs have matured, a number have encouraged property owners to cooperate in abatement actions by sponsoring workshops that inform owners about their responsibilities under abatement laws and provide them with suggestions on screening prospective tenants and improving building security (Davis and Lurigio 1998).

When drug dealers are evicted or buildings padlocked, innocent family members or neighbors might become homeless. Accordingly, some programs have developed procedures to minimize the number of innocent parties evicted as a result of abatement actions and to resettle innocent parties who are evicted. The use of court suits and building closures only as a last resort is key to reducing the numbers of innocent parties evicted.

Sending warning letters rather than padlocking buildings reduces the possibility that targeted properties will be abandoned. Targeted buildings are typically in poor condition and are located in deteriorating neighborhoods. Closing them for an extended period invites vandalism and deprives owners of the rental income necessary to cover mortgage payments.

A final concern about abatement programs is whether they reduce drug sales or merely move them to another neighborhood. Limited evidence suggests that abatement actions might actually reduce, not just displace, drug sales. The most comprehensive look at displacement is reported in Davis and Lurigio (1996). The researchers worked with the Milwaukee Police Department to track one hundred persons who had been evicted as a result of abatement actions. Of sixty-three whom they traced to new locations (the remaining thirty-seven were either incarcerated, deceased, untraceable, or gone from the jurisdiction), just nineteen continued to sell drugs, based on attempts to make undercover buys. Davis and Lurigio suggested that abatement may have been an effective deterrent because it made business more difficult for "opportunists" (Buerger 1992) or "occasional sellers" (Reuter et al. 1990) who sell small quantities of drugs. When relocation prompted by abatement actions made it harder for buyers and sellers to connect, these marginal sellers were encouraged to turn to other means of support.

Conclusions

Drug abatement programs have been established as an effective community anti-drug initiative. They are particularly cost effective in curtailing drug sales on private properties and may actually reduce, not just displace, drug sales. Abatement strategies that directly involve owners in the process can minimize the unbidden consequences that property closures can have on owners such as the threat of physical assault and property damage and the leveling of unfair legal penalties. To be effective, abatement programs must also be cognizant that property closures can exacerbate urban blight in already run-down communities.

ROBERT C. DAVIS

See also **Crime Control Strategies: Alcohol and Drugs; Crime Prevention; Drug Markets; Hot Spots; Situational Crime Prevention**

References and Further Reading

Buerger, M. 1992. Defensive strategies of the street-level drug trade. *Journal of Crime and Justice* 15: 3–51.

Cheh, M. 1991. Constitutional limits on using civil remedies to achieve criminal law objectives: understanding and transcending the criminal-civil law distinction. *The Hastings Law Journal* 42: 1325–1413.

———. 1988. Blurring the law: Civil remedies to control crime. In *Civil remedies and crime prevention*, ed. L. Green-Mazaerolle and J. Roehl. Vol. 9 of *Crime prevention studies*, series ed. R. V. Clarke. Monsey, NY: Criminal Justice Press.

Davis, R. C., and A. J. Lurigio. 1996. *Fighting back: Neighborhood drug strategies*. Thousand Oaks, CA: Sage.

———. 1998. Civil abatement as a tool for controlling drug dealing in rental properties. *Security Journal* 11: 45–50.

Eck, J., and J. Wartell. 1998. Improving the management of rental properties with drug problems: A randomized experiment. In *Civil remedies and crime prevention*, ed. L. Green-Mazaerolle and J. Roehl. Vol. 9 of *Crime prevention studies*, series ed. R. V. Clarke. Monsey, NY: Criminal Justice Press.

Finn, P., and M. Hylton. 1994. *Using civil remedies for criminal behavior: Rationale, case studies, and constitutional issues*. Washington, DC: U.S. Department of Justice.

Green-Mazerolle, L., J. Roehl, and C. Kadleck. 1998. Controlling social disorder using civil remedies: Results from a randomized field experiment in Oakland, California. In *Civil remedies and crime prevention*, ed. L. Green-Mazaerolle and J. Roehl. Vol. 9 of *Crime prevention studies*, series ed. R. V. Clarke. Monsey, NY: Criminal Justice Press.

Higgins, D. 2000. *Controlling gang and drug house nuisances in Chicago*. Chicago: Illinois Criminal Justice Authority.

Lurigio, A., R. Davis, T. Regulus, V. Gwisada, S. Popkin, M. Dantzker, B. Smith, and A. Ouellet. 1998. More effective place management: An evaluation of the Cook County State's Attorney's Office narcotics nuisance abatement program. In *Civil remedies and crime prevention*, ed. L. Green-Mazaerolle and J. Roehl, 187–218. Vol. 9 of *Crime prevention studies*, series ed. R. V. Clarke. Monsey, NY: Criminal Justice Press.

Rengert, G. F. 1990. *Drug marketing, property crime, and neighborhood viability: Organized crime connections*. Report to the Pennsylvania Commission by the Department of Criminal Justice. Philadelphia, PA: Temple University.

Reuter, P., R. MacCoun, and P. Murphy. 1990. *Money from crime: A study of the economics of drug dealing in Washington, DC*. Santa Monica, CA: RAND Corp.

Smith, B. E., and R. C. Davis. 1998. What do landlords think about drug abatement laws? In *Civil remedies and crime prevention*, ed. L. Green-Mazaerolle and J. Roehl. Vol. 9 of *Crime prevention studies*, series ed. R. V. Clarke. Monsey, NY: Criminal Justice Press.

Smith, B. E., R. C. Davis, S. W. Hillenbrand, and S. R. Goretsky. 1992. *Ridding neighborhoods of drug houses in the private sector*. Washington, DC: American Bar Association.

Welsh, B. C., D. P. Farrington, L. W. Sherman, and D. L. MacKenzie, 2002. What do we know about crime prevention? *International Annals of Criminology* 40: 11–31.

ABUSE OF AUTHORITY BY POLICE

Police officers in the United States are asked by the general public to intervene in multiple types of critical incidents. Whether it is responding to a bank robbery or trying to calm a complainant in a domestic disturbance call, police officers are occupationally mandated to assume to variable degrees the roles of law enforcement agents, psychologists, legal advisers, and even parents. The reason for this omnibus social service/public safety role likely resides in Egon Bittner's (1970) now-classic explanation of why we have police in a democratic society: because "something-ought-not-to-be-happening-about-which-something-ought-to-be-done-now!" To facilitate the rapid response to diverse exigent situations, the American public has voluntarily given the police the general right to use coercive force—something that no other members of the public possess (Bittner 1970; Klockars 1985). While many (perhaps most) officers exercise their coercive authority judiciously and with appropriate restraint, others abuse their authority in violation of their office of public trust. This chapter identifies a framework for understanding police abuse of authority, describing the most common types of abuse, as well as several conventional mechanisms of police accountability.

The Nature of Police Abuse of Authority

David Carter (1985, 322) offers perhaps the most comprehensive definition of police abuse of authority, arguing that it is best described as "any action by a police officer without regard to motive, intent, or malice that tends to injure, insult, tread on human dignity, manifest feelings of inferiority, and/or violate an inherent legal right of a member of the . . ." public. Carter's definition considers three broad areas of police abuse including physical, psychological, and legal domains.

Physical Abuse

Since the early 1990s, police violence has become perhaps the most widely discussed and debated form of abuse committed by police. While extralegal use of force is often considered a single dimension of police abuse of authority, Fyfe (1986) made an important distinction between extralegal (i.e., physical abuse) and unnecessary (i.e., professional incompetence) police violence. (Like Binder and Scharf [1980], Fyfe [1986] defined unnecessary force as force that was legitimately used at the time of application, but which could have been avoided had officers used tactics and strategies to keep the potentially violent encounter from becoming violent. In this regard, unnecessary force is regarded as professional incompetence as opposed to abuse of authority.) For present purposes, Fyfe argued that extralegal force represents intentional physical abuse properly described as police brutality committed with a certain degree of malice toward the victim—who is typically "guilty" of committing an affront to police authority (see

also Van Maanen 1978). In this context, brutality is analogous to punishment and is generally justified as such among officers who engage in putatively violent behavior. For example, Worden (1996) found that suspects who attempt to evade police when commanded to yield generally place themselves at high risk for violence when caught by pursing officers.

Two types of brutality have been historically associated with American policing, occurring at two distinct points of contact between police and citizens. *External brutality* is any form of excessive force—or "street justice" (Klockars 1985; Sykes 1986) that occurs within a public setting before any formal disposition (e.g., arrest) is made. *Custodial coercion* is brutality that occurs after an arrest has been made, generally during the interrogation process. In early American policing (i.e., prior to 1900), because officers typically minimized the use of arrest largely due to the limited availability of efficient modes of transporting suspects to jail, external brutality was a normative "tool" of neighborhood-level peacekeeping (Haller 1976). As the police, however, evolved into a more formalized institution of social control and began relying on "scientific" detection methods, the arrest disposition became a more common component of the policing process. With more suspects being taken into physical custody, it was natural that the police would question suspects regarding their alleged crimes for the purposes of obtaining confessions. As custodial interrogations became a more common feature of the policing paradigm, so too did custodial coercion—particularly in the years through the 1930s when the third degree was widely used (Skolnick and Fyfe 1993). The Wickersham Commission's 1931 *Report on Police* argued that the use of the "third degree" during interrogation of suspects was widespread (if not universal) throughout police departments in the United States. The authors of the police volume of the report referred to the third degree as "torturous," and publicly called for the police to use less physically abusive tactics during interrogations (see also Chevingy 1995).

As America entered the decade of the 1960s, crime rates were increasing, riots were taking place in major and minor cities across the country, and the police appeared largely ill prepared to respond to these new urban "threats" (LaFree 1998). President Lyndon Johnson appointed a special commission to investigate the current state of the police, and the National Advisory Commission on Civil Disorders, known as the Kerner Commission, found several severe problems with American police practices. Most notable, brutality was reportedly standard practice in policing; and it was the aggressive use of police coercion that triggered many of the urban riots that would occur during the decade (Uchida 1997).

The legacy of policing from the 1960s is that social scientists gained interest in policing as an academic pursuit, applying their expertise to a relatively unstudied field (see Skolnick 1966; Wilson 1968; Westely 1970). As a result, many traditional methods of training, deployment, and officer selection were subsequently questioned (e.g., Kelling et al. 1974), and as time has progressed through the 1990s, many police departments have tried to stay current with research and the application of the latest methods and ideas. Brutality still has been a problem in the past few decades, but it has been slight in comparison to the institutionalized brutality found in the 1960s. Indeed, when the Knapp Commission (1972) published its report on allegations of police misconduct in the New York City Police Department, the focus on police deviance largely shifted from brutality to profit-motivated corruption. Interest in police brutality gained renewal with the 1991 beating of motorist Rodney King by officers of the Los Angeles Police Department, initiating a wave of scholarly attention as to the causes and implications of police violence, as well as its control (see Skolnick and Fyfe 1993; Geller and Toch 1996).

Psychological Abuse

Carter (1985) notes that psychological abuse by police historically has been rooted primarily in police interview practices, largely developing in response to the prohibition of the use of physically compelling tactics during interrogations. As del Carmen (1991) noted, the Supreme Court's decision in *Brown v. Mississippi* (1936), which banned the police use of physical coercion during interrogations, led officers to begin a reliance on psychological coercion as a means of obtaining confessions. Though the Court officially ended the use of "intense psychological" coercion of suspects in police custody (see *Spano v. New York*, 1959), it is likely that such abuse endures (see Chevingy 1995; del Carmen 1991)—particularly because the police continue to rely on the confession as their primary form of evidence during custodial interrogations (Skolnick and Fyfe 1993).

Legal Abuse

Generally, legal abuse relates to police officers violating criminal statutes, or the rights of citizens (typically, accused offenders) in order to achieve some organizational goal (Kappeler et al. 1994). This is often expressed in the form of committing perjury on the witness stand to ensure that an accused offender is adjudicated guilty; it may also involve officers setting up illegal wiretaps in order to surreptitiously gather incriminating information on police suspects. Certainly, these examples are not exhaustive.

It is important to note that although the framework discussed here provides a context for conceptualizing perhaps the most egregious types of police abuse, it ignores what is likely the most common—and most difficult to redress—type of abuse: verbal. Although Carter's (1985) definition of police abuse appears to include (or at least make room for) verbal mistreatment by police officers, few if any scholars (and practitioners) have addressed verbal abuse as a form of police malpractice. This omission is likely due to the difficulty of defining and measuring the prevalence of verbal abuse. The importance of considering verbal abuse, however, is difficult to overstate because cumulative verbal abuse may be a primary cause of decreased police legitimacy and increased noncompliance among citizens—particularly in communities that experience social and political marginalization.

Legitimizing Police Abuse of Authority

As noted, the core of the police role resides in the general right to use coercive force, and no other member or group in American society enjoys such a legal privilege. It is therefore paradoxical that the same legal authority allowing police to engage in crowd control, take physical custody of citizens, and search for evidence in private residences also provides a structural framework that may facilitate police abuse of authority. For several reasons the criminal law has been implicated as a mechanism that gives police officers a unique opportunity to engage in occupational deviance. For example, Brodeur (1981) noted that many actions routinely practiced by police officers, which are part of their legal mandate, would be considered violations of criminal law if they were practiced by private citizens. Moreover, for each of these "practices" of legal policing, there exists an illegal analogue that moves the activity into a category of police deviance (Brodeur 1981). These activities fall into both personal and property violations and are described next.

In terms of personal actions, Brodeur (1981) indicated that citizens who kill would be generally held to answer for homicide, but that police officers who kill are often engaging in the legitimate police practice of "deadly force." The analogue to

deadly force in the police deviance arena is police executions, killings not authorized by law. Next, Brodeur suggested that if private citizens detain other citizens, they may be guilty of kidnapping; but that when police officers engage in liberty deprivation, they are generally legally detaining or arresting criminal suspects. Such police detentions may become abusive if officers make false arrests. Some forms of personal invasion are legal for police, such as when they conduct strip and body cavity searches. This behavior becomes deviant when these searches escalate to sexual exploitation. Police officers may use force to seize property. In most cases, citizens who engage in this practice would be guilty of robbery. When police officers abuse their authority to seize property, it is generally described as extortion or bribe taking. Finally, what may be considered assault and battery between private citizens is often reasonable force when practiced by police officers. Reasonable force becomes deviant when officers engage in police brutality.

In terms of property-related activity, Brodeur (1981) wrote that police searches and seizures often involve conduct that if committed by private citizens would be considered theft and/or burglary. These behaviors become deviant among police officers when they steal and/or convert the seized property to money or money's worth. Finally, police officers are allowed to seize and possess illegal drugs for arrest and investigative purposes. Private citizens who engage in such activity would likely be guilty of violating criminal drug statues (Brodeur 1981).

Brodeur's (1981) observations are important because they show not only that police are given special authority to engage in what would be normally considered rule-breaking behavior among private citizens, but that this special authority also provides police officers with unique opportunities to engage in abusive behavior. Indeed, several researchers have noted that the structure of policing in America creates virtually unlimited opportunities for police deviance and abuse of authority (Barker 1990; Bryant 1974). Ericson (1981) wrote, "substantive laws are written broadly enough, and with sufficient ambiguity, that they can be applied across a range of circumstances" (p. 91). He goes on to argue that criminal laws provide police with such vast discretionary power that officers in the field may rely on a number of possible charges for making arrests and taking suspects into custody. Ericson (1981, 91) noted that public order offenses and obstructing the police are two widely relied on charges that police officers use as a pretext for accomplishing individual or organizational goals.

Redressing Police Abuse of Authority

The history of police abuse of authority in the United States has foreshadowed the development of mechanisms designed to hold the police accountable when officers have grossly violated the dignity of members of the public. Macro-level mechanisms, typically in the form of Supreme Court decisions, have been used to articulate the outer boundaries of police authority in both custodial and public settings. Micro-level mechanisms of accountability have been developed to respond precisely to individual officers accused of committing acts of brutality or excessive force. For present purposes, the term *accountability* is used to describe the mechanisms available to private citizens and the government to redress police malpractice and abuse of authority.

Case Law: The Macro-Level Mechanism

Regulating the methods by which police obtain information from suspects during custodial interrogations has been legally complex because the Supreme Court has historically appealed to the Due Process Clause of the Fourteenth Amendment,

the Self Incrimination Clause of the Fifth Amendment, and the Right to Counsel Clause of the Sixth Amendment. As previously noted, the increased reliance on confessions became associated with custodial brutality through the Prohibition era and into the 1930s. In 1936, however, the Supreme Court ruled in *Brown v. Mississippi* that the police use of physical coercion to obtain confessions from suspects was unconstitutional because such confessions could be regarded only as "involuntary." Some researchers have argued that *Brown v. Mississippi* led the police to switch from physically coercive methods to psychologically abusive methods in the quest to obtain confessions (see Walker and del Carmen 1997). With its decision in the case *Spano v. New York* (1959), however, the Supreme Court prohibited psychologically abusive tactics during custodial interrogations.

To date it has been impossible to determine the extent to which physical and extreme psychological coercion have been eliminated during custodial interrogations given that police still rely heavily on the use of confessions to prove the guilt of criminal suspects. The increased use of audio and video recording technologies during interrogations may do much to ensure both legal and ethical methods of interrogation, but only to the extent that such devices are employed systematically.

In addition to attempting to regulate police coercion in custodial contexts, the Court has also addressed police coercion (i.e., violence) in general police–citizen encounters. For example, the landmark decision in *Tennessee v. Garner* (1985) made impermissible the common law police practice of using deadly force against nondangerous fleeing felons. Specifically, the Court ruled that officers were allowed to use deadly force only to prevent the escape of suspects believed to pose a "significant threat of death or serious physical injury to the officer or others" if not immediately apprehended. The Court concluded that deadly force was tantamount to a seizure of the person and therefore subject to regulation under the reasonableness requirement of the Fourth Amendment to the U.S. Constitution. Interestingly, although *Garner* automatically invalidated laws in states that had legalized the "feeling felon" rule (del Carmen and Walker 1997), the decision may have had only limited impact on street-level police practices, because many metropolitan police departments by 1985 had already adopted highly restrictive deadly force policies in response to the threat of civil liability (Fyfe 1986).

In a case that may have had a more direct impact on police accountability in the United States, the Court in *Graham v. Connor* (1989) ruled that police officers may be held liable under the Constitution for using excessive force. Under *Graham*, the test for liability is "objective reasonableness" as opposed to a more rigorous "substantive due process" standard because, as the Court reasoned, excessive force should be judged "from the perspective of a reasonable officer at the scene rather than with the 20/20 vision of hindsight." With the objective reasonableness standard (also regulated by the Fourth Amendment), the Court recognized that police officers often must make quick decisions during critical incidents without the benefit of time to fully reflect on the potential implications of their actions.

Micro-Level Mechanisms

As Klockars (1996) notes, most states have civil rights statutes that make it illegal for police officers to commit acts of brutality under color of authority. The most widely known statutes by the public, however, are the federal civil rights laws incorporated into the United States Code, which include both criminal (Title 18 §242 USC) and civil (Title 42 §1983 USC) versions. These statutes, which are almost identical in phrasing, make it a federal crime and tort, respectively, for police officers to violate citizens' civil rights under color of authority. Because of the lower evidentiary threshold required in civil court (a "preponderance of evidence" versus the "beyond a reasonable doubt" required in criminal court), officers accused of brutality or abuse of authority are often sued rather than prosecuted. In many cases, they are both sued *and* prosecuted in federal court.

Administrative mechanisms usually include restrictive policies and procedures, as well as internal affairs investigative units. Many of America's large police departments—such as those in New York City and Chicago—have developed highly formalized disciplinary review processes analogous to courts-martial of military justice. In such systems, officers are processed through administrative trials during which they may use counsel, where charge and plea negotiations occur, and where administrative "due process" must be maintained.

Emerging Issues Regarding Police Abuse of Authority

Since the United States "declared" war on crime in the 1960s—which escalated into a war on drugs in the 1980s—local police have increasingly appealed to military symbolism, tactics, and strategies to fulfill their enforcement mandate. As both Walker (2001) and Kennedy (2003) have noted, the consequences of the war on drugs paradigm have been felt primarily by residents of socially dislocated urban ghettos as young black males have become the archetype of the urban criminal offender (see also Wilson 1987; Massey and Denton 1993; Skolnick and Fyfe 1993; Anderson 1999). Since September 11, 2001, the war on terrorism has given renewed legitimacy to aggressive police tactics that bring with them the increased potential for abuse of authority. This may be especially true as the fear of terrorism outweighs the American public's concerns for civil liberties and due process protections. The post-9/11 era presents special challenges to policing and public policy because every increase in police authority (such as in the areas of search and seizure, internal surveillance, and enforcement of federal statutes) brings with it new ways for motivated officers and departments to abuse their offices of public trust.

ROBERT J. KANE

See also **Accountability; Civil Restraint in Policing; Community Attitudes toward the Police; Deadly Force; Excessive Force; History of American Policing; Knapp Commission; Minorities and the Police; Police Misconduct: After the Rodney King Incident; Role of the Police**

References and Further Reading

Barker, T. 1990. Peer group support for police occupational deviance. In *Police deviance*, ed. T. Barker and D. Carter. Cincinnati, OH: Anderson Publishing Company.

Bartollas, C., and L. Hahn. 1999. *Policing in America*. Boston: Allyn and Bacon.

Binder, A., and P. Scharf. 1980. The violent police–citizen encounter. *Annals of the American Academy of Political and Social Science*, 452: 111–21.

Bittner, E. 1970. *The functions of the police in modern society*. Washington, DC: U.S. Government Printing Office.

Brodeur, J. 1981. Legitimizing police deviance. In *Organizational police deviance*, ed. C. D. Shearing. Toronto: Butterworth and Company.

Brown v. Mississippi, 297 U.S. 278 (1936).

Bryant, C. D. 1974. *Deviant behavior: occupational and organizational biases*.

Carter, D. L. 1985. Police brutality: A model for definition, perspective, and control. In *The ambivalent force*, ed. A. S. Blumberg and E. Neiderhoffer. New York: Holt, Rinehart and Winston.

Chevigny, P. B. 1995. *Edge of the knife: Police violence in the Americas*. New York: Free Press.

del Carmen, R. 1991. *Civil liabilities in American policing: A text for law enforcement personnel*. Englewood Cliffs, NJ: Brady.

Ericson, R. V. 1981. Rules for police deviance. In *Organizational Police Deviance*,

Shearing, C. D. ed. Toronto: Butterworth and Company.

Fyfe, J. J. 1986. The split-second syndrome and other determinants of police violence. In *Violent Transactions*, ed. A. Campbell and J. Gibbs. New York: Basil Blackwell.

Geller, W., and H. Toch, eds. *Police violence: Understanding and controlling police abuse of force*. New Haven, CT: Yale University Press.

Haller, M. 1976. Historical roots of police behavior, Chicago 1890–1925. *Law and Society Review* 10: 303–23.

Kappeler, V., R. Sluder, and G. Alpert. 1994. *Forces of deviance: Understanding the dark side of policing*. Prospect Heights, IL: Waveland.

Kelling, G., A. Pate, and C. Brown. 1974. *The Kansas City preventive patrol study*. Washington, DC: U.S. General Accounting Office.

Kennedy, J. 2003. Drug wars in black and white. *Law and Contemporary Problems* 66: 153–81.

Klockars, C. 1985. *The idea of police*. Beverly Hills, CA: Sage.

Knapp Commission. 1972. *Commission to investigate allegations of police corruption and the city's anti-corruption procedures*. New York.

LaFree, G. 1998. *Losing legitimacy: Street crime and the decline of social institutions in America*. Boulder, CO: Westview Press.

Skolnick, J. H. 1966. *Justice without trial: Law enforcement in democratic society*. New York: Macmillan.

Skolnick, J. H., and J. J. Fyfe. 1993. *Above the law: Police and excessive use of force*. New York: The Free Press.

Spano v. New York, 360 U.S. 315 (1959).

Van Maanen, J. 1978. The asshole. In *Policing: A view from the street*, ed. P. K. Manning and J. Van Maanen, 221–38. Santa Monica, CA: Goodyear.

Walker, S. 2001. *Sense and nonsense about crime and drugs: A police guide*. Belmont, CA: Wadsworth.

Westley, W. 1970. *Violence and the police*. Cambridge, MA: The MIT Press.

Wilson, J. Q. 1968. *Varieties of police behavior*. Cambridge, MA: Harvard University Press.

Worden, R. E. 1996. The causes of police brutality: Theory and evidence on police use of force. In *Police violence: Understanding and controlling police abuse of force*, ed. W. A. Geller and H. Toch, 23–51. New Haven, CT: Yale University Press.

ACADEMIES, POLICE

Police training has come a long way since the days when officer candidates simply paid the going rate to local politicians, received the tools of their job (a badge, a club, and a list of local ordinances), and hit the streets. Today, police officers typically receive about 720 hours of formal academy training on a wide variety of subjects, including firearms skills, criminal law and procedure, investigations, human relations, ethics and integrity, and several other topics that form the foundations of policing. Getting to this point took more than one hundred years of effort by police reformers, national commissions, legislators, and many others.

Largely spearheaded by August Vollmer, the "father" of police professionalism, reform movements in the early twentieth century sought to increase police personnel standards and training, in addition to numerous other reforms. Vollmer brought attention to the problem of inadequate training and advanced the goals of the reform agenda in a volume of the Wickersham Commission reports (National Commission on Law Observance and Enforcement 1931). In particular, a survey of 383 cities reported in that volume found that only 20% conducted formal training for new officers.

The next major commission to study the police, the 1967 President's Commission on Law Enforcement and Administration of Justice, noted significant changes since the Wickersham Commission reports. The 1967 commission report on the police cited studies showing that the majority of surveyed agencies were conducting some type of recruit training, but that the content of the training was still lacking: "Current training programs, for the most part, prepare an officer to perform work mechanically, but do not prepare him to understand his community, the police role, or the imperfections of the criminal justice system." The commission also noted wide variation in the length of training programs; whereas large city departments typically had programs running eight weeks, smaller departments averaged less than three weeks. Large proportions of officers in small cities still received no training at all.

The National Advisory Commission on Criminal Justice Standards and Goals (1973) subsequently recommended that each state establish mandatory minimum standards for basic training (including at least four hundred hours of academy training and four months of field training), as well as a state commission to develop and administer the standards. Seventeen states already had a state commission at the time, and by 1981, all states had a Peace Officer Standards and Training (POST) organization.

Until just recently, however, relatively little was known about the operations and outputs of individual training academies across the country. Basic but essential information, such as the number of academies, number of annual graduates, curriculum content, and academy resources, were unavailable on a national scale. The remainder of this entry is a review of key findings from a recent national study of law enforcement training in the United States (Hickman 2005). This study, a comprehensive census of state and local law enforcement training academies, collected information about academy personnel, expenditures, facilities and equipment, trainees, and training curricula.

General Characteristics

At year-end 2002, a total of 626 state and local law enforcement academies were operating in the United States. These academies offered basic law enforcement training to individuals recruited or seeking to become law enforcement officers. This overall figure does not include academies that provide only in-service training, corrections/detention training, or other special types of training. Included are 274 county, regional, or state academies, 249 college, university, or technical school academies, and 103 city or municipal academies.

In addition to basic recruit training, many academies provided additional types of training such as in-service training for active duty, certified officers (88% of academies), specialized training such as K-9 and SWAT (84%), and managerial training for police supervisors (70%). Some academies also provide training for other public safety and emergency personnel. For example, 23% of academies provided training for probation/parole officers, 14% provided training for firefighters, and 13% for emergency medical technicians.

Academy Personnel

Overall, academies in 2002 employed about 12,200 full-time and 25,700 part-time trainers or instructors. Most academies, about three-quarters, employed fewer than fifty full-time equivalent (FTE) training personnel. Just 8% of academies had one hundred or more FTE trainers, but these academies accounted for nearly half (47%) of all full-time trainers.

Academies typically had an education and/or experience requirement for their full-time trainers. About two-thirds of academies had a minimum education requirement for full-time trainers, most commonly a high school degree or GED (33%), followed by a two-year (12%) or four-year (11%) college degree. Likewise, about two-thirds required their full-time trainers to have a minimum number of years of law enforcement experience, ranging from one to ten years, with three and five years being the most common minimum requirements.

Trainees/Recruits

Training academies in 2002 typically held two basic recruit academy classes (i.e., a cohort of recruits) during the year. Larger academies (those with one hundred or more FTE trainers) typically held four academy classes during the year. Average class sizes ranged from about twenty to thirty recruits.

Among basic law enforcement academy classes that completed training during 2002, an estimated 53,302 trainees successfully completed their training program. Just over half (55%) of those individuals completed their training in county, regional, or state academies. Twenty-nine percent graduated from college, university, or technical school academies, and 15% from city or municipal academies.

Seventeen percent of recruits who completed training in 2002 were female, and 27% were members of a racial or ethnic minority, including 12% Hispanic or Latino, 12% black or African American, and 3% from other racial categories (including American Indian/Alaska Native, Asian, Hawaiian or Pacific Islander, and any other race).

Attrition

The 53,302 individuals who completed their training during 2002 represent 87% of those who started training (i.e., an overall attrition rate of 13%). Recruit attrition varied only slightly by size of academy (ranging from 12% to 14%) and type of academy (12% among county, regional, or state academies; 13% among college, university, or technical school academies; and 16% among city or municipal academies).

Overall, males had a lower attrition rate than females (12% versus 19%). By racial/ethnic categories, whites (12%) had a lower attrition rate than Hispanics or Latinos (17%), blacks or African Americans (19%), and other racial categories (22%). White males comprised 63% of the recruits who completed training, and had the lowest attrition rate (11%). Females in the "other" race category comprised less than half a percent of those completing training, and had the highest attrition rate (26%).

Curriculum

A typical academy in 2002 provided about 720 hours of basic academy training, excluding any field training component. The greatest amount of instruction time was in firearms skills (median 60 hours), followed by health and fitness (50 hours), investigations (45 hours), self-defense (44 hours), criminal law (40 hours), patrol procedures and techniques (40 hours), emergency vehicle operations (36 hours), and basic first-aid/CPR (24 hours). Other common training topics included domestic violence (median 12 hours), constitutional law (11 hours), ethics and integrity (8 hours), juvenile law and procedures (8 hours), and cultural diversity (8 hours). Ninety-five percent or more of all academies provided training in these areas.

Thirty-eight percent of academies provided field training as part of their basic recruit training program, typically about 180 hours.

Training Environment

The training environments of state and local academies are quite varied. The training environment in some academies is similar to a military boot camp (often referred to as a "stress" model), while others are more like an academic campus (often referred to as a "nonstress" model). Just over half (54%) of basic academies in the United States, providing training to 49% of recruits, indicated that their training environment was best described as following some type of stress model, with the remainder indicating some type of nonstress model. Perhaps not surprisingly, most college, university, or technical school academies (62%) had some type of nonstress

model. In contrast, most city or municipal academies (68%) and county, regional, and state academies (62%) had some type of stress model.

Cost of Training

During fiscal year 2002, training academies expended an estimated total of $725.6 million. Expenditures averaged about $1.2 million per academy, ranging from about $6.3 million among the largest academies (those with one hundred or more FTE trainers), to about $261,000 among the smallest (those with fewer than ten FTE trainers).

Based on annual academy expenditures, per trainee costs during 2002 were estimated to be about $13,100 overall, ranging from $5,400 per trainee among smaller academies to $18,800 per trainee among the largest. Per trainee expenditures were much higher in city or municipal academies, at about $36,200 per trainee. In contrast, county, regional, or state academies spent about $11,200 per trainee, and college, university, or technical school academies, about $4,600 per trainee.

MATTHEW J. HICKMAN

See also **American Policing: Early Years; Education and Training; History of American Policing; Police Reform: 1950–1970; Police Standards and Training Commissions; Professionalism; Vollmer, August; Wickersham, George W.; Wilson, O. W.**

References and Further Reading

Hickman, M. 2005. *State and local law enforcement training academies, 2002.* Washington, DC: Bureau of Justice Statistics.

National Advisory Commission on Criminal Justice Standards and Goals. 1973. *Police.* Washington, DC: U.S. Government Printing Office.

National Commission on Law Observance and Enforcement. 1931. *Report on the police.* Washington, DC: U.S. Government Printing Office.

President's Commission on Law Enforcement and Administration of Justice. 1967. *Task force report: The Police*. Washington, DC: U.S. Government Printing Office.

ACCIDENTAL DEATHS/ ASSAULTS AGAINST POLICE AND MURDER OF POLICE OFFICERS

On an almost daily basis, law enforcement officers in jurisdictions of all sizes encounter individuals and circumstances that pose a high risk of personal injury, assault, and sometimes death. The continuum of risks and the circumstances in which they arise are as broad as they are varied. Officers can receive anything from minor cuts and contusions while attempting to restrain a combative suspect to more serious and life-threatening injuries at the hands of a desperate individual who believes that he or she has nothing to lose and everything to gain by harming the police. The fact that police make almost fourteen million arrests and engage in nearly forty-five million face-to-face contacts with the public on an annual basis no doubt creates an environment that provides ample opportunity for injurious, and sometimes deadly, altercations to erupt.

With little room for disagreement, policing is a dangerous line of work. While it may be true that other occupations (e.g., timber cutters, mining) pose a statistically higher risk of job-related injury or death, such examples are qualitatively distinct from police work on the basis that they generally involve unintentional mishaps or negligence, whereas the risks confronted by officers generally involve acts of aggression committed by someone who intends to do them harm. In simple terms, police work is uniquely dangerous because it is one of only a few professions whose employees must acknowledge and reconcile the fact that any injury inflicted on them is typically the result of an aggressive act by someone who intends to hurt or perhaps even kill them.

Official Sources of Information on Police Officer Deaths

With this distinction in mind, the question that logically arises is one of assessing the frequency with which police officers are injured, assaulted, or killed while on the job. In making this determination, the most widely recognized source of official information on what can be best characterized as "line-of-duty" assaults and deaths is the Federal Bureau of Investigation's publication *Law Enforcement Officers Killed and Assaulted*. The report, released annually since 1960, relates aggregate-level data regarding the number of officers who are assaulted or killed during the previous calendar year. While informative, the report is not without its weaknesses. First, it fails to reflect the less serious everyday injuries that are incurred (e.g., a jammed finger, twisted knee, or broken bone) because it focuses only on those instances involving the use of a dangerous weapon. Consequently, little is known about the "dark figure" of less-than-deadly assaults on the police. Second, the report is based on data that have been voluntarily submitted by participating agencies. This potential weakness is offset somewhat by the fact that FBI field offices attempt to follow up on assaults against the police as such instances come to their attention. Third, larger agencies that experience a high frequency of assaults on officers may not report such instances due to the additional burden that is placed on what may be an already overtaxed and sometimes antiquated record-keeping system.

Because of these and other practical considerations, there are no firm official estimates from the FBI regarding the frequency with which less serious injuries are inflicted on officers—thus the reason for such a narrow focus within the report on only those instances where an officer has lost her or his life under accidental or intentional circumstance.

Research into the Prevalence and Correlates of Violence against the Police

Fortunately, this lack of official attention regarding the frequency of nonlethal assaults on the police has been acknowledged and, to a certain extent, reconciled by a small number of researchers who, also since the early 1960s, have conducted their own inquiries using data gleaned from various agencies. The first and arguably most influential of these studies was that conducted by Bard (1970), which asserted that officers are most likely to be seriously injured while responding to calls of a domestic nature.

Although this early finding has since been reconsidered due to its reliance on statistical methods of limited sophistication, it nonetheless seems reasonable to credit the assertions made therein with drawing attention to the general problem of assaults on the police as well as highlighting the specific risks that domestic disturbance calls pose for officer safety. More recent research, such as that conducted by Ellis et al. (1993), Garner and Clemmer (1986), Grennan (1987), Hirschel et al. (1994), Kaminski (2004), Kaminski and Sorensen (1995), Lester (1978, 1982), Margarita (1980), Stanford and Mowry (1990), Uchida et al. (1987), and Wilson and Meyer (1990), has identified a much broader range of circumstances and factors both temporally and statistically related to assaults on police officers.

Although these studies are too numerous and detailed to summarize in the immediate context, several practical implications have arisen from this line of research. One implication is the acknowledgment that nonlethal assaults against the police far exceed the number of officers who are murdered. Another is the increased emphasis that they have placed on the need for training on topics as varied as communication and problem solving to defensive tactics. Yet another is the recognition that assaults on the police not only pose obvious physical consequences for those directly involved, but also for the figurative "health" of the agency in terms of morale, recruitment, retention, productivity, and police–community relations to name but just a few areas of administrative concern. Given these consequences, the need for continued and sophisticated research on the topic, particularly that which is as broad based and generalized as possible, remains strong.

Accidental Deaths of Police Officers

While personal injury as the result of an intentional assault is indeed widespread and disconcerting, perhaps even more so are the accidental deaths incurred by the profession. During the ten-year period from 1994 to 2003 (the most recent time frame for which data are available), 697 officers died accidentally in the line of duty. The fewest accidental deaths occurred in 1996 (fifty-two cases) and the greatest number of losses occurred in 2000 (eighty-three cases).

The most frequent circumstance giving rise to the accidental death of police officers across the ten-year period without exception involved automobile accidents. The second most common cause of accidental death among officers is being struck by a vehicle, generally during a traffic stop, while directing traffic, or while investigating an accident. Far less common, but still prevalent, are other situations such as training mishaps, accidental discharge of firearms, and mistaken identity. To be sure, these unfortunate instances are significant insofar as they provide a unique learning opportunity intended to prevent or, at least minimize, their future occurrence.

Murders of Police Officers

Of greatest concern to both the public and the profession are those instances in which a police officer is feloniously killed in the line of duty. Over the ten-year period from 1994 to 2003, 616 officers were intentionally killed while performing their duties. The greatest number of officers was killed in 1994 (seventy-nine murders) with the fewest number of occurrences in 1992 (forty-two murders). On average, approximately sixty-one officers have been killed annually between 1994 and 2003. Interestingly, the FBI does not include the seventy-two law enforcement personnel who were killed in conjunction with the events of September 11, 2001, in this ten-year longitudinal analysis on grounds that including these cases would skew the data. Excluding this particular instance, a police officer's risk of being murdered has steadily decreased during the past thirty-five years from 1 in 4,000 to over 1 in 12,000. Several potential explanations for this trend might include improved training and tactics as well as the increased use of protective body armor.

Situational Characteristics

The type of situation most frequently giving rise to the murder of a police officer for the ten-year period from 1994 to 2003 was that involving an attempted arrest (187) followed by traffic pursuits/stops (101) and ambushes (100). Other situations in which officers were killed included responding to disturbance calls (e.g., domestic assaults or bar fights) (98) or investigating suspicious persons (96). Far less frequent were instances involving prisoner transport (20), handling the mentally ill (14), or civil disturbances/riots (0). Interestingly, the distribution of these instances does not appear to fluctuate greatly from year to year. Simply stated, arrest situations, suspicious person calls, and traffic stops seem to consistently dominate the contexts in which officers are most frequently killed.

Research conducted by Cardarelli (1968) in the early 1960s revealed that arrests related to robbery or suspicious person calls posed the greatest risk for officers in urban areas, whereas prisoner transport was the more common cause of fatality in nonurban settings. Research conducted by Konstanin (1984) supports the threat posed by "suspicious persons," especially where the contact is officer initiated, but failed to find the elevated risk associated with robbery calls/arrests as previously reported by Cardarelli. Yet another study focusing on the murder of New York City police officers from 1844 to 1978 by Margarita (1980) revealed that only 28.5% of such incidents occurred in the context of robbery investigations. Although evidence regarding the prevalence of robbery-related deaths is somewhat contradictory in the context of these historically and geographically bound studies, the fact remains that offenses involving the use of a weapon pose a substantial risk to officer safety.

Common knowledge abounds in law enforcement circles regarding the fact that nighttime hours are the most dangerous for an officer's personal safety. While this contention is in fact supported by the available data, such narrow focus detracts attention from the risk that officers face during the daytime hours when, quite surprisingly, a significant number of killings occur in broad daylight. Although variation exists from year to year, the most dangerous days of the week are Tuesday through Friday, with the fewest officer killings occurring on Sundays. No readily distinguishable differences exist indicating that any one season or month of the year is more or less dangerous than the next.

Weapons Involved

Contrary to expectation and the understandable fear of most officers, very few officers were killed with their own weapons. Rather, most officers are killed by other weapons already in the possession of those who would do them harm. Practically speaking, this means that officers should be more cognizant of weapons other than their own that might be readily used against them. Without exception across the ten-year period from 1994 to 2003, most officers who were feloniously killed in the line of duty (320) did not make use of their own weapon for defensive purposes, and most (516) did not have their weapon stolen by the assailant. A clear majority of officers are killed by a handgun (425), with very few being killed by a rifle (109) or shotgun (34). Edged weapon (knife) attacks (7) occur even less frequently. Thus, although weapon retention is indeed an important part of the training officers receive regarding street survival, the available data strongly suggest that attention should also be paid to the early detection and securing of other weapons (i.e., handguns) that might be used for assaultive purposes.

Officer Characteristics

Particular attention is frequently given to the characteristics of victim officers—surviving officers like to think that they are somehow different from those who have fallen and are therefore at lower risk for meeting the same fate. This rationalization can, however, lead to a false sense of safety in light of the available data, which suggest that although officers between thirty-one and forty years of age comprise the largest number of victims (227), those in the age ranges of twenty-one to thirty (200) and forty-one and above (186) remain at almost equal risk. White male officers are at higher risk than their female and racial counterparts. This pattern may be due, at least in part, to the fact that law enforcement continues to be a profession largely dominated by this particular demographic (i.e., white males). The typical victim officer is between thirty-six and thirty-eight years of age with an average of ten years of service—two

particular characteristics that have not changed much, if any, over the years. Again, however, officers in other age groups with fewer or greater years of service remain at risk, albeit to a slightly lesser extent.

Offender Characteristics

Of the 748 suspects involved in the killings of police officers over the ten-year period from 1994 to 2003, most were white (407) males (721) between the ages of eighteen and twenty-four (284). This profile should not, however, be interpreted to mean that other races, genders, or age groups are harmless—members of other groups still account for a significant number of suspects involved in police killings and should not be taken any less seriously. Similarly, although individuals with prior arrests and convictions accounted for the largest portion of suspects, there remain significant numbers of individuals who fatally strike out at the police in the absence of any real past criminal record.

Clearance Rates

To be sure, the killing of a police officer receives considerable media attention and public outcry. This reaction, combined with the fervent determination of fellow officers to capture the suspect, likely accounts for the exceptionally high clearance rate of police murders. Of the 816 individuals identified as suspects in police killings from 1992 to 2001, only 11 evaded arrest at the time of the report publication (and may very well have been since killed or captured). Most suspects (629) were arrested and brought to trial. Others were justifiably killed by police (103), and some committed suicide (64). Thus, the clearance rate for the murder of police officers is especially high given that surviving officers and investigators take a very "personal" interest in these types of cases.

Benefits for Survivors

While local communities and agencies both suffer from the accidental loss or felonious killing of an officer, those who experience the most long-term effects of a life cut short in the line of duty are immediate family members. Initially emerging in response to isolated instances at the local and then state level, there exist today a number and variety of support networks for police survivors. Some of these, such as the Concerns of Police Survivors, are privately created and funded, while others like the Bureau of Justice Administration's Public Safety Officers' Benefits Program are taxpayer supported and, as such, government administered. Clearly, the purpose of these programs is to provide emotional and financial support for survivors through a network of local chapters, peer support groups, benefit coordinators, and programmatic offerings.

Commemorating Fallen Officers

The legacy of those who are killed in the line of duty is preserved by the National Law Enforcement Officers' Memorial Fund, which not only maintains a memorial wall visited by more than 150,000 people annually, but has successfully lobbied for several public acknowledgments of police sacrifice such as Police Officer Memorial Day (on May 15 each year) and the minting of five hundred thousand commemorative silver dollars, which has generated more than $1.5 million for maintenance and repair of the facility. Most recently, the fund successfully lobbied Congress for the appropriation of land at Judiciary Square in Washington, D.C., on which a national law enforcement museum is expected to be constructed.

R. ALAN THOMPSON

See also **Crime, Serious Violent; Danger and Police Work; Deadly Force; Stress and Police Work**

References and Further Reading

Bard, M. 1970. *Training police as specialists in family crisis intervention.* Washington, DC: U.S. Government Printing Office.

Cardarelli, A. 1968. An analysis of police killed by criminal action: 1961–1963. *Journal of Criminal Law, Criminology and Police Science* 59: 447–53.

Ellis, D., A. Choi, and C. Blaus. 1993. Injuries to police officers attending domestic disturbances: An empirical study. *Canadian Journal of Criminology* 352: 149–68.

Federal Bureau of Investigation. 2004. *Law enforcement officers killed and assaulted—2003.* Washington, DC: U.S. Government Printing Office.

Garner, J., and E. Clemmer. 1986. *Danger to police in domestic disturbances: A new look.* Washington, DC: U.S. Department of Justice, National Institute of Justice.

Grennan, S. A. 1987. Findings on the role of officer gender in violent encounters with citizens. *Journal of Police Science and Administration* 15: 78–85.

Hirschel, D., C. Dean, and R. Lumb. 1994. The relative contribution of domestic violence to assault and injury of police officers. *Justice Quarterly* 11: 99–116.

Kaminski, R., and D. Sorensen. 1995. A multivariate analysis of individual, situational and environmental factors associated with police assault injuries. *American Journal of Police* 14: 3–48.

Konstantin, D. 1984. Law enforcement officers feloniously killed in the line of duty: An exploratory study. *Justice Quarterly* 1: 29–46.

Lester, D. 1978. A study of civilian-caused murder of police officers. *International Journal of Criminology and Penology* 6: 373–78.

———. 1982. Civilians who kill police officers and police officers who kill civilians: A comparison of American cities. *Journal of Police Science and Administration* 10: 384–87.

Margarita, M. 1980. *Criminal violence against police.* Ann Arbor, MI: University Microfilms International.

Stanford, R., and B. Mowry. 1990. Domestic disturbance danger rate. *Journal of Police Science and Administration* 174: 244–49.

Uchida, C., L. Brooks, and C. Koper. 1987. Danger to police during domestic encounters: Assaults on Baltimore County police. *Criminal Justice Policy Review* 2: 357–71.

Wilson, L., and C. Meyer. Violence at the street level: Police casualties and fatalities. *The Police Journal* 64: 28–45.

ACCOUNTABILITY

The power of police in any society is derived from the communities they serve. The public invests responsibility in its police to enforce the laws and, in some rare cases, to use force against citizens. This is an extremely important set of responsibilities that police must use with caution and care. In cases where police overstep their responsibilities and engage in misconduct, they can be removed from their positions and, in the most extreme cases, prosecuted for violating the law. The major way in which citizens ensure that police are exercising their responsibilities within the parameters set by the community is through police accountability measures.

Samuel Walker, one of the leading researchers of police accountability, describes two main levels at which the police can be held accountable: the *individual* level where police officers are held accountable for their actions and the *organizational* level where law enforcement agencies are held accountable for the services they deliver to their communities. Additionally, within each of these levels there are two main avenues for ensuring police accountability. Community members or other government actors may act through *external* mechanisms, while departmental leadership and supervisors may target *internal* influences (Walker 2005). A number of models or practices are being used in each area by law enforcement agencies across the country. In the following sections, we review some of the most promising of these models.

External Police Integrity

Citizen Involvement Models

Citizen involvement models refer to organizational accountability bodies, composed wholly or in part of citizens, that provide some level of oversight over police operations. Traditionally, citizen involvement models have focused on how police departments investigate complaints filed by citizens against officers. In recent years, however, some citizen involvement models have expanded their focus to include overseeing use-of-force investigations, issuing annual reports, providing outreach to citizens in the community, facilitating mediation between police and citizens, and providing policy analysis of local police policies.

There are roughly four different types of citizen review agencies that engage in varying levels of involvement in the police complaint investigation process (Bobb 2003; Finn 2001; Walker 2001). Although scholars and justice professionals vary in the ways in which they classify each model, the types of models generally include the following categories:

- *External citizen oversight models.* These organizations are generally separate from the police department, with offices in a separate location. They often take citizen complaints and perform their own investigations. Many of these organizations are composed entirely of private citizens, although some also have police employees play a role in the process.
- *External auditors/ombudsman.* These organizations are usually led by a single individual who is an employee of the city, county, or state and is not affiliated with the police. This individual has access to and may audit police investigations. In some cases this individual may participate in the investigation by asking additional questions or requesting to speak with different witnesses. The auditor/ombudsman evaluates the investigation as it unfolds and can request that the police conduct an additional investigation.
- *Appellate review models.* These organizations generally review the complaints that citizens file against the police once the internal affairs office

has made a finding on the complaint. They serve as a way in which individuals who file a complaint can appeal the findings of the police department. However, their review is limited to the process of the investigation itself; they generally have limited powers and do not conduct their own investigations.

- *Hybrid models.* These organizations contain different elements from several of the models.

There is no one national model of citizen involvement. Rather citizen participation models are organic, emerging from a host of local variables, and the model is largely dependent on the police and the community and the history of the relationship between these two groups. Luna and Walker (2000) have posited that different cities throughout the United States have created models of citizen participation not from trying to replicate a specific model but through focusing on the local aspects of the community. They characterize the development of these other models as "an ad hoc experimental" process that "reflect[s] . . . the vagaries of local leadership and political compromise" (p. 88). Therefore, different models across the country have different levels of power and different functions that reflect local community expectations.

Consent Decrees

During the past decade, more than twenty police departments have entered into consent decrees with the U.S. Department of Justice after they were found to have fostered a "pattern or practice" of civil rights violations. A consent decree is a settlement agreement entered into by the "consent" of the party subject to its terms. The decree is submitted in writing to a court and gains legal authority once approved by a judge. These settlements are the result of federal investigations into allegations of ongoing civil rights violations by the departments. Consent decrees are intended to promote organizational accountability by providing agencies with the incentive to avoid litigation by implementing what are considered "best practices" in the field. These can include such initiatives as enhancement of use-of-force policies and the implementation of an early intervention system.

Once a police agency enters into a consent decree, it is obligated to take specific steps involving policy and practice, as described in the decree, so that the agency comes into compliance with the law. For example, the consent decree the New Jersey State Police entered into in 1999 mandated policy changes to specifically proscribe the use of race, national, or ethnic characteristics to make traffic stops; to document traffic stops and provide supervisory review of individual traffic stops and of patterns of conduct; to conduct comprehensive investigations into allegations of misconduct; to improve training for recruits and incumbent troopers; to submit to auditing by the New Jersey attorney general; to issue regular reports on certain law enforcement activities; and to be evaluated by a court-appointed monitor. Other departments that have entered into consent decrees during the past ten years include the Pittsburgh Police Bureau, Pennsylvania; Steubenville Police Department, Ohio; and Los Angeles Police Department, California (U.S. Department of Justice 2006b).

Use-of-Force Reporting

Among topics of police accountability, officer use of force has attracted the most attention. The authority to use physical coercion and deadly force distinguishes the police from other types of organizations. Despite the consequences for citizens when this authority is misused or abused, use of force has only been subject to meaningful organizational constraints since the 1970s, before which most police agencies did not have policies governing officers' use of force or the collection of data on use of force.

Only relatively recently have police received training and guidance in how they use force on the job (Walker 2005). The policy developed in 1972 by the New York City Police Department (NYPD) provided an original model for other departments. The NYPD made several important decisions, which included a clarification of the rules for when the use of force is appropriate, changing the standard from when a felon is fleeing to when force must be used in defense of the officer's or another person's life. Rules about discharging weapons were also restricted. Officers could not fire warning shots, shoot to wound, or shoot at or from a moving vehicle (Walker 2005).

In an overview of prior studies of use of force, McEwen (1996) notes that "the research over the last 30 years . . . consistently calls for improved data collection at the local and national level" (p. 26). The Violent Crime Control and Law Enforcement Act of 1994 represents the first effort to do so nationally, providing the attorney general with the authority to bring litigation against agencies engaging in a "pattern or practice" of civil rights violations. This legislation also requires the attorney general to "acquire data about the use of excessive force by law enforcement officers" and "publish an annual summary of the data acquired."

In response to this mandate, in 1995 the National Institute of Justice (NIJ) and Bureau of Justice Statistics (BJS) convened a workshop to discuss how best to collect data on excessive use of force. Participants, which included police practitioners, lawyers, researchers, and civilians, noted that there was no single accepted definition of what constitutes "excessive force." The legal test, which comes from the 1985 U.S. Supreme Court case *Tennessee v. Garner*, limits the use of deadly force to when "it is necessary to prevent the escape and the officer to believe that the suspect poses a

significant threat of death or serious physical injury to the officer or others." However, the policies and procedures developed to comply with these requirements differ widely.

Another important issue raised concerned the lack of a single source of information (e.g., court records, citizen complaints, police reports) that would provide the complete picture (McEwen 1996). Additionally, participants agreed that data collection should include incidents of police use of force in general rather than the limited scope of excessive force (McEwen 1996). Following the workshop, the NIJ and BJS jointly funded the International Association of Chiefs of Police (IACP) to develop a National Police Use of Force Database. Because of the sensitivity of the subject, data contributions would be voluntary and anonymous to promote participation and accurate reporting (Henriquez 1999).

As agencies continue to implement use-of-force policies, these policies have developed in four important ways: Written policies cover an increasing range of actions, the content of policies has become increasingly detailed, the review of use-of-force reports is the subject of greater attention, and increasingly departments are analyzing use-of-force reports in the aggregate to determine if patterns exist (Walker 2005). In particular, report and review has become the best practice for critical incidents, defined by Walker (2005) as "any police action that has a potentially adverse effect on the life, liberty, or dignity or a citizen" (p. 44).

Practitioners and researchers increasingly understand police–citizen encounters as fluid and composed of multiple stages that can be analyzed and prepared for. De-escalation techniques such as "verbal judo" and training and policies on responding to people with mental disorders are examples of efforts to control proactively the outcome of situations. Today, departments use a force continuum to train officers to apply force in a way that approximately matches the level of resistance offered by the suspect and changes incrementally based on how the interaction progresses. Some researchers (e.g., Alpert and Dunham 1999; Terrill et al. 2003; Terrill 2005) are working to improve the analytical and training capabilities of the force continuum.

Internal Police Integrity

COMPSTAT

COMPSTAT, which stands for computer-driven statistics, has been described as "a goal-oriented strategic management process that uses computer technology, operational strategy and managerial accountability to structure the manner in which a police department provides crime-control services" (Walsh 2001). After developing the fundamentals of the system while chief of the New York City Transit Police, William Bratton introduced COMPSTAT to the NYPD when he became commissioner in 1994. Many departments throughout the country have implemented COMPSTAT-type systems. COMPSTAT has since rapidly diffused through larger police departments (Weisburd et al. 2003).

COMPSTAT employs geographic information systems (GIS) and crime analysis to provide a data-driven and visual representation of a particular problem in a timely manner so that an intervention can be crafted in real time. The system is meant to promote accountability through the focused use of these data in regular police staff meetings. In these meetings, those in leadership positions are held accountable for addressing problems within their area of geographic responsibility. The emphasis of COMPSTAT is on assisting mangers to deploy rapid follow-up to the problems in their patrol beats and to then address those efforts in these regular meetings.

Departments using COMPSTAT may note the difference in where COMPSTAT locates responsibility for problem solving as opposed to its locus in community policing. Whereas community policing seeks to empower the patrol officer because of his or her proximity to the street, many departments using COMPSTAT programs give responsibility for problem prioritization and strategy to supervisors and managers, who, its proponents argue, possess the experience and resources to marshal change. It is then up to the local manager to identify the best approach to solving the problem that has been identified.

Some observers (e.g., Scott 2000) have noted that COMPSTAT's effectiveness is highly dependent on how it is practiced. Overreliance on technology, to the detriment of both analytical thinking and selection by commanders of problems from a "limited and conventional set" of responses (e.g., increased patrol), is not the problem-solving capability touted by the system's proponents. Some police practitioners note that their daily routine has been completely co-opted by COMPSTAT. Departments with strong unions may face obstacles when implementing meaningful accountability measures, although some police executives have come up with creative alternatives. Anecdotal evidence also indicates that COMPSTAT meetings must find a happy medium between an accountability-free staff meeting and a gratuitously harsh or demeaning atmosphere that many COMPSTAT programs have embraced (Dewan 2004). Although the pressure to produce results is great, COMPSTAT's advocates argue that accountability should address the quality of the efforts made in targeting a problem, not its amelioration.

Early Intervention Systems

Early intervention (EI) systems are computer programs that provide police administrators with the ability to monitor officer performance across a variety of fields.

The two types of EI systems are the Comprehensive Personnel Assessment System (CPAS) and the Performance Problem System (Walker 2005). The first system collects information from a wide range of fields and, as a result, provides a window into a broad variety of performance issues. However, these systems need a "sophisticated technological infrastructure and an enormous amount of administrative oversight" (Walker 2005, 105). The Performance Problem System, on the other hand, collects information from a smaller set of fields and provides a more limited view of officer performance. This system is easier to manage, is less expensive, and requires less technological support than the CPAS.

The origin of the EI system derives from the long-held, but previously little tested, belief that a small number of officers are responsible for the majority of complaints made against a police department (Walker 2005). During the 1970s, some departments began to track officers who used force on the job, especially those involved in shootings. Several controversial incidents between police officers and racial minorities also served as precipitating events (Walker 2005). One such event occurred in Miami-Dade, Florida, in 1980 when four police officers beat to death an African American citizen, Arthur McDuffie, and significant community violence ensued. Following the violence, a local ordinance directed Miami-Dade to create the Employee Profile System to allow for a detailed examination of each officer (Walker 2005).

Another controversial incident occurred in Los Angeles in 1991 when, at the end of a pursuit, police officers beat Rodney King, an unarmed motorist who resisted arrest. Examining the Los Angeles Police Department (LAPD), the Christopher Commission found that forty-four officers accounted for a high percentage of complaints and that all of these officers could be identified through readily available forms of data. Despite the fact that a system could be constructed to track these data, the LAPD did not develop an EI system. The next year the Kolt Commission found exactly the same situation with sixty-seven deputies in the Los Angeles County Sheriff's Office. In this case, however, the Sheriff's Office did develop an early intervention system in response.

Originally, EI systems were referred to as early warning (EW) systems. The original terminology bothered many officers, because it had "a negative connotation" (Walker 2005, 102), making it sound as if these systems focused on singling out officers for discipline. The name change also emphasizes that the EI system is intended as a tool for supervisors to use to spot officers who may be engaging in potentially problematic behavior and intervene before there is a larger problem—not to impose discipline. Specifically, the EI system is "intended to highlight poor officer performance and provide a system to correct behavior, thus potentially saving a career rather than destroying one" (Davis et al. 2002, 25). These systems track police performance in a variety of areas in addition to use of force. Moreover, some of these systems have the ability to examine officers who are performing their jobs better than their peers in addition to those officers perhaps engaged in troublesome behaviors (Davis et al. 2002).

The EI system uses a two-step process: identification and selection. Identification occurs when an officer is flagged by the system. At this point, the system has merely identified the officer for the supervisor to take a closer look at so the supervisor can determine whether there is reason for concern. This occurs when an officer reaches a threshold in one or a combination of the fields (e.g., citizen complaints, use-of-force incidents, line-of-duty injuries). The supervisor looks at official records of the tasks that the officer does during his or her shift, discretionary decisions that involve controversial actions (e.g., use of force), and personnel records (e.g., how many sick days the officer has taken). As an extra level of supervision, the administrator examines "the context of an officer's work assignment and performance history" to identify possible counter-explanations for the officer being selected by the EI system (Walker 2005, 111). The second step, selection, refers to the act of the supervisor's decision to intervene. At this phase, the supervisor determines that there is a reason to intervene and take action with the officer. Importantly, it is the *supervisor* rather than the EI system making the determination of whether some sort of intervention is necessary.

Officers who are selected enter into the intervention stage. The intervention stage is important because it is "where the department delivers the 'treatment' designed to improve an officer's performance" (Walker 2005, 116). Despite its importance, however, the intervention stage has received scant attention from researchers and practitioners (Walker 2005). Once the intervention is administered, the department often monitors the officer.

The EI system has two additional functions besides merely identifying problematic behavior from officers (Walker 2005). First, EI systems communicate to officers that their behavior on the job is being monitored and that the department will hold them accountable for their work performance. Second, in some EI systems, officers have access to observe their score. In these systems, officers can observe their performance and take action in advance to enhance their performance and bring it into compliance with the threshold of their fellow officers.

In-Car Video

The introduction of in-car video (ICV) units into police departments represents a potentially exciting advance in police supervision. The ICV system is a video camera system mounted in the patrol car for the purpose of filming police–citizen contacts—including criminal incidents, car accidents, and drunk driving arrests—and

for offering increased protection to both officers and citizens. The ICV also provides supervisors with access to the decision making that officers conduct during the delivery of police services to citizens.

The literature traces the first experimental uses of cameras to record police–citizen contacts to the mid-1980s (Kubiovak 1997; Schrest et al. 1990). Schrest et al. note that in 1984 police administrators began to consider outfitting patrol cars with cameras after an analysis of *Uniform Crime Reports* (UCR) data found that four out of every five officers attacked (both fatally and nonfatally) had been on uniformed patrol. The ICV unit was suggested as a reactive tool to serve as a means of capturing police assaults on video so that the assailant could eventually be held criminally responsible (Liquori and Perry 1988, 35, in Schrest et al. 1990).

Despite the interest in equipping patrol cars with cameras, police departments still faced barriers when trying to implement ICV units. In particular, ICV systems were unfeasible due to the technological limitations of the time—large cameras that recorded poorly (Schrest et al. 1990). Police departments also faced financial constraints (Schrest et al. 1990). One agency, the Georgia Department of Public Safety, funded their ICV unit through a partnership with the Drug Enforcement Administration that provided them with federal money and money from drug seizures (Johnson 1992). Improvements in technology and the decrease in cost have now made ICV units a viable tool for many police departments.

The ICV assists law enforcement officers in the performance of their job by recording evidence, police–citizen interactions, and criminal incidents or investigations that result in arrest. The units are ideal for creating an "objective" record of drug seizures and automobile accidents to supplement the written police report (Cook 1993; Pilant 1995). Johnson (1992) reports that Georgia had a 100% conviction rate for drug-related cases after implementing their ICV system. Additionally, should the police incident report be called into question, police departments can provide the video record of the original incident (Vetterli 1996). Ultimately, this "objective record" of the incident serves as a check on the accuracy and veracity of a police report.

In particular, the ICV unit is also well suited for capturing officer–citizen interactions during traffic patrol (Pilant 1995). Police officers can record traffic incidents in two ways (Maxfield and Andresen 2001). First, when a police officer turns on his patrol lights to signal a motorist to pull over to the side of the road, the camera automatically begins filming. The camera records the officer–citizen interaction until the officer turns off the camera. This allows a supervisor to examine the officer's manner of interacting with a citizen in a particular stop. Second, a police officer can film the offender actually committing the traffic offense by manually activating the camera before turning on his police lights. In recording a traffic offense, an objective record of the infraction is created for the officer and supervisor to examine later. In certain cases, officers have taken the additional step of providing voiceover narration as the event unfolds, thereby indicating in word and on video his or her reasons for stopping the motorist (Maxfield and Andresen 2001).

It is important to remember that the ICV unit is still only a tool, useful in specific situations. Though the ICV unit shows promise for improving certain aspects of police work, it is clearly inappropriate for some police operations. For example, since the camera is mounted, or at least located, in the patrol car, officers on foot patrol cannot use an ICV unit (Pilant 1995). Also, the fixed location of the camera makes the ICV unit ineffective for incidents that occur off of roadways, such as those that are the result of police calls for service and where officers leave their cars and travel outside the view of the camera and out of range of the microphone. Finally,

initial experiences with these systems have found their use as a training tool to be limited. Few agencies with ICV systems have supervisors regularly monitor the tapes of their reporting officers, so to date many of the ongoing training opportunities associated with ICV have been unfulfilled.

External versus Internal Models

Many law enforcement agencies utilize both external and internal models of ensuring police accountability. While effective internal systems reduce the demand for external models of law enforcement oversight, it appears to be the case that a blend of internal and external models offers an agency the best approach for monitoring its officers and ensuring members of the community that they are receiving enforcement efforts in the most fair and equitable manner.

Supervision

The key to the effectiveness of any of the police accountability models cited above is the role of the supervisor. The first-level supervisor must be trained and inclined to use the information that comes from these various models to influence the behavior of her or his officers. Initial training is essential because in many law enforcement agencies training in employee supervision is extremely limited when officers are promoted to supervisory positions. In many cases officers simply try to replicate the behavior of their prior supervisors whom they respected.

In the area of police accountability, the role of the supervisor is critical. When supervisors ignore difficult employees or fail to effectively intervene in cases of employee misconduct, the resulting situation not only affects the future behavior of that employee but negatively affects the attitudes and orientation of all employees, who quickly identify a double standard between what an organization says are its values and policies and what happens to employees who fail to carry out these policies or reflect the organizational values.

JACK MCDEVITT, RUSSELL WOLFF, and W. CARSTEN ANDRESEN

See also **Abuse of Authority by Police; Civilian Review Boards; Codes of Ethics; COMPSTAT; Corruption; Deadly Force; Deviant Subcultures in Policing; Discretion; Ethics and Values in the Context of Community Policing; Excessive Force; Integrity in Policing; Performance Measurement; Professionalism**

References and Further Reading

Alpert, G. P., and R. G. Dunham. 1999. The force factor: Measuring and assessing police use of force and suspect resistance. In *use of force by police: Overview of national and local data*. Washington, DC: National Institute of Justice and Bureau of Justice Statistics.

Bobb, M. 2003. *Civilian oversight of the police in the United States*. Paper presented at Global Meeting on Civilian Oversight of Police, Rio de Janeiro.

Cook, V. O., Jr. 1993. Improving the capability to monitor police field behavior. *Journal of California Law Enforcement* 26: 29–31.

Davis, R. C., C. Ortiz, N. J. Henderson, J. Miller, and M. K. Massie. 2002. *Turning necessity into virtue: Pittsburgh's experience with a federal consent decree*. New York: Vera Institute of Justice.

Dewan, S. K. 2004. New York's gospel of policing by data spreads across U.S. *New York Times*, April 28.

Finn, P. 2001. *Citizen review of police: Approaches and implementation*. Washington, DC: National Institute of Justice.

Henriquez, M. A. 1999. IACP national database project on police use of force. In *Use of force by police: Overview of national and local data*. Washington, DC: National Institute of Justice and Bureau of Justice Statistics.

Johnson, J. M. 1992. *The Georgia State Patrol's in-car video system*. Lexington, KY: Council of State Governments.

Kuboviak, J. 1997. *Legal application of mobile videotaping to criminal interdiction patrol*. Jacksonville, FL: Institute of Police Technology and Management.

Liquori, W., and J. Perry. 1988. The video observer: A friend on the side of law enforcement. *The Florida Police Chief*, February, 35–41.

Luna, E., and S. Walker. 2000. Institutional structure vs. political will: Albuquerque as a case study in the effectiveness of citizen oversight of the police. In *Civilian oversight of police: Governance, democracy and human rights*, ed. A. J. Goldsmith and C. Lewis, 83–104. Oxford: Hart Publishing.

Maxfield, M. G., and W. C. Andresen. 2001. *Evaluation of New Jersey State Police in-car mobile video recording system*. Unpublished draft final report, New Jersey Department of Law and Public Safety.

McEwen, T. 1996. *National data collection on police use of force*. Washington, DC: Bureau of Justice Statistics and National Institute of Justice.

Pilant, L. 1995. In-car video systems. *Police Chief* 62 (4): 30–37.

Racial Profiling Data Collection Resource Center. 2006. *Legislation and litigation: DOJ investigations*. Boston: Institute on Race and Justice, Northeastern University. http://www.racialprofilinganalysis.neu.edu (accessed February 7, 2006).

Schrest, D. K., W. Liquori, and J. Perry. 1990. Using video technology in police patrol. In *The media and criminal justice policy: Recent research and social effects*, ed. Ray Surette. Springfield, OH: Charles C Thomas.

Scott, M. 2000. *Problem-oriented policing: Reflections on the first 20 years*. Office of Community-Oriented Policing Services.

Tennessee v. Garner, 471 U.S. 1 (1985).

Terrill, W. 2005. Police use of force: A transactional approach. *Justice Quarterly* 22: 107–38.

Terrill, W., G. P. Alpert, R. G. Dunham, and M. R. Smith. 2003. A management tool for evaluating police use of force: An application of the force factor. *Police Quarterly* 6: 150–171.

U.S. Department of Justice, Civil Rights Division, Special Litigation Section. 2006. *Conduct of law enforcement agencies settlements and court decisions*. http://www.usdoj.gov/crt/split/findsettle.htm#Settlements (accessed February 7, 2006).

———. 2006. *Frequently asked questions*. http://www.usdoj.gov/crt/split/faq.htm#pppmp.htm (accessed February 7, 2006).

Vetterli, G. 1996. In-car video provides ultimate back-up. *Law and Order* 44: 196.

Violent Crime Control and Law Enforcement Act of 1994 (P.L. 103-322).

Walker, S. 2001. *Police accountability: The role of citizen oversight.* Belmont, CA: Wadsworth.

———. 2005. *The new world of police accountability.* Thousand Oaks, CA: Sage.

Walsh, W. F. 2001. COMPSTAT: An analysis of an emerging police managerial paradigm. *Policing: An International Journal of Police Strategies and Management* 24: 347–62.

Weisburd, D., S. D. Mastrofsky, A. M. McNally, R. Greenspan, and J. J. Willis. 2003. Reforming to preserve: COMPSTAT and strategic problem solving in American policing. *Criminology and Public Policy* 2: 421–56.

ADMINISTRATION OF POLICE AGENCIES, THEORIES OF

Theories of police administration have been largely derived from the more general fields of organization theory, public administration, and business administration. Police administration textbooks and training programs have changed over the years, sometimes in response to new developments in the practice of police administration, and sometimes in response to new ideas and concepts from research and literature. Today, several approaches can be identified that differ primarily in the emphasis they give to particular components of police administration and factors affecting police organizations.

The Classical Approach

The classical approach to police administration dominated textbooks and training into the 1960s; it was and is closely associated with the professional model of policing and probably still has more influence over practice than any other. This approach is best illustrated by the pioneering textbooks *Police Administration* (first edition by O. W. Wilson, 1950) and *Municipal Police Administration* (1938, edited under the general direction of the International City Management Association; now re-titled *Local Government Police Management*). The classical approach emphasizes structure and management: organizational principles (unity of command, chain of command, delegation of authority), management functions (planning, directing, controlling), and functional components of policing (patrol administration, traffic supervision, jail management).

The classical approach remains popular and influential today for several reasons. It provides the most straightforward approach to holding police officers accountable. It is at the heart of the law enforcement agency accreditation program now in its third decade of operation. It is the primary means of risk management for minimizing a police agency's civil liability exposure. It has been encouraged by developments in administrative law that require more and more documentation in support of disciplinary actions. It is consistent with the Incident Command System (ICS) and National Incident Management System (NIMS) that are being federally mandated for response to major homeland security crises, and it provides an appearance, at least, of close control over police power and discretion that is comforting to citizens and police administrators alike.

The Human Relations Approach

The human relations approach was developed as an alternative to the classical approach when research and experience demonstrated that the performance of people in organizations was significantly affected by attitudes, feelings, beliefs, peer pressure, and organizational culture—not just structure, principles, and functions. The human relations approach came to dominate police administration textbooks and training, although its impact on actual police management is harder to gauge.

The underlying rationale is that the performance of a police organization is almost entirely a function of people productivity and that police management is almost entirely people management. The approach focuses on morale, communications, motivation, group dynamics, and leadership. Most of the police administration textbooks published since 1970 place substantial emphasis on the human relations approach.

In recent decades, police agencies have shown considerable interest in a variety of popular management techniques affiliated with the human relations approach, including situational leadership, effective habits of leaders, quality circles, principles of excellence, management by values, and total quality management. The rise of community policing also gave a push to the human relations approach to police administration. Community policing tends to advocate extending police officer discretion, encouraging officers to work closely with the public, and expecting officers to implement creative solutions to community problems. Some police executives have argued that police management must establish better human relations in its dealings with its own employees before it can reasonably expect those employees to treat the public with increased care and respect, let alone innovation and creativity.

The Strategic Management Approach

The strategic management approach to police administration emphasizes objectives, tasks, and resources. Police administration is conceived primarily as a rational adaptation of means to ends, of planning and designing tasks that will lead to the achievement of organizational objectives. Police evaluation research, exemplified by the Kansas City Preventive Patrol Experiment, the RAND study of criminal investigation, and the PERF study of police response time, focused on police operational tasks and their effectiveness and gave rise to such programs as "Managing Patrol Operations," "Managing Criminal Investigations," and "Differential Police Response Strategies." More recently, community policing, problem-oriented policing, COMPSTAT, and intelligence-led policing have emerged as leading new police strategies.

The strategic management approach gained considerable stature during the last two decades as resource constraints forced police administrators to focus more and more on the efficiency and effectiveness of police programs and strategies. The "Perspectives on Policing" series prepared at Harvard University and distributed by the National Institute of Justice was influential in popularizing this approach, as were the books *Beyond 911: A New Era for Policing* (Sparrow et al. 1990) and *Beyond Command and Control: The Strategic Management of Police Departments* (Moore and Stephens 1991). The heightened concern over efficiency and effectiveness has greatly elevated the roles of policy analysis, program evaluation, and other analytical aspects of police administration. Most recently, the "Measuring What Matters" program has focused attention on the importance of specifying and then measuring the most important services and outcomes of police agencies. The book *Recognizing Value in Policing: The Challenge of Measuring Police Performance* (Moore et al. 2002) represents this approach.

The Institutional Approach

The institutional approach to police administration emphasizes the external environment of police organizations, policy making, and decision making more than internal management duties. The two books that best illustrate this approach are Herman Goldstein's *Policing a Free*

Society (1977) and the anthology *Police Leadership in America* (Geller 1985). These books consider the police administrator's external relations with political leaders, city managers, the media, labor unions, and community groups. They also emphasize such matters as defining the police function, developing alternatives to formal legal processing, and structuring police discretion, all of which are extremely important in the big picture of executing government policy, but are likely to be overlooked when the focus is exclusively on the internal management of the police department.

One contemporary issue that illustrates the value of the institutional approach is racial profiling. The classical approach might respond to racial profiling with a rule prohibiting discrimination and increased supervision to discourage it. The human relations approach might tend to rely on sensitivity or diversity training for officers to change their attitudes and beliefs. The strategic management approach might analyze tactics and strategies in order to identify one, perhaps community policing, that would produce fewer complaints and more nuanced police service. The institutional approach would tend to focus on policies and training that guide officer decision making about how to choose vehicles and pedestrians to stop and how to decide when to search people and cars. These are discretionary decisions made by individual officers day in and day out, and in many police departments they are not guided to any significant degree by clear policies, training, or other guidelines. As a result, in many departments, stops and searches are carried out by individual officers based on inconsistent criteria, resulting in under-policing, overpolicing, and/or patterns of discrimination. The institutional approach recognizes the importance of the cumulative impact of these individual decisions and specifically tries to structure discretion in order to achieve more consistency and less discrimination.

Conclusion

The theoretical and practical emphases of police administration have evolved over the years. Initial reform efforts stressed professional administration, structure, and control based on the classical approach to administration. In the 1960s, increasing attention was paid to improving police performance through inspired leadership and paying attention to employee needs—the human relations approach. In recent years increased emphasis has been placed on improving the effectiveness of police tactics and strategies and on the police agency's relations with its external environment—the strategic management and institutional approaches. More attention is still needed on the institutional approach's focus on structuring discretion. Also needed are textbooks and training programs that effectively integrate all of these approaches into a more comprehensive treatment of the theory and practice of police administration.

GARY CORDNER

See also **Accountability; Intelligence-Led Policing and Organizational Learning; Police Chief Executive; Problem-Oriented Policing; Professionalism; Wilson, O. W.**

References and Further Reading

Cordner, G. W., K. E. Scarborough, and R. Sheehan. 2004. *Police administration.* 5th ed. Cincinnati, OH: Anderson/Lexis-Nexis.

Fyfe, J. J., J. R. Greene, W. F. Walsh, O. W. Wilson, and R. C. McLaren. 1997. *Police administration.* 5th ed. New York: McGraw-Hill.

Geller, W. A., ed. 1985. *Police leadership in America: Crisis and opportunity.* New York: Praeger.

Geller, W. A., and D. W. Stephens, eds. 2003. *Local government police management.* 4th ed. Washington, DC: International City Management Association.

Goldstein, H. 1977. *Policing a free society.* Cambridge, MA: Ballinger.

Moore, M. H., and D. W. Stephens. 1991. *Beyond command and control: The strategic management of police departments.* Washington, DC: Police Executive Research Forum.

Moore, M. H., with D. Thatcher, A. Dodge, and T. Moore. 2002. *Recognizing value in policing: The challenge of measuring police performance.* Washington, DC: Police Executive Research Forum.

Roberg, R. R., J. Kuykendall, and K. Novak. 2002. *Police management.* 3rd ed. Los Angeles: Roxbury Publishing.

Sparrow, M. K., M. H. Moore, and D. M. Kennedy. 1990. *Beyond 911: A new era for policing.* New York: Basic Books.

Swanson, C. R., L. Territo, and R. W. Taylor. 2005. *Police administration: Structures, processes, and behavior.* Upper Saddle River, NJ: Pearson Prentice Hall.

AGE AND CRIME

The relationship between aging and criminal activity has been noted since the beginnings of criminology. For example, Adolphe Quetelet (1833) found that the proportion of the population involved in crime tends to peak in adolescence or early adulthood and then decline with age. This age–crime relationship is remarkably similar across historical periods, geographic locations, and crime types. That the impact of age on criminal involvement is one of the strongest factors associated with crime has prompted the controversial claim that the age–crime relationship is invariant (Hirschi and Gottfredson 1983). However, considerable variation exists among offenses and across historical periods in specific features of the age–crime relationship (for example, peak age, median age, rate of decline from peak age). A claim of "invariance" in the age–crime relationship therefore overstates the case (Steffensmeier et al. 1989).

Arrest data from the FBI's *Uniform Crime Reports* (UCR) on ordinary crimes (e.g., robbery, assault, burglary, larceny-theft, auto theft) document the robustness of the age effect on crime and also reveal a long-term trend toward *younger* age–crime distributions in more modern times. Today, the peak age (the age group with the highest age-specific arrest rate) is younger than twenty-five for most crimes reported in the FBI's UCR program, and rates begin to decline in the late teenage years for more than half of the UCR crimes. The *National Crime Victimization Survey* (NCVS), self-report studies of juvenile and adult criminality, and interview data from convicted felons also corroborate the robust effect of age on crime patterns (Rowe and Tittle 1977; Elliott et al. 1983).

Explaining Youthful Offending

A variety of social, cognitive, and physical factors can help explain the rapid rise in age-specific rates of offending around mid-adolescence. Teenagers generally lack strong bonds to conventional adult institutions, such as work and family (Warr 1998). At the same time, teens are faced with strong potential rewards for offending: money, status, power, autonomy, identity claims, strong sensate experiences stemming from sex, natural adrenaline highs or highs from illegal substances, and respect from similar peers (Wilson and Herrenstein 1985; Steffensmeier et al. 1989). Further, their dependent status as juveniles insulates teens from many of the social and legal costs of illegitimate activities, and their stage of cognitive development limits prudence concerning the consequences of their behavior. At the same time, they possess the physical prowess required to commit crimes. Finally, a certain amount of misbehavior is often seen as natural to youth and seen as simply a stage of growing up (Jolin and Gibbons 1987; Hagan et al. 1998).

For those in late adolescence or early adulthood (roughly ages seventeen to twenty-two, the age group showing the sharpest decline in arrest rates for many crimes), important changes occur in at least six spheres of life (Steffensmeier et al. 1989):

1. *Greater access to legitimate sources of material goods and excitement:* jobs, credit, alcohol, sex, etc.
2. *Patterns of illegitimate opportunities:* with the assumption of adult roles, opportunities increase for crimes (for example, gambling, fraud, and employee theft) that are less risky, more lucrative, or less likely to be reflected in official statistics.
3. *Peer associations and lifestyle:* reduced orientation to same-age–same-sex peers and increased orientation toward persons of the opposite sex or persons who are older or more mature.
4. *Cognitive and analytical skill development*, leading to a gradual decline in egocentrism, hedonism, and sense of invincibility; becoming more concerned for others, more accepting of social values, more comfortable in social relations, and more concerned with the meaning of life and their place of things; and seeing their casual delinquencies of youth as childish or foolish.
5. *Increased legal and social costs for deviant behavior.*
6. *Age-graded norms:* externally, increased expectation of maturity and responsibility; internally, anticipation of assuming adult roles, coupled with reduced subjective acceptance of deviant roles and the threat they pose to entering adult status.

As young people move into adulthood or anticipate entering it, most find their bonds to conventional society strengthening, with expanded access to work or further education and increased interest in "settling down." Leaving high school, finding employment, going to college, enlisting in the military, and getting married all tend to increase informal social controls and integration into conventional society. In addition, early adulthood typically involves a change in peer associations and lifestyle

routines that diminish the opportunities for committing these offenses. Furthermore, at the same time when informal sanctions for law violation are increasing, potential legal sanctions increase substantially.

Variations in the Age Curve

Although crime tends to decline with age, substantial variation can be found in the parameters of the age–crime curve (such as peak age, median age, and rate of decline from peak age). "Flatter" age curves (i.e., those with an older peak age and/or a slower decline in offending rates among older age groups) are associated with at least two circumstances: (1) cultures and historical periods in which youth have greater access to legitimate opportunities and integration into adult society and (2) types of crime for which illegitimate opportunities increase rather than diminish with age.

Cross-Cultural and Historical Differences

In nonindustrial societies, the passage to adult status is relatively simple and continuous. Formal rites of passage at relatively early ages avoid much of the status ambiguity and role conflict that torment modern adolescents in the developed world. Youths begin to assume responsible and economically productive roles well before they reach full physical maturity. It is not surprising, therefore, to find that such societies and time periods have significantly flatter and less skewed age–crime patterns (for a review, see Greenberg 1979; Steffensmeier and Allan 2000).

Much the same is true for earlier periods in the history of the United States and other industrial nations, when farm youth were crucial for harvesting crops and working-class children were expected to leave school at an early age and do their part in helping to support their families. By contrast, today teenagers typically work at marginal jobs that provide little self-pride or opportunities for adult mentorship, and instead segregate them in a separate peer culture. Although youth has always been seen as a turbulent time, social processes associated with the coming of industrialization and the postindustrial age have aggravated the stresses of adolescence, resulting in increased levels of juvenile criminality in recent decades. The structure of modern societies, therefore, encourages crime and delinquency among the young because these societies "lack institutional procedures for moving people smoothly from protected childhood to autonomous adulthood" (Nettler 1978, 241). Unfortunately, reliable age statistics on criminal involvement are not available over extended historical periods.

Crime Types

The offenses that show the youngest peaks and sharpest declines are crimes that fit the low-yield, criminal mischief, "hell-raising" category: vandalism, petty theft, robbery, arson, auto theft, burglary, and liquor law and drug violations. Personal crimes such as aggravated assault and homicide tend to have somewhat "older" age distributions (median age in the late twenties), as do some of the public order offenses, public drunkenness, and certain of the property crimes that juveniles have less opportunity to commit, like embezzlement, fraud, and gambling (median age in late twenties or thirties).

Older people may also shift to less visible criminal roles such as bookie or fence (Steffensmeier and Ulmer 2005). Or as a spinoff of legitimate roles, they may commit surreptitious crimes or crimes that, if discovered, are unlikely to be reported to the authorities, such as embezzlement, stock fraud, bribery, or price-fixing.

Unfortunately, we know relatively little about the age distribution of persons who commit these and related lucrative crimes, but the fragmentary evidence that does exist suggests that they are likely to be middle age or older (Shapiro 1984; Pennsylvania Crime Commission 1991). Evidence also suggests that the age curves for lucrative crimes in the underworld such as racketeering or loan-sharking not only peak much later but tend to decline more slowly with age (Steffensmeier and Allan 2000; Steffensmeier 1986).

Sex Differences in the Age–Crime Relationship

There appears to be considerable similarity in the age–crime relationship between males and females (Steffensmeier and Streifel 1991). To the extent that age differences between the sexes exists for certain crimes (e.g., prostitution), the tendency is for somewhat lower peak ages of offending among females—apparently because of their earlier physical maturity, the gendered age effects of marketability of sexual services, and the likelihood that young adolescent females might date and associate with older delinquent male peers. Also, the trend toward younger and more peaked age–crime distributions holds for both sexes.

"Aging Out" of Crime

Research suggests that exiting from a criminal career is more likely with the acquisition of meaningful bonds to conventional adult individuals and institutions such as a good job or strong adult relationship (Irwin 1970; Shover 1983, 1996). Other bonds that may lead people away from crime include involvement in religion, sports, hobbies, or other activities (Steffensmeier and Ulmer 2005). The development of conventional social bonds may be coupled with burnout or a belated deterrent effect as offenders grow tired of the hassles of repeated involvement with the criminal justice system and the hardships of a life of crime (Meisenhelder 1977; Shover 1983, 1996). They may also have experienced a long prison sentence that jolts them into quitting or that entails the loss of street contacts that make the successful continuation of a criminal career difficult. Or offenders may develop a fear of dying alone in prison, especially since repeated convictions yield longer sentences. Still other offenders may quit or "slow down" as they find their abilities and efficiency declining with increasing age, loss of "nerve," or sustained narcotics or alcohol use (Prus and Sharper 1977; Adler and Adler 1983; Shover 1983, 1996; Steffensmeier 1986; Steffensmeier and Ulmer 2005).

Older offenders who persist in crime are more likely to belong to the criminal underworld. These are individuals who are relatively successful in their criminal activities or who are extensively integrated into subcultural or family criminal enterprises. They seem to receive relational and psychic rewards (e.g., pride in their expertise) as well as monetary rewards from lawbreaking and, as a result, see no need to withdraw from lawbreaking (Steffensmeier and Ulmer 2005). Alternatively, such offenders may "shift and oscillate" back and forth between conventionality and lawbreaking, depending on shifting life circumstances and situational inducements to offend (Adler and Adler 1983; Adler 1993; Steffensmeier and Ulmer 2005). These older offenders are also unlikely to see many meaningful opportunities for themselves in the conventional or law-abiding world. Consequently, "the straight life" may have little to offer successful criminals, who will be more likely to persist in their criminality for an extended period. But they, too, may slow down eventually as they grow tired of the cumulative aggravations and risks of criminal involvement, or as they encounter the diminishing capacities associated with the aging process.

Conclusion

Age is a consistent predictor of crime, both in the aggregate and for individuals. The most common finding across countries, groups, and historical periods shows that crime—especially "ordinary" or "street" crime—tends to be a young person's activity. However, the age–crime relationship is not invariant; in fact, it varies in its specific features according to crime types, the structural position of groups, and historical and cultural contexts. On the other hand, relatively little is known about older chronic offenders. Clearly, the structure, dynamics, and contexts of offending among older individuals is a rich topic for future research.

DARRELL STEFFENSMEIER and
STEPHEN DEMUTH

See also **Elderly and Crime; Juvenile Crime and Criminalization; Juvenile Delinquency; Youth Gangs: Definitions**

References and Further Reading

Adler, P. 1996. *Wheeling and dealing: An ethnography of an upper level drug dealing and smuggling community*. New York: Columbia University Press.

Adler, P., and P. Adler. 1983. Shifts and oscillations in deviant careers: The case of upper-level drug dealers and smugglers. *Social Problems* 31: 195–207.

Akerstrom, M. 1985. *Crooks and squares: Lifestyles of thieves and addicts in comparison to conventional people*. Piscataway, NJ: Transaction.

Federal Bureau of Investigation. 1935–1997. *Crime in the United States*. Washington, DC: U.S. Government Printing Office.

Greenberg, D. 1979. Delinquency and the age structure of society. *Contemporary Crisis* 1: 66–86.

Hagan, J., G. Heffler, G. Classen, K. Boehnke, and H. Merkens. 1998. Subterranean sources of subcultural delinquency beyond the American dream. *Criminology* 36: 309–42.

Hirschi, T., and M. Gottfredson. 1983. Age and the explanation of crime. *American Journal of Sociology* 89: 522–84.

Jolin, A., and D. Gibbons. 1987. Age patterns in criminal involvement. *International Journal* of *Offender Therapy and Comparative Criminology* 31: 237–60.

Nettler, G. 1978. *Explaining crime*. New York: McGraw-Hill.

Pennsylvania Crime Commission. 1991. *1990 report—Organized crime in America: A decade of change*. Commonwealth of Pennsylvania.

Quetelet, A. 1833/1984. *Research on the propensity for crime at different ages*. Trans. S. Sylvester. Cincinnati, OH: Anderson Publishing Co.

Shapiro, S. 1984. *Wayward capitalists: Target of the Securities and Exchange Commission*. New Haven, CT: Yale University Press.

Shover, N. 1983. The later stages of ordinary property offender careers. *Social Problems, 30*, 208–218.

———. 1996. *Great pretenders: Pursuits and careers of persistent thieves*. Boulder, CO: Westview Press.

Steffensmeier, D. 1986. *The fence: In the shadow of two worlds*. Totowa, NJ: Rowman and Littlefield.

Steffensmeier, D., and E. Allan. 2000. Criminal behavior: Gender and age. In *Criminology: A contemporary handbook*, ed. J. Sheley, 83–114. Belmont, CA: Wadsworth.

Steffensmeier, D., A. Allan, M. Harer, and C. Streifel. 1989. Age and the distribution of crime. *American Journal of Sociology* 94: 803–31.

Steffensmeier, D., and C. Streifel. 1991. Age, gender, and crime across three historical periods: 1935, 1960, and 1985. *Social Forces* 69: 869–94.

Steffensmeier, D., and J. Ulmer. 2005. *Confessions of a dying thief: Understanding criminal careers and criminal enterprise*. New Brunswick, NJ: Aldine Transaction.

Warr, M. 1998. Life-course transitions and desistance from crime. *Criminology* 36: 183–216.

Wilson, J. Q., and R. Herrnstein. 1985. *Crime and human nature*. New York: Simon and Schuster.

AIRPORT SAFETY AND SECURITY

How safe are airports and commercial airplanes? The aftermath of the terrorist attacks on September 11, 2001, has shed light on the lax standards of airport safety and security throughout the United States. After all, the hijackers were able to board four different U.S. flights with box cutters either on their person or in their carry-on luggage. With these box cutters (which, prior to 9/11, would not commonly have been considered "weapons"), the terrorists were able to hijack four flights and ultimately kill thousands of innocent Americans. Since the tragic event, recommendations have been brought forth to help make airports safer and more secure. Proposals have included changes in training and staffing, restructuring airport access points, elevating standards and regulations, utilizing various technological advancements to detect explosives and weapons in baggage, and preventing unauthorized access to secure parts of airports, to name just a few. A combination of changes have been planned and implemented, ensuring a safer flying experience and greater airport safety at the growing number of airports throughout the United States.

The 9/11 terrorist attacks have prompted us to revisit airport safety and security standards from new perspectives and with the intent to employ an even more proactive approach to prevent attacks. Security prior to the attacks was much more lax in various ways. There was no requirement to screen all checked-in baggage on domestic flights. Additionally, there were no stringent restrictions preventing access to secure areas within airports. A number of reports indicated that individuals with fake badges were allowed access to secure areas seven out of ten times. Traffic control devices, plane cockpits, and facilities were not safe from attack. Criminal background checks and fingerprints were not always performed on flight crews and security workers employed by airports. Also, the screening of passengers and carry-on baggage failed to detect numerous threat objects. The crux of the problem was that there were no true uniform safety standards and security measures to begin with. Each airline carrier was given the responsibility of handling safety issues for itself, in some cases with a few loose guidelines set forth by individual airports. Generally, the airline carrier would either hire individual screeners or use a contracted security company. It is possible that a number of airline carriers (especially in times of low estimated threats) followed more lax safety standards in order to cut expenses, thereby increasing corporate profits.

Prior to the 9/11 attacks, and even thereafter in many instances, passenger screening consisted of three major components: X-ray machines, metal detectors, and manual baggage checks (the third for baggage that required extra attention). The X-ray machines that were utilized before and continued to be used after the hijackings were not capable of detecting every single type of threat object, because certain hazardous substances or objects may not have stood out as being suspicious. Metal detectors, likewise, failed to detect threat objects that were not made out of metal; plastic knives, for example, would easily pass through the metal detector. Finally, manual baggage checks, being the only human factor, led to many problems. Approximately 20% of all threat objects pass through manual baggage inspection unnoticed. Clearly, this percentage was found to be unsatisfactory by the Federal Aviation Administration (FAA).

There are a plethora of reasons for this unsatisfactory level of work. First and foremost, the screeners are essentially unskilled workers. By 2004, the turnover rate of screeners in the United States had risen to levels ranging from 100% to more than 400%, in comparison to Europe, which has had turnover rates ranging from 10% to 50%. Minimum wages and low benefits are partially accountable for this, as is the monotony of the job. Until screeners can maintain their positions, have adequate training, and gain experience in finding threat objects, less-than-optimal effectiveness will endure. On a positive note, according to the Transportation Security Administration (TSA), by December 2005, there were forty-three thousand newly classified transportation security officers trained to detect and combat terrorist threats deployed to all of the major airports and about four hundred TSA Explosives Detection Canine Teams deployed to more than eighty U.S. airports.

There are many ways in which airport security can be improved. In fact, many of these steps have already been taken. Incompetent passenger screeners can be replaced with more skilled screeners. Cockpit areas on aircrafts can be made secure with reinforced doors for the protection of the pilot and copilot. Pilots can be trained and licensed to carry firearms—by the end of 2005, about one-third of the pilots of commercial planes had been trained to carry firearms. More federal air marshals can be deployed for every flight. Airports can be restructured to promote safety. Most importantly, various technological advancements such as biometrics for airport access control and identification of authorized personnel can be employed, which would significantly increase airport safety and potentially expedite the screening process. Also, important is the training and deployment of Explosives Detection Canine Teams to all 420 commercial airports nationwide, not just to 80 or 85 airports at random.

In the wake of the September 11, 2001, terrorist attacks, action has been taken at the federal level to prevent such a tragedy from occurring again in the future. The Aviation and Transportation Act of November 2001 formed the Transportation Security Administration, which would be held responsible for overall mass transportation security. Since its creation, the TSA has come up with various ways to heighten security at airports throughout the United States.

So, what has the TSA done so far? By December 2002 the TSA had hired approximately 40,000 screeners to help make passenger screening more effective. By the following month, most "marked" bags (those that required additional security attention) were being screened. Technology to detect traces of explosives, or ETD, an acronym for Explosives Trace

Detection, has been utilized on 90% of all baggage. As of December 2005, as a result of increased training and enhanced standards, all forty thousand screeners hired since 2002 plus all three thousand newly hired screeners were reclassified as transportation security officers. Alternative measures such as canine explosive sniffing teams, hand searches and pat downs, and passenger–bag matches have also been randomly employed to ensure security. Additionally, the U.S. Air Marshal Program has been expanded, allowing for air marshals to be deployed on more commercial flights. Furthermore, approximately 98% of all commercial fleets have an approved design in place for the installation of secure cockpit doors; 80% of all commercial fleets already have this secure door installed. Air traffic control systems have been made more secure from attack and intrusion. All contractors are now required to have criminal history background checks performed. Air cargo safety is also on its way to heightened security. A database of known shippers is in the process of being compiled to increase the safety of the cargo being transported. General aviation, which encompasses private fleet and air travel, is also in the process of being scrutinized to increase security. Perimeter access to airports has also been under restriction. The number of access points in airports has been reduced. Background checks are now more frequently performed on airports workers.

Much is yet to come. The TSA has laid out a five-year plan covering the period from 2003 to 2008 to measure the effectiveness of the changes put into place. This plan includes both random and scheduled reviews of the security process, oversight of compliance with standards and regulations, the measure of performance against the standards set forth, and the collection and communication of performance data.

To address the competency of the passenger screeners, TSA is working on the Threat Image Projection (TIP) system.

The TIP system randomly places threat objects on the screen during actual passenger baggage screening to see if screeners are able to identify them. Once the screener "marks" the baggage for further security attention, he or she is informed that it was only a test. This system had actually been in place prior to the terrorist attacks but was halted in the effort to prevent screening delays. Overall, the TIP system is an excellent way to measure a screener's alertness and ability to identify threat objects.

The government is seeking to create uniformity in standards and training for all transportation screeners and security officers. An annual security officer recertification program is also under development for security personnel hired by the federal government. This program will measure the security officer/screener's ability to recognize images of threat objects, the screener's knowledge of standard operating procedures, as well as the screener's practical demonstration of these skills. For screeners other than those hired by the federal government, studies are being conducted to compare their ability in comparison with the ability of federally hired security officer-screeners. Screening companies will also have to measure up to federal performance standards and will be subject to automated readiness tests.

Another technology in the development stage is CAPPS II, also known as the Computer Assisted Passenger Prescreening System, which will replace the CAPPS system already in place. The system in place now was launched in 1998, operated by air carriers in conjunction with reservation systems. The original CAPPS system helps to identify high-risk passengers. Passengers who express strange or suspicious behavior are marked in the system as high risk (to be placed under a watchful eye from then on). Unfortunately, however, the system is now out of date and is difficult to modify. Many of the suspicious behavioral traits examined by the system have now become public knowledge, making the system less effective. The new CAPPS II program will be different from the existing system in quite a few ways. It will be government run, which will allow it to be more up to date and effective. CAPPS II will prescreen all passengers, tabulating a risk score for each. The system plans to increase the authenticity of identity, to prevent identity theft or fraud. Further, the system hopes to identify high-risk flights, airports, and geographic regions. As of the start of 2006, the system was not quite ready for launch because many of its facets were still being studied. The accuracy of the system has not yet been determined. Once development is complete, CAPPS II is expected to provide an enhanced computer-assisted prescreening system. The implementation of CAPPS II has been delayed primarily due to privacy laws and concerns about obtaining passenger data as well as high costs and the continued attempts to develop a proven method of preventing unauthorized access and identity theft.

Advanced scanning technology has been put into use in some airports even as they continue being developed. This includes machines that are able to detect explosives. The Explosives Detection System (EDS) and Explosives Trace Detection (ETD) are both systems that help security officers to detect explosives contained in baggage. The ETD system has already been deployed in many airports. The system, as its name suggests, helps to detect traces of explosives and hazardous materials in baggage. The Explosives Detection System, which detects explosives carried in bulk, is still under research and development. Fine-tuning still needs to be done for EDS to find out how much of an explosive needs to be carried in order to be detected.

The perimeters of airports have also been under more scrutiny. The TSA plans on randomly checking people to make sure that they are legitimate employees. Because access points to perimeter areas have become more limited, this in combination with random checks will heighten security in those areas. Ensuring the safety of the airports requires that no area of an airport is overlooked.

The future will pave the way for even more advanced technological equipment. One of the most advanced technologies in consideration for use in the future is biometrics. Biometrics is one of the most recent technological innovations for identifying authorized personnel at airports, seaports, railways, and other mass transit facilities. When examining the advantages and most promising aspects of biometrics, it is important to point out that automated biometrics recognizes and identifies a person based on his or her facial features, hand geometry, iris, retina, handwriting, body odor, heartbeat, inner ear bones, and voice. According to Don Philpott's article entitled "Physical Security—Biometrics," published in the *Homeland Defense Journal* in May 2005, biometrics links the identification of a person to his or her own individual physical and/or physiological features, which cannot be faked. Biometrics utilizes an individual's physical characteristics and personal character traits to assist in the identification of an individual. In *Biometrics: Facing Up to Terrorism*, the author, John Woodward, describes biometrics:

> Fingerprints, faces, voices, and handwritten signatures are all examples of characteristics that have been used to identify us in this way. Biometric-based systems provide automatic, nearly instantaneous identification of a person by converting the biometric—a fingerprint, for example—into digital form and then comparing it against a computerized database. In this way, fingerprints, faces, voices, iris and retinal images of the eye, hand geometry, and signature dynamics can now be used to identify us, or to authenticate our claimed identity, quickly and accurately.

Thus, we can see that there are various different ways in which we can employ the use of biometrics. Fingerprinting and palm printing have been common practice in many different areas and would be a useful way to enhance security at airports.

Passengers, for example, can have their prints taken at the time of reservation (or some other time prior to their arrival at the airport) and airport personnel can have their prints taken at the time of hire. These prints can then be used to gain access through secure checkpoints or before boarding a plane. Similar to finger and palm printing, a scan of facial characteristics can be employed to allow access to secure areas, by previously having photos of individuals on file. Woodward also addresses a system called FaceCheck, which can scan a crowd to find an individual who may be flagged in the system as a possible suspect.

The use of biometrics will also enable the use of smart cards. Smart cards are capable of storing biometric data such as finger or palm prints and facial characteristics, as well as other data such as name, address, and so on. Passengers can bring their smart cards to the airport for use during check-in, security check points, passenger–bag matches, and for boarding the plane. Likewise, airport personnel could use smart cards to access secure areas. A smart card can even be a unified card that can be used on all modes of mass transit, or perhaps even beyond transportation. The card can be linked up to other agencies such as the state department of motor vehicles or the IRS—the possibilities are endless. Use of smart cards will allow control over access to secure areas, may assist in preventing identity theft, and can help to identify suspicious suspects. Therefore, utilization of smart cards can both secure and expedite individuals' experiences at the airport and elsewhere. Despite the numerous benefits, some challenges do exist. The main barrier is that many people may feel that the smart cards represent an invasion of privacy and may feel hesitant to disclose personal information. It may also be a challenge to get the system in place. How will the data for the smart cards be gathered, and where will it be stored? How will the system be implemented? Are the costs feasible? If the challenges are overcome, it will be an invaluable asset to the enhancement of airport security.

On March 4, 2005, the TSA requested help and guidance from representatives from the aviation industry, the biometric identifier industry, and the National Institute of Standards and Technology for using biometric technology in American airports. TSA is planning for comprehensive technical and operational system requirements and performance standards and procedures for implementing biometric systems that prevent the use of assumed identities and resolve false matches and false nonmatches. According to Section 4011(a)(5)of the Intelligence Reform and Terrorism Prevention Act of 2004, electronic privacy issues must be safeguarded by the Electronic Privacy Information Center (EPIC). EPIC encourages TSA not to test its use of biometric technology until it conducts a comprehensive privacy impact assessment. The purpose of this assessment would be to ensure protection of privacy rights of program members to meet legal requirements, legislative oversight, and government standards for privacy protection of federal data banks and personal information systems. TSA has agreed to follow the Privacy Act when they begin to test biometric technology with flight crew members. TSA also said they would provide a "privacy impact statement" so that they could ensure all data collected would not be misused.

Conclusion

As this encyclopedia was going to press, both the TSA and *The New York Times* reported on several noteworthy advances in aviation and airport security taking place beginning on December 22, 2005, right before the holiday travel rush: random explosive screening of shoes, hand-wanding of passengers, enhanced pat-down searches, and more than four hundred TSA explosive detection canine teams deployed to more than eighty U.S. airports. An additional thirty canine teams were to be deployed to ten mass transit rail systems in early 2006. Finally, an article appeared on January 4, 2006, in New Jersey's *Star-Ledger* newspaper reporting on TSA's plan to implement voluntary biometric iris, facial, and fingerprint imagery at about fifty airports nationwide by the summer of 2006. The combination of iris scans with fingerprints has been more than 99% successful in identifying low security risk frequent flyer passengers who have enrolled in the program. With the cost of each iris-scanning camera being only $3,700, the program seems to be cost effective as well.

ALBERT R. ROBERTS and PIA BISWAS

See also **Crime Prevention; Terrorism: Overview**

References and Further Reading

Atkinson, R. D. 2001. *How technology can help make air travel safe again.* Washington, DC: Progressive Policy Institute. http://www. ncjrs.gov (accessed November 26, 2005).

Berrick, C. A. 2003. *Aviation security: Efforts to measure effectiveness and address challenges.* Testimony before the Committee on Commerce, Science and Transportation, U.S. Senate. Washington, DC: U.S. General Accounting Office.

Coughlin, K. 2006. Security in the blink of an eye. *The (Newark, NJ) Star-Ledger,* January 4, 43, 47.

Dillingham, G. 2000. *Aviation security: Slow progress in addressing long-standing screener performance problems.* Washington, DC: U.S. General Accounting Office.

———. 2003. *Transportation security: Post-September 11th initiatives and long-term challenges.* Washington, DC: U.S. General Accounting Office.

Evans, P. 2005. Three-dimensional x-ray imaging for security. *Security Journal* 18: 19–28.

Philpott, D. 2005. Physical security—biometrics. *Homeland Defense Journal,* May.

Poole, R. W., Jr. 2001. *Learn from experience on airport security.* Washington, DC: The Heritage Foundation.

Rabkin, N. J., and D. A. Powner. 2004. *Aviation security: Challenges delay implementation of computer-assisted passenger prescreening system.* Testimony before the Subcommittee on Aviation, Committee on Transportation

and Infrastructure, U.S. House of Representatives. Washington, DC: U.S. General Accounting Office.

Raffel, R. T. 2001. Airport policing: Training issues and options. *FBI Law Enforcement Bulletin* 70 (9): 26–29.

Schell, T. L., B. G. Chow, and C. Grammich. 2003. *Designing airports for security.* Santa Monica, CA: RAND Corporation.

Woodward, J. D., Jr. 2001. *Biometrics: Facing up to terrorism.* Santa Monica, CA: RAND Corporation.

ALARMS AS CRIME PREVENTION

Intrusion or burglar alarms have been around for more than seventy-five years (Michael 1931). Commercial establishments such as banks use them to protect their vaults. Airports use alarms to control and restrict access to secured locations. Residential homeowners use them to guard against home burglary. At issue is whether alarms can prevent crime.

Security systems can be categorized as either access control or perimeter control systems (Kobza and Jacobson 1997). Access control refers to gate-keeping that limits access to a designated area to authorized personnel. For example, in 1991, the Federal Aviation Administration (FAA) defined the Security Identification Display Area (SIDA) with requirements for use of airport identification badges in designated areas. Following the tragedy of September 11, 2001, when hijacked airplanes crashed into prominent buildings in the United States, the FAA regulations were updated significantly. Worldwide, most modern airports use an identification badge as an access control system card.

Access control systems record all access attempts, who went through particular doors, and whether access was granted or denied, and may be used to generate a list for individuals, doors, groups such as attendants, passengers, cleaning, and maintenance crews. Higher security for access control in critical areas can be obtained with fingerprint readers or other biometric devices. No matter what type of identification is used, the basic issue of access control is limiting access to secured areas to authorized personnel. When access control is violated, an alarm will go off.

Perimeter security is defined as protection of a facility or area from external intruders (or internal escapees). A typical home burglar alarm system is a perimeter security system designed to protect the entire home using door alarms and a motion detector to sound an alarm when an intruder enters the home. For an airport, perimeter security is slightly more complicated because the airport runways may be the only area of concern. Chain-link fence with barbed wire may surround and protect the exterior of the airport aprons, taxiways, and runways. However, access control within the secured terminal area faces dual objectives of security and safety. The fact that anyone can open exit doors provides the possibility that someone may gain access to the runways. Gated loading doors and exit doors inside the terminal need to be easy to open, large enough to accommodate wheelchairs, and numerous so that everybody can easily exit the terminal in the event of a fire. These exit doors and the fire alarm doors may be alarmed with or without loud sirens. Yet, gated loading doors can not be controlled easily because keys, personal identification numbers, or ID cards can be borrowed or easily copied. The hard truth is that perimeter security alarms in a home or business actually can do little to stop a threatening offender from entering an area.

One unintended consequence of access control systems is false alarms that sound when users fail to properly close doors, enter using incorrect procedures, or tamper with a system so that it sends a false signal. User error is the most common cause of false alarms in commercial and home environments (Alarm Industry Research and Educational Foundation 1999). False home burglar alarms are a problem because police may be responding to a false burglar alarm while a crime is occurring elsewhere.

Alarms are intended to deter a potential offender from choosing a target. A key question about the benefits of alarms is whether a potential offender will choose another target because of an alarm (displacement) or choose not to commit a crime (diffusion). Displacement may mean different things such as an offender choosing another target (bank or home) because it does not have an alarm; an offender using another tactic to enter a location, for example, going in a window because the door is alarmed; or the offender coming back at a different time when the alarm is not on. Research as a whole seems to suggest that alarms lead to diffusion. Nonetheless, the debate over displacement versus diffusion remains complicated because studies use imperfect definitions in setting geographical boundaries and they use time limits for evaluation that are too short (Bowers and Johnson 2003).

Hakim, Rengert, and Shachmurove (1995) suggest that home burglar and fire alarms provide a net benefit to society. The household with false alarms does cost the community because there is an expense involved anytime police respond to an incident, yet the home alarms provide a social benefit in terms of fewer rapes, assaults, and burglaries and reduced fire damage due to earlier detection. Quite clearly, the hijackings of September 11, 2001, show that the costs of a single security breach in an airport can be substantial for the incident, consumer confidence, and lost business.

Graham Farrell (1995) argues that crime prevention policy should advocate the use of rapid response alarms. His work in Great Britain finds that people (and places) who are victimized have very high likelihoods of revictimization. Farrell makes a convincing argument that quick response alarms may deter revictimization and that they may be used to efficiently locate offenders, which prevents additional crime.

By installing and managing an alarm system to first prevent unauthorized access to secured areas, deterrence, detection, and response may follow. The stronger the security system is, the more it will act as a deterrent, and the need to respond to (false positive) security breaches is reduced. Improving access control through enhanced technology and training will reduce false system alarms and ultimately enhance crime prevention.

DAVID R. FORDE

See also **Computer Technology; Crime Prevention; Routine Guardianship; Situational Crime Prevention**

References and Further Reading

Alarm Industry Research and Educational Foundation. 1999. Model states report: Best practices in reducing false dispatches. http://www.airef.org/modelstates.htm (accessed December 2005).

Bowers, K. J., and S. D. Johnson. 2003. Measuring the geographical displacement and diffusion of benefit effects of crime prevention activity. *Journal of Quantitative Criminology* 19: 275–301.

Farrell, G. 1995. Preventing repeat victimization. *Crime and Justice* 19: 469–534.

Hakim, S., G. F. Rengert, and Y. Shachmurove. 1995. Burglar and fire alarms: Costs and benefits in the locality. *American Journal of Economics and Sociology* 54: 145–61.

Kobza, J. E., and S. H. Jacobson. 1997. Probability models for access security systems architectures. *Journal of the Operational Research Society* 48: 255–63.

Michael, H. B. 1931. Modern burglary and robbery prevention methods. *American Journal of Police Science* 2: 20–29.

Transportation Security Administration. 2005. *Security technologies—Physical security.* http://www.tsa.gov/public (accessed December 2005).

ALCOHOL, DRUGS, AND CRIME

Overview

The association between drug use and crime is complex. Little research support can be found for a single, specific, or direct cause-and-effect relationship between drug use and criminal activity, which is neither an inevitable consequence of illicit drug use (apart from the illegal nature of drug use itself), nor a necessary or sufficient condition for criminal behavior. Many illegal drug users commit no other kinds of crimes, and many persons who commit crimes never use illegal drugs. Furthermore, it is possible for people to commit crimes while using illegal drugs without a causal connection between the two activities. Most crimes result from a variety of factors (personal, situational, cultural, and economic); hence, even when drug use is a cause, it is more likely to be only one factor among many. In short, no evidence suggests drug use alone inexorably leads to criminal activity. The same conclusion applies to the link between alcohol use and crime, which is also influenced by multiple factors.

However, at the most intense levels of drug use, drugs and crime are directly and highly correlated. Among crime-prone individuals, illegal drug use intensifies criminal activity. As illegal drug use increases in frequency and amount, so does criminal behavior. Persons who are criminally inclined tend to commit both a greater number and more serious crimes after they become dependent on drugs. As their drug use decreases, so do the number of crimes they commit. In addition, illicit drug use and criminal activity often occur simultaneously and are mutually reinforcing aspects of a deviant lifestyle.

The propensity for crime-prone, drug-using persons to commit property or violent crimes might be expressed only after they cross the threshold from use to abuse or dependence.

Yet an unknown number of illegal drug users, perhaps even dependent users, are able to maintain steady employment and never commit crimes, other than the crime of illicit drug use itself. Because drug use is an illegal and socially undesirable behavior, accurate, self-reported estimates of the size and nature of this "hidden" population are difficult to garner from national prevalence surveys.

Types of Drug Crimes

Illegal drugs are involved in different types of crimes: drug-defined, drug-related, and drug-induced crimes. Drug-defined offenses are violations of laws that prohibit the manufacture, distribution, or possession of illegal substances such as amphetamines, cocaine, heroin, or marijuana. Drug-related offenses are motivated by an individual's need for money to purchase drugs (e.g., property crimes and prostitution) or are occasioned by conflicts that surround the illicit drug trade (e.g., violence among competing drug dealers). The pharmacological effects of illicit substances (and alcohol) can encourage reckless or violent behaviors or result in drug- or alcohol-induced offenses, such as driving under the influence and domestic battery.

Substance Use and Crime

The annual National Youth Survey has found that juveniles who commit serious crimes are significantly more likely to use drugs than juveniles who commit minor crimes or no crimes at all. Other long-term studies of youth have also found that those delinquents who commit more serious offenses are heavier drug users than those with less serious offenses. Consistent with research on the relationship between drugs and crime among youths, a survey of adult drug users indicated they had engaged in numerous criminal activities (excluding drug-law violations) in the 90 days before they were interviewed for the study. A national survey of prison inmates also indicated that more than half were under the influence of drugs when they committed their current offenses.

Substance use, abuse, and dependence are more common in the criminal justice population than in the general population. For example, in 2000, the Arrestee Drug Abuse Monitoring Program demonstrated that nearly two-thirds of male and female arrestees tested positive for illicit drugs at the time of arrest. Similarly, a study of jail detainees demonstrated that two-thirds had been abusing or were dependent on drugs or alcohol before they were detained. Among jail detainees convicted of a crime, 55% reported they had used illegal drugs at the time of their current offense. More than half of state and federal prisoners in the late 1990s indicated they were under the influence of alcohol or drugs while committing their offenses. Among state prison inmates nationwide in 2000, 25% of property and drug offenders reported they committed their crimes to get money to buy drugs; 59% of all inmates reported they had used drugs in the month before they committed their most recent crimes; and 45% of all inmates reported they were under the influence of drugs when they committed their most recent crimes.

Serious drug use can also amplify and perpetuate preexisting criminal activity. Although substance use itself is not necessarily the cause of criminal behavior, as noted earlier, the need for money to purchase drugs can be a motivating factor for criminally active drug users. Two types of studies support an income-generating explanation for the drug–crime nexus: studies of the relationship between illegal income and drug purchases, and studies of the relationship between drug use intensity and criminal activity.

Offenders' income from property crime increases proportionately with their drug use. In a jail survey, nearly 20% of detainees reported they had committed their most recent offenses for money to buy drugs. In another study, heroin users reported that 90 cents of every illegal dollar they earned was spent on drug purchases. Researchers have found a direct relationship between illegal income and drug spending among cocaine users. The need to have an income to purchase illegal drugs often leads to prostitution among drug-addicted women. Researchers estimate that between 40 and 70% of female narcotic addicts maintain their drug habits through the sex trade. The exchange of sex for drugs seems to be especially common among women who use crack cocaine.

Persons addicted to heroin often increase their criminal activities dramatically during periods of accelerated drug use, with the onset of their addictions coinciding with a sharp rise in their criminal activities. Conversely, a study of heroin-dependent persons found their criminal activities decreased by more than 80% during the months and years in which they refrained from heroin or other opiate use. A very large percentage of jail inmates (85%) convicted of burglary were assessed as abusing or dependent on drugs, suggesting a strong link between drug use severity and income-generating crime.

Other research has shown that criminal activity is substantially greater among frequent drug and polydrug users (i.e., users of two or more substances at the same time) than among sporadic or nonusers of drugs. Thus, drug-using offenders, especially those with substance abuse and dependence problems, commit both more and a greater variety of income-generating crimes and also commit crimes at higher rates than offenders without drug-use problems.

Drug Trafficking and Violent Crime

Drug users frequently participate in the production, distribution, and sales of illicit drugs in order to earn money for their own drug use. In a study of drug sellers in Washington, D.C., researchers estimated that in one year, street drug sales generated approximately $350 million, more than twice the estimated earnings from robbery and property crimes such as burglary and shoplifting. Heavy drug users commit relatively fewer violent offenses, including violent predatory crimes, compared with income-generating property crimes; however, studies show cocaine use is associated with a higher-than-average likelihood of violent crimes among both men and women offenders. Violent cocaine users often commit robbery, a high-risk but expedient means of obtaining ready cash. In 2004, the Federal Bureau of Investigation reported that of the homicides in which the circumstances were known, 4% were drug related. A survey of the nation's victims of violent crime demonstrated that nearly 30% believed the offender was using drugs or alcohol (or a combination of the two) at the time of their victimization.

Drug trafficking and violence are associated in several ways. The violence that accompanies illicit drug use can be related to the drug trade; it occurs because of the conflicts that stem from the importation, distribution, or sale of illicit substances. Competition for drug markets and customers can encourage violence among drug sellers. Public drug selling in particular is associated with high rates of violent crime. In addition, disputes and "ripoffs" in drug-cash transactions can erupt among individuals involved in the illegal drug market. Individuals who participate in drug trafficking frequently use violence to resolve conflicts. Locations where street drug markets proliferate tend to be disadvantaged economically and socially, and legal and social controls against violence in those areas tend to be ineffective.

The systemic violence of the drug trade was first recognized as a serious problem in 1985 when crack cocaine sales became widespread in major metropolitan areas such as New York City and Washington, D.C. Well-armed and violent drug dealers led the struggle to protect or gain control over initially unstable, highly lucrative drug markets. At that time, the proliferation of automatic weapons had also made drug violence more lethal. When the drug markets stabilized, homicide rates fell in most major cities.

Contrary to common beliefs about the direction of the relationship between drugs and crime, researchers have suggested that overall criminal involvement causes drug use by providing situations that are conducive to drug use and sales. In this perspective, criminals start using drugs before committing offenses to lower their anxiety, or after committing offenses to celebrate their success. Delinquent and criminal behaviors can predate drug use among juveniles. For example, the National Youth Survey showed that minor delinquency led to alcohol consumption and more serious offenses, which led to marijuana and polydrug use (in that order). Minor delinquency preceded drug use in nearly all the cases studied. In general, the theory that crime precedes drug use suggests drug use is simply another form of deviant behavior, with involvement in crime affording many opportunities for drug-use initiation.

The relationship between drug use and crime can be bidirectional, that is, reciprocal and mutually reinforcing. Specifically, as persons commit more income-generating crimes, they find it easier to buy drugs. Then, as they begin to use drugs more frequently, they are compelled to commit more crimes in support of their escalating addiction. In this theory, drug use and offending are interrelated, with the correlation between drug use and criminality being at the intersection between the two lifestyles.

However, for many youth, drug use and delinquency are not causally related in either direction; instead, they are contemporaneous, as both behaviors arise from common causes such as social disaffection, poor relationships with parents, school failure, and deviant peers. Among adult offenders, the connection between drug use and crime can be explained by the criminal subculture theory. In this framework, members of criminal subcultures are described as self-indulgent, hedonistic, materialistic, and risk seeking, as they are committed to living the "fast life." For these individuals, drug use and crime operate along parallel lines, because they are components of a larger constellation of destructive behaviors that also include high-risk sexual practices.

Alcohol Use and Crime

Because alcohol use is legal and pervasive, it contributes greatly to crime and other social problems. Other than driving offenses, alcohol use is associated mostly with violent and public order offenses. Similar to illicit drug use, alcohol use facilitates or multiplies criminal behaviors among persons who are predisposed to commit offenses.

In a survey conducted in the late 1990s, nearly three million crime victims reported that they perceived the offender in their case had been drinking at the time of the incident. A large percentage (two-thirds) of the victims of intimate violence perceived their partners' alcohol use as precipitating the episode. Nearly 70% of alcohol-related violent incidents occurred in the victim's own residence, while the use of firearms was involved in 4% of alcohol-related violent incidents.

Alcohol abuse occurs disproportionately among juveniles and adults who report violent behaviors. A study of convicted offenders estimated that more than one-third had been drinking at the time of their offense. Among persons in jails and on probation, public order offenses, such as disorderly conduct, disturbing the peace, and trespassing, were the most common crimes reported by those who had been drinking at the time of the offense. Approximately one-third of prison inmates and 40% of probationers and jail detainees report they had been drinking alcohol at the time of the offense, with nearly 60% of convicted jail inmates reporting they had been drinking regularly in the year before their conviction and incarceration. Adults who are lifetime alcohol users are also nearly five times more likely to use illicit substances, compared with lifetime nondrinkers.

Finally, alcohol use is responsible for thousands of traffic fatalities each year. More than one million people are arrested annually for driving while intoxicated (DWI), which is the third most commonly reported crime in the United States. In the late 1990s, more than five hundred thousand individuals were on probation or in jail and prison for a DWI conviction.

ARTHUR J. LURIGIO

See also **Crime Control Strategies: Alcohol and Drugs; Drug Abuse Prevention Education; Drug Abuse Resistance Education (D.A.R.E.); Drug Enforcement Administration (DEA); Drug Interdiction; Drug Markets; Drunk Driving**

References and Further Reading

Bureau of Justice Statistics. 1998a. *Alcohol and crime.* Washington, DC: U.S. Department of Justice.
———. 1998b. *Substance abuse and treatment of probation on probation, 1995.* Washington, DC: U.S. Department of Justice.
———. 1999a. *DWI offenders under correctional supervision.* Washington, DC: U.S. Department of Justice.
———. 1999b. *Substance dependence, abuse, and treatment of state and federal prison inmates.* Washington, DC: U.S. Department of Justice.
———. 2005a. *Criminal victimization in the United States, 2003.* Washington, DC: U.S. Department of Justice.
———. 2005b. *Drugs and crimes facts.* Washington, DC: U.S. Department of Justice.
———. 2005c. *Substance dependence, abuse, and treatment of jail inmates, 2002.* Washington, DC: U.S. Department of Justice.
Leshner, A. I. 1998. Addiction is a brain disease and it matters. *National Institute of Justice Journal* 237: 2–6.
Lurigio, A. J., and J. A. Swartz. 1999. The nexus between drugs and crime: theory, research, and practice. *Federal Probation* 63: 67–72.

National Institute of Justice. 2003. *2000 annual report on drug use among adult and juvenile arrestees, arrestee drug abuse monitoring program.* Washington, DC: U.S. Department of Justice.
Office of National Drug Control Policy. 2001. *Drug treatment in the criminal justice system.* Washington, DC: U.S. Government Printing Office.

AMERICAN POLICING: EARLY YEARS

Early American Policing (1600–1860)

Police departments as we know them—organized, salaried bureaucracies, most of whose members wear uniforms—began in the United States in the generation before 1860. From the outset, the police department has been a multipurpose agency of municipal government, not just a component of the criminal justice system. New York police officers in the 1850s spent more time on stray horses and lost children than they did on burglaries, just as their counterparts a century later labored to keep traffic moving and initiated the paperwork on fender benders. Understanding the origins of American policing, therefore, requires attention to the general context of urban government, as well as official responses to crime and disorder.

The earliest inhabitants of colonial cities in the seventeenth century still had at least one foot in the Middle Ages. Their worldview was dominated by scarcity. Government's most important task was to regulate economic life so that strangers did not usurp work rightfully belonging to residents, or wandering poor gain the right to local relief, or greedy men take undue advantage of consumers. Public officials did not think of government as a provider of services financed through the collection of taxes. Government did encourage private interests to undertake necessary projects, like streets and wharves, for which the public purse was inadequate. In New York City one mechanism to achieve such goals was to transfer public land to private ownership in return for specific commitments to the construction of public facilities.

In the late eighteenth and early nineteenth centuries, a new worldview came to prevail, at least among the elite, one characterized by the prospect of growth and perhaps even of abundance rather than scarcity. Adam Smith's *Wealth of Nations*, published in 1776, gave a convincing theoretical statement about how the pursuit of individual interests could lead to general economic growth if the market were free of government-granted monopolies or private combinations in restraint of trade. In this intellectual climate, government would be more a promoter of growth than a regulator of scarcity by helping provide what modern economists know as *social overhead capital* and what the nineteenth century called *improvements*. Thus government now paid for new wharves and streets, built canals, and promoted the development of railways. Tax-supported schools, at least in theory, produced a disciplined and literate labor force; gas lamps made night a little less gloomy and fearful; and publicly equipped, although not yet paid, fire companies provided some protection against this major urban hazard. By 1860 twelve of the sixteen largest cities had public water systems to aid in firefighting and to give residents something to drink other than alcohol or possibly fouled well water.

Urban Growth and the Need for Police

Between 1820 and 1860 American cities attracted unprecedented numbers of migrants from rural America, Ireland, and Germany. Growth was the reality as well as a theoretical possibility. Whereas only one of twenty Americans lived in an urban settlement in 1790, the ratio was one in five in 1860. New York and Brooklyn together accounted for more than a million people, Philadelphia more than one-half million, while Chicago, incorporated only in 1833, had more than one hundred thousand residents in 1860. By the early 1870s the city of Chicago was spending in a day what had sufficed for an entire year in the late 1840s.

When municipal governments examined growth and its consequences, they were both exhilarated and fearful. Historian Edward Pessen has demonstrated that the business elite exercised disproportionate influence on urban government throughout the so-called age of the common man. When city councils became less patrician and more plebeian in the late 1840s and 1850s, they also lost many of their former functions. Independent boards and commissions replaced council committees as the overseers of public services while the mayor, almost invariably a leading business or professional man, became a more powerful figure. Councils, usually elected by wards, more often reacted to external initiatives than proposed measures of their own, at least for anything that went beyond the neighborhood level. Most members of the elite liked growth; their businesses and real estate holdings appreciated in value with more people and higher levels of economic activity. They did not like some of the negative consequences, such as larger numbers of strangers, immigrants of alien tongue, customs, and religion who did not always recognize the cultural superiority and natural goodness of old-stock American Protestants. Some members of the elite were also troubled by the visible increase in the number of poor and dependent people who neither benefited from the city's growth nor seemed able to cope with its complexity.

Establishing a police department was one response to these concerns. When New York created its modern department in 1845, the city made the police responsible for a wide range of services, from inspecting hacks and stages to lighting the gas lamps in the evening. Over time many of these functions were transferred to other agencies, but the point remains that the police were never thought of exclusively as a crime-fighting and order-maintaining group.

The police did have important responsibilities in keeping the peace and dealing with criminals. In the colonial period order maintenance and crime fighting were more individual and communal responsibilities than the purview of a bureaucratic agency. The colonists brought with them such traditional English institutions as elected constables and the night watch. In theory constables had extensive legal responsibilities and powers, although rarely did their prestige and authority match their legal position. The watch, often made up of reluctant citizens, kept a lookout for fire as well as crime and disorder. In the case of crime the aggrieved party bore the burden of initiating the processes of apprehension and prosecution. By the early nineteenth century, New York had more than one hundred persons with police powers, either as elected constables or appointed mayor's marshals. These officers spent much of their time in the service of civil processes, although they were available for hire by victims of theft. They made a specialty of returning stolen property in exchange for a portion of the recovery. Early nineteenth-century police officers were thus fee-for-service professionals rather than salaried bureaucrats.

Riots, often with specific political targets and goals, were recognized features of pre-industrial urban life. Rioters rarely took life, although they often destroyed considerable property. The most famous riots were those associated with the American Revolution, such as the protests over the Stamp Act of 1765, the Boston Massacre of 1770, and the Boston Tea Party of 1773. The decades before the revolutionary agitation also experienced periodic urban disorders. The most savage reprisals were directed at slaves thought to be plotting against whites, such as in New York City in 1712 and 1741. In most instances rioters seemed content to disperse once they made their point, whether it was antipopery or a protest against body snatching by doctors and medical students. But by the 1820s, middle- and upper-class urbanites no longer seemed willing to accept levels of unseemly behavior in public places previously thought unavoidable.

From the early eighteenth century onward, urbanites like Benjamin Franklin organized voluntary societies to achieve desirable social goals. The pace of this activity accelerated in the generation after 1815, especially under the auspices of religious groups that wished to spread the good news of salvation through the publication and distribution of bibles and tracts, to reach children in Sunday schools, to uplift the poor, and to reform juvenile delinquents and fallen women. Whenever families failed in their tasks of nurturing and disciplining their members, other institutions had to step in to remedy the deficiencies. A case in point is New York's House of Refuge, founded by the privately established Society for the Reformation of Juvenile Delinquents in 1825, which received state support for this purpose.

The English Example

In these activities American institution builders looked to England for both general inspiration and specific models to emulate. The American elite considered the Atlantic to be a highway as well as a barrier (indeed in the early nineteenth century it was cheaper to cross the Atlantic than to move any distance at all on land), so that books, ideas, and people moved freely between London, Boston, New York, and Philadelphia.

One of these ideas was that government in some instances would have to assume direct responsibility for social well-being. In 1829 Sir Robert Peel put through

Parliament a bill for the creation of the London Metropolitan Police, a salaried bureaucracy responsible for the maintenance of order and the prevention and detection of crime. The London Metropolitan Police served as a direct model for police departments subsequently established in American cities.

Peel's bill was preceded by a half-century of debate and discussion, parliamentary inquiries, and the creation of numerous voluntary societies to reform public morals. During these decades London also relied on fee-for-service police officers while the watch was organized and paid for on a parish-by-parish basis with consequent wide variations in numbers and effectiveness. Civil authorities were virtually helpless to deal with such outbreaks as the Gordon Riots of 1780, while senior army officers objected to being called upon to suppress riots because of the possible impact on morale and discipline. As evangelical religious ideas became more popular in England, there was greater concern for the state of public morality. Prostitution and drunkenness came to be thought of as social problems to a greater extent than they had been in earlier decades. This is not to say that rates of disorder, crime, or behavior contrary to evangelical notions of propriety were necessarily rising, but that influential figures were less tolerant, accepting, or stoic about such matters. The French Revolution and its aftermath seems to have convinced the upper classes that they needed to exercise firmer control over the lower. To some extent, the more orderly people became, the higher the level of expectations among the propertied and respectable.

The London Metropolitan Police Bill thus represented the convergence of three streams of social concern. The first was for a public agency other than the army that could be mobilized to deal with civil disorder. Policemen would be uniformed, subject to quasi-military discipline, and sufficiently removed from civilians to act as a riot-repressing force, but there would not be the potential morale problems associated with the use of the army or the possible class bias of the militia. If the militia were recruited from the same groups as rioters, it might join in. If, like England's mounted yeomanry, the militia came from landowners, urban workers and farm laborers would hardly accept it as legitimate. The police would be recruited from the people, but not locally, so that their loyalties would be more to their organization and their superiors than to the people they policed.

The second stream of concern was crime. Pre-Peel police officers, such as the famous Bow Street Runners, might deal efficiently with property crimes after victims hired them. Unfortunately, they also found consorting and conspiring with criminals to be in their interests. The line between cops and robbers was a fuzzy one at best and easily crossed. Moreover, even the best officers acted only after the crime had occurred and when there was sufficient monetary incentive. Peel's police were to be preventive, a word used frequently and loosely. Ideally the very presence of such a force would lead criminals to accept honest toil as a way of life and would keep young people from ever straying from that path.

Finally, the police could deal with the "police" of the city in its generic sense. When early nineteenth-century figures referred to the "police" of the city, they had a broad conception in mind, akin to the later judicial notion of police power, the ability to legislate for the public welfare. Policing involved keeping city streets clean as well as the good order and discipline of its residents. The presence of a police officer might deter residents from airmailing their garbage into the streets and keep streetwalkers from plying their trade. We can subsume these activities under the heading of "preventing unseemly behavior in public places." In the absence of salaried bureaucrats entrusted with keeping the peace and imposing a moral code, what could sober people do about drunks except step over them or avoid where they congregated? The establishment of the police meant an active group patrolling the streets on the lookout for breaches of the moral code as well as common-law crimes, thus extending the authority of the state into the daily lives of the people.

The London police were not universally accepted in their first years. The slang term *crushers* gives some sense of the response of the lower class. The leaders of the force worked hard to get citizens to acknowledge the moral authority of the police. The first commissioners, recruited from outside London where possible, dismissed many of their early appointees for drunkenness and tried to maintain tight administrative control. The lines of authority ran to a cabinet minister, the home secretary, not to locally elected officials.

The Rise of American Urban Police Departments

The existence of the London police stimulated American urban leaders to think about establishing similar institutions, especially since their own cities were experiencing rapid growth and social change. New York City's population had grown almost four times between 1790 and 1820; between 1820 and 1860 the growth was more than sevenfold. Before the mid-1820s, city officials considered their problems of crime and disorder to be manageable, but by the mid-1830s they worried about endemic street violence. Indeed, 1834 was long remembered in the city's history as the year of riots. When the great fire struck a year later, authorities could neither fight the fire effectively nor control looting without calling out the militia. Sensational murder cases went undetected and largely uninvestigated unless someone put up substantial reward money. Periodic economic panics and crises meant thousands of unemployed men and women on the margins

of subsistence would fall below it without some form of assistance. Boston and Philadelphia also experienced conflict among religious, ethnic, and class rivals, while cities with substantial slave populations were concerned above all else with controlling their blacks.

After a decade of debate and the forging of a consensus that New York City needed a police force, the state legislature adopted legislation in 1844 creating the police department and setting forth its powers and structure in detail. The law required municipal approval before it became effective. This approval was granted in 1845. Increasingly, both legal theorists and municipal officials took the position that any extension of municipal powers required direct action by the state legislature. For the remainder of the nineteenth century, state legislatures sometimes exercised their prerogative to intervene in urban police departments in a heavy-handed fashion.

The New York Police Department, established in 1845, was a salaried bureaucracy, but it differed in significant ways from the London police, even though its first set of rules and regulations was largely copied from London's. The New York police were not uniformed, although members did carry a star-shaped badge for identification. Originally the term of office was one year, raised to two in 1846 and four in 1849. The alderman of the particular ward had the most to say about who should serve as police officers. If an alderman was voted out of office, most of the police officers he appointed lost their jobs. The force was decentralized in that each ward constituted a patrol district with little central supervision.

A new state law in 1853 made major changes in the organization and administration of the police. It established a board of police commissioners, consisting of the mayor, the city judge, and the recorder (a judicial official), thus reducing the aldermen's role in appointments and administration. Police officers now could be removed only for cause, thus making police work a career. The practice of naming people to senior positions without prior police experience died out, and the standard became entry at the bottom and promotion from within. The new commissioners put the police into uniform, an innovation resisted without success by some men who cherished their anonymity.

Although the New York police now looked like their London counterparts, there were still substantial differences between the two departments. London's administrators stressed careful control of the use of police powers and tried to keep the police from having to perform unpopular tasks like closing drinking places on Sunday. In New York ultimate authority over the police lay in the hands of locally elected officials who, along with New York's judges, were more prone to let the police take a tougher approach than their counterparts in London. Historian Wilbur Miller, Jr., has documented how the New York police were more inclined to use force and make arrests on suspicion than London's. Despite police rhetoric about judicial intervention or not being backed up, they were rarely disciplined for such actions or discouraged from using such tactics. London's police were generally more circumspect in their dealing with citizens because their superiors wanted them to be embodiments of the moral authority of the state, with the uniform accepted as its legitimate symbol.

An obvious and very important difference was the unarmed police of London compared with the armed police of New York. Throughout the nineteenth century and for most of the twentieth, English police officers were not armed; in recent years a rising volume of violent crime has led to serious questioning of this policy. In New York the police were not armed early in their history. Officers began to carry weapons without legal authorization to do so because they perceived their working environment as dangerously unpredictable. Samuel Colt's technological innovations made handguns cheaper and more readily available in the 1850s. New York newspapers complained in the mid-1850s that the streets of New York were more dangerous than the plains of Kansas, while historians Roger Lane and David Johnson have noted the prevalence of violent crime in Philadelphia during these years.

The arming of American police, begun by officers without legal authorization, soon became enshrined in custom. Unlike their British counterparts, American public authorities took the position that the tough, armed cop was the best response to the pervasive problems of crime and disorder within their cities.

Police departments joined other public institutions such as school systems as instruments of order, stability, and uplift to cope with an explosively growing and often disorderly urban environment. Within the ranks, station house socialization passed the norms of the veterans along to the rookies, norms that had less to do with law enforcement than with maintenance of group solidarity and respect. "Don't talk about police business to outsiders" and "Don't take any guff from civilians" were more important than the statute books or the rules and regulations of the department set forth in such minute details.

At top levels, such as among board members and commissioners, political winds could blow harshly. In 1857 the New York state legislature abolished the municipal police and substituted a new department, the Metropolitan Police, with responsibilities for an enlarged district. New York City still had to pay for the officers assigned within its boundaries. This arrangement lasted for thirteen years. In other states as well, legislatures stepped in and replaced individuals holding senior administrative positions. These interventions were usually related to some hope of partisan advantage or distaste for the way city police were or were not enforcing liquor and vice laws.

One branch not always provided for in the first stages of a bureaucratic policy were the detectives. If a preventive police were fully effective, there would be no need for detectives. Establishing a detective squad was an admission that the police had not lived up to expectations. And there was the old fear that detectives and criminals were much too close. Roger Lane has shown how slow Philadelphia was in assigning police officers to work as homicide specialists.

Marxist scholars treat American police within a conceptual framework of class analysis. Historians such as Sidney Harring and Sean Wilentz look at the police as an instrument created by the owners of the means of production to control workers' behavior. The most obvious instances of such control came in strikes, where the police aided owners who wished to keep operating despite turnouts of their workforce. In such situations, say these scholars, the naked realities could not be disguised under such formulas as enforcing the law or protecting life and property. One does not have to be a Marxist to acknowledge that in large cities at least local police departments were seldom neutral in labor disputes.

Just as London provided the model for New York, Boston, and Philadelphia, these eastern cities served as models for other American communities. Historian Eric Monkkonen sees the establishment of bureaucratic police departments as an innovation beginning in the older and larger cities and then diffusing surprisingly quickly out and down the urban hierarchy. According to Monkkonen, fifteen cities had adopted uniforms—his key indicator of a bureaucratic police—by 1860 while another twenty-four joined them in the following decade. Evidently, the salaried, bureaucratic police was an idea whose time had come between 1840 and 1870. Later decades were to see the maturation and expansion of the patterns established during these formative years.

JAMES F. RICHARDSON

See also **British Policing; History of American Policing**

References and Further Reading

Jonson, D. R. 1979. *Policing the urban underworld: The impact of crime on the development of the American police, 1800–1887.* Philadelphia, PA: Temple University Press.

——. 1981. *American law enforcement: A history.* St. Louis, MO: Forum Press.

Lane, R. 1967. *Policing the city: Boston, 1822–1885.* Cambridge, MA: Harvard University Press.

——. 1979. *Violent death in the city: Suicide, accident, and murder in nineteenth century Philadelphia.* Cambridge, MA: Harvard University Press.

Miller, W. R. 1977. *Cops and robbers: Police authority in New York and London, 1830–1870.* Chicago: University of Chicago Press.

Richardson, J. 1970. *The New York police: Colonial times to 1901.* New York: Oxford University Press.

——. 1974. *Urban police in the United States.* Port Washington, NY: Kennikat.

Walker, S. 1977. *A critical history of police reform: The emergence of professionalism.* Lexington, MA: Lexington, 1977.

——. 1980. *Popular justice: A history of American criminal justice.* New York: Oxford University Press.

ARREST POWERS OF THE POLICE

The word *arrest* is derived from the French *arrêter*, "to stop, to obtain, to hinder, to obstruct." Arrest is "an ordinary English word" (Lord Eilhorne in *Spicer v. Holt*, 1976, 71), but it has acquired multiple meanings and measures for various criminal justice agencies, particularly the police.

Arrest is legally defined as "the apprehending or restraining of one's person in order to be forthcoming to answer all alleged or suspected crimes" (Blackstone 1979; Warner 1983). Arrest occurs whenever the following elements are present: (1) a police officer has reason to believe that a crime has been committed (probable cause); (2) the officer intends to take the suspect into custody; and (3) the person arrested experiences loss of freedom and restriction of movement.

Legal determination of whether a given contact is an arrest can be difficult (Whitebread and Slobogin 2000), which poses a practical problem for police. On the one hand, seizures accompanied by handcuffing, drawn guns, and the use of words to the effect that one is under arrest constitute arrest; on the other, brief questioning of a citizen on the street is generally not considered an arrest. Between the two extremes lie many types of police detentions, whose legal nature must be determined by the courts (Whitebread and Slobogin 2000).

The meaning attached to the term *arrest* is dependent on the purpose and context of its use. The definition or determination of arrest is complex because of the ramification for the person arrested and the emotional context in which it often takes place. The U.S. Supreme Court, however, has focused on freedom of movement. The Court, in the case of *U.S. v. Mendenhall* (1980), put forth the "free to leave" test. Justice Potter Stuart wrote, "A person has been seized within the meaning of the Fourth Amendment, only if, in view of all the circumstances surrounding the incident, a reasonable person would have believed that he is not free to leave." The Court, again, used the "free to leave" test in the 1994 case of *Stansbury v. California* saying the key factor in determining whether an arrest had been made was the suspect's freedom of movement.

Probable Cause

The quantum of knowledge required to justify an arrest for probable cause has been defined by the Supreme Court as "whether at that moment [of arrest] the facts and circumstances within [the officers'] knowledge and of which they [have] reasonable trustworthy information [are] sufficient to warrant a prudent man in believing that the [suspect] had committed or was committing an offense" (*Beck v. Ohio*, 379 U.S. 89, 91 [1964]). When the arresting officer's own observations are the basis for the arrest, only indicators of criminality noted prior to the arrest or evidence obtained as a result of a legitimate patdown based on reasonable suspicion (*Terry v. Ohio*, 1968) may be used to develop probable cause. Failure to identify oneself, protest one's innocence, or distance oneself from criminal suspects is, by itself, insufficient in constituting probable cause (Whitebread and Slobogin 2000).

In addition to the officer's personal knowledge, other sources for probable cause are information from credible informants whose input is reasonably corroborated, "respected citizens" or typical witnesses to or victims of crime, or reports from other police jurisdictions. Mere suspicion of criminal activity is not sufficient to justify arrest. Once the probable-cause requirement is met, subsequent discovery of information that casts doubt on whether probable cause existed at the time of the arrest will not invalidate the arrest (*Henry v. United States* 1959).

Taking a Person into Custody

An arrest can be carried out with or without an arrest warrant. An arrest warrant is an order to arrest a specific individual, signed by an impartial magistrate, if he or she feels that the proof presented by the police or the district attorney constitutes probable cause. Most magistrates require a written affidavit outlining the reasons for the arrest. Since the Fourth Amendment prohibits arbitrary arrests, the probable-cause requirement applies to both warrant and warrantless arrests.

Whenever feasible, police should obtain a warrant before making an arrest. Warrantless arrests occur mostly in "emergency" situations and are often made by patrolmen at the scene of a crime or when citizens apprehend the suspect before the police arrive. The courts, however, have allowed the police greater latitude in making warrantless arrests in recent years. For example, the Supreme Court in 2001 upheld the warrantless arrest of a woman for a seat-belt violation (*Atwater v. Largo Vista*).

The police can make an arrest in a number of ways. In a "mild arrest" an officer will announce that a person is under arrest and tap the arrestee's shoulder to reinforce the verbal statement. The officer may use an appropriate amount of force, depending on the degree of resistance offered by the suspect, to accomplish the arrest, ranging from physical subjugation to deadly force.

The police must provide the arrestee with specific statutory and constitutional protections. The Federal Rules of Criminal Procedure require that the arrested person be taken before the nearest available magistrate without any unnecessary delay, in order to prevent possible abuses by police during interrogation. The police must read the arrestee the Miranda warning, in which the suspect is informed of his or her Fifth Amendment right against self-incrimination, his or her right to be silent, and his or her Sixth Amendment right to be represented by counsel. The police are responsible for the physical well-being of the arrestee while the person is in their custody.

powers of the police may be exercised (Creamer 1980).

Some events, including placing someone in custody for mental health–related reasons, taking a minor younger than eighteen under certain conditions to a police station, or placing intoxicated persons under protective custody, that involve restrictions on one's liberty and being taken into custody are not considered arrest (Gless 1980, 281).

A definitional difficulty is the distinction between detention and arrest. The two concepts have certain elements in common: (1) the actual or constructive apprehension of an individual at a particular point in time, and (2) the continued retention of that person for a period of time to be determined (Telling 1978, 324). The concepts differ in the degree that the police may intrude on an individual's rights and interests as protected by the Fourth, Fifth, and Sixth Amendments. In analyzing and determining whether a detention is an arrest, the courts have considered that key factors are the purpose of the detention (e.g., fingerprinting versus questioning), its manner (police detention versus grand jury subpoenas), location (stationhouse confrontations versus seizures in the "field" or at the border), and duration. None of these factors, by itself, is determinative; rather, the "totality of circumstances" is the test of whether the detention amounted to an arrest (Whitebread and Slobogin 2000).

Arrest and Detention

A review of arrest and other types of contact between police and citizens indicates that restraint or restriction of a citizen's liberty does not necessarily constitute arrest. Police encounters with citizens range from those in which citizens are not compelled to respond to a stop (prompted by reasonable suspicion), detention short of arrest, and finally arrest, at which point all

Arrest and Police Practices

Because arrest has certain legal requirements (probable cause) and creates significant legal risks for the police (e.g., being liable for false imprisonment and being subject to a civil suit for damages), and because evidence gathered in the course of wrongful arrest may not be admissible in court, officers may sometimes avoid arrest and use field interrogation techniques (or detention) to accomplish their purposes (for examples and cases, see Telling 1978, and Zander 1977). Detention for investigation describes a broad category of police activities, which range from stopping individuals on the street to holding persons for interrogation for a few minutes to a few hours (Abrams 1967, 1103–1113). Detention, for purposes such as interrogation, is often an established police practice (La Fave 1965, ch. 16; Markowitz and Summerfield 1952, 1202, 1204). One study indicated that "though it constitutes an arrest, persons detained are not booked . . . and no record is kept of such cases" (Markowitz and Summerfield 1952, 1204; see also Telling 1978, 321; La Fave 1965, ch. 16). The legal classifications of such encounters do not arise unless the citizen is subsequently charged with an offense and the fruits of the detention—confessions—are introduced at the trial.

Behaviorally, arrest has been defined as the transporting of a suspect to a police station (Black 1971; La Fave 1965, 3–4), which is distinct from other preliminary investigative devices such as stopping and questioning, frisking, or other on-the-spot checks. The degree of interference is substantially greater when a suspect is taken to the station—whatever the purpose of the custody (for investigation or prosecution, or to realize other deterrent, rehabilitative, or punitive functions). The person being transported also views such extended custody as different from on-the-street investigation, because the consequences of being taken to the police station (an arrest record, often including photographing and fingerprinting) may be more serious.

Suspects, however, are sometimes taken to the station for investigation under circumstances that do not constitute an arrest, such as taking the suspect in without telling him that he is arrested and without recording the detention as an arrest. Or, a suspect could be "invited" to headquarters (La Fave 1965, 302). Some police officers believe that they have not "arrested" a suspect until he or she has formally been booked on the police blotter.

The definition of arrest and numerous court decisions (Cook 1971, 180) suggest that a critical factor in determining whether an arrest has occurred is the officer's intent to take custody of the individual in order to charge him or her with a crime. In practice, police often arrest citizens for other purposes such as harassment or taking offenders off the street (La Fave 1965, 150), as a peacekeeping device in certain neighborhoods, as a means to enforce and legitimize their authority (Reiss 1971), and to demonstrate to superiors or to the public that they are doing their jobs (Markowitz and Summerfield 1952, 1202). In short, arrest has come to have meaning and importance as a form of immediate intervention in dealing with various exigencies that is independent of the rest of the criminal justice system.

The understanding of the person suspect is also an important legal element of arrest. Generally, an individual is not under arrest if he or she has no knowledge or reason to suspect that he or she has been arrested (Cook 1971, 177). The law recognizes that arrest is primarily a personal and subjective experience that must be felt by the individual being arrested.

The understanding of citizens concerning the nature of a confrontation with the police and their freedom to leave the place of the encounter has, therefore, often been the subject of criminal trials and legal discussions. For instance, it has been argued that a person detained for field interrogation "will undoubtedly not consider himself under arrest, and consequently can in all honesty answer in the negative if later asked whether he has been arrested" (La Fave 1965, 347).

Research has indicated, however, that citizens are unable to distinguish between arrest and other types of police contact and often admit to having been arrested when they actually have no arrest record (Erez 1984).

Arrest Records and Recording

Empirically, it has been demonstrated that ambiguity concerning the nature of various types of contacts between citizens and police also results in multiple definitions of arrest for purposes of data recording, reporting, and statistical tabulation. "Whether a youngster obtained an arrest record or not could be a function of different officers' conceptions of what constituted the meaning of arrest" (according to Klein, Rosenweig, and Bates 1975, 83). These conceptions resulted in definitions that ranged from "booking" through "brought into the station," "any detention (or citation, too) at the station," and even "field contacts" (Klein et al. 1975, 85–86; Sherman 1980b, 471):

> . . . in the San Jose, California department arrest was defined as charging, but in Denver . . . all persons brought to a station house were counted as arrested. Cincinnati was reported to make frequent use of investigative detention, in which suspects were kept in custody at a police station for up to twenty-four hours without being counted as having been arrested. In Detroit, arresting patrol officers turn everything over to detectives at the station house, where the detectives . . . released an estimated 50% of the persons arrested for major felony offenses because of weak evidence or other reasons. . . .

The Police Foundation (Sherman 1980a, 1980b) suggests that the counts of arrests in different cities may be based on as many as five different points of reference: contacting suspects on the street, transporting suspects to a police station, detaining a suspect at a police station, booking a suspect at a police station, or filing charges against a suspect with a prosecutor.

The booking process, the external or formal proof of arrest, is usually a clerical activity performed soon after the suspect has been delivered to the station. Booking results in an arrest record with a detrimental effect on the person booked. Booking constitutes a check on police abuse, because friends, counsel, and others may learn of the suspect's arrest (La Fave 1965, 380). Important legal rights and privileges arise at booking such as the right to counsel and the right against self-incrimination. Although the suspect has Fifth and Sixth Amendment protections at the time of arrest, police may delay the booking process hoping that such rights will not be demanded until booking occurs. In some cases the police may refrain from booking the suspect/arrestee in order to give him the opportunity to exculpate himself before his involvement is recorded and publicized.

Factors Influencing Police Discretion to Make an Arrest

Police are vested with wide discretionary power in their decision to arrest. Conflicting organizational goals, the dependence of police on the communities they serve, and various situational factors make full enforcement of the law neither possible nor desirable. The primary legal factor influencing police use of discretion is the seriousness of the offense (Terry 1967, 179) because the police are more likely to arrest adults and juveniles when the offense is a felony rather than a misdemeanor (see, e.g., Black 1971).

Situational factors influencing the decision to arrest include the demeanor of the suspect, because antagonistic suspects have a greater risk of being arrested (Black 1971; Reiss 1971). The presence and action of a complainant will also influence police to make an arrest. A preexisting victim–suspect relationship will reduce the likelihood of arrest (Black 1971; La Fave 1965). The way the police enter the scene is a factor, because arrest is more likely in reactive encounters than in proactive ones (Black 1971; Reiss 1971). Location of the encounter is another factor, because arrest is more likely in public places than in private ones (Black 1976).

Extralegal factors that influence the arrest decision include age (juveniles are arrested more often than adults), gender (Visher 1983) (males are arrested more often than females), race (blacks are arrested more often than whites), and socioeconomic status (Smith et al. 1984) (the poor are arrested more often than the wealthy). Many of these characteristics have been associated with the "symbolic assailant," who is viewed by police as being potentially violent and a great threat to the police and the public.

Another extralegal factor that influences the arrest decision is a department's "style" of policing. Departments that follow a "legalistic" style will produce more arrests than those that adopt a "service" style, while the departments that follow a "watchman" style will produce the fewest arrests.

Judicial Review of Arrest Practices and the Police

Police arrests are inevitably subject to judicial review. When the courts rule that the officers have violated procedural law, the police feel that their professional competence is being questioned and that they are hamstrung because the guilty go free (Reiss 1971). Because the rules governing police work are in constant flux, the police continuously test the limits of their arrest authority in their daily efforts to control crime, while the courts limit this authority in order to protect individual rights and civil liberties.

EDNA EREZ and DANIEL PRICE

See also **Autonomy and the Police; Civil Restraint in Policing; Constitutional Rights: In-Custody Interrogation; Liability and the Police; Presumptive Arrest Policing**

References and Further Reading

Abrams, G. H. 1967. Constitutional limitations on detention for investigation. *Iowa Law Review* 52:1093–1119.
Black, D. 1971. The Social organization of arrest. *Standard Law Review* 23: 1087–1111.
———. 1976. *The behavior of law*. New York: Academic Press.
Blackstone, W. 1979. *Commentaries on the laws of England*. 4 vols. Chicago: University of Chicago Press.
Cook, J. G. 1971. Subjective attitudes of arrestee and arrestor as affecting occurrence of arrest. *Kansas Law Review* 19: 173–83.
Creamer, J. S. 1980. *The law of arrest, search and seizure*. New York: Holt, Rinehart and Winston.
Erez, E. 1984. On the 'dark figure' of arrest. *Journal of Police Science and Administration* 12: 431–40.
Gless, A. G. 1980. Arrest and citation: Definition and analysis. *Nebraska Law Review* 26: 279–326.
Klein, M. W., S. L. Rosenweig, and R. Bates. 1975. The ambiguous arrest. *Criminology* 13: 78–89.
La Fave, W. R. 1965. *Arrest: The decision to take a suspect into custody*. Boston: Little, Brown.
Markowitz, P. R., and W. Summerfield. 1952. Philadelphia police practice and the law of arrest. *University of Pennsylvania Law Review* 100: 1182–1216.
Reiss, A. J. 1971. *The police and the public*. New Haven, CT: Yale University Press.
Sherman, L. 1980a. Enforcement workshop: Defining arrests—The practical consequences of agency differences, part I. *Criminal Law Bulletin* 16: 376–80.
———. 1980b. Enforcement workshop: Defining arrests—The practical consequences of agency differences, part ii. *Criminal Law Bulletin* 16: 468–71.
Smith, D., C. A. Visher, and L. A. Davidson. 1984. Equity and discretionary justice: The influence of race on police arrest decisions. *Journal of Criminal Law and Criminality* 75: 234–49.
Telling, D. 1978. Arrest and detention: The conceptual maze. *Criminal Law Review*, June, 320–31.
Terry, R. 1967. The screening of juvenile offenders. *Journal of Criminal Law, Criminology and Police Science*, 173–81.
Visher, C. 1983. Gender, police arrest decisions, and notions of chivalry. *Criminology* 21 (1): 5–28.

Warner, S. B. 2000. The Uniform Arrest Act. *Virginia Law Review* 28: 315–47.

Whitebread, C. H., and C. Slobogin. 2000. *Criminal procedure*. New York: Foundation Press.

Zander, M. 1977. When is arrest not an arrest? *New Law Journal* 127: 352–54, 379–82.

ARSON AND ITS INVESTIGATION

Magnitude of the Problem

According to the 2002 *Uniform Crime Reports* (UCR), as compiled by the Federal Bureau of Investigation, 12,454 law enforcement agencies reported 74,921 arson offenses. In 1991, 11,845 law enforcement agencies reported 99,784 arson offenses. Since 1993, arson arrests have declined 20.5%. Average damage per arson offense in 2002 was $11,253, an amount that has decreased by $700 since 1991. The national arson clearance rate for 1991 was 16%; for 2022 it was 16.5%, showing little change.

Forty-three percent of arsons cleared in 2002 involved juvenile offenders, and 71.8 of offenses involving juveniles involved community/public structures. Almost half (49.4%) of arrestees for arson were under age eighteen; 67.8% were under twenty-five. Males accounted for 84.8% of arrestees; 76.8% of arrestees were white and 21.5% were black.

It seems as though arson, like all crimes, has declined during the past decade. However, it should be noted that there is limited reporting of arson offenses by law enforcement, so generalizations from UCR data must be made with care.

Purpose of the Arson Investigation

The purpose of an arson investigation is to determine the origin and cause of a fire that has been purposefully set to burn down the property of another or to incinerate one's own property for some illegal purpose. The desired outcome of an arson investigation is the arrest of the perpetrator. The 2002 UCR defined arson as "any willful or malicious burning or attempt to burn, with or without intent to defraud, a dwelling house, public building, motor vehicle or aircraft, personal property of another, etc." Obviously, not all fires are arson. The UCR does not consider suspicious fires or fires of unknown origin. It is the investigator's duty to gather all the facts and evidence at the fire scene, then to decide whether the fire was of incendiary, natural, or accidental origin.

The arson investigation focuses first on determining the point or points of origin of the fire, and second on determining how the fire started. The trained arson investigator, and indeed the vast majority of firefighters, can easily determine the point of origin of a fire. Generally, the fire burns hottest at the point of origin. Incendiary fires tend to burn quicker and at a higher heat than natural or accidental fires due to the use of an accelerant. Incendiary fires also often have distinctive burn patterns. As the fire burns, it spreads away from the point of origin, creating noticeable burn patterns.

Handling the Arson Crime Scene

Every type of crime scene presents investigators with particular challenges that must be overcome, or at least accounted for, in order for the investigation to be successful. Unlike many other crime scenes, which can remain relatively intact from the time of the commission of the crime until investigators arrive, arson scenes suffer considerable damage prior to the start of the investigation. First and foremost, fire is very destructive. Although it is highly unlikely that a fire will completely destroy objects at the scene, it does alter them considerably. Second, the water that is generally used to extinguish fires is also very destructive to evidence. Third, when firefighters are called to the scene of a fire, their first concern is not preserving the scene for the arson investigators. Their first concern is rescuing any victims that may be present and extinguishing the fire. These goals may be contradictory to preserving the crime scene.

Proper crime scene handling dictates a systematic (to ensure that no evidence is missed) and controlled (to minimize the possibility of contamination) approach to the collection, preservation, and processing of evidence. The search of an arson scene should begin at the furthest point at which debris is found and progress toward the origin of the fire. The search should be conducted in a predetermined pattern so that no area remains unsearched.

Most evidence will be found near the origin of the fire. This area naturally receives the most focus and material from this area should be sent to the laboratory. Generally a significant amount of ash and charred remnants from this point should be submitted to the laboratory for analysis since this debris is most likely to contain chemical residue from any accelerant used. This area may also contain partially burned items that may reveal fingerprints, fibers, or hair that can be linked to the suspect. Depending on how the fire was started, any devices used to ignite the fire may not be completely destroyed and may reveal evidence that can be used to successfully link a suspect to the crime scene.

Arson evidence is packaged differently from other evidence because it often contains residues that require laboratory analysis. It should not be air dried and packaged in a breathable, paper bag like other wet, crime scene evidence. To ensure that chemical residues do not deteriorate, the evidence must be packaged in airtight, plastic containers. These containers will not allow vapors to escape; these vapors may be the only indication of what sort of accelerant or explosive was used. As with any evidence, these containers should be appropriately marked and the chain of custody should be observed. Burnt evidence may be submitted in whole or part to the laboratory, depending on the size of the object.

At the scene chemical color tests may be used to test for accelerant residue. Some departments also have canines trained to detect accelerant residue. At the laboratory, a variety of tests may be performed to determine the chemical makeup of any residue found at the scene. The gas chromatograph is the most reliable way to determine the chemical makeup of flammable residues in the laboratory.

Motives for Arson

Although there are a variety of motives for arson, by far, the most common is financial gain through insurance fraud. In determining whether or not the fire was motivated by insurance fraud, the investigator must determine who, if anyone, would stand to gain from the damage or destruction of a particular piece of residential or commercial property. This motive may become apparent when the investigator discovers that the building was insured for more than its value, that the insurance was recently increased, and that expensive equipment, important papers, personal items, and the like were removed from the building just prior to the fire.

The second most common motive is vandalism and revenge. These motives may occur separately or in conjunction with each other. Revenge can be easy to determine. Generally, the perpetrator will have made specific threats toward the victim or victims. Even in the absence of a specific threat, it may be generally known that the perpetrator had a grudge against the victim. An act of vandalism may be carried out as a form of revenge, or vandalism may be perpetrated for fun. Most juvenile instances of arson fall into this category.

Arson may be committed as a secondary crime, in an attempt to disguise another offense. The primary crime, for example, may be murder, fraud (not related to arson-related insurance fraud), or organized criminal activity, to name a few.

Fires may be set by highly pathological adults who enjoy setting fires. Serial arsonists frequently derive a sexual enjoyment from the fires that they set. Many will remain at or near the scene and many prefer to burn unoccupied buildings.

Fires may also be set by children. Generally children who set fires can be placed into one of three groups. The first group is comprised of children with very limited knowledge of fire and for whom the fire-setting was an accident. This group is comprised mostly of very young children. The second group is comprised of children who were experimenting with fire out of curiosity and the resultant fire was an accident. The third group sets fires as part of a larger pathology—they also frequently exhibit aggression and social skill deficits. This latter group is referred to as childhood firesetters.

Similarity between Arson Investigations and Explosive Investigations

Arson and explosive investigations are remarkably similar. Both of these types of investigations focus on these specifics:

- The point of origin
- How the explosion/fire was set
- Where to begin the scene search (It should begin at the furthest point at which debris is found and progress toward the origin.)
- Gathering evidence, most of which will be found near the point of origin
- The devices used to ignite the explosion (These may not be completely destroyed and may reveal fingerprints, fibers, hairs, and other particles that can be used to successfully link a suspect to the crime scene.)
- Packaging of evidence (It should be packaged to protect chemical residues that may deteriorate.)
- Determining in the laboratory the chemical makeup of any residue found at the scene.

Training for Investigators

To become an expert in arson investigation, an individual must have on-the-job experience as a firefighter, police officer, or both and must be broadly trained. The arson investigator must also be involved in ongoing training. Courses are available from local police academies, fire academies, private agencies, and colleges and universities. Some courses are even being offered in an online format.

Courses cover such areas as:

- Law
- Chemistry of fire
- Behavior of fire
- Building construction
- Fire-scene investigation
- Initial fire attack and suppression
- Interviewing and interrogation
- Fire typology
- Courtroom testimony
- Motives of the arsonist
- Fire modeling
- Arson fraud
- Report writing
- Scene reconstruction

AYN EMBAR-SEDDON and
ALLAN D. PASS

See also **Clearance Rates and Criminal Investigations; Criminal Investigation; Forensic Investigations;** *Uniform Crime Reports*

References and Further Reading

Battle, Brendan P., and Paul B. Weston. 1975. *Arson*. New York: Arco Publishing.
Boudreau, J. F., et al. 1977. *Arson and arson investigation: Survey and assessment.*

Washington, DC: National Institute of Law Enforcement and Criminal Justice.

Bouquard, Thomas J. 1983. *Arson investigation: The step-by-step procedure*. Springfield, IL: Charles C Thomas.

DeForest, P. R., R. E. Gaensslen, and H. C. Lee. 1983. *Forensic science: An introduction to criminalistics*. New York: McGraw-Hill.

Icove, D. J. 2003. *Forensic fire scene reconstruction*. New York: Prentice Hall.

International Association of Arson Investigators. 1976. *Selected articles for fire and arson investigators*. Springfield, IL: IAAI Publishers.

Kirk, P. L., and J. D. Dehaan. 2002. *Kirk's fire investigation*. New York: Prentice Hall.

Kolko, D. J., and A. E. Kazdin. 1991. Motives of childhood firesetters: Firesetting characteristics and psychological correlates. *Journal of Child Psychology and Psychiatry* 32: 535–50.

O'Conner, J. 1993. *Practical fire and arson investigation*. Boca Raton, FL: CRC Press.

Tuck, Charles A., Jr. 1976. *NFPA inspection manual*. 4th ed. Boston: National Fire Protection Association.

Uniform Crime Reports: Arson. 2002. http://www.fbi.gov/ucr/cius_02/html/web/offreported/02-narson11.html (accessed November 15, 2005).

ASIAN POLICING SYSTEMS

As the largest and most populous continent, Asia is merely a geographic term. Asia can be divided into six regions. Our focus is confined to East Asia and Southeast Asia because these peoples as well as their cultures resemble each other more than any other regions of Asia. Like the concept of Asia, East Asia and Southeast Asia are more geographic terms than homogeneous concepts, and the use of the terms to describe these vast areas always carries the potential of obscuring the enormous diversity among the two regions. Because of space limitations, the discussion of Asian policing systems is limited to selected law enforcement agencies in East Asian and Southeast Asia.

East Asia and Southeast Asia are regarded separately mainly because of the level of industrialization, cultural traditions, and geographic influences. East Asia includes China (Hong Kong and Macao), Korea (North and South), Mongolia, and the islands of Japan and Taiwan. Historically, these countries were under the influence of Buddhism and Confucianism, with Islamic and Christian impacts being marginal. Buddhism and Confucianism interacted with the local culture and mixed with shamanism and Taoism in China and Korea and with Shinto in Japan. Southeast Asia embraces Brunei, Cambodia, Indonesia, Laos, Malaysia, Myanmar (formerly known as Burma), Philippines, Singapore, Thailand, and Vietnam. Traditionally, these nations were greatly influenced by Buddhism, Hinduism, and Islam. Modern history saw the conversion to Catholicism in the Philippines, East Timor, and Vietnam.

Politically, many nations are communist states, such as China, Laos, North Korea, and Vietnam. Others have liberal democratic regimes such as Japan. The rest of the nations sit between these two extremes with South Korea and Taiwan having recently joined the liberal democratic regimes. There are also three constitutional monarchies—Cambodia, Japan, and Malaysia—and one constitutional sultanate—Brunei (Central Intelligence Agency 2005).

East Asian societies are more homogeneous than countries in Southeast Asia. The common philosophical Confucianism and Buddhism, reinforced by centuries of tradition, have molded these societies into accepting patriarchal, hierarchical, authoritarian order. People are bound by notions of reciprocal duty, informal resolution of conflict, and great reliance on collectivism. The resulting legal systems are unlike those found in the West, and in the eyes of Western scholars, these legal systems hold little respect for procedural niceties or individual rights. They do not recognize the existence of an autonomous, rights-bearing individual who is an isolated being, related solely to God or to nature. Instead, the individual in East Asia from birth to death and beyond is defined in the context of a hierarchical collective (Cao and Cullen 2001; Dutton 1992). These societies place emphasis on intertwining bonds of human relationship to maintain the social fabric and to prevent crime and disorder. In other words, these intertwining bonds have been the basic unit of informal policing over the centuries.

It is impossible to describe each of the police forces in these regions. The current entry, therefore, only describes the police organizations in five nations in these regions: China, Japan, Korea, Malaysia, and Singapore.

Policing in China

Although China has a very long history of bureaucracy, the police agency was not part of this long tradition. Before the twentieth century, Confucian China had no professional police force. Some forms of forerunners of secret police can be found in the Ming Dynasty's (1368–1644) dong-chang and xi-chang, and the county magistrate, who was a chief executive and judge in one, employed "runners" to perform some duties of law enforcement. The first modern sense of a professional police force was created in Tianjin in 1901 under the command of General Yuan Shi-kai as a compromised solution to maintain law and order in the concessions of Western powers. Soon the police as a paramilitary government agency spread to all major cities, and the government of the Qing Dynasty (1644–1911) in Beijing established a bureau to manage this force in 1905.

After the overthrow of the Qing Dynasty in 1911, more systematic ways of organizing and training police, which imitated the police of Germany, Japan, and the Soviet Union, were introduced in the Republic of China (1912–1949). The process was interrupted in 1949 when the communists took over the government. The new regime, The People's Republic of China,

under Mao, developed a total proletarian dictatorship that modeled the Soviet practice exclusively. The police were highly centralized and were loyal only to the Communist Party. Its power is ubiquitous, absolute, and unchallengeable.

After Mao's death in 1976, the reform-minded Deng Xiaoping introduced many changes in an attempt to decentralize the police apparatus. The Ministry of Justice was established under the new constitution of 1982, which removed the duty of managing the prisons and most other correctional institutions from the police. The Ministry of State Security was established in June 1983 with the mandate "to ensure China's security and strengthen the struggle against espionage." The military police, however, were established in the following year as a separate unit within the Public Security Ministry. As a result, the Public Security Ministry has become more focused on crime prevention, criminal investigation, fire control, traffic, census responsibilities, and border control. In 1995, the Police Law came into effect (Ma 1997). The law defines the police organization, duties, recruitment, training, powers, disciplinary procedures, and citizen complaint mechanism.

The many levels of police are controlled in a top-down manner by the Ministry of Public Security in Beijing with the approval of the provincial and city governments. In each province and in each city, there are four major divisions of the police: military police, which guard the important government buildings; fire police; traffic police; and public security police. The unique characteristics of Chinese policing are that crime prevention and crime investigation are largely shouldered by the public security police at the neighborhood station, working closely with the neighborhood committee. Since 1978, there has been a slow but steady shift from a force (imposer of order) to a service (servant of the community) orientation. The police officers have more discretionary power than their counterparts in the West as well as more responsibilities.

overhaul the department's activities. In 1991, the ACU was disbanded and replaced with the Anti-Gang Violence Unit (AGVU), which was charged with disrupting ongoing gang conflicts rather than mounting an aggressive campaign to arrest as many offenders as possible. In 1992, the St. Clair Commission released its report and cited extensive corruption and incompetent management of the Boston Police Department. Commissioner Mickey Roache was replaced with William Bratton, a former Boston Police officer who was the chief of the New York City Transit Police. Commissioner Bratton immediately replaced the old command staff with new officers who were known to be innovative and hardworking, made investments in developing the department's technology to understand crime problems, developed a neighborhood policing plan, and commenced training of beat-level officers in the methods of community and problem-oriented policing (Bratton 1998). In 1993, Bratton left the Boston Police Department to become the commissioner of the New York Police Department. Paul Evans, a career Boston Police officer, became the new leader of the Boston Police. Commissioner Evans expanded the initial groundwork laid by Bratton to institute a formal neighborhood policing plan and led the department in its efforts to prevent youth violence and to repair the department's badly damaged relationship with the community.

A cornerstone of Commissioner Evans' neighborhood policing strategy was the Same Cop Same Neighborhood (SC/SN) plan to deliver public safety services to every neighborhood in Boston (http://www.cityofboston.gov/police). Under SC/SN, the same officers were assigned to a neighborhood beat and required to spend no less than 60% of their shift in that designated beat. SC/SN beat officers were encouraged to form working relationships with community members and engage in problem-oriented policing strategies to deal with crime and disorder problems in their neighborhood. Beat officers developed relationships with community members by participating in community meetings and attending neighborhood activities and events, many of which are sponsored by the city of Boston. An important idea underlying the SC/SN plan was to increase ownership and accountability for problems in specific neighborhoods by beat officers and, through this sense of responsibility, to promote increased coordination among the various units within the Boston Police Department as well as with the community.

While this general strategy seems straightforward, it required fundamental changes in the way the Boston Police Department operates internally and delivers public safety services to citizens (http://www.cityofboston.gov/police). It also required changes in the attitude of every officer in the department from patrolman to the highest command levels. Work processes and reporting procedures were redesigned and new uses of technology were developed. For instance, local crime conditions in each of Boston's eleven police districts were analyzed on a monthly basis at Crime Analysis Meetings (CAM). CAMs were similar to the New York Police Department's COMPSTAT meetings. Boston police crime analysts used crime maps and trend analysis to uncover emergent crime and disorder problems. District commanders were held accountable for developing problem-oriented strategies to deal with changes in neighborhood conditions. These changes mandated shifts in the assignment and deployment of personnel. Some of the noteworthy changes included reconfiguring boundaries for police districts and sectors, training and education sessions with supervisory personnel, the identification of potential roadblocks and suggestions on how to avoid them by middle managers, and an ongoing dialogue about implementation issues across the varying ranks of the department.

The Boston Police Department credits their neighborhood policing strategy with improving their relationships with the community and positioning them to deal more effectively with crime problems when compared to their policing strategies and practices of the past. Between 1990 and 2000, the FBI index crime rate in Boston fell by nearly 50%, from 11,850 per 100,000 residents to 6,088 per 100,000 residents (http://bjsdata.ojp.usdoj.gov/dataonline/Search/Crime/Crime.cfm). While Boston is known for its serious commitment to community policing, it has been nationally recognized for its innovative approach to youth violence prevention and its unusually strong working relationship with black churches. These success stories flow from the department's commitment to changing their ineffective practices of the past.

Preventing Youth Violence

Under the leadership of Commissioner Evans, the Boston Police Department focused its efforts on dealing with the upswing in youth violence that devastated Boston's inner-city neighborhoods. During the early 1990s, the AGVU evolved into the Youth Violence Strike Force (YVSF) and its mandate was broadened beyond controlling outbreaks of gang violence to more general youth violence prevention. With a range of criminal justice and community-based partners, the YVSF developed many innovative programs including "Operation Nightlight," a police-probation partnership to ensure at-risk youth were abiding by the conditions of their release into the community; a partnership with the Bureau of Alcohol, Tobacco, and Firearms (ATF) and the U.S. Attorney's Office to identify and apprehend illegal gun traffickers who were providing guns to violent gangs; and the "Summer of Opportunity" program, which provides at-risk youth with job training and leadership skills that can be transferred to workplace, school, or home

settings. Although these programs were certainly innovative and added to the Boston Police Department's array of tools to prevent youth violence, in 1995, the city still suffered from high rates of youth homicide fueled by conflicts between street gangs.

The Boston Gun Project was a problem-oriented policing exercise expressly aimed at taking on a serious, large-scale crime problem: homicide victimization among young people in Boston. The Boston Gun Project proceeded by (1) assembling an interagency working group of largely line-level criminal justice and other practitioners; (2) applying quantitative and qualitative research techniques to create an assessment of the nature of, and dynamics driving, youth violence in Boston; (3) developing an intervention designed to have a substantial, near-term impact on youth homicide; (4) implementing and adapting the intervention; and (5) evaluating the intervention's impact (Kennedy et al. 1996). The project began in early 1995 and implemented what is now known as the "Operation Ceasefire" intervention, which began in the late spring of 1996.

The trajectory of the project and of Operation Ceasefire has been extensively documented (see, e.g., Kennedy, Braga, and Piehl 2001). Briefly, the working group of law enforcement personnel, youth workers, and researchers diagnosed the youth violence problem in Boston as one of patterned, largely vendetta-like ("beef") hostility among a small population of chronically criminal offenders, and particularly among those involved in some sixty loose, informal, mostly neighborhood-based groups (these groups were called "gangs" in Boston, but were not Chicago- or LA-style gangs). The Operation Ceasefire "pulling levers" strategy was designed to deter gang violence by reaching out directly to gangs, saying explicitly that violence would no longer be tolerated, and backing up that message by "pulling every lever" legally available when violence occurred (Kennedy 1997, 1998). These law enforcement levers included disrupting street-level drug markets, serving warrants, mounting federal prosecutions, and changing the conditions of community supervision for probationers and parolees in the targeted group. Simultaneously, youth workers, probation and parole officers, and later churches and other community groups offered gang members services and other kinds of help. If gang members wanted to step away from a violent lifestyle, the Operation Ceasefire working group focused on providing them with the services and opportunities necessary to make the transition.

The Operation Ceasefire working group delivered their antiviolence message in formal meetings with gang members, through individual police and probation contacts with gang members, through meetings with inmates of secure juvenile facilities in the city, and through gang outreach workers. The deterrence message was not a deal with gang members to stop violence. Rather, it was a promise to gang members that violent behavior would evoke an immediate and intense response. If gangs committed other crimes but refrained from violence, the normal workings of police, prosecutors, and the rest of the criminal justice system dealt with these matters. But if gang members hurt people, the working group focused its enforcement actions on them.

A central hypothesis within the working group was the idea that a meaningful period of substantially reduced youth violence might serve as a "firebreak" and result in a relatively long-lasting reduction in future youth violence (Kennedy et al. 1996). The idea was that youth violence in Boston had become a self-sustaining cycle among a relatively small number of youth, with objectively high levels of risk leading to nominally self-protective behavior such as gun acquisition and use, gang formation, tough "street" behavior, and the like—behavior that then became an additional input into the cycle of violence (Kennedy et al. 1996). If this cycle could be interrupted, a new equilibrium at a lower level of risk and violence might be established, perhaps without the need for continued high levels of either deterrent or facilitative intervention. The larger hope was that a successful intervention to reduce gang violence in the short term would have a disproportionate, sustainable impact in the long term.

A large reduction in the yearly number of Boston youth homicides followed immediately after Operation Ceasefire was implemented in mid-1996. A formal evaluation of Operation Ceasefire revealed that the intervention was associated with a 63% decrease in the monthly number of Boston youth homicides, a 32% decrease in monthly number of shots-fired calls, a 25% decrease in monthly number of gun assaults, and, in one high-risk police district given special attention in the evaluation, a 44% decrease in monthly number of youth gun assault incidents (Braga et al. 2001b). The evaluation also suggested that Boston's significant youth homicide reduction associated with Operation Ceasefire was distinct when compared to youth homicide trends in most major cities in New England and nationally.

Boston Cops and Black Churches

Operation Ceasefire benefited from strong community support emanating from a strong relationship with black churches in neighborhoods suffering from gang violence. In 1992, a key partnership developed between the Boston Police Department and members of the city's black clergy. A loosely allied group of activist black clergy formed the Ten Point Coalition after a gang invasion of the Morningstar Baptist Church. During a memorial for a slain rival gang member, mourners were attacked with knives and guns (Kennedy et al. 2001; Winship and Berrien 1999). In the wake of that outrage, the Ten Point Coalition expanded their existing ministries to include all at-risk youth in the Roxbury, Dorchester, and Mattapan sections of

Boston. The ministers decided they should attempt to prevent the youth in their community from joining gangs, and also that they needed to send an antiviolence message to all youth, whether gang involved or not.

To do this, the clergy had to make two adjustments to their normal ministry. First, they had to define all youth as their responsibility regardless of the parish the youth lived in or the youth's denominational affiliation. Previously, young people who did not participate in church activities were not viewed as part of the ministry's mission; henceforth, the protection of these young people would be the primary mission of many churches. The second adjustment involved taking the ministry to the streets. It was clear that if the ministers wanted to get involved with the community's youth they could not wait in their churches for the youth to come to them. They had to go "where the kids were." This meant that the clergy had to spend time on the streets at night, getting to know the kids they were attempting to protect. This was a very different and often frightening new approach to providing ministry services, but they found the Boston Streetworkers, city-employed gang outreach workers, were natural allies. Quickly the streetworkers and the Ten Point clergy came to work closely together to provide at-risk youth with alternatives to gang violence.

Working with the Boston Police Department, the Ten Point Coalition provided another important dimension to the development of Operation Ceasefire: credibility for the Boston Police Department with the communities of color in Boston, which in Boston, as in many other cities, had a lengthy history of tension with the police. Although the Ten Point Coalition had initially been very critical of the Boston Police Department, they eventually forged a strong working relationship with the YVSF (Winship and Berrien 1999). Ten Point clergy and others involved in the faith-based organization accompanied YVSF police officers on home visits to the families of troubled youth and also acted as advocates for youth in the criminal justice system. The presence of former adversaries working together toward a common goal dramatically enhanced the legitimacy of the entire effort.

ANTHONY A. BRAGA

See also **Community-Oriented Policing: Effects and Impacts; Community-Oriented Policing: Practices; Community-Oriented Policing: Rationale; COMPSTAT; Crime Control Strategies; Minorities and the Police; Problem-Oriented Policing; Youth Gangs: Interventions and Results**

References and Further Reading

Braga, Anthony A., and David M. Kennedy. 2002. Reducing gang violence in Boston. In *Responding to gangs: Evaluation and research*, ed. W. L. Reed and S. H. Decker, 265–88. Washington, DC: National Institute of Justice, U.S. Department of Justice.

Braga, Anthony A., David M. Kennedy, and George Tita. 2002. New approaches to the strategic prevention of gang and group-involved violence. In *Gangs in America*, 3rd ed., ed. C. R. Huff, 271–86. Thousand Oaks, CA: Sage Publications.

Braga, Anthony A., David M. Kennedy, Anne M. Piehl, and Elin J. Waring. 2001a. Measuring the impact of Operation Ceasefire. In *Reducing Gun violence: The Boston Gun Project's Operation Ceasefire*, 55–71. Washington, DC: National Institute of Justice, U.S. Department of Justice.

Braga, Anthony A., David M. Kennedy, Elin J. Waring, and Anne M. Piehl 2001b. Problem-oriented policing, deterrence, and youth violence: An evaluation of Boston's Operation Ceasefire. *Journal of Research in Crime and Delinquency* 38: 195–225.

Bratton, William. 1998. *Turnaround: How America's top cop reversed the crime epidemic*. New York: Random House.

Kennedy, David M. 1997. Pulling levers: Chronic offenders, high-crime settings, and a theory of prevention. *Valparaiso University Law Review* 31: 449–84.

———. 1998. Pulling levers: Getting deterrence right. *National Institute of Justice Journal* 136: 2–8.

Kennedy, David M., Anthony A. Braga, and Anne M. Piehl 1997. The unknown universe: Mapping gangs and gang violence in Boston. In *Crime mapping and crime prevention*, ed. D. L. Weisburd and J. T. McEwen, 219–62. Monsey, NY: Criminal Justice Press.

———. 2001. Developing and implementing Operation Ceasefire. In *Reducing gun violence: The Boston Gun Project's Operation Ceasefire*, 5–54. Washington, DC: National Institute of Justice, U.S. Department of Justice.

Kennedy, David M., Anne M. Piehl, and Anthony A. Braga. 1996. Youth violence in Boston: Gun markets, serious youth offenders, and a use-reduction strategy. *Law and Contemporary Problems* 59: 147–96.

McDevitt, Jack, Anthony A. Braga, Dana Nurge, and Michael Buerger. 2003. Boston's Youth Violence Prevention Program: A comprehensive community-wide approach. In *Policing gangs and youth violence*, ed. S. H. Decker, 53–76. Belmont, CA: Wadsworth Publishing Company.

Winship, Christopher, and Jenny Berrien. 1999. Boston cops and black churches. *The Public Interest* 136: 52–68.

BOSTON POLICE DEPARTMENT

Boston is credited with being home to the very first modern American police force in 1838. The Boston Police Department (BPD) consisted of nine officers identified only by a distinctive hat and badge. Instead of carrying guns, officers protected themselves using six-foot blue and white poles and "police rattles," which they used to call for assistance. Also, police communicated through a telegraph system that linked the central office and area police stations.

Boston, like many of the other police forces forming across the nation at the time, structured itself nominally after the London model of modern policing created by Sir Robert Peel. This British model consisted of three elements: the mission of crime prevention, the strategy of visible patrol over fixed beats, and the quasi-military organizational structure. However, the American police force differed from its British counterpart in that politics dominated nearly every facet of American policing in the nineteenth century, which led to inefficiency, corruption, and a lack of professionalism. In Boston, for example, the mayor frequently rewarded loyal campaign workers by appointing them as members of the police force. Boston Police also took on a more multifunctional role than London police, carrying out a host of civic activities that were not necessarily crime related. Some of these additional responsibilities included snow removal, street repair, and animal control. Finally, since Boston police officers served at the pleasure of the mayor, large numbers of police officers were terminated each time a new mayor took office.

Widespread police corruption planted the seeds for the Reform Era in the twentieth century, which introduced an organized movement for police professionalism nationally. The Professionalism Movement defined policing as a profession; thereby, raising standards for police departments especially with regards to recruiting and training. It also called for taking power away from politicians and captains in neighborhood precincts and centralizing command and control within police departments. Specialized units such as traffic, juvenile, and vice emerged out of this movement, and departments began to employ female officers. The Boston Police Department hired its first female officers in 1921.

On the other hand, reformers alienated the rank-and-file in their campaign to recruit strong leaders, and this helped to bring about one of the most infamous events in police history, the 1919 Boston Police strike. At the time, the department consisted of mostly Irish-Catholic rank-and-file and was under the control of a Protestant police commissioner described as "an uncompromising martinet with no previous experience in police administration and no great affection for the Boston Irish" (Russell 1975, 43). Also, new officer pay had remained the same for sixty years despite a nearly 80% increase in the cost of living, and officers worked between seventy-three and ninety-eight hours a week. The police turned to the American Federation of Labor, but Police Commissioner Edwin U. Curtis condemned the formation of a police union, which ultimately resulted in nearly three-quarters of the city's police going on strike. The absence of police brought out the worst in people, and massive rioting ensued followed by Governor Calvin Coolidge summoning the entire State Guard. All of the strikers lost their jobs, and the Boston Police Department lost its reputation as being one of the most respected police forces in the country.

The wounds of the strike were slow to heal. Department morale suffered following the strike, and there were rumors of large-scale police corruption and inefficiency. The Boston strike also killed police unionism around the nation for the next twenty years. It would take forty-six more years before Boston police, triggered by a collective bargaining law giving state and municipal workers the right to organize, launched its own union, the Boston Police Patrolmen's Association. In those years, and in large part due to the Reform Era, the BPD became much more insular, shifting from a decentralized organizational design influenced by politics and patronage to an organization centralized in both command and control. It was around this time that the changing social climate of the 1970s and 1980s ushered in a new era of policing, the Community Problem-Solving Era.

In the 1980s Massachusetts legislators, following a national trend, enacted tax reduction measures that resulted in officer layoffs and reductions in overall staffing within the Boston Police Department. Around this time, Boston began to experience a significant increase in violence fueled by gang rivalries that increasingly involved firearms. The city averaged 95 homicides per year in the 1970s and 1980s, but the number of homicides increased to 152 in 1990. This unprecedented level of violence persuaded the Boston Police Department to develop partnerships with community groups, most notably members of the African American clergy, to deal with this extraordinary level of violence.

A broad array of partnerships developed with community groups, many for the first time. The clergy formed a group called the Ten Point Coalition, and worked in conjunction with area academics and city-funded Boston Streetworkers. The Boston police attempted to send a message to the community that any future violence would not be tolerated, and any future shootings would be dealt with by the full force of the law, including for the first time the possibility of federal prosecution. Police officials delivered their message in face-to-face meetings with young men from area gangs, who were most at risk of becoming victims or offenders of future gun violence. Most importantly, this message of deterrence was delivered in conjunction with an offer to help those at-risk young people turn their lives around through employment and job readiness training, educational support, substance abuse counseling, life skills workshops, and mentorship programs.

During the course of the next ten years, gun violence in the city of Boston dropped dramatically. The number of homicides dropped from 152 in 1990 to 34 in 1998. In addition, the city of Boston enjoyed a two-and-a-half-year period with no juvenile homicides. This represented a first for the city at least since homicide records had been maintained.

The Boston Police Department received national recognition for its success, most notably from U.S. Attorney General Janet Reno and also garnered a number of national awards. In addition, the crime reduction efforts in Boston, dubbed "the Boston Miracle" by some in the media, was replicated in cities across the country and became the backbone of a number of federal initiatives, including most recently the $1 billion Project Safe Neighborhoods Program.

JACK MCDEVITT and STEPHANIE FAHY

See also **Accountability; Boston Community Policing; Boston Police Strike; British Policing; Civil Restraint in Policing; Community Attitudes toward the Police; Deadly Force; Excessive Force; History of American Policing; Knapp Commission; Minorities and the Police; Police in Urban America, 1860–1920; Police Misconduct: After the Rodney King Incident; Role of the Police**

References and Further Reading

City of Boston. 2005. B.P.D. at a glance. http://www.cityofboston.gov/police/glance.asp.
Kenney, D. J., and R. P. McNamara. 1999. *Police and policing: Contemporary issues.* Westport, CT: Praeger.
Russell, F. 1975. *A city in terror: 1919, The Boston Police strike.* New York: Viking Press.
Walker, S. 1977. *A critical history of police reform: The emergence of professionalism.* Lexington, MA: Lexington Books.
———. 1999. *The police in America: An introduction.* Boston, McGraw-Hill College.

BOSTON POLICE STRIKE

Prelude to the Strike

The Boston (Massachusetts) Police Department boasts of being the oldest police department in the nation. It has roots that go back to 1635 when the country's first "night watch" was established. It also possesses the distinction of engaging in one of the most noteworthy and historic work stoppages in the history of organized labor. The Boston Police Strike of 1919 increased the interest in police reform and helped to catapult then-Governor Calvin Coolidge into the national spotlight, and ultimately into the White House.

Though often regarded as an obscure event in American history, the Boston Police Strike of 1919 was one of the most significant events in the history of policing. While other professions were organizing, unionizing, and generally improving their standards of living, policing as a profession seriously lagged behind, and police officers were becoming increasingly unhappy with their diminished status in society. In Boston, the largely Irish-American police force had seen its wages lag badly during World War I, and their respect from average citizens was declining as well.

There was a general consensus that the Boston policemen of 1919 had a great deal of validity in their work-related complaints and demands. Their substantive grievances fell into three primary categories: length of working shifts, working conditions, and, most importantly, pay. After getting a raise in 1913, the policemen asked for another raise in 1917 to compensate for the high wartime inflation. In the summer of 1918, they asked for a $200 increase in the patrolmen's annual salary, which was then $1,200. By the time that raise was finally granted in May 1919, steady inflation had eroded buying power so that even with the raise, policemen were still having difficulty making ends meet.

Another point of contention was the long, tormenting hours the men were forced to work, including special details and one night in the stationhouse each week. Finally, the policemen objected to the conditions under which they were forced to work, particularly in the crowded decay and disrepair of the police station. Police officers in Boston had to sleep in beds infested with bedbugs and cockroaches and on the soiled sheets left over from the previous occupant. The officer's primary means to voice their complaints was the Boston Social Club, a fraternal organization founded by Police Commissioner Stephen O'Meara in 1906.

Attempts at Unionization

By the fall of 1919, a series of strikes hit the United States as unions attempted to gain higher wages to adjust for wartime inflation. Collective bargaining had long been viewed with suspicion by many Americans, whose suspicions were heightened by the worker revolution in Russia and efforts to spread communism throughout the Western world. Efforts were made to organize in order to gain not only higher pay, but also shorter hours and better working conditions. The Boston police officers endured a month-long labor dispute arising from an attempt to form a union affiliated with the American Federation of Labor (AFL).

On the opposing side of the negotiation, representing the city of Boston, was newly appointed Police Commissioner Edwin U. Curtis. Curtis had only been commissioner since December 1918, when his predecessor Commissioner O'Meara had died. Since 1885, police commissioners had been appointed and removed not by the mayor, but by the governor of the Commonwealth of Massachusetts, who in 1919 was a terse Republican named Calvin Coolidge. Though the mayor of Boston helped determine the police department's annual budget, he could not override a decision by the commissioner.

Curtis believed himself to be sympathetic to the policemen's demands, but he refused to deal with the Social Club and instead established a Grievance Committee comprised of men from each station. Curtis believed that if allowed to unionize, the police department would take orders from the AFL, thereby hampering discipline and, ultimately, his authority to command the officers. Curtis banned the officers from associating with any outside organization and refused to sanction a police union. On July 29, Curtis, responding to the rumor that the police were seeking a union, issued a statement detailing O'Meara's objection to a police union and proclaiming his own objection as well. Seeing no other option, the fraternal association of Boston police officers voted to become a union affiliated with the American Federation of Labor. On August 9, 1919, the policemen, through the Social Club, applied for a charter from the AFL.

On August 11, Commissioner Curtis followed up with an amendment to Rule 35 of the department's Rules and Regulations, barring the policemen from forming any organization within the department with ties to an outside group, except for veterans' groups. This order initiated the showdown that led to the strike: The policemen's insistence on a union clashed with Curtis's demand for obedience. The Boston police officers' application was accepted and on August 15 they formed Local 16,807 of the AFL: the Boston Policemen's Union.

As the weeks passed, the situation grew tenser. On August 26 and 29, Commissioner Curtis began the process of suspending nineteen Boston police officers, including the president and other officers of the union, for violation of his amendment to Rule 35. Meanwhile, former police superintendent William Pierce began recruiting a volunteer police force as insurance against a strike. Boston Mayor Andrew J. Peters attempted to effect a settlement between the two sides by forming a Citizens Committee composed of prominent residents of Boston and its suburbs. This committee drafted a compromise, which Curtis rejected. On Monday, September 8, saying that the compromise had nothing to do with his legal obligation to punish violators of the antiunion clause of Rule 35, Curtis announced the suspension of the nineteen officers. That evening, the Policemen's Union voted to protest the suspensions by striking at evening roll call the next day: Tuesday, September 9.

The Strike

At 5:45 P.M. on Tuesday, September 9, 1919, at the beginning of the evening shift, 1,117 Boston policemen conducted a work stoppage. This action removed 70% of the police force from protecting the city's streets. This was the first strike by public safety workers in U.S. history. With the city of Boston virtually unprotected, petty crimes escalated into looting, and rioting took place. As Boston residents absorbed the reality of the policemen's absence, assaults, rapes, vandalism, and looting went unpunished as the city struggled to get replacement police in place. Checked only by a small coalition of nonstriking Boston police, metropolitan police, and a few private watchmen, the riots continued throughout the city. The immediate consequence was about forty-eight hours of looting and rioting in Boston and sporadic, uncontrolled violence during the next few days. Mayor Peters summoned local militia units, which managed to restore order the next day. In the process of pacifying the city and quelling nocturnal disturbances, the guard forces killed five residents and wounded several others. Civilians killed three more, and dozens were injured and wounded. The riots also destroyed hundreds of thousands of dollars worth of property.

The Aftermath

Angered by the violence in Boston, Governor Calvin Coolidge decided to take matters into his own hands after having passed up several earlier opportunities to intercede in the police dispute. Coolidge summoned the entire Massachusetts Guard to take over protection of Massachusetts' capital city. This overwhelming show of force rapidly caused the strike to collapse and earned for the governor the reputation of a strict enforcer of law and order. Meanwhile, in the face of public disapproval of their actions and the uncompromising stance of Curtis and Coolidge, the police began considering cutting their losses and returning to work. But when the American Federation of Labor president sent a telegram to Governor Coolidge asking that the striking Boston policemen be reinstated and their grievances negotiated later, he was rebuffed on September 14 by Coolidge's immediately famous reply that "there is no right to strike against the public safety by anybody, anywhere, any time."

Striking officers were fired, and the collapse of the strike sounded the death toll for the early police labor movement. Coolidge's strong action was soothing to a fearful public and led to his nomination for the vice presidency in 1920. Most of the postwar strikes in the United States were unsuccessful and ushered in a decade of declining union membership. The striking policemen in Boston were not allowed to recover their jobs, which went overwhelmingly to returning servicemen. Despite repeated appeals from the American Federation of Labor requesting reinstatement of the striking officers, they were not allowed to return to work. By December 13, the new force had reached its desired strength. Eight days later, the last state guard unit was dismissed, bringing Boston back to some semblance of "normalcy." The new officers were granted higher pay and additional holidays, and gained the additional benefit of free uniforms. The irony is that the Boston Police Strike was effective in obtaining its objectives, just not for the striking police officers.

LORENZO M. BOYD

See also **American Policing: Early Years; Boston Police Department; Strikes and Job Actions; Unionization, Police**

References and Further Reading

Dempsey, John S., and Linda S. Forst. 2005. *An introduction to policing*. 3rd ed. Belmont, CA: Thomson/Wadsworth.

Russell, Francis. 1975. *A city in terror: 1919 the Boston Police strike*. New York: Viking Press.

BRITISH POLICING

By the end of the twentieth century, the police service in England and Wales was likely to experience the greatest change it had ever encountered. According to one author:

> The police institution is beset by innovation and undergoing changes which seem momentous since the establishment of the Metropolitan Police. The tacit contract between police and public, so delicately drawn between the 1850s and 1950s had begun to fray glaringly by 1981. The still open question is whether current efforts will suffice to repair it. (Reiner 1985, 62)

Various central government commissions examined such diverse issues as:

- The practices and procedures to be adopted by the police with regard to the criminal justice process
- The current and future structure of the service
- The political and managerial control of forces

These commissions were created at least partially in response to serious difficulties that had faced the service since the 1980s, including both external relations between police and public and internal revelations of scandal and wrongdoing.

The purpose of this article is fourfold. First, it provides a brief historical description of the development of the police service in England and Wales since its inception in 1829. Second, it examines the structure, including the political and managerial controls under which it operates. Third, it discusses some of the difficulties that the service experienced and, finally, comments on three major initiatives promulgated by central government to address those perceived problems.

The History and Development of British Police Forces

The first formal professional police force in England and Wales was the London Metropolitan Force, which was created following enactment of the Metropolitan Police Act in 1829. This act provided for a single force for the metropolis and ensured that policing would cover a radius of approximately seven miles from the city center.

In 1835, the Municipal Corporations Act required new towns and boroughs in England and Wales to establish police forces. This act applied to 178 corporate towns, although not all towns took advantage of the act to establish police forces. The problem of rural police forces was addressed in the County Police Act of 1839, which was intended to permit regular police forces for the fifty-six existing counties in England and Wales. Because the Municipal Corporations Act gave virtual unlimited discretion to local authorities in setting standards of pay, recruitment, and service, the result was the creation of forces widely differing in quality. To avoid this result among counties, the County Police Act of 1839 retained significant powers given by central government, a condition that still exists today. The home secretary was empowered to regulate the conditions of pay and service of county forces and provided that the appointment of the chief constable of each force be approved by him. Again, because this act was "enabling" rather than "obligatory," only twenty-eight counties created police forces under it.

By 1848, there were 182 police forces in Great Britain. However, over time, a number of smaller forces were amalgamated with either the county force in which they were situated or with larger city departments. According to Stead (1985):

> The next principle measure was the County and Borough Police Act of 1856, known as the "Obligatory Act." This is the major landmark in the making of Britain's modern police system. . . . The Act of 1856 produced a model for the nationwide standardization of police that characterizes the British system today. (p. 49)

This legislation placed on central government, for the first time, the responsibility of ensuring that a police force was established in every county and borough throughout the United Kingdom and to ensure that they were operating in an efficient manner. In addition to the home secretary's responsibilities, as stated earlier, a further important provision was that the central government undertook the obligation of providing a proportion of financing for those forces certified as efficient. As a result, central and local government became partners in providing police service in Britain—a model that continues to exist in contemporary policing. By 1939, England and Wales had 183 police forces.

The watershed for the development of the modern police service came with the Royal Commission on Police in 1962. The outcome of the commission's deliberations was the Police Act of 1964, which sets the structure of policing in England and Wales and is the basis on which modern policing is formulated. Stead (1985) notes:

> The Police Act of 1964 marks a decisive stage in police development. It reaffirmed the principle of local participation in police governance. It gave Parliament a whole range of subjects on which it can question the Home Secretary and it makes possible the consolidations of the 1960s. (p. 103)

Following the local government reorganization in 1974, the number of forces was reduced to forty-three. As of 1992 there were fifty-two police forces in the United Kingdom with 29,243 special constables to assist in law enforcement. These forces vary in size from 798 sworn officers (City

of London Police) to more than 28,000 (Metropolitan Police Force). These totals take no account of civilian staff whose numbers have swelled considerably during the past few years as forces have implemented extensive civilianization programs to ensure that police officers are not tied down with clerical and administrative tasks.

Although the geographic area that each force covers varies, the boundaries are coterminus with the principal local government areas. Each force has the total responsibility for policing policy and operations taking place within its area.

Although this reorganization was hailed by many as promoting greater economy and efficiency through the elimination of many small forces, it was not without its critics. Stead (1985) indicates:

> Whether greater size really brought greater efficiency was doubted, when it kept the command too remote from the front line. One major disadvantage was felt in the most important sphere of all—that of the police's relationship to the public. . . . The change entailed some loss on the human side of policing and must be seen in the context of a wholesale reshuffling of local government structures, from which the country has yet to recover. (p. 95)

In short, the readjustment of forces in 1974, while encouraging efficiency by creating larger forces resulting in greater economy, also created problems in service delivery. Larger police forces resulted in both greater separation between the administration and those at the sharp end of policing, and greater personal distance between the forces and the public they served. The latter problem was no small issue for a police service that prided itself on service delivery and relied heavily on its personal relationship with the people it served.

The Structure of Police Authority

The chief officer of each force (i.e., a chief constable in all forces except the

Metropolitan and City of London forces, each of which is headed by a commissioner) is totally responsible for the operational policing in his area. However, in all forces except the two outlined above, the local authority has the responsibility under the Police Acts of 1964 and 1976 to maintain an adequate and efficient police force for its area. In this regard, they appoint a police committee composed of local politicians and magistrates to oversee policing issues. They also have the responsibility for appointing the chief constable and serve as his disciplinary authority.

On a national basis, the secretary of state for home affairs (the home secretary), who is a senior member of the government, has a direct responsibility for the police service. He or she exercises control through the home office and his or her role is primarily to maintain a consistent national policy on policing. This responsibility is undertaken primarily through the medium of home office circulars, which do not have the force of law, but which provide chief officers with advice and guidance on a variety of policing issues. In addition, central government through the home office funds 51% of all policing costs and, as a result, maintains a considerable level of control. In effect, therefore, police forces are controlled by what is called a tripartite arrangement among:

- The home office, which maintains a consistent national policy
- The local authority, which is responsible for maintaining an adequate and efficient police force for its area
- The chief constable, who is responsible for the operational efficiency and the day-to-day management of the force

In summary, therefore, although the home secretary possesses administrative power and control over the police service, he or she tends to limit the use of such authority. Thus, the chief constables and the local authorities are afforded a good deal of discretion to operate their police

force in a manner suitable to local needs and requirements.

While this system has withstood the test of time, questions were raised as to whether the same arrangement should continue in the future. Vize (1992) indicates that the review of police organizations, which was commenced on the instructions of the home secretary in the summer of 1992 and which is commented on later in this article, would include a detailed examination of the powers of police authorities, including their control of constabulary budgets. This review raised issues of principle, particularly that of the accountability of local forces.

Having commented on issues concerning the control of police forces, we now propose to look at the rank structure. With the exception of the Metropolitan and City of London forces, the rank structure for sworn personnel is identical in all police forces in England and Wales. (In the Metropolitan Police the rank structure above chief superintendent is commander, deputy assistant commissioner, assistant commissioner, deputy commissioner, and commissioner. In the city of London, it is assistant commissioner, deputy commissioner, and commissioner.) The standard rank structure is outlined below:

- Chief constable
- Deputy chief constable
- Assistant chief constable
- Chief superintendent
- Superintendent
- Chief inspector
- Inspector sergeant constable

Note that there are a considerable number of layers of management in this structure, which results in an average of one supervisor to every three constables.

Contemporary Issues

At no other time since its inception has the police service in England and Wales come under greater scrutiny than in the 1980s. Gone were the days when it enjoyed the support of virtually all the community, a fact evidenced by the results of the British Crime Surveys of 1983 and 1988. These surveys revealed that while there was continuing support for the police, it had been declining over time. This situation was brought about, in part, by the adverse publicity the service attracted due to malpractice on the part of some of its members. It was also a consequence of social, political, and economic changes experienced by British society.

One of the most significant factors that contributed to the erosion of public support for the police service was the outbreak of serious urban disturbances across England in the 1980s. Just as the United States experienced rioting in a number of major cities in the 1960s, rioting in English cities broke out in the early 1980s. The first of these occurred in the St. Paul's District of Bristol in April 1980. Almost one year to the day later, serious disorders in Brixton resulted in widespread damage and injury to 279 police officers and 45 citizens (Benyon 1984, 3). Other cities that experienced rioting in 1981 included Birmingham, Sheffield, Leeds, Leicester, and Derby.

In response to the Brixton disturbances, Parliament appointed the Rt. Hon. Lord Scarman, OBE, a highly respected appeals court judge, to head an inquiry into the causes of the disorders. The results of the investigation were released in November 1981. According to the Scarman Report:

> . . . a combination of a high incidence of deprived groups in the population, the difficulties of living in the inner cities, the economic, social, and political disadvantages of the ethnic minorities, and the latter's complete loss of confidence in the police . . . constituted a potential for collective violence. Scarman regarded "Operation Swamp" . . . a massive and visible police presence as the accelerator event which triggered actual political violence. (Benyon 1984, 28)

With respect to the role of the police:

> Lord Scarman came to the view that the "history of relations between the police and the people of Brixton during recent years has been a tale of failure." (Benyon 1984, 100)

Further disorders were experienced in 1982 and again in 1985. The most serious of these took place in London in October 1985:

> The rioting began at about 7 p.m. on Sunday 6 October 1985, and during a night of extraordinary violence PC Keith Blakelock was stabbed to death, 20 members of the public and 223 police officers were injured and 47 cars and some buildings were burned. (Benyon and Solomos 1987, 7)

Commenting on the observation that the 1981 and 1985 urban disturbances were fundamentally antipolice, David Smith notes:

> It does appear that racism and racial prejudice within the police, and the concentration of certain kinds of policing on young people generally and particularly young black people, has brought forth a response both at the individual level and also at a more collective level. (Benyon and Solomos 1987, 72)

Certainly, just as the Scarman Report indicated, the cause of these riots, similar to those in the United States in the 1960s, goes much deeper than simply the attitudes of individual police officers and different styles of policing in predominantly minority communities. Widespread discrimination, poverty, and high rates of unemployment in the inner cities were the locus of urban unrest, whereas distrust and dissatisfaction with the police service provided the spark. Nevertheless, as a consequence, the spotlight was thrown on the British police service resulting in the most serious adverse publicity and strain with the public than it had experienced in many decades.

The public image of the police service was further eroded by violent confrontations between the police and picketers during a number of notorious industrial disputes, especially the Miner's Dispute in 1984–1985. In another notorious event, on April 15, 1989, a large and unruly crowd attending a soccer game at Hillsborough caused a disaster in which ninety-five persons lost their lives with many more injured. In this latter incident, the police were severely criticized for their crowd-control tactics and a lack of command control. The investigations that followed produced further negative publicity for the police service.

While all of these incidents (the riots, industrial disputes, and the soccer disaster) involved serious criticisms of the relationship between the police and the public in order-maintenance functions, the integrity of the service was still widely acclaimed for its efficiency and dedication in fighting crime. Much of this confidence eroded as a consequence of two major scandals involving the police and the activities of the Irish Republican Army. In the early 1970s, a series of pub bombings resulted in the deaths of twenty-six persons in Guilford and Birmingham. Four persons were convicted in the Guilford incident and six in the Birmingham bombing. Following a series of inquiries and appeals, the Guilford Four were released in 1989 and the Birmingham Six in 1991 on the grounds of tainted evidence. In each case, the convicted individuals served more than fourteen years in prison, based on evidence produced by alleged coerced confessions, uncorroborated testimony, and faulty scientific investigations. Once again, the public image of the police service was rocked, morale was seriously affected, and public inquiry into police behavior was initiated.

In sum, throughout the decade of the 1980s, the British police service faced greater adversity and met with more public criticism than it had faced in half a century. Public trust declined while the central government's interest in policing increased. Graef (1990), who addressed many of these issues, concluded that

"Perhaps the management of Police Forces throughout the Western world was faltering, jaded, unimaginative, inert, and shy on accountability" (p. 456).

Interest on the part of central government was demonstrated through home office circulars, the Audit Commission, the Home Affairs Select Committee, and the Police Complaints Authority. These bodies demonstrated an ever-increasing interest in policing issues to ensure not only greater accountability but also that a more effective, efficient, and value-for-money service was provided. For example, the Home Affairs Select Committee (1989) commented that:

> The Police Service of England and Wales commands considerable public resources which demand exceptional management skills if Forces are to respond to the needs of the public. The fundamental questions which arose during our enquiry concern whether the current system of training and career development for police officers based on a 19th-Century system and constrained by the separate organisation of each is adequate for the Police Service as it approaches the 21st Century.

Clearly, the concentration of interest in policing in the United Kingdom was more than just a passing phenomenon likely to disappear once the initial enthusiasm had worn off. It was symptomatic of a change in relationships among police, their masters, and their customers.

All of these issues necessitated a change in the role of police managers at all levels of the organization, and, in consequence, emphasis was placed on identifying the skills those officers require to undertake these new responsibilities. However, despite the efforts made in this regard, considerable debate took place within Parliament, the service, and the media on the quality of senior police managers. For example, Johnson (1990) indicated that events within the service encouraged the ordinary public to think that the police were not really able to provide a professional service and that radical proposals were needed to improve police management. On the other hand, Robertson (1990) reported that it would be easy to conclude that police executives were either disinterested in pursuing efficiency and general excellence or that they were simply ill equipped to administer large and complex organizations. To endorse either assumption would be patently unfair, because, although particular chief officers may suffer lethargy in one direction or the other, such a rash generalization would be inaccurate.

Nevertheless, in a world where the theory and practice of business administration and human resource management are undergoing constant refinement, it is essential that today's police managers, particularly those at a senior and executive level, should be attuned to both private and public sector management developments to avoid accusations of inertia and stagnation.

It is against the background outlined above that central government implemented three important reviews, likely to greatly affect the police service and the criminal justice system. The first was the Royal Commission on Criminal Justice, which had the following extensive terms of reference:

> To review the effectiveness of the Criminal Justice System in England and Wales in securing the conviction of those guilty of criminal offences and the acquittal of those who are innocent, having regard to the efficient use of resources.

In particular, they were asked to consider whether changes were needed regarding:

- The conduct of police investigations and their supervision by senior police officers
- The role of the prosecutor in supervising the gathering of evidence and deciding whether a case should proceed
- The right of silence for the accused
- The powers of the courts to direct proceedings

- The role of the Court of Appeal in considering new evidence on appeal
- The arrangements for considering and investigating allegations of miscarriages of justice when appeal rights have been exhausted

During the course of its work, the commission examined many aspects of the criminal justice system and in that regard received submissions from many interested individuals and bodies including the police service.

The second was the review undertaken by the local government commission into the future of local government. Its terms of reference were to examine all relevant issues and make recommendations concerning the future structure, boundaries, and electoral changes to particular local government areas. The review took the form of a rolling program and, in consequence, it took some time to cover the whole of the country. However, the results could have major implications for the police service. For example, if local authority boundary changes took place, it could result in the demise of many of the smaller forces, the amalgamation of others, and even the breaking up of some of the larger forces. The possibility of such changes was a fact recognized by Chief Constable O'Dowd in a speech at an international police conference in London on the future of the police service in England and Wales. He concluded that there would be fewer police forces. Many people believed that the restructuring of forces was high on the hidden political agenda.

The final review and probably the most important as far as the police service is concerned was that which the home secretary established in May 1992, under the chairmanship of Sir Patrick Sheey, to review police responsibilities and rewards. The inquiry team, which had to report by May 1993, comprised management consultants, academics, and industrialists who addressed a variety of policing issues including the following:

- The structure of forces to ensure that they meet the management needs of today's police service
- The roles and responsibilities of the various ranks within the service
- The salaries of police officers to ensure the salary reflects the responsibilities of the particular individuals
- Rewards and sanctions for good and bad performance
- The conditions of service, work practices, and the improvement of professional standards

This review was quite clearly very wide in its scope and affected every officer in the country in one way or another.

Summary and Conclusions

Although the results of these three major commissions should produce significant changes in policing in England and Wales, the changes that occur must preserve both the traditional relationship between the British police service and its public and the internal morale and cohesion of the forces. As Reiner (1985) notes:

> An adequate approach to police reform must be grounded in an understanding of police culture and practices, not a simplistic view that if only the right authorities were in charge all would be well. (p. 198)

Two particular areas of concern likely to arise as a consequence of these commissions are the reduction in the number of forces, which would produce larger forces, and the "flattening" of the rank structure through the elimination of some current ranks. The former change was a likely outgrowth of the Local Government Commission and the latter from the deliberations of the Sheehy Commission.

Changes in the size of forces, which may alter the relationship between police and community, appear especially critical. Wells clearly anticipated these problems:

If the police organisation is, or appears to be, a centrally imposed anonymous body, as in many states of Europe and elsewhere, there will be little sense of the "familia": rather than intimate and integrated, the police will seem remote and out of sympathy with local needs. (Benyon and Solomos 1987, 81)

Further he noted:

Force policy and philosophy should be aimed at making ranks from commissioner to constable more obviously tied to community structures. . . . Any move which makes the police appear as impersonal, external to the community and, accordingly, anonymous must be resisted. (Benyon and Solomos 1987, 79)

Clearly, any forthcoming recommendations from the Local Government Commission, which would create larger forces responsible for wider geographic areas and containing greater population heterogeneity, must address these concerns.

Another set of concerns involving the internal cohesion of the forces was likely to emerge from the Sheehy Commission. One recommendation nearly certain to be made was the elimination of certain current ranks thus collapsing the rank structure. While one possible result of this change could produce a closer integration of command and line officers, thus improving communication in both directions, it would also raise issues of professional development and promotional opportunities that could affect the morale of younger officers. An article, which appeared in one of Great Britain's national newspapers, took note of this concern:

The ranks of chief inspector, chief superintendent, deputy chief constable and possibly commander seem certain to disappear and the status of constables, sergeants and inspectors enhanced. . . . Abolition of chief inspectors and chief superintendent posts would seriously diminish promotion prospects for thousands of officers and create career bottlenecks. Existing chief inspectors and chief superintendents are also worried about what would happen to them. (Darbyshire 1993, 1)

Another controversial recommendation likely to occur was "performance-based pay increments." While the concept of reward for those officers who are effective in carrying out their duties and no reward for those who demonstrate subpar performance is attractive in theory, there are serious questions regarding the translation of theory into practice. What criteria are to be used to measure performance? What norm will be established for satisfactory performance so that those who fall above and below that norm can be recognized? Clearly these are crucial questions that beg easy answers. These questions are imbedded in the much larger question of the functions of policing, which has been the center of controversy since the establishment of professional police forces. A related issue is the fact that policing produces a qualitative product rather than one that is quantitative in nature. The president of the Association of Chief Police Officers, Mr. John Burrow, is quoted as saying:

We agree in principle with the concept, but our dilemma is that there are many aspects to performance-related pay. It clearly can't be based on the number of arrests or traffic summonses issued. That would do more damage to public relations than the improvement in police performance it would achieve. (Darbyshire 1993, 1)

In conclusion, therefore, it is apparent that the police service in England and Wales had entered a period of great uncertainty by the end of the twentieth century. There is no doubt that changes will be extensive and wide ranging and will result in considerable conflict, particularly with respect to local accountability vis-à-vis centralized control, a change in the traditional relationship between the police and the communities that they serve, and changes in police practices and procedures brought about as a result of the changes in the criminal justice process as a whole.

Such conflict will hopefully be the catalyst to reorganize the service to meet the changing circumstances and the ever-increasing demands that are likely to be placed on it. Many managers at all levels will no doubt have difficulty coming to terms with the changes and will fall by the wayside, but for those willing to accept the challenge that will be forthcoming, the future should be very interesting and exciting.

DONALD B. WALKER and
MALCOLM RICHARDS

See also **Rowand and Mayne, First Police Commissioners, United Kingdom**

References and Further Reading

Benyon, John. 1984. The riots, Lord Scarman and the political agenda. In *Scarman and after*, ed. J. Benyon, 3–19. New York: Pergamon Press.

Benyon, John, and John Solomos. 1987. British urban unrest in the 1980's. In *The roots of urban unrest*, ed. J. Benyon and J. Solomos, 3–21. New York: Pergamon Press.

Darbyshire, Nell. 1993. Merit only pay plan for the police. *Daily Telegraph*, January 22, 1.

Graef, R. 1990. *Talking blues*. London: Fontana/Collins.

Home Affairs Select Committee. 1989. *Higher police training and the police staff college*. London: Home Affairs Select Committee.

Hough, M., and P. Mayhew. 1983. *The British crime survey: First reports*. London: Home Affairs Select Committee.

Johnson, P. 1990. Change or be changed. *Police Review*, August 10.

Mayhew, P., D. Elliott, and L. Dowds. 1988. *The British Crime survey*. London: Home Affairs Select Committee.

Reiner, Robert. 1985. *The politics of the police*. New York: St. Martin's Press.

Robertson, W. W. 1990. Your money and your life. Unpublished paper. Bramshill, England: Police Staff College.

Smith, David. 1987. Policing and urban unrest. In *The roots of urban unrest*, ed. J. Benyon and J. Solomos, 69–74. New York: Pergamon Press.

Stead, Philip. 1985. *The police of Britain*. New York: Macmillan.

Taylor, Stan. 1984. The Scarman Report and explanations of riots. In *Scarman and after*, ed. J. Benyon, 20–34. New York: Pergamon Press.

Vize, R. 1992. Fears grow for survival of police authorities. *Local Government Chronicle*, October 23.

Wells, Richard. 1987. The will and the way to move forward in policing. In *The roots of urban unrest*, ed. J. Benyon and J. Solomos, 75–89. New York: Pergamon Press.

BROKEN-WINDOWS POLICING

Broken-windows policing is a style of policing generally associated with the broken-windows theory—namely, the idea advanced by James Q. Wilson and George L. Kelling that tolerating minor physical and social disorder in a neighborhood (such as graffiti, litter, aggressive panhandling, or turnstile jumping) encourages serious violent crime. Although the broken-windows theory itself did not compel a particular policing strategy, most policy makers interpreted the broken-windows theory as implying a form of aggressive disorder policing that has come to be known under several names, including not only broken-windows policing but also "order-maintenance policing," "quality-of-life policing," and "zero tolerance policing." George Kelling, for instance, the coauthor of the original *Broken Windows* essay, suggests that the most effective way to address disorder and reduce crime is to increase the number of misdemeanor arrests. There has been a lot of social scientific research conducted to test the efficacy of broken-windows policing—including important work by Jeffrey Fagan, Bernard Harcourt, Jens Ludwig, Stephen Raudenbush, Robert Sampson, and Wesley Skogan—but, to date, there is no reliable empirical support for the proposition that disorder causes crime or that broken-windows policing reduces serious crime.

The Emergence of Broken-Windows Policing

The broken-windows theory was first articulated by James Q. Wilson and George L. Kelling in a short, nine-page article titled *Broken Windows* that appeared in the *Atlantic Monthly* in 1982. The theory is premised on the idea that "disorder and crime are usually inextricably linked, in a kind of developmental sequence" (p. 31). According to Wilson and Kelling, minor disorder (such as littering, loitering, public drinking, panhandling, and prostitution), if tolerated in a neighborhood, produce an environment that is likely to attract crime. It signals to potential criminals that delinquent behavior will not be reported or controlled—that no one is in charge. One broken window, left unrepaired, invites other broken windows. These progressively break down community standards and leave the community vulnerable to crime.

From a policy perspective, the broken-windows theory was, in principle, consistent with a variety of potential policy levers, ranging from neighborhood beautification programs to community organizing. Nevertheless, the theory was soon deployed by influential policy makers in support of aggressive misdemeanor policing and became associated with the type of policing that focuses on minor disorder offenses. New York City mayor Rudolph Giuliani was at the forefront of this development. Under the rubric of the "quality-of-life initiative," Giuliani and Police Commissioner William Bratton began enforcing municipal ordinances against minor disorder offenses, such as loitering, panhandling, graffiti writing, turnstile jumping, public drinking, and public urination, through arrest, detention, and criminal charges.

The New York City quality-of-life initiative produced what many observers called a revolution in policing and law enforcement. Today, the three most populous cities in the United States—New York, Chicago, and, most recently, Los Angeles—have all adopted at least some aspect of Wilson and Kelling's broken-windows theory. In addition to the strategies of former New York City Mayor Rudolph Giuliani, the city of Chicago implemented an antigang loitering ordinance in the early 1990s that it vigorously enforced during the period from 1993 to 1995 resulting in misdemeanor arrests of more than 42,000 individuals. In October 2002, Los Angeles Mayor James Hahn appointed William Bratton police commissioner on a platform that promised a broken-windows approach. According to the *New York Times*, "Mr. Bratton said his first priority after being sworn in on Oct. 28 [2002] would be ending the smile-and-wave approach to crime fighting. He said he wanted policing based on the so-called broken-windows theory." The popularity of broken-windows policing in the United States is matched only by its appeal abroad. In 1998 alone, representatives of more than 150 police departments from foreign countries visited the New York Police Department for briefings and instruction in order-maintenance policing. For the first ten months of 2000, another 235 police departments (85% of them from abroad) sent delegations to the New York City police headquarters.

The Lack of Empirical Evidence

Despite the widespread policy influence of the 1982 *Atlantic Monthly* essay, remarkably little is known about the effects of broken windows. A number of leading researchers in sociology, law, and police studies have compiled datasets from different urban areas to explore the broken-windows hypothesis, but the evidence remains, at best, mixed. In 2000, John Eck and Edward Maguire reviewed the empirical evidence and studies on broken-windows policing in their contribution to Alfred Blumstein and Joel Wallman's *The Crime Drop in America* (2000), and found that there is little evidence to support the claim that broken-windows policing contributed to the sharp decrease in crime during the 1990s.

To date, empirical testing of the broken-windows idea has taken one of two forms. A first approach attempts to measure neighborhood disorder and crime, as well as other correlates of criminality, such as poverty and residential instability, in order to determine whether there are statistically interesting correlations between these variables. A second approach has focused on measures of broken-windows policing—for instance, rates of misdemeanor arrests—and conducts relatively similar statistical analyses on these variables in order, again, to identify significant correlations.

Disorder and Crime

Early on, many proponents of the broken-windows hypothesis pointed to the research of Wesley Skogan, especially his monograph *Disorder and Decline: Crime and the Spiral of Decay in American Neighborhoods* (1990), and argued that it empirically verified the broken-windows theory. *Disorder and Decline* addressed the larger question of the impact of neighborhood disorder on urban decline, but in one section, Skogan discussed the broken-windows hypothesis, ran a regression of neighborhood disorder on robbery victimization, and concluded that "'Broken windows' do need to be repaired quickly" (p. 75). Many observers interpreted this as an endorsement of the broken-windows theory and accepted this view of the evidence. George Kelling contended that Skogan "established the causal links between disorder and serious crime—empirically verifying the 'Broken Windows' hypotheses" (Kelling and Coles 1996, 24). Subsequent research by Bernard Harcourt (2001), however, cast doubt on Skogan's findings and raised significant questions as to what conclusions could properly be drawn from Skogan's analysis.

A few years later, Ralph Taylor (2001) conducted research in sixty-six neighborhoods in Baltimore using longitudinal data. Taylor attempted to determine the relationship between neighborhood crime and what he termed social and physical "incivilities"—panhandlers, public drunks, trash, graffiti, and vacant lots, among other things. What he found was that, while certain types of incivilities were associated with crime or urban decay, others were not. He concluded from his data that different types of incivilities may require different policy responses: "Researchers and policy-makers alike need to break away from broken windows per se and widen the models upon which they rely, both to predict and to preserve safe and stable neighborhoods with assured and committed residents" (p. 22).

In a 2005 study, *Broken Windows: Evidence from New York City and a Five-City Social Experiment*, Bernard Harcourt and Jens Ludwig explore the empirical results from an important social experiment known as Moving to Opportunity (MTO) that is under way in five cities: New York, Chicago, Los Angeles, Baltimore, and Boston. Under the MTO program, approximately 4,600 low-income families living in high-crime public housing communities characterized by high rates of social disorder were randomly assigned housing vouchers to move to less disadvantaged and disorderly communities. Harcourt and Ludwig compare the crime rates among those who moved and those who did not—using official arrests and self-report surveys—and the results are clear, though disappointing: Moving people to communities with less social or physical disorder on balance does not lead to reductions in their criminal behavior. Neighborhood order and disorder do not seem to have a noticeable effect on criminal behavior.

The implications of MTO for the ongoing debates about the broken-windows theory are significant and suggest that moving people to communities with less social or physical disorder—the key intervening factor in the original broken-windows hypothesis—on balance does not lead to reductions in their criminal behavior. Taken together, the data from MTO provide no support for the idea that "broken-windows" activities, including broken-windows policing or other measures designed to reduce the level of social or physical disorder within a community, represent the optimal use of scarce government resources.

Another comprehensive study of the broken-windows theory is Robert Sampson and Stephen Raudenbush's 1999 study, *Systematic Social Observation of Public Spaces: A New Look at Disorder in Urban Neighborhoods*. Their study grew out of the Project on Human Development in Chicago Neighborhoods and was based on systematic social observation: Using trained observers who drove a sports utility vehicle at five miles per hour down every street in 196 Chicago census tracts, and randomly selecting 15,141 street sides, they were able to collect precise data on neighborhood disorder. With regard to the disorder-crime nexus, they found that disorder and predatory crime are only moderately correlated, but that, when antecedent neighborhood characteristics are taken into account, the connection between disorder and crime "vanished in 4 out of 5 tests—including homicide, arguably our best measure of violence" (p. 637). On the basis of their extensive research, they conclude that "[a]ttacking public order through tough police tactics may thus be a politically popular but perhaps analytically weak strategy to reduce crime" (p. 638). As an alternative to the broken-windows theory, they suggest that disorder is of the same etiology as crime—being, so often, forms of minor crime—and that both crime and disorder have the same antecedent conditions. "Rather than conceive of disorder as a direct cause of crime, we view many elements of disorder as part and parcel of crime itself" (p. 608). Thus, "a reasonable hypothesis is that public disorder and predatory crimes are manifestations of the same explanatory process, albeit at different ends of a 'seriousness' continuum" (p. 608).

Studies of Aggressive Misdemeanor Arrest Policing

Another strand of research, focusing on studies of aggressive arrest policies, has also been brought to bear on the broken-windows hypothesis. Here, too, James Q. Wilson sparked the debate, primarily with his 1968 book on the *Varieties of Police Behavior*, and his research with Barbara Boland on the effects of police arrests on crime. Wilson and Boland hypothesized that aggressive police patrols, involving increased stops and arrests, have a deterrent effect on crime. A number of contributions ensued, both supporting and criticizing these findings, but, as Robert Sampson and Jacqueline Cohen suggested back in 1988, the results were "mixed" (p. 166). There have been strong contributions to the literature, such as the 1999 study led by Anthony Braga, titled "Problem-Oriented Policing in Violent Crime Places: A Randomized Controlled Experiment," published in *Criminology*. But still, most of this research is unable to distinguish between the broken-windows hypothesis and more traditional explanations of incapacitation and deterrence associated with increased police arrests, presence, contact, and surveillance. The problem is somewhat endemic to the design of these studies. As Sampson and Cohen conclude with regard to their own work, "[i]t is true that our analysis was not able to choose definitely between the two alternative scenarios" (p. 185).

The most recent study here, Harcourt and Ludwig's article *Broken Windows: New Evidence from New York City and a Five-City Social Experiment*, reanalyzes and assesses the best available evidence from New York City about the effects of broken-windows policing. They demonstrate that the pattern of crime changes across New York precincts during the 1990s that has been attributed to broken-windows policing is more consistent with what statisticians call mean reversion: Those precincts that experienced the *largest drop* in crime in the 1990s were the ones that experienced the *largest increases* in crime during the city's crack epidemic of the mid- to late-1980s. They call this *Newton's law of crime*: What goes up, must come down, and what goes up the most, tends to come down the most.

In this vein, Jeffrey Fagan and Garth Davies (2003) also test, in *Policing Guns: Order Maintenance and Crime Control in New York*, whether quality-of-life policing in New York City contributed to the reduction in lethal violence in the late 1990s. They analyze precinct crime rates from 1999 and try to determine whether these crime rates can be predicted by the amount of stop-and-frisk activity that occurred in the precinct in the preceding year. Based on their research, they find that "[f]or both violence arrests broadly and homicide arrests specifically, there is no single category of citizen stops by police that predicts where crime will increase or decrease in the following year." When they examine homicide fatalities, they observe different effects by type of stop and by victim race. "Stops for violence are significant predictors of reductions in both gun homicide deaths and overall homicide deaths, but only among Hispanics." In contrast, for African Americans, no type of arrests predicts homicide victimization a year later; and for whites, the results are not reliable because of the low white homicide victimization rate. Why is it that there may be effects for Hispanics, but not for African Americans? Fagan and Davies suggest that it may have to do with what they call "stigma saturation" in black communities: When stigma is applied in ways that are perceived as too harsh and unfair, it may have reverse effects. They write, "When legal control engenders resistance, opposition or defiance, the opportunity to leverage formal social control into informal social control is lost. The absence of crime control returns from [order-maintenance policing] may reflect just such a dynamic among African Americans, who shouldered much of the burden of [order-maintenance policing]."

Steve Levitt's 2004 *Journal of Economic Perspectives* review essay similarly suggests that policing practices probably do not explain much of the crime drop in the 1990s because crime went down everywhere, even in places where police departments did not implement new policing strategies. Instead, Levitt attributes the massive period effects on crime throughout the United States during the 1990s to some combination of increased imprisonment, increases in the number of police, the ebbing of the crack epidemic that started in many big cities in the mid-1980s, and the legalization of abortion in the United States during the early 1970s.

Criminological Evidence

The criminological evidence surrounding New York City is not any more helpful to the broken-windows theory. A number of large U.S. cities—Boston, Houston, Los Angeles, San Diego, San Francisco, among others—have experienced significant drops in crime since the early 1990s, in some cases even larger proportionally to the drop in crime in New York City. Several of these cities did not implement the type of aggressive order-maintenance policing that New York City did. Applying a variety of different tests, one recent study found that New York City's drop in homicides, though not very common, is not unprecedented either. Houston's drop in homicides of 59% between 1991 and 1996 outpaced New York City's decline over the same period of 51%, and both were surpassed by Pittsburgh's 61% drop in homicides between 1984 and 1988 (Fagan, Zimring, and Kim 1998). Another study looked at the rates of decline of homicides

in the seventeen largest U.S. cities from 1976 to 1998 in comparison to each city's cyclical peaks and troughs, using a method of indexed cyclical comparison. With regard to the most recent cyclical drop in homicides, New York City's decline, though above average, was the fifth largest, behind San Diego, Washington, D.C., St. Louis, and Houston (Joanes 1999).

A straight comparison of homicide and robbery rates between 1991 and 1998 reveals that, although New York City is again in the top, with declines in homicide and robbery rates of 70.6% and 60.1%, respectively, San Diego experienced larger declines in homicide and robbery rates (76.4% and 62.6%, respectively), Boston experienced a comparable decline in its homicide rate (69.3%), Los Angeles experienced a greater decline in its robbery rate (60.9%), and San Antonio experienced a comparable decline in its robbery rate (59.1%). Other major cities also experienced impressive declines in their homicide and robbery rates, including Houston (61.3% and 48.5%, respectively) and Dallas (52.4% and 50.7%, respectively) (Butterfield 2000).

What is particularly striking is that many of these cities did not implement New York–style order-maintenance policing. San Diego and San Francisco bear perhaps the greatest contrast. The San Diego police department implemented a radically different model of policing focused on community–police relations. The police began experimenting with problem-oriented policing in the late 1980s and retraining their police force to better respond to community concerns. They implemented a strategy of sharing responsibility with citizens for identifying and solving crime. Overall, while recording remarkable drops in crime, San Diego also posted a 15% drop in total arrests between 1993 and 1996, and an 8% decline in total complaints of police misconduct filed with the police department between 1993 and 1996 (Greene 1999).

San Francisco also focused on community involvement and experienced decreased arrest and incarceration rates between 1993 and 1998. San Francisco's felony commitments to the California Department of Corrections dropped from 2,136 in 1993 to 703 in 1998, whereas other California counties either maintained or slightly increased their incarcerations. San Francisco also abandoned a youth curfew in the early 1990s and sharply reduced its commitments to the California Youth Authority from 1994 to 1998. Despite this, San Francisco experienced greater drops in its crime rate for rape, robbery, and aggravated assault than did New York City for the period 1995 through 1998. In addition, San Francisco experienced the sharpest decline in total violent crime—sharper than New York City or Boston—between 1992 and 1998 (Taqi-Eddin and Macallair 1999).

Other cities, including Los Angeles, Houston, Dallas, and San Antonio, also experienced significant drops in crime without as coherent a policing strategy as other large cities. There was a remarkable decline in crime in several major cities in the United States during the 1990s. Depending on the specific time frame of the "before-and-after" comparison, New York City's drop in crime can be characterized anywhere from the biggest decline to a very high performer. Time frames can be easily manipulated, but what is clear is that numerous major U.S. cities have experienced remarkable declines in crime and have employed a variety of different policing strategies. It is too simplistic to attribute the rate of the decline in New York City to the quality-of-life initiative.

Moreover, criminologists have suggested a number of factors that have contributed to declining crime rates in New York City, including a shift in drug use patterns from crack cocaine to heroin, favorable economic conditions in the 1990s, new computerized tracking systems that speed up police response to crime, a dip in the number of eighteen- to twenty-four-year-old males, as well as possible changes in adolescent behavior. There have also been important changes at the New York Police Department (NYPD), including a significant increase in the raw number of police officers. Former Mayor Dinkins hired more than two thousand new police officers under the Safe Streets, Safe City program in 1992, and Giuliani hired another four thousand officers and merged about six thousand Transit and Housing Authority officers into the ranks of the NYPD. As a result, from 1991 to 2000, the NYPD force increased almost by half, up by 12,923 police officers (including those transferred from Transit) from a force of 26,856 police officers in 1991 to 39,779 police officers in 2000. Excluding the Transit merger, the police force grew by almost a quarter. As a result, the New York Police Department now has the largest police force in the country with the highest ratio of police officers per civilian of any major metropolitan area.

The bottom line is that the broken-windows theory—the idea that public disorder sends a message that encourages crime—is probably not right, and there is no reliable evidence that broken-windows policing is an effective law enforcement tool. As Sampson and Raudenbush (1999) observe, "bearing in mind the example of some European and American cities (e.g., Amsterdam, San Francisco) where visible street level activity linked to prostitution, drug use, and panhandling does not necessarily translate into high rates of violence, public disorder may not be so 'criminogenic' after all in certain neighborhood and social contexts" (p. 638).

BERNARD E. HARCOURT

See also **Accountability; COMPSTAT; Crackdowns by the Police; Crime Control Strategies; Order Maintenance; Quality-of-Life Policing; Role of the Police; Zero Tolerance Policing**

References and Further Reading

Braga, Anthony A. 2002. *Problem-oriented policing and crime prevention*. Monsey, NY: Criminal Justice Press.

Eck, John E., and Edward R. Maguire. 2000. Have changes in policing reduced violent crime? An assessment of the evidence. In *The crime drop in America*, ed. A. Blumstein and J. Wallman. Cambridge, MA: Cambridge University Press.

Fagan, Jeffrey, and Garth Davies. 2003. Policing guns: Order maintenance and crime control in New York. In *Guns, crime, and punishment in America*, ed. B. E. Harcourt. New York: New York University Press.

Harcourt, Bernard E. 2001. *Illusion of order: The false promise of broken windows policing*. Cambridge, MA: Harvard University Press.

Harcourt, Bernard E., and Jens Ludwig. Forthcoming. Broken windows: New evidence from New York City and a five-city social experiment. *University of Chicago Law Review* 73.

Kelling, George, and Catherine Coles. 1996. *Fixing broken windows: Restoring order and reducing crime in our communities*. New York: The Free Press.

Kelling, George L., and William H. Sousa, Jr. 2001. Do police matter? An analysis of the impact of New York City's police reforms. Civic Report No. 22. Manhattan, NY: Manhattan Institute Center for Civic Innovation.

Ludwig, Jens, Jeffrey R. Kling, and Maria Hanratty. 2004. *Neighborhood effects on crime over the life cycle*. Working paper, Georgetown University Public Policy Institute.

Sampson, Robert J., and Stephen W. Raudenbush. 1999. Systematic social observation of public spaces: A new look at disorder in urban neighborhoods. *American Journal of Sociology* 105: 603–51.

Skogan, Wesley. 1990. *Disorder and decline: Crime and the spiral of decay in American cities*. Berkeley, CA: University of California Press.

Taylor, Ralph B. 2001. *Breaking away from broken windows: Baltimore neighborhoods and the nationwide fight against crime, guns, fear, and decline*. Boulder, CO: Westview Press.

Wilson, James Q., and George Kelling. 1982. The police and neighborhood safety: Broken windows. *Atlantic Monthly* 127: 29–38.

BUDGETING, POLICE

In the most general sense, police budgeting is merely an agency-specific form of public administration budgeting, and its development corresponds to budgetary development throughout the public sector. The only way in which police budgeting might be distinguished from other public budgeting is in the programmatic materials required to support budget requests within the most recent forms of budgeting: planning, program, budgeting systems, and zero-based budgeting.

The historical derivation of modern budgeting has been a cumulative working-out process resulting from the sequential emergence or "discovery" of fiscal management problems and solutions to those problems. As each problem has become clearly identified and resolved by means of new approaches to the management of public funds, the older techniques, by and large, have been absorbed and continued within the new techniques and formats. The following description of events and concepts rests on this view of a derived, evolutionary, and cumulative public-budgeting system.

Major Periods of Budgetary Development

Allen Schick (1982) has identified three periods of budgetary reform, each named after the major *purpose* of the reform or the *problem* that led to the reform. Those three periods are reviewed after a brief discussion of the pre-reform era.

The Pre-Reform Spoils Era

Although the local, state, and national governments of the United States have collected taxes and expended revenues since Revolutionary times, budgeting as we conceive of the term today was not practiced until early in the twentieth century. Prior to that, the collection and spending of public funds were pretty much ad hoc practices, with little attention given to accounting for funds, at either the points of collection or expenditure. The lack of controls permitted carelessness and more than a little dishonesty in the handling of public funds at all levels of government. Fiscal abuses (as well as nepotism) during President Grant's administration gave rise to major reform efforts during the Reconstruction era, but it was not until 1906 that budget reform became a serious force in public administration.

Reform for Control

New York City was the first American city to establish a consolidated line-item budget, following the creation of the New York Bureau of Municipal Research in 1906. President Taft appointed a Commission on Economy and Efficiency in 1909, whose work prompted Congress to pass the Budget and Accounting Act in 1921. The first consolidated federal budget was realized soon afterward. These earliest line-item budgets were designed almost solely to establish *control* over public funds—to require *accountability* of public funds from collection through expenditure. Although controls were focused primarily on integrity problems, there were also increased efforts to ensure that funds were spent for the purposes intended by the appropriating officials. The expenditure categories of *personnel, equipment, supplies, contractual services*, and *capital expenditures* were devised at this time for control purposes.

This initial period of budgetary reform extended from approximately 1910 to the mid-1930s. The *line-item budget* was originated during this period, and the skills of *accountants* were predominantly required to support the new system.

Reform for Management

For about three decades, beginning in 1930, public administration burgeoned with the invention, development, and refinement of management techniques. The emphasis was on efficiency, and the primary budgetary format that emerged was the *performance budget*. The control emphasis of the previous era was continued and absorbed into a new mode of budgeting, which required the administrator to submit budget documentation showing efficient programmatic elements, in addition to the line-item controls of the previous era.

Reform for Planning

Systems theory contributed to the development of administrative concepts in both business and the public sector after World War II. By 1954 the Rand Corporation had presented *program budgeting* to the U.S. Department of Defense, and DOD Comptroller Charles Hitch had instituted the *planning, programming, budgeting system* (PPBS) by 1961. Although this new system included the former requirements of *control* and *management*, it emphasized the clear statement of agency objectives and expectations of results, all quantifiable as inputs and outputs. It also required cost/benefit analyses of alternative approaches to the accomplishment of agency goals.

President Lyndon Johnson generalized PPBS to most departments of the federal government and the new system soon spread to some progressive state and local governments.

Zero-based budgeting (ZBB) was originated at Texas Instruments by Peter Phyrr and introduced into the Georgia state government and then the federal government by Jimmy Carter. It is a derivative of PPBS, but an elaborate one, emphasizing the setting of objectives, detailed planning, and essentially placing all program elements of an agency in competition with each other for funding on the basis of their comparative contributions to the agency's goals.

PPBS and ZBB are said to raise the visibility of an agency's operations and the level of the political debate over the allocation of fiscal resources.

State-of-the-Art Budgeting and Current Police Practices

In most respects police agencies are required to use whatever budgeting format has been adopted by the city, county, or state government of which they are a part. Following the initiative of the federal government in the early 1960s, some of the more progressive states, counties, and cities, large and small, adopted varied forms of PPBS, often applying a localized name to the new approach. As this increasingly occurred, the police administrators in those jurisdictions were required to make strategic decisions about the goals of their departments, to quantify those goals in multiyear formats, and to relate proposed expenditures to expected levels of goal achievement (e.g., a patrol plan would specify a percentile reduction in business burglaries for the next budget cycle, if funded at a requested level; a new investigative unit, a specific clearance rate for a given offense; a traffic enforcement unit, a reduction in fatal collisions). This new practice was found to be difficult, time consuming, and expensive in terms of analysis and data requirements.

As those local police agencies gained experience with programmatic budgeting, they built the requisite databases and adapted to the system's greater requirements of data and administrative work. Soon, however, ZBB overtook PPBS and was considered by many to be more useful than PPBS, while costing no more to administer.

Many state and local governments have adopted only a few elements of PPBS or ZBB, avoiding their more ponderous analytic requirements, and thus have produced hybrids of line-item and programmatic budgeting techniques under a variety of localized titles. Some sophisticated police chiefs and sheriffs have adopted the analytic techniques associated with PPBS and ZBB even though their parent governments have been unable to adopt the advanced budgeting systems jurisdiction-wide. In these cases, it should be pointed out, the benefits to the agency consist largely of internal improvements in administrative quality, rather than improved budgeting practices of the jurisdiction.

Despite almost three decades of adaptation to the PBBS and ZBB systems by many sophisticated local governments, both large and small, indications are that most of the approximately seventeen thousand local police and sheriff's departments continue to utilize *line-item* budgeting systems, consistent with the practices of their parent governments.

All governmental budgeting systems require the adoption of a fiscal calendar, which generally includes the following elements: (1) adoption of a fiscal year, which establishes the date on which a new annual budget law becomes effective; (2) distribution of budget request forms to operating agency managers for the next fiscal year; (3) submission of completed budget request forms to the fiscal manager of the jurisdiction; (4) analysis and adjustments of operating agency requests by the fiscal manager; (5) submission of the fiscal manager's budget recommendations to the jurisdiction executive (mayor, supervisor, governor); analysis and adjustments of the fiscal manager's recommendations into an executive budget; (6) submission of the executive budget to the legislative branch (council, legislature); (7) legislative consideration and presentation to the public; (8) enactment of a budgetary ordinance or statute by the legislative branch; (9) approval or veto of the budget law by the jurisdiction executive; and (10) enactment of the budget at the beginning of the fiscal year.

In most governmental jurisdictions, agency administrators are simultaneously working with three different budgets.

They are executing the current fiscal year budget (spending it), they are fine-tuning the next fiscal year's budget prior to its formal consideration and adoption, and they are roughing-in a budget for a year and a half hence. The need for this multi-year perspective often perplexes police administrators who are new to their role in fiscal management.

In summary, police budgeting in the United States is a rich mix of all the conceptual approaches, methods, and techniques devised since the founding of the nation, with the greater number of local governments continuing to stress *control* of public funds over the more recent concerns with *management* and *planning*. It is expected that the more recent concepts of budgeting will continue their diffusion into the many thousands of local law enforcement agencies of the United States.

VICTOR G. STRECHER

References and Further Reading

Kelly, Joseph A., and Joseph T. Kelley. 1984. *Costing police services*. Washington, DC: National Institute of Justice.

Lyden, Fremont J., and Ernest G. Miller. 1982. *Public budgeting*. 4th ed. Englewood Cliffs, NJ: Prentice-Hall.

Miron, Jerome H. 1979. *Managing the pressures of inflation in criminal justice: A manual of selected readings*. National Criminal Justice Executive Training Program. Washington, DC: National Institute of Law Enforcement and Criminal Justice.

Sabo, Lawrence D., and Peter C. Unsinger. 1977. Zero-based budgeting: Its application in a patrol division of a small department. *Police Chief* 44 (May): 60–62.

Schick, Allen. 1982. The road to PPB: The stages of budget reform. In *Public budgeting*, ed. F. J. Lyden and E. G. Miller, 46–68. Englewood Cliffs, NJ: Prentice-Hall.

BUREAU OF ALCOHOL, TOBACCO, FIREARMS, AND EXPLOSIVES

In 1972 the Alcohol, Tobacco, and Firearms Division was separated from the Internal Revenue Service by Treasury Department Order No. 120-1 and became its own independent bureau within the Department of Treasury. Prior to that point the Bureau of Alcohol, Tobacco, and Firearms' (ATF's) mission had been shaped by series of major federal legislation acts and regulations relating to alcohol, firearms, and tobacco. These included the National Firearms Act of 1934, the Federal Alcohol Administration Act of 1935, the Federal Firearms Act of 1938, and the 1968 Gun Control Act, in addition to other legislative acts, amendments, and provisions. These acts and regulations provided ATF with authority over the regulation and collection of taxes for the alcoholic beverages, cigarette, and firearms industries and established new categories of criminal offenses involving firearms and explosives under federal jurisdiction. (See ATF n.d.; Vizzard 1997; and http://www.atf.treas.gov/about/history.htm for information on the organizational and legislative history of ATF and its predecessor agencies.)

The Homeland Security Act of 2002, signed by President Bush on November 25, 2002, split the Bureau of Alcohol, Tobacco, and Firearms into two entities. The newly created Tobacco Tax and Trade Bureau (TTB) remained in the Department of Treasury with responsibility for collecting alcohol, tobacco, firearms, and ammunition excise taxes, and for ensuring that these products are labeled and marketed in accordance with the law (see http://www.ttb.gov/about/index.htm). ATF transferred as a bureau to the Department of Justice and was renamed the Bureau of Alcohol, Tobacco, Firearms and Explosives. The mission of the realigned ATF carried forth the law enforcement component of its predecessor agency including the enforcement of federal criminal laws relating to firearms, explosives, arson, alcohol, and tobacco. In addition ATF retained the regulatory responsibility of the firearms and explosives industries, which include licensing and inspection functions (ATF n.d.). Finally, a provision in the Homeland Security Act titled the Safe Explosives Act (SEA) gave ATF additional responsibilities for regulating explosives. SEA requires all persons obtaining explosives materials to obtain a federal permit issued by the ATF and to be screened by ATF.

Today, ATF's efforts are organized into three major strategic program areas: (1) firearms, (2) explosives and arson, and (3) alcohol and tobacco diversion (ATF 2005). ATF's firearms program is designed to (1) enforce federal firearms laws in order to keep firearms away from persons who are prohibited from possessing firearms (felons, underage persons, etc.), and remove violent offenders from communities; (2) monitor and increase compliance with firearms licensing laws and regulations in order to prevent the illegal transfer of firearms; and (3) collaborate with community organizations, local law enforcement, and the firearms industry to implement initiatives to reduce firearms crime.

In pursuit of these objectives ATF assists law enforcement in identifying firearms trafficking patterns and trends and in resolving violent crimes by providing crime gun tracing support, ballistics imaging technology, and advanced firearms investigative techniques. ATF firearms programs, resources, and expertise also support efforts to prevent terrorism and, as part of this function, ATF serves on the National Security Coordinating Committee and assists Joint Terrorism Task Forces throughout the nation. In its firearms regulatory role, ATF oversees compliance with federal policies regarding the production and distribution of alcohol, tobacco, and firearms. As part of ATF's regulatory firearms program, the agency inspects firearms dealers, monitors the accuracy of dealer records required for tracing, reviews applicants for firearms dealer licenses to ensure they meet legal eligibility requirements, and monitors firearms imported into the United States to ensure they are legally importable and properly marked and recorded by the importer for sale in the United States. Finally, the agency regulates and enforces federal civil penalties and criminal laws relating to firearms production, import sales, transport, use, carrying, and possession (ATF 2005; http://www.atf.gov/firearms/index.htm).

ATF's explosives and arson program is responsible for administering and enforcing the regulatory and crime provisions of federal laws pertaining to explosives and arson (including the Antiarson Act of 1982, the Antiterrorism and Effective Death Penalty Act of 1996, and the Safe Explosives Act of 2002). As part of this program, the agency also promotes new methods of investigation into fire and explosives-related crime and acts of terrorism. In support of these objectives ATF supports and conducts investigations of bombing, explosions, fire, and other incidents to determine whether they are criminal acts; conducts investigations of missing explosives; shares intelligence with the counterterrorism community; assists and trains federal, state, and local law enforcement in investigation techniques relative to explosives and fires; and promotes standardized reporting practices regarding explosives, bombings, and fires.

In its role as a regulator, ATF screens applicants for licenses in the explosives industry to ensure that prohibited persons, such as felons and potential terrorists, are denied access to explosives; inspects explosive storage facilities; works with holders of federal explosives licenses and permits to ensure proper record keeping and business practices; assists in the enforcement of federal and state regulations governing explosives; and educates relevant actors in the public sector and private industry regarding ATF policies and regulations. Finally, ATF is also charged with fostering innovation in the fire and explosives investigative community (ATF 2005; http://www.atf.gov/explarson/index.htm).

ATF's alcohol and tobacco diversion program recognizes that the proliferation of large-volume trafficking of alcohol and tobacco products (particularly counterfeit and lawfully manufactured cigarettes) across international borders and in interstate commerce, without the payment of taxes, provides increasing funding and support to traditional organized criminal enterprises and to terrorist organizations. To address these problems, ATF's alcohol and tobacco diversion program seeks to enforce laws that prohibit the diversion of alcohol and tobacco from legitimate commerce and to provide law enforcement and regulatory agencies with methods to identify trafficking schemes and enterprises.

To support the ATF program of activities, the bureau has developed and/or promoted a broad range of innovative technologies, information and intelligence systems, laboratories, and initiatives. Among the most prominent of these innovations and systems are ATF's National Laboratory, the U.S. Bomb Center, the Bomb Arson Tracking System (BATS), the National Tracing Center, the National Integrated Ballistics Information Network (NIBIN), and the National Licensing Center (for firearms dealers and manufacturers). In addition, ATF supports a range of national response teams (including rapid response laboratories designed to support examination of evidence at the scene of a fire or explosion) to support law enforcement investigations and respond to firearm, arson, and explosives-related incidents or threats.

GLENN L. PIERCE and ROBERTA GRIFFITH

See also **Crime Control Strategies: Gun Control; Federal Police and Investigative Agencies; Firearms Regulation and Control; Firearms Tracing; Firearms: History**

References and Further Reading

Anti-Arson Act of 1982. Pub. L. No. 97–298, § 1, 96 Stat. 1319 (October 12, 1982).
Antiterrorism and Effective Death Penalty Act of 1996. Pub. L. No. 104-132, 110 Stat. 1214 (1996).
Bureau of Alcohol, Tobacco, Firearms and Explosives. (n.d.). *ATF 2003 Performance and Accountability Report*, 7. Washington, DC: U.S. Department of Justice.
———. (n.d.). *Working for a safer and more secure America . . . Through innovation and partnerships: Strategic plan for 2004 to 2009*, 4. Washington, DC: U.S. Department of Justice.
Federal Alcohol Administration Act of 1935. 27 USC §§ 201.
Federal Firearms Act of 1938. Pub. L. No. 75-785, 52 Stat. 1250 (1938).
Gun Control Act of 1968. Pub. L. No. 90-618, 82 Stat. 1213, 18 U.S.C. Sec. 921, et seq. (1968).
Homeland Security Act of 2002. Pub. L. No. 107–296 (2002).
National Firearms Act of 1934. 48 Stat. 1236, 26 U.S.C. Chapter 53 (2000).
Vizzard, W. J. 1997. *In the cross fire: A political history of the bureau of alcohol, tobacco and firearms*. Boulder, CO: Lynne Rienner Publishers.

BURGLARY AND POLICE RESPONSE

Definition of Burglary

Burglary is defined by the Federal Bureau of Investigation (FBI) as ". . . the unlawful entry of a structure to commit a felony or theft. The use of force to gain entry is not required to classify an offense as burglary." The FBI recognizes three distinct types of burglary: (1) forcible entry, (2) unlawful entry where no force is used, and (3) attempted forcible entry. Burglary is one of three major property crimes counted by the FBI's Uniform Crime Reporting (UCR) Program, along with larceny-theft and motor vehicle theft.

Data on Burglary

The two major sources of burglary data in the United States are the UCR and the

National Crime Victimization Survey (NCVS). The UCR is a nationwide law enforcement effort coordinated by the FBI that provides annual crime statistics on the city, county, and state levels through the voluntary submission of statistics by agencies across the country. The Bureau of Justice Statistics produces the NCVS estimates of the number of households victimized each year by surveying a nationally representative sample of households. Thus, the NCVS provides a valuable alternative to the UCR on crime whether or not the crimes are reported to the police. Like crime in general, and specifically other types of property crime, both sources show a sharp decline in burglary during the last several decades. However, even though burglary has experienced a sharp decline, it remains a persistent problem.

In 2003, the UCR estimated that 2,153,464 burglaries occurred, a 0.1% increase from the 2002 estimate of 2,151,252. Despite the slight increase in burglaries between 2002 and 2003, the burglary rate per 100,000 citizens experienced a slight decrease. The burglary rate in 2003 was 740.5. For 2003, 62.4% of burglaries were forcible entry burglaries, 31.2% were unlawful entry burglaries, and the remaining 6.3% were attempted forcible entry burglaries. In 2003, residential burglaries accounted for 65.8% of all burglaries and the remaining 34.2% of burglaries occurred in nonresidential locations. For residential burglaries, the majority, 62%, occurred during the day, while for nonresidential burglaries, the majority, 58.4%, occurred at night. The estimated loss for all burglaries combined in 2003 is $3.5 billion, with and average of $1,626 per offense. The average of $1,600 for residential burglaries is slightly less than that of $1,676 for nonresidential burglaries.

The residential burglary estimate provided by the 2003 NCVS is 3,395,620 victimizations (29.9 burglaries per 1,000 households), up from the 2002 estimate of 3,055,720 (27.7 burglaries per 1,000 households). The NCVS estimates that 54.1% of residential burglaries are reported to police. According to the NCVS data, the burglary rate varies depending on annual household income, ownership of household (owned or rented), location of household (urban, suburban, or rural), and region of household (Northeast, Midwest, South, or West). For households with an income of $7,500 or less, the rate is 58 burglaries per 1,000, while the rate for households with an income of $75,000 or more is 20.8. The rate is 24.5 for those who own their homes, while those who rent have a rate of 41.2. For households in urban areas, the burglary rate is 38.7 per 1,000 households, in suburban areas the rate is much lower at 24.0, and in rural areas the rate is 30.5. The Northeast experienced burglaries at the lowest rate of 20.5, and the Midwest has the highest rate of 32.5. The South and West are not far behind with rates of 32.2 and 30.6, respectively.

In 2003, 13.1% of burglaries reported to police were cleared, meaning that arrests were made. Of cleared burglaries, 16.8% of arrestees were under the age of eighteen and 70.5% were male. Whites accounted for almost three-quarters of arrestees.

Etiology

The etiology of burglary can be found in the needs of offenders, whether perceived or actual. This need is often immediate in nature, thus requiring an equally immediate solution such as burglary, as opposed to legitimate work or some other form of crime.

The bulk of research on burglary indicates that the need for money is the primary motivation for its commission (Bennett and Wright 1984; Cromwell, Olson, and Avary 1991; Rengert and Wasilchick 1985; Wright and Decker 1994). While the motivation is generally financial, it varies from the need for money for legitimate expenses to the necessity for the material constructs of the lifestyle of most burglars. Wright and Decker (2004) describe the motivation of burglars as largely falling into the purposes of "keeping the party going," in other words being able to have or buy drugs and/or alcohol; "keeping up appearances," including having stylish clothes or cars; and "keeping things together," or simply being able to pay the rent or any other necessary responsibility. Burglary causes offenders to engage in behaviors that promote the maintenance of short-term goals and future offending.

Police Response

Police respond to burglaries and also attempt to prevent future burglaries. There are two ways in which burglaries can come to the attention of the police. The first is to actually observe the burglary taking place, and the second, and far more frequent, way is to respond to reported burglaries. Once a burglary has been called to the attention of the police, and it has not been directly observed by the police, an investigation begins. The primary purpose of the investigation is to identify, locate, and apprehend the burglar. Once an offender has been identified, it is necessary for the police to prepare a case that can be successfully prosecuted.

The police can also respond to burglary in an attempt to prevent it. While the statement sounds paradoxical, police can respond to patterns of burglary that exist on their beats or in their cities. By understanding and being cognizant of the trends of burglary, they can react by increasing visibility and presence as well as by forming relationships with members of the community, namely, the youth, creating a mutual respect in the neighborhood.

Recent police efforts to prevent burglary (and crime in general) have included such policies/programs as problem-oriented policing (POP) and community-oriented policing (COP). POP involves identifying specific problems and developing strategies to solve those problems. This type of policing can be useful in the prevention of burglary because often those involved in burglary are both offenders and victims of this crime, allowing for the reduction of a significant portion of these crimes with the removal of recidivists. COP, on the other hand, is a law enforcement approach that seeks to work closely with the residents of the community. In the case of burglary, citizens can inform police of specific problem areas and patterns of burglarizing.

Conclusion

Because burglary involves the entering into ones place of residence or business, it holds particular fear for potential victims. While police can help to prevent burglaries, residents and business owners can implement strategies such as using proxies for occupancy and installing locks and alarm systems. Although the burglary rate has declined significantly in the past several decades, it remains a problem and the second most frequently occurring serious offense, after only larceny-theft. If for no other reason than its frequency, it is important for police to strategically respond to committed burglaries and attempt to prevent its occurrence in the future.

LINDSEY GREEN and SCOTT H. DECKER

See also **Clearance Rates and Criminal Investigations; Community Watch Programs; Crime Prevention; National Crime Victimization Survey (NCVS); Problem-Oriented Policing;** *Uniform Crime Reports*

References and Further Reading

Bennett, T., and R. Wright. 1984. *Burglars on burglary: Prevention and the offender.* Aldershot, England: Gower.

Catalano, S. M. 2004. *Criminal victimization, 2003.* Washington, DC: Bureau of Justice

Statistics, U.S. Department of Justice, Office of Justice Programs.

Cromwell, P., J. Olson, and D. Avary. 1991. *Breaking and entering: An ethnographic analysis of burglary.* Newbury Park, CA: Sage.

Federal Bureau of Investigation. 2003. *Crime in the United States.* Washington, DC: Federal Bureau of Investigation.

Rengert, G., and J. Wasilchick. 1985. *Suburban burglary: A time and a place for everything.* Springfield, IL: Charles C Thomas.

Wright, R. T., and S. Decker. 1994. *Burglars on the job: Streetlife and residential break-ins.* Richmond, VA: Northeastern University Press.

BUSINESS DISTRICTS, POLICING

Business districts represent social environments that differ substantially from residential areas in cities. They are key to local economic development strategies, offering employment as well as a range of goods and services. They generally include a mix of retail and service office space, as well as restaurants, theaters, and other cultural institutions. Because of their concentration on commerce, they are also prime targets for crime and forms of social disorder including vagrancy, panhandling, and other types of street-level disturbance behaviors. Business districts are often characterized by dense and congested traffic patters (vehicular and pedestrian) as well. From the standpoint of crime, business or commercial districts also provide substantial opportunities for crime—the victimization of the businesses themselves, as well as those who work in the business districts and visitors to these areas of cities.

Business districts also represent economic and political power in that they provide substantial support for local government through employment and the goods and services they sell to the public. In many respects they anchor local government, and their decline inevitably affects the ability of local governments to provide wider services outside of the business district.

While business districts within central cities have always been acknowledged as important to the fiscal health of cities, over many years, particularly in the period between 1970 and 1990, urban central cities faced considerable decline. The advent and growth of suburban life in the 1950s and beyond resulted in many local businesses leaving the central city for suburban communities. The strip mall and later the mega-mall replaced city centers as centers of commerce, and "office parks" emerged, drawing office and service support industries away from the cities. Many city centers were abandoned, inhabited by the dispossessed, and unable to provide economic support for themselves or their hosting cities. Urban decline in general and in business districts in particular fueled concerns for rising crime and social disorder in these places (Skogan 1990).

Business districts also present different problems for policing. As indicated, and in contrast to residential areas, business districts require a high order of traffic management and are vulnerable to a range of emergencies. In many communities, central business districts are often also some of the oldest parts of the city, requiring substantial investments in infrastructure, including a wide range of public safety services: fire, emergency medical response, and police.

Beginning in the late 1980s and into the 1990s, a business improvement district (BID) movement emerged as an effort to recapture the vitality of central business districts (Frieden and Sagalyn 1989). The BID concept emerged first in the 1960s in the form of special purpose, special assessment, and special zoning districts. Although each of these had slightly different purposes, their similarities include the ideas of focused attention on business districts, self-taxing to provide funding to supplement but not replace city funding for local services (e.g., police, fire, street cleaning, and other

public works functions), and some degree of legal independence from local government.

BIDs tend to provide services under three broadly defined categories: clean, safe, and attractive. This approach often is modeled on the broken-windows concept (Wilson and Kelling 1982) of addressing small and visible problems before they become more significant. BIDs generally focus their attention on removing the signs of crime, graffiti, unclean streets and sidewalks, poor lighting and signage, public panhandling, and the like, while at the same time marketing and promoting public use of the downtown area and its commercial base.

Clean activities include street cleaning, graffiti control, and other physical place issues (e.g., repair of small parks and sidewalks, improved lighting and signage). Safety is focused on public disorder and public crime, thereby removing, monitoring, or deterring those who create a climate of fear of crime as well as those who would engage in criminal acts. These activities involve ideas associated with situational crime prevention, particularly the idea of place management and the creation of capable guardians to "keep an eye" on the downtown area.

Marketing involves increasing use of downtown businesses, restaurants, and cultural activities and attracting businesses back to the city centers. The BID movement has produced well over 1,200 business improvement districts nationally, perhaps the most notable being the Times Square Partnership in New York City (Rogowsky and Gross 1999).

Central business districts often have higher crime and disorder problems in comparison to residential areas (Wikstrom 1995) and they offer distinct problems for policing because they are most often characterized as being highly transient, evidencing considerable variation in populations by hours of the day and day of week (Reiss 1985). Additionally, the level

of "social control" in business districts is often lower than that in residential areas in that "ownership" for public space is made more complicated by the transience in populations that use business districts (Kelling and Coles 1996). They are most often heavily populated during traditional working periods (Monday through Friday, between the hours of 7 a.m. and 7 p.m.), and are at times "abandoned" during the late evenings and on weekends.

In a critique of crime and disorder crimes in business districts, Reiss (1985) suggested that these areas in cities have become a place where homeless persons have congregated and where "soft crimes" (harassment, aggressive panhandling, loitering, and threatening behaviors) have flourished, resulting in increased fear of crime and disorder on the part of those who work, but do not live, in these areas. Moreover, Reiss suggests that "control" of business districts has often been taken over by private security interests, making the coordination of public safety in these areas, particularly with the local police, more complex.

Wikstrom (1995), in a major critique of crime and crime prevention in business districts, suggests that the central crime prevention strategy to be employed is that focused on the "routine activities" (Felson 1987) found in these areas and by addressing problems created by youth, public disorder, drinking and drug use, and violence associated with entertainment opportunities provided in city center areas. He further suggests that the best partnerships available to the police for these purposes are the businesses themselves and private security agents that provide security and surveillance to center city areas.

JACK R. GREENE

See also **Broken-Windows Policing; Crime and Place, Theories of; Crime Prevention; Routine Guardianship; Situational Crime Prevention; Zero Tolerance Policing**

References and Further Reading

Briffault, Richard. 1999. A government for our time? business improvement districts and urban governance. *Columbia Law Review*, March, 365–477.

Council of the City of New York. 1995. *Cities within cities: Business improvement districts and the emergence of the metropolis.* New York: Council of the City of New York.

Felson, Marcus. 1987. Routine activities and crime in the developing metropolis. *Criminology* 25: 911–31.

Frieden, Bernard, and Lynn B. Sagalyn. 1989. *Downtown Inc.: How America rebuilds cities.* Cambridge, MA: The MIT Press.

Hoyt, Lorlene. 2005. Do business improvement districts make a difference? Criminal activity in and around commercial areas in Philadelphia. *Journal of Planning Education and Research* 25: 185–99.

Kelling, George L., and Catherine M. Coles. 1996. *Fixing broken windows: Restoring order and reducing crime in our communities.* New York: The Free Press.

Lloyd, M. G., J. McCarthy, S. McGreal, and J. Berry. 2003. Business improvement districts, planning and urban regeneration. *International Planning Studies* 8: 295–321.

Rogowsky, Edward, and Jill Simone Gross. 1999. Managing development in New York City: The case of business improvement districts. In *Managing capital resources for central city revitalization*, 81–87. New York: Garland Publishing.

Skogan, Westley G. 1990. *Disorder and decline: Crime and the spiral of decay in American cities.* New York: The Free Press.

Wikstrom, Per-Olof H. 1995. Preventing city-center street crimes. In *Building a safer society: Strategic approaches to crime prevention*, vol. 19, ed. Tonry and Farrington, 429–68. Chicago: University of Chicago Press.

Wilson, James Q., and George L. Kelling. 1982. Broken windows. *Atlantic Monthly*, March, 29–38.

C

CALLS FOR SERVICE

Calls for service are requests from citizens for police assistance. Most calls for service originate when a citizen dials either an emergency number such as 911 or a non-emergency number for the local police department. Calls for service range from minor problems in the neighborhood (traffic complaints, loud neighbors, and graffiti) to the most serious crimes (burglaries, robberies, and homicides). The obligation of a police department is to respond to calls for service in an efficient and effective manner.

Reporting Calls for Service

Historically, Great Britain introduced a "9-9-9" number in 1938 for its citizens to contact the police. In the United States the first 911 system became operational in Haleyville, Alabama, in 1968, replacing the need for citizens to dial a seven-digit number or to press zero so that a telephone company operator could connect them to the police. The 911 number quickly became adopted across the country as a universal emergency number; today virtually all jurisdictions have established it for emergency calls to police. The advantage of 911 is that is it not an area code, and it is easy to remember and dial.

By the 1990s, an overload of nonemergency calls on 911 had created serious problems in some cities, with 911 callers receiving busy signals or getting placed on hold at peak times. Indeed, the three-digit number became a victim of its own success as citizens found it easier to dial 911 instead of looking up the nonemergency seven-digit number. In February 1997, the Federal Communications Center designated 311 as a national, voluntary, nontoll phone number for nonemergencies. The two most common types of 311 systems that are emerging are police-operated systems, where 311 is for nonemergency calls, and 311 systems operated by a jurisdiction for general services, including nonemergency police calls for service. As examples, Chicago and Dallas have implemented 311 for citywide services, with Chicago describing the number as "your call to city hall." The police department in Las Vegas started its service by encouraging citizens to call 311 "when there's urgency but no emergency."

A related technological impact on calls for service is the evolution of the wireless cell phone as a means of communication. Police departments receive calls for service more quickly than in the past, with traffic accidents and crimes in progress as good examples. Someone seeing a traffic accident or a crime in progress may immediately dial 911 with a cell phone to report what has occurred. In fact, police departments frequently receive several calls immediately after a major incident occurs. The result is faster response time by the police.

In reverse manner, officers in some police departments have been issued cell phones for making work-related calls during their shift. An unanticipated result is that citizens who find out about this number call the officer directly for service—an occurrence that completely bypasses normal reporting avenues.

Call Classification Schemes

Regardless of how calls arrive, they are classified by police departments by call type and priority. Call type is based on the caller's information elicited through question-and-answer protocols from call takers. Police departments prioritize incoming calls based on the department's established policies on the emergency nature of the call (for example, harm to a person imminent, crime in progress), response time, need for backup units, and

other local factors. Although call priority schemes vary across the country, most have three to five levels. A typical three-priority scheme might look like that shown in Table 1.

Emergency calls include crimes in progress, serious traffic accidents, and other types of calls for which the presence of police is needed as quickly as possible. These calls usually account for less than 5% of a department's total volume. Immediate calls include less serious crimes (for example, trespassing, loitering, minor traffic accidents) and routine calls that do not require immediate police presence (for example, vandalism, noise disturbance, suspicious vehicle).

Calls that do not require a patrol officer at the scene represent another call category. With some types of calls, the citizen can report the problem to the police department in an alternate manner such as connecting to the department's telephone report unit (TRU). Police departments establish TRUs for the specific purpose of allowing citizens to provide information about an incident by telephone. Policies are established on the types of incidents for which telephone reporting is applicable. Evaluations of TRUs consistently find that citizen satisfaction is dependent on the courtesy of the call taker, including the call taker's willingness to explain the reason for taking the report over the phone and how long it will take.

The Arlington County (Virginia) Police Department provides another example of an alternate way to report minor crimes. The department maintains a website

Table 1

Priority	Designation	Response	Number of Units
1	Emergency	Immediate; lights and siren; exceed speed limit	Two
2	Immediate	Immediate; lights and siren; maintain speed limit	One or two depending on call type
3	Routine	Maintain speed limit; response may be delayed	One

(http://www.co.arlington.va.us/police) for reporting destruction of property, fraud, simple assault, eight types of theft (vehicle license plate, bicycle, cell phone, and so on), and threatening or harassing phone calls. Citizens complete an online form giving the type of incident, address, estimate of when it occurred, and other information.

Calls for service include incidents an officer comes across while on patrol. An officer may directly observe an incident or a citizen may flag down a patrol car because an incident has taken place in the neighborhood. These situations fall under the rubric of "self-initiated activities" because it is the patrol officer who is starting the contact with citizens. In these instances, a citizen eventually would have called the police for assistance, and it is in this sense that these activities are calls for service.

Call classification schemes can range from having twenty different call types in some agencies to sixty or more different call types in others. They include broad categories, such as "suspicious persons" and "heard shots," because the citizen contacting the department may not be able to provide more specific information. It is only after investigation by a responding patrol officer that the final determination can be made, and an officer can respond back to the dispatcher with a more accurate call type.

Interestingly, in many jurisdictions, alarm calls are the most frequent type of call based on their classification schemes. These calls are given a high priority with two patrol units dispatched to the scene. Unfortunately, the vast majority—usually 97% or more—are false alarms. That is, they have been set off accidentally. Many jurisdictions have established programs to reduce the volume of false alarms. For example, the Montgomery County Police Department established a False Alarm Reduction Section in 1994 to address the large number of false alarms it had been receiving. Between 1995 and 2004, the

county experienced a 55.2% reduction in false alarms due to programs established by the section.

Analysis of Calls for Service

Police departments depend heavily on their classifications of calls for service for strategic and tactical analysis. Analysis inevitably shows that a minority of calls for service are serious crimes (homicide, sexual assault, aggravated assault, burglary, auto theft, larceny), reflecting the reality that the daily job of patrol officers centers on problems happening on their beats. Calls for disorderly conduct, traffic complaints, suspicious vehicles, noise disturbances, disputes between neighbors, and other noncrime incidents are at the core of what patrol officers do each day.

Analysis of calls for services blends nicely into departments that have transitioned to community-oriented and problem-oriented policing. Examples of analysis of calls that support those policing approaches include the following:

- Analyze calls by call type and problem location
- Conduct "hot spot" analysis
- Identify repeat callers

As a problem-solving activity, the aim of the analysis is to determine the underlying causes of the problems and enlist community support for solutions. Resolving a local problem and freeing up patrol time are the main benefits of problem-solving activities centered on calls for service.

Analysis of calls for service also plays a key role in determining the allocation of patrol officers in the field. This analysis is based on information captured in a department's computer-aided dispatch (CAD) system. Call takers and dispatchers employ a CAD system to capture information from citizens and track patrol officers who are responding to calls for service. A CAD system is the automated backbone of a communications center. Data in a CAD system include the type of call for service, priority, address, beat, unit(s) responding, time of dispatch, time of a unit's arrival on the scene, and time the call was completed.

By analyzing data on calls for service in a CAD system, a department can determine:

- Number of calls by day of week and hour of day
- Number of calls by beat
- Calls requiring backup units
- Patrol officer time devoted to call by type and priority
- Patrol officer time on calls by day, shift, and geographic area

The analysis leads to determinations on how many patrol officers are needed and where they should be allocated both spatially and temporally.

Issues about calls for service center on the impact of technology on how calls come into a police department and the need to merge disparate sources of information about calls. The impact of technology on calls for service has yet to be fully determined. Calls are made by citizens and handled by police in many different ways—seven-digit telephone numbers, 911 or 311 numbers, online incident reports, TRUs, and direct calls to officers. The diversity of reporting methods makes it challenging for a department to paint a complete picture of its activities. Departments must find ways to merge the information sources together for a richer analysis of calls for service.

J. THOMAS MCEWEN

See also **Community-Oriented Policing: Practices; Computer-Aided Dispatching (CAD) Systems; Differential Police Response; Performance Measurement; Personnel Allocation; Problem-Oriented Policing; SARA, the Model; Technology, Records Management, and Calls for Service**

References and Further Reading

Baltimore Police Department. 1997. *Baltimore Police Department Communications Division 311 non-emergency telephone number first annual program evaluation (October 1996/ September 1997)*. Baltimore, MD: Baltimore Police Department.

Cohen, Marcia, and J. T. McEwen. 1984. *Handling calls for service—Alternatives to traditional policing*. NIJ Research in Action Report. Washington, DC: U.S. Department of Justice, National Institute of Justice.

Diez, L. 1984. *Use of call grading: How calls to the police are graded and resourced*. Police Research Series Paper 13, September. London: United Kingdom Home Office Police Research Group.

Eck, John, and W. Spelman. 1987. *Problem-solving: Problem-oriented policing in Newport News*. Washington, DC: Police Executive Research Forum.

Goldstein, Herman. 1990. *Problem oriented policing*. New York: McGraw-Hill.

Hoover, Larry, ed. 1996. Assessing alternative responses to calls for service. In *Quantifying quality in policing*, ed. L. T. Hoover, 153–66. Washington, DC: Police Executive Research Forum.

Jolowicz, C., and T. Read. 1995. *Telephone demand on the police: The 90's picture?* Briefing Note, May. London: United Kingdom Home Office Police Research Group.

McEwen, Tom, E. F. Connors, and M. I. Cohen. 1986. *Evaluation of the differential police response field test*. Alexandria, VA: Research Management Associates.

McEwen, Tom, D. Spence, R. Wolff, J. Wartell, and B. Webster. 2003. *Call management and community policing: A guidebook for law enforcement*. Washington, DC: U.S. Department of Justice, Office of Community Oriented Policing Services.

Ommen, T. L. 1988. *What will be the police response to non-emergency calls for service by the year 2000?* Sacramento: California Commission on Peace Officer Standards and Training.

Scott, Mike. 2001. *Problem oriented policing: reflections on the first 20 years*. Washington, DC: U.S. Department of Justice, Office of Community Oriented Policing Services.

Sumrall, R. O., J. Roberts, and M. T. Farmer. 1981. *Differential police response strategies*. Washington, DC: U.S. Department of Justice.

CAMPUS POLICE

The first documented presence of law enforcement personnel on college and university campuses occurred when Yale University hired two city of New Haven police officers to walk foot patrol on its campus in 1894 (Bordner and Peterson 1984; Powell 1994; Sloan 1992). As we enter the twenty-first century, campus police agencies now form the core of specialized protection and law enforcement at postsecondary institutions in the United States and Western Europe. This evolution has seen the campus police shift from providing little more than a campus watch function to one in which highly trained and specialized professional law enforcement officers engage in law enforcement, crime prevention, and service-related functions. This century of evolution also saw the number of agencies grow to nearly one thousand as of 2002 (http://dpsw.usc.edu/UnivPDWeb.html).

Campus police agencies developed as a direct outcome of returning World War II veterans and the arrival of the baby boomers at college during the 1960s. Additionally, although sharing many of the organizational and operational characteristics of local police agencies, they also face some unique challenges. Finally, with expansion and increased specialization of their role on campus, the future of campus police agencies involves further adaptation to changing needs and circumstances.

The Development of Modern Campus Police Agencies

The development of campus police agencies during the twentieth century involved an evolution in the role the agency played on the campus. The first decades of the century saw no university-based formal police entity on college or university campuses. Rather, the campus "watchman" or guard became a familiar presence at many postsecondary institutions. These individuals were part of the campus maintenance department, were typically retired, worked only at night or on weekends, had no law enforcement training, and expected only to secure campus buildings.

During the 1930s and 1940s, campus "watchmen" began enforcing college and university rules and monitoring violations of codes of conduct. Again, however, these individuals had no formal law enforcement training and were little more than security guards. During the late 1940s and early 1950s, an influx of WWII veterans flooded the college campus, forcing campus administrators to recognize a need for a more formal presence of security officials on campus. During this period formal "campus security departments" or "campus police departments" began appearing on college campuses. Separated from campus maintenance, these units were typically headed by administrators who were either ex-police officers or whom universities had hired away from local police departments. These individuals then turned to an organizational model with which they were most familiar—municipal police agencies—to structure the operational and tactical aspects of the department. Although more formalized in appearance, the individuals who worked for these departments did not differ greatly from their predecessors—poorly trained and educated, often retired, and generally not in a position to engage in true law enforcement functions.

With the coming of the baby boom generation to college during the 1960s and 1970s, colleges and universities faced a variety of pressures, including tremendous increases in the sheer numbers of students attending school; active political environments on campus that included protests; wide acceptance of drug use; and a much freer lifestyle among students. Because of these factors, college and university presidents were under increasing pressure to ensure order and prevent harm to property. They responded by allocating unprecedented resources to the campus police, including funding to hire additional officers, as well as approving enhancements to officers' responsibilities. Concurrently, colleges petitioned the states to grant full police powers to campus officers and when the states agreed, it paved the way for the emergence of a true campus police entity on campuses.

During the 1980s, campus police agencies sought further "professionalization" of officers. This was achieved by upgrading prospective officers' qualifications and training requirements, developing specialized units within departments (for example, SWAT teams, detectives), and increasingly adopting not only the tactical, but the operational characteristics of municipal police departments. Officers relied heavily on automobiles to patrol campus, response time was emphasized, and crime control and order maintenance were stressed as key functions of the department. Some campus law enforcement agencies pursued—and were granted—national accreditation, further enhancing their stature.

By the 1990s, according to Jackson (1992), Lanier (1995), and Sloan, Lanier, and Beer (2000), campus law enforcement agencies, like their municipal counterparts, began to experiment with community-oriented policing (COP) or problem-oriented policing (POP) as new "organizational models."

Thus, the twentieth-century saw formal law enforcement on college campuses evolve from "officers" performing little more than a campus watch function to officers receiving training comparable to that received by municipal police officers. Further, the evolution saw campus police move from being housed in the campus maintenance division to being housed in a separate unit within the larger organization, headed by a "chief" or a "director." Finally, as local police agencies began exploring new organizational models, campus police agencies began looking to models such as COP and POP to determine their applicability on the college campus.

Organizational Characteristics and Functions of Campus Police Agencies

The single most important source of data on campus law enforcement is the Justice Department's *Campus Law Enforcement and Administrative Statistics* (CLEMAS). In 1995, the Bureau of Justice Statistics (BJS) surveyed more than six hundred police agencies located at a random sample of four-year institutions of higher education in the United States with twenty-five hundred or more students to determine the nature of law enforcement services at these campuses (Reaves and Goldberg 1996; http://www.ojp.usdoj.gov/bjs/pub/pdf/clea95.pdf). The survey described the agencies in terms of their personnel, expenditures and pay, operations, equipment, computers and information systems, policies, and special programs.

Several studies using these data (for example, Bromley and Reaves 1998a, 1998b; Paoline and Sloan 2003; Reaves and Goldberg 1996) have shown that campus police agencies "mirror," in many ways, traditional municipal police departments. Similarities include a well-defined and paramilitary-based rank structure; comparable operational practices and written policies; equivalent levels of training; use of technology, including computers, 911 systems, and advanced communications capabilities; analogous service functions, including provision of emergency medical services and search and rescue operations; and comparable use of officer protective equipment such as body armor, batons, and pepper spray. Additionally, Paoline and Sloan (2003) found strong similarities between the organizational structure of campus agencies and that of municipal police agencies.

The Unique Challenges Facing Campus Police Agencies

Although campus and municipal police departments share many of the same tactical and organizational characteristics, and both focus on engaging in crime control, order maintenance, and service to the community, campus police do face challenges not encountered by local law enforcement.

One unique challenge faced by campus law enforcement involves federal crime reporting requirements. Unlike their municipal counterparts who may choose to release local crime statistics to the FBI each year, campus police agencies are under strict mandate from the Clery Act to make campus crime statistics available to current and prospective students, parents, and university employees each year. Failure to do so may result in sanctions, including reductions in federal financial aid for the college or university. Thus, careful record keeping and dissemination of information involving campus crime are tasks to which campus law enforcement must devote far more resources than do local police agencies.

Another unique challenge faced by campus law enforcement is the transitory nature of the college campus. While certain areas of a municipal police agency's jurisdiction may be transitory, a college campus experiences large numbers of students graduating and new students arriving each year, along with the departure and hiring of faculty and staff and the large numbers of visitors on campus each day. This more transitory environment, particularly when combined with a large physical plant, creates unique problems that campus police must address daily through tactical and administrative considerations.

Finally, despite efforts to professionalize itself, including upgrading training and education requirements, pursuing accreditation, and transforming itself into a "modern law enforcement agency (Sloan 1992),

campus law enforcement too often confronts the perception that somehow officers are little more than "door shakers" (Peak 1995). Because modern campus police agencies evolved from campus maintenance departments and for most of the twentieth century "officers" were little more than security guards, old stereotypes remain. By adopting new organizational models such as the COP model, campus law enforcement will slowly help the campus community overcome its stereotypes of who campus officers are and what they represent.

Modern campus police agencies serve as the foundation for security, crime control, order maintenance, and service on college and university campuses around the nation. The twentieth century saw the growth, development, and eventual arrival of formal law enforcement entities on campus whose officers receive training not only on par with, but sometimes exceeding, the training received by municipal police officers. As we move into the new century, campus law enforcement agencies began involving themselves even more with the campus community via new "models" of policing such as COP and POP. Such models may prove invaluable in helping campus agencies address the unique challenges they face and continue to grow and develop.

JOHN J. SLOAN, III

See also **Community-Oriented Policing: Practices; Problem-Oriented Policing**

References and Further Reading

Bordner, D. C., and D. M. Peterson. 1984. *Campus policing: The nature of university work*. Lanham, MD: University Press of America.

Bromley, M. L., and B. Reaves. 1998a. Comparing campus and city police operational practices. *Journal of Security Administration* 21: 41–54.

———. 1998b. Comparing campus and municipal police: The human resource dimension. *Policing: An International Journal of Police Strategies & Management* 21: 534–46.

Gelber, S. 1972. *The role of security in the campus setting*. Washington, DC: U.S. Government Printing Office.

Jackson, E. 1992. Campus police embrace community-based approach. *The Police Chief* 59: 63–64.

Lanier, M. 1995. Community policing on college campuses: Tradition, tactics, and outlook. In *Campus crime: Legal, social, and policy perspectives*, ed. B. S. Fisher and J. J. Sloan, 360–86. Springfield, IL: Charles C Thomas.

Paoline, E. A., and J. J. Sloan. 2003. Variability in the organizational structure of contemporary campus law enforcement agencies: A national-level analysis. *Policing: An International Journal of Police Strategies & Management* 26: 612–39.

Peak, K. 1995. The professionalization of campus law enforcement: The 1990s and beyond. In *Campus crime: Legal, social, and policy perspectives*, ed. B. Fisher and J. Sloan, 246–74. Springfield, IL: Charles C Thomas.

Powell, J. 1994. The beginning—Yale campus police department—1894. *Campus Law Enforcement Journal* 24: 2–5.

Reaves, B., and A. Goldberg. 1996. *Campus law enforcement agencies, 1995*. Washington, DC: U.S. Department of Justice.

Sloan, J. J. 1992. The modern campus police: An analysis of their evolution, structure, and function. *American Journal of Police* 11: 85–104.

Sloan, J. J., M. M. Lanier, and D. L. Beer. 2000. Policing the contemporary university campus: Challenging traditional organizational models. *Journal of Security Administration* 23: 1–17.

CANADIAN POLICING

Introduction

Policing in Canada has evolved into a separate and distinct form of professional practice that reflects elements from many sources throughout the Western world. In a country that prides itself on multicultural and officially bilingual public policies, it is not surprising that Canada's police organizations demonstrate characteristics that derive from external influences. It would be a mistake to focus exclusively on the evocative image of the red-coated officer of the Royal Canadian Mounted Police (RCMP) as the central symbol of Canadian policing. The reality is significantly more nuanced and diverse than this compelling figure would imply. Indeed, Canadian policing presents an array of complexities and qualities that warrant careful attention.

Early Developments

The lands that became Canada were colonized by French and British interests. Those interests have fundamentally informed Canadian institutions. The impact of these dominating powers remains evident in the cultural, religious, linguistic, and legal systems present in contemporary Canada, including policing.

The French presence has important concentrations in the provinces of Québec and New Brunswick. Imperial Britain's penetration of institutional life is emblematized by the office of the governor-general, who constitutes the British monarch's official representative in the Dominion of Canada. In policing, the figure of Sir Robert Peel stands in bold outline on the landscape. His principles and practice, as manifest in the London Metropolitan Police, were assiduously adopted by Canadian police departments and remain a touchstone for police officers at all levels. Also, the model of the Royal Irish Constabulary, as embodied in the person of Inspector General John R. McCowen of the former Newfoundland Constabulary, remains embedded in Canadian policing.

Indeed, the office of the constable is central to an understanding of policing across Canada. To this day in several jurisdictions the chief of police is referred to as "chief constable." The role of police constable is a direct inheritance from British practice and remains a strong sign of

Canada's attachment to British policing tradition. Dating from medieval England, constables were agents of the Crown who also held responsibility for representing their communities. The constable held a range of duties that indicated the broad complexity of police officers' engagement in their towns and villages. The overriding allegiance of the constable to the Crown was of high significance and has informed a great deal of thinking about this position in Canadian jurisprudence. Accordingly, the constable occupies a unique position with respect to the law and the chief of police. The constable does not occupy a typical master–servant relationship, and Canadian legal tradition has operated to preserve a high degree of independence for this office. The British influence is also apparent in the creation of the Chief Constables' Association of Canada (CCAC) in 1905. This body was formed to advance the interests of chiefs of police across the nation and became known as the Canadian Association of Chiefs of Police in 1953.

The World at War (1914–1945)

During the period of the two world wars, Canadian policing was on heightened alert to preserve and protect national security. In the interwar years it was not uncommon for military leaders to be appointed as chiefs of police. This, of course, had an abiding impact on the nature of Canadian policing. One reality of the war effort was a significant depletion of the ranks in many police departments as officers volunteered to fight abroad. Cooperation among different levels of policing increased during these years as a consequence of the external threat to civil order and stability.

In 1932, Alberta, Manitoba, New Brunswick, Prince Edward Island, and Nova Scotia entered into contracts with the RCMP for provincial police services. Saskatchewan had already done so in 1928. Today, the only provinces that have their own provincial police services are Newfoundland and Labrador, Québec, and Ontario.

Decades of Change

Following World War II technology has played an increasingly important role in modern Canadian policing. The widespread introduction of the automobile, telecommunications systems, computers, and other means of automating police functions has brought about both challenge and change for Canada's police departments. However, the basic structure of policing across Canada has persisted. Beginning with a strong federal presence in policing, there are also ten provincial governments that have significant levels of responsibility for local law enforcement. Also, Canada has three territorial jurisdictions (Nunavut, Northwest Territories, and the Yukon) with a degree of policing responsibility delivered by the RCMP. At the community level, municipalities (or regional municipalities) have direct responsibility for the delivery of police services across Canada. Several municipalities have entered into contracts with the RCMP and/or the Ontario Provincial Police (OPP) for the provision of police services within their jurisdiction.

Increasingly, the governance of policing by civilian bodies has become an important issue within Canada. Based on early experience in Upper Canada (that is, Ontario) the model of the board of commissioners of police has been extrapolated across the country with certain local modifications. Today, the most popular model of civilian governing authority appears to be the police services board, which is characterized by appointees from both the provincial and the municipal levels of government. However, other models of civilian governance exist, including committees of municipal council or the direct reporting of the chief of police to a city manager. In addition to this growing concentration on civilian governance of police departments, increased attention is being paid in Canada to the oversight of police activities. This has resulted in the creation of police complaint commissions, special investigation units, and other civilian agencies mandated to investigate, inquire into, and often adjudicate public complaints about police behavior.

In the 1980s, police services across Canada became devoted to the philosophy of "community policing" and made great efforts toward institutionalizing the principles of this philosophy. Today, many departments have moved away from that particular label, although many have adapted the problem-oriented policing model first articulated by Professor Herman Goldstein. Along with such innovations in progressive policing, Canadian departments have internalized race relations, employment equity, freedom of information, and protection of privacy initiatives. During the last few decades, women and visible minorities have come to play a more equitable role within police services. First Nations policing has also become an important issue on the national political agenda. Also, police unions or associations have grown in stature and capacity as they continue to organize to represent the collective interests of their membership.

Essential Legal Aspects

It is important to highlight the national nature of criminal law in Canada. The federal government holds responsibility for enacting the Criminal Code of Canada, as well as the Controlled Drugs and Substances Act, antiterrorism legislation, and a wide range of other statutes that affect policing and public safety across the country. Furthermore, as part of the Canadian Constitution, the Canadian Charter of Rights and Freedoms sets out a series of fundamental freedoms that profoundly influence the manner in which Canadian police officers will function. The Supreme Court of Canada is the final court of appeal on matters pertaining to search and seizure, arrest and release, interrogation, and other essential police functions. Virtually every police action may be scrutinized through the lens of the charter, and police officers in every Canadian jurisdiction are bound by the rulings of the Supreme Court of Canada.

Each province has enacted its own legislation for the establishment and administration of local police services. Of course, there are many similarities among these pieces of legislation and the core functions of any police department typically include law enforcement, emergency response, assistance to victims of crime, public order maintenance, and crime prevention. Many provincial jurisdictions have adopted formal standards for their police services and have enshrined those standards in the form of regulations. This approach is similar to the framework first developed in the 1980s by the U.S. Commission for the Accreditation of Law Enforcement Agencies (CALEA).

Canada's Response to 9/11 and Its Aftermath

Following the events in the United States pertaining to the September 11, 2001, terrorist attacks, integration in Canadian policing has become an essential issue. The goal of integrating the operational, tactical, and strategic elements of police services is now paramount among Canada's police leaders. Developing a capacity to respond in a coordinated manner with high levels of interoperability is a high priority. An enormously active series of national bodies continue to work diligently to provide leadership for policing issues and priorities. The Canadian Association of Chiefs of Police, the Canadian Association of Police Boards, the Canadian Professional Police Association, and the Canadian Association for Civilian Oversight of Law Enforcement are some of the distinct but often convergent interests relevant to their individual constituencies. Furthermore, the Criminal Intelligence Service of Canada (CISC) operates on a national basis to coordinate the tactical and strategic operational levels of police agencies with direct concerns about organized crime.

The federal Department of Public Safety and Emergency Preparedness Canada was launched in December 2003. The clear intent behind the creation of this department was to elevate issues of national security and antiterrorism to a strategic level. This department has responsibility for the RCMP, the Canadian Security Intelligence Service (CSIS), Correctional Service of Canada, the Canadian Border Services Agency, the Canadian Firearms Centre, and the National Parole Board. This new entity seeks to demonstrate Canada's recognition of global conditions that require a steadfast focus on public safety preparedness. Increasing integration with American law enforcement agencies is an inevitable by-product of this recognition. However, not everyone sees this trend as desirable. Civil liberties groups have been vocal in their critique of pending antiterrorism legislation and what is perceived as an erosion of individual privacy and human rights.

There have been welcome changes in the area of Canadian police leadership development. One example of a growing trend toward university-based police learning is the Centre for Excellence in Police, Fire and Security Management, which has been developed at the Schulich School of Business, York University. This is an effort to provide high-quality, flexible, and relevant educational development for police personnel across Canada. Also offering a range of courses, programs, and seminars for police officers at all levels is the Canadian Police College in Ottawa (Ontario). Consistent with the principles of continuous learning, at both the individual and organizational levels, police services in Canada will be called on to address socioeconomic, cultural, technological, legislative, operational, administrative, and international challenges within an infinitely variable and complex world.

PAUL F. MCKENNA

See also **Accountability; British Policing; Role of the Police**

References and Further Reading

Biro, Fred, et al. 2000. *Police executives under pressure: A study and discussion of the issues.* Ottawa: Canadian Association of Chiefs of Police.

Ceyssens, Paul. 1994. *Legal aspects of policing.* Scarborough, Ontario: Carswell.

Kelly, William, and Nora Kelly. 1976. *Policing in Canada.* Toronto: Macmillan of Canada.

Macleod, R. C., and David Schneiderman, eds. 1994. *Police powers in Canada: The evolution and practice of authority.* Toronto: Centre for Constitutional Studies, University of Alberta and University of Toronto Press.

Marquis, Greg. 1998. *Policing Canada's century: A history of the Canadian Association of Chiefs of Police.* Toronto: The Osgoode Society.

McKenna, Paul F. 1998. *Foundations of policing in Canada.* Scarborough, Ontario: Prentice-Hall Canada Career and Technology.

———. 2000. *Foundations of community policing in Canada.* Scarborough, Ontario: Prentice-Hall Allyn and Bacon Canada.

Stenning, Philip C. 1981. *Police commissions and boards in Canada.* Toronto: Centre of Criminology.

———. 1982. *Legal status of the police: A study paper prepared for the Law Reform Commission of Canada.* Ottawa: Law Reform Commission of Canada.

Talbot, C. K., C. H. S. Jaywardene, and T. J. Juliani. 1985. *Canada's constables: The historical development of policing in Canada.* Ottawa: Crimcare Inc.

CANINE UNITS

The use of canine units in law enforcement has become a prominent feature in policing today. The use of dogs in law enforcement can be traced back to the ancient Egyptians, and it now borders on the impossible to go through police road blocks without being exposed to a canine sniff search. The same is true in airports across the country, where dogs are used to search for bombs and drugs in a post-9/11 world; dogs were used in airports prior to the September 11, 2001, terrorist attacks, but their use since has more than doubled.

Searches are not the only purpose that canine units serve in police work. Canines are also used as an alternative avenue of less-than-lethal violence, as additions in patrol work, and as a means to locate missing persons or stolen goods. While canine units have become a hallmark of modern police forces, they have done so through numerous judicial reviews in which the courts have helped in identifying and determining the proper role of canines in law enforcement. This article reviews the evolution of canine units in police work, the canine unit role, and constitutional challenges to the use of canines in relation to individual due process rights.

The Historical and Contemporary Role of Canine Units in Law Enforcement

The use of dogs in policing dates back to ancient Egypt, where dogs were used to patrol and protect the pyramids. While used in relation to police work throughout the intervening centuries, it was not until the 1960s that dogs began to make a significant mark on law enforcement. As of then, dogs were being used for patrol, searches, apprehending suspects, and finding stolen property and missing persons. The utilization of canines has not changed much since this time period.

Today, the canine unit's primary role comes in the form of searches. Dogs are used by law enforcement to search for suspects, evidence, drugs, and bombs. So-called detector dogs can be trained to find drugs, bombs, and humans. Sniffing for bombs has been a key role for dogs in law enforcement after the 9/11 terrorist attacks, although dogs are still employed as a means of sniff searching for drugs on individuals and vehicles. Indeed, dogs are an important feature of police roadblocks. Canine units can also be used to track down suspects who have eluded the police and to find homicide victims/cadavers, crime or disaster victims in need of rescue, or those who have been lost. All of these functions of canines serve to decrease the risk to officers' safety, allow for the arrest of suspects who may have temporarily escaped, or increase the likelihood of finding lost individuals or dead bodies.

Searching is not the only role that dogs can play in police work. Canine units can be used as less-than-lethal force to control crowds, break up fights, or chase down fleeing suspects. Again, these services provided by canine units can greatly add to police officer safety. Although the use of canines as less-than-lethal force has been debated by the courts, no official consensus has yet been reached. However, the use of dogs in this respect makes a certain level of sense; a dog handler can recall a dog, but a police officer cannot stop a bullet.

Although many different breeds of dogs have been employed in police canine units (bloodhounds, Doberman pinschers, Labradors, mastiffs, and retrievers to name a few), the type of dog most associated with canine units is the German shepherd. German shepherds are preferred to other dog breeds because of their ability to engage in various tasks, ranging from searches for illicit materials to their abilities to use less-than-lethal force due to their size.

While canine units are now indispensable components of law enforcement, they do have both drawbacks and limitations. First, canine units require both a trainer and the appropriate amount of training time to be successful (usually ten to twelve weeks). The bond between the trainer and the dog is imperative. If the trainer transfers, quits, or retires, the dog must be retrained with a new trainer. Second, as with humans, dogs have good and bad days. Although considered unexplainable by trainers, sometimes canine sniff searches will miss evidence, such as drugs. Therefore, canine units are not successful 100% of the time. Third, when using dogs as less-than-lethal force against suspects, both the dog and the police officers (nonhandlers) want to get to the individual first. If a police officer reaches the suspect first, it is possible that the dog will bite the officer as well as the suspect. All of these limitations can lead to a police department being vulnerable to potential lawsuits.

As stated earlier, the key feature of canine units is their ability to search for multiple objects (individuals and evidence). The search function inherent in any canine unit makes them inherently subject to the Fourth Amendment's ban on unreasonable searches and seizures and thus judicial review. Although lower courts have been somewhat divided on the use of canines in searches and subsequent seizures, the Supreme Court has continually sustained their usage. In *Florida v. Royer* (1983), the Court actually maintained that if a dog had been present then the search and seizure of drugs would be lawful. This support of canines has been shown in relation to luggage (*United States v. Place*), vehicles (dominated by a host of lower court rulings), roadblocks/highway checkpoints (*City of Indianapolis v. Edmond*), and persons (*Horton v. Goose Creek Independent School District*). While the Supreme Court has not ruled on every aspect of canine searches, the Court has shown considerable support for various issues with regards to canine searches in the past.

Conclusion

The use of dogs in police work dates back to the Egyptians, and canine units are an integral part of law enforcement agencies today. Their ability to search for suspects and evidence expedites police work and adds another level of safety for officers. The integration of canine units in police work is further seen in the development of canine bulletproof vests. Canine units are now seeing the implementation of body armor to better protect the dogs. Manufactured to the same specification as human body armor to protect against small firearms and stab wounds, the canine body armor costs around a thousand dollars, but is money well spent when compared to the cost of raising, feeding, and training the dog in the first place. With canines receiving better protection and continued judicial support, it is clear that canine units will continue as support for law enforcement officials into the future.

SEAN MADDAN

See also **Airport Safety and Security; Constitutional Rights: Search and Seizure; Drug Interdiction; Nonlethal (or Less-Than-Lethal) Weapons: History**

References and Further Reading

City of Indianapolis v. Edmond, 531 U.S. 32 (2000).
Florida v. Royer, 460 U.S. 491 (1983).
Golden, J. W., and J. T. Walker. 2002. That dog will hunt: Canine-assisted search and seizure. In *Policing and the law*, ed. J. T. Walker, 71–90. Upper Saddle River, NJ: Prentice-Hall.
Hess, K. M., and H. W. Wrobleski. 2003. *Police operations: Theory and practice*. 3rd ed. New York: Tomson-Wadsworth.
Horton v. Goose Creek Independent School District, 690 F.2d 470 (1982).
O'Block, R., S. E. Doeran, and N. J. True. 1979. The benefits of canine squads. *Journal of Police Science and Administration* 7 (2): 155–60.
Trojan, C. 1986. Egypt: Evolution of a modern police state. *CJ International* 2 (1): 15–18.

United States v. Place, 462 U.S. 696 (1983).

U.S. Marine Corp. 2004. Body armor going to the dogs. *Marines*, January–March. http://usmc.mil.

CAPITAL CRIMES AND CAPITAL PUNISHMENT

Capital punishment remains one of the most controversial issues in the American criminal justice system. Although precise figures are unknown, scholars estimate that some twenty-one thousand executions have occurred in our history. Since the 1960s all those executed have been convicted murderers, but earlier in the twentieth century there were executions for rape, burglary, robbery, and kidnapping; prior to that criminals were also executed for a wide array of property crimes.

Precise counts on the numbers of executions began in 1930. Between then and 1967 there were 3,859 people executed in the United States, 54% of whom were African American. The racial disparities were especially evident in executions for rape, where 90% of the 455 executed during that period were African American. Prior to 1967 only 30 whites were executed for crimes against blacks; no white person was ever executed for the rape of an African American woman.

Executions declined in the 1950s and 1960s, and came to a halt after two men were executed in 1967. Five years later, largely because of what it saw as the arbitrary administration of the death penalty, the Supreme Court effectively invalidated all existing death penalty statutes, and 630 death row inmates had their sentences commuted to prison terms. However, this 5–4 decision was very complex (and one of the longest decisions in the history of the Court), and states quickly began to rewrite capital statutes that they hoped would pass Supreme Court scrutiny. In a series of cases in 1976, the Court gave its stamp of approval to some of these new statutes.

In 1977, a Utah prisoner, Gary Gilmore, dropped his appeals and asked to be executed, ending the ten-year moratorium on the death penalty. Between then and mid-2004, 915 additional prisoners were executed, all of whom were convicted of murder. Thirty-five percent of those executions occurred in Texas and 82% in the South. In mid-2004 the death penalty was legal in thirty-seven states (the New York statute was ruled unconstitutional in June 2004); the federal government and the U.S. military also had active capital statutes.

Also in mid-2004, there were 3,500 inmates on America's death rows, including 50 women and 79 inmates sentenced to death for crimes that predated their eighteenth birthdays. The largest death rows were in California (635 inmates), Texas (454), and Florida (381); Pennsylvania, Ohio, and North Carolina also had more than 200 inmates each on their death rows.

The accelerating use of the death penalty in the United States in the past quarter century is in direct contradiction to what is happening in most of the rest of the world, especially in those countries that are America's closest allies. Amnesty International counted 118 abolitionist countries in 2004, including all Western democracies except the United States, all European countries, and most countries in the Western Hemisphere. Another 78 countries retained the death penalty. In 2003, 84% of all executions worldwide occurred in just four countries: China, Iran, Viet Nam, and the United States.

Arguments supporting the death penalty have undergone significant changes during the past generation. A few decades ago, the leading argument in favor of the death penalty was deterrence: Executing offenders sends a message to potential murderers, who will be discouraged from killing when they realize that murder might result in their own executions. Today virtually no criminologists support this argument, and a decreasing proportion of death penalty supporters base their opinion on deterrence grounds. In part, this is because the death penalty is far from a certain punishment given a murder. (Less than 1% of those who commit murder can expect to be executed.) In addition, while the typical punishment in the mid-twentieth century for those convicted of murder and *not* sentenced to death was a moderate prison term, today in thirty-five of the thirty-seven death penalty states those convicted of capital crimes and not sentenced to death are sentenced to terms of life imprisonment with no chance of parole. The deterrent effects of a punishment tend to increase with the severity of the penalty, but once a penalty is already severe, further increases in severity do not add to the deterrent effect. There is little reason to believe that those who are not deterred by the threat of life imprisonment would be deterred by the remote possibility of execution.

A second pro-death penalty argument of a generation ago was fiscal: Offenders should be executed to save the massive costs of long imprisonment. Today's capital trials, however, have increased significantly in complexity and length, and combined with the costs of appellate review, the costs of each execution, on average, quickly amount to millions of dollars. Several recent studies (by legislators, state supreme courts, newspapers, and academics) have examined these expenditures, and though they use different data sources and methodologies, all agree that the costs of the death penalty are three to five times higher than the costs of life imprisonment. Supporters of the death penalty argue that bringing justice to the offender is well worth these costs; opponents claim that abolishing the death penalty would allow more resources to be used for helping families of homicide victims and funding programs that offer more effective solutions to America's high rates of criminal violence.

A third argument used in past generations to support the death penalty was religious; there is no shortage of biblical passages (primarily Old Testament) that can be quoted to support this position. In the past two decades, however, more and more leaders of the major American religious faiths (for example, Jewish, Catholic, Episcopalian, Presbyterian, Lutheran, and Methodist) have spoken out against the death penalty, so that today only the most conservative and fundamentalist branches of each religion (with some exceptions) support capital punishment.

In place of the preceding arguments, the leading pro-death penalty justification today is retribution: Murderers deserve to suffer for the immense suffering they have caused, and life imprisonment without parole is simply insufficient to pay for the crimes. Such arguments are often made in the name of families of homicide victims ("survivors" or "co-victims"), who in recent years have had an increased role in capital cases. (For example, in most jurisdictions they are now permitted to testify in the sentencing phases of capital trials and/or to witness the execution of the killer of their loved one.) Abolitionists respond by claiming that executions do not provide long-term relief (and point to many families of homicide victims who oppose the death penalty), and contend that death penalty cases focus far too many resources on only a small proportion of homicides cases, leaving fewer resources for remaining families.

Two additional points about retribution enter the debate. First, approximately 11% of those executed in the past twenty-five years have dropped their appeals and asked to be put to death, raising the question of whether death is significantly different than life without parole in its retributive impact. Second, for the past century America has seen an effort to make executions more "humane." This movement was first seen in the 1890s with the emergence of the electric chair, in the 1920s with the gas chamber, and in the 1980s with the first uses of lethal injection. Today almost all executions are performed by lethal injection; the only prisoners who are put to death by other means (hanging, gas chamber, firing squad, or electric chair) are those who decline the opportunity to select lethal injection. Americans may want retribution, but they want it to be "humane," perhaps revealing an underlying ambivalence about the death penalty itself.

To counter the retributive arguments, those who oppose the death penalty point to continued inequities in who is executed and the ever-present danger of executing the innocent. Inequities are linked with social class (and inability to hire a high-quality defense team) and race. Several recent studies in a variety of states have found that for similar crimes, those who kill whites are several times more likely to be sentenced to death than those who kill blacks. Also of concern is pure arbitrariness (for example, when two similar defendants are convicted of two similar crimes, but for mysterious reasons—or pure luck—one is sentenced to death and the other is not).

Opponents of the death penalty contend that as long as we retain the death penalty, innocent people will occasionally be executed. Supporters of the death penalty acknowledge this risk, but contend that the net retributive benefits of capital punishment outweigh this liability. Between 1972 and mid-2004, 114 inmates were released from America's death rows after significant doubts about their guilt surfaced. Florida leads the United States with 23 exonerations, and in second place is Illinois with 18. These cases led former Illinois Governor George Ryan to impose a moratorium on executions in 2000. While several major reforms have since been implemented, in 2004 the moratorium remained in place while the effects of those reforms could be evaluated.

MICHAEL L. RADELET

See also **Crime, Serious; Crime, Serious Violent**

References and Further Reading

Acker, James R., Robert M. Bohm, and Charles S. Lanier, eds. 2003. *America's experiment with capital punishment*. 2nd ed. Durham, NC: Carolina Academic Press.

Baldus, David C., and George Woodworth. 2003. Race discrimination in the administration of the death penalty: An overview of the empirical evidence with special emphasis on the post-1990 research. *Criminal Law Bulletin* 39: 194–226.

Banner, Stuart. 2002. *The death penalty: An American history*. Cambridge, MA: Harvard University Press.

Bedau, Hugo Adam, ed. 1997. *The death penalty in America, current controversies*. New York: Oxford University Press.

Bedau, Hugo Adam, and Paul Cassell, eds. 2004. *Debating the death penalty: Should America have capital punishment? The experts from both sides make their case*. New York: Oxford University Press.

Death Penalty Information Center. 2004. http://www.deathpenaltyinfo.org (accessed July 2004).

Hood, Roger. 2002. *The death penalty: A worldwide perspective*. 3rd ed. New York: Oxford University Press.

Justice for All. 2004. http://www.prodeathpenalty.org (accessed July 2004).

Prejean, Helen. 1993. *Dead man walking: An eyewitness account of the death penalty in the United States*. New York: Random House.

Radelet, Michael L., and Marian Borg. 2000. The changing nature of death penalty debates. *Annual Reviews of Sociology* 26: 43–61.

Zimring, Franklin E. 2003. *The contradictions of American capital punishment*. New York: Oxford University Press.

CARIBBEAN POLICING

Caribbean policing is now caught between a series of forces, the major ones being the rising rate of serious crimes, relentless public pressures for Caribbean governments "to do something quickly," the increasing politicization of crime, low public confidence in the police, and governments' hurried quests for effective and corruption-free policing.

Largely derived from a history of slavery and indentured labor in the eighteenth century and mores in the nineteenth century, Caribbean states have also inherited, especially from the British, a very authoritarian and centralized colonial policing structure. Part of this policing culture was further derived from the need to protect and serve the property and safety of plantation owners, mainly British, some French and Spanish. The social and economic interests between the masses and the colonial rulers were therefore quite divergent, so Caribbean policing was inevitably a rather unfriendly, very coercive exercise across the colonial Caribbean. To some extent, it still is even though most Caribbean states are now politically independent.

The three major issues in Caribbean policing are (1) governance, (2) police effectiveness, and (3) police–citizen relationships. Before dealing with these issues, it is helpful to clarify what is the "Caribbean," at least as used in this article. The Caribbean region is located in the Caribbean Sea, bounded by the United States in the north, Central America on the west, the Atlantic Ocean on the east, and having two of its states (Guyana and Suriname) lodged in its southern border of South America.

The Caribbean region consists of twenty-one states that exhibit considerable diversity in political, social, legal, and judicial structure. Puerto Rico and the U.S. Virgin Islands are U.S. dependencies, while Bermuda is still under British jurisdiction. French influence is still present in Guadeloupe, Martinique, and, to a great extent, the Dominican Republic. Fourteen of these Caribbean states, mainly English-speaking and part of the Commonwealth, have formed themselves into a legal regional body called the Caribbean Community (Caricom).

The information provided in this article will generally refer to the following fourteen states with a total population of about seven million: Antigua and Barbuda, Bahamas, Barbados, Belize, Dominica, Grenada, Guyana, Jamaica, Montserrat, St. Lucia, St. Kitts and Nevis, St. Vincent and the Grenadines, Suriname, and Trinidad and Tobago. In addition, some reference will be made to Haiti, a French-speaking country, with a population of more than seven and a half million.

Apart from trade and economic cooperation, there is increasing movement among the English-speaking Caribbean toward common policing and security strategies, a movement no doubt inspired by the serious crime facing the region, especially drug trafficking, kidnapping, and terrorism threats. Even once peaceful, tourist-dependent Barbados is now experiencing an upsurge of crime and visible public discomfort. The governments of these English-speaking Caribbean states have established a Caricom Task Force on Crime and Security that helps shape policy recommendations to these governments. One of the important recommendations to help improve police–citizen relations is the establishment of a National Crime Commission in each Caribbean state; so far only St. Lucia and Barbados have implemented this.

The complex challenges of effective policing and crime reduction are very important for the economic well-being of Caribbean states, especially those smaller states that depend almost exclusively on tourism. The repeated failures during the last twenty years of numerous "crime committees" and inquiries to improve police effectiveness help to diminish the credibility of the relevant authorities in the matters of policing and national security.

Two major, related Caribbean initiatives have recently been undertaken. The first is the Caribbean Institute for Security and Law Enforcement Studies (CISLES), a centralized training and educational police center located in Barbados. The second is a Regional Crime and Research Institute at the University of the West Indies, which has also recently established a graduate program in criminology and criminal justice at its St. Augustine campus in Trinidad and Tobago (through its Centre for Criminology and Criminal Justice) for police officers and other members of the protective services across the Caribbean.

Governance

Police departments in the Commonwealth Caribbean are in varying degrees under the control of a civilian minister of government. The commissioner of police, who heads the police department (also called police force in St. Lucia, police service in Trinidad and Tobago, and constabulary force in Jamaica), must be first approved or directly appointed by the country's cabinet. This matter of appointing a police commissioner has become a controversial public issue. On one side there are strong views that the government should have a direct role in such an appointment since it is the government that is ultimately held responsible for crime management and crime reduction. On the other hand, there are perhaps stronger views that the office of police commissioner and the police service for that matter should be kept as far as possible from political control and interference. This debate is now light in the smaller states, such as St. Lucia, St. Kitts and Nevis, and Grenada, but quite intense in the larger states of Jamaica and particularly Trinidad and Tobago.

It is necessary to note two related issues. One, the relationship between the political directorate and the police service depends on what the respective constitutions allow. In the smaller states, there is no constitutionally independent body to appoint, promote, or discipline police officers. The body that performs such functions largely operates as an administrative body and under the hand of the relevant government minister. Generally, the cabinet appoints the members of this body. In Trinidad and Tobago, it is different. The constitution established a Police Service Commission whose members are appointed by the country's president after consultations with the prime minister and leader of the opposition. On several occasions, the prime minister has tried to impress on the Police Service Commission the need to dismiss a police commissioner, but the commission resisted amidst intense public controversy.

The second issue is the low confidence that the populations in the various states have in the police service. Overall, survey data show that across the Caribbean more than 50% of the population have low confidence in their respective police departments, a situation that no doubt creates great apprehension over any sign of political control over police departments.

The jurisdictional issue is different from that of the United States where Congress and its oversight committees have statutory powers of inquiry over the FBI, CIA, and other policing and intelligence agencies. In other words, the countervailing and even veto powers of the U.S. Congress are not present in the legislatures of the Caribbean. The concept and practice of the separation of powers are different. These Caribbean legislatures (the parliaments) function as pale imitations of the British Westminster-type system of government, that is, with the country's cabinet generally having numerical and statutory domination over each legislature. And so, in the smaller Caribbean states particularly, the cabinet, which is itself dominated by the prime minister, virtually governs the police. Even in the larger states, where there is an independent Police Service Commission, the prime minister must first give his approval to the service commission's appointment of a police commissioner or a deputy commissioner of police.

Quite interestingly, however, in two larger countries, Jamaica and Trinidad/Tobago, there is a slight but discernable move toward increased transparency in police governance, mainly through the constitutional establishment of a Joint Parliamentary Select Committee to inquire and report on the Police Service Commission and the agencies falling under this commission, such as the police service. The select committee reports are presented to parliament, and the minister of national security is required to respond within ninety days.

Public Confidence

The second issue, low public confidence in Caribbean police, is mixed with the public's rather high fear of crime across the Caribbean. Again, survey data show that as much as 50% of the population is afraid to go out at night, with significant proportions also afraid of being "murdered," "kidnapped," or having their homes "broken into." Then there are strong suspicions and even validating court cases that point to police corruption. For example, in Jamaica, in early 2005, the police commissioner publicly complained about "drug and bribery" corruption existing among some officers in the Jamaica Constabulary Force and pledged to clean up his force. In Guyana, around the same time, alleged complicity between a government minister regarding police brutality has led to an official inquiry. This reminds us of the infamous "mongoose gang," a group of officers used in the 1970s by Grenada's then prime minister against his political opponents.

In Trinidad and Tobago, the Police Service Commission, under a new chairman, and the cabinet itself have expressed strong views about "cleaning up the police service." The Joint Parliamentary Select Committee is also pursuing this matter because it has such serious implications for improving public confidence and police accountability and for facilitating the supply of strategic information by citizens for effective policing.

Police Effectiveness

When detection and especially conviction rates are used as indicators of police effectiveness, the picture is not very encouraging and certainly shows a need for quick improvement. The detection rate for serious crimes generally ranges from 25% to 40% of reported crimes. The conviction rate for reported serious crimes is generally between 10% and 15%. These crime statistics imply that thousands of criminals are either not caught by the police or are acquitted for a number of reasons, the disturbing ones being the unreliability, inefficiency, and even the total absence of police evidence in many cases. In fact, citizens' complaints against the police in all Caribbean states, especially the larger states of Jamaica, Trinidad and Tobago, and Guyana, have been increasing and without the expeditious adjudication required.

In fact, several attempts are now being made, especially in Jamaica, Trinidad and Tobago, Guyana, St. Lucia, and Barbados, to improve police effectiveness mainly through legislation, seeking foreign expertise, training, and providing increased amounts of physical, technical, and manpower resources. The Caribbean country with the smallest population is St. Kitts and Nevis having a 450-strong police service. The largest, Jamaica has a population of more than 2.5 million and a police service with 13,000 now. Though Jamaica and Trinidad and Tobago have recently made significant increases in the size of their respective police departments (Jamaica from an estimated 10,000 to 13,000, Trinidad and Tobago from an estimated 7,000 to 8,000), the police–citizen ratio looks quite reasonable from an international viewpoint. For example, in St. Lucia it is 1:285, Barbados 1:166, Jamaica 1:200, Trinidad and Tobago 1:162, Guyana 1:212, Grenada 1:128, and Bahamas 1:120. Haiti is understandably lopsided with a ratio of 1:1,153. Given its very unsettled political condition, Haiti is crippled by waves of police violence and partisanship, political rivalries, and escalating crime and civil strife. In Jamaica, political patronage to gang leaders has perpetuated "garrison violence" in several districts.

The alliance between politicians and gang leaders in Jamaica and Trinidad and Tobago, in particular, has been severely criticized by civic organizations because it subverts effective policing.

The current means of recording, compiling, reporting, and analyzing crime data within the police departments across the Caribbean is not very effective for data-driven day-to-day operations, police accountability, and policy development. In fact, there have been repeated complaints from researchers, opposition members of parliament, and even international funding agencies (for example, IDB, World Bank) about the inefficient, nontransparent, and very inadequate manner of collecting and reporting police statistics. All this is apart from the fact that, similar to other countries, many crimes, both serious and minor, are not reported to the police across Caribbean states.

The official crime statistics therefore do not tell the full story of crime and policing in the Caribbean. For example, one study found that more than "60%" of robbery, break-in, burglary, and dwelling-house larceny crimes—as a category—do not get reported to the police. A similar proportion of rapes, incest, and domestic violence also do not get reported. For drug abuse and trafficking, the unreported figure is more than 70%, and growing especially since the use of cocaine and marijuana is also on the increase across the Caribbean. Two related solutions have been made to improve both the reliability and validity of police statistics. The first is the systematic use of victimization surveys, which has already begun in Barbados, and secondly the establishment of professionally independent, well-staffed, technologically supported, and easily accessible crime analysis and policy development centers.

The police commissioners from all Caribbean states, singly and collectively through the Association of Caribbean Commissioners of Police, have admitted that traditional law enforcement has not been effective in reducing the crime rate and increasing public confidence in the police. During the last ten years, each Caribbean state, with vacillating amounts of financial, manpower, and training support, has adopted community-oriented policing as an alternative or supplementary approach to traditional law enforcement. With much ambivalence still residing in police operations, community-oriented policing has not been effectively incorporated, practiced, or evaluated in the Caribbean.

Several training programs and citizen surveys have shown viable support from citizens and junior officers for community-oriented policing. However, the managerial support and operational configuration required for the essential practices of community policing, beyond the rhetorical stage, are largely lacking across the Caribbean. This deficiency is accompanied by quick relapses into traditional law enforcement. Such relapse is tightly connected to the mounting public concerns over serious crime and subsequent public pressures, especially from the business sector, in all Caribbean states for quick, drastic law enforcement.

RAMESH DEOSARAN

See also **Academies, Police; Attitudes toward the Police: Overview; Autonomy and the Police; Clearance Rates and Criminal Investigations; Community-Oriented Policing: Effects and Impacts; Corruption; Criminology; Deadly Force; Excessive Force; Fear of Crime; National Crime Victimization Survey (NCVS); Politics and the Police; Public Image of the Police**

References and Further Reading

Caribbean Journal of Criminology and Social Psychology. Vols. 1–3. Trinidad: UWI, Centre for Criminology and Criminal Justice.
Danns, George. 1982. *Domination and power in Guyana: A study of police in a third world context.* New Brunswick, NJ: Transaction.

De Albuquerque, Klaus, and Jerome McElroy. 1999. A longitudinal study of serious crime in the Caribbean. *Caribbean Journal of Criminology and Social Psychology* 4 (1 & 2): 32–70.

Deosaran, Ramesh. 2000. *The dynamics of community policing: Theory, practice and evaluation.* Trinidad: UWI, Centre for Criminology and Criminal Justice.

———. 2001. *Crime statistics, analysis and policy action: The way forward.* Trinidad: UWI, Centre for Criminology and Criminal Justice.

———. 2002. Community policing in the Caribbean: Context, community and police capability. *Policing: An International Journal of Police Strategies and Management* 25: 125–46.

Deosaran, Ramesh, and Derek Chadee. 1997. Juvenile delinquency in Trinidad and Tobago: Challenges for social policy and Caribbean criminology. *Caribbean Journal of Criminology and Social Psychology* 2 (2): 36–83.

Harriott, Anthony. 2000. *Police and crime control in Jamaica.* Kingston, Jamaica: University of the West Indies Press.

Harriott, Anthony, Farley Braithwaite, and Scot Wortley, eds. 2004. *Crime and justice in the Caribbean.* Kingston, Jamaica: Arawak Publications.

Headley, Bernard. 1994. *The Jamaican crime scene: A perspective.* Mandeville, Jamaica: Eureka Press.

Mars, Joan. 2002. *Deadly force, colonialism and the rule of law: Police violence in Guyana.* Westport, CT: Greenwood Press.

Trotman, David. 1987. *Crime in Trinidad: Conflict and control in a plantation society (1838–1900).* Englewood Cliffs, NJ: Prentice-Hall.

CASE SCREENING AND CASE MANAGEMENT FOR INVESTIGATIONS

The concept of managing criminal investigations (MCI) from a "scientific" perspective has its roots in a Rochester Police Department project in the 1970s and in several other reports by the RAND Corporation and the Police Executive Research Forum. Over the years, and with the introduction of computer technology, more effective methods of managing the investigative process have been developed. Among the criteria developed to better manage investigations are:

- Number of cases handled
- Number and percentage of cases cleared
- Number and percentage of cases accepted for prosecution
- Number and percentage of convictions

Cases handled and cases cleared are largely the responsibility of the investigative unit and individual investigators, and serve as a measure of the effectiveness of the crime investigation process. A case may be cleared by an arrest or exceptionally when it can be determined that more than one crime may have been committed by a one or more individuals, but the suspect is deceased or is only charged with one crime. A case may also be cleared as unfounded.

The number of cases accepted for prosecution and the number of convictions are largely under the auspices of the prosecutor or the judiciary, which may involve a jury. An important consideration in evaluating investigators has been the premise that placing responsibility for prosecution on an investigator can unduly influence or pressure an individual detective to go beyond accepted legal and procedural methods in order to obtain a conviction. Further, if a prosecution is unsuccessful it is frequently difficult to determine who might have been responsible for a dismissal or an acquittal.

Several other components of managing criminal investigations include the elements of the process and case screening methods. In evaluating an MCI program the following points are important:

- The initial investigation
- Case screening
- Management of ongoing investigations
- Police–prosecutor relations
- Ongoing monitoring of the process

Solvability Factors

Case screening is an important aspect of both effectiveness and efficiency, because experience indicates that not all cases are solvable, at least at the outset of an investigation. For this reason managers frequently rely on so-called solvability factors, which have proven to be instrumental in an investigation. These include:

- Is there a witness to the crime?
- Is a suspect named?
- Is there a description of the suspect?
- Can a suspect be located?
- Can a vehicle be identified?
- Is stolen property traceable?
- Is physical evidence present?
- Is there a distinguishable *modus operandi*?
- Can crime analysis help identify a perpetrator?

These elements form the basis for MCI. Coupled with a monitoring system they make it possible for administrators to better manage resources devoted to crime investigation. Generally, it should be noted that this model is designed largely for more "common" types of cases, such as theft, burglary, and robbery, whereas cases involving murder, rape, organized crime, and terrorism will involve more than a preliminary investigation.

By focusing on the solvability of most criminal cases that come to the attention of law enforcement, better utilization of investigative resources can be attained. However, it should be noted that improved technology and better training of investigators has made it possible to "keep an eye" on cases that might not appear to be solvable following a preliminary investigation. For example, in a burglary where there is not enough evidence or information to pursue an immediate investigation, the information about the crime can be stored in a computer that may later serve to link a suspect arrested or identified in a future crime. Advances in crime analysis

have made it possible to store information on *modus operandi* (MO or method of operation), prior arrests for similar crimes, identification of property that may turn up later, and persons released from prison who committed similar crimes in the past.

MCI is also used by administrators to assess the effectiveness of investigative operations and to a lesser degree the effectiveness of investigators. By monitoring such variables as the percentage of crimes solved or cleared, the effectiveness of individual investigators (when compared with other investigators handling similar cases), and resources employed, it is frequently possible to identify the need for additional training, better allocation of human resources, equipment and technology needs, and better preparation of cases.

Experience has shown that some investigators are better prepared, through experience, education, training, and motivation, to handle certain types of cases. For example, some investigators are better at handling interviews and interrogations, whereas others may be more suited to use a computer or to collect evidence that may have gone unnoticed. Other investigators may be more familiar with geographic locations and the use of informants or surveillance techniques.

Criminal investigation has become more complex over time as offenders have become more mobile, more aware of investigative methods, more familiar with the legal system, and more adept at "covering their tracks." At the same time investigative expertise has been enhanced by better training; new technology, such as single-digit computer systems (AFIS, the Automated Fingerprint Identification System); advances in forensic science (such as DNA); and the adoption of relational databases.

Procedural Aspects of MCI

Of particular importance is the recognition that not all categories of crime are similar. Homicide investigations, for example, are different from burglary investigations. Thus, in developing a program it is important not to mix "apples and oranges" during the design phase. This has proven to be one of the drawbacks of MCI, because in many organizations more experienced investigators are frequently assigned the more difficult cases, and it may appear that their productivity is lower than that of an investigator who handles cases that are easier to solve. Strong-arm robberies, for example, are generally more difficult to solve than armed robberies, and residential burglaries may be more difficult to solve than business burglaries. Nevertheless, over time MCI provides a methodology for evaluating a unit's effectiveness and efficiency, as well as assisting in better case assignments.

Of particular concern in the MCI model is the assignment of "weighting" factors, and very little research has been done to test the effectiveness of the scores assigned to each category. For example, one of the more popular models of case screening uses the point scores shown in Table 1.

Table 1   Assignment of Weighting Factors

Gravity of offense	Points
Felony	5
Misdemeanor	3
Probability of solution	
Suspects	
Suspect named	10
Suspect known or described	10
Witness available	4
Vehicle identified	5
Physical evidence recovered	1
Undeveloped leads available	1
Urgency of action	
Danger to others	4
Immediate action required	3
Pattern or frequency of crime	1

In the model shown in Table 1, the number of points generated dictates the following priority levels and points necessary to assign a priority:

Priority Level	Points
1	20+
2	12–19
3	6–11
4	0–5

There is likely to be some room for subjectivity, and the scores are open to question. For example, a crime scene that yields latent prints that might be matched by AFIS would seem to have a fairly high priority of solution if a match should occur. Should the availability of a witness be important if the witness can provide no information? How does one determine the need for "immediate action"?

Such questions place great responsibility on the investigative review officer or supervisor, who should have the knowledge and expertise to "overrule" the point count if necessary. One must keep in mind that MCI is a tool, generally designed to assist in prioritizing caseloads, with a view toward identifying those cases that have the highest probability of solution. It should help improve decision making, especially in units where there are high caseloads.

The MCI model has proven to be an important tool in law enforcement administration when used as a means of better deploying resources, improving investigative effectiveness, evaluating individuals over time, and increasing the probability of solving crimes. Utilized as a means of improving investigations—and not as a tool solely to put pressure on investigators to make arrests—the MCI model can contribute to improving criminal investigations.

RICHARD H. WARD

See also **Clearance Rates and Criminal Investigations; Computer Forensics; Computer Technology; Detective Work/Culture;**

Detectives; Forensic Evidence; Forensic Investigations; Homicide and Its Investigation; Investigation Outcomes

References and Further Reading

Carroll, B. P. 2001. Major case management: Key components. *FBI Law Enforcement Bulletin* 70: 1–4.

Eck, John E. 1983. *Solving crimes: The investigation of burglary and robbery.* Washington, DC: Police Executive Research Forum.

Greenberg, Ilene, and Robert Wasserman. 1979. *Managing criminal investigations.* Washington, DC: U.S. Department of Justice.

Greenwood, Peter W., and Joan Petersillia. 1976. *The criminal investigation process, vol. 1: Summary and policy implications; vol. III: Observations and analysis.* Santa Monica, CA: RAND Corporation.

Osterburg, James W., and Richard H. Ward. 2004. *Criminal investigation: A method for reconstructing the past.* 4th ed. Cincinnati, OH: LexisNexis.

Swanson. C. R., L. Territo, and N. C. Chamelin. *Criminal investigation.* 8th ed. Boston, MA: McGraw-Hill.

CHANGING DEMOGRAPHICS IN POLICING

During the last quarter of the twentieth century, some noteworthy organizational changes in American police organizations occurred, and their influences were significant for the direction of American policing in the twenty-first century. Two significant changes in particular deserve special mention (Zhao, Herbst, and Lovrich 2001). First, the presence of minorities and women in policing is associated with the broad goal of social equity in a democratic society. The real change took place with the passage of the Equal Employment Opportunity Act of 1972, an amendment to Title VII of the Civil Rights Act of 1964 (Steel and Lovrich 1987). For example, the International Association of Chiefs of Police (IACP) and the Law Enforcement Assistance Administration (LEAA) conducted a survey in 1973 and found that minorities accounted for about 4% of police employment in the nation. Since then, the representation of minorities in the public service sector has received much attention in the media and from government officials. In addition, the employment of women in policing highlights the gendered nature of public services where occupational segregation and exclusively male workforces in public safety and criminal justice have been the established tradition (Brown and Pechman 1987). The change toward gender equity may be as difficult as racial equity in police agencies. Accommodation of gender equity is complicated by the need for the occasional use of force required in the line of duty, which is believed to require an emphasis on the physical strength of officers and, as a consequence, has become an important component in police selection (Morash and Haarr 1995).

A second significant change affecting the demographics of policing concerns the implementation of community policing, emphasizing elements of crime prevention, victim assistance, and police partnership in the community. All of these initiatives and associated activities reflect the need for representatives of the police to engage in collaborative (versus enforcement) activities. This is an area of work in which gender and racial differences can be a decidedly positive factor in policing. In some situations female officers are preferable to males for tasks that require empathy and sensitivity rather than a credible threat of use of physical force (Martin 1993). Walker (1985) has pointed out that virtually every major national report on the police in the post–World War II period has explicitly recommended hiring more minorities and women in policing for these specific reasons.

Data Sources

Two primary data sources offer information on minority and female employment in policing. Each has its merits and shortcomings. The first source is Police Employee Data (LEOKA), which is part of the annual *Uniform Crime Reports* (UCR) published by the Federal Bureau of Investigation. In these data there are questions about the number of male and female sworn officers in each department. Because the UCR includes more than seventeen thousand reporting agencies, researchers can obtain a global picture about the extent of female employment in law enforcement including employment in municipal, township, and special-purpose police agencies (for example, school district and port authority police) as well as sheriff's offices. Another advantage of the employee data found in the UCR is that they are published annually. Therefore, researchers can examine change over a period of time. However, a major disadvantage is that although there is a breakdown of the number of male and female officers, no racial or ethnic breakdowns are provided.

The second source of information on police employment is the Law Enforcement Management and Administrative Statistics (LEMAS), published periodically by the Bureau of Justice Statistics (BJS). About every three years throughout the 1990s, BJS conducted surveys of large police agencies (those hiring more than one hundred sworn officers). In the 1990 LEMAS survey, 387 municipal police departments fit this definition. The number increased to 495 in the 2000 LEMAS survey. In each LEMAS data series (1990, 1993, 1997, and 2000) information on gender and racial breakdowns is available. For example, the total number of female officers is broken down by racial/ethnic categories to show the numbers of female officers who identify themselves as white, Hispanic, black/African American, Asian/Pacific Islander, and other races/ethnicities. This detailed information on race and gender is the primary advantage of LEMAS data. A major drawback of LEMAS data concerns the sporadic timing of the survey. It seems that the survey is administered at the convenience of the BJS. Since the 2000 LEMAS survey, for example, there has been no additional data posted by the Inter-University Consortium for Political and Social Research (ICPSR) for five years. Therefore, only LEMAS data from the 1990s is currently available to researchers. However, both LEOKA and LEMAS data for past surveys are available on the ICPSR website and can be easily downloaded.

Current Status of Change in Demographics in Policing

How much did the demographics of large police agencies change during the 1990s? Table 1 compares the percentage changes in three racial and ethnical groups for both male and female officers as reported

Table 1 Percentage of Racial and Ethnical Groups in Large Police Agencies

Groups	1990	2000	% Change
White male officers	78.64%	73.05%	−7.11%
African American male officers	8.03	8.64	+7.6
Hispanic male officers	5.01	7.00	+39.7
White female officers	5.37	6.88	+28.1
African American female officers	1.46	1.74	+19.1
Hispanic female officers	0.40	0.72	+80.0

Note: Number of police agencies surveyed = 387 in 1990 and 495 in 2000.
The base numbers are small, so that the changes appear to have great magnitude, whereas in reality they represent very small overall increases.

in the first (1990) and, as of this writing, most recent (2000) LEMAS surveys of large police departments.

The percentages of each category listed Table 1 clearly show that some significant changes took place during the 1990s. First, the percentage of white male officers declined from 78.64% in 1990 to 73.05% in 2000, a drop of 7.11%. In comparison, all other racial and ethnical groups appeared to have sizable gains during the same period. This is particularly true for the increase in the proportion of Hispanic officers. There were 39.7% and 80% increases in the number of Hispanic male officers and Hispanic female officers, respectively. Overall, the change in the 1990s closely resembled the 1970s and 1980s regarding an increase in the representation of minority and female officers in the police force. It is important to note that the increase in representation varied by racial and ethnical groups during the 1990s. In the meantime, the UCR data show that female officers employed in cities with populations of more than twenty-five thousand in 1990 (1,953 cities) accounted for 7.12% of all sworn officers. In 2002 UCR data on police employment, female officers made up 9.0% of sworn officers in cities with a population of more than twenty-five thousand (2,307 cities), a 26.4% increase in twelve years.

Factors Associated with Hiring Minority and Female Officers

A considerable body of literature has accumulated since the 1980s regarding the hiring of minority and female officers in U.S. law enforcement agencies (see, for example, Zhao, He, and Lovrich 2005; Zhao, Herbst, and Lovrich 2001; Ramirez 1997; Felkenes, Peretz, and Schroedel 1993; Felkenes and Schroedel 1993; Martin 1991; Zhao and Lovrich 1998; Potts 1983; Poulos and Doerner 1996; Warner et al. 1989; Lewis 1989; Steel and Lovrich 1987).

Four primary factors have been identified in the empirical study on minorities and women in policing (see Walker 1985). The research revealed factors that are consistently significant with respect to the hiring of minority and female officers. The first factor concerns minority representation in the population. This explanation is simple and straightforward: The increase in minority officers is positively associated with increases in minority populations in cities. The representation of minority populations is the most significant predictor of hiring minority police officers. For example, the presence of a large African American population is the most significant predictor of the hiring of African American officers, whereas a large Hispanic population is correlated with the employment of Hispanic officers (Zhao, He, and Lovrich 2005; Zhao, Herbst, and Lovrich 2001; Zhao and Lovrich 1998; Martin 1991).

The next factor is related to city size. In particular, several studies found that city size is a significant predictor of the rate of employment of female officers after controlling for other city demographics such as percentage of young population, minority population, and single-mother households (see, for example, Zhao, Herbst, and Lovrich 2001). The LEOKA data on workforce composition in the 2002 UCR, for example, indicated that the percentage of female officers relative to males is higher in larger cities as compared to smaller ones.

The third factor is related to the unique political environment in each city. Elected public officials are inclined to represent the interests of the people who elect them to office. Following this line of thinking, there is a positive relationship between the presence of a black mayor, for example, and the likelihood of the provision of noteworthy collective benefits to African Americans. Because top municipal administrators have considerable discretionary power in determining the outcome of personnel policies in a local police agency, a minority mayor may advocate for additional hiring of minority officers. Furthermore, female council members and mayors are also highlighted in previous studies as possible predictors of increases in the number of female police officers. (Note, however, that the variables that attempt to measure local political influence such as the leadership of a minority mayor or the percentage of female council members have produced mixed findings.)

The final significant predictor is the presence of an affirmative action program. The passage of the Equal Employment Opportunity Act of 1972 made a vast number of federal, state, and local agencies subject to requirements for "good faith effort" affirmative action programs as defined by the federal courts and the Equal Employment Opportunity Commission (EEOC), pursuant to the legislative intent of Title VII of the Civil Rights Act of 1964. A key aspect of affirmative action programs is their focus on a set of specific goals and timetables keyed to the pools of qualified applicants. These programs frequently feature specific goals in numerical terms with respect to the hiring of minority and female candidates, particularly when reflecting a federal court mandate issued on a substantiated claim of historical underrepresentation or manifesting discriminatory personnel practices. The availability of an affirmative action program in a police department is a significant determinant of the hiring of female and minority officers (Zhao, He, and Lovrich 2005; Zhao, Herbst, and Lovrich 2001; Martin 1991; Steel and Lovrich 1989).

JIHONG ZHAO

See also **Community-Oriented Policing: Rationale; Diversity in Police Departments; Minorities and the Police; Personnel Selection; Women in Law Enforcement**

References and Further Reading

Brown, C., and A. Pechman, eds. 1987. *Gender in the workplace.* Washington, DC: Brookings Institute.

Felkenes, G. T., P. Peretz, and J.R. Schroedel. 1993. An analysis of the mandatory hiring of females: The Los Angeles Police Department experience. *Women and Criminal Justice* 4: 65–89.

Felkenes, G. T., and J. R. Schroedel. 1993. A case study of minority women in policing. *Women and Criminal Justice* 4: 31–63.

Lewis, W. G. 1989. Toward representative bureaucracy: Blacks in city police organizations: 1975–1985. *Public Administration Review* 49: 257–67.

Martin, S. E. 1991. The effectiveness of affirmative action: The case of women in policing. *Justice Quarterly* 8: 489–504.

———. 1993. Female officers on the move: The status report on women in policing. In *Critical issues in policing: Contemporary readings,* ed. R. Dunham and J. Alpert, 2nd ed., 327–74. Prospect Heights, IL: Waveland Press.

Morash, M., and R. N. Haarr. 1995. Gender, workplace problems, and stress in policing. *Justice Quarterly* 12: 113–40.

Potts, L. W. (1983). Equal employment opportunity and female employment in police agencies. *Journal of Criminal Justice* 11: 505–23.

Poulos, T. M., and W. G. Doerner. 1996. Women in law enforcement: The distribution of females in Florida police agencies. *Women and Criminal Justice* 8: 19–33.

Ramirez, E. J. 1997. Hispanic policing in local government. Ph.D diss. Arizona State University, Tempe.

Steel, Brent, and Nicholas Lovrich. 1987. Equality and efficiency trade-offs in affirmative action—real or imagined? The case of women in policing. *The Social Science Journal* 24: 53–70.

Walker, Samuel. 1985. Racial minority and female employment in policing: The implications of "glacial change." *Crime and Delinquency* 31: 565–72.

Zhao, J., N. He, and N. Lovrich. 2005. Predicting the employment of minority officers in U.S. cities: OLS fixed-effect panel model results for African American and Latino Officers for 1993, 1996, and 2000. *Journal of Criminal Justice* 33: 377–86.

Zhao, Jihong, Leigh Herbst, and Nicholas Lovrich. 2001. Race, ethnicity and the female COP: Differential patterns of representation. *Journal of Criminal Justice* 23: 243–57.

Zhao, Jihong, and Nicholas Lovrich. 1998. Determinants of minority employment in American municipal police agencies: The representation of African American officers. *Journal of Criminal Justice* 26: 267–77.

CHARLOTTE–MECKLENBURG POLICE DEPARTMENT

Charlotte, North Carolina, located in the southwestern region of the state in Mecklenburg County, experienced steady growth over time. Developing from just 1,500 citizens in 1861, Charlotte quickly grew to 9,000 by 1881 (Kiser et al. 1990) and continued growing for the next 150 years, including a particularly rapid growth period between 1980 and 2005. Much of the late twentieth-century population surge resulted from significant expansion of banking and financial industries, where Charlotte ranked second only to New York City. Local census counts indicated that the city population had doubled from an estimated 315,000 citizens in 1980 to 632,760 by 2005. The Mecklenburg County population also nearly doubled within that time frame, growing from an estimated 404,000 citizens in 1980 to 829,978 by 2005. As a result, the Charlotte Metropolitan Statistical Area housed more than 1.5 million citizens by 2005 (Charlotte Chamber of Commerce 2005).

Meanwhile, Charlotte law enforcement efforts slowly evolved from informal to transitional to formalized policing. Prior to 1816 citizen volunteers enforced the law, and in that year the town commissioner appointed a Town Watch to protect the streets, patrol businesses, and enforce local ordinances. Charlotte was soon divided into two wards (an early precursor to modern district systems). Each ward was assigned a captain of the watch who was responsible for assigning citizens to serve on patrol. In 1827, the city hired its first constable, and by 1850 the Town Guard included ten paid positions at a salary of fifteen dollars a month. Following the Civil War, North Carolina established a provisional government, which appointed Charlotte's mayor as the first "Intendant of Police," although duties were shared with the Mecklenburg County sheriff who had primary law enforcement

authority. Finally, on January 11, 1866, town commissioners formally created the Charlotte Police Department (CPD), adding eight officers to the payroll. On May 5, 1881, the CPD hired their first police chief through a political appointment by the town council. This appointment practice continued until 1970 when a city manager was hired (Kiser et al. 1990).

Consistent with Charlotte's late twentieth-century population growth, the Charlotte Police Department also grew. By 1934, CPD had 91 employees on the payroll, including a surgeon and a dog catcher (Kiser et al. 1990). By 1980 the department (prior to a merger with the Mecklenburg County Police Department) had grown to 594 sworn officers and 152 civilian employees for a total of 746 full-time staff. The Mecklenburg County Police Department (not to be confused with the Mecklenburg County Sheriff's Office) had about 160 sworn and civilian staff. In 1993, following years of planning, financial considerations, and political negotiations, the Charlotte Police Department merged with the Mecklenburg County Police Department, and the Charlotte–Mecklenburg Police Department (CMPD) provided primary law enforcement services for the metropolitan area going forward. By 2002, CMPD had grown to 1,501 sworn officers and 501 civilians for a total of 2,002 employees, the largest local law enforcement agency in North Carolina (Federal Bureau of Investigation 2005).

The mission of CMPD is "to build problem-solving partnerships with our citizens to prevent the next crime. Preventing the next crime is a lofty goal, worth striving to reach. And we believe that through the successes of these partnerships, the contributions of officers and citizens, crime can be reduced and the quality of life within our community can be improved" (http://www.charmeck.org).

In pursuing this mission, CMPD embraced the community-oriented and problem-oriented policing practices that evolved from the team policing of the 1970s (Goldstein 1990). CMPD was widely recognized as a national leader in community policing, problem solving, community partnerships, and crime prevention (National Institute of Justice 1999). From 1995 to 2005, CMPD received almost two dozen federal grants for more than $38 million from the Office of Community Oriented Policing Services (COPS) to hire additional officers, develop an effective technology-based infrastructure, train officers in community policing, ensure officer and agency integrity, and engage the community in law enforcement planning and practices (Office of Community Oriented Policing Services 2005). While the effectiveness of community policing in reducing crime and fear remained an ongoing debate, studies suggested that COPS community policing hiring grants generated significant crime reductions in cities (like Charlotte) with populations of more than ten thousand (Zhao, Scheider, and Thurman 2002).

Despite their attempts at innovation, CMPD faces several future challenges. First, the growth of the Charlotte metropolitan area continues to present resource, geographical (CMPD has twenty-two facilities spread across the city and county), and criminal challenges for the department. Gang crime slowly emerged as a local concern and "twenty-first century" crimes such as identity theft, cybercrimes, and terrorism threats required CMPD to continually reconsider and balance officer and civilian allocations, improve departmental training, and increase specialization within the agency. Further, new crimes require ongoing improvements in police technology, hiring of technology specialists (crime mapping experts or data analysts, for example), and increased operating budgets for technology implementation, maintenance, and information dissemination.

Second, Charlotte is home to an increasing numbers of Hispanics, Asians, American Indians, and African Americans. More than 28% of the county population is African American, although African Americans comprised only 13% of the U.S. population in the early twenty-first century. Increased diversity is vitally important for communities, but diversity requires that police officers learn new languages and cultures. Police departments must work to ensure diversity in recruitment, hiring, and promotional processes, and community members and leaders must work with police to maintain public trust in law enforcement.

Finally, like many large local police departments, CMPD continues to examine ways to enhance its reputation within the community and within law enforcement, reduce crime and disorder, maintain officer and organizational integrity, and enforce laws fairly and consistently. CMPD has publicly addressed potential concerns with racial profiling (Smith et al. 2004), use of force and excessive force (National Institute of Justice and Bureau of Justice Statistics 1999), academy recruits cheating on exams (Stephens 2004), deaths related to high-speed pursuits (*North Carolina v. Lee Taylor Farrar* 2002; Beshears, Moore, and Wellin 2003), and other such challenges. The future success of the Charlotte Mecklenburg Police Department rests with their ability to adapt to new challenges, operate efficiently given increasing demands and limited resources, address emerging crime patterns and trends, and maintain positive police–community relationships.

JOSEPH B. KUHNS, III

See also **American Policing: Early Years; Boston Police Department; Community-Oriented Policing: History; Community-Oriented Policing: Practices; Crime Prevention; Integrity in Policing; Technology and the Police**

References and Further Readings

Beshears, Erica, Robert Moore, and Kathryn Wellin. 2003. Police: Chase followed policy. *Charlotte (NC) Observer*, December 30.

http://www.centredaily.com/mld/observer/
7595992.htm (accessed January 2005).

Charlotte Chamber of Commerce. 2005. *2005 population demographics*. http://www.charlottechamber.com/content.cfm?category_level_id=134&content_id=187 (accessed January 2005).

Charlotte-Mecklenburg Police Department. 2005. *About us*. http://www.charmeck.org/Departments/Police/About+Us/Home.htm (accessed January 2005).

Federal Bureau of Investigation. *Crime in the United States—2002*. http://www.fbi.gov/ucr/02cius.htm (accessed January 2005).

Goldstein, Herman. 1990. *Problem-oriented policing*. New York, McGraw Hill.

Kiser, D., P. Beatty, M. Casey, J. Maxwell, M. Berry, R. Burgess, M. Callaham, F. Coley, W. Hilderman, J. Kelley, et al. 1990. *Charlotte Police Department: 1866–1991*. Dallas, TX: Taylor Publishing Company.

National Institute of Justice. 1999. *Measuring what matters: Proceedings from the Policing Research Institute Meetings*. July, pp. 151–227. Washington, DC: U.S. Department of Justice.

National Institute of Justice and the Bureau of Justice Statistics. 1999. *Use of force by police: Overview of national and local data series research report*. October. Washington, DC: U.S. Department of Justice.

North Carolina v. Lee Taylor Farrar, North Carolina Court of Appeals; Mecklenburg County Superior Court: NO. COA01-1569 (December 2002). http://www.aoc.state.nc.us/www/public/coa/opinions/2002/unpub/011569-1.htm (accessed January 2005).

Office of Community Oriented Policing Services. 2005. *Grants by agency*. http://www.cops.usdoj.gov/mime/open.pdf?Item=1228 (accessed January 2005).

Smith, William, Elizabeth Davidson, Matthew Zingraff, Kennon Rice, and Denis Bissler. 2004. *An empirical investigation of the possible presence and extent of arbitrary profiling in the Charlotte-Mecklenburg Police Department*. January. Charlotte: Department of Sociology and Anthropology, North Carolina State University.

Stephens, D. *Police academy investigation report: Charlotte Mecklenburg Police Department*. May. Charlotte, NC: Charlotte Police Department.

Zhao, Jihong, Matthew Scheider, and Quint Thurman. 2002. Funding community policing to reduce crime: Have COPS grants made a difference? *Criminology and Public Policy* 2 (1): 7–32.

CHICAGO COMMUNITY POLICING

In 1993, Chicago inaugurated an experimental community policing program in five of its twenty-five police districts. Known as CAPS (for Chicago's Alternative Policing Strategy), it became a citywide program in 1995, after some of the kinks were worked out of the plan.

What cities actually do when they implement community policing varies a great deal. In some places it is in the hands of special teams run from police headquarters, while in others it involves transforming the entire department. Under the heading "community policing," officers patrol on foot and bicycles, and departments open small neighborhood storefront offices, conduct surveys to measure community satisfaction, and work with municipal agencies to enforce health and safety regulations.

However, community policing is not a set of specific projects. Underneath these tactics lies a deeper organizational strategy that involves changing decision-making processes in a way that leaves the setting of many priorities and the means for achieving them in the hands of residents and the police who serve in their area. As a result, community policing projects should look different in different cities, and even in different neighborhoods, because crime and the resources that police and the community can bring to bear on it differ from place to place. Underlying these seemingly different programs are three core strategic elements: community engagement, decentralization, and problem solving. These three elements are closely interrelated, and departments that shortchange even one of them will not field a very effective program. Police in Chicago established an effective program, especially for a large and unwieldy city, and this article describes what they did to turn each of these elements of community policing into reality.

The first common feature of departments adopting this new model of policing is community engagement. Community policing calls for developing mechanisms for constructively sharing information with the public, and for accommodating citizen input in setting priorities and evaluating whether or not they have been successful in addressing local concerns. To accomplish this, departments hold community meetings, form advisory committees, and survey the public in order to identify their priorities. In some places police share information with residents through educational programs or by enrolling them in citizen police academies that give them in-depth knowledge of law enforcement. Engagement usually extends to involving the public in some way in efforts to enhance community safety. Residents are certainly asked to assist the police by reporting crimes promptly when they occur and cooperating as witnesses, but community policing also promises to strengthen the capacity of communities to fight and prevent crime on their own. Residents may get involved in the coordinated or collaborative crime prevention projects, and even participate in officially sanctioned neighborhood patrol groups, though this is less common because of the legal liabilities it threatens if someone gets hurt. Even where these are old ideas, moving them to center stage as part of a larger strategic plan can showcase the commitment of police departments to resident involvement.

In Chicago's plan, beat community meetings are the most important mechanism for building and sustaining close relationships between police and the public. Beats are the department's smallest administrative unit, and each month an average of 6,700 residents attend about 250 evening beat community meetings. They are held in church social halls, park district buildings, hospital cafeterias, condominium party rooms, and other venues located in the beats. Residents meet with an average of five police officers, most of whom regularly patrol in the area. Officers working on other shifts are paid overtime to attend, to ensure that day watch and late-night problems are also discussed. Officers serving in specialized units, such as gang officers or detectives, are often present as well, along with a representative of the police district's neighborhood relations unit. Meetings are sometimes attended by representatives of the city's service departments and area community organizations, and the local aldermen's staff.

The purpose of the meetings is to provide a forum for exchanging information and a venue for identifying, analyzing, and prioritizing problems in an area. Local crime maps, "Top Ten" lists of the most frequent crimes, and other informational materials are distributed at the meetings. There is always a discussion of what has happened with regard to issues raised at the last meeting, and this provides a bit of community oversight of police activity. Chicagoans are not shy, and an observational study found that criticism of the police was voiced at about half the meetings. The new business segments of the meetings focus on identifying new issues and debating whether they are general problems or just the concern of one resident. Beat meetings are also a very convenient place to distribute announcements about upcoming community events, circulate petitions, and call for volunteers to participate in action projects. Importantly, they also provide occasions for residents and police who work in the area and will likely answer residents' calls to meet face to face and get acquainted.

The city invests a great deal of energy in turning residents out for the monthly meetings. District officers distribute flyers and hang posters in businesses and apartment building entryways. District neighborhood relations offices encourage organizations to get involved and send their members to the meetings, and they maintain mailing lists from sign-in sheets completed at the meetings. One district arranged to have beat maps and a list of upcoming meetings stapled to the lids of pizza boxes delivered in their area. Low-turnout beats often raffle off donated smoke detectors and crime prevention equipment at the conclusion of their meetings, to reward attendees. In an attempt to reach out more effectively to the city's growing Latino population, beginning in 2002, the department began circulating Spanish-language beat meeting schedules and maps at hundreds of Catholic churches. On occasion, schoolchildren have brought home announcements of beat community meetings. Computer-savvy residents can check the meeting schedule for their beat via the Internet. The city's two cable television channels feature a fifteen-minute "Crime Watch" infomercial each week that highlights neighborhood "success stories" and urges watchers to "get with the beat" and attend the meetings. In addition, about forty community organizers staff a civilian CAPS Implementation Office that is charged with sustaining turnout at beat meetings, marches, assemblies, and problem-solving projects. They go door to door in selected areas, trying to form block clubs and encouraging residents to attend beat meetings.

Beat meetings are one of the most distinctive features of Chicago's community policing program, and observers come from all over the world to see how they work. It turns out that meeting attendance rates are generally highest in the beats that need the most help. An early concern was that attending beat meetings and forming alliances with the police would be popular in better-off, white, home-owning areas of the city, but a tough sell elsewhere. However, beat meetings—and CAPS more generally—are most well known and widely attended in predominantly African American neighborhoods. Surveys indicate that about 80% of Chicagoans are aware of the city's community policing program and 60% know about neighborhood beat meetings, and that this awareness is highest

among African Americans. Their enthusiasm for the program is bad news as well as good news, for beat meeting attendance rates are principally driven by concern about violent crime, social disorder, street drug markets, and other neighborhood problems. But the result is that attendance is highest in the city's poorest, most disorganized, and highest crime neighborhoods.

A second common feature of community policing departments is that they attempt to decentralize responsibility and authority. Decentralization strategies are partly managerial and partly operational. In management terms, many departments try to delegate more responsibility for identifying and responding to chronic crime and disorder problems to midlevel district commanders. This has forced them to experiment with how to structure and manage decentralization in a way that holds midlevel managers accountable for measures of their success. Here community policing intersects with another movement in policing, one toward a culture of systematic performance measurement and managerial accountability. At the same time, more responsibility for identifying and responding to community problems is typically delegated to individual patrol officers and their sergeants, who are encouraged to take the initiative in finding ways to deal with a broad range of problems specific to the communities they serve. Decentralization, paired with a commitment to consultation and engagement with local communities, allows the police to respond to problems that are important to particular communities, and it legitimates having one priority in one part of town, and allocating resources some other way somewhere else.

Chicago completely reorganized the work of its patrol division in order to support community policing. The department formed teams of officers with responsibility for each of the city's 279 beats. Each team consists of nine officers, which is about the number it takes to staff a beat 24/7, plus a sergeant who is assigned to coordinate their activities. The 911 system was reconfigured to concentrate officers' activities in their assigned beat, effectively restructuring the daily work of thousands of patrol officers. The system prioritizes dispatching in a way that keeps them in their beat about 70% of the time, with some "unassigned" time available for getting out of their cars to attend meetings and talk with residents, merchants, and building managers. Calls in their beat that they cannot answer are forwarded to rapid response cars, which take up the slack.

The goal of engaging with the public was directly supported by this operational decentralization. Beat cars are identifiable by their beat number, which is posted on the top of the vehicle, and they have become very familiar to local residents. Team members regularly attend meetings in "their" beat, and they have a sense of ownership of place that did not exist before the teams were created. Residents complain when they don't see "their" beat officers around, a reciprocal sense of ownership that certainly did not exist before CAPS. The entire team meets quarterly to discuss priorities and strategies.

One of the tasks officers are supposed to attend to is working on their beat's priority problems. Under the watchful eye of their sergeant, each team maintains a list of about three priority problems that they have identified based on crime reports and 911 calls, complaints voiced at beat meetings, and their own observations of their assigned beats. They create a formal beat plan for each that describes the nature of the problem and records major actions they have taken to counter it. The plan form tracks reported crimes and 911 calls regarding the problem. All of this is maintained online, where it can be reviewed by their sergeant and the sergeant's boss, the "CAPS lieutenant." The district's CAPS lieutenant must approve each plan, and must later approve closing it when the problem has receded. These plans provide major input into the crafting of district-level plans, so senior managers at that level also review them on a regular basis. A 2002 study of a sample of sixty-eight beat plans found that in a year about half of them were successfully resolved. Because the department's definition of a "problem" includes that it cannot be resolved by the regular routines of patrol work, this was a respectable accomplishment.

A third feature of many community policing departments is that they embrace a broad-ranging, problem-solving orientation toward much of their work. Other chapters in this encyclopedia address problem solving as an organizational strategy. Community policing problem solving involves the public in identifying and prioritizing a broad range of chronic neighborhood conditions, and it may involve the public in solving them. Departments doing both community policing and problem solving also find that they must take on a much broader range of issues than they did before. This is one of the consequences of opening themselves up to the public. At community meetings residents complain about bad buildings, noise, and people draining their car radiators at the curb, not just about burglary. If police reply "that's not our responsibility" and try to move on, no one will come to the next meeting. As a result, they need to form partnerships with other agencies of government who can help them out, because even though loose garbage and rats in an alley may be a big issue for residents, police are not organized to do the cleanup. Their partners frequently include bureaucracies responsible for health, housing, and even street lighting. Community policing also involves the public in solving problems. Neighborhood residents can paint over graffiti, walk their dogs in areas frequented by prostitutes, and hold prayer vigils in the midst of street drug markets.

Problem solving is one of the key components of CAPS. In Chicago, a "problem" is defined as "a group of related incidents or an ongoing situation that concerns a significant portion of those who live or work in a particular area." Links between incidents can arise because they share common victims, offenders, or methods of operation, but most are defined by their concentration in specific locations. Problems are also persistent: They are unlikely to disappear without an intervention of some significance, because they typically have survived routine efforts by the police to resolve them. Because they are persistent, repeated incidents probably share causes, so dealing with these underlying sources may prevent future problems. Problems chosen by the residents and police to work on should be capable of being solved using the resources that police and the community can bring to bear on them; the team cannot take on society's largest problems at the beat level. Finally, while dealing with crime remains at the heart of the police mission, problems can include a broad range of community concerns. They range from noise to the dilapidated condition of many of the city's older rental buildings, and include a host of social disorders, municipal service shortcomings, and a broad range of code enforcement matters.

Chicago police and thousands of residents have been trained to respond to local problems using a five-step process. They have been taught to identify problems and prioritize them, and then analyze them by gathering information about offenders, victims, and locations of crimes. Subsequently, they are to design strategies that might deal with the chronic character of priority problems. They are asked to "think outside the box" of traditional police enforcement tactics and to use new tools that have been developed to support their problem-solving efforts. Chicago's model also recognizes a stage during which the community, police, and other city departments implement strategies. This highlights the special skill and effort required to actually set plans in motion. Finally, police and residents are to evaluate their own effectiveness by assessing how well they carried out their plan and how much good they accomplished.

Public participation in problem solving is fairly widespread. Residents are prominently involved in weekend graffiti clean-ups and "positive loitering" campaigns, which attempt to reclaim the streets from street prostitutes and public drinking. The mayor heads a CAPS take-back-the-neighborhood march almost every Saturday morning. A survey of participants at beat meetings found 53% reporting being involved in one or more CAPS-related problem-solving projects or bringing problems to the attention of their alderman. Other groups sponsor neighborhood patrols, which the department does not officially support because of the risk of lawsuits, and 20% of beat meeting participants reported being active in those. All of this activism was more frequent in higher crime, predominantly African American neighborhoods.

Agency partnerships are another key feature of an effective program. In cities where community policing is the police department's program, problem solving typically addresses only a narrow range of issues, not the broad range of problems that CAPS has taken on. In Chicago, CAPS is the city's program, and every relevant agency is making an effort to support problem solving at the beat and district level. The CAPS Implementation Office provides the interagency coordination that is required to address the most significant problems. The city attorney's office and a multiagency inspection task force support district efforts to deal with gang and drug houses by using building, fire, and health codes to force landlords to take action.

Community policing, Chicago style, thus involves all of the major elements of this model of policing. It was intended to be transformational; that is, it was designed to change the way in which the entire department and even city government did its business, and not just special units or even just the police department. It weaves responsibility for problem solving into the daily routines of beat officers and integrates them into the fabric of the community. It created a mechanism by which the public can influence and monitor the work of officers in their neighborhood, and do so in a constructive and collaborative way, and it is probably here to stay. Immensely popular with the public, community policing has become the routine way in which Chicagoans expect police services to be delivered, giving the program the political support it might require to survive budgetary downturns and changes in administration.

WESLEY G. SKOGAN

See also **Accountability; Administration of Police Agencies, Theories of; Community-Oriented Policing: Practices; Crime Control Strategies; Problem-Oriented Policing; SARA, the Model**

References and Further Reading

Skogan, Wesley G., ed. 2003. *Community policing: Can it work?* Belmont, CA: Wadsworth.
Skogan, Wesley G., and Susan Hartnett. 1997. *Community policing, Chicago style.* New York: Oxford University Press.

CHILD ABUSE AND ITS INVESTIGATION

Police departments and social service agencies witnessed a dramatic increase of criminal cases involving children in the 1980s. This increase, driven by shifts in societal attitudes and the resulting legal and policy reforms, left forensic interviewers searching for optimal ways to elicit accurate testimony from child witnesses. More than a quarter century of research now demonstrates that children can, when interviewed with certain methods, give accurate accounts of previously experienced events.

Most of this forensic developmental research has focused on interview procedures for cases involving alleged child victims of sexual abuse (CSA). Because incidents of CSA rarely involve witnesses or physical evidence, garnering accurate reports in these cases is especially important. Before continuing it should be noted that, although the true prevalence of CSA is unknown, it is well agreed that child abuse is a pervasive societal problem.

History of Forensic Interviews with Children

Prior to the 1970s, children under age fourteen typically were not allowed to give uncorroborated testimony in the courtroom. The courts reasoned that children were neither able to distinguish fact from fantasy nor able to accurately remember past events. In the 1980s, as the reality of the frequency of CSA became more apparent, and as a wave of hysteria swept over the United States regarding mass (and sometimes ritualistic) sex abuse rings, views of children's competency took a polemic shift. Many child protective workers adopted the belief that children do not make false allegations, and never lie, especially about sexual abuse. Some interviewers adopted the belief that children are reluctant to disclose sexual abuse; some went as far as to consider denial of abuse a sign that the child was abused. Because of these views, some investigators adopted forceful interview styles, doggedly pursuing children with techniques such as bribery, selective reinforcement, repeated suggestive interviewing, peer pressure, and negative stereotyping during interviews lasting several hours (and sometimes over several days or weeks) until the child finally assented to abuse. During the past several decades, however, a corpus of studies demonstrates that interviewer bias manifests in suggestive questioning that leads to false reports from children (see Bruck and Ceci 1999).

Suggestive interviewing extends beyond simply asking children misleading questions. For example, studies have found that negative stereotyping can produce inaccurate accounts in children. Leichtman and Ceci (1995) told children a story about a man, Sam, who was very messy and clumsy. Sam later visited their classroom and engaged in a few neutral actions with the children. When suggestively interviewed about the visit after a ten-week delay, many children made false claims about Sam that were consistent with the stereotype of being clumsy and messy (for example, that he tore pages out of a book). Studies have also found that selective reinforcement (for example, telling the child he is a good boy only when making abuse disclosures) may lead children to provide false information. The scientific literature indicates that children sometimes agree with false statements about central actions involving bodily touch. While preschoolers are particularly prone to acquiescing to suggestive questions, studies are emerging that find suggestibility effects in older school-aged children.

Despite studies showing that suggestive techniques are detrimental to children's reports, some interviewers justified their continued use of such techniques by claiming that such methods were necessary to elicit disclosures from reticent children. However, a comprehensive review of the literature revealed that while children often delay disclosing abuse (or never disclose to anyone during childhood), the evidence does not support the notion that abused children commonly deny or recant abuse allegations when asked directly about abuse (London et al. forthcoming). In short, the evidence does not support the practice of interviews characterized by suggestive techniques; rather such methods have been shown to produce erroneous reports.

As a result of research showing the detrimental influences of suggestive interviewing techniques, a number of different teams have developed "suggestion-free" protocols (for example, NICHD protocol

[see Lamb 1994]; Poole and Lamb 1998). These protocols provide detailed accounts of empirically supported interview techniques, which are briefly summarized next.

Empirically Supported Techniques for Interviewing Children

The first interview is crucial in that it provides the first opportunity for the child to provide his or her account of the event. In the absence of suggestive techniques (or some overt motive for the child to employ deception), children as young as age three can provide accurate details about past experienced events.

The interview should start with brief, open-ended rapport building (for example, "Tell me everything about a recent holiday"). Rapport building helps establish the conversational style of the interview (see Sternberg et al. 1997). The interviewer should explain to children that because the interviewer was not there, he or she does not know what happened, and that the child can respond "don't know." If the interviewer conducts a truth/lie ceremony, it should be brief and he or she should avoid asking children to explain the difference between a truth and a lie. Rather, the interviewer can ask children to identify examples of truths and lies (for example, "If John said that he was a girl, is that the truth, a lie, or something else?"; see London and Nunez 2002).

Next, the interviewer must introduce the topic of abuse without mentioning a specific event or suspect. Sternberg et al. (1997) found that the following prompt elicited disclosure in 96% of alleged victims: "Now that we know each other a little better I want to talk about the reason you are here today. I understand that something may have happened to you. Please tell me everything that happened, every detail, from the very beginning to the very end" (p. 1146). The key point is to raise the topic of abuse without suggesting a specific incident or suspect.

Research has found that children give the most accurate reports to open-ended questions (for example, "Tell me everything you can remember" and "What else?"). Children should be allowed to make disclosures in their own words. While research has found that open-ended questions lead to the most accurate reports for children, particularly for young children, their open-ended reports are sometimes sparse. The interviewer should be patient and exhaust open-ended prompts. After the child has provided a free narrative, the interviewer should continue to prompt with open-ended questions to get additional information and clarification. More direct questions may be necessary to elicit information from the child. Even so, the interviewer should return to open-ended questions. (For example, an assent to "Were your clothes on or off?" can be followed with "Tell me about that.") Yes/no questions should be avoided as much as possible and only introduced at the end of the interview to clarify statements the child has made. *Wh-* questions are not necessarily neutral. (For example, the interviewer might ask "What did he say to you when he touched your penis?" when the child had not made any statements about touching.) The interviewer must be careful not to embed suggestions within a direct question (for example, "When he took your pants off, were you in the bedroom or the living room?" when the child previously said nothing about having clothes off), but rather only ask direct questions about topics the child has already mentioned.

There is mixed evidence on whether interview props such as dolls and drawings facilitate children's reports (for a review, see Salmon 2001). If props are used, they should be introduced toward the end of the interview (but only among children who have made disclosures). The use of props should be avoided with preschoolers,

because studies suggest that they do not have the cognitive prerequisites to appreciate the props' symbolic quality. At this time, the safest practice would be to avoid or minimize the use of props during forensic interviews with children.

Best practice guidelines recommend audiotaping and videotaping the interview. Typically, children's disclosures comprise the sole evidence in CSA cases, so it is crucial for fact-finders to be able to evaluate the quality by which this evidence was collected. Also, by recording interviews, prosecutors can counter unfounded criticisms that shoddy interview techniques were used.

Conducting quality forensic interviews with children requires specialized and continued training. Lamb and colleagues found that intensive training in using highly standardized interview procedures alone was insufficient for maintaining quality interview methods. Additional monthly supervision and individual feedback, however, greatly bolstered the quality of interviewers' methods.

Forensic interviewers have a weighty job. The stakes of reaching correct decisions are high. Furthermore, once false statements are elicited from children, evidence suggests that children come to believe these false claims, and adults cannot reliably distinguish children's narratives about true versus false events. In the laboratory, researchers have knowledge of the experimental events; in the real world, however, interviewers, experts, and the jury members do not know whether statements are true or false in most cases.

On a positive note, there is a growing body of empirically supported guidelines for conducting forensic interviews with children. Previously, interviewers were basically being asked to build a house with no tools in their toolbox. These forensic manuals provide the best tools that we have today to promote disclosure among truly abused children while minimizing false reports.

KAMALA LONDON

See also **Domestic (or Intimate Partner) Violence and the Police; Forensic Evidence; Forensic Investigations; Police Social Work Teams and Victim Advocates**

References and Further Reading

Bruck, M., S. J. Ceci, and E. Francoeur. 1999. The accuracy of mothers' memories of conversations with their preschool children. *Journal of Experimental Psychology: Applied* 5: 1–18.

Bruck, M., S. J. Ceci, E. Francoeur, and A. Renick. 1995. Anatomically detailed dolls do not facilitate preschoolers' reports of a pediatric examination involving genital touch. *Journal of Experimental Psychology: Applied* 1: 95–109.

Bruck, M., S. J. Ceci, and H. Hembrooke. 2002. The nature of children's true and false narratives. *Developmental Review* 22: 520–54.

Bruck, M., K. London, J. Goodman, and R. Landa. Forthcoming. Autobiographical memory and suggestibility in children with autism spectrum disorder.

Bruck, Maggie, and Laura Melnyk. Forthcoming. Individual differences in children's suggestibility: A review and synthesis.

Ceci, Stephen J., and Maggie Bruck. 1995. *Jeopardy in the courtroom: A scientific analysis of children's testimony.* Washington, DC: American Psychological Association.

Jones, Lisa M., and David Finkelhor. 2003. Putting together evidence on declining trends in sexual abuse: A complex puzzle. *Child Abuse and Neglect* 27: 133–35.

Lamb, Michael E. 1994. The investigation of child sexual abuse: An interdisciplinary consensus statement. *Expert Evidence* 2: 151–63.

———. 2002. The effects of intensive training and ongoing supervision in the quality of investigative interviews with alleged sex abuse victims. *Applied Developmental Science* 6: 114–25.

Lamb, M. E., Y. Orbach, and K. J. Sternberg. 2000. Accuracy of investigators' verbatim notes of their forensic interviews with alleged child abuse victims. *Law and Human Behavior* 24: 699–708.

Lamb, M. E., K. J. Sternberg, and P. Esplin. 1994. Factors influencing the reliability and validity of statements made by young victims of sexual maltreatment. *Journal of Applied Developmental Psychology* 15: 255–80.

———. 1995. Conducting investigative interviews of alleged sexual abuse victims. *Child Abuse and Neglect* 22: 813–23.

Leichtman, Michelle D., and Stephen J. Ceci. 1995. The effects of stereotypes and suggestions on preschoolers' reports. *Developmental Psychology* 31: 568–78.

London, K., M. Bruck, S. J. Ceci, and D. Shuman. Forthcoming. Children's disclosure of sexual abuse: What does research tell us about the ways that children tell? *Psychology, Public Policy, and the Law.*

London, Kamala, and Narina Nunez. 2002. Investigative and courtroom interviews of children: Examining the efficacy of truth/lie discussions in increasing the veracity of children's reports. *Journal of Experimental Child Psychology* 83: 131–47.

Salmon, Karen. 2001. Remembering and reporting by children: The influence of cues and props. *Clinical Psychology Review* 21: 267–300.

Sternberg, K. J., M. E. Lamb, I. Hershkowitz, L. Yudilevitch, Y. Orbach, P. Esplin, and M. Horaw. 1997. Effects of introductory style on children's abilities to describe experiences of sexual abuse. *Child Abuse and Neglect* 21: 1133–46.

CITIZEN COMPLAINTS IN THE NEW POLICE ORDER

A dynamic tension exists in the role of government in a society that aspires to be democratic. On one hand, government is created to provide citizens with safety, security, and service, while on the other it serves as an instrument that organizes many aspects of social life bringing a sense of order, stability, and conformity to social interactions. The tension between service and control has been dramatized in the writing of political philosophers. Political philosophers expressed this tension in terms of a "social contract," attempting to present the proper balance between government as "service provider" and as "citizen controller." By entering into the social contract, citizens are thought to surrender certain natural rights and vest government with the power to maintain social stability and to ensure citizen interests. In exchange for relinquishing the right to use physical force, for instance, citizens expect government to provide effective systems for regulating conduct and forums for resolving social conflict.

The police institution is the most visible of the government's formal social control creations. The tension between the dual roles of government is no better portrayed than in the actions of social control agents, who continually struggle with the conflict that arises when balancing their governmental role as service provider and citizen controller. Historically, police have provided little in terms of social service and much in state-sanctioned social control. Yet, if the contemporary rhetoric of leading police administrators, the printed words of scholars, and the remarks of politicians are to be believed, the role police play in society is changing. Spokespersons from both policing and academe are addressing citizens and their colleagues on an emerging philosophy of policing. This new philosophy and its operationalization are usually spoken of as "community" and "problem-solving" policing. While these role strategies differ in implementation, they are driven by reconceptualizing the police as service providers rather than citizen controllers. While many scholars question the viability of instituting such a reconceptualization (Strecher 1991; Williams and Wagoner 1992), the rhetoric from the trenches is certainly permeated with expressions of a shift in police role strategy.

As with any significant philosophical or political change, this reform movement has been accompanied by a new language. Police chiefs are now referred to as "executives"; citizens are referred to as "clients" or "consumers"; and the control that police provide is shrouded in the jargon of "service." Remarks of Los Angeles Chief Willie Williams capture the essence of the role strategy: "I liken the L.A. police to a business. . . . We have 3 1/2 million customers . . ." (Wickerham 1993, 13A). In like fashion, the actions of the New York City Police Department in placing a twelve-page guide on how to use departmental services in a local news source reflects attempts to transform rhetoric into reality (*USA Today* 1993). As these examples show, police are invoking the language of business and capitalism (Manning 1992). Perhaps because they are relinquishing their "monopoly on legitimate violence," they are embracing "the language of economics and management . . . to reconceptualize the police mandate" (Manning 1992, 1). This fundamental shift in philosophy and its attendant rhetoric, if accompanied by operational change, promises to have profound consequences on virtually every aspect of policing.

One aspect of policing that provides insight into the integration of the "new" service rhetoric and the "old" control reality is how police respond to citizen complaints. Few other aspects of policing provide a more direct and empirical link between the emerging language of service and actual practices than does the police response to citizen complaints. Within this context, this article explores citizen complaints against police. Highlighted first are some assumptions that drove the development of the current citizen complaint system. Second, the nature of citizen complaints levied against the police is reviewed and assessment is made of the responsiveness of the police institution to these challenges to their control authority. By examining police responses to citizen complaints, an assessment can be made of the division between the emerging rhetoric of service and the reality of citizen control. Finally, the article explores the possible transformations that citizen complaint systems might find if the new police role strategy is institutionalized.

Traditional Views and Responses to Citizen Complaints

The history of citizen complaints against police has been a quest to develop a system of ensuring accountability to the citizenry that empowers it. Fundamental in establishing police accountability was the creation of a system from which assessments could be made as to whether police abused their powers and authorities as citizen controllers. The desire to develop a system of accountability for police deviations in control practices is best expressed in this report: "In 1903, a New York City police commissioner turned judge noted that his court had seen numerous citizens with injuries received when the police effected their arrest. He felt that many of them had done nothing to deserve an arrest but most of them made no complaint" (Wagner and Decker 1993, 276). Implicit in this judicial observation is that there existed no effective mechanism for citizens to levy complaints against police or even a desire by police officials to encourage citizen complaints. What transpired in the ninety-some years since this observation was the development of a police-controlled citizen complaint system in every major law enforcement organization.

With an overriding concern about police abuse, the emerging system focused on technical rule violations by police—especially physical abuse. To ensure police accountability, the resulting system had to allow agencies to document and investigate citizen complaints so that some assessment of performance could be obtained to demonstrate that police are accountable to and controlled by the government and its citizens. Unfortunately, like many aspects of modern policing, the citizen complaint system was born of two fundamental legalistic precepts: accountability and control. The current citizen complaint system was modeled after, and founded on, assumptions that permeate the larger legal system. Because it stressed localized accountability and patterned itself after other legal forums, the citizen complaint system became legalistic in form and adversarial in nature, therefore mirroring the criminal justice system. With an emphasis on accountability and control, a focus on legally and organizationally defined abuse, and driven by the assumptions that underpin an adversarial model of justice, the citizen complaint system became a quasijudicial

forum. From its inception, then, the process pitted police against public in a quasi-legal forum that focused not on the adequacy of police as service providers but on technical violations of legal and organizational rules.

Given a legalistic framework, the system's twin focal concerns became the establishment of the validity of citizen allegations and the disposal of complaints in finite fashion. The system was constructed with all the safeguards of a due process model of justice, but failed to benefit from its neutrality. Police agencies adopting citizen complaint systems provided an array of shields similar to those offered defendants in criminal trials, thus insulating themselves from sanction by housing investigative and adjudicative functions in stationhouses. Approximately 84% of the nation's largest police departments use a complaint system that relies exclusively on internal investigation and adjudication (West 1988). The system allowed law enforcement to control the types of citizen complaints it accepted; the extent to which police investigated complaints; the weight given to evidence uncovered by police investigations; the burden of proof required for adjudication; and ultimately the disposition of citizen complaints.

In developing the system, police have erected formidable barriers to citizen complaints. Suffice it to mention just a few obstacles police have used to bar the flow of citizen complaints. First, there are inherent deterrents to citizen complaints against police. These include a lack of citizen knowledge that they can and should complain; a lack of citizen knowledge concerning actionable police conducts; the time and energy needed to complain; and a fatalistic citizen attitude concerning the effectiveness of complaining. While these barriers are inherent in any system of accountability, historically police have done little to remove these obstructions. Second, police have employed a deterrent "strategy" to reduce the number of citizen complaints. Although differences in complaint systems abound, many police departments have adopted tactics that effectively block a large proportion of potential citizen complaints. These tactics have generally included requiring citizens to file complaints in person rather than anonymously; requiring citizens to file complaints at stationhouses; restricting access to the complaint system (either through location or language barriers); requiring citizens to sign written formal statements (often accompanied by warnings of criminal prosecution for falsely reporting); requiring citizens to take polygraph tests before beginning an investigation; and limiting complaints to only those behaviors recognized by police as falling within their self-defined areas of accountability. Finally, and hopefully to a lesser extent, police have used some draconian measures to prevent citizen complaints. Some of these measures have included making citizens wait at stationhouses for hours (hoping they will forego complaining); threatening minority citizens with notification of the immigration and naturalization service; making it known that police will run warrant checks on anyone filing a complaint; and threatening citizens with defamation lawsuits (see generally Christopher 1991; Kolts 1992; Mayor's Citizen Commission 1991). In short, police have not only availed themselves of the protections of a legalistic system of citizen complaints, but they have used many tactics to discourage challenges to their control authority. Many of these tactics undermine the integrity of the citizen complaint system.

Those citizen complaints that reach disposition are classified according to a typology developed by police officials. This classification functions to sustain police concern with reducing the volume of viable complaints that enter the system and limits the effectiveness of the system as a mechanism of accountability and control. Most police organizations classify the citizen complaints they decide to investigate into one of the following categories:

- Unfounded—the act complained of did not occur. This classification results when the investigators find noninvolved citizens or police witnesses who contradict the allegations of the complainant.
- Not sustained—the evidence is insufficient to clearly prove or disprove the allegations made. This classification almost always results when the only witnesses to the allegations were the accused officer and the complainant, or witnesses in some way affiliated with the complainant, such as the complainant's family or friends.
- Exonerated—the event of alleged conduct occurred but it was justified, lawful, and proper.
- Sustained—the police officer engaged in the alleged conduct and the conduct was out of policy. Excessive force and improper tactics complaints are rarely sustained unless there are noninvolved, independent witnesses who corroborate the complainant's version of the facts (Christopher 1991, 155).

Inherent in this classification, as with the entire complaint process, is the assumption that citizens bring improper or false complaints against police. Although false complaints do occur, the existing classification weights more heavily the desire to determine whether a citizen complaint is valid than it does understanding the reason for the complaint. A second intent reflected in the current classification is the desire to dispose of complaints in a finite fashion with the least disruption to the institution. This means that complaints must be disposed of with a designation that generally vindicates police conduct to avoid other legal entanglements. Vindication can take the form of an "exoneration" of the conduct as proper, it can call into question the validity of the citizen's complaint by labeling it "unfounded," or it can fail to sustain the complaint by challenging the sufficiency of misconduct evidence. The vast majority of complaints lodged against police are disposed of through this vindication process. A national self-report survey of the largest police agencies found that on average only 11% of citizen complaints are classified as sustained (West 1988).

The police have generally failed to establish either accountability or control of abuse of authority under the present system. Nor does the present system seem able to handle the bulk of concerns citizens have with the police institution. The manner in which citizen complaints are disposed of reflects these shortcomings. Consider how few citizen complaints are sustained by select law-enforcement agencies in various cities.

Table 1 indicates that only a very small percentage of all complaints filed against the police are sustained. The research demonstrates that of all types of citizen claims, physical abuse claims are sustained at the lowest rates (see table footnotes), whereas complaints of rudeness, verbal abuse, or improper attitude are sustained at higher rates (Kappeler, Carter, and Sapp 1992). There are several ironies in this finding. First, a system designed to provide accountability and control of physical abuse has been shown to be the least effective in dealing with this area of police conduct. Second, the system seems most conducive to controlling nonphysical abuse when one would suspect that these forms of abuse would produce the least credible evidence of police misconduct. Finally, of all the sustained complaints reported in Table 1, relatively few officers

Table 1   Police Response to Citizen Complaints in Select Agencies

Jurisdiction	Year(s)	Total	Sustained	Source of Data
Columbia, MO	1985–90	413	92 (22%)	Kappeler, Sapp, and Carter 1992[a]
Los Angeles, CA (PD)	1986–90	3,419	171 (5%)	Independent CA Commission on LAPD 1991[b]
Los Angeles, CA (SD)	1990–92	514	27 (6%)	Special Counsel on LASD 1992[c]
Metro City	1971	304	16 (5%)	Wagner 1980[d]
	1972–73	280	32 (11%)	
Milwaukee, WI	1985–90	206	1 (.05%)	Mayor's Citizens Commission 1991[e]
Omaha, NE	1989	255	26 (10%)	Walker 1992[f]
Philadelphia, PA	1959–68	868	145 (17%)	Hudson 1972
St. Louis, MO	1980–90	2,218	202 (9%)	Official Records[g]
Truck Stop City	1971	253	40 (16%)	Culver 1975
	1973	279	13 (5%)	

[a] Includes complaints initiated by police officials, which inflates the percentage of sustained complaints.

[b] Includes only allegations of excessive force and improper tactics. LAPD sustained only 2% of its citizen complaints for excessive force, but since the commission report contains conflicting percentages, the most conservative figure is reported.

[c] Includes only citizen complaints of excessive use of force.

[d] Only 2% of citizen complaints for physical abuse were sustained.

[e] Includes four complaints against the city fire department.

[f] Sustained rate was derived from disciplinary actions taken and may be an underestimate.

[g] The official reports claim a much higher rate of sustained complaints due to the inclusion of complaints brought against civilian employees and excluding unfounded, exonerated, and withdrawn complaints from analysis. The authors' independent analysis of the official data, however, indicates only 9% of citizen complaints are sustained. In 1990, 12.6% of physical abuse complaints were sustained, whereas 36% of improper attitude complaints were sustained.

ever received the sanction of suspension, demotion, or termination from duty (see original sources of data). It is hard not to conclude that the citizen complaint system, as employed by many police organizations, has failed to establish either accountability to the citizenry or governmental control of the police.

Citizen Complaints in the New Police Order

If police adopt a service orientation to citizen complaints, one that fashions its approach on the rhetoric of the business community, police may find that the general assumptions that underpin the existing system will have to be altered. First, a system built around an ethos of service would require police to accept more citizen complaints. Not only would police be obliged to accept complaints in greater volume, they would be required to accept a greater variety of complaints including those that challenge the quality of service and the adequacy of police as service providers. The police would also have to be concerned with the outcome of complaints not as possible disruptive forces to the integrity of the institution, but, rather, as measures of the effectiveness of police in providing service to a consumer population that could go elsewhere for service. Additionally, the process by which police handle citizen complaints would have to be altered under the new police order. The investigation of citizen complaints against police could no longer focus on establishing the validity of the citizen's complaint, but rather on the underlying concern the citizen had with the police. Police departments might find themselves adopting the business adage that the "citizen is always right" rather than requiring citizen complaints to meet the current police-imposed burden of proof, as under the existing system. Finally, police would have to abandon the vision of the complaint system as an adjudicative process in favor of negotiation or mediation processes designed to satisfy its "customers." Such outcomes if followed by "imposed service improvements" rather than "departmental sanctions" could alter both police and public perception of the citizen complaint system.

The likelihood of such a transformation is open to debate. It is questionable whether one can expect substantive changes in the police handling of citizen complaints, given the increasing litigious environment in which they operate and the protective nature of police subcultures. The more important question, therefore, is what consequences can we expect from police attempts to tailor the citizen complaint system to the new police order.

Such an attempt to transform the citizen complaint system has both possibilities and perils. Developing a consumer approach, for example, has the definite possibility of opening up the institution of policing to greater and more detailed public scrutiny and control, an appealing possibility for those who value a government guided by democratic principles and a service orientation. By expanding what constitutes a recognizable citizen complaint, by investigating complaints based on responding to "consumer" needs, and by processing cases in a mediation format, the citizen complaint system could become a critical component in promoting the new police order.

A realistic peril of this new order and its attendant role strategy is that reform may only appear to seriously address citizen complaints by spotlighting those that coincide with the police definition of service provider. While the police institution focuses the community's attention on its "new" role, the handling of complaints associated with the previous role of police as citizen controllers may remain unchanged. This situation is evidenced by some police departments' attempts to integrate community police with drug enforcement efforts in hopes of generating more intelligence information. As with attempts

171

to reform other organizational practices that threaten members' security, the envisioned complaint processing practices may end up being only superficially service driven and sustaining, instead of challenging the original problem of police abuses as citizen controllers. Another peril lies in how police might define "service" and "customer." One can envision police definitions that exclude certain segments of society from the distinction of "customer." Such a system might develop "preferred" customers who receive preferential treatment based on their ability to differentially influence the type, quality, and distribution of police services. Whatever the possibility and perils, clearly the citizen complaint system will play a dominant and strategic role in the new police order.

VICTOR E. KAPPELER and PETER B. KRASKA

See also **Complaints against Police**

References and Further Reading

Christopher, W. 1991. *Report of the independent commission on the Los Angeles Police Department*. Los Angeles: Los Angeles Police Department.

Culver, J. H. 1975. Policing the police: Problems and perspectives. *Journal of Police Science and Administration* 3 (2): 125–35.

Dugan, J. R., and D. R. Breda. 1991. Complaints about police officers: A comparison among types and agencies. *Journal of Criminal Justice* 19: 156–71.

Hudson, J. R. 1972. Organizational aspects of internal and external review of the police. *Journal of Criminal Law, Criminology, and Police Science* 63: 427–33.

Kappeler, V. E., D. Carter, and A. Sapp. 1992. Police officer higher education, citizen complaints and departmental rule violation. *American Journal of Police* 11 (2): 37–54.

Kolts, J. G. 1992. *The Los Angeles County Sheriff's Department: A report by special counsel*. Los Angeles: Los Angeles County Sheriff's Department.

Manning, P. K. 1992. Economic rhetoric and policing reform. *Criminal Justice Research Bulletin* 7 (4): 1–8.

Mayor's Citizen Commission. 1991. *A Report to Mayor John Norquist and the Board of Fire and Police Commissioners*. Milwaukee, WI: Mayor's Citizen Commission.

Strecher, V. G. 1991. Histories and futures of policing: Readings and misreadings of a pivotal present. *Police Forum* 1 (1): 1–9.

USA Today. 1993. Across the nation. April 2.

Wagner, A. 1980. Citizen complaints against the police: The complainant. *Journal of Police Science and Administration* 8 (3): 247–52.

Wagner, A. E., and S. H. Decker. 1993. Evaluating citizen complaints against the police. In *Critical Issues in Policing: Contemporary Readings*, ed. R. Dunham and G. Alpert, 275–89. Prospect Heights, IL: Waveland Press.

Walker, S. 1992. *The police in America*. 2nd ed. New York: McGraw-Hill.

West, P. 1988. Investigation of complaints against the police: summary of a national survey. *American Journal of Police* 7 (2): 101–22.

Wickerham, D. 1993. L.A. police chief: Treat people like customers. *USA Today*, March 29, 13A.

Williams, F. P., and C. P. Wagoner. 1992. Making the police proactive: An impossible task for improbable reasons. *Police Forum* 2 (2): 1–5.

CITIZEN POLICE ACADEMIES

Citizen police academies (CPAs) are police programs intended to educate members of the public about the general duties and problems of policing their community. CPAs are intended to improve police–community relations by informing citizens about the structure and operation of their local police department. Using a common curriculum and structure, CPA programs teach citizens about the challenges and realities of police work. It is hoped that CPA graduates will become more sympathetic to the difficulties of modern police work, both in general and within their own community. CPA graduates are expected to serve as informal advocates for the local police, exponentially increasing the benefits of these programs.

CPA programs are based on the theory that educating small groups of citizens on how local police agencies and officers operate will improve broader community support. The idea dates back to 1977, when the Devon and Cornwall Constabulary in the United Kingdom established a ten-week "Police Night School." Select citizens from the area were invited to attend the school. Students and their police instructors met one night a week, with different police personnel volunteering to teach various topics to the citizen-students. The school and its curriculum were created to educate attendees about general issues in British policing, as well as the challenges faced by the local constabulary. The night school was well received by both constables and citizens, and similar programs were implemented in other British constabularies.

The first American CPA program was sponsored by the Orlando (Florida) Police Department in 1985 (Greenberg 1991). The Orlando program based its structure and curriculum on the British model; it also offered attendees the opportunity to observe an officer during a "ride-along" and to receive basic training in the use of police firearms. In the following years, CPA programs were adopted by a number of agencies across the United States. CPAs are now a common programmatic element that agencies use to educate the public about the challenges and realities of crime and police work. As the label implies, these programs expose citizens to an accelerated course about police work; in many ways they are similar to some of the topics new police officers will learn in their training academy.

Although their exact structure, content, organization, and length might vary, American CPAs tend to be alike in many regards (Bumphus, Gaines, and Blakely 1999). Most programs meet one evening a week for three hours and last a total of ten to twelve weeks. It is common to have a voluntary weekend meeting where citizens can learn basic firearm usage and safety, while being exposed to the policy and legal frameworks within which police officers use deadly force. Many programs also offer students the opportunity to "ride along" with an officer to observe

police work with their own eyes. Course materials are delivered by a variety of speakers, including patrol officers, detectives, police leaders, prosecutors, judges, and social service providers. Common lecture topics include an overview of the community and its crime problems, an introduction to the sponsoring agency and its structure, patrol operations, investigative operations, the prosecution and adjudication of criminal cases at the local level, special weapon and tactic teams, canine and special service units, and criminal law and police policy. Programs typically end with a graduation ceremony in which those completing the program are given a certificate and other commemorative memorabilia.

By exposing citizens to CPA programs, it is hoped that departments will generate more support and understanding within their community. Much of the focus of CPAs can be on differentiating between the media image of police work and the realities of policing in a community. For example, discussions of patrol operations provide insights into the realities of how officers spend their time. Lectures on law and policy shed light on the complex decisions officers must make and the context within which they do so. Courses on firearms use and safety are also mechanisms for introducing citizens to the complexity of using deadly force in a legal, ethical, and moral manner. In the end, agencies hope to create "goodwill ambassadors" within their community; in this way, CPAs can be seen to serve important public relations functions.

Another objective of CPAs is to build citizen support for, and involvement in, local police operations. Graduates of some CPA programs have created "alumni associations" that volunteer in support of other departmental efforts and raise money to support departmental needs and causes. For example, alumni might hold a car wash to raise money for a bulletproof vest for an agency's canine. In other communities, CPA graduates are encouraged to volunteer their time doing basic clerical work, answering nonemergency phone calls, and staffing information desks. Even in the absence of volunteer involvement, it is expected that CPA graduates will be more informed citizens who can serve as an agency's "eyes and ears" within a community.

Some agencies have experimented with CPA programs targeting select populations, including youth, senior citizens, and business leaders. These focused CPA programs modify their content to present important information for their specific audience. A youth academy might focus more on policing as a career and the importance of cooperating with the police. A senior's academy could explore issues of public safety and crime awareness, and could also encourage retirees to volunteer their time and talents to support the sponsoring agency. A business academy may serve a crime prevention function by discussing facility security, how to avoid being the victim of fraud, and how to train staff members to respond to criminal events.

Despite their strong potential, we know little about the actual outcome of CPA programs. One of the greatest problems CPAs have is attracting participants from segments of the population that mistrust the police. In one community, the average CPA graduate began the program with a positive view of the sponsoring agency (Schafer and Bonello 2001). Although including "pro-police" citizens has many merits, the absence of "anti-police" citizens limits the ability of CPA programs to truly improve police–community relations, particularly where such improvements are needed the most. In this same agency (Schafer and Bonello 2001), it was found that 56% of CPA participants had already volunteered their time prior to entering this program. Although both volunteerism and positive attitudes toward the police increased after participants graduated, it is reasonable to ask whether the program was reaching deep enough into the community in an effort to achieve its goals.

CPAs hold the promise of being effective dimensions of departmental efforts, but whether they are having the impact agencies hoped to achieve remains unclear. In addition, CPA programs can be moderately expensive, costing agencies several hundred dollars per participant in addition to the time personnel must devote to operate the program and deliver lectures. It is reasonable to ask whether the resulting benefits are worth the associated expenses.

JOSEPH A. SCHAFER

See also **Academies, Police; Attitudes toward the Police: Overview; Media Images of Policing; Public Image of the Police**

References and Further Reading

Bumphus, V. W., L. K. Gaines, and C. R. Blakely. 1999. Citizen police academies: Observing goals, objectives, and recent trends. *American Journal of Criminal Justice* 24 (1): 67–79.

Greenberg, M. A. 1991. Citizen police academies. *FBI Law Enforcement Bulletin* 60 (8): 10–13.

Schafer, J. A., and E. M. Bonello. 2001. The citizen police academy: Measuring outcomes. *Police Quarterly* 4: 434–48.

CIVIL RESTRAINT IN POLICING

In a democratic society, everyone is constitutionally equal; police officers are not above the law and may find themselves in the midst of civil litigation. An average-size lawsuit against a large department, with deep pockets, can be monetarily devastating to the department and the community it serves. In some civil cases, jury awards exceed $30 million. When you calculate jury awards and out-of-court settlements in police liability cases, the sum may reach hundreds of millions annually.

Consider the following hypothetical scenario: Two police officers drink coffee to stay awake while working the midnight shift. A red sports car unexpectedly appears and speeds past their location at approximately one hundred miles an hour. The officers, in full pursuit, follow the reckless driver. Without warning, the driver attempts to navigate a bridge, goes airborne, and spins out of control in the intersection. The officers repeat the same misfortune; however, they strike a pedestrian, and immediately stop to render aid. The speeding sports car pursuit continues, involving several jurisdictions and approximately twenty police cars.

Suddenly, the driver navigates several bootleg turns and drives in the direction of the pursuing police cars. The officers quickly divide to avoid impact, turn around, and pursue the driver once again. The officers engage the sports car in pursuit for over an hour. Finally, the operator abandons the vehicle and tries to run on foot. One officer pursues on foot at the location where he is likely to pass. The officer catches the offender by surprise as he turns the corner of a building and runs directly in his path.

There are three general types of torts against police officers: (1) negligence torts, (2) intentional torts, and (3) constitutional torts. The officers learn later that morning that the pedestrian at the intersection died of multiple injuries; that is a negligence tort. After being transferred to another jurisdiction, several police officers assault the handcuffed sports car driver. The assault represents an intentional tort, in this case, assault and battery. The emotionally drained officers neglect to advise the violator of his right to remain silent and legal counsel, which is a constitutional tort.

This police pursuit scenario characterizes the most frequent types of lawsuits against law enforcement agencies. Officers who operate police vehicles in violation of their department's policies or state law or who place others in danger may find themselves subject to lawsuits. High-liability behaviors typically involve reckless or negligent operation of a police vehicle. The courts may consider strict liability, that is, acts used by the courts to infer

intent or omit state of mind considerations. For example, the officer failed to use flashers and sirens, or did not consider alternatives to vehicle pursuit. Moreover, the officer's failure to consider traffic control devices can fall under strict liability. In strict liability cases, the court focuses on proving the act, that is, not stopping to assist innocent injured bystanders. Moreover, suits may surface in cases where officers follow correct protocols.

Civil Restraint: Lawsuits

Numerous options are available for citizens to sue law enforcement officers and their agencies. A lawsuit may be filed in state court as a tort claim against local or regional governments. Local governments offer an excellent means for financial return, because their tort settlements present more opportunities beyond addressing constitutional issues. Many opportunities exist to sue police officers and their agencies, including arrest, indifference to training and supervision requirements, abuse of authority, and use of force. Some suits may involve civil rights issues, directed at changing the way agencies treat minorities and women. A related lawsuit may be filed in federal court as a violation of Title 42 of the United States Code, Section 1983:

> Every person who, under color of any statute, ordinance, regulation, custom, or usage of any State or Territory, subjects, or causes to be subjected, any citizen of the United States or any other person within the jurisdiction thereof to the deprivation of any rights, privileges, or immunities secured by the Constitution and laws, shall be liable to the party injured in an action at law, suit in equity, or other proper proceeding for redress....

Section 1983 requires due process of law, protects life, liberty, or property, and provides redress for the violation of one's constitutional rights by officials acting under "color of law." State municipalities, regional governments, and sheriffs are vulnerable if (1) acting under color of state law and (2) violating the U.S. Constitution.

Under Color of Law Requirement

"Under color of law" means that a police officer is acting or actually carrying out his or her official duties or acting in a manner that makes it seem appropriate according to the law. Off-duty officers are liable while working in security positions, because they are acting "under color of law" while performing a police/security function, for example, arresting shoplifters or enforcing state law. An off-duty police officer identifying him- or herself as a police officer is acting under "color of law." There are numerous situations in which police officers are working for what appears to be a private corporation. They may come under the authority of the "color of law" in that private capacity and meet the criteria for violating a citizen's constitutional rights. Opportunities for "conflicts of interest" for police officers acting in a double capacity are considerable.

Constitutional Rights Violations

Provisions under the U.S. Constitution and Bill of Rights, including the first ten amendments, are primary areas of concerns. Freedom from unreasonable searches and seizures, a Fourth Amendment violation, is frequently cited in Section 1983 suits. In addition, citizens have a right to assistance of counsel under the Sixth Amendment, another frequent violation. Moreover, the Bill of Rights is applicable to the states and provides freedom from deprivations of life, liberty, or property without due process and equal protection under the Fourteenth Amendment to the U.S. Constitution.

Bivens Actions: Federal Agents

In the case of *Bivens v. Six Unknown Federal Agents,* 456 F.2d 1339 (1972), the precedent for civil legal remedies for agents who abuse the constitutional rights of citizens is noted. The decision reaffirmed the importance of constitutional rights and Section 1983. The plaintiff alleged that agents of the Federal Bureau of Narcotics acting under the "color of law" entered the plaintiff's apartment without probable cause. He was humiliated and handcuffed in front of his wife and children during the illegal search. The agents threatened to arrest the entire family, causing fear and alarm.

The plaintiff was then transported to the courthouse. He was immediately subjected to a visual strip search and interrogated. The petitioner sued in Federal District Court. In addition to the allegations above, his complaint asserted that the arrest and search were without a warrant, and claimed officers used unreasonable force while making the arrest. The plaintiff cited great humiliation, embarrassment, and mental suffering because of the agents' unlawful conduct.

The U.S. Supreme Court held that a citizen could sue federal agents for financial damages. Citizens have U.S. Constitutional and Bill of Rights protections. In the *Bivens'* case, the Fourth Amendment prevailed, not the agents. Citizens have the right to sue federal agents.

State Court: Civil Restraints

If the plaintiff does not prevail in federal court, he or she may seek remedies under state law. Moreover, the standard of proof is only a "preponderance of the evidence," a standard much lower than a "reasonable doubt" standard in criminal cases. There are three types of torts under state law, each with different levels of proof:

1. *Strict liability* means the injury or damage is severe and it is reasonably certain that the harm could have been foreseen. The law dispenses with the need to prove intent or mental state, for example, excessive force in tactical operations.
2. *Intentional torts* mean that the officer's intent must be proven, using a foreseeability test. This test determines whether the officer knowingly engaged in behavior that was substantially certain to bring about injury, for example, in wrongful death cases. It must be proven that the officer wanted to severely injure or cause death.
3. In *negligence cases*, intent or mental state does not matter. What matters is whether some inadvertent act or failure to act created an unreasonable risk to citizens, for example, speeding resulting in a traffic accident, while not responding to an emergency.

Civil Restraints: Defenses to Liability

1. *Contributory negligence:* The government may prove that the plaintiff contributed to his or her own injury or damage.
2. *Qualified immunity doctrine:* Protects public officials and government agents from undue interference with their duties.
3. A reasonable belief that probable cause exists and the police officer is entitled to immunity.

There are many other defenses, including good faith exceptions.

In Summary

There are many civil constraints on law enforcement officers' behaviors. Civil tort actions seek remedies for the plaintiff against the police officer, supervisors, and department. The injured person brings the tort civil action before the court. Generally, the plaintiff is seeking money damages from the defendant(s). Police officers and their departments often have scarce financial resources; the real targets are the law enforcement agencies and taxpayers. In the future, lawsuits will likely increase. Solutions to this legal quagmire will evolve from better trained and educated officers; eventually, the cost of civil litigation will improve.

THOMAS E. BAKER

See also **Arrest Powers of the Police; Complaints against Police; Deadly Force; Liability and the Use of Force; Traffic Services and Management**

References and Further Reading

Del Carmen, Rolando. 1991. *Civil liabilities in American policing.* Upper Saddle River, NJ: Prentice-Hall.

Kappeler, V. 2001a. *Critical issues in police civil liability.* Prospect Heights, IL: Waveland Press.

———. 2001b. *Police civil liability: Supreme Court cases and materials.* Prospect Heights, IL: Waveland Press.

CIVILIAN REVIEW BOARDS

During the 1970s, civilian review boards (CRBs) were thought to provide a means to control police misconduct. In effect, CRBs permitted an appointed group of outsiders (nonpolice) to judge—exonerate or condemn—officers suspected of wrongdoing. The public credo was that police would not police themselves. Therefore, an autonomous body of adjudicators given the power to decide misconduct cases appeared to be the answer. More and Wegener (1990) state that the CRB concept began to flourish in the late 1950s. Most likely, the concept of citizen or civilian review of police antedated that time period. The reason for assigning an earlier date is because the impetus for CRBs is usually a flagrant, or even a shocking, instance of police misconduct. Long before the 1950s victimized and/or enraged citizens would have demanded a say in police matters and exerted pressure in some way.

If a police officer issues such orders to a percolating crowd as "Move on" or "Break it up," citizens complain. If a police officer is not completely respectful of everyone involved, citizens complain. If a police officer appears to engage in discriminatory enforcement of minor laws and ordinances—causing citizens to cry "Why me?"—citizens complain. Because these examples of perceived abuses of power are somewhat daily occurrences, any CRB would have its hands full hearing all citizen complaints. For that matter, any police internal affairs department would be so handcuffed by the same looping complaints as to be ineffective. More officers would sit in line for review than would be out on the streets to protect the public from itself. For a CRB to be responsible, it would have to concentrate on real wrongdoers, what used to be called "crooked cops." But even that mandate is dubious because an officer suspected of committing a felony should go to regular court, not to a citizens' review board.

In the mid-1970s a survey conducted by the National Opinion Research Center found that 45% of the respondents favored CRBs, 35% opposed them, and the remaining 20% were undecided. The less-than-half in favor is perplexing. During the late 1960s and into the early 1970s, police seemed to be barbarians. The televised mayhem in Chicago at the 1968 Democratic Convention and the Kent State killings did nothing to uplift law enforcement's image. If at any point in recent history CRBs could have gained a foothold, the mid-1970s should have been optimal. Unified police resistance to CRBs and a good deal of persuasive talk, however, curtailed the movement. In an article written for *Police Chief* (1977), Gary F. Stowell posed the critical question:

> Reaction to a CRB in police circles is clear: Almost any decision made by a police officer in a crisis situation could conceivably leave him open to charges before a CRB. How could a civilian sit in judgment on a police officer's actions any more than he could sit in judgment on a doctor's actions in an operating room?

New York Police Commissioner Vincent Brodrick added another dimension: "It is vital that when a police officer's action is reviewed, it be reviewed by one who has the capacity to evaluate the propriety of the action, but also to its complement, the propriety in the same situation with the officer having failed to take the action." FBI Director J. Edgar Hoover had long before made his opinion known. CRBs "undermine the morale and sap the efficiency of the police. They deter officers in the proper performance of their duties for fear of having charges placed against them, which will be judged by individuals wholly unfamiliar with police work." Also a decade earlier, Chief O. W. Wilson had warned, "A review board in this city would destroy discipline in the Chicago Police Department. If we would have a civilian review board, it would create a situation where I, as the head of the police department, would be confronted by an adversary group, which the entire department would tend to unite against." On-and-off the record most police alluded to CRBs as witch hunts of benefit to no one.

The Hartford Study

The Hartford Institute of Criminal and Social Justice published an influential study in 1980 entitled "Civilian Review of the Police—The Experiences of American Cities." The institute prepared the study in response to a proposal by the Hartford, Connecticut, City Council to establish a civilian review board. A shocking incident confirmed the council's resolve. In February 1980 the council endorsed the concept of a CRB. But in March after Guy Brown, who turned out to be innocent, was shot by a Hartford police officer, public outcry forced the council to act on its endorsement. On October 17 the council passed an amendment calling for the immediate creation of a permanent civilian review board. To advise the council of what to do next, the institute surveyed literature on the topic and conducted interviews to determine how other municipalities set up their CRBs and with what success.

In all, the institute was able to collect information in detail from seven cities and on a limited basis from several more. The cities surveyed, the type of review board, and the date established were as follows:

1. *Chicago, Illinois:* Office of Professional Standards; physically within the police department but separate from the Internal Affairs Division; operated by three civilian administrators appointed by the superintendent of police; one black, one white, one Hispanic—all lawyers. Started in 1974.
2. *Detroit, Michigan:* Board of Police Commissioners; administered by the Office of the Chief Investigator; composed of five civilians appointed by the mayor with the approval of the city council; minority representation, including one woman. Started in 1974.
3. *Kansas City, Missouri:* Office of Citizen Complaints; five-person civilian staff appointed by the Board of Police Commissioners. Started in 1970.
4. *Memphis, Tennessee:* Police Advisory Commission; composed of no more than eighteen and no less than ten civilian members; appointed annually by the director of police and the mayor from a list of candidates provided by the commission; commission members represented both extremes, for and against police. Started in 1977.
5. *New York City, New York:* Civilian Complaint Review Board; located within the police department with seven members: three police appointed by the police commissioner and four community representatives assigned by the mayor; ethnic mixture. 1953 forward—police members only; after 1966—addition of civilians.
6. *Oakland, California:* Citizens Complaint Board; mayor appoints seven citizens to one-year terms subject to approval by the city council; cross section of the community. Started in 1980.
7. *Philadelphia, Pennsylvania:* Police Advisory Board; five, then eight civilian members appointed by the mayor with no fixed length of term; cross section of the community with two retired police officers to add balance. 1958–1969.
8. *Baltimore, Maryland:* Complaint Evaluation Board; unstated membership, all were government employees or elected officials with one active police officer as member. Started around 1965.
9. *Miami, Florida:* Office of Professional Compliance; four members with a director appointed by the city manager and the police chief. Started in 1980.
10. *Minneapolis, Minnesota:* Minneapolis Civil Rights Commission; unstated membership staffed by the city council; short lived due in part to the commission subpoenaing the president of the city council. 1965.
11. *Rochester, New York:* Civilian Review Board; nine members

appointed by the city manager; disbanded when no longer funded. 1963–1971.

12. *Washington, D.C.:* Civilian Review Board; seven members including two attorneys, how appointed not stated. 1948–1965; in 1965 completely restructured, then oddly disbanded the same year; reproposed in 1980.

13. *York, Pennsylvania:* Police Review Board; city council appointed five York residents to act as a board and also to advise the mayor and other officials about police "oppressiveness." 1960–1962.

The civilian review boards also differed in the amount of authority granted them. Some of the boards had investigatory power and could issue subpoenas, while others subsisted as advisory only. Another prominent fact from the institute's study is that either the boards were adversarial beyond normal expectations, or suspiciously agreed in nearly every instance with the police review. In conclusion, the institute listed arguments for and against CRBs.

In Favor:

- CRBs are a means to create more effective relationships with the public.
- Courts cannot handle every legitimate complaint leveled at police.
- Civilians are traditionally less strict in reviewing police misconduct.
- An officer exonerated by a CRB is less likely to be thought of as having been white-washed.
- CRBs are useful as public relations vehicles.
- Police have too much discretion in carrying out their duties and must be watched.
- CRBs are a safety valve for both police and citizens to get at the facts.
- CRBs increase respect for the law when reviews are handled promptly.

- CRBs increase public confidence in police departments by demonstrating police agreement to undergo civilian review.
- CRBs often aid in dispelling the belief that police are brutal and arbitrary.
- Police appear less isolated and more accountable.
- CRBs deter misconduct before it happens because police fear public review.
- Citizens want some form of settlement (an apology) even if the complaint does not merit court action.
- Police cannot deal fairly with complaints against their fellow officers.

Against:

- Only police know their business.
- Internal, not external, review places the responsibility for handling misconduct with those who best know how to cure it.
- CRBs destroy morale.
- CRBs are redundant to police review.
- Other adequate means are available to citizens with legitimate complaints, for example, the courts.
- Every profession should have the right to discipline itself.
- Criminals or anyone can harass police to get them in trouble.
- CRBs are unlawful; the police powers of a city cannot be delegated.
- CRBs fail to provide for procedural safeguards, for example, rules of evidence, protection against double jeopardy, and so on.
- CRBs entertain minor to frivolous complaints.
- CRBs by their very existence continue to polarize police and citizens.
- The history of CRBs is lackluster.
- Emotional catharsis takes place more often than dispassionate inquiry.

- Police job security hangs in the balance.
- Police are less efficient, knowing the CRB can call them in for anything.

Of the reasons for and against, the third "for" reason—civilians are traditionally less strict in reviewing police misconduct—stands out. If true, logic dictates the reason should be in the "against" list. The whole rationale behind civilian review is to convene a group of citizens who will do a better job of reviewing police misconduct (more punitive) than the supposed buddy system does in the department. If police are harder on themselves than the public would be, then why involve citizens at all? This reason alone does much to defeat the CRB concept.

Current Accountability

Even though civilian review boards have not worked out well, the need for greater accountability external to police control is still a burning issue. The Rodney King beating incident in Los Angeles fueled the debate. Other King-type cases occur with regularity, whether the police are at fault or not. Any show of force by police usually guarantees citizen backlash and a cry for investigation—if not the head(s) of the officer(s) involved. Because an alert citizen videotaped Rodney King being beaten or subdued, depending on individual perception, no one could deny it happened exactly as filmed. The shock value of the incident and the lawless aftermath reinvigorated discussion of civilian review boards and other accountability mechanisms. The ombudsman or "citizen advocate" is one such control. As a government official, the ombudsman investigates abuse and/or misconduct in the police department and elsewhere throughout city government. He or she is a grievance commissioner who chooses which complaints to investigate. With such a broad jurisdiction, the ombudsman oversees a general complaint office, not focusing on any single department. Therefore, police do not feel they are the only ones under scrutiny. The Hartford study credited a number of cities with adopting the ombudsman concept, though it could not obtain enough information from those cities to clarify types of operation.

A second external control combines the civilian review board with the office of ombudsman. Independent review panels, as they are called, investigate public complaints directed at any city department and/or employee. Thus all city employees, not just police, are held accountable for their actions. Naturally, many police officers and public employee unions dislike the panels and will resist them. Until one or both of these controls achieves success or a better concept arises, internal discipline administered by police to police will continue to suffice.

WILLIAM G. BAILEY

See also **Accountability; Complaints against Police**

References and Further Reading

Barton, Peter G. 1970. Civilian review boards and the handling of complaints against the police. *University of Toronto Law Journal* 20: 448–69.

Brent, David J. 1977. Redress of alleged police misconduct: A new approach to citizen complaints and police disciplinary procedures. *University of San Francisco Law Review* 11 (Summer): 587–621.

Broadaway, Fred M. 1974. Police misconduct: Positive alternatives. *Journal of Police Science and Administration* 2 (June): 210–18.

Carrow, Milton M. 1969. Mechanisms for the redress of grievances against the government. *Administrative Law Review* 22: 1–37.

Hartford Institute of Criminal and Social Justice. 1980. Civilian review of the police—The experiences of American cities. Hartford, CT: Hartford Institute of Criminal and Social Justice.

Hudson, James R. 1971. Police review boards and police accountability. *Law and Contemporary Problems* 36 (Fall): 515–38.

Lenzi, Margaret A. 1974. Reviewing civilian complaints of police misconduct—Some answers and more questions. *Temple Law Quarterly* 48 (Fall): 89–125.

More, Harry W., and W. Fred Wegener. 1990. Effective police supervision. Cincinnati, OH: Anderson Publishing Company.

Olson, Robert W. 1969. Grievance response mechanisms for police misconduct. *Virginia Law Review* 55 (June): 909–51.

Stowell, Gary F. 1977. Civilian review boards. *Police Chief* 44 (April): 63–65.

Yeager, Matthew G., and William P. Brown. 1978. Police professionalism and corruption control. *Journal of Police Science and Administration* 6 (Sept.): 273–82.

CLEARANCE RATES AND CRIMINAL INVESTIGATIONS

The work of investigators has been the subject of various empirical studies seeking to provide systematic evidence regarding their practices (for example, Greenwood 1970; Bloch and Bell 1976; Greenwood, Chaiken, and Petersilia 1977; Waegel 1981; Eck 1992; Horvath, Meesig, and Lee 2001). These studies have debunked the mythical portrayals of "super-sleuths" who can solve any crime through careful investigation. In contrast, research shows that most crimes go unsolved and that investigators perform a wide variety of tasks not directly related to this outcome.

Additionally, a number of studies have considered the effectiveness of investigations (for example, Isaacs 1967; Cordner 1989; Eck 1992; Davenport 1999; Wellford and Cronin 2000). Various measures have been used to assess effectiveness, including victim/citizen satisfaction and prosecution results. However, the one most commonly employed is the clearance rate.

The clearance rate is used as a measure for a variety of reasons. Most importantly, it provides direct assessment of the goal of "crime management"—dealing with crime that has occurred and is reported (Wycoff 1982). This measure also reflects the internal goals of police departments and investigators. As such, this measure is highly valued by practitioners (Horvath, Meesig, and Lee 2001; Davenport 1999). Furthermore, clearance data has been systematically collected through the *Uniform Crime Reports* (UCR), permitting long-term trend analysis. Virtually every other source of data restricts researchers to cross-sectional analyses.

Defining Clearances

The terminology and requirements for clearing crimes are derived from the guidelines of the UCR program. Clearing a crime occurs in two ways. Most commonly, a crime is cleared by the arrest of one or more suspects. This may occur with or without a warrant. By UCR guidelines, this requires that the arrestee(s) be "charged with the commission of an offense and turned over to the court for prosecution" (Federal Bureau of Investigation 2004, 255). Alternatively, a crime may be "exceptionally cleared" when sufficient evidence exists to justify an arrest and prosecution, but the agency is prevented from making the arrest due to circumstances beyond its control. The guidelines require that the exact location of the suspect be known in order to clear a crime by exceptional means.

Clearance statistics are gathered and reported to the FBI regarding the eight Part I offenses: murder and non-negligent manslaughter, rape, robbery, aggravated assault, burglary, larceny, auto theft, and arson. The clearance rate is calculated as the percentage of Part I index crimes reported as cleared by arrest or exceptional means.

Clearance rates are highest for violent crimes (murder, rape, robbery, and aggravated assault). Since 1971, an average of 46.1% of violent crimes have been cleared annually. In contrast, clearance rates for property crimes (burglary, larceny-theft, auto theft, and arson) have averaged 17.5% during that same time period (data drawn from UCR annual reports).

Problems Using Clearance Rates to Examine Performance

Despite the apparent utility of clearance data for measuring investigative effectiveness, the measure is not without its problems. Greenwood, Chaiken, and Petersilia (1977) argued that variations in defining and recording clearances by individual agencies make the clearance rate an inappropriate measure for comparing investigative effectiveness of agencies. Additionally, Sherman and Glick (1984) found that agencies operationally define arrests in various ways, further undermining the reliability of clearance data to examine investigative performance.

In contrast to Greenwood, Chaiken, and Petersilia (1977), Davenport (1999) found that police departments strictly adhered to the UCR coding guidelines for recording clearances. These agencies also indicated that their reporting and coding practices had not changed over time. Thus, it is not clear that interagency variations are necessarily widespread or that they preclude using the data for cross-sectional analyses.

An alternative concern revolves around the potential for agencies to distort their clearance data to reflect either more or less crime solved. It is possible that politically motivated police administrators might manipulate data to secure more funding or improve the appearance of organizational success. However, the concern regarding distortion is more generally applied to reported crime, rather than solved crime, and there is no systematic evidence that it occurs.

Factors Affecting Clearance Rates

Because of the importance of solving crime, researchers have sought to identify the factors that influence clearance rates. Generally speaking, studies focus on environmental factors (underlying community characteristics), contextual factors (event-specific circumstances), and investigative factors (effort and resources).

Because policing occurs in a community context, the characteristics of that environment will have important effects on police performance. Pogue (1975) looked at aggregated clearance rates for metropolitan areas and found that population density had a significant, negative effect. Upon examining clearance data for Part I offenses from a group of Maryland police departments, Cordner (1989) found that geographic region explained most of the variation. Further examination revealed that agencies outside the Washington or Baltimore metropolitan areas had statistically significantly higher clearance rates.

Davenport (1999) used environmental characteristics to analyze Texas clearance data. He found that community complexity and turbulence had modest but significant effects on clearance rates. Both violent and property crime clearance rates were lower where complexity was higher, while turbulence negatively affected property clearance rates. While such factors have only indirect effects on police performance, they clearly constrain the ability of agencies to significantly improve clearance rates.

In the landmark RAND Corporation study, Greenwood, Chaiken, and Petersilia (1977) examined the effects of investigative effort (amount of time spent) on clearance rates. They found that only about 3% of clearances were due to the work of investigators; the vast majority were cleared based on arrests made by patrol officers at the scene or through positive identification of the suspects at the time of occurrence. Thus, they argued that there is no evidence that investigative activities have any substantial effect on clearances. Instead, clearance rates are primarily a function of the circumstances present at the time of the event.

These findings supported the prior research of Isaacs (1967) and Greenwood

(1970). Isaacs reviewed a group of case files from the Los Angeles Police Department and found that only 8% of the arrests were due to the activities of detectives. Far more likely was an arrest based on the victim naming the suspect in the initial report. Greenwood considered burglary, robbery, and grand larceny cases in New York City. His research indicated that only 2% of the arrests resulted from investigative follow-up. Most frequently, arrests occurred when a suspect was named by the victim.

However, additional studies have suggested that the relationship between investigative effort and clearances is more complex. Eck (1992) reviewed burglary and robbery cases in three jurisdictions, distinguishing between the information derived from the preliminary investigation and information obtained during the follow-up investigation. Eck hypothesized that if circumstances predicted outcomes, then follow-up activities would not have a significant effect. However, Eck found that both preliminary and follow-up investigatory actions were significant. To further explain these findings, Eck (1992, 103) proposed a "triage hypothesis," whereby investigators sort cases based on the strength of preliminary information (solvability factors). Those cases that cannot be solved with reasonable effort receive less activity, as do those cases that have already been solved by circumstances. However, cases that may be solved with reasonable effort (but would not be solved otherwise) receive the most effort. This explanation relies on circumstances for identifying which cases would most likely benefit from activity, but affirms the relative importance of investigative effort for clearing crime.

Further support was provided by Brandl and Frank (1994). They examined burglary and robbery cases for a medium-sized municipal police department and compared the relative effects of two factors: the strength of suspect information emerging from the preliminary investigation and the amount of time spent on the follow-up investigation. For both robberies and burglaries, time spent on cases with moderate suspect information significantly increased the probability of an arrest.

Studies have also focused on clearance rates for homicide, due to the dramatic nature of the crime and the public attention the events receive. Wellford and Cronin (1999) found that various factors, including investigative effort, are important in clearing these crimes. Wellford and Cronin examined more than two hundred factors in 798 homicide investigations from four large municipal police departments. Several case characteristics were significant predictors of clearance status, including factors regarding the victim, the suspect, and general crime circumstances. Detective and investigative variables that influenced clearance status include the number of detectives assigned to the case, time taken to arrive at the scene, and following up on witness information. Consistent with other research, Wellford and Cronin found that information provided by witnesses at the scene has a significant impact on clearance status.

Overall, research has consistently pointed to the importance of witness identifications and cooperation for clearing cases. Though the RAND study (Greenwood, Chaiken, and Petersilia 1977) largely dismissed the role of follow-up investigations, additional research has demonstrated that focused efforts on selected cases produce successful outcomes. It is also clear that careful work at the crime scene (by investigators and responding patrol officers) increases the likelihood of solving crime. Thus, clearance rates are not simply the by-product of circumstances, but are constrained by them in many ways. Investigative effectiveness can be improved, but only within limits created by the context of the criminal event.

DOUGLAS DAVENPORT

See also **Case Screening and Case Management for Investigations; Criminal Investigation; Homicide and Its Investigation; Investigation Outcomes; Managing Criminal Investigations**

References and Further Reading

Bloch, Peter, and James Bell. 1976. *Managing investigations: The Rochester system.* Washington, DC: Police Foundation.

Brandl, Steven, and James Frank. 1994. The relationship between evidence, detective effort, and the disposition of burglary and robbery investigations. *American Journal of Police* 13:149–68.

Cordner, Gary. 1989. Police agency size and investigative effectiveness. *Journal of Criminal Justice* 17:145–55.

Davenport, Douglas. 1999. Environmental constraints and organizational outcomes: Modeling communities of municipal police departments. *Police Quarterly* 2:174–200.

Eck, John. 1992. *Solving crimes: The investigation of burglary and robbery.* Washington, DC: Police Executive Research Foundation.

Federal Bureau of Investigation. 2004. *Crime in the United States.* Washington, DC: U.S. Government Printing Office.

Greenwood, Peter. 1970. *An analysis of the apprehension activities of the New York City Police Department.* New York: RAND Corporation.

Greenwood, Peter, Jan Chaiken, and Joan Petersilia. 1977. *The criminal investigation process.* Lexington, MA: Heath.

Horvath, Frank, Robert T. Meesig, and Yung Hyeock Lee. 2001. National survey of police policies and practices regarding the criminal investigations process: Twenty-five years after RAND. East Lansing: Michigan State University.

Isaacs, Herbert H. 1967. A study of communications, crimes and arrests in a metropolitan police department. Appendix B in the President's Commission on Law Enforcement and Administration of Justice. In *Task force report: Science and technology.* Washington, DC: Government Printing Office.

Sherman, Lawrence and Barry Glick. 1984. *The quality of police arrest statistics.* Washington, DC: Police Foundation.

Simms, B., and E. Petersen. 1989. The economics of criminal investigation in a municipal police force. *Journal of Criminal Justice* 17:199–224.

Waegel, William. 1981. Case routinization of investigative police work. *Social Problems* 28: 263–75.

Wellford, Charles, and James Cronin. 1999. *An analysis of variables affecting the clearance of homicides: A multistate study.* October. Washington, DC: Justice Research and Statistics Association.

Wycoff, Mary Ann. 1982. Evaluating the crime-effectiveness of municipal police. In *Managing police work: Issues and analysis,* ed. Jack R. Greene. Beverly Hills, CA: Sage.

CLOSED-CIRCUIT TELEVISION APPLICATIONS FOR POLICING

Although it is common to talk about closed-circuit television (CCTV) as if there were just one type, nothing could be further from the truth; indeed, it is doubtful whether any two systems or schemes are ever the same. For example, the technical specifications of cameras differ markedly, so they vary considerably in terms of what and how much they can "see" and how reliable they are. Also, the process of transmitting images from a camera to a place where they can be viewed and analyzed affects the quality of the images, and there are a variety of ways to do the analysis. Then there is the ability of the operators—those who watch the screens and act on what they see. They have vastly different skill levels and commitment to the job; and the quality of management of both the equipment and the people involved varies.

The different types of cameras have different capabilities. Redeployable cameras move around a location and can be positioned at hotspots. The term *mobile cameras* usually refers to those that are located in vehicles. Then there are cameras that are static in one location, although some of these may "pan, tilt and zoom" or rotate 360 degrees and so on. This is by no means an exhaustive list of all the features of CCTVs, but it does indicate reasons why CCTV systems are unlikely to be the same and why the police, like anyone else, need to be wary of a casual approach to supporting or denigrating CCTV systems (see, for example, Gill 2006; Gill and Spriggs 2005; Nieto 1997; Nieto, Johnston-Dodds, and Simmons 2002; Pierce 2002).

In discussing CCTV, therefore, one has to be aware of these differences. Unfortunately, studies of CCTV have not always been explicit about the characteristics of the schemes in question and this complicates comparisons. Nevertheless, there is now a rich body of research that offers important insights and this has helped us to understand how CCTV can be used. This is especially the case in Europe where some countries—the United Kingdom being a case in point—have embraced CCTV wholeheartedly such that CCTV is commonplace in workplaces, public areas including nearly all city centers and most town centers, and many residential streets. Therefore, although privacy issues loom large in concerns about the use of CCTV (see, for example, Davies 1998; Goold 2004; McCahill 2002; McCahill, and Norris 2003; Norris and Armstrong 1999), this does not amount to a collective view that it is a bad thing. Most evidence suggests the public likes cameras, and the speed with which the police issued pictures of those suspected of the Summer 2005 London transit bombings appears to have reminded the public in the United Kingdome of their value. But just how effective is CCTV, and how useful is it to the police?

The Effectiveness of CCTV

The research evidence on the effectiveness of CCTV produces mixed findings. Of course, one has to be careful about what is meant by "effectiveness." There are a variety of ways of measuring effectiveness. The most commonly used is that of impact on crime rates, something with which the police would clearly identify. However, one review that assessed the most scientifically rigorous studies found that CCTV was wanting in this respect (Welsh and Farrington 2002). It concluded that CCTV did have some impact on crime rates in some American apartment blocks and when implemented alongside other measures in car parks, but overall supporters of CCTV had little to be positive about.

But there are many other measures of CCTV as a variety of studies have shown (Gill and Turbin 1999; Tilley 1993) and as the police have discovered over time. For example, CCTV can make people feel safer and can be used to manage crowds and (controversially) to monitor staff. Its images can be used to track suspects, and this may help deter offenders because they fear they will be caught. These are but a few examples; the real question is, do they work?

Recently a major study of CCTV, sponsored by the British Home Office, reported its findings (Gill and Spriggs 2005) and they were instructive. For example, of the thirteen project areas studied, six showed a reduction in overall crime relative to the surrounding area, but in only one of these could the reduction be confidently attributed to CCTV, and that project was a car park scheme focused on reducing vehicle-related crime. There were a number of successes across the schemes although few distinct trends were apparent. In general, alcohol-related offenses were less likely to be reduced than theft and other premeditated offenses.

In general, fear of crime was found to be reduced after the implementation of CCTV yet rarely at a rate greater than experienced in each project's respective control area (that is, in a comparison area that did not have CCTV). Generally, public support for CCTV decreased after the public had experience with it, mainly because members of the public became more realistic about what it could do. For example, the number of individuals who believed CCTV would lower crime went down substantially postimplementation. For the most part, good studies of CCTV have painted a somewhat less than favorable impression of its effectiveness.

But examining why such a mixed bag of results occurs gives clues, and important ones, as to how CCTV may be used in the future. The truth about CCTV is that it is quite a complex measure, there is a lot to get right, and it is a relatively new measure and one about which there is very little information. Many of those who have used CCTV have done so with little experience and little guidance, and this has certainly contributed to disappointing results (Gill and Spriggs 2005). However, as a knowledge base grows, so does the opportunity to influence improved performance.

Policing and CCTV: The Future

Although the police at a strategic level have long endorsed CCTV in the fight against crime, at lower levels they have experienced problems. Offenders who have been interviewed about CCTV have tended to play down its effectiveness, because they can wear disguises, because all too often no one is looking at the screens, and most importantly because the images are not of a sufficient quality to support a prosecution of them (Gill and Loveday 2003). Of course, where the image is good, it is a good friend of the police, but often images are not that good. There is another problem, there are so many images—many cameras generate images 24/7—that to both assess them all and respond to each incident would be impossible. The police have to prioritize, and this can cause disquiet. Certainly some British residents were disappointed that CCTV had not marshaled a police response more often, and this in part led some to lessening of their support for it (Gill and Spriggs 2005).

In a different way, the police are still learning to trust CCTV. They have certainly been skeptical about the quality of operators, and some police just don't trust them. Remember also that the police perform a range of duties in public space, and these can now be monitored. Every decision police officers make can be scrutinized in detail in court later. This can work both ways: It can protect the police, but it can also magnify their errors.

CCTV in Perspective

Whole books have now been written about CCTV, and in this short article it has been possible to discuss just a few issues about its use in policing. What is clear is that CCTV is a valuable tool with enormous potential to assist good policing and highlight poor practice. But there are a few things that need to be underlined. First, it is a technical measure and technology is moving fast; its usefulness is likely to be enhanced along the way, but there is a need to keep abreast with developments in technology. Second, although a technical solution, CCTV needs people to help make it work, and those people need special preparation to act as operators. Third, CCTV is complex to use, there is a lot to do to get it right, and the police and society generally are only just beginning to understand how to use it for the best. So while there are advocates of CCTV who herald it as the silver bullet in the fight against crime, in truth, it is still maturing and we have to do a lot more to integrate it into mainstream policing if its full potential is ever to be realized.

Martin Gill

See also **Crime Prevention; Surveillance; Technology and the Police; Video Technology in Policing**

References and Further Reading

Davies, S. 1998. *Big brother: Britain's web of surveillance and the new technological order.* London: Pan Books.

Gill, M. 2006 CCTV: Is it effective? In *The handbook of security*, ed. M. Gill. London: Palgrave, MacMillan.

Gill, M., and K. Loveday. 2003. What do offenders think about CCTV? In *CCTV*, ed. M. Gill. Leicester: Perpetuity Press.

Gill, M., and A. Spriggs. 2005. *Assessing the impact of CCTV*. Home Office Research Study No. 292. London: Home Office. http://www.homeoffice.gov.uk/rds/pdfs05/hors292.pdf.

Gill, M., and V. Turbin. 1999. Evaluating "realistic evaluation": Evidence from a study of CCTV. In *Surveillance of public space: CCTV, street lighting and crime prevention*, ed. K. Painter and N. Tilley. Vol. 10 of *Crime prevention studies*. Monsey, NY: Criminal Justice Press.

Goold, B. J. 2004. *CCTV and policing: Public area surveillance and police practices in Britain*. Oxford: Oxford University Press.

McCahill, M. 2002. *The surveillance web: The rise of visual surveillance in an English city*. Collumpton: Willan.

McCahill, M., and C. Norris. 2003. *Four CCTV systems in London*. UrbanEye Working Paper No. 10. http://www.urbaneye.net/results/ue_wp10.pdf.

Nieto, M. 1997. *Public video surveillance: Is it an effective crime prevention tool?* Sacramento: California Research Bureau, California State Library.

Nieto, M., K. Johnston-Dodds, and C. Simmons. 2002. *Public and private applications of video surveillance and biometric technologies*. Sacramento: California Research Bureau. http://www.library.ca.gov/crb/02/06/02-006.pdf.

Norris, C., and G. Armstrong. 1999. *The maximum surveillence society: The rise of closed circuit television*. Oxford: Berg.

Pierce, C. 2002. *The professional's guide to CCTV*. Boston: Butterworth-Heinemann.

Welsh, B., and D. Farrington. 2002. *Crime prevention effects of closed circuit television: A systematic review*. Home Office Research Study No. 252. London: Home Office.

CODES OF ETHICS

In 1957, the International Association of Chiefs of Police (IACP) adopted a document entitled *Law Enforcement Code of Ethics*. Except for the 1956 California code on which it was modeled, this IACP document seems to have been the first "code of ethics" for police. Behind the IACP code lay a century-and-a-half of police "rules and regulations," "oaths," "pledges," "guiding principles," and other documents containing similar provisions (as well as an even longer line of "codes" in other professions, the earliest in medicine). Among the more important of police codes today are the Interpol Code of Conduct for Law Enforcement Officers, the U.S. Military Police Code of Ethics, the United Nations Code of Conduct for Law Enforcement Officers, and the current IACP Code (adopted in 1989).

Names and Kinds

Attempts have been made to distinguish between short, general, or uncontroversial codes ("code of ethics") and longer, more detailed, or more controversial ones ("code of conduct," "guidelines," and so on). While some such distinction may sometimes be useful in practice (as in the Interpol code), it is hard to defend in theory. A "code of conduct" is as much a special standard of conduct as a "code of ethics"—except where the "code of ethics," being a mere restatement of morality, is just "a moral code." "Codes of conduct" are also (generally) as morally binding as "codes of ethics."

Whatever it is called, a code of police ethics will belong to one of three categories: (1) *professional* code applying to all, and only, members of a certain profession, such as the IACP code for police; (2) *employer's* code applying only to members of a particular police department (like the Police Code of Conduct and Ethics of New South Wales for the NSW Police Department); or (3) *organizational* code applying only to members of some professional, fraternal, or technical organization. Codes of ethics may include ordinary moral rules such as "Don't steal" or "Don't lie." They may also be enacted into law. For example, in many police departments, the code of ethics has been adopted as a regulation. But a code of ethics is not simply law or morality. What then is it?

Code

The word *code* comes from Latin. Originally, it referred to any wooden board, then to boards covered with wax that were written on, and then to any book (*codex*). That was the sense it had when first applied to the book-length systemization of Roman statutes that the Emperor Justinian enacted in 529 C.E. Justinian's *Code* differed from an ordinary compilation of law in one important way: He had the legal authority to make his a law, replacing all that preceded it.

Since 529 C.E., any document much like Justinian's *Code* could also be called "a code." Sometimes the analogy with Justinian's *Code* is quite close, as it is, for example, in the *Illinois Criminal Code*. Sometimes it is not. For example, a spy's "code" is a system of rules for concealing (and then revealing) the meaning of a message. Unlike Justinian's *Code* (and Illinois'), a spy's code imposes no obligations.

One important feature of Justinian's *Code* was that it was written. Could a code be *unwritten*? Since the point of codification (strictly speaking) is to give law (and, by analogy, any similar system of guidance) an authoritative formulation, an unwritten code might seem to be no code at all. Nonetheless, there are at least two interesting ways in which codes can be unwritten. First, a code might have an authoritative *oral* formulation. Second, a code, though unformulated, might be so obvious to those who know the practice that the formulation need only be stated to be accepted. While some police departments may have a few unwritten rules in one of these two exceptional ways ("the code of silence," for example), no substantial department (or larger organization) of police seems to have enough such rules to constitute an unwritten *code*. Nor is it likely that they would. How could so many individuals differing in age, education, and experience—with some arriving as others leave—reach and maintain agreement on a complex set of rules without putting the rules in writing?

Ethics

Ethics has at least four senses in common English usage. In one sense, *ethics* is a synonym for ordinary morality (those universal standards of conduct that apply to moral agents simply because they are moral agents). Etymology fully justifies this first sense. The root for *ethics* (*ēthos*) is the Greek word for "habit" (or "character") just as the root of *morality* (*mores*) is the Latin word for it. Etymologically, *ethics* and *morality* are twins (as are *ethic* and *morale*). In this first sense of *ethics*, codes of ethics would just be systematic statements of ordinary morality.

In at least three other senses of *ethics*, *ethics* differs from *morality*. In one, ethics consists of those standards of conduct that moral agents *should* follow ("critical morality"); morality, in contrast, is said to consist of those standards that moral agents generally do follow ("positive morality"). *Morality* in this sense is very close to its root *mores*; it can be unethical (in the first sense of *ethics*). What some believe is morally right (for example, that torturing suspects is justified) can be morally wrong. *Morality*, in this sense, has a plural. There can be as many moralit*ies* as there are moral agents. Even so, ethics, in this sense, can be a standard common to everyone. Hence, this second sense of *ethics* is as irrelevant here as the first.

Ethics is sometimes contrasted with *morality* in another way. Morality then consists of those standards every moral agent should follow. Morality is a universal minimum, our standard of moral right and wrong. Ethics, in contrast, is concerned with moral good, with whatever is beyond the moral minimum. This is another sense that seems not to fit codes of ethics, for at least two reasons. First, this ethics of the good is still universal, applying outside professions, employing departments, and other organizations as well as within. Second, codes of ethics consist (in large part at least) of *requirements*, the right way to conduct oneself rather than just a good way to. Any sense of *ethics* that does not include the right cannot be the sense relevant to "codes of ethics."

Ethics can be used in a fourth sense to refer to those morally permissible standards of conduct governing members of a group simply because they are members of that group. In this sense, business ethics is for people in business and no one else; engineering ethics, for engineers and no one else; and so on. Ethics (in this sense) is relative even though morality is not; it resembles law and custom, which can also vary from group to group and over time. But ethics (in this sense) is not mere *mores*. By definition, ethics in this sense must be at least morally permissible. There can be no thieves' "ethics" or torturers' "ethics," except with scare quotes around "ethics" to signal an analogical or perverted use.

Ethics resembles law and custom in another way: It sets a standard to guide and evaluate conduct. Unlike "scientific law," ethical rules do not describe conduct—except insofar as people act as they should (which they generally do only for the most part).

The Moral Force of Ethical Codes

A code of ethics, though not a mere restatement or application of ordinary morality, can be morally binding on those to whom it applies (that is, can impose new moral obligations or requirements). How is that possible? Some codes of ethics are morally binding, in part, because of an oath, promise, or other express commitment (for example, one's signature on a contract making acceptance of the employer's code of ethics a condition of employment). In general, though, codes of ethics bind in the way rules of a (morally permissible) game bind while one is a voluntary participant. While one voluntarily receives the benefits of a code of ethics, one has a moral obligation, an obligation of fairness, to do what the code says. Because a code of ethics applies only to voluntary participants in a special practice, not to everyone, a code (if generally followed) can create trust beyond what ordinary moral conduct can. It can create a special moral environment. For example, a code of ethics can justify trust in "professional law officers" beyond what they would be entitled to if they were known simply to do no more than law, market, morality, and public opinion required of them.

Because law applies to its subjects whether they wish it or not, law (as such) cannot bind in the way a code of ethics (a voluntary practice) can. A code of ethics is therefore always distinguishable from a mere statute even when the code is embedded in a statute. One need only ask, "Does this code state a (morally permissible) standard of conduct I (at my rational best) want everyone covered by it to follow so much that I would be willing to follow it too if that were the price of everyone else doing the same?" If everyone the code governs can answer yes, then it is a code of ethics. If some (at their rational best) answer no, then the code will have the same status as other statutes. There will be no moral obligation to fellow officers resulting from participation in a cooperative practice (an obligation of fairness). There will be no *ethical* obligation (in the fourth sense of *ethics*).

Uses (and Misuses) of Police Codes of Ethics

Codes of ethics have at least six uses: First, and most important, a code of ethics can establish special standards of conduct where experience has shown common sense is no longer adequate. Second, a code of ethics, being an authoritative formulation of the rules governing a practice, can help those new to the practice learn how they should act. Third, a code can remind those with even considerable experience of what they might otherwise forget. Fourth, a code can provide a framework for settling disputes, even disputes among those with considerable experience. Fifth, a code can help those outside the group ("the public") understand what may reasonably be expected of those in the group. Sixth, a code of ethics can justify discipline. The discipline must, however, aim at helping those disciplined to understand the code, not at deterring or punishing misconduct. Deterrence or punishment would turn the code into ordinary (criminal) law. A code of ethics is for the honest; the criminal law, for the dishonest.

Codes of ethics may also be *misused* in at least two ways. First, codes of ethics may be proposed as "window dressing" to fend off regulation, closer supervision, or public criticism. A code of ethics should never be used in that way. Where it is not a serious attempt to raise standards, a code of ethics is a deceptive practice to be avoided precisely because it is deceptive. Nonetheless, one by-product of a code of ethics that is well written, sufficiently demanding, and (generally) followed should be an increased trust in (and respect for) those subject to it.

Second, well-meaning advocates often defend a code of ethics as a way to raise the status or income of police by making law enforcement a profession like law or medicine. While adopting a code of ethics can help change law enforcement from an ordinary honest occupation into a profession, it probably cannot raise the social status or income of law enforcement officers. A profession is simply a number of individuals in the same occupation voluntarily organized to earn a living by openly serving a certain moral ideal in a morally permissible way beyond what law, market, morality, and public opinion would otherwise require. In no society in the world does law enforcement have the social status or income of law or medicine. A code of ethics probably will not change that. Ethics has little to do with social status or income.

MICHAEL DAVIS

See also **International Association of Chiefs of Police (IACP); Professionalism**

References and Further Reading

Bossard, Andre. 1981. Police ethics and international police cooperation. In *The social basis of criminal justice: Ethical issues for the 1980's*, ed. F. Schmalleger and R. Gustafson, 23–37. Washington, DC: University Press of America.

Coady, M., and S. Block, eds. 1996. *Codes of ethics in the professions*. Carlton South, Victoria: Melbourne University Press.

Davis, Michael. 2002. *Profession, code, and ethics*. Aldershot, England: Ashgate.

———. 2003. What can we learn by looking for the first code of professional ethics? *Theoretical Medicine and Bioethics* 24: 433–54.

Institute for Criminal Justice Ethics. 2005. *Codes*. http://www.lib.jjay.cuny.edu/cje/html/codes.html (accessed June 2005).

Johnson, A., and G. Copus. 1981. Law enforcement ethics: A theoretical analysis. In *The social basis of criminal justice: Ethical issues for the 1980's*, ed. F. Schmalleger and R. Gustafson, 39–83. Washington, DC: University Press of America.

Kleinig, John. *The ethics of policing*. Cambridge: Cambridge University Press.

Kleinig, John, with Yurong Zhang. 1993. *Professional law enforcement codes: A documentary collection*. Westport, CT: Greenwood Press.

Kultgen, John. 1988. *Ethics and professionalism*, 201–51. Philadelphia: University of Pennsylvania Press.

COMMUNITY ATTITUDES TOWARD THE POLICE

Public views about the police are central to effective law enforcement efforts. Law enforcement agencies often measure public attitudes toward police and try to improve their image with the public because their job requires public trust and cooperation. The British government, for example, created a policy that emphasized a "customer orientation among police forces" (Skogan 1996), which thus may increase the importance of national and local surveys about public evaluations of police performance. Much of police work is reactive, occurring after citizens have reported crimes or suspicious behavior. The police thus rely on public assistance to obtain accurate reporting of crimes so that they may catch criminals and prevent future crimes. In addition to reporting crimes, citizens often are witnesses of criminal activity; in order to identify suspects and report crucial information, they must believe that the police are competent at protecting them from violent crime and are honest, law-abiding professionals. The shift toward more community policing and foot or bicycle patrols has heightened the importance of positive public attitudes toward the police because such methods require working closely with the public to prevent and reduce criminal activity (Huang and Vaughn 1996).

Public views of the fairness of the police also affect their compliance with the law. Based on systematic survey research, individuals who judge the police as less trustworthy are more likely to steal, speed, and drive under the influence of alcohol or drugs (Tyler 1990), and they are less likely to report crimes, work with the police in community policing activities, or report accidents or suspicious behavior to the police (Sunshine and Tyler 2003). Furthermore, it is important for the police to increase public support of the policing institution so that when corrupt or biased officers are caught the public does not lose their trust in the law enforcement institution as a whole.

A law enforcement system that stops, searches, and arrests minorities in a discriminatory way, or a system in which many officers lack integrity or are out of touch with community values, will not be seen as legitimate in the eyes of the public, and will not have authority to enforce the law. Legitimacy means that the public believes the police have the authority to enforce the law and should be obeyed because the citizens trust and respect their power to do so; thus, legitimacy is the linchpin of successful law enforcement. Discrimination, lack of integrity, and even incompetence at solving crimes can undermine legitimacy. Several studies have demonstrated that how fairly officers treat citizens and respect them is the most important determinant of legitimacy (Sunshine and Tyler 2003).

This article provides a brief review of the literature on public attitudes toward the police. The review focuses on published research using systematic, reliable surveys of community members primarily in North America, although, where available, European and Latin American surveys are covered. Public attitudes toward the police cover two distinct, related dimensions: how fairly the police treat citizens and how competent they are at controlling and preventing crimes. Fairness of treatment involves friendliness, respect, honesty, concern for citizens' welfare, and nondiscriminatory and ethical behavior toward citizens and suspects. Competence includes several instrumental issues: How well can the police protect citizens from violent crime? How much effort do they exert to solve crimes? Are the police priorities consistent with what the public wants? Do they use force only in circumstances that the public would support? Before covering specific dimensions, public confidence in the police and evaluations of police performance in general are reviewed. Racial differences in attitudes toward the police are then covered and explanations for these differences examined. Linked to racial differences in attitudes is the police use of racial profiling to stop and search potential suspects, and police use of force. Public views on these topics are discussed.

Confidence in the Police

National surveys in many countries have asked the public whether they have a great deal, quite a lot, a little, or no confidence in many institutions such as the police, the criminal justice system, the military, religious organizations, public schools, the media, legislators, and big business. The police generally receive much higher confidence ratings than other institutions. Moreover, across countries, public confidence or trust ratings in the police compared to other branches of criminal justice such as the courts or prison system were at least twenty percentage points higher. For example, 64% of Americans, 76% of Australians, and 83% of Canadians indicated that they had a great deal or quite a lot of confidence in the police, and these ratings were higher than all institutions except the military. Citizens in Latin American countries, however, have more negative views of the police. Across seventeen Latin American countries, representative national surveys found that only 30% expressed a great deal or some confidence in the police, whereas 72% were confident about the church and 50% expressed this view about television (Public Perceptions of Justice 2004).

The police also receive the most positive ratings from the public in surveys in which respondents are asked to provide a performance rating, such as excellent, good, fair, or poor, of how well they are doing their job. In general, the public holds positive views about police performance. American surveys during the last two decades indicate that between 50% and 60% of respondents have confidence in the police to protect them from violent crimes (Bureau of Justice Statistics 2003; Roberts and Stalans 2000). National surveys in America indicate that public support for expanding police monitoring of cell phones and e-mails to intercept communications has declined from 54% in 2001 to 36% in 2004 (Bureau of Justice Statistics 2003). This decline is in direct conflict with recent federal policies to engage in more wiretapping of suspected terrorists without legal warrants. Most Americans, however, do favor expanding undercover activities to penetrate terrorist groups, stronger security checks at airports, use of facial recognition technology to scan for suspected terrorists, and closer monitoring of banking and credit card transactions. However, there is disagreement among the public about police performance and fairness, which is covered in a later section.

Public Views of the Ethical Standards of the Police

Across three decades, two to three times as many minorities (20% to 30%) compared to Caucasians in national American polls have rated the police as having low or very low ethical standards (Ackerman et al. 2001). Views of police integrity and honesty also vary across countries. Based on the 2004 Transparency International Corruption Barometer given to large, randomly selected samples of adult citizens in each country, the United States, England, and Canada receive an average rating of 2.9 on a five-point scale where 1 is equal to not at all corrupt and 5 is equal to extremely corrupt. The police are seen as more corrupt in countries that have a short history of democracy and more internal conflicts such as Russia, Lithuania, Ukraine, Latvia, Romania, Bulgaria,

Poland, and South Africa, with these countries receiving a rating of 3.8 to 4.3. The citizens of the socialist countries of Iceland, Denmark, and Finland perceived the police as the least corrupt providing an average rating of 2 or less, whereas the more established European democratic or socialist countries such as Germany, Austria, Netherlands, and Spain receive a rating between 2.5 and 3. Research shows that exposure to media stories about police misconduct lowers public views of the police's honesty and integrity (Weitzer and Tuch 2005).

Racial Differences in Attitudes toward the Police

Research during the last fifty years has consistently documented that African Americans distrust and have more negative views of the police than do Caucasian Americans (Sunshine and Tyler 2003; Roberts and Stalans 2000; Huang and Vaughn 1996). Fewer studies have examined Hispanic American attitudes and this group holds more complex views of the police, though additional research is required to draw more definitive conclusions on Hispanic Americans' views (Weitzer and Tuch 2005). Whereas 70% of Caucasians expressed high confidence in the police, only 43% of minorities held this view in a 2004 Gallup poll (Bureau of Justice Statistics 2003). Other polls find that a substantial minority (17% to 30%) of African Americans, compared with 10% or fewer Caucasians, have little or no confidence in the police (see Roberts and Stalans 2000). Hispanic Americans and African Americans have similar and more negative views of the police's honesty, ethical standards, and unfair treatment than do Caucasian Americans. However, Caucasians and Hispanics both rate officers as excellent or very good on helpfulness, friendliness, and solving crimes (see Roberts and Stalans 2000).

African Americans' discontent covers all areas of policing such as dishonest and discriminatory treatment and ineffectiveness at responding to crimes in a timely manner, helping victims, or solving crimes. Hispanics are more discontent about the fairness of police officers' treatment and their integrity.

Explanations for Racial Differences

What can explain minorities' more negative views of the police? Studies have found that the neighborhood context shapes the public's perceptions of police performance. Irrespective of race, individuals living in neighborhoods that have higher levels of disorder and crime have less positive views of police performance than individuals living in neighborhoods that have low levels of disorder or crime (Dunham and Alpert 1988; Maxson, Henning, and Sloane 2003). Individuals living in high-crime and disorderly neighborhoods rate police performance much lower, and racial differences in these ratings are not evident. Thus, the level of neighborhood disorder explains why African Americans rate police performance lower, because they are more likely to live in more disordered and crime-ridden neighborhoods. However, in both minimally and highly disordered neighborhoods, African Americans, as compared to Caucasians, believed that the police were substantially less respectful, concerned, fair, or trustworthy (Maxson, Henning, and Sloane 2003).

One of the largest disagreements across racial groups concerns whether the police treat minorities worse than Caucasians. The majority of African Americans and Hispanics believe that the police treat both African Americans and Hispanics worse than Caucasians, whereas the majority of Caucasians disagree. Only about one-quarter to one-third of Caucasians believe the police show discriminatory behavior toward minorities and treat Caucasians better than they do minorities (Weitzer and Tuch 2005). Most Caucasians do not acknowledge widespread and systematic discriminatory behavior of the police toward minorities, whereas most minorities do. Other national surveys replicate this wide divide between minorities' and Caucasians' views of discriminatory behavior by the police. The police use of race as an indicator of a higher likelihood of involvement in criminal activity has been labeled *racial profiling* and is controversial. In the 2004 Gallup poll, more than half of Caucasians and about two-thirds of African Americans and Hispanic Americans indicated that racial profiling is widespread in traffic stops. Thirty percent of Caucasians and Hispanics believed racial profiling was justified, whereas 23% of African Americans held this view. Based on a 2002 national survey on contact between police and the public, this perception of racial profiling in traffic stops does not result in a greater number of minority drivers being stopped by the police. The survey revealed that the likelihood of a traffic stop did not vary across race, with about 9% of Caucasians, Hispanics, and African Americans being stopped. However, once stopped by the police, minorities are significantly more likely to experience a "pat-down" of their person for weapons or have their cars searched. Moreover, searches of African American compared to Caucasian drivers or their vehicles were more likely to be without the consent of the driver, but the police were less likely to find evidence of a crime in searches of African Americans than in searches of Caucasian drivers (Durose, Schmitt, and Langan 2005). Minorities thus may perceive the police's greater propensity to search them as disrespectful and unfair treatment. Given the fact that more than 80% of searches do not yield evidence of criminal activity and more evidence is found against Caucasians (Durose,

Schmitt, and Langan 2005), these public views should shape police behavior. Based on a 2002 national police–public contact survey, minorities also report that the police are more likely to threaten the use of force or to use force during their contact (Durose, Schmitt, and Langan 2005). Research shows that minorities' and Caucasians' differential direct experiences with the police as well as their vicarious experiences from their conversations with others may explain why minorities rate the police as providing less fair and respectful treatment (Weitzer and Tuch 2005).

Conclusions

The literature on public attitudes toward the police is vast and covers many aspects. The public holds more positive views of the police than any other justice institution and most public institutions. The public places great importance on respectful and fair treatment in their interactions with the police. The amount of disorder and criminal activity in their neighborhood shapes their views of police performance, whereas personal victimization has little effect. Victims and nonvictims do not have significantly different views of police performance in most studies (Roberts and Stalans 2000). Moreover, whether the police provided respectful treatment and took the time to listen to their experience, rather than whether the case was solved or the response time, shapes victims' evaluations of the police. Negative direct encounters, stories of negative encounters with the police from family and friends, and media reports of misconduct all lower public views of the fairness and integrity of the police. Because minorities are more likely to live in neighborhoods with high levels of disorder or crime and are more likely to have negative direct or vicarious experiences, they are more distrustful of the police.

LORETTA J. STALANS

195

See also **Attitudes toward the Police: Measurement Issues; Minorities and the Police; Victims' Attitudes toward the Police**

References and Further Reading

Ackerman, G., B. Anderson, S. Jensen, R. Ludwig, D. Montero, N. Plante, and V. Yanez. 2001. Crime rates and confidence in the police: America's changing attitudes toward crime and police, 1972–1999. *Journal of Sociology and Social Welfare* 28 (1): 43–54.

Bureau of Justice Statistics. 2003. Various tables from *Sourcebook of criminal justice.* http://www.albany.edu/sourcebook.

Durose, M. R., E. L. Schmitt, and P. A. Langan. 2005. Contacts between police and the public: Findings from the 2002 national survey. NCJ 207845. http://www.ojp. usdoj.gov/bjs/abstract/cpp02.htm.

Huang, W. S., and M. S. Vaughn. 1996. Support and confidence: Public attitudes toward the police. In *Americans view crime and justice: A national public opinion survey*, ed. T. J. Flanagan and D. R. Longmire, 31–45 Thousand Oaks, CA: Sage Publications.

Maxson, C., K. Henning, and D. C. Sloane. 2003. Factors that influence public opinion of the police. NCJ 197925. http://www. ncjrs.gov/txtfiles1/nij/197925.txt.

Public perception of justice: Democracy and public confidence in institutions: Latinobarometo. 2004. Report of the Justice Studies Center of Americas. http://www.cejamericas. org/reporte/muestra_seccion.php?idioma= ingles&capitula=indsubje&tipreport= reporte0&seccion=ENCUCIUD

Roberts, J. V., and L. J. Stalans. 2000. *Public opinion, crime, and criminal justice.* Boulder, CO: Westview Press.

Skogan, W. G. 1996. The police and public opinion in Britain. *American Behavioral Scientist* 39 (4): 421–32.

Sunshine, J., and T. R. Tyler. 2003. The role of procedural justice and legitimacy in shaping public support for policing. *Law and Society Review* 37 (3): 513–47.

Transparency International corruption perceptions index. 2004. http://www.transparency. org/cpi/2004/cpi2004.en.html#cpi2004.

Weitzer, R. 2002. Incidents of police misconduct and public opinion. *Journal of Criminal Justice* 30 (5): 397–408.

Weitzer, R., and S. Tuch. 2005. Racially biased policing: Determinants of citizen perceptions. *Social Forces* 833: 1009–30.

COMMUNITY-ORIENTED POLICING: EFFECTS AND IMPACTS

Defining Community-Oriented Policing

Community-oriented policing (also known as community policing or CP) is an omnibus term. It can stand for (1) a contrast to rapid response, enforcement-oriented policing, involving long-term beat assignment so police are closer to the community; (2) a process by which crime control is shared with the public, as in Neighborhood Watch programs; or (3) a means of developing communication with the public and interest groups, for example, consultation meetings (Weatheritt 1983). CP has an enduring appeal to the public and is found in many jurisdictions in the English-speaking world and elsewhere. The term evokes images of police–community relations in stable, consensus-based, and homogenous neighborhoods where crime is occasional and disorder largely consists of petty vandalism. This idealized view is one where police define, and strive to enact, a posited common good.

Early initiatives emerged in the United States and United Kingdom in the 1970s (Trojanowicz and Moore 1988). Initially CP represented short-term tactics to repair police–minority relations and was regarded by many as a cosmetic exercise masking reluctance to change unsuccessful established law enforcement methods (Bucqueroux 1988). Contemporary efforts, such as the reassurance policing initiative in the United Kingdom and a brace of programs funded by the Office of Community-Oriented Policing Services (COPS) of the U.S. Department of Justice, have addressed fundamental change in the organization and delivery of policing services and have extended CP's scope from police–minority relations to policing in relation to the general community. COPS (2004) defines CP as "a policing philosophy that promotes and supports organizational strategies to address the causes and reduce the fear of crime and social disorder through problem-solving tactics and police–community partnerships." The seminal U.K. statement was made by a chief constable; CP would exist in its purest form where all elements in the community, official and unofficial, would conceive of the common good and combine to produce a social climate and an environment conducive to good order and the happiness of all those living within it (Alderson 1978, 9). At officer level, the CP role emphasizes public contact and reassurance along with deterrence, prevention, intelligence gathering, and reducing fear of crime (Bennett 1994).

COPS was founded in 1994 and provides resources and grants promoting CP, dispensing some $635 million in 2003. Between 1994 and 2003, its total investment was $10.6 billion. Much of the budget goes toward funding more police posts (more than 118,500 at the end of 2003). COPS also provides technologies that enhance the police–community interface and funds CP initiatives for tribal lands. Some 64% of U.S. law enforcement agencies, serving 86% of the population, currently have some engagement in CP. In the United Kingdom, CP initiatives are funded by a range of central and force-specific programs, and all U.K. police forces are engaged in CP. In England and Wales the Crime and Disorder Act of 1998 created a statutory requirement for police–community partnerships and mandated community consultation. The principal force-level programs are Crime and Disorder Reduction Partnerships, which bring together police and other local agencies from the public sector (for example, health service, probation service), private sector (via business forums), and voluntary sector.

Community-oriented policing takes a number of forms and incorporates a range of initiatives. At the organizational level,

CP emphasizes the desirability of adopting an organization-wide CP ethos, decentralized decision making, locale-based accountability, and the involvement of volunteers as auxiliaries. It pursues proactive tactics oriented to crime prevention and a problem-solving approach. It encourages interagency partnerships and public involvement. This diffuse character makes a tidy evaluation of its effects and impact elusive. Rather than think in terms of a uniform, generic entity, research-based evaluations have focused on specific initiatives and programs, although beat-level engagement is a key feature in many.

Effects and Impacts: Overview

Research on CP is both voluminous and dominated by policy-oriented evaluation research. Evaluations must be mindful of whether a given CP initiative aims to increase arrests (for example, by more effective information gathering as a result of regular and forthcoming contact with citizens), prevent opportunities for crime (for example, by providing target-hardening advice), or manage reported crime rates (Manning 2001). Evaluations also have to take into account displacement.

A major interest has been to examine the role of police managers, frontline officers, and community residents as factors in the success of CP initiatives. These strands of research have established a myriad of organizational, operational, and officer-level factors that may facilitate or hinder CP. Research suggests that successful CP heavily depends on frontline officer commitment and motivation, which is itself reliant on managerial support (see Bayley and Rosenbaum 1994; Lurigio and Skogan 1994).

Another strand of research is field studies of CP in practice, evaluating the efforts to get close to the community to garner information and respond to community needs. One such study found that what police did was to develop a neighborhood consensus among both the "good" citizens and the troublemakers about appropriate behavior that became self-enforcing over time (Kelling 1998, 4). In a U.K. context, Fielding (1995) documented a police division where CP had achieved a tangible impact on crime detection and identified the close effect that enhanced autonomy, discretion, senior officer support, and protection from redeployment to non-CP duties had on effective CP. This line of research suggests that to bring about CP, frontline officers need to be granted more discretion and authority, with more backing from command, and the best safeguard against abuse is their relationship with the community.

However, evaluation research on the impact of increased police patrol is pessimistic. Sherman (1992) examined the effects of increased, directed patrol on levels of reported "hard" (predatory) crime and "soft" crime and disorder at 110 crime "hotspots." A 250% increase in directed patrol had only a modest deterrent effect on robbery calls and no significant impact on "hard" crime calls generally. However, when the much larger number of "soft" crime calls were added, a 13% reduction in total calls for service was observed. Enhanced, visible police presence appears to have little impact on crime but a tangible impact on disorder. Moreover, Bennett (1991) found in the United Kingdom that a scheme involving the police seeking more direct contact with citizens had little effect on crime or reporting rates but did substantially improve public satisfaction with police.

CP draws on conceptual foundations including design for secure built environments (Otto Newman's "defensible space"); the impact on public fear and confidence of signs of physical dereliction (George Kelling's "broken windows" hypothesis); and the need to configure the police organization and services to reflect public demand rather than internal organizational imperatives (Herman

Goldstein's "problem-oriented policing"). These conceptual roots help to draw together what may otherwise seem a panoply of unrelated initiatives. Trojanowicz and Bucqueroux (1989) reported CP interventions against drug dealing involving posting officers outside known dealing premises or doing routine paperwork in front of them. CP initiatives have seen housing code violations used more aggressively and the instruction of landlords on screening prospective tenants and adding instant eviction clauses to leases in response to drug taking (McLanus 1990, 6–7). In the United Kingdom, partnership work between police, local government, and environmental authorities in red light districts of London led to increased convictions and a two-thirds reduction in drug dealing (*Guardian* February 16, 1994), and a campaign by police, schools, and community forums against street robbery, including the designation of safe routes through high-crime locations and a "crime shop" offering preventive advice on a high-crime estate, saw a 38% decrease in robbery (*Guardian* April 4, 1994). These interventions suggest that CP can impact on serious crime and social problems in difficult environments. However, in these examples the interventions were by the police, with a subsidiary role for partner agencies. The evidence is that more active citizen involvement is hard to achieve. CP initiatives also often involve teamwork across ranks and functions, challenging established organizational practices.

Effects and Impacts: Crime, Disorder, and Social Cohesion

One of the most sustained CP initiatives is Chicago's CAPS (Chicago Alternative Policing Strategy) program. It emphasized integrating city services—police, housing, social services—and involving residents in efforts against disorder and crime. As it developed, the policing element of the police/city services/civilian trio actually delivered least well, while it would be fair to speak in terms of a transformation of city services and of real improvement in civilian involvement.

City workers and police led problem-solving training sessions for the public, in which tens of thousands of residents participated. Beat officers were required to participate in community meetings to ensure community input when setting their priorities. Between 1995 and 1997 most patrol officers and thousands of civilians were taught to analyze how offenders and victims coincide at particular locations to create crime/disorder hotspots. CP expands the police mandate: Citizens raised social disorder problems dominated by unlawful activities police had customarily not prioritized—graffiti, public drinking, vandalism, truancy—and activities on the fringe of legality—loitering, begging, noisy domestic discord. Police found themselves involved in neighborhood cleanups by inventorying dilapidated structures and tracing the owners. Police accompanied residents at prayer vigils where drug-related shootings had occurred, guarded barbecue "smoke-outs" on drug-selling corners, and noted broken streetlights and trees that needed trimming. The police department had to change its dispatch system to protect beat cars for beat calls. The proportion of calls to beat officers that involved their own beat rose to an average of 75%.

After two years of CAPS, about a third of residents had attended a beat community meeting and three-quarters of these reported that actions were taken or that they noticed a change in their neighborhood as a result of the meetings. Those reporting police doing a good job increased with participation in CAPS programs. Those who were better off and homeowners were most likely to participate in the training on problem diagnosis. Some 65% of participants were already involved in community groups—they were "joiners." The beat meetings chiefly provided information to police on the basis that it was for them to act. Residents proved most active and successful in tackling troublesome or abandoned buildings. They contacted landlords, worked with city legal departments to evict problem tenants or secure demolition of abandoned buildings, and put addresses on the backs of buildings so officers in alleys could specify their location. A key instrument was a one-page city service request form that covered all service requests and was available online or from police and community organizations. Thus, interventions focused on the physical environment rather than direct interventions against "problem people," seen as a police responsibility.

Problem measures declined about 7% over the period from inception to 1999, with a 10% fall (to 45%) in residents reporting gang violence problems. The property and street crime index fell (from 40% to 31%), the largest decline being reports of problems with robbery and assault on the street. Burglary, car theft, and car vandalism declined by 8%. The physical decay index fell 6%. These are not spectacular improvements but disproportionately registered with those most in need, particularly African Americans. There was a modest increase in perceived neighborhood safety. From 1994 onward there were sustained if unspectacular decreases in fear of crime. Feeling safe outdoors while alone after dark increased nearly 10%. Reports that nearby areas were safe increased from 45% to 56%.

Before CAPS, fewer than 40% of Chicagoans had an optimistic view of police responsiveness to community concerns. Under CAPS, perceptions of police responsiveness to community concerns improved steadily (the index rose 20%). Those who thought police were doing a good job working with residents to solve problems rose 20% (to 59%). Chicagoans rating police as doing their job well rose from 36% to 50%. Reports that police were doing a good job assisting crime victims rose 20% (to 57%). Highest marks were given for keeping order: Positive scores hit 66% by 1999, from 56% in 1993.

The gains seen under CAPS do not imply that CP's focus on social disorder will directly impact on serious crime (the "broken windows" hypothesis). Wilson and Kelling (1982) argued that disorder—even if relatively minor—attracts predatory crime because potential offenders assume that residents do not care what happens in their neighborhood. Both physical and social disorder are seen as environmental cues that entice potential predators (Greenberg and Rohe 1986; Skogan 1990). Sampson and Raudenbush (1999) offer a dissenting assessment, in which the relationship between public disorder and crime proves to be spurious, except for robbery. Their alternative hypothesis is that disorder and crime have similar causes and that social cohesion reduces disorder and crime by disabling the forces that produce them.

Sampson and Raudenbush (1999) found that disorder is a moderate correlate of predatory crime but varies consistently with antecedent neighborhood characteristics. Once these characteristics are taken into account, the connection between disorder and crime vanishes in four out of five tests, including the best indicator of violence, homicide. Eradicating disorder may indirectly reduce crime by stabilizing neighborhoods, but a direct link to crime is absent. Sampson and Raudenbush found that neighborhoods high in disorder do not have higher crime rates than neighborhoods low in disorder once collective efficacy and structural antecedents are held constant. That it would be fanciful to expect CP interventions against social disorder to yield significant returns against serious crime is further evidenced by CAPS, which was premised on the link between social disorder and serious crime. During the 1990s, serious crime declined in American cities, including Chicago. In the ten cities with a population of more than one million (excluding New York, where the decline was atypically large), robbery declined 45%, auto theft 39%, and murder 46%. In Chicago the rates of decline were 47%, 38%, and 23%, respectively. CAPS appeared to have had little impact on serious crime, and indeed Chicago closed the decade with a higher homicide rate than New York, a city with 60% more residents.

The message should not end with skepticism about CP's impact on serious crime. Community-oriented policing can bring benefits of social integration, responsiveness of city services to residents' needs, and improved handling of urban decay. While the best research tells us that working against social disorder does not affect serious crime rates, it also tells us that working against social disorder impacts positively on public reassurance.

Evaluating Community-Oriented Policing

Empirical research into the effects of CP is abundant, but largely program specific. Our understanding of community policing could gain from more investment in conceptualizing the findings from the field's rich tradition of empirical research. A systematic attempt to assess the overall effects and impacts of community-oriented policing, as opposed to evaluating specific initiatives, would require attention to the macro, mezzo, and micro levels of CP as a system of service delivery (Fielding 2002). The policy maker and police manager looking to CP to address crime and disorder problems has a wealth of studies to guide decisions and investment. If one finding rises above the rest from the evaluative effort that has gone into CP, it is that program integrity, and the commitment of the organization and its officers, are vital for success.

NIGEL G. FIELDING

See also **Accountability; Autonomy and the Police; Boston Community Policing; Broken-Windows Policing; Calls for Service; Chicago Community Policing; Community-Oriented Policing: History; Community-Oriented Policing: International; Community-Oriented Policing: Practices; Community-Oriented Policing: Rationale; Discretion; Dispute Resolution, Community; Foot Patrol; Kansas City Preventive Patrol Experiment; Neighborhood Watch; Office of Community-Oriented Police Services, U.S. Department of Justice; Patrol, Types and Effectiveness of; Policing Multiethnic Communities; Problem-Oriented Policing; Styles of Policing; Weed and Seed; Zero Tolerance Policing**

References and Further Reading

Alderson, John. 1978. *Communal policing*. Exeter: Devon and Cornwall Constabulary.

Bayley, David, and Dennis Rosenbaum. 1994. The impact of community policing on police personnel: A review of the literature. In *The challenge of community policing: Testing the promises*, ed. Rosenbaum, 147–66. London: Sage.

Bennett, Trevor. 1991. The effectiveness of a police-initiated fear reducing strategy. *British Journal of Criminology* 31: 11–14.

———. 1994. Recent developments in community policing. In *Police force, police service: Care and control in Britain*, ed. Stephens and Becker, 107–29. London: Macmillan.

Bucqueroux, Bonny. 1988. Executive session on community policing. *Footprints* (Spring/Summer): 2–7.

Community-Oriented Police Services. 2004. What is community policing? http//www.cops.usdog.gov/default.asp?Item=36 (accessed October 2004).

Fielding, Nigel. 1995. *Community policing*. Oxford: Clarendon.

———. 2002. Theorizing community policing. *British Journal of Criminology* 42 (1): 147–63.

Greenberg, Stephanie, and William Rohe. 1986. Informal social control and crime prevention in modern urban neighborhoods. In *Urban neighborhoods: Research and policy*, ed. Taylor, 79–118. New York: Praeger.

Kelling, George. 1998. The evolution of broken windows. In *Zero tolerance: What does it mean and is it right for policing in Britain?*, ed. Weatheritt, 3–12. London: Police Foundation.

Lurigio, Arthur, and Wesley Skogan. 1994. Winning the hearts and minds of police officers: An assessment of staff perceptions of community policing in Chicago. *Crime and Delinquency* 40: 315–30.

Manning, Peter K. 2001. Community policing: Milestones and fundamentals. In *The police and the community*, ed. Carter and Radelet, 54–88. London: Prentice-Hall.

McLanus, Theodore. 1990. Tactics to target troubled neighborhoods. *Footprints* III (1): 6–7.

Sampson, R., and S. Raudenbush. 1999. Systematic social observation of public spaces: A new look at disorder in urban neighborhoods. *American Journal of Sociology* 105 (3): 603–51.

Sherman, Lawrence. 1992. Attacking crime: Police and crime control. In *Modern policing*, ed. Tonry and Morris, 159–230. Chicago, IL: University of Chicago Press.

Skogan, Wesley. 1990. *Disorder and decline: Crime and spirals of decay in American neighborhoods*. New York: The Free Press.

Trojanowicz, Robert, and Bonny Bucqueroux. 1989. What community policing can do to help. *Footprints* II (2): 2–15.

Trojanowicz, Robert, and Mary Moore. 1988. *The meaning of community in community policing*. East Lansing: Michigan State University.

Weatheritt, Mollie. 1983. Community policing: Does it work and how do we know? In *The future of policing*, ed. Bennett, 3–15. Cambridge: Institute of Criminology.

COMMUNITY-ORIENTED POLICING: HISTORY

Community policing and variations on it have become the operating philosophy and underlie much of police practice today. Moreover, community policing has become a powerful organizing theme that continues to shape how police departments deliver services, particularly at the local level of government. The range and complexity of programs associated with community policing are broad and have often evaded systematic scientific investigation. Nonetheless, community policing has and continues to transform modern policing in the United States and elsewhere. This article reflects on how community policing came about and was originally formed. Most importantly, this assessment is focused on the historical roots of community policing, and how it has set a premise for a more "user-friendly" and community-sensitive form of local law enforcement.

Historical Roots of Community Policing

Since their earliest inception in the nineteenth century in the United States and England, the police have struggled with balancing the need to be efficient and effective, while also being lawful (Walker 1994). Police practice is indeed rooted in Western political philosophy, which emphasizes equity, fairness, and justice (Critchley 1967). The police originally started as "thief takers," but their more traditional role has been to preserve local order. In their historic role of maintaining the public peace, the police have focused their efforts mostly on maintaining social order, controlling violence, and minimizing civil unrest. More recently the police have also been associated with reducing the public's fear of crime and improving community "quality of life" (Greene 2000). Although the goals of the police to preserve the public peace and maintain order are indeed laudable, in practice policing has often been criticized for its negative impacts—being inefficient, brutal, corrupt, and political.

This has led in the United States to several efforts to reform the police. Such reforms have shaped policing over many years, and have set the precedent for what is now called community-oriented policing. These reforms, however, were not always associated with "good policing"; rather they sought to minimize and control what was seen as "bad police behavior."

In a review of the shifts in police strategy in the twentieth century, Kelling and Moore (1988) suggest that the earliest organizational strategy of the police was essentially political. Police were primarily concerned with maintaining the political power of those in office (who appointed the police), and were consequently corrupted by their close association with those in power. At the time, policing was directly associated with the rise of political machines in the late 1800s and early 1900s and their dominance in large American cities (Fogelson 1977).

During this era police were directly tied to the political patronage systems of the times, and their actions helped those in power, often by punishing political enemies and the underclass, generally defined as those of a different ethnic heritage. At this time, the police problem was not one of the police overenforcing the law, but rather one in which the police selectively underenforced the law, particularly within political patronage systems of the era. In many respects it was the police who were "lawless" (Walker 1977); they were often seen as an adjunct to the local political machine, using violence and brutality against those who were not in political favor, and were themselves otherwise lazy and corrupt. During this same period (roughly, 1890 to 1930) the local police, particularly in large urban cities, encountered several waves of immigration. How immigrants were to be socialized to their new living arrangements, most particularly to the political processes that shaped those living arrangements, was often left to the uneven hand of the police—and the police nightstick.

Reformers in the early 1900s began to challenge the political corruption of much of local government. A "good government" movement followed these efforts and the strategy to reform the police was to "take the politics out of policing." This strategy was built on efforts aimed at administrative reform (Fogelson 1977), wherein administrative control, distance from political and social communities, and law and professionalism guided the police response, not political partisanship or party loyalty. Today this idea of police reform still dominates much American police administrative thinking.

The reform era sought to first make the police legally accountable; it was not so much a concern with public accountability, but rather in having a lawful police. The "lawlessness of the police" had become legend by the beginning of the twentieth century. Reformers sought to divide the police from political control and subject their actions to greater administrative review. All of this was done in the name of controlling the political tendencies of the police, while introducing efficiencies into police administration.

During this reform era of policing (roughly the 1920s to 1960s), the police expanded on their models of organization and administration (typically borrowed from the military); improved response technology through the introduction of telephones, radio cars, and dispatch systems; and attempted to instill uniformity in police practice through more uniform training. These reforms all sought to build a foundation for policing and to raise the status of the police from political hacks to professionals.

Perhaps the success of these reforms was also their failure. In embracing administrative reform, the police drifted away from the public, often seeing the public as an unnecessary interference. Institutionally, the police became inward looking, and cloaked their business in secrecy. Speed of response overtook policing neighborhoods, and secondary measures of effort eclipsed those of effectiveness. Routinely the police presented themselves as uniformed, selectively organized, and capable of rapid response to emergencies. Such a presentational strategy was thought to help maintain the public legitimacy of the police (Crank and Langworthy 1992) and is still an important way the police present themselves to the public, but such a presentational strategy may actually be one of the major obstacles to

overcome in the implementation of community-oriented policies.

Beginning in the late 1950s and continuing into the 1970s, the institution of policing encountered its most formidable challenge—a direct and frontal assault on the legitimacy of the police and indeed of the legal system itself. The civil rights and Vietnam antiwar movements effectively merged two groups who had heretofore been socially and politically separated: minorities, particularly blacks, and urban and suburban middle-class white youth. The convergence of these two social and political movements confronted American policing in very direct ways.

In response to these confrontations, the police, generally speaking, became militant. They were often so confrontational when dealing with these groups that they produced what Stark (1972) has termed "police riots." The nationally televised Chicago Democratic Convention and the riots that ensued for the first time portrayed the police as institutionally unaccountable. Moreover, the National Advisory Commission on Civil Disorder concluded that the spark of most urban riots occurring in the late 1960s was poor or aggressive police action, generally taken in a minority community. Riots in Los Angeles, Detroit, Philadelphia, Newark, and elsewhere portrayed a disintegrating social structure, often precipitated by police action. The police were at once the cause and the solution to social unrest. Liberals saw them as the cause of problems, conservatives as the solution. The country was divided on these issues, and the police were caught between significant ideological shifts occurring in American political and social life (National Advisory Commission on Civil Disorder 1968).

The American police were sorely in need of reform yet again. Beginning in the early 1970s, the police began to experiment with ways that put them into closer interaction with the public. The community relations movement, begun in the late 1940s and into the 1950s (Greene and

Pelfry 1997), influenced this transition for policing, as did the rise of alternative forms of policing such as team policing (Sherman, Milton, and Kelly 1973). In both the community relations movement and team policing, there was an attempt to create more public support for the police, while at the same time providing them with a clearer role in community public safety. Police–community relations programs sought to sensitize the police to neighborhood ethnic and cultural differences, while team policing was an import initial attempt to change the focus and structure of the police. It is from these early roots that the community-oriented policing movement in the United States can trace its roots.

The more current trends in U.S. police reform, falling under the broad label of community policing, began in the mid-1980s and continue to the present. These trends stress a contextual role for the police, one that emphasizes greater interaction with the community toward the resolution of persistent neighborhood crime and disorder problems (Wilson and Kelling 1982; Goldstein 1987; Kelling and Moore 1988). This newest in a long tradition of reforms has many implications for police role definitions, strategic and tactical operations, and understanding about the limits of formal and informal social control.

Conclusion

The organizing themes of community policing suggest that law enforcement can be more focused, proactive, and community sensitive. Moreover, community policing portends significant changes to the social and formal organization of policing. On the level of social organization, community policing is thought to break down the barriers separating the police from the public, while inculcating police officers with a broader community service set of ideals. Organizationally, community policing is thought to shift police decision making from what was a traditional bureaucracy to one emphasizing greater organizational–environmental interaction. Simultaneously, the shift to community policing is said to be accompanied by a flattening of the police hierarchy and the development of coordinated service delivery with any number of agencies that affect public safety. These are indeed profound changes to policing, as they continue to be implemented and shape the institution of American policing.

JACK R. GREENE

See also **Boston Community Policing; Chicago Community Policing; Community-Oriented Policing: Effects and Impacts; Community-Oriented Policing: Practices; Community-Oriented Policing: Rationale; History of American Policing; Minorities and the Police; Multiethnic Communities: Interactive Model; National Advisory Commission on Civil Disorder; Police Reform in an Era of Community and Problem-Oriented Policing; Police Reform: 1950–1970; Politics and the Police**

References and Further Reading

Crank, J. P., and R. Langworthy. 1992. An institutional perspective of policing. *Journal of Criminal Law and Criminology* 83 (2): 338–63.

Critchley, T. A. 1967. *History of police in England and Wales, 900–1966.* London: Constable and Company.

Fogelson, R. 1977. *Big city police.* Cambridge, MA: Harvard University Press.

Goldstein, H. 1987. Toward community-oriented policing: Potential, basic requirements, and threshold questions. *Crime and Delinquency* 33 (1): 6–30.

Greene, J. R. 2000. Community policing in America. In *Policies, processes and decisions of the justice system, criminal justice 2000,* vol. 3, ed. J. Horney. Washington, DC: National Institute of Justice, Office of Justice Programs.

Greene, J. R., and W. V. Pelfrey, Jr. 1997. Shifting the balance of power between police and community: Responsibility for crime control. In *Critical issues in policing:*

Contemporary readings, ed. R. G. Dunham and G. P. Alpert, 3rd ed. Prospect Heights, IL: Waveland Press.

Kelling, G. W., and M. Moore. 1988. From political to reform to community. In *Community policing: Rhetoric and reality*, ed. J. R. Greene and S. Mastrofski. New York: Praeger.

National Advisory Commission on Civil Disorder. 1968. *Report of the National Advisory Commission on Civil Disorder*. Washington, DC: U.S. Government Printing Office.

Sherman, L., C. Milton, and T. Kelley. 1973. *Team policing: Seven case studies*. Washington, DC: Police Foundation

Stark, R. 1972. *Police riots*. Belmont, CA: Wadsworth.

Walker, S. 1994. *A critical history of police reform*. Lexington, MA: Lexington Books.

Wilson, J. Q., and G. L. Kelling. 1982. The police and neighborhood safety: Broken windows. *Atlantic Monthly* 127 (March): 29–38.

COMMUNITY-ORIENTED POLICING: INTERNATIONAL

Community-oriented policing has emerged as the dominant model of democratic policing in the world. The core notions of partnership with communities, orientation to service, problem solving and crime prevention, organizational decentralization of personnel, and permanent deployment of officers to a defined area (leaving aside the devolution of authority to lower echelons within the organization) have an ideological resonance and legitimating utility that transcend national boundaries, especially for countries that are democracies or are seeking to democratize. Additionally, non–state security providers, for example, private and corporate police, community groups, and self-protection militias, have expanded dramatically in all societies. The decline of state capacity and the expansion of informal social control raise the question of how the state can harness the energy and normative power of informal control efforts to state-centered policing. Community-oriented policing (COP) does that.

The COP model has been adopted in domestic settings in Western democracies for similar reasons: dissatisfaction with police performance and negative police relations as the consequences of prior models, a decline of government resources available to support policing services, changes in the political climate favoring local governance, and technological advances in communications and information processing. The ideology of COP has been diffused around the globe by scholarly writings, the missionary activities of advocates and reformers, the growing networks of interactions and exchanges among police from different countries, the international legitimacy of reform commission recommendations (such as those from the Patten Commission in Northern Ireland), the efforts of nongovernmental organizations (NGOs) promoting reforms (such as the Justice Initiative of the Open Society Foundation), and by international policing missions and assistance programs.

COP has many ideological parents, ranging from traditional and socialist ideologies of the need for both informal and formal social control to social science-based performance evaluations of specific policing practices, and is reborn in many organizational permutations in its global travels, in effect rendering the ideology of COP, except for core values and themes, an illusory guide to policies and tactics. Currently, it is not readily apparent, beyond the rhetoric, what it means to do COP and how COP can be recognized in practice. The specific ways in which the goals of partnership, crime prevention through problem solving, and decentralization have structured the activities of the police have varied significantly, shaped by the historical trajectory of how policing developed in different countries. New ideas and practices have been fitted into existing policing patterns. In addition, the desire by individual police organizations to be acknowledged by other police organizations elsewhere as modern, efficient, and up to date has led to the adoption of competitors, or variations on the COP model, such as zero tolerance policing, COMPSTAT, or the marriage of soft and hard (militarized) policing to suit local conditions. In the end, every variation of COP is still a variation of policing—that is, the use of coercive persuasion to maintain social control. That justification for state policing still dominates the social control discourse in all countries, and policing will continue to be judged by communities on how well it protects the safety and sense of security of the public.

Policing systems all over are continually being reformed in ways that fit changing local political and social conditions. In the United Kingdom, which has a long political tradition of central control of the police combined with local input, advice, and supervision, policing has always been based on community support and consent, a tradition that goes back to the Peelian origins of the police. Recent reforms have both centralized control over local policing through oversight, performance demands and direction from the Home Office and expanded community participation by parceling out some aspects of police work to volunteer constables who are entitled to report deviations from community norms.

In the Netherlands community policing policies have been integrated into a tradition of interagency cooperation in municipalities and are now elaborated in contracts between the central government and municipalities on how to incorporate all local agencies, which have some responsibility and can make a contribution to the quality of life and well-being of the community, into a joint effort. In France, "proximity policing" is the national version of COP. Local communities were allowed to create local police forces (to supplement the existing two national police forces) as a way of bringing policing closer to the local level and under the influence of local governments. Cooperation among the three police forces has been institutionalized in local security contracts, which require that the national police share information and responsibilities with the local police.

Policing practices in Asian communities are surrounded and supported by a vast system of volunteerism and respect by communities for the authority of the police and the power of the government. The most widely cited example of a COP practice, the *koban* in Japan, along with the street policing units in China have integrated the police into the everyday lives of their communities and have provided an inspiration for one of the few common organizational changes anywhere—local police–community forums, such as community policing centers (Israel), community policing forums (South Africa), storefronts (United States), or district policing boards (Northern Ireland).

Issues

The rhetoric of COP dominates national and transnational policing discourses among police officials, academics, and policy makers. It is less clear whether that rhetoric is being translated into practice on a consistent basis. In many countries, for example, South Africa and Hungary, the COP model has lost its luster under the onslaught of organized local and transnational crime against which it seems too soft and ineffective a model. People demanded more repressive policies than those delivered by COP.

Because the model has little organizational and policy specificity, it has been fairly easy for some police to claim that they are doing COP by pointing to specific programs or by symbolic changes such a relabeling themselves a police service, when in reality they are continuing conventional and nondemocratic practices. Policing in China has been organized by streets and small neighborhoods and the police routinely and systematically collect and evaluate information on everyone who lives or visits their territory. This looks like COP, and clearly the Chinese police and their communities know each other intimately, but the ideology that drives familiarity is not partnership but state control. Assisting the police is an obligation, not a choice. In Singapore, intimate police–community relations serve an authoritarian state and harness the communities to state-approved self-control activities. In Japan the police are supported in their invasion of privacy (such as twice annual census visits) by a cultural values system based on respect for authority, tradition, and the dominance of group identity over individual wants. In many developing countries in which the state and the police are under-resourced, ineffective, and perceived to be corrupt, much of policing has drifted toward community and vigilante forms of enforcing social order, which are condoned or encouraged by the state, with the formal police being minor and distant partners. This looks like community-based policing but partakes little of the sprit or the practices of problem solving or respect for the rule of law. Where the police and society have become habituated to corruption—giving and receiving as a normal part of life— community policing will only enhance corruption's salience and intensity.

Some scholars and police have questioned whether COP is suited to all political, cultural, and economic environments into which it is being introduced. COP assumes particular environmental conditions to be workable, such as the level of social capital and trust to enable communities to partner with the police; a progressive police leadership willing to devolve more authority to its street police, and a street police sufficiently trained and capable of doing COP work; access to other governmental agencies or civic society organizations, which can be called on and are willing to participate in problem-solving programs; a minimum level of social order and safety (when insecurity is massive and pervasive, it is quite unlikely that the police or the community will

support COP); or a history of police submission to the demands of the powerful and the state and the repression of society. New COP practices will lack meaning and legitimacy for the police and the public. Such legacies of distrust cannot be overcome, except (possibly) in the long term, by shifting the rhetoric and some policing practices to a COP model.

OTWIN MARENIN

See also **Accountability; Asian Policing Systems; Attitudes toward the Police: Overview; Autonomy and the Police; Community-Oriented Policing: Effects and Impacts; Community-Oriented Policing: History; Community-Oriented Policing: Practices; Community-Oriented Policing: Rationale; Problem-Oriented Policing**

References and Further Reading

Bayley, David H. 1991. *Forces of order. Policing modern Japan.* Berkeley: University of California Press.

Brogden, M. 1999. Community policing as cherry pie. In *Policing across the world*, ed. R. I. Mawby, 167–86. London: UCL Press.

Brogden, Mike, and Preeti Nijhar. 2005. *Community policing. National and international models and approaches.* Cullompton, Devon, UK: Willan Publishing.

Caparini, Marina, and Otwin Marenin, eds. 2004. *Transforming police in Central and Eastern Europe.* Münster, Germany: LIT Verlag.

Dixon, Bill. 2000. *The globalisation of democratic policing: Sector policing and zero tolerance in the New South Africa, Cape Town.* Occasional Paper. Cape Town: Institute of Criminology, University of Cape Town.

Findlay, Mark, and Uglješa Zveki, eds. 1993. *Alternative policing styles: Cross-cultural perspectives.* Boston: Kluwer Law and Taxation Publishers.

Friedman, Robert R. 1992. *Community policing. Comparative perspectives and prospects.* New York: St. Martin's Press.

Haberfeld, M. R. 1997. Poland: The police are not the public and the public are not the police. *Policing: An International Journal of Police Strategies and Management* 20: 641–54.

Independent Commission on Policing for Northern Ireland Patten Commission. 1999. *A new beginning: Policing in Northern*

Ireland. http://www.belfast.org.uk/report. html.

Lab, Steven, and Dilip Das, eds. 2003. *International perspectives on community policing and crime prevention*. Upper Saddle River, NJ: Prentice-Hall.

Mawby, R. I. 1990. Community involvement in policing: A comparative analysis. In *Comparative policing issues: The British and American experience in international perspective*, ed. R. I. Mawby, 168–89. London: Unwin Hyman.

Mobekk, Eirin. 2002. Policing from below: Community policing as an objective in peace operations. In *Executive policing. Enforcing the law in peace operations*, ed. Renata Dwan, 53–66. Oxford: Oxford University Press.

Punch, Maurice, K. van der Vijver, and M. Zoomer. 2002. Dutch "COP": Developing community policing in the Netherlands. *Policing* 25 (1): 60–79.

Shaw, Mark. 2002. *Crime and policing in post-apartheid South Africa: Transforming under fire*. Bloomington: Indiana University Press.

Skolnick, Jerome, and David H. Bayley. 1988. *Community policing: Issues and practices around the world*. Cambridge, MA: ABT Associates.

South Eastern Europe Clearinghouse for the Control of Small Arms and Light Weapons (SEESAC). 2003. *Philosophy and principles of community-based policing*. Belgrade: SEESAC.

Wong, Kam C. 2001. The philosophy of community policing in China. *Police Quarterly* 4 (2): 186–214.

COMMUNITY-ORIENTED POLICING: PRACTICES

Those who have led the professional change away from the crime fighting model of policing toward the community policing model so well known today have alternately referred to it as a paradigm shift, a major reform, or an evolutionary outcome stemming from precursor efforts in American law enforcement. In the literature on community policing the terms *community policing, community-oriented policing,* and *problem-oriented policing* are used quite interchangeably, both among practitioners and scholars; we follow that practice here. To many leaders in professional law enforcement, community policing is viewed as an outgrowth of progressive policing practices attempted in the early 1970s when teams of officers focused on building public support through police–community relations efforts of various sorts. Reflecting this commonplace viewpoint, William Tafoya (2000, 306) was moved to ask: "What could be done to correct the commonly held perception among practitioners that community policing is 'Old Wine in a New Bottle'?"

Despite this common view, most scholars who have studied community policing in depth have come to view community policing as much more than a continuation of earlier experiments with community outreach; they see it as a fundamental change from doing police business as usual (Kelling and Moore 2000; Thurman, Zhao, and Giacomazzi 2001). Careful observers commonly note that the underlying philosophy of public outreach, citizen-centered service, citizen engagement in crime prevention, and active partnership with community-based groups and organizations leads to the adoption of new political elements, new professional norms, new crime fighting tools, new community relations efforts, and a range of new interagency collaborations intended to manage crime and public safety–related problems. The practical implementation of community policing can be seen at the individual officer level, at the specially designated unit level, and at the organizational level alike.

Given this degree of change in how police work is to be carried out, it shouldn't be much of a surprise that the implementation of community policing in a quasi-military organizational setting steeped in rich traditions has been challenging virtually everywhere it has been instituted. Dennis Rosenbaum offered the following telling comments about how community policing was affecting police agencies in the United States by the end of the 1990s (1998, 4): "This reform movement is both promising and threatening; it promises to improve public safety, yet it offers no simple formula or road map to get there; it promises to reform police agencies and stimulate community involvement in public safety, yet police officers and community residents are often left to imagine how this will happen."

public schools—both in the form of special officer-led instruction (for example, Drug Awareness Resistance Education) and in the form of school resource officers—uniformed officers who are assigned to specific schools without direct classroom curricular roles.

Police Practices Reflecting a Commitment to Community Policing

Officers involved in the practice of implementing a community policing agency commitment engage in a variety of activities spread across a wide range of specific circumstances. Community policing practices typically feature the purposeful planning of positive, trust-building, non-enforcement contacts between police and law-abiding citizens and community youth. A quite common problem-solving effort of community policing-oriented agencies is to address the public safety concerns of citizens occasioned by the presence of serious habitual offenders, violent youth gangs, or persons selling/using illegal drugs through neighborhood-based meetings and the development of collaborative action plans linking citizen coproduction of public order with supportive police activities.

The planning process of Crime Prevention Through Environmental Design (CPTED) is another frequently used tool for the formation of police–community collaboration. Community policing and such problem-solving practices have been used to address violent street crime in specific areas, as well as to address quality-of-life issues such as vandalism, loitering, drunk driving, unwanted noise, litter, and abandoned vehicles. The assignment of officers to fixed beats and/or shifts has also become a key feature of community policing in many places. Finally, a quite common community policing program involves ongoing direct contact with

Resources Available to Support Community Policing Practices

The Center for Problem Oriented Policing (POP) was the primary early influence behind nascent community policing practices arising in the early 1970s when police executives and researchers alike focused attention on improving police effectiveness after researchers took note of the serious limitations of foundational police practices. A nonprofit organization comprised of affiliated police practitioners, researchers, and universities, the POP Center is dedicated to the systematic application of problem-solving practices, principally situational crime prevention, and the commonly used SARA (Scanning, Analysis, Response, and Assessment) problem-solving model. The primary institutional affiliates of the POP Center include the University of Wisconsin–Madison Law School; the Rutgers University–Newark School of Criminal Justice, where a library houses most of the compiled research literature for *Problem Oriented Guides for Police;* and SUNY Albany, where the POP Center's website is maintained.

The Community Policing Consortium (CPC) represents another early-day influence on the institutionalization of community policing practices. Established in 1992 under the auspices of the Bureau of Justice Assistance, the CPC represents a partnership of five of the leading police organizations in the United States: the International Association of Chiefs of Police (IACP), the National Organization of Black Law Enforcement Executives (NOBLE), the National Sheriffs' Association (NSA), the Police Executive Research Forum (PERF), and the Police Foundation. Training modules, technical assistance, and resource "toolboxes" were provided to law enforcement agencies by the consortium across the entire country. Seminal publications from the CPC include such titles as *Understanding Community Policing: A Framework for Action* and *The Police Organization in Transition.* Later publications, such as *Community Policing Exchange, Sheriff Times,* and *Community Links,* have been distributed to more than two hundred thousand practitioners and community members across the country. Currently, the consortium assists the COPS Office with enhancing law enforcement and community engagement processes to develop specific action plans promoting trust in law enforcement, reducing community fear of crime, and enhancing homeland security through terrorism countermeasures.

Although researchers, politicians, and law enforcement practitioners express a wide range of opinion about the overall impact of the COPS Office, it is beyond dispute that no other entity has had the breadth of influence on the practices of local, state, and tribal policing as this organization—a relatively small federal agency located within the enormous confines of the U.S. Department of Justice. Roberg, Crank, and Kuykendall (2000, 402) correctly note that "the Violent Crime Control and Law Enforcement Act of 1994 (The Crime Control Act) is the most comprehensive federal crime legislation since the Omnibus Crime Control and Safe Streets Act of 1968." That statute established the COPS Office, and that duly authorized agency has allocated approximately $30 billion to a wide range of criminal justice agencies, with almost $11 billion being directed to state and local law enforcement—including almost $9 billion to hire an additional one hundred thousand police officers "doing community policing" under guidelines set forth

by the agency. According to the agency's "Reports from the Field" web page, since its inception, the COPS Office has awarded more than thirty-eight thousand grants to assist more than thirteen thousand local law enforcement agencies in order to implement community policing practices through eighty innovative grant programs. Among these programs are Universal Hiring; Making Officer Deployment Effective; Distressed Neighborhoods; COPS in Schools; School-Based Partnerships; Problem Solving Partnerships; Tribal Government Resource Grants; Domestic Violence Grants; Methamphetamine Initiatives; Technology Adoption; Justice-Based After School Activities; Anti-Gang Initiatives; Value-Based Initiatives; and the creation of a network of twenty-seven regional community police institutes in 1997 for the dissemination of community policing training and technical assistance. The "Reports from the Field" web page lists law enforcement entities in all fifty states, the territories of Guam and Puerto Rico, and a multitude of tribal governments—all of which have received COPS Office funds to implement community policing practices.

Community policing practices, now into their third decade of operation, have become firmly institutionalized into the profession of law enforcement in the United States, and increasingly in police work in democratic nations worldwide (Skogan 2004). It can be fairly stated that the capacity of the police and the public they serve to work together to manage local public safety issues has never been greater, and many police–community partnerships are now in place effectively promoting the coproduction of public order and public safety in their communities.

MICHAEL J. ERP and NICHOLAS P. LOVRICH

See also **Accountability; Community-Oriented Policing: History; Crime Control Strategies; Problem-Oriented Policing; SARA, the Model**

References and Further Reading

Kelling, G., and M. Moore. 2000. The evolving strategy of policing. In *Community policing: Classical readings*. Upper Saddle River, NJ: Prentice-Hall.

Roberg, R., J. Crank, and J. Kuykendall. 2000. *Police & society*. 2nd ed. Los Angeles: Roxbury Publishing.

Rosenbaum, Dennis P. 1998. The changing role of the police: Assessing the current transition to community policing. In *How to recognize good policing: Problems and issues*, ed. Jean-Paul Brodeur. Washington, DC: Police Executive Research Forum, and Thousand Oaks, CA: Sage Publications.

Skogan, Wesley G., ed. 2004. *Community policing (can it work)?* Belmont, CA: Wadsworth-Thomson Learning.

Tafoya, William L. 2000. The current state and future of community policing. In *Policing communities: Understanding crime and solving problems*, ed. R. Glensor, M. Correia, and K. Peak. Los Angeles: Roxbury Publishing. Also includes an insightful chapter (chap. 5) by Wesley Skogan examining the role of the public in community policing.

Thurman, Quint, Jihong Zhao, and Andrew L. Giacomazzi. 2001. *Community policing in a community era: An introduction and exploration*. Los Angeles: Roxbury Publishing.

COMMUNITY-ORIENTED POLICING: RATIONALE

Police Reform and the Professional Era

Several important developments provided the rationale for the contemporary community policing and problem-solving era in America. First, reformers attempted to remove the police from political influences that prevailed from the 1840s to the 1930s by creating civil service systems to eliminate patronage and ward influences in hiring and firing police officers (Goldstein 1977). August Vollmer, a pioneer of police professionalism, also rallied police executives around the idea of reform during the 1920s and 1930s. Vollmer believed that police officers should do more than merely arrest offenders, and that they should actively seek to prevent crime by "saving" potential or actual offenders. The focus on prevention instead of repression was an important step in police reform (Goldstein 1977).

During this reform period of the 1930s to 1980s, however, police organizations evolved into law enforcement agencies that primarily emphasized controlling crime. Thus, during this period the "professional era" of policing was in full bloom, with officers expected to remain in their "rolling fortresses," going from one call to the next with all due haste (Manning 1971); officers were typically judged by factors such as the number of arrests they made or the number of miles they drove during a shift. The crime rate became the primary indicator of police effectiveness—personified by television's Sgt. Friday on *Dragnet*: "Just the facts, ma'am." Citizens' responsibility in crime control was limited, and police were the "thin blue line" (Walker 1977) that separated residents from crime problems.

Problems Overwhelm the Professional Model

Problems with the professional model of policing began to arise during the late 1960s due to the following reasons:

1. *Crime began to rise and research suggested that conventional police methods were not effective.* The 1960s were a time of political and social unrest. Inner-city residents rioted in several major cities, protesters denounced military involvement in Vietnam, and many questions were raised about the role of the police and their ability to effectively control crime.

2. *Increased fear of crime.* Citizens abandoned parks, public transportation,

211

neighborhood shopping centers, churches, and entire neighborhoods. Researchers found that fear was more closely associated with disorder than with actual crime. Ironically, order maintenance was one of the functions that police had been downplaying over the years, choosing instead to focus on crime control.

3. *Minority citizens did not perceive their treatment as equitable or adequate.* They protested not only police mistreatment, but lack of treatment. The legitimacy of police was questioned: Students resisted police, minorities rioted against what they represented, and the public began to question the effectiveness of police tactics.

4. *Some of the premises on which the reform era was founded could no longer be sustained.* Police studies highlighted the use of discretion at all levels of policing and reported that law enforcement comprised but a small portion of police activities. Other research findings shook the foundations of old assumptions about policing (some of which are discussed below) (Skolnick and Bayley 1986).

5. *Although managers had tried to professionalize policing, line officers continued to have low status.* Police work continued to be routinized and petty rules governed officer behavior. Meanwhile, line officers received little guidance in the use of discretion and had little opportunity for providing input concerning their work.

6. *Police began to acquire competition: private security and the community crime control movement.* Businesses, industries, and private citizens began turning to private police agencies to protect themselves and their property, reflecting a lack of confidence in public policing.

Changing the Conventional Wisdom of Policing

As a result of the above-described problems, studies of policing provided a new "common wisdom" of policing (Goldstein 1977). For example, it was learned that two-person patrol vehicles were no more safe or effective than one-person cars; response time had very little to do with whether or not an arrest was made at the scene; detectives were greatly overrated in their ability to solve crimes (Peak and Glensor 2005); and less than 50% of an officer's time was committed to calls for service (CFS), and of those calls handled, more than 80% were noncriminal incidents (Cumming, Cumming, and Edell 1965; Bercal 1970; Reiss 1971). Such findings demonstrated that many "sacred cow" beliefs about police methods were erroneous (Goldstein 1990). Officers who were glued to their police car radios, flitting like pinballs from one call for service to the next as rapidly as possible, were not effective in the long term, and learned very little about the underlying causes of problems in the neighborhoods on their beats.

Three Generations of COPS

The elements just discussed made it clear that police agencies had to change their methods, management practices, and how they viewed their work. First, they had to reacquaint themselves with members of the community by involving citizens in the resolution of neighborhood problems. The public, as well as other government and social services organizations, were to be considered "a part of," as opposed to "apart from," their efforts.

Crime control remains an important function, but equal emphasis is given to *prevention.* Police officers return to their wide use of discretion under this model, with decision making being shared across all levels of the organization, including line officers. Participative management is thus greatly increased, and fewer levels of authority are required to administer the organization. In essence, middle-management layers are reduced.

COPS is now the culture of many police organizations, affecting and permeating their hiring processes, recruiting academies, in-service training, promotional examinations, and strategic plans. Significantly, the Violent Crime Control and Law Enforcement Act of 1994 authorized $8.8 billion over six years to create the Office of Community Oriented Policing Services (COPS) within the U.S. Department of Justice, in order to add one hundred thousand more police officers to communities across the country and to create thirty-one regional community policing institutes.

COPS has now moved through three generations (Oliver 2000). The first generation, *innovation,* spans the period from 1979 through 1986. It began with the aforementioned seminal work of Herman Goldstein concerning needed improvement of policing (Goldstein 1979) and with the "broken windows" theory of James Q. Wilson and George L. Kelling (1982). Early trials of community policing during this period—called "experiments," "test sites," and "demonstration projects"—were usually restricted to larger metropolitan cities. The style of policing that was employed was predominantly narrow in focus, emphasizing foot patrols, problem-solving methods, or community substations.

In its second generation, *diffusion* (from 1987 through 1994), the COPS philosophy and practice spread rapidly among police agencies. In 1985, slightly more than three hundred police agencies employed some form of community policing (Walker 1985), and by 1994 it had spread to more than eight thousand agencies (McEwen 1995). The practice of community policing during this generation was still generally limited to large- and medium-sized cities,

and the strategies normally targeted drugs and fear-of-crime issues while improving police–community relations. Much more emphasis was placed on evaluating outcomes through the use of appropriate research methodologies. These evaluations demonstrated the benefits and pitfalls of various strategies, allowing more efficient and targeted police work.

The third generation, *institutionalization,* began in 1995 and continues to the present. Nearly seven in ten (68%) of the nation's seventeen thousand local police agencies, employing 90% of all officers, have adopted this strategy (U.S. Department of Justice 2003). Today, COPS includes programs that address youth firearm violence, gangs, and domestic violence, and involves crime mapping techniques and applies the principles of crime prevention through environmental design.

In Sum: "What Works?"

Following a systematic review of more than five hundred scientific evaluations of criminal justice and crime prevention practices, a prestigious team of researchers including Lawrence Sherman, John Eck, and others stated in their 1998 report to Congress that "*problem solving analysis is effective when addressed to the specific crime situation*" (emphasis added).

While many more impact evaluations are needed before conclusions can be reached about COPS, it is clear that this strategy is now an established and accepted approach to policing for the twenty-first century.

KENNETH J. PEAK and EMMANUEL P. BARTHE

See also **Community-Oriented Policing: Effects and Impacts; Community-Oriented Policing: History; Community-Oriented Policing: International; Community-Oriented Policing: Practices; Crime Prevention; Problem-Oriented Policing**

References and Further Reading

Bercal, T. 1970. Calls for police assistance. *American Behavioral Scientist* 13: 682.

Cumming, Elaine, Ian Cumming, and Laura Edell. 1965. Policeman as philosopher, guide, and friend. *Social Problems* 12: 285.

Goldstein, Herman. 1977. *Policing a free society*. Cambridge, MA: Ballinger.

———. 1979. Improving policing: A problem-oriented approach. *Crime and Delinquency* 25: 236–58.

———. 1990. *Problem-oriented policing*. New York: McGraw-Hill.

McEwen, T. 1995. *National assessment program: 1994 survey results*. Washington, DC: National Institute of Justice.

Oliver, Willard M. 2000. The third generation of community policing: Moving through innovation, diffusion, and institutionalization. *Police Quarterly* 3 (December): 367–88.

Peak, Kenneth J., and Ronald W. Glensor. 2005. *Community policing and problem solving: Strategies and practices*. 4th ed. Upper Saddle River, NJ: Prentice-Hall.

Reiss, Albert J., Jr. 1971. *The police and the public*. New Haven, CT: Yale University Press.

Sherman, Lawrence W., Denise C. Gottfredson, Doris L. MacKenzie, John Eck, Peter Reuter, and Shawn D. Bushway. 1998. *Preventing crime: What works, what doesn't, what's promising*. Research in Brief, pp. 1–27. Washington, DC: National Institute of Justice.

Skolnick, Jerome H., and David H. Bayley. 1986. *The new blue line: Police innovation in six American cities*. New York: The Free Press.

U.S. Department of Justice, Bureau of Justice Statistics. 2003. *Law enforcement management and administrative statistics: Local police departments 2000*. January, p. iii. Washington, DC: U.S. Department of Justice, Bureau of Justice Statistics.

Walker, Samuel. 1977. *A critical history of police reform: The emergence of professionalism*. Lexington, MA: Lexington Books.

———. 1985. *The police in America: An introduction*. New York: McGraw-Hill.

Wilson, J. Q., and G. L. Kelling. 1982. The police and neighborhood safety: Broken windows. *Atlantic Monthly* 127 (March): 29–38.

Wycoff, Mary Ann. 1982. *The role of municipal police research as a prelude to changing it*. Washington, DC: Police Foundation.

COMMUNITY WATCH PROGRAMS

The term *community watch* covers several programs based on the idea of crime prevention through citizen surveillance. These include neighborhood watch programs, block watch, home watch, and apartment watch. The term can also be used to cover citizen surveillance in nonresidential areas, such as boat watch, farm watch, park watch, and car watch.

The idea of watch programs emerged in the United States during the 1960s and 1970s out of a broader movement to involve citizens in crime control. Other collective responses to crime introduced at that time were citizen patrols, police–community councils, citizen alerts, and citizen anticrime crusades. One of the earliest community watch programs in the United States was established in 1966 in Oakland under the name of Home Alert. Participants in the scheme attended regular meetings, displayed window stickers, marked their property, and acted as the "eyes and ears" of the police (Washnis 1976). Perhaps the best known of these early programs was the Seattle Community Crime Prevention Project launched in 1973 (Cirel et al. 1977). The Seattle program encouraged citizens to obtain home security inspections, mark their property, organize block watches, and "augment the range of vision" of traditional policing.

Community watch programs were also developed in other countries about the same time. Most of these drew on the U.S. model and incorporated similar components and terminology. One of the earliest neighborhood watch schemes in the United Kingdom was established in 1982 in Mollington, Cheshire. The program was based on the American model and comprised neighbors keeping their eyes and ears open for suspicious persons and reporting anything suspicious to the police, property marking, and improvements in physical security. The first scheme in

Australia was launched in Victoria in 1984 and the first scheme in New Zealand began in 1980.

Structure

Community watch programs are usually made up of a number of component parts. The typical package in the United States is sometimes referred to as the "Big Three" and includes community watch, property marking, and home security. In the United Kingdom, the typical package is similar and comprises neighborhood watch in conjunction with property marking and home security surveys.

Comprehensive packages sometimes include other crime prevention measures in addition to the "Big Three." A notable difference between schemes is the choice of these additional elements. They are often idiosyncratic and fit the needs of particular communities. A community watch program in Wilmington, Delaware, for example, included in its package a "Senior Citizen's Educational Program" and an "Auxiliary Police Unit" to support the watch groups (Decampli 1977). A Block Watch program in Philadelphia included providing emotional support for victims of crime during court proceedings (Finn 1986).

There is also some variation in the size of the schemes. Block watches and block clubs in the United States typically cover a small number of households (sometimes less than fifty), whereas neighborhood watch programs in the United Kingdom typically include entire residential areas, covering perhaps thousands of households. While there was some early interest in "cocoon" watch schemes in the United Kingdom, based on just a handful of households, the dominant form has tended to be much larger than this. Schemes in Australia are more variable and sometimes cover entire residential areas and sometimes smaller locations such as high-rise apartment blocks and specific institutions such as hospitals.

There is also some variation in the way schemes are established and funded. Watch schemes in the United States and the United Kingdom are sometimes police initiated and sometimes public initiated. The choice is often a result of the stage in the development of watch schemes in the area. Early schemes tend to be police initiated to assist their establishment, whereas schemes launched at a later stage, after the program has become well developed, are often public initiated. However, police involvement may continue for other reasons. The police in Detroit, for example, continued to launch police-initiated schemes to ensure that disadvantaged areas that were unlikely to generate requests from the public were also covered.

Function

There is a clear consensus in the literature that the main aim of watch programs is to prevent crime. There are some variations in terms of which crimes are to be prevented. The most commonly identified crime targeted is residential burglary. Programs sometimes aim to reduce street robbery, auto thefts, and vandalism. Schemes also report supplementary aims such as reduction of fear of crime and improvements in police–community relations, crime reporting, and the quality of life.

Watch schemes are typically operated by local citizens who watch out for suspicious incidents and behavior and report these to the police. There are many references in the publicity material to the idea of citizens becoming "the eyes and ears" of the police. Some police departments ask the public to look out only for crimes rather than anything else suspicious.

Others encourage reporting of anything suspicious and issue recording cards for the public to complete when identifying suspects. Some programs include additional activities that the public can take to prevent crimes in their area. In some areas, community watch residents are encouraged to ensure that neighbor's homes look occupied while they are away.

Mechanisms

The most frequently recorded mechanism by which watch programs are supposed to reduce crime is as a result of residents looking out for suspicious activities and reporting these to the police. There are at least three ways in which surveillance and reporting might reduce crime. First, visible surveillance might reduce crime as a result of its effect on the perceptions and decision making of potential offenders. Watching and reporting might deter offenders if they are aware of the propensity of the local residents to report suspicious behavior and if they believe that this increases their risks of being caught.

Second, community watch schemes might reduce crime as a result of an increase in the flow of useful information from the public to the police. This might involve reports of crimes in progress and early warning of suspicious persons and events. These reports might then lead to a greater number of arrests and convictions, which might in turn result in individual deterrence or (when a custodial sentence is passed) incapacitation of local offenders.

Third, watch programs might reduce crime through the mechanisms of social control. Community watch might enhance a sense of community cohesion, community activism, and collective efficacy, which might in turn increase the ability of communities to control crime in their neighborhoods.

Effectiveness

Several evaluations of community watch programs have been conducted. One of the earliest conducted in the United States was by Titus (1984) who summarized the results of nearly forty community crime prevention programs. Most of these included elements of community watch. The majority of the studies were conducted by police departments or included data from police departments. Nearly all of the studies found that community watch areas were associated with lower levels of crime. However, most of the evaluations were described as "weak" in terms of research design.

Another review of the literature looked mainly at community watch programs in the United Kingdom (Husain 1990). The study reviewed the results of nine existing evaluations and conducted an original analysis of community watch in six additional locations using police-recorded crime data. The review of existing evaluations concluded that "the published evidence to suggest that [neighborhood watch] can prevent crime is extremely thin." The results of the original analysis in six locations concluded that there was strong evidence of a reduction in crime in one location, but weak or no evidence of a reduction in the remaining five.

One of the most recent reviews of the literature on the effectiveness of community watch programs selected only evaluations with the strongest research designs (Sherman et al. 1997). The authors included only studies that used random assignment or studies that monitored both watch areas and similar comparison areas without community watch. The review found just four evaluations that matched these criteria. The results of these evaluations were mainly negative. The authors concluded, "The oldest and best-known community policing program, Neighborhood Watch, is ineffective at preventing crime."

These three reviews of the literature have produced mixed results. One explanation for this is that the nature of the findings might be affected by the quality of the research methods used. Evaluations based on "before" and "after" measures only with no comparison area can provide false results because they do not show what might have happened in the absence of the scheme. Evaluations based on a comparison of community watch and non–community watch areas at a single point in time can also produce false results because they do not show whether there were preexisting differences between the areas. The best research designs are either random allocation studies or carefully controlled "before" and "after" studies using matched comparison areas. Unfortunately, there are very few studies of these kinds. More research needs to be done, therefore, before the effectiveness of community watch can be finally determined.

TREVOR BENNETT

See also **Attitudes toward the Police: Measurement Issues; Crime Prevention; Situational Crime Prevention**

References and Further Reading

Cirel, P., P. Evans, D. McGillis, and D. Whitcomb. 1977. *Community crime prevention, Seattle, Washington: An exemplary project*. Washington, DC: U.S. Department of Justice.

Decampli, Thomas R. 1977. *Wilmington Neighborhood Security Project: A project evaluation*. Wilmington, DE: Wilmington Bureau of Police.

Finn, Peter. 1986. *Block watches help crime victims in Philadelphia*. Rockville, MD: National Criminal Justice Reference Service.

Husain, Sohail. 1990. *Neighborhood watch and crime: An assessment of impact*. London: Police Foundation.

Sherman, L. W., D. Gottfredson, D. MacKenzie, P. Reuter, J. Eck, and S. Bushway. 1997. *Preventing crime: What works, what doesn't, what's promising*. Washington, DC: U.S. Department of Justice.

Titus, R. 1984. Residential burglary and the community response. In *Coping with burglary*, ed. Clarke and Hope, 97–130. Boston: Kluwer-Nijhoff.

Washnis, George. 1976. *Citizen involvement in crime prevention*. London: Lexington Books.

COMPLAINTS AGAINST POLICE

To put complaints against the police into perspective, it is necessary to briefly outline why police exist or, rather, the functions of the police in society. According to the American Bar Association's *Standards Relating to the Urban Police Function* (as in Peak 1997), the functions of the police in modern society are as follows:

1. To identify criminals and criminal activity and, where appropriate, apprehend offenders and participate in court proceedings
2. To reduce the opportunities for the commission of crime through preventive patrol and other measures
3. To aid individuals who are in danger of physical harm
4. To protect constitutional guarantees
5. To facilitate the movement of people and vehicles
6. To assist those who cannot care for themselves
7. To help resolve conflict
8. To identify problems that are potentially serious law enforcement or governmental problems
9. To create and maintain a feeling of security in the community
10. To promote and preserve civil order
11. To provide other services on an emergency basis.

To this list, the authors would like to add that the police are responsible for identifying and controlling situations that have the propensity of becoming problematic and to locate missing persons and help recover missing and/or stolen property.

According to Oliver (2001), the preceding functions can be summarized into two broad categories: enforcing the laws and maintaining order. Between these two broad functions, order maintenance constitutes the bulk of police officers' daily activities (Senna and Siegel 1999) and therefore presents many opportunities for face-to-face contact with the public and complaints against the police.

Relative to their functions, it is obvious that the police are the most visible symbol of authority in society. Such visibility, coupled with the complexity and ambiguity of their role and the heterogeneity of the modern society in which they operate, not only makes law enforcement a dangerous profession but also increases the chance that similar conduct by police officers in varying communities would result in different responses in different parts of the community, thereby increasing complaints against the police. Also, police organizations are the only governmental agency authorized to use force—including lethal force—when necessary, to carry out their responsibilities. How wisely or judiciously police officers use their powers is the primary determinant of how free and open a society is (O'Connor 2005), and how open and free a society is determines the types and number of complaints citizens have and/or file against police officers. The number and types of complaints against the police reflect differences in behavior of police officers, the willingness of the department to receive and act on complaints, and a political climate that either discourages or encourages citizens to complain (Roberg and Kuykendall 1993).

According to Bennett and Hess (2001), citizen complaints against police officers can be classified as sustained, not sustained, unfounded, or the officer is exonerated. Sustained complaints, they say, are those that, as a result of an investigation, are determined to be justified. That is, it has been determined that the claim made by the citizen is true. Unsustained complaints are those that, in the opinion of those making the determination, cannot be substantiated as either true or false. Unfounded complaints, they continue, are those that the investigation has determined did not occur as alleged by the complainant, whereas exoneration means that investigation of a complaint showed that the allegation is essentially true but that the officer's behavior was found to be justified, legal, or consistent with departmental policy.

Although research concerning police behavior and the number, types, and dispositions of citizens' complaints against the police is scanty, studies (Bennett and Hess 2001; Bittner 1975; Bobb 2002; Christopher 1991; Dugan and Breda 1991; Fogel 1987; Human Rights Watch 1998a, 1998b, 1998c, 1998d, 1998e, 1998f, 1998g, 1998h, 1998i, 1998j, 1998k, 1998l, 1998m, 1998n; Lersch and Mieczkowski 1996; Petterson 1991; Rojek, Wagner, and Decker 2001; Terrill and McCluskey 2002; Walker 1992, 2001) provide some useful insights:

1. Whereas less than 1% of all citizens who come in contact with the police complain about police methods and behavior, as many as 10% to 15% may feel they have something to complain about. For the most part, citizens' complaints against the police are in relation to what the officer did or failed to do.

2. Whereas there is little agreement among researchers regarding whether African Americans are overtly discriminated against by the police in their enforcement tactics, there is no doubt that they constitute the majority of complainants against the police. African Americans make up between 50% and 60% of complainants against the police.

3. The rate of complaints varies between six and eighty-one complaints per one hundred officers among police departments.

4. The number of complaints sustained by police departments varies between 0% and 25% mostly due to shoddy police internal affairs investigations, the blue wall of silence, powerless citizens' review boards, lack of "credible" witnesses, and police corruption.

5. The most common complaint concerns excessive use of force.

6. Complaints of excessive use of force are usually sustained less often than other types of complaints.

7. "Conduct unbecoming a police officer" is sustained more often than other forms of complaints.

8. In instances where complaints are sustained and the city or the police department pays out a huge sum of money to the complainant, police officers are not disciplined mostly due to political infighting within the police department, attitudes of city officials toward complaints against police officers, resistance by a strong police union, complainants' criminal history, state immunity laws, and short-term statutes of limitation on complaints against the police.

9. A small number of police officers account for a disproportionate number of complaints. This is referred to as the "bad apple" theory. (For a brief summary of the problem officer hypothesis, see Walker, Alpert, and Kennedy 2000.) Although the number varies from one department to another, it is estimated that between 5% and 10% of officers in most departments account for between 20% and 35% of complaints.

10. It seems that a disproportionate number of complaints against the police are filed against younger, less experienced officers. As many as two-thirds of all complaints in some departments involve officers who are thirty years of age or younger and who have five or fewer years of experience.

11. The blue wall of silence exists in all police departments and contributes immensely to incidents of abuse of citizens by the police. Police officers who are aware of misconduct by other officers do not come forward for fear of reprisal by fellow officers or the department. Those who report misconduct are ostracized and harassed, become targets of complaints and even physical threats, and are made to fear that they will be left alone on the streets in a time of crisis. This situation has given rise to what has been termed the "subculture" theory of police misconduct.

12. There is a general flaw in the supervision and evaluation of police officers. Officers with long records of alleged misconduct, including some with histories of alleged physical abuse of citizens, are allowed to remain on the street largely unidentified and unsupervised and consistently receive perfect performance evaluations each year and are rewarded with promotion.

13. Although use of excessive force (especially, deadly force) by the police is a rare occurrence, there nonetheless is heightened concern among citizens about excessive force. The public has increasingly become aware that law enforcement agencies cannot police themselves. The public believes that the power to investigate police misconduct should be ceded by the police in whole or in part to qualified, independent investigative bodies.

14. Abusive police officers sometimes use excessive force just to show who was in charge. Some keep guns and drugs seized during raids. The guns are used as "throwaway" guns to plant on a suspect in the event of a questionable arrest

or police shooting, and the drugs can be used to frame suspects.

15. It is more difficult to prosecute and/or fire police officers who are the subject of sustained citizen complaints or who have a pattern of alleged misconducts both on and off duty than other city employees due in part to lack of witnesses, a strong police union that is willing to defend even officers with a pattern of citizens' complaints, skewed internal investigation techniques, and special immunity laws that protect police officers from prosecution.

16. Cities and sometimes police departments pay out huge sums of money each year to settle lawsuits and awards dealing with police use of excessive force, wrongful death, false arrests, and false imprisonment.

17. Many police departments are not in compliance with international human rights standards or with the 1985 U.S. Supreme Court ruling in *Tennessee v. Garner,* which requires that police officers only shoot fleeing felony suspects when necessary to prevent escape and when there is probable cause to believe that they pose a significant danger to the officer or members of the public.

Although it is a small percentage of officers in any police department that engages in abuse of citizens, some researchers believe that the establishment of civilian review boards with real powers to ensure that investigations of complaints are full, fair, and thorough would further reduce the number of such complaints. The benefits of such boards are already being reaped by the Los Angeles Sheriff's Department (LASD), which, since being subject to ongoing independent outside investigation and monitoring, has noticed a decrease in the number of officers killed or wounded in the line of duty from a high of ten in 1991 to three in 2001, while the number of arrests remained the same. Between 1991 and 2000, the number of suspects killed or wounded by LASD officers also decreased from a high of sixty-three people in 1991 to a low of eighteen in 2000 (Bobb 2002). Also during the ten years of outside independent monitoring and reporting, the total docket of excessive force cases on file against LASD officers dropped from a high of 381 cases in 1992 to a low of 93 in 2001, and the amounts paid out in settlements and judgments in excessive force cases during the same period dropped from a high of $17 million to a low of $2 million in 2001. In today's economic climate and budget cuts, cutting this expense would save taxpayers money and improve community–police relations.

GODPOWER O. OKEREKE, TOM JORDAN, and GEORGE PARANGIMALIL

See also **Accountability; Attitudes toward the Police: Measurement Issues; Attitudes toward the Police: Overview; Autonomy and the Police; Citizen Complaints in the New Police Order; Corruption; Deviant Subcultures in Policing; Excessive Force; Integrity in Policing; Minorities and the Police; Public Image of the Police**

References and Further Reading

Bennett, Wayne W., and Karen M. Hess. 2001. Management and supervision in law enforcement. 3rd ed. Belmont, CA: Wadsworth-Thomson Learning.

Bittner, Egon. 1975. *The functions of the police in modern society.* New York: Jason Aronson.

Bobb, Merrick. 2002. *Civilian oversight of the police in the United States.* Paper presented at the Global Meeting on Civilian Oversight of Police, Rio de Janeiro.

Christopher, W. 1991. *Report of the independent commission on the Los Angeles Police Department.* Los Angeles: City of Los Angeles.

Dugan, John R., and Daniel R. Breda. 1991. Complaints about police officers: A comparison among types and agencies. *Journal of Criminal Justice* 19: 165–71.

Fogel, David. 1987. The investigation and disciplining of police misconduct: A comparative view. *Police Studies* 10: 1–15.

Human Rights Watch. 1998a. *Shielded from justice: Police brutality and accountability in the United States—Atlanta*. http://www.hrw.org/reports98/police/uspo41.htm (accessed October 10, 2005).

Human Rights Watch. 1998b. *Shielded from justice: Police brutality and accountability in the United States—Boston*. http://www.hrw.org/reports98/police/uspo46.htm (accessed October 10, 2005).

Human Rights Watch. 1998c. *Shielded from justice: Police brutality and accountability in the United States—Chicago*. http://www.hrw.org/reports98/police/uspo54.htm (accessed October 10, 2005).

Human Rights Watch. 1998d. *Shielded from justice: Police brutality and accountability in the United States—Detroit*. http://www.hrw.org/reports98/police/uspo60.htm (accessed October 15, 2005).

Human Rights Watch. 1998e. *Shielded from justice: Police brutality and accountability in the United States—Indianapolis*. http://www.hrw.org/reports98/police/uspo65.htm (accessed October 16, 2005).

Human Rights Watch. 1998f. *Shielded from justice: Police brutality and accountability in the United States—Los Angeles*. http://www.hrw.org/reports98/police/uspo72.htm (accessed October 20, 2005).

Human Rights Watch. 1998g. *Shielded from justice: Police brutality and accountability in the United States—Minneapolis*. http://www.hrw.org/reports98/police/uspo84.htm (accessed October 20, 2005).

Human Rights Watch. 1998h. *Shielded from justice: Police brutality and accountability in the United States—New Orleans*. http://www.hrw.org/reports98/police/uspo92.htm (accessed October 21, 2005).

Human Rights Watch. 1998i. *Shielded from justice: Police brutality and accountability in the United States—New York*. http://www.hrw.org/reports98/police/uspo99.htm (accessed October 25, 2005).

Human Rights Watch. 1998j. *Shielded from justice: Police brutality and accountability in the United States—Philadelphia*. http://www.hrw.org/reports98/police/uspo108.htm (accessed October 25, 2005).

Human Rights Watch. 1998k. *Shielded from justice: Police brutality and accountability in the United States—Portland*. http://www.hrw.org/reports98/police/uspo116.htm (accessed October 25, 2005).

Human Rights Watch. 1998l. *Shielded from justice: Police brutality and accountability in the United States—Providence*. http://www.hrw.org/reports98/police/uspo123.htm (accessed October 26, 2005).

Human Rights Watch. 1998m. *Shielded from justice: Police brutality and accountability in the United States—San Francisco*. http://www.hrw.org/reports98/police/uspo130.htm (accessed October 26, 2005).

Human Rights Watch. 1998n. *Shielded from justice: Police brutality and accountability in the United States—Atlanta*. http://www.hrw.org/reports98/police/uspo136.htm (accessed October 26, 2005).

Lersch, Kim M., and Tom Mieczkowski. 1996. Who are the problem-prone officers? An analysis of citizen complaints. *American Journal of Police* 15 (3): 23–44.

O'Connor, Tom. 2005. *Justice, society, and law*. http://www.faculty.ncwc.edu/toconnor/111/111lect05.htm (accessed December 2, 2005).

Oliver, Willard M. 2001. *Community-oriented policing: A systemic approach to policing*. 2nd ed. Upper Saddle River, NJ: Prentice-Hall.

Peak, Kenneth J. 1997. *Policing America: Methods, issues, challenges*. 2nd ed. Upper Saddle River, NJ: Prentice-Hall.

Petterson, Werner E. 1991. Police accountability and civilian oversight of policing: An American perspective. In *Complaints against the police: The trends to external review*, ed. A. J. Goldsmith, 259–89. Avon, Great Britain.

Roberg, Roy R., and Jack Kuykendall. 1993. *Police and society*. Belmont, CA: Wadsworth-Thomson Learning.

Rojek, Jeff, Allen E. Wagner, and Scott H. Decker. 2001. Addressing police misconduct: The role of citizen complaints. In *Critical issues in policing*, ed. Roger G. Dunham and Geoffrey P. Alpert, 4th ed. Prospect Heights, IL: Waveland Press.

Senna, Joseph P., and Larry Siegel. 1999. *Introduction to criminal justice*. 8th ed. Belmont, CA: Wadsworth-Thomson Learning.

Terrill, William, and John McCluskey. 2002. Citizen complaints and problem officers: Examining officer behavior. *Journal of Criminal Justice* 30 (2): 143–55.

Walker, Samuel. 1992. *The police in America: An introduction*. 2nd ed. New York: McGraw-Hill.

———. 2001. *Police accountability: The role of citizen oversight*. Belmont, CA: Wadsworth-Thomson Learning.

Walker, Samuel, Geoffrey P. Alpert, and Dennis J. Kennedy. 2000. Early warning systems for police: Concept, history, and issues. *Police Quarterly* 3 (2): 132–52.

COMPSTAT

The crime analysis and management approach known as COMPSTAT is widely heralded and frequently imitated. The tributes describe COMPSTAT as "perhaps the single most important organizational/administrative innovation in policing during the latter half of the 20th century" (Kelling and Sousa 2001, 6). A *Criminology and Public Policy Journal* editor termed COMPSTAT "arguably one of the most significant strategic innovations in policing in the last couple of decades" (*Criminology and Public Policy* 2003, 419). The authors of a major study note that COMPSTAT "has already been recognized as a major innovation in American policing" (Weisburd et al. 2003, 422). In 1996, COMPSTAT was awarded the prestigious Innovations in American Government Award from the Ford Foundation and the John F. Kennedy School of Government at Harvard University. Former New York City Mayor Rudy Giuliani proclaims COMPSTAT as his administration's "crown jewel" (Giuliani 2002, 7).

Because most people only observe its most visible elements, COMPSTAT is frequently misunderstood. These visible elements include up-to-date computerized crime data, crime analysis, and advanced crime mapping, which serve as the bases for regularized, interactive crime strategy meetings in which managers are held accountable for specific crime strategies and solutions in their areas. It is fair to say that the widespread diffusion of COMPSTAT refers to these most noticeable elements. Since COMPSTAT was first unveiled by the New York City Police Department (NYPD) in 1994, a Police Foundation's 1999 survey for the National Institute of Justice (NIJ) revealed that a third of the nation's 515 largest police departments had implemented a COMPSTAT-like program by 2001 and 20% were planning to do so. The same survey found that about 70% of police departments with COMPSTAT programs reported attending a NYPD COMPSTAT meeting (Weisburd et al. 2001).

This process has continued in subsequent years. Gootman (2000, B1) reported that 219 police agency representatives visited NYPD COMPSTAT meetings in 1998, 221 in 1999, and 235 in the first ten months of 2000. Attendance at a COMPSTAT meeting, while a useful introduction, does not provide adequate preparation for introducing and establishing COMPSTAT into one's own department. In fact, the presentations at such meetings may be misleading because attendees often become mesmerized by the flashy overhead display of multiple crime maps synchronized with technologically advanced portrayals of computerized crime statistics. In the vernacular, it is only necessary to display computer-generated crime maps and pressure commanders "to make the dots go away" (Maple 2000, 38). This more elaborate but superficial approach is emblematic of the quick managerial fix approach, thus contributing to the misunderstanding and misapplication of COMPSTAT.

Performance Management Comes to Policing

More importantly, COMPSTAT is, in many ways, emblematic of the application of business-oriented managerial reforms to modern policing. Enhancing accountability for performance by adopting business and professional practices has repeatedly emerged as the holy grail of police managerial reform. Early twentieth-century police reformers such as O. W. Wilson sought to upgrade the quality of police performance through the introduction of sound business practices.

In recent years, the goal of refashioning police agencies so that they more closely mirror private organizations has been extended to entire police departments.

For example, Herman Goldstein's path-breaking work advocated new managerial structures capable of reading and responding to internal and external work environments (Goldstein 1990, p.162).

By 1994, there was a clear trend within government to emulate business practices and "reinvent" themselves by dramatically altering administrative structures and operational processes in order to enhance efficiency and the overall quality of performance. This all-embracing view is now shared by many police scholars urging police adoption of "corporate strategies" and "entrepreneurial" approaches (Burns and Stalker 1961; Moore and Trojanowicz 1988).

For police, as with other public organizations, performance measures were viewed as integral to the adoption of and accountability for these business characteristics (Kravchuk and Schack 1996; Wholey and Hatry 1992). The Government Performance and Results Act of 1993 (GPRA) and Osborne and Gaebler's *Reinventing Government* (1992) promoted the reinventing government movement as the "public sector analogue to the corporate 'business process engineering' movement, which has been described as 'one of the most influential management ideas of the nineties'" (Case 1999, 419, as cited in O'Connell 2002).

Performance measures are supported by concepts linked to the reengineering process. "Benchmarking" and "best practices" cherish objectives and standards that are shared throughout the entire organization (Bowerman and Ball 2000; Coe 1999).

The New York City Police Department

The introduction and spread of these business concepts and practices in American police departments is revealed through an examination of post-1993 COMPSTAT and related changes in the New York City Police Department (NYPD). Modern business management provided the orchestral score for these changes; *reengineering* was its name. Contemporary management literature explains that reengineering requires "radical change," a "starting over" throughout the entire organization, nothing less than a "reinvention of how organizations work."

New York's police commissioner at this time, William Bratton, was portrayed by the *Economist* as "a fan of the reengineering rhetoric of Michael Hammer and James Champy" (*Economist* 1995, 50). *Business Week* lauded the NYPD's "innovative turnaround artists" who used "private-sector" techniques (*Business Week* 1995, 83). Each of twelve reengineering teams was dedicated to a specific topic and was asked to determine what was broken and how to fix it—or, perhaps more accurately, what would be used to replace it. Each committee was supplied with a copy of Hammer and Champy's *Reengineering the Corporation*, which advocates "abandoning outdated rules and fundamental assumptions" (Hammer and Champy 1993, 31).

The NYPD's reengineering reports questioned the department's operating procedures. What current policy yields, they claimed, was inadequate. The precinct organization report, for example, noted:

> . . . 2 or 3% reduction in crime is not good enough. We need to change the organization to do more. The need to reengineer precincts is not immediately apparent. Citywide crime continues to decline year after year. Every annual precinct state of command report, without exception, includes evidence of neighborhood improvements. Bureau and Special Unit Commanders to a man, or a woman, will vigorously defend the effectiveness of the present system. Why fix what's not broken?

The answer is in the new mission of the department to dramatically reduce crime, fear, and disorder. Slow, continuous improvement doesn't cut it, and that is all the present system can deliver. . . . [R]e-engineering in its simplest form means starting all over, starting from scratch (New York City Police Department 1994, v).

COMPSTAT acted like a booster cable to the NYPD's battery, providing the cranking power needed to activate decentralization and command accountability. Relinquishing control of daily ground operations was the most fundamental yet difficult challenge facing the new administration. Traditionally, the person at the apex of the NYPD pyramid would retain control through standardized procedures and policies. But in order to hold precinct commanders accountable for crime prevention, the new leadership knew the organization must grant them more discretion. Rather than allow headquarters to determine staffing and deployment on a citywide basis, it was decided that reducing crime, fear of crime, and disorder would flow from patrol borough and precinct coordination of selected enforcement efforts.

COMPSTAT emerged as the central mechanism with which up-to-date crime performance measures were developed, and precinct commanders were held accountable for crime in their areas. In the parlance of business management, performance standards were set for the whole department and its subunits. Entrance to Bratton's higher echelon was restricted to commanders committed to double-digit crime reduction. Establishing a specific objective—a 10% reduction in crime for 1994—was the initial propellant for change. While target setting is the norm for the private sector, it usually is anathema for public organizations because it offers a yardstick against which performance can be more accurately measured and, if deficient, condemned.

The commissioner and his top aides recognized that data needed to be gathered and analyzed in a timely manner if effective crime reduction strategies were to be implemented. These statistics constituted the first COMPSTAT book in February 1994. Subsequently, periodic meetings were scheduled at headquarters whereby precinct commanders were required to report and react to crime data generated from their areas of responsibility (that is, their commands). Over time, these data-based informal discussions between department executives and field commanders developed into formal biweekly strategy meetings (known as COMPSTAT meetings) at which all levels of the department participate to identify precinct and citywide crime trends, deploy resources, make assessments, and are held accountable for crime control strategies and results. (For details, see Silverman 1999.)

The first three years of the NYPD's COMPSTAT program corresponded with dramatic declines in the city's crime rate. According to the FBI's *Unified Crime Reports,* the city's 12% decline in index crime in 1994 (compared to a national drop of less than 2%) grew to 16% in 1995 and yielded another 16% in 1996. These decreases accounted for more than 60% of the national decline during this period.

Although these figures, of course, do not prove a causal relationship between COMPSTAT and a decrease in crime, they received extraordinary law enforcement and national attention. The New York model (COMPSTAT) was offered as the road to rapid crime reduction (Gootman 2000, B1). A *Time* magazine 1996 observation is still applicable ten years later: "COMPSTAT has become the Lourdes of policing, drawing pilgrim cops from around the world . . . for a taste of New York's magic" (Pooley 1996, 55–56).

Response to COMPSTAT Critiques

In a valuable national study, the Police Foundation identified COMPSTAT's "six key elements." They are "mission clarification, internal accountability, geographic organization of operational command, organizational flexibility, data driven problem identification and assessment, innovative problem solving tactics, and external information exchange" (Weisburd et al. 2003, 427).

The study found many of these key elements lacking in many police COMPSTAT programs. In their comparison of COMPSTAT and non-COMPSTAT agencies, the study concludes that the COMPSTAT agencies "have opted for a model much heavier on control than on empowerment" (Weisburd et al. 2003, 448). Moreover, despite its virtues, the authors found that:

> COMPSTAT agencies were largely indistinguishable from non-COMPSTAT agencies on measures that gauged geographic organization of command, organizationally flexibility, the time availability of data, and the selection and implementation of innovative strategies and tactics. . . . COMPSTAT departments are more reluctant to relinquish power that would decentralize some key elements of decision making geographically . . . enhance flexibility, and risk going outside of the standard tool kit of police tactics and strategies. The combined effect overall, whether or not intended, is to reinforce a traditional bureaucratic model of command and control. (Weisburd et al. 2003, 448)

This analysis fails to address the fact that the study's COMPSTAT programs are self-designated. There is no evidence that these police agencies underwent the self-diagnosis, reengineering, and organizational and managerial overhaul processes that preceded the New York COMPSTAT experience. In reality, COMPSTAT is a revolution in thinking about the role and ability of the police to address crime as opposed to reacting to social and economic conditions that breed crime. COMPSTAT, then, is a performance management mind-set that some have likened to a paradigm change in policing. In accordance with classic bureaucratic structure, the overall orientation of managers within the department was "downward," rather than outward (toward the external environment) or upward. Precinct commanders "did not see crime reduction as their foremost responsibility" and were "essentially on their own in combating crime" (Silverman 1999, 98). Commissioner Bratton quickly altered this mindset by making a variety of high-level personnel changes and by redefining the department's overall purpose and mission (Bratton 1998).

Both Henry and Wash follow Kuhn (1996) in their adoption of the "paradigm" concept. Henry and Bratton (2002, 15) posit that paradigms are a sort of mindset or a collection of organizing principles and fundamental viewpoints around which we organize our basic understanding of the world. Paradigms can be compared to ideologies, belief systems, philosophical principles, or cognitive models that shape our understanding of something.

Walsh, in 2001, adopted this approach when he depicted COMPSTAT as representing an "emerging police organizational management paradigm" (p. 1). Three years later, Walsh and Vito (2004) characterized COMPSTAT's "paradigm shift" as a "goal-oriented, strategic-management process that uses information technology, operational strategy, and managerial accountability to guide police operations" (p. 57).

What started out as a computer file and a book to satisfy crime informational needs has evolved and been reconstructed into a multifaceted forum for coordinated, reenergized, and accountable organizational crime fighting strategies. Its strength lies in its adaptability and compliance mechanisms. It is vitally important to recognize that COMPSTAT's initial and prime raison d'etre was and is to measure and hold managers accountable for performance. In Moore's words:

It becomes a powerful managerial system in part because the technical capacity of the system allows it to produce accurate information on important dimensions of performance at a level that coincides with a particular manager's domain of responsibility. . . . [COMPSTAT] is, in the end, primarily a performance measurement system. (Moore 2003, 470, 472)

The Future of COMPSTAT

Today, COMPSTAT crime reduction efficacy is frequently advocated by police administrators, several of whom moved from the NYPD to head other city police departments. COMPSTAT's introduction in New Orleans, for example, corresponded with a decline in murders from 421 in 1994, diving 55% in 1999 to 162. Minneapolis's version of COMPSTAT, CODEFOR (Computer Optimized Deployment–Focus on Results), has been credited with a double-digit decrease in homicides, aggravated assaults, robberies, burglaries, and auto thefts between 1998 and 1999 (Anderson 2001, 4). In 2000 COMPSTAT was introduced in Baltimore by its new chief, a former NYPD deputy police commissioner. By the end of the year, there had been fewer than 300 homicides in Baltimore for the first time in twenty years as well as an overall crime drop of 25% (Anderson 2001, 4; Clines 2001, 15; Weissenstein 2003, 27). Between 1999 and 2001, Baltimore's overall violent crime declined 24%, homicides dropped 15%, shootings fell 34%, robberies dropped 28%, rapes 20%, and assaults 21% (Henry and Bratton 2002, 307). Philadelphia's former police commissioner, another former NYPD deputy police commissioner, attributed a decline in the city's crime to COMPSTAT-driven policing. "Social conditions in the city have not changed radically in the two years and we have the same police department, the same number of officers.

Nothing has changed but how we deploy them and utilize them" (Anderson 2001, 3).

Similar crime reduction assertions have been made for police agencies around the world. Two Australian scholars, for example, recently published an evaluation of the New South Wales COMPSTAT-modeled Operation and Crime Review (OCM). The authors found that this process was effective in reducing three of the four offense categories studied (Chilvers and Weatherburn, 2004). Omaha's year-old COMPSTAT is credited with improving cooperation among all units. "Instead of one unit tackling a problem, everyone gets involved. . . . The entire culture has changed now" (*Law Enforcement News* 2004, 11).

In 1996, New York City's Corrections Department modeled its TEAMS (Total Efficiency Accountability Management System) program on COMPSTAT with an examination of the department's "most fundamental practices and procedures" (O'Connell 2001, 17). Again, accountability is a major theme, which, when fused with more accurate and timely statistical reporting and analysis and interunit cooperation, has been credited with a dramatic reduction in inmate violence. Between 1995 and 1999, stabbings and slashing declined from 1,093 to 70 (Anderson 2001, 3).

TEAMS has evolved and now addresses more than just jail violence. Its accountability system has been continually expanded to retrieve and assess almost six hundred performance indicators addressing such issues as religious service attendance, maintenance work orders, health care, overtime, compliance with food service regulations, completed searches conducted, and the performance of personnel who have been the subject of the department's civility tests (O'Connell and Straub 1999a, 1999b, 1999c).

COMPSTAT accountability mechanisms, long a staple of the private sector, have also become increasingly attractive to non–law enforcement public agencies.

There are numerous examples. The New York City Department of Parks and Recreation, for instance, developed its own version of COMPSTAT, calling it Parkstat. When parks officials visited NYPD COMPSTAT meetings in 1997, they realized that they could utilize this system to develop and refine their Parks Inspection Program (PIP), which oversees the maintenance and operation of more than twenty-eight thousand acres of property throughout New York City. Now Parks Department data analysis and managerial accountability are combined with monthly meetings to assess overall conditions; cleanliness of structural features such as benches, fences, sidewalks, and play equipment; and landscape features such as trees, athletic fields, and water bodies (O'Connell 2001, 20). The percentage of parks rated acceptably clean and safe increased from 47% in 1993 to 86% in 2001 (Webber and Robinson 2003, 3).

One observer's assessment of Parkstat ranks it comparable to COMPSTAT's high rating:

> The Parkstat program is continually developing. Indeed, the department recently renamed it Parkstat Plus and has expanded it to include a broader range of performance measures . . . relating to personnel, vehicle maintenance, resource allocation and enforcement activity to ensure superior service delivery. Parkstat stands as an excellent example of how the COMPSTAT model can be adopted and successfully implemented outside the field of criminal justice. (O' Connell 2001, 21, 22)

Perhaps the most ambitious extension of COMPSTAT's managerial accountability and informational exchange processes began in the city of Baltimore in mid-2000 when its mayor was delighted with the results of the Baltimore Police Department's first year with COMPSTAT. Baltimore's program, called Citistat (first developed by the COMPSTAT architect, the late NYPD Deputy Commissioner Jack Maple), is an attempt to evaluate and coordinate performance on a citywide basis whereby supervisors report every two weeks (as opposed to the previous quarterly basis) on their departments' performances. Citistat's timely data permit the assessment and coordination of diverse social services dealing with graffiti, abandoned vehicles, vacant housing, lead paint abatement, urban blight, and drug use and drug treatment. Discussions are based on up-to-date information. Citistat meetings are similar to those of COMPSTAT whereby data, graphs, and maps are projected to track and display department performance.

So far, the city is pleased with Citistat's development. There has been a 40% reduction in payroll overtime with a savings of more than $15 million over two years. Its director of operations maintains that "The charts, maps and pictures tell a story of performance, and those managers are held accountable" (Webber and Robinson 2003, 4). The fact that the prestigious Innovations in American Government Award was awarded to Baltimore's Citistat ten years after NYPD's COMPSTAT received the same award speaks to the enduring concepts embedded in this managerial and organizational approach. Speaking for an audience at Harvard University's Kennedy School, Stephen Goldsmith (2004) stated, "Citistat is a management tool for public officials that translates into real, tangible results for citizens. Government leaders across the country and around the world are taking notice of its success—and for good reason."

Citistat, like most COMPSTAT-type programs, seeks to lower the informational barriers that generally hinder intra- and interagency collaboration. Baltimore is constantly expanding the number of agencies included in the data analyses and its Citistat meetings. It appears that Citistat is the ultimate test of COMPSTAT's ability to serve as the informational cement of reform, the central mechanism that provides communication links to traditionally isolated specialized units. Fragmentation plagues many organizations. Harvard management expert Rosabeth Kanter (1983, 301) calls it "segmentalism" and notes, "The failure of many organization-change efforts has more to do with the lack . . . of an integrating, institutionalizing mechanism than with inherent problems in an innovation itself." Without COMPSTAT, fragmentation would continue to rule supreme. COMPSTAT's confrontation of informational splintering can be indispensable to organizational well-being. COMPSTAT can serve as the organizational glue that bonds many changes together.

COMPSTAT lends itself to a variety of law enforcement and non–law enforcement contexts. Numerous additional agencies are currently adopting their own versions of COMPSTAT. These include New York's Office of Health Insurance with its Healthstat, which is designed to assist uninsured New Yorkers enroll in publicly funded health insurance programs. "In the first 18 months, participating agencies enrolled about 340,000 eligible New Yorkers" (Webber and Robinson 2003, 4). The Department of Transportation instituted MOVE, an accountability and performance management system that meets twice a month to assess operational performance. The cities of Miami, Pittsburgh, and New York are pursuing comprehensive COMPSTAT-like systems similar to Baltimore's Citistat.

Societal needs for information sharing, data analysis, and effective organizational-managerial performance will only continue to proliferate and even expand COMPSTAT's rapid diffusion. Two and a half years before the terrorist attacks of September 11, 2001, on the United States, COMPSTAT's architect, the late Jack Maple, was asked about the future of COMPSTAT. He replied:

> This should not be limited to the police department. It should involve every city agency, the fire department, the building department, the transportation department; everybody should be contributing and coordinating. And other law enforcement

agencies need to participate fully. The FBI, DEA and ATF offices in a city should be running their own number and then bring those to COMPSTAT meetings at the police department. (Dussault 1999, 2)

Now in this post-9/11 era, there are numerous calls to overcome institutional barriers by federalizing the COMPSTAT process in order to combat terrorism.

The intelligence and accountability mechanism known as COMPSTAT is tailor-made for combating terrorism. Applying this mechanism to America's new war, however, requires solving one of the most enduring problems in policing: turf jealousy, especially between the FBI and local law enforcement agencies.

The FBI's antiterrorism efforts should be COMPSTATed in every city where the bureau operates. Where a Joint Terrorism Task Force (JTTF) exists, the commanders of the agencies should meet on a biweekly basis to interrogate task force members about the progress of their investigations. Where JTTFs do not exist, the FBI should assemble comparable meetings with all relevant agency heads. The new Fedstat meetings would have two purposes: to ensure that each ongoing investigation is being relentlessly and competently pursued, and to share intelligence (MacDonald 2001, 27).

ELI B. SILVERMAN

See also **Accountability; Administration of Police Agencies, Theories of; Autonomy and the Police; Community-Oriented Policing: Practices; Computer Technology; Crime Analysis; Crime Mapping; New York Police Department (NYPD); Technology and the Police**

References and Further Reading

Anderson, D. C. 2001. Crime control by the numbers: COMPSTAT yields new lessons for the police and the replication of a good idea. *Ford Foundation Report.*

Bowerman, M., and A. Ball. 2000. Great expectations: Benchmarking for best value. *Public Money and Management* 20 (2): 21–26.

Bratton, W. 1998. *The turnaround*. New York: Random House.

Burns, T., and G. M. Stalker. 1961. *Management of innovation*. London: Routledge, Keegan and Paul.

Business Week. 1995. A safer New York City. December 11.

Case, P. 1999. Remember re-engineering: The rhetorical appeal of a managerial salvation device. *Journal of Management Studies* 36: 419–45.

Chilvers, M., and D. Weatherburn. 2004. The New South Wales COMPSTAT process: Its impact on crime. *Australian and New Zealand Journal of Criminology*.

Clines, F. X. 2001. Baltimore gladly breaks 10 year homicide streak. *New York Times*, January 3, A11.

Coe, C. 1999. Local government benchmarking: Lessons learned from two major multi-government efforts. *Public Administration Review* 59 (2): 110–30.

Dussault, R. 1999. Jack Maple: Betting on intelligence. http://govtech.net/publications (accessed April 2006).

Economist. 1995. July 29.

Giuliani, R. W. 2002. *Leadership*. New York: Hyperion.

Goldsmith, S. 2004. *The innovations in American government awards*. July 28. Cambridge, MA: John F. Kennedy School of Government, Harvard University.

Goldstein, H. 1990. *Problem oriented policing*. New York: McGraw-Hill.

Gootman, E. 2000. A police department's growing allure: Crime fighters from around world visit for tips. *New York Times*, October 24, B1.

Hammer, M., and J. Champy. 1993. *Reengineering the corporation*. New York: Harper Collins.

Henry, V. E., and W. J. Bratton. 2002. *The COMPSTAT paradigm: Management accountability in policing, business and the public sector*. New York: Looseleaf Law Publications.

Kanter, R. M. 1983. *The change masters*. New York: Simon and Schuster.

Kelling, G. L., and W. H. Sousa. 2001. *Do police matter? An analysis of the impact of New York City's police reforms*. Civic Report No. 22. New York: Manhattan Institute.

Kravchuk, R. S., and R. W. Schack. 1996. Designing effective performance-measurement systems under the Government Performance and Results Act of 1993. *Public Administration Review* 56 (4): 348–58.

Kuhn, T. 1996. *The structure of scientific revolution*. 3rd ed. Chicago, IL: University of Chicago Press.

Law Enforcement News. 2004. COMPSTAT is doing more than just driving down Omaha's rate. March.

MacDonald, H. 2001. Keeping New York safe from terrorism. *City Journal*, Autumn.

Maple, J. 2000. *Crime fighter*. New York: Broadway.

Moore, M. 2003. Sizing up COMPSTAT: An important administrative innovation in policing. *Criminology and Public Policy* 2 (3): 469–94.

Moore, M. H., and R. C. Trojanowicz. 1988. *Policing and the fear of crime*. Perspectives on Policing. June 3. Washington, DC: National Institute of Justice.

New York City Police Department. 1994. Re-engineering team. *Precinct Organization*. New York: New York City Police Department.

O'Connell, P. E. 2001. *Using performance data for accountability*. August. Arlington, VA: Price Waterhouse Coopers.

———. 2002. An intellectual history of the COMPSTAT model of police management. Ph.D. diss. City University of New York.

O'Connell, P. E., and F. Straub. 1999a. For jail management, COMPSTAT's a keeper. *Law Enforcement News*, September 30, 9.

———. 1999b. Managing jails with T.E.A.M.S. *American Jail* (March/April): 48–54.

———. 1999c. Why the jails didn't explode. *City Journal* 2 (Spring): 28–37.

Osborne, D., and T. Gaebler. 1992. *Reinventing government*. New York: Addison Wesley.

Pooley, E. 1996. One good apple. *Time*, January, 55–56.

Silverman, E. B. 1999. *NYPD battles crime: Innovative strategies in policing*. Boston: Northeastern University Press.

———. 2001. Epilogue. *NYPD battles crime: Innovative strategies in policing*. Boston: Northeastern University Press.

Silverman, E. B., and P. O'Connell. 1999. Organizational change and decision making in the New York City Police Department. *International Journal of Public Administration* 222.

Walsh, W. 2001. COMPSTAT: An analysis of an emerging police managerial paradigm. *Policing: An International Journal of Police Strategies and Management* 24 (3): 347–62.

Walsh, W., and G. Vito. 2004. The meaning of COMPSTAT. *Journal of Contemporary Criminal Justice* 20 (1): 51–69.

Webber, R., and G. Robinson. 2003. Compsta-mania. *Gotham Gazette.* July 7. New York: Citizens Union.

Weisburd, D., S. D. Mastrofski, A. M. McNally, and R. Greenspan. 2001. *COMP-STAT and organizational change: Findings from a national survey.* Report submitted to the National Institute of Justice by the Police Foundation.

Weisburd, D., S. D. Mastrofski, A. M. McNally, R. Greenspan, and J. J. Willis. 2003. Reforming to preserve: COMPSTAT and strategic problem solving in American policing. *Criminology and Public Policy* 2 (3): 421–56.

Weissenstein, M. 2003. Call on NY's top cops: NYPD brass recruited by other cities to lower crime rates. *Newsday,* January 2.

Wholey, Joseph S., and Harry P. Hatry. 1992. The case for performance monitoring. *Public Administration Review* 52, (6): 604–10.

COMPUTER-AIDED DISPATCHING (CAD) SYSTEMS

Computer-aided dispatching (CAD) systems were developed in the 1960s as part of the first major wave of police department computerization (Colton 1978). By the mid-1980s CAD had become nearly universal in medium and large-sized police departments (Hickman and Reaves 2002a; McEwen et al. 2002). By the late 1990s CAD systems were used to a lesser extent by sheriff's offices and local police departments. In these agencies computers were used for managing calls for police services by 47% of sheriff's offices and 32% of local police departments (Hickman and Reaves 2003b). Today, along with 911 emergency call systems, CAD systems are the primary information technology supporting police communications centers in almost all medium and large-sized police departments.

The first generation of CAD systems was developed to manage the calls for service and the dispatching functions of police departments (Colton, Brandeau, and Tien 1983). These systems were designed to monitor large fleets of patrol units and calls for service, to centralize the patrol function, and to reduce the response time of patrol units to citizens' requests for assistance (Colton, Brandeau, and Tien 1983). These systems were also intended to operate as online work order systems that kept track of calls for police assistance and coordinated these calls with available patrol units (McEwen et al. 2002; Pierce, Spaar, and Briggs 1988).

To support the goal of coordinating requests for assistance and patrol units, a CAD system operates by first defining a set of items/data that call-takers collect when they receive requests for assistance. The CAD system then transfers the call-taker information to a police dispatcher's computer screen who has responsibility for the geographic area associated with the request for assistance. The CAD system provides information to the dispatcher on available patrol units and recommends a unit(s) to dispatch to the request for assistance. The dispatching recommendations are usually based on a set of rules/guidelines, such as patrol unit availability, location of the incident, and type of request for assistance (McEwen et al. 2002). Finally, CAD systems also often collect information from the patrol unit(s) responding to requests for service regarding the disposition of the request and availability of the unit(s) for service.

The central role of CAD systems in police communications centers makes it possible for these systems to collect and computerize a broad range of public safety–related data for police departments. The computerization of calls for service data is a product of CAD systems' ability to track and store digitized data on the actions and activities of call trackers, police dispatchers, and patrol units responding to request for assistance. Based on a national survey of police departments, McEwen et al. (2002) found that the range of data routinely collected (and also often computerized) by CAD systems includes data on (1) requests for police assistance (for example, time, location, and nature of problem or incident as identified by individuals requesting assistance), (2) police officer responses to requests for assistance (for example, time of dispatch, arrival, and completion of service), (3) recorded comments between responding officers and dispatchers, and (4) information on the disposition of the request for service (for example, office provided final disposition information, formal incidents reports, data on additional responding units, arrest reports). Importantly, many CAD transactions between callers, dispatchers, and patrol units are essentially time stamped by the CAD system and addresses are typically verified by the CAD system's geographic database.

Although CAD systems have successfully enabled police to more systematically manage calls for service and patrol unit dispatching, earlier generations of CAD systems also may have caused police to think too narrowly about the potential uses of CAD systems (Dunworth 2000). First-generation CAD systems (with little reserve computing capacity to support other law enforcement functions) encouraged many police departments to focus on one of the primary performance indicators these systems routinely generated—response time—at the expense of other less easily measured performance indicators, such as fear of crime (Gruber, Mechling, and Pierce 1991). In addition, the introduction of CAD systems along with the implementation of the 911 emergency call systems in the 1960s and 1970s both supported and encouraged the centralization of police services and the professional model of policing, thus rapid response became a primary strategy for addressing serious crime (Maguire 1997; McEwen et al. 2002). Finally, the advent of CAD systems combined with the emergence of 911 emergency phone systems in the early 1970s provided the technological foundation for the development of the preventive patrol emergency response strategy of policing in major American cities during the 1970s and 1980s.

During the last two decades, however, CAD systems have evolved to support potentially a much broader range of law enforcement strategies and tactics, including problem-oriented policing and community-oriented policing strategies, which rely on a more proactive approach to policing. CAD systems have evolved to incorporate "intelligent" decision support capabilities that can triage requests for assistance based on call priorities, manage multiple unit dispatches, coordinate with fire and emergency medical services, link to criminal history inquiry systems and/or motor vehicle registry systems, and support mobile digital terminals in patrol units (Gruber, Mechling, and Pierce 1991; McEwen et al. 2002). As a result, current CAD systems often incorporate a broad range of data that is important to dispatchers directing the calls and to officers responding to calls (Morgan 2003).

A major challenge for the future development of CAD systems lies in the more productive use of the data that these systems collect to support more proactive policing tactics and strategies. A major national study of the potential of CAD systems to support community policing identified several areas where CAD data are either underutilized or need significant enhancement (McEwen et al. 2002). The study concluded that future CAD systems should increase the scope (for example, collect data on officer time devoted to problem solving, expand call classification schemes to incorporate data on community concerns and perceptions) and precision (for example, refine call classification schemes), and that CAD systems need to continue to increase links with other sources of public safety information. The report also concluded that CAD data must become more accessible to potential users (for example, patrol officers, crime analysts, police supervisors, and administrators), and that there is a need for a greater application of CAD to problem-solving tactics and strategies.

Finally, as CAD systems continue to evolve, they also need to coordinate with (and take advantage of) advancements in other types of law enforcement–related technologies. These include advances in global positioning systems (Casey et al. 1996) and geographic information systems, and evolving applications for wireless communications (Douglas 2004; Dunworth 2000; Diemert 2005).

GLENN L. PIERCE

See also **Calls for Service; Patrol, Types and Effectiveness of; Technology and the Police**

References and Further Reading

Casey, R., L. Labell, R. Holmstrom, J. LoVecchio, C. Schweiger, and T. Sheehan. 1996. *Advanced public transportation systems: The state of the art update '96*. Washington, DC: U.S. Department of Transportation, Federal Transit Administration.

Colton, Kent W. ed. 1978. *Police computer technology: Implementation and impact*. Lexington, MA: Lexington Books.

Colton, B., M. Brandeau, and J. Tien. 1983. *A national assessment of police command, control, and communication systems*. Washington, DC: U.S. Department of Justice.

Diemert, M. 2005. Is your CAD system ready for wireless E911 phase II? *Law Enforcement Technology* 32 (2): 84.

Douglas, M. 2004. Bringing CAD into the field. *Mobile Radio Technology* 22: 11.

Dunworth, T. 2000. Criminal justice and the IT revolution. In *Policies, processes, and decisions of the criminal justice system*, vol. 3, 371–426. Washington, DC: U.S. Department of Justice.

Gruber, C., J. Mechling, and G. Pierce. 1991. Information management and law enforcement. Chap. 11 in *Local government police management*.

Hickman, M. J., and B. Reaves. 2003a. *Local police departments 2000*. NCJ 196002. Washington, DC: Bureau of Justice Statistics, U.S. Department of Justice.

———. 2003b. *Sheriffs' offices 2000*. NCJ 196534. Washington, DC: Bureau of Justice Statistics, U.S. Department of Justice.

McEwen, T., J. Ahn, S. Pendleton, B. Webster, and G. Williams. 2002. *Computer aided dispatch in support of community policing, final report*. Washington, DC: U.S. Department of Justice.

Pierce, G., S. Spaar, and L. Briggs. 1988. *The character of police work: Implications for the delivery of police service, final report*. Washington, DC: National Institute of Justice.

COMPUTER CRIMES

The phenomenon of computer crime is not new; it has actually been around in one form or another for more than thirty years. Despite this, dealing effectively with computer crime cases is proving problematic for prosecutors and investigators. Society's ever increasing reliance on technology and the pervasiveness of the Internet has resulted in the majority of people owning or having access to a computer or computer-like device (for example, personal digital assistants, cell phones, or digital music devices). This has resulted in a significant increase in the amount of evidence that is now digital or electronic, as opposed to being document based (for example, paper files, notes).

Computer crime has traditionally been categorized with other white collar criminal activities (for example, fraud, embezzlement). This aggregation makes it difficult to determine the exact impact that computer crime has. The fact that technologies such as the Internet have no real geographical boundaries means that this is truly an international issue. The internationalization of computer crime has serious implications for investigators and prosecutors. With the global scope of computer crime, elements such as motive, opportunity, means, and jurisdiction take on new and different meanings.

Definition

Although attempts have been made to define computer crime, the courts do not appear to have adopted one universal definition. At its most basic level, computer crime involves the use of a computer or computer-like device in the furtherance of some criminal activity. The computer can be a tool used to enhance the criminal's tradecraft (for example, child pornography, identity theft) or the victim of the crime itself (for example, virus attacks, and hacking).

Traditionally computer crime has been categorized by the nature in which the computer was used. The categories are computer-assisted/computer as a tool, computer specific or computer targeted, or computer is incidental to the activity (see Table 1). This categorization reflects the distinction of the computer as being either passive or active in the commission of the offense. While the category of being incidental has been included in most definitions, the fact that we as a society increasingly communicate with the aid of computers or computer-like technology (for example, e-mail, cell phones, Internet messaging) may lead to this category being dropped from future definitions of computer crime because it will no longer be a discriminating element of the criminal activity.

Common Offenses

We will confine our discussion to the first two and most primary categories of computer crime (that is, computer-assisted and computer-targeted crime). Several offenses are included in these categories. Offenses include but are not limited to copyright infringement, trademarks and trade secrets violations, hacking and cracking, mail and wire fraud, sexual exploitation of children, sending obscene, abusive or harassing communications, online stalking and threats, identity theft, fraud, theft, and forgery.

Various federal statutes directly or indirectly address computer crimes, but the most often cited and used are those contained within Title 18 of the U.S. Code:

- Computer Fraud and Abuse Act, 18 U.S.C. §1030
- Mail and Wire Fraud, 18 U.S.C. §1341
- Child Pornography and Protection Act, 18 U.S.C. §§ 2251–2260

Another less common but equally important statute is the Economic Espionage Act of 1996 (18 U.S.C. §1831). This deals with theft of trade secrets and economic espionage by foreign governments.

The Uniting and Strengthening America by Providing Appropriate Tools Required to Intercept and Obstruct Terrorism Act (USA PATRIOT Act) amended the 18 U.S.C. wiretap and pen register and trap-and-trace sections and also broadened the reach of court orders and other investigative tools.

Table 1   Computer Crime General Categories

Category	Characteristics
Computer-assisted/computer as a tool	Criminal activities that are not unique to computers, but use computers as tools to assist the criminal endeavor (for example, fraud, child pornography)
Computer specific/computer targeted	Crimes directed at computers, networks, and the information stored on these systems (for example, denial of service, password sniffers, attacking passwords)
Computer as incidental to the activity	Criminal activity in which evidence is of a digital/electronic nature, but the use of a computer or computer-like device is not directly involved in the crime (for example, customer lists for traffickers)

Other commonly used statutes deal specifically with software piracy and have been codified in Title 17 of the U.S. Code—Copyright. The Digital Millennium Copyright Act (DMCA) passed in 1998 amended Title 17 U.S.C. §1201–1205 to make it an offense to circumvent or tamper with copyright protection. This also added penalties for these offenses.

In response to the rise in computer crimes, most states have passed laws dealing with criminal computer activity. These laws reflect 18 U.S.C. §1030 definitions and specified activities.

Motivations

Although the criminal tradecraft of computer crime is relatively new, the motivations of those committing computer crimes appear to be similar to those motivations of criminals committing more "traditional" crimes. Computer criminals are motivated by greed, revenge, anger and other emotions, political motives, sexual impulses, and psychiatric disorders.

Research to date indicates that there are no significant sociodemographic differences between computer criminals and traditional criminals. Contrary to popular myths computer criminals are not more intelligent, introverted, or socially inept than the general public or other criminals. Although computer criminals tend to be younger (twelve to twenty-five years old) than traditional criminals, and male, this demographic profile fits the majority of individuals engaged in risky and criminal behaviors and, like traditional criminals, computer criminals tend to age out of this behavior.

Specific computer criminal activities such as those directed at corporations (for example, intellectual property theft, fraud, embezzlement) are correlated with certain categories of offenders. Here the greatest risk comes from employees and "insiders" as opposed to those external to the organizations. This is consistent with white collar crime in general. Within the insider category of offenders, disgruntled employees account for the greatest financial impact to businesses. These employees often operate behind any computer security controls and have intimate knowledge of information and intellectual property whose loss would severely damage the company either financially or be publicly embarrassing to the company.

Scope

The actual impact of computer crime is unknown but is estimated to be in the hundreds of millions of dollars annually, and this seems to be increasing year to year. Despite numerous attempts to collect meaningful data regarding the number of computer crimes and their financial impact, most businesses refuse to report the incident to authorities or take part in studies. These businesses are reluctant to report the crimes for several reasons including fear of bad publicity, loss of consumer confidence, negative impact to share value/price, and fear of lawsuits and official inquiries.

Computer crime is an international problem that crosses borders and jurisdictional boundaries. Computer criminals can sit behind a system and, using the Internet, attack a computer or network halfway around the world as quickly and as easily as they could a computer system located right next door. The global nature of this type of criminal activity has complicated and hampered the successful investigation and prosecution of those engaging in these behaviors. Issues related to investigative standards, rules of evidence, jurisdictional authority, and the actual codification and definition of criminal statutes have added to the difficulty.

As individuals, businesses, and governments become more connected and technology dependent, more evidence will become digital in nature and the prevalence and frequency of computer crimes will continue to increase.

Law Enforcement Response

Traditionally federal agencies such as the Federal Bureau of Investigation (FBI), U.S. Postal Inspectors, and the U.S. Secret Service have primarily dealt with computer and computer-related crimes. This is changing as more states pass criminal statutes targeting computer crimes and more state and local law enforcement agencies develop the capacity to conduct computer forensic investigations. This capacity includes laboratory facilities and trained technicians and investigators. The American Society of Crime Laboratory Directors/Laboratory Accreditation Board (ASCLD/LAB)—the body tasked with accrediting forensic laboratories in the United States—has begun to accredit crime labs that include the processing of digital evidence.

The international law enforcement response has somewhat paralleled developments in the United States. Various countries are struggling with passing effective legislation and educating the judiciary, lawyers, and investigators.

Investigative Issues

Although there are several issues related to computer crime, the most pressing can be classified as issues related to resources, legislation, and the rapid rate of technological change. Resource issues include the lack of properly trained investigators, technicians, and laboratory personnel.

Almost all agencies from federal to state and local are finding it difficult to keep pace with the increasing demand of computer crime cases. The costs associated with education and training are significant, as is keeping these trained individuals up to date with new technologies, tools, and techniques. Computer crime is very dynamic in nature and staying abreast of new developments is vital. Although several private sector, government, and academic institutions are starting to provide education and training in this field, there is no single standard or curriculum that is nationally recognized as the *de facto* standard. The American Academy of Forensic Sciences (AAFS) also has yet to officially recognize the discipline of computer forensics as a unique scientific/technical area.

Once investigators are trained, there are problems retaining them because the private sector is becoming very heavily involved in investigating computer crime for criminal, civil, and contract law cases. Private-sector organizations are typically much more able to pay competitive salaries with which public-sector organizations simply cannot compete.

Legal issues encompass problems related to the admissibility of digital evidence derived from the investigations. The federal and state courts are struggling to come to terms with computer crimes and have not fully articulated how they will deal with the authenticity and integrity of digital evidence. The courts have also chosen not to express an opinion on what credentials they require in order to consider a computer crime investigator an expert witness. While the federal courts have opted to follow the FRE §702 *Daubert* considerations for scientific evidence, several state courts have decided to use other criteria (for example, *Frye*) or have adopted a hybrid approach that relies on the judge to determine if there is a general consensus regarding the validity of the methods used to derive the scientific evidence.

Other legal issues are related to clarifying the exact jurisdiction to both try the case in and which jurisdiction should issue court orders related to the search and seizure of computer system, wiretaps, and Internet service provider user subscription information. The recently passed USA PATRIOT Act has simplified matters somewhat by extending court orders across state borders. However, dealing with international cases is more difficult and usually requires involvement by a duly designated international liaison legal officer. Investigators often run into questions regarding the exact equipment to be named in a warrant, the proper information to request in court orders directed to Internet service providers, and how to apply for wiretap and pen register/trap-and-trace orders. These legal tools are covered under sections of the Electronic Privacy and Communications Act of 1986 that amended several sections of Title 18 U.S.C. §2500. It is very important for investigators to be familiar with these sections and the subtle differences between stored and live data, and what constitutes "addressing information" and actual content of communications (that is, data).

The ever changing nature of technology may be the largest issue faced by investigators. Technology is changing at a rate unseen at any other time in history. New storage devices (for example, thumb drives, memory sticks), changing computer operating and file systems, increased storage capacity (for example, terabyte hard drives), the move from magnetic-based storage media to flash-based memory, faster computers, and storage area networks (SANs) all make the job of an investigator extremely difficult. Tools and investigative protocols must be updated and the searching of storage media has to be automated in order to deal with the increased volume of potential digital evidence on the average home computer system (to speak nothing of the business systems). Other computer-like devices such as cell phones, personal digital assistants (PDAs), and digital music players are becoming more common and have new features added almost monthly. These devices must be considered within the context of a computer crime investigation, because they can store digital evidence directly or indirectly related to the case in question.

As mentioned, the sheer volume of digital evidence to be analyzed and examined during the course of a computer crime investigation is quickly outpacing the tools and protocols available. To date, most investigations require a manual examination of data/files that could be of potential evidentiary importance. This worked well when storage media capacities were small, say, five to ten megabytes. Today's hard drives are in the range of five hundred to eight hundred gigabytes and in some cases terabytes. This very large jump in storage capacity and its consequences—vast increases in data—make the old methods impractical. It would take months if not years to manually sift through all the data available on current computer hard drives and other commonly available storage media (for example, thumb drives, external drives). Unfortunately the current computer forensics tools are also feeling the effects of this explosion in data volume and need to be drastically improved to remain an effective investigative tool for officers.

Encrypted data and encrypted file systems present another significant challenge to investigators because none of the current investigative tools can handle data that are in an encrypted format. With encrypted data, the data have to first be decrypted into plaintext before a determination of its significance can be made. Depending on the encryption scheme used, decrypting the data without the password or key can take anywhere from hours to years, depending on the strength of the encryption used. This raises Fifth Amendment issues related to the suspect being obligated to assist investigators in cases were encryption has been used to protect data.

Conclusion

Computer crime is an artifact of the technology and Internet revolution. This dark side of technology is here to stay and it is predicted that computer crime will only continue to grow in prevalence and frequency, as we as a society become increasingly dependent on technology. The same features that make computers and computer technology attractive to businesses and individuals make them attractive to criminals. Criminals have discovered that technology can help them to reach more victims more quickly, have access to victims they would traditionally not have access to (that is, geographically distant), make them harder to locate and prosecute, and overall help them improve their criminal trade craft. Investigators and prosecutors need to be sensitive to the various issues surrounding computer crime and the difficulty involved in dealing with a relatively new criminal phenomenon (for example, immature laws, a judiciary struggling to understand the nuances of technology).

Obstacles such as jurisdictional authority, lack of consistent domestic and international laws, changing technology, and lack of properly trained resources are part of the computer crime landscape. These issues should not overshadow the fact that the investigation of computer crimes is as much a part of modern-day policing as telegraph, wire, and phone fraud investigations were in the older days. Technology has always been a double-edged sword for law enforcement; for every benefit gained, someone finds a way to misuse and abuse technology for personal gain and/or criminal enterprise.

MARCUS K. ROGERS and
KATHRYN E. SCARBOROUGH

See also **Computer Forensics; Computer Technology; Forensic Evidence; Fraud Investigation; Identify Theft**

References and Further Reading

Carrier, B., and E. Spafford. 2003. Getting physical with digital forensics investigation. *International Journal of Digital Evidence* (Winter).

Casey, E. 2002. *Handbook of computer crime investigation: Forensic tools and technology.* San Diego, CA: Academic Press.

Clifford, R. D. 2001. *Cybercrime: The investigation, prosecution, and defense of a computer-related crime.* Durham, NC: Carolina Academic Press.

Digital Forensics Research Workshop. 2001. *A road map for digital forensic research.* Paper presented at the First Digital Forensic Research Workshop, Utica, New York.

Kovacich, G., and W. Boni. 2003. *High-technology crime investigators handbook.* New York: Butterworth Heinemann.

Kruse, W. G., and J. G. Heiser. 2001. *Computer forensics: Incident response essentials.* Boston: Addison-Wesley.

Marcella, A. J., and R. Greenfield. 2002. *Cyber forensics: A field manual for collecting, examining, and preserving evidence of computer crimes.* Boca Raton, FL: Auerbach Publications.

Parker, D. B. 1983. *Fighting computer crime.* New York: Scribner.

Prosise, C., and K. Mandia. 2003. *Incident response and computer forensics.* 2nd ed. Berkeley, CA: Osborne.

Reith, M., C. Carr, and G. Gunsch. 2002. An examination of digital forensic models. *International Journal of Digital Evidence* 1 (3): 1–12.

Rogers, M. 2005. DCSA: Digital crime scene analysis. In *Handbook of information security management*, ed. H. Tipton and M. Krause. Boca Raton, FL: Auerbach Publications.

Slade, R. M. 2004. *Software forensics: Collecting evidence from the scene of a digital crime.* New York: McGraw-Hill.

Stephenson, P. 2000. *Investigating computer-related crime.* Boca Raton, FL: CRC Press.

Vacca, J. R. 2002. *Computer forensics: Computer crime scene investigation.* Hingham, MA: Charles River Media.

Whitcomb, C. 2002. A historical perspective of digital evidence: A forensic scientist's view. *International Journal of Digital Evidence* 1 (Spring).

COMPUTER FORENSICS

With the advent of technology, law enforcement has seen a change in the types of crimes committed as well has how crimes are committed. Officers are still faced with what are perceived as "traditional" crimes that involve tangible, physical evidence left at a crime scene with an oftentimes unknown suspect. In addition to those traditional crimes, however, officers on the street today are faced with the less familiar computer crimes, which do not conform as well to classic processes and procedures that have been the foundation of criminal investigation for years. Consequently, individual officers and organizations must meet the challenges that technology has brought, by ensuring that appropriate measures are taken to effectively deal with computer crime, including adequate training, dedication of resources, and comprehensive laboratory and examination support, in addition to familiarity with significant issues and appropriate policies and procedures for legal testimony.

Although law enforcement has become more intimately familiar with computer crime during the last decade, it is apparent that consensus regarding the scope of computer crime has not been completely reached and that the perception of the scope is affected by one's occupation, such as a law enforcement officer or a computer scientist. Computer crime, unlike traditional crimes, is one that necessitates multidisciplinary efforts to investigate and solve cases. While law enforcement is accustomed to working with forensic scientists in a crime lab, and perhaps evidence technicians in the field, no other crime requires multidisciplinary efforts of this magnitude. For instance, law enforcement must potentially work with computer professionals, security professionals, information technologists, and forensic scientists to solve these complex crimes. Some of the law enforcement skills, such as basic investigation skills, are useful for computer crime cases, but issues such as digital evidence collection require personnel who are more specially trained than basic investigators.

Computer Crime and Digital Evidence

It is essential to have an understanding of computer crime and digital evidence prior to further exploring computer forensics. The most consensus-based types of computer crime include the following: (1) the computer as a target of crime, (2) the computer as a tool to commit a crime, and (3) the computer as incidental to crime. An example of a computer as a target of crime would be a case in which a perpetrator hacks into a computer network. An example of a computer being used as a tool to commit a crime would be online fraud or the dissemination of child pornography. Finally, an example in which a computer is incidental to crime would be a case in which a computer is used to write a threatening letter to someone (Brenner 2001).

The term *digital* implies the representation of information using numbers, specifically binary digits (bits) and hexadecimal values. Digital evidence, then, is "any and all digital data that can establish that a crime has been committed or can provide a link between crime and its victim or a crime and its perpetrator" (Casey 2004, 668). So one goal of an investigation of computer crime would be to identify and seize any digital evidence associated with the criminal activity.

Scope and Activities of Computer Forensics

Literally, computer forensics is "computer science for answering legal questions." Nelson et al. (2004) describe computer forensics as "obtaining and analyzing digital information for use as evidence" in court cases. Lacks and Bryce (2005) propose a definition of computer forensics that incorporates policing, forensic, and legal aspects, and further demonstrates the multidisciplinary nature of the work. Further they indicate that "Computer forensics draws upon not only technical skills and criminal investigative skills, but also on the combination and effective utilization of both of these skills sets within the court system" (Lacks and Bryce 2005, 246). In contrast, what is sometimes missed, however, is that computer forensics applies basic investigative principles in a digital environment. Hence, the basic methodologies reflect long-accepted tenets of the criminal investigation process and include the following:

- Acquire the evidence without altering or damaging the original.
- Authenticate that your recovered evidence is the same as the originally seized data.
- Analyze the data without modifying it (Kruse and Heiser 2002, 3)

In addition to the definition of computer forensics, it is important to recognize activities associated with computer forensics and used for the investigation of computer crime. These include (1) media and electronic device analysis, (2) data communication and analysis, and (3) research and development activities (Lacks and Bryce 2005, 247). Practically speaking, the analysis of media and electronic devices includes more that analyzing computers or computer media, such as CDs and thumb drives; other media include personal digital assistants (PDAs), pagers, and cell phones. Data communication analyses emphasize Internet-based analyses, including but not limited to network intrusions and data acquisition. Computer forensic research and development is the most important of these three activities because these processes serve as the "crime analysis" for computer crime and

allow investigators to identify trends in computer crimes (Lacks and Bryce 2005).

Training and Support for Computer Forensics

Despite advancements in technology and the increase in computer crime during the last decade, law enforcement struggles with limited resources with which to respond. Not only is technology for responding to computer crime limited, qualified human resources are limited as well. For law enforcement to be qualified to respond to computer crimes using computer forensics, the assumption is made that the officers have received adequate training and/or education. What is happening, however, is that computer crime and computer forensics are not part of most basic police academy instruction and are a limited part of in-service training. Therefore, officers currently employed in law enforcement agencies have minimal opportunities for training, and those that are "qualified" are often self-taught computer aficionados.

Casey (2004) proposes that persons who specialize in computer crime in law enforcement organizations should be classified into three groups based on their levels of knowledge and training: digital crime scene technicians, digital evidence examiners, and digital investigators. Digital crime scene technicians are essentially first responders to a crime scene and are responsible for identifying and collecting evidence, specifically digital evidence. Digital evidence examiners are responsible for processing digital evidence, and would use computer forensics to perform this examination; Casey recommends that those personnel who perform this kind of examination should be certified in this area. Finally, digital investigators are those who are responsible for reconstructing the crime using information from the technicians and examiners. Ideally digital investigators would be a multidisciplinary team consisting of law enforcement officers, forensic examiners, attorneys, and computer security professionals, each of which plays a key role in solving computer crimes.

Typically law enforcement organizations recognize certifications, as Casey (2004) proposes, from state training bodies or POST commissions. What appears to be a trend for computer crime and forensics is the development of professional organizations that support law enforcement in these areas and sometimes offer certifications. The International Association of Computer Investigative Specialists (IACIS), for example, is an international volunteer nonprofit corporation composed of law enforcement professionals dedicated to education in the field of forensic computer science, and includes members from federal, state, local, and international law enforcement organizations. IACIS members have been trained and certified in the forensic science of seizing and processing computer systems. IACIS also assists in the creation of policies and procedures, training personnel, and certifying forensic examiners in the recovery of evidence from computer systems (http://www.cops.org).

Another useful organization that is currently helping law enforcement respond to these challenges is the High Technology Crime Investigators Association (HTCIA), which encourages, promotes, aids, and effects the voluntary interchange of data, information, experience, ideas, and knowledge about methods, processes, and techniques relating to investigations and security in advanced technologies (http://www.htcia.org).

Future Prospects

Unfortunately, as law enforcement begins to make strides in addressing computer crime with computer forensics—and becomes more technologically savvy in the process—perpetrators of these crimes are simultaneously embracing technological advancements. Law enforcement must make a concerted effort and maintain a strong commitment if computer crime prevention, as opposed to just computer crime response, will ever be the norm. Understanding the phenomena and dedicating adequate resources to response efforts can greatly benefit those who must deal with these contemporary issues in an acceptable manner.

KATHRYN E. SCARBOROUGH

See also **Computer Crimes; Computer Technology; Constitutional Rights: Search and Seizure; Crime Scene Search and Evidence Collection; Criminal Investigation; Forensic Evidence; Forensic Investigations**

References and Further Reading

Brenner, Susan W. 2001. Defining cybercrime: A review of state and federal law. In *Cybercrime: The investigation, prosecution and defense of computer-related crime*, ed. Ralph D. Clifford, 11–69. Durham, NC: Carolina Academic Press.

Britz, Marjie T. 2004. *Computer forensics and cyber crime*. Upper Saddle River, NJ: Pearson Education.

Casey, Eoghan. 2004. *Digital evidence and computer crime: Forensic science, computers and the Internet*. 2nd ed. Boston, MA: Elsevier Academic Press.

Kruse, Warren G., and Jay G. Heiser. 2002. *Computer forensics: Incident response essentials*. Boston, MA: Addison-Wesley.

Lacks, Robyn Diehl, and Christine E. Bryce. 2005. Computer forensics. In *Criminal justice technology in the 21st century*, ed. Laura J. Moriarty. Springfield, IL: Charles C Thomas.

Nelson, Bill, Amelia Phillips, Frank Enfinger, and Chris Steuart. 2004. *Guide to computer forensics and investigations*. Boston, MA: Course Technology.

COMPUTER TECHNOLOGY

The use of computer technology in policing has increased during the last few years primarily due to the rapid adoption and development of technology in today's society. Gilbert (2004) contends that law enforcement's use of the computer is as significant as was the adoption of the police radio or the use of the motorized patrol car. When technology is mentioned nowadays, it does not necessarily refer to a desktop PC computer as has been the case historically. Today, many different types of equipment are dependent on computers and computer technology in order to function (for example, radar guns, breathalyzer machines, cell phones). It will become apparent how Gilbert's contention regarding technology is supported by the variety and prevalence of computer technology in contemporary law enforcement organizations.

Nunn (2005) developed a broad categorization of technological systems that can be applied to computer technology in general. He classifies technology into seven different categories based on its usage: communications, database and record keeping, decision support, biometrics, monitoring, imaging, and weaponry and personal defense. Following are examples of law enforcement uses of each type of technology.

Communications technology includes analog and digital radios, digital wireless mobile terminals, and cell phones. Database and record-keeping technology includes criminal histories, warrants, NCIC, and property and evidence room inventories. Link analysis software, data mining software, and case management software are examples of decision support computer technology that is useful to law enforcement. Access control systems and pattern recognition systems are examples of biometric technology currently used by law enforcement. Monitoring computer technology includes video cameras, passive scanning thermography, and in-car video recording. Imaging technology includes facial recognition software, aerial photography, geographic information systems (GIS), thermographics, and passive scanning devices. Finally, for weaponry and personal defense, law enforcement uses taser stun guns, laser dazzlers, and laser heating weapons.

Foster (2005) offers another useful means of examining computer technology. He categorizes law enforcement's use of computers as strategic, tactical, and administrative and management. Strategic uses of computers are those that might be used in planning and include communications via the dispatch center, agency systems, external systems, the Internet, information exchange, and crime analysis. Tactical uses of the computer, on the other hand, are those used in the field. These are typically for immediate decision making and include technology used in investigations, wiretaps, tracking and surveillance, major incident and disaster response, and technology on the street. Administrative and management uses are those that enable the organization to operate systematically using standard operating procedures and include personnel functions, training, and implementing and managing of technology (Foster 2005).

Computer technology can also be viewed as being used internally and externally. Internal uses of computer technology include paperless report writing, rapid report review by supervisors, case status communication between patrol and detective units, crime analysis projection, artificial intelligence, training, crime scene reconstruction, and personnel communication within the organization—usually via e-mail. External uses of computer technology include interagency Internet communication with local, state, federal, and foreign jurisdictions regarding an entire range of facts, communication of fingerprints, DNA and other forensic identification data, and posting of community information through agency home pages and websites (Gilbert 2004,186).

Even though significant advancements have been made with computer technology, not all agencies routinely use computer technology. A lack of resources is often cited as a reason for not adopting technology. Furthermore, while technology is much less expensive today than it was ten years ago, many agencies, especially smaller ones, still cannot currently afford various computer technologies. Additional reasons include concerns about the right to privacy, lack of training, and a resistance by officers who do not have a good understanding of the computer's capabilities (Osterberg and Ward 2004).

The right to privacy is highly valued by citizens; they are reluctant to support any technology that appears to infringe on that right, such as surveillance technology. Even though law enforcement's intentions in using surveillance technology are typically acceptable, some are concerned that law enforcement will abuse those capabilities and "spy" on them. Adequate training for computer technology is somewhat limited. Training for computer technology in basic academy training is minimal, as is the case in in-service training. Absence of training makes officers reluctant to embrace the technology for fear of not using it appropriately or effectively. Resistance to using computer technology is also a by-product of some officers not wanting to change the way things "have always been done." For reasons already stated, veteran officers are not generally willing to try these new technologies. On the other hand, newer officers tend to be more comfortable with computer technology and, therefore, are more willing to use it.

Aside from the uses listed earlier, computers are now used for criminal investigative purposes. Specifically, computers can be used to efficiently access existing records, record new information and store it for immediate transmission to like systems, analyze the information for patterns and trends, manipulate digital representations of people with respect to age, and recreate and visually track a series of events (Bennett and Hess 2004, 16). Computer technology has dramatically increased the information-gathering/sharing and the electronic document management capabilities of law enforcement; today information can be obtained from paper, fax, e-mail, and handwritten documents (Bennett and Hess 2004).

Additional uses of computers in investigations include developing analytical timelines and performing link analysis that allows officers to generate intelligence from raw data. The use of computer-assisted drawing has also increased greatly during the last few years and has enabled law enforcement to improve their accuracy, repeatability, simplicity, and the ability of files to be inserted into crime scene reports (Bennett and Hess 2004, 57).

While training on the use of computers is sporadic, training using computers is becoming more commonplace. For example, computer-based training and Internet-based training are being used as alternatives to the more traditional platform-based instruction. Given the resource constraints faced by most agencies, providing training that officers can do independently and without having to leave the organization for weeks at a time is an attractive option to some law enforcement administrators.

Baggett, Collins, and Cordner (2005) evaluated the efficacy of computer-based training compared to platform-based instruction with officers taking a DNA evidence collection training course. They found that students taking both courses significantly increased their scores from the pretests to the post-test; the researchers concluded that computer-based training was as effective as the platform-based training. An important point to note is that the computer-based training was also conducted in less time, for less money. Additionally, officers expressed a generally positive attitude toward the use of computer-based training. Computer-based training may not be a panacea for law enforcement, but it certainly offers a viable alternative to administrators who find it difficult to send personnel away from the organization for training.

A multitude of computer technologies that are useful for law enforcement are available today. Many of these technologies help law enforcement perform their jobs more efficiently and effectively. However, computer technologies are not readily available to or adopted by all law enforcement agencies. As technology becomes cheaper and more readily available, it is incumbent on police administrators to equip their personnel with the most advanced technologies available today in order to meet the new and dynamic challenges of twenty-first-century policing.

KATHRYN E. SCARBOROUGH and
MARCUS K. ROGERS

See also **Accountability; COMPSTAT; Computer-Aided Dispatching (CAD) Systems; Crime Mapping; Criminal Investigation; Technology and the Police**

References and Further Reading

Baggett, R. K., P. A. Collins, and A. Cordner. 2005. Evaluation of computer-based training for DNA evidence collection. In *Criminal justice technology in the 21st century*, ed. L. Moriarity. Springfield, IL: Charles C Thomas.

Bennett, W. W., and K. M. Hess. 2004. *Criminal investigation*. Belmont, CA: Wadsworth-Thomson Learning.

Foster, R. E. 2005. *Police technology*. Upper Saddle River, NJ: Pearson/Prentice-Hall.

Gilbert, J. N. 2004. *Criminal investigation*. Upper Saddle River, NJ: Pearson/Prentice-Hall.

Nunn, S. 2005. The technology infrastructure of criminal justice. In *Criminal justice technology in the 21st century*, ed. L. Moriarity. Springfield, IL: Charles C Thomas.

Osterberg, J. W., and R. H. Ward. 2004. *Criminal investigation: A method for reconstructing the past*. 4th ed. Cincinnati, OH: LexisNexis.

CONFLICT MANAGEMENT

Police officers can be injured when they try to intervene in conflicts between individuals who know each other. For example, police officers who are called to the scene of a domestic violence incident face potential violence-related injuries themselves (Morewitz 2003, 2004). Law enforcement officers also face injuries when they try to intervene in conflicts between strangers. The highly stressful nature of police work and the associated difficulties of managing anger increase the risks for law enforcement officers (Novaco 1977; Sarason et al. 1979; Mearns and Mauch 1998).

Conflict management training programs have been developed for police to enhance their skills in managing conflict (Zacker and Bard 1973; Consortium for Research on Emotional Intelligence in Organizations 2006). Initially, some police departments were resistant to these training programs because of their deeply ingrained military culture. However, these conflict management training programs have gained acceptance over time, and today many large urban police departments use such training programs.

In fact, law enforcement agencies have operational conflict management units. For example, the Delaware State Police (2006) uses a Conflict Management Team to assist in hostage negotiation, kidnap mediation, and other crises. In addition, law enforcement agencies have early warning systems in place to identify and respond to officers who have problems managing conflicts and other difficulties (U.S. Department of Justice 2001).

A discussion follows of the elements of conflict, different approaches to conflict management, interpersonal skills needed to manage conflict, and research on the effectiveness of police training in conflict management.

Elements of Conflict

Social scientists have identified five elements of conflict:

1. *Needs.* All of us have needs that are essential to our well-being. When we ignore our own needs and/or the needs of others, conflicts can occur. Needs should not be confused with

desires, which are things that we want, but are not essential to our well-being.

2. *Perceptions*. Conflicts occur because different people interpret reality differently and perceive problems in different ways. Self-perceptions, others' perceptions, differing perceptions of situations, and perceptions of threat may lead to misperceptions and conflicts.

3. *Power*. Conflicts may arise depending on how we define and use power. The ways in which we define and use power can determine the frequency and types of conflicts that arise. In addition, our use of power can affect how we manage conflict. When people try to take advantage of others or make others change their actions, conflict can emerge.

4. *Values*. We are influenced by our values—beliefs or principles that we consider to be essential to our well-being. When values are incompatible or not clear, conflicts can ensue. Moreover, when one refuses to accept that others consider something as a value rather than a preference, conflicts can develop.

5. *Feelings and emotions*. Conflicts arise when individuals allow their feelings and emotions to affect how they resolve problems. In addition, when individuals ignore their own or others' feelings and emotions, conflicts can ensue. The fact that our feelings and emotions may differ over a particular issue also results in conflicts (Managing conflict 2006).

Conflict Management

Social scientists have noted that conflicts can be managed in five ways:

1. *Collaboration*. This "win/win" strategy is considered the best way for dealing with conflict. The goal of collaboration is to reach agreement over goals. Collaboration can lead to commitment to goals and reduce bad feelings. The disadvantage of collaboration is that it can be time consuming and requires energy.

2. *Compromise*. This "win some/lose some" approach is used to reach temporary solutions, to avoid conflicts, or when there is not enough time to resolve problems. A disadvantage of this strategy is that persons can ignore important values and long-term goals. In addition, this strategy can lead individuals to ignore the importance of an issue and can lead to cynical attitudes toward an issue.

3. *Competition*. This "win/lose" strategy involves attempts to defeat your opponents in order to acquire scarce resources. Bargaining is one form of competition. Competition can lead to an escalation of conflicts, and losers may try to retaliate against the winners.

4. *Accommodation*. This "lose/win" approach is used when the problem is more important to others than to you. This strategy promotes goodwill. It is also effective when you have made a mistake. The disadvantage is that your views are secondary to others. In addition, you may lose credibility and the ability to influence people in the future.

5. *Avoidance*. This "lose/lose" strategy is employed when the issue is not important or other issues are more important. Avoidance is also used when conflict can be very dangerous or where more information is needed to resolve the problem. The disadvantage of this strategy is that issues may be decided by default (Managing Conflict 2006).

Interpersonal Skills Needed to Manage Conflict

Whatever strategies police officers choose to manage conflicts, they should understand their own feelings about conflict. Police officers should identify triggers, for example, a tone of voice or words that immediately cause negative emotional responses. Once police officers identify these triggers, they can better control their emotions and the emotions of others.

In addition, police officers should do more than just *hear* what another person is saying (Beyond Intractability.org 2003). They should attempt to *understand* what the other person is saying. Police officers should take the time to listen carefully, instead of thinking about what they are going to say next. As an active listener, a police officer should concentrate on what the other person is saying.

Law enforcement officers also should collect all of the relevant information. The law enforcement officers should come up with ideas that might help resolve the conflict.

Effectiveness of Police Training in Conflict Management

Morton Bard designed a training program to assist police officers in managing interpersonal conflict and using other interpersonal skills, such as empathy and self-awareness (Zacker and Bard 1973; Consortium for Research on Emotional Intelligence in Organizations 2006). Police officers were trained using group discussions, real-life simulations of interpersonal conflicts, role plays, and lectures. Police officers who participated in this conflict management training program had higher clearance rates, decreased absenteeism, and other improvements compared to controls.

STEPHEN J. MOREWITZ

See also **Critical Incidents; Danger and Police Work; Discretion; Domestic (or Intimate Partner) Violence and the Police; Mental Illness: Improved Law Enforcement Response; Police Social Work Teams and Victim Advocates; Stress and Police Work**

References and Further Reading

Beyond Intractability.org. 2003. Empathic listening. http://www.beyondintractability.org/m/empathic_listening.jsp (accessed April 2006).

Consortium for Research on Emotional Intelligence in Organizations. 2006. Training in conflict management for police officers. http://www.eiconsortium.org (accessed April 2006).

Delaware State Police. 2006. Conflict Management Team. http://www.state.de.us/dsp/conflict.htm (accessed April 2006).

Managing conflict: A guide for watershed partnerships. 2006. http://www.ctic.purdue.edu/KYW/Brochures/ManageConflict.html (accessed April 2006).

Mearns, J., and T. G. Mauch. 1998. Negative mood regulation expectancies predict anger among police officers and buffer the effects of job stress. *Journal of Mental and Nervous Disease* 186 (2): 120–5.

Morewitz, S. 2003. *Stalking and violence: New patterns of trauma and obsession.* New York: Springer.

———. 2004. *Domestic violence and maternal and child health.* New York: Springer.

Novaco, R. W. 1977. A stress inoculation approach to anger management in the training of law enforcement officers. *American Journal of Community Psychology* 5 (3): 327–46.

Sarason, I. G., et al. 1979. Helping police officers to cope with stress: A cognitive-behavioral approach. *American Journal of Community Psychology* 7 (6): 593–603.

U.S. Department of Justice. 2001. Early warning systems: Responding to the problem officer. Research in Brief, July. Washington, DC: Office of Justice Programs, National Institute of Justice. http://www.ojp.usdoj.gov/nij.

Zacker, J., and M. Bard. 1973. Effects of conflict management training on police performance. *Journal of Applied Psychology* 58 (2): 202–8.

CONSTABLES

In many respects constables perform duties similar to sheriffs. They serve criminal and civil legal papers, transport prisoners, collect back taxes and debts owed the government, and provide emergency assistance when needed. Different from sheriffs, constables no longer retain the peacekeeping or criminal investigatory powers they once had. Thirty-seven states mandate the office of constable; nine states never recognized the office; and the remaining states employed constables at one time, but no longer. In some states the office is elective; in others, appointive. Constables serve in both urban and rural areas and, like sheriffs, have the power to deputize.

History

The word *constable* comes from the Latin *comes stabuli*, meaning "head of the stables." In ancient Rome the first men to perform the role of constable were trustworthy servants who guarded the royal stable and armaments. The French introduced the position of constable into British common law, following the Norman invasion of the British Isles in 1066. With more expansive duties than stable groom, the transported constables kept the militia and the king's armaments in a state of readiness to defend village communities throughout England. Before long the Lord High Constable emerged to represent the king in all military affairs and wield considerable power. In France the same elevated personage enjoyed even greater authority. The French constable stood next in line to the king on matters of state. On a lower level English constables, public civil officers as opposed to military, acted as a legion of enforcers for the Lord High Constable. The *Blackstone Commentaries on the Common Law* provided for a broad range of constable duties and powers. Constables were entrusted with collecting taxes, arresting lawbreakers, conducting searches, transporting prisoners, and serving all criminal and civil papers. Even the local apothecary had to open his books and records to the constable.

In the American colonies the constable was the first law enforcement officer. His duties varied from place to place according to the particular needs of the people he served. Usually, the constable sealed weights and measures, surveyed land, announced marriages, and executed all warrants. Additionally, he meted out physical punishment and kept the peace. The first constable on record was Joshua Pratt of Plymouth colony (1634). His primary responsibility was to maintain vigilance against disorder by overseeing the Watch and Ward, the Ward during the day and the Watch at night. Curiously, New England settlers went so far as to appoint Indian constables who supervised Indian deputies under their command. In populated cities like New York, a large contingent of constables went about their duties. The indomitable Jacob Hays served as high constable in New York for more than forty years and built a reputation for stringent law enforcement. Farther west in youthful cities like St. Louis, the constabulary was the precursor of regular police forces. Being the first law enforcement officers in the colonies did not guarantee job security. As with sheriffs, the rise of centralized police departments by the mid-1800s appeared to diminish the need for their services. Nevertheless, constables have survived another 150 years.

Lack of Cohesion

The National Constables Association (NCA) was founded in 1973 in New Jersey as the National Police Constables Association (NPCA). Little came of the NPCA, so in 1976 several dedicated members moved the association to Pennsylvania where it was incorporated as the NCA. Dropping *Police* from the title was a show of independence that may have estranged cordial relations. Seemingly, police, sheriffs, and constables cannot get along with one another. If government funding is low, police believe they should get the lion's share. Not only money but authority and jurisdiction are at stake. Some police see sheriffs as too power hungry and constables as taking bread from their mouths, while sheriffs and constables remind police of their rich heritages and cannot understand why their brethren are so monopolistically bent. Speaking on behalf of the NCA, Pennsylvania representative Peter H. Kostmayer underscored the value of constables to the nation:

> More and more local municipalities are finding it increasingly difficult to pay for the salary and benefits of new patrolmen. Constables are legally self-employed contractors who provide their own liability insurance, health insurance, the use of their own emergency vehicles, and their own uniform and radio communications equipment. . . . In all cases, the constable can be paid for services on a salaried basis, an hourly basis, or on a fee plus mileage basis at almost no cost to the taxpayer.

Because constables are sanctioned by law to carry out non–crime prevention duties under the direction of the chief of police, to serve court papers, and to perform a myriad of other duties for the county commissioners and local municipalities, they should be in great demand. Those are jobs regular police disdain and should not have to do anyway given their main charge of crime prevention. However, sporadic friction continues to separate constables, police, and sheriffs. The national census of constables and deputy-constables is unknown. Estimates for Pennsylvania, the home state of the National Constables Association, run as high as five thousand professionals. The NCA proposed to President Bill Clinton that constable positions be made part of a jobs package to stimulate the economy (1993). The proposal asked for three million new positions that would ensure the continuance of constables and in

the bargain be cost effective to government. If today the United States still adhered to the English model, constables would be full-fledged police as they once were. Throughout Great Britain police forces are called constabularies and the highest ranking officer is the chief constable. The exception is the London Metropolitan Police Force, New Scotland Yard, administered by a commissioner, his deputies and assistants, along with a group of commanders.

Information provided by the
NATIONAL CONSTABLES ASSOCIATION

See also **American Policing: Early Years; British Policing; Sheriffs**

Reference and Further Reading

National Constables Association (NCA) website. http://www.angelfire.com/la/nationalconstable.

CONSTITUTIONAL RIGHTS: IN-CUSTODY INTERROGATION

The case of *Miranda v. Arizona* (384 U.S. 436, 1966) is arguably one of the most influential Supreme Court decisions of the latter twentieth century. The practical effects of this narrow 5–4 decision on criminal procedure and police practice are so far reaching that even today, some forty years later, questions and debate persist regarding the scope and manner of its application. This is somewhat surprising given that the Court very clearly spelled out the prophylactic measures to be taken in administering what has since come to be known as the *Miranda warning*. Specifically, the Court stated:

> To summarize, we hold that when an individual is taken into custody or otherwise deprived of his freedom by the authorities in any significant way and is subjected to questioning, the privilege against self-incrimination is jeopardized. Procedural

safeguards must be employed to protect the privilege, and unless other fully effective means are adopted to notify the person of his right of silence and to assure that the exercise of the right will be scrupulously honored, the following measures are required. He must be warned prior to any questioning that he has the right to remain silent, that anything he says can be used against him in a court of law, that he has the right to the presence of an attorney, and that if he cannot afford an attorney one will be appointed for him prior to any questioning if he so desires. Opportunity to exercise these rights must be afforded to him throughout the interrogation. After such warnings have been given, and such opportunity afforded him, the individual may knowingly and intelligently waive these rights and agree to answer questions or make a statement. But unless and until such warnings and waiver are demonstrated by the prosecution at trial, no evidence obtained as a result of interrogation can be used against him.

Although unambiguous on this particular dimension, the continually evolving case law surrounding *Miranda* and its progeny is anything but clear. This ambiguity stems from the fact that at times the Supreme Court has rendered various decisions strengthening the case and its protective measures, while at other times delivering opinions that serve to weaken them. In the years since the *Miranda* decision was initially rendered, subsequent cases have clarified the circumstances under which the warning must be given and, once the attending protections have been invoked, the measures that must be taken to prevent their violation. For example, in *Edwards v. Arizona* (1981), the Court ruled that once a suspect invokes her or his *Miranda* rights, not only must all questioning immediately cease, but officers are strictly prohibited from reinitiating contact with the suspect even if only to inquire whether or not the person has had a change of mind and wants to confess. This rule was further expanded by the decision in *Arizona v. Roberson* (1988) where the Court held that police are also prohibited from reinitiating contact with a suspect even where the subsequent interrogation focuses on altogether separate offenses. Interestingly, not only do these and other decisions serve to restrict the actions of police interrogators, but they also go so far as to effectively render a suspect incapable of retracting her or his right to remain silent once invoked. In simple terms, even if a suspect later changes her/his mind and freely decides to talk to the police, s/he is expressly prohibited from doing so. Thus, while a suspect is capable of invoking the protections afforded by Miranda, s/he cannot rescind them later even if they wanted to until such time as an attorney is physically present (*Minnick v. Mississippi*, 1990).

By comparison, other cases serve to weaken the protections initially afforded under the *Miranda* decision. For example, the case of *New York v. Quarles* (1984) created what is now referred to as the public safety exception. In this case, a woman reported to police that she had been raped at gunpoint by a man who only minutes later was apprehended inside a grocery store. Before reading Quarles his rights, the officer asked and discovered where the gun had been hidden. On appeal, the Supreme Court ruled that the public safety interest of an unattended gun in a public location outweighed the officer's failure to immediately inform Quarles of his *Miranda* rights. Another case loosening restrictions associated with the initial decision is *Davis v. United States* (1994), which stands for the principle of law that authorities may continue to question a suspect who has knowingly and voluntarily waived her or his Miranda rights until such time as she or he clearly asks for assistance of counsel. Stated differently, a suspect must clearly and unequivocally indicate a request for counsel before the police are required to stop an interrogation. Under this ruling, statements such as "I better ask an attorney" or "Maybe I should talk to a lawyer" do not constitute a clear request for counsel as does the statement: "I'd like to speak with (or want to see) an attorney before answering your questions."

With little room for disagreement, television programs centering on law enforcement, investigative, or other law-related themes have undeniably influenced pubic perception regarding when the *Miranda* warnings must be given and the form they must take. While some might argue that such dramatized depictions serve to heighten public awareness thereby dissuading unscrupulous officers from taking advantage of uninformed individuals, it might also be argued that such television shows have created a gross misunderstanding of the law as it relates to Fifth and Sixth Amendment jurisprudence. To illustrate, many individuals possess the erroneous belief that they have an absolute right to remain silent in all verbal exchanges with the police. This is not the case and, in fact, many states criminalize the refusal to provide officers with certain information such as name, date of birth, and place of residence under what are generally referred to as "failure to I.D." or "obstruction" statutes so that individuals who do not provide this information where the officer has probable cause to believe that a crime has been or is being committed become subject to immediate arrest. Additionally, the protections do not extend to routine booking questions when a person is being processed at the jail upon arrest.

Several Supreme Court cases supporting these little-known and often overlooked exceptions to the *Miranda* rule include *Berkemer v. McCarty* (1984) and *Pennsylvania v. Muniz* (1990). In *Berkemer*, the Court ruled that the roadside questioning of a motorist who is detained pursuant to a lawful traffic stop does not constitute a custodial interrogation. Consequently, officers are not required to inform traffic violators of their *Miranda* rights. In the *Muniz* case, the Court ruled that not only are police allowed to ask routine questions of a DWI suspect during booking procedures, but they are also allowed to videotape the responses without having to first inform the

arrestee of her or his *Miranda* rights. Additionally, many people erroneously believe that officers are required to read them their rights exactly as they appeared in the original Supreme Court opinion. Although countless television shows have employed the *Miranda* warnings so frequently that even casual observers are themselves capable of restating them almost verbatim, the Court has since adopted a more relaxed standard by no longer requiring the police to recite the warnings exactly as they appeared in the original opinion (*Duckworth v. Eagan*, 1989).

As the preceding review makes clear, case law surrounding the Fifth and Sixth Amendment rights of criminal suspects during custodial interrogation is indeed confusing. While the decision in *Miranda* was no doubt intended to draw a bright line rule for protecting the rights of suspects during such encounters with the police, it has in many ways created more confusion than expected. Consequently, the Supreme Court still finds itself today, some forty years after its initial attempt to standardize the rule of law on such matters, hearing cases related to *Miranda* on a regular basis. While crime control advocates would argue that, like the exclusionary rule, the decision in *Miranda* serves to figuratively handcuff the police thereby making it difficult for them to obtain confessions from criminals who enjoy greater rights than those who they have victimized, others would assert that the protections are necessary to prevent overzealous officers from using coercive methods to obtain confessions from individuals who are truly innocent or of diminished capacity. In either instance, one fact that becomes exceedingly clear is that, for better or for worse, *Miranda* and its progeny are so solidly rooted in both American culture and jurisprudence that the only question that remains is how to effectively manage its future evolution and application to an ever widening context of contacts between the public and police or other agents of government in a post-9/11 era.

R. Alan Thompson

See also **Arrest Powers of the Police; Interrogations, Criminal; Supreme Court Decisions**

References and Further Reading

Arizona v. Mauro, 481 U.S. 520 (1987).
Arizona v. Roberson, 486 U.S. 675 (1988).
Berkemer v. McCarty, 468 U.S. 420 (1984).
Brewer v. Williams, 430 U.S. 387 (1977).
Brown v. Mississippi, 297 U.S. 278 (1936).
Colorado v. Spring, 479 U.S. 564 (1987).
Davis v. U.S., 512 U.S. 452 (1994).
del Carmen, Rolando V. 2004. *Criminal procedure: Law and practice.* 6th ed. Belmont, CA: Wadsworth-Thomson Learning.
del Carmen, Rolando V., and J. T. Walker. 2004. *Briefs of leading cases in law enforcement.* 5th ed. Cincinnati, OH: Anderson Publishing Company.
Duckworth v. Eagan, 492 U.S. 195 (1989).
Edwards v. Arizona, 451 U.S. 477 (1981).
Escobedo v. Illinois, 378 U.S. 478 (1964).
Hemmens, C., J. Worrall, and R. A. Thompson. 2004. *Criminal justice case briefs: Significant cases in criminal procedure.* Los Angeles: Roxbury Publishing.
Israel, Jerold H., Y. Kamisar, and W. LaFave. 2005. *Criminal procedure and the Constitution.* 5th ed. St. Paul, MN: West Publishing.
Michigan v. Jackson, 475 U.S. 625 (1986).
Minnick v. Mississippi, 498 U.S. 146 (1990).
Miranda v. Arizona, 384 U.S. 436 (1966).
New York v. Quarles, 467 U.S. 649 (1984).
Oregon v. Elstad, 70 U.S. 298 (1985).
Pennsylvania v. Muniz, 496 U.S. 582 (1990).
Rhode Island v. Innis, 446 U.S. 291 (1980).
Zalman, Marvin. 2006. *Essentials of criminal procedure.* Upper Saddle River, NJ: Pearson/Prentice-Hall.

CONSTITUTIONAL RIGHTS: PRIVACY

This article provides readers with a basic conceptual framework to serve as a launch pad from which they can enter the various areas covered by the title with a working knowledge of the case law in these areas.

Our initial question is this: What protection, if any, does the U.S. Constitution provide for the individual right to privacy? Note that, stated this way, the question accepts that there is an individual right to privacy and focuses on the scope of protection, if any, afforded by the U.S. Constitution. In the U.S. legal system, the institutional body charged with answering this question is the U.S. Supreme Court. The Court has said that the Constitution only protects the individual's privacy against violations by governmental action (state or federal). It does not protect him or her against the actions of private individuals. ". . . [T]he protection of a person's general right to privacy—his right to be let alone by other people—is, like the protection of his property and his very life, left largely to the law of the individual states" (*Katz v. United States*, 389 U.S. 347, 88 S. Ct. 507, 19 L. Ed. 576 [1967]).

How then does the Constitution protect the individual's right to privacy against governmental action? We must look to the Court's cases for the answer to this question. Sometimes the answer is not so clear and, on occasion, has been and continues to be controversial.

Our basic conceptual framework will be enhanced if we divide all governmental action into two categories: (1) governmental actions that involve the process of administering the laws (this includes all administering activities whether they are statutes, rules, regulations, or other activities), which we shall call *procedural due process*; and (2) governmental actions that regulate or prohibit conduct that is *not* involved with the administration of the laws; this we shall call *substantive due process*. An example of the first is the rules relative to the issuance and execution of a warrant. An example of the second is a law prohibiting an abortion.

The Court has recognized that the right to privacy against government interference has two zones: the spatial zone and the decisional zone (*Bowers v. Hardwick*, 478 U.S. 186, 106 S. Ct. 2841, 92 L. Ed. 2d 140, dissenting opinion, Justice Blackman). Privacy issues in the first category usually involve the First, Fourth, Fifth, Sixth, and Eighth Amendments and the Due Process Clause of the Fourteenth Amendment but could include other amendments. Privacy issues in the second category usually involve the Due Process Clauses of the Fifth and Fourteenth Amendments but could also include other amendments.

Privacy and Procedural Due Process

In the first area we will focus on the Court's cases interpreting the Fourth and Fourteenth Amendments. The Court has decided that the Fourteenth Amendment applies the Fourth Amendment to the states. This means that the Fourth Amendment's requirements are, essentially, the same for the state as they are for the federal government. See *Wolf v. Colorado*, 338 U.S. 25, 69 S. Ct. 1359, 93 L. Ed 1782 (1949), and *Mapp v. Ohio*, 367 U.S. 643, 81 S. Ct. 1684, 6 L. Ed. 2d 1081 (1961). Note here the distinction between actual requirements of the Constitution and the Court's use of its supervisory powers over the federal courts to promulgate desirable rules of operating the courts.

In the Fourth Amendment area, the Court has said that "The security of one's privacy against arbitrary intrusion by the police—which is at the core of the Fourth Amendment—is basic to a free society" (see *Wolf*). The cases before and after *Wolf* struggled with efforts to give meaning to this principle in trying to decide when and under what circumstances the requirements of the Fourth Amendment's protections come into play. *Katz v. United States* is the major signpost in these efforts. Here the Court rejected the locational theory of protection and held that ". . . the Fourth Amendment protects people, not places. What a person knowingly exposes to the public, even in his own home or office, is not a subject of Fourth Amendment protection. . . . But what he seeks to preserve as

private, even in an area accessible to the public, may be constitutionally protected" (*Katz*).

Now came the task of explaining what this means and of applying it to the facts of individual cases. This has not been an easy task. The process started with the concurring opinion of Justice Harlan in *Katz*: "My understanding of the rule that has emerged from prior decisions is that there is a twofold requirement, first that a person have exhibited an actual (subjective) expectation of privacy and, second, that the expectation be one that society is prepared to recognize as 'reasonable'" (*Katz*).

The Court quickly adopted this formulation and went further by using the phrases "legitimate expectation of privacy" and "justifiable expectation of privacy" interchangeably with, in addition to, and, sometimes, instead of the phrase "reasonable expectation of privacy." The Court often also uses the phrase "an expectation of privacy society is prepared to recognize as legitimate." The end result seems to be a continuous stream of confusing and contradictory Court decisions severely denying Fourth Amendment protection in situations where one would expect privacy and the circumstances indicate the expectation is a reasonable one.

A review of some of the precedent cases in this area, from the last thirty years or so, indicates the problem. *Rakas v. Illinois*, 439 U.S. 128, 99 S. Ct. 421, 58 L. Ed. 387 (1978) is a good place to start. In *Rakas*, petitioners were convicted of armed robbery. At their trial, the prosecution offered into evidence a sawed-off rifle and rifle shell that had been seized by police during a search of an automobile, which included the locked glove compartment and the area under the front seat in which petitioners had been passengers. The petitioners moved to suppress this evidence. Neither petitioner was the owner of the automobile and neither had ever asserted that he owned the rifle shells seized.

The Court cites, with approval, the language of *Katz*, and yet appears not to follow it. It stated:

> The Court in *Katz* held that capacity to claim the protection of the Fourth Amendment depends not upon a right in the invaded space but upon whether the person who claims the protection of the Amendment has a *legitimate* [sic] expectation of privacy in the invaded space." *Emphasis added.*

The Court then went on to hold:

> [The] . . . petitioner's claims must fail. They asserted neither a property or a possessory interest in the automobile, nor an interest in the property seized. And as we have previously indicated, the fact that they were "legitimately on the premises" in the same sense that they were in the car with the permission of its owner is not determinative of whether they had a legitimate expectation of privacy in the particular areas of the automobile searched. (*Katz*)

The Court's recent cases indicate that the Court is more likely to find a reasonable expectation of privacy where an individual's home is involved. See *Kyllo v. United States*, 553 U.S. 27, 121 S. Ct. 2038, 150 L. Ed. 94 (2001) where the Court prohibited the use of a thermal imager to obtain ". . . information regarding the interior of the home that could not otherwise have been obtained without physical 'intrusion into a constitutionally protected area' . . . at least where, as here, the technology in question is not in general public use."

Although it has been more protective of the home traditionally, the Court has stepped back from this position when the facts of a case permit. See *California v. Carney*, 471 U.S. 386 (1985), in which the Court decided to permit automobile warrantless probable searches of motor homes instead of requiring a warrant as is the rule for the traditional home. See also *California v. Ciraolo*, 476 U.S. 207, 106 S. Ct. 1809, 90 L. Ed. 210 (1986), in which the Court permitted police officers to conduct surveillance of the defendant's fenced backyard from a private plane flying at an altitude of a thousand feet, even though it had two years earlier declared this area (the curtilage) to be part of the home. See *Oliver v. United States*, 466 U.S.170 (1984).

The reasonable expectation of privacy issue is critical because it determines when the protections of the Fourth Amendment must be enforced in specific situations. However, if the Court decides that a reasonable expectation of privacy does exist, it does not mean the government will not be able to conduct the search. It simply means that the government activity is a search within the meaning of the Fourth Amendment and must meet the requirements of the Fourth Amendment (warrant requirement, probable cause requirement, or some objective standard of reasonableness, and so on) before the search is conducted. See *Payton v. New York* 445 U.S. 573, 100 S. Ct. 1371, 63 L. Ed. 639 (1980); *United States v. Place*, 462 U.S. 696 (1983); *Illinois v. Caballes*, 125 S. Ct. 834 (2005).

The Court has addressed the "reasonable expectation of privacy" issue extensively in many areas other than the home. In *United States v. Place,* supra, it saw no violation of a person's Fourth Amendment's privacy interest in the contents of personal luggage in permitting the temporary seizure of luggage at an airport so that it could be brought into contact with a drug detection dog.

In *Illinois v. Caballes,* supra, the defendant was stopped by a state for driving 71 mph on an interstate highway with a posted speed limit of 65 mph. Another trooper assigned to the Drug Interdiction Team heard a radio transmission reporting the stop and without any request immediately traveled to the scene and walked his dog around the defendant's car while the defendant was in the patrol car awaiting a warning ticket. The dog alerted, and, in a subsequent search of the car's trunk, marijuana was found. The Court found that ". . . conducting a dog sniff would not change the character of a traffic stop that is lawful at its inception and otherwise executed in a reasonable manner, unless the dog sniff itself infringed respondent's constitutionally protected interest in privacy. Our cases hold that it did not" (*Caballes, supra*).

In *United States v. Knotts*, 460 U.S. 276 (1983) and *United States v. Karo*, 468 U.S. 705 (1984), the Court gave wide latitude to police use of electronic tracking to assist in their visual surveillance and tracking of a container but limited it to situations where the police would have a right to make visual observations. The Court specifically prohibited its use in the home absent a valid warrant or exigent circumstances.

In *Smith v. Maryland*, 442 U.S.735 (1979), the Court held ". . . that the police did not violate the Fourth Amendment by causing a pen register to be installed at the telephone company's offices to record the telephone numbers dialed by a criminal suspect. An individual has no legitimate expectation of privacy in the numbers dialed on his telephone . . . because he voluntarily conveys those numbers to the telephone company when he uses the telephone. Again, we observed that 'a person has no expectation of privacy in information he voluntarily turns over to third parties.'"

In *Dow Chemical Co. v United States*, 476 U.S. 227 (1986), the Court held that the Environmental Protection Agency's aerial photographing of Dow Chemical's industrial complex was not a Fourth Amendment search. "It may well be, as the Government concedes, that surveillance of private property by using highly sophisticated surveillance equipment not generally available to the public, such as satellite technology, might be constitutionally proscribed absent a warrant. But the photographs here are not so revealing of intimate details as to raise constitutional concerns."

If the Court decides, on the facts of a case, that there is "a reasonable expectation of privacy," then the protections of the Fourth Amendment come into play and the Court has to decide which ones are applicable to the facts of the case. The protections include, but are not limited to, the warrant requirement, the probable cause requirement, the reasonableness requirement, the Court's diminished or lesser expectation of privacy doctrine, and the Court's balancing test. These are seen as methods of protecting constitutionally recognized reasonable expectations of privacy by setting standards for when the government will be able to infringe on a person's reasonable expectation of privacy. (They are not covered in this article.) It may be argued that the last two are methods of diluting the protections. Our focus is on the Court's decisions of what expectations of privacy will have the benefits of these methods of "protections" and which will not.

Privacy and Substantive Due Process

In our second area of government action set out earlier, *substantive due process*, the cases indicate very clearly that the constitution recognizes and protects the individual's right to privacy. The government is not free to regulate and/or prohibit any and all private conduct:

> Our cases long have recognized that the Constitution embodies a promise that a certain private sphere of individual liberty will be kept largely beyond the reach of government. See *Thornburgh v. American Coll. of Obst. & Gyn.*, 476 U.S. 747, 106 S. Ct. 2169, 2184, 90 L. Ed. 2d 779 (1986); *Bowers v. Hardwick*, 478 U.S.186, 106 S. Ct. 2841, 92 L. Ed. 2d 140, dissenting opinion, Justice Blackman.

Here we focus on the decisional zone of privacy, the right of the individual to make certain private decisions and take certain private actions in his or her life without government interference. This became explicit in *Griswold v. Connecticut*, 381 U.S.

479, 85 S. Ct. 1678, 14 L. Ed. 510 (1965); however, it was also affirmed in earlier cases on freedom of association and freedom to marry outside one's ethnic group. See *NAACP v. Button*, 371 U.S. 415; *NAACP v. Alabama*, 357 U.S. 469; and *Loving v. Virginia*, 388 U.S. 1, 87 S. Ct. 1817, 18 L. Ed. 2d 1010 (1967). It is also generally accepted that the government may not decide what an individual's religion will be.

> In construing the right to privacy, this Court has proceeded along two somewhat distinct, albeit complementary, lines. First, it has recognized a privacy interest with reference to certain decisions that are properly for the individual to make. Second, it has recognized a privacy interest with reference to certain places without regard for the particular activities in which the individuals who occupy them are engaged. *Bowers v. Hardwick*, 478 U.S.186, 106 S. Ct. 2841, 92 L. Ed. 2d 140, dissenting opinion, Justice Blackman.

More recent cases indicate the continuing and growing debate over the scope of the right to privacy against government intrusion.

In *Stanley v. Georgia*, 394 U.S. 557, 89 S. Ct. 1243 (1969), the Supreme Court, Justice Marshall, held that the First and Fourteenth Amendments prohibit making mere private possession of obscene material a crime.

In *Roe v. Wade* the Court ruled that a woman's right to privacy as protected by the due process clause of the Fourteenth Amendment gives her the right to make the decision on continuing or terminating her pregnancy during the first trimester of her pregnancy. The Court employed its three-step analysis process to arrive at its decision. This process is used when the denial of a fundamental right is claimed. Step one, what is the right claimed to have been violated? Is it a fundamental right? Step two, if it is a fundamental right, is the conduct involved encompassed by the right? Simply put, in the case of the right of privacy, is it private or public conduct? Step three, does the government have a compelling state interest in regulating or prohibiting the conduct? After reviewing the medical knowledge and the legal precedents, the Court found that the government did not have a compelling state interest that could override the woman's right to decide until the end of the first trimester. The compelling state interest after the first trimester is the medical dangers to the woman and the state's interest in preventing them. See *Roe. V. Wade*, 410 U.S. 113, 93 S. Ct. 705, 35 L. Ed. 147 (1973).

In *Lawrence v. Texas* 539 U.S. 558, 123 S. Ct. 2472 (U.S. 2003), the Supreme Court, Justice Kennedy, overruled its prior decision in *Bowers v. Hardwick*, 478 U.S. 186, 106 S. Ct. 2841, 92 L. Ed. 2d 140 (1986), and held that a Texas statute making it a crime for two persons of the same sex to engage in certain intimate sexual conduct was unconstitutional, as applied to adult males who had engaged in consensual act of sodomy in the privacy of home.

A wide variety of laws impinging on personal autonomy or privacy have been challenged under the due process clause, including laws prohibiting homosexuality, adultery, and cohabitation; forbidding the use of recreational drugs; imposing dress and appearance standards; and requiring motorcyclists to wear protective helmets. This is an ongoing process and promises to be a major area of development for constitutional law into the foreseeable future and beyond. See generally, Lawrence Tribe, *American Constitutional Law*, chap. 15 (1978), cited by Brest and Levinson, *Processes of Constitutional Decisionmaking*, p. 683 (2d ed., 1983).

WALLACE W. SHERWOOD

See also **Constitutional Rights: In-Custody Interrogation; Constitutional Rights: Search and Seizure; Exclusionary Rule; Informants, Use of; Police Legal Liabilities: Overview**

References and Further Reading

Bowers v. Hardwick, 478 U.S. 186, 106 S. Ct. 2841, 92 L. Ed. 2d 140, *reh. denied* 107 S. Ct. 29.92 L. Ed. 2d 779 (1986).

California v. Carney, 471 U.S. 386 (1985).

Dow Chemical Co. v United Stated, 476 U.S. 227 (1986).

Griswold v. Connecticut, 381 U.S. 479, 85 S. Ct. 1678, 14 L. Ed. 510 (1965).

Illinois v. Caballes, 125 S. Ct. 834 (2005).

Katz v. United States, 389 U.S. 347, 88 S. Ct. 507, 19 L. Ed. 576 (1967).

Kyllo v. United States, 553 U.S. 27, 121 S. Ct. 2038, 150 L. Ed. 94 (2001).

Lawrence v. Texas, 539 U.S. 558, 123 S. Ct. 2472 (U.S. 2003).

NAACP v. Alabama, 357 U.S. 469.

NAACP v. Button, 371 U.S. 415.

Oliver v. United States, 466 U.S. 170 (1984).

Rakas v. Illinois, 439 U.S. 128, 99 S. Ct. 421, 58 L. Ed. 387 (1978).

Roe. v. Wade, 410 U.S. 113, 93 S. Ct. 705, 35 L. Ed. 147 (1973).

Smith v. Maryland, 442 U.S. 735 (1979).

Stanley v. Georgia, 394 U.S. 557, 89 S. Ct. 1243 (1969).

Thornburgh v. American Coll. of Obst. & Gyn., 476 U.S. 747, 106 S. Ct. 2169, 2184, 90 L. Ed. 2d 779 (1986).

U.S. v. Karo, 468 U.S. 705 (1984).

U.S. v. Knotts, 460 U.S. 276 (1983).

U.S. v. Place, 462 U.S. 696 (1983).

Wolf v. Colorado, 338 U.S. 25, 69 S. Ct. 1359, 93 L. Ed. 1782 (1949).

CONSTITUTIONAL RIGHTS: SEARCH AND SEIZURE

The law of search and seizure derives primarily from interpretation by the U.S. Supreme Court of the Fourth Amendment to the U.S. Constitution. The Fourth Amendment provides that "[t]he right of the people to be secure in their persons, houses, papers, and effects, against unreasonable searches and seizures, shall not be violated, and no Warrants shall issue, but upon probable cause, supported by Oath or affirmation, and particularly describing the place to be searched, and the persons or things to be seized." The amendment was proposed by the first Congress assembled under the newly ratified Constitution in 1789 and was approved by the required number of states in 1791.

During the debate in the states about whether to ratify the new Constitution (written at a convention held in Philadelphia in 1787), much concern was expressed about whether the federal government created by the instrument was too strong. In particular, there was considerable concern about the absence of a list of rights that people possessed with respect to this new national government. The Bill of Rights (the first ten amendments to the Constitution) was written to address this concern. Thus, the Fourth Amendment was intended to be a limit on the national government, not on the states, and the Supreme Court held in 1833 that the Bill of Rights applied only to the federal government (*Barron v. Baltimore*).

In 1868, the Fourteenth Amendment was ratified. That amendment includes a provision that prohibits the states from depriving anyone "of life, liberty, or property without due process of law." In 1949 in *Wolf v. Colorado*, the Supreme Court held that the due process clause requires that the states comply with the Fourth Amendment, although it also held that states did not have to exclude at trial evidence obtained in violation of the amendment. Twelve years later, however, the Court reversed itself in a very controversial decision, holding that in state criminal prosecutions evidence obtained in violation may not be introduced at the criminal trial of the person whose reasonable expectation of privacy was violated in obtaining the evidence to prove that person's guilt (*Mapp v. Ohio*). (The evidence may be introduced to contradict any testimony given at trial by that person, *Murray v. U.S.*)

Scope of the Amendment

The Fourth Amendment prohibits unreasonable searches *and* seizures. The Supreme Court has held that the police are not necessarily searching, for purposes of the Fourth Amendment, just because they are looking for contraband, evidence, or a suspect. The Fourth Amendment provides no definition of "searches," but the Court has indicated that the police are searching, as that term is used in the Fourth Amendment, only when their actions intrude upon a reasonable expectation of privacy (*Katz v. U.S.*). The Court has also indicated that even when the police are on private property, they do not intrude upon a reasonable expectation of privacy when they walk about the "open fields" outside the residence and the area immediately surrounding the residence (*Oliver v. U.S.*).

The Fourth Amendment also does not indicate whose actions are covered. The Supreme Court has determined that the actions of law enforcement officers and some other government officials, such as public school principals, are subject to Fourth Amendment requirements (*N.J. v. T.L.O.*). The Court has also held that the actions of private individuals are covered when such persons are acting jointly with the police, at the direction of the police, or under the influence of the strong encouragement of the police (*Coolidge v. N.H.*).

When the police arrest someone, they have seized that person; thus the Fourth Amendment applies to arrests. The Supreme Court has indicated that persons are seized when reasonable persons under the circumstances would conclude that they are not free to ignore the police or otherwise terminate the encounter (*Florida v. Bostick*). This definition includes arrests, but it also includes temporary detentions of people for purposes of a brief investigation where the police have reasonable suspicion to think that the person stopped has committed, is committing, or is about to commit a crime (*Terry v. Ohio*).

The Warrant Requirement

The Fourth Amendment has two distinct components: (1) a prohibition against unreasonable searches and seizures and (2) a requirement that warrants be specific and based on probable cause. The relationship between the two components is not obvious. The two parts could be viewed as essentially separate from and unrelated to each other. They could also be read as requiring the use of warrants (absent unusual circumstances) in order for searches and seizures to be reasonable. Over the years, justices have supported both positions, but most justices and scholars have favored the warrant requirement. Consequently, discussions of the law of search and seizure have typically been organized around a discussion of warrant requirements, followed by a discussion of the most common exceptions to that requirement.

Requirements for Obtaining and Executing Warrants

When a warrant to search or arrest is required, the police must obtain it from a neutral and detached judicial officer and must have probable cause to think that contraband or evidence of a crime will be found at the place to be searched or to think the person they want to arrest has committed a crime (*Coolidge v. N.H.*). The Supreme Court has defined probable cause as circumstances that would cause a reasonable person to think that seizable items are at the place to be searched or to think that the person to be arrested has committed a crime (*Brinegar v. U.S.*).

The warrant itself must specify the things for which the police may search and state the place to be searched with sufficient precision that a police officer can determine, with reasonable effort, where to search (*Maryland v. Garrison*). Before executing the warrant at a residence (or before entering the residence without a warrant, where an exception to the warrant requirement exists), the police must knock at the residence and announce their purpose and then wait a reasonable time before entering if no one responds to the knock (*Wilson v.*

Arkansas). The police may dispense with knocking and announcing if they have reasonable suspicion to think that doing so would result in the destruction of evidence, would place the officers in danger, or would permit a suspect to escape (*Richards v. Wisconsin*).

Exceptions to the Warrant Requirement

The Supreme Court has long recognized several situations in which the police may search or arrest without a warrant. For example, in English common law, arrests for felonies could be made without a warrant. The Supreme Court held in 1976 that this common law rule is part of the Fourth Amendment, at least if the arrest occurs in public (*U.S. v. Watson*). In 1980, the Supreme Court ruled that if the felony arrest is made in a residence, a warrant is required because "physical entry of the home is the chief evil against which the wording of the Fourth Amendment is directed" (*Payton v. New York*).

Another important exception to the warrant requirement allows the police to search an arrested person for a weapon or evidence of a crime (*Chimel v. California*). The Court justifies the need for such searches without a warrant in order to protect the arresting officer and to protect against the destruction of evidence. While the police do not need probable cause to think they will find either a weapon or evidence of a crime, the search is limited to a search of the arrestee's body and the area within his immediate control where he could reach for a weapon or evidence (*U.S. v. Robinson; Chimel v. California*). The Court condoned pretext arrests (where the arrest is made so the officer can search incident to the arrest) when it held that, so long as there is a lawful basis for an arrest, the officer's motivation in making the arrest is immaterial.

JACK E. CALL

See also **Arrest Powers of Police; Courts; Criminal Investigation; Exclusionary Rule; PATRIOT Acts I and II; Police Pursuits; Racial Profiling; Supreme Court Decisions; Undercover Investigations**

References and Further Reading

Barron v. Baltimore, 32 U.S. 243 (1833).
Brinegar v. U.S., 338 U.S. 160 (1949).
Call, Jack. 2000. The United States Supreme Court and the Fourth Amendment: Evolution from Warren to post-Warren perspectives. *Criminal Justice Review* 25: 93–118.
Chimel v. California, 395 U.S. 752 (1969).
Coolidge v. N.H., 403 U.S. 443 (1971).
Florida v. Bostick, 501 U.S. 429 (1991).
Katz v. U.S., 389 U.S. 347 (1967).
LaFave, Wayne. 2004. *Search and seizure*. 5th ed. St. Paul: MN: West Publishing.
Mapp v. Ohio, 367 U.S. 643 (1961).
Maryland v. Garrison, 480 U.S. 79 (1987).
Murray v. U.S., 487 U.S. 533 (1988).
N.J. v. T.L.O., 469 U.S. 325 (1985).
Oliver v. U.S., 466 U.S. 170 (1984).
Payton v. New York, 445 U.S. 573 (1980).
Richards v. Wisconsin, 520 U.S. 385 (1997).
Terry v. Ohio, 392 U.S. 1 (1968).
U.S. v. Robinson, 414 U.S. 218 (1973).
U.S. v. Watson, 423 U.S. 411 (1976).
Wilson v. Arkansas, 514 U.S. 927 (1995).
Wolf v. Colorado, 338 U.S. 25 (1949).

CONTINENTAL EUROPE, POLICING IN

Continental Europe stretches from the Atlantic to the Urals, from the North Sea to Turkey. It is comprised of many different countries, twenty-five of them being part of the European Union (EU). We cannot account for the diversity of policing in Continental Europe within a relatively short article. We chose to exclude Russia and the former countries of the Eastern bloc, because policing there is still in transition. We shall focus on the largest countries—France, Germany, Italy, and Spain—to which we have added three others—Belgium, the Netherlands, and Sweden—for comparison purposes.

Although security and intelligence services are involved in political policing, we will not deal with them in any detail, because such work is of a specialized nature. The article is divided into five parts: the structure of policing in the seven countries that we mentioned, history, common aspects of police organizations in these countries, selected features of the police personnel and of the environment in which they operate, and, finally, police cooperation in Continental Europe. We will briefly conclude with a comparison between public and private policing. We also contrast Continental European policing with Anglo-American policing.

The Structure of Policing

To provide some factual ground to our analyses, we briefly describe the organizational structure of policing in the seven selected countries:

- *Sweden*. Like the Irish Republic, Sweden has only one national police force (*Rikspolis*), which answers to the Ministry of Justice. Within this police force, twenty-one police authorities are responsible for policing the counties of the country. The counties are further subdivided into police districts, of which there are several hundreds. The National Security Service is integrated into the national police. There is also a national crime investigation department and a special unit for crowd control.
- *France*. France has two national police agencies. The *Police nationale* is under the authority of the Ministry of the Interior (Home Secretary) and the *Gendarmerie nationale* answers to the Ministry of Defense. The *Police nationale* operates in cities, whereas the *Gendarmerie* polices rural areas and small towns. There is a third force—the *Compagnies républicaines de sécurité*—that is part of the national police, but is organized like a military unit, with its members living

in barracks. This unit specializes in crowd control and riot policing. There is a national criminal investigation department—*police judicaire*—and an intelligence service that is part of the national police (there are several other security and intelligence services). In some cities, mayors have set up municipal policing agencies (*polices municipales*).
- *Italy*. The Italian structure of policing is similar to that of the French. Italy has three national police agencies, the State Police (*Polizia di Stato*), the Corps of Carabineers (*Corpo Carabinieri*), and the Treasury Guard (*Guardia di Finanze*). All three are under the authority of the Ministry of the Interior and they are organized like military forces. Among other functions, the *Carabinieri* are responsible for criminal investigation, the repression of organized crime, and counterterrorism. All cities and larger towns have municipal forces (*Vigili Urbani*) that enforce municipal regulations and police traffic.
- *Spain*. Spain's police forces are organized very much like those of the two previous countries. It has two national police agencies, the National Police (*Policia Nacional*), which is responsible for most police duties, and the Civil Guard (*Guardia Civil*), which is a militarized force that patrols rural areas and is also specialized in the protection of national security (counterterrorism) and crowd control. There are also municipal police forces (*Policia Municipal*) that enforce local bylaws and traffic regulations.
- *Germany*. Although they are also highly centralized, the German police forces are structured differently. There are two federal police forces: the Federal Criminal Police Office (*Bundeskriminalamt*), which might be termed a German FBI, and the Federal Border Guard (*Bundesgrenzschutz*). Both are under the authority

of the Ministry of the Interior. However, the basic policing structure rests on the sixteen state or province police agencies (*Landespolizei*), which are similarly structured.

- *The Netherlands.* The Dutch structure is similar to the German. There is a National Police Agency (*Rijkpolitie*) that is under the authority of the central government (Ministry of the Interior) and twenty-five regional police forces that provide the backbone of the policing system. There is also a military police force, the Royal Dutch Constabulary (*Koninklijke Marechaussee*), that operates in rural areas and polices the Dutch borders.
- *Belgium.* The Belgian police underwent a complete reform in 2001 that moved it closer to an Anglo-American decentralized model. It is comprised of a federal police force that brought together the former *Gendarmerie* and the national criminal investigation unit and of 196 local police forces answering to a mayor.

This sample of continental police forces was selected because it displays the various types of police structure found in Europe: (1) complete centralization in one police force (Sweden); (2) high centralization, with no more than four police forces (France, Italy, and Spain); (3) regional centralization (Germany and the Netherlands); and (4) an experiment into decentralized local policing, with a strong national agency (Belgium). Most police systems in Europe fall under these categories. Except in Belgium, the municipal police forces enforce various local bylaws, regulate traffic, and are unarmed. They are closer to a private security agency accountable to the local mayor than to a private police force.

History

The first policing system was founded in 1667, in France, with the creation of the office of the general lieutenant of police. The French system migrated throughout Continental Europe, particularly in Austria and the German states. The crucial feature of this system was that policing originally meant governance, the police mandate encompassing nearly all public services (for example, garbage collection) and all matters of interest to the state. This was particularly true of the German states, where *Policeywissenschaft*—the first German concept of policing—coincided with what would be called today the welfare state. The redefinition of policing as criminal law enforcement occurred only in the late 1800s, under the influence of the British reform of policing.

Common Structural Aspects

The most prominent feature of the police systems just described is their high level of centralization, Belgium being in part an exception. Centralization means that there is a single source of command that flows from the top and that there is a drastically limited number of police organizations. It entails several other characteristics of Continental European policing:

- *Policing for the state.* According to Max Weber, the state is defined by its monopoly over the use of force. This reflects the reality of Continental Europe, where the state is "the monopoly" and the military and police are the force. The police forces of Continental Europe were originally created by the state on its behalf, and consequently all of them harbor a security intelligence service, which performs work similar to that of independent national security agencies. There is now a growing debate in Europe on what the police should be doing: either preserving the state's sovereignty against threats (for example, political dissidence) or providing security to the community, the latter alternative being increasingly favored.

- *Militarization.* Military forces are prototypes of centralized organizations. Expectedly, centralized police forces also have a military structure. In Continental Europe, many police agencies are effectively under the authority of the Ministry of Defense. The police are even more militaristic in Eastern bloc countries.
- *Specialization.* The larger the organization is, the more it can afford to have specialized units. This is the case in Continental Europe, where police forces have a wealth of specialized units (for example, gambling police). The crucial specialization is crowd control, because of Continental Europe's strong historical tradition of mass demonstrations that could threaten the state.
- *Friction.* In Continental Europe, large agencies take the form of a pyramid, where hierarchy plays an overwhelming role. This hierarchy not only ranks individual members of organizations, but it also scales the prestige of the constituent parts of these agencies. For instance, criminal investigation units staffed with plainclothes inspectors have a higher status than other units staffed with personnel in uniform. These marked differences in status generate friction between the different components of the police apparatus. Hence, high centralization may maximize conflict rather than unity of purpose.
- *Accountability.* In the mind of their Anglo-American critics, the police of Continental Europe have a bad reputation with respect to accountability. This reputation is largely undeserved but reflects the symbiosis between the state and its police. Scandinavian countries, which have invented the concept of an *ombudsman*—a government authority receiving citizens' complaints—are not lacking in accountability. France cuts an exemplary figure in this respect. The police are subject to several accountability mechanisms: their own hierarchy, two kinds of inspectors (police and administration), the courts, three national commissions (on data banks, electronic surveillance, and police ethics), and parliament. The French National Commission on the Ethics of Security (*Commission nationale de déontologie de la sécurité*) provides an insight into the system. It receives complaints against all main government agencies involved in security (the police, customs, the national railroad police, and the prison system). However, a citizen cannot complain directly to the commission but must instead typically go through an elected official, such as a member of parliament or senator. Despite this limitation, complaints have risen from 19 in 2001 when the commission was established to 107 in 2004, an increase of five times. The situation in France reflects the mixed nature of police accountability in other Continental European countries.
- *Prosecution.* Another feature of police accountability is found in countries such as France, Italy, and Spain. The criminal investigation of serious offenses—notably murder, organized crime, or terrorism—is supervised by a judge. Some of these magistrates have achieved celebrity in their fight against organized crime, particularly in Italy (judges Falcone and Borselllino).

Police Personnel

Several features of police personnel in Continental Europe are in contrast with Anglo-American policing. Having police forces that represent the ethnic makeup of the society is a concern that began to emerge around the end of the twentieth century, if at all. Here are some more structural features:

- *Lateral entry.* Police forces having a quasi-military structure recruit their staff in two ways, as do military organizations. The rank-and-file officers are recruited into the organizations at the bottom entry level through recruitment centers. Individuals who satisfy certain criteria, such as having a university degree (generally in law), are recruited as commissioned officers and undergo special training. Thus, many forces have a dual system of promotion. The rank-and-file can move up the organization by succeeding at examinations. Commissioned officers have their own promotion files. The chief of police is generally a political appointee, often without any previous experience in policing.
- *Unionization.* Police unions in Continental Europe do not follow the "one shop for all" model that is current in North America. There are different unions for the rank-and-file and for officers. Furthermore, there are various police unions at a given level, which recruit members on the basis of their politics. This fragmentation pits unions against each other and undermines their force.
- *Local posting.* In large policing organizations, the members are not posted in a particular place on the basis of where they originate from, but according to the needs of the organization. Hence, a police officer recruited in the south of the country may be assigned to the north, with the consequence that the local knowledge of recently posted recruits is limited.
- *Ratio of police.* The number of police per 100,000 population is significantly higher in the south of Continental Europe than in Anglo-American countries. For New Zealand, the United Kingdom, and the United

States, this number is respectively 195, 318, and 321. This compares with 379 police per 100,000 population in Greece, 394 in France, 440 in Portugal, 477 in Spain, and 488 in Italy.

The Environment

Europe is admittedly very different from the countries of North and South America. We single out two features that have special relevance for policing:

- *The urban environment.* Historians of policing have emphasized that policing was essentially an urban affair, the policing of cities being a defining feature of the police mandate. The cities of Continental Europe and the United Kingdom are generally old, and their beginnings can be traced back to the middle ages and even before for ancient Greek and Roman cities. The streets of these cities are generally narrow, some even feature stairs, and their layout is irregular. Consequently, the urban topography in Europe requires a deployment of police forces that is markedly different from the cruiser-based police patrol common to many North American cities. Random car patrols and high-speed car chases are not tactics adapted to the European urban setting.
- *The legal environment.* The legal environment of Continental Europe is complex. However, one simple and general feature of this environment is of paramount importance for policing: In nearly all the countries of Continental Europe, citizens are compelled to carry an identity card. The control of identity affords the police with a pervasive way to initiate contacts with citizens—particularly youths—whenever they suspect that something ought to be checked.

Police Cooperation and Transnational Policing

Police cooperation is rapidly developing among the members of the EU. Cooperation is different from the U.S. model, according to which federal agencies open offices in various countries (for example, the U.S. Drug Enforcement Administration has had some sixty offices in more than forty countries). In the EU, cooperation is based on various transnational pieces of legislation enacted by the European Parliament, such as agreements and conventions against terrorism, drug trafficking, trafficking in human beings, money laundering, and organized crime. Interpol excepted, cooperation was formally launched in 1976 by the TREVI (Terrorism, Radicalism, Extremism, and International Violence) minister group. Now the main instruments of transnational police cooperation in the EU are the Schengen agreements signed in 1985 and 1990 and Europol.

The Schengen agreements were followed by the creation of the Schengen Information System (SIS), which allows the member states to obtain information regarding certain categories of persons and properties. A more powerful SIS II was expected to be developed by 2006. Europol functions as a support for the law enforcement agencies of all countries in the EU by gathering and analyzing information and intelligence specifically about people who are members or possible members of criminal organizations that operate internationally. Europol was first established as the European Drug Unit in 1992, which evolved into the European Police Office (Europol) with a much broader mandate. Europol's headquarters is in The Hague and it employs some 130 members and forty-five liaison officers. Europol is still far removed from police field operations and its priority is building trust among the hundreds of law enforcement organizations with which it liaisons.

Private Security Forces

This article has essentially focused on the public police forces and nothing has yet been said about the private sector. The EU countries differ greatly from Anglo-Saxon countries with respect to the size of their private security sector. Australia, Canada, and New Zealand have at least as much private police as public, and the United States has more than twice as much (some figures for the United States are much higher). In the EU, only the United Kingdom and Denmark have a private security sector that is approximately the same size as their public police forces. In other countries of the EU—Italy, Spain, Portugal, France, Greece, Austria, and Belgium—the ratio between the numbers of privately and publicly employed police is rather small and ranges from 0.16 and 0.32. Nevertheless, it is to be expected that the private sector will increase in the years to come.

Conclusion

It is difficult to foresee what the future of policing has in store. Still, it is safe to predict that the police systems of Continental Europe and of Anglo-American countries will increasingly share common features rather than widening their differences.

JEAN-PAUL BRODEUR

See also **Community-Oriented Policing: International; International Police Cooperation; International Police Missions; Terrorism: International**

References and Further Reading

Amir, Menachem, and Stanley Einstein. 2004. *Police corruption: Challenges for developed countries—Comparative issues and commissions of inquiry.* Hunstville, TX: Sam Houston State University.

Anderson, Malcolm, and Joanna Apap. 1989. *Policing the world: Interpol and the politics of international police co-operation*. Oxford: Clarendon Press; New York: Oxford University Press.

———. 1995. *Policing the European Union*. Oxford: Clarendon Press; Toronto: Oxford University Press.

———. 2002. *Police and justice co-operation and the new European borders*. New York: Kluwer International.

Bayley, David H. 1985. *Patterns of policing: A comparative international analysis*. New Brunswick, NJ: Rutgers University Press.

———. 1994. *Police for the future*. New York: Oxford University Press.

Bigo, Didier. 2000. Liaison officers in Europe: New officers in the European security field. In *Issues in transnational policing*, ed. J. W. E Sheptycki, 67–99. New York: Routledge.

Brodeur, Jean-Paul. 1997. *Comparisons in policing: An international perspective*. Brookfield, IL: Avebury.

De Ward, Jan. 1993. The private security sector in fifteen European countries: Size, rule and legislation. *Security Journal* 4 (2): 58–63.

———. 1999. The private security industry. *European Journal on Criminal Policy and Research* 7 (2): 143–74.

Einstein, Stanley, and Menachem Amir. 2003. *Police corruption: Paradigms, models and concepts—challenges for developing countries*. Hunstville, TX: Sam Houston State University.

Fosdick, R. B. 1969. *European police systems*. Montclair, NJ: Patterson Smith.

Liang, Hsi-Huey. 1992. *The rise of the European state system from Metternich to the Second World War*. New York: Cambridge University Press.

Mawby, Rob I. 2003. Models of policing. In *Handbook of policing*, ed. Tim Newburn, 15–40. Cullompton (Devon): Willan Publishing.

Sheptycki, James W. E., ed. 2000. *Issues in transnational policing*. New York: Routledge.

———. 2002. *In search of transnational policing: Towards a sociology of global policing*. Burlington, VT: Ashgate.

Tupman, Bill, and Alison Tupman. Policing in Europe: Uniform in diversity. http://www.NetLibrary.com/urlapi.asp?action=summary&v=1&bookid=20905.

Walker, Neil. 2003. The pattern of transnational policing. In *Handbook of policing*, ed. Tim Newburn, 111–35. Cullompton (Devon): Willan Publishing.

CORRUPTION

According to Dean J. Champion (2005, 61), corruption is defined as "behavior of public officials who accept money or other bribes for doing something they are under a duty to do anyway." In terms of law enforcement, police officers engage in corrupt actions when, for money or other favors, they fail to do something when they have a lawful duty to act or when the officer does something that he or she should not have done (Dempsey and Forst 2005, 296). Also, if officers incorrectly use their discretion, they are engaging in corruption (Champion 2005, 61). An example of an officer's failure to perform his or her duty is when an officer accepts a small bribe in exchange for not issuing a traffic citation. An example of a law enforcement officer doing something that he or she should not do would be an officer's protection of criminals who engage in unlawful actions. Finally, an example of an officer misusing his or her discretion involves letting personal values, biases, and beliefs interfere with the performance of the job, such as when an officer issues traffic tickets only to African Americans because of personal discrimination against this ethnic minority.

Dimensions of Corruption

Types of Corruption

Most researchers identify nine main types of corruption by law enforcement officers: (1) corruption of authority, (2) kickbacks, (3) opportunistic theft, (4) shakedowns, (5) protection of illegal activities, (6) case fixing, (7) direct criminal activity, (8) internal payoffs, and (9) padding (Types and dimensions 2005). Corruption of authority is defined as "when an officer receives some form of material gain by virtue of their position as a police officer without violating the law per se" (Types and dimensions 2005). An example of this form of corruption occurs when an officer accepts a gratuity, such as a free meal. Kickbacks occur when, in exchange for referring an offender to a business, the officer receives a fee. When defense attorneys pay a police officer a fee for referring everyone he or she has arrested to their offices, this is an example of a kickback. When a police officer steals from a crime scene or an arrestee, this is known as opportunistic theft.

According to Champion (2005, 231), a shakedown is defined as "a form of police corruption in which money or valuables are extorted from criminals by police officers in exchange for the criminals not being arrested." Protection of illegal activities involves, as the name suggests, the officer using his or her position to protect those individuals engaging in illegal conduct (Types and dimensions 2005). An example of this is an officer protecting organized crime figures who are engaging in prostitution rings. Fixing cases is also a problem within policing, and it involves officers using their position to get someone that they know out of trouble, such as out of a traffic ticket. Directed criminal activity involves officers actively committing crimes for money or property. The key to directed criminal activity is the officer's planning of the criminal offense. The final two forms of corruption are padding and internal payoffs. Padding involves interfering in the investigation of crime by planting evidence, and its purpose is to ensure the prosecution of an offender (Types and dimensions 2005). Internal payoffs are associated with the police department itself. It includes things such as paying other officers for their holiday or vacation times.

Levels of Corruption

There are three general categories or levels of corruption within police departments (Lawrence Sherman, as cited in Dempsey and Forst 2005, 299). The first level is "the rotten apples and rotten pockets" theory of police corruption, which holds that only one officer or a very small group of officers in a department or precinct is corrupt. With this theory, because there is no widespread corruption within the police department, the organization might not do anything to combat these corruption acts. The second level of corruption that occurs in departments is known as "pervasive, unorganized corruption" (Dempsey and Forst 2005, 299). With this form of corruption, many officers within a department might be engaging in corrupt actions, but they are not working together. The final level of corruption occurs when the entire police department is working together and protecting each. This type of corruption is known as "pervasive, organized corruption" (Dempsey and Forst 2005, 299).

Issues Associated with Gratuities

One of the most controversial issues in terms of police corruption is the acceptance of gratuities by officers. Accepting gratuities is defined as happening when an officer accepts an incentive in exchange for favors (Champion 2005, 114). *Gratuities* can be free items, discounts, or gifts. Many law enforcement administrators do not allow their officers to accept any form of gratuities; some departments allow them to accept some things such as a free meal. Those departments that allow officers to accept gratuities usually rationalize it by letting the persons offering the gratuities know that they will not received any special privileges, which is more like the officer accepting a gift rather than a gratuity. Those departments that do not allow gratuities believe that it opens the officer up to committing corrupted acts, and administrators believe gratuities are never offered without the expectation of something in return (Delattre 1996, 77). These departments believe that officers will start justifying stealing and other major corruptions if they accept small incentives for services. Stuart MacIntrye and Tim Prenzler (1999) found that officers are more likely to respond favorably to those individuals who have offered them some form of special privilege.

With regards to the issue of gratuities, there are different arguments for and against their use. Because most gratuities are small, many people do not see a problem with officers accepting them (White 2002, 22). According to Mike White (2002, 21), other reasons why those who support the use of gratuities believe that it is safe to do so is because not only do the officers who receive the gratuities benefit, but the community is also helped. The relationship between the police and the citizens within their policing community is improved when officers feel appreciated and rewarded for their work. Also, officers might feel that their supervisors do not trust them to make a decision on unacceptable and acceptable behavior if the department has guidelines against the acceptance of gratuities.

In addition to the reasons previously stated, critics of the use of gratuities believe that other people are at a disadvantage when they are offered (White 2002, 22). For example, if one restaurant offers police officers free meals in exchange for patronage and another restaurant owner cannot afford to offer the same service, then problems might arise. If there were a sudden string of robberies in the area, the owner who could not afford the gratuity would be at a disadvantage. Many people believe that officers can be placed in situations where they encounter such conflicts (White 2002, 21). This conflict could occur when individuals expect officers to ignore certain unlawful behavior, such as driving while under the influence of alcohol, because of the special services that the officer received. Pollock and Becker (1996, 172) look at the issue from a different perspective. If other governmental professions cannot accept gifts or services, then police officers should not be allowed to accept them.

The Corruption Process

Many theories have been proposed for why officers or police departments become corrupt. One explanation involves the increased drug use and distribution in today's society. With the current war on drugs, police are encountering more money than ever before (Carter 1990). Because of the lack of supervision that occurs when an officer comes into contact with criminals, this can increase the likelihood that officers will take money from the offender because they are not likely to get caught. Officers can further become involved in drug-related corruption through the sale of drugs for money or the protection of those criminals engaging in the drug trade for a bribe.

The Police Subculture and the Cop Code

Another reason for the amount of corruption among law enforcement personnel is the nature of police work and, particularly, the nature of the police subculture. Dean J. Champion (2005, 195) defined the police subculture as "the result of socialization and bonding among police officers because of their stress and job-related anxiety" and the "unofficial norms and values possessed" by those working in the field of law enforcement. These values that officers learn as part of their job are different from the values of non–law enforcement people. New recruits learn quickly what is expected of them in terms of their fellow officers. They learn the cop code that is discussed by John P. Crank and Michael A. Caldero. These authors identified the following relationships that exist within police department between peers and supervisors. The following rules apply to law enforcement:

Rules Defining Relationships with Other Cops:

1. Watch out for your partner first and then the rest of the guys working that tour.
2. Don't give up another cop.
3. Show toughness.
4. Be aggressive when you have to, but don't be too eager.
5. Don't get involved in anything in another guy's sector.
6. Hold up your end of the work.
7. If you get caught off base, don't implicate anybody else.
8. Make sure the other guys know if another cop is dangerous or unsafe.
9. Don't trust a new guy until you have checked him out.
10. Don't tell anybody else more than they have to know; it could be bad for you and it could be bad for them.
11. Don't talk too much or too little. Both are suspicious.
12. Don't leave work for the next tour.

Rules Defining Relationships of Street Cops with Bosses:

1. Protect yourself. (If the system wants to get you, it will.)
2. Don't make waves. Supervisors pay attention to troublemakers.
3. Don't give them too much activity. Don't be too eager.
4. Keep out of the way of any boss from outside your precinct.
5. Don't look for favors just for yourself.
6. Don't take on the patrol sergeant by yourself.
7. Know your bosses. Who's working and who has the desk?
8. Don't do the bosses' work for them.
9. Don't trust bosses to look out for your interests (Crank and Caldero 2000, 144).

The cop code demonstrates how the police subculture can foster corruption through protecting those who are engaging in criminal acts and not reporting them to supervisors and the public.

Corruption Continuum

Neal Trautman (2000, 65) developed the *corruption continuum* to explain the unethical actions of police officers. This continuum involves four levels. The first one is the implementation of policies that ensure that officers know the ethical rules that they have to follow. If the administrator fails to do this, then officers will believe that they can be corrupt and no one will do anything about it. The next phase of the process involves police supervisors not doing anything when they know of unethical acts committed by officers or when they try to cover for those officers who engage in corruption. The next step involves officers become indifferent or fearful of becoming involved in the situation. They may feel that if they come forward, they will be punished. After a period of time, when these officers become unhappy with their job, they are more likely to become corrupt. The final step of the corruption continuum involves officers doing anything they can to survive within the corrupt environment of the police organization, even if that means they have to become corrupt themselves.

Combating Corruption in Police Organizations

When faced with the issue of combating police corruption, law enforcement agencies and administrators can try various means to deal with the problem. J. Kevin Grant (2002) listed four means of dealing with this issue. The first method of fighting police corruption is through leadership. Police agencies must have a strong administrator that is willing to assess the problems, come up with solutions, and monitor the success of their implementations. Strong leadership is very important in terms of handling corruption because officers will typically look to their leaders to determine how they should behave (Pollock 1996, 220). If officers see that their supervisors are engaging in corruption, they are more likely to engage in it themselves, but if they see that administrators are following the law, punishing violations, and behaving ethically, then they would learn that to do otherwise is unacceptable.

Two other ways that J. Kevin Grant (2002) developed for combating corruption involved the hiring process and departmental procedures. Grant believed that if administrators selected quality applicants through high standards, then corruption would likely decrease. The use of psychological tests can help in the selection process because they are designed to determine characteristics of individuals. The administrator can decline those applicants that do not meet the standards set by the department. With regard to department standards, Grant believed that by providing training, setting up codes of conduct, making sure the officers are punished when violations occur, and encouraging officers to work together, a lot of the problems with corruption would disappear in police agencies. One of the main forms of training that police departments can provide is ethics training. Joycelyn Pollock (1996, 217) stated that "ethics training in the academy, as well as offering in-service courses, is common and recommended for all police departments today." This training will give officers the opportunity to understand the different ethical issues that are a part of the job, and, it is hoped, they will learn how to deal with these conflicts in a moral and ethical manner.

Civilian Review Boards

A final way to combat corruption in law enforcement is through civilian review boards (Dempsey and Forst 2005, 311). It is the job of law enforcement civil review boards to investigate allegations of corruption. The board can also make recommendations for change in terms of punishment meted out and policies on dealing with corruption. Many people like review boards that are independent of police departments because of the increase in impartiality that is associated with them. They believe that these types of boards are able to fully investigate issues of corruption and look at everyone's side of the story.

TINA L. LEE

See also **Accountability; Civilian Review Boards; Codes of Ethics; Discretion; Ethics and Values in the Context of Community Policing; "Good" Policing; Mollen Commission; Occupational Culture; Personnel Selection**

References and Further Reading

Carter, David L. 1990. Drug-related corruption of police officers: A contemporary typology. *Journal of Criminal Justice* 18: 85–98.

Champion, Dean J. 2005. *The American dictionary of criminal justice: Key terms and major court cases.* 3rd ed. Los Angeles: Roxbury Publishing.

Crank, John P., and Michael A. Caldero. 2000. *Police ethics: The corruption of a noble cause.* Cincinnati, OH: Anderson Publishing Company.

Delattre, Edwin J. 1996. *Character and cops.* 3rd ed. Washington, DC: The AEI Press.

Dempsey, John S., and Linda S. Forst. 2005. *An introduction to policing.* 3rd ed. Belmont, CA: Wadsworth-Thomson Learning.

Grant, J. Kevin. 2002. Ethics and law enforcement. *FBI Law Enforcement Bulletin* 71 (12).

MacIntryre, Stuart, and Tim Prenzler. 1999. The influence of gratuities and personal relationships on police use of discretion. *Police and Society* 9 (April).

Pollock, Joycelyn M., and Ronald F. Becker. 1996. Ethics training. *FBI Law Enforcement Bulletin* 65 (11).

Sherman, Lawrence. 1982. Learning police ethics. In *Justice, crime, and ethics*, ed. Braswell, McCarthy, and McCarty, 4th ed., 49–67. Cincinnati, OH: Anderson Publishing Company.

Trautman, Neal. 2000. How organizations become corrupt: The corruption continuum. *Law and Order* 48 (5): 65–68.

Types and dimensions of police corruption. 2005. http://www.rouncefield.homestead.com/files/a_soc_dev_31.htm (accessed November 2005).

White, Mike. 2002. The problem with gratuities. *FBI Law Enforcement Bulletin* 71 (7): 20–24.

COSTS OF POLICE SERVICES

This article examines the direct financial cost of public police services. A broad interpretation of the term *costs* could include various other costs and benefits such as crimes prevented and detected, the resultant costs of criminal justice services, and quality-of-life issues for society. However, these are not the present focus. In what follows, the discussion of costs of police services in both the United States and the United Kingdom sheds light on the significant differences in the composition, sources, and nature of the costs in two industrialized countries. To provide a broader context, that discussion is located alongside coverage of the rise in private police services as well as the most recent estimates of the global costs of public police services.

Public and private police expenditures change to reflect supply and demand. Demand from society changes as crime patterns change with socioeconomic, technological, and political developments. Supply of police services adapts to changes in labor markets as well as technological and other change. Generally speaking, industrialized countries have seen an increase in police salaries and numbers at the same time as increasing expenditure on technology. In many countries, private policing, that is, the private security industry, has been a major growth area in recent years (National Archives 2005; Home Office 1999; Jones and Newburn 2002).

Costs of Police Services in the United States

Estimating total expenditure on public policing in the United States is logistically difficult due to the existence of around eighteen thousand law enforcement agencies of varying sizes (Maguire et al. 1998; Reaves and Hickman 2002). Federal government expenditure on justice, funneled via the U.S. Department of Justice (DOJ), trebled in real terms between 1981 and 2001 to reach $25.3 billion. Direct expenditure on state and local agencies increased 230% in real terms between 1982 and 2001.

This article was written in 2005, when the estimated relevant DOJ budget for 2006 was $19.1 billion, down from $20.2 billion for 2005. The reduction was sought from state and local law enforcement grants deemed to have little impact on crime. At the same time, however, increases in spending on federal agencies was expected, including increases for the Federal Bureau of Investigation and the Drug Enforcement Administration (Office of Management and Budget 2005).

At the state and local levels, the Law Enforcement Management and Administrative Statistics (LEMAS) surveys of 1993 and 2000 found rising annual operating expenditure per officer (Hickman and Reaves 2003). Although the 2004 census of state and local law enforcement agencies was under way, results were not available at the time of this writing (*Police Chief* 2004); the 2000 census found just under eight hundred thousand full-time sworn staff in various agencies (Table 1) and more than three hundred thousand nonsworn police staff in 2000 (Reaves and Hickman 2002). Average cost per officer, including equipment, was around $100,000 in 2000 (Table 2).

A significant part of rising police costs is attributable to increased use of technology including radios and other communications, vehicles, computers, and digital equipment. LEMAS found that in 1990 only 14% of state and 19% of local agencies

Table 1 Number of Police Agencies and Staff in the United States

Type of agency	Number of agencies	Number of full-time officers
Local police	12,666	440,920
Sheriff	3,070	164,711
Primary state	49	56,348
Special jurisdiction	1,376	43,413
Texas constable	623	2,630
All state and local	17,784	708,022
Federal		88,496
Total		796,518

Source: Bureau of Justice Statistics (2004c).

Table 2 Annual Operating Expenditure per Officer per Annum 1993–2000

	1993	2000
State	$76,300	$108,000
Sheriff	$64,400	$108,000
Municipal	$65,900	$83,638
County	$66,500	$90,237

Source: Reaves and Smith (1995); Hickman and Reaves (2003).

used car-mounted computers compared to 59% and 68% respectively by 2000 (Reaves and Hickman 2002).

Costs of Police Services in the United Kingdom

In England and Wales in 2005, police were organized into forty-three area police forces, while in the process of consolidation to as few as a dozen (BBC 2005a, 2005b). Officially, 51% of police costs are met by central government grants and 49% by local government (Police grant report 2005). In practice, due to supplementary small grants, the central government funds around 80% of U.K. policing (Mellows-Facer 2003; Home Office 2004). Central government expenditure is established on a needs-based formula with additional funding received from three central sources: police grants, revenue support grants including business rates, and council tax (Her Majesty's Inspectorate of Constabulary 2004). Because central government keeps a tight hold on the funding reins, it has far more control and influence over the nation's policing than exists in the United States. Together with the different structure, this way of meeting the costs of police services is arguably one of the key differences between the organization of U.S. and U.K. policing.

U.K. government spending on policing increased by around a quarter from 2000 to nearly £12 billion ($21 billion at a 1.75 exchange rate) for 2005–2006 (Home Office 2004). Recent increases in spending were mainly due to increased staff. In 1971 there were ninety-seven thousand police officers and twenty-eight thousand civilian staff (Census 2001). By 2005 there were more than one hundred and forty thousand police officers and more than seventy thousand civilian staff (Home Office 2005b). In the region of 85% of police budgets are taken up by staffing costs (Her Majesty's Inspectorate of Constabulary 1998/99; Newing 2002).

Prior to U.K. government allocation of police funding, a proportion is retained to fund science and technology initiatives. This increased from £35 million in 2001–2002 to £164 million in 2002–2003 (Home Office 2004, 2005a). The government funds various agencies such as the Police Scientific Development Branch (PSDB) and the Forensic Science Service (FSS). Their science and technology budget varies with priorities. For example, the introduction of Airwave—a radio communications system—was supported by £500 million of central funding, and £34 million was provided in 1999 to expand the national DNA database (Home Office 2000).

Local police force expenditure in the United Kingdom is difficult to calculate because costs are based on local needs and priorities. Total government expenditure on science and technology is estimated to have declined from £900 million in 2001–2002 to £748 million in 2002–2003 (Home Office 2004, 2005a). The majority of that budget was spent on equipment for forensics, information technology, and transport (Table 3).

Private Policing

The growth of the private security industry during the last thirty years threatens the

state monopoly (Jones and Newburn 2002; Maguire et al. 2002). Private security policing covers three main areas: manned security services, detention/professional security services, and security products (George and Button 2000, cited in Danby 2001). However, estimates of spending appear infrequent and are not comprehensively examined here. In the United States, state and local government spending on private security increased from $27 billion in 1975 (Cunningham et al. 1990, cited in Golsby 1998) to an estimated $40 billion for local, state, and federal law enforcement agencies combined in 1996 (Gage 1998). By 2002, annual expenditure for security products and services was estimated to be around $45 billion (Gage 1998). In the United Kingdom, estimated turnover of the private security industry increased from £130 to £140 million in 1979 to around £2.1 billion by 1992 (Home Office 1999). The British Security Industry Association (2004) estimated the annual turnover of the private security industry in the region of £4.8 billion for 2004.

Table 3   Average Percentage Spent on Science and Technology Services and Equipment 2001–2002 to 2002–2003

	2001–2002	2002–2003
Forensics	21%	20%
Helicopters	2%	2%
Information technology	26%	28%
Office equipment	2%	5%
Other science and technology	2%	1%
Police national computer	5%	2%
Radio	8%	9%
Telephone	13%	13%
Transport	21%	20%

Note: Figures from the average total force spent on science and technology by six representative forces. Figures exclude expenditure on centrally funded science and technology projects (Home Office 2004, 2005a).

The Cost of Global Public Police Services

While industrialized countries such as the United States and the United Kingdom often have the administrative ability and public accountability that produces public estimates of the costs of police services, this is far from true for the world as a whole. The most recent estimates of the global cost of public police services were based on a global survey by the United Nations and relate to 1997 (Farrell and Clarke 2004). Expenditure on public police services tends to reflect the overall strength of a country's economy. Based on a survey of seventy countries, that relationship was used to predict spending for countries where the expenditure data were unavailable. It was estimated that the world spent

$223 billion in 1997 or the equivalent of $268 billion in 2005 prices (adjusted for inflation using the Bureau of Labor Statistics inflation calculator, though it would be expected that actual spending would have increased along with economic growth during this period).

Whereas the costs of public police services per capita in the United Kingdom and the United States were roughly similar at around $215 per annum, significant variations were seen across the world. Switzerland had the highest estimated per capita expenditure on police services at $277. It is also the case that costs were notably lower than expected for a simple GDP–expenditure relationship in some industrialized countries such as Japan and Belgium. For many of the less affluent countries of the world, per capita expenditure on policing was less than $50, although that would go further if labor and other costs were lower. While such issues require further research and exploration, it is clear that while the economy (and thus the availability of public funds) is an important determinant, other factors also play a role in determining expenditure on public police services.

Conclusion

The costs of police services are met from different sources in different countries. Costs of public policing have increased significantly in recent years in industrial countries (highlighted here by the United States and the United Kingdom), reflecting both increased expenditure on technology and demands for more police officers. Globally, however, the costs of police services vary enormously. A key determinant of overall public policing expenditure appears to be the strength of a country's economy, which drives tax revenues on which public service expenditures are based. Over time, existing technologies will become cheaper and more readily available, while new technologies will require additional expenditure.

The expansion of private policing is likely to continue to play an increasingly important role in the overall costs of police services. However, the introduction of market-based innovations such as sponsorship could play an increasingly prominent role in generating revenue for public services. It is not inconceivable that such market-based funding sources could lead to increased investment in public (and publicly accountable) police services without requiring commensurate increases in the allocation of public revenues. Advertising on police cars could increase if it brings resources that allow public policing to compete in the marketplace.

FAIZA QURESHI and GRAHAM FARRELL

See also **Accountability; Administration of Police Agencies, Theories of; Budgeting, Police**

References and Further Reading

BBC. 2005a. *Plan to cut police forces to 12.* BBC News Online. http://news.bbc.co.uk/1/hi/uk_politics/4426106.stm (accessed November 10, 2005).

———. 2005b. *Police merger plans are unveiled.* BBC News Online. http://news.bbc.co.uk/1/hi/england/west_midlands/4551284.stm (accessed December 22, 2005).

Bowling, B., and J. Foster. 2002. Policing and the police. In *The Oxford handbook of criminology,* ed. M. Maguire, R. Morgan, and R. Reiner, 3rd ed. Oxford: Oxford University Press.

British Security Industry Association. 2003. *Interesting facts and figures in the U.K. security industry.* http://www.bsia.co.uk/industry.html.

Bureau of Justice Statistics. 2004a. *Direct expenditure by criminal justice function 1982–2001.* Washington, DC: U.S. Department of Justice, Office of Justice Programs. http://www.ojp.usdoj.gov/bjs/glance/exptyp.htm (accessed May 4, 2005).

———. 2004b. *Direct expenditure by level of government 1982–2001.* Washington, DC: U.S. Department of Justice, Office of Justice Programs. http://www.ojp.usdoj.gov/bjs/glance/expgov.htm (accessed May 4, 2005).

————. 2004c. *Law enforcement statistics: Summary findings*. Washington, DC: U.S. Department of Justice, Office of Justice Programs. http://www.ojp.usdoj.gov/bjs/lawenf. htm#Programs (accessed May 4, 2005).

Bureau of Labor Statistics. 2005. *Consumer price indexes—Inflation calculator*. http:// www.bls.gov/cpi/home.htm (accessed May 4, 2005).

Chicago Tribune. 2003. To serve and advertise. http://www.commercialalert.org/policead-stribune.html (accessed May 4, 2005).

Danby, G. 2001. *The private security industry bill*. Research Paper 01/34. London: House of Commons.

Farrell, G., and K. Clarke. 2004. *What does the world spend on criminal justice?* HEUNI Paper Series No. 20. Helsinki: United Nations Institute for Crime Prevention and Crime Control. http://www.heuni.fi/ uploads/qjy0ay2w7l.pdf (accessed May 4, 2005).

Gage, B. 1998. Kiss those Miranda rights goodbye. *Salon Newsreal*, September. http://archive.salon.com/news/1998/09/ 24news.html (accessed May 4, 2005).

Golsby, G. 1998. *Police and private security working together in a co-operative approach to crime prevention and public safety*. Australia: SRM Australia Pty Ltd.

Her Majesty's Inspectorate of Constabulary. 2004. *Modernising the police service*. London: Home Office.

Hickman, M. J., and B. A. Reaves. 2003. *Local police departments 2000*. Washington, DC: Bureau of Justice Statistics, U.S. Department of Justice. http://www.ojp.usdoj.gov/ bjs/pub/pdf/lpd00.pdf.

Home Office. 1999a. *The government's proposals for the regulation of the private security industry in England and Wales*. London: The Stationery Office. http://www.archive.offi-cial-documents.co.uk/document/cm42/ 4254/4254-00.htm.

————. 2001. Policing a new century: A blue-print for reform. London: Home Office.

————. 2004. *£750 million cash boost for law and order*. Home Office Press Release, December 2. London: Home Office.

————. 2005a. *£982 million two year boost for policing*. Home Office Press Release, December 6. London: Home Office.

————. 2005b. *Police numbers reach record high*. Home Office Press Release, July 25. London: Home Office.

Home Office Science Policy Unit. 2003. *Police science and technology strategy 2003–2008*. London: Home Office Science Policy Unit.

————. 2004. *Police science and technology strategy 2004–2009*. London: Home Office Science Policy Unit.

Maguire, E. R., J. B. Snipes, C. D. Uchida, and M. Townsend. 1998. Counting cops: Estimating the number of police departments and police officers in the USA. *Policing: An International Journal of Police Strategies and Management* 21 (1): 97–120.

Matthew Good Band. 2001. Advertising on police cars. *Audio of being*. Universal International.

Mellows-Facer, A. 2003. *Social indicators*. London: House of Commons.

National policing plan 2004–2007. London: Home Office.

Newing, J. 2002. Money today, cuts tomorrow? http://www.sourceuk.net/indexf.html? 00761 (accessed May 4, 2005).

Office of Community Oriented Policing Services. 2002. *Making officer redeployment effective (MORE): Using technologies to keep America's communities safe*. COPS Factsheet, December. Washington, DC: Office of Community Oriented Policing Services. http://www.cops.usdoj.gov/mime/open.pdf? Item=319 (accessed May 5, 2005).

Office of Management and Budget. *2005 Budget of the United States Government fiscal year 2006: Department of Justice*. Washington, DC: Office of Management and Budget. http://www.whitehouse.gov/ omb/budget/fy2006/budget.html (accessed May 2005).

Parry, W. 2002. *Police cars may feature advertising*. http://www.centredaily.com/mld/cen-tredaily/news/4556145.htm (accessed May 2005).

Police Chief, The. 2004. *2004 Census of state and local law enforcement agencies*. http:// policechiefmagazine.org/magazine/index. cfm?fuseaction=display&article_id=432& issue_id=102004 (accessed May 2005).

Police grant report (England and Wales) 2005/06. London: The Stationery Office.

Reaves, B. A., and M. J. Hickman. 2002. *Census of state and local law enforcement agencies, 2000*. Washington, DC: U.S. Government Printing Office.

————. 2004. *Law enforcement management and administrative statistics, 2000: Data from individual states and local agencies with 100 or more officers*. Washington, DC: Bureau of Justice Statistics, U.S. Department of Justice.

Reaves, B. A., and P. Z. Smith. 1995. *Law enforcement and management administrative statistics: Data for individual state and local agencies with 100 or more officers.* http://www.ojp.usdoj.gov/bjs/pub/pdf/lemas93.pdf.

Suiru, B. 2003. Funding patrol cars with advertising. *Police and Security News*, April–March. http://www.policeandsecuritynews.com/marapr03/Advertising.htm.

National Archives. 2005. *Crime and punishment: The police and new technology.* http://www.learningcurve.gov.uk/candp/prevention/g11/g11cs1.htm (accessed May 2005).

COURTROOM TESTIMONY AND "TESTILYING"

"Testilying," police fabricating evidence or lying in court, is a type of police corruption. It involves the interactions between the police and criminal offenders. A police officer, while generally honest, can also think that it is legitimate to commit illegal searches or to commit perjury because he or she is fighting an evil. For example, the officer reaches inside a suspect's pocket for drugs and later testifies that the suspect "dropped" the package. This type of testilying is called "dropsy testimony" and covers up an illegal search. The practice of testilying has different names in different cities. While in New York, it is called "testilying," in Los Angeles it is called "joining the Liars Club." Other cities call the practice "white perjury."

Nature of Testifying

Testilying can occur at any stage of the criminal process. It is more likely to take place during the investigative and pretrial stages, with much of it as an attempt to cover up illicit evidence gathering. Police fabricate their reports, knowing that these reports may be dispositive in a case resolved through plea bargaining. This form of perjury is called "reportilying." For example, it was found that narcotics officers in New York City falsified arrest papers to make it appear as if an arrest had occurred out on the street rather than inside a building, which would have made the arrest illegal.

Testilying can also occur during the warrant application process, which takes place under oath. A frequent form of testilying is the invention of a "confidential informant" to obtain a warrant. By using this strategy, the officer essentially covers up any irregularities in developing probable cause. In the 1990s, the Mollen Commission found that information from a nonexistent "unidentified civilian informant" was used to cover up unlawful entrances in New York's 30th Precinct.

Testilying can occur at the suppression hearing, and the most frequent type is post hoc (after the fact) fabrication for probable cause. In this type of testilying, a multitude of tales can be manufactured. Traffic violations that led to contraband in plain view are a common story. A bulge in the person's pocket or money changing hands is used to conceal unlawful searches of an individual.

Police Response

Alan Dershowitz has suggested that policemen are indirectly taught to commit perjury when they are in the academy. Their training implicitly supports attitudes that perjury is not serious. This training, in combination with both a police officer's job expectations and peer pressure, contributes to testilying. Officers that have testilied have frequently cited a desire to see the guilty brought to justice. The officer does not want a person that they know to be a criminal to escape because of a technical violation. And indirectly related, their desire is to produce results by securing convictions. Job productivity, for which an officer is rewarded, is obtaining results through arrests. A "code of silence" among police further supports testilying. Knowledge that other officers commit perjury condones the practice. Because other officers commit perjury to obtain an end, testilying is acceptable.

Police officers may also disagree with laws that curtail their discretion, such as the exclusionary rule. Judges have publicly stated that the exclusionary rule influences police to lie in order to prevent someone they think is guilty from going free. As a consequence, a police officer may not perceive that, when stretching an incident to fit it into the legal requirements, this is committing perjury. To circumvent the exclusionary rule, the officer may fabricate details about the arrest, the search, or the evidence. This type of testilying became apparent after the imposition of the exclusionary rule. In particular, "dropsy testimony," in which the officers testified that the offender dropped the drugs before being arrested, increased in drug-related cases.

It has also been suggested that the police think that they can get away with testilying because police supervisors implicitly accept the practice. For example, the Mollen Commission found that in New York's 30th Precinct, there was either an absence of supervision or supervisors who turned a "blind eye" to testilying. Higher rank officers in New York advocated that those officers who testilied should not be prosecuted because testilying was a police tradition

Further complicity by prosecutors and judges not only supports testilying, it legitimizes it as well. Prosecutors use a technique of steering police testimony by informing the officer as to what courtroom scenarios lead to winning and what courtroom scenarios lead to losing. If the prosecutor is determined to win, trial preparation can be geared to leading the police witness. By doing so, impressionable officers learn to tailor their testimony to the prosecutor's expectations. Judges have acknowledged that testilying occurs; however, they also acknowledge that it would not happen without their complicity. A judge's rationalization to tolerate perjury stems from sympathy for the officer's ultimate goal.

Prevalence

Research supports that courtroom workgroups are aware of testilying. In one survey that included prosecutors, defense attorneys, and judges, the courtroom workgroup perceived that perjury occurs 20% of the time in court. The workgroup believed that it occurred more frequently at suppression hearings, between 20% and 50% of the cases. Only 8% of these professional workgroups believed that police do not lie in court.

In another study of the Chicago court system, extensive evidence of prosecutorial and judicial acceptance toward police perjury was found. The research found that nearly 50% of each group believed that prosecutors had knowledge of perjury at least half the time. An even greater percentage of the groups believed that prosecutors tolerate perjury.

Key Events

Two famous cases involving police perjury occurred in the 1990s. One of the most damaging cases of policy perjury and testilying was in the New York Police Department's 30th Precinct during 1994. William J. Bratton, then police commissioner, retired the officers' badges; however, the scandal reverberated throughout the city. The Mollen Commission was formed to investigate the extent of police corruption. One hundred and twenty-five convictions against ninety-eight defendants were thrown out because the convictions were based on untruthful testimony by officers from the Harlem stationhouse. About seventy of these defendants admitted that they were committing crimes when they were arrested. The officers who were involved in the scandal gave different explanations for testilying. Some officers reported that they wanted to counterbalance loopholes used by dealers to evade conviction, and other officers lied to protect their own drug business. The chain of command accepted the testilying by their officers. Prior to the prosecution of the officers, some ranking police commanders argued that the officers who had "testilied" should not be prosecuted. They indicated that police tradition allowed officers to occasionally "shade" their testimony by changing details of an arrest to meet search and seizure standards.

In another well-known case, the O.J. Simpson trial for the murders of Nicole Brown Simpson and Ronald Goldman, police perjury affected the outcome for the prosecution. Detective Marc Fuhrman was exposed as a liar by the defense when he asserted that he had not used the word "nigger." In addition, Judge Ito found that Detective Vannatter demonstrated a "reckless disregard for the truth" in the warrant application for the search of Simpson's house. The prosecution's response to the perjury was that these lies were well-intentioned efforts, though improper, to convict a guilty person. They proposed that Furhman's denial at trial was meant to avoid a topic that would distract the jury, and that Vannatter's lies were designed to cover up irregularities in the evidence-gathering process that could have led to exclusion of incriminating information. The defense differed and obtained an acquittal.

Effects and Public Opinion

The corrosive effects of "testilying" are widespread. Testilying damages the credibility of police testimony in a trial. After the Simpson case, prosecutors indicated that their cases then had to begin with bringing the jury around to the opinion that cops are not lying. The perjury can extend to law enforcement's effectiveness in the streets, as the public feel a lack of trust. This distrust can further extend into the criminal justice system. Because other actors, such as prosecutors and judges, are perceived to be condoning police perjury, the system is viewed as corrupt. Essentially by acting in complicity with the police officers, the effectiveness of the entire criminal justice system is called into question.

In addition, convictions can be overturned, and departments, then, bear the liability for unwarranted prison sentences. Monetary considerations can have significant effect on a municipality. Several of the drug dealers and perjury victims from the 30th Precinct scandal sued New York City for unlawful imprisonment. They won six-figure settlements—the eventual financial toll for the city could be up to $10,000,000.

Unresolved Issues

Remedies for testilying focus on law enforcement and the law. Training has been a major focus as a remedy. In New York City, police cadets receive extensive training about perjury and about appearing credible without resorting to embellishment. Commanders and assistant district attorneys receive training on how to identify questionable police testimony.

Other suggested remedies include requiring police to produce their informant in front of the magistrate rather than rely on an unidentified confidential informant. In addition it has been suggested that police, when conducting a house search, be accompanied by lay citizens who observe the search. This is a practice that is used, with success, in other countries. Videotaping police activities, though time consuming and expensive, has also been recommended. All of these efforts focus on corroborating testimony, and it has been suggested that when an officer uses such measures, the officer should be commended and promoted for such behaviors.

Legal scholars have suggested that "probable cause" should be approached as a "commonsense" concept. At the same time, this gives the officer greater discretion. However, if there is a more stringent warrant requirement, the officer's discretion is curtailed. A more controversial suggestion has been to abolish the exclusionary rule, which would mean that officers would no longer make adjustments to their testimony. Then, if an officer were committing perjury, prosecutors and judges would be more willing to expose and prosecute such perjury.

KRISTEN J. KUEHNLE

See also **Accountability; Codes of Ethics; Complaints against Police; Corruption; Cynicism, Police; Ethics and Values in the Context of Community Policing; Informants, Use of; Integrity in Policing; Mollen Commission; Occupational Culture; Police Solidarity**

References and Further Reading

Daley, Robert. 1978. *Prince of the city*. Boston: Houghton Mifflin.
Dershowitz, Alan M. 1982. *The best defense*. New York: Random House.
Mollen, Milton, chair. 1994. Commission to Investigate Allegations of Police Corruption and the Anti-Corruption Practices of the Police Department.
Slobogin, Christopher. 1996. Testilying: Police perjury and what to do about it. 67 *University of Colorado Law Review* 67 (Fall): 1037.

COURTS

Courts both symbolize justice and administer it. Courthouse architecture—often classic, stately, imposing—is meant to inspire awe and reverence among those who pass and enter the building. Judges, too, are symbols of the law's majesty, sitting on an elevated bench, wearing black robes, wielding a gavel, and being addressed as "Your Honor." The formal language of the law, with its frequent use of Latin, reinforces the pomp and solemnity.

Only in court are the aura and mystique of the law made manifest, expressing the collective mores and will of society. Not surprisingly, judges rank high in studies of prestige, with justices of the U.S. Supreme Court standing first among all occupations. High prestige implies high expectations; many people criticize judges for not living up to them. Critics include the press, defendants, lawyers, police—even other judges. A common criticism is that judges are too lenient with offenders; other criticisms include dismissing cases for legal, technical reasons; reducing felony charges to misdemeanors; and letting convicted offenders go free or nearly free with fines, short jail terms, and probation.

The public generally rates judicial performance low and police performance high. Police gain notoriety by being overly assertive: arresting the innocent, abusing suspects, plating evidence, and entrapping. People who think judges are too soft on criminals are likely to applaud, if only tacitly, police who err in the opposite direction.

Judicial leniency is publicized; police leniency is not (Wheeler et al. 1968). The police often have probable cause for making an arrest but choose not to use it. On the other hand, more judges are prosecution rather than defense minded in their leanings and decisions (Wice 1985). For example, in *voir dire* (examination of potential jurors before trial), judges sometimes make only the most perfunctory attempts to determine whether veniremen are prejudiced against the defendant (Kairys et al. 1975).

Prosecution

Much lay criticism of judges is based on misunderstanding. The general public holds judges responsible for dismissing charges; in fact, the prosecutor is responsible for more dismissals. One study showed that the prosecutor typically rejected twenty out of one hundred felony arrests after initial screening. Thirty more were dismissed later by the prosecutor or judge (Boland et al. 1982). Of the remaining fifty, forty-five offenders pleaded guilty, and only five went to trial. Prosecutors thus play a pivotal part in the determination of a case.

Prosecutors bargain for guilty pleas in many cases. Hence, they do not usually go to trial or push for the maximum sentence. Several reasons have been offered for this unwillingness to push for severity: (1) Prosecutors do not want to risk losing a case at trial, (2) prosecutors face a large backlog of cases, (3) some suspects are initially overcharged, (4) some cases are routine and easily disposed of, and (5) some cases are too weak to pursue very far. Weaknesses may be due to various factors. Problems with witnesses or victims are particularly common. Either their stories are implausible or they keep changing them, or they are unwilling to testify—perhaps because they fear reprisal or perhaps they know the offenders personally (such offenders are of course easiest to identify and therefore to find and arrest).

Police and prosecutors are often assumed to be like minded and to have the same goals. But this is true only in the most exiguous sense. Often their relations are tense, sometimes breaking into overt conflict. Police think that their arrests should be prosecuted vigorously and result in conviction and punishment. Law enforcement for them is both a career and a moral commitment; hence, they accept the idea that they are the "thin blue line." No one imputes such qualities to assistant prosecutors, who typically are recent law school graduates who plan to leave the job in a few years for more lucrative fields. Controlling offenders is neither their career nor their passion. They want a reputation for achievement, which in the prosecutor's office means handling a large number of cases expeditiously, securing guilty pleas, and not losing cases at trial. Prosecutors have limited resources, so they pursue cases only if the evidence appears strong enough to produce convictions were the cases to go to trial. In addition, prosecutors face pressures not only from police, but also countervailing ones from defense attorneys and judges.

Complaints about courts' dismissing so many cases filter up to the state legislatures, which assume that judges are at fault—hence, the new laws mandating determinate sentencing. When such laws are combined with the many guilty pleas and the prosecution-minded juries, they result in a population explosion in American prisons. Even before the wave of laws on determinate sentencing, American laws were tougher than those in Western Europe. Perhaps this is because legislators pass these laws with the most serious career criminals in mind.

Defense

Defense attorneys are important members of the judicial process, but have far less power than prosecutors or judges. Defense attorneys may be hired by defendants or appointed by the judge when defendants are indigent. In some urban courts, as many as 90% of defendants are considered indigent by the judge. Therefore, the case is turned over to the public defender or assigned counsel. Public defenders predominate in urban courts; assigned counsel in rural ones.

Studies indicate that on the whole public defenders are consistently adequate or capable. Private defense attorneys hired by the defendants are much more variable, ranging from the brilliant to the ineffective. The public, long nurtured on Perry Mason television reruns or the headline exploits of F. Lee Bailey, Edward Bennett Williams, and Melvin Belli, continues to believe in the myth of brilliant, vigorous defense advocates. Few lawyers live up to this standard, however, perhaps because the pay is uncertain and the status low compared with that of other lawyers.

The life of a public defender is frustrating: (1) Few cases can be won at trial, so success in the conventional sense is elusive; and (2) clients are notoriously unsupportive. Like the general public, clients entertain the idea that defense attorneys should fit the Clarence Darrow or F. Lee Bailey mold. Defendants rarely cooperate with public defenders by telling them the truth, and defendants refuse to believe that public defenders are bona fide defense lawyers. This is because public defenders spend so little time counseling them, because there is a different public defender at each stage of the court process, and because public defenders are paid by the state and function as part of the same workgroup with judges and prosecutors every day. Resentful clients and poor pay make the life of public defenders unattractive; many leave after a few years on the job.

Most people arrested for felonies are poor, so they tend to be powerless. In the cities, many of them are young and either black, Hispanic, or members of some other minority. Thus they have little in common with judges, who are usually white, non-Hispanic, middle class, and older; but most researchers find that such extralegal factors are relatively unimportant in sentencing decisions (Hagan 1974; Kleck 1981; Lotz and Hewitt 1977). Seriousness of offense and past record are the factors that matter most.

Juries

Finally, there are the jurors. Trials are costly, time consuming, and unpredictable—three reasons why few cases go to a jury and many are instead disposed of via dismissals and guilty pleas. But the United States holds more trials by jury than any other nation, indeed more than all others combined. And what transpires in these trials forms a baseline for the rest of the cases: Defense attorneys and prosecutors first try to anticipate how a jury will react to their case, then they decide what kind of plea bargain to make. Three kinds of cases are more likely than others to result in a trial: first, very serious crime (murder, kidnapping, and forcible rape), which would be likely to draw a stiff penalty even if there were a plea bargain; second, those cases where the defense attorney thinks there is a good prospect of gaining an acquittal; and, third, those cases where the defendant ignores the public defender's advice and stubbornly insists on a trial.

Over the centuries juries have been both praised and castigated, called the palladium of liberty, and damned as the apotheosis of amateurs selected for their lack of ability. Such rave and critical reviews abound, but juries were little understood because for a long time researchers ignored them. In 1966 Kalven and Zeisel brought forth a compendium of findings in *The American Jury*. They discovered among other things that (1) in about 80% of the cases where juries are not hung, they reach the same verdict as judges (to convict or acquit); (2) juries apparently understand the facts of a case, because their verdicts are no more likely to disagree with the judges' in difficult-to-understand cases than in easy ones; (3) many of the judge–jury disagreements are due to jury values—jurors go outside the law sometimes in search of equity; and (4) very rarely does a minority persuade the majority to switch its votes in jury deliberations.

Pretrial Publicity

The same year *The American Jury* was published, the U.S. Supreme Court took up the issue of fair trial versus free press and overturned the conviction of Dr. Sam Sheppard for murder. It said that his trial had been marred by pretrial publicity, and that during the trial the press had been allowed to dominate the courtroom. Subsequently, commentators have consistently maintained that pretrial publicity affects jurors in a minuscule fraction of cases, if ever. Researchers, however, have discovered that (1) a majority of crime stories in the press violate fair trial standards (mentioning, for example, that the defendant has a prior record or has made a confession) and (2) jurors exposed to prejudicial publicity are more likely to vote for conviction (Padawer-Singer and Barton 1975; Tankard et al. 1979). The more informed people are about a case, the more likely they are to regard the suspect as guilty—and such information usually comes from the media.

Some jury trials are big events, attended by the national media and followed closely by a large number of citizens. They help to put the courts in the best light, by showing the due process model at work. The lawyers are in their attacking mode, the judge is dignified as he or she rules on points of law, and the jury makes the final decision (democracy in action). But while all of this press attention may promote interest in the law and support for the adversary process, it may be carried too far if the police and prosecutor feed the media damaging information about the defendant, diminishing his or her chance of getting a fair trial.

ROY LOTZ

References and Further Reading

Boland, Barbara, et al. 1982. *The prosecution of felony arrests*. Washington, DC: Institute for Law and Social Research.
Hagan, John. 1974. Extra-legal attributes and criminal sentencing. *Law and Society Review* 8 (Spring): 357–83.
Kairys, David, et al. 1975. *The jury system*. Cambridge, MA: National Jury Project and National Lawyers Guild.
Kalven, Harry, Jr., and Hans Zeisel. 1966. *The American jury*. Boston: Little Brown.
Kleck, Gary. 1981. Racial discrimination in criminal sentencing. *American Sociological Review* 46 (December): 783–805.
Lotz, Roy. 1976. *Public attitudes toward crime and its control*. Pullman: Washington State University.
Lotz, Roy, and John Hewitt. 1977. The influence of legally irrelevant factors on felony sentencing. *Sociological Inquiry* 47 (January): 39–48.
Padawer-Singer, Alice M., and Allen H. Barton. 1975. The impact of pretrial publicity on jurors' verdicts. In *The jury system in America*, ed. Rita James Simon, 123–39. Beverly Hills, CA: Sage.
Tankard, James W., et al. 1979. Compliance with American Bar Association fair trial–free press guidelines. *Journalism Quarterly* 56 (Autumn): 464–68.
Wheeler, Stanton, et al. 1968. Agents of delinquency control. In *Controlling delinquents*, ed. Stanton Wheeler, 31–60. New York: John Wiley and Sons.
Wice, Paul B. 1985. *Chaos in the courtroom*. New York: Praeger.

CRACKDOWNS BY THE POLICE

Police have utilized variants of the crackdown tactic for decades. Crackdown measures are often employed in response to demands from the community or political leaders for the police to take action against a particular crime problem that receives significant attention from the media or is severely degrading the quality of life in a particular area.

Crackdown is a frequently used term in the television and print media that loosely describes a wide variety of police initiatives aimed at particular types of enforcement. More specifically, a crackdown may be defined as a dramatic and measurable increase in police enforcement activity directed at a particular crime problem in a defined area or areas, generally with concomitant publicity and threats of severity in prosecution.

The problems addressed by a crackdown can range from speeding vehicles on residential streets, to prostitution, drug dealing, armed robberies, or other serious offenses. Generally, police crackdowns result in increased numbers of arrests—often for offenses that would only result in a warning or be ignored by the police under ordinary circumstances.

Other terms that are used to describe this type of activity include *sweep, raid, saturation,* and *zero tolerance policing,* each of which is briefly outlined next. The driving force behind the police crackdown has always been the notion that vigorous enforcement activity will serve to suppress a specific crime problem. Additionally, the crackdown demonstrates positive action being undertaken by the police. A publicized campaign of aggressive enforcement and increased arrests can heighten the visibility of the police, reassure citizens, and provide political benefits for the police department and the governing administration.

Of concern to professional police practitioners, however, is the critical question of whether or not crackdowns produce any measurable amount of crime reduction and how long any benefits may last once the police activity returns to normal. The academic and professional communities have studied these types of police operations in an effort to determine their effectiveness, both in the short term and over the long run.

Types of Crackdowns

A police crackdown can take many forms, from simply placing an emphasis on certain violations of the vehicle and traffic laws, to a city or county-wide sweep of search and arrest warrants directed against a particular set of offenders or an organized crime operation. Different terms are sometimes used that informally differentiate between types of police crackdowns.

A sweep typically refers to one particular police action on a particular day, although it may be followed up with additional sweeps. A sweep may involve a highly co-ordinated operation assisted by numerous officers and even multiple agencies, or may be as simple as arresting a large number of vagrants occupying a city park.

A raid is generally a tactic of a larger police action directed at particular premises where criminal or nuisance activity is taking place.

Saturation describes increased patrol activity in a given area. This may be intended to target a particular violation or to address a problem of disorder more generally. This is sometimes referred to as aggressive patrol or aggressive enforcement.

Zero tolerance policing is a term popularized by its implementation in New York City under Commissioner William Bratton during the 1990s. This form of policing can be implemented as part of a crackdown in a particular area or for a particular offense. It may involve suspension of the discretion that officers normally exercise when dealing with a certain offense, or it may be part of a strategy targeting minor incivilities in general, as in the case of New York City's program.

The police can initiate a crackdown as a direct response to a problem identified by the agency, or a crackdown may be precipitated by public outcry or pressure from government officials. To be effective, the methods selected by the police must be appropriate for the community and for tackling the particular problem at hand. Unintended consequences must be anticipated and planned for to the extent practicable.

Elements of Successful Crackdowns

In order for a police crackdown operation to be effective, several elements should be present. Generally, these actions should include:

- Heightened police visibility

- Increases in arrests
- Intensive prosecution
- Significant publicity

These elements help to ensure both initial and more lasting efficacy of the police action. Visibility provides both a deterrent to criminals as well as feelings of confidence among citizens. Increased numbers of arrests both remove offenders from the area and act as a deterrent. Cooperation from prosecutors to aggressively prosecute offenders can have the effect of removing offenders for longer periods of time, and publicity deters criminals, informs the public, and demonstrates that officials are taking action to improve conditions. Obviously, some crackdowns may not require all of these elements; for example, a narcotics sweep involving undercover officers may want visibility and publicity only as the operation comes to a close.

In addition to these basic elements, effective crackdowns select the appropriate method of police operation and include other governmental agencies in a multifaceted approach to entrenched problems. For example, police in New York City and Richmond, Virginia, initiated operations known as "Operation Pressure Point" and "Blitz to Bloom," respectively. These operations involved intensive police efforts to remove drug dealers, vagrants, and petty criminals from blighted areas, combined with cooperation from city agencies concerned with code enforcement, abandoned vehicle removal, and litter disposal. The results in both cities were a dramatic reduction in both observable and reported crime and disorder in the targeted districts. Moreover, the crime and disorder suppression also occurred in neighborhoods adjacent to the area of interest. This phenomenon of benefits accruing to areas surrounding a crackdown is known as *diffusion.*

The existing body of research leaves little doubt that police crackdowns have been proven to be an effective means of reducing crime and disorder, and that these positive benefits persist beyond the conclusion of such initiatives. This residual benefit is important, given the fact that police crackdowns tend to consume significant manpower, equipment, and financial resources, and cannot generally be maintained for long periods of time. Although less definitive research exists, it appears that strategies employing a multifaceted approach that includes a holistic, problem-oriented approach, coupled with an initial crackdown, enjoy longer-term success.

Determining Effectiveness

It is important for police officials to determine in advance how they will measure or evaluate the effectiveness of a crackdown operation. Specific goals should be enumerated before plans are put into effect. Postoperatively, the value of an initiative can be measured in a number of ways, including reductions in reported crime, increased (good-quality) arrests for targeted offenses, improved perceptions of safety on the part of neighborhood residents, reduction in calls to the police, lack of complaints about the operation from citizens, and no evidence that the problems were merely displaced to another location. Police officials who wish to continue to employ this tactic should be prepared to convincingly demonstrate their viability in the face of budgetary and other pressures on the police administration.

Consequences of Crackdowns

Unintended consequences can sometimes attend a police crackdown. These can be positive as well as negative, and should be given careful consideration by administrators and planners considering such a strategy.

One of the most obvious considerations about the impact of a crackdown in a specific area or neighborhood is that the criminal activity will simply be forced into neighboring areas or adjacent jurisdictions, a phenomenon researchers call *displacement*. This can be difficult to accurately measure, because researchers cannot be certain how far the newly deterred perpetrators may travel to commit their offense of choice. Moreover, there are other forms of displacement that include such aspects as changes in the time offenders operate, the targets they select, the methods they use, and even a shift in the crimes they choose to commit. Depending on the type of crime targeted and the geography of the area, these concerns may present a greater or lesser challenge to evaluating a crackdown's effectiveness.

Civil rights concerns are also important for police and political leaders to contemplate. Citizens who find themselves in an area targeted for aggressive patrol or zero tolerance enforcement may feel that the police are treating them unfairly. When offenses that have been ignored or given low priority by police in the past are suddenly rigorously enforced, citizens may become sensitive to police actions and ascribe economic class or racial motives to a crackdown initiative. Although these charges may be without merit, public perception of unfair treatment from the police can have negative political consequences and undermine the efforts of law enforcement to improve those same citizens' communities. Careful consideration should be given to communicating with the public in the area that is to receive intensive enforcement, so as to avoid misunderstandings that can sabotage the best laid plans.

Positive consequences of a crackdown—aside from a reduction in the targeted violations—can include improved police–community relations, a reduction in crimes and nuisances other than those targeted by the crackdown, and an improved sense of security among citizens,

regardless of the true effect of the police action.

Police crackdowns have been demonstrated to be a useful tactic. Careful planning and a strategy for avoiding pitfalls and conducting an effective post-operational evaluation can help to ensure a successful undertaking.

TODD D. KEISTER

See also **Abatement of Nuisance Property Seizure; Broken-Windows Policing; Hot Spots; Kansas City Preventive Patrol Experiment; Problem-Oriented Policing; Weed and Seed; Zero Tolerance Policing**

References and Further Reading

Center for Problem-Oriented Policing website. http://www.popcenter.org.

Fritsch, E., T. Caeti, and R. Taylor. 1999. Gang suppression through saturation patrol, aggressive curfew, and truancy enforcement: A quasi-experimental test of the Dallas anti-gang initiative. *Crime and Delinquency* 45: 122–39.

Greene, Judith. 1999. Zero tolerance: A case study of policies and practices in New York City. *Crime and Delinquency* 45: 171–87.

Green, Lorraine. 1995. Cleaning up drug hot spots in Oakland, California: The displacement and diffusion effects. *Justice Quarterly* 12: 737–54.

Hakim, Simon, and George Rengert. 1981. *Crime spillover*. Beverly Hills, CA: Sage, 1981.

Scott, Michael. 2003. The benefits and consequences of police crackdowns. Washington, DC: U.S. Department of Justice, Office of Community Oriented Policing Services. http://www.popcenter.org/Responses/response-crackdowns.htm.

Sherman, Lawrence, and David Weisburd. 1995. General deterrent effects of police patrol in crime "hot spots": A randomized, controlled trial. *Justice Quarterly* 12: 625–48.

Smith, Michael. 2001. Police-led crackdowns and cleanups: An evaluation of a crime control initiative in Richmond, Virginia. *Crime & Delinquency* 47: 60–83.

Weisburd, D. 1994. Diffusion of crime control benefits: Observations on the reverse of displacement. In *Crime Prevention Studies*, vol. 2, ed. R. V. Clark, 165–84. Monsey, NY: Criminal Justice Press.

CRIME ANALYSIS

Definition

Crime analysis is the collection and manipulation of crime-related information and data to discern patterns within that data with the goal of predicting, understanding, or empirically explaining crime and criminality, evaluating justice agency performance, or creating tactical and strategic deployment for criminal justice personnel. Although crime analysis has become more regularly used by police agencies, its development and utility can be found in other criminal justice agencies, as well as among the work of social scientists particularly in the field of criminology, who have used multiple crime analytic approaches to study crime and to assist police agencies. Each concept within this definition is explored next.

Information and Data Collection

Crime analysis begins with collecting information to analyze. While this first step to any type of analysis might seem obvious, accurate and useful crime analysis depends on the quality and sometimes the quantity of information that is gathered. Locating and collecting information to be analyzed is therefore an essential and often time-consuming starting point for crime analysis. Further, because crime analysis involves discerning patterns from large amounts of seemingly disparate pieces of information, computerized and automated forms of data can be a convenient and abundant source of data.

The most commonly used forms of computerized information collected for the purposes of analyzing crime are police calls for service or 911 calls, computerized records of written police reports, and computerized records of arrest. These three sources are most widely used by police analysts and criminologists when attempting to discern crime patterns, predict criminality, or develop crime prevention schemes.

Calls for Service

Computerized calls for service are generated each time a citizen calls the police for assistance or when the police proactively generate enforcement activity. Information is often collected by a computer-aided dispatch (CAD) system and can include the date, time, location, and type of call as the citizen or dispatcher interprets it. Calls-for-service information databases usually contain large amounts of records because they are generated each time an individual calls for police, fire, or ambulance service. For large cities, the number is often hundreds of thousands of records per year. Thus, calls-for-service information confounds analysis because these data can be repetitive, represent false calls, and include crimes that are misrepresented by citizens or are not crime related.

In addition to these problems, calls-for-service information also contains systematic errors that are generated by emergency personnel who initially record the data. These include multiple data entrants who use different styles and abbreviations when entering data, spelling errors, or purposely created errors, which may be generated according to unwritten rules of the police service. For example, homicides are often not found in calls-for-service databases because dispatchers and responding officers are specifically ordered not to label or announce an incident a homicide until deemed so by a detective.

However, given these limitations, calls for service are often a useful source of information when conducting crime analysis. For example, a number of crime-related incidents are found in calls for service that are not found in other data sources, which may provide police departments with a better understanding of crime in a particular neighborhood. These may include calls about disorder and quality-of-life incidents, ranging from noise complaints and public drunkenness to drug use and distribution, prostitution, street gambling, or fighting. Many of these crimes are either "victimless" (or go unreported by participants) or may not be formally recorded into a police report once the police respond. Yet, these incidents provide analysts with a better understanding of crime and disorder in a city or neighborhood, and can help direct deployment efforts.

Computerized Records of Written Reports

Another widely used source of information for crime analysis is computerized databases of written reports. These computerized records usually begin as manually written, paper forms that police personnel fill out in the field. Recently, some police departments have adopted computerized systems in which reports are automatically entered into a computerized database. Manually written reports may later be entered into an automated information system by other personnel, and the entire population of crime incident reports over a particular time period may then be downloaded by crime analysts.

Computerized records of written reports have been viewed as useful to analysts and researchers alike because they represent a filter of incidents that may be recorded in the calls-for-service database that are not crime related, are duplicate calls, or have other systematic errors and misrepresentations. At the same time, police culture, departmental practices, and the personal styles of individual officers and detectives will also create systematic biases and errors as to the types of incidents in which a report is written. Usually, when police respond to more serious crimes, this increases the likelihood that an incident report will be written. Because of this, computerized records of written

reports vastly underreport disorder and quality-of-life incidents or may only be generated if an arrest is made (for example, a report related to drug dealing).

However, computerized records of written reports are a rich data source for crime analysis because more information is often collected in these records compared to the information collected in calls-for-service databases. For example, not only are the date, time, and location of the incident collected (and perhaps more accurately than the date, time, and location of when and where a call for service was generated), but more specific information about the crime incident may also be recorded. These specifics may include whether a weapon was used, what type of building the crime took place in, what relation, if any, was the suspect to the victim; in some cases, the entire narrative of the report may be entered into the computer database. All of this information might be used in crime analysis to gain a better understanding of crime patterns and to assist with future predictions about where, when, how, or why crime will occur.

Computerized Records of Arrest Reports

Crime analysis has also been commonly conducted on computerized records of arrest reports. In some cases, the arrest report and the incident report may be the same report, or the arrest information may be added to the incident database as additional information connected to a specific incident. Computerized records of arrest can be especially useful to analysts in ascertaining who the repeat offenders are in a particular community, evaluating officer productivity, or examining co-offending. However, because a large percentage of crimes do not result in arrest, arrest records can also be less useful for certain types of crime analysis (for example, in determining "hot spots" of criminal activity).

Other Information Sources

The sources of information collected and used for crime analysis, however, are not limited to computerized records of calls for service, written reports, or arrest. In addition to these three primary sources of information, crime analysis is conducted on a wide variety of data sources depending on the goals of the analyses. For example, information may be garnered for crime analysis from these sources:

- Surveys of residents in a community
- Information about the modus operandi for a set of crimes
- Sentencing dispositions and other court records
- Self-reports of victimization or offending
- Ethnographic observations
- Police officer daily written logs of minute-by-minute activities ("run sheets")
- Detective case folders
- Parole and probation case folders
- Police personnel files
- Ad hoc databases generated by specialized units
- Field interview cards
- Data collected by evidence-submission units
- Traffic citations or accident reports
- Pawnshop tickets
- Surveys of police personnel
- Census, demographic, economic, or land use information

Information Manipulation and Analysis

Once data and information have been collected, crime analysis involves the manipulation of that data toward some goal. The term *manipulation* is used here to connote a wide variety of approaches in which data can be aggregated, combined, reshaped, related, reordered, or transformed in order to ascertain patterns within the data. The manipulation of collected information may involve a number of steps that make up the "analysis."

First, information may need to be prepared, "cleaned," extracted, or made into a form that can be analyzed because of aforementioned errors within the data. Raw intelligence may need to be coded and entered into a computerized system in order to systematically analyze it. Or, as already mentioned, data entrants of computerized crime information may make a number of systematic and nonsystematic errors that need to be fixed in order for analysis to continue. Often, data entrants are not entering crime data with the goal that such information will be analyzed in the future, which further confounds the standardization of the data. For example, in geographic crime analysis, computerized records of the locations of crimes are digitally mapped to determine clusters of crime for deployment purposes. If addresses are misspelled or include more information (for example, an apartment number) than a geographic information system can interpret, the crime cannot be digitally mapped. Further, if data entrants or field officers use and record common names for a particular location (for example, "Central Park") repeatedly for multiple crimes, entire groups of records may never be digitally mapped if a geographic information system does not understand where "Central Park" is. The systematic correction or "cleaning" of addresses is a fundamental and time-consuming job of crime analysts who conduct geographic crime analysis.

Once information has been cleaned or standardized, data manipulation and analysis can utilize a range of descriptive, statistical, qualitative, econometric, and/or geographic tools depending on the purpose of analysis, the skills of the analyst, and the data extraction and analytic tools that are available. Examples of data manipulations that have been conducted include the following:

- Geographic "hot spot" analysis, in which a geographic information system is used to create computerized maps of the locations of different types of crime incidents to ascertain clustering of these incidents
- Descriptive temporal analysis to determine the most likely times of the day or year in which crime will occur
- Statistical comparison methods to analyze data from randomized controlled experiments to evaluate the effectiveness of a particular crime prevention strategy that the police want to implement
- The use of time series analysis to determine the effects of a police after-school program on juvenile delinquency or the effects of a police deployment against terrorism
- Measures of productivity of police officers or supervisors (for example, examining changes in crime rates over time in a particular officer's beat) to evaluate officer performance
- The analysis of long-term crime trends across a neighborhood, city, state, nation, or world region, to determine the development of crime and its possible relationship with police activity or other social and economic trends
- The analysis of modus operandi of a group of crimes to determine patterns or commonalities for purposes of investigation
- The drawing of patterns from qualitative surveys of residents or ethnographies to better understand a community's concerns about crime.
- Surveys can be used to gauge officer satisfaction with their jobs or the level of brutality in a police department
- Statistical analyses of field interviews or traffic tickets to determine if police are racially profiling individuals
- Analysis of police activity logs to determine the productivity of certain officers or to monitor corruption

- Determining the major streets and pathways between locations of stolen automobiles and locations in which they are recovered to set up tactical or covert checkpoints of stolen automobiles
- The analysis of the price or purity of cocaine or crack sold on the street to determine trends of international drug trafficking

Purposes and Goals of Crime Analysis

The wide variety of analyses given in the preceding examples emphasizes that crime analysis does not point to any specific set of analytic tools, systems, or information sources. The only constraining factors that might determine what type of analysis is conducted is the availability of data, the purpose for which it was collected, or the analytic abilities of the crime analyst. For example, qualitative ethnographic observation data might require triangulation analysis or the use of software developed specifically to determine patterns in narratives. One might use logistic regression to determine what factors contribute to whether or not an individual is likely to be rearrested after his or her first domestic violence assault (for use by repeat offender units). Spatial statistical software might be utilized to determine whether drug events in a particular neighborhood exhibit any statistically significant clustering. Geographic information systems might be used to map the locations of robberies in a city. Link/network analysis can help to analyze organized crime networks, gang affiliations, and co-offending. Analysis can also incorporate noncrime data as well, to determine correlates to crime patterns or crime problems or to explore alternative answers to initial questions and hypotheses.

Thus, crime analysis is not limited to a certain set of tools, data, or perspectives.

Like any police investigation, crime analysis requires the exploration of multiple sources, views, and manipulations of data in order to reach a particular goal or purpose. Although crime analysis may have a number of goals, these can be generalized under the following four categories:

1. *To understand and predict.* One of the primary, if not central purposes of crime analysis is to ascertain patterns from information with the goal of understanding crime phenomena or to make predictions about crime patterns. Spatial, temporal, behavioral, and correlational patterns provide analysts with a better understanding of what types of crime might occur in the future, as well as when, how, where, and why they might occur. Common questions in crime analysis might include these: Which offenders are responsible for committing a large proportion of crimes? Where are crimes occurring? Why are these crimes occurring? What environmental factors are influencing crime occurrence? How are these crimes related? Which officers are at higher risk for health problems or corruption? Which areas of a city are most prone to terrorist or drug activity?

2. *To strategize and deploy.* Police are concerned with predicting and understanding crime patterns, often with the explicit goal of determining how to prevent crime in the future through strategic and tactical deployment schemes. Crime analysis may be conducted to create cluster maps of the locations of crimes to direct general preventive patrol efforts. Information from arrest or incident records can be analyzed to determine where an individual might be hiding or how best to apprehend someone. Or officer run sheets may be analyzed to detect corruption or laziness so that internal investigations might be generated.

Analysis might be used for both short-run, immediate deployment actions (sometimes referred to as "tactical" crime analysis) and more long-run strategies ("strategic" crime analysis). Tactical crime analysis is conducted on short time periods, perhaps examining crime incidents in a specific location over a week or month. Additionally, this type of analysis is conducted to obtain an up-to-date understanding of specific types of crime patterns in order to better inform a current police operation. While the use of crime analysis for tactical deployment may seem logical, this is a new and recent development for police agencies. Law enforcement agencies have evolved into reactive, calls-for-service–driven organizations in which officers and detectives respond to requests on an individual, case-by-case basis. Tactical deployment is rarely based on analysis of past information, but rather on tradition, "experience," hunches, what officers did in the past, or on "common sense." The use of tactical crime analysis stands in sharp contrast to these approaches. Tactical crime analysis uses information and intelligence to inform decision making, and groups past crimes together to discern patterns in order to take a proactive and preventive approach to dealing with a current crime problem.

Strategic crime analysis is conducted for the purposes of long-run police planning (perhaps to create a yearly plan of action). Although strategic and tactical analyses have a number of overlapping goals and applications, strategic crime analysis may examine long-run crime trends in a particular city, or can be used to allocate personnel or finances for an upcoming year. At its most basic level, strategic crime analysis is the collection of crime information for the purposes of collecting descriptive statistics on yearly crime data (for example, for the *Uniformed Crime Reports* collected by the Federal Bureau of Investigation). However, strategic crime analysis can also include time series analysis of the effects of major changes in general policing strategies (for example, patrol or investigations strategies) across multiple months or understanding crime displacement and geographic shifts across a city after a change in the physical or social environment of that city.

3. *To evaluate the effectiveness of police deployment schemes.* Crime analysis is also used in policing to evaluate the effects of police tactics and strategies. Crime statistics, experiments, and maps can provide useful ways for police to see whether their efforts are having any discernible effect on crime, criminality, disorder, or quality of life. This type of analysis is a subset of evaluation research, often conducted by social scientists to examine the effects of social programs on a particular problem. A wide variety of evaluation techniques are available to crime analysts conducting evaluations including randomized controlled experiments, quasi-experiments, time series analysis, statistical regression analysis, or the examination of satisfaction interviews. As with any type of analysis, evaluation methods are not created equal; some analytic methods are considered more accurate than others and thus are more reliable when making decisions about what police deployment schemes work.

4. *To evaluate the performance of police personnel.* Along similar lines of evaluating the effectiveness of police deployment is evaluating the performance of police personnel. For example, the New York City Police Department's COMPSTAT strategy is an explicit effort to use analytic tools including geographic information analysis and descriptive statistics about crime to monitor the efforts of supervisors, detectives, and officers (as well as the performance of other criminal justice agencies, such as probation and parole). Monthly crime statistics (and changes from previous months) are presented by supervising commanders in front of senior command staff and other supervising commanders in monthly administrative meetings. In these COMPSTAT meetings, information is then used by senior command staff to ask officers and commanders to provide reasons why crime has increased or to give reports on what they have done to deal with last month's crime problems. COMPSTAT has been replicated in a variety of forms across numerous police agencies who utilize crime analysis and statistics to keep track of police productivity.

Is Crime Analysis Useful and Effective?

In general, crime analysis is believed to be a positive policing development because its central function is to facilitate a proactive policing style in both administrative and deployment matters. Traditionally, police have focused on crime (as well as disciplinary issues) on a case-by-case basis, reacting to crime after its occurrence with the goal of arresting the offender. This reactive approach has been increasingly discounted in terms of being useful in reducing crime rates in cities or neighborhoods. As mentioned earlier, analytic results might help to predict the locations of future crime events and/or offenders, which may help police more efficiently target deployment. Crime analysis may also be useful in evaluating the effectiveness of policing strategies and the performance of police officers, thus serving as a way to more directly and strongly supervise officers and motivate them to be diligent.

Although little research is available that directly evaluates whether crime analysis is effective in reducing crime, there is evidence that preventive, proactive policing approaches that rely on crime analysis work better in reducing crime than those that are reactive and address crime incidents on a case-by-case basis. Often, crime analysis is not evaluated because it is seen as a technical aspect of a prevention program rather than the program itself. Yet, the intelligence that is generated by manipulating seemingly separate pieces of information might make deployment more effective, efficient, logical, feasible, or politically acceptable.

An excellent example of where crime analysis has been central to the reduction of crime is in one of the most common uses of crime analysis—hot-spot patrol. Hot-spot patrol, as made most famous by Lawrence Sherman and David Weisburd's experiments, is arguably a direct and logical extension of hot-spot crime mapping. However, it is the deployment (that is, hot-spot patrol), not the information or information technology (that is, maps generated by geographic information systems that indicate crime clustering) that is often promoted as achieving the outcome sought (crime reduction). Yet, in hot-spot policing, the generation of maps is a direct part of this deployment strategy. Further, the development of computerized crime mapping as well as hot-spot work conducted by a number of criminologists, social scientists, and crime analysts have helped facilitate the adoption of this deployment innovation.

Three important theoretical developments in policing have provided a foundation and justification for why improving information collection, analysis, proces-sing, and use by police may help improve police deployment effectiveness. These include problem-oriented policing, evidence-based policing, and information-driven management strategies.

Problem-Oriented Policing

Problem-oriented policing was formally introduced by Herman Goldstein in 1979 and represents the first structured framework for incorporating the collection, manipulation, and analysis of crime-related information into an organized police deployment strategy. Problem-oriented policing suggests that police can be more effective when deployment is based on the combination and manipulation of information about multiple incidents rather than separately focusing on individual incidents.

The centrality of crime analysis in problem-oriented policing was well articulated by Eck and Spelman in 1987 when they introduced the acronym SARA to describe the problem-oriented process. Respectively, SARA stands for a problem-oriented process in which police should "scan" for common crime problems within a community by collecting information from multiple sources (crime and noncrime related) about that community, "analyze" multiple sources and records of these problems to discern patterns, "respond" to problems *according to the results of the analysis*, and then "assess" the effectiveness of the response in reducing the problem.

The problem-oriented policing model suggests that the proactive use of information and analysis in policing to better understand overarching problems is directly connected to police effectiveness and evaluation efforts. Although evidence as to the effectiveness of problem-oriented policing can best be described as moderately strong, the few empirical tests that have been conducted show much promise to the hypothesis that crime analysis can directly help police to reduce crime.

Evidence-Based Policing

Evidence-based policing, as articulated by Lawrence Sherman in 1998, is another foundation for the usefulness and effectiveness of crime analysis in policing. Evidence-based policing refers to the idea that deployment and prevention decisions should be based on strong evidence that a particular police strategy is effective in reducing crime. Program effectiveness is directly determined by evaluation research, a particular type of crime analysis carried out by both criminologists as well as police analysts. Through this type of analysis, effectiveness is determined by collecting information about the outcomes of police prevention programs and then scientifically testing whether these outcomes are linked to the program.

Like problem-oriented policing, evidence-based policing suggests a new perspective with regard to the use of information that goes beyond examining information related to a specific crime for the sole purpose of clearing a case. In evidence-based policing, crime information is combined and analyzed to evaluate programs as well as the productivity of personnel. Thus, it not only contributes to determining better responses in the SARA process, but also emphasizes the need to collect information for the purpose of guiding decisions and assessing effectiveness. Like problem-oriented policing, evidence-based policing also indirectly suggests that improvements in information collection technologies and more scientifically rigorous analysis are important mechanisms in facilitating police effectiveness.

Information-Driven Management Strategies

As already mentioned, police agencies are beginning to use crime analysis as a tool in which to evaluate personnel and carry out strategic meetings to motivate officers and supervisors. While the aforementioned COMPSTAT strategy used by the New York City Police Department has been the most visible manifestation of this administrative use of crime analysis, information-driven management strategies more generally have placed crime analysis at the center of management strategies. These strategies utilize crime maps, crime rate statistics, and other analyzed information on personnel (complaints by citizens, trends of medical leave, analysis of the use of overtime by officers, and so on) to uncover inefficiencies and problems in police behavior. Here, information and analysis are used in an attempt to improve police services, uncover racial profiling, or root out corruption and brutality.

The Realities of Crime Analysis in Police Agencies

These broad definitions, theoretical justifications, and general overviews suggest that crime analysis is a positive, effective development in police agencies. Yet, the realities of the current state of crime analysis suggest a number of challenges and shortcomings. Furthermore, how crime analysis is conducted, who carries out crime analysis, and how analysis might be disseminated and used suffer from a number of myths that should be dispelled. At the time of this entry, these realities are as follows:

1. *The types of crime analysis conducted in policing are limited.* The types of analyses used in policing have been restricted primarily to descriptive statistics on crime trends per week, month, or year or the compilation of *Uniformed Crime Reports* (UCR) statistics. Although the use of geographic crime analysis and hot-spot mapping has become more widely diffused in policing, crime analysis continues to be a relatively new innovation. Other types of statistical, qualitative, ethnographic, evaluative,

network, or modus operandi analysis are rarely conducted.

2. *The use of crime analysis in policing is limited.* Not only are the methods and types of analysis used by law enforcement rudimentary in nature, but law enforcement still primarily relies on a reactive, case-by-case mentality in which to tackle crime problems. Often, hunches, officer experience, "word on the street," or "common sense" (however vague the term) are seen as more reliable than other forms of information. Crime analytic units in police agencies are not only small and poorly funded, but are believed by other police personnel, from patrol officers to sometimes the chief executive officer, to have utility only in the collection of UCR statistics or to assist senior supervisors in gathering crime statistics for monthly management meetings. It is rare to find tactical crime analysis being conducted at the precinct or stationhouse level, and there is clearly a gap between the generation of crime analysis and its dissemination as a regular tool in police deployment. More generally, the use of proactive and innovative policing approaches has generally been eschewed by policing culture, which continues to support a reactive, procedure-based approach.

3. *Crime analysis is primarily not conducted by crime analysts.* It is clear that the vast majority of crime analysis that is conducted is not conducted by crime analysts in police agencies. Rather, researchers doing work in criminology, environmental criminology, criminal justice evaluation, policing, geography, economics, and public policy have been the primary supporters, providers, and facilitators of the crime analysis movement. For example, consultation, research, and pro bono work

by environmental and place-based criminologists and geographers have helped facilitate hot-spot analysis and partnerships that have helped develop crime analysis and mapping units in police agencies. Police agencies have partnered with researchers from universities, research foundations, or government agencies to understand crime distributions within a jurisdiction or situational features that may lead to the availability of crime opportunities in a city. Police departments also have received crime analysis training, assistance, and products from academic and other research entities.

Further, crime analysts in police agencies have often been "one-person shops." Many crime analysts in police agencies are uniquely innovative individuals who have been identified by chief executive officers as being able to provide (or who can learn very quickly to provide) analytic services to police commanders. Their function, however, still remains ambiguous and they are widely underutilized in terms of tactical or strategic functions. Crime analysts in police agencies often rely on on-the-job training or support from outside individuals; because the use of analysis in policing is relatively new, very little mentorship or apprenticeship is available to train crime analysts in the tools needed for analysis. Recently, police agencies have begun to hire civilians to conduct crime analysis, including students with graduate degrees in criminology, statistics, geography, and computer science.

4. *The purpose and function of crime analysis are often misunderstood.* Crime analysis is often mistaken for other police functions, including forensics, crime scene processing, or computer-aided dispatch systems by

both police personnel and those outside of the police agency. One primary difference between forensics/crime scene processing and crime analysis is that crime analysis is not conducted on one single incident for the purposes of finding a perpetrator to make an arrest. While this might be one specific goal of a particular type of crime analysis, crime analysis is primarily focused on discerning patterns from multiple pieces of data in order to create prevention programs, tactical or strategic deployment schemes, evaluate officers, or determine the effectiveness of programs. Crime analysis might be used with the goal of arresting an individual by examining multiple crimes that individual is believed to have committed. However, the key difference and discerning characteristic of crime analysis is that it is the analysis of multiple pieces of information, often with proactive goals.

5. *Police culture is often suspicious of analysis.* It is also clear that crime analysts are seen as outsiders within the police agency. For analysts who work for administrative purposes to evaluate other officers (such as its use in COMPSTAT meetings at the New York City Police Department), crime analysts might be seen along similar lines as detectives in internal affairs units. In many cases, crime analysts are academic researchers volunteering their services to police agencies. This further places the crime analyst at the peripheries of the police service. Police culture continues to be suspicious of any activity that seems academic, proactive, or preventive, and this will be a major obstacle to overcome if crime analysis is to become a regularly used investigative and patrol tool.

Overall, crime analysis is a promising and useful tool for police agencies.

However, it remains to be seen whether proactive approaches that involve the collection and manipulation of multiple sources of information can become incorporated into police practice and culture.

CYNTHIA M. LUM

See also **Accountability; Calls for Service; COMPSTAT; Computer-Aided Dispatching (CAD) Systems; Computer Technology; Crackdowns by the Police; Crime Control Strategies; Crime Mapping; Crime Prevention; Hot Spots; Intelligence-Led Policing and Organizational Learning; Performance Measurement; Police Reform in an Era of Community and Problem-Oriented Policing; Problem-Oriented Policing; Research and Development; SARA, the Model; Strategic Planning; Technology and Police Decision Making; Technology, Records Management, and Calls for Service**

References and Further Reading

Mamalian, C., N. LaVigne, and E. Groff. 1999. *The use of computerized crime mapping by law enforcement: Survey results.* NIJ Research Preview. Washington, DC: National Institute of Justice.

Sherman, Lawrence, and David Weisburd. 1995. General deterrent effects of police patrol in crime "hot spots": A randomized, controlled trial. *Justice Quarterly* 12 (4): 625–48.

U.S. Department of Justice, Bureau of Justice Statistics. 1999. *Law enforcement management and administrative statistics (LEMAS): 1999 sample survey of law enforcement agencies.* http://www.icpsr.umich.edu.

Weisburd, David, and Cynthia Lum. Forthcoming. The diffusion of computerized crime mapping in policing: Linking research and practice. *Police Practice and Research: An International Journal.*

CRIME AND PLACE, THEORIES OF

Theories of crime and place understand crime in a physical or spatial environment. They explain crime patterns by the location of targets, offenders' choice of travel routes, use of space for various activities, and the innate ability of a place or target to defend itself. Theories of crime and place can be described as belonging together under the umbrella of what is called "environmental criminology" (Brantingham and Brantingham 1981). Theories of crime and place trace their origins to the work of the Cartographic School in the mid-1800s. Henry Mayhew, who is considered to be the founder of the Cartographic School, pioneered the use of maps in the analysis of crime. Mayhew's maps of counties of London showed spatial relationships between crime and rates of illiteracy, teenage marriage, and number of illegitimate children. Other statisticians, including Andre Guerry and Adolphe Quetelet, were also working with statistics and maps to represent crime patterns in France in the mid-1800s.

In the United States, the analysis of crime and place is rooted in the work done by the members of what is known as the "Chicago School" early in the twentieth century. Robert Park and Ernest Burgess, founders of the Chicago School, borrowed from plant ecology to explain the development of cities. According to Park and Burgess, cities developed in a process they called "succession" whereby competition for scarce resources, primarily land, drove the development of the city outward from the city core. They proposed that cities would develop in a series of successive concentric zones with the zones at the interior being the most deteriorated.

Based on their analysis, Park and Burgess proposed a theory of crime known as *concentric zone theory*. They showed that the zones closest to the inner city had the highest prevalence of social ills, notably, unemployment, poverty, reliance on social assistance, and rates of disease. Park and Burgess said that the prevalence of these social problems in the inner zones of the city where social conflict was high led to a condition they called *social disorganization*.

Other work by members of the Chicago School, notably Clifford Shaw and Henry McKay (active from the early to mid-1900s), explored the theory of social disorganization. Shaw and McKay (1969) divided the city into "natural areas." These areas shared social and demographic characteristics. They examined the locations of residences of juvenile delinquents and noted that areas with the highest rates of juvenile delinquents were geographic areas with weak community controls. Shaw and McKay did not attribute crime problems to the people who lived in these areas, but instead to characteristics of the areas including physical deterioration, ethnic heterogeneity, and low rental costs.

Shaw and McKay (1969) showed that social disorganization peaked in the central business district (CBD) (the first zone) and the zone of transition (the second concentric zone where recent immigrants first moved to and where industries were located). Social disorganization was shown to decrease in a linear fashion as one proceeds through the remaining concentric zones outward from the CBD. With each progressive zone away from the CBD, housing became more desirable and household income increased.

From these origins, much of criminology has sought to explain or predict crime based on factors ("causes") external to the individual and the individual's interaction with them. The ecological or areal tradition of criminology is concerned with the environmental, contextual, community, physical, or situational correlates of crime—or their interactions. Together, these theories aim to explain the relationships between crime and place at three different levels of spatial aggregation: the micro-level, the meso-level, and the macro-level. Often, though not always, the micro-level refers to the actual location of a crime. The meso-level often refers to a neighborhood or community. The macro-level, on the other hand, may refer to a city, or an area even larger such as a country.

Macro-Level

Theories of crime and place at this level of spatial aggregation explain crime patterns across larger areas. Examples of macro-level crime and place theories include the crime prevention through environmental design (CPTED) perspective, routine activity theory, and behavioral geography and crime pattern theory.

Crime Prevention through Environmental Design (CPTED)

According to this perspective, areas within the city emit "cues" about their characteristics that offenders use to select suitable targets. Urban settings can discourage crime and limit the number of targets that are perceived as "suitable" by motivated offenders through physical design that incorporates cues that show how the living space is well maintained, well cared for, and hence well controlled. Under such conditions, the potential offenders realize that (1) she or he will be easily recognized and (2) not tolerated (Newman 1972).

Routine Activity Theory

Routine activity theory suggests that each successful crime has at least one motivated offender and at least one personal or property target and requires the absence of an effective "guardian" capable of preventing its occurrence (Cohen and Felson 1979). Routine activity theory was originally intended to explain the spatial nature of crime on a citywide basis (Cohen and Felson 1979). The theory as originally conceptualized addresses how the movement of motivated offenders throughout a city shapes spatial patterns of crime when this movement overlaps with places where suitable targets or victims congregate and where there is no person or entity to properly guard the target.

Behavioral Geography and Crime Pattern Theory

Closely related branches of crime and place theory to routine activity theory are behavioral geography and crime pattern theory. In general, behavioral geography and crime pattern theory propose that offenders, in choices of victims and targets, use mental maps and cues. Places are said to exhibit special cues that elicit specific responses from motivated offenders and others (Brantingham and Brantingham 1981; Rengert and Wasilchick 1985).

Like routine activity theory, behavioral geography and crime pattern theory focus in part on movement throughout and travel paths within the city. A motivated offender's choice of targets and locations is based on his or her travel paths and awareness or activity spaces in a city. Awareness and activity spaces are part of mental maps. Cues are located within awareness spaces. Brantingham and Brantingham (1991) suggest that it is through travels from home to work and places of recreation ("nodes of activity") that an offender develops an "awareness space" within the environment. It is within the awareness space that an offender will search for "suitable" targets.

Meso-Level

Explanations of crime at the meso-level explain crime at an intermediate level of spatial aggregation. Examples of crime and place theories at the meso-level include territorial functioning, social disorganization, and collective efficacy.

Territorial Functioning

Territorial functioning is a perspective within environmental criminology that links the presence of fear of crime to the amount of crime. From this perspective, the occurrence of crime and fear of crime are associated with three particular elements: (1) attitudes of residents (responsibility and perceptions of control); (2) behaviors (responding to intrusions or potential intrusions and exercising control over activities in the territory); and (3) markers (signs and embellishments) (Taylor and Brower 1985). The territorial functioning perspective is clearly helpful to the examination of crime in residential neighborhoods. The applicability of this theoretical perspective to the examination of crime in other types of land use (for example, retail and commercial) is more difficult to establish.

According to the territorial functioning perspective, the perceptions and behaviors of residents of a residential setting act in combination with physical characteristics of a place to influence crime in that area. Local social ties not only increase territorial functioning, for example, but more cohesive social culture on the street block mitigates both crime and fear of crime among residents (Taylor, Gottfredson, and Brower 1984).

Social Disorganization

Social disorganization is a meso-level theory and was described earlier in this article. This theory serves as the underpinning for a more recent development in crime and place theory, Sampson and Raudenbush's theory of collective efficacy.

Collective Efficacy

Where social cohesion between residents is high, they are more likely than those who do not have good social cohesion to have control over what happens on their block and in their neighborhood, and they are more likely to intervene in problematic events (Taylor, Gottfredson, and Brower 1984). Sampson and Raudenbush (1999) measured social cohesion and levels of

social control among residents in Chicago neighborhoods and combined these indicators to develop a measure of what they refer to as *collective efficacy*. Specifically, collective efficacy includes three elements: informal social control, organizational participation of residents, and the willingness of neighbors to intervene in problematic situations. In neighborhoods where collective efficacy was strong, signs of disorder and crime were lower, regardless of sociodemographic characteristics of the residents.

Micro-Level

Theories at the micro-level focus on explanations of crime at the individual level or at the actual location of the crime. Examples of these theories include rational choice theory, revised routine activity theory, the situational crime prevention perspective, and the criminal events perspective.

Rational Choice

The existence of motivated, rational offenders is an underlying assumption of many theories included under the rubric of environmental criminology. In a majority of these theories, the motivated offender is portrayed as a rational actor choosing, based on a weighing of costs and benefits, suitable targets (Cornish and Clarke 1986).

Routine Activity Theory (Revised)

John Eck (1995) expanded routine activity theory to include more elements about the nature of the crime event and shifted the focus of routine activity theory to the micro-level. He expanded the routine activity into six "subtheories" of targets, guardians, offenders, handlers, places, and managers. Eck argues that each of these micro-level "subtheories" functions systematically to form a theory that has macro-level implications.

Situational Crime Prevention

As a type of crime prevention activity, situational crime prevention (Clarke and Homel 1997) targets specific places and seeks to change physical characteristics of places in order to reduce or prevent crime. This perspective is designed to reduce opportunities for crime as well as to reduce criminal motivation. More specifically, situational crime prevention aims to change the routine activities associated with clearly targeted places.

Criminal Events Perspective

The criminal events perspective posits that criminal acts and criminal events are two separate and distinct phenomena (Meier, Kennedy, and Sacco 2001). This approach considers not only the offenders and victims, but also "the contexts within which they interact," or in other words, the specific conditions that may influence the likelihood of a crime occurring (Meier, Kennedy, and Sacco 2001, p. 1). Ekblom (1994, 197) notes that criminal events should be viewed "more like a dynamic process," rather than a "single episode."

The criminal events perspective requires one to consider a number of conditions or components. According to Meier, Kennedy, and Sacco (2001, 3), they are "the immediate parties to the event, the possible history between them, the social situation in which they find themselves, and the rules that define their actions as legal and illegal." Other conditions may also be taken into consideration, such as "interpersonal context: how individuals define situations, their expected role, and acceptable responses to others' actions," as well as, "time (weekends, at night), geography (inner-city areas), economic and political

pressures, and community characteristics that increase the likelihood of crimes" (Meier, Kennedy, and Sacco 2001, 4). Brantingham and Brantingham (2001, 278) refer to these components, or "vectors of the criminal event," as "the *law*, the *offender*, the *target* (or victim), the *site* of the crime, the social *situation* obtaining at the site at the time of the crime, and the *mechanics* of the criminal act." The authors also stress that "every vector provides potential crime prevention intervention points" (Brantingham and Brantingham 2001, 290).

Police Response

Beginning with Block's (1979) work, much of the research that is focused from a policing perspective on the spatial nature of crime in environmental criminology on the specific locations characterized by high rates of crime or calls for service have used the term *hot spot* to describe these places. Although explanations for spatial patterns of crime are often associated with the term *hot spot,* this term is problematic for the following three reasons. First, there is no single, accepted definition in criminology for the term *hot spot.* Second, because of this lack of definitional consensus, as a term for characterizing places that have high rates of crime or police calls for service the term *hot spot* is unclear. Third, the inherently resulting elasticity of the hot-spot concept poses methodological problems in research focused on the spatial nature of crime.

Nevertheless, hot-spot and other place-based research has led a number of police departments to implement strategies that target these hot-spot areas. Use of the hot-spot approach allows police to concentrate on manageable challenges (Sherman 1995). Hot-spot policing is based on empirical findings that may allow police to maximize effectiveness and productivity by concentrating on manageable challenges

(Farrell and Sousa 2001; Sherman 1995; Taylor 1997).

Sherman and Weisburd (1995), for example, evaluated the effectiveness of a hot-spot patrol experiment in Minneapolis. Half of the city's hot spots received twice as much police patrol than the other half over a one-year period. Analyses revealed significant reductions in total calls and disorder in the areas that received the extra police patrol. Similarly, Sherman et al. (1995) evaluated the effect of police raids on crack houses in Kansas City, Missouri. Police executed raids at 98 of 207 identified crack house locations within the city. Results showed that although some crime and disorder appeared to be prevented, the deterrent effects of the raids disappeared quickly.

Place-based theories have also led to the development of new technologies for the police including crime mapping and geographic profiling. The use of computerized crime mapping can assist police departments in a number of ways. In its simplest form, mapping allows police to clearly visualize, identify, and target criminal problem areas within their jurisdictions. Police also benefit from the use of geographic profiling. According to Rossmo (1995, 218), the geographic profiling strategy takes, compiles, and analyzes information from "crime site locations, their geographic connections, and the characteristics and demography of the surrounding neighborhoods" in an attempt to locate and apprehend suspects.

Many community and problem-oriented policing strategies benefit from place-based criminological theory. To illustrate an example of a place-based problem-oriented policing tactic, Green (1995) examined the effects of the Specialized Multi-Agency Response Team (SMART) program in Oakland, California. The SMART program involved using "municipal codes and drug nuisance abatement laws to control drug and disorder problems" (Green 1995, 737). The police department partnered with other agencies and members of the community in order to combat neighborhood drug problems. Evaluation of the SMART program revealed that the combined efforts of police, landlords, and municipal code enforcement can reduce crime and improve the appearance of targeted places.

Conclusion

In short, theories of crime and place, in different ways, suggest factors apart from attributes of individuals or in interaction with individual attributes that explain crime occurrence or offending.

JENNIFER B. ROBINSON and
LAUREN GIORDANO

See also **Broken-Windows Policing; Community-Oriented Policing: Practices; COMPSTAT; Crime Analysis; Crime Control Strategies: Crime Prevention Through Environmental Design; Crime Mapping; Criminology; Hot Spots; Intelligence Gathering and Analysis: Impacts on Terrorism; Neighborhood Effects on Crime and Social Organization; Problem-Oriented Policing; Social Disorganization, Theory of**

References and Further Reading

Block, Richard. 1979. Community, environment, and violent crime. *Criminology* 17: 46–57.

Brantingham, Patricia, and Paul Brantingham. 1981. Introduction. In *Environmental criminology*, ed. Brantingham and Brantingham. Prospect Heights, IL: Waveland Press.

———. 2001. The implications of the criminal event model for crime prevention. In *The process and structure of crime: Criminal events and crime analysis,* Vol. 9, ed. Robert F. Meier, Leslie W. Kennedy, and Vincent F. Sacco, 227–303. New Brunswick, NJ: Transaction.

Clarke, Ronald, and R. Homel. 1997. A revised classification of situational crime prevention techniques. In *Crime prevention at a crossroads*, ed. S. Lab, 17–27. Cincinnati, OH: Anderson Publishing.

Cohen, Lawrence, and Felson, Marcus. 1979. Social change and crime rate trends: A routine activity approach. *American Sociological Review* 44: 588–608.

Cornish, D., and R. Clarke. Eds. 1986. *The reasoning criminal, rational choice perspectives on offending*. New York: Springer-Verlag.

Eck, John. 1995. Examining routine activity theory: A review of two books. *Justice Quarterly* 12: 783–97.

Ekblom, Paul. 1994. Proximal circumstances: A mechanism-based classification of crime prevention. In *Crime prevention studies*, Vol. 2, ed. Ronald V. Clarke, 185–232. Monsey, NY: Criminal Justice Press.

Farrell, Graham, and William Sousa. 2001. Repeat victimization and hot spots: The overlap and its implications for crime control and problem-oriented policing. In *Repeat victimization: Crime prevention studies*, Vol. 12, ed. Graham Farrell and Ken Pease, 221–40. Monsey, NY: Criminal Justice Press.

Green, Lorraine. 1995. Cleaning up drug hot spots in Oakland, California: The displacement and diffusion effects. *Justice Quarterly* 12: 737–54.

Meier, Robert F., Leslie W. Kennedy, and Vincent F. Sacco. 2001. Crime and the criminal event perspective. In *The process and structure of crime: Criminal events and crime analysis*, Vol. 9, ed. Robert F. Meier, Leslie W. Kennedy, and Vincent F. Sacco, 1–27. New Brunswick, NJ: Transaction.

Newman, Oscar. 1972. *Defensible space*. New York: Macmillan.

Rengert, George, and J. Wasilchik. 1985. *Suburban burglary: A time and a place for everything*. Springfield, IL: Charles C Thomas.

Rossmo, D. Kim. 1995. Place, space, and police investigations: Hunting serial violent criminals. In *Crime and place: Crime prevention studies,* Vol. 4, ed. John E. Eck and David Weisburd, 259–84. Monsey, NY: Criminal Justice Press.

Sampson, Robert, and Steve Raudenbush. 1999. Systematic social observations of public spaces: A new look at disorder in urban neighborhoods. *American Journal of Sociology* 105: 603–51.

Shaw, Clifford, and Henry McKay. 1969. *Juvenile delinquency and urban areas: A study of rates of delinquency in relation to differential characteristics of local communities in American cities*. Chicago: University of Chicago Press.

Sherman, Lawrence W. 1995. Hot spots of crime and criminal careers of places. In *Crime and place: Crime prevention studies*, Vol. 4, ed. John E. Eck and David Weisburd, 35–52. Monsey, NY: Criminal Justice Press.

Sherman, Lawrence W., et al. 1995. Deterrent effects of police raids on crack houses: a randomized, controlled experiment. *Justice Quarterly*, 12: 755–82.

Sherman, Lawrence W., and David Weisburd. 1995. General deterrent effects of police patrol in crime hot spots: A randomized controlled trial. *Justice Quarterly* 12: 625–48.

Taylor, Ralph B. 1997. Crime and small-scale places: What we know, what we can prevent, and what else we need to know. In *Crime and place: Plenary papers of the 1997 Conference on Criminal Justice Research and Evaluation*, 1–22. Washington, DC: National Institute of Justice, U.S. Department of Justice.

Taylor, Ralph B., and Sidney Brower. 1985. Home and near-home territories. In *Human behavior and environment: Current theory and research 8: Home environments*, ed. I. Altman and C. Werner. New York: Plenum, 1985.

Taylor, Ralph, Steve Gottfredson, and Sidney Brower. 1984. Understanding block crime and fear. *Journal of Research in Crime and Delinquency* 21: 303–31.

CRIME COMMISSIONS

Crime commissions can fit a variety of different descriptions. Some are privately funded and provide citizens, especially the civic-minded business and political elites, opportunities to participate in criminal justice. Others are affiliated with the government and perform a variety of functions. Some are instruments of criminal justice reform. Others thwart progressive change, deflect blame, and delay action. The main types of crime commissions are citizens' crime commissions, survey commissions, state crime commissions, truth commissions, and presidential crime commissions.

Citizens' Crime Commissions

Citizens' crime commissions are independent, privately funded agencies that serve as public watchdogs—they observe judges in courtrooms, investigate public corruption, and conduct research on the administration of justice. In contrast to state crime commissions and presidential crime commissions, citizens' crime commissions have neither governmental status nor official power. Instead, they serve as pressure groups, attempting to alter the practices and policies of criminal justice agencies and to articulate the public interest. A citizens' crime commission's importance in any community cannot be measured simply by the results obtained in the particular problems it addresses. Its very presence in a community serves as a potentially powerful force for good government and accountability.

The first citizens' crime commission in America was the Chicago Crime Commission (CCC). Formed in 1919 by the Chicago Association of Commerce, the CCC is the oldest, most active, and most respected citizens' crime commission in the United States. Influential businessmen and civic leaders established the organization to prevent crime and to wage war against corruption and inefficiency within the criminal justice system. Over the years, the CCC has advocated a more punitive criminal justice system that deters crime. Its leadership describes the CCC's role as that of a "watchdog" that monitors police, courts, and correctional institutions for lenience, laxity, and corruption. The commission's main claim to fame rests on a clever publicity stunt it pulled during the Prohibition era in order to arouse public indignation against Chicago's gangs. When the CCC released the first "public enemies list" in 1930, Chicago's newspapers published this list and labeled Al Capone as "Public Enemy Number One." Although the CCC has not been in the limelight in recent decades, it has remained active in Chicago, monitoring the justice system, campaigning against legalized gambling, and pressing authorities to take a punitive response to crime.

The CCC was one of more than two dozen citizens' crime commissions operating in the United States in 2006. Atlanta, Dallas, Kansas City, Los Angeles, New Orleans, New York, Philadelphia, San Diego, and Wichita are some of the other communities that had citizens' crime commissions in 2006.

Survey Commissions

Survey commissions were in vogue in America during the 1920s. These commissions mobilized the talents of experts from different fields, focused their energies on investigating the state of criminal justice in a particular city or state at a specific moment in time, prepared reports, used those reports to arouse public opinion to win support for the commission's recommendation, and then went out of existence. In terms of their politics, these commissions reflected the crime control perspective that dominated thinking in the 1920s. They stressed the importance of improving the bureaucratic efficiency of criminal justice agencies and gave short shrift to the question of whether or not the legal system was achieving equal justice for all.

The Cleveland Survey of Criminal Justice was the single most important crime commission of its type. It put forth the model of criminal justice as a system, a model that other crime commissions copied. Codirectors of the survey were Roscoe Pound and Felix Frankfurter, two of the most famous figures in American criminal law in the 1920s. The final seven-hundred-page report, published in 1922, represented the best thinking about criminal justice in the United States. The section on the police, for instance, was written by Raymond B. Fosdick, author of *American Police Systems.*

The Missouri Crime Survey (1926) and the Illinois Crime Survey (1929) replicated the Cleveland Survey's approach. These commissions differed from the Cleveland Survey, however, insofar as they were studies of criminal justice at the state level rather than the city level. Both the Illinois and Missouri surveys were started by respective state bar associations, were funded by business interests, and retained social scientists to do the research. The Illinois Survey also included an extraordinary study of organized crime in Chicago.

State Crime Commissions

State crime commissions are state agencies whose responsibilities range from investigation to planning and coordination. The examples of Nebraska and New York capture the diversity of state crime commissions.

The Nebraska Crime Commission provides comprehensive planning of activities leading to the improvement of the criminal justice system. Through the direction of a board comprised of criminal justice and juvenile justice professionals, this crime commission serves a leadership role by providing expertise, technical assistance, training, financial aid, enforcement of jail standards, research and evaluation, and informational resources to criminal justice and juvenile justice programs across the state.

The New York State Crime Commission investigates public corruption, labor racketeering, fraud, and organized crime. When evidence of criminal involvement is developed during an investigation, the commission refers the case to an appropriate prosecutor. Of equal importance is the commission's role as a "sunshine agency." To focus public attention on particular problems of local or statewide importance, the commission has the authority to conduct public hearings and issue public reports. As a result of playing this role, the commission has been a catalyst for the passage of new laws and changes in existing laws.

Truth Commissions

Truth commissions are ad hoc bodies formed to research and report on human rights abuses in a particular country or in relationship to a specific conflict. These commissions permit victims, victims' relatives, and the alleged perpetrators of human rights violations to present evidence. Usually truth commissions prepare recommendations on how to prevent a recurrence of human rights abuses. Governments and international organizations sponsor and fund truth commissions.

During the twenty-first century the international community has favored the idea of truth commissions as an alternative to prosecutions in order to document abuses and facilitate national reconciliation. Some shortcomings of truth commissions are that they lack prosecutorial power to subpoena witnesses or punish perjury and they are vulnerable to politically imposed limitations and manipulation.

A prominent example of a truth commission is Nelson Mandela's Truth and Reconciliation Commission. Following the end of apartheid and Mandela's election, South Africa sought to come to grips with its violent past. The Truth and Reconciliation Commission was established to address human rights abuses during the time of apartheid and minority rule. The commission emphasized collecting information over assigning blame and guilt. It even extended pardons to those willing to cooperate. This commission did not bring any perpetrators of injustice to justice, but it did begin the dialogue necessary for ethnic healing and national unity.

Presidential Crime Commissions

Presidential crime commissions are corporate bodies of civilians created by the president to operate for a short period of time and to focus on a discrete task. Two types of presidential crime commissions are agenda commissions and information commissions. Agenda commissions direct their efforts toward a mass audience and try to marshal support for new presidential policy initiatives. Information commissions target a much narrower group of officials. Their goal is to improve policy making by providing new ideas, new facts, and new analysis to policy makers. Both types can be either proactive or reactive.

Examples of proactive presidential crime commissions include the Reagan administration's Presidential Commission on Drunk Driving and the Attorney General's Commission on Pornography (the Meese Commission), which was created in 1985 to bring greater public attention to the harms associated with pornography. An example of a reactive agenda commission is the Wickersham Commission. It responded to a hotly debated issue already in the public eye, prohibition, and its task was to control political damage, defuse the issue of prohibition enforcement to allow political passions to cool, deflect blame, and provide some sort of official administration response.

Proactive information presidential crime commissions feature a forward focus. These commissions are meant to get out in front of a policy problem and anticipate future developments. One of the most significant proactive crime commissions has been the U.S. Commission on National Security in the Twenty-First Century (better known as the Hart–Rudman Commission after its cochairs, former Senators Gary Hart and Warren Rudman), which was created in 1998 to review U.S. national security challenges after the Cold War. This commission's final report made the most accurate prediction ever made by a presidential crime commission: The report warned in January 2001 that terrorists would attack America on U.S. soil.

In their reactive form presidential crime commissions assess what went wrong, investigate policy failures, and report on lessons learned. Examples of reactive information commissions are the Warren Commission on President Kennedy's assassination, the Kerner Commission on the 1967 race riots, and the 9/11 Commission.

DENNIS E. HOFFMAN

See also **Accountability; Federal Commissions and Enactments; Fosdick, Raymond B.; National Advisory Commission on Civil Disorder; Wickersham, George W.**

References and Further Reading

Hoffman, Dennis E. 1993. *Scarface Al and the crime crusaders: Chicago's private war against Capone.* Carbondale, IL: University of Southern Illinois Press.

Nebraska Commission on Law Enforcement and Criminal Justice. 2005. *Nebraska Crime Commission's mission statement.* http://www.ncc.state.ne.us/Mission.htm (accessed November 2005).

Peterson, Virgil. 1945. *Crime commissions in the United States.* Chicago: Chicago Crime Commission.

U.S. Institute of Peace. *Truth commissions digital collection.* http://www.usip.org/library/truth.html (accessed November 2005).

Walker, Samuel. 1980. *Popular justice: A history of American criminal justice.* New York: Oxford University Press.

CRIME CONTROL STRATEGIES

Whereas crime prevention efforts seek to thwart crimes from occurring, attempts at crime control concentrate on restraining, monitoring, supervising, and incapacitating those who have already committed a crime. Crime control in the United States has historically emphasized the use of legislative measures as well as various other mechanisms of incapacitation, surveillance, and restraint. Debates arguing the benefits of both punitive sanctions and rehabilitative treatments each carry political undertones, but the critical question as to what will keep communities safe remains to be answered.

The effort to control criminal misdeeds has been referred to as a "war on crime," yet Walker explains that "'war' is the wrong metaphor to use for reducing crime [since] it raises unrealistic expectations . . . promising a 'victory'" (Walker 2001, 11). According to Walker, fighting crime consists of a political process in which "liberals and conservatives begin with different assumptions about crime, the administration of justice, and human nature" (p. 11). Whether each side proposes harsher punishments or more treatment, "crime control politics makes criminal law a particularly attractive area of law reform" (Coker 2001, 802) for politicians seeking the approval of their constituency. Afraid of being victimized, voters turn to their leaders for solutions to the crime problem. As revealed by Cohen et al.'s 2001 study of 1,300 residents living in the United States, "the typical household would be willing to pay between $100 and $150 per year for crime control programs that reduced specific crimes by 10% in their communities." Unfortunately, despite the residents' eagerness to pay for a safer community, Walker (2001) claims that "both liberal and conservatives are guilty of peddling nonsense about crime" (p. 17) by espousing solutions that "rest on faith rather than facts" (p. 18). Still, the majority of the crime control efforts in the United States are initiated through federal legislative action, state crime control measures, or local surveillance efforts by community corrections agencies.

Crime Control Legislation

As a result of increased crime rates during the 1960s, Congress passed the Omnibus Crime Control and Safe Streets Act, which created the Law Enforcement Assistance Administration (LEAA) to encourage and fund the recruitment, training, and education of law enforcement officers. In addition, the Violent Crime Control and Law Enforcement Act of 1994 lengthened the list of federal crimes eligible for capital punishment, added a "three-strikes" condition mandating life imprisonment for third-time recidivists in federal cases, and prohibited the manufacture of semiautomatic assault weapons for a ten-year period. Until it expired, the ban barred the

manufacturing of semiautomatic weapons except for military or police use.

Since that time, the Omnibus Act has been revised to revamp the sentencing systems (1984), build new prisons, and develop community-based alternatives to incarceration (1990). Furthermore, the Violence Against Women Act, which was renewed in 2000, allocated federal funds to investigate and address violence against women, hire an additional one hundred thousand police officers, and build new prisons. More recently, the September 11, 2001, plane hijackings and terrorist attacks on the World Trade Center in Manhattan and the Pentagon led to the signing of the USA PATRIOT Act on October 26, 2001. Along with several expansions of law enforcement powers, the PATRIOT Act enhanced the powers of the Federal Bureau of Investigation to monitor phone and Internet communications as well as detain noncitizens under suspicion for extended periods of time.

At the state level, Megan's law, three-strikes laws, mandatory minimum sentences, and capital punishment all exemplify efforts to control crime through limiting anonymity, increasing the length of incarceration, or completely incapacitating offenders. Megan's law extends a sex offender's responsibility for his or her crime beyond the incarceration period by publicly notifying the community of his or her returned residency in a community neighborhood. Upon the offender's release, the sex offender will register with local law enforcement and, whenever deemed a high risk of recidivating, local residents will be notified of the offender's return to the community. Three-strikes policies mandate that offenders of a third violent offense serve a life sentence, and mandatory minimum sentences require that offenders, particularly drug offenders, complete a specified minimum amount of incarceration prior to their eligibility for release.

Unfortunately, crime control efforts that lengthen the incarceration period for offenders such as three-strikes laws and mandatory minimum sentences have "actually backfired in many states. As prisons become overcrowded, correctional officials are forced to release many offenders earlier than they normally would just to make room for new arrivals" (Walker 2001, 11). With the increasing prison overcrowding, critics claim that nonviolent drug offenders sentenced to mandatory minimum sentences are being held in correctional facilities, while more dangerous offenders are released. Furthermore, besides elongating the length of incarceration and turning to life sentences, the ultimate sanction is the use of capital punishment. While the controversy against the use of the death penalty continues, at the beginning of 2006, more than 3,300 death row inmates awaited their executions in thirty-eight states (Death Penalty Information Center 2006).

As with the unanticipated consequences of three-strikes laws and mandatory minimum sentences, other crime control policies have also resulted in adverse effects despite their good intentions. The "one strike and you're out" policy targeting drug dealers, gang members, and violent offenders implicated in unlawful activities within public housing sites became effective in March 1996. According to the Department of Housing and Urban Development, all public housing residents must sign an assurance that they will forfeit their housing contract if they, another member of the household, or a guest engages in drug-related activities within proximity of the property. In the case *Department of Housing and Urban Development v. Rucker et al.* (2002), the U.S. Supreme Court upheld the right of the housing authority to evict an entire household as a result of a drug or criminal conviction. In this particular case, three sets of elderly tenants brought suit against the housing authority. Despite years of law-abiding behaviors, senior citizens Pearlie Rucker, Barbara Hill, and Herman Walker were all evicted from their home as a result of a daughter, grandchild, or caretaker being apprehended in possession of marijuana or cocaine. Barbara Hill had lived in public housing in Oakland, California, for thirty years when she was evicted as a result of her grandson smoking marijuana with his friends in the parking lot of the public housing site. While the "one-strike" policy sought to control gang and drug activity within public housing, those who were most disadvantaged and vulnerable became the casualties.

Incarceration

Whether crime control efforts are the result of legislative initiatives or state measures, the greatest impact of these policies has been felt within the correctional system. Crime control tactics have mainly included punitive attempts at lengthening incarceration sentences and toughening terms of release; therefore, "imprisonment rates have skyrocketed since the 1970's to levels not seen anywhere else in the world, except South Africa and Russia" (Rosenfeld 2003, 296). The United States is currently housing more than two million inmates within its correctional facilities while "more than twice that number are under some form of correctional supervision in the community" (Rosenfeld 2003, 296). According to Clear and Dammer (2003, 3), "five million Americans are under some form of correctional control. Four-fifths of them are *not* in prison or jail; they are on probation or parole or in another community program." Clear and Dammer estimate that one in forty-seven adults is under community supervision.

Both probation and parole, the most frequently used types of community-based corrections, involve the supervision of offenders within a community context. Whereas probation represents an alternative sentence to incarceration, parole embodies the supervised release of an offender prior to the conclusion of his or her full sentence of incarceration. While under supervision, parolees sign a contract agreeing to abide by the conditions that they maintain regular contact with their probation or parole officer, abide by a curfew, secure regular employment, remain substance free, and refrain from involvement in illicit activities. In some cases, additional conditions such as geographic limitations or restricted contact with particular individuals may be added depending on the parolee's circumstances. For some, halfway houses are offered to aid offenders in transitioning back into society. While in these residential programs, offenders and ex-offenders experience more freedom than while incarcerated, yet they are still held to higher standards of control than the general public. They live and work within the community, but they must follow the conditions of the program or risk returning to jail or prison. Often, those supervised within the community are monitored using various technologies and surveillance equipment. "Most states now use some form of electronic monitoring to manage offenders in the community, and some have begun to use Global Positioning Satellite (GPS) systems to track their whereabouts twenty four hours a day" (Rosenfeld 2003, 297).

Technology used to monitor, restrain, or apprehend individuals assists in capitalizing on limited resources. In situations in which an offender has fled, technology has been used to locate and disable the offender. In Australia, "a variety of technologies are under development for the incapacitation of motor vehicles" (Grabosky 1998, 4) fleeing a scene. Controlling crime often entails immobilizing absconding vehicles. "One such method involves transmitting a short electromagnetic pulse which can damage the electronic components of a vehicle's ignition system and cause it to stall" (Grabosky 1998, 4) in the same manner as if the vehicle had consumed all its gasoline. Furthermore, the increasing efficacy of GPS allows for the use of a "small adhesive projectile containing a radio-frequency transmitter" (Grabosky 1998, 4) to be propelled at the escaping vehicle and used in determining its location at a later time.

While technological advances provide assistance in apprehending, monitoring, and controlling offenders, technology alone cannot fight crime. Bryne and Taxman (2005) believe that both treatment and control must be utilized to achieve the desired results. Countless others suggest that "with the burgeoning explosion of incarcerated individuals throughout the country, and the proliferation of prisons in which to house them . . . [one must examine the] current policies on crime control in conjunction with issues of social justice" (Pomeroy, 213), social change, and community involvement. Boyum and Kleiman (2001, 1) state that "one of the few universally accepted propositions about crime in the United States is that active criminals are disproportionately substance abusers. In Manhattan, urine tests indicate that over three-quarters of those arrested have recently taken one or more illicit drugs." For these exact reasons, drug courts were established in 1989 in Dade County, Florida, in an effort to specifically address the special needs of drug-abusing offenders. "Drug courts recognize the atypicality of drug abusers and their need for special services provided only through an integrated community program involving several helping agencies" (Champion 2005, 535). According to Boyum and Kleiman (2001):

> It is our view that current reentry initiatives also need to incorporate both treatment and control features to be (even marginally) successful in reducing the number of offenders who continually move back and forth from institutional to community control. The challenge is to develop initiatives (for example, a civic engagement model of restorative justice) that focus on individual and community change (Bazemore and Stinchcomb, 2004) because it is becoming increasingly clear that the system can not realistically expect offenders to change unless it begins to change the long-standing problems in offenders' communities (for

example, poverty, collective efficacy, culture). Ultimately, our choice of crime control policies should reflect our recognition of the inexorable link between individual and community change (Bryne and Taxman, 2005: 291–310).

While some hesitate about adding more therapeutic and restorative elements to crime control methods, one has to evaluate and consider the effects of current efforts to control crime through restraining, monitoring, supervising, and incapacitating offenders. Both nationally and globally, alternate justice models including therapeutic justice and restorative justice are recording successes. With the increasing problem of prison overcrowding and countless offenders under community supervision, data on these alternate justice models will be needed to develop the next wave of crime control approaches.

Conclusion

Crime control in the United States has emphasized the use of legislative measures to incapacitate, monitor, and restrain individuals. Various legislative crime control measures have lengthened incarceration sentences, expanded the list of federal crimes eligible for capital punishment, notified the public of sex offenders residing in their neighborhoods, prohibited the manufacture of semiautomatic assault weapons, and ejected individuals involved in illicit activities on public housing grounds.

Although it is clear that citizens are eager to solve the crime problem, one cannot discount the unintended consequences and adverse effects of some crime fighting initiatives. Furthermore, the problem of the increasing number of individuals under correctional control must be addressed. While the number of incarcerated individuals in the United States has surpassed two million, the numbers of individuals under community supervision continues to grow. The use of technology has provided assistance in monitoring probationers and parolees within the community, yet other solutions for controlling crime may require greater use of drug treatment programs, restorative justice endeavors, and additional community-based alternatives. Although it is unrealistic to expect that all crime will cease, new approaches to crime control will need to be developed.

SILVINA ITUARTE

See also **Crime Prevention; Criminology; Domestic (or Intimate Partner) Violence and the Police; Federal Commissions and Enactments; PATRIOT Acts I and II; Prisoner Reentry, Public Safety, and Crime; Repeat Offender Programs**

References and Further Reading

Boyum, David A., and Mark A. R. Kleiman. 2001. Substance abuse policy from a crime-control perspective. In *Crime: Public policies for crime control*, ed. James Q. Wilson and Joan Petersilia, 2nd ed. San Francisco: Institute for Contemporary Studies.

Bryne, James M., and Faye S. Taxman. 2005. Review essay: Crime (control) is a choice: Divergent perspectives on the role of treatment in the adult corrections system. *Criminology and Public Policy* 4 (2): 291–310.

Champion, Dean J. 2005. *Probation, parole, and community corrections*. Upper Saddle River, NJ: Pearson/Prentice Hall.

Clear, Todd R., and Harry R. Dammer. 2003. *The offender in the community*. Belmont, CA: Wadsworth-Thomson Learning.

Cohen, Mark A., et al. 2001. Willingness-to-pay for crime control programs, November.

Coker, Donna. 2001. Crime control and feminist law reform in domestic violence law: a critical review.

Grabosky, Peter. 1998. Technology and crime control. *Australian Institute of Criminology Trends and Issues in Crime and Criminal Justice* No. 78 (January).

Pomeroy, Elizabeth C. Book review of *Crime control and social justice: The delicate balance*. *Journal of Sociology and Social Welfare*.

Rosenfeld, Richard. 2003. Book review of *The limits of crime control. The Journal of Criminal Law and Criminology* 93 (1): 289–97.

Van Zyl Smit, Dirk. 2000. The place of criminal law in contemporary crime control strategies. *European Journal of Crime* 8 (4): 361–76.

Walker, Samuel. 2001. *Sense and nonsense about crime and drugs: A policy guide*. Belmont, CA: Wadsworth-Thomson Learning.

CRIME CONTROL STRATEGIES: ALCOHOL AND DRUGS

The social control of alcohol and illegal drug use dominates policing activities in the United States. Twice as many arrests for driving under the influence occur each year than they do for all violent crimes combined. During 2004, 12.4% of all arrests were for drug abuse violations, defined as the manufacture, sale, possession, or use of specified controlled or prohibited psychoactive substances. More arrests are made for drug abuse violations each year than for any other specified offense category (Federal Bureau of Investigation [FBI] 2004).

Policing Alcohol

The Volstead Act outlawed the sale or distribution of alcohol in the United States from 1920 to 1933. In the wake of its repeal a "control of consumption" model emerged. Today each state is given the authority to regulate the manufacture and distribution of alcohol, including hours and days of sale, allowable points of purchase and consumption, and drinking age (Hanson 1995). In 2004 there were 360,825 arrests for "liquor law violations" related to these various statutes. This compares with 374,499 arrests for all violent crimes *combined*. Liquor law violations have increased by 10% since 1995, reflecting efforts to suppress underage drinking (FBI 2004; National Highway Traffic Safety Administration 2002). Enforcement duties are the purview of state-level alcohol beverage control agencies and local police.

Public drunkenness is a second major category of alcohol-involved offenses. There were 355,495 such arrests in 2004, reflecting a 28% decrease over 1995 (FBI 2004). During the 1960s, arrests for public drunkenness comprised almost 40% of the nontraffic arrests in the United States, primarily involving "skid-row" men (Nimmer 1971, 1). Public drunkenness was decriminalized in thirty-seven states throughout the 1970s (Whitford 1983). Earlier federal court decisions such as *Easter v. District of Columbia* found that because alcoholism was considered a disease then it did not technically constitute a crime. Such findings influenced the 1967 President's Crime Commission, which recommended that public drunkenness be treated as a public health and not a criminal justice concern (Hutt 1968). In 1971 the Uniform Alcoholism and Intoxication Treatment Act developed guidelines for developing treatment diversion models at the state level in response to the federal Alcohol Rehabilitation Act of 1968 and the Comprehensive Alcohol Abuse and Alcoholism Prevention, Treatment and Rehabilitation Act of 1970 (Whitford 1983; Room 1976). St. Louis, New York, and other major cities established detoxification facilities designed for police diversion (Nimmer 1971). While arrests for public drunkenness have declined over time, current proportions of arrests reflect the conflation of drunkenness with disorderly conduct and varying levels of police discretion in support of diversion (Pastore 1978; Aaronson, Dienes, and U.S. Department of Justice 1982).

Finally, driving under the influence (DUI) currently absorbs the most amount of policing attention as this pertains to alcohol-involved offending. This was not always the case. Lundman (1998, 529) reports that police used to treat DUI as a "relatively minor problem." Social movements were definitive in changing laws and policing attitudes pertinent to DUI offenses. Organizations such as Mothers Against Drunk Driving mobilized nationally to require that twenty-one be the legal drinking age in all fifty states, to lower legal alcohol blood content levels for operating motor vehicles, and to demand more enforcement (Wagenaar and Toomey 2002; McCarthy and Wolfson 1996). Sobriety checkpoints for random drivers emerged as a constitutionally acceptable method of control (Ross 1994; Pellicciotti 1988). During the 1970s and 1980s, arrests for DUI steadily increased from less than 225 per 100,000 to almost 900 per 100,000. In 2004 there were 842,704 DUI arrests, a 4.6% decline from 1995, but still roughly 10% of all arrests (FBI 2004).

The policing of DUI remains problematic. Officers need to be adequately trained to collect evidence, and there have been difficulties in sustaining officer commitment to enforcement (Mastrofski and Ritti 1992; Lacey and Jones 1991).

Policing Illegal Drugs

There was a time in the United States when anyone could purchase grams of morphine or heroin from his or her corner druggist for just a few pennies (Duster 1970). This changed with the dawn of the twentieth century. "Moral entrepreneurs" from government and religious groups drew increasing attention to the dangers of addiction as both a public health concern and socially degenerative phenomenon (Becker 1963). Fears related to opium use and its links to Chinese immigration, and the belief that cocaine was a "public menace," especially among African Americans, led to the passage of local and state laws against recreational drug use (Faupel, Horowitz, and Weaver 2004, 41). Among the Western industrialized nations, the United States has been the most decidedly prohibitionist (MacCoun and Reuter 2001).

The passage of the Harrison Act in 1914 in the midst of concerns over the global opium trade signaled greater federal involvement in drug control. Largely a revenue measure, Harrison also stipulated that the distribution of narcotics and cocaine be for medical purposes only, effectively prohibiting the legal purchase and use of these psychoactive substances (Duster 1970).

U.S. Treasury agents were responsible for enforcing the Harrison Act, focusing particularly on distributors such as physicians and pharmacists. Supreme Court decisions in 1919 narrowed the definition of medical intervention and allowed for crackdowns on "narcotics clinics" devoted to drug maintenance therapies. Increasing numbers of users and physicians filled America's prisons throughout the 1920s. Eventually prison wardens and the U.S. Justice Department raised concerns about mixing addicts with the rest of the offender population, leading to the creation of so-called narcotics farms (Musto 1999; King 1953). The establishment of the Federal Bureau of Narcotics in 1930 and its first commissioner, Harry Anslinger, further intensified America's prohibitionist control regime, working to pass the Marijuana Tax Act of 1937, which effectively outlawed the sale and use of cannabis (Musto 1999).

The immediate post–World War II era represented a period of "relative calm" where the policing of drugs was concerned (Faupel, Horowitz, and Weaver 2003, 54). Increasing drug use and the discovery of psychedelic substances such as LSD in the 1960s created a resurgence of government concern. In 1968 President Nixon called recreational drug use the "modern curse of the youth" (Goode 2005, 105), and in 1970 the passage of the federal Controlled Substances Act "scheduled" drugs according to the severity of legal sanctions. The Department of Justice became the lead federal agency in combating drugs through the formation of the Drug Enforcement Administration. On the local level, drug enforcement that once targeted inner-city neighborhoods was shifted to the youth counterculture and focused in particular on the use of marijuana. Federal drug control costs increased substantially during the Nixon administration

(1968–1974), although a surprising two-thirds of this went to treatment, primarily methadone maintenance (Massing 1998).

During the 1980s the Reagan and Bush administrations launched a "war on drugs," despite indications that use patterns were declining (Goode 2005; MacCoun and Reuter 2001). Drug arrests for adults, in particular, doubled between 1980 and 1990 (FBI 2004). In 1984 the federal government stipulated mandatory minimum sentences for drug offenders convicted in the federal courts. Fears over the scourge of "crack" cocaine within African American communities led to the passage of differential federal sentencing guidelines in relation to powder cocaine in 1986, and in 1988 the Anti-Drug Abuse Act allowed the death penalty to be applied to drug traffickers tried in federal courts (Musto 1999; Lusane 1990). The drug war emphasized supply or "source reduction" strategies aimed at stopping importation at the border and at the street level through "buy and bust" operations and arrest crackdowns (Kleiman 1992; Moore 1990). Other efforts included targeting trafficking "kingpins" and confiscating the property of traffickers (Moore and Kleiman 2003; Worrall 2003).

Critics of the drug war have argued that supply reduction models have failed to reduce the demand for illegal drugs while at the same time leading to a tripling of America's prison population since 1980 (Harrison 2001). The drug war has also been blamed for exacerbating racial inequities in the criminal justice system (Tonry 1996; Lusane 1990). In 1989 blacks comprised 40% of drug arrests while only 12% of the population. The proportion of blacks or Hispanics charged with drug violations rose from 55% in 1983 to 73% in 1989 (Currie 1993).

Increasing opposition to punitive drug control prompted a vigorous debate over legalizing drugs in the 1990s (Massing 1998; Currie 1993). Twelve states decriminalized the possession of small amounts of marijuana (Goode 2005). The community policing movement was seen as a "third way" to drug policy reform emphasizing "problem-oriented" control strategies, for example, using housing code enforcement to abate trafficking (Green 1996; Uchida and Forst 1994). Some programs also supported harm reduction initiatives such as needle exchange programs and treatment diversion (Goetz and Mitchell 2003).

Despite reforms, drug arrests still increased by 21% between 1995 and 2004. In 2003 roughly one-half of all federal prison inmates and one of five state inmates were drug offenders (Harrison, Page, and Beck 2005). Recent increases reflect "zero tolerance" policing models that caused a surge in misdemeanor arrests during the 1990s (Conklin 2003).

The Future

Drug treatment courts have changed the ways that many drug and alcohol-involved offenses are now adjudicated (Nolan 1999). Nevertheless, drug courts do not necessarily impact policing behaviors or policies. Therapeutic interventions for drug and alcohol users and strategies to suppress drug supplies "beyond arrest" represent some innovations in the policing of alcohol and drugs. Nevertheless, arrests continue to dominate as the primary social control strategy used by police to regulate the distribution and use of psychoactive substances in the United States.

BARRY GOETZ

See also **Alcohol, Drugs, and Crime; Bureau of Alcohol, Tobacco, Firearms and Explosives; Community-Oriented Policing: Effects and Impacts; Crime Control Strategies; Drug Enforcement Administration (DEA); Drunk Driving**

References and Further Reading

Aaronson, David E., Thomas Dienes, and U.S. Department of Justice. 1982. *Decriminalization of public drunkenness: The implementation of a public policy*. Washington, DC: U.S. Government Printing Office.

Becker, Howard. 1963. *The outsiders*. London: Free Press of Glencoe.

Conklin, John. 2003. *Why crime rates fell*. Boston: Allyn and Bacon.

Currie, Elliott. 1993. *Reckoning: Drugs, the cities, and the American future*. New York: Hill and Wang.

Duster, Troy. 1970. *The legislation of morality: Law, drugs and moral judgment*. New York: The Free Press.

Faupel, C., A. M. Horowitz, and G. S. Weaver. 2004. *The sociology of American drug use*. Boston: McGraw-Hill.

Federal Bureau of Investigation. 2004. *Crime in the United States*. Washington, DC: U.S. Government Printing Office.

Goetz, Barry, and Roger Mitchell. 2003. Community-building and reintegrative approaches to community policing: The case of drug control. *Social Justice* 30: 222–47.

Goode, Erich. 2005. *Drugs in American society*. 6th ed. New York: McGraw-Hill.

Green, Lorraine A. 1996. *Policing places with drug problems*. Thousand Oaks, CA: Sage.

Hanson, David J. 1995. *Preventing alcohol abuse*. Westport, CT: Praeger.

Harrison, Lana. 2001. The revolving prison door for drug-involved offenders: Challenges and opportunities. *Crime and Delinquency* 47: 462–84.

Harrison, Paige M., and Allen J. Beck. 2005. *Prisoners in 2004*. October. Washington, DC: Bureau of Justice Statistics.

Hutt, Peter B. 1968. Perspectives on the report of the President's Crime Commission on the Problem of Drunkenness. *Notre Dame Lawyer* 43: 857–64.

Joint Committee of the States to Study Alcoholic Beverage Laws. 1960. *Alcohol beverage control*. Washington, DC.

King, Rufus. 1953. The narcotics bureau and the Harrison Act: Jailing the healers and the sick. *Yale Law Journal* 62: 784–87.

Kleiman, Mark. 1992. *Against excess: Drug policy for results*. New York: Basic Books.

Lacey, John H., and Ralph K. Jones. 1991. *Assessment of changes in DWI enforcement/level*. Washington, DC: National Highway Traffic Safety Administration.

Lundman, Richard J. 1998. City police and drunk driving: Baseline data. *Justice Quarterly* 15: 527–46.

Lusane, Clarence. 1990. *Pipe dream blues: Racism and the war on drugs*. Boston: South End Press.

MacCoun, Robert J., and Peter Reuter. 2001. *Drug war heresies*. Cambridge: Cambridge University Press.

Massing, M. 1998. *The fix*. Berkeley: University of California Press.

Mastrofski, Stephen D., and Richard R. Ritti. 1996. Police training and the effects of organization on drunk driving enforcement. *Justice Quarterly* 13: 290–320.

McCarthy, John D., and Mark Wolfson. 1996. Resource mobilization by local social movement organizations: Agency, strategy and organization in the movement against drinking and driving. *American Sociological Review* 61: 1070–88.

Moore, M. 1990. Supply reduction and drug law enforcement. In *Crime and justice: A review of research: Drugs and crime*, ed. Tonry and Wilson, 109–58. Chicago: University of Chicago Press.

Moore, M., and M. A. R. Kleiman. 2003. The police and drugs. In *Drugs, crime and justice*, ed. Gaines and Kraska, 2nd ed., 248–67. Prospect Heights, IL: Waveland Press.

Musto, David. 1999. *The American disease*. New York: Oxford University Press.

National Highway Traffic Safety Administration. 2002. *Partners in prevention: State alcohol agencies' approach to underage drinking prevention*. Washington, DC: U.S. Department of Transportation and Pennsylvania Liquor Control Board.

Nimmer, Raymond T. 1971. *Two million unnecessary arrests: Removing a social service concern from the criminal justice system*. Chicago: American Bar Foundation.

Nolan, James L. 1999. *Reinventing justice: The American drug court movement*, pp. 437–44. Princeton, NJ: Princeton University Press.

Pastore, Paul A. 1978. Mobilization in public drunkenness control: A comparison of legal and medical approaches." *Social Problems* 25: 373–84.

Pellicciotti, Joseph M. 1988. The law and administration of sobriety checkpoints. *Journal of Police Science and Administration* 16: 84–90.

Room, Robin. 1976. Comment on the Uniform Alcoholism and Intoxication Treatment Act. *Journal of Studies on Alcohol* 37: 113–44.

Ross, H. Laurence. 1994. Sobriety checkpoints, American style. *Journal of Criminal Justice*.

Tonry, Michael. 1996. *Malign neglect: Race, crime and punishment in America*. New York: Oxford University Press.

Uchida, C., and B. Forst. 1994. Controlling street-level drug trafficking: Professional and community policing approaches." In *Drugs and crime: Evaluating public policy initiatives*, ed. MacKenzie and Uchida, 77–94. Thousand Oaks, CA: Sage.

Wagenaar, Alexander C., and Traci L. Toomey. 2002. Effects of minimum drinking age laws: Review and analyses of the literature from 1960 to 2000. *Journal of Studies on Alcohol* Suppl 14: 206–25.

Whitford, David. 1983. Getting police off the skid-row merry-go-round. *Police* 6: 12–22.

Worrall, John. 2003. Civil asset forfeiture: Past, present and future. In *Drugs, crime and justice*, ed. Gaines and Kraska, 2nd ed., 268–87. Prospect Heights, IL: Waveland Press.

CRIME CONTROL STRATEGIES: CRIME PREVENTION THROUGH ENVIRONMENTAL DESIGN

Origins

The origin of crime prevention through environmental design (CPTED) dates back to the 1960s. The term *crime prevention through environmental design* was first coined by criminologist C. Ray Jeffery in a book by the same name (1971). However, it has an earlier beginning in Jane Jacob's book, *The Death and Life of Great American Cities* (1961). Jacobs drew on her observations of Greenwich Village in New York. She saw that well-used streets were more likely to be safe from serious crime. She felt crime opportunities could be minimized by a clear demarcation between public and private areas and by plenty of legitimate "eyes on the street." She thought this was accomplished by encouraging diverse urban places and creating opportunities for positive social interactions. The core of this idea was Jacob's belief that a sense of neighborliness and caring can lead to safer neighborhoods.

Beginning in the mid-1970s, CPTED was taught to police and crime prevention officers as a specific strategy, the main principle of which was the idea of *territoriality*, or physical areas where legitimate users of a place exert influence and take ownership over places. Architect Oscar Newman expanded these ideas during his work in public housing and wrote *Defensible Space*

(1972). Newman broke the concept down into four basic strategies:

1. *Territorial control*—the design or modification of a place so that legitimate users can exert influence. Property owners might separate their front door from public areas by symbolic landscaping, such as terracing and different pavement treatments. Another way to accomplish this was to divide the lawn space in front of apartments into semiprivate courtyards with overlooking windows. Pedestrians entering this area walk from the public sidewalk into the realm of the apartment prior to entering the building foyer. Residents can then monitor and control the area more easily.

2. *Access control*—controlling entrance and exits into buildings or neighborhoods. This can be done through physical designs such as fences and gates, or through softer approaches such as entrance signs. In recent years technological devices, such as electronic card readers, have become part of building security.

3. *Natural surveillance*—opening up natural sightlines into vulnerable areas to give potential offenders the impression they cannot offend with impunity. Although many forms of surveillance can have effect, natural surveillance is preferred to organized surveillance (security patrols) or mechanical surveillance (closed-circuit television).

4. *Image and maintenance*—Newman called this concept *milieu* (the total impression of one's surroundings). It refers to the cleanliness and maintenance of properties. In recent years this has become known as the "broken-windows" effect. Improving the maintenance and cleanliness in a neighborhood can help to confer to potential offender that residents care and control the public areas where

they live. Potential offenders feel unable to offend with impunity and are less likely to victimize residents in that area.

Throughout the 1970s and 1980s these basic CPTED concepts, now known as first-generation CPTED, were tested in numerous field studies, such as the Hartford Anti-Crime Project (Gardiner 1978). Gardiner summarized how his research team successfully reduced crime by applying CPTED to urban planning. Because the strategies in these approaches aim to minimize the opportunity for crime by making it more difficult for the potential offender, they became known as *opportunity reduction strategies.*

Conceptual Debates

In the 1980s and 1990s the criticism against CPTED was environmental determinism—the concept that the physical environment determines human behavior in spite of other social and cultural influences. Criticism also arose regarding displacement, or moving problems from one geographical location to another. In response, research in the geography of crime and situational crime prevention showed that displacement was not as big a problem as originally thought (Clarke 1997). It also led to the development of more advanced first-generation CPTED strategies.

Advanced strategies involve looking at opportunity reduction in places, but at a more complex and larger scale. Deflecting offenders, movement predictors (walkways in isolated subway platforms), and conflicting land uses (porn shops near daycare facilities) are among advanced concepts. Environmental criminology is the academic study of such topics. Using these advanced notions, planners and developers can properly locate different land uses in a new development to minimize the conflicts between users of that space. For example, avoiding placing a seniors' home next to a

skateboard park can minimize opportunities for potential conflict between two legitimate users of each space.

Armed with the new strategies, crime prevention specialists in some locations have had success implementing these ideas into new urban developments. For example, in 1987 Florida passed the Safe Street Act (Zahm, Carter, and Zelinka 1997) to provide funds for local crime prevention improvements and collaboration between police and planners. In British Columbia CPTED-trained police officers sit in city hall on urban design panels when new developments are being planned and then recommend changes to enhance safety long before construction begins.

Key Events

In response to growing demand for more professional CPTED practice, police, CPTED planners, and criminologists gathered in Calgary, Alberta, for a 1996 international conference on CPTED. Emerging from that event was the International CPTED Association (http://www.cpted.net), a nonprofit semiprofessional organization dedicated to professionalizing the practice of CPTED worldwide in annual conferences. Emerging at one such conference was the concept of second-generation CPTED (Saville and Cleveland 2003). Second-generation CPTED further expands CPTED by combining the reduction of crime opportunities with reducing the motives for crime in the first place.

This aligns with successful crime prevention and problem-oriented policing projects in recent years. For example, a theme emerging from successful problem-oriented policing projects is that they typically employ a wide range of strategies for maximum effect, many including first- and second-generation CPTED (Saville and Clear 2000). As Scott (2000) notes in his twenty-year summary of problem-oriented policing, the most successful projects typically combine a minimum of five or more strategies including social programs, enforcement, education, situational prevention, and CPTED.

Second-generation CPTED seizes on that reality and revisits Jacob's original formulation that a sense of neighborliness and community is at the core of safe streets (Colquhoun 2004). It incorporates a wide range of social crime prevention strategies in a holistic way. Police officers have long used similar strategies such as Neighborhood Watch and Community Crime Prevention.

Second-generation CPTED employs four new strategies—the four C's: enhancing social *cohesion* (for example, mediation skills, conflict resolution training); expanding local *connections* (for example, networks with outside agencies such as governments for fund-raising); community *culture* (for example, street fairs and festivals); and neighborhood *capacity* (for example, creating activities that support positive relations).

Other policing strategies adopting an approach somewhat similar to second-generation CPTED include quality-of-life policing, insofar as it hinges on the idea that safety emerges from community cohesion and neighborliness—all of which contribute to shared standards of behavior and values that bring people together in common purpose.

GREGORY SAVILLE

See also **Broken-Windows Policing; Crime and Place, Theories of; Crime Control Strategies; Crime Prevention; Neighborhood Effects on Crime and Social Organization; Neighborhood Watch; Quality-of-Life Policing; Routine Guardianship; Situational Crime Prevention**

References and Further Reading

Clarke, Ronald V., ed. 1997. *Situational crime prevention: Successful case studies.* 2nd ed. Albany, NY: Harrow and Heston.
Colquhoun, Ian. 2004. *Design out crime: Creating safe and sustainable communities.* Oxford, England: Elsevier Architectural Press.
Gardiner, Richard. 1978. *Design for safe neighborhoods.* Washington, DC: U.S. Government Printing Office.
Jacobs, Jane. 1961. *The death and life of great American cities.* New York: Vintage Books.
Jeffery, C. Ray. 1971. *Crime prevention through environmental design.* Beverly Hills, CA: Sage.
Newman, Oscar. 1972. *Defensible space: Crime prevention through urban design.* New York: Macmillan.
Saville, Gregory, and Todd Clear. 2000. Community renaissance with community justice. *The Neighborworks Journal* 18: 19–25.
Saville, Gregory, and Gerry Cleveland. 2003. An introduction to 2nd generation CPTED: Part 2. *CPTED Perspectives* 6: 7–10.
Scott, Michael S. 2000. *Problem oriented policing: Reflections on the first 20 years.* Washington, DC: U.S. Department of Justice, Office of Community Oriented Policing Services.
Zahm, Diane, Sherry Carter, and Al Zelinka. 1997. Safe place design. http://www.asu.edu/caed/proceedings97/zahm.html.

CRIME CONTROL STRATEGIES: GUN CONTROL

The use of guns in crime is a major problem in the United States. Cook (1982) counted 682,000 violent crimes in 1977 in which a gun had been used, including 11,300 homicides, 367,000 assaults, 15,000 rapes, and 289,000 burglaries. Guns have several features that make them more dangerous than other weapons. They can be used by weak and unskilled assailants, they kill impersonally at a distance and quickly, and sometimes merely the display of a gun can immobilize the victim.

Guns are also responsible for a large number of deaths each year. From 1979 to 1987, an average of 32,639 deaths resulted from firearms each year (encompassing suicides, homicides, and accidental deaths). The average overall death rate from firearms ranged from 4.6 per 100,000 per year in Massachusetts to 26.4 in Alaska (Centers for Disease Control, n.d.).

Focusing on the use of guns in crime and death leads to strong support for gun control. However, guns are also owned by many Americans who have not committed and will not commit a crime. Guns are used for sport and competition and to give the owner a sense of security against enemies. Many gun owners belong to the National Rifle Association (NRA), which has become a powerful lobby against any restrictions on the purchase and ownership of guns. However, organizations in favor of gun control, such as Handgun Control, have become more effective as lobbyists even though the membership of Handgun Control was only about two hundred thousand in 1995.

In fact, polls conducted for the NRA and the Center for the Study and Prevention of Handgun Violence have produced similar results, although their sponsors differed in their views on the issue (Wright 1981). The majority in both polls (whether they owned a gun or not) favored registration of handguns, but there was little support for an outright ban on handguns, except for cheap small handguns, the so-called Saturday night specials. The majority in both polls felt that the right to own guns was a constitutional right, but that registration of guns would not violate that right. The majority also favored strict mandatory sentences for crimes committed with a gun, and many states have now introduced such laws. Other proposed gun control measures have included prohibiting certain individuals from owning guns (such as criminals and those psychiatrically disturbed) and prohibiting the ownership of particular types of guns (such as cheap handguns and semiautomatic and automatic assault weapons). Others have suggested using product liability laws to force manufacturers to limit the kinds of weapons they sell.

Police are among those supporting stricter gun control laws. In a study conducted by Lester (1984), both state and municipal police favored stricter handgun laws, bans on the manufacture of Saturday night specials and on forbidding citizens from carrying guns in cars, mandatory sentences for crimes committed with a gun, stricter

requirements for commercial gun dealers, and longer waiting periods between obtaining a permit and taking ownership of a gun in order to permit a more thorough search of the buyer's background. Though many police officers are members of the NRA, the opposition of the association even to restrictions on armor-piercing ("cop-killer") ammunition has increased police support for stricter gun control laws.

Schuman and Presser (1981) discovered that opponents of stricter gun control laws are more active in their opposition than proponents. For example, they donate more money and write more letters. Hence, stricter gun control laws are difficult to pass.

The Use of Guns in Crime

Wright and Rosi (1986) surveyed felons in prison and found that half had used guns in their crimes. Of the gun-using criminals, 28% had used a gun once, 28% had used guns sporadically, and 44% had used them regularly. Of these regular users, handguns were more than three times as common as shoulder weapons for the weapon of choice. The gun-using felons had committed every type of crime more frequently, and though representing only about 22% of the total sample they accounted for nearly one-half of the violent crimes.

The most common sources of handguns for these felons were friends (40%), the street (14%), and gun shops (11%). The most common sources for shoulder weapons were friends (33%), family (22%), gun shops (17%), and hardware/department stores (11%). Thirty-two percent of the handguns and 23% of the shoulder weapons were stolen.

Guns in the United States and the Netherlands

It is revealing to compare data on guns in the United States with data from a country where gun ownership is rare. Colijn, Lester, and Slothouwer (1985) estimated that there were approximately three hundred guns per thousand people in the United States as compared to nine per thousand in the Netherlands. The rate of robbery with violence in 1980 in the Netherlands was 37 per 100,000 adults as compared to 303 in the United States, and the percentage of guns used in crimes is also lower in the Netherlands. For example, 13% of the crimes of robbery with violence in the Netherlands involved guns as compared to 45% in the United States.

Do Stricter Handgun Control Laws Prevent Crime?

The issue of gun control in America arouses powerful emotions on both sides of the issue. The National Rifle Association lobbies against any strengthening of gun control laws, appearing to believe that allowing any change in the laws governing the purchasing or ownership of guns would lead inexorably to the banning of all gun ownership. Proponents of stricter gun control, led by Sarah Brady, are often represented in public by her disabled husband, James Brady, who was seriously wounded in the assassination attempt on President Reagan.

The strong opinions involved in this issue render evaluations of the research on the effectiveness of gun control on firearm deaths suspect. Kleck (1991) did not think that research had demonstrated that stricter gun control prevents firearm deaths. Lester (1984, 1993) reviewed the same research and concluded that strict gun control had prevented suicide and that even stricter gun control would prevent murder. It is difficult, therefore, to draw unambiguous conclusions from past research.

Although two of the three studies from the 1960s and 1970s argued that stricter gun control laws did reduce the homicide rate, they can be criticized on methodological

grounds. Lester and Murrell (1982) found that states with the stricter handgun control laws in the 1960s did not have lower homicide rates in 1960 or 1970 or less of an increase in the homicide rate from 1960 to 1970. (They did, however, have a smaller proportion of homicides committed with guns.)

On the other hand, Lester and Murrell (1982) also found that states with the stricter handgun control laws did have lower suicide rates, both by gun and overall. They concluded that stricter handgun control laws may prevent suicide, possibly by restricting the means available for committing suicide. Restrictions on the buying and selling of handguns were the critical variables here, while restrictions on the carrying of guns were not. Lester (1993) concluded that more recent research conducted in the 1980s and 1990s supported the conclusion that restricting gun availability would reduce the use of firearms for suicide and possibly for murder. Lester has urged that researchers move on to the study of why (and under what circumstances) some individuals would switch to a different weapon for suicide, murder, or criminal acts while others would not.

The apparently weak (or possibly nonexistent) effect of strict gun control laws on the prevention of crime is understandable given the relatively weak controls even in those states with the strictest gun control laws. Gun control laws in the United States are much weaker than corresponding laws in Europe, for example. Thus, it is not surprising that these laws have not been conclusively shown to have any impact on the use of guns in crimes. Furthermore, even when stricter gun controls are passed, compliance with and enforcement of those laws is often lax.

DAVID LESTER

See also **Bureau of Alcohol, Tobacco, Firearms and Explosives; Firearms Availability and Homicide Rates; Firearms Regulation and Control; Firearms Tracing; Firearms: Guns and the Gun Culture**

References and Further Reading

Centers for Disease Control. n.d. *Injury mortality atlas*. Atlanta, GA: Centers for Disease Control.

Colijn, G. G., D. Lester, and A. Slothouwer. 1985. Firearms and crime in the Netherlands. *International Journal of Comparative and Applied Criminal Justice* 9: 49–55.

Kleck, G. 1991. *Point blank*. New York: Aldine de Gruyter.

Lester, David. 1984. *Gun control: Issues and answers*. Springfield, IL: Charles C Thomas.

———. 1993. Controlling crime facilitators. In *Crime Prevention Studies*, ed. R. V. Clarke. Monsey, NY: Criminal Justice Press.

Lester, David, and M. E. Murrell. 1982. The preventive effect of strict gun control laws on suicide and homicide. *Suicide and Life-Threatening Behavior* 12: 131–40.

Schuman, H., and S. Presser. 1981. The attitude–action connection and the issue of gun control. *Annals of the American Academy of Political and Social Science* 455: 40–47.

Wolfgang, M., and N. A. Weiner, eds. 1982. *Criminal violence*. Beverly Hills, CA: Sage.

Wright, J. D. 1981. Public opinion and gun control. *Annals of the American Academy of Political and Social Science* 455: 24–39.

Wright, J. D., and P. H. Rossi. 1986. *Armed and considered dangerous*. New York: Aldine de Gruyter.

CRIME CONTROL STRATEGIES: MORE POLICE

When crime rates begin to increase; when residents, business owners, tourists, or visitors begin to feel unsafe; when local politicians want to appear tough on crime; and when high-profile violent crimes are splashed across the headlines, the most common policy response is to hire more cops. For example, in his 1992 presidential campaign, Bill Clinton promised to "fight crime by putting 100,000 new police officers on the streets" (Clinton 1992, 72). Once in office, he fulfilled that campaign promise with the enactment of the 1994 Crime Act. Clinton's rationale for wanting to hire more police was simple and intuitively appealing:

> Our crime bill fulfilled a commitment I made to the American people to put 100,000 new police officers on the street in community policing. It's an old-fashioned idea, really. It means put the police back on the street, in the neighborhood, working with neighbors to spot criminals, shutting down crack houses, stopping crime before it happens, getting to know children on the street and encouraging them to stay away from crime. (Clinton 1996)

In a 1995 *Atlantic Monthly* article, one prominent police reformer, Adam Walinsky, suggested that the United States needs at least 500,000 new police officers to protect us from rising crime rates.

This affinity for hiring more police officers to reduce crime appears to transcend time and place—it is a universal instinct for achieving safer communities. From tiny developing nations to heavily populated industrial democracies, the pressure to hire more police is omnipresent. Research has shown that growth in the world's policing industry has outpaced population growth, which means the ratio of police to citizens is increasing worldwide (Maguire and Schulte-Murray 2001).

Although the idea of hiring more police to control crime is understandable, the evidence for its effectiveness is weak. Social scientists have studied the relationship between the number of police officers (known as "police strength") and crime rates for many years. If we look closely at this body of research, we find that it is exceedingly complex and often reaches unclear or contradictory conclusions.

Why is the research on the relationship between police strength and crime so complex? One reason is that it suffers from what statisticians call an "identification" problem. In other words, the statistical equations used to model the relationship between police and crime often lack sufficient information for the model to be identified or solved. The reason for this statistical difficulty is that the relationship between police and crime is reciprocal or simultaneous—the amount of police may influence the crime rate, and the crime rate may influence the amount of police. If we find a positive relationship between police and crime (as one increases, so does the other), is it because places with high crime hire more police, or because there are more police officers available to detect and report crime? If we find a negative relationship (as one increases, the other decreases), is it because places with high crime cannot afford to hire a sufficient number of police, or because more police means less crime? For these reasons, merely finding a statistical relationship (or a correlation) between police and crime is not enough to conclude that one "causes" or exerts an influence on the other.

Due to the model identification problem, complex statistical methods are often used to assess the relationship between police strength and crime. These studies are difficult to understand and evaluate for somebody without advanced statistical or econometric training, thus they are often inaccessible to those who can use them most such as police chiefs, politicians, and the media.

In 2000, a pair of university criminologists, John Eck and Edward Maguire, reviewed every published study that had ever investigated the relationship between police strength and violent crime. These twenty-seven studies contained eighty-nine separate estimates of the effects of police on violent crime. Of these estimates, 49.4% found no relationship, 30.3% found a positive relationship (more police, more crime), and 20.2% found a negative relationship (more police, less crime). The authors concluded that they "could not find consistent evidence that increases in police strength produce decreases in violent crime" (Eck and Maguire 2000, 217).

One of the most well-known papers reviewed by Eck and Maguire was written by the popular economist Steven Levitt (1997), who found that hiring more police results in less crime. In a replication of Levitt's (1997) analysis, McCrary (2002) criticized his methods and concluded "In the absence of stronger research designs,

or perhaps heroic data collection, a precise estimate of the causal effect of police on crime will remain at large." Levitt (2002) then replied by using different methods and finding the same results as his previous study. Though social scientists continue to use better data and more sophisticated methods, the results are often not very illuminating for practitioners and policy makers trying to decide how to spend taxpayer's money to reduce crime.

Two more recent studies took advantage of the increase in police presence during periods of terrorist threat—a sort of "natural" experiment—to examine the effects of police on crime rates. Klick and Tabarrok (2005), for instance, found that the heightened police presence associated with terror alerts resulted in no effect on violent crime, but a substantial decrease in auto thefts and thefts from autos. That analysis relied on daily crime data from Washington, D.C. Similarly, DiTella and Schargrodsky (2003) found that auto thefts decreased significantly during the heightened police presence that occurred in the aftermath of a terrorist incident at a Jewish center in Buenos Aires. In another recent study, Corman and Mocan (2003) used data collected over time in New York City, and found that increased police presence had an effect on motor vehicle thefts, but not on other types of offenses. Thus, three careful, recent studies have now found that increased police presence can reduce auto theft.

Taken together, the studies that were completed after Eck and Maguire's review of the research suggest that police strength may have effects on some offenses but not others. Altogether, combining the most recent research with the earlier findings summarized by Eck and Maguire, it seems that the scientific evidence on the effects of police strength on overall crime rates and violent crime rates is unclear.

Why are the research findings inconsistent and often contradictory? One reason is that different research methods often produce different findings. Another reason might simply be that increasing the number of police officers may have a dramatic effect in some places and times but not in others. Moreover, it may deter some offense types, such as those committed outdoors (like auto theft), but not others. In other words, this universal "cure" for unsafe communities may only work in some places, at some times, and under some conditions.

There are good reasons to support this interpretation of the evidence. As Sherman (1997) notes:

Hiring more police to provide rapid 911 responses, unfocused random patrol, and reactive arrests does not prevent serious crime. Community policing without a clear focus on crime risk factors generally shows no effect on crime. But directed patrols, proactive arrests and problem-solving at high-crime "hot spots" has shown substantial evidence of crime prevention. Police can prevent robbery, disorder, gun violence, drunk driving and domestic violence, but only by using certain methods under certain conditions.

The research evidence suggests that what police *do* may be far more important than how many of them there are. Hiring more police may have a large effect when the officers are assigned to perform the tasks of problem-oriented policing or hot-spot policing that have been found highly effective in reducing crime. When officers are deployed inefficiently or they are asked to perform tasks having a low probability of reducing crime, then the number of police may not matter. This conclusion is consistent with the findings of a committee of social scientists convened recently by the National Research Council to review research on policing. The committee found that previous research on the effects of police strength "are confounded with . . . the effects of changes in the strategies of policing" (National Research Council 2004, 225).

Some communities in the United States are chronically understaffed and could benefit from hiring more police officers. Other communities have too many police—where scarce community resources might be used to greater benefit by hiring more teachers or social workers or investing in more effective crime prevention strategies. There is no magic number of police—no ratio of police to citizens that is right for every community. The challenge is looking carefully at police operations, making sure that police are using the right tactics and strategies in the right places at the right times—and then hiring a sufficient number of police to get those things done.

EDWARD R. MAGUIRE

See also **Attitudes toward the Police: Overview; Computer-Aided Dispatching (CAD) Systems; Costs of Police Services; Differential Police Response; Fear of Crime; Homeland Security and Law Enforcement; Hot Spots; Performance Measurement**

References and Further Reading

Clinton, W. J. 1992. *Putting people first: How we can all change America.* New York: Three Rivers Press.

———. 1996. *Remarks by the president, Pennsylvania State University Graduate School Commencement.* Speech presented at Pennsylvania State University, University Park, May.

Corman, H., and N. Mocan. 2003. *Carrots, sticks, and broken windows.* Working Paper. National Bureau of Economic Research.

DiTella, R., and E. Shargrodsky. 2003. *Do police reduce crime? Estimates using the allocation of police forces after a terrorist attack.* Working paper 01-076. Cambridge, MA: Harvard Business School.

Eck, J., and E. R. Maguire. 2000. Have changes in policing reduced violent crime? An assessment of the evidence. In *The crime drop in America*, ed. Blumstein and Wallman, 207–65. New York: Cambridge University Press.

Klick, J., and A. Tabarrok. 2005. Using terror alert levels to estimate the effect of police on crime. *Journal of Law and Economics* 48 (1): 267–79.

Levitt, Steven D. 2002. Using electoral cycles in police hiring to estimate the effects of police on crime: Reply. *American Economic Review* 92 (4): 1244–50.

———. 2003. Using electoral cycles in police hiring to estimate the effect of police on crime. *American Economic Review* 87 (3): 270–90.

Maguire, Edward R., and Rebecca Schulte-Murray. 2001 Issues and patterns in the comparative international study of police strength. *International Journal of Comparative Sociology* XLII (1–2): 75–100.

McCrary, Justin. 2002. Do electoral cycles in police hiring really help us estimate the effect of police on crime? Comment. *American Economic Review* 92 (4): 1236–43.

National Research Council. 2004. *Fairness and effectiveness in policing: The evidence.* Washington, DC: National Academies Press.

Sherman, L. W. 1997. Policing for crime prevention. In *Preventing crime: What works, what doesn't, and what's promising*, ed. Sherman, Gottfredson, MacKenzie, Eck, Reuter, and Bushway. Washington, DC: U.S. Department of Justice, Office of Justice Programs.

Walinsky, Adam. 1995. The crisis of public order. *Atlantic Monthly* 276 (1): 39–50.

CRIME CONTROL STRATEGIES: SELECTIVE PROSECUTION/ INCARCERATION

Selective prosecution and incarceration is a tool used in the criminal justice system to identify those offenders who pose the greatest risk to society and impose stiff sentences on them with the goal of incapacitating them from committing future harm. Supporters argue that incarcerating habitual offenders early, even if it is for a minor offense, will reduce crime in the future. Persistent offenders, as well as offenders who present certain risk factors such as drug users, are generally the targets of selective prosecution and incarceration.

Policies that support this notion were created in response to the Philadelphia birth cohort studies. In these studies, Marvin Wolfgang and his colleagues followed a cohort of Philadelphia residents and described a group of them who were habitual offenders at high risk of offending again.

These offenders came to be known as "career criminals" (Wolfgang, Figlio, and Sellin 1972). Policies were then created with which prosecutors, judges, legislators, and probationers could identify, prosecute, and incarcerate others who fit this "career criminal" description.

While prosecutorial discretion influences the rigorous prosecution of certain groups of offenders, discretion among legislators, judges, and probation officers influences the selective incarceration of certain groups of offenders. The prosecutor can decide whether to file charges at all and which charges to file. More severe charges generally come with harsher penalties such as longer periods of incarceration. Thus, the prosecutors can select certain types of offenders that they feel are deserving of more serious charges and longer periods of incarceration. Judges are also important because they ultimately decide the severity of the sentence an offender receives upon conviction and have some discretion in their decisions. As such, they can selectively target particular groups of offenders with their decisions.

Legislators may also influence this process by creating sentencing guidelines for certain offenses and offenders. For example, one of the main contributors to the increased percentages of offenders incarcerated at the federal level for drug-related offenses that began in the 1980s and continues until today resulted directly from the sentencing changes at the federal level that require a mandatory five-year sentence for crimes involving five hundred grams of powder cocaine or five grams of crack cocaine (U.S. Sentencing Commission 1995). Finally, probation officers can also influence the sentencing process because they generally conduct presentence investigations and subsequent reports for the court. This report provides information on the offender and a sentencing recommendation that can greatly influence a judge's decision.

Most scholars suggest that there are five goals of punishment: deterrence, retribution, rehabilitation, restoration, and incapacitation. Selective prosecution and incarceration seek to achieve deterrence, retribution, and, to some extent, rehabilitation, but the main goal of this strategy is incapacitation. With incapacitation, the idea is to deprive offenders of the ability to commit crimes against society, usually by detention of the offender in prison. It is not clear whether prison achieves deterrence, rehabilitation, or retribution, but what is clear is that it incapacitates offenders from future crime, at least for as long as they are incarcerated. Because most of the targets of selective incarceration are persistent offenders who have not been responsive to previous attempts to achieve other goals of punishment, incapacitation is often seen as a last resort.

Selective prosecution and incarceration are also seen as ways to ease some of the practical problems faced by the corrections system. Proponents argue that by reserving incarceration for the most serious and persistent offenders, selective incarceration can reduce overcrowding and prison costs. It also prevents the cost of prosecuting and the cost to the victim for crimes committed by "career criminals" who would otherwise be in the normal population.

Greenwood (1982) provides some evidence that selective incarceration has the potential to be an effective strategy. Using data from almost 2,200 prison inmates in California, Texas, and Michigan incarcerated for burglary or robbery, Greenwood classified inmates into low-, medium-, and high-risk offenders based on their previous juvenile and adult arrest and drug use records and their employment histories. He demonstrates that reducing the time served by low- and medium-risk inmates and increasing the time served for high-risk inmates could simultaneously reduce both the crime rate and incarceration rate for specific crimes. This study has been criticized by a number of researchers; however, it does offer some promise that

selective incarceration has the potential to reduce crime.

Although selective prosecution and incarceration may incapacitate criminals and reduce the cost of corrections, critics argue that it actually widens the net of corrections. In many cases, selective incarceration is used in addition to, not in place of, incarceration of other offenders, thus increasing the number of people in prison. There are also questions surrounding the overall efficacy of selective incarceration. Some studies reveal that selective incarceration has little or no effect on arrest rates. In fact, some suggest that there must be an extremely large increase in incarceration to achieve even a small reduction in arrest rates (Visher 1986).

A further net-widening effect occurs in the use of sentencing guidelines. Those who have committed an offense and are on probation or parole have a higher likelihood of being arrested for an offense, but are not necessarily more likely to offend than their counterparts who are not under supervision. Selective incarceration may also reduce civil liberties and rights because (1) individuals are by definition treated unequally under the law and (2) the system may unfairly target groups that are defined by characteristics that have nothing to do with future criminality (for example, prior criminal history, type of offense).

The overarching criticism of selective prosecution and incarceration, however, concerns the inability to predict future behavior in the criminal justice area. Criminal justice researchers have identified certain risk factors whose presence increases the likelihood that one will engage in criminality, but have not been able to identify any single factor that consistently and unfailingly predicts criminal behavior. Thus, the idea of incarcerating people for longer sentences based on what they might do is highly controversial.

Selective prosecution and incarceration in practice currently target repeat offenders, drug offenders, and offenders who use firearms in commission of their crimes. "Three strikes and you're out" laws mandate that an offender be sentenced to a long period of incarceration on a third felony offense no matter how severe the offense(s). While the proponents of this legislation argue that it will deter both the offender and society from future crime, they also argue that it will incapacitate those with proven records of criminality and incorrigibility. Policy makers have also created mandatory sentences for certain drug-related crimes (for instance, the crack/cocaine sentences mentioned earlier). Drug users and sellers face selective incarceration in the war on drugs, partly because drug use and drug distribution are often linked to other types of crime. Therefore, drug use and distribution are often used as a signal in sentencing decisions to suggest to the sentencing authority that a longer, more stringent sentence is warranted. The goal of selective incarceration and prosecution is thus not only to incapacitate drug users and sellers from committing future drug crimes, but also from committing crimes that are tied to drug use and sales. Finally, a number of legislative efforts have centered on harsher sentences for those who use firearms in commission of crime and who possess firearms when they are legally prohibited from doing so (for example, probationers, parolees). Although the evidence is still far from conclusive, a number of authors suggest that these efforts reduce firearm-related crime (National Research Council, 2005).

While the practice of selective prosecution and selective incarceration remains highly controversial, most jurisdictions use it regularly, often for widely disparate crimes and sentences. Until legislators, judges, and prosecutors are convinced that these practices do not provide greater protection for the public, it is likely that selective prosecution and incarceration will continue to be used widely throughout many jurisdictions by many of the aforementioned actors in the criminal justice system.

TIMOTHY E. MCCLURE and DAVID C. MAY

See also **Crime Control Strategies; Crime Control Strategies: Alcohol and Drugs; Crime Control Strategies: Gun Control; Criminal Careers**

References and Further Reading

Greenwood, Peter. 1982. *Selective incapacitation*. Santa Monica, CA: RAND Corporation.

National Research Council. 2005. *Firearms and violence: A critical review*. Washington, DC: National Academies Press.

U.S. Sentencing Commission. 1995. *Special report to Congress: Cocaine and federal sentencing policy*. February. Washington, DC: U.S. Sentencing Commission.

Visher, Christy A. 1986. Incapacitation and crime control: Does a "lock 'em up" strategy reduce crime?" *Justice Quarterly* 4: 513–44.

Wolfgang, Marvin E., Robert M. Figlio, and Thorsten Sellin. 1972. *Delinquency in a birth cohort*. Chicago: University of Chicago Press.

CRIME LABORATORY

Police rely heavily on the positive identification of evidence in a case and its link to the suspect in solving a crime. In fact, this identification alone often secures a conviction. The police department crime laboratory is, therefore, of singular importance and houses a necessary array of highly trained individuals and technology.

Forensic science is the application of science to the law. It is in the crime laboratory that the forensic scientist plies his or her craft. The field of forensic science is new and hence is constantly growing and changing. Today's crime laboratory has many specialists. This was not so just a few years ago. In the early days of forensic science, a few scientists had to wear many hats and examine a variety of evidence types. Whereas before one scientist might have tested controlled substances, analyzed blood alcohols and bloodstains, and compared hairs and fibers, now there are specialists, especially in the areas of serology—the study of body fluids—and toxicology—the study of toxic substances (usually drugs) in body fluids. Specialization has come about because of the vast store of knowledge needed to interpret myriad evidence resulting in a final answer.

Lab Requirements

The basic equipment and supplies needed for a crime laboratory vary with the types of analyses performed. Before equipment is purchased, some considerations and a commitment must be made. Qualified forensic scientists are hired, with degrees in chemistry, biology, or one of the related sciences. Support personnel are also hired to type affidavit reports, file, and so forth. An area for the laboratory must be designated that is safe for the storage of hazardous chemicals, well ventilated, and secured by alarms, with entry allowed only to the forensic scientists. A separate area is set aside with its own alarm and lock for the securing of evidence and controlled substances.

The funding agency for the laboratory should underwrite any ongoing training expenses. Approximate cost for this additional training was $3,000 per person per year as of 1995. At no cost to the agency, though, are training seminars given at the FBI Academy in Quantico, Virginia. The FBI seminars cover a multitude of forensic subjects. One training course that does have a fee, but is invaluable, is the Forensic Chemist's Seminar at the Drug Enforcement Administration Training Center in McLean, Virginia; this excellent course deals with controlled substance identification methodologies. Because forensic science is currently evolving at a fast pace, membership in forensic societies is essential to keep abreast of new developments. Two such societies are the American Academy of Forensic Sciences and the American Society of Crime Laboratory Directors. Besides the national ones, regional forensic societies offer many learning opportunities.

A Drug Enforcement Administration (DEA) license is needed to purchase, handle, use, and store controlled substances, as is a state license. General laboratory supplies cost approximately $20,000 in 1995. In a typical police crime lab a visitor sees lab coats, test tubes, racks, microscope slides, spot plates, scissors, weighing papers, spatulas, tweezers, gloves, chemicals, a safety shower and eyewash station, spill pillows, safety blankets, safety goggles, a refrigerator/freezer, a burn station, a first-aid kit, a flammable storage cabinet, an acid storage cabinet, and fire extinguishers. The controlled substances acquired are for use as primary and secondary standards. The equipment and supplies listed next pertain to specific types of examination:

- *Marijuana identification:* stereo microscope, reagents, thin-layer chromatography tanks, sprayers, silica gel plates
- *Blood alcohol analyses:* blood alcohol kits, gas chromatograph, column, compressed gases, recorder, miscellaneous supplies (an automated headspace gas chromatograph is expensive, but the best)
- *Controlled substance analysis: Physicians' Desk Reference*, analytical balance, ultraviolet viewer, microscope, fume hoods, infrared spectrometer, compilation of known spectra, pellet maker
- *Firearms:* comparison microscope with fiber optics, workstation complete with tools and supplies, shooting tank (horizontal), reference collection of firearms for parts, subscriptions to firearms journals/magazines, membership in Association of Firearm and Toolmark Examiners
- *Library:* forensic texts, catalogs from laboratory supply companies

Evidence Submission Procedure

The police crime lab devises and enforces a procedure so that evidence is always submitted in the same manner and to the same place. Evidence envelopes and seals are provided to the submitter for packaging the evidence. Evidence envelopes contain the following information: suspect's name, report number, incident, date of incident, submitting officer's name, date of submission, and completed chain of custody. After the evidence is packaged, it is sealed with an evidence seal, on which are placed the sealer's initials, service number, and date. The chain of custody is a most important step in the process. Depending on the laws of evidence endorsed by courts in the area, it might be required that every person who has custody of the evidence—no matter for how brief a time—must sign the chain of custody. An alternative might be that every person who opens the evidence must sign the chain. The officer who collects the evidence at the scene of the crime is the first name on the chain, and next to his or her name is the date. On the next line is the name of the second person to receive the envelope, and so forth. Defense attorneys look for a broken chain of custody or a shoddily done envelope to discredit the evidence.

Evidence must also be packaged properly, so that no part of it is damaged or lost. Controlled substances must be tightly sealed to avoid leakage, arson evidence put in cans to avoid evaporation, blood tubes protected from breakage, and wet evidence completely dried before packaging. Evidence of any type is never packaged in plastic because it promotes mold formation; paper is used. An evidence analysis request form should clearly state what analysis the forensic scientist is to perform. The properly filled-out request accompanies the evidence, is logged in the master log book, stamped with the date, and placed in the evidence vault for safekeeping. Cases are then assigned for evidence analysis on a first-come, first-served basis, unless a certain urgency exists. The evidence stays in the evidence vault until called for by the examiner, who opens the package without damaging the collecting officer's seal, if at all possible. After analysis, another seal is affixed by the examiner, with his or her initials, service number, and date. The evidence is then returned to the vault, awaiting either pickup by the law enforcement agency or destruction.

In any case where source is to be determined, such as blood or semen, known samples must be submitted. This requirement is critical in homicides and sexual assaults. Known blood and semen must be collected from both victim and suspect for proper identification of origin.

Court Testimony

By the very nature of their work, forensic scientists are expert witnesses in court. They possess knowledge and skill outside of the range of the average person when it comes to identification of evidence. But to be a good expert witness requires skill of a different sort—a skill in communication. Complex chemical and biological reactions must be explained to a jury of "peers," who might possess knowledge of varying degrees, from that of a high-school dropout to that of a nuclear scientist. So it is imperative that the forensic scientist in the role of expert witness make eye contact with the jury and communicate his or her laboratory findings plainly, accurately, and unequivocally.

CARLA M. NOZIGLIA

See also **Forensic Evidence; Forensic Investigations; Forensic Medicine; Forensic Science**

References and Further Reading

Maehly, Andreas C., and Lars Stromberg. 1981. *Chemical criminalistics.* New York: Springer-Verlag.

Osterburg, James W. 1982. *The crime laboratory: Case studies of scientific criminal investigation.* 2nd ed. New York: Boardman.

Peterson, Joseph L., et al. 1978. *Crime laboratory proficiency testing research program.*

Washington, DC: National Institute of Law Enforcement and Criminal Justice.

Steinberg, Harold L. 1977. *Standard reference collections of forensic science materials: Status and needs*. Washington, DC: National Institute of Law Enforcement and Criminal Justice.

U.S. Federal Bureau of Investigation. *Handbook of forensic science*. Washington, DC: U.S. Government Printing Office.

CRIME MAPPING

Crime mapping is a tool used by the police, other agencies in the criminal justice system, and researchers to visualize locations of criminal events and related phenomena. The practice of crime mapping has evolved over time from the plotting of points on paper maps by hand to the use of computer software programs known as geographic information systems (GIS). The following discussion of crime mapping will explore its development over time, major principles, practice, techniques, unresolved issues, and future directions.

Development over Time

The origins of the practice of crime mapping and spatial analysis of crime can be traced to the work of French sociologists Andre Guerry and Adolphe Quetelet in the early to mid-1800s. In the United States, principles of crime mapping and crime analysis hail primarily from the work conducted by sociologists in the early to mid-1900s at the University of Chicago. Now referred to as members of the "Chicago School," Robert Park, Ernest Burgess, Clifford Shaw, Henry McKay, and others performed research that comprises the basis for crime mapping today. Today, crime mapping is used by law enforcement agencies in many countries including Australia, Brazil, Canada, India, Japan, Norway, the United Kingdom, and the United States.

One of the earliest official examples of crime mapping in the United States is the Illinois Crime Survey of Homicides performed by the city of Chicago in 1926. The city of Chicago researchers reproduced the patterns of homicides via pin maps (Block 2000). What was most likely the first use of computerized crime mapping occurred in St. Louis in the mid-1960s (Harries 1999). Official recognition of the value of crime mapping by the U.S. federal government came in 1997 when the National Institute of Justice (NIJ) established the Crime Mapping Research Center (CMRC), now known as the Mapping and Analysis for Public Safety (MAPS) office. MAPS serves as a clearinghouse of information for crime mapping–related funding, research, software, conferences, and practice.

By the mid-1990s, computerized crime mapping became more widely used and accepted in large police departments, most notably by the New York City Police Department (NYPD) and the Chicago Police Department (CPD). COMPSTAT, computer-aided statistical analysis, for example, was first introduced to policing in 1994 by the NYPD. Since then many police departments have adopted the COMPSTAT program or developed a similar program. COMPSTAT has been heralded as a successful tool for law enforcement leading to increased communication between departmental units and outside agencies. The use of COMPSTAT by police is related to reductions in crime and improvement in community policing (Weisburd et al. 2004).

By 1998, 75% of law enforcement agencies performed at least some crime analysis but only 13% of those agencies used some form of crime mapping (Mamalian and LaVigne 1999). In 1999, approximately 11% of small police departments (fifty to ninety-nine sworn personnel) and 32.6% of large police departments (one hundred plus sworn personnel) had implemented a COMPSTAT-like program, with approximately 60% of departments with five hundred or more sworn personnel having implemented such a program (Weisburd et al. 2004, 6, 12).

Major Principles

Current techniques of spatial analysis of crime, including crime mapping, are based on an area of criminological theory known as environmental criminology. The theories of environmental criminology state that crime is predictably located in place and in time (Brantingham and Brantingham 1991). According to this perspective, the locations of crime can be explained through a number of factors, including the road and transportation network of a city and the ecological and demographic characteristics of places. Crime mapping is a natural tool, therefore, not just for law enforcement agencies, but also for criminologists.

Crime mapping relies principally on police data—calls for service and arrest data. Data used for crime mapping analysis must contain, at the very minimum, specific location data, incident types, and dates of occurrence. Accuracy of the data is of paramount importance. Without accurate data meaningful analysis cannot be performed. Before crime location data can be mapped, careful procedures must be in place to ensure the accuracy of recorded data and the thoroughness of recording (Casady 1999). In other words, for crime mapping to be a truly useful tool for the police there need to exist databases that integrate accurate and useful information from a variety of sources, the proper infrastructure to support it, and an efficient method for distributing the information to the officers and management (Manning 2001, 93).

Practice

Improvement in the capabilities of desktop computers is one explanation for the increased use of crime mapping by the police. The basic tool of crime mapping is the GIS. Modern desktop computer GISs permit the depiction and analysis of spatial phenomena in ways that were not possible before their widespread introduction. The ultimate reason for using a GIS is to provide a medium for geographic analysis. Traditional statistical analyses cannot do this.

A GIS spatially codes data and attaches attributes to the features stored to analyze these data based on those attributes. Data that are spatially coded have geographic coordinates associated with each data point. This process is called *geocoding*. The location of arrests may be coded to, for example, a street address, a zip code, or a police precinct, among other types of locations. A GIS is an increasingly flexible analytic tool that is limited only by the imagination of the analyst or researcher and the availability of spatially coded data.

Because a GIS organizes data in a way similar to maps it is an excellent tool for examining multidimensional, multifaceted crime problems. In other words, GISs are able to examine and clarify the spatial relationships that exist between general social indicators in an environment and the crime patterns that also exist there (Rich 1995). Due to their flexible analytic capabilities, GISs are used by the police for more than crime analysis and resource planning. GISs are also used for intelligence dissemination (Ratcliffe 2000, 315), to inform residents about crime problems in their area (Mamalian and LaVigne 1999, 3), and to support court testimony (Travis and Hughes 2002, 3).

A 1997 survey of law enforcement agencies in the United States found that of the departments that did not use GIS, 20% reported having budgeted funds to purchase hardware and software in the following year (Mamalian and LaVigne 1999, 1). The survey also found that of the departments that possessed crime mapping capability, ". . . 88 percent use commercially available software packages, 38 percent have customized . . . application[s], 89 percent use . . . desktop computers, 82 percent use the Internet [and] 16 percent use [Global Positioning Systems] to assist in their operations" (Mamalian and LaVigne 1999, 2). Ninety-one percent of the agencies reported mapping offense data and 52% reported mapping vehicle recovery data (Mamalian and LaVigne 1999, 2).

An example of a sophisticated use of GIS for crime mapping is the Information Collection for Automated Mapping (ICAM) program used by the Chicago Police Department (Rich 1995, 1996). This system allows patrol officers to create their own maps. The ICAM system is easy for the officers to use; it requires only the use of a mouse where the officer selects the crimes of interest by clicking on incident types, districts or patrol beats, location types, and ranges of dates (Rich, 1995, 5; 1996). ICAM is installed in each of the district stations as well as in patrol cars.

Agencies other than the police use GISs to map crime. Two examples are the Wisconsin Department of Correction and the Office for Victims of Crime. The Wisconsin Department of Corrections uses GISs to map probationers and parolees as a means of targeting increased neighborhood supervision in areas where their residences congregated (Mixdorf 1999). The Office for Victims of Crime (2003) suggests the mapping of services for crime victims to compare them with the locations of crime victims' homes.

Crime mapping is also used in criminological research to describe a number of different phenomena including, but not limited to, gang activity (Block 2000), drug arrests and interventions (Robinson 2003), crimes of serial rapists (LeBeau 1992), residential burglary (Rengert and Wasilchik 1985), and the home addresses of juvenile delinquents (Shaw and McKay 1969).

Techniques

Techniques of crime mapping are of two types, exploratory or confirmatory. Unlike exploratory techniques, which simply describe spatial and temporal patterns in the data, confirmatory spatial statistics explain the interdependence of spatial phenomena as well as their heterogeneity. To explore and confirm spatial patterns of crime, crime mapping generally assumes one of the following forms: point pattern analysis (electronic pin mapping), hot spots (clusters of crimes near to one another), and density mapping (for example, choropleth mapping uses color intensities to indicate crime density in places) (Vann and Garson 2003).

As technology improves and practical knowledge among analysts develops, techniques are increasing in complexity. Digital images (raster images) rather than simple point and line data (pin maps and street networks), temporal weighting (aoristic analysis—the recognition of patterns of crime based on time of day as well as in space), dasymetric mapping (for revealing patterns obscured with traditional choropleth mapping), and spatial autocorrelation (taking into account the criminogenic influence of adjoining places) are a few examples of the increasing complexity in current crime mapping techniques.

Techniques and tools for the mapping of crime for use by communities have also been developed. An example of this type of tool is the *GeoArchive*. A GeoArchive contains address-level data from both community and law enforcement sources, linked to a GIS capability (Block 1998). This tool brings crime mapping to community residents and multiagency task forces, thus allowing them to tackle their respective crime problems.

Unresolved Issues

Many agencies experience barriers to using crime mapping (Mamalian and LaVigne 1999; Rich 1995). These barriers include the acquisition of tools (computer hardware and software), technical expertise, sharing data across jurisdictional boundaries, duties of crime analysts, data accuracy, and data privacy issues.

The costs of computer hardware and software can be prohibitive to smaller departments (Rich 1995). Although street maps and maps of census blocks and census tracts are likely to be available from local and state agencies, if an agency purchases these maps from commercial sources, the financial costs can be high. A related issue to cost is training. Training personnel is costly. Without proper training for crime analysts and proper tools available for their use, including software and computer hardware, crime mapping will not be useful to the police.

Another unresolved issue involves mapping crimes across jurisdictional boundaries. Mapping across jurisdictional boundaries necessitates the sharing of spatial data between neighboring agencies. City limits and other boundaries can create artificial crime hot spots and can also limit the analytical utility of a GIS. Barriers to sharing data across boundaries often stem from political and organizational reasons rather than simply budgetary reasons (Eck 2002).

The type and quantity of duties assigned to crime analysts comprise a fourth unresolved issue in crime mapping. The amount of time a crime analyst spends conducting overall analysis for the department, generating reports, and responding to individual officer inquiries will affect the quality of analysis and crime mapping. Information technology (IT) can also become a problem for crime analysts, either when IT is not able to provide proper support to crime analysis software and hardware or when crime analysts are responsible for IT duties. Problems with IT can become a source of frustration for crime analysts (Ratcliffe 2000, 319).

A fifth unresolved issue involves data quality. Street maps become outdated on a regular basis, and a number of costs are associated with keeping them up to date. These costs can be financial in nature—for example, purchasing new software—but

also involve personnel costs, to maintain the databases. Data recording lag time also affects the timely relevance of crime mapping reports. The amount of time between the filing of an officer report and accurate data entry affects the ability of crime analysts to provide useful information to their departments.

Privacy concerns are a sixth unresolved issue. The dissemination of spatial crime data can be problematic when the locations of crimes can be linked to specific addresses and, therefore, specific individuals. Police reports are public record. A number of police departments offer Internet crime mapping tools on their website. Suggested measures undertaken to address privacy issues when releasing crime data to the public include employing disclaimers, mapping to polygons rather than specific locations, eliminating exact street addresses, and limiting underlying information in data tables about the incident (Casady 1999).

Future Directions

The "relative utility" of crime mapping to law enforcement will determine its viability as a resource (Travis and Hughes 2002, 4). To ensure continued use among law enforcement agencies, future directions and considerations for crime mapping include the following: professional standards, funding, global positioning systems (GPSs), data accessibility for patrol officers and for the public, cross-jurisidictional alliances, and crime forecasting.

The development of professional standards is a clear directive for the future (Wartell 1999). Standards may help to counteract misinterpretation of and misuse of information presented in maps (Idsvoog 1999). The amount of funding for the use of GIS by law enforcement agencies is a clear second future directive. To promote the use of GIS for crime analysis, funding will need to be increased.

A third directive for the future involves the use of GPS coordinates. GPS has many potential uses for law enforcement including locating officers to increase their safety and evaluating officers' performance. GPS can also be used in conjunction with other place-related data and officer activities (Rich 1995; Travis and Hughes 2002). Corrections agencies have also begun to experiment with the use of GPS in electronic monitoring (Rich 1999).

The accessibility of spatial data to patrol officers is a fourth issue to be addressed in the future. If crime mapping is to be useful to the police, it must be available to patrol officers who can use maps to identify current problems or issues in the areas they patrol and to react accordingly. An example of where this type of crime mapping is being used is the ICAM system employed by the CPD. Fifth, the public should be granted increased access to crime mapping. A number of police departments currently offer crime mapping applications on their websites. Examples include the Portland (Oregon) Police Bureau, the Sacramento (California) Police Department, the Redlands (California) Police Department, and the Austin (Texas) Police Department. Cross-jurisdictional alliances and collaboration between agencies at different levels of government comprise a sixth area to be addressed in the future in order to ensure the continued viability of crime mapping for crime analysis. The GeoArchive described earlier is an example of this. Last, crime mapping and analysis must focus on the development of methods to predict (forecast) crime patterns rather than simply display and explain current patterns.

Conclusion

Crime mapping is becoming widespread throughout law enforcement as technology improves and costs to purchase requisite software and hardware decrease. Whether law enforcement is able to overcome unresolved issues to allow crime mapping as a tool for crime analysis to realize its full potential remains to be seen.

JENNIFER B. ROBINSON

See also **Boston Police Department; COMPSTAT; Crime Analysis; Crime and Place, Theories of; Criminology; Intelligence Gathering and Analysis: Impacts on Terrorism; Neighborhood Effects on Crime and Social Organization; New York Police Department (NYPD); Problem-Oriented Policing; Social Disorganization, Theory of**

References and Further Reading

Block, Carolyn. 1998. The GeoArchive: An information foundation for community policing. In *Crime mapping and crime prevention*, ed. Weisburd and McEwen, 27–82. Monsey, NY: Criminal Justice Press.

Block, Richard. 2000. Gang activity and overall levels of crime: A new mapping tool for defining areas of gang activity using police records. *Journal of Quantitative Criminology* 16: 36–51.

Brantingham, Patricia, and Paul Brantingham. 1991. Introduction. In *Environmental criminology*, ed. Brantingham and Brantingham. Prospect Heights, IL: Waveland Press.

Casady, Tom. 1999. *Privacy issues in the presentation of geocoded data.* Paper presented at the Crime Mapping and Data Confidentiality Roundtable Sponsored by the Crime Mapping Research Center. Washington, DC: National Institute of Justice.

Eck, John. 2002. Crossing the borders of crime: Factors influencing the utility and practicality of interjurisdictional crime mapping. *Overcoming the Barriers: Crime Mapping in the 21st Century* 1: 1–16.

Harries, Keith. 1999. *Mapping crime: Principle and practice.* Washington, DC: National Institute of Justice.

Idsvoog, Karl. 1999. *When information passes from one agency to another, who is liable or accountable for the inappropriate use of crime maps or the sharing of inaccurate geocoded data? What kind of statements should be made?* Paper presented at the Crime Mapping and Data Confidentiality Roundtable Sponsored by the Crime Mapping Research Center. Washington, DC: National Institute of Justice.

LeBeau, James. 1992. Four case studies illustrating the spatial-temporal analysis of serial rapists. *Police Studies* 15: 124–45.

Mamalian, Cynthia, and Nancy LaVigne. 1999. *The use of computerized crime mapping by law enforcement: Survey results.* NIJ Research Preview. Washington, DC: National Institute of Justice.

Manning, Peter. 2001. Technology's ways: Information technology, crime analysis and the rationalization of policing. *Criminal Justice the International Journal of Policy and Practice* 1: 83–103.

Office for Victims of Crime. 2003. *Using geographic information systems to map crime victim services.* Washington, DC: U.S. Department of Justice.

Ratcliffe, Jerry. 2000. Implementing and integrating crime mapping into a police intelligence environment. *International Journal of Police Science and Management* 2: 313–23.

Rengert, George, and J. Wasilchik. 1985. *Suburban burglary: A time and a place for everything.* Springfield, IL: Charles C Thomas.

Rich, Thomas. 1995. *The use of computerized mapping in crime control and prevention programs.* Washington DC: U.S. Department of Justice, Office of Justice Programs.

———. 1996. *Chicago Police Department's Information for Automated Mapping (ICAM) program.* Washington, DC: U.S. National Institute of Justice.

———. 1999. *Mapping the path to problem solving.* Washington, DC: U.S. National Institute of Justice.

Robinson, Jennifer. 2003. *The drug free zones, the police, locations, and trends of drug sales in Portland, Oregon, 1990–1998.* Diss., Graduate School of Temple University, Philadelphia, PA.

Shaw, Clifford, and Henry McKay. 1969. *Juvenile delinquency and urban areas: A study of rates of delinquency in relation to differential characteristics of local communities in American Cities.* Chicago: University of Chicago Press.

Travis, Lawrence, and Kenneth Hughes. 2002. Mapping in police agencies: Beyond this point there be monsters. *Overcoming the Barriers: Crime Mapping in the 21st Century* 2: 1–16.

Wartell, Julie. 1999. *Should professional standards or guidelines be developed for crime mapping as it pertains to privacy and freedom of information issues? If so, what should these standards look like and who should promote them?* Paper presented at the Crime Mapping and Data Confidentiality Roundtable Sponsored by the Crime Mapping Research Center. Washington, DC: National Institute of Justice.

Weisburd, David, Stephen Mastrofski, Rosann Greenspan, and James Willis. 2004. *The growth of COMPSTAT in American policing.* Washington, DC: Police Foundation.

CRIME PREVENTION

While the concept of crime prevention is familiar to most people, traditional definitions have focused on the role of police protecting the public from law violators (Rush 2000) or groups engaging in activities intended to deter individuals from committing crimes (Champion 1998). While others connote crime prevention with deterrence, incapacitation, and rehabilitation (Rosenbaum, Lurigio, and Davis 1998, 9), this analysis explores various approaches to the prevention of crime. Some of these include innovative policing strategies (that is, problem-oriented policing), situational crime prevention (lighting and access control), legislative mandates (civil remedies), delinquency programs (family-based programs, mentoring, and so on), and public awareness (media campaigns, citizen patrols, and Neighborhood Watch). For the purposes of this analysis, *crime prevention* and *crime control* will be distinguished according to efforts to *prevent* criminal events from occurring in the first place, versus *controlling* the behaviors of those who have already committed criminal acts.

How crime prevention efforts are viewed, implemented, and preferred relies heavily on the political emphasis of the era and the inclination of those in command. "Ingrained in the very process of designing crime prevention strategies are certain core assumptions and political choices" (White 1996, 97) defined by whether a crime prevention strategy assumes a conservative, liberal, or radical view of crime. Each of these three models "identifies the key focus and concepts of a particular approach, preferred strategies of intervention, dominant conception of 'crime', the role of the 'community' as part of the crime prevention effort, and relationship to 'law-and-order' strategies" (White 1996, 98).

The *conservative model* focuses heavily on opportunity reduction theories that seek to deter crime through increased costs to offenders and reduced opportunities for crime commission. In the *liberal model*, the emphasis is placed on addressing social problems and improving opportunities for disadvantaged groups through creating self-help and community development programs. Finally, the *radical model* embraces a social justice approach that confronts the problem of marginalization, social alienation, and inequality (White 1996, 100) by seeking to improve social conditions for every member of society. Throughout the most recent decades, the political inclinations and public outcry have leaned toward a "law and order" approach that concentrates on police taking the lead in the prevention of crime.

Police Strategies of Crime Prevention

Traditionally police work was reactive in nature with the expectation that officers would respond to calls for service, rather than take a proactive approach to crime fighting. In the 1970s, efforts to improve policing practices led to a new approach that focused on fostering positive police–community relations: the birth of community policing (Cordner and Biebel 2005, 158). While this was an improvement over traditional policing approaches, a need for proactive crime prevention strategies was needed. As a result, in 1979, Herman Goldstein introduced the concept of problem-oriented policing (POP) in which officers became the problem solvers of recurring crime problems.

In problem-oriented policing, officers, in coordination with skilled crime analysts and community members, work together to develop effective strategies for reducing crime. Problem-oriented policing shifts police efforts away from reactive policing to more proactive and preventive efforts. "By focusing more on problems rather than incidents, police address causes rather than mere symptoms and consequently have a greater impact" (Cordner and Biebel 2005, 156) on public safety. The focus of POP is to find patterns and resolve problems utilizing the "most targeted, analytical, and in-depth approach" (Cordner and Biebel 2005, 158) to uncover the "underlying conditions that give rise to incidents, crime, disorder, and other substantive community issues" (Cordner and Biebel 2005, 156).

Officers have incorporated a systematic four-stage approach to problem solving called the SARA Model (scanning, analysis, response, and assessment), which allows police to conduct in-depth analyses of crime problems and seek creative alternative strategies to prevent crime. In the *scanning phase,* officers identify recurring problems through a cursory review of data including, but not limited to, calls for service, arrest rates, recurring acts of vandalism, requests from store owners for assistance, or other indicators of crime and disorder.

The *analysis phase* delves further into the crime problem and identifies the problem's underlying causes and characteristics. The focus is to gather information about the problem such as finding answers to questions such as "Where is the problem most concentrated?" "When are the crimes occurring?" "Why does the problem persist?" "Who is responsible?" and "How is it affecting the community?" Quite often, this phase involves officers interviewing neighborhood leaders, business owners, and residents for their input.

During the *response stage*, officers devise custom-fitted responses best suited to address the community's problem. In the selection of a prevention strategy, officers most frequently use the *problem analysis triangle,* which targets the three components of a crime to be altered: the victim, offender, and location of the crime. Through the use of this triangle, officers select strategies that protect probable victims, ward off likely offenders, or reduce opportunities for crime at given locations.

Finally, the strategy is *assessed* to ensure its effectiveness, make improvements, and create a foundation of knowledge for police everywhere. This evaluation utilizes measures taken before and after the intervention was introduced to assess the impact of the response.

The advent of new technologies that increase communication between agencies, handle large sources of data, and identify crime patterns have also aided police in the prevention of crime. Technologies including, but not limited to, the geographic information systems (GISs) used for crime mapping and advances such as AMBER Alerts help police identify and respond to problems more quickly than ever before. While crime mapping is used to mark the sites of recent crimes in order to ascertain patterns and trends occurring within specific neighborhoods, AMBER (America's Missing: Broadcast Emergency Response) Alerts utilize media broadcast systems to quickly distribute information about missing children among an assortment of law enforcement agencies as well as to the public.

At the same time that policing strategies underwent a transformation, another multidisciplinary approach to crime prevention originated. Crime prevention through environmental design (CPTED) was established in the early 1970s as a multidisciplinary approach intended to alter the physical environment in ways that discourage offenders from committing crimes (Jeffrey 1971; Newman 1972). Careful attention to design details was said to lead to a "reduction in the fear and incidence of crime, and an improvement in the quality of life" (Poyser 2004, 123). Now, "it is widely accepted that the design of buildings and their surroundings can influence the commission of crime and nuisance behavior" (Poyser 2004, 123) through the creation or elimination of opportunities for the commission of crime. Although this approach did not gain popularity rapidly, some criminologists incorporated elements of CPTED into new ways of fighting crime.

James Q. Wilson and George Kelling's broken-windows theory (1982) examined the effects of how visible signs of decay in neighborhoods impacted the behavior of both abiding and non–law-abiding community members. According to the authors, signs of disorder including both physical indicators of disorder such as broken windows, vacant lots, deteriorating buildings, litter, and graffiti as well as social indicators such as loitering, public drunkenness, gangs, drugs, panhandling, and prostitution (Lab 2000, 42) instill fear in law-abiding citizens and communicate a host of available criminal opportunities to non–law-abiding offenders. Wilson and Kelling "suggest that neighborhood incivilities are fear-inspiring because they indicate a lack of concern for public order and suggest the inability of officials to cope" (Poyser 2004, 124) with the negative influences that are leading to the incivilities in the first place. Law-abiding members respond to these indicators with fear, whereas potential offenders welcome the increasing opportunities of limited risk of apprehension since frightened citizens are too afraid to leave their homes, confront strangers, or call the police.

Situational Crime Prevention

In yet another perspective, Cohen and Felson's (1979) *routine activity* approach states that three components must converge in time and space for a crime to occur. A suitable target, a motivated offender, and a lack of a capable guardian must all converge at one time in a specific place. Cohen and Felson's routine activity approach focuses more on the elements of the crime than on the characteristics of the offender. The authors claim that crime is the result of everyday activities and interactions and assume motivated offenders exist everywhere. Cohen and Felson originally developed their perspective as a result of the rising crimes between the 1960s and 1980s. Their controversial perspective focused on the changing number of women working outside of the home who were leaving residences unoccupied and therefore unguarded against possible offenders. For them, the key to crime prevention rests with limiting the number of suitable targets and increasing the number of capable guardians.

The routine activities approach uses the term *target* instead of *victim* to indicate the fact that the victim of a crime may be a person or thing as in the case of a stolen wallet. The four main factors that make targets more attractive from the offender's perspective may be summarized by the acronym VIVA: value, inertia, visibility, and access. Typically, offenders want to obtain the most valuable item through exerting the least amount of effort. Items such as CDs, iPods, and other small items with a high monetary value exemplify these principles. The item should be *valuable*, whether it be for resale purposes, or for personal use. Inertia refers to the weight of the item and the ease with which to steal it. For example, *inertia* would explain why a thief would choose to steal a small laptop that can be easily concealed in a backpack as opposed to a traditional desktop computer system, which must be carried in multiple pieces in a less secretive fashion. *Visibility* and *access* both refer to the principles of witnessing the availability of an item and the ease with which to remove it. If a thief witnesses a college student place an expensive iPod in the pocket of a coat placed on a chair next to the aisle in a café, the offender has the advantage of visibility and access. He or she has seen the item and knows exactly where it is placed. Furthermore, the fact that the chair is located next to an aisle provides easy accessibility to make an attempt to remove it without being noticed (Felson 1998).

Much like Cohen and Felson's approach, an economist and a psychologist began viewing crime from a perspective they coined *rational choice theory.* They viewed crime from the perspective of the offender's decision making. According to the authors, offenders make rational choices and decisions as to who is a suitable target based on the possible gains achieved and the risks suffered. In viewing crimes according to the opportunities for offenders, Cornish and Clarke (1986) concluded with five techniques by which to alter situations in a manner that limits opportunities for offenders. These techniques focus on limiting the opportunities for offenders by increasing the effort in carrying out the crime, increasing the risk of being apprehended, reducing the benefits expected from the desired target, removing the possible rationalizations to justify a criminal act, and reducing provocations that tempt or incite offenders. Applying a cost–benefit analysis to rational decision making about crime, Clarke turned these five categories of altering situations into twenty-five techniques of situational crime prevention that include, but are not limited to, target hardening, controlling access entries, identifying property, and countless other techniques (Clarke 2003) that limit crime opportunities and constrain the decisions of offenders.

Civil Remedies

Legislative measures such as civil remedies, also known as civil injunctions, also serve as a tool for law enforcement to address crime. Civil remedies represent a wide array of "procedures and sanctions found in civil statutes and regulations [designed] to prevent or reduce criminal problems and incivilities, such as drug dealing, disorderly behavior, panhandling, and loitering" (Mazerolle and Roehl 1999, 1). Police and prosecutors gather evidence of public nuisances in neighborhoods using "evidence used to support an injunction [which] includes the criminal history of gang members, written declarations by officers familiar with the neighborhood, and sometimes, declarations from community members that describe the effects of specific nuisance activities on neighborhood residents" (Maxson, Hennigan, and Slone 2005, 580). Using this evidence, restraining orders are filed against the defendants for "illegal activities such as trespass, vandalism, drug selling, and public urination, as well as otherwise legal activities, such as wearing gang colors, displaying hand signals, and carrying a pager or signaling passing cars; behaviors associated with drug selling. Nighttime curfews are [also] often imposed" (Maxson, Hennigan, and Slone 2005, 579). These civil injunctions, or restraining orders, create a vehicle by which lawbreakers can be "prosecuted in either civil or criminal court for violation of a valid court order and fined up to $1000 and/or incarcerated for up to six months" (Maxson, Hennigan, and Slone 2005, 581).

Civil remedies are also intended to encourage law-abiding individuals to assist in fighting crime. "Police often apply civil remedies to persuade or coerce non-offending third parties to act against criminal or nuisance behaviors" (Mazerolle and Roehl 1999, 1), by encouraging store owners to file reports against loiterers or anyone engaged in illicit behaviors. In a gang prevention attempt initiated by the Chicago Police Department, unresponsive owners were forced to respond by the Municipal Drug and Gang Enforcement (MDGE) program. "Before the program, according to CPD, building owners or managers were not forced to manage their properties in a manner that contributed to the vitality rather than the decay of the neighborhood. The MDGE program strategy attempt[ed] to engage building owners as proactive partners in corrective measures—and present[ed] powerful deterrents against those owners who are unresponsive" (Higgins 2000, i). In many cases in which ordinary citizens are too afraid to intervene, police place the

responsibility for illicit behaviors on landlords and store owners. Typically, a specifically designated task force

> . . . identifies city buildings . . . [and] documents drug and gang problems, conducts inspections for code violations, provides information and recommendations for improving the properties, and conducts administrative proceedings to bring landlords into compliance. . . . [The task force also] refers some cases to city attorneys at the Department of Law for prosecution under the modified city nuisance abatement ordinance allowing the city to hold landlords accountable for some criminal activities of their tenants. (Higgins 2000, i–ii)

While civil remedies demonstrate some promise in preventing crime, studies have shown the effects to be short lived (Green 1996) and many fear the potential abuses of mishandling such a tool. "Stop-and-frisk practices and anti-loitering laws cause concern because they circumscribe the rights of individuals . . . [and] are used disproportionately against minorities (Rosenbaum, Lurigio, and Davis 1998, 117). According to White (2004, 3), many "attempts to restrict the street presence of gangs have taken the form of youth curfews or anti-loitering statutes . . . [that] have been struck down by the Supreme Court as being unconstitutional," yet when legislators have clarified specific types of loitering, such as blocking traffic, the courts have accepted the injunctions (White 2004, 3). Nonetheless, countless individuals are troubled by "the commonly applied prohibitions [that] any two or more named gang members associating with one another" (Maxson, Hennigan, and Slone 2005, 580) be questioned.

Delinquency Prevention

A challenge of crime prevention is to recognize which techniques are effective and which show little, if any, effectiveness despite their popularity. Though widely popular, Scared Straight and boot camps have not shown the type of effectiveness suggested by their popularity. Scared Straight was designed to take young offenders to a maximum security men's institution in hopes of frightening the juveniles into ceasing their criminal activities (Finkenhauer 1978). While this may sound logical, Scared Straight has consistently failed to show deterrent effect on juveniles (Finkenhauer and Gavin 1999).

Similarly, in a meta-analysis of boot camp participants, the results show "no overall difference in recidivism between boot camp participants and their control group counterparts" (Welsh and Farrington 2005, 345). Only those boot camp programs incorporating counseling and therapeutic programming show positive results among boot camps" (Welsh and Farrington 2005, 345). On the other hand, research has cited numerous programs that have demonstrated effective results in preventing delinquency including family-based techniques such as home visiting programs, day care/pre-school programs, parent training, treatment foster care and multisystemic therapy (Farrington and Welsh 2003), cognitive-behavioral techniques (Tong and Farrington 2005; Wilson et al. 2001), and drug courts (Wilson et al. 2005).

In a meta-analysis of 200 program evaluations, Lipsey and Wilson (1998) determined that "overall, the most effective programs were cognitive-behavioral skills training programs" (Farrington 2005, 242). "Other programs showing evidence of effectiveness included individual counseling, restitution, employment programs, academic programs, and family counseling (for noninstitutionalized offenders) and teaching family homes and community residential programs such as therapeutic communities (for institutional offenders)" (Farrington 2005, 243). The programs showing the least effectiveness at preventing delinquency were programs emphasizing deterrence, challenges (that is, wilderness camps), increased supervision, and drug and alcohol self-restraint (Farrington

2005). Of the community-based prevention programs, gang member intervention, mentoring, and after-school recreation programs offer the greatest success (Farrington 2005, 243).

While some family-based and community-based programs offer hope for prevention, lack of evaluation research of other types of programs makes it difficult to assess the effectiveness of many programs. In some cases, the most effective crime prevention method may involve more than one mode of intervention. In a study by Whitted and Dupper (2005), "the most effective approaches for preventing or minimizing bullying in schools involve[d] a comprehensive, multilevel strategy that targets bullies, victims, bystanders, families, and communities" (Whitted and Dupper 2005, 169).

Community and Individual Self-Protection

Citizens have sought participation in proactive crime prevention efforts through increased awareness, Neighborhood Watch, citizen patrols, and property marking projects. Several efforts involving mass media campaigns have sought to empower citizens through increased awareness. In October 1979, the "Take a Bite Out of Crime" campaign was initiated as a joint venture involving various agencies (Rosenbaum, Lurigio, and Davis 1998, 61). This campaign encouraged citizens to take a more active role in the prevention of crime through their participation in Neighborhood Watch. As the times and the crime problem changed, so did the emphasis of the campaigns (Rosenbaum, Lurigio, and Davis 1998). At first the focus was to increase awareness about crime, but as the need changed, the stress shifted to reducing drug use. More recently, the "Friends Don't Let Friends Drive Drunk" campaign renewed its message to target the casual drinker who consumes one or two drinks with the new slogan "Buzzed

Driving Is Drunk Driving." According to Rosenbaum, Lurigio, and Davis (1998, 64), "mass media crime prevention programs have produced mixed results," which have raised public awareness and at times led to increased fear of crime.

On a more individual level, Rosenbaum, Lurigio, and Davis (1998) have identified two distinct self-protective measures for individuals to protect themselves from victimization: "(1) those behaviors intended to *reduce* the risk of victimization, and (2) those behaviors intended to *manage* the risk of victimization when crime is unavoidable" (p. 81). Risk avoidance behaviors encourage individuals to focus on, and often alter, their routine activities by avoiding certain places, activities, or people that may lead to increased risk of victimization. This may include activities such as not staying out in the evenings, avoiding bars, and avoiding persons who have a propensity to cause harm. In contrast, risk management focuses on reducing the opportunity for victimization in a different way. Because it may not always be possible to avoid specific places or activities, one can manage the risk by not carrying cash or by driving instead of walking (Rosenbaum, Lurigio, and Davis 1998, 85).

It may be possible that self-defense training or other individual efforts to defend oneself provide individuals with the confidence to take better measures to protect themselves (Brecklin and Ullman 2005, 738). "From 1992 to 1996, nonfatal assaults on nurses, others in health care, and those in mental health settings were similar in frequency to those in law enforcement, well over 200,000 annually" (*Massachusetts Nurse* 2005, 12). While encouraged to attend self-defense and crisis intervention courses, nurses are also encouraged to protect themselves with a few small behavioral changes such as not carrying any keys or pens that can be used as a weapon against them or wearing things around their necks that could be used in confrontations.

Conclusion

While problem-oriented policing, situational crime prevention, civil remedies, socially based programs, public awareness projects, and self-defense represent some of the most popular current crime prevention trends, these do not embody an exhaustive list of all existing crime prevention efforts. Unfortunately, fighting crime presents an interesting dilemma in that crime prevention efforts require a significant amount of resources, yet provide few substantial measures to confirm that a criminal act was prevented. Political pressures often lead to a misuse of time, energy, and resources on efforts that have not been proven to work, and forego the resources needed to design new approaches for preventing crime. For prevention efforts to succeed, careful planning, implementation, and evaluation are required. For these reasons, there is a growing need for more research into which programs work, for whom, and under what circumstances.

SILVINA ITUARTE

See also **Broken-Windows Policing; Crime and Place, Theories of; Crime Control Strategies; Criminology; Quality-of-Life Policing; Situational Crime Prevention; Social Disorganization, Theory of; Zero Tolerance Policing**

References and Further Reading

Brecklin, Leanne R., and Sarah E. Ullman. 2005. Self-defense or assertiveness training and women's responses to sexual attacks. *Journal of Interpersonal Violence* 20 (6): 738–62.

Champion, Dean J. 1998. *Dictionary of American criminal justice: Key terms and major Supreme Court cases*. Chicago: Fitzroy Dearborn Publishers.

Clarke, Ronald. 1980. Situational crime prevention: Theory and practice. *British Journal of Criminology* 20: 136–47.

Cohen, Larry, and Marcus Felson. 1979. Social change and crime rate trends: A routine activity approach. *American Sociological Review* 44 (588).

Cordner, Gary, and Elizabeth P. Biebel. 2005. Problem-oriented policing in practice. 2: 155–80.

Cornish, Derek, and Ronald Clarke. 1986. *The reasoning criminal: Rational choice perspective on offending.* New York: Springer-Verlag.

Farrington, David P. 2005. Early identification and preventive intervention: How effective is this strategy? 2: 237–48.

Felson, Marcus. 1998. *Crime and everyday life.* Thousand Oaks, CA: Pine Forge Press.

Finkenhauer, James, and Patricia Gavin. 1999. *Scared straight: The panacea phenomenon revisited.* Prospect Heights, IL: Waveland Press.

Hastings, Ross. 2005. Perspectives on crime prevention: Issues and challenges. *Canadian Journal of Criminology and Criminal Justice* (April): 209–19.

Jeffrey, C. Ray. 1971. *Crime prevention through environmental design.* Beverly Hills, CA: Sage.

Lab, Steve. 2000. *Crime prevention: Approaches, practices and evaluations.* Cincinnati, OH: Anderson Publishing.

Linden, Rick, and Renuka Chaturvedi. 2005. The need for comprehensive crime prevention planning: The case of motor vehicle theft. *Canadian Journal of Criminology and Criminal Justice* (April): 252–70.

Massachusetts Nurse. 2005. Workplace violence prevention and intervention: Being assaulted is not part of the job no matter where you work.

Maxson, Cheryl L., Karen M. Hennigan, and David C. Slone. 2005. It's getting crazy out there: Can a civil injunction change a community? 3: 577–606.

Newman, Oscar. 1972. *Defensible space: Crime prevention through urban design.* New York: Macmillan.

Poyser, Sam. 2004. Shopping centre design, decline and crime. *International Journal of Police Science and Management* 7 (2): 123–36.

Quigley, Richard. 2005. Building strengths in the neighborhood. *Reclaiming Children and Youth* 14 (2) (Summer): 104–06.

Rosenbaum, Dennis P., Arthur J. Lurigio, and Robert C. Davis. 1998. *The prevention of crime: Social and situational strategies.* Belmont, CA: Wadsworth Publishing.

Rush, George E. 2000. *The dictionary of criminal justice.* Guilford, CT: McGraw-Hill/Dushkin.

White, Robert. Situating crime prevention: Models, methods, and political perspectives, 97–113.

Whitted, Kathryn S., and David R. Dupper. 2005. Best practices for preventing or reducing bullying in schools. *Children and Schools* 27 (3): 167–75.

Wilson, James Q., and George Kelling. 1982. Broken windows: The police and neighborhood safety. *Atlantic Monthly*, March, 29–38.

CRIME SCENE SEARCH AND EVIDENCE COLLECTION

Crime scene searches and evidence collection are the backbone of criminal investigation. If the crime scene boundaries are not adequately identified, with an appropriate search and *systematic* identification and collection of evidence to follow, then cases may not be prosecutable.

Crime scenes are sources of evidence, and therefore must be painstakingly examined for both visible and latent evidence. Searches may vary by type of crime, geography, human resources, and availability of equipment. Of particular note is that the size of an organization, which directly affects human resources, dictates who conducts a crime scene search and collects evidence. In small organizations, which represent approximately 90% of local police agencies, it is common for one officer to be responsible for not only responding to a crime scene, identifying and searching the scene, but also for identifying and collecting the evidence. In medium and large organizations, however, where there tends to be more specialization among duties, one or more officers might be responsible for each of the preceding tasks.

Purpose of a Crime Scene Search

The primary purpose of a crime scene search is to develop associative evidence that could link a suspect to the scene or a victim, and to answer questions crucial to the investigation, such as who perpetrated the crime, how the crime was committed, the circumstances surrounding the commission of the crime, and why the crime was committed. Additionally, police search crime scenes to identify evidence through which a psychological profile of the suspect can be developed, to identify an object(s) that does not logically belong at the crime scene and that could potentially be linked to a suspect, and to identify the suspect's modus operandi (MO), or motive for committing the crime (Osterburg and Ward 2004; Swanson, Chamelin, and Territo 2003). It is important to note that although these principles apply to all crime scenes, more specific tasks may be undertaken, depending on what type of crime has been committed.

Swanson, Chamelin, and Territo (2003, 51–55) indicate that there are five primary considerations for conducting a crime scene search: (1) boundary determination, (2) choice of search pattern, (3) instruction of personnel, (4) coordination of efforts, and (5) processing of the evidence. Again, it should be noted that depending on human resources available, one officer or a number of officers might be responsible for these tasks.

Determining the boundary of the crime scene is critical. Numerous factors affect boundary determination, such as whether the crime scene has more than one location, and whether the crime scene is indoor or outdoor. Crime scenes may be categorized into primary and secondary, though secondary crime scenes do not always exist when the crime occurred in only one area. Typically when a crime scene is inside a physical structure (indoors), boundaries are restricted and more easily identifiable. In contrast, with an outdoor crime scene, determining accurate boundaries is more challenging.

Additionally, crime scenes are divided into inner and outer perimeters, with the inner perimeter being where the actual crime took place and the outer perimeter being the boundary for maintaining control of the crime scene (Swanson, Chamelin, and Territo 2003).

Choosing a search pattern is critical and depends on the locale, size of the area, and the apparent actions of the suspect, victim, and any others having access to the scene, that is, witnesses (Saferstein 2004). The number of personnel available also affects the type of search, with some methods requiring more personnel than others.

Types of Crime Scene Searches

Common search patterns include the spiral, strip/line, grid, zone/quadrant, and pie/wheel. The spiral search is used most often for outdoor crime scenes, is conducted by one person, and is done by walking in a circle from the outermost point of the inner perimeter toward the center of the circle. The strip/line search is done by dividing the crime scene into a series of lanes in which personnel search up and down the lanes until the scene is completely searched. A grid search is similar to a strip/line search but is also divided into lanes perpendicularly, thereby constituting a more systematically thorough search from multiple perspectives. A zone/quadrant search is one in which the crime scene is divided into four quadrants and searched using another method, such as a strip or line search. In a pie/wheel search, the crime scene is divided into a large circle with numerous sectors, and searched using another method, such as a strip/line search. Practically speaking, a strip/line or grid search is used most often (Swanson, Chamelin, and Territo 2003).

Careful instruction of personnel, when more than one officer is involved, is of the utmost importance. When numerous individuals are involved in searching a crime scene, it is imperative to delineate responsibilities to provide for a thorough, systematic search, but also to ensure that efforts are not duplicated. Additionally, continuous coordination of tasks may provide for effective and efficient completion of searches, regardless of how many people are involved. Comprehensive instruction and coordination of crime scene search efforts result in optimal conditions for the identification and collection of evidence, which can ultimately lead to a successful prosecution.

Evidence Collection

The type of evidence officers look for will typically be determined by the circumstances surrounding the crime. Physical evidence may be visible and easily identified in some cases, and in other cases evidence may be invisible and only detected using advanced technologies. While evidence is typically searched for at a crime scene, evidence may also be found in other places, such as on a suspect or victim, or at a morgue or laboratory. Therefore, it is extremely important to examine less obvious places and/or items that might contain potential evidence, such as a vehicle or a victim's clothing (Saferstein 2004).

Physical evidence may be collected so that it is not altered from the time it is removed from the scene or other receptacle, until it is transferred to the crime laboratory. However, changes in the state of the evidence may occur due to contamination, breakage, evaporation, scratching, bending, or improper packaging. Also critical to the evidence collection process is the proper packaging of evidence, which means that each item must be collected and placed in a separate container to prevent damage and maintain the integrity of the evidence (Saferstein 2004).

Although digital evidence is a form of physical evidence and is commonplace in many crime scenes today, the identification and collection of digital evidence presents unique challenges for law enforcement. Digital evidence, or electronic evidence, is

"any data stored or transmitted using a computer that support or refute a theory of how an offense occurred or that address critical elements of the offense such as intent or alibi" (adapted from Chisum 1999, as cited in Casey 2004). Digital data is the binary numerical representation of information such as text, images, audio, or video. Digital evidence is typically the product of crimes such as fraud, child pornography, and computer intrusions.

Even though digital evidence is prevalent today, many police organizations have limited capabilities when it comes to not only handling, but simply identifying digital evidence. Particular challenges regarding digital evidence include but are not limited to these: (1) Digital evidence is difficult to handle, (2) digital evidence represents only an abstraction or part of what occurred during the criminal activity, and (3) digital evidence is easily manipulated (Casey 2004). With technology advancements occurring every day, it is likely that handling digital evidence will increasingly become a major part of crime scenes in the future.

Another important consideration when collecting evidence and subsequently transferring it to the crime laboratory is chain of custody, which means "continuity of possession" (Saferstein 2004, 45). Practically speaking what this means is that all personnel who have handled the evidence must have maintained its integrity and provided no means through which the evidence could have been altered. When evidence is finally presented in court, if the chain of custody cannot be established, then the evidence will probably not be allowed to support the prosecution's case.

Following identification and collection, evidence is submitted to a crime laboratory for analysis. Transferring of the evidence may take place by personnel delivering the evidence themselves or, in some cases, transferring may occur by mail or other means of shipment. Regardless of the method of transferring the evidence to the crime laboratory, the chain of custody must be maintained throughout the process.

Crime scene searches and evidence collection constitute a vital part of the duties of law enforcement. Strict adherence to policy and procedure, as well as thoughtfulness and common sense, contribute significantly to not only a successful prosecution, but also to the effectiveness and efficiency of police operations.

KATHRYN E. SCARBOROUGH

See also **Computer Crimes; Computer Forensics; Constitutional Rights: Search and Seizure; Criminal Investigation; Forensic Evidence; Forensic Investigations**

References and Further Reading

Casey, Eoghan. 2004. *Digital evidence and computer crime: Forensic science, computers and the Internet*. Boston: Elsevier Academic Press.

Chisum, J. W. 1999. *Crime reconstruction and evidence dynamics*. Paper presented at the Academy of Behavioral Profiling Annual Meeting, Monterey, CA.

Fisher, Barry A. J. 2004. *Techniques of crime scene investigation*. 7th ed. New York: CRC Press.

Gilbert, James N. 2004. *Criminal investigation*. 6th ed. Upper Saddle River, NJ: Pearson/Prentice-Hall.

Lee, Henry C., Timothy Palmbach, and Marilyn T. Miller. *Henry Lee's crime scene handbook*. San Diego, CA: Academic Press.

Osterburg, James W., and Richard H. Ward. 2004. *Criminal investigation: A method for reconstructing the past*. Cincinnati, OH: Anderson Publishing.

Saferstein, Richard. 2004. *Criminalistics: An introduction to forensic science*. Upper Saddle River, NJ: Pearson/Prentice-Hall.

Swanson, Charles R., Neil C. Chamelin, and Leonard Territo. 2003. *Criminal investigation*. New York: McGraw-Hill Higher Education.

CRIME, SERIOUS

Serious crime is a term that shows up everywhere today: in the news, political speeches, radio and television talk shows, policy white papers, courses at universities, movies, music, magazines, and so forth. Oddly, despite the prevalence of the term, its meaning is far from clear. For example, many would argue that only so-called street crime—murder, assault, rape, robbery, burglary, larceny-theft, auto theft, and arson—is serious crime. Others would contend that polluting streams and rivers with dangerous chemicals by major corporations is serious crime. Still others would include organized crime and belonging to various types of criminal syndicates or gangs under the umbrella of serious crime. Some would include computer hacking as serious crime. And, of course, no post-9/11 discussion of serious crime can ignore terrorism (see Siegel 2004, 354–64). The fact of the matter is that the problem of fully defining "serious crime" is itself a very knotty problem and could easily occupy a full volume (see, for example, Henry and Lanier 1988, 2001).

This article focuses on the traditional definition, the "street crime" approach, used by the majority of U.S. law enforcement agencies. Those agencies participate in a national crime reporting system, the FBI's Uniform Crime Reporting System (commonly known as "the UCR"). Serious crimes in the UCR include the following violent and property crimes: murder and non-negligent manslaughter, forcible rape, robbery, aggravated assault, burglary, larceny-theft, motor vehicle theft, and arson. The first seven of these offenses were originally chosen in 1929 during the early development of the UCR because they were considered "generally serious in nature"; arson was added to the list in 1970 (Bureau of Justice Statistics 2004; Maltz 1999, 4–15). These eight crimes are referred to as index crimes or Part I offenses.

How Much Serious Crime Exists?

This seems like an easy question to answer, but it is not. Crime measurement, while certainly no "sexy" topic for most people, lies at the heart of our thinking, decision making, and policies regarding serious crime. Listening to contemporary politicians, talk show hosts, police chiefs, and other commentators on crime and crime policy, one easily gets the impression that reliable and exact numbers/rates of crime are readily known and available. The *appearance of certainty* that some of these spokespersons are able to generate is quite impressive in terms of persuasive skills. However, those skills aside, the unfortunate fact is that the data foundation is not nearly as solid as some would have us believe: Unhappily, in the case of serious crime, we only have a rough idea about how much exists. What we do have is a collection of indicators, each flawed in its own ways and useful in others.

Four main measures of crime are in common use by academic and government researchers/policy analysts. These four measures may be subclassified into two broad categories: the first category includes crime measurement based on government data—specifically, law enforcement information—and the second category includes crime measurement based on scientific sampling and survey research techniques. The crime measurement based on government agency data includes these two important instances: (1) the Federal Bureau of Investigation's Uniform Crime Reporting Program, representing nearly 18,000 law enforcement agencies' reports of crimes known to police and (2) the FBI's National Incident-Based Reporting System, a modernized and more comprehensive but, as of yet, not completely implemented version of the UCR (cf. Bureau of Justice Statistics 2004; Lindgren 2001). The crime measurement based on scientifically based survey information includes (1) the Bureau of Justice Statistics' National Crime Victimization Survey (NCVS), a nationwide sample of some forty-two thousand households and about seventy-five thousand individuals begun in 1973; and (2) self-report surveys of offending by various academic research institutes (for example, *Monitoring the Future* [Survey Research Center 2005]), policy researchers, and others (Cantor and Lynch 2000; Junger-Tas and Marshall 1999).

Current available information for the UCR estimates a violent crime rate of 465.5 per 100,000 inhabitants in 2004. That means that for every 100,000 people living in the United States in 2004, about 465 cases of murder and non-negligent manslaughter, forcible rape, robbery, and aggravated assault were reported to the police. This rate was down slightly (–2.2%) from the 2003 estimate. An important additional statistic provided by law enforcement data is the *clearance rate,* which describes the level of reported crimes that are resolved by arrest. For 2004, 46.3% of the reported violent crimes were cleared by arrest (Federal Bureau of Investigation [FBI] 2005; see also web page "Offenses Reported, Violent Crime"). With respect to property crime, in 2004, the UCR estimates a property crime rate of 3,517.1 or about 7.6 times greater than the violent rate. That is, about 3,517 cases of burglary, larceny-theft, motor vehicle theft, and arson were reported to the police for every 100,000 persons living in the United States in 2004. The property crime rate was also down slightly (–2.1%) from the 2003 estimate. The 2004 property crime clearance rate was—at 16.5%—much lower than the clearance rate for violent crime (FBI 2005).

The total volume of serious crime measured by victimization surveys always is considerably larger than that measured by official agency statistics. This is not surprising in view of the fact that many crimes are never reported to the police for a variety of reasons (for example, the belief that nothing can be done about it or fear of retaliation by the offender). The NCVS follows the UCR's definition of index crimes as closely as possible with one important exception: Homicide is not included in the victim surveys and thus homicide is not included in the violent victimization estimates provided by the

NCVS. The 2003 National Crime Victimization Survey estimate of the level of victimization by personal crimes—defined as both attempted and completed rape/sexual assaults, robberies, and assaults—is 23.5 per 1,000 persons ages 12 and older. In other words, based on interviews with a representative sample of U.S. households and persons, it is estimated that about 23 out of every 1,000 people ages 12 and older were the victim of rape/sexual assault, robbery, or assault in 2003. For property crimes—attempted and completed household burglaries, motor vehicle thefts, and personal thefts—the rate is 161.1 per 1,000 persons ages 12 and older (Catalano 2004, 3).

An important quality of the NCVS enables crime victimization comparisons between important subgroups of society. For instance, in 2003, males were more likely than females to be victims of robbery and assault (26.3 males per 1,000 persons ages 12 and older and 19.0 females). Also, black citizens are more likely than white citizens to be victimized by violent crime (29.1 blacks per 1,000 persons ages 12 and older and 21.5 for whites) (Catalano 2004, 6). As one moves upward through the household income levels of Americans, NCVS data show that the likelihood of violent victimization diminishes. Specifically, those having less than $7,500 annual household incomes are about three times as likely as those having greater than $75,000 annual household incomes to be victimized by a violent criminal act; this inverse relationship generally holds true for the intervening income categories as well (Catalano 2004, 6).

With respect to property crime, the 2003 NCVS estimates that property crime is more likely in the Western region of the United States (213.5 per 1,000 households) and in an urban setting (215.8 per 1,000 households) and in rented households (206.7 per 1,000 households) (Catalano 2004, 6). Once again, as one moves upward through the household income levels of Americans, the likelihood of property victimization of the household diminishes, though not as dramatically as for personal victimization. Specifically, those households having less than $7,500 annual incomes are about 1.1 times more likely to be victimized by a property crime than those households having an annual household income greater than $75,000; that inverse relationship generally holds true for the intervening income categories as well (Catalano 2004, 6).

What Are the Trends in Serious Crime?

Main data sources demonstrate a general decline, beginning around 1993, in three categories of serious crime (including homicide): total violent crime, victimizations reported to the police, and crimes recorded by the police (Bureau of Justice Statistics 2002a, slide 1). Furthermore, the NCVS reports declining household victimization rates since the early 1970s (Bureau of Justice Statistics 2002a, slide 2).

With respect specifically to homicide and personal violence, while regrettably the United States remains atop the industrial nations in terms of lethal violence (that is, homicide and gun-related robberies), the levels of homicide and other violence in the United States have generally declined through the 1990s; furthermore, the rates have remained relatively stable in the early 2000s (Blumstein and Wallman 2000, 1). After peaking in the early 1980s and then again in the early 1990s, the homicide rates declined through the 1990s to mid-1960s levels (Bureau of Justice Statistics 2002b; U.S. Census Bureau 2005). At its highest peak in 1991, the U.S. homicide rate was at 10.1 per 100,000 population; by 2002 this rate has been almost cut in half to 5.9 homicides per 100,000 population (U.S. Census Bureau 2005). Much effort has been made to explain this drop in violence in the United States. Respected analysts

Alfred Blumstein and Joel Wallman (2000) argue that no single cause accounts for this drop; instead, a credible explanation should incorporate a combination of factors including demographic factors, the decline of crack cocaine markets, the rejection of crack cocaine as the drug of choice by a new generation of young people (see the particularly interesting discussion in Johnson, Golub, and Dunlap 2000), aggressive police tactics, the strength of the economy, the growth of incarceration, and local and federal efforts to control gun crime.

The Globalization of Serious Crime

We have focused on what is variously called "street crime" or "ordinary crime" or, for some, "serious crime." Most of the time, when thinking of this kind of crime, we formulate the discussion in terms of one-criminal-and-one-victim. However, a fact that has become ever clearer in the twenty-first century is the *global interconnectedness* of many serious criminal acts. Dick Hobbs (2000, 172) comments that ". . . [t]he political economy of contemporary crime links street dealers with private armies in the Far East, market traders in provincial cities with sweat shops producing counterfeit designer clothing in Asia, and weekend cocaine, ecstasy, and amphetamine users with rogue governments and men of marketable violence all over the globe." The topical areas of international criminology or transnational crime are becoming more and more popular in the academic disciplines of criminal justice and criminology. The reason for this growing popularity is straightforward: Much serious crime *is* international in a fundamental sense. Also, it is not unreasonable to expect that serious crime will be increasingly examined from an international perspective as we move further into the twenty-first century. As Hobbs has made clear, a sale of cocaine on any ordinary street corner on any ordinary day in any ordinary city is anything but simple,

and can only be fully understood as an action embedded in a broader and interconnected world.

CHRIS E. MARSHALL

See also **National Crime Victimization Survey (NCVS);** *Uniform Crime Reports*

References and Further Reading

Blumstein, Alfred, and Joel Wallman. 2000. The recent rise and fall of American violence. In *The crime drop in America*, ed. Alfred Blumstein and Joel Wallman, 1–12. Cambridge, England: Cambridge University Press.

Bureau of Justice Statistics. 2002a. Key crime and justice facts at a glance. In Key crime and justice facts at a glance slide show charts. Washington, DC: U.S. Department of Justice. http://www.ojp.usdoj.gov/bjs/glance.htm. (accessed November 25, 2005).

———. 2002b. *Key crime and justice facts at a glance (crime trends): Homicide rate, 1900–1999.* Washington, DC: U.S. Department of Justice.

———. 2004. The nation's two crime measures. Washington, DC: U.S. Department of Justice, Bureau of Justice Statistics.

Cantor, David, and James P. Lynch. 2000. Self-report surveys as measures of crime and criminal victimization. In *Measurement and analysis of crime and justice*, 85–138. Washington, DC: U.S. Department of Justice, Office of Justice Programs.

Catalano, Shannan M. 2004. *Criminal Victimization, 2003*, 1–12. Washington, DC: U.S. Department of Justice, Bureau of Justice Statistics.

Federal Bureau of Investigation. 2005. *Crime in the United States 2004*. Washington, DC: U.S. Department of Justice. http://www.fbi.gov/ucr/cius_04/ (accessed November 25, 2005).

Henry, Stuart, and Mark M. Lanier. 1988. The prism of crime: Arguments for an integrated definition of crime. *Justice Quarterly* 15 (4): 609–27.

———, eds. 2001. *What is crime? Controversy over the nature of crime and what to do about it*. Boulder, CO: Rowman and Littlefield.

Hobbs, Dick. 2000. Researching serious crime. In *Doing research on crime and justice*, ed. Roy D. King and Emma Wincup, 153–82. Oxford, England: Oxford University Press.

Johnson, Bruce D., Andrew Golub, and Eloise Dunlap. 2000. The rise and decline of hard drugs, drug markets, and violence in inner-city New York. In *The crime drop in America*, ed. Alfred Blumstein and Joel Wallman, 164–206. Cambridge, England: Cambridge University Press.

Junger-Tas, Josine, and Ineke Haen Marshall. 1999. The self-report methodology in crime research: Strengths and weaknesses. In *Crime and justice*, ed. Michael Tonry, 291–367. Chicago: University of Chicago Press.

Lindgren, Sue A. 2001. Bureau of Justice Statistics' technical report: Linking Uniform Crime Reporting data to other datasets, 1–9. Washington, DC: U.S. Department of Justice, Bureau of Justice Statistics.

Maltz, Michael D. 1999. Bridging gaps in police crime data: A discussion paper from the BJS fellows program, 1–78. Washington, DC: U.S. Department of Justice, Bureau of Justice Statistics.

Siegel, Larry J. 2004. *Criminology: Theories, patterns, and typologies.* 8th ed. Belmont, CA: Wadsworth-Thomson Learning.

Survey Research Center. 2005. *Monitoring the future: A continuing study of American youth.* Ann Arbor: University of Michigan, Institute for Social Research. http://monitoringthe future.org/ (accessed November 27, 2005).

U.S. Census Bureau. 2005. Vital statistics: Table No. 102, Deaths by major causes, 1960 to 2002. In *Statistical abstract of the United States: 2004–2005, the national data book [CD-ROM Version]*, ed. Economics and Statistics Administration of the U.S. Department of Commerce. Washington, DC: U.S. Census Bureau, 2005.

CRIME, SERIOUS VIOLENT

Definitions

In general usage, serious violent crime consists of the crimes of murder/non-negligent manslaughter, rape, robbery, and aggravated assault. Other behaviors have been defined as serious violent crimes, including everything from terrorism to the sale of drugs, but these are usually merely different classifications of the four major types just listed.

Murder and non-negligent manslaughter involve the criminal killing of a human being. As reported in the *Uniform Crime Reports* (UCR), this category does not include attempted murder, nor does it include noncriminal homicides, so self-defense, justifiable homicide, capital punishment, and combat deaths do not fall under this category. The essential features defining murder and non-negligent manslaughter are intent and premeditation. When both intent and premeditation are present, the homicide is classified by the UCR as murder. When there is intent to kill, or an awareness at the point of attack that one's actions could have a lethal outcome, but no premeditation, the homicide is classified as non-negligent manslaughter. These distinctions are standardized for these definitions through the reporting standards of the UCR, and the specific name of the crime varies by jurisdiction, so that non-negligent manslaughter may be murder two, manslaughter, voluntary manslaughter, non-negligent manslaughter, or any other name within a particular state.

Rape, as defined in the *Uniform Crime Reports,* is the carnal knowledge of a female forcibly and against her will. In this UCR classification, as in all others except murder, assaults are included. Because this definition is based on the common law definition of rape and is limited to females, states have passed laws creating the category of sexual assault. Sexual assault brings a broader range of sexual behaviors under its umbrella, and covers male victims as well as female victims.

Robbery involves taking something from someone by the use of force, the threat of force, or putting the victim in fear for themselves or another. While it involves a theft, it is necessarily a confrontational crime and requires that the victim and offender be in some direct contact. As a consequence, although one may speak of a bank being robbed late at night, or a house being robbed when no one is home, these do not constitute robbery as legally defined and are not considered serious violent crimes.

Aggravated assault is a personal attack for the purpose of inflicting severe or aggravated bodily injury. Attempts to cause this degree of injury are also included, so assaults that involve a weapon capable of causing this degree of injury, even if the victim is not so injured, are regularly included. Both aggravated assault and murder involve an attack on another with the potential for a lethal outcome. The attacker seldom has the real ability to control the degree of injury inflicted, so that one of the primary distinctions between these crimes is the lethality of the weapon used. This fact has consequences for theories on these crimes and for practical policies that have reduced the incidence of violent crimes.

Rates and Rate Changes

Rates of specific violent crimes change annually, of course, so for the latest rate information one must refer to the *Uniform Crime Reports* or to the data available at http://www.fbi.gove under *Crime In the United States*. However, the rates of all violent crimes displayed the same pattern during the last half of the twentieth century. From 1950 to around 1965 the rate for each of the violent crimes was stable. Around 1965 the rates began a steady increase, which peaked between 1975 and 1980. The rates then showed little variation until around 1990, when they all began to go down steadily. By 2000, murder had reached its 1965 level. Rape, robbery, and aggravated assault all showed exactly the same pattern of increase, stability, and then decline, but never returned fully to their 1965 levels and remain closer to rates found in the 1970s.

This pattern is important because it reflects some of the major features that we believe contribute to violent crime. Chief among these are changes in demographic factors (primarily age composition), and changes in policy and social conditions that have an impact on violent crime. The pattern of these changes also

supports the idea based on medical models of disease transmission that violence is somehow "contagious" within a community. As rates of violent crime increase, they develop their own inertia, and will continue to increase because of that inertia until some other factors intervene to bring a change in the direction of the rates (Loftin 1986; Jones and Jones 2000). If this is true, it suggests that early intervention as violent crimes begin to increase may be critical in preventing their long-term increase.

Major Features of Violent Crime

Every crime is unique, but overall the offenders and victims in violent serious crimes have some significant features in common. Two factors stand out: age and gender. Statistically speaking, violent crime is a young man's game. Consistently, more than 80% of all violent offenders are male. Also with notable consistency, more than 40% of those arrested for violent crimes are under the age of twenty-five (44.3% in 2003).

Minority groups also tend to have higher rates of violent crime, and one of the major debates in research and theory on violent crime concerns the roles that race, the structure of poverty, and the culture of the South play in violence. Since the 1930s researchers have reached very different, and often contradictory, answers on whether racial and ethnic differences in violent crime are reflections of differing poverty rates among racial and ethnic groups in the United States, or whether those differences reflect a cultural difference in the tolerance or acceptance of violence within the South and populations with Southern origins in other parts of the United States. (Hawley and Messner [1987] provide the best general review of this argument.) Quite simply, there is no definitive answer on this even today, and one has to go to the research and reach an individual conclusion based on reading of that work.

Significant debate also surrounds the role of firearms, and whether either their presence or the nature of the laws regarding them contribute to an increase or a decrease in violent crime. Both sides of the debate, however, agree that firearms are lethal weapons that change the nature of an interpersonal conflict, whether in the hands of the offender or of the potential victim. Although aggravated assault and murder are sibling crimes in that they involve very similar sets of offenders and victims in very similar situations, they are vastly different in weapon involvement, with more than 65% of all murders, but only about a third of aggravated assaults, involving a firearm.

Understanding these characteristics, and how they play out in differing types of violent crimes, provides us with clues as to how to explain and then to reduce violent crime.

Theory and Policy Impacts on Serious Violent Crime

The goal of research, theory, and policy is either to prevent or to reduce the harm produced by violent crime. History teaches us that attempting to prevent all violent crime is an unrealistic goal. The more pragmatic approach is to try to figure out ways to reduce the level of violent crime, or to reduce the harm or damage following from violent crime.

There are a multitude of theories attempting to explain violent criminal behavior on biological, psychological, or sociological frameworks. (Englander [1997] provides a good basic overview.) However, at least one approach, called routine activities theory, does not concern itself with the origin of the violent behavior, but pragmatically considers the structures in which violence is more likely to occur (Cohen and Felson 1979). This theory suggests that violent crime occurs because of the convergence in the same place and at the same time of people with the motivation to commit the crime, suitable victims, and the absence of capable guardians to prevent the crime. Basic police work attempts to place suitable guardians in the right places at the right times, and to remove motivated offenders from the picture. However, there are other ways to prevent this convergence of all the wrong factors. The principle of target hardening in burglary or robbery, for example, reflects this approach by reducing the "suitability" of victims (see Wright and Decker 1994, 1997). And anything that keeps offenders and potential victims apart in space or in time, that makes targets less suitable, that places capable guardians in the picture, or that reduces the motivation of offenders can have an impact.

The Boston Gun Project is one example of a program that attempts to change the dynamic of motivation, offenders, and structure, in this case by focusing on the role of firearms in increasing the seriousness of violent crimes (Braga et al. 2001). The goal was not to prevent all violent crimes, but rather to form a workable policy to reduce the harm following from levels of violent crime by reducing the use of firearms among problematic groups in the city, and the attempt seems to have paid positive dividends.

In devising policies to reduce the level of violent crime, it helps to remember that violent crime is only one outcome in a situation that could have had a number of other results. Whether those involved in any situation are male or female, young or old, whether they are armed, whether they are drunk, and so on, all change the odds that a situation may result in violence. Obviously, whether the individuals are male or female, young or old, cannot be changed, but police practices that change the probability that one or both of these people will be armed, that they will be drunk, or that they will have no other outlet to settle their dispute can have an impact (White et al. 2003). As a result, policies and practices that address the significant features that increase the probability of violent outcomes can be effective in reducing the occurrence of serious violent crime at every level from political decisions to street level policing.

DERRAL CHEATWOOD

See also **Attitudes toward the Police: Overview; Capital Crimes and Capital Punishment; Crime Control Strategies: Gun Control; Crime, Serious; Domestic (or Intimate Partner) Violence and the Police; Firearms: Guns and the Gun Culture; Homicide and Its Investigation; Homicide: Unsolved; Offender Profiling; Responding to School Violence; Robbery; School Violence; Serial Murder;** *Uniform Crime Reports*

References and Further Reading

Braga, Anthony A., David M. Kennedy, Elin J. Waring, and Anne Morrison Piehl. 2001. Problem-oriented policing, deterrence, and youth violence: An evaluation of Boston's Operation Ceasefire. *Journal of Research in Crime and Delinquency* 38: 195–225.

Cohen, Lawrence E., and Marcus Felson. 1979. Social change and crime rate trends: A routine activity approach. *American Sociological Review* 44: 588–608.

Englander, Elizabeth Kandel. 1997. *Understanding violence*. Mahwah, NJ: Lawrence Erlbaum Associates.

Hawley, F., and Steven Messner. 1987. The Southern violence construct: A review of arguments, evidence, and the normative context. *Justice Quarterly* 6: 481–511.

Jones, M. B., and D. R. Jones. 2000. The contagious nature of antisocial behavior. *Criminology* 38: 25–46.

Loftin, Colin. 1986. Assaultive violence as a contagious social process. *Bulletin of the New York Academy of Medicine* 62: 550–55.

White, Michael D., James J. Fyfe, Suzanne P. Campbell, and John S. Goldkamp. 2003. The police role in preventing homicide: Considering the impact of problem-oriented policing on the prevalence of murder. *Journal of Research in Crime and Delinquency* 40: 194–225.

Wright, Richard T., and Scott H. Decker. 1994. *Burglars on the job: Streetlife and residential break-ins*. Boston: Northeastern University Press.

———. 1997. *Armed robbers in action: Stickups and street culture*. Boston: Northeastern University Press.

CRIMESTOPPERS

Crimestoppers is a program that is designed to utilize citizens in the criminal justice process. The role of the citizen is to contribute to the capture of felony offenders who have escaped the law. Citizens can help the police solve a crime in various ways. When the police do not have any clues as to who committed the act, information that citizens provide can be the key to solving the crime. Citizens can also help officers recapture those individuals who fled after becoming known to the police. The key premise of the Crimestoppers programs is that in exchange for information that leads to the arrest and conviction of an offender, the person that volunteered the information receives a cash reward (Dempsey and Forst 2005, 215).

According to the Crimestoppers USA website, there are three impediments to officers obtaining information on offenders, the nature of the crime, and witnesses to the crime: (1) the fear that if a citizen comes forward with information about a crime or criminal, there will be some form of retaliation or reprisal; (2) a general sense of apathy or lack of concern on the part of the citizens; and (3) an aversion or reluctance, of the community, to get involved in the issue of crime (Crimestoppers USA 2005). Crimestoppers programs around the world have taken several steps to overcome these problems. One is to ensure that tips given to the program are anonymous. To accomplish this goal, Crimestoppers programs provide telephone hotlines that anyone can call and leave a tip on without giving his or her name. Providing cash rewards to individuals for information is another method of increasing public participation in criminal justice (Crimestoppers USA 2005). The premise behind providing cash rewards is that people are more likely to become involved with the criminal justice system if they are getting something in return. (This, of course, would require forgoing anonymity.)

The stated mission of Crimestoppers is "to develop Crimestoppers as an effective crime-solving organization throughout the world, with the primary objective of this tri-partite organization of the community, media and law enforcement being 'Working Together to Solve Crime'" (M. Cooper, personal communication, October 10, 2005). There are three elements of every Crimestoppers program that help to ensure the mission of this agency is accomplished: the community, the media, and law enforcement personnel. The role of the community in Crimestoppers programs is the involvement of citizens who "are responsible for forming a Crimestoppers non-profit corporation, whose directors establish policy, determine amount and method of reward payments, work closely with the police and the media and generally oversee the program" (Crimestoppers USA 2005). Without the community, Crimestopper programs cannot be effective because the members of the community are responsible for raising money and volunteering their time. The role of the media in the continued success of Crimestoppers programs is to provide information about the goals, objectives, methodology, and phone numbers to the public (Crimestoppers USA 2005). The media also contribute by relaying to the public which offenders are under investigation through newspapers and television programs. The job of law enforcement personnel is the investigation of tips and the arrest of suspects.

Currently, about 1,200 Crimestopper programs are in existence in twenty countries including the United States, Australia, and the United Kingdom (Worldwide importance of Crimestoppers 2005). Although there are many different Crimestoppers programs around the world, Crimestoppers International, Inc., is the central agency that encompasses all programs. The main goal of Crimestoppers International, Inc., is the creation of programs around the world, and they provide training, support, publications, and useful information to established programs as well as to those communities that are interested in starting a Crimestoppers program of their own (What is Crimestoppers International?).

Tips from citizens have led to the capture of many fugitives. As of October 2005, about 1,142,717 cases have been solved internationally, and citizens have helped in the arrest of 611,807 felons (Worldwide importance of Crimestoppers 2005). In terms of property and drugs, Crimestoppers programs have succeeded in the recovery of an estimated $1,543,997,725 in property and $5,640,370,838 in drugs seizures (Worldwide importance of Crimestoppers 2005). The total amount of money received from drugs and property recovery was $7,184,368,563. Crimestoppers program have paid an estimated $68,556,831 in reward money to those individuals who gave information that helped lead police to the arrest and capture of felons (Worldwide importance of Crimestoppers 2005). The statistics reported on Crimestoppers programs "show an average conviction rate of 95% and tips to Crimestoppers save law enforcement agencies thousands of dollars in investigation time" (Worldwide importance of Crimestoppers 2005). This indicates that once citizens become involved with helping the police solve crime through reporting tips, the rate of solving that crime increases. This means that police officers must indeed rely on the help of the community to solve some crimes.

Crimestoppers programs are very effective, and there are many benefits of having Crimestoppers programs throughout the world. Some of these benefits include (1) making the community aware of the crime problems within their area, (2) helping citizens in the fight against crime, and (3) ensuring that the community, law enforcement officers, and the media work together to solve crime (The tri-partite concept 2005).

Although no recent study could be located on the effectiveness of Crimestopper programs today, some studies evaluated these programs in the past. According to Challinger (2004, 9), three studies, in addition to the current one that the author was conducting, evaluated Crimestoppers programs. The three evaluations were conducted by the United States in 1987, the United Kingdom in 2001, and Canada in 1989. These past studies found it hard to evaluate the true effectiveness of Crimestopper programs because of the nature of the program itself. Because these programs are based on anonymity, there is no way to collect data on informants and how they obtained their information about the crime or the criminal suspect (Challinger 2004, 9). Most Crimestoppers programs only evaluate the number of cases that are solved by the police based on tips and the amount of property seized, and this is not a true measure of effectiveness because it is not known if the police would have solved the case eventually without the help of the informant (Challinger 2004, 9). The true effectiveness of Crimestopper programs might not ever be fully evaluated as long the program is based on anonymous tips.

TINA L. LEE

See also **Crime Prevention; Criminal Investigation**

References and Further Reading

Challinger, Dennis. 2004. *Crimestoppers Victoria: An evaluation*. Canberra: Australian Institute of Criminology.

Crimestoppers USA. 2005. http://www.crimestopusa.com/ (accessed November 2005).

Dempsey, John S., and Linda S. Forst. 2005. *An introduction to policing*. 3rd ed. Belmont: Wadsworth-Thomson.

The tri-partite concept—public, police, and press all working together. 2005. http://www.c-s-i.org/concept.php (accessed November 2005).

What is Crimestoppers International? 2005. http://www.c-s-i.org/about.php (accessed November 2005).

Worldwide importance of Crimestoppers. 2005. http://www.c-s-i.org/ (accessed November 2005).

CRIMINAL CAREERS

The term *criminal career* describes an individual's total involvement in criminal activity, from the point of onset, through continuation, ending at the last incident of criminal activity. Specifically, a criminal career charts an individual's long-term sequences and patterns of criminal behaviors. Instead of focusing on aggregate crime rates, the criminal career perspective explores the causes of criminal behavior by placing emphasis on individuals and individual long-term patterns of offending (Blumstein et al. 1986). This perspective is an important framework within which the life-course perspective can be studied with regard to crime. While life-course perspectives are concerned with the duration, timing, and ordering of transition events and their effects on long-term social development and trajectories (Sampson and Laub 1992), the criminal career perspective focuses on the origins, continuation, and cessation of an individual's criminal activity. Although the criminal career perspective is interested in the causes and patterns of criminality, another goal central to this perspective is to aid in developing crime control policies that would focus on interrupting or altering criminal careers (Blumstein and Cohen 1987).

There are four main components to the criminal career paradigm: participation, frequency, seriousness, and career length. The first two, participation and frequency, are considered the primary components. Participation separates those who have offended from those who have not. In other words, this component operates as a filter, making the necessary distinction between those individuals who engage in crime from those individuals who do not (Blumstein et al. 1986). The point at which the criminal career begins is referred to as the age of onset. The end of the criminal career is generally called desistance. Research on the participation component of criminal careers has shown that males have higher participation rates than females, that blacks have higher participation rates than whites, and that the probability of onset is strongest between the ages of thirteen and eighteen (Piquero, Farrington, and Blumstein 2003). Once the subset of criminally active individuals has been identified, the other components of the criminal career perspective can be utilized to characterize the offender population.

Among those who have criminal careers, there is variation in the intensity of offending. Therefore, the second component, frequency (represented by the Greek letter lambda, λ), indicates the rate of criminal activity for an active offender. It is measured by the number of criminal offenses committed during a specified period of time (Blumstein et al. 1986). Often, it is measured as the number of crimes committed during a one-year period per individual offender. This dimension of the criminal career is often considered to be the most significant of the four components, and research on criminal careers has identified notable variation in individual offender frequencies. While some criminal careers are marked by low frequencies of offending, other individuals have high frequency rates. Criminal career research has indicated a relationship between age of onset and offending frequency, with individuals exhibiting an earlier at age first offense having higher offending frequencies. In terms of gender, research on frequency has indicated that, among active offenders, frequency rates are similar for males and females (Piquero, Farrington, and Blumstein 2003).

The third component, seriousness, describes the severity of offenses. This element of the criminal career perspective refers to the severity of the criminal act committed, as well as the patterns and sequences of seriousness from one offense to another (Blumstein et al. 1986). In other words, this dimension focuses on whether, during an individual's criminal career, criminal acts escalate in severity, de-escalate in severity, or are intermixed and display no apparent patterns. Within this element, there is also a concern about crime type and crime specialization. The term *generalist* refers to offenders who commit a variety of crimes, while the term *specialist* refers to offenders who tend to repeat and engage in the same type of offense (Benson 2002). Research in this area of the criminal career perspective has found that while there exists some small tendency to specialize in a small range of crimes, most offenders display generality in their offenses. The research has also indicated differences in crime type specialization among adults and juveniles, with adult offenders being more likely to specialize than juvenile offenders (Piquero, Farrington, and Blumstein 2003).

The fourth and final component of the criminal career is career length, which describes how long the offender is actively committing crimes. This dimension is measured as the time between age of onset and desistance (Vold, Bernard, and Snipes 2002). Criminal career lengths can vary to a large extent. For one-time offenders, the duration of the career is short, whereas for chronic offenders the duration of the criminal career is much longer (Blumstein et al. 1986). The research on this dimension has suggested that most criminal careers are brief, and begin and end during the teenage and late teenage years. For a smaller number of individuals, however, career lengths are longer and can continue through the adult years (Piquero, Farrington, and Blumstein 2003).

The criminal career perspective is guided and shaped by two pieces of criminological knowledge. The first is the largely accepted aggregate age–crime relationship. This relationship was first observed in the 1800s, and describes crime rates as reaching their peak during the late adolescent years and subsequently declining with age. Although this finding is accepted at the aggregate level, the interpretation is at the center of criminological debate (Piquero and Mazerolle 2001). While certain scholars view the decline in the aggregate age–crime curve as the result of active offenders experiencing declining offending rates with time, the criminal career perspective holds that this does not necessarily have to be the case. According to the criminal career paradigm, the decline in the aggregate age–crime relationship may also be the result of a change in participation rates. As individuals age, the numbers of criminally active offenders declines, but those who continue to offend, offend at high or stable frequencies (Vold, Bernard, and Snipes 2002).

Second, and also guiding the criminal career perspective, is the knowledge that a small percentage of offenders is responsible for the majority of crime. This piece of information was first identified in a seminal birth cohort study by Wolfgang, Figlio, and Sellin (1972). Similar findings have emerged in many other longitudinal studies that utilize different samples from different cohorts and contexts (Piquero, Farrington, and Blumstein 2003). On this score, the criminal career perspective directs focus to identifying the chronic offenders who are accountable for the largest proportion of crime, and to use this information in order to develop crime control policies (Blumstein and Cohen 1987). These chronic offenders are often referred to as *career criminals,* but terms such as *habitual offenders* and *persistent offenders* are also used (Svensson 2002). Several public policy implications stem from the combination of these two pieces of criminological knowledge.

Policy Implications

The criminal career framework identifies three crime control policies. The first is deterrence, which is a prevention strategy. The goal of deterrence is to dissuade nonoffenders from becoming offenders in the first place. The second crime control strategy is modification. The goal of this strategy is to reduce offending among active offenders by modifying their current behaviors. The third crime control strategy is incapacitation. The criminal career perspective has given incapacitation the greatest amount of consideration and attention. The goal is to separate active offenders from general society, normally through incarceration, during the duration of the criminal career.

Incapacitation efforts can be either general or selective. In other words, collectively incapacitating all offenders, or selectively incapacitating chronic offenders (Blumstein et al. 1986; Piquero, Farrington, and Blumstein 2003). Selective incapacitation, in theory, would identify and confine those offenders who commit a high frequency of more serious offenses. According to Blumstein and Cohen (1987), this method of crime control could reduce "wasted" sentencing on offenders who would desist from crime naturally and end their criminal careers. Instead, selective incapacitation would target "career criminals," those offenders who have longer and more active criminal careers. Unfortunately, it has been difficult to identify prospective career criminals.

Unresolved Issues

There are a number of unresolved issues in the criminal career literature. Five of them are highlighted here. First, due to lack of longitudinal data, there exists very little information on patterns of participation, frequency, and desistance past the third decade of life. To obtain true estimates of desistance, lengthier data collection efforts are required. Second, because much of the early data collection efforts in criminology employed samples of white male offenders, there exists no long-term information on patterns of offending across sex and race. Third, much of the information about criminal careers comes from official records (arrests and convictions). Self-reported information obtained from individuals over the life course is necessary. Fourth, the effect of incapacitation policies shows that offenders are oftentimes incarcerated for lengthy periods when they would otherwise likely not offend. A review of current sentencing policies appears relevant. Finally, very little information on the nature of criminal careers exists in a cross-national context. Future studies should attempt to document the natural history of offending using data from around the world.

ZENTA GOMEZ-SMITH and
ALEX R. PIQUERO

See also **Crime Control Strategies; Criminology**

References and Further Reading

Benson, M. L. 2002. *Crime and the life course: An introduction.* Los Angeles: Roxbury Publishing.

Blumstein, A., and J. Cohen. 1987. Characterizing criminal careers. *Science* 238: 985–91.

Blumstein, A., J. Cohen, J. Roth, and C. Visher. 1986. *Criminal careers and "career criminals."* Washington, DC: National Academy Press.

Piquero, A. R., D. P. Farrington, and A. Blumstein. 2003. The criminal career paradigm: Background and recent developments. In *Crime and justice: A review of research*, vol. 30, ed. Michael Tonry, 359–506. Chicago: University of Chicago Press.

Piquero, A. R., and P. Mazerolle. 2001. *Life course criminology: Contemporary and classic readings.* Belmont, CA: Wadsworth.

Sampson, R. J., and J. H. Laub. 1992. Crime and deviance in the life course. *Annual Review of Sociology* 18: 63–84.

Svensson, R. 2002. Strategic offences in the criminal career context. *British Journal of Criminology* 42: 395–411.

Vold, G. B., Bernard, T. J., and J. B. Snipes. 2002. *Theoretical criminology.* New York: Oxford University Press.

Wolfgang, M. E., R. M. Figlio, and T. Sellin. 1972. *Delinquency in a birth cohort.* Chicago: University of Chicago Press.

CRIMINAL HISTORY INFORMATION

Criminal history information (CHI) is defined as "a record, or system for maintaining records, that includes individual identifiers and that describes an individual's arrests and subsequent dispositions" (Search Group Inc. 2001, 3). Records generally reflect arrests and subsequent processing for the most serious of crimes including serious misdemeanors and felonies. Criminal history records include a variety of information about personal characteristics of individuals, and characteristics of criminal events for which individuals were arrested.

Individual personal identifiers include name, address, date of birth, Social security number (SSN), sex, race, and other physical characteristics such as hair color, eye color, height, weight, scars, marks, and tattoos. Other personal information such as place of employment and automobile registration is included in some situations. There has been an emphasis on also including biometric identifiers such as fingerprints. The completeness of biometric identifiers varies by state. The most recent statistics indicate that approximately thirty-seven states include fingerprint support for 100% of criminal history records (Barton 2003, 3).

Records also include characteristics of criminal incidents for which individuals were arrested including date, type of offense, and court disposition. Disposition information generally refers to final disposition such as a police decision to drop all charges, prosecutorial decision not to prosecute, or trial court disposition such as "guilty" or "not guilty." In 2001 more than sixty-four million criminal history records were maintained in state systems (Bureau of Justice Statistics [BJS] 2003, 3).

It is important to note that not all states include juvenile records as part of adult criminal history records due to increased privacy protections over juvenile criminal records. One of the categorical exceptions relates to crimes involving juveniles who are charged in adult courts. Although juveniles still maintain increased levels of privacy compared to their adult counterparts, there is an increased tendency among states and the federal government to relax such standards.

Creating Criminal History Records

A number of agencies throughout the criminal justice system are responsible for the generation, collection, maintenance, and dissemination of criminal history information. Police agencies complete arrest reports as part of booking processes, which include demographics, personal descriptors, and arrest charges. In addition, arrestees are typically fingerprinted when charged with felonies or serious misdemeanors. The collected data along with captured fingerprints are subsequently forwarded to state central repositories once the booking process is completed. A state central repository is either a law enforcement or criminal justice agency within state government that has been charged with the responsibility of collecting, maintaining, and disseminating criminal history information. Today all fifty states plus the District of Columbia and Puerto Rico have central repositories (Search Group Inc. 2001, 23). Additional data elements are subsequently updated to arrest records by prosecutors, courts, and correctional facilities as cases progress through the criminal justice system.

What Are the Uses of CHI?

Criminal history information is a critical decision-making tool used by both criminal justice and non–criminal justice agencies alike. Criminal history information is used by law enforcement during investigations as well as in the field when assessing the potential risk a person may present based on a past criminal history. The courts utilize criminal history information in a number of key decisions such as bail, pretrial release, trial decisions, and sentencing. Prosecutors rely heavily on criminal history throughout a case whether or not to impose enhanced charging or charge a person as a habitual or career criminal. Correctional institutions use criminal history to complete presentencing reports. In addition, corrections consider criminal history information when making classification decisions.

Criminal history information is also used to determine an individual's eligibility to purchase firearms or possess a license to carry firearms. Provisions in both state and federal legislation place restrictions on individuals previously convicted of certain offenses (primarily felonies) from purchasing or possessing firearms. In 2001, nearly eight million background checks were conducted to verify a person's eligibility to purchase firearms (Bureau of Justice Statistics 2003, 3).

Increasingly, criminal history information is also used by employers for screening applicants who work in occupations that have access to sensitive information or are responsible for the care of vulnerable populations such as children, the elderly, or populations with disabilities. Some returning convicts may even be restricted from reentering professions in which they were employed before incarceration. Surprisingly, nearly all states go so far as to restrict individuals with serious criminal histories from employment as barbers and beauticians even though many correctional facilities provide this type of training (Petersilia 2003).

Initiatives to Improve the Quality of the Information and Its Utility

Given the importance of criminal history information to the criminal justice community, a number of initiatives have been dedicated to improving the completeness, accuracy, and timeliness of criminal history information. In 1995, the U.S. Department of Justice's Bureau of Justice Statistics (BJS) initiated the National Criminal History Improvement Program (NCHIP). Under this program, all states have been the "recipient of direct funds and technical assistance to improve the quality, timeliness, and immediate accessibility of criminal history and related records" (see BJS 2003, 1).

As a direct result of NCHIP, a number of significant accomplishments have been realized. These accomplishments include increased state participation in the Interstate Identification Index, increased record automation, increased record completeness, increased state participation in the FBI's Integrated Automated Fingerprint Identification System (IAFIS), increased submissions by states to the National Protection Order File, the development of sex offender registries, participation of all fifty states plus Guam, District of Columbia, and the Virgin Islands in the National Sex Offender Registry, and support of nearly eight million background checks annually for firearms purchases (BJS 2005).

Future Issues

Federal and state governments have worked earnestly during the past two decades to improve criminal history records systems. Improvement of these systems is critical to the criminal justice community and public alike. The need for timely and accurate data is particularly important in the wake of national security concerns related to terrorism.

The future of criminal history information lies in two core areas. The first relates to issues of data quality. More specifically, it is imperative for the criminal justice system to work to ensure criminal history records are timely, accurate, and complete. Tremendous efforts have been made in recent years to reduce administrative backlogs and rectify technical problems that

hinder such quality. The NCHIP has been an effort directed solely at these problems.

The second major issue that needs to be addressed in the upcoming years relates to levels of automation and accessibility of data. Criminal history data must be electronically stored and easily accessible by local as well as other agencies. The FBI, for example, has implemented the Interstate Identification Index in order to serve as a national repository of criminal history records to improve the level of interstate sharing of criminal history information. Such initiatives hold the potential for dramatically improving the usefulness of such information.

TRACY A. VARANO and SEAN P. VARANO

See also **Computer Technology; Criminal Investigation; Fingerprinting; Information within Police Agencies; Terrorism: Police Functions Associated with**

References and Further Reading

Barton, Sheila J. 2003. *State criminal history information systems, 2001.* Washington, DC: U.S. Department of Justice.

Bureau of Justice Statistics. 2001. *Survey of state criminal history information systems, 2001.* Washington, DC: U.S. Department of Justice.

———. 2003. *Improving criminal history records for background checks.* Washington, DC: Bureau of Justice Statistics.

———. 2005. *National criminal history improvement program (NCHIP).* http://www.ojp.usdoj.gov/bjs/nchip.htm#impact (accessed April 27, 2005).

Petersilia, Joan. 2003. *When prisoners come home.* New York: Oxford University Press.

Search Group Inc. 2001. Use and management of criminal history record information: A comprehensive report, 2001 update. Washington, DC: U.S. Department of Justice.

CRIMINAL INFORMANTS

The acquisition and organization of legally reliable evidence is the essence of the criminal investigation process. Evidence is usually obtained through the use of one or more of the three I's of investigation: interviewing, instrumentation, and information. Information provides direction to investigation. Information about a crime may be obtained from many sources. However, people motivated by the desire to improve the community usually have only limited knowledge of crime. Investigators must often turn to another, more questionable source of information: the criminal informant.

American law enforcement agencies have long made use of informants. In the nineteenth and early twentieth centuries, detectives concentrated on identifying suspects and set about building a case from testimony of witnesses and confessions, or from actually catching offenders in the act (Lane 1967; Richardson 1970).

In time, investigators began to concentrate less on suspects and more on crimes. The shift away from suspects came because investigators began to view the collection of physical evidence as the most essential part of their job. However, an interest in the use of informants has reemerged. A major conclusion from a study of investigation methods suggested a need for both patrol officers and investigators to make greater use of informants (Eck 1983).

Using an Informant's Information

The concept of probable cause is at the heart of American law enforcement. Of particular importance is the hearsay method for establishing probable cause most commonly used by officers relying on informants.

In *Aguilar v. Texas*, the Supreme Court created what became known as the two-pronged test for establishing probable cause on hearsay evidence. This test required that two things be done: (1) that the credibility of the informant be established, and (2) the reliability of the informant's information also be established.

The establishment of an informant's credibility was usually satisfied in one of two ways. First, if the informant made statements that led to prosecution this was generally considered proof of an informant's reliability. This technique is particularly valuable when using informants for the first time.

Multiple use of an informant establishes a "track record," the second means used to demonstrate an informant's credibility. A police officer preparing an affidavit for a warrant can cite the track record as proof that the informant has provided accurate information leading to a specified number of arrests and convictions. Demonstrating the reliability of an informant's information, the second prong of the test, is most commonly accomplished by stating the informant's direct knowledge of the facts.

In *Spinelli v. United States*, the Supreme Court approved the technique of corroboration as a means to establish probable cause. Under this concept, the Court suggested that facts, when combined in sufficient number, could establish probable cause. Thus, traditional investigative techniques such as surveillance, record checks, and neighborhood canvasses could be of value in obtaining warrants.

In 1983, the Supreme Court handed down a decision that impacted the use of informants. In *Illinois v. Gates*, the Court established a totality of the circumstances test to determine the existence of probable cause. In *Gates*, a police officer received an anonymous letter so detailed that a judge felt the information contained in the letter was adequate to establish probable cause and issued a search warrant. At no point in the letter did the informant identify himself or provide information as to his credibility, from the perspective of *Aguilar*. The judge inferred the informant's credibility from the detailed information provided in the letter. The Court had eliminated the "first prong" of the two-pronged test, that of establishing credibility of the informant. Presently, the techniques set forth in

Aguilar, Spinelli, and *Gates* affect use of an informant's information.

Protecting an Informant's Identity

Investigators must make every effort to protect informants. The reasons are obvious: No one can be expected to provide information if it leads to his or her injury, death, or ostracism. Two cases have established principles that determine circumstances under which courts can compel disclosure of an informant's identity. In a 1957 case, *Roviaro v. United States,* the Supreme Court held that when an informant is a material witness in a case, such as a participant, his or her identity must be revealed to the defendant. This requirement stems from the Sixth Amendment, the right of a criminal defendant to confront his accusers. Thus, if an informant is actually making drug buys, for example, this activity must be undertaken with the informant aware that he or she might have to testify in court. In a later decision, however, the Supreme Court held that where an informant, whose reliability has already been established, only provides information that establishes probable cause, the informant's identity need not be disclosed (*McCray v. Illinois*).

In some states, the identity of an informant may be protected as a privileged communication between police officer and informant. Where that privilege exists, a police officer may refuse to disclose the identity of an informant who has only provided information leading to probable cause. In those states where privilege does not exist, an informant's identity may be treated as a matter of relevancy. A prosecutor may argue that as long as the informant is not a material witness, revealing his or her identity is not relevant. The trial judge will then make an *in camera* determination on the need to reveal the informant's identity.

Problems Related to the Use of Informants

By its very nature, the use of informants requires secrecy. The potential for abuse is therefore enormous. One of the most complex problems concerns to whom informants should provide information. Should they provide it only to specified police officers who will then have exclusive use of the information or should the informants' names and their information be maintained in a master informant file?

Proponents of individual control argue that informants are developed on a personal basis. A working relationship, based on a degree of trust, facilitates the flow of information. Once the relationship has been altered by inclusion of the informant's name in a master file, the informant's fear of exposure may hinder the acquisition of any further information. Another argument is that once the informant's identity is known to others it may become impossible to protect his or her identity, despite the most stringent security measures.

Arguments in support of centralized control hold that centralization reduces the potential for corruption either by police or informants. Administrative review may serve as a check on police officers engaging in corrupt and illegal acts. Centralization also makes an informant's information available to other investigators.

Use of informants also presents problems vis-à-vis the system as a whole. The American criminal justice system is rooted in the concepts of accountability and punishment; that is, persons are to receive their just desserts for violating the law.

The "buy–bust–flip" procedure by which informants are developed reduces the certainty of being held accountable for violating the law. The "buy–bust–flip" technique of developing informants is well documented (Jacobson 1981; Wilson 1978). In its simplest form, the technique involves hand-to-hand purchases of drugs:

the *buy*. The buy results in an immediate arrest, the *bust*. The arrestee is then given an unpleasant choice: going to prison or becoming an informant (the *flip*). While it could be argued that being compelled to perform in the sometimes risky role of informant is a form of punishment, it is equally likely that the person will feel it to be the more attractive option. But the threat of punishment cannot be effective as a deterrent unless it is certain. As long as law violators believe that an avenue of escape as an informant exists, there can be no certainty of punishment.

Another problem of informant use relates to the selection of a target. Investigations tend to focus on individuals and activities already known to the informant, not necessarily on the most serious offenders. Allocation of resources should be made only after careful sifting of all available information, rather than on only the idiosyncratic knowledge of an informant. The decision to investigate someone is also tied to the amount of "buy money" available. For example, if an agency's resources are limited, purchases will be small. The larger the budget, the larger the prize. Eventually, however, the prize becomes too expensive and the person making the last transaction becomes the target. Thus, money, not criminal activity, determines who is prosecuted.

Informant Control

The Commission on Accreditation for Law Enforcement Agencies requires that agencies seeking accreditation establish policies governing the use of informants. Although it is unrealistic to expect law enforcement agencies to develop an all-encompassing policy, it is necessary to promulgate a series of workable guidelines. The policy statement should begin with a frank declaration that informants are a valuable resource to be used. Information provided by informants will be kept in a master file, but access must be tightly controlled. The policy must state that neither the agency's administration nor its individual members will allow informants to commit crimes, and those who do will be prosecuted. Officers must be prohibited from offering immunity without review by the prosecuting attorney. Informants must be briefed on entrapment laws and warned that they cannot present themselves as sworn or nonsworn employees of the agency. Finally, the commission emphasizes the need for special efforts to protect juvenile informants.

Conclusion

The use of criminal informants is an essential aspect of criminal investigations. It is also an area in which the potential for abuse is enormous. An understanding of the issues associated with informant use and a policy regulating the use of informants can reduce the possibility of informant misuse. The solution, however, lies not in the creation of rigid policies, but in the continual reevaluation of the goals of the police and the extent to which those goals are appropriate in a democratic society.

MICHAEL F. BROWN

See also **Detective Work/Culture; Sting Tactics; Undercover Investigations**

References and Further Reading

Brown, Michael F. 1985. Criminal informants: Some observations on use, abuse, and control. *Journal of Police Science and Administration* 13 (3): 251–56.

Eck, John E. 1983. *Solving crimes: The investigation of burglary and robbery*. Washington, DC: Police Executive Research Forum.

Jacobson, Ben. 1981. Informants and the public police. In *Criminal and civil investigations handbook*, ed. Joseph J. Graw. New York: McGraw-Hill.

Kleinman, David Marc. 1980. Out of the shadows and into the files: Who should control informants? *Police* 13 (6): 36–44.

Lane, Roger. 1967. *Policing the city: Boston, 1822–1908*. Cambridge, MA: Harvard University Press.

Morris, Jack. 1983. *Police informant management*. Orangevale, CA: Palmer Enterprises.

Richardson, James. 1970. *New York police: Colonial times to 1901*. New York: Oxford University Press.

Van den Haag, Ernest. 1982. The criminal law as a threat system. *Journal of Criminal Law and Criminology* 73: 709–85.

Wilson, James Q. 1978. *The investigators*. New York: Basic Books.

Wilson, O. W. 1972. *Police administration*. New York: McGraw-Hill.

CRIMINAL INVESTIGATION

Criminal investigation is defined as "a reconstruction of a past event," through which police personnel solve crimes (Osterberg and Ward 2004, 5). Detectives or other investigative personnel take numerous factors into consideration when reconstructing a case in order to determine who committed the crime and under what circumstances the crime was committed. Personnel who perform criminal investigations must have certain characteristics and abilities in order to do the job successfully. Great care is taken in selecting those who perform criminal investigations.

Very broadly, the objectives of the criminal investigation process are (1) to establish that a crime was actually committed, (2) to identify and apprehend the suspect(s), (3) to recover stolen property, and (4) to assist in the prosecution of the person(s) charged with the crime (Swanson et al. 2006, 50).

The three major functions performed at the crime scene as part of the investigative process are overall coordination of the scene, technical services, and investigative services (Swanson et al. 2006). Most crime scenes require someone who coordinates the crime scene, due to the numerous responsibilities involved in the process. This person is ultimately responsible for everything that goes on at the crime scene. Technical services are performed by crime laboratory personnel, civilian evidence technicians, or sworn law enforcement personnel who are responsible for collecting and processing evidence. Investigative services include gathering information from people, including victims, witnesses, or other people who were in the vicinity of the criminal activity, but may not have necessarily known that.

Various factors affect the criminal investigation process. The more significant factors include the size of the organization, type of the organization, geographical location of the organization, and the philosophy of the organization. Most agencies are affected by more than one of these factors simultaneously, in varying degrees. The size of the organization may affect the resources of the organization, thereby dictating how many personnel might be allocated to perform criminal investigation duties. In larger organizations, there tends to be more specialization of duties, which means that there is a great likelihood that criminal investigation might consist of an entire unit. In contrast, in smaller organizations, which constitute roughly 90% of local police organizations, the likelihood that criminal investigation will comprise an entire unit is minimal. In small organizations, it is not unusual for all personnel to perform criminal investigations. In the larger, more specialized organizations, it is unusual for several personnel to be involved in the criminal investigation process.

The type of organization affects the criminal investigation process as a result of its mission. For example, local organizations are more likely to perform all general criminal investigations, whereas federal organizations have a narrower focus, such as the Drug Enforcement Administration, which focuses primarily on drug investigation and interdiction.

The geographical location of the organization can also affect the type of criminal investigations that the agency performs. Agencies that have coastal borders would be more than likely to have a greater number of crimes that involve the coastline or water. In other states, in the Midwest for example, crimes involving farming and agriculture would be more prevalent.

The philosophy of the organization may also affect the criminal investigation process, both in formal and informal ways. Policies will dictate some of the investigation process and could be additionally affected by the internal and external politics of the community. Informally, if the administration lets its desires be known with respect to types of investigations to pursue, this could also have an effect on the criminal investigation process.

Phases of Criminal Investigation

The criminal investigation process consists of two primary phases: the preliminary investigation and the follow-up investigation.

Preliminary Investigation

The steps of the preliminary investigation are (1) receipt of information, initial response, and officer safety procedures; (2) emergency care; (3) secure and control persons at the scene; (4) issue a be-on-the-lookout; (5) evidence procedures generally; and (6) the incident/offense report (Swanson et al. 2006, 53–58).

Information typically originates with the victim or a witness to a police dispatcher and then to whomever is responding to the call, which is usually a uniformed patrol officer. Regardless of the size of the organization, a uniformed patrol officer usually makes the initial response. At the scene, if an organization has a criminal investigation unit, it is determined whether or not to turn the case over to a detective. The initial response will vary based on the type of case, and officer safety is paramount regardless of the type of call. Emergency care for anyone at the scene, including the suspect, is a primary consideration. Prior

to taking further action, the responding officer must identify and control the crime scene, followed by issuing a "be-on-the-lookout" order as needed. In most organizations, even the smaller ones, an officer will be joined by additional personnel to help identify and gather evidence. Finally, an offense report must be completed documenting the circumstances of the criminal activity, which is basically the reconstruction of events, as stated previously. The offense report serves as the foundational basis for further follow-up of the investigation.

Follow-Up Investigation

Procedures vary from organization to organization regarding whether or not to continue the preliminary investigation with a follow-up investigation, which is the secondary information gathering phase following the preliminary investigation and prior to the closing of the case (Swanson et al. 2006). Typically the larger the organization, the more elaborate the process is for determining whether or not to proceed with a follow-up. Some organizations use solvability factors to determine whether or not to pursue a case. Solvability factors use a system of weighting in which values are assigned to certain case characteristics. The total of the weights have to meet a certain numerical value, or threshold, in order for the case to be pursued. Examples of case characteristics that are considered include, but are not limited to, the naming of a suspect, the presence of physical evidence, whether or not there are any witnesses, and whether or not the crime fits an established modus operandi (MO) (Swanson et al. 2006).

As with the preliminary investigation, certain steps must be adhered to during the follow-up investigation: (1) further examination of physical evidence, (2) neighborhood and vehicle canvasses, (3) checking pertinent databases, and (4) interviewing victims and witnesses (Swanson ct al. 2006).

Further examination is typically performed at a crime lab unless the organization is large enough to have its own lab. Neighborhood and vehicle canvasses provide detectives the opportunity to gather information from people in proximity to where the event occurred. Oftentimes, citizens provide useful information to police without even knowing that the information is related to a crime. Numerous databases are available to police personnel for the follow-up investigation. The National Crime Information Center (NCIC), which is maintained by the Federal Bureau of Investigation, is one of the most comprehensive sources of information. The NCIC database includes information such as a stolen vehicle file, a stolen gun file, a wanted persons file, and a terrorist file.

Research

Oftentimes, research will be conducted to evaluate the effectiveness of certain procedures or practices in order to improve the work that is being evaluated. The most significant work examining the process of criminal investigation was the RAND study by Greenwood, Chaiken, and Petersilia (1975). This study found that 80% of serious crime cases were never solved, and of those that were solved, most of the cases were solved because of information gathered from witnesses and patrol officers rather than because of detectives or forensic science. Greenwood and colleagues also found that physical evidence was often collected at crime scenes, but most of it was never analyzed and it was rare for physical evidence to lead the police to a suspect.

Following the RAND study, Eck (1983) and the Police Executive Research Forum (PERF) came to similar conclusions. Eck examined robberies and burglaries in three jurisdictions. He found that follow-up work performed by detectives contributed to solving some cases. Use of

physical evidence, though, while readily available, was still limited. The detective activities that contributed the most to crime solving were searching for additional witnesses, contacting informants, talking to other officers, and using police records—not using physical evidence or forensic science. Consequently, it appears that gathering information from people appears to be more valuable than using physical evidence recovered at a crime scene.

Processing the Crime Scene

Processing the crime scene should follow routine protocol under most circumstances. Following a systematic process provides for the likelihood of the most thorough collection of evidence at the scene. Comprehensive crime scene processing consists of the following components: (1) developing a plan of action, (2) note taking, (3) crime scene search, (4) crime scene photography, (5) sketching the crime scene, and (6) collection of evidence (Fisher 2004).

The plan of action will vary from crime to crime, but it is important to do an initial assessment of the scene to ensure that all aspects of the crime are covered. Note taking should be done throughout the entire process. These notes may be used in court by both the prosecution and the defense. The crime scene search should cover the entire area within the crime scene boundaries, but also should take into consideration the areas surrounding the crime scene. Although it is ideal to control the entire crime scene, evidence might leave the crime scene as personnel go in and out of it. So, it is wise to search whatever is within reasonable proximity to the crime scene.

Photographing the crime scene with multiple views of relevant items is necessary. Photographs provide visuals of objects in their original states and also aid in demonstrating size, with the use of measuring tools that are also present in the photographs. Sketching the crime scene as it appears upon the first responder's arrival is imperative because objects or even people may be moved during the course of processing the scene. Typically a rough sketch is done at the crime scene and a final sketch, usually for use in court, is done after the scene is processed and sometimes with technological aids for computer-aided drawing.

Finally, collecting and packaging evidence must be done. This is tedious work that requires strict adherence to policies and procedures in order to not damage the evidence. Criminalistics, the science dealing with the interpretation of physical evidence, is used frequently when trying to solve crimes. Some form of physical evidence is always present at a crime scene whether it is visible to the naked eye or not. The examination of the crime scene for physical evidence often constitutes a major part of the tasks that must be performed by various personnel.

Physical Evidence

One of the most important considerations regarding physical evidence is that every crime scene has to be treated individually, with its own particular history and challenges. So those who collect evidence at the crime scene must have a very broad knowledge base when it comes to not only how to collect evidence, but also how evidence is processed at a crime scene (Saferstein 2004).

The examination of physical evidence is undertaken for two reasons: identification or comparison. Identification provides a substance's chemical or physical identity; comparison is the process through which it is determined whether or not two or more objects have a common origin (Saferstein 2004).

The following is a list of common types of physical evidence found at crime scenes.

Although this list is comprehensive, it is not exhaustive. Common physical evidence includes blood, semen and saliva, documents, drugs, explosives, fibers, fingerprints, firearms and ammunition, glass, hair, impressions, organs and physiological fluids, paint, petroleum products, plastic bags, plastic, rubber and other polymers, powder residues, serial numbers, soil and minerals, tool marks, vehicle lights, and wood and other vegetative matter. Those who collect evidence must be familiar with the many different types of processing and packaging associated with the previous types of evidence.

Digital Evidence

With current technological advances, crimes nowadays are often committed with the use of technology. In these cases, in addition to physical evidence as identified earlier, digital evidence is left at crime scenes, ready to be collected. Digital evidence is "any data stored or transmitted using a computer that supports or refutes a theory of how an offense occurred or that address critical elements of the offense such as intent or alibi" (Casey 2004, 12). Unlike traditional physical evidence, police are not as familiar with digital evidence and often overlook it at the crime scene, or sometimes are aware of its existence but are unable to process it due to insufficient knowledge and lack of training. As was with the case of DNA, police must become more familiar with digital evidence in order to successfully solve crimes of the future.

Conclusion

Criminal investigation is a complex and tedious process that requires a certain knowledge base, skills, and attention to detail. This process is perhaps the single most important action performed by police because it starts the action of a case in the entire criminal justice system. Criminal investigation varies from agency to agency based on numerous factors. Regardless of the variation, each case must be treated individually while simultaneously adhering to consistent standard policies and procedures in order to facilitate the solving of crimes and improvement of the quality of life in contemporary society.

KATHRYN E. SCARBOROUGH

See also **Case Screening and Case Management for Investigations; Clearance Rates and Criminal Investigations; Computer Forensics; Crime Scene Search and Evidence Collection; Detective Work/Culture; Detectives; Federal Bureau of Investigation; Forensic Investigations; Investigation Outcomes**

References and Further Reading

Casey, E. 2004. *Digital evidence and computer crime: Forensic science, computers and the Internet*. Boston: Elsevier Academic Press.

Fisher, B. A. J. 2004. *Techniques of crime scene investigation*. 7th ed. Boca Raton, FL: CRC Press.

Greenwood, P. W., J. M. Chaiken, and J. Petersilia. 1975. *The criminal investigation process*. Santa Monica, CA: RAND Corporation.

Osterberg, J. W., and R. H. Ward. 2004. *Criminal investigation: A method for reconstructing the past*. 4th ed. Cincinnati, OH: LexisNexis.

Saferstein, R. 2004. *Criminalistics: An introduction to forensic science*. 8th ed. Upper Saddle River, NJ: Pearson/Prentice-Hall.

Swanson, C. R., N. C. Chamelin, L. Territo, and R. W. Taylor. 2006. *Criminal investigation*. 9th ed. Boston: McGraw-Hill.

CRIMINOLOGY

Definition

The study of crime and criminals is the province of the field of criminology. As the late Edwin Sutherland wrote in his classic work *Principles of Criminology* (1939, 1): "Criminology is the body of knowledge regarding crime as a social phenomenon. It includes within its scope the processes of making laws, of breaking laws, and of reacting toward the breaking of laws." Although Sutherland's definition of criminology is commonly accepted and widely quoted, it is not quite accurate because it declares that the study of crime is solely focused on *social* factors. In fact, the study of crime by criminologists has encompassed several fields of knowledge that are not primarily social in nature.

It is also necessary to add that criminology has been generally defined as the *scientific* study of crime and criminals. Thus, not all those who comment on crime and criminals (such as forensic experts, lawyers, judges, and those who work in the criminal justice system) are criminologists. This distinction of a scientific approach to the subject is, however, not as simple as it seems. There are scholars who consider themselves criminologists and yet do not embrace a scientific method of study. Instead, they generally practice a methodology that studies crime and criminals from a dynamic, historical perspective. Further, these scholars usually focus on the "making of laws" and "reaction to the breaking of laws" rather than on the actual behavior of the lawbreaker.

As a final note on the definition of criminology, the terms *crime* and *criminal* are not as clear as they might seem. Much debate has surrounded what constitutes crime and criminals. Some have argued that the definition of crime is fully a legal matter; that is, if something is prohibited by law it is then and only then a crime. Others answer that because the laws are not really concerned with behavior itself, a legal definition does not provide a clear-cut focus for behavioral distinctions. The act of taking a life, for example, is not necessarily murder because states perform executions and nations go to war. They suggest that a *social* definition more tuned to deviance, in all of its forms, is a better approach. Yet other scholars point out that if a crime or deviant act is not noticed, then for all intents and purposes the act might as well not have occurred and the individual involved is not deemed criminal or deviant. Thus, the legal or social definitions of crime and criminals capture only those acts and persons to whom we react. This problem makes it quite difficult to talk of criminals and "noncriminals" and obscures the subject matter of the field.

Disciplinary Focus

Criminology is generally understood to be an offspring of the discipline of sociology. While this is arguably the case, such a statement slights both the history of criminology and the various disciplines that comprise the breadth of the field. At one time or another, the disciplines of philosophy, history, anthropology, psychology, psychiatry, medicine, biology, genetics, endocrinology, neurochemistry, political science, economics, social work, jurisprudence, geography, urban planning, architecture, and statistics have all played prominent roles in the development of criminological theory and research. Since the 1930s, however, sociology departments have been the primary source of academic training for most criminologists and there have been very few free-standing academic departments of criminology in the United States. Nevertheless, in spite of this sociological focus, it should be recognized that criminology is characterized by a relative integration of materials from several disciplines. The advent and rise, through the last four decades, of the multidisciplinary field of criminal justice has challenged sociology as the training ground for criminology.

Within the general discipline of criminology lie several interest areas. In their more general forms they are allied with such fields as philosophy of law, sociology

of law, sociology of deviance, penology/corrections, police science, administration, and demography. It is possible, then, to identify oneself as a criminologist and yet spend an entire career working within a relatively small area of the field, such as policing.

The Development of Criminology

Criminology, as a generic form of study relating to crime and criminals, can be traced far back into history. It is only recently, however, that a systematic study developed. Perhaps the best estimate of the "birth" of criminology lies with the rise of the European Classical Period in the eighteenth century. The real thrust of the period was not so much the study of the criminal, but the system of justice itself. With relatively capricious and arbitrary law in effect, the writers of the day criticized the system of justice and proposed massive reform. Referred to as the Classical School of criminology, the ideas of these reformers became the basis for today's criminal law and justice systems, and originated the modern concept of deterrence.

In the nineteenth century the study of crime and criminals began in earnest. Scholars began mapping the distribution of crimes in what were the first real studies using so-called social statistics. Other scholars engaged in the study of head shapes and produced some of the first scientific studies of criminals. The generally accepted beginning of scientific criminology, however, occurred in the 1870s with the work of an Italian physician, Cesare Lombroso.

Drawing on the positive science methods of the day (thus the generic name "the Positive School"), Lombroso's work on the relationship between physical features, personality, and criminals led to theories of a "born" criminal and spurred both genetic and hereditary studies. It was during this period that the term *criminology* itself came into popular usage. Followed by others, this work was extended into the arena of social and environmental factors. With the rise of sociology as a discipline in the 1890s, scientific criminology expanded under a number of fronts.

The first two decades of the twentieth century saw an assortment of criminological explanations rise, most notably the social varieties, the emotional/psychoanalytic, and the combined product of then-new intelligence testing and heredity research. By the 1920s, sociological studies were in full swing and the Sociology Department of the University of Chicago began to dominate criminology. The major explanations of criminality became tied to the transmission of values from one person to another, especially in areas that were culturally different and socially disorganized. In addition, statistical studies that placed crime and delinquency in particular areas of the city became popular.

By the 1940s criminology had become concerned with the effect of social conditions on people in general and began an examination of the relationship among social structure, social class, and crime. Commonly known as "structural functionalist" theories, their focus was on differing rates of criminality or delinquency among groups of people in society. This approach held sway until the 1960s, when criminology, along with the rest of society, became concerned with civil rights and liberal political issues. The focus shifted away from the criminal and toward the way in which the criminal justice system reacted to and processed people.

Following the federal government's crusade and "war" against crime during the late 1960s and early 1970s, which culminated with the creation of the Law Enforcement Assistance Administration (LEAA; now the National Institute of Justice), criminology became much more concerned with studying the criminal justice system itself. Under the aegis of LEAA funding, criminologists examined the operation of the police, the courts, and correctional systems with an eye to evaluating their effectiveness.

Where the criminal was concerned, explanations of behavior favored an assumption that people made rational choices and that crime was simply a rational choice decision.

Relationship between Criminology and Police Science

Along with the rise of academic criminology in the United States came the field of police science. Actually, police science departments preceded criminology departments in the colleges and universities. While often difficult to distinguish from each other, police science departments usually focus more on the technical aspects of policing: administration, management, crime analysis, and the "doing" of law enforcement. Criminology, when it deals with the police province, more often uses a "system in action" focus. Thus, criminological approaches to the problem of policing are apt to be sociological in nature and to focus on informal structures and relationships.

Contributions of Criminology to Police Work

Because it is difficult to separate early criminology from early police science, one may argue that some of the first scientific contributions could have come from either source. Nonetheless, a review of the first three decades of the *Journal of Criminal Law and Criminology* suggests that much of contemporary policing was developed from research of the early twentieth century. Articles include training, personnel selection, psychological testing, use of technology, fingerprinting, and so forth. Obviously, too, the various techniques of crime analysis have their origins in early work on crime statistics and geographic mapping.

During the 1960s and 1970s the criminological work of Egon Bittner, Albert

Reiss, Jerome Skolnick, and Peter Manning found its way into police training and community relations work. Similarly, the work of political scientist James Q. Wilson, who some view as a criminologist, had an effect on police administration practices. The products of civil disobedience research and victimization studies changed police selection processes and created an emphasis on education.

George Kelling and colleagues' Kansas City Preventive Patrol Experiment caused police departments nationwide to restructure their patrol procedures. Several response time studies suggested that immediate response to all citizen calls was not necessary and that response time was not as critical to making an arrest as was thought. Lawrence Sherman and Richard Berk's research on response to spousal assault calls (Minneapolis Domestic Violence Experiment) led to changes in response and arrest policies for disturbance calls. Studies by RAND Corporation and the Police Executive Research Foundation on detective work and crime solving resulted in patrol officers being given more responsibility in the investigative process and in new ways to screen cases. A criminological theory, the routine activities approach, precipitated a new analytical approach to locating crime, known as *hot spots*. Finally, Herman Goldstein's work on problem-oriented policing influenced many police departments to give up traditional policing for variations on community policing. This latter influence gained momentum from Wilson and Kelling's "broken-windows" essay and is now the dominant approach to policing.

In short, criminology is not focused on the police by any means, but it has had a profound effect, which ranges from the Classical School's reform of criminal justice operation and philosophy to the techniques and crime control styles in use by police departments today. Indeed, of all the components of today's criminal justice system, it is the police who rely most heavily on criminological research to make substantial changes in basic structure and methods of operating.

FRANK WILLIAMS

See also **Bittner, Egon; Broken-Windows Policing; Community-Oriented Policing: Effects and Impacts; Crime Analysis; Crime Mapping; Criminal Careers; Fingerprinting; Hot Spots; Kansas City Preventive Patrol Experiment; Minneapolis Domestic Violence Experiment; Police Reform: 1950–1970; Problem-Oriented Policing; Reiss, Albert J., Jr.; Vollmer, August; Wilson, James Q.**

References and Further Reading

Goldstein, Herman. 1977. *Policing a free society*. Cambridge, MA: Ballinger.
———. 1990. *Problem-oriented policing*. Philadelphia, PA: Temple University Press.
Kelling, George L., Tony Pate, Duane Dieckman, and Charles E. Brown. 1974. *The Kansas City Preventive Patrol Experiment: A summary report*. Washington, DC: The Police Foundation.
Manning, Peter K. 1977. *Police work: The social organization of policing*. Cambridge, MA: The MIT Press.
Martin, Susan E., and Lawrence W. Sherman. 1986. *Catching career criminals: The Washington, D.C. repeat offender project*. Washington, DC: The Police Foundation.
Pate, Tony, Amy Ferrara, Robert Bowers, and Jon Lorence. 1976. *Police response time: Its determinants and effects*. Washington, DC: The Police Foundation.
President's Commission on Law Enforcement and Administration of Justice. 1976. *Task force report: The police*. Washington, DC: U.S. Government Printing Office.
Reiss, Albert J., Jr. 1971. *The police and the public*. New Haven, CT: Yale University Press.
Sherman, Lawrence, and Richard Berk. 1984. *The Minneapolis Domestic Violence Experiment*. Washington, DC: The Police Foundation.
Skolnick, Jerome. 1966. *Justice without trial: Law enforcement in a democratic society*. New York: John Wiley and Sons.
Sutherland, Edwin H. 1939. *Principles of criminology*. Philadelphia, PA: Lippincott.
Wilson, James Q. 1968. *Varieties of police behavior: The management of law and order in eight communities*. Cambridge, MA: Harvard University Press.

Wilson, James W., and George L. Kelling. 1982. Broken windows: Police and neighborhood safety. *Atlantic Monthly* 249 (March): 29–38.

CRITICAL INCIDENTS

Until the mid-1990s most studies of stress in law enforcement focused exclusively on post-shooting trauma. Kureczka (1996) identified a number of other traumatic events, collectively known as *critical stress incidents*. His definition encompasses any event that has a stressful impact sufficient to overwhelm the usually effective coping skills of an individual. Among the events listed are a line-of-duty death or serious injury of a coworker, a police suicide, an officer-involved shooting in a combat situation, a life-threatening assault on an officer, a death or serious injury caused by an officer, an incident involving multiple deaths, a traumatic death of a child, a barricaded suspect/hostage situation, a highly profiled media event, or any other incident that appears critical or questionable.

According to Kureczka, the definition of a critical incident must remain fluid because what affects one officer might not affect another. This particular assumption is extremely valid for the expanded definition of critical incident stress (CIS), which will be presented in the next section of this article.

In 1980, the American Psychiatric Association formally recognized the existence of a disorder, similar to what was frequently referred by the military as "battle fatigue," that became known as post-traumatic stress disorder (PTSD). Symptoms of the disorder include intrusive recollections, excessive stress arousal, withdrawal, numbing, and depression. Pierson (1989) claims that critical stress affects up to 87% of all emergency service workers at least once in their careers. Critical incident stress manifests itself physically, cognitively, and emotionally.

Walker (1990) provides a slightly different definition of a critical incident and describes it as ". . . any crisis situation that causes emergency personnel, family members, or bystanders to respond with immediate or delayed stress-altered physical, mental, emotional, psychological, or social coping mechanisms." She recognizes the need for critical incident stress debriefing procedures, using Mitchell's (1983) process, which includes the elements of factual description of the event, emotional ventilation, and identification of stress response symptoms.

Stress Management Training as a Function of an Ill-Defined Problem

The approaches to the CIS, as defined earlier, are among the prevalent definitions of the problem, and the stress management training modules, devised by and for various law enforcement training academies, rely heavily on those definitions. Finn and Esselman Tomz (1997) published a thorough manual about developing law enforcement stress programs; however, this publication seems to "suffer" from a similar disease—the multiple and intangible definitions. The overreliance on fluid and elusive terms on one hand, and on an infinite host of traditional traumatic events (such as shootings, deaths, injuries) on the other, provides for a misguided approach to training.

The problems enveloped in the CIS are ill defined and inadequate. First, one cannot devise an effective training module if one cannot define—and define precisely—what it is that you would like your recruits to be trained in, against, for, and so on. Undoubtedly there are a number of good definitions, offered by the researchers; however, those definitions cover only a small percentage of the problematic issues involved in a critical stress incident. If, as the researchers claim, the definition must remain fluid, since what constitutes a critical incident for one officer might not affect another, then the only rational conclusion is that we must abandon stress management training since we are targeting only a very small percentage of our audience.

It is extremely difficult to identify with certain situations that are supposed to generate feelings and emotions, when one cannot generate those feelings and emotions if the situations presented are not relevant to one's emotional buildup. The theoretical depiction of the events, in a given training environment, no matter how realistic and potent, remains theoretical for a significant segment of the audience. The examples, mentioned by the researchers, such as the death of your partner, death of a child, traumatic media event, and so on, remain in the sphere of "unreal," since the training is offered to the recruits who still do not have a partner, most of them do not have a child, and they cannot possibly envision the power and influence of the media on their daily performance. When stress management training is offered only to the officers who are already on the force, then the new recruits enter the workforce exposed to the dangers of being affected by CIS and having no coping mechanism whatsoever, nor the ability to recognize the danger (Haberfeld 2002).

Redefining CIS: "It's a Cop Thing; You Wouldn't Understand"

The new, and expanded, definition of critical incident stress offered in this article is based on the assumption that police officers, en masse, join law enforcement agencies to serve and protect the public from the so-called bad guys. These sentiments were adequately defined by researchers. Crank (1998) believes that police see themselves as representatives of a higher morality embodied in a blend of American traditionalism, patriotism, and religion. According to Sykes (1986), as moral agents, police view themselves as guardians whose responsibility is not simply to make arrests but to roust out society's troublemakers.

They perceive themselves to be a superior class (Hunt and Magenau 1993), or as people on the side of angels, the sense of "us versus them" that develops between cops and the outside world forges a bond between cops whose strength is fabled (Bouza 1990). Police believe themselves to be a distinct occupational group, apart from society (Van Maanen 1974). This belief stems from their perception that their relationship with the public, with brass, and with the courts is less than friendly, sometimes adversarial. As outsiders, officers tend to develop a "we–them" attitude, in which the enemy of the police tends to shift from the criminal element to the general public (Sherman 1982).

"To serve and protect" entails, at least in an officer's mind, to deliver justice. In other words the "good guys" (the police officers) are here to enable "us" (members of the society) to live in a civilized manner, protected, or at least being under constitutional certainty entitled to the protection, from the "bad guys." This profound, sometimes taken for granted, subconscious belief enables "us" to function on a daily basis, without looking over our shoulders for predators and enemies. This sense of security is almost built into our civilized systems; we "know" that around us there is this invisible fence of protection provided by law enforcement officers. Of course, sometimes, we do experience some erosion in the sense of this built-in security, predominantly when we are involved in an incident, from which we emerge injured physically, psychologically, or both, since there was nobody out there to protect us, on an immediate basis. This sense of insecurity could be extremely traumatic, for the rest of the person's life, and frequently one cannot regain the "built-in" feeling of security.

Police officers, despite serving as protectors from evil and messengers of justice, no matter how symbolic, have the same "built-in" need for security and justice, even though they are supposed to provide these needs for themselves. They are fully prepared, at least mentally to do so;

however, very frequently, as opposed to a citizen, they face the reality of danger and injustice. From these assumptions, a new and expanded definition for CIS is presented as follows:

A critical stress incident can be generated by any situation /encounter with a citizen, peer, organization, or others, from which a police officer emerges with a feeling/perception that "justice has not been served" for him and or the others.

The sense of being on the "right side," on the "side of the angels," crumbles when the officer realizes that, although he or she is expected to provide justice for others (again in a symbolic way by serving and protecting the "good citizens" from the "bad ones"), there is no justice for him or her. The "built-in" mechanism that produces the faulty, but effective, sense of safety and security disintegrates, the sense of "fairness" disappears, leaving a residue of fear and cynicism, a proven formula for stress.

Future Recommendations

Crank (1998) asserts that danger is a poorly understood phenomenon of police work. Police officers believe that their work is dangerous, although they perceive it in a different way than the one depicted by the media. It is not necessarily the actual danger but rather the potential for danger. The reality is that anything could happen on the streets.

A counseling session, therapy, a peer support group, or any other environment that contains a potential "stigma" for being weak and fearful is usually and rather routinely met with complete resentment on the part of law enforcement officers. They spend their days and night preparing to deal with danger, to protect others and themselves; a sign of weakness (which can be associated with any reaching out for help—whether external or internal) will immediately decrease an officer's perceived

ability to face danger in a boisterous and forceful way. The officers who are willing to admit that they need the offered "support" inadvertently admit their weakness; they are stigmatized not so much in the eyes of the others but first and foremost in their own view and perception. This is the reason why counseling and support sessions, in the format offered today, are not as effective as they might have been had they been approached from a different angle.

Time must be set aside for all members of a given agency to participate in meetings during which individuals will take turns revealing their feelings of injustice. Time should be provided for inputs from other participants, as well as tips and tactics about how to deal with a given injustice in the future. Nobody should be excluded from those meetings, or excused for any reason. Even members who feel that they have nothing to share with others have to participate, the same way as in any other mandatory meeting or activity, regardless of the enthusiasm or willingness. Only by securing the attendance of the entire personnel of a given agency will it be possible to get rid of the stigma, the label, and provide for a productive and preventive forum. Mandatory, in-service stress management training for police personnel is no longer a luxury; it is a necessity in a law enforcement environment that is more stressful than ever.

M. R. HABERFELD

See also **Danger and Police Work; Psychological Fitness for Duty; Psychological Standards; Psychology and the Police; Stress and Police Work**

References and Further Reading

Bouza, A. 1990. *The police mystique: An insider's look at cops, crime, and the criminal justice system.* New York: Plenum Press.
Crank, J. P. 1998. *Understanding police culture.* Cincinnati, OH: Anderson Publishing Company.
Finn, P., and J. Esselman Tomz. 1997. *Developing a law enforcement stress program for officers*

and their families. March. Washington, DC: National Institute of Justice.

Haberfeld, M. R. 2002. *Critical issues in police training*. Upper Saddle River, NJ: Prentice-Hall.

Hunt, R. G., and J. M. Magenau. 1993. *Power and the police chief: An institutional and organizational analysis*. Newbury Park, CA: Sage.

Kureczka, A. W. 1996. Critical incident stress in law enforcement. *FBI Law Enforcement Bulletin* 65 (3): 10–16.

Maslow, A. H. 1954. *Motivation and personality*. New York: Harper and Brothers.

———. 1970. *Motivation and personality*. 2nd ed. New York: Harper and Brothers.

Mitchell, J. T. 1983. When disaster strikes . . . the critical incident stress debriefing process. *Journal of Emergency Medical Services* 8: 36–39.

Olson, D. T. 1998. Improving deadly force decision making. *FBI Law Enforcement Bulletin*, February, 4.

Pierson, T. 1989. Critical incident stress: A serious law enforcement problem. *The Police Chief*, February, 32–33.

Sherman, L. 1982. Learning police ethics. *Criminal Justice Ethics* 1: 10–19.

Sykes, G. W. 1986. Street justice: A moral defense of order maintenance policing. *Justice Quarterly* 3: 497–512.

Van Maanen, J. 1974. Working the street: A developmental view of police behavior. In *The potential for reform in criminal justice*, vol. 3, ed. H. Jacob, 83–84, 87, 100–10. Beverly Hill, CA: Sage.

Walker, G. 1990. Crisis care in critical incident debriefing. *Death Studies* 14: 121–33.

Sections of this entry quoted from Haberfeld, M. R., *Critical Issues in Police Training*, 1st ed., © 2003, pp. 32, 33, 35, 58, 59, 313, 122, 123, 124, 130. Reprinted by permission of Pearson Education, Inc., Upper Saddle River, NJ.

CROWD/RIOT CONTROL

Any large gathering of people presents special challenges to law enforcement agencies regardless of the type of crowd or its reasons for assembling. Problems associated with crowds range from minor acts of public disorder and vandalism to large-scale riots. Understanding the dynamics of crowds and crowd behaviors is essential in formulating and implementing appropriate law enforcement responses.

Explanations of Crowd Behavior

Traditional crowd theory was originated with the work of Gustave Le Bon (1885). He believed that individuals in a crowd lose their "conscious personality" and become enmeshed into the crowd mentality and behavior. When this occurs, crowds become irrational, impulsive, and destructive. Le Bon argued that there were three stages to crowd behavior: (1) when people lose their individuality and take on the crowd mentality (submergence), (2) when people seem to lose their ability to make sound decisions and begin to follow others in the crowd (contagion), and (3) when the crowd ideas and emotions become unruly and violent and then become group mentality (suggestion).

Self-categorization theory extends traditional crowd theory by attempting to understand the relationship of the individual to the crowd along with the relationship of the crowd to the individual (Turner 1987). When identifying oneself in a crowd, individuals do not lose their conscious personality; they simply shift their values and identity to that of the crowd. A person's social identity fluctuates depending of their social context. For instance, a person may think of themselves as a Boston Red Sox fan while at a baseball game, a Democrat while voting in the national election, and a Catholic while attending church. Self-categorization theorists argue that there is a shared collective understanding among individuals in a crowd that drives the crowd's behavior. Moreover, crowd behavior is greatly influenced by the actions of other groups or crowds with differing collective understandings (for example, the police or opposing political protest groups). A key aspect of understanding crowd behavior is to include the role and behaviors of other groups (Stott and Reicher 1998).

Mob sociology is similar to traditional crowd theory and is based on the belief that any crowd can become lawbreaking and violent (Schweingruber 2000). Crowds become mobs when a significant event occurs that causes "spiral stimulation" (Momboisse 1967). As the excitement or tension created by the significant event increases, individuals lose their self-consciousness and respond to the influences of the group. During this time strangers within the crowd develop camaraderie or shared bonds. The resulting unruly behavior is attributed to the crowd rather than the individual, who has temporarily lost the ability to make rational decisions and has become an anonymous component of the crowd.

Raymond Momboisse (1967) has identified four types of crowds: casual, conventional, expressive, and hostile or aggressive. The casual crowd is defined as a large gathering of people who happen to be at the same place and have no type of organization or purpose (for example, crowded city streets during rush hour). Conventional crowds have a specific purpose but are not organized (for example, spectators at sporting events or parades). Expressive crowds also have a specific purpose but are not organized. They differ from conventional crowds because expressive crowds are participating in an expressive behavior, such as singing or dancing. Hostile or aggressive crowds lack formal organization but have come together for a specific purpose (such as political protests). Hostile or aggressive crowds are the most unpredictable and raise the most concern to law enforcement agencies because the individuals in these crowds may already have destructive or unlawful intentions prior to joining the crowd.

Crowd Control Goals and Law Enforcement Responsibilities

As stated earlier, any crowd has the potential to become unruly and violent. Police responses to crowds and riots have been developed from components of the previously discussed theories. Regardless of the response, law enforcement agencies dealing with crowd situations need to consider several goals and responsibilities (California Commission on Peace Officer Standards and Training 2003).

There are four overarching goals and responsibilities of law enforcement agencies when creating and implementing crowd control policies and practices (these are not listed in any priority). First, it is very important that any response does not jeopardize the constitutional rights of anyone involved, especially individuals in the crowd. While it may be difficult for police officers to allow protesters to express controversial or inflammatory beliefs, these lawful activities are considered free speech and are protected by the First Amendment of the U.S. Constitution.

Second, another important goal and responsibility is to protect life and property. This goal involves not only maintaining the safety of innocent bystanders and their property, but also the lives of those individuals participating in the crowd. Police officers responding to aggressive crowds are placed in vicarious situations because they are being asked to protect the general citizenry from the rioters, and the rioters from other rioters, all while using the least amount of force possible in order to minimize police-induced injuries to the rioters.

Third, police agencies must develop crowd control strategies that include the protection of critical facilities in or near the crowded areas. These critical facilities include but are not limited to hospitals, power and telecommunication companies, police stations, chemical factories, and government buildings.

Fourth, crowd control policies and procedures must maximize police officer safety. This goal includes supplying responding police officers with the proper equipment, establishing clear procedures for engaging crowds and using force, maintaining constant communication with all officers involved, deploying a sufficient number of police officers to the area, and having adequate medical and emergency services personnel nearby.

Common Approaches to Crowd Control

Several different types of crowd control and crowd management strategies can be used depending on the type and behavior of the crowd. In any case, the best approach is one that is well thought out, includes various community stakeholder agencies and groups (for example, prosecutors, town elected officials, emergency services agencies, hospitals, social service agencies, hospitals, local businesses, and religious officials), and is proactive rather than reactive.

Proactive strategies seek to understand the type and behavior of the crowd, coordinate activities with community stakeholders, and establish procedures for when and how to engage the crowd, if necessary. Some of these activities include the following:

- Coordinate incident planning and preparation
- Host prearranged meetings with group organizers
- Coordinate preincident training
- Conduct preincident community education
- Designate public assembly areas when reasonable
- Separate opposing factions
- Provide effective means of communication
- Establish rules of conduct
- Define illegal activity
- Create a photo/video chronology of events
- Ensure on-the-scene incident command (California Commission on Peace Officer Standards and Training 2003)

Given the nature of crowds, it is not always possible to be proactive to individual events or have firm knowledge of crowd activity. Therefore, it is necessary to establish crowd control policies and procedures that are also reactive. The primary reactive activities are:

- Establishing contact with the crowd
- Implementing dispersal orders
- Using force

Police tactics have often been seen as the contributing factor in crowd aggression and hostility (Schweingruber 2000; Stott and Reicher 1998). Therefore, crowd control policies and procedures need to explicitly state who is to establish contact with the crowd and the format in which this contact will take place, how and when dispersal orders will be carried out, and, most importantly, when and what types of physical force will be used.

Physical force should be viewed as the last viable option but one that must be applied to minimize the likelihood of police officers needing to use deadly force. Types of nondeadly physical force vary but generally consist of nonlethal chemicals (for example, pepper spray, mace), electrical control devices (for example, tasers, stun guns), and less lethal options (for example, bean bags, rubber bullets). In using force for crowd control purposes, the legal standard is based on reasonableness of the force used. That is, consider whether the amount and type of force used reflect the overall circumstances presented to the law enforcement agency (California Commission on Peace Officer Standards and Training 2003).

The unpredictable nature of crowds raises serious concerns of law enforcement officials, elected officers, and the general public. However, these concerns can be greatly minimized with the creation of proactive crowd management strategies between law enforcement agencies and community stakeholders, the establishment of detailed police policies and procedures regarding crowd engagement and use of force, and extensive training of law enforcement personnel.

STEPHEN M. COX

See also **Codes of Ethics; Conflict Management; Critical Incidents; Emergency Management and Planning; Excessive Force; Liability and the Police; Nonlethal (or Less-than-Lethal) Weapons: History; Nonlethal Weapons: Empirical Evidence; Order Maintenance**

References and Further Reading

California Commission on Peace Officer Standards and Training. 2003. *Crowd management and civil disobedience guidelines.* Sacramento: California Commission on Peace Officer Standards and Training.

Le Bon, Gustave. 1885. *The crowd.* New York: Viking Press.

Momboisse, Raymond. 1967. *Riots, revolts, and insurrections.* Springfield, IL: Charles C Thomas.

Schweingruber, David. 2000. Mob sociology and escalated force: Sociology's contribution to repressive police tactics. *The Sociological Quarterly* 41: 371–89.

Stott, Clifford, and Stephen Reicher. 1998. Crowd action as intergroup process: Introducing the police perspective. *European Journal of Social Psychology* 28: 509–29.

Turner, J. C. 1987. Introducing the problem: Individual and group. In *Rediscovering the social group: A self categorization theory*, ed. Turner, 1–18. Oxford: Basic Blackwell.

CYNICISM, POLICE

Police cynicism is a widely acknowledged, little quantified property of the police subculture. It is a belief that the world—or at least the criminal justice system—operates according to rules that are opposite to its publicly articulated principles. The concept summarizes an ingrained belief that there is no altruism, everyone is out for themselves at the expense of anyone who gets in the way, and everyone lies—especially to the police.

It may be that police cynicism is little different than any other form of occupational cynicism. On the surface, there is an apparent relation between cynicism and "burnout." A cynical individual is jaded, seemingly no longer devoted to professional ideals, simply "going through the motions" and making judgments based on an impaired, narrow interpretation of the facts available. Citizens and policy makers have real concerns that cynical individuals will make erroneous decisions that are life changing for citizens.

Most police officers enter the work with idealism, however, and never really lose it. There is reason to understand police cynicism as a pressure valve, something that allows officers to deal with their frustrations through verbal outlets that are not connected to their official actions. Another recognizable widespread trait of police culture, "gallows humor," performs the same function, and is only a step away from the realm labeled "cynicism." Police speak vividly and directly, and their viewpoints are continuous sources of interest to social scientists and other observers, who may misinterpret the relationship between verbal expressions and any actions they may actually commit in their capacity as officers. In modern systematic observations of police behavior, scholars have noted a dissonance between the privately held views police officers express toward particular groups and the professional manner with which the officers deal with members of those groups in the field.

Contemporary police agencies are not monolithic, but staffed with individuals representing a wide range of backgrounds and outlooks. Cynicism in such a setting represents the voice of past experience at one level, giving words to alternative interpretations that otherwise might be suppressed as "politically incorrect." At the same time, the cynic's voice is but one of many, leavened by (and a leaven for) others with alternative views.

Early Research

The subject was first explored scientifically by Arthur Niederhoffer (1967), using an instrument called the F-scale to examine the tendency of police subculture to foster cynicism and authoritarianism. His observation that "[a]s the cynic becomes increasingly pessimistic and misanthropic, he finds it easier to reduce his commitment to the social system and its values" (Niederhoffer 1976, 208 [1967]) is in accord with the perceived alienation of the police from society. Cynicism is "learned as part of socialization into the police occupation," which Niederhoffer identifies as taking a full five years to complete (Niederhoffer 1976, 209 [1967]). Progressing from benign, affected pseudo-cynicism in the police academy through the resentment and hostility of "aggressive cynicism" around the ten-year mark of an officer's career, cynicism becomes a resigned acceptance of the foibles of humanity and the criminal justice system. Viewing cynicism as "a mode of adaptation to frustration" (209), Niederhoffer noted other dimensions of variance as well, including position and status within the organization, recognition and achievement factors, and socioeconomic background.

Cynicism is a hard-shelled attitude, one of the by-products of the conditions in which the police work. Much of Jerome Skolnick's concept of a "working personality" forged by constant potential danger, a craft based on suspicion, and imposed expectations of "efficiency" holds true today, despite considerable gains in raising education levels and diversifying the police force. Cynicism arises from similar factors of suspicion, conflicting demands, and unrealized expectations. The tension between stated goals and observed factual conditions—in public life and within police organizations themselves—produces a belief that "the job ain't on the level."

Police suspicions are based on more than just potential danger: To do police work is to deal constantly with liars. "Liars" are not just people who tell bald-faced untruths, but also people who shade the truth to their advantage, omit important facts that might work against them,

provide false rationales for questionable actions, deny accusations, and grudgingly admit only to things that the police can already prove. These behaviors are expected when dealing with the criminal element, but police officers encounter the same behaviors among respectable citizens. In response to a steady diet of lies, immersed in a web of half-truths and indeterminate evidence, the police develop an operational cynicism, the willing suspension of belief.

Police also endure periodic intrusion by moral entrepreneurs who demand that the police devote resources to a specific target of choice, then move on to other pursuits or different venues. Other sources of disdain are politicians, especially high-profile ones whose positions shift with the winds or the public opinion polls. The feet of clay of these reputed leaders, and the periodic scandals that erupt in other echelons of the justice system, are major sources of cynicism. In politicized departments, the phrase "the job ain't on the level" summarizes officers' disdain for processes where connections and influence take precedence over merit.

The view also extends to those higher up in the police hierarchy, those superiors who—in the view of the line officer and those who still think like line officers—have "forgotten what it's like to be a cop." An attitude heard in one form or another in many police agencies around the country denigrates the process of promotion: Line officers may scoff that a supervisor had been a failure when she or he was on patrol, and that's considered grounds for promotion in this department.

Consequences of Cynicism

One of the outgrowths of a cynical outlook is a tendency to look for the down side of everything: Well-connected crooks will go free despite overwhelming evidence, programs are launched only for political capital, funding will disappear, or whatever process is established will quickly be co-opted and manipulated to the selfish advantage of a few, sometimes even by the nominal targets the program is intended to suppress. Cynicism is one of the major obstacles to new initiatives or meaningful reform of unethical or outdated practices.

(In this regard, police cynicism also embodies a certain amount of irony: There are a number of cases in which the public has succeeded in establishing a police review board to deal with allegations of police misconduct, and the police and their supporters have rushed to try to "stack the deck" with police sympathizers, but this is not subject to the same police scrutiny as the motives of those who advocate for the board in the first place.)

In day-to-day encounters, visible cynicism can be damaging to police–community relations. If citizens detect subtle or overt indicators that the police do not believe them, they may interpret the cues as products of bias or contempt. Individual and public support of the police can be damaged, and valuable information withheld.

The Sources of Cynicism

Unrealistic expectations on the part of the police themselves may be a major contributor to the formation of cynicism. Despite vigorous attempts to transform the occupation, most of line-level police culture defines police work in terms of "law enforcement," the detection, apprehension, and successful prosecution of criminals. That worldview subscribes to an intuitive version of Herbert Packer's "crime control" model, an assembly-line process of justice wherein decision makers at each stage rely on the judgment of the decision maker at the prior stage. The police, as the gatekeepers to the criminal justice system, expect that supervisors, prosecutors, judges, and juries will accept and confirm the officer's original judgment. Whenever that

expectation is thwarted, cynicism attributes the result to incompetence or corruption.

Such a view ignores (sometimes willfully) the other realities of the system. Officers who recognize the primacy of the presumption of innocence, strength of evidence, how well the police "make their case" in the report, and the occasional triage of cases demanded by prosecutors' workloads are less vulnerable to developing cynical attitudes.

Similarly, police cynicism about new programs also has a firm grounding in reality, and a counterpart in the community outlook: "innovation fatigue." Officers who invested personally in new programs, as well as those who took a wait-and-see approach, have seen projects fail from lack of resources, misguided political interference, or personnel changes. A pattern of false starts creates an expectation that all programs will suffer the same fate; therefore, there is no reason to invest in them. The attitude is certainly not universal: New ideas and new programs invariably attract acolytes who see the possibility of doing something good. Nevertheless, cynicism impedes agencies' ability to obtain the buy-in needed to expand a good project beyond its original champions.

Complaints about the department's promotional policy may have a variety of sources. Not every negative assessment of an agency's practices is a product of cynicism alone. Despite advances in professionalization, politicized departments remain places where "who you know" determines career paths. There are departments that are poorly structured and managed, marked by cronyism or burdened with a legacy of past mistakes.

Not every officer necessarily appreciates the demands of the upper or special positions, and they may be unable to appreciate the judgments of those who make promotion decisions. Complaining officers may have an unrealistic view of their own knowledge, skills, and abilities (KSAs) for certain positions. Some foreign police prepare potential supervisors and others with training courses prior to the promotional process, including training achievements in their promotability assessment. American police tend to promote on standardized test scores (a marginal improvement over the seniority system that existed before the modern reform era), and occasionally on performance in the previous assignment. Critics of the process suggest that it is not suited to selecting the best candidates, or even those amenable to the subsequent training.

To dismiss all criticisms as the whining self-pity of no-hopers would be cynical in itself. Promotions and desired assignments are hard won in an occupation that has few of the private sector's reward opportunities. Disappointments and perceived injustices may be more keenly felt, and past errors magnified.

Additional Research

The utility of the F-scale has been challenged. Bayley and Mendelsohn's (1969, 15–18) personality scales indicated that Denver police, at least, were "absolutely average people" and found police recruits to be "somewhat more idealistic" than community members. That finding echoed McNamara's (1967, 195) conclusion that police recruits were less authoritative than the general public. These studies actually bolster Niederhoffer's argument that cynicism and authoritarianism are the result of the socialization process, not an inherent quality that a recruit brings to the work. Because they examined only the rookie year, however, they do not address the development of cynicism over time.

Regoli (1976, 237) criticized the F-scale used to measure cynicism, on the grounds that "cynicism is a multidimensional phenomenon" and "it is possible that police can be cynical toward one aspect of the

occupation and not others, or toward any combination of aspects simultaneously." Additional studies failed to validate the F-scale on measurement grounds, yielding only mixed results with modest effects and low reliability (Regoli et al. 1987; Langworthy 1987). Niederhoffer's original cohort has long since retired; recruitment, management, and the sociolegal environment have all changed. Current research has all but abandoned trying to validate cynicism as a concept, in favor of examining the multiple factors affecting police job satisfaction.

MICHAEL E. BUERGER

See also **Accountability; Danger and Police Work; Deviant Subcultures in Policing; Knapp Commission; Media Images of Policing; Personnel Selection; Police Solidarity; Theories of Policing**

References and Further Reading

Bayley, D., and H. Mendelsohn. 1969. *Minorities and the police.*

Langworthy, Robert H. 1987. Have we measured the concepts of police cynicism using Niederhoffer's cynicism index? Comment. *Justice Quarterly* 4 (2): 277–80.

McNamara, J. H. 1967. Uncertainties in police work: The relevance of police recruits' background and training. In *The police: Six sociological essays*, ed. D. J. Bordua, 207–15. New York: John Wiley.

Niederhoffer, Arthur. 1967. *Behind the shield: The police in urban society.* New York: Doubleday.

Packer, Herbert L. 1968. *The limits of the criminal sanction.* Stanford, CA: Stanford University Press.

Regoli, Robert. 1976. The effects of college education on the maintenance of police cynicism. *Journal of Police Science and Administration* 4 (3): 340–57.

Regoli, Robert M., John P. Crank, Robert G. Culbertson, and Eric D. Poole. 1987. Police professionalism and cynicism reconsidered: an assessment of measurement issues. *Justice Quarterly* 4 (2): 257–75.

Skolnick, Jerome H. 1967. *Justice without trial: Law enforcement in a democratic society.* New York: John Wiley & Sons.

DALLAS POLICE DEPARTMENT

The Dallas Police Department (DPD) is one of the nation's largest municipal police forces, employing more than 2,900 sworn officers and 550 civilians who collectively serve as the primary law enforcement agency for the city of Dallas, Texas (population 1,188,580). The department originated more than 120 years ago and is one of the oldest law enforcement agencies in the southwestern United States. The historical development of the DPD into one of the nation's largest and most comprehensive police agencies has paralleled the explosive population growth that has occurred within the Dallas region, and the department has incorporated many of the technological advances that have marked the history of the law enforcement industry in the United States during the course of the last century (Fogelson 1977).

History of the Department

The origins of formalized policing in the Dallas region can be traced to the formation of "vigilance committees" that were created to protect early settlers from skirmishes with the native population during the 1840s and through the incorporation of Dallas as a town in 1856 (Stowers 1983). Later in the nineteenth century, the city adopted a formal charter, and the Dallas Police Department came under the control of the Texas governor, who appointed the police chief through the police commissioner. The DPD instituted formal uniforms and mounted patrols during the 1880s. Similar to other newly formalized police agencies during this period, the department was understaffed and overworked (Stowers 1983). By the turn of the twentieth century, Dallas had grown from a frontier outpost into a city of 45,000 inhabitants, and the DPD had expanded to serve the increasing needs of a growing population. The department numbered forty-seven sworn officers by 1903, and it instituted its first motorized patrol units and had created a substation in the city's newly incorporated Oak Cliff section by the end of the decade (Stowers 1983).

The 1920s and 1930s has been described as a crucial period for law enforcement agencies in general and the Dallas Police Department in particular. Like many other police agencies during this period, the DPD struggled to control the growth of organized crime and other criminal elements during prohibition by utilizing many of the new technologies that had recently emerged. The department became increasingly "professionalized," with the creation of training classes for new recruits, a rudimentary radio dispatch system, and the creation of a detective section and a special traffic division to deal with the increasing presence of automobiles within the city (Fogelson 1977; Stowers 1983).

The creation of the Texas Department of Public Safety in 1932 led to a much greater exchange of information among Texas's various police agencies, as well as the expanded use of fingerprint files and ballistics tests in the investigation of criminal suspects (Stowers 1983). Although the advent of World War II worked to cut the number of sworn officers and resources of the Dallas Police Department during the 1940s, the postwar years saw a resumption in growth for the DPD. By the end of the 1950s, the department employed 966 sworn officers, who patrolled a city with a population of close to 700,000 (Stowers 1983).

The department was put into the national spotlight with the assassination of President John F. Kennedy on November 22, 1963, in Dallas. Kennedy's presidential motorcade was traveling through Dallas's central business district when he was hit in the head and the throat by gunman Lee Harvey Oswald. Texas Governor John Connelly was also wounded in the attack. As the nation watched, the Dallas Police Department served as the primary investigative agency in the death of the president. Members of the Dallas police force and federal agents recovered the rifle used in the attack from the Texas School Book Repository. Oswald was apprehended later that same day, but only before killing Dallas police patrolman J. D. Tippett. Oswald himself would be killed by gunman

Jack Ruby two days after the Kennedy assassination in a parking garage adjacent to Dallas Police headquarters.

The Modern Era

As the nation emerged from the 1960s and a period of civil unrest associated with rising violent crime rates, the struggle for civil rights, and the antiwar protests of the Vietnam war era, law enforcement executives began to recognize the need to improve the relationship between police agencies and members of the public and improve the quality of police services. Beginning in the 1970s, the Dallas Police Department initiated numerous tactics and programs associated with the nationwide movement toward community-oriented policing (COP). These initiatives include the creation of an Interactive Community Policing Coordination Unit designed to manage community crime prevention and educational programs. In addition, the department has strived to tailor police services to the local neighborhood level by creating nine "storefront" ministations to make the department and its officers more accessible to citizens. As a result of these and other community-based initiatives, the department has been generally regarded as one of the most progressive law enforcement agencies in the United States.

Despite these developments, the city and the department continue to struggle with a violent crime rate that has been among the nation's highest in recent years. The region's persistently high violent crime rate has been associated with many of the social problems that plague most urban areas in the United States, including shrinking municipal tax bases and resources, problems associated with the trade in illegal drugs, and rising levels of youth gang membership in the city. The department continues to recover from a highly publicized scandal involving the alleged false arrest of Mexican immigrants on drug possession charges in 2001.

These issues led to the appointment of a new chief and an administrative reorganization in 2004 designed to refocus the department toward community policing and addressing the city's chronic crime problems. As part of this shake-up, the department reorganized its patrol operations in order to become more responsive to local community problems. These initiatives were recently aided by the acquisition of a $15 million private grant to be used for the purchase of new equipment and to implement innovative strategies designed to reduce the city's persistently high violent crime rate. The grant is thought to be one of the largest ever awarded to a municipal police department by a private donor in the United States.

JOHN LIEDERBACH

References and Further Reading

Fogelson, R. 1977. *Big city police*. Cambridge, MA: Harvard University Press.

Stowers, C. 1983. *Partners in blue: The history of the Dallas Police Department*. Dallas, TX: Taylor Publishing.

DANGER AND POLICE WORK

It is common wisdom both within and outside law enforcement circles that policing is dangerous business. While workers in several other U.S. occupations (for example, timber cutting, commercial fishing, and construction) are killed on the job at rates higher than police officers, policing is one of the few lines of work that include an ever-present threat of being attacked and killed by fellow humans. In addition, the fact that officers are regularly involved in hazardous activities that do not involve criminal activity directed at them (for example, emergency driving, handling vehicle mishaps, search and rescue) means that police work involves an elevated risk of being accidentally injured or killed. The degree of danger officers face can be seen in records kept by the Federal Bureau of Investigation (FBI), which indicate that in the decade ending in 2003, 697 officers died in accidents, another 688 were murdered, and tens of thousands of officers suffered injuries in the 550,000-plus assaults that citizens perpetrated against U.S. cops (the FBI does not keep records on officers who are accidentally injured).

Despite the fact that officers are more likely to die in accidents than to be slain in the line of duty, popular conceptions (both within policing and among the general public) of the dangers inherent in police work focus on the threat from criminal attack. This outlook has profound consequences for how officers think about and carry out their duties, which, in turn, have profound consequences for public perceptions of the police. We provide an empirical sketch of key points related to the threat officers face from criminal attack and discuss how officers' perceptions about the dangers of being attacked shape both how police work is done and how the public views the police.

The aforementioned FBI data include a good deal of information about numerous aspects of assaults perpetrated against police officers. This information indicates that officers are killed and assaulted in a wide variety of circumstances and ways and that the circumstances and means of attack vary markedly between lethal and nonlethal assaults. While the vast majority of nonfatal assaults (some 80%) involved no weapon and fewer than 4% were perpetrated with firearms, more than 90% of the officers murdered (excluding the seventy-two officers who perished in the terrorist attacks on September 11, 2001) were killed with firearms. Fewer than 1% died in unarmed attacks.

Regarding the circumstances of attacks, the FBI data (again excluding the 9/11 deaths) indicate that the single most dangerous sort of activity during the past decade was attempting to take suspects into custody, with just above 30% of the officers killed trying to make arrests when they were murdered. Four other types of activities each accounted for about 16% of fatal attacks: traffic stops and pursuits, handling disturbance calls, investigating suspicious persons, and ambushes. Finally, about 3% of murdered officers were killed while handling or transporting prisoners, and 2% were killed while dealing with mentally deranged individuals.

The FBI data provide more precise information about three of the sorts of circumstances in which officers were murdered—disturbance calls, arrests, and ambushes—and a closer look discloses some interesting patterns. The FBI differentiates between family quarrels and all other types of disturbances. Fifty-seven of the ninety-eight officers slain during disturbance calls were handling family quarrels, which indicates that domestics are the most dangerous sort of disturbance that officers are called upon to deal with. The FBI divides arrest situations into those involving burglaries, robberies, drugs, and all other sorts of crimes. More officers, sixty four, were killed while attempting arrests for robbery than any other single crime. Drug-related arrests cost thirty-six officers their lives, twenty-three officers were murdered while trying to arrest burglars, and sixty-four others were killed while attempting to make arrests for crimes besides robbery, burglary, and drug offenses. Finally, the FBI identifies two different types of ambush: spontaneous and premeditated attacks. Sixty-three of the one hundred officers who were killed in ambushes died in unprovoked attacks, while the other thirty- seven were murdered by assailants who had a premeditated plan to kill them.

The patterns evident in the FBI data on attacks on officers show that some police tasks are more dangerous than others. They also indicate that officers are susceptible to being attacked in virtually any situation. These two features of the police environment have important implications for how officers approach their jobs.

Because the threat of assault is ever present, officers seek ways to mitigate the risks they face by employing a variety of tactics designed to lower the chances they will be hurt. This approach to the job begins in the academy when young officers are taught that they must always be vigilant in all their dealings with citizens, so as to not be taken by surprise. Recruits are also taught what the FBI statistics show about the relative danger of various law enforcement actions: that they are more likely to be killed when making arrests, dealing with disturbances, and so on, and that they should be especially cautious when called upon to handle these sorts of situations.

When rookie officers take to the streets upon completing their academy training, they learn additional lessons from veteran officers about how to protect themselves in their dealings with citizens. One of the things that young officers learn as they work with their more experienced peers is to look for signs that the people, situations, and places they encounter might pose a greater than normal risk to them. In this way then, officers are constantly sizing up the potential for danger as they go about their business. When officers perceive that a specific person, place, or situation involves heightened danger, they take steps to mitigate it. Such action might involve conducting a "pat down" search of a suspicious individual, parking some distance away from and observing a dwelling that is known as a drug den when dispatched to investigate a disturbance therein, or calling for assistance before getting involved in certain sorts of situations. Thus do perceptions of danger influence how officers behave in the field.

One of the first commentators to recognize how the threat of physical harm shapes the outlook and actions of police officers was Jerome Skolnick, who studied a group of California detectives in the early 1960s. Extrapolating from the observations he made, Skolnick asserted that officers' concerns about the danger inherent in their job was a key determinant of the occupational orientation—or "working personality"—of police officers. One danger-driven aspect of the police working personality, according to Skolnick, is the development of a perceptual shorthand for identifying those individuals who were most likely to attack them. Individuals who exhibit the signs of increased danger—"symbolic assailants" as Skolnick dubbed them—are more likely to be stopped and dealt with carefully.

Unfortunately, the cues that officers sometimes use to identify citizens as potentially dangerous (for example, dress and status characteristics) are features that are shared by many individuals who have no intention of harming the police. When officers view and treat innocent citizens as symbolic assailants, both the citizens in question and members of the public at large can take offense, which can lead to problems such as heightened racial tensions and damage to police–community relations. That innocent citizens can (and do) take offense at some of the practices that officers use to protect themselves from the very real dangers they face presents a challenge to our society. On the one hand, citizens have the right to expect to be free from government intrusion in the form of unreasonable police intervention in their lives. On the other, officers must be able to behave in ways that reduce their exposure to danger.

In recent years, many police agencies have taken steps to reduce the fallout potential posed by officers' protective posture. One component of this is to educate members of the public through means such as citizen police academies about the dangers officers face and how they are trained to deal with these dangers. Another is to provide officers with training that is designed to ensure that the self-protective steps they employ violate neither citizens' rights nor their sense of probity. Despite such actions, however, police officers do not always comport themselves at the highest level of police professionalism, and some members of the public take offense even when officers do their jobs 100%

correctly. As a consequence, the down side of the protective actions that officers take cannot be eliminated entirely from police work. Because of this, the danger that officers face on the streets of America will continue to be a source of tension between the police and the public.

DAVID KLINGER

See also **Civil Restraint in Policing; Conflict Management; Crime, Serious Violent; Cynicism, Police; "Good" Policing; Occupational Culture; Stress and Police Work**

References and Further Reading

Bureau of Labor Statistics. 2003. *Census of fatal occupational injuries.* http://stats.bls.gov/iif/oshcfoi1.htm.

Federal Bureau of Investigation. 2003. *Law enforcement officers killed and assaulted.* http://www.fbi.gov/ucr/killed/leoka03.pdf.

Schafer, Joseph A., and Elizabeth M. Bonello. 2001. The citizen police academy: measuring outcomes. *Police Quarterly* 4: 434–48.

Skolnick, Jerome. 1966. *Justice without trial.* New York: Wiley.

DEADLY FORCE

Significance

The use of deadly force by the police remains a national issue. The deadly force issue has found its way to the U.S. Supreme Court, and Court decisions have altered related laws across the nation. Ironically, criminal law itself could not resolve the emerging issues and problems revolving around the "fleeing felon statutes" in various state jurisdictions. Eventually, citizens sought civil damages under 42 U.S.C. 1983 and other landmark decisions that restructured criminal statutes, the police use of deadly force, and law enforcement protocols.

The following scenario was part of a larger pattern and problem unfolding across America prior to the 1983 Supreme Court case. An officer in one car calls, "Send some backup, a possible burglary in progress." Another officer following closely behind responds to the announcement, "Car 239 responding as backup." An unarmed suspect attempts to flee the scene by running away from the rear exit of the building. The first arriving officer warns the offender, "Halt, or I will shoot"; the burglar continues to run at an even faster pace. The officer fires his revolver and kills the fleeing suspect.

This kind of shooting occurred within the legal guidance across the United States. This was a legal shooting under the state "Fleeing Felon Statute." Eventually, the U.S. Supreme Court decisions modified the legalities of the use of deadly force and formulated new policies concerning constitutional standards. As a result, the justification and application of deadly force by law enforcement officers revolves around two basic components: (1) dangerousness and (2) necessity.

Supreme Court Intervention: Deadly Force

It would take years for the U.S. Supreme Court to address this kind of deadly force. It took the legal controversy surrounding the fatal police shooting of an unarmed teenage boy to precipitate the Court's consideration. A Tennessee police officer responded to the scene of a residential burglary and intercepted the juvenile who was fleeing from an unoccupied house at the time of the crime. The officer ordered the suspect to stop, then fired his weapon and killed the juvenile as he attempted to escape.

In this landmark 1985 case, *Tennessee v. Garner* (105 S. Ct. 1694), the U.S. Supreme Court reviewed the following facts of the case: While Garner (the fleeing juvenile) was crouched at the base of the fence, the officer called out "Police! Halt!"

and took a few steps toward him. Garner then began to climb over the fence. Convinced that if Garner made it over the fence, he would elude capture, the officer shot him. The responding ambulance crew quickly transported Garner to a local hospital, where he died on the operating table.

The Supreme Court ruled that laws authorizing the police use of deadly force against unarmed and nonviolent felony suspects violated the Fourth Amendment's guarantees against unreasonable seizure. The U.S. Supreme Court cited as unconstitutional the use of deadly force laws of numerous states. The thirty-one states and law enforcement agencies followed the legal guidance provided by the U.S. Supreme Court. Police departmental policies authorizing deadly force to apprehend nonviolent fleeing felony suspects changed significantly.

Before the Tennessee case, state law guided the use of deadly force by law enforcement officers. The Tennessee statute required police officers to warn a fleeing felon that they would shoot if they continued their flight. The officer could then use all necessary means to make an arrest. The main weakness of these state statutes centered on the fleeing felon sections. Many statutes stemmed from the old common law rule concerning fleeing felons. The law was antiquated and failed to meet contemporary standards.

Many law enforcement agencies developed guidelines that stated that "deadly force" may not be used unless (1) necessary to prevent escape and the officer has probable cause to believe that the fleeing felon poses significant threat of death or serious physical injury to officers or others, and, (2) if practical and feasible, a warning should precede using deadly force. However, firing verbal warning shots is a controversial practice and can lead to unintended consequences. Many law enforcement agencies are concerned about injuries that may result from stray bullets.

Law enforcement agencies responded to these concerns by implementing new policies and protocols to address the use of deadly force. As a consequence, the use of deadly force was restricted to instances in which the offender had (1) the ability and capacity to kill the officer or another, (2) the ability and capacity to cause great bodily harm, and (3) the opportunity to cause great bodily harm to the officer or another. Additionally, the threat must be imminent, and the preclusion factor requires the exhaustion of other avenues of action. Deadly force against violent fleeing felons who do not meet these requirements are not within the protection of the law, and the emphasis is on using the least amount of force necessary to stop the aggressor's violence.

Supreme Court Intervention: Nondeadly Force

Officers must be able to distinguish between nondeadly and deadly force. In police street confrontations this is no easy task, especially when dealing with intense emotional situations. Generally, nondeadly force requires nondeadly strategies; for example, when a citizen engages in passive resistance during a demonstration, generally two officers simply restrain and handcuff the individual and place him or her in the police van to be transported to jail.

Active resistance requires the appropriate level of force for the situation; for example, if a suspect tears the badge off the officer's uniform, the officer may respond with a nondeadly physical response that requires restraining techniques. If the resistance continues to escalate, the officer's response may include the use of mace, a nightstick, or other nondeadly strategies. However, after the subject is subdued, a nondeadly or deadly force response would not be appropriate. Once resistance ceases and the subject is handcuffed, the use of additional force would be illegal.

A scenario involving nondeadly force may escalate to deadly force under certain circumstances; for example, an offender may attempt to seize the arresting officer's weapon during a struggle. What appears to be a nonviolent situation can quickly turn into a deadly force incident. Consider, for example, the following scenario: An off-duty officer responds to a scene of disorderly conduct, identifies himself as a police officer, and attempts to detain one of the suspects. The officer enters into a physical struggle with the suspect, now the arrestee, who soon overpowers and begins to strangle the officer. The officer starts to lose consciousness and fears that he may lose his weapon and die in the struggle. In the twilight of semiconscious, the officer reaches for his revolver, shoots the resisting subject, who falls over and dies.

As noted above, deadly force is appropriate if the officer has probable cause to believe that the suspect poses significant threat of death or serious physical injury to officers or others. In addition, the severity of the crime, uncertain conditions or rapidly evolving circumstances, and a suspect actively resisting arrest may enter into the "objective reasonableness" standard. In other words, the Court views the situation from the officer's perspective, evaluating the objective reasonableness of the officer's response to the unfolding events.

Directly related to the police deadly force issue is nondeadly force, occasionally interconnected and evolving from the same scenario. In 1989, the issue of nondeadly force emerged in *Graham v. Connor,* 490 U.S. 386. The U.S. Supreme Court established the standard of "objective reasonableness" where the use of deadly force applied by an officer could be evaluated by the "reasonableness at the moment." The Court ruled that the evaluation of the decision to use force should be judged from the perspective of a reasonable officer on the scene, not with the benefit of retrospective analysis.

The following example from the case illustrates the objective reasonableness standard. The police officer focused on what he believed to be suspicious behavior.

The officer conducted an investigative stop of the vehicle operated by Graham's friend. During the stop, a physical altercation developed between the officer and Graham. The officer checked with the employees of a store where Graham had been prior to the stop, discovered that there was no criminal activity, and released Graham. However, during the investigative stop, Graham sustained injuries and filed suit, 42 U.S.C. 1983. Graham's argument alleged that excessive force was applied maliciously and sadistically to cause harm. The U.S. Supreme Court applied the *Johnson v. Glick* test, 481 F.2nd 1028 to his case evidence and did not find that the force applied was constitutionally excessive. The objective reasonableness test justified the officer's vehicle stop and the questioning of its occupants.

Event Phase: Deadly Force

While the media and public focus on victims of police shootings, comparatively less concern is shown for police victims of deadly force. The exception was the televised Los Angles bank robbery shootout in which suspects fired high-powered automatic weapons and wore bulletproof vests. While most shootings of police officers are not as dramatic or highly publicized as this event, approximately fifty officers lose their lives in deadly force confrontations every year.

The public becomes outraged when a citizen encounters physical abuse from a police officer. The officer is in a position of trust and the criticism is justified and fair. However, a considerable amount of non-deadly force is directed at police officers, though the same level of outrage is rarely forthcoming.

Wearing a police uniform and making arrests increase an officer's risk for becoming a victim. Officers may become complacent (less vigilant) and expose their weapon. Criminals may seize an officer's weapon, without warning, and escape by shooting the officer or threatening to use violence. Unfortunately, such incidents often turn deadly for the officer. Appropriate training and recognizing identifiable behaviors enhance survival skills and help officers anticipate unfortunate dangerous field experiences.

Postevent Phase: Deadly Force

Even if an officer survives a deadly assault and prevails over an attacker, there often remains a price to be paid after the shooting incident. The emotional response of an officer who uses deadly force may secondarily impact the officer psychologically. Posttraumatic stress disorder (PTSD) may follow the event phase, and the emotional aftermath may create problems for the officer, the officer's family, and the law enforcement agency.

The officer may experience a heightened sense of danger, vulnerability, fear, and anxiety about future encounters. PTSD has been linked to combat and violent personal assault. Aftereffects of such traumatic events can be experienced in various ways. Most often, the officer suffering from PTSD has recurring and intrusive recollections of the shooting event.

An officer who has been at either end of a shooting may develop a pattern of employment problems that did not exist before the incident, exhibit signs of the trauma and noticeable behaviors that require professional intervention, and experience nightmares, flashbacks, and disruptive sleep patterns.

PTSD requires early proactive intervention to avoid additional violence and post-trauma-related problems. Officers need appropriate information and referral services. Psychological defenses may develop in post-shooting incidents. Counseling and the retraining of these officers may assist in the adjustment process.

Research: Use of Force

Gathering and analyzing use-of-force statistics and related data in the United States remains problematic; however, the methodology has been improving in recent years. Additional research would prove helpful in identifying how often use-of-force incidents, as well as possible legal or policy transgressions, occur. According to the National Institute of Justice (NIJ) and the Bureau of Justice Statistics (BJS) in *Use-of-Force by Police: Overview National and Local Data,* research is critically needed to determine the reliability and validity of use-of-force data. The weakness of the current data is that police agencies often self-report. The main argument against police self-reporting is that filtering and bias may cause underreporting. According to NIJ and BJS (1999), 2.1% of the 7,512 arrests studied involved the use of weapons by the police.

The research moderately supports that the use of force occurs more frequently when police officers encounter suspects who are under the influence of alcohol or drugs or individuals with mental health problems. Generally, the police use of force results while officers are attempting to make arrests and the suspects resist. The moment of arrest continues to be a hazardous time for citizens and officers. According to NIJ, BJS, and Kenneth Adams, the use of force appears to be unrelated to an officer's age, gender, and ethnicity. However, other studies indicate that female officers tend to use less force.

The research on the type of officer who might be prone to use excessive force is beginning to focus on the problem officer and early warning signs. According to an NIJ 2001 research report, a small percentage of police officers constitute high-risk employees. Early warning signs might identify future police officers with problematic behaviors. According to police administrators, this population constitutes less than 10% of the officer corps, yet the group causes 90% of the problems. According to the research, these police officers are easily identified by supervisors, citizens, and peers as being conflict oriented.

Problematic police officers have a high grievance reporting level and discipline-oriented behaviors. The application of early warning systems assists law enforcement agencies in identification, monitoring, and intervention strategies. Some of the performance indicators of problematic behaviors include citizen complaints, use-of-force complaints, resisting arrest incidents, high-speed pursuits, and firearms discharge reports. In addition, civil litigation and civil rights violations are other strong indicators.

The predictive ability of the present warning tools has problems with reliability and validity. The danger is that contrary to what the data indicate, individual officers may be correct concerning their behaviors, especially if the officers are working in high-profile crime areas, with high-risk working conditions, or in socioeconomically and culturally deprived neighborhoods. Moreover, the leadership in the agency may create a climate that produces hostile and aggressive behaviors.

A hostile work environment is not conducive to promoting an ethical climate and effective social bonds between officers and the communities they serve. The individual is part of a larger police culture; the starting point is with the organizational climate and its leadership. However, mentoring, counseling, and timely interventions can provide some of the solutions.

Use-of-Force Training

Mastery of diverse use-of-force situations is the result of excellent training. Excellent training increases an officer's level of performance and confidence. Officers who control their emotions and practice critical tasks have a high probability of success. Moreover, they will increase the probability of survival in deadly confrontations. Realistic deadly force training saves lives, citizens, and officers.

The department's use-of-force training philosophy provides the foundation for positive outcomes. The value of human life is of extreme importance in our society. Therefore, life is to be respected and protected by the police and serves as the foundation of law enforcement service. The philosophy of minimum force emphasizes the safety of citizens. Officer training serves as the basis for effective action. Teaching effective and ethical decision making improves clarity of thought concerning the use of force.

The Federal Law Enforcement Training Center (FLETC) has developed a use-of-force model. The FLECT use-of-force continuum describes a variety of circumstances relating to the ethical application of the use of nondeadly and deadly force. The FLECT learning-organizing center serves as a frame of reference, emphasis, and focal point for conceptualizing the application of force and describes the various levels of force applied to basic scenarios.

Police learning occurs most efficiently and effectively when the officer has the opportunity to engage in active learning behaviors. The learning simulation or practical scenario is the best format. The ultimate test for judging a learning experience demands evidence that the learning opportunity or instructional invention is actually creating the desired responses. All learning experiences should evoke desired change in the learner. If a given learning experience does not create the expected or desired outcomes, then the experience is considered invalid.

The FBI Hogan's Alley deadly force shooting range is an excellent example of simulated shooting scenarios. This active learning simulation approximates field situations. This shooting range applies tactical training and is located at the FBI Training Academy. The simulated scenario includes the actors, such as terrorist bank robbers and drug dealers, and innocent bystanders in realistic town locations. Simulated gunfights add to the realism and lessons learned. In short, most officers learn best by doing, not by listening to long lectures that do not meet diverse learning needs.

Law enforcement agencies must train and execute well thought out training plans to achieve mission effectiveness. The element of surprise in certain situations will favor the offender. An officer may face superior firepower or encounter multiple criminals. For these officers, even excellent training may not help them survive. There will be inevitable casualities in the war against crime. However, excellent and realistic training may save many lives.

In summary, a significant part of the solution remains the psychology of violence and performance under stress. Training police officers to perform in stressful situations is a difficult task. Law enforcement officers must perform efficiently in situations that are a matter of life and death.

What does it take to survive a deadly confrontation or avoid civilian casualties? An officer must have the discipline and ability to stay focused in the moment and must anticipate the emotional response of citizens. Finally, excellent training is important, but the quality of the person behind the badge remains the deciding factor when faced with deadly force scenarios.

THOMAS E. BAKER

See also **Accidental Deaths/Assaults against Police and Murder of Police Officers; Arrest Powers of the Polices; Civil Restraint in Policing; Complaints against Police; Excessive Force; Liability and Use of Force; Post-Shooting Review**

References and Further Reading

Alpert, Geoffrey P., and Lorie A. Fridell. 1992. *Police vehicles and firearms: Instruments of deadly force.* Long Grove, IL: Waveland Press.

Blum, Lawrence W. 2000. *Force under pressure: How cops live and why they die.* New York: Lantern Books.

Klinger, David. 2004. *Into the kill zone: A cop's eye view of deadly force.* San Francisco: Jossey-Bass.

National Institute of Justice and Bureau of Justice Statistics. 1999. *Use of force by police: Overview of national and local data.* Research report, October. Washington, DC: U.S. Government Printing Office.

Walker, Samuel, Geoffrey P. Alpert, and Dennis J. Kenney. 2001. *Early warning systems: Responding to the problem police officer.* Research in Brief Series. Washington, DC: U.S. Department of Justice, Office of Justice Programs, National Institute of Justice.

DEPARTMENT OF HOMELAND SECURITY

Background

On November 25, 2002, President George W. Bush signed the Homeland Security Act of 2002 into law. The act restructured and strengthened the executive branch of the federal government to better meet the threat to the United States posed by terrorism. In establishing the new Department of Homeland Security, the act, for the first time, created a federal department whose primary mission is to help prevent, protect against, and respond to acts of terrorism on American soil. Some historians believe that this act is the most significant law to be passed by Congress since the approval of the National Security Act in 1947, which combined the War and Navy departments into a single Department of Defense headed by a civilian secretary appointed by the president, established the Central Intelligence Agency to coordinate all foreign intelligence activities, and created the National Security Council in the White House to coordinate all foreign and defense policy initiatives. While the National Security Act was necessary to face the Cold War, the Homeland Security Act was required for America's new war on terrorism.

The New Department

The new Department of Homeland Security is supposed to make Americans safer because the nation now has one department whose primary mission is to protect the nation. More security officers are in the field working to stop terrorists. The goals and responsibilities of the department are as follows:

- Securing borders, the transportation sector, ports, and critical infrastructure
- Synthesizing and analyzing homeland security intelligence from multiple sources
- Coordinating communications with state and local governments, private industry, and the American people about threats and preparedness
- Coordinating efforts to protect the American people against bioterrorism and other weapons of mass destruction
- Helping train and equip first responders
- Managing federal emergency response activities

In order to achieve these goals, this department was organized into four divisions: Border and Transportation Security; Emergency Preparedness and Response; Chemical, Biological, Radiological, and Nuclear Countermeasures; and Information Analysis and Infrastructure Protection. Other key components include increased federal, state, local government, and private sector coordination; the Secret Service was moved to this new department; and the White House Office of Homeland Security and the Homeland Security Council are to continue to advise the president. Although not directly related to homeland security, the Federal Emergency Management Agency (FEMA) and the U.S. Coast Guard were also transferred to this new department.

A Slow Start

Congress approved the new department in November 2002, and some critics felt that the federal government took too much time to create a national mechanism for responding to possible future terrorist attacks, and some feel that it is still stumbling over efforts to better coordinate preventive measures at the federal level. For example, it was not until October 2003 that the new secretary of this department, Tom Ridge, approved the Initial National Response Plan (INRP), an interim plan designed to help develop a unified approach to domestic incident management across the United States. The INRP represents a significant first step toward the overall goal of integrating the current family of federal domestic prevention, preparedness, response, and recovery plans into a single all-hazards national response plan.

The initial plan was developed in conjunction with state and local governments, law enforcement officials, fire and emergency management agencies, tribal associations, the private sector, and other nongovernmental organizations. The objective of the INRP was for the United States to be better prepared by integrating emergency response plans that cover terrorist attacks, major disasters, and other emergencies. This led to the development of the National Incident Management System (NIMS). NIMS serves as the model for all state and local governments in America for responding to significant emergency incidents, including acts of terrorism.

The Homeland Security Act also designated the secretary of the Department of Homeland Security as the principal federal official for domestic incident management. The secretary is responsible for coordinating federal operations to prepare for and respond to terrorist attacks and for coordinating the use of the federal government's resources during recovery from terrorist attacks, major disasters, and other emergencies. For this action to take place, one of four conditions must apply:

- A federal department or agency acting under its own authority has requested the assistance of the secretary of the Department of Homeland Security.
- The resources of state and local authorities have been overwhelmed, and the appropriate state and local authorities have requested federal assistance.
- More than one federal department or agency has become substantially involved in responding to the incident.
- The secretary of the Department of Homeland Security has been directed to assume responsibility for managing the domestic incident by the president of the United States.

The USA Patriot Act

Congress passed the USA Patriot Act in response to the terrorist attacks of September 11, 2001. The act gives federal officials greater authority to track and intercept communications, both for law enforcement and foreign intelligence gathering purposes. It vests the secretary of the Treasury with regulatory powers to combat corruption of U.S. financial institutions for foreign money laundering purposes. It also seeks to further close U.S. borders to foreign terrorists and to detain and remove those within U.S. borders.

It also creates new crimes, new penalties, and new procedural efficiencies for use against domestic and international terrorists. Although it is not without safeguards, critics contend some of its provisions go too far. Although it grants many of the enhancements sought by the Department of Justice, others are concerned that it does not go far enough. The future will require finding and maintaining a tight balance between effectively "cracking down" on terrorism and doing so at the expense of the civil liberties of Americans in all walks of life.

Local Officials Are First Responders

Federal and state officials have made substantial progress in the field of homeland security since September 2001. City and county managers and locally elected officials, however, are at the forefront of this movement. After all, local governments were the first responders to the terrorist acts of September 11. While national and state leadership are essential, the future of security will depend on preparedness initiatives at the local level. Fire, public health, and law enforcement officials have developed new emergency management practices, applied new computer software to the field, and begun to initiate new security measures and safeguards to protect citizens. All of these new measures fall into one or more of the four phases of emergency management: *mitigation, preparedness, response*, and *recovery*.

The national government has responded with a new agency, the first in a half-century, the Department of Homeland Security. As this department evolves, coordination among federal agencies in the area of homeland security will improve. Equally important, federal departments are initiating training programs to educate public safety personnel in the many facets of homeland security. In only a few years, state law enforcement agencies have standardized many of their practices in emergency management for those cities and counties within their respective boundaries. Some of the more important state-of-the-art practices and major

homeland and police service trends are as follows:

Mitigation
New federal assistance programs
U.S. Homeland Security advisory system
Threat analysis and assessment practices
Measures to improve building safety
Designation of pedestrian and vehicular evacuation routes.

Preparedness
New emergency plans and possible hazards
Mutual aid agreements
Simulated disaster exercises
Training for police personnel
Use of the National Incident Management System.

Response
New early-warning public notification system
Evacuation procedures and practices
Geographic information systems
Public information and the news media.

Recovery
Crime scene security
Crisis counseling for police personnel
Management of fatalities
Restoration of public infrastructure and open spaces.

Some acronyms commonly used in homeland security and by the police are as follows:

ARC	American Red Cross
ATAC	Anti-Terrorism Advisory Council
ATF	Bureau of Alcohol, Tobacco, and Firearms
CBRN	Chemical, Biological, Radiological, Nuclear
CB-RRT	Chemical and Biological Rapid Response Team
CBW	Chemical and Biological Weapons
CCP	Civilian Corps Program

CISM	Critical Incident Stress Management
DHS	Department of Homeland Security
DMAT	Disaster Medical Assistance Team
DMORT	Disaster Mortuary Response Team
DOJ	Department of Justice
EOP	Emergency Operations Plan
ERRT	Emergency Rapid Response Team
FEMA	Federal Emergency Management Agency
FRERP	Federal Radiological Emergency Response Plan
IRZ	Immediate Response Zone
LETPP	Law Enforcement Terrorism Prevention Program
NAS	National Advisory System
NDPO	National Disaster Preparedness Office
NECC	National Emergency Coordination Center
NIMS	National Incident Management System
PDA	Preliminary Damage Assessment
PTE	Potential Threat Elements
RAP	Radiation Assistance Program
RERT	Radiological Emergency Response Team
SRT	Search Response Team
WMD	Weapons of Mass Destruction

Some Internet resources for homeland security and police services are

American Red Cross (http://www.redcross.org)

Centers for Disease Control and Prevention (http://www.cdc.gov)

Central Intelligence Agency (http://www.odci.gov/terrorism)

Counter-terrorism Office (State Dept.) (http://www.state.gov/s/ct)

Domestic Terrorism Research Center (http://www.ksg.harvard.edu/terrorism)

Department of Homeland Security (http://www.dhs.gov)

Emergency Management Institute (FEMA) (http://training.fema.gov/emiweb)

Federal Bureau of Investigation (http://www.fbi.gov)

Federal Emergency Management Agency (http://www.fema.gov)

International City/County Management Association (http://www.icma.org)

National League of Cities (http://www.nlc.org)

National Association of Counties (http://www.naco.org)

National Infrastructure Protection Center (http://www.nipc.gov)

Office of Domestic Preparedness (Dept. of Justice) (http://osldps.ncjrs.org)

U.S. Conference of Mayors (http://www.usmayors.org)

U.S. Department of Health and Human Services (http://www.hhs.gov)

U.S. Department of Justice (http://www.usdoj.gov)

Local public safety and health officials throughout the nation should be aware of these evolving practices, because the public expects those local officials to take the necessary steps to safeguard their life and property during times of disaster.

Against this backdrop of increased security and safeguards comes the loss of personal freedom that Americans commonly take for granted. Many Americans feel their world has changed since the terrorist attack on September 11, 2001. In a less secure world, Americans are reexamining the delicate balance between protecting the public safety and preserving individual civil liberties. Also, government officials are revisiting policies that some consider intrusive or discriminatory. The public's attention has shifted, at least temporarily, to several public policy debates, including racial profiling, Internet privacy, and the rights of noncitizens. These sensitive issues will be sorted out in state capitols, by the federal government, and in the court systems, as America's security practices continue to evolve.

Conclusion

After the terrorist attacks on September 11, 2001, the federal government coined the phrase "homeland security" to describe the actions of all levels of government to protect citizens from future actions of this type. While the emergency management practices that evolve during the coming years will be different from those of the past, the goal of these initiatives will still be the same, that is, to minimize the loss of life and property when such acts occur. FEMA's NIMS approach to emergency management enables public safety officials to prepare plans that encompass all potential hazards, including man-made ones such as terrorist acts.

Law enforcement and fire officials are taking the dangers posed by the threat of a possible terrorist attack seriously and have implemented many state-of-the-art homeland security practices since 2001. New practices continue to be developed and tested by public safety officials at all levels of government. The trends examined above are at the promising forefront of this new field. Police and fire personnel, along with health and public works officials, are now working together in preparing homeland security plans in safeguard the United States from a future terrorist attack.

As future homeland security practices emerge, the challenge will be to maintain democracy and accountability while attempting to protect the nation and its citizens from terrorist acts. The challenge is to develop a framework in which liberty and order can coexist while public officials take steps to increase domestic security. In the less secure world we all live in, Americans are beginning to reexamine that fine line between protecting the public safety and maintaining individual civil liberties. Evolving homeland security practices should fit the nation's long-standing philosophy of maintaining security while at the same time protecting the rights of citizens from the overzealous actions of their government.

ROGER L. KEMP

See also **Emergency Management and Planning; Homeland Security and Law Enforcement; PATRIOT Acts I and II; Terrorism: Domestic; Terrorism: International**

References and Further Reading

Allbaugh, Joe M. 2001. *Terrorism preparedness and response* Brochure L255, March. Washington, DC: Federal Emergency Management Agency.

Clewett, Laurie. 2001. Protecting freedom: Public safety vs. civil liberty. *State Government News*. October.

Grano, Joseph J. 2003. *Statewide template initiative*. March. Washington, DC: President's Homeland Security Advisory Council.

Howitt, Arnold M., and Robyn L. Pangi, eds. 2003. *Countering terrorism: Dimensions of preparedness*, Cambridge, MA: The MIT Press.

Jacobs, Lee Anne. 2001. What Makes a Terrorist? *State Government News*, October.

Kayyem, Juliette N., and Robyn L. Pangi, eds. 2003. *First to arrive: State and local responses to terrorism*. Cambridge, MA: The MIT Press.

Kemp, Roger L., ed. 2003. *Homeland security: Best practices for local government*. Washington, DC: International City/County Management Association.

Larsen, Randall, and Dave McIntyre. 2004. Dissecting the 9/11 Commission Report. *Homeland Security*, 1 (4).

Mariani, Michele. 2002. Exposure to risk. *Governing*, 15 (8).

Mayer, Harry. 2003. Homeland security: Collaborative planning in readiness enhancement. *Public Management* 85 (5).

McEntire, David A., Robie Jack Robinson, and Richard T. Weber. 2001. Managing the threat of terrorism. *IQ Report* 33 (12).

Morial, Marc H. 2001. *A National Action Plan for Safety and Security in America's Cities*. December. Washington, DC: U.S. Conference of Mayors.

Murphy, Gerard R., and Martha R. Plotkin. 2003. *Protecting your community from terrorism: Strategies for local law enforcement*. Vol. 1, March. Washington, DC: Police Executive Research Forum.

Nicholson, John. 2001. Collapse: World Trade Center aftermath. *NFPA Journal* 95 (6).

Raymong, Gary, and Rick Wimberly. 2002. Obtaining and using high-speed notification technology in a cross-jurisdictional setting. *Police Chief* LXIX (6).

Reimer, Dennis J. 2004. The private sector must be a partner in homeland security. *Homeland Security* 1 (4).

Rothman, Paul. 2002. Setting Priorities to Protect the Nation's Infrastructure. *Government Security*, April.

DETECTIVE WORK/CULTURE

Introduction

Contemporary detectives are information processors who investigate, define, clear, and otherwise manage the tension between "the case" as their property (Ericson 1981/1991) and the case as an organizational object of concern. The first work is constrained by rules and the second varies by the type of case or detecting involved. The process of managing the case within the organization may involve how to document it, what relations with other units are required (for example, concerning handling informants or "deals" made with the suspect). Detectives investigate reported incidents that may be founded or established as crimes, instigate crime by making it happen (vice, drugs, internal affairs), take cases to court if required, process arrested prisoners, and attempt to clear founded crimes. To do this, they may interview suspects, witnesses, and victims; interrogate citizens (interview intensively with the purpose of extracting a confession or revelation); gather evidence; visit crime scenes; process forms (the disliked paperwork); carefully track or observe citizens or their communications; and clear, solve, or otherwise close cases. They make numerous phone calls. In recent years in the United States and the United Kingdom there has been more pressure to develop informants and to be concerned with homeland security. While carrying out these functions, the modern detective, at best, is a careful and skillful bureaucrat who fits the organizational demands to "produce" (clear cases) with career aims and the extant detective (occupational) culture. As Ericson (1993, 213) observes dryly, while this process was designed to meet the needs of the citizenry and sometimes does, it does well ". . . meet the needs of the detectives, facilitating their working designs." There are at least four sorts of local, city, or state detective work: general investigation (Ericson 1993); vice/drugs (Manning 1989); homicide (Innes 2000; Simon 1991); and political intelligence (Brodeur 1999; Marx 1981). Much more is known about local general investigation and homicide operatives than about those in other specialized investigative work, and we know almost nothing about federal investigators (forty-three U.S. federal agencies do investigations, and there is little known about the workings of the FBI and the investigators attached to the services, for example, nor about those attached to the congressional, court, and executive branches of the federal government) and private investigators. This suggests that as in most other matters, the knowledge social scientists possess is inversely related to the power, status, and authority of the segment or subgroup studied, both within and across occupations.

Historical Perspective

While crime detection as a social function has been known since the sixteenth century in England, it was in the middle of the eighteenth that it became a socially organized, state-based role. Even at that time, detection of villains was a mixed public/private activity with fees, rewards, and paid private investigations entwined with public policing. It was not until 1878 that private fees as a supplement to a police salary were abandoned in London (Kuykendall 1986, 177). It is important to note that it was assumed that the burden of detection and identification was an obligation of the citizen, not the state. This collective burden for investigating serious crime, especially murder, was not assumed by the state until the late nineteenth century in the United Kingdom (Kuykendall 1986, 178). The resistance to public police detectives was very strong in the United Kingdom and less so in the United States. This was rooted in a concern for privacy, the corruption potential of such work, and its alliance with thieves, associations that have haunted detectives since (see Kuykendall 1986, 175, for a summary).

The transition to public policing began in the late 1840s in the United States (Johnson 1979, 48–50). The impetus was not only the rising crime figures but concerns that entrepreneurship and public duties were in some conflict. Also encouraging the transition were the development of the insurance industry, techniques used by private detectives, and perhaps a shift to crime control concerns rather than prevention via citizens' mobilization of the reaction. This mixture of control modes remains in the Anglo-American world, where private detectives, the private security industry, and public police may investigate crimes against persons or property, but only public police can enter a case into the criminal justice system as police.

Kuykendall (1986, 179–193) argues using ideal types that the detective role has evolved from a "secretive rogue" to an "inquisitor" and thence to a "clerk" or bureaucrat. The secretive rogue was an entrepreneur in league more with criminals than responsible citizens and is corrupt, venial, and inefficient. The inquisitor was an interrogator whose apex was in the early part of the twentieth century and whose skills lay in pressing suspects to confess or betray others. Solving crime was arrived at via confessions, betrayals, informants, and intense physical and psychological abuse.

The reform movements of the 1920s and 1930s brought new constraints, and the detective, according to Kuykendall, became a bureaucrat, a clerk, and a "paper pusher" in the mid-twentieth century. While they became no more efficient in clearing or solving crimes and more scientific investigation was urged by reformers, constraints of supervision, procedural innovations in criminal law, and the professionalism movement within policing did reshape detective work. The aim of reform, as with policing in general, was to create a clean-living, scientifically oriented, rational, competent, and incorruptible officer (Kuykendall 1986, 186), but the effort focused on control and restraint rather than improved capacity to influence and reduce crime. The general structural approach to criminal investigation has not changed, formal selection criteria for entry into detective work have not changed, and the role of detective work in reducing crime is unknown. There is some indication that female detectives experience the job differently, have innovative detection styles, and suffer different sources and kinds of stress.

Detectives Subculture

The role of the detective in contemporary police departments stands in contrast to the visible, well-known uniformed patrol officer, and the subculture of the detective differs as well. Ironically, of course, the detective is dependent upon the patrol officers' acuity, memory, and reports for constructing a case. Patrol officers who want to "make detective" often cultivate detectives' friendship and "hang around" the detective unit. The occupational culture of policing is shared by detectives. An occupational culture is a means for coping with the vicissitudes of the job: a reduced, selective, and task-based version of culture that includes history and traditions, etiquette and routines, rules, principles, and practices that serve to buffer practitioners from contacts with the public. The sources of the occupational culture are the repeated, routinized tasks incumbent on the members, a technology that is variously direct or indirect in its effects (mediated by the organizational structure within which the occupation is done), and the reflexive aspects of talking about the work.

The following are distinguishing features or hypotheses about this context:

- The detective works in plain clothes, not a uniform, and has considerably low visibility and high autonomy.
- The detective learns the job, following brief (generally a few weeks') training, via apprenticeships and partnerships between junior and senior agents.
- The detective has flexible hours, guided by the individual's energies and imagination, current caseload, and pressures to produce clearances for the particular shift or unit.
- The detective is generally paid more than a uniformed officer and has many opportunities for earning money via overtime through court appearances, longer hours approved by supervisors, and special investigations that may be required, such as for manhunts for escaped prisoners, "moral panics" associated with a series of homicides, or crimes by or upon major political or social figures in the city.
- The workload is variable and the demand episodic. While most cases are simple, the demands associated with some cases are complex. The weighting of such cases with respect to workload and their political significance is not easily resolved and makes comparisons across organizations and cases difficult.
- Skill level varies among detectives, and the stratification system (vertical ranking by skill) within a unit is generally well known and shared.
- Detectives have higher status than patrol officers in the department, although SWAT units are also highly respected because of their equipment, public respect, and visibility in media-covered occasions.
- There is a hierarchy within the detective world from homicide detectives to general investigators working primarily auto thefts and burglaries, a scale that reflects the importance attached to actually catching the villain.
- Cases present various degrees of "trouble" in that victims, witnesses, and evidence can all be problematic to manage. Homicide cases are the most likely to produce media concern, pressure for solution, and paperwork tracking decisions made.
- Supervision is democratic and less rule-bound than in uniform patrol.
- The mode of selection of detectives, transfers in and out, as well as rank promotion within the unit are political, based on sponsorship and reputation more than on exam results, seniority, or even the selection interview. The networks of sponsorship extend outside the unit and may involve city politicians.
- Paperwork and interviewing skills are admired and required, even though paperwork is viewed ambivalently or disdained (see Manning 1980).

The detective subculture is omitted in conventional descriptions of the police occupational culture (Reiner 2000; Crank 1998). It is possible, however, to draw some generalizations about the work and its rewards, evaluative standards, values, and divisions.

The criteria and bases for selection vary across departments but generally include an interview, approval of the transfer, and a good reputation. Being chosen to be a detective requires personal skill, good interpersonal networks within the organization, or "politics," support from present detectives, and "fit" with local traditions.

A detective soon has a network of informal power relations inside and outside the unit. The prestige of a detective rests in part upon the boundary spanning and networking work that is essential to carry out the job well. This "politicking" is necessary but is viewed ambivalently within the department. Selection to a unit signifies that the person has the potential to be trusted and loyal, a "team player," and has investigative skills.

Status accrues as a result of accomplishing the possible with style, in a collegial and egalitarian organizational environment. This is mitigated by gender and ethnicity as factors in interaction and evaluation. Failure to carry the load, "ducking cases," failing to clear conventional crimes, and adding to others' workload all decrease a detective's status with his peers. Rank or formal position is rarely used to define social relations (Corsianos 1999). The stratification and differentiation within detective units is greater than in the patrol division. Fine status distinctions based on skill and experience are observed in the work that is done in teams or collectively.

The values of detectives are shaped by the insulated position of the unit in the police organization. They are dependent on their investigative colleagues and to a lesser degree on the public but view themselves as independent operators, skilled artisans, and puzzle solvers. Detectives are much less threatened by rules, supervision, and public complaints than are patrol officers, so their autonomy is less salient, and collective obligations are emphasized. Their authority is rarely challenged except in court. To an important degree, detectives view the uncertainties they encounter as controllable.

The subculture of detectives is gender and ethnicity biased in dramatic fashion (Simon 1991; Martinez 1996; Corsianos 1999). Females, African Americans, and Latinos who are selected enter a white male world. This subcultural bias manifests itself in gossip about these officers being lazy, not being hustlers, being unable to clear cases. In Latino-based units, it is believed that Anglos cannot investigate cases properly because they cannot get people to talk with them, have no informants, and do not know African American or Latino neighborhoods (Martinez 1996). In Boston, for example, the clearance rate of below 35% in homicide cases in 2005 was at least in part attributable to the absence of experienced African American investigators and distrust of police in disadvantaged areas of the city. Where ethnicity divides the unit, racial stereotypes also shape the prestige of officers. A corollary of this is that sponsorship to the unit is difficult for those from stereotypic categories, and power shifts among ethnic groups are revealed in the composition of the unit. When police organizations are divided by conflict between ethnic groups and this division exists between the top command and detectives, transfers and promotions indicate additional ethnically based power relations.

Detective Work as Casework

Modern detective work, television and movies not withstanding, has been transformed into a bureaucratic function, constrained by procedural constraints, public intolerance of direct efforts to produce confessions, and supervision to reduce corruption, and is less reliant on paid informants, undercover work, and citizen-paid investigations. While the pressures toward intelligence work are extant in the United States, they have been made visible through the creation of the national intelligence model and specialist intelligence units in the United Kingdom. They are primarily, but not exclusively, reactive (to crime brought to their attention) agents of the state, or public servants. Kuykendall (1986, 192) rather unkindly writes that ". . . the role of the police detective [has been] gradually changed to that of a clerk." This suggests a routinized, impotent, and highly constrained manqué.

This view is contested by Ericson (1981/ 1993), who argues that detectives deal with suspects, witnesses, and victims quite differently, depending on the police detective's definition of the outcomes to be achieved. The game is defined by the officer and played to achieve his or her ends. Further, Ericson sees the detective not as constrained by rules and law but facilitated by them. The officer uses various definitions of the case's features (who is a victim, who is a suspect) and rules to achieve desired outcomes. These are but two sides of the same process. Detective work is a case-focused enterprise, and preparing cases for court is a demanding aspect of the job.

Officers are assigned cases on a regular basis, either weekly or on a one by one basis as in homicide units. Typically, officers make a first cut. They set aside cases that have little or no chance of being solved: those with no witness, no physical evidence, no suspects or confession, no arrest on the scene. These cases are treated superficially, with only a few calls or interviews. A second set of cases involves those that have some potential to be cleared as a result of further investigation. How these cases are typified varies by the unit (burglary, robbery, homicide, other crimes). For example, in homicide work, a binary division was reported in two departments (Miami and Baltimore) between "dunkers" or "smoking gun" cases (immediate arrest or confession) and "whodunits" ("WDIs"). The time spent on such "solvable" cases varies but is typically brief. From an instrumental perspective, or the workers' view of efficiency, screening has three aims: to reduce the workload, to focus effort on those cases most likely to be cleared, and to avoid legal or "bureaucratic" complications. Concern that these bureaucratic complications may arise leads to failures to complete paperwork or to avoiding it altogether.

The police occupational culture emphasizes the capacity to cope creatively with the unexpected, especially events of social importance but of low statistical probability such as a child kidnapping, a mass murder, or a series of rapes of elderly women. Such matters are central to policing because they are highly visible in the media, raise public anxieties about police effectiveness, and produce enormous goodwill if cleared.

There are therefore exceptions to the screening and focusing activity of detectives. These arise when the case involves a child or an old person, becomes a media case, or involves a politician or notable figure in the city. These are "high-profile" cases. High-status victims, if they received media attention, are also subject to additional police time and attention. If the victim is a police officer or relative of a police officer, the case will receive special attention, and often special task forces are assigned (Simon 1991; Corsianos 1999). Clearing high-profile cases conveys lasting respect.

Cases do not have equal weight, as the exceptions noted above imply. The time and attention given to a case will depend on the status, gender, and age of the victim.

Detectives, like all officers, are especially sensitive to cases that might reveal any "dirty laundry"—crimes involving other officers, cover-ups of controversial decisions, or corruption more generally (Corsianos 1999).

Case knowledge is personal, a kind of property not easily shared with others. Knowledge developed and synthesized is not always written and accessible. What might be called collective or institutional memory, facts and associations possessed by individual officer's that are not written down nor shared, increase iniquitous practices. The occupational culture assumes that information is virtually personal property, and secrecy is highly valued. This is magnified by the absence of articulated databases within departments and (especially in homicide) the absence of easy, known, and trusted modes of data sharing, accessible informant files and records, and access to the case files or databases of other squads, for example, gang, juvenile, drug, or warrant-serving squads.

"Case-focused" means that the efforts of detectives are organized and framed by the named case at hand. For detectives, the "case" is the key concept. It is not just a named manila file folder; it is a concept, itself a social creation, constituted by tradition, by unspoken and tacit knowledge, and by organizational processes. The definition of a case is very subtle. This is certainly true of proactive investigations, such as watching and tracking members of a drug-dealing network in which any transaction, individual, or group of two or more persons could be the target and any number of tactics could be used, such as informants, a buy bust, or tracking back to the wholesaler. In proactive cases, the flexibility of the concept of a case is clear, and the deciding done by agents shapes who will be the target, how the case will be worked, the tactics employed, and what the hoped-for results will be.

In reactive investigations, on the other hand, such as a stranger-stranger rape, it is rare for officers to see the incident reported as being connected to outstanding domestic violence cases, other rapes unless they are dramatic and occur in a short time span, and drug cases. The aim is to narrow the quest for a clearance and close the case, not widen or deepen it. The case is the center; connections to other cases (unless after the fact to clear cases "taken into consideration"), multiple victims of the villain, or direct links between the case of someone arrested and another case are of secondary concern.

The day-to-day work of a detective illustrates some combination of a walk in bureaucratic doldrums and occasioned, situational rationality. This type of rationality is case based, craftlike, and often stylistic and is sensitive to the changing horizon of possibilities that a case represents. The detective's "case" is defined by the layered meanings it denotes and connotes in the subjective and objective forces in the surround (the social structure of the city) and the field (the occupational values, routines, and tacit knowledge).

By "working a case well," detectives mean the flair, the aesthetics one brings to the work. It is assumed that things will go wrong: Witnesses disappear or recant testimony, evidence will be overlooked or contaminated, interrogations will go badly, and errors in procedure will arise (see Simon 1991, 195–220). While some officers do not work much or are incompetent (and known to be incompetent), most officers use their past experience, tacit or intuitive knowledge, and understanding of typical areas and practices to construct what might be done and why. Officers develop their cases privately and restrict access to their cases, thus reducing the capacity of crime analysts or other officers to infer patterns of cooffending or to identify multiple victims of the same murderer or links between crimes. While they may try to clear a series of cases with similar features by eliciting a confession or agreement to cooperate, thus clearing several, they are working from a perpetrator to cases, not by examining diverse cases that may link a set of co-offenders or, least likely, working from "raw intelligence" to discover a yet unknown suspect or set of suspects. The individual detective is seen as the defining "expert" in a case unless it is reassigned. "Working" a homicide case begins with a crime and usually a body. It seems to involve a combination of substantive and concrete local knowledge—of offenders, settings, and types of offenses—associational thinking, responding to intuitive hunches, and following leads. It would be difficult to devise an expert system version of such detecting.

Performance or success is indicated traditionally by unit clearance rates, arrests, and seizures in drugs units. Court convictions are of little interest unless the case is an important one politically in the city. Clearance is an organizational term not to be confused with solved (in the conventional sense of arresting a perpetrator), closed (which means investigative efforts were abandoned), or closely investigated to the point of exhausting the clues. A case may be cleared in a variety of ways. These include clearance by issuing a warrant, either by name or a John Doe warrant, cases being transferred to another jurisdiction or force (for example, the FBI or tribal or state police), and those cleared by exception (two men shoot each other, a murder-suicide combination). There are local variations about what is an excepted clearance. In short, the term is context dependent. Homicide is considered the most consistently measured and investigated crime and of greatest public concern. However, criteria for clearing a homicide are neither universal nor universally applied. While the Bureau of Justice Statistics compiles the *Uniform Crime Reports* and defines and sets standards for homicides and clearances, practices in individual departments vary, as do the warranted processes of producing an organizationally acceptable clearance.

Officers and squads keep records of clearances, and sergeants and lieutenants seek to increase the clearance rate or the percentage of homicides cleared. The personnel, size of the unit, number of homicides, and percentage "cleared" (an organizational label) vary in urban departments. Most reported crimes, unlike homicide, are processed quickly and given little attention. The clearance rate for homicide varies across the country; estimates are from 60+% to more than 90%. The homicide clearance rate itself appears to have low association with reported crime rates in general (JCRS research). It is a powerful reflexive indicator used generally to assess the performance of the unit, even while it is routinely manipulated, and is insensitive to the quality of the investigation and court results (Martinez 1996). While there are pressures to "produce" and a focus on clearances (Waegel 1982; Simon 1991, 197 ff.), clearances result for the most part from the structural, political,

economic, social, and psychological forces that shape the event more than from how the detective works the case as paperwork that has to be cleared. Research (Greenwood, Petersilia, and Chaikin 1977) suggests that a few key elements—physical evidence, witnesses present, or a confession—are of critical importance in determining the probability of a clearance. These are rarely under the officer's control. In many respects, social scientists have been taken in by the oral culture of detectives that emphasizes this pressure.

Clearances, although a standard measure of police detective work, like arrests, are not always sought. It depends. Closing a case, clearing it from organizational records, is but one of several functions of a homicide investigation. While conventional wisdom would elevate the instrumental aim, a closure, there are expressive or socioemotional aspects of the investigation, such as the quality of the police work involved or the wish to hold a case to obtain witness cooperation or confession or to protect the families of the witnesses or victims. Even in a matter as serious as murder, charges are laid to discipline people, to force them to confess to acknowledge complicity in other crimes or to a lesser charge. Thus, the present topic is merely background to other moral and political issues (Corsianos 1999, 98) and a focus for a repertoire of tactics. While police detectives deal with many crimes, these crimes are clustered in areas of large cities where witnesses are reticent and revenge and retaliation operate, areas that are crime dependent insofar as types of crimes (burglaries and drug use) and criminals are linked. Because detectives see themselves as catching criminals and putting them in jail, the failure to clear crimes causes morale variations and cynicism among detectives.

Detective work remains a complex subspecialty within policing, and the culture reflects some of its self-created nuances and tactics. It stands midway between the citizen and the organization, a kind of buffer that expands and contracts its tactical reservoir as need be.

PETER K. MANNING

See also **Attitudes toward the Police: Overview; British Policing; Case Screening and Case Management for Investigations; Clearance Rates and Criminal Investigations; Criminal Informants; Criminal Investigation; Detectives; Informants, Use of; Investigation Outcomes; Managing Criminal Investigations; Occupational Culture**

References and Further Reading

Brodeur, J. P. 1999. Cops and spooks: The uneasy partnership. In *Policing: Key readings*, ed. T. Newburn Cullompton, Devon: Willan.

Corsianos, M. 1999. Detective work. Ph.D. diss. Department of Sociology, York University, Toronto.

Crank, John. 1998. *Occupational culture*. Cincinnati, OH: Anderson.

Ericson, Richard. 1981/1993. *Making Crime*. Toronto: Butterworth and Company.

Greenwood, P., J. Petersilia, and J. Chaikin. 1977. *The criminal investigation process*. Lexington, MA: D. C. Heath.

Innes, Martin. 2000. *Investigating murder*. Oxford: Clarendon Press.

Kuykendall, K. 1986. The municipal police detective. In *Police and policing: Contemporary issues*. Westport, CT: Praeger.

Manning, Peter K. 1989/2004. *The narcs' game*. Prospect Heights, IL: Waveland Press.

Marx, Gary. 1981. *Undercover*. New York: Russell Sage.

Reiner, Robert. 2000. *The politics of the police*. 3rd ed. Oxford: Oxford University Press.

Simon, David. 1991. *Homicide*. New York: Simon and Schuster.

Waegel, W. 1982. Patterns of police investigation of urban crimes. *Journal of Police Science and Administration* 10: 452–65.

DETECTIVES

Since the earliest use of detectives, there has been somewhat of a mystique surrounding them and their jobs. Unlike patrol officers and most other personnel in the police organization, detectives typically do not wear uniforms, work primarily during the day shift, and in the case of undercover detectives may be covert operatives unknown to many people, even in the police organization.

Detectives are responsible for starting the entire criminal justice process, because if an arrest is not made based on probable cause, with grounds to further pursue investigative inquiry, then nothing happens. A series of questions must be answered using logical, systematic processes in order to facilitate the criminal investigative activity. As will be evident, these processes are complex, necessitate great responsibilities, and require dedicated individuals with numerous characteristics that support these processes.

Origin

Detectives play an important role in the criminal investigation process. While some organizations do not have detectives, someone, usually patrol officers, must perform the investigative function in the police organization. In larger organizations, which tend to be more specialized, entire units of detectives, which are called criminal investigative units, exist. Oftentimes criminal investigative units are even subdivided into smaller units that focus more specifically on certain types of crimes such as homicide or sex crimes (Gilbert 2004).

The American police organization, and consequently the American detective, were greatly influenced by English policing. In fact, the origin of the American detective can be traced back to the early English police organizations. The "Bow Street Runners" were the first organized group of detectives in England and became professionalized with the passage of the Metropolitan Police Act of 1929, which also called for the Metropolitan Police Force.

Thieves were often used as early detectives due to their access to information and knowledge of the criminal lifestyle (Osterberg and Ward 2004). Early detectives, some of whom were criminals, initially also mingled with the criminal element in order to perform the investigative function. As time passed, the role of the detective became more professional, resulting in detectives spending less time with criminals and gathering information from other sources and in different ways. Consequently, thieves were used less frequently as detectives, used instead as informants.

In 1845 in New York City, there were more than eight hundred plainclothes police officers functioning as detectives. It was not until 1857, however, that the police department officially designated twenty officers as detectives. Shortly after the officers were designated as detectives, the New York City Police created the "rogues' gallery" to assist detectives in doing their jobs. The rogues' gallery was a systematic set of photographs of known criminals that were coded by criminal specialty and height. Then in 1884, New York City created the first formally recognized Criminal Investigation Bureau, with Atlanta following suit in 1885 (Swanson et al. 2006).

While these efforts were undertaken in municipal policing, both state and federal governments were trying to establish investigative capabilities in their jurisdictions. In 1865, Congress created the U.S. Secret Service. In 1908, the U.S. attorney general created a small police organization, which years later, in 1924, became the Federal Bureau of Investigation (FBI) under the direction of J. Edgar Hoover. Federal investigative agencies were typically responsible for more specific duties than the more generalized local agencies. During the same period in 1905, California became the first state to set up a state bureau of investigation, followed quickly by Pennsylvania, which created the Pennsylvania State Police. New York, Michigan, and Delaware developed state police organizations during the early twentieth century also. State police organizations quite often assisted local organizations in investigations and still do this today (Swanson et al. 2006).

While American police organizations such as New York's were evolving, the private sector saw a need for investigators that the public sector police organizations simply could not fill. Allan Pinkerton, along with Edward Rucker, formed the first private detective agency in response to the overabundance of graft and corruption, the limited jurisdiction of the public police, and the lack of communication of vital information between police organizations. In fact, in 1849, the mayor of St. Louis appointed Pinkerton as the first city detective. Pinkerton's detectives were known as the only "consistently competent" detectives for more than fifty years and set a good example for public sector detectives.

Detective's Responsibilities

As stated previously, whether or not an organization has a criminal investigative unit depends primarily on the size, type, and level of specialization within the police organization. Regardless of whether the organization has a criminal investigative unit, personnel still have the same responsibilities if they are performing the investigative function. Very broadly, a detective is an officer who gathers, documents, and evaluates evidence in order to solve crimes (Swanson et al. 2006), but more specific responsibilities of a detective include the following:

1. Determine whether a crime has been committed.
2. Decide if the crime was committed within the investigator's jurisdiction.
3. Discover all facts pertaining to the complaint.
4. Gather and preserve physical evidence.
5. Develop and follow up all clues.
6. Recover stolen property.
7. Identify the perpetrator or eliminate a suspect as the perpetrator.
8. Locate and apprehend the perpetrator.

9. Aid in the prosecution of the offender by providing evidence of guilt that is admissible in court.
10. Testify effectively as a witness in court (Osterberg and Ward 2004, 5–6).

Desirable Traits of a Detective

As is apparent, a detective's responsibilities are extensive, and if the case is prosecutable, working on a single case can take weeks, months, and sometimes even years. Obviously, to be a successful detective requires certain attributes. These attributes are two-fold: the ability, both physical and mental, to conduct an inquiry, together with those skills necessary to reach the intended objectives (Osterberg and Ward 2004, 11). More specifically, Osterberg and Ward (2004) indicate that the following traits of a criminal investigator are desirable:

1. Intelligence and reasoning ability
2. Curiosity and imagination
3. Observation and memory
4. Knowledge of life and people
5. Technical "know-how"
6. Perseverance, "stick-to-itiveness," and energy
7. Ability to recognize and control bias and prejudice in one's self and on the job
8. Sensitivity to people's feelings, acting with discretion and tact; showing respect and confidence
9. Honesty and courage enough to withstand temptation and corruption
10. Ability to testify well in court, being neither overzealous nor committing perjury
11. Miscellaneous characteristics, such as physically fit appearance, report-writing skills, awareness of good public relations as a future source of cooperation and information (Osterberg and Ward 2004, 12–13)

In addition to these traits, Swanson et al. (2006) include other essential qualities of an investigator. These are knowing that investigation is more of a science than an art due to its systematic method; using inductive reasoning, knowing that both inductive and deductive reasoning can be distorted; having empathy, sympathy, and compassion; and finally, avoiding becoming calloused and cynical due to the nature of the work. While all of these traits are not likely to be characteristic of many detectives, ideally detectives can develop some of these traits over time with more experience in their jobs.

Gilbert (2004) adds that of all the desirable traits of a detective, critical thinking is the most important to the criminal investigation process. Without adequate critical thinking in the investigative process, it does not matter how many of the other traits you have or how well you perform certain tasks. Critical thinking allows one to differentiate between fact and opinion, determine cause and effect relationships, determine the accuracy and completeness of information, recognize logical fallacies and faulty reasoning, and develop inferential skills using deductive or inductive reasoning. The importance of using the appropriate type of reasoning, deductive or inductive, cannot be understated. It is imperative that a detective know which to emphasize based on the facts available.

Weston and Lushbaugh (2003) contend that there are certain standards to which detectives must be held. These are reasonable care, self-discipline, and judgment. Reasonable care is "care fairly and properly taken in response to the circumstances of a situation, such care as an ordinary prudent person would take in the same time frame, conditions, and act(s)" (p. 5). Self-discipline is that quality that enables a person to monitor his or her activities to ensure that all activities are aboveboard. Using sound judgment, then, is a product of taking reasonable care and being self-disciplined.

The comprehensive knowledge base that a detective must have, along with certain traits, helps him or her to facilitate successful prosecutions. Without the thorough job of the detective, the criminal justice system would cease to function. The importance of the job should never be underestimated, because detectives are relied upon tremendously by numerous individuals who would not be able to perform their jobs without the work of the detective.

KATHRYN E. SCARBOROUGH

See also **British Policing; Criminal Investigation; Detective Work/Culture; Federal Bureau of Investigation; Investigation Outcomes**

References and Further Reading

Gilbert, J. N. 2004. *Criminal investigation*. 6th ed. Upper Saddle River, NJ: Pearson/Prentice-Hall.

Osterberg, J. W., and R. H. Ward. 2004. *Criminal investigation: A method for reconstructing the past*. 4th ed. Cincinnati, OH: LexisNexis.

Swanson, C. R., N. C. Chamelin, L. Territo, and R. W. Taylor. 2006. *Criminal investigation*. 9th ed. Boston, MA: McGraw-Hill.

Weston, P. B., and C. A. Lushbaugh. 2003. *Criminal investigation: Basic perspectives*. 9th ed. Upper Saddle River, NJ: Pearson/Prentice-Hall.

DEVIANT SUBCULTURES IN POLICING

Subcultures are collections of "norms, values, interests (and associated artifacts) that are derivative of, but distinct from the larger" dominant culture; deviant or criminal subcultures consist of the norms, values, artifacts, and interests that revolve around deviant or criminal behavior (Anderson and Short 2002, 499). Within police departments, supervisors and colleagues who tolerate violent or corrupt behavior set the standard for and encourage misbehavior. Most police departments have a fraternity of officers who find and support each other in their deviant or corrupt activities, as well as in the ideology that rationalizes these behaviors. Police often view themselves as an isolated fraternity, alienated from both the criminals and the public. This alienation is often rationalized by suggesting that the stresses and pressures of the job lead officers to be embittered about the criminal justice system and create an attitude that the ends can justify the means (see especially Kappeler and Potter 2005, chap. 10).

Even if a few officers are responsible for most of the brutal and corrupt acts in a police department, fellow officers' reaction to the behavior, either overtly or in passive acceptance, allows it to flourish. A common phenomenon termed the "code of silence" is an excuse for otherwise noncorrupt officers to tolerate the misbehavior of their fellow officers. From very early in their careers young policemen are discouraged from reporting misbehavior by their colleagues, thus creating an environment in which officers act as a type of fraternity or close-knit family. As corrupt NYPD cop Michael Dowd would say, "You kick some punk down the stairs in front of 10 cops and you have 10 friends, . . . how much bad could you be trusted to see, the old-timers wanted to know, before you ratted on another cop" (McAlary 1994). "Two cops ['bad apples'] can go berserk, but 20 cops embody a subculture ['rotten barrel'] of policing" (Skolnick and Fyfe 1993, 25).

If an officer arrests a criminal, even though it might not be a technically correct arrest, it is generally acceptable to his colleagues, supervisor, and society that the "bad guy" be punished. Police perjury is rationalized as hiding technicalities (such as illegal searches), and officers often cover for each other. Judges and juries make it easier because they generally give police officers the benefit of the doubt. Police rationalize their main task as removing criminals from society and often justify violating citizens' rights as an unfortunate by-product of that goal.

Many rationalize that going "by the book" leads to fewer arrests and less jail time for criminals. Police become frustrated by the expansion of laws that provide increased protection of criminal suspects.

Low Salaries and Police Corruption

Low wages provide a popular rationalization for corruption. "When police see dealers with $300,000 in the back seat of their car and know if they arrest them the court's going to turn them out anyway, it may seem a better form of justice to hit them in the pocketbook and take their money—especially if the policeman has a big mortgage" (At Issue 1995). The reality that some criminals make much more money than the officers sworn to apprehend them provides yet another rationalization for extorting or accepting bribes from crooks. The New Orleans police have a long history of low pay and corruption. One-third of its entire police force abandoned their posts during 2005's Hurricane Katrina.

Two independent commissions have been organized to investigate New York's problems, the Knapp Commission of the 1970s and the Mollen Commission of the 1990s (*The Economist* 1994). New York police earn relatively low salaries. The Knapp Commission report of 1972 exposed major corruption in virtually every NYPD precinct and found that some corrupt officers rationalized that taking "clean" money from illegal gambling operations was morally superior than taking "dirty" money from traffickers who sold narcotics to children.

The Mollen Commission report in 1994 described rampant police corruption, especially in the West Harlem precinct. Officers terrorized minorities in neighborhoods and participated in drug trafficking. One particularly surprising charge was the shooting and serious wounding of a drug dealer when officers stole the dealer's cocaine supply and $100,000 in cash while illegally searching an apartment. An officer testified that police would keep guns that had been seized from suspects and use them as "throwaway" guns to plant on suspects in the event of a questionable arrest. The report claimed that officers found to be corrupt were more likely to be brutal (violate citizens' rights) as well. Perjury by NYPD officers was so common that some officers referred to it as "testilying" (*The Economist* 1994).

The central figure in the Mollen investigation, Officer Michael Dowd, organized groups of officers in raids on Brooklyn drug dealers' apartments for cash and drugs. The officers extorted protection money from dealers and sold cocaine to youths.

Undercover officers are especially susceptible to corruption because of the corrupt nature of the job. Their role involves deception and risk taking, and they often possess corruption-prone personalities, especially if they are undercover long term. Officers start believing the criminals are their friends and become alienated from law-abiding society.

Conclusion

There is little evidence that police departments discourage all types of police deviance and corruption. If a department takes a no-tolerance stance, it may be able to discourage the behavior that leads to corruption. Most departments allow some corruption to exist within the department. Police officers often alienate themselves from society by spending their time almost entirely with other officers. They often do not see their deviant or corruptive behavior as a problem. Potentially deviant or corrupt officers are influenced by their fellow officers and, hence, view their behavior as socially acceptable. Those officers who insist on honesty are often themselves viewed as deviant within corrupt departments.

DAVID R. SIMON

See also **Accountability; Attitudes toward the Police: Overview; Codes of Ethics; Corruption; Cynicism, Police; Danger and Police Work; Discretion; Integrity in Policing; Knapp Commission; Mollen Commission; Police Solidarity; Undercover Investigations**

References and Further Reading

Anderson, Elijah, and James F. Short. 2002. Delinquent and criminal subcultures. In *Encyclopedia of Crime and Justice*, ed. Joshua Dressler, 2nd ed., 499–507. New York: Gale Group.

At Issue. 1995. *CQ Researcher*. November 24.

Kappeler, V., and G. Potter. 2005. *The mythology of crime and criminal justice*. 3rd ed. Prospect Heights, IL: Waveland Press.

McAlary, M. 1994. *Good cop, bad cop: Detective Joe Trimboli's heroic pursuit of NYPD officer Michael Dowd*, p. 25. New York: Pocket.

New York University School of Law. 2005. *Shielded from justice: New York: Background.* http://www.law.nyu.edu/mirskyc/uspohmt/uspo10.htm.

Rorty, A. O. 1998. How to harden your heart: Six easy ways to become corrupt. *Yale Review* 86 (April): 104.

Scrivner, E. M. 1994. Controlling police use of excessive force: The role of the police psychologist. *National Institute of Justice Research*, October.

Simon, David R. 2004. *Tony Soprano's America: The criminal side of the American dream*. New York: Westview Press.

———. 2006. *Elite deviance*. 8th ed. Boston: Allyn & Bacon.

Skolnick, J. H., and J. J. Fyfe. 1993. *Above the law: Police and the excessive use of force*. p. 13. New York: Free Press.

DIFFERENTIAL POLICE RESPONSE

Differential police response (DPR) is a management tool that extends the range of options for responding to requests for police service, intended to optimize the match between the service required and the response made. Rather than dispatching a patrol unit to every call, on an as-available basis, police agencies that practice DPR allow for systematically delayed responses by patrol units to some types of calls and for "relief" responses, which do not involve a patrol unit, to other types of calls. This practice builds on research that has shown that much of the time an immediate response by patrol units does not improve the prospects for desirable outcomes: the apprehension of suspects, the prevention of injuries, the collection of evidence, or even the satisfaction of callers. Furthermore, the time saved or restructured through the use of DPR is a resource that can be put to more productive uses.

Research in the 1970s and 1980s found that police response time is in most instances unrelated to key outcomes (Kansas City Police Department 1978; Spelman and Brown 1984). Some crimes are "cold," having been perpetrated long before they are discovered (thefts from automobiles would be one example), and sometimes the victims of personal crimes (such as a robbery) delay contacting the police, as they assess their situations, decide whether to contact the police, cope with the immediate problems that their victimization has caused, and seek advice or support from friends or family. Thus, even successful efforts by the police to minimize the two components of response time—dispatch time, the lag between receipt of a call and the dispatch of a patrol unit, and travel time, the lag between dispatch and the arrival of the unit at the scene—often cannot have beneficial results. Spelman and Brown (1984) found that a rapid police response was instrumental in apprehending the offender in only 2.9% of reported serious crimes, mainly incidents that were in progress at the time of the call or that were reported with a short delay.

Furthermore, and contrary to the conventional wisdom of police administration, citizen satisfaction with the police response does not turn on response time by itself. Research has shown that citizens' satisfaction is shaped by the speed of the police response relative to their expectations, and that their expectations are malleable. When citizens expect an immediate response, they tend to be dissatisfied with anything less. But when they are told that police will arrive in thirty minutes (or an hour), and the police do arrive in that time, they tend to be satisfied (Pate et al. 1976; Percy 1980). Citizens are also receptive to relief responses, though not equally receptive to all forms (McEwen, Connors, and Cohen 1986; Worden 1993).

DPR systems may include a number of response options. One of those is a delayed response by patrol units. For any of the types of calls to which a rapid response is not essential—when neither lives nor property are in jeopardy and neither serious offenders nor evidence will vanish—a dispatcher can place the call in a queue, awaiting the availability of the unit assigned to the beat in which the call originated. Response may be deliberately delayed for thirty minutes, an hour, or longer. Responses to such calls are often delayed even without DPR, but with DPR the delay is by design, and the response protocol specifies that the caller be informed of the likely delay. Other options are relief responses, which divert calls from the patrol dispatch queue altogether. Some kinds of calls may be handled by dispatching nonsworn (civilian) personnel or a sworn specialist (such as community policing officers), while others may be referred to other agencies for assistance.

To other types of requests, callers may be asked to give reports over the phone, to mail a report to the police, to come to the police station to complete a report, to complete a report over the Internet, or to schedule an appointment with a specialist. Reports may be of minor motor vehicle accidents or of minor crimes—typically, offenses in which the loss (for example, from theft) or damage (for example, from vandalism) is under a specified dollar threshold and in which no physical evidence or other leads are available. Research has shown that in such cases, the likelihood of apprehending offenders is very low, and in many departments cases with such low solvability are not even assigned to detectives for follow-up investigation (Greenwood and Petersilia 1975; Eck 1983).

Delayed responses do not save patrol time but reallocate it in what might be more productive ways. A substantial fraction of the time that patrol officers have at their discretion, free of dispatched calls and other administrative assignments, is in blocks that are too small to be put to constructive use. In Indianapolis, for example, one study showed that in a sample of beats 71% of patrol officers' time was "unassigned," but only 44% was unassigned time in blocks of an hour or more (Mastrofski et al. 1998). The more that dispatchers "clear their screens" by assigning calls as quickly as possible to the nearest available patrol unit, the more likely that officers' unassigned time will be fractured into pieces too small for problem solving or other proactive work. When dispatchers are able to "stack" low-priority calls, however, officers are better able to go out of service to engage in activity at their initiative, uninterrupted by dispatches.

Relief responses save patrol officers the time that they would spend handling the diverted calls, at the cost of the time of the personnel who staff the alternative responses. A field test of DPR in three police departments in the 1980s suggested that 15% to 20% of calls were eligible for relief responses, which could yield net time savings of substantial magnitude (McEwen, Connors, and Cohen 1986). In one department (Garden Grove, California), the evaluators estimated that alternative responses to selected types of calls could free patrol officers from five hundred hours on dispatched calls each month, while other personnel (for example, telephone report takers) would spend 162 hours handling those diverted calls.

The field test, and other research, also shows that the implementation of DPR is not simple or straightforward. When normal practice provides for dispatching a patrol unit in response to most calls, the information demands at call receipt are minimal: the location, the general nature of the problem, and the identity of the caller. Many police agencies provide for only a small number of call categories (signified by "10" codes) to characterize the nature of the problem. When DPR is adopted, call takers must gather more information, including not only the nature (and seriousness) of the problem but also when it occurred, whether an offender remains at the scene, and so forth so that they can determine what kind of response is appropriate. Often the information that call takers can obtain is fragmentary or ambiguous. Any doubt about the nature of the response that is required tends to be resolved in favor of dispatching a patrol unit, because mistakes are not symmetrical in their consequences: The consequences of underresponding (for example, referring the call to a telephone report unit when a patrol unit should be dispatched) are potentially much more serious than the consequences of overresponding.

The call classification burden might be eased somewhat if citizens were to play a greater part in differentiating between calls that require an immediate dispatch and calls that do not, especially where this differentiation is facilitated by a 311 system. These systems, designed to field nonemergency calls, emerged in the mid-1990s as an alternative to 911, with the expectation that they would reduce the volume of 911 calls. One study of 311 systems in four cities (focusing primarily on Baltimore) found these expectations fulfilled: Citizen reporting changed dramatically, with the newly established 311 system absorbing about 30% of the calls previously made to 911, and there was widespread community acceptance to using 311 as an alternative number. However, the new system did not have a great impact on policing strategies. Officers continued to be dispatched to all calls (except for priority five), whether the call was placed through 911 or 311. Response

times to most categories of 911 calls were the same as before. Further, more than two-thirds of officers surveyed noticed little change in how much discretionary time they had available (Mazerolle et al. 2005).

Police are "slaves to 911" not only when they run from call to call but also, and much more commonly, when they keep themselves "in-service"—by doing nothing other than driving around—and available for the next call (Cordner 1982; Kessler 1993). Although some departments actually may be understaffed, in most agencies the deployment of patrol resources is inefficient (Bouza 1990). DPR enables police to meet public demands more economically, and it frees some patrol resources for more productive purposes, including community policing, problem-oriented policing, and other proactive strategies such as directed/aggressive patrol (Worden 1993). Thus, DPR enables police managers to exercise more managerial influence over what their officers do.

ROBERT E. WORDEN and HEIDI S. BONNER

See also **Accountability; Administration of Police Agencies, Theories of; Calls for Service; COMPSTAT; Costs of Police Services; Hot Spots; Kansas City Preventive Patrol Experiment; Problem-Oriented Policing; Technology, Records Management, and Calls for Service**

References and Further Reading

Bouza, Anthony. 1990. *The police mystique: An insider's look at cops, crime, and the criminal justice system.* New York: Plenum.

Cordner, Gary W. 1982. While on routine patrol: What the police do when they're not doing anything. *American Journal of Police* 1: 94–112.

Eck, John. 1983. *Solving crimes: The investigation of burglary and robbery.* Washington, DC: Police Executive Research Forum.

Greenwood, Peter W., and Joan Petersilia. 1975. *The criminal investigation process. Vol. 1: Summary and implications.* Santa Monica, CA: RAND Corporation.

Kansas City Police Department. 1978. *Response time analysis: Executive summary.*

Washington, DC: U.S. Department of Justice.

Kessler, David A. 1993. Integrating calls for service with community- and problem-oriented policing: A case study. *Crime and Delinquency* 39(4): 484–508.

Mastrofski, Stephen D., Roger B. Parks, Albert J. Reiss, Jr., and Robert E. Worden. 1998. *Policing neighborhoods: A report from Indianapolis*. Washington, DC: National Institute of Justice.

Mazerolle, Lorraine, Dennis Rogan, James Frank, Christine Famega, and John E. Eck. 2005. *Research for practice: Managing calls to the police with 911/311 systems*. Washington, DC: National Institute for Justice.

McEwen, J. Thomas, Edward F. Connors III, and Marcia I. Cohen. 1986. *Evaluation of the differential response field test: Research report*. Washington, DC: National Institute of Justice.

Pate, Tony, Amy Ferrara, Robert A. Bowers, and Jon Lorence. 1976. *Police response time: Its determinants and effects*. Washington, DC: Police Foundation.

Percy, Stephen L. 1980. Response time and citizen evaluation of police. *Journal of Police Science and Administration* 8: 75–86.

Spelman, William, and Dale K. Brown. 1984. *Calling the police: Citizen reporting of serious crime*. Washington, DC: Police Executive Research Forum.

Worden, Robert E. 1993. Toward equity and efficiency in law enforcement: differential police response. *American Journal of Police* 12: 1–32.

DISCRETION

Defining and Discovering Discretion

Any discussion of police discretion must first begin with defining the construct and charting its historical recognition and acceptance in criminal justice. In general terms, discretion involves the ability to make a decision, choosing from several different alternatives. Police officers can choose from alternatives in a wide range of circumstances, from relatively minor incidents to those involving potential loss of liberty or life. Examples of police discretion include issuing a speeding ticket, resolving a domestic dispute, handling an encounter with a mentally ill person in crisis, and using deadly force.

Although discretion is widely accepted and considered an important part of policing today, this has not always been the case. Many scholars attribute the "discovery" of discretion in criminal justice to survey research conducted by the American Bar Association in the 1950s (American Bar Association 1956). Much of the early research and emphasis on discretion focused on its abolition; many argued that the decisions in criminal justice are too important to be made subjectively by criminal justice officials, including police. Law enforcement officials were especially reluctant to acknowledge the existence of discretion, arguing instead that laws were enforced consistently and equally all of the time (the myth of total enforcement). However, the President's Commission on Law Enforcement and the Administration of Justice (1967, 106) argued that discretion is an essential element of criminal justice and with regard to discretion in policing stated that "the police should openly acknowledge that, quite properly, they do not arrest all, or even most, offenders they know of."

The Context for Police Decision Making

Police officers do not make decisions in a vacuum. As we will see later, police decision making can be influenced by a wide range of factors involving the suspect, the officer, their encounter, the police department, and the external environment. Before examining the panoply of factors that influence police discretion, one should consider more broadly the general context of police decision making. More specifically, there are several defining features of policing that provide an important back-drop for officers' use of discretion.

The Complex Police Role

It is difficult to understand police discretion and decision making without considering the complex role of the police in society. Research has demonstrated that the role of the police goes far beyond chasing criminals and solving crimes. Instead, the primary functions of the police are considered to be order maintenance (or peacekeeping) and service-related tasks (Wilson 1968; Manning 1978). "Police spend most of their time attending to order-maintaining functions, such as finding lost children, substituting as ambulance drivers, or interceding in quarrels of one sort or another" (Manning 1978, 107). The police have traditionally emphasized the crime-fighting element of their job, which has created a distorted image of their role, exacerbated their role conflict, and devalued the other elements of their role (Walker and Katz 2002).

Police and Politics

One of the fundamental early differences between Robert Peel's London Metropolitan Police Department and early American departments involved the role of politics. While London "Bobbies" were representatives of the Crown, American police officers were tied to local politics. In many places during the last half of the nineteenth century, police functioned at the whim of local political leaders, leaving a legacy of poor performance, brutality, and corruption. In fact, one of the primary tenets of the Professional Reform effort—led by August Vollmer and others—centered on removing politics from policing. Many police scholars, however, argue that politics is an intrinsic part of American policing (see, for example, Manning 1978).

Force as the Core of the Police Role

Police officers have the legal authority to use force in certain situations including to protect themselves, to make an arrest, to overcome resistance, and to gain control of a potentially dangerous situation (Walker and Katz 2002). Research generally shows police use of force to be a rare event (Bureau of Justice Statistics 2001). However, Bittner (1970) argues that force is the core of the police role. Accordingly, police use of discretion occurs in this context. Their ability to resort to force defines each police–citizen encounter and shapes the decisions that citizens and police officers make during each situation.

The Factors That Influence Police Decisions

During the past forty years, much research has focused on identifying the primary determinants of police behavior, and three sets of potentially influential variables emerge from prior research: environmental, organizational, and situational. Each set of influential factors is described below (see referenced sources for more in-depth discussion).

Environmental Variables

"Environmental" variables refer to factors outside the police organization and can be separated into two basic categories: community-level characteristics that indirectly affect police behavior, such as variations in local levels of crime and violence, and direct external efforts to control police behavior (such as court rulings):

- Formal action such as arrest and use of force appears more likely in minority neighborhoods (Wilson 1968; Swanson 1978; Smith, 1986).

- The community's political culture helps shape police behavior (Wilson 1968; Rossi, Burke, and Edison 1974; Wilson and Boland 1978).
- Social class of a community affects police behavior (Wilson 1968; Westley 1970; Swanson 1978).
- The prevalence of community crime and violence affects police behavior (Kania and Mackey 1977; Mastrofski 1981; Geller and Karales 1981; Fyfe 1980).
- Direct external efforts to control police behavior—such as changes in law and court rulings—can influence police behavior, if there is departmental support of those external efforts (Skolnick and Fyfe 1993; White 2003).

Organizational Variables

Organizational variables refer to factors that are within the realm of the police agency, such as administrative policy, informal norms, and the police subculture:

- The departmental philosophy influences police officer behavior—that is, aggressive crime fighting, community-oriented policing, and order maintenance (Skolnick 1966; Wilson 1968; Skolnick and Fyfe 1993).
- The size of the department can influence police officer behavior (Ostrum, Parks, and Whitaker 1978; Mastrofski 1981; Brown 1981).
- The degree of supervision and accountability that a department provides will affect police officer behavior (Reiss 1971; Walker and Katz 2002).
- Organizational structure—such as the degree of bureaucracy or professionalism, adherence to the military model, rotating shifts and assignments, and patrol strategy—can influence police officer behavior (Boydstun and Sherry 1975; Brown

1981; Murphy and Pate 1977; Skolnick and Fyfe 1993);
- Informal norms and rules affect police officer behavior (that is, police subculture) (Skolnick 1966; Brown 1981; Reuss-Ianni 1983; Skolnick and Fyfe 1993).

Situational Variables

Last, situational variables refer to contextual factors specific to each police–citizen encounter. These contextual factors may involve the suspect (such as race), the officer (such as the number of years on the job), or the characteristics of the encounter (such as when others citizens are present):

- Citizen hostility toward police increases the likelihood of formal police action (Westley 1970; Reiss 1971; Black and Reiss 1967; Lundman 1974, 1996; Worden 1989).
- Suspects in lower socioeconomic classes are more likely to be subject to formal police action (Black 1970; Reiss 1971; Black and Reiss 1967).
- Police tend to treat juveniles and the elderly more severely than middle-aged citizens (Friedrich 1980; Black 1970).
- Some research has shown that minority citizens are treated more harshly than whites, though findings are mixed (Black and Reiss 1967; Black 1970; Smith and Visher 1981).
- Some research has shown that female citizens are treated differently than males, though findings are mixed (Smith and Visher 1981; Klinger 1996).
- The degree of relational distance between suspects and complainants can influence police officer behavior—formal action is more likely when they are strangers (Black 1970; Friedrich 1980).
- The seriousness of the alleged offense is an important influence on

police officer behavior (Black and Reiss 1967; Black 1970; Ricksheim and Chermak 1993).

- Police may be more likely to act harshly toward suspects in public places than in private (Friedrich 1980; Reiss 1971).
- Police often follow a polite complainant's wishes (Black 1970; Friedrich, 1980; Lundman, Sykes, and Clarke 1978; Smith and Visher 1981; Smith 1984).
- The presence of others appears to affect police behavior (Friedrich 1980; Smith and Visher 1981).
- Decisions made earlier in the encounter—by the officer and citizen—influence subsequent decisions—wielding a weapon or physically assaulting an officer will increase likelihood of a formal response (Binder and Scharf 1980; Bayley 1986).
- Overall, officer characteristics—education, race, gender, attitudes—appear to exert little influence on police officer behavior (Worden 1989; Fyfe 1980; Geller and Karales 1981; Brooks 2001).

Clearly, a wide range of both legal and extralegal factors have been linked to police discretion. Although it is difficult to assess or compare the relative importance of these factors, several overriding themes emerge. First, the police department itself plays a critically important role in guiding and controlling police officer discretion. The department can provide this guidance through a range of different means, including official policies and procedures, training, effective supervision, and setting an overall organizational tone that officers will be held to account for the decisions that they make. Second, police decision making appears to be affected by the environment in which officers work. Levels of community violence, socio-economic status, politics, and even the level of disorder and disorganization all may influence police officer discretion. Quite simply, police

officers are aware of and affected by their surroundings. Third, the police–citizen encounter is a fluid event with numerous decision points, and the decisions made by both participants at each of those points affect the final outcome. In many ways, the police–citizen encounter resembles a chess match, with each participant making "moves" to which the other participant then responds. Any number of characteristics of the encounter—and either participant—can play a role in shaping how the incident is ultimately resolved.

The Role of Perceived Danger in Police Decision Making

Understanding how environmental, organizational, and situational factors explain or influence police discretion is complicated because of their interaction. For example, consider why an officer may make an arrest in a domestic dispute. Was the arrest decision made because of department policy, the suspect's demeanor, the socio-economic status of the neighborhood, or some combination of these factors? Teasing apart the relative contributions of factors is extremely difficult. However, one critical element in determining the relative role of each set of factors is the perceived danger or threat facing the officer. As the perceived danger in the encounter increases, situational factors tend to play a more prominent and important role and organizational and environmental factors become secondary.

For example, the officer responding to a "man with a gun" call will be most influenced by the situational characteristics of the encounter: Is there an armed suspect? Formal organizational rules and environmental characteristics may still play a role in decision making (such as, is this also a high-crime neighborhood?), but the relative influence of those factors will be mediated by the situational variables. Alternatively, in less dangerous encounters organizational and environmental factors typically become more influential. Clearly, there are no hard-and-fast rules for interpreting the importance of specific factors since police–citizen encounters are complex, but perceived danger often plays a critical role.

Building on What We Know: Increasing the Rationality of Police Decision Making

Police departments and police scholars have begun to think about ways to improve police decision making, that is, to reduce the likelihood that police officers will make bad decisions. Given their tremendous amount of discretion and the potentially devastating consequences of poor police decisions—strained police–community relations, riot and disorder, and even loss of liberty and life—it is critically important to think about ways to structure police discretion.

The Three-Legged Stool

Gottfredson and Gottfredson (1988) argue that each decision is composed of three parts: goals, alternatives, and information. The goal represents the objective the decision maker would like to achieve. For a police officer, that goal may be any number of things, such as deterrence, order maintenance, or incapacitation. Alternatives represent choices, which are central to the concept of discretion. For a police officer, alternatives may include taking no action or making an arrest, using force or not, issuing a traffic citation or not. Finally, the decision maker has information to help him or her select from the alternatives (Gottfredson and Gottfredson 1988). Information about previous tickets may influence the officer to issue another ticket.

Gottfredson and Gottfredson (1988, xii) consider "goals, alternatives, and information as three legs of the stool on which the decision maker sits." The central issue for police departments then is to ensure that none of the legs are weak: Goals must be clearly stated and known among all personnel; alternatives must be identifiable and understood; and officers must possess relevant information to guide their decision making.

Fostering the Rational Use of Police Discretion

There are five major areas a police department can target to improve the rationality of police decision making. First, departments must be careful and selective in who they hire as police officers. A rigorous recruitment and selection process can weed out those who will be ill equipped to make good decisions under pressure. Second, departments must ensure that their officers are properly trained and adequately prepared for the situations they will encounter on the job. Police officers will be more likely to make rational and fair decisions if their training, both in the academy and while in service, has prepared them to do so.

Third, police departments should develop clear and understandable administrative guidelines for structuring police discretion in certain types of encounters. Davis (1971) argued that administrative rule making is the most effective method for controlling discretion, and research has supported his position in a number of critical areas of policing: use of deadly force, automobile pursuits, domestic violence encounters, handling the mentally ill, and the use of police dogs (see, for example, Fyfe 1979, 1988; White 2001; Alpert 2001; Walker and Katz 2002). Fourth, administrative policies are meaningless if not enforced. Police officers must be held accountable for the decisions they make, especially if the decision violates departmental policy. When officers are not held to account by management for their decisions, the informal message sent to line officers is that regardless of the decisions they make, their use of discretion is essentially unfettered.

Last, rational decision making by police is facilitated when there are mechanisms to supply systematic feedback (Gottfredson and Gottfredson 1988). Traditionally, police officers hear very little about the consequences of their decisions after the case or suspect moves farther along in the criminal justice system. Did an arrest result in the prosecutor filing charges? Was there a conviction? Did the officer's decisions have anything to do with a negative outcome (case dropped, acquittal, or the like)? These are important questions that are typically not answered for police, but they go to the central issue of whether the alternative that was selected achieved the stated goal (Gottfredson and Gottfredson 1988). Although the decision "stool" has three legs, the information leg is perhaps most critical for rational decision making, and a feedback mechanism provides officers with a constant flow of information about their use of discretion.

Conclusion

In the context of a poorly defined, inherently political role in which each citizen interaction is shaped by the potential use of force, police officers exercise tremendous discretion in carrying out their duties. Four decades of research have demonstrated that their use of discretion is influenced by a wide array of factors—legal and extralegal—and that police decision making is a complex process. The factors that influence police discretion have led to recommendations for enhancing the use of discretion in the context of a "decision stool" metaphor. There are no guaranteed methods for eliminating poor decisions, but departments can reduce their occurrence by attending to all three legs of the decision stool—goals, alternatives, and information—and by holding officers accountable when they make poor decisions.

MICHAEL D. WHITE

See also **Accountability; Attitudes toward the Police: Overview; Clearance Rates and Criminal Investigations; Crime Commissions; Crime, Serious Violent; Discrimination; Early Warning Systems; Ethics and Values in the Context of Community Policing; "Good" Policing; Integrity in Policing; Knapp Commission; Minorities and the Police; Post-Shooting Review; Styles of Policing**

References and Further Reading

Alpert, G. P. 2001. Managing the benefits and risks of pursuit driving. In *Critical issues in policing*, ed. R. G. Dunham and G. P. Alpert, 4th ed. Prospect Heights, IL: Waveland Press.

American Bar Association. 1956. *American Bar Association survey of the administration of justice*. Chicago: American Bar Association.

Bayley, D. H. 1986. The tactical choices of police patrol officers. *Journal of Criminal Justice* 14: 329–48.

Binder, A., and P. Scharf. 1980. The violent police–citizen encounter. *Annals of the American Academy of Political and Social Science* 452: 111–21.

Bittner, E. (1970). *The functions of police in modern society*. Chevy Chase, MD: National Institute of Mental Health.

Black, D. 1970. The production of crime rates. *American Sociological Review* 35: 733–48.

Black, D., and A. J. Reiss, Jr. 1967. *Studies of crime and law enforcement in major metropolitan areas*. Vol. 2, *Field surveys III, Section 1: Patterns of behavior in police and citizen transactions*. Washington, DC: U.S. Government Printing Office.

Boydstun, J. E., and M. E. Sherry. 1975. *San Diego community profile: Final report*. Washington, DC: Police Foundation.

Brown, M. K. 1981. *Working the street: Police discretion and the dilemma of reform*. New York: Russell Sage Foundation.

Bureau of Justice Statistics 2001. *Contacts between police and the public*. Washington, DC: U.S. Government Printing Office.

Friedrich, R. J. 1980. Police use of force: Individuals, situations, and organizations. *Annals of the American Academy of Political and Social Science* 452: 82–97.

Fyfe, J. J. 1979. Administrative interventions on police shooting discretion: An empirical examination. *Journal of Criminal Justice* 7: 309–24.

———. 1980. Geographic correlates of police shooting: A microanalysis. *Journal of Research in Crime and Delinquency* 17: 101–13.

———. 1988. Police use of deadly force: Research and reform. *Justice Quarterly* 5: 165–205.

Geller, W., and K. Karales. 1981. Shootings of and by Chicago police: Uncommon crises: Part I. Shootings by Chicago police. *Journal of Criminal Law and Criminology* 72(4): 1813–66.

Gottfredson, M. R., and D. M. Gottfredson. 1988. *Decision making in criminal justice.* New York: Plenum Press.

Kania, R. E., and W. C. Mackey. 1977. Police violence as a function of community characteristics. *Criminology* 15: 27–48.

Klinger, D. A. 1996. More on demeanor and arrest in Dade County. *Criminology* 34: 61–82.

Lundman, R. J. 1974. Routine police arrest practices: A commonweal perspective. *Social Problems* 22: 127–41.

———. (1996). Demeanor and arrest: Additional evidence from previously unpublished data. *Journal of Research in Crime and Delinquency* 33 (3): 306–23.

Lundman, R. J., R. E. Sykes, and J. P. Clark. 1978. Police control of juveniles. *Journal of Research in Crime and Delinquency* 15(1): 74–91.

Manning, P. K. 1978. The police: Mandate, strategies, and appearances. In *Policing: A view from the street*, ed. Peter K. Manning and John Van Maanen. Santa Monica, CA: Goodyear Publishing.

Mastrofski, S. 1981. Policing the beat: The impact of organizational scale on patrol officer behavior in urban residential neighborhoods. *Journal of Criminal Justice* 9: 343–58.

Murphy, P. V., and T. Pate. 1977. *Commissioner: A view from the top of American law enforcement.* New York: Simon and Schuster.

Ostrum, E., R. B. Parks, and G. Whitaker. 1978. *Patterns of metropolitan policing.* Cambridge, MA: Ballinger.

President's Commission on Law Enforcement and Administration of Justice. 1967. *Task force report: The police.* Washington, DC: U.S. Government Printing Office.

Reiss, A. J., Jr., 1971. *The police and the public.* New Haven, CT: Yale University Press.

Reuss-Ianni, E. 1983. *Two cultures of policing.* New Brunswick, NJ: Transaction Books.

Ricksheim, E. C., and S. M. Chermak. 1993. Causes of police behavior revisited. *Journal of Criminal Justice* 21: 353–82.

Rossi, P., R. Berk, and B. Edison. 1974. *The roots of urban discontent: Public policy, municipal institutions, and the ghetto.* New York: Wiley.

Skolnick, J. H. 1966. *Justice without trial: Law enforcement in a democratic society.* New York: Wiley.

Skolnick, J. H., and J. J. Fyfe. 1993. *Above the law: Police and the excessive use of force.* New York: Free Press.

Smith, D. 1984. The organizational context of legal control. *Criminology* 22: 19–38.

———. 1986. The neighborhood context of police behavior. In *Crime and Justice: Annual Review of Research*, Vol. 8, ed. A. Reiss and M. Tonry.

Smith, D., and C. Visher. 1981. Street level justice: Situational determinants of police arrest decisions. *Social Problems* 29: 167–78.

Swanson, C. 1978. The influence of organization and environment on arrest policies in major U.S. cities. *Policy Studies Journal* 7: 390–418.

Walker, S., and C. M. Katz. 2002. *The police in America: An introduction.* New York: McGraw-Hill.

Westley, W. A. 1970. *Violence and the police: A sociological study of law, custom, and morality.* Cambridge, MA: The MIT Press.

White, M. D. 2001. Controlling police decisions to use deadly force: Reexamining the importance of administrative policy. *Crime and Delinquency* 47 (1): 131–51.

———. 2003. Examining the impact of external influences on police use of deadly force over time. *Evaluation Review* 27 (1): 50–78.

Wilson, J. Q. 1968. *Varieties of police behavior.* Cambridge, MA: Harvard University Press.

Wilson, J. Q., and B. Boland. 1978. The effect of the police on crime. *Law and Society Review* 12: 367–90.

Worden, R. E. 1989. Situational and attitudinal explanations of police behavior: A theoretical reappraisal and empirical assessment. *Law and Society Review* 23: 667–711.

DISCRIMINATION

Introduction

The equal and just application of law is central to the mission of criminal justice in the United States. Despite this goal, law enforcement has historically struggled with race and gender discrimination. The fourteenth amendment of the constitution protects citizens from state actions that "deprive any person of life, liberty, or property, without due process of law; nor deny to any person within its jurisdiction the equal protection of the laws." Since the 1960s, courts have used evidence of disparate treatment and outcomes based on race and gender as a means to evaluate whether various law enforcement practices are unconstitutionally biased.

Addressing the challenges of discrimination, both real and perceived, has become critical as local law enforcement agencies across the country embrace community policing models, which depend on the trust and confidence of all members of the community. We explore public perceptions of discriminatory treatment in the enforcement of justice and racial and gender disparities that have emerged in statistics regarding traffic stops, arrests, and use of force as well as the legal and legislative responses to discriminatory treatment of citizens by the police. Such treatment in the hiring and promotion of employees within police agencies also is discussed.

Racial Discrimination in the Application of Criminal Law

Perceptions of Police by the Public

Perceived disparate treatment of groups in the enforcement of justice strongly shapes the public trust and confidence in the police and may lead to legal claims of discrimination. The loss of public trust, particularly among minority groups, has led to legal challenges of discrimination against the police. In general, a majority of Americans express confidence in the police; however, non-whites consistently demonstrate lower confidence levels than do whites. In 2004, according to Gallup Poll results, 90% of U.S. citizens had at least some confidence in the police. Seventy percent of white Americans had a "great deal" of confidence in the police, compared to 43% of non-white Americans. In addition, non-whites were almost twice as likely to indicate that they had "very little" confidence in the police when compared to whites (Bureau of Justice Statistics 2003).

In general, race tends to influence public perception of police injustice. Blacks are considerably more likely to perceive criminal injustice (Hagan and Albonetti 1982). More recently, Weitzer (2000) demonstrated that a majority of all individuals, regardless of race, believed that being black made a difference in how an individual was treated by the police. Ultimately, however, research indicates that although non-whites are more likely to believe the police are unjust, these attitudes are affected by factors other than race exclusively.

A variety of factors negatively influence non-white perceptions of the police, including marital status, income, and neighborhood crime rate (Parker, Onyekwuluke, and Murty 1995). Class inequality appears to be a significant factor in blacks' experience of social institutions. Research indicates that perceptions of blacks from a middle class neighborhood more closely paralleled those of middle class whites than those of blacks from a lower class neighborhood (Weitzer 1999, 2000). Ultimately, in examining police perception, neighborhood and class characteristics appear to play a more significant role than race alone.

Racial Profiling

During the past decade, concern about racial profiling and the disparate treatment of drivers during routine traffic stops has become a critical issue for law enforcement. Although there have long been allegations of police targeting people of color, aggressive crime control strategies utilized by police in an effort to reduce crime rates throughout the 1980s and

1990s heightened the perception that police may use traffic offenses as a pretext to conduct disproportionate numbers of roadside investigations of black or Hispanic drivers and their vehicles. The term "racial profiling" was derived from the use of a "profile" of drug couriers developed by the Drug Enforcement Agency during the mid-1980s to interdict interstate drug trafficking. Allegations of racial profiling become so common that the phenomenon was popularly labeled "driving while black" or "driving while brown."

Racial profiling is generally understood as any "police-initiated action that relies upon the race, ethnicity, or national origin of an individual rather than the behavior of that individual or information that leads the police to a particular individual who has been identified as being engaged in or having been engaged in criminal activity" (Ramirez, McDevitt, and Farrell 2000). Using this definition, it is appropriate for police to use race or ethnicity to determine whether a person matches a specific description of a particular suspect but not appropriate to use racial or ethnic stereotypes as factors in selecting whom to stop and search.

National surveys indicate that a majority of Americans, regardless of race, believe that racial bias in police stops is a significant social problem. In Gallup Polls from 1999, 2001, and 2003, almost 60% of Americans surveyed believe that the practice of racial profiling is widespread. For black respondents, the perception that racial profiling is widespread actually increased from 77% in 1999 to 85% in 2003.

In April 1999, the issues of racial profiling took the national spotlight when the New Jersey attorney general released a report concluding that the New Jersey State Police illegitimately used race as a basis for stopping drivers on interstate highways in an attempt to make drug arrests. The attorney general's findings followed public outcry over several high profile incidents, including the shooting and wounding of three unarmed black and Hispanic men during a traffic stop by New Jersey state troopers. In the same year, the U.S. Department of Justice brought a federal civil rights suit against the New Jersey State Police based on "pattern and practice" of discrimination. Ultimately, the New Jersey State Police and the Department of Justice came to an agreement memorialized in a federal consent decree.

Arrest

Suggestions of racial disparity and discrimination in policing have also been attributed to arrest discretion. Black and Hispanic individuals are disproportionately likely to be arrested, compared to their representation in the general population. In 2002, blacks comprised 12.9% of the population but 26.9% of all arrests. Whites represented 77.1% of the population but made up 70.7% of arrests (Bureau of Justice Statistics 2003). Further, blacks perceive that they are more likely than whites to be hassled by police, both personally and vicariously (Browning et al. 1994).

Although research does indicate the veracity of at least some level of disparity in arrest discretion, there exists no consensus or clear indication of the presence of specific racial discrimination. As with other components of police work, the decision to arrest involves a multitude of factors, and thus disparity may in fact be attributable to other confounding variables. Arrest discretion has been attributed to situational factors, and further, it has been suggested that disparity could be accounted for by factors such as increased disrespectfulness to the police or greater involvement in more serious crimes (Walker, Spohn, and Delone 2004). The neighborhood in which an incident occurred may also play a more significant role than race alone in determining arrest decision.

It is possible that discrimination exists but has little to do with the suspect. Some research indicates that even when no evidence of racial bias against suspects is ascertained, police appear more inclined to arrest in the event that a white complainant is involved. Thus, it becomes unclear as to whether disparities can be attributed to the existence of racist practices or to other criteria such as seriousness of offense, neighborhood characteristics, age, suspect history, behavior and demeanor, or presence of a complainant.

Research also suggests that differential treatment by police occurs in relation to female suspects. The presence of chivalry, where women receive preferential treatment, has been suggested and examined. Visher (1983) found that women were treated differently than males in arrest situations, with the decision to arrest a female being made more on the basis of individual factors than larger situational cues. Results also indicate that females who violate stereotypical female characteristics and behaviors are less likely to be afforded chivalry. Here, young, black, and hostile women did not receive preferential treatment, while calm older white women were granted leniency. The presence of a complainant or victim appeared to influence chivalry, with victim request for arrest discouraging chivalry. Further research has supported the discrepancy between arrest decisions for black and white female suspects (Smith, Visher, and Davidson 1984).

Additional research is needed in the area of disparity and discrimination in police arrest discretion. Research has been used to both support and to refute the presence of discriminatory practices. It is possible that disparities may be more attributable to where a suspect lives or to the nature of the suspect's interaction with police than to specifically race in and of itself. However, gender does appear to play a role in arrest discretion. Ultimately, conclusions cannot be drawn until further experimentation is conducted and confounding variables are more specifically examined.

Use of Force by the Police

From the Wickersham Commission's 1931 examination of the practice of using the "third degree" and infliction of pain in order to obtain confessions to reactions to the 1991 beating of Rodney King by Los Angeles police officers, police use of force has and continues to represent an issue of fundamental concern in the United States. This concern is heightened by the suggestion that force may be used disproportionately on certain groups.

It is estimated that police use force in approximately 1% of police–citizen interactions (Langan et al. 2001). Use of force is relatively infrequent, typically occurs at the lower end of the spectrum of force, and typically occurs when a suspect is resisting arrest. Research has shown that minorities have an increased likelihood of experiencing police use of force. For example, a 1999 Bureau of Justice Statistics national survey of contact between the police and public suggests that blacks and Hispanics were more likely than whites to have reported police use of force, or threatened use of force (Langan et al. 2001).

Discerning the extent and nature of use of force is challenging. Recent empirical research examining local police departments supports prior findings that use of force is infrequent and that when it does occur, it usually involves a low level of force. Factors previously thought to influence use of force, such as the race of both officers and suspects, do not appear to significantly predict police use of force (Garner et al. 1996). Research also indicates that officers tend to use higher levels of force against suspects of the same ethnicity as the officer (Alpert and Dunham 1999).

A more specific subcategory of police use of force that receives significant public attention is the use of deadly force by officers. Public outcry, such as the Cincinnati riots following the shooting of a black man in April 2001, heightens social concern about disparate uses of force. Although there is evidence of racial disparity in fatal shootings by police, there appears to be no consensus as to whether the disparity that does exist is indicative of discrimination. Data suggest that a growing percentage of felons killed by police are white, while a declining percentage are black. In 1978, blacks were killed at a rate of eight black to every one white victim. By 1998, such discrepancy had decreased by half (Brown and Langan 2001).

Ultimately, it is unclear as to the extent to which discriminatory use of force exists and, if present, what the nature of such discriminatory practices is. As with other components of policing and discrimination, there potentially exist other factors (such as age, class, or suspect behavior) that may additionally explain findings. Further research is necessary, specifically research that examines both the explicit nature of use of force as well as the dynamic interaction of confounding variables that might exist.

Legal Responses to Discriminatory Treatment

Lawsuits against the Police

A number of laws protect individuals from discriminatory conduct by the police in arrests, traffic stops, and use of excessive force, in the use of racial slurs, or in the refusal of an agency to respond to complaints alleging discriminatory treatment by its officers. The Omnibus Crime Control and Safe Streets Act of 1968 and Title VI of the Civil Rights Act of 1964 together prohibit discrimination on the basis of race, color, sex, or national origin by police departments receiving federal funds. These laws prohibit both individual acts and patterns or practices of discriminatory misconduct by state and local law enforcement agencies that receive any financial assistance from the federal government. Departments found to have engaged in discriminatory practices risk losing all federal funding.

Individuals who are subject to police discrimination can also bring civil litigation against police officers or municipalities for violations of 42 U.S.C. § 1983. To establish a legal claim of discrimination under § 1983, a citizen must show that the action occurred "under color of law" and that they were deprived of a constitutionally protected right. Over time, however, it has become more difficult for citizens to succeed in § 1983 claims against police officers or agencies. The courts have consistently ruled that the citizen must prove that discriminatory treatment by the police was intentional, not merely a practice with a disparate impact on a particular group. Additionally, state and local law enforcement agencies have largely escaped liability under § 1983 because citizens must additionally show that the leadership of an agency either promoted, condoned, or had knowledge of discriminatory practices within the organization and failed to prevent such practices.

Prior to 1994, the federal government primarily prevented discrimination by the state and local police through legal action to withhold federal funding if discriminatory treatment was found. Following the high profile beating of Rodney King by Los Angeles Police Department officers, Congress passed legislation amending the federal code under 42 U.S.C. § 14141, which made it unlawful for state and local law enforcement officers to engage in a pattern or practice of conduct that deprives persons of their constitutional civil rights. Section 14141 allows the U.S. Department of Justice to mandate structural changes within law enforcement agencies to end patterns of abusive and discriminatory practices.

Commissions and Civil Rights

Perceived police misconduct and racial discrimination by the police has historically led to racial turmoil in many minority communities. In response to these high profile events, numerous government sponsored commissions have addressed the impact of disparate treatment and discrimination. Following urban race riots of the 1960s, President Johnson appointed the Kerner Commission to investigate community upheaval and offer recommendations. The commission identified deep hostility between the police and the minority communities as a primary cause for the public disorder and a glaring lack of minority representation in policing as a primary cause of the negative relationship between communities of color and the police. The conclusion of the commission was that predominately large city police departments employed few individuals of color and "loomed as virtually all-white occupying armies" in urban neighborhoods (Walker, Spohn, and Delone 2004, 197).

Since that time, numerous commissions have found that discriminatory treatment by the police in the application of justice and employment practices has led to community distrust and instability. More recently, the Christopher Commission was formed to investigate the beating of Rodney King by members of the Los Angeles Police Department. The commission concluded that "the problem of excessive force [was] aggravated by racism and bias within the LAPD" (Commission, 54).

To address the concerns raised by these commissions and other public outcry, law enforcement has largely moved from reactive patrols to more proactive models of community policing. Under a community policing model, police agencies are expected to solicit input and participation from citizens and communities in order to determine what neighborhoods or individuals should be targets of law enforcement attention. As a result of this shift, minority representation in the police force has gained increased attention since it constitutes an important tool for helping police departments gain the trust of minority community members who might not otherwise serve in a police–community partnership. The underrepresentation of minorities among the police ranks has historically signified a lack of sensitivity and understanding of minority concerns and culture within law enforcement, which threatens to reduce the support for community policing within the communities where partnerships are needed the most.

Bias and Discrimination in Employment

Prior to the 1960s, there were very few women or racial minorities employed in law enforcement professions. Employment discrimination through formal requirements and informal practices kept many qualified individuals out of the police ranks. Changes in employment law since the 1960s have largely reversed biased practices that were codified in departmental hiring policies. Despite these legal advances and the widespread acceptance and support for diversifying the law enforcement profession, the majority of law enforcement agencies continue to struggle with issues of recruiting a diverse workforce—particularly people of color and women. A 2002 Bureau of Justice Statistics report on police departments nationally indicated that more than three-quarters (77.4%) of officers were white males (Reaves and Hickman 2002). The same report estimated that, as of June 2002, 10.6% of all full-time officers were female and 22.6% members of a racial/ethnic minority.

Historically, physical requirements, including height-weight proportion and physical strength, prevented women from advancing through the recruitment process, thus limiting the pool of qualified female applicants (Milton 1972; Sulton and Townsey 1981; Police Foundation Report 1989). Although many of these tests have been modified to test the true occupational requirements of law enforcement, the ability of female recruits to pass physical agility tests remains a concern for administrators interested in diversifying the police workforce. In a 1998 study by the International Association of Chiefs of Police looking at women in policing, physical strength was listed as the top concern (28%) regarding women's skills. Among the explanations provided for the under-representation of minorities are a lack of education, including higher dropout rates (Winter 1991), and the use of drugs and arrest rates (Clark 1989). Thus, the criminal background check has limited the pool of minority recruits.

Despite these barriers, one of the primary reasons for the small proportion of women and minorities available within the applicant pool is a lack of interest or perceived lack of interest in law enforcement careers by women and racial and ethnic minorities. Life experiences, including higher education and familial obligations, of both women and minorities vary from the conventional model of a police officer. Due to the traditional all-white, all-male environment, there is also a low probability of mentors or support for female or minority officers within the upper echelons of police organizations.

Legal Remedies to Discrimination in Law Enforcement Hiring and Promotion

The legal landscape has changed dramatically since 1960, protecting the rights of persons seeking employment and enabling applicants facing discrimination to seek compensatory and punitive damages from employers or potential employers. Most prominent among these changes were the Civil Rights Acts of 1964 and 1970, which provided explicit protection of employees from discrimination based on race, sex, religion, or ethnicity. Title VII of the Civil Rights Act states that it is unlawful for an employer ". . . to limit, segregate, or classify his employees or applicants for employment in any way which would deprive or tend to deprive any individual of employment opportunities or otherwise adversely affect his status as an employee, because of such individual's race, color, religion, sex, or national origin." The Supreme Court has subsequently interpreted disparate treatment of individuals based on these protected categories as a violation of Title VII. Therefore, employers must not engage in hiring or promotion practices that have a disparate impact on certain groups, which might be indicative of a pattern of discrimination.

The Equal Employment Opportunity Act of 1972 amended Title VII and created the Equal Employment Opportunity Commission (EEOC). The EEOC has been the primary governmental agency to investigate disparate hiring and promotion practices that may violate employees' civil rights. Employers may also face liability for discriminatory treatment when they "use employment practices that although apparently unbiased on their face, operate to the disadvantage of groups of persons based on race, color, sex, religion, or national origin" (Sustra et al. 1995). In essence, standards set forth by departments and to be applied to all applicants, such as written exams, cannot have a purposefully disparate effect.

More recently, federal law and the courts have expanded the protected categories of individuals who can be protected from discrimination in hiring. The Age Discrimination Act of 1967 prohibits discrimination in hiring and promotion against people older than forty. The Americans with Disabilities Act of 1990 again amended Title VII of the Civil Rights Act of 1964, providing significant protections against discrimination for people with handicaps, mental impairments, or medial illness. The 1990 act provided compensatory and punitive damages, which had previously been available only to racial and ethnic minorities but can now be sought by any victim of intentional discrimination based on sex, religion, or disability.

As courts continue to expand and clarify the protections to citizens facing discrimination by law enforcement in either the administration of justice or professional employment, fair and equitable enforcement will be central to the operational mission of law enforcement agencies seeking public trust.

AMY FARRELL and DANIELLE ROUSSEAU

See also **Accountability; Attitudes toward the Police: Overview; Community-Oriented Policing: Rationale; Discretion; Excessive Force; Independent Commission on the Los Angeles Police Department (The Christopher Commission); Minorities and the Police; National Advisory Commission on Civil Disorder; Personnel Selection; Racial Profiling; Women in Law Enforcement**

References and Further Reading

Alpert, G. P., and R. G. Dunham. 1999, The force factor: Measuring and assessing police use of force and suspect resistance. In *Use of force by police: Overview of national and local data*, ed. J. Travis, J. M. Chaiken, and R. J. Jaminski, 45–60. NCJ 176330, October. Washington, DC: U.S. Department of Justice, National Institute of Justice and Bureau of Justice Statistics.

Brown, J. M., and P. A. Langan. 2001. *Policing and homicide, 1976–1998: Justifiable homicide by police, police officers murdered by felons*. NCJ 18087, March. Washington, DC: U.S. Department of Justice, Bureau of Justice Statistics.

Browning, S. L., F. T. Cullen, L. Cao, R. Kopache, and T. J. Stevenson. 1994. Race and getting hassled by the police: A research note. *Police Studies* 17 (1): 1–11.

Bureau of Justice Statistics. 2003. *Sourcebook of criminal justice statistics 2003*. Washington, DC: Bureau of Justice Statistics.

Garner, J., J. Buchanan, T. Schade, and J. Hepburn. 1996. *Understanding the use of force by police and against police*. November. Washington, DC: U.S. Department of Justice, National Institute of Justice.

Hagan, J., and C. Albonetti. 1982. Race, class, and the perception of criminal injustice in America. *American Journal of Sociology* 88 (2): 329–55.

Langan, P. A., L. A. Greenfeld, S. K. Smith, M. R. Durose, and D. J. Levin. 2001. *Contacts between police and the public: Findings from the 1999 national survey*. NJC 184957, February. Washington, DC: U.S. Department of Justice, Bureau of Justice Statistics.

Parker, K. D., A. B. Onyekwuluke, and K. S. Murty. 1995. African Americans' attitudes toward the local police: A multivariate analysis. *Journal of Black Studies* 25 (3): 396–409.

Smith, D. A., C. A. Visher, and L. A. Davidson. 1984. Equity and discretionary justice: The influence of race on police arrest decisions. *The Journal of Criminal Law & Criminology* 75 (1): 234–49.

Visher, C. A. 1983. Gender, police arrest decisions, and notions of chivalry. *Criminology* 21 (1): 5–28.

Walker, S., C. Spohn, and M. Delone. 2004. *The color of justice: Race, ethnicity, and crime in America*. Belmont, CA: Wadsworth/Thompson Learning.

Weitzer, R. 1999. Citizens' perceptions of police misconduct: Race and neighborhood context. *Justice Quarterly*, 16 (4): 819–46.

———. 2000. Racialized policing: Residents' perceptions in three neighborhoods. *Law and Society Review* 31 (1): 129–55.

DISPATCH AND COMMUNICATIONS CENTERS

As society has become more mobile, so police dispatch and communications centers have become increasingly important to the social organization of policing. They are crucial in terms of how members of the public contact the police and also in relation to the command and control processes by which police organizations manage public demand and coordinate their responses to it.

Calling the Police

The impact that the telephone has had upon policing is a comparatively neglected issue, but it is a pivotal technology in terms of understanding the trajectory of change of police–community interactions. Prior to the widespread availability of telephones, people were limited in terms of how they could make the police aware of an issue that potentially required a policing intervention. But with the spread of landline telephones to most domestic addresses and subsequently the adoption of mobile phones by much of the population, it has become much easier for the public to make contact with the police. Therefore, dispatch and communications centers are often one of the first points of contact that members of the public have when trying to engage with the police, whether they are reporting a "hot" emergency, requiring immediate response, or making contact for some other reason.

Particularly as a result of the adoption of single emergency number systems that make it easy for citizens to establish a contact, police dispatch and communications centers are typically responsible for handling large numbers of calls for service from the public. Indeed, in most police organizations the total volume of calls being handled has increased significantly, a pattern amplified in the late twentieth and early twenty-first centuries with the spread of mobile phones. In both U.S. and U.K. policing agencies, a number of efforts to manage this gap between the public demand for services and the police capacity to supply them have been instigated through reforming the organization of dispatch and communications centers. Of particular note is a trend toward the regionalization of call centers or the sharing of them with other emergency services. Utilizing advances in information and communication technologies, such reforms offer the promise of increased efficiency in managing public demands, but it is not clear whether this translates into improved public experiences of contacting the police.

Given that public demand for police services now routinely outstrips police resources, important organizational decisions are implemented through the dispatch and communications centers in terms of which incidents will receive what response. Thus, although working in these centers is typically seen as being a comparatively low status occupation in many police organizations, the operators are actually involved in making significant decisions that determine both how the organization responds to individual incidents and also the ways that it manages its overall workload.

Peter Manning's research has demonstrated that members of the public in trying to communicate information to police often do so in a confused, complex, and unclear fashion (Manning 1988). Consequently, the first task for the police organization, through the individuals working in the dispatch and communications center, is a sense-making one. Upon receiving a call from the public, the operator has to interpret the information provided by the caller, fit the information to some form of meaningful organizational classification, and on this basis arrange for an appropriate response to be made. To aid in this complex decision-making task, many police organizations have adopted formal graded response criteria for establishing what form of response is required to different situations. Nevertheless, the presence of such bureaucratic protocols does not eradicate the important interpretative work that is performed by human operators.

The decision making of the operators working in dispatch and communications centers is structured to varying degrees by a number of organizational imperatives. A particularly important one is the "just in case" rule. If the situation is ambiguous in terms of how much trouble might be present, operators will often decide to send officers to attend just in case the problem should escalate or just in case the incident is more serious than is immediately apparent from the information being provided to them by the caller.

A similar outcome results from the need of the organization to "demonstrate concern." Thus, in many instances when police are called, there is little probability of them catching the perpetrator as a result of a fast response, but it is nevertheless felt important that they respond quickly in order to demonstrate concern for someone's personal crisis, especially where the individual concerned is deemed vulnerable in some way. Consequently, although dispatch and communications workers can often exercise considerable discretion in the performance of their role, their decision-making power is not completely unfettered. Other organizational and political imperatives directly impact upon and influence their work.

Command and Control

Just as the development of communications technologies has transformed how the public contacts the police, so they also changed how the police have organized themselves to respond to such calls for service. The ability of dispatch and communications centers to relay publicly provided information to police officers who are not co-present establishes a capacity, at least in principle, for a faster and more flexible response to be provided. This is certainly the case when contrasted with the "fixed point system" of patrol that was used in many forces prior to the widespread use of personal radios. Because officers can be contacted via their radios, they do not need to return to the station to be assigned new tasks, nor do they have to be sought out by a citizen wanting to contact them. As such, the dispatch and communications center is vital to an increasing flexibility in terms of the organization of policing and needs to be understood as a central component of the command and control systems by which modern police bureaucracies seek to coordinate their resources.

Given the well-established research finding that a police patrol officer often operates in conditions of comparative low visibility in respect to their supervisors, something that is facilitated in part by dispatch and communications centers, it is perhaps unsurprising that increasingly these centers have come to perform a surveillance function over officers on the streets. The conduct of officers is increasingly monitored through the communications technologies that are used to stay in contact with them. This information is used for monitoring the performance of individual officers but also, in a more aggregated form, the organization as a whole.

Research has demonstrated that it is important not to overstate the efficacy of the police command and control systems (Waddington 1993). The promise of the command and control system to effect better oversight over police activity has only been partially realized. It is also the case that with advances in information and communication technologies and a growing realization about how consequential the work in dispatch and communications centers is, the conduct of those in these centers likewise is increasingly subject to surveillance. The number of calls being handled and how they are handled by individuals is routinely monitored by supervisors.

MARTIN INNES

See also **Calls for Service; Computer-Aided Dispatching (CAD) Systems; Technology and Police Decision Making; Technology and the Police; Technology, Records Management, and Calls for Service**

References and Further Reading

Manning, Peter. 1988. *Symbolic communication: Signifying calls and the police response.* Cambridge, MA: The MIT Press.
Waddington, Peter. 1993. *Calling the police: The interpretation of and response to calls for assistance from the public.* Aldershot, England: Avebury.

DISPUTE RESOLUTION, COMMUNITY

Although community dispute resolution can refer to a wide range of initiatives aimed at addressing community conflicts and undertaken by many very diverse local entities (Auerbach 1983), since the early 1970s the phrase has become associated with a variety of eclectic, innovative community-based centers that focus their attention on how to better manage conflict situations involving citizens in their respective local communities.

Known by many different names, such as community mediation programs, restorative justice programs, neighborhood justice centers, community peacemaking programs, community justice programs, victim–offender mediation programs, dispute settlement programs, and conflict or dispute resolution programs, all of these efforts aim to provide local citizens with more accessible, less adversarial, more appropriate, less time-consuming, and less expensive or even free services, handling an extensive variety of conflicts, many of which would otherwise be handled by the legal system. In many instances, these centers are closely associated with the civil and criminal courts, from which they receive referrals. The community dispute resolution centers also partner with other components of the criminal justice system, particularly the police, for access to cases that come to their attention or to conduct conflict resolution training.

Community Dispute Resolution and Mediation

Central to most community dispute resolution initiatives has been the use of mediation and related collaborative problem-solving processes such as conciliation and facilitation. Mediation, the best known and most widely used process, relies on a third party known as a mediator, who assists disputing parties to resolve their differences. Through face-to-face meetings, parties have an opportunity to exchange information and work through their differences voluntarily (Moore 2003). Mediation is viewed as especially useful in those situations where parties have an ongoing relationship.

Key recognizable characteristics of the mediation process are self-determination by the parties, impartiality by the interveners, and confidentiality of process (Association for Conflict Resolution 2005). Self-determination means that the parties are empowered to make informed choices about their situation and can choose to terminate the process at any point. Mediators do not make decisions for parties. They use techniques and skills to help the parties share their perspectives, clarify concerns, generate possible options, and craft a working arrangement for the future. Impartiality refers to the need for mediators to pay careful attention to any conduct implying any partiality on their part. Their actions should not show any biases or preferences. Confidentiality assures the parties that they can speak candidly in a safe, respectful setting. It means that information exchanged during the mediation sessions will not be discussed with others or used in future court or administrative hearings. Depending on the context, there are some exceptions to the confidentiality provisions. A few widely recognized exceptions include child abuse, domestic violence, or imminent harm to a person.

While it is generally understood that mediation is a process in which parties are assisted to work through their differences, there is no one way to do it. Mediation reflects the mediator's personality, styles, training, and philosophy as well as the context in which the mediation is being conducted. Despite mediation's sensitivity to nuances of practitioners and milieu, as its use has expanded, several dominant styles have evolved. The style most common to community dispute resolution is facilitative, in which facilitative mediators ask questions to identify, reframe, and analyze issues and options. They rely on the parties to play an active role in identifying their needs and interests and shy away from making recommendations or expressing opinions.

The Development and Growth of Community Dispute Resolution Centers

Community dispute resolution centers have flourished since the early 1970s. The growth of these centers has been attributed to a number of factors. Chief among them are dissatisfaction with the cost, slowness, and inappropriateness of the traditional adversarial processing of cases and the desire for greater social justice (Wahrhaftig 2004).

Because community dispute resolution centers are very decentralized and highly dispersed, comprehensive and accurate data about them are elusive. Despite the paucity of available data, what is evident is that community dispute resolution centers have proliferated throughout the United States (McGillis 1997). Although there were only a handful of such centers in the early 1970s, by the end of that decade the U.S. Department of Justice had begun formally funding experimental neighborhood justice centers in Atlanta, Kansas City, and Los Angeles. According to estimates made by the National Association for Community Mediation (NAFCM), the number of centers has swelled to more than 550. NAFCM also reports that over the years more than 76,000 citizens have been trained as mediators and that each year more than 97,500 disputes are referred to community dispute resolution centers (NAFCM 2005).

Increasingly, community dispute resolution centers have focused on restorative justice, an umbrella concept that refers to a variety of responses to criminal wrongdoing, including victim–offender mediation, circle sentencing, community reparative boards, and family group conferences. Restorative justice involves rectifying harm and restoring relationships by providing victims, offenders, and community members with an opportunity to actively participate in the justice process.

The best known of the restorative justice efforts is victim–offender mediation, which formally began in Kitchener, Ontario, in 1974 and increasingly has been adopted in a variety of communities and contexts worldwide (Umbreit 2001). As an informal, nonadversarial process bringing victims and offenders together face to face, victim–offender mediation allows the victims to share their concerns about the impact of the crime, the offenders to give information about the offense, and in some instances, community members an opportunity to participate. This approach to community dispute resolution assists the victim to recover and the offender to be restored to the community. Minor criminal matters such as vandalism, theft, burglary, and minor assaults tend to be referred to victim–offender mediation by the courts. However, violent crimes are also mediated, usually when so requested by victims or by a surviving family member (Umbreit 2000).

Finally, hybrid versions of community dispute resolution centers have emerged. For example, community or victim impact panels provide offenders with an opportunity to meet face to face with members of the community, not necessarily the victims themselves, to discuss the impact of their offense on the community. In New York City, the offenses brought to impact panels consist of those involving quality of life offenses, where a summons from the police has been issued for a misdemeanor crime or violation.

The Eclectic Community Dispute Resolution Landscape

Community dispute resolution centers can be quite diverse (McGillis 1997). In general, they tend to be operated by nonprofit organizations and funded by a variety of sources, including government, private foundations, fund-raisers, and fees from special services such as training programs. They tend to be low budget centers, providing the bulk of their services gratis, for a nominal fee, or on a sliding scale basis. Program costs are kept low since virtually all of the centers utilize volunteer citizens who are trained to mediate cases. The citizens come from very diverse backgrounds in each community, often mirroring the local population.

There are no universally accepted guidelines for training mediators. As a result, training is quite varied, ranging from little formal training to precisely defined criteria identifying specific topics and activities. New York State, for example, which has one of the nation's most comprehensive statewide community dispute resolution networks, has identified standards and requirements for community mediators. To be certified by a local dispute resolution center, mediators must attend a thirty-hour basic mediation training program that includes skills practice and "role plays," followed by an apprenticeship with two role plays, the observation of one actual mediation, the mediation or comediation of at least five cases with an experienced mediator, and the mediation or comediation of one case that is debriefed by staff or through a self-evaluation instrument. Additionally, each year, mediators must participate in at least six hours of continuing education and mediate or comediate at least three mediations. Finally, mediators who mediate any special cases must complete additional training (New York State Unified Court System 2003).

The types of cases handled by the community dispute resolution centers are quite varied and reflect local context. Generally speaking, they process both civil and criminal cases, including neighborhood conflicts involving noise, barking dogs, lifestyle differences, family conflicts over custody disputes and parenting, landlord–tenant complaints about leases and repairs, business disputes about consumer complaints, and minor criminal matters such as harassment, assaults, and trespassing.

The community dispute resolution centers have been viewed as providing a wide range of benefits. Some of the benefits widely attributed to the centers include highly satisfied parties, faster and less expensive processing of cases than in conventional court processing, and creative outcomes defined by the parties.

Ongoing Challenge: Need for Rigorous Research

While community dispute resolution centers have proliferated throughout the country and are staffed by very enthusiastic mediators, these centers are significantly underresearched (Hedeen 2004). Most of the data are dated, filed in the wide range of local program reports and newsletters, or based on fragmented anecdotal and descriptive accounts from program staff and participants. Information is needed to fully understand what works, what does not, and why the centers are underutilized in their respective communities. Since virtually all centers are staffed by volunteers and run by nonprofit organizations operating on very limited budgets, research is particularly important for funding and policy-making purposes. Of particular note, research could also help shed light on questions regarding the specific role of the community dispute resolution centers vis-à-vis the criminal justice system.

MARIA R. VOLPE

See also **Conflict Management; Crime Prevention; Police Social Work Teams and Victim Advocates; Public Safety, Defined; Victim Rights Movement in the United States**

References and Further Reading

Association for Conflict Resolution. 2005. *Model standards of conduct for mediators.* http://www.acrnet.org.

Auerbach, Jerold. 1983. *Justice without law: Resolving disputes without lawyers.* New York: Oxford University Press.

Hedeen, Timothy. 2004. The evolution of community mediation: Limited research suggests unlimited progress. *Conflict Resolution Quarterly* 22 (1–2): 101–33.

McGillis, Daniel. 1986. *Community dispute resolution programs and public policy.* Washington, DC: U.S. Department of Justice.

———. 1997. *Community mediation programs: Developments and challenges.* Washington, DC: U.S. Department of Justice, Office of Justice Programs, National Institute of Justice.

McKinney, Bruce, William D. Kimsey, and Rex M. Fuller. 1996. A nationwide survey of mediation centers. *Mediation Quarterly* 14 (2): 155–66.

Moore, Christopher W. 2003. *The mediation process: Practical strategies for resolving conflict.* 3rd ed. San Francisco: Jossey-Bass.

National Association for Community Mediation (NAFCM). 2005. http://www.nafcm.org.

New York State Unified Court System Office of Alternative Dispute Resolution Programs. 2003. *Standards and requirements for mediators and mediation trainers.* http://www.courts.state.ny.us/ip/adr/cdrc.shtml (accessed June 11, 2003).

Tomasic, Roman, and Malcolm M. Feeley, eds. 1982. *Neighborhood justice: An assessment of an emergent idea.* New York: Longman.

Umbreit, Mark S. 2000. The restorative justice and mediation collection. *Office for Victims of Crime Bulletin*, July. Washington, DC: U.S. Department of Justice, Office of Justice Programs.

———. 2001. *The handbook of victim offender mediation.* San Francisco: Jossey-Bass.

Wahrhaftig, Paul. 2004. *Community dispute resolution, empowerment and social justice: The origins, history and future of a movement.* Washington, DC: NAFCM Press.

DIVERSITY IN POLICE DEPARTMENTS

As the political landscape and social conditions of American society have changed, so have the personnel policies and practices of local law enforcement departments and, ultimately, the racial and gender makeup of American police departments. We trace the growing diversity that now

exists in American police departments and conclude by offering general, yet pertinent, policy implications to better facilitate public safety and public order in the present-day mosaic of post-9/11, twenty-first century American society.

Introduction: The Functions and Reformations of American Policing

Police have played and will continue to play a pivotal role in the development of American society and the life of American communities. As one of the most visible branches of civil government, police departments are called on to enforce the laws and maintain public safety and public order. However, the guiding philosophy, strategic designs, tactical approaches, and organizational structuring of police departments have changed with the ever expanding notion of American democracy and its more inclusive classification of, and regard for, American citizens, regardless of racial, ethnic, gender, and other differences.

Current attempts to redesign and restructure the police role have been guided by the identification of four dimensions—the philosophical, the strategic, the tactical, and the organizational (Cordner 1999). These dimensions seek to: (1) increase citizen involvement and input, (2) expand the role of law enforcement from one exclusively addressing crime fighting to one that fights crime in the context of enhancing the community welfare, (c) reintroduce more positive interactions and experiences with the public, as well as (d) build and facilitate active partnerships between the police and their constituents.

Consequently, these dimensions have played a key role in the ongoing efforts to compensate for the darker side of American policing, inclusive of the compelling evidence that identifies the old slave patrols as the progenitor and forerunner of contemporary policing (Williams and Murphy

1990; Walker 1977, 1980). Moreover, these dimensions have ushered in a more coactive function of local law enforcement by facilitating the partnering or integration of the police with the community in the coproduction of public safety and order. This coactive function blends the more traditional reactive role (responding to calls for service) and proactive functions (police-initiated activities) with community partnering (police and citizens regularly meeting, listening, discussing, planning, and evaluating concerns that relate to public safety, broadly conceived) (Ottemeier and Wycoff 1997; Koven 1992).

However, the success of this coactive function (with its coproduction implications), especially when considering the multiethnic realities of post-9/11 America, is dependent upon more diverse police personnel who are sensitive to the cultures, traditions, and perceptions of others who make up and contribute to the present-day American mosaic (MacDonald 2003; Culver 2004).

The Changing Face and Responsive Nature of American Policing

The face of American policing traditionally has been white and its gender male. Even taking into account the growing racial and gender diversity of full-time sworn personnel in local police departments during the past twenty-five years, this historical description generally holds true today. The most recent national statistics compiled by the U.S. Department of Justice's Bureau of Justice Statistics on the gender and racial makeup of full-time sworn personnel in local police departments reveal that of the 440,920 full-time sworn officers, 89.4% were male and 10.6% were female (Hickman and Reeves 2003). In 2000, the estimated 46,569 female officers represented an increase of nearly 60% (or 17,300 officers) from 1990 figures (Hickman and Reeves 2003).

In terms of race and ethnicity, 22.7% of all full-time local police officers in 2000 were minorities. This represented an increase of about 61%, or 38,000 officers, from the 1990 levels. African Americans, Hispanics or Latinos, and other ethnic groups (that is, Asians, native Hawaiians, American Indians, and Alaska natives) accounted for 11.7%, 8.3%, and 2.7%, respectively, of all local police officers in 2000 (Hickman and Reeves 2003). In terms of numbers, the number of Hispanic or Latino officers represented an increase of 17,600 officers from the 1990 level, while that of African American officers represented an increase of 13,300 (Hickman and Reeves 2003).

Based upon the analysis of Hickman and Reeves (2003), much of the growing diversity in local police departments is taking place in larger police agencies. For example, in local agencies that serve a million or more citizens, women make up 16.5% of all full-time sworn police officers, compared to 15.5% in departments serving a population of 500,000 to 999,999, 14.2% in those serving 250,000 to 499,999, but only 8.2%, 7.0%, and 5.7% in those serving 50,000 to 99,999, 25,000 to 49,999, and 10,000 to 24,999, respectively.

Similarly, employment of blacks (25.2%) in 2000 was highest in those departments serving a population of 500,000 to 999,999, followed by 19.0% and 16.1% in those serving 250,000 to 499,999 and a million or more, respectively. Furthermore, Hispanic or Latino representation at 17.3% in 2000 was highest in those departments serving a population of a million or more, followed by 10.7% and 8.0% in those serving 250,000 to 499,999 and 100,000 to 249,999, respectively (Hickman and Reeves 2003).

These statistics reflect the growing diversity in local police departments; however, they fail to reflect the more responsive nature of local law enforcement to a more diverse American society. The American landscape has changed from the more idealistic analogy of the melting pot into the more realistic view of a salad bowl.

As such, police departments, both large and small, have become more responsive to the changing demands of their more diverse communities of constituents. For example, such police departments as those in Atlanta, metropolitan Washington, D. C., Cambridge, Massachusetts, and Missoula, Montana, have implemented and utilized gay and lesbian liaison officers and units to better understand and address the concerns of the gay, lesbian, and transgender community.

Similarly, the Chicago Police Department, through its Chicago Alternative Policing Strategy (CAPS) model, like other local police departments has embraced a preventive problem-solving approach (Goldstein 1990) and increased its efforts to overcome various language, cultural, and other barriers to connect with immigrants and other new residents of the community (Skogan et al. 2002). These efforts represent only a small sample of what is being done by local police departments to better learn from, understand, connect with, serve, and protect a more diverse American society.

Conclusion

Egon Bittner has noted that "the role of the police is best understood as a mechanism for the distribution of nonnegotiable, coercive force employed in accordance with the dictates of an intuitive grasp of situational exigencies" (1970, 46). Similarly, MacDonald (2003) acknowledges that the growing "challenge for police in multiethnic, liberal, democratic societies is to find the correct balance among the public goods at stake. They must enforce the law but also maintain racial and ethnic peace. These goals are incompatible to some extent . . . enforcing the law may disrupt the peace" (p. 233).

Both Bittner (1970) and MacDonald (2003) speak to the need for police to be adept at operating from a dichotomous

nature—they must be able to employ coercive force when needed while understanding the very infrequent conditions that warrant such behavior. This is of greater import when considering the coactive function of contemporary law enforcement and its efforts to coproduce public safety and public order when coupled with the post-9/11 conditions facing a more multiethnic America.

Considering the perspectives of Bittner, MacDonald, and others, one viable approach to embrace this paradigm is to continue to exert more effort and energy in recruiting and retaining more diverse police officers—officers who are more sensitive toward and have a greater appreciation for diversity. However, for this approach to be most effective, local police departments must continue to tailor their approach to public safety and public order in a fashion that best fits with the changing nature of American society and that facilitates a symbiotic relationship.

Progress in terms of greater representation and enhanced sensitivity to the American mosaic is evident. The personnel policies and practices of local law enforcement departments have changed dramatically since the successful efforts by the American Federation Reform Society to install female "matrons" in prisons in 1845, the utilization of African Americans as police officers in Washington, D.C., in 1861, and the subsequent hiring of Alice Stebbins Wells, America's first female police officer, by the Los Angeles Police Department in 1909 (Cox 1996). The more recent hiring practices and personnel policies have been aided by presidential and legislative assistance, including the President's Commission on Law Enforcement and the Administration of Justice in 1967, the 1972 congressional amendment to Title VII of the 1964 Civil Rights Act, as well as the social and occupational ramifications of World War II and the civil rights movement (Cox 1996).

However, due to the present-day realities of a more heterogeneous, multiethnic, post-9/11 America, local police departments have many miles to go before they can rest. They must continue to seek greater diversity within their ranks and at all levels of the organizational hierarchy. Likewise, they must continue to find ways to better learn from, understand, connect with, and eventually serve the dynamic and ever-changing social landscape of the American mosaic by devising and implementing tailored approaches that foster a more collaborative and coproductive approach to public safety and public order.

BRIAN N. WILLIAMS

See also **Accountability; Attitudes toward the Police: Overview; Community-Oriented Policing: History; Community-Oriented Policing: Practices; Community-Oriented Policing: Rationale; Immigrant Communities and the Police; Minorities and the Police; National Association of Women Law Enforcement Executives (NAWLEE); National Organization of Blacks in Law Enforcement; Women in Law Enforcement**

References and Further Reading

Bittner, E. 1970. *The functions of the police in modern society: A review of background factors, current practices, and possible role models*. Chevy Chase, MD: National Institute of Mental Health.

Cordner, G. W. 1999. Elements of community policing. In *Policing perspectives: An anthology*, ed. Larry K. Gaines and Gary W. Cordner, 137–49. Los Angeles: Roxbury.

Cox, S. 1996. *Police practices, perspectives, problems*. Boston: Allyn and Bacon.

Goldstein, H. 1990. *Problem-oriented policing*. New York: McGraw-Hill.

Hickman, M. J., and B. A. Reeves. 2003. *Local police departments 2000*. Washington, DC: Bureau of Justice Statistics.

Koven, S. 1992. Co-production of law enforcement services: Benefits and implications. *Urban Affairs Quarterly* 27 (3): 457–70.

MacDonald, W. 2003. The emerging paradigm for policing multiethnic societies: Glimpses from the American experience. *Police & Society* 7: 231–53.

Ottemeier, T., and M. A. Wycoff. 1997. *Personnel performance evaluation in the community policing context*. Washington, DC: Police Executive Research Forum.

Skogan, W. G., L. Steiner, J. DuBois, J. E. Gudell, and A. Fagin. 2002. *Community policing and "the new immigrants": Latinos in Chicago*. Washington, DC: National Institute of Justice.

Websdale, N. 2001. *Policing the poor: From slave plantation to public housing*. Boston: Northeastern University Press.

Williams, H., and P. V. Murphy. 1990. The evolving strategy of policing: A minority view. *Perspective on policing*, No. 13. Washington, DC: National Institute of Justice.

DNA FINGERPRINTING

Background

Prior to the mid-1980s, crimes were solved by criminal investigators who compared evidence collected from crime scenes to known or suspected offenders. Evidence commonly consisted of fingerprints, hair, teeth marks, blood or semen samples, and fingernail scrapings. Fingerprints were often considered by investigators to be the best lead for the identification of a suspect and for connecting the suspect to the crime scene. Fingerprints are unique markers to an individual, but they have limited value in impacting crime because they can be altered through surgery. Evidence such as hair, teeth marks, blood, and semen likewise suffer in their ability to convince juries to the standard of "beyond a reasonable doubt" because their uniqueness is subjective. In many criminal cases it can be shown that a suspect's hair or blood type was similar to that found at a crime scene, but not to the exclusion of all other hair or blood. A paradigm shift occurred in the mid- to late 1980s that changed the way criminal investigators impact crimes. The change was the result not of the type of evidence collected but, rather, of the way the evidence was forensically examined.

DNA and the Criminal Identification Process

Sir Alec Jeffreys and associate Victoria Wilson successfully proved in 1985 that in the DNA (deoxyribonucleic acid) of human beings, "hypervariable" regions that they called "minisatellites" exist in which core sequences of DNA repeated (Jeffreys, Wilson, and Thein 1985). They determined that the repetitive sequences were unique to each individual (except in the case of identical twins), and thus the term "DNA fingerprinting" was born.

For forensic criminologists, this discovery was monumental. They knew that if they could examine evidentiary samples from crime scenes that contained nucleated cells left by a perpetrator, they would have a basis on which to build a case that would be more unique to an individual than previous evidence such as fingerprints. In essence, this discovery could be deemed as genetic fingerprinting. Since much of the evidence left at crime scenes includes nucleated cells, including hair follicles, semen, white blood cells, saliva, and perspiration in the ridges of fingerprints, it was widely thought that crimes would be easier to solve. The effectiveness of forensic evidence, however, is limited by the proper collection, storage, and analysis of the evidence.

Criminal Justice Application of DNA Fingerprinting

Police agencies, through their regional or state crime labs, submit crime scene DNA profiles for inclusion in the national DNA database CODIS (or combined DNA index system). Following a pilot database program in 1990, the CODIS database became effective in 1994 and is maintained by the Federal Bureau of Investigation. The CODIS database contains both crime scene DNA samples and DNA from known offenders. Officers from local law enforcement agencies run queries on the CODIS database based on crime scene evidence. When a match is made between evidentiary DNA and a DNA profile in CODIS, the match is known as a "hit." According to the CODIS information website maintained by the FBI, there were 119,782 forensic files and 2,643,409 offender profiles housed in the National DNA Index System as of November 2005. As a measure of success, the FBI reports that the CODIS database has "produced over 25,900 hits assisting in more than 27,800 investigations" (Federal Bureau of Investigation 2005).

Criminal justice agencies use DNA fingerprinting in the course of their duties in various ways. Consider for a moment that the attacks on the World Trade Centers on September 11, 2001, constituted the largest crime scene in the history of the United States. DNA fingerprinting was used to identify perpetrators and victims of that crime. DNA fingerprinting is also used to identify human remains in other disasters, such as airplane crashes. A growing field of concern and study for criminal justice agencies concerns missing children and adults. DNA fingerprints are used not only by criminal prosecutors to identify offenders but also by prosecutors and defense attorneys to aid in the exclusion of specific people as suspects in specific cases. Although the absence of DNA samples from seminal fluids in a rape case does not mean that a suspect did not commit the offense, the presence of such evidence could exonerate a suspect if it does not match that of the suspect. As of November 2005, the Innocence Project reports that 163 people have been exonerated of crimes they had previously been convicted of after postconviction DNA sampling was conducted on their behalf (Scheck 2005).

Because DNA samples can be obtained from a wide variety of evidentiary sources, police officers are trained in ever-changing methods of collection and preservation of crime scene evidence. For example, it was once thought that evidence should be preserved in plastic bags. The common practice in use today is to place dried samples in paper bags so that contamination or degradation of the evidence is not facilitated due to the development of moisture. Additionally, the amount of evidence necessary in order to collect a usable DNA sample has decreased due to new technologies and methodologies in the processing of DNA. Crime labs nationwide are increasingly becoming certified to handle and process DNA evidence using industry-accepted protocols. Uniformity in the handling and processing of DNA samples helps to ensure judicial acceptance of the evidence when presented in criminal cases.

Issues Facing Law Enforcement

As the probability of discovering DNA evidence left by a suspect at a crime scene increases, so too does the demand for the storage and processing of evidence. Police agencies, in anticipation of someday clearing reported crimes through the matching of DNA fingerprint profiles from evidence to those housed in CODIS, are forced to create additional storage space for crime scene evidence. Frustration mounts as officers wait for results of DNA analysis from crime labs that have been inundated with extremely high numbers of requests for analysis. A recent National Institute of Justice study conducted by researchers at Washington State University, in cooperation with the law firm Smith, Alling, Lane, P.S., reported that state and local crime laboratories claimed they maintain more than 57,000 unanalyzed DNA cases (Lovrich et al. 2003). The backlog was attributed to the lack of manpower to conduct DNA analysis. In addition, the researchers discovered that there are more than half a million cases nationwide in which DNA evidence could exist but has not yet been submitted to the crime lab for analysis (Lovrich et al. 2003).

Many people involved in the criminal justice system agree that increasing the volume of DNA fingerprint analysis at various crime labs and the inclusion of such analyses in massive databases such as CODIS will improve the quality of life in the United States by making the identification of offenders quick and certain. Others, however, argue that the improvement in DNA fingerprinting technology may lead to the restriction of personal liberties.

Legal Challenges

Among the questions surrounding the inclusion of DNA fingerprint profiles are, Which profiles are to be included, and which are not? Are the DNA fingerprint profiles of misdemeanants to be included, or only those of felons? Which felonies qualify for inclusion, violent only or nonviolent also? How long are the profiles to be maintained in the database? Are they to be purged upon the completion of the corresponding prison sentence by the offender? When are the profiles to be collected? Are they collected and entered into CODIS on conviction, on prison entrance, or on exit?

All of those questions have been the basis of lawsuits filed by civil libertarians. On a more technical note, concerns about near misses have sounded with respect to disclosure of a match probability when a suspect in a criminal action has a sibling who has not been excluded as a possible suspect (Buckleton and Triggs 2005). To summarize the argument, it is contended that when a crime lab returns the results of DNA fingerprinting, an obligation is owed that goes beyond simply making notification that a suspect's DNA fingerprint is or is not the donor of origin. If possible, the argument goes, crime labs should make notification if a relative of the suspect is the donor.

Future of DNA Fingerprinting in Criminal Justice

Legal wrangling surrounding the collection, preservation, and analysis of DNA evidence and the presentation of DNA fingerprints as unique personal identifiers will highlight criminal justice forensics during the next few decades. Criminal justice agencies and crime laboratories will adapt to newly defined protocols as the demand for improved DNA fingerprint profiling increases. Crime labs will continue to need increased funding to meet the ever-increasing demands placed on them by the law enforcement community. New discoveries in the methodology of DNA fingerprint analysis will put additional pressure on the FBI's CODIS database to improve in both capacity and classification capability. As DNA fingerprint typing becomes more prolific due to improved methodologies and as the CODIS database capacity increases in numbers of both crime scene profiles and offender profiles, the ability of law enforcement to impact crime should increase.

CHARLES L. JOHNSON

See also **Crime Laboratory; Crime Scene Search and Evidence Collection; Forensic Evidence; Forensic Investigations; Forensic Science; Technology and the Police**

References and Further Reading

Buckleton, John, and Christopher M. Triggs. 2005. Relatedness and DNA: Are we taking it seriously enough? *Forensic Science International* 152: 115–19.

Federal Bureau of Investigation. 2005. *CODIS: Measuring success*. http://www.fbi.gov/hq/lab/codis/success.htm (accessed November 14, 2005).

Jeffreys, Alec C., Victoria Wilson, and S. L. Thein. 1985. Individual-specific "fingerprints" of human DNA. *Nature* 316: 76–79.

Lovrich, Nicholas P., Travis C. Pratt, Michael J. Gaffney, and Charles L. Johnson. 2003. *National Forensic DNA Study Report*. Pullman: Washington State University.

Scheck, Barry. 2005. *The Innocence Project 2005*. http://www.innocenceproject.com (accessed November 14, 2005).

DOMESTIC (OR INTIMATE PARTNER) VIOLENCE AND THE POLICE

In the 1970s, domestic (or family) violence, in particular spousal or intimate partner violence (IPV), was transformed from a private issue into a public concern that warrants intervention by the criminal justice system. Societal acceptance of family violence as a criminal matter has made demands on the police to change their traditional (or nonintervention) practices of handling victims and offenders of IPV, resulting in reforms that include proarrest policies. We provide a definition of domestic violence or IPV and describe its patterns, reviewing the history of domestic violence laws, traditional police practices in responding to it, and reforms in police response. Research on police responses to domestic violence, factors that influence victims' calls to police, and the effectiveness of proarrest practices are presented, and remaining concerns in this area are discussed.

Definition and Extent of Domestic (Intimate Partner) Violence

Domestic violence is defined as "the willful intimidation, assault, battery, sexual assault, or other abusive behavior perpetrated by one family member, household member, or intimate partner against another" (National Center for Victims of Crime 2005). It includes physical, sexual, and psychological abuse of a family member, as well as the destruction of property, which is why the term "intimate partner abuse" is now more widely accepted than "domestic violence." Physical abuse commonly includes rape or sexual assaults on the victim (Johnson and Sigler 1997). In most cases of domestic violence, mental and physical abuse occur together. Verbal abuse includes threats regarding the woman's welfare and the welfare of the children and degrading comments.

In most state laws criminalizing domestic violence, a charge of this offense requires that the parties are spouses, former spouses, cohabiting persons, or those who have resided together within the previous year, or persons who share a common child. A significant number of states also include dating relationships within the scope of domestic violence. Research confirms that a substantial amount of abuse occurs among persons who are not married to each other (for example, who are dating, cohabiting, ex-spouses, or ex-cohabitants [Erez 1986; Tjaden and Thoennes 2000]). Research has consistently found that the majority (more than 90%) of the victims are women. There is currently an academic debate as to the extent to which domestic violence is gendered, but the most careful research designs report it as being predominantly male offenders and female victims, and this is most pronounced when the measures include high levels of fear, injury, and abuse (Belknap and Melton 2005).

Domestic violence data are typically derived from calls to the police or national survey data. The severity of the injuries and the danger facing the victims of abuse are often high. Weapons are used in about a third of all domestic violence incidents. Almost a third of all women murdered in the United States are killed by their husbands, ex-husbands, or lovers, making IPV the largest cause of injury to women in the United States (Tjaden and Thoennes 2000).

Historical Background

Domestic violence appears to be a cultural universal; its historical roots are ancient and deep. In many societies the woman was essentially defined as her husband's property; her sole purpose to satisfy his needs—bearing his children and tending to his household (Martin 1976). In medieval times, husbands had the power of life and death over their dependents and the right to unrestrained physical chastisement of the wife and other family members (Pleck 1987). Physical cruelty, including murder of the wife, was allowed as long as it was inflicted for disciplinary purposes (Davis 1971). Men killed their wives for reasons such as talking back, scolding and nagging, miscarrying, or sodomy (Martin 1976).

For "family protection" purposes, the English common law provided husbands the right to chastise their wives "moderately"; it excluded death (Blackstone 1987, 177). This law was brought to the American colonies, which allowed husbands to physically chastise their wives, as long as they did not use a stick larger than their thumb. Courts did not consider family violence incidents proper matters for court intervention, arguing that family arguments were best left inside the walls of the home. Exceptions to this rule were when the violence was excessive, was exercised merely to gratify "bad passions," or resulted in lasting injury. The economic and legal dependency of women on their husbands "justified" the state's nonintervention, which had an overriding interest in keeping the family intact. The sanctity of the family home and the maxim that "a man's home is his castle" were major reasons for a de facto decriminalization of wife abuse. They led to police treating spouse abuse differently than assaults between persons who were not intimate, resulting in policy of nonintervention in domestic violence cases.

The husband's right to use necessary force to make the wife "behave" and "know her place" was not challenged in court until the end of the nineteenth century. At that time many of the legal restrictions on married women were lifted, and the right of the husband to chastise his wife was abolished. Yet, the belief that physical abuse in spousal relationships does not constitute a crime continued to guide the police in their responses. Until the 1970s, police officers treated domestic violence as a private matter, unsuitable for the intervention of the criminal justice system. At that time, the women's movement began calling attention to the problem, and victim advocates initiated actions designed to bring about a change in police handling of domestic violence cases.

Police Attitudes and Changing Practices Concerning Domestic Violence

Until the 1980s, arrest in misdemeanor domestic violence cases was rarely made since police attached low priority to domestic violence. In the police culture, intervention in domestic situations was not viewed as "real" police work; the police perceived intervention in it as unglamorous and unrewarding. Thus, police often ignored these calls, or if they did respond, treated it as a "family dispute" where everyone needed to calm down.

The low level of enforcement of domestic violence incidents, however, was primarily attributed to legal requirements that the offense be committed in the presence of an officer, which technically barred officers who did not witness the abuse from making warrantless arrests. Other possible explanations include the erroneous police perception that domestic violence incidents are dangerous situations for the police, victim preferences against arrest, and possible police officers' support or sympathy for the abusive male partner (Sherman 1992). This attitude was reinforced by the long-held belief that family conflict is a private matter and that taking action against abusers will hurt their families, particularly if they are economically dependent on the abuser. Female complainants were also viewed as uncooperative, making arrest (and prosecution) a waste of time in the eyes of the police (Parnas 1967).

This policy of avoiding making arrests received some professional attention in the 1960s, when social scientists and psychologists began to advocate mediation in "family disturbance" incidents as the appropriate measures to handle IPV. Police officers received training in mediation, and many police departments established family crisis intervention units or police crisis teams that included social workers. This approach resulted in a further decrease in arrests in cities in which crisis intervention was practiced. Mediation resulted in keeping domestic violence out of the criminal justice system (Hirschel et al. 1992).

Mediation was soon rejected by both the police and women's groups. For police officers, mediation seemed like social work rather than activities suitable for being considered police work. There was also no evidence to show that mediation was useful in the long run. Women's groups objected to this approach because it ignored or underplayed the danger to women in abusive relationships. Mediation assumes equality of culpability between the parties to a dispute and fails to hold the offender accountable for his actions, inadvertently contributing to a dangerous escalation of the violence. In some jurisdictions (California, New York, and Connecticut) women's groups filed suits against police departments on behalf of abused women whom the police failed to protect by arresting their abusers. The victims in these cases were awarded large sums of money for police negligence in protecting them. This litigation put pressure on the police to adopt a full enforcement policy in domestic violence. Arrest was now advocated as domestic violence began to be perceived as a criminal act, to be treated like assaults among nonfamily members. The pressure of litigation alone, however, could not resolve the problem of the "in presence" requirement for warrantless misdemeanor arrests. Legislative action was necessary to provide officers with the power to arrest in misdemeanor domestic violence cases (Sherman 1992).

The preferred (or presumptive) arrest policy advocated slowly began to be transformed into laws in several states, and by 1984 the number of police departments that had adopted such policies had increased fourfold. Nonetheless, the actual implementation of this policy remained problematic, since there was no evidence to show that arrest in fact deters recidivism by abusive partners. And research still reports troubling responses by police to battered women (Erez and Belknap 1998).

Deterrent Effect of Arrest on Repeated Domestic Violence

Despite not being necessary to justify arrest in criminal offenses, the deterrent effect of arrest has become a central issue in attempts to convince policy makers to change the traditional police nonintervention practices in domestic violence cases. To provide evidence that arrest deters batterers, a scientific study of the effect of arrest on domestic violence recidivism rates was needed. In the early 1980s in Minneapolis, Sherman and Berk (1984) conducted an experimental design study comparing the effects of the traditional responses of the police (separation of the parties and mediation or advising) and arrest on subsequent battering by intimates ("the Minneapolis experiment"). Analysis of the data showed that arrest was more effective than the other two responses in deterring repeat abuse.

The Minneapolis experiment received national attention and was instrumental in promoting arrest as the preferred response to domestic violence cases across the country. By 1989, about three-quarters of the large city police departments had adopted a mandatory arrest policy and more than 80% a preferred arrest policy (Hirschel et al. 1992). Predictably, the

national arrest rate for misdemeanor domestic violence rose by 70% from 1985 to 1989 (Sherman 1992). However, this did not amount to a full compliance with proarrest policies. Research shows that despite official proarrest policies by many police departments, the arrest rate continues to be low (for example, Buzawa and Buzawa 1996; Ferraro 1989).

Several factors may account for this low compliance: persistent negative attitudes of the police concerning the seriousness of the abuse (Belknap 1992) or the appropriateness of intervention in family matters, identification with the abuser, fear of being sued in civil court for wrongful arrest (Hirschel et al. 1992), and the erroneous perception that intervention is highly dangerous to the police. The perception about higher probability of injury or death to the officers who intervene in domestic violence has been a part of police folklore for a long time and was often promoted in crisis intervention training to convince recruits who were reluctant to adopt the mediation approach. This perception was also supported by misinterpretation of "disturbance calls" data, which grouped family violence with all other types of disturbances, such as fights in bars (Garner and Clemmer 1986). While an in-depth analysis of police injury and death rates has raised serious doubts about such danger to officers, some studies continue to suggest that in some locations domestic calls may still constitute the most dangerous category for police, both in assault and injury (Hirschel et al. 1992).

To overcome remaining resistance to the preferred arrest policy by some police officers and departments and to provide further evidence of the superiority of the arrest response, the National Institute of Justice (NIJ) funded replications of the Minneapolis experiment. These six studies, known collectively as the NIJ's Spouse Assault Replication Program (SARP) field experiments, were carried out between 1981 and 1991 by police departments and research teams in Omaha, Nebraska,

Charlotte, North Carolina, Milwaukee, Wisconsin, Colorado Springs, Colorado, Dade County, Florida, and Atlanta, Georgia. The combined results of five studies (all except Atlanta; see Maxwell, Garner, and Fagan 2001) show that arresting batterers was related to reduced subsequent aggression against female intimate partners, although not all comparisons met the standard level of statistical significance. The impact of arrest on repeat offending (that is, the deterrent effect of arrest) was also found to be modest when compared to such factors as the batterer's prior criminal record or age. It showed that regardless of whether the batterer was arrested, more than half of the suspects committed no subsequent criminal offense against the original victim during the follow-up period, and a minority of suspects continued to commit intimate partner violence regardless of whether they were arrested, counseled, or temporarily separated from their partner (Maxwell, Garner, and Fagan 2001).

Legal experts, feminist scholars, social activists, and researchers have criticized the attention to the deterrent effect of arrest on batterers and the interpretation of the Minneapolis experiment and its replications. Practitioners and women's advocates argue that arrest alone is ineffective in halting the long-term expected progression of violence by socially marginal offenders. Research has documented that domestic violence escalates in spousal relationships whether or not the abuser is arrested (Frisch 1992). Social activists argue that the heavy emphasis on arrest as a panacea for domestic violence detracts from the role of community attitudes and practices in determining the scope and nature of the problem. The preoccupation with pro-arrest policies results in focusing on the individual rather than acknowledging societal factors that perpetuate the dependency of women on batterers (Ferraro 1989). They also point out the need for coordination among the police, the judiciary, and social services in responding to domestic

violence, for additional resources to pursue IPV cases through the legal system, and for higher probability of abusers' prosecution (Hirschel et al. 1992).

Feminists have argued that the experiments' effects were interpreted from the viewpoint of the abuser and ignored the perspective of the battered woman. For instance, the importance of the employment status of victims has not been taken into account; employed women are more able to successfully leave battering relationships than their unemployed counterparts. Generally, the Minneapolis experiment and its replications have centered on police response almost exclusively in terms of the arrest versus mediation decision. Other police actions, such as referrals made by the police for battered victims and their offenders for programs, shelters, and rights are critical and need to be addressed. The research on the deterrent effect of proarrest policies has also limited the definition of "success" to whether arresting batterers reduces their recidivism rates. This view ignores other influences that arrest might have, such as providing victims and their children an opportunity to escape, as well as communicating to offenders and victims and their children that the batterers' behavior is reprehensible.

Mandatory or presumed arrest policies and practices have been criticized. Research shows that many victims would prefer to resolve the incident without an arrest (Kingsnorth and Macintosh 2004). When victims do call the police, many merely want the violence to end, not to have their abuser arrested. In some cases, police are called to the scene by a third party rather than the victim. The majority of IPV victims do not even call the police (Buzawa and Buzawa 1996; Hoyle and Sanders 2000). Fear of reprisal, perceived social stigma, and a belief that nothing can be accomplished by reporting all reduce victim willingness to call the police.

Some researchers have attributed the drop in calls to the police for assistance in domestic violence cases following the passage of mandatory arrest laws to women's fears that their abusers will be arrested (Felders 2001). From the victim's perspective, the costs of involving the police (for example, losing the abuser's financial support or fear of loneliness or of future problems such as retaliatory violence) outweigh the benefits. In many cases, however, arrest accomplishes what the victim wanted in terms of changes in the offender's behavior, and prosecution is not necessary. A major criticism of mandatory arrest policies is that they deprive women of choice. It is argued that despite victims' emotional involvement and trauma, they are usually in a better position than patrol officers to determine the likely impact of an offender's arrest on their safety.

Finally, the implementation of pro-arrest policies led to the unprecedented large numbers of women arrested for domestic violence, even though they were not the primary aggressor. Most of these women appeared to be the victims, but police arrested them based on the male offender claiming they were abusive or the police simply arresting both the man and woman (dual arrests) when a woman resisted the abuse in any way (see Belknap and Melton 2005).

Conclusion

The gradual changes in societal attitudes toward spousal abuse and recognition of its criminal nature have led to a reevaluation of state law concerning domestic violence and reforms in police response to it. Currently, most police departments throughout the country adopt either preferred or mandatory arrest policies, although this reform did not result in a substantial increase in arrest rates. Police response to domestic violence and the amount of discretion they may or should use in making arrests in misdemeanor incidents remains an open question. The magnitude of the IPV problem justifies attention to the deterrent capability of arrest from a victim safety perspective. Arrest, which is mainly a response to criminal conduct, also serves as the gateway to the justice system. On the other hand, pre-occupation with its deterrence capability ignores the fact that arrest alone may not be a panacea and that policy makers need to explore other avenues to handle this persistent social problem.

EDNA EREZ and JOANNE BELKNAP

See also **Accountability; Arrest Powers of the Police; Community Attitudes toward the Police; Conflict Management; Minneapolis Domestic Violence Experiment; Presumptive Arrest Policing; Victim Rights Movement in the United States; Victims' Attitudes toward the Police**

References and Further Reading

Belknap, Joanne. 1992. Perceptions of woman battering. In *The changing roles of women in the criminal justice system*, ed. Imogene L. Moyer, 181–201. Prospect Heights, IL: Waveland Press.

Belknap, Joanne, and Heather Melton, 2005. *Are heterosexual men also victims of intimate partner abuse?* Harrisburg, PA: National Electronic Network on Violence Against Women, Pennsylvania Coalition Against Domestic Violence. http://www.vawnet. org/DomesticViolence/Research/VAWnet-Docs/AR_MaleVictims.pdf.

Blackstone, William. 1987. *Commentaries on the laws of England,* ed. W. Hardcastle Brown. St. Paul, MN: West.

Buzawa, Eve, and Carl G. Buzawa. 1996. *Domestic violence: The criminal justice response*. Newbury Park, CA: Sage.

Erez, Edna. 1986. Intimacy, violence and the police. *Human Relations* 39: 265–81.

Erez, Edna, and Joanne Belknap. 1998. In their own words: Battered women's assessment of system's responses. *Violence and Victims* 13 (1): 3–20.

Ferraro, Kathleen J. 1989. Policing woman battering. *Social Problems* 36: 61–74.

Garner, Joel, and Elizabeth Clemmer. 1986. *Danger to police in domestic disturbance: A new look*. Washington, DC: U.S. Department of Justice.

Hirschel, J. David, Ira W. Hutchison, Charles W. Dean, and Ann Marie Mills. 1992.

Review essay on the law enforcement response to spouse abuse: Past, present, and future. *Justice Quarterly* 9: 247–83.

Hoyle, C., and A. Sanders 2000. Police response to domestic violence—From victim choice to victim empowerment? *British Journal of Criminology* 40 (1): 14–36.

Johnson, Ida M., and Robert T. Sigler. 1997. *Forced sexual intercourse in intimate relationships*. Aldershot, England: Dartmouth Publishing.

Kingsnorth, R. E., and R. C. Macintosh. 2004, Domestic violence: Predictors of victim support for official action. *Justice Quarterly* 21 (2): 301–28.

Martin, Del. 1976. *Battered wives*. San Francisco: Glide.

Maxwell, C. D., J. H. Garner, and J. A. Fagan. 2001. *The effects of arrest on intimate partner violence: New evidence from the spouse assault replication program*. Research in Brief Series, July. Washington, DC: National Institute of Justice.

National Center for Victims of Crime (NCVC). http://www.ncvc.org/ncvc/main.aspx/documentID=32347 (accessed April 28, 2005).

Parnas, Raymond I. 1967. The police response to the domestic disturbance. *Wisconsin Law Review* (Fall): 914–60.

Pleck, Elizabeth. 1987. *Domestic tyranny: The making of social policy against family violence from colonial times to the present*. New York: Oxford University Press.

Sherman, Lawrence W. 1992. *Policing domestic violence*. New York: Macmillan.

Sherman, Lawrence W., and Richard A. Berk. 1984. The specific deterrent effects of arrest for domestic assault. *American Sociological Review* 49: 261–72.

Tjaden, P., and N. Thoennes. 2000. *Extent, nature, and consequences of intimate partner violence: Findings from the National Violence Against Women survey*. July. Washington, DC: U.S. Department of Justice, Office of Justice Programs, National Institute of Justice.

DRUG ABUSE PREVENTION EDUCATION

National statistics on drug use show there is truly cause for alarm. After decades of progress in the war on drugs, the number of young people using drugs began to increase in 1992; use among young kids showed the sharpest increase. LSD use reached its highest level since 1975, when it was first measured. Since 1992, the number of children between the ages of twelve and seventeen using marijuana has nearly doubled. To put the problem in perspective, in the average class of 25 eighth graders (thirteen- and fourteen-year-olds), five (20%) are now using marijuana. Portman (2005) describes a horrific event, wherein a sixteen-year-old boy died from a lethal combination of "huffing" gasoline and smoking marijuana. This is just one of the tragic stories of 2005.

Drug abuse, of course, is implicated in other social problems such as violent crime, dropout rates, and domestic violence. According to the National Institute on Drug Abuse (NIDA), most successful antidrug programs share the following five features: (1) They target all forms of drug abuse, including tobacco, alcohol, marijuana, cocaine, steroids, and inhalants with a focus on whatever their communities' primary drug problems are. (2) They use interactive methods, such as peer discussion groups, skits, or public service projects. (3) They teach skills to resist offers to use drugs, helping to strengthen commitments against drug use in general, and helping to build social skills such as communication, peer relationships, and self-evaluation. (4) They offer opportunities for families or caregivers to participate if they wish to do so. (5) They have components that are appropriate for all age levels. However, they give special emphasis to young people moving from grade school to middle school and from middle school to high school. According to most research these are the times when young people are most likely to make poor choices about smoking, drinking, or using other drugs (Ingram 2005).

Between 2001 and 2004, the use of illicit drugs among teenagers declined almost 7%. This trend translates into about six hundred thousand fewer adolescent drug abusers than in 2001 and has advanced President George W. Bush's initiative to decrease drug use among adolescents by

25% in five years. Other statistics show a drop of 41.0% to 36.4% between 2001 and 2004. Several key abuse patterns emerged. Between 2001 and 2004, cigarette smoking declined among adolescents. Marijuana abuse has declined by 18.1%, and from 2003 to 2004, amphetamine abuse dropped from 9.6% to 7.6% and LSD and Ecstasy (MDMA) use dropped by 60%. However, between 2001 and 2004, the use of inhalants among eighth graders and of OxyContin among students increased (National Institute on Drug Abuse Statistics 2005).

Project D.A.R.E.

Project D.A.R.E. began in Los Angeles when Chief of Police Daryl Gates approached Superintendent of Schools Dr. Harry Handler in January 1983 to explore how they could collaborate to deal more effectively with the problem of drug and alcohol use among adolescents. Law enforcement efforts to control the distribution and sale of illicit drugs on school campuses in Los Angeles, primarily through undercover work and periodic drug busts, had made little impact and had alienated students and school personnel from police. Chief Gates viewed project D.A.R.E. as a priority and offered to reassign officers to the program.

After examining current drug abuse education and prevention programs, a joint police–school task force made its recommendations. First, the program would address the broad spectrum of substance abuse, including drugs, alcohol, and tobacco. Second, it would extend from kindergarten through high school. Third, veteran police officers, recognized by the students as experts in the field of substance abuse, would serve as full-time instructors. And fourth, emphasis would be placed on teaching the skills and developing the strength of character that enable students to make responsible decisions regarding substance use (Brown 2001).

For more than twenty years, D.A.R.E. programs have been run collaboratively by schools and police departments throughout the United States and more recently in other Western countries as well. Despite wide dissemination and broad acclaim, there is little scientific evidence to show that D.A.R.E. is effective. Generally, by eighth grade more than 50% of children and by high school more than 80% of adolescents have consumed alcohol. Eighteen- to twenty-nine-year-olds drink 45% of the alcohol in the United States, and 63% of the heaviest drinkers (consuming more than six drinks per day) are under thirty years of age (Brown 2001).

It is sometimes argued that although alcohol use is illegal for teenagers, it is not realistic to expect total abstinence. A number of programs educating adolescents to drink responsibly or advocating "safe drinking" have included helping teens understand the direct toxic effects of alcohol and poor judgment that results from intoxication and often leads to violent and destructive behavior and dangerous risk taking, including unsafe sex and driving. Public service announcements broadcast on television caution, "Friends don't let friends drive drunk." It is interesting to note that no matter how much information seems to be forthcoming, most individuals under the age of thirty will still drink alcohol and use illicit drugs.

Project SHAHRP

The theory behind harm reduction is that the best should not become the enemy of the good. Examples of such programs are the life skills training programs and the Alcohol Misuse Prevention Study in the United States and Australia's School Health and Alcohol Harm Reduction

Project (SHAHRP) (McBride et al. 2003) These programs generally use cognitive behavioral methods. Their goals are to reduce anticipation of positive drug effects, explain the negative effects, promote self-esteem and social skills, and teach young people how to resist peer pressure. Another thematic shift is an emphasis on the advantages, even the pleasures, that come from choosing healthy alternatives to drugs and alcohol. Several controlled studies have shown that the shift of emphasis lowers the rate of alcohol-related problems.

Australian researchers have recently had some success reaching thirteen- and fourteen-year-olds with the SHAHRP approach. In several group sessions spanning two years, the students in the SHAHRP program group rehearsed skills, put their heads together about decision making, and discussed scenarios of their own devising. These students reported less use of alcohol than a control group receiving standard alcohol education. Interestingly, that difference almost disappeared once the course was completed. A year and a half after the program's completion, it was reported that the adolescents in the SHAHRP program group had experienced 23% less harm than the control group.

One part of the study pointed out that the retention rate for the study remained at 75.9% over a thirty-two-month period. It should be noted that the intervention used evidence-based approaches to enhance behavioral changes in the target population. The intervention was classroom based, with goals that minimized explicit harm and work conducted in two phases during a two-year period. This study indicates that a school drug education program needs to be offered in several phases in order to enhance success. Findings also indicate that program components are included to meet the needs of different groups and that early unsupervised drinkers need these programs in order to reduce harmful alcohol effects (McBride et al. 2003).

Motivational Therapies for Success in Drug Abuse Programs

A motivational interviewing (MI) approach (Miller and Rollnick 2002) suggests that motivation to change can be increased by increasing an individual's awareness of personal negative consequences of substance abuse. MI involves using a nonconfrontational, empathic, therapist style and highlighting discrepancies between the patient's goals for life and effects of drug use to increase the likelihood that personal feedback of the effects of the substance abuse will be absorbed. This approach first showed significant effects on drinking for non-treatment-seeking adolescents (Miller, Sovereign, and Krege 1988; Miller, Benefield, and Tonigan 1993) and demonstrated that the empathic patient-centered approach was crucial as compared to a confrontational style (Miller, Benefield, and Tonigan 1993). Non-treatment-seeking older adolescents in emergency care for an alcohol-related incident had fewer alcohol-related problems during follow-up when provided with this type of therapy than when given referral resources (Monti et al. 1999). As preparation for treatment, MI resulted in more alcoholism treatment attendance and better drinking outcomes than no preparation (Bien, Miller, and Buroughs 1993; Brown and Miller 1993; Connors, Walitzer, and Dermen 2002) plus greater retention in addiction treatment after incarceration. A second part of this is coping skills training (CST), which is a promising approach that focuses on anticipating and coping with situations that pose a high risk for relapse (Monti et al. 2002).

Summary of Programs

D.A.R.E. and other "just say no" programs are a legitimate police initiative, similar in intent to neighborhood watch,

"Officer Friendly," and other crime prevention efforts. Yet, the reassignment of officers from patrol and other essential law enforcement work to teach in classrooms is a profound step. Every veteran officer, whose training represents a significant financial investment, is an important weapon in the fight against crime. In communities where public concerns about crime are especially great, it may be politically impossible for the police department to staff a drug prevention program. Ultimately, of course, the wisdom of redeploying officers must emerge from evaluation data. Unfortunately, the police may reject this program as not being "real police work," not recognizing that many of the crimes committed are done under the influence of drugs, alcohol, or mind-altering substances.

In a 2001 study conducted by Brown, it was noted that students who completed 60% or more of the life skills training studies were less likely to be prone to drug use. Interestingly, when the participation level of the students was 59% or less, the program did not decrease their drug use, and some students even had a higher incidence of drug use.

D.A.R.E. officials likewise tried to counter bad publicity by falling back on beliefs, trumpeting that 97% of teachers rated D.A.R.E. as being good to excellent, 93% of parents believed D.A.R.E. teaches children to avoid drugs, and 86% of school principals believed students would be less likely to use drugs after D.A.R.E. With only beliefs to cite and not actual research data, D.A.R.E. was left off the federal governments "exemplary" and "promising" prevention curricula in 2000. Desperate to retain its dominance in the prevention market, D.A.R.E. has begun a dramatic overhaul of its curriculum to keep up with the current emphasis on scientific research, decision making skills, and resistance techniques. It remains to be seen whether this new D.A.R.E. curriculum is going to be more successful than the old one (Brown 2001).

None of these programs accomplishes all we might wish for. They are not designed to address mental disorders or family conflict and other environmental stressors that may contribute to alcohol and drug use. As research continues to refine our knowledge, it may be hoped that positive changes and improved efficacy may impact the adolescent culture of drugs abuse.

JOSEPHINE A. KAHLER and SHIRLEY GARICK

See also **Crime Control Strategies: Alcohol and Drugs; Drug Abuse Resistance Education (D.A.R.E.); Juvenile Crime and Criminalization; Juvenile Delinquency; Juvenile Diversion**

References and Further Reading

Bien, T. H., W. R. Miller, and Y. M. Boroughs. 1993. Motivational interviewing with alcohol outpatients. *Behavioral and Cognitive Psychotherapy* 21: 347–56.

Brown, Y. 2001. Six year evaluation of life skills training. *Journal of Drug Education*. http://vnweb.hwwilsonweb.com.

Brown, Y. M., and W. R. Miller. 1993. Impact of motivational interviewing on participation and outcome in residential alcoholism treatment. *Psychology of Addictive Behaviors* 7: 211–18.

Connors, G. Y., K. S. Walitzer, and K. H. Dermen. 2002. Preparing patients for alcoholism treatment: Effects on treatment participation and outcomes. *Journal of Consulting and Clinical Psychology* 70: 1161–69.

Ingram, W. Scott. 2005. *Teaming up against drug abuse*. http://vnweb.hwwilsonweb.com.

McBride, N., F. Farringdon, R. Midford, L. Meuleners, and M. Phillips. 2003. Early unsupervised drinking: Reducing the risks. The School Health and Alcohol Harm Reduction Program. *Drug and Alcohol Review* 22: 263–76.

Miller, W. R., and S. Rollnick. 2002. *Motivational interviewing: Preparing people for change*. 2nd ed. New York: Guilford Press.

Miller, W. R., G. S. Benefield, and J. S. Tonigan. 1993. Enhancing motivation for change in problem drinking: A controlled comparison of two therapist styles. *Journal of Consulting and Clinical Psychology* 61: 455–61.

Miller, W. R., R. G. Sovereign, and B. Krege. 1988. Motivational interviewing with problem drinkers. 11. The drinker's check-up as a preventive intervention. *Behavioral Psychotherapy* 16: 251–68.

Monti, P. M., S. M. Colby, et al. 1999. Brief intervention for harm-reduction with alcohol-positive older adolescents in a hospital emergency department. *Journal of Consulting and Clinical Psychology* 67: 989–94.

Monti, P. M., R. Kadden, et al. 2002. *Treating alcohol dependence: A coping skills training guide*. 2nd ed. New York: Guilford Press.

National Institute on Drug Abuse Statistics. 2005. *Teen Drug Abuse Continues Its Three Year Decline*. May. http://www.dare.com/home/Resources/NIDA.asp.

Portman, Rob. 2005. *Addicted to Failure*. http://vnweb.hwwilsonweb.com.

DRUG ABUSE RESISTANCE EDUCATION (D.A.R.E.)

Drug Abuse Resistance Education (D.A.R.E.) is one of the most popular prevention strategies utilized to educate children about the impact of drug and alcohol abuse. According to Dr. Herb Kleber, chairman of D.A.R.E. America's Scientific Advisory Board, D.A.R.E. currently reaches twenty-six million children a year in 75% of all school districts (D.A.R.E. 2005). It has also been implemented in more than fifty foreign countries.

The underlying philosophy of D.A.R.E. is that exposure to information regarding the impact of drug and alcohol abuse coupled with skills training in areas such as self-esteem and decision making during the formative years will significantly reduce the likelihood that a child will experiment with and possibly abuse drugs and alcohol. D.A.R.E. seeks to improve the lives of children through the cooperative efforts of law enforcement, schools, parents, and the community. It has thrived, in large part, due to generous donations from the business community, private foundations, and government (D.A.R.E. 2005). Corporate sponsors include General Mills, Polaroid, Sam's Club, and Warner Brothers. Private foundations that contribute to D.A.R.E. include the Horn Foundation, the American Express Philanthrophic Program, and the Brener Family Foundation.

The U.S. Departments of Defense, Justice, and State are among government agencies that have provided funding.

Origins of D.A.R.E.

D.A.R.E. was the result of the dedication of a parent whose child struggled with drug addiction. Daryl Gates, better known as the chief of the Los Angeles Police Department (1979–1992), was frustrated by the prevailing wisdom toward the problems associated with drug abuse. Gates' frustration led him to approach the Los Angeles County School Board for support (Gates and Shaw 1992). The board agreed and Gates instituted the first D.A.R.E. program in 1983 in fifth grade classes within the Los Angeles County School District. The combination of Gates' motivation and a leap of faith by the board transformed an idea of a concerned parent into a national program. Less than a decade later, the D.A.R.E. program was operational in all fifty states (U.S. House of Representatives 1990; Wysong, Aniskiewicz, and Wright 1994; Rosenbaum et al. 1994; Harmon 1993).

The D.A.R.E. Curriculum

The traditional D.A.R.E. program involves the use of uniformed law enforcement officers within the public schools to provide instruction to middle school students. The curriculum was developed by Dr. Ruth Rich, a curriculum specialist with the Los Angeles Unified School District (Lundman 2001; Harmon 1993). The foundation for the original D.A.R.E. curriculum was Project SMART (Self-Management and Resistance Training), which was designed by researchers at the University of Southern California (Lundman 2001; Harmon 1993) to instruct middle school students regarding resistance to drugs and as such served as an excellent model from which to develop the D.A.R.E. curriculum. Moreover, the programs are philosophically similar in their belief that children can be taught the necessary skills that will enable them to resist drugs and alcohol.

In essence, D.A.R.E. is an instructional program designed to teach students the skills necessary to resist the lure of drugs, alcohol, and violence. As such, D.A.R.E. is quick to distinguish itself from other programs that use scare tactics to convey their message. Moreover, while uniformed officers provide D.A.R.E. instruction, officers are not in the classroom to perform law enforcement–related functions. For example, officers do not elicit information from students regarding family or friends who may be involved with drugs or other criminal activity. In addition, the D.A.R.E. curriculum does not include specific information regarding the mechanics of drug use.

The traditional D.A.R.E. curriculum is delivered over a seventeen-week period during the academic year (Lundman 2001; Rosenbaum and Hanson 1998/ 2003). Students receive instruction for fifty-minute periods once per week by uniformed law enforcement officers. Officers are required to undergo intensive training prior to certification as a D.A.R.E. instructor. Training is intended to provide the officers with a foundational understanding of the D.A.R.E. program, skills necessary to relate to children in the classroom environment, and basic educational strategies. The traditional D.A.R.E. curriculum includes topics such as resistance techniques, the consequences of drug abuse, stress management, self-esteem enhancement, role modeling, assertiveness, and personal safety (D.A.R.E. 2005; Lundman 2001; Rosenbaum and Hanson 1998/2003).

While the traditional D.A.R.E. program has been received well, ongoing evaluation of program effectiveness has led to curriculum modifications. Such actions demonstrate the willingness of D.A.R.E.

to continually evaluate and modify its program in order to best meet the needs of the children who participate. The new D.A.R.E. program is designed to address not only substance abuse but violence prevention as well. According to D.A.R.E., the new program is designed to assist the educational system with "ever-evolving federal prevention program requirements and the thorny issues of school violence, budget cuts, and terrorism" (D.A.R.E. 2005). In addition to the inclusion of violence prevention and terrorism, the modern curriculum minimizes the use of traditional lecture-based instruction and emphasizes the use of group exercises such as role playing and group discussions. The modern reliance on group techniques is believed to enhance the ability of children to develop skills that facilitate positive social interaction, coordination, and critical thinking skills (D.A.R.E. 2005).

The role of law enforcement officers is also modified in the new D.A.R.E. program. Traditional D.A.R.E. programs utilized officers in teacher-mentor roles, whereas officers are now trained to function as coaches for the children in the program. Officer coaches are trained to assist children in the development of skills using "refusal strategies in high-stakes peer-pressure environments" (D.A.R.E. 2005). In addition, modern D.A.R.E. officers are also certified as School Resource Officers.

Evaluation and Results

Despite generous funding and continued development of the D.A.R.E. curriculum, researchers and policy analysts continue to debate the effectiveness of D.A.R.E. and other drug prevention programs. The ongoing debate is fueled by rising rates of drug abuse among adolescents and young adults. As such, the question most policy makers and parents want answered is whether drug prevention programs work.

Moreover, with the passage of the Drug-Free Schools and Communities Act (1986) and the more recent Safe and Drug-Free Schools and Communities Act (SDFSCA), Congress is also concerned with the effectiveness of school-based drug and violence prevention.

There have been numerous studies designed to evaluate the effectiveness of drug abuse prevention programs. Due to its widespread popularity, D.A.R.E. receives much of the critical attention. Interestingly, despite its popularity, many evaluation efforts have questioned the effectiveness of the D.A.R.E. program (Dukes, Stein, and Ullman 1997; Wysong, Aniskiewicz, and Wright 1994; Rosenbaum et al. 1994; Becker, Agopian, and Yeh 1992).

However, researchers have noted the methodological flaws present in many of the evaluations. Such flaws diminish the scientific rigor of the designs and therefore potentially undermine the results. For example, Rosenbaum and Hanson (1998/2003) suggest that most of the prior evaluations are ". . . of limited scientific value because of their weak research designs, poor sampling and data collection procedures, inadequate measurement and analysis problems." They also note the failure of prior research to evaluate the impact of school-level effects on youth who are exposed to drug prevention programs. Rather, previous studies tend to limit their analysis to individual-level variables that may "lead to overly liberal estimates of program effects."

In response to the identified flaws that plagued prior evaluation efforts and with a desire to obtain valid information regarding the effectiveness of the D.A.R.E. curriculum, Rosenbaum and Hanson (1998/2003) designed a six-year multilevel analysis of D.A.R.E. programs in Illinois. In an effort to remedy many of the methodological issues present in prior evaluations, the analysts utilized a randomized field experiment with one pretest and multiple posttests. Eighteen pairs of elementary schools (rural, urban, and suburban) were included in the sample. Each school was matched with a similar counterpart (in terms of type of school, ethnic composition, number of students with English proficiency, and number of students in low income families) to form the pair. Schools were assigned either to a control group that did not provide the D.A.R.E. program or to an experimental group that did.

The primary means through which data were collected was the administration of a survey instrument to students. Surveys were administered to participants over a six-year period and thus allowed the analysts to perform a longitudinal evaluation. The survey instrument specifically included items designed to assess the drug use behaviors of students, attitudes toward the use of specific drugs, onset of alcohol use, perceived benefits and costs of using drugs, self-esteem, attitudes toward police, peer resistance skills, and other measures.

Like other studies, the Rosenbaum and Hanson evaluation did not find that exposure to D.A.R.E. instruction resulted in long-term drug use prevention. However, the study revealed that the primary effects of D.A.R.E. were realized in the two-year period following participation in the program. As such, additional drug prevention programming in subsequent school years may enhance the long-term effects of the initial training. In addition, the authors found that D.A.R.E. had the most significant impact on urban as compared to suburban children. The authors suggest that this difference may be attributed to the amount of time that D.A.R.E. officers spent on school campuses. The authors suggested that the officers spent considerably more time on campus in urban schools, which in turn provided children more opportunity to bond with and relate to the officers.

The Future of D.A.R.E.

Despite the ongoing debate regarding the long-term effects of D.A.R.E., its future looks bright. D.A.R.E. continues to enjoy widespread community and parental support and as such has not declined in number or strength. Moreover, with the modification of the curriculum, continuing evaluation is needed.

LISA S. NORED

See also **Crime Control Strategies: Alcohol and Drugs; Crime Prevention; Juvenile Delinquency; School Resource Officers**

References and Further Reading

Becker, H. R., M. E. Agopian, and S. Yeh. 1992. Impact evaluation of Drug Abuse Resistance Education (DARE). *Journal of Drug Education* 22: 283–91.

Drug Abuse Resistance Education (DARE). (2005). http://www.DARE.com.

Drug-Free Schools and Communities Act. 1986. 20 U.S.C. § 5964.

Dukes, R., J. Stein, and J. Ullman. 1997. The long term effects of DARE. *Evaluation Review* 21: 473–500.

Gates, Daryl, and Diane K. Shaw. 1992. *Chief: My life in the LAPD*. New York: Bantam Books.

Harmon, Michele A. 1993. Reducing the risk of drug involvement among early adolescents: An evaluation of Drug Abuse Resistance Education (DARE). *Evaluation Review* 17: 223.

Lundman, Richard J. 2001. *Prevention and control of juvenile delinquency*. 3rd ed. New York: Oxford University Press.

Rosenbaum, Dennis P., and Gordon S. Hanson. 1998/2003. Assessing the effects of school-based drug education: A six-year multilevel analysis of Project D.A.R.E. In *Readings in juvenile delinquency and juvenile justice*, ed. Thomas Calhoun and Constance L. Chapple. Upper Saddle River, NJ: Prentice-Hall.

Rosenbaum, Dennis P., Robert L. Flewelling, Susan L. Bailey, Chris Ringwalt, and Deanna L. Wilkinson. 1994. Cops in the classroom: A longitudinal evaluation of Drug Abuse Resistance Education (DARE). *Journal of Research in Crime and Delinquency* 31: 3–31.

Safe and Drug-Free Schools and Communities Act. (2005). 20 U.S.C. § 7101.

U.S. House of Representatives. 1990. *Oversight hearing on drug abuse education programs*. Committee on Education and Labor, Subcommittee on Elementary, Secondary and Vocational Education, 101st Congress, First Session. Serial No. 101–129. Washington, DC: U.S. Government Printing Office.

Wysong, Earl, Richard Aniskiewicz, and David Wright. 1994. Truth and DARE: Tracking drug education to graduation and as symbolic politics. *Social Problems* 41(3): 448–72.

DRUG ENFORCEMENT ADMINISTRATION (DEA)

The Drug Enforcement Administration (DEA) enforces the law and regulations relating to narcotic drugs, marijuana, depressants, stimulants, and the hallucinogenic drugs. Its objectives are to reach all levels of source of supply and to interdict illegal drugs before they reach the user. To achieve its mission, the administration has stationed highly trained agents along the many and varied routes of illicit traffic, both in the United States and in foreign countries. DEA's enforcement program is aimed at disruption of the highest echelons of the traffic in the priority drugs of abuse. Drug enforcement action by state and local agencies is also an essential part of the national drug enforcement strategy.

Inception

The earliest federal drug enforcement efforts can be traced organizationally to the Internal Revenue Service. In 1915, 162 collectors and agents placed in the IRS Miscellaneous Division were assigned responsibility under the Harrison Narcotics Act for "restricting the sale of opium." Over the years a number of agencies became involved in federal drug law enforcement. In 1973, the U.S. attorney general was given overall federal responsibility for drug law enforcement. The DEA was established July 1, 1973, by Presidential Reorganization Plan No. 2. It resulted from the merger of the Bureau of Narcotics and Dangerous Drugs, the Office for Drug Abuse Law Enforcement, the Office of National Narcotics Intelligence, those elements of the Bureau of Customs that had drug investigative responsibilities, and those functions of the Office of Science and Technology that were related to drug enforcement. Clearly, reorganization was needed.

On January 21, 1982, the attorney general gave the Federal Bureau of Investigation concurrent jurisdiction with DEA over drug offenses. The DEA's administrator now reports to the director of the FBI, who was given general supervision of the drug enforcement effort. DEA agents work side by side with FBI agents throughout the country in major drug cases—a significant change in narcotics law enforcement.

Mission

Enforcement of drug laws by the DEA emphasizes the reduction of available cocaine, phencyclidine (PCP), illicit and legally produced but diverted stimulants such as amphetamines and methamphetamines, as well as barbiturates and other depressants and sedative-hypnotics. Trafficking in multiton quantities of marijuana and other types of cannabis such as hashish and "hash oil" receives similar enforcement attention. The DEA's response to the varying patterns, methods, and international routes of the traffic in illicit drugs must be flexible and timely. After the "French connection" for heroin from Marseilles was cut off in 1973, Mexican brown heroin began to replace it. To counter the new threat, the DEA instituted interdiction and eradication programs that resulted in a reduction of both opium production and level of purity of heroin on the streets of the United States. In anticipation of possible smuggling from Southeast Asia, measures to slow its progress were undertaken immediately. Cocaine, imported illegally from South America, is an increasing problem now receiving special attention through programs designed to reduce the illicit traffic and the cultivation of coca leaf, from which cocaine is derived.

The DEA never lacks for business, whether it has to identify type and variety of drug or plan some new way of seizing the contraband. The animal tranquilizer and hallucinogen PCP has replaced other hallucinogens such as LSD as the most abused of this type of drug. Because of the serious psychological effects of using PCP, including violent and irrational behavior, clandestine manufacturing and trafficking in PCP have become an important target of the DEA's enforcement operations. PCP laboratories, difficult to detect but easily set up, have been discovered and dismantled in increasing numbers.

Compliance and Regulatory Affairs

The DEA is also responsible for regulating the legal distribution of narcotics and dangerous drugs. This includes monitoring all imports and exports of controlled substances and establishing manufacturing quotas for all Schedules I and II controlled substances. All individuals handling controlled substances are required to register with the DEA and are periodically investigated by DEA compliance investigators, who ensure that record keeping and security safeguards of all controlled substances comply with existing federal regulations. Other responsibilities of the DEA's regulatory program include monitoring various drug abuse patterns and determining whether a drug should be controlled, based on its abuse potential.

Training

The DEA's National Training Institute conducts intensive training in narcotics and dangerous drug law enforcement for law enforcement officers from agencies throughout the United States and the world. Ten-week schools allow police officers to receive training similar to that received by DEA special agents. In addition, they are introduced to management concepts that will enable them to develop and lead drug investigative units and organize drug traffic prevention programs in their own communities. Specialized two-week schools offer eighty hours of instruction in the basic techniques of narcotics and dangerous drugs investigation to state, county, and city officers. These schools are held at the DEA's National Training Institute in Washington, D.C., and at field locations across the United States. The programs conducted in foreign countries range from a few days to three weeks and are presented in the native languages.

Interagency Cooperation

The DEA's global agents provide intelligence information to Bureau of Customs and Border Patrol agents so that they can intercept illegal drugs and traffickers at entry points into the United States. The DEA also coordinates EPIC (the El Paso Intelligence Center), the first joint fact-finding operation in the annals of federal law enforcement. This interagency group, located in the southwestern border area, receives and disseminates information on drug trafficking and illegal alien activity along the southern border. The DEA Mobile Task Forces (MTF), another cooperative effort, have been successful in removing illicit drugs from the streets through coactive planning tailored to the specific assignment. The DEA State and Local Task Forces (SLTF) ensure that drug enforcement ventures do not stagnate and acts as an impetus for nonfederal law enforcement assaults on drug trafficking. The administration regularly responds to requests for investigative assistance from state and local authorities and through its six regional laboratories provides analyses of drug evidence and also supplies related expert testimony. Additionally, DEA-FBI task forces have been established to identify potential organized crime narcotics activities.

Achievements Mid-1980s

Acting Administrator John C. Lawn, appearing before a House Subcommittee on Crime, May 1, 1985, reported the following notable achievements of the DEA:

> The DEA rate of arrests has gone from less than 1,000 per month in FY 1980 to nearly 1,100 per month in FY 1984. Arrests in those cases targeted at the top echelon, or Class I cases, have increased approximately 40 percent. Convictions are up from about four hundred per month in FY 1980 to more than nine hundred per month in FY 1984.

Cocaine removals were up 380% and totaled 11.7 metric tons in FY 1984. Marijuana seizures increased 270% and heroin seizures increased 80 percent. During FY 1984, DEA investigations also accounted for the seizure of 190 clandestine laboratories, including 120 methamphetamine, 18 PCP, and 17 cocaine laboratories.

Other impressive figures accrued for task force operations, the cannabis eradication program, EPIC, and international control of illicit drugs. For example, based on DEA information, the Colombian government seized seven cocaine laboratory complexes and ten tons of cocaine, later described as the "largest drug raid ever in the world." The DEA's budget and employee request for fiscal year 1986 was for a total of $345,671,000 and 4,564 permanent positions. That represented a net increase of 134 positions and $15,683,000 above the 1985 enacted level.

Total Federal Effort

The DEA has primary responsibility for enforcing federal drug laws and policies, but it does not and cannot carry the entire burden for enforcement. A number of other federal departments assist in the effort. The Federal Bureau of Investigation has concurrent jurisdiction with the DEA over federal drug laws focusing on complex conspiracy investigations. The ninety-three U.S. attorneys are the chief federal law enforcement officers in their districts; they are responsible for investigating and prosecuting federal drug offenses and are often involved in drug task forces and asset forfeiture cases. The Immigration and Naturalization Service performs interdiction duties through its Border Patrol and is responsible for deporting aliens convicted of drug crimes. The U.S. Marshals Service manages the Department of Justice Asset Forfeiture Fund, serves warrants on federal drug suspects and fugitives, and escorts them when in custody. The Customs Service interdicts and seizes contraband, including illegal drugs that are smuggled into the United States. The Internal Revenue Service assists with the financial aspects of drug investigations, particularly money laundering. The Bureau of Alcohol, Tobacco, Firearms and Explosives investigates federal drug offenses that involve weapons. The U.S. Coast Guard enforces federal laws on the high seas and waters subject to U.S. jurisdiction and is involved with the interdiction of drugs smuggled via water into the United States. The Federal Aviation Administration's radar system detects suspected air smugglers. The Department of Defense detects and monitors aerial and maritime transit of illegal drugs into the United States. The State Department formulates international antidrug policy and coordinates drug control efforts with foreign governments. The Postal Inspection Service of the U.S. Postal Service enforces laws against the use of the mails in transporting illegal drugs and drug paraphernalia.

International Narcotics Control

The DEA has more than 343 employees in fifty countries throughout the world. Under the policy direction of the secretary of state and the U.S. ambassadors, the DEA provides consultation, technical assistance, and training to drug law enforcement officials in those countries. The DEA also collects and shares international drug data and assists in drug control activities and investigations where authorized. The United States encourages foreign governments to control cultivation and production of illegal drugs.

Success has been modest but promising; the following figures are for 1990: In Bolivia an estimated 8,100 hectares of coca were eradicated, representing 14% of coca cultivation. In Mexico and Guatemala about half of the opium poppy crop was destroyed. Eradication of opiates is more difficult in other areas of the world due to the lack of government support for such efforts. In Belize 84% of the estimated marijuana crop was destroyed, as was 46% in Jamaica, 25% in Colombia, and 16% in Mexico. Colombian authorities seized fifty metric tons of cocaine and destroyed more than three hundred processing labs. They also arrested seven thousand traffickers and extradited fourteen drug suspects to the United States for prosecution. Mexico seized 46.5 metric tons of cocaine and destroyed twelve heroin labs. Bolivia destroyed thirty-three cocaine hydrochloride labs and 1,446 maceration pits that produce cocaine paste. India seized twelve heroin labs and Turkey, seven labs.

The War on Drugs

The combined federal effort and the promise of greater international cooperation continue to bolster the DEA in its pursuit of the seemingly impossible. Drug control figures are always disappointing to cite. Domestically, no matter how large a confiscation or bust might be, it is a mere token of what is left out on the street. The modest international figures for 1990 are for that year only and do not carry over. Drug crops destroyed one year can return even twofold the next year. Current political and law enforcement thinking believes that since supply cannot be cut off, much more effort should go into stemming demand.

Given that new emphasis, the DEA will still conduct business as usual, although there was some worry in 1993. The Clinton administration, wanting to streamline the federal bureaucracy, considered merging the DEA and FBI. Furthermore, it was argued that such a merger would eliminate disputes that hindered both agencies in their ability to combat and prosecute drug traffickers. FBI Director Louis J. Freeh favored the merger, which also included placing the Bureau of Alcohol, Tobacco, Firearms and Explosives (BATF) under FBI control. Naturally, the DEA and BATF put up strong resistance. On October 21, 1993, Attorney General Janet Reno announced that the Clinton administration would abandon its proposal. The FBI would not become the sole federal law enforcement agency for the United States.

WILLIAM G. BAILEY

See also **Bureau of Alcohol, Tobacco, Firearms and Explosives; Crime Control Strategies: Alcohol and Drugs; Drug Interdiction; Drug Markets; U.S. Border Patrol**

References and Further Reading

Drug Enforcement Administration, Office of Planning and Evaluation. 1981. *Drug Enforcement Administration: A profile.* Washington, DC: U.S. Department of Justice.

Rachal, P. 1982. *Federal narcotics enforcement: Reorganization and reform*. Boston: Auburn House.

U.S. House of Representatives. 1982. *Federal drug law enforcement coordination*. Hearing before the House Select Committee on Narcotics Abuse and Control. Washington, DC: U.S. Government Printing Office.

———. 1984. *Efficacy of the federal drug abuse control strategy—State and local perspectives*. Report of the House Select Committee on Narcotics Abuse and Control. Washington, DC: U.S. Government Printing Office.

———. 1986. *Drug Enforcement Administration reauthorization for fiscal year 1986*. Hearing before the subcommittee on crime. Washington, DC: U.S. Government Printing Office.

U.S. Senate. 1981. *International narcotics trafficking*. Hearings before the Senate Permanent Subcommittee on Investigations, November 10, 12, 13, 17, and 18. Washington, DC: U.S. Government Printing Office.

Wilson, James Q. 1978. *The investigators: Managing FBI and narcotics agents*. New York: Basic Books.

DRUG INTERDICTION

Drug interdiction is designed to prevent the importation of illegal drugs into the United States from foreign source countries. The intent of the policy is to intercept and seize drug contraband. In practice, interdiction consists of five categories of activity: (1) intelligence, (2) command and control, (3) surveillance, (4) pursuit, and (5) capture. Most drug interdiction efforts focus on major points of entry and the twelve-mile "customs search" radius surrounding the U.S. border. The major agencies involved in interdiction efforts are the U.S. Coast Guard, Customs Service, and Border Patrol, with support from the Department of Defense and the Federal Aviation Administration (Lyman and Potter 2003, 301–306).

Interdiction policies assume that with sufficient resources, drugs can be stopped from entering the United States by controlling the borders. However, using the most optimistic claims of interdiction success, only about 8% to 15% of the heroin and about 30% of the cocaine in international drug shipments is seized (United Nations 1999, 32, 40).

Certainly interdiction policies are complicated by the massive increases in both international travel and trade in the late twentieth century. In the last half of the twentieth century, the ability of people to easily move across large distances has increased dramatically, as has the ability of people to move materials across equally large distances. In 1999, some 395 million people entered the United States overland from Mexico and Canada, 76 million people arrived on more than 928,000 commercial airline and private flights, and 9 million arrived by sea. In addition, 135 million vehicles—including automobiles and commercial trucks—crossed U.S. borders with Mexico and Canada, and more than 200,000 merchant and passenger ships and other maritime vessels docked at U.S. seaports or coastal harbors. Those seaports handled more than 4.4 million shipping containers and 400 million tons of cargo in 1999. U.S. Customs is able to inspect only about 3% of the goods entering the United States, a figure that will drop to about 1% by the end of the first decade of the twenty-first century as the volume of trade continues to grow.

The difficulty with interdiction strategies can be illustrated by taking a quick look at the cocaine market. The entire U.S. demand for cocaine, the largest market in the world, can be satisfied by thirteen pickup truck loads of cocaine per year.

The only minor success that the interdiction campaign can claim is with marijuana, a bulky commodity that is difficult to transport. However, the net effect of that success has been an even bigger problem. Marijuana smugglers and growers in other countries have simply moved to cocaine and heroin as substitutes for marijuana, meaning even more of those drugs are being imported to the United States, and marijuana production in the United

States has increased dramatically in the past ten years.

A RAND Corporation evaluation study of interdiction determined that "even massively stepped up drug interdiction efforts are not likely to greatly affect the availability of cocaine and heroin in the United States" (Reuter, Crawford, and Cace 1988).

The primary problem with interdiction is that it is based on two false assumptions. First, it assumes a stable and static supply of illegal drugs. That assumption is wrong. The supply of drugs is infinitely elastic: "Suppliers simply produce for the market what they would have produced anyway, plus enough extra to cover anticipated government seizures" (Rydell and Everingham 1994, 5). Second, it is based on a similarly incorrect assumption that drug traffickers do not adjust to the exigencies of new enforcement strategies. In reality, U.S. drug enforcement efforts in Colombia in the 1980s and 1990s resulted in the creation of hundreds of small, decentralized drug trafficking organizations, organizations that are virtually impossible to find, let alone control. In addition, these new traffickers have altered their product in a significant manner. They began producing "black cocaine" by using a chemical process that evades detection by drug sniffing dogs and chemical tests. The process is simple and inexpensive, primarily requiring adding charcoal and a couple of chemicals to their cocaine shipments (GAO 1999, 4–5).

The idea that interdiction will impact the supply and cost of drugs, thereby simultaneously hurting both traffickers and users, is simply wrong. After several decades of intensive interdiction campaigns, the facts are that heroin and cocaine are cheaper, more readily available, and of higher quality than ever before.

For example, in 1982, the cost of a gram of heroin at the retail level on the streets of an American city was $3,295.01. In 2000, the cost was $2,087.86. But the huge price reduction is only part of the story. In 1982, that gram of heroin at the retail level was at 4% purity. By 2000, that much cheaper gram of heroin was at 25% purity. At the wholesale level the impact is even more dramatic. In 1981, the wholesale price of a gram of heroin (the price paid by drug dealers) was $865.21 at 59% purity. In 2000, the wholesale price per gram had fallen to $112.51 at 59% purity (Abt Associates 2001, 43). In 1987, the average purity level of heroin in the United States was 6%; by 1997, it was 37% on average and in New York City it had reached 60% (United Nations 1999, 86). The net effect of interdiction and the drug war on heroin consumers is obvious, a 63% drop in price and a 635% increase in quality.

What about cocaine? In 1981, at the retail level a gram of 36% pure cocaine cost $423.09. In 2000, a gram of 61% pure cocaine at the retail level cost $211.70. For retail customers, the net impact of the drug war has been cocaine at twice the quality and half the price. At the wholesale level the differences are truly enormous. The wholesale price of a gram of 70% pure cocaine fell from $125.43 in 1981 to $26.03 in 2000 (Abt Associates 2001, 43). In the 1990s alone, the inflation-adjusted prices for cocaine and heroin fell 50% and 70% respectively in the United States (United Nations 1999, 86).

GARY W. POTTER

See also **Alcohol, Drugs, and Crime; Crime Control Strategies: Alcohol and Drugs; Drug Enforcement Administration (DEA); Federal Police and Investigative Agencies**

References and Further Reading

Abt Associates. 2001. *The price of illicit drugs: 1981 through the second quarter of 2000*. Washington, DC: Office of National Drug Control Policy.
Lyman, M., and G. Potter. 2003. *Drugs in society*. 4th ed. Cincinnati, OH: Anderson.
Reuter, P., G. Crawford, and J. Cace. 1988. *Sealing the borders: The effects of increased military participation in drug interdiction*. Santa Barbara, CA: RAND Corporation.
Rydell, C. P., and S. S. Everingham. 1994. *Controlling cocaine*. Prepared for the Office of National Drug Control Policy and the United States Army. Santa Monica, CA: Drug Policy Research Center, RAND Corporation.
United Nations Office of Drug Control and Crime Prevention (UNODCCP). 1999. *Global illicit drug trends 2000*. New York: UNODCCP.
U.S. Government Accountability Office. (1999). *Drug control: Threat from Colombia continues to grow*. Washington, DC: U.S. Government Accountability Office.

DRUG MARKETS

Both licit and illicit drug use and dealing continue to present serious challenges for law enforcement and for our communities. Criminal justice and law enforcement responses to drug markets, drug abuse, and drug dealing at all levels vary significantly depending on the substance, the defined user base, and the dealing and distribution structure. We examine the drug distribution process, consider various local and national law enforcement responses to drug markets, and explore the impact of law enforcement on drug markets.

Drug Distribution Processes, Dealers, and Users

Drug markets may operate differently depending on the nature of the substance being marketed, the user base, the presence and impact of federal and local law enforcement, and a myriad of other social factors. However, the general distribution process of illicit drugs is somewhat consistent and requires the active participation of many different players across different venues. Farmers (or chemists, in the case of synthetic drugs such as methamphetamine) must initially grow and harvest the base plant or ingredient(s) and fully prepare the substance(s) for the manufacturing process. Manufacturers must then transform the base plant(s) or ingredient(s) into a usable form that can be eventually consumed through drinking, eating, smoking, snorting, injecting, or inhaling the substance (some substances, such as cocaine, can be consumed in many different ways). The manufacturing process typically involves the introduction of additional components, compounds, and chemicals, a cooking, drying, heating, or chemical process, and subsequent packaging of the product for shipment. The manufacturers must then transfer the drugs to various traffickers, who are typically responsible for transferring larger quantities of drugs to wholesale movers, regional distributors, and street-level dealers, who ultimately sell the substances to end users.

In addition to the drug distribution process, illicit drug markets rely on the ongoing participation of a variety of support staff, including accountants and bankers (who manage the money and property), security personnel or enforcers (who ensure that payments are made on time, handle disputes, and manage other responsibilities that require force), lawyers, and others with a financial or political stake.

Illicit drug markets also operate in different ways, again depending on a variety of factors. "Open markets" are markets where anyone can buy or sell within any of the designated buying/selling locations. Open markets are often located in heavily trafficked areas (street corners, neighborhoods, bars, and so on), where users can easily find dealers and vice versa (Harocopos and Hough 2005). "Semiopen markets" develop when dealers restrict their sales to known customers or to customers who are referred by other acquaintances or dealers in an effort to reduce risk, minimize botched deals, and avoid transaction conflicts. "Closed" or "discreet markets" are those where a finite number of individuals buy, sell, and use the drugs and access to the dealers is strictly controlled (Rengert 2003). City

areas with extensive drug market activity have also been referred to as "hot spots," and police often focus significant enforcement and prevention efforts on these particular zones in an effort to disrupt routine deals, apprehend dealers and users, and minimize drug-related harm to communities (Ratcliffe 2004; Weisburd and Green 1996; Green 1995).

Final sale and transfer of drugs to the end user and use of the drug can also occur in a variety of settings and is often a function of the substance, the marketing strategy, the targeted audience, and the method of ingestion. Ecstasy and other "club drugs" are frequently distributed at nightclubs or at "rave" parties to mostly younger users. Crack cocaine (which is smoked) and heroin (which is either smoked or injected) are typically sold on the streets or in abandoned buildings turned into "shooting galleries" or "crack houses." Methamphetamine is often manufactured and sold out of temporary apartments, rented hotel rooms, or even from moving vans or trucks that are difficult to detect given their mobility. Marijuana may be distributed essentially anywhere, including at schools and colleges, at parties, and during concerts. OxyContin and other prescription-based drugs are often disseminated through illegal prescription services, stolen out of doctors' offices or clinics, or ordered online (Drug Enforcement Administration 2005). In fact, the evolution of the Internet has had a significant impact on traditional drug markets because drug transactions can simply be set up online, payments transferred wirelessly, and products simply shipped via mail or other courier services.

Drug Market Impact on Local Crime and Violence

There is little doubt that illicit drug markets contribute to, and in some situations cause, various crimes to occur and facilitate increases in overall crime rates. First, casual or excessive users of various substances are at increased risk of being victimized, engaging in dangerous sexual activity, being involved in automobile accidents, committing property crimes, engaging in violence, and participating in other illegal and high-risk behaviors (McBride and McCoy 1993; Thornberry, Huizinga, and Loeber 1995; Kuhns 2005). Further, involvement in drug dealing and participation in illicit drug markets also facilitates increased criminal involvement (beyond those crimes that are associated with drug use and dealing), including prostitution, violent crime, property crime, and financial crime (Elliott, Huizinga, and Menard 1987).

The risk of drug-related crime and violence also rises and falls depending on the nature and stability of the selling market, real and perceived levels of local enforcement, and other ecological and economic factors. Open drug markets are usually more susceptible to drug-related systemic violence, including robberies, homicides, and assaults. Open markets are often less stable, which generates increased uncertainty during transactions due to the lack of established trust between buyers and sellers, ongoing fears of undercover police operations, emergence of new users who are often younger and less self-controlled, and lack of defined territories among competitive dealers who will quickly resort to violence to enforce market rules.

Open markets can also introduce new drugs, which can also bring in new users, inexperienced dealers, and uncertainty regarding drug-induced behaviors. The emergence of crack cocaine in the late 1980s and early 1990s was directly related to increased violence rates during that time frame (Inciardi 1990), and the cross-country spread of methamphetamines from the southwest is also thought to be a significant contributor to increased violence.

Law Enforcement Responses to Drug Markets

A number of law enforcement responses to drug markets have been implemented, with varying degrees of success. Drug, vice, or narcotics squads have been established in many small and large law enforcement agencies. Their measure of success is often based on arrest rates and quantity of drug seizures. Vice squads utilize a variety of strategies and tactics, including undercover work, buy-bust operations (where police agents purchase drugs and subsequently arrest dealers), and buy-bust campaigns (which are more strategic extensions of buy-bust operations that involve identification of numerous drug dealers before numerous arrests begin). Sting and reverse-buy operations involve having police pose as dealers and subsequently arresting purchasers and users. Interagency task forces draw on the collaborative resources of a number of agencies to conduct large-scale investigations and stings (Green 1996). Police crackdowns involve intensive suppression-focused operations designed to quickly maximize arrests and clean up the streets (Scott 2003). Crackdowns are often effectively implemented in drug hot spots (Weisburd and Green 1995), although such efforts are not always successful for extended periods of time (National Institute of Justice 1996).

Problem-oriented policing and community policing, "weed and seed" operations, and other nontraditional approaches have been attempted in various drug market settings, including dilapidated neighborhoods, open air markets, public housing complexes, and schools. Increased emphasis on the physical environment, including enforcement of code violations for crack house and shooting gallery landlords and crime prevention through environmental design, are other nontraditional tactics that have been successful in some settings.

Issuing citations, in lieu of making arrests, for possession of minor amounts of marijuana is gaining popularity in some areas of the country, although processing offenders through the court system is still both time consuming and costly.

The Impact of Law Enforcement on Drug Market Disruption

Crackdowns can be a viable approach to drug market disruption, but many suppression efforts are effective only for a short time, with the positive impacts typically not being sustainable unless additional long-term measures are in place (for example, community policing, community engagement and support, infrastructure improvements, job placement opportunities, or the like). Drug markets controlled by street gangs have been effectively disrupted (permanently in some situations), particularly when police, prosecutors, probation officers, and others worked collaboratively to disable the entire organizational structure at one time (Decker 2003).

Displacement, which occurs when illicit drug markets adapt to law enforcement techniques and subsequently migrate elsewhere and/or change the methods of dealing, remains an ongoing challenge for law enforcement (Johnson and Natarajan 1995). Although mapping and other innovative technologies sometimes allow researchers and police to anticipate and predict displacement patterns and develop effective strategies and responses accordingly, drug markets will nevertheless persist where demand continues to exist. Demand reductions strategies, including education, family services, drug treatment availability, mental health services, and career counseling, are all important supportive measures that can deter excessive drug use and abuse.

JOSEPH B. KUHNS, III

See also **Alcohol, Drugs, and Crime; Community-Oriented Policing: History; Community-Oriented Policing: Practices; Crime Control Strategies: Alcohol and Drugs; Drug Enforcement Administration (DEA); Drug Interdiction; Hot Spots; Informants, Use of; Sting Tactics; Undercover Investigations**

References and Further Reading

Decker, Scott. 2003. *Policing gangs and youth violence*. Belmont, CA: Wadsworth/Thompson Learning.

Drug Enforcement Administration. 2005. http://www.dea.gov.

Elliott, Delbert, David Huizinga, and Scott Menard. 1987. *Multiple problem youth: Delinquency, substance use, and mental health problems*. New York: Springer Publishing.

Green, Lorraine. 1996. *Policing places with drug problems*. Vol. 2 of *Drugs, health, and social policy series*. London: Sage.

Harocopos, Alex, and Mike Hough. 2005. *Drug dealing in open-air markets*. Vol. 31 of *Problem-oriented guides for police, problem-specific guide series*. Washington, DC: U.S. Department of Justice, Office of Community-Oriented Policing Services.

Inciardi, James. 1990. The crack-violence connection within a population of hard-core adolescent offenders. In *Drugs and violence: Causes, correlates and consequences*, ed. M. de la Rosa, E. Y. Lambert, and B. Gropper. Rockville, MD: U.S. Department of Health and Human Services, National Institute on Drug Abuse.

Johnson, Bruce, and Mangai Natarajan. 1995. Strategies to avoid arrest: Crack sellers' response to intensified policing. *American Journal of Police* 14: 49–69.

Kuhns, Joseph, III. 2005. The dynamic nature of the drug use/serious violence relationship: A multi-causal approach. *Violence and Victims* 20: 433–54.

McBride, Duane, and Clyde McCoy. 1993. The drug–crimes relationship: An analytical framework. *The Prison Journal* 73: 257–78.

National Institute of Justice. 1996. *Policing drug hot spots*. January. Washington, DC: U.S. Government Printing Office.

Rengert, George. 2003. The distribution of illegal drugs at the retail level: The street dealers. In *Drugs, crime, and criminal justice*, ed. Gaines and Kraska, 175–93. Prospect Heights, IL: Waveland Press.

Scott, Michael. 2003. *The benefits and consequences of police crackdowns*. Vol. 1 of

Problem-oriented guides for police responses series. Washington, DC: U.S. Department of Justice, Office of Community Oriented Policing Services.

Thornberry, Terry, David Huizinga, and Rolf Loeber. 1995. The prevention of serious delinquency and violence: Implications from the program of research on the causes and correlates of delinquency. In *Sourcebook on Serious Violent and Chronic Juvenile Offenders,* ed. J. Howell, B. Krisberg, D. Hawkins, and J. Wilson. Thousand Oaks, CA: Sage.

Weisburd, David, and Lorraine Green. 1995. Policing drug hotspots: The Jersey City drug market analysis experiment. *Justice Quarterly* 12: 711–35.

DRUNK DRIVING

Introduction

Just over a hundred years have passed since the first scientific report on drunk-driving crashes of motorized wagons in 1904 (U.S. Department of Transportation 1968). The number of alcohol-related deaths in that year is unknown, but in 2004, a century later, 16,694 Americans died on the nation's highways in alcohol-related crashes. That is a 36% decline from the 26,173 alcohol-related fatalities in 1982 [National Highway Traffic Safety Administration (NHTSA) 1998]. The number of non-alcohol-related crashes has risen as the number of cars on the road (vehicle miles of travel) has increased, yet alcohol-related crashes have declined, saving an estimated 270,000 lives in the past two decades. Even so, drunk driving costs the nation $110 billion annually: $40 billion in direct costs and $70 billion in quality of life costs (Miller et al. 1997).

A Bit of History

Today, enforcement of drunk-driving laws is technologically complex, involving standardized behavioral tests and procedures for measuring blood alcohol concentration (BAC). These scientific techniques developed slowly over the twentieth century. Early in the century, a number of scientists worked on methods for detecting alcohol in blood (Jones 2000). A pioneer in the field was Widmark, a Swedish scientist, who between 1914 and 1932 described the relationship between BAC and the amount of alcohol consumed, based on the process by which the body absorbs and eliminates alcohol. Widmark developed his famous eponymous formula to calculate BAC from the amount of alcohol consumed (Andreasson and Widmark 1985).

In 1934, Heise published the first scientific paper directly relating alcohol consumption to driving. This, along with the work of Widmark, led Norway to adopt a per se BAC limit (0.05) in 1936, which defined impaired driving in terms of alcohol in the blood rather than the appearance and behavior of the driver. Even earlier, while the United States relied on officer testimony to obtain impaired-driving convictions, Scandinavian officers brought suspects to the police station to be examined by a physician who made the impairment decision.

Three important milestones occurred in the United States. In 1954, Robert Borkenstein, a professor at the University of Indiana, invented the *Breathalyzer,* the first practical, easily used breath-testing device (Borkenstein and Smith 1961). A decade later, he conducted the Grand Rapids study that compared crash-involved drivers with non-crash-involved drivers. This provided the means for plotting the relative risk of crash involvement as a function of BAC level (Borkenstein et al. 1974). The Grand Rapids study was repeated in 1995 and produced similar results. In 1977, Burns and Moskowitz (1977) developed a set of three standardized field sobriety tests (SFSTs) that are now widely used by officers to measure driver impairment.

These technological developments during the past twenty years have led to the passage of approximately 2,300 drunk-driving laws by state legislatures (NHTSA 2001). The National Committee on Uniform Traffic Codes and Laws (NCUTLO) issued a model state traffic law in 2000 (NCUTLO 2000) reflecting two decades of progress. Four laws formed the foundation for the current impaired-driving criminal justice system:

1. *Implied consent laws,* first adopted by New York in 1953, provide that accepting a driver's license obligates the driver to submit to a BAC test if the officer has probable cause to believe that the driver is impaired. The penalty for refusal is administrative suspension of the driver's license.
2. *Administrative license suspension laws* allow the officer to confiscate and the Motor Vehicle Department to suspend the license of any driver arrested for impaired driving with a BAC at or higher than the legal limit (currently 0.08). This law, adopted by Minnesota in 1976, responded to the courts' inability to consistently suspend impaired drivers.
3. *Driving-while-impaired (DWI) laws,* which make it an offense to drive while impaired, were first adopted by New York in 1910. These laws require descriptive evidence of impairment from an officer (such as how the vehicle was operated and the appearance and behavior of the driver).
4. *Per se laws* make it an offense to drive with a BAC higher than a prohibited level. Indiana passed the first per se law in 1939, setting the limit at 0.15 BAC. As more and more states passed per se laws, that limit was gradually lowered to 0.10 BAC and then to 0.08 in 2000, following a congressional action. Now, all fifty states have adopted 0.08 as their legal BAC limit.

Based on these four primary laws, the standard impaired-driving arrest procedure follows four steps: (1) Identify and stop a vehicle likely being driven by an impaired driver; (2) interview the driver at the driver's window to determine whether there is sufficient evidence to invite the suspect to step out of the car; (3) perform SFSTs to determine whether there is probable cause to make an arrest; and (4) arrest and transport the suspect to the police station for an evidential breath test. During the past three decades, the NHTSA has sponsored research on each of these steps to engender procedures useful to officers enforcing drunk-driving laws. This includes the development of observable signs that a vehicle is being driven by an impaired driver (Harris, Howlett, and Ridgeway 1979), the development of SFSTs (Burns and Moskowitz 1977), preliminary breath-test devices (PBTs) to be used in the field (Cleary and Rodgers 1986), and finally, standards for evidential breath-test devices (NHTSA 1992).

The current DWI enforcement system is substantially limited by several problems. Two recent reviews, one funded by NHTSA (Hedlund and McCartt 2001) and the other by the Traffic Injury Research Foundation of Canada (Simpson and Robertson 2001), have highlighted some issues faced by police in enforcing DWI laws. Hedlund and McCartt (2001) point to the need to (1) simplify arrest procedures to reduce the time required to apprehend and process offenders; (2) increase penalties to discourage breath-test refusals; and (3) provide improved training on the use of SFSTs and PBTs.

Hedlund and McCartt also emphasize the need for greater use of PBTs, particularly passive sensors that can detect alcohol in the expired air from a distance of six inches to identify heavy drinkers who are tolerant to alcohol and show few behavioral signs of intoxication. Sobriety checkpoints, where all drivers can be stopped and examined for impairment by the police under controlled conditions, have been strongly supported by the NHTSA and safety advocates. Police departments have been less enthusiastic, viewing them as expensive and as yielding too few DWI arrests (Fell, Lacey, and Voas 2004). Proponents argue that if the checkpoints were run with minimum personnel using passive sensors, they would be cost effective and produce greater deterrence to DWI than the traditional enforcement procedures (Voas, Lacey, and Fell 2005).

Recently, there has been an increasing concern with high BAC first offenders becoming repeat offenders, based on work by Simpson and colleagues (1996). They argue that most crash-involved drinking drivers have high BACs and that many are repeat offenders. This has stimulated interest and legislation aimed at controlling such drivers by increasing the DWI offense penalties and, ultimately, has led to lengthier license suspensions and, for multiple offenders, longer jail sentences. It also has increased the use of vehicle sanctions, such as vehicle impoundment, vehicle forfeiture, and registration suspension with license plate seizure or special plates (Voas and DeYoung 2002). Of these sanctions, vehicle impoundment has produced the strongest evidence for effectiveness in reducing recidivism rates.

Ignition alcohol interlocks, which prevent a driver with a BAC greater than 0.03 from starting a car, have been proved to reduce recidivism by 50% to 90% when installed on an offender's vehicle (Voas et al. 1999).

Unfortunately, this positive impact is lost after the unit has been removed, and only 10% to 20% of eligible DWI offenders install the units (Voas and Marques 2003). Only when coerced by the threat of house arrest do as many as two-thirds of offenders agree to install the units (Voas et al. 2002).

Following prohibition, most states adopted twenty-one as the minimum legal drinking age (MLDA) (Toomey, Rosenfeld, and Wagenaar 1996). When the voting age was lowered to eighteen in response to the Vietnam War, however,

twenty-nine states followed this trend between 1970 and 1975 and lowered their MLDA to younger than twenty-one (Mosher 1993). A series of research studies followed, demonstrating that the lower drinking ages increased crash involvements for the affected youth. This led to a reversal of the low MLDA trend and culminated in federal legislation—the Uniform Drinking Age Act—that resulted in all states adopting twenty-one as the MLDA by 1988 (Toomey, Rosenfeld, and Wagenaar 1996). Since that time, NHTSA has estimated that 900 lives are saved each year by the MLDA (NHTSA 2004).

Aside from the traffic safety benefit, the MLDA led to an increase in the attention to primary prevention of impaired driving through control of alcohol availability (Wagenaar and Holder 1996), price (Cook 1981; Chaloupka, Saffer, and Grossman 1993), and server interventions to promote "responsible sales" practices (McKnight 1996). This was characterized by an expansion of the traditional drunk-driving prevention programs into the broader public health field. Consequently, police departments became more involved in enforcing "zero tolerance" laws, which make it an offense for drivers age twenty and younger to have any alcohol in their systems. Police also began conducting "cops in shops" programs (Century Council 2005), in which officers in civilian clothes act as clerks to apprehend underage alcohol purchase attempts. In addition, alcohol outlet "stings" (University of Minneapolis 2000) are held, in which underage police cadets attempt to purchase alcohol, and party patrols are formed to break up teenage keg parties. Some police departments have a low enthusiasm for enforcing such underage and alcohol sales laws; however, recent research has shown that early onset of drinking (before age sixteen) leads to increased probability that the individual will be an impaired driver as an adult and will be more likely to become dependent on alcohol (Grant, Stinson, and Harford 2001; Hingson et al. 2002).

ROBERT B. VOAS

See also **Alcohol, Drugs, and Crime; Traffic Services and Management**

References and Further Reading

Andréasson, R., and E. Widmark. 1985. *Widmark's micromethod and Swedish legislation on alcohol and traffic.* Stockholm, Sweden: The Information Center for Traffic Safety.

Baker, S. P., and L. H. Chen. 2001. Determination of characteristics of fatally injured drivers. Washington, DC: National Highway Traffic Safety Administration and Johns Hopkins School of Public Health, Center for Injury Research and Policy.

Borkenstein, R. F., and H. W. Smith. 1961. The Breathalyzer and Its Application. *Medicine, Science and the Law* 1: 13.

Borkenstein, R. F., R. F. Crowther, R. P. Shumate, W. B. Ziel, and R. Zylman. 1974. The role of the drinking driver in traffic accidents. *Blutalkohol* 11 (Suppl. 1): 1–132.

Burns, M., and H. Moskowitz. 1977. *Psychophysical tests for DWI arrest*, 126. Springfield, VA: National Technical Information Service.

Century Council. 2005. *Cops in shops.* http:\\www.centurycouncil.org\underage\cops.html (accessed November 30).

Chaloupka, F. J., H. Saffer, and M. Grossman. 1993. Alcohol-control policies and motor-vehicle fatalities. *Journal of Legal Studies* 22 (1): 161–86.

Cleary, J., and A. Rodgers. 1986. *Analysis of the effects of recent changes in Minnesota's DWI laws: Part III. Longitudinal analysis of policy impacts.* St. Paul, MN: Minnesota House of Representatives, Research Department.

Cook, P. J. 1981. The effect of liquor taxes on drinking, cirrhosis, and auto accidents. In *Alcohol and public policy: Beyond the shadow of Prohibition*, ed. M. Moore and D. Gerstein, 255–85. Washington, DC: National Academy Press.

Fell, J. C., J. H. Lacey, and R. B. Voas. 2004. Sobriety checkpoints: Evidence of effectiveness is strong, but use is limited. *Traffic Injury Prevention* 5 (3): 220–27.

Harris, D. H., J. G. Howlett, and R. G. Ridgeway. 1979. *Visual detection of driving while intoxicated. Project interim report: Identification of visual cues and development of detection methods.* Washington, DC: Department of Transportation, National Highway Traffic Safety Administration.

Hedlund, J. H., and A. T. McCartt. 2001. *Seeking additional solutions.* Washington, DC: AAA Foundation for Traffic Safety (AAAFTS).

Heise, H. A. 1934. Alcohol and automobile accidents. *Journal of the American Medical Association* 103: 739–41.

Jones, A. W. 2000. Measuring alcohol in blood and breath for forensic purposes—A historical review. *Forensic Science Review* 12 (1/2): 151–82.

McKnight, A. James. 1996. Server intervention to reduce alcohol-involved traffic crashes. *Alcohol Health and Research World* 20 (4): 227–29.

Miller, T. R., M. S. Galbraith, D. C. Lestina, T. Schlax, P. Mabery, and R. Deering. 1997. United States passenger–vehicle crashes by crash geometry: Direct costs and other losses. *Accident Analysis and Prevention* 29 (3): 343–52.

Mosher, J. F. 1993. Implementing alcohol policy. *Addiction* 88 (1): 17–19.

National Committee on Uniform Traffic Codes. 2000. Millennium DUI prevention act. In *Drunk driving: Seeking additional solutions*, ed. J. Hedlund and A. T. McCarrt, 53. Washington, DC: AAA Foundation for Traffic Safety.

National Highway Traffic Safety Administration (NHTSA). 1992. Model specifications for breath alcohol ignition interlock devices (BAIIDs). *Federal Register* 57 (67): 11772–87.

———. 1998. *Fatality analysis reporting system data files, 1982–1997.* Washington, DC: National Highway Traffic Safety Administration.

———. 2001. *Digest of state alcohol-highway safety related legislation.* 19th ed. Washington, DC: National Highway Traffic Safety Administration.

———. 2004a. *Fatality Analysis Reporting System (FARS).* Washington, DC: National Center for Statistics and Analysis.

———. 2004b. Strategies for addressing the DWI offender: 10 promising sentencing practices. In *A compendium of promising practices proposed at the NHTSA National DWI Sentencing Summit at the National Judicial College*, ed. W. Brunson and P. Knighten. Washington, DC: National Highway Traffic Safety Administration.

Ross, H. L. 1984. *Deterring the drinking driver: Legal policy and social control.* 2nd ed. Lexington, MA: Lexington Books.

Shults, Ruth A., Randy W. Elder, David A. Sleet, James L. Nichols, Mary O. Alao,

Vilma G. Carande-Kulis, Stephanie Zaza, Daniel M. Sosin, Robert S. Thompson, and Task Force on Community Preventive Services. Reviews of evidence regarding interventions to reduce alcohol-impaired driving. *American Journal of Preventive Medicine* 21 (4 Suppl): 66–88.

Simpson, H. M., and R. D. Robertson. 2001. *DWI system improvements for dealing with hard core drinking drivers: enforcement*, 32. Ottawa, Canada: Traffic Injury Research Foundation.

Simpson, H. M., D. R. Mayhew, and D. J. Beirness. 1996. *Dealing with the hard core drinking driver*. Ottawa, Canada: Traffic Injury Research Foundation.

Toomey, Traci L., Carolyn Rosenfeld, and Alexander C. Wagenaar. 1996. The minimum legal drinking age: History, effectiveness, and ongoing debate. *Alcohol Health and Research World* 20 (4): 213–18.

University of Minneapolis Alcohol Epidemiology Program. 2000. *Alcohol compliance checks: A procedures manual for enforcing alcohol age-of-sale laws*. Minneapolis, MN: University of Minneapolis.

U.S. Department of Transportation. 1968. *1968 Alcohol and highway safety. Report to the U.S. Congress*. Washington, DC: U.S. Government Printing Office.

Voas, R. B., and P. R. Marques. 2003. Commentary: Barriers to interlock implementation. *Traffic Injury Prevention* 4 (3): 183–87.

Voas, R. B., J. H. Lacey, and J. C. Fell. 2005. The "Paspoint" system—Passive sensors at mini-checkpoints: Bringing Australia's random breath-test system to the United States. In *Implementing impaired driving countermeasures: Putting research into action*. Washington, DC: Transportation Research Board of the National Academies.

Voas, Robert B., and David. J. DeYoung. 2002. Vehicle action: Effective policy for controlling drunk and other high-risk drivers? *Accident Analysis and Prevention* 34 (3): 263–70.

Voas, Robert B., K. O. Blackman, A. S. Tippetts, and P. R. Marques. 2002. Evaluation of a program to motivate impaired driving offenders to install ignition interlocks. *Accident Analysis and Prevention* 34 (4): 449–55.

Voas, Robert B., Paul R. Marques, A. Scott Tippetts, and D. J. Beirness. 1999. The Alberta interlock program: The evaluation of a province-wide program on DUI recidivism. *Addiction* 94 (12): 1849–59.

Wagenaar, A. C., and M. Wolfson. 1995. Deterring sales and provision of alcohol to minors: A study of enforcement in 295 counties in four states. *Public Health Reports* 110 (4): 419–27.

Willis, C., S. Lybrand, and N. Bellamy. 2004. Alcohol Ignition interlock programmes for reducing drink driving recidivism. *Cochran Database of Systematic Reviews* 4: CD004168.

Zwicker, T. J., J. Hedlund, and V. S. Northrup. 2005. *Breath test refusals in DWI enforcement: An interim report*. Washington, DC: National Highway Traffic Safety Administration.

E

EARLY WARNING SYSTEMS

It has become a truism among the police that 10% of their officers cause 90% of their disciplinary problems. Investigative journalists have found police departments where as few as 2% of all officers are responsible for at least half of all citizen complaints. As early as the 1970s, Herman Goldstein observed that problem officers were well known to all, but that all too little was often done to alter their conduct. In 1981, the U.S. Commission of Civil Rights recommended that all police departments implement an early warning system to identify those officers generating frequent citizen complaints or demonstrating identifiable patterns of inappropriate behavior. Still, what are early warning systems and do they work?

An early warning system is a data-based police management tool designed to identify officers whose behavior is problematic. Once problem behaviors are identified, some form of intervention is offered to correct the performance. An early response means the police department is able to intervene before the officer's behavior damages the department's efforts

or requires formal disciplinary action. The idea is that by alerting the department and assisting the officer, the employee, his or her agency, and the citizens they both serve can all benefit.

While little is known about the use of early warning systems, a 1999 survey by the Police Executive Research Forum (PERF) found that about one-fourth of police and sheriff's departments serving populations of 50,000 or more had an early warning system in place; half of those had been created since 1994 while more than one-third of departments had introduced theirs after 1996. Another 12% of agencies had planned to introduce a system within a few years of the survey date. Municipal agencies were more likely than county police or sheriff's departments to have such systems.

Basically, most early warning systems have three distinct phases: selection, intervention, and postintervention monitoring. First, of course, officers have to be selected for the program. Although no standards exist as to how this should be done, there is general agreement about the criteria that should be used. Among these criteria are citizen complaints, discharges of fire-arms, uses of force by police, involvement in civil litigation, a disproportionate number of resisting-arrest incidents, involvement in high-speed pursuits, and the occurrence of incidents causing vehicular damage.

Although a few police departments rely on citizen complaints alone to identify problem officers, most use a combination of factors such as those just noted instead. The PERF survey showed that among those agencies relying on citizen complaints as at least a factor in their early warning system, most (67%) require three complaints within a specified time frame (overwhelmingly twelve months) for an officer's inclusion.

Once identified, the primary goal of an early warning system is to intervene with the officer to correct his or her problem behavior(s). Usually this means some combination of deterrence and education. Simply put, it is assumed that the process of being identified and included will induce officers to change their behavior so as to avoid some anticipated punishment. General deterrence assumes that even those officers not selected will alter their behaviors to remain outside of the system's concern. In addition, any training that follows has the potential to correct officers' mistakes and help them improve their performance.

For nearly two-thirds of the police departments in the PERF survey, the initial response consisted of a review by the selected officer's immediate supervisor. Command officers participated at least in counseling selected officers in nearly half (45%) of the surveyed departments, while an equal percentage (45%) made training classes available for groups of officers identified.

Once they have intervened, nearly all (90%) of the agencies in the PERF survey reported that they monitored the selected officer's conduct so as to determine if the effort had been successful. Although the officer's immediate supervisor often informally did the monitoring, some departments have instituted formal methods of continued observation, evaluation, and reporting of the officer's actions. Nearly half (47%) continued to monitor the officer's performance for at least three years after the initial intervention. The remaining half either did not specify the length of follow-up or noted that monitoring decisions were made on a case-by-case basis.

While there are no experimental evaluations of the impact of early warning systems, case studies of the systems in place in Minneapolis, New Orleans, and Miami-Dade County are instructive. Overall, the systems in place in these cities appear to have been successful at reducing citizen complaints against officers as well as other indicators of problematic police performance. In Minneapolis, for example, complaints against selected officers dropped by 67% within one year of the initial intervention. In New Orleans, the reduction was 64%, while in Miami-Dade the numbers of selected officers having no uses of force went from only 4% to at least 50% following the early warning intervention.

Further, from the New Orleans data it appears that the officers themselves generally had a positive mind-set toward the early warning intervention. In that city, selected officers participated in a Professional Performance Enhancement Program (PPEP) class designed to address the concerns that had led to their selection by the system. In anonymous evaluations of those classes, participating officers gave them an average rating of 7 on a 1 to 10 scale. All officers had at least one positive thing to say about the class experience, and some added specific comments about how the class had helped them. Observations of the PPEP classes found officers most engaged in those components most directly related to the practical problems of policing—especially those incidents that often generate citizen complaints—and least engaged in the more abstract or moralistic components.

Although the use of early warning systems appears to offer some potential benefits, each of the system's three phases involves a number of complex policy issues. For example, while the criteria involved in officer selection can vary, most systems appear to rely significantly on citizen complaints. The problems related to official data on citizen complaints—including under-reporting—have long been documented. As such, a broad range of indicators of problem behaviors is more likely to effectively and accurately identify officers requiring department intervention.

The intervention also can be problematic. In many systems the initial intervention relies on informal counseling between the selected officer and his or her immediate supervisor. Some of these systems required no documentation of the content of that counseling, raising concerns about whether the supervisors know, and delivered, the desired content. Some supervisors may choose to minimize the importance of the intervention by telling the officer not to worry. If so, the selected officer's behavior may be reinforced rather than corrected. Clearly, further research on the most effective forms of intervention is necessary.

Finally, the types and methods of post-intervention monitoring vary widely. Since the department's follow-up may be critical to the success of the system and how it is perceived both inside and outside of the department, more research here is important as well.

An effective early warning system is likely to involve a complex, high-maintenance effort that requires a significant investment of administrative and supervisory resources. Unfortunately, some systems appear to be little more than symbolic efforts with little substantive content. It is unlikely that these systems can be effective, especially if the agency otherwise lacks a serious commitment to accountability. When taken seriously, however, the limited information available suggests that early warning systems can become effective management tools. We should remember, however, that an early warning system is but one of many tools needed to raise standards of performance and improve the quality of policing.

SAMUEL WALKER, GEOFFREY P. ALPERT, and DENNIS JAY KENNEY

See also **Abuse of Authority by Police; Accountability; Civilian Review Boards; Corruption; Deadly Force; Deviant Subcultures in Policing; Discretion; Ethics and Values in the Context of Community Policing; Excessive Force; Integrity in Policing; Performance Measurement; Professionalism**

References and Further Reading

Kansas City Police Go After Their 'Bad Boys. 1991. *New York Times*, September 10.

Kappeler, V., R. Sluder, and G. Alpert. 1998. *Forces of deviance: Understanding the dark side of policing*. Prospect Heights, IL: Waveland Press.

U.S. Commission on Civil Rights. 1981. *Who Is Guarding the Guardians*? Washington, DC: U.S. Commission on Civil Rights.

Walker, S. 2001. *Police accountability: The role of citizen oversight*. Belmont, CA: Wadsworth Thompson.

Walker, S., G. Alpert, and D. Kenney. 2001. *Early warning systems: Responding to the problem officer*. Washington, DC: National Institute of Justice.

Waves of Abuse Laid to a Few Officers. 1992. *Boston Globe*, October 4.

EDUCATION AND TRAINING

The preparation of police recruits for their profession includes practical training as well as classroom education. For example, it would be almost impossible to train officers to use firearms through educational approaches only. This particular skill will always remain in the domain of police training. However, as a concept, the use of force and implications of the use of firearms can never be learned through the training approach alone. It should and must be approached from a more academic and educational angle.

History

Although the profession of policing can be traced back thousands of years, the concept of training is a relatively new phenomenon; the education of officers is even more revolutionary in nature. Although larger police departments in the United States trace their training academies to the nineteenth century, training became mandatory for all police departments only in the late 1960s. A training council in California led the way, establishing the Police Officers Standards and Training guidelines in 1959. Although this was a state rather than a federal initiative, within approximately four years, many states throughout the country had developed their own standards for training (Christian and Edwards 1985).

In 1967, the President's Commission on Law Enforcement and Administration of Justice recommended that a Peace Officer Standards and Training (POST) commission be established in every state. These POST commissions or boards were empowered to set mandatory minimum requirements and appropriately funded so that they might provide financial aid to governmental units for the implementation of established standards. The two important charges of the POST commissions were as follows:

1. Establish mandatory minimum training standards (at both the recruit and in-service levels), with the authority to determine and approve curricula, identify required preparation for instructors, and approve facilities acceptable for police training.
2. Certify police officers who have acquired various levels of education, training, and experience necessary to adequately perform the duties of the police service (Bennett and Hess 1996).

In the 1960s and 1970s a number of blue-ribbon committees furthered the goals of police training and education. One of the outcomes of these activities was creation of the Law Enforcement Education Program (LEEP), which was funded by Congress to provide financial assistance for police officers who enrolled in various academic courses offered at more than a thousand academic institutions around the country. Although it was considered to be a major push in the direction of furthering the goal of professionalism in the field of policing, it had a relatively short life span and was removed from the federal budget, though without real justification.

Education

Education involves the learning of general concepts, terms, policies, practices, and theories. The subject matter taught is often broad in scope. Typical relationships and practices within a given field are discussed, as well as hypotheses as to why these particular relationships and practices exist. Among the types of skills stressed in education are correctly analyzing different situations; communicating information and defending one's opinion effectively, both orally and in writing; drawing insights from related situations in different settings; gathering information using various methods of research; creating alternative approaches and solutions to diverse problems; and learning new facts and ideas from others through various media (for example, lectures, books, articles, conversations, or video presentations).

The goals of education include teaching people to recognize, categorize, evaluate, and understand different types of phenomena; to interact and communicate effectively with others; to think for themselves; and to predict the probable outcomes of competing solutions (Haberfeld 2002).

Training

The goal of training is to teach a specific method of performing a task or responding to a given situation. The subject matter taught is usually narrow in scope. Training usually involves two stages:

1. Prescribed procedures are first presented and explained.
2. Prescribed procedures are then practiced until they become second nature or reflexive.

Training is focused on how to most effectively accomplish a task whenever a particular situation arises. Training is experiential and goal oriented.

Among the skills associated with most training programs are the ability to determine whether or not the circumstances warrant following a prescribed course of action, the physical and verbal skills associated with those actions, and the cognitive abilities needed to recall what steps should be followed and in what order for each of the situations covered in the training program (Timm and Christian 1991).

The Role of Training and Education in Law Enforcement

Both training and education appear to be essential regardless of the law enforcement position one holds within an organization (Timm and Christian 1991). Both play important roles in the field of law enforcement. Training provides unambiguous instructions on how to perform many of the tasks that an officer is expected to complete. As a result, trained officers often respond both consistently, using proven techniques, and automatically, even under emergency conditions. Education, by contrast, helps prepare officers to solve problems independently, as well as to communicate and interact effectively with others.

Different law enforcement positions may require different levels of education and training; however, a combination of both is needed in every position. Law enforcement officers, for example, often interact with people from a wide range of backgrounds, exercise considerable discretion in many critical situations (such as deciding whether or not to arrest someone, to shoot or not to shoot, whether or not to evacuate an area in an emergency situation, and so on), and must prepare written incident reports. These tasks can be effectively performed only through acquisition of some general evaluative and decision-making skills traditionally taught through various educational programs. Officers also need hands-on training in a wide range of specific physical tasks directly related to their positions (such as arresting people, shooting firearms, operating equipment, and handling emergency situations).

Middle- and top-level administration personnel also need practical training in certain areas, even though in performing most of their tasks they rely more heavily on knowledge and mental skills generally acquired and/or developed through formal education. For example, middle and senior police executives often need training in how to operate computers, use new software (such as crime mapping software) and other technologies that they will need personally, what reporting procedures to follow, and a number of other essentials that will enable them to complete the tasks for which they are responsible. Law enforcement executives may also participate in training programs to familiarize themselves with new evaluation tools and research findings.

Merging Training and Education

The term *police academy* usually refers to three main types of police academies in the United States: agency, regional, and college sponsored. Agency schools are generally found in large municipal areas or are established for the state police or highway patrol. Regional academies handle the training functions for both large and small departments located in a designated geographical area. The college-sponsored training academies operate on the premises of postsecondary institutions, particularly community colleges. These college-sponsored academies allow a person to take police training courses for college credit (Thibault et al. 1998).

There is no international consensus on the best possible model for police training and education, and even within jurisdictions several models may be employed. As one example of an approach from a diverse democracy, the Canadian police used four models of basic training for police recruits in the early 2000s:

- *Model 1:* Education and training in a police academy, separated from mainstream adult education.
- *Model 2:* Education and training on a university campus (with adult mainstream education).
- *Model 3:* A holistic approach, exposing recruits to the entire criminal justice system rather than just to the field of policing. It alternates classroom learning with field experience in a bloc program.
- *Model 4:* Police education integrated with adult education (the Quebec model). New recruits must complete a three-year college program to obtain a diploma of collegial studies, which includes general academic courses and instruction in criminology, policing, and law (Griffits et al. 1999).

The United States has more than nineteen thousand autonomous police agencies and thus a myriad of training and educational approaches, ranging from as little as eight weeks of training to as much as thirty-two weeks. On average, departments require 640 training hours of their new officer recruits (425 classroom training hours and 215 field training hours). While minimum hours are determined by the respective state's POST, academies may add extra sessions to reflect particular agencies' areas of emphasis or need.

In the United States, there is a lack of consensus on what constitutes the most important skills and requirements for police officers to acquire and hone. Lawyers, accountants, social workers, and medical doctors—all are required to be educated and trained in a consistent manner in order to practice in their profession. However, in the United States policing is subject to an enormous variety of educational and training requirements. Critics believe that in order for policing to be looked on as a true profession, its apprentices need to be educated and trained in a consistent manner. They disagree, however, on whether it should be done through training, education, or some combination of both. The academic community tends to push for more education for officers, while practitioners tend to emphasize the value of training. One approach toward bridging this schism would be focused on identifying the basic and mandatory standards that reflect police qualifications, but customizing them to reflect local need. If basic professional standards can be identified, then developing the methods to refine those skills will be a less controversial process.

The overall impact of education and training on quality of policing cannot be overstated. Modern police training has come a long way in just three decades. In 1975, the grim state of the police profession was reflected by the following quote: "Ignorance of police duties is no handicap to a successful career as a policeman" (Reith 1975). This statement no longer holds true. Progress has come primarily from the recognition that police officers must and will be trained and educated as professionals. The increasing sophistication of crime and criminals has made essential the development of academically oriented training, to enable officers to cope with the complexity of various criminal activities they may confront. Furthermore, as society has become more sophisticated, it increasingly resents the notion that force alone can solve problems. Policing is, first and foremost, about the use of force. Improved training and education means that officers now wield this ultimate tool in a more balanced and nonthreatening manner.

M. R. HABERFELD

See also **Academies, Police; Personnel Selection; Police Standards and Training Commissions; Professionalism**

References and Further Reading

Bennet, W. W., and K. M. Hess. 1996. *Criminal investigation*. St. Paul, MN: West.

Christian, K. E., and S. M. Edwards. 1985. Law enforcement standards and training councils: A human resource for planning force in the future. *Journal of Police Science and Administration* 13: 1–9.

Griffits, C. T., B. Whitelaw, and R. B. Parent. 1999. *Canadian police work*. Scarborough, Ontario, Canada: International Thomson Publishing.

Haberfeld, M. R. 2002. *Critical issues in police training*. Upper Saddle River, NJ: Prentice-Hall, 2002.

Reith, C. 1975. *The blind eye of history: A study of the origins of the present police era*. Montclair, NJ: Patterson Smith.

Timm, H., and K. E. Christian. 1991. *Introduction to private security*. Pacific Grove, CA: Brooks/Cole.

ELDERLY AND CRIME

Statistics show that in general people are living longer. With this longevity comes the increased likelihood of victimization at some point in the life course. Many seniors are fearful that they will be victimized as they age even though the crime victimization rate for seniors has continued to decline over the years. The elderly as a group are the least likely of all age categories to experience crime. Still, the elderly are vulnerable to certain types of crimes. According to the National Crime Prevention Council, the most common types of crimes committed against seniors are (1) financial crime, (2) property crime, (3) violent crime, and (4) elderly abuse/mistreatment.

Concern about the victimization of elderly persons increased in the early 1980s after British medical researchers drew attention to a phenomenon they called "granny battering." Eventually, the granny battering term was replaced with less offensive concepts such as elder mistreatment and elder abuse. Elder mistreatment is a broader concept used to characterize a range of violations against elderly persons. The National Center on Elder Abuse cites six types of elder mistreatment: physical abuse, sexual abuse, financial exploitation, emotional/psychological abuse, neglect, and self-neglect. Although these forms of abuse are discussed separately below, they usually occur simultaneously or in some combination.

Physical abuse is likely the type of elder abuse that comes to mind when people use the phrase *elder abuse.* Examples include acts such as hitting, slapping, cutting, punching, or kicking an elderly person. Also included are instances in which elderly persons are overmedicated or undermedicated. Overmedication usually occurs because caregivers want to make their elderly care recipient passive and easy to manage. Undermedication generally occurs because caregivers are stealing drugs or money that would be used to purchase drugs.

Sexual abuse likely conjures up images of elderly individuals being forcibly raped. However, such acts make up only a very small proportion of the cases of elder sexual abuse. More common are instances of groping during bathing, voyeurism, obscene language, and other behaviors in which genital–genital contact does not occur. Studies using social services samples have found that family members are more likely to be the offenders in these cases, while those using self-report strategies have found that nonfamily members are more likely to be the offenders.

Financial exploitation occurs when individuals steal from elderly persons using any number of strategies. Examples range from instances when family members misuse an elderly person's Social Security check to cases in which loved ones convince elderly persons to sign over their property. Power-of-attorney fraud (for example, signing an elderly person's name for fraudulent purposes) is among the most popular types of elder financial exploitation. In such exploitation, individuals gain complete access to all of the elderly person's assets once they are granted power of attorney. Unfortunately, some misuse this power. One problem that arises is proving that the actions were fraudulent.

Verbal and nonverbal acts that torment the senior, such as verbal abuse, rights violations, and harassment, are considered to be acts of emotional abuse. Emotional abuse is the most difficult form of elder abuse to prove and among the least reported forms of elder mistreatment. Neglect occurs when individuals fail to provide adequate care to the elderly care recipient. Experts distinguish between active and passive neglect. Active neglect refers to instances of intentional neglect, whereas passive neglect refers to instances when care providers unintentionally fail to provide care.

Self-neglect is perhaps the most controversial type of elder mistreatment. It refers to instances in which elderly persons fail to provide adequate care to themselves and adult protective services intervenes to provide or recommend improvements in care. Although self-neglect is arguably the most common form of elder mistreatment, it is also the least studied form of elder mistreatment.

Some researchers have focused specifically on types of elder abuse occurring in nursing homes or other long-term care settings. These forms of abuse include the same forms noted earlier, but also include a form called *duty-related abuse.* Duty-related abuse refers to instances in which a worker's failure to perform a particular job-related duty ultimately results in harm to the elderly person. Failing to report abuse, lifting residents without the help of coworkers, and ignoring the medical needs of residents are examples of duty-related abuse.

Estimates suggest that anywhere from five hundred thousand to two million elderly persons are victims of elder abuse each year. However, it is difficult to determine the true extent of elder abuse for a number of reasons. First, different states may define *elderly* in different ways. Some states define elderly as more than fifty years of age while other states use the age of 65. The way a state defines *elderly* in its elder abuse legislation will influence official estimates about the extent of elder abuse.

Second, victims may not report instances of abuse for a number of reasons. Some may be afraid of repercussions for reporting abuse. Concerns about being placed in a long-term care setting inhibit community-residing residents from reporting abuse, and fear of increased abuse by caregivers keeps many nursing home residents from notifying authorities. Also, some elderly victims may be cognitively unable to report abuse.

Third, the failure of authorities to recognize elder abuse and set into motion a response system has made it difficult to determine the extent of abuse. In some cases, failure to report is intentional and stems from a culture of silence that exists in families and the health care field. In other cases, the failure to report is unintentional and stems from the lack of understanding about risk factors and causes of elder abuse among practitioners and policy makers. Indeed, not knowing what to watch for allows cases of elder abuse to go unnoticed. The importance of understanding the causes and risk factors of elder abuse goes beyond the need to identify and intervene in elder abuse cases. In fact, understanding the risk factors and causes of elder abuse potentially sheds light on effective prevention strategies.

Crime prevention strategies have been developed that focus primarily on educating the elderly. The best defense against any type of crime is an awareness of the crime with some commonsense ways to avoid certain behaviors that make one more vulnerable to victimization. Many senior organizations such as AARP (American Association of Retired Persons) or NCPEA (National Committee for the Prevention of Elder Abuse) provide elaborate websites with lists of publications and other resources to provide information to seniors about how to avoid becoming a victim of crime, and also to explain how to report being a victim of crime with clear and detailed information about what to do to overcome the victimization. Workshops and presentations are given to seniors in local community settings such as senior centers, club houses, and so forth. These presentations focus on senior victimization and how to avoid it. These educational programs usually focus on financial crimes with some consideration given to personal crimes, such as violent crimes. Most programs spend a great deal of time talking about fraud. The elderly are particularly vulnerable to acts of deception (for example, fraud) resulting in financial loss for the victim. Generally, the types of fraud discussed include home/auto repairs, overseas investments, lottery winnings, and work-at-home schemes. The elderly are especially vulnerable to telemarketing scams because this group often is the sole target of such fraud. The first line of defense to prevent these types of crime is to question the proposal—and if "it sounds too good to be true," it probably is too good, meaning that the senior should be very suspicious of the offer. Anytime money must to be exchanged to get the "big winnings" or prize package, often, fraud is involved.

Law enforcement agencies often have Senior Victim Assistance Units or some similarly named units that deal specifically with elderly crime victims. Often volunteers work in these units to assist victims. The units serve as advocates for victims over a certain age, usually fifty-five or above. Police departments that have such units often also have special training for the police officers that includes empathy training so that police officers can understand what seniors are experiencing in terms of the decline in their physical and mental abilities in an effort to help police be more sensitive and understanding when trying to assist senior crime victims. They are also trained on the warning signs of elder abuse including but not limited to new or unexplained bruises, broken bones, or other physical injuries; changes in routine activities, such as not participating in daily activities; quick financial hardships; and uncared for medical conditions.

In 2000 then-attorney general of the United States, Janet Reno, called for a justice system that responded in helpful ways to the aging population. She challenged police departments to work with other agencies to develop an inclusive, well-coordinated, and well-funded national plan to address elder abuse. To date, such a national plan is not in effect; however, more national level organizations are working with local and regional police departments to ensure the aggressive prosecution of crimes against the elderly, and to provide crime prevention awareness programs to educate seniors about how to avoid becoming a victim of crime.

LAURA J. MORIARTY and BRIAN K. PAYNE

See also **Crime Prevention; Fear of Crime; Uniform Crime Reports**

References and Further Reading

Harris, D. K., and M. L. Benson. 1998. Nursing home theft: The hidden problem. *Journal of Aging Studies* 12 (1): 57–67.

National Center on Elder Abuse. 2002. *Fact sheets*. http://www.preventelderabuse.org.

National Crime Prevention Council. 2005. *Seniors and crime prevention*. Powerpoint slide show available at http://www.ncpc.org (accessed November 23, 2005).

Payne, B. K. 2005. *Crime and elder abuse*. 2nd ed. Springfield, IL: Charles C Thomas.

EMERGENCY MANAGEMENT AND PLANNING

After World War II, U.S. military personnel and citizens were highly involved in civil defense initiatives. Citizens would assist the military and other government agencies by checking borders for illegal immigrants, observing coastlines for foreign vessels, and watching the skies for foreign aircraft. Any transgressions would be immediately reported to the government, typically the military. These efforts were typical following the war, even during the years of the Cold War, but slowly waned as life returned to normal in America. Over time, civil defense gave way to emergency management, and the focus became both human-made and natural disasters. Emergency management was the byword for disaster preparedness until only a few short years ago.

The world was shocked on September 11, 2001, when terrorists used commercial airplanes owned by U.S. airline companies in a well-planned attack on the Pentagon in Washington, D.C., and the World Trade Center towers in New York City. The loss of life caused by this terrorist attack was the largest to take place on American soil since the Civil War. In total, nearly three thousand people died, including police officers, firefighters, and other emergency personnel.

Levels of Responsibility

The responsibility for responding to emergencies and disasters, both natural and human-made, begins at the local level—in cities and towns. The next level of response is activated when the resources and capabilities of a municipality have been exhausted, and help is still needed. After this, a city or town calls on its county for assistance in coping with the disaster or emergency at hand. If all local efforts fail, and help is still needed, assistance is requested from the state. Most cities and towns, counties, and states have mutual aid agreements, whereby they provide assistance to one another, if necessary, when a natural or human-made disaster takes place, and these resources are also tapped in the event of an emergency. Once available local, state, and regional resources have been exhausted, the resources of the federal government are requested.

Table 1 illustrates the four levels of disaster and emergency management, from citizens through the federal government. While citizens are directly involved in level 1, other levels of involvement require the actions of public officials, at the local, state, and federal levels. Each level of government, once its resources and capabilities have been exhausted, must request assistance from the next higher level of government. This burden falls on municipal, county, and state officials.

Four Phases of Emergency Management

The terrorist acts of September 11, 2001, have launched a new wave of efforts by cities, counties, and states throughout the

Table 1 Emergency Management: Levels of Responsibility

Level 1—Citizens
Level 2—Local Response
. . . Cities and towns
. . . Counties
. . . Mutual aid agreements
Level 3—State Government
. . . Mutual aid agreements
Level 4—Federal Government

country to enhance their emergency management programs. Specifically, local, state, and federal officials have focused their attention on the four primary phases of emergency management: mitigation, preparedness, response, and recovery, which are explained in greater detail next.

- *Mitigation:* Mitigation includes efforts to prevent a human-made or natural disaster or to reduce its impact on the community. Mitigation involves an assessment of the threats facing a community, such as the likelihood of a natural disaster, such as a snowstorm, hurricane, or flooding, or a human-made disaster, such as a terrorist attack. This initial phase of emergency management involves an assessment of the possible venues, or sites, where a disaster would likely take place. Mitigation is an ongoing process, with continual reassessments done as needed to ensure proper preparedness by local officials.

- *Preparedness:* City and county officials must be prepared to respond properly to disasters of all types, including terrorist attacks. Preparedness includes proper planning, resource allocation, training, and conducting simulated disaster response exercises. It is important to conduct simulated disaster exercises to ensure that skills, equipment, and other resources can be effectively coordinated when an emergency occurs. Simulated disaster exercises also provide a good opportunity to identify organizational and departmental shortcomings, and provide time to take corrective action before an actual event takes place.

- *Response:* A local government's response to a human-made or natural disaster has many components. If possible, the jurisdiction must issue appropriate warnings to the public and keep citizens informed of an agency's ongoing recovery efforts.

Donations from the public must be accepted and properly managed. Mass care and sheltering may also be necessary, depending on the type and magnitude of the disaster. Proper incident management and coordination are essential. Emergency services and hospital/medical care must be provided. Other important aspects of the response phase include search and rescue operations, evacuation of citizens according to established procedures, damage assessments, and the proper handling and management of on-site fatalities.

- *Recovery:* After a natural or human-made disaster takes place, the cleanup of debris, the restoration of the environment, the reinstitution of public services, and the rebuilding of the public infrastructure are all necessary to restore civic life to a community. This phase of the emergency response typically also includes disaster assistance, for both citizens and their local governments, and crisis counseling, for both civilians and public safety employees (for example, typically those on-site emergency response employees such as police and fire personnel).

Departmental Responsibilities

Local government employees from numerous departments are involved in the four phases of emergency management. They include executive-level personnel, public safety employees (for example, sworn police officers and firefighters), public health officials, public works employees, as well as those employees working for non-for-profit public utility companies. Traditionally, police and fire personnel have been involved in responding to disasters, both natural and human-made. After September 11, 2001, other local public officials have been actively involved in a local government's response (for example, public works and public health officials).

The public officials involved in emergency planning and management at the local level are several. Cities and towns most likely designate the position of emergency management coordinator to an existing full-time police or fire employee. This function winds up as one of his or her collateral duties. In larger cities, there may be a part-time or even a full-time emergency management coordinator or director. Most county governments have full-time emergency management directors. In both smaller cities and counties, this person would report to the police or fire chief. In the case of larger cities and towns, this person would report to the city or town manager. In larger cities and counties, this person would report directly to his or her chief executive officer.

The emergency management coordinator or director is assisted by, and coordinates the efforts of, several employees in departments that perform disaster-related services (that is, mitigation, preparedness, response, and recovery). These departments contain sworn personnel, such as police officers and firefighters, as well as other employees who work in public works and health departments. It is also a common practice for local governments to have a citizens' advisory committee that works with the emergency management coordinator or director. The names of these departments, as well as the titles of their

directors, change from city to county government. The most common titles given to these emergency management personnel are shown in Table 2. Note that the functions of local governments, and the names of their departments, change from state to state. Some services may also be provided by special districts or private utility companies.

Most states throughout the nation have a full-time director of emergency services, or an official with a similar title, who is appointed by the state government. Since September 11, 2001, the titles of these positions have changed to reflect additional duties related to homeland security. These officials, in some states, may even be called director of homeland security. However, they typically still perform the duties and responsibilities of a director of emergency management or director of emergency services. With the advent of the national focus on homeland security, the various facets of emergency management at the state and local level are now being reviewed and expanded to include human-made disasters, in addition to natural disasters, which had traditionally been the focus of emergency management after the Cold War.

Managing Emergency Incidents

The way the United States prepares for and responds to emergency incidents changed in the wake of the 2001 terrorist

Table 2   City and County Departments Involved in Emergency Management

Cities	Counties
(for incorporated areas)	(for unincorporated areas)
City manager	County manager
Fire chief	Fire chief
Police	Sheriff
Public works	Public works
None	Health director
Public utilities	Public utilities

attacks. It was not designed to be an abrupt change, but a gradual one. The best practices that have evolved over the years are part of the new comprehensive national approach known as the National Incident Management System (NIMS). NIMS was developed by the Department of Homeland Security (DHS) in March 2004. NIMS represents a core set of doctrines, principles, terminology, and organizational processes to enable effective, efficient, and collaborative incident management at all levels of government to properly respond to emergencies. The role of the private sector is also included in this model. The role of responders is defined in advance, along with common sets of protocols, so that all agencies work together seamlessly when responding to a disaster. NIMS training is now commonplace in the federal and state governments. An increasing number of training programs are also being offered to local governments throughout the nation with funds provided by the federal government. NIMS will enable responders from all levels of government, and across all functional jurisdictions, to work together more effectively and efficiently when responding to emergencies. In fact, beginning in 2006, all federal funding for state and local government preparedness grants will be tied to compliance with the NIMS requirements.

One of the most important "best practices" that has been incorporated into NIMS is the Incident Command System (ICS). ICS is a standard, on-scene, all-hazards incident management system already in use by firefighters, hazardous materials teams, rescuers, and emergency medical teams. The ICS has been established by NIMS as the standardized incident organizational structure for the management of all incidents. This model of emergency response was developed to facilitate coordination of on-site activities by all agencies when responding to a disaster. All levels of government have ICS plans in advance that include common terminology, the organizational structure of on-scene personnel, how to deal with the press and public, and designating an on-scene chain of command. Reliance is also placed on an incident action plan. On-scene personnel may also assume other roles, different from their regular job titles, such as public information officer, safety officer, and liaison officer. ICS classes are now being offered by the Department of Homeland Security to state and local government officials. The implementation of the NIMS approach to dealing with emergencies will essentially institutionalize the use of ICS throughout the nation as the response system for all levels of government as they work together to respond to disasters.

In case of a large disaster, either natural or human-made, all responding agencies, at all levels of government and in the private sector, must work closely together to limit the loss of life and property. The purpose of the ICS is to have an established and standardized local response to emergencies within the national framework provided by NIMS. In fact, the DHS has established the NIMS Integration Center (NIC) to develop a common understanding and application of the ICS process among all stakeholders, including tribal nations and the private sector. This focus will continue in future years.

Individual public agencies are now conducting more disaster exercises than ever before to test their skills. The number of multiple public agency disaster exercises is also on the increase. It is better for officials in public agencies to fine-tune their skills before an actual disaster takes place. Here are a number of major national trends in emergency planning and management:

- Advanced training for public safety employees
- Crisis counseling for public safety employees
- Designation of building evacuation routes

- Early warning public notification systems
- Expanded geographic information systems
- Greater use of the Incident Command System
- Immediate public assistance to the needy
- Measures to improve building safety
- Mutual aid agreements for public safety services
- New federal assistance programs
- Simulated disaster exercises
- Threat analysis and assessment practices
- Updated emergency response plans
- Use of the National Incident Management System

As citizens become increasingly aware of the resources and agencies involved in emergency planning and management, it is helpful to familiarize themselves with the acronyms by which these resources and agencies are commonly known:

ARC	American Red Cross
ATF	Bureau of Alcohol, Tobacco, Firearms and Explosives
CBRRT	Chemical and Biological Rapid Response Team
CISM	Critical Incident Stress Management
DHS	Department of Homeland Security
DMAT	Disaster Medical Assistance Team
DMORT	Disaster Mortuary Response Team
DOJ	Department of Justice
EOP	Emergency Operations Plan
ERRT	Emergency Rapid Response Team
FEMA	Federal Emergency Management Agency
ICS	Incident Command System
IRZ	Immediate Response Zone
NDPO	National Disaster Preparedness Office

NECC	National Emergency Coordination Center
NIMA	National Incident Management System
NIMS	National Incident Management System
PDA	Preliminary Damage Assessment
PTE	Potential Threat Analysis
RERT	Radiological Emergency Response Team
SRT	Search Response Team

The Future

In the era of homeland security, the field of emergency management once again has a civil defense focus. Citizens and the private sector are being encouraged to assist governments in their efforts to prevent a possible terrorist attack, such as the one that took place on September 11, 2001. The emphasis is not only on being prepared to respond, but on proper planning that includes citizens, the private sector, and non-for-profit organizations. New emergency planning and management practices will continue to evolve, and the existing practices will continually be fine-tuned to limit the loss of life and property during an emergency.

During the last half of the twentieth century and into the twenty-first century, the United States has evolved from civil defense, to emergency management, to the new field of homeland security. Both public and private sectors are working closely together in the new field of homeland security, which has incorporated major aspects of emergency management. The principles and practices of emergency management will be with us forever, notwithstanding what the government agencies are called that oversee them.

ROGER L. KEMP

See also **Terrorism: Domestic; Terrorism: Overview**

References and Further Reading

Alexander, David. 2002. *Principles of emergency planning and management*. New York: Oxford University Press.

Compton, Dennis, and John Granito. 2002. *Managing fire and rescue services*, Washington, DC: International City/County Management Association.

Drabek, Thomas E., and Gerard J. Hoetmer. 1991. *Emergency management: Principles and practices for local government*. Washington, DC: International City/County Management Association.

Erickson, Paul A. 1999. *Emergency response planning for corporate and municipal managers*. Alexandria, VA: ASIS International.

Green III, Walter G. 2000. *Exercise alternatives for training emergency management command center staff*. Washington, DC: Federal Emergency Management Agency.

Haddow, George D., and Jane A. Bullock. 2005. *Introduction to emergency management*. Burlington, MA: Butterworth Heinemann.

Kemp, Roger L. 2003. *Homeland security: Best practices for local government*, Washington, DC: International City/County Management Association.

Posner, Richard A. 2004. *Catastrophe: Risk and response*. New York: Oxford University Press.

Schneid, Thomas D., and Larry Collins. 2001. *Disaster management and preparedness*. Boca Raton, FL: CRC Press.

ENTRAPMENT

The defense of entrapment is one of the most familiar defenses within criminal law. However, the ability of criminal defendants to successfully establish entrapment through proof at trial is uncommon. Although the defense of entrapment did not exist at common law, modern courts have easily embraced this defense. Legal scholars suggest that the entrapment defense has been widely accepted by the judiciary due to the common use of informants and undercover agents in law enforcement coupled with the increasing focus during the twentieth century on drug-related offenses and other crimes that are commonly described as "victimless," such as offenses ranging from prostitution and pornography to gambling (Samaha 1999).

Entrapment is generally defined as the inducement of an individual by government agents to commit a crime that the defendant would not otherwise commit. Generally, the motivation to induce individuals to commit criminal behavior is the need to obtain a criminal conviction (21 Am. Jur. 2d., § 246). Thus, the defense of entrapment exists to prohibit law enforcement from inducing otherwise innocent persons to commit crimes for the purpose of securing a criminal conviction. However, entrapment does not occur when law enforcement officers simply provide an otherwise willing participant with an opportunity to engage in criminal behavior.

A review of the literature and appellate court decisions reveals several theoretical justifications for the entrapment defense (Colquitt 2004). Many courts have held that the defense exists to deter unethical or overzealous behavior of law enforcement agents, whereas others suggest that sound public policy requires a defense such as entrapment to protect law-abiding individuals from unscrupulous law enforcement tactics. Still others cite the lack of the element of *mens rea* in true entrapment situations as a sufficient justification for the defense. However, regardless of the basis for the entrapment defense it is currently allowed in all federal and state jurisdictions (21 Am. Jur. 2d., § 246).

Entrapment is considered an affirmative defense. Generally speaking, defendants who assert the entrapment defense must establish two critical elements: the lack of predisposition to commit the crime and inducement by government agents. The majority of American jurisdictions require the defendant to admit that the criminal acts occurred prior to proceeding with an entrapment defense. Thus, an admission by the defendant is a prerequisite to presenting evidence to establish the defense. While a defendant must admit his or her participation in the criminal acts, a guilty plea to the offense is not required.

Currently, two tests are used to determine whether the defendant has established the elements of entrapment. The first is a subjective test and is used in the majority of American jurisdictions and in the federal courts (Samaha 1999). The focus of this approach is the state of mind of the defendant. The defendant must establish that he or she was not predisposed to commit the crime, but rather was induced into doing so by the conduct of government agents. Thus, the defendant must prove that, absent the inducement by government agents, the defendant would not have participated in the criminal behavior. Courts have developed criteria to assist the jury with this determination. These include the following: the character or reputation of the defendant, including prior criminal convictions; whether the initial suggestion regarding criminal behavior was made by government agents or the defendant; whether the defendant engaged in criminal behavior for financial gain; whether the defendant displayed initial reluctance to participate in the suggested activity that was overcome by the actions of government agents; and last, the nature of the conduct of government agents alleged to constitute inducement (21 Am. Jur. 2d., § 263).

The second test used to establish the elements of entrapment is an objective test. The impetus for the use of the objective test is the deterrence of unethical law enforcement practices that serve to entrap otherwise innocent individuals. With this approach, the primary focus is on the nature of the police conduct as opposed to the predisposition of the defendant. Thus, the proper line of inquiry asks whether the conduct of law enforcement was sufficient to induce a reasonable *law-abiding* person to commit a crime.

Unlike the subjective test, the jury is not obligated to determine whether the conduct of law enforcement would have induced the particular individual on trial, but rather, whether the conduct would have induced a hypothetical person of reasonable intelligence (Colquitt 2004). As such, the predisposition of the defendant is not a central issue in jurisdictions that utilize the objective test, and juries are not instructed to consider the particular characteristics of the defendant, which would normally be relevant to determine predisposition.

In the most recent ruling by the U.S. Supreme Court on the issue of entrapment, the Court reversed a conviction of a Nebraska farmer for a violation of the Child Protection Act of 1984 due to the inability of the government to clearly establish the predisposition of the defendant. In *Jacobson v. United States*, 503 U.S. 540 (1992), the Supreme Court emphasized the distinction between merely offering or providing an individual with the opportunity to commit the crime with which he or she is charged and conduct by government agents which either due to its nature or frequency actually induces the individual to commit a crime he or she would not otherwise commit. In *Jacobson*, the Court concluded the prosecution failed to establish that the actions of the defendant were the result of an independent predisposition as opposed to the result of the twenty-six months of solicitations through the mail by government agents. The Court concluded that the evidence presented by the government ". . . merely indicates a generic inclination to act within a broad range, not all of which is criminal, [and] is of little probative value in establishing predisposition." Other entrapment cases decided by the U.S. Supreme Court include *Sorrells v. United States* (1932), *Sherman v. United States* (1958), *United States v. Russell* (1973), and *Hampton v. United States* (1976).

An example of law enforcement tactics that have been condemned by many courts is the practice of "supply and buy." Supply and buy was once a common practice within the field of drug enforcement. In the typical supply and buy case, government agents or informants supply the drugs that the defendant is eventually encouraged to sell to undercover government agents. Once the "sale" is complete, the defendant is arrested. Many courts have characterized the practice of supply and buy as official misconduct. However, in some jurisdictions, evidence that clearly establishes the predisposition of the defendant to engage in the criminal act will avoid acquittal. However, absent such clear proof of predisposition in supply and buy cases, entrapment is established and the defendant discharged. Other examples of police conduct that have been deemed unacceptable include cases involving "extreme pleas of desperate illness, appeals based primarily on sympathy, pity or close personal friendship and offers of inordinate sums of money" (21 Am. Jur. 2d., § 267: 326).

Regardless of the test utilized by the courts, there is ongoing debate regarding the propriety of the entrapment defense within modern American jurisprudence. However, despite this debate, law enforcement officers must understand the essential elements of entrapment and continue to strive to maintain the delicate balance that exists between the use of proper law enforcement practices and those that may snare otherwise law-abiding citizens.

LISA S. NORED

See also **Accountability; Arrest Powers of the Police**

References and Further Reading

American jurisprudence. Vol. 21, 2nd ed., Entrapment, §§ 247–67.
Colquitt, J. A. 2004. Rethinking entrapment. *American Criminal Law Review* 41: 1389–1437.
Greaney, G. M. 1992. Crossing the constitutional line: Due process and the law enforcement justification. *Notre Dame Law Review* 67: 745–97.
Hampton v. United States, 425 U.S. 484 (1976).
Jacobson v. United States, 503 U.S. 540 (1992).
Samaha, Joel. 1999. *Criminal law*. 6th ed. Belmont, CA: Wadsworth Publishing.
Schultze, J.R. 1996. United States v. Tucker: Can the Sixth Circuit really abolish the outrageous government conduct defense? *DePaul Law Review* 45: 943–85.
Sherman v. United States, 356 U.S. 369 (1958).
Sorrells v. United States, 287 U.S. 435 (1932).
Stevenson, D. 2004. Entrapment and the problem of deterring police misconduct. *Connecticut Law Review* 37: 67–153.
United States v. Russell, 411 U.S. 423 (1973).

ENVIRONMENTAL CRIME

Background

Crimes against the environment of the United States have occurred since the country's beginning. During colonization, indiscriminate removal of trees and resulting unchecked erosion and sedimentation polluted our environment. Westward expansion brought the slaughter of buffalo herds, placer mining utterly destroyed streams of the Sierra Nevada, and mining of lands for minerals forever changed our landscape. Activists such as Henry David Thoreau and John Muir teamed with then-President Theodore Roosevelt to pass federal legislation to protect wild lands—technically the first environmental legislation passed in the United States aimed specifically to protect the environment.

Twentieth-century industrialization and chemical waste production, land use expansion, and urbanization radically changed the environment in the United States. Some, such as Rachel Carson, decried the harmful effects of chemical use, particularly horrors from pesticides such as DDT, instigating a chain reaction of events leading to the establishment of Earth Day in 1970 and a subsequent avalanche of environmental legislation. The National Environmental Policy Act (NEPA) created national environmental awareness through the Council on Environmental Quality (CEQ) within the Executive Office of the President. The Clean Air Act (CAA) and Clean Water Act (CWA) followed as major environmental legislation protecting the environment. With this legislation it became a crime to pollute without governmental oversight.

Modern environmental protection is rooted in statutory law—the passing of legislation by congress and state legislators to protect the environment. Legislation sets out the framework such as protection of air or water. Federal and state regulators mold legislation creating rules. Rules carry the full weight of the law. Courts carry final interpretation often deciding the meaning of vague environmental legislation, settling disputes generated from rules, or setting the precedents we follow today. All branches of government are involved as the president appoints key environmental posts such as EPA director and secretary of the interior. Within the states, governors appoint top posts such as secretary of natural resources. These posts set and enforce the policy framework legislators develop as environmental law.

Enforcement

Once an environmental crime is suspected, investigators and prosecutors at the federal and state levels become involved. The Environmental Protection Agency (EPA), Federal Bureau of Investigation (FBI), Defense Criminal Investigative Service (DCIS), and the U.S. Coast Guard regulate and enforce federal law. Specifically, EPA's Office of Criminal Enforcement, Forensics and Training (OCEFT) investigates environmental crime for all EPA programs along with the FBI through the attorney general of the United States. Individual state environmental protection agencies, attorneys general offices, or the state police prosecute crimes within individual states.

The EPA began initial enforcement in 1982 with full law enforcement authority by 1988. The 1990 Pollution Prosecution Act greatly expanded the EPA's enforcement authority. The National Enforcement Training Institute was founded to provide training to federal, state, and local personnel with regard to both criminal and civil enforcement. To further strengthen the EPA's enforcement capabilities, the Environmental Crimes and Enforcement Act was introduced into Congress in 1992, 1996, and again in 1999. The act's intent was to amend the federal criminal code to require that, on motion of the United States, a person convicted of an environmental crime (defined as a violation of specified statutes, including provisions of the Toxic Substances Control Act, Solid Waste Disposal Act, and Community Right-to-Know Act of 1986) be ordered to pay the costs incurred by a state, local, or tribal government when assisting in the investigation and prosecution of the case by the United States.

Enforcement may be divided into three distinct areas of environmental law. Civil enforcement brings violators into compliance with existing laws. Typically fines are imposed and permits revoked to force compliance. The effort is toward prevention and elimination of illegal pollution into the air, water, and soil. Cleanup enforcement forces responsible parties to clean up hazardous waste sites or pay the government for the cleanup. Both federal and state governments have created priority lists for the cleanup of contaminated areas. Criminal enforcement brings criminal sanctions against the most serious environmental violators. Serious environmental crimes involve negligent, knowing, or willful violations of law. These acts are deliberate—not an accident or a mistake.

Local governments develop, investigate, and prosecute a limited number of environmental crimes. Budget limitations dictate the breadth of environmental enforcement possible by a local government. Typically issues of land use, erosion, and water/sewage disposal are covered by the local municipality. Any violation is subject to local, state, and federal prosecution.

Prosecution

Many legal questions arise during the prosecution of an environmental crime. The most difficult question surrounds standing or right to sue in criminal litigation. Because the environment does not have rights under our constitution, individuals must show harm or loss of use from an environmental crime to prosecute. Administrative charges must show violation of rules set by the regulating authority.

Different means exist to prosecute under the law. Charges of assault and battery by means of a dangerous weapon from hazardous materials, criminal trespass for leachate from underground storage tanks, or felony convictions for illegal fishing activities in closed waters are examples of charges relating to environmental crime. Many environmental statutes contain provisions for citizen suits allowing anyone to bring charges against purported environmental violators. Courts view these provisions as a necessary and vital component of environmental enforcement.

Punishment

Punishment for convictions takes three forms: notice of violation, permit revocation or fines, and community service and/or incarceration. Stemming from some of the earliest convictions in 1979 to current punishments, the courts show a pattern of increasing fines and jail sentences indicating a greater level of seriousness associated with environmental crime.

Corporate Crime

Of the top one hundred corporate crimes committed during the 1990s, thirty-eight were environmental:

- Exxon Corporation and Exxon Shipping pled guilty to federal criminal charges in connection with the March 24, 1989, *Exxon Valdez* oil spill. The company was assessed a $125 million criminal fine, possibly the largest single environmental criminal recovery ever enacted.
- Louisiana-Pacific Corporation pled guilty to eighteen felonies for tampering with pollution control equipment, was fined $37 million, and was placed on five years of probation.
- The Summitville Consolidated Mining Co., Inc., pled guilty to forty counts of violating the Clean Water Act and other federal statutes at its Summitville Gold Mine operation in southwestern Colorado from 1984 to 1992. The company was fined $20 million.
- Rockwell International pled guilty to four felony violations of the Resource Conservation and Recovery Act and to one felony and five misdemeanors of the Clean Water Act for illegally stored and treated hazardous wastes generated during the production of plutonium "triggers" and other components of nuclear weapons at Rocky Flats.
- Royal Caribbean Cruises Ltd., one of the world's largest passenger cruise lines, pled guilty to twenty-one felony counts and agreed to pay a record $18 million criminal fine for dumping waste oil and hazardous chemicals and lying to the U.S. Coast Guard.

Individual Criminal Violations

Courts are becoming less tolerant of environmental crimes by the individual. While the criminal threshold still demands willful knowledge of the crime, punishment is increasingly becoming more severe.

- Father and son owners of asbestos abatement companies in New York State were sentenced to twenty-five years of imprisonment with forfeiture to the United States of America of more than $2 million in assets for violation of the Clean Air Act and the Toxic Substances Control Act. Their illegal asbestos abatement activities took place over a ten-year period at more than 1,550 facilities throughout New York State—including elementary schools, churches, hospitals, military housing, theaters, cafeterias, the New York State Legislature Office Building, public and commercial buildings of nearly every sort, and private residences. Each was sentenced to serve the two longest federal jail sentences for environmental crimes in U.S. history.

- A Connecticut businessman who made millions by illegally importing and selling ozone-depleting chlorofluorocarbon (CFC) gases was sentenced to six years and six months in prison with $1.8 million in restitution. The businessman concealed more than $6 million in profits from the sale of more than a million pounds of CFCs between 1996 and 1998. The defendant admitted smuggling about 660 tons of CFCs into the United States, and importing another 1,100 tons without paying excise taxes. These chemicals are subject to an excise tax of about $5 per pound, which is imposed to discourage their use and to promote the transition to more ozone-friendly replacement products.

- A Mississippi man was sentenced to six years and six months in prison for his conviction on forty-five counts of spraying the pesticide methyl parathion without a license and three counts of illegally distributing methyl parathion in violation of the federal Insecticide, Fungicide and Rodenticide Act. Methyl parathion is approved only for outdoor agricultural use in uninhabited fields. Human exposure to methyl parathion can produce convulsions, coma, and death.

- A Connecticut metal finisher pleaded guilty to discharging wastewater containing excessive amounts of cyanide and acid into a public sewer system between November 1993 and April 1995, operating without a permit, and making false monitoring reports to environmental officials. The metal finisher was sentenced to six months of home confinement, three years of probation, and a $15,000 fine.

Lab Fraud

Environmental protection is dependent on accurate and reliable reporting by laboratories. All regulators rely on this reporting to determine if polluting entities are in compliance. Lab fraud cases go to the heart of a regulatory system that relies on accurate reporting.

- Intertek Testing Services, Inc., was fined $9 million for falsifying the results of environmental tests. ITS conducted environmental sample analysis, primarily as a subcontractor, for environmental consulting firms, engineering firms, and federal, state, and local governments nationwide. The test results were used for decision making at Superfund sites, Department of Defense facilities, and hazardous waste sites to determine site safety and to monitor the migration of hazardous wastes, including cancer-causing petrochemicals. The migration could affect groundwater, drinking water, and soil conditions in places where people might be exposed.

- The owner of a Baton Rouge laboratory known as Enviro-Comp was sentenced to serve forty-six months in federal prison and was ordered to pay $13,359 in public defender fees for mail fraud and obstruction of justice. The owner admitted to witness tampering and making false statements in an EPA Criminal Investigation Division (EPA-CID) lab fraud investigation.

THOMAS D. SHAHADY

See also **Criminal Investigation; White Collar Crime**

References and Further Reading

Brunner, H. J. 1992. Environmental criminal enforcement: A retrospective view. *Environmental Law* 22: 1315–46.

Clifford, M., ed. 1998. *Environmental crime: Enforcement, policy and social responsibility.* Gaithersburg, MD: Aspen Publishers.

Helland, E. 1998. The enforcement of pollution control laws: Inspections, violations and self reporting. *The Review of Economics and Statistics* 80: 141–53.

Kubasek, N. K., and G. S. Silverman. 2005. *Environmental law.* Upper Saddle River, NJ: Prentice Hall.

U.S. Environmental Protection Agency. 2006. *EPA newsroom.* http://www.epa.gov/newsroom/index.htm.

U.S. Code. Washington, DC: U.S. Government Printing Office.

ETHICS AND VALUES IN THE CONTEXT OF COMMUNITY POLICING

In the late 1980s and early 1990s, it became evident that police departments would have to implement various forms of community policing programs to assist in the fight against ever increasing crime rates. Departments were, for the most part, chronically short of resources and, when coupled with a developing siege mentality, continued to reinforce an "us" versus "them" attitude against the communities they were paid to serve. There was increasing realization that police departments could not by themselves manage the crime scene in their communities without assistance, input, and cooperation from other partners such as community associations, individual citizens, and municipal, state/provincial. and federal agencies.

It also became evident that a paramilitary, hierarchical policing service would have difficulty participating in such programs without significant changes to its organizational culture and behavior. Police officers were obligated to comply with inflexible operational policies and procedures. This severely restricted their ability to collaboratively develop and implement practical solutions to community problems and supported the perception by police officers that their police services were isolated from the communities they served.

As mentioned earlier, community policing emphasizes individual initiative rather than compliance with inflexible operational policies and procedures. Legal frameworks emphasize the individual rights of citizens with corresponding limitations on police powers. There is a demonstrated need for peace officers to recognize this dichotomy and to be able to resolve ethical issues and ethical dilemmas. To institute an ethics dialogue within an organization, it is necessary to change the culture of an organization.

The adoption of the philosophy of community policing as a service delivery model requires a proactive collaborative approach in partnership with key elements of the communities of interest. The ability to deal proactively with the root causes of crime and social problems should be the desired outcome rather than the traditional reactive response associated with the professional policing model, which emphasizes command and control as the dominant response. A shared leadership style of management should be identified as the sought after approach and the optimum model for the organization.

The initial step would be to establish a working group comprised of a cross section of employees to review existing policy structures with the objective of establishing guidelines to streamline and eliminate redundant policy directives that inhibit the ability of employees to operate in a shared leadership environment. This review would also send the message within an organization that senior management is serious about implementing the required changes and willing to champion the process.

To achieve a shared leadership approach in its service delivery model, a second internal grassroots initiative should be considered. The objective is to develop a mission statement for a department supported by a corporate vision and underlying organizational core values aligned in all respects with the community policing philosophy. This process can take several months and involve extensive consultation and discussion with many employees and other stakeholders representing all categories, from police officers to support staff.

This process can be accomplished by initially training a number of employees in facilitation methods with each facilitator subsequently working in their own units or sections in sessions with individual groups of twenty or thirty people. Each group's members would look at how they saw themselves within the organization and how the organization was seen within their communities. At the same time, employees would be encouraged to identify contentious issues of concern to them that they felt needed to be addressed. Their concerns would cover a wide spectrum and include everything from administrative issues through to communications and on to operational issues. These issues would be subsequently reviewed by the relevant policy centers. Their responses would then be communicated to all employees in the form of a staff newsletter or other appropriate form of communication.

Training in principle-based leadership such as the Stephen Covey approach on the four roles and seven habits of effective leaders should be implemented. This could be complemented by community policing workshops at which officers discuss issues among themselves and with citizens of the community they serve.

Most police departments have extensive discipline and grievance processes in place. However, in a shared leadership environment, there should be an opportunity for employees and management to work out their differences in an informal environment. An informal, alternative dispute resolution (ADR) initiative should be put in place. It provides a simple formula for building stronger relationships and is another way of doing business. It offers a fresh approach to finding sensible resolutions to internal conflict. With ADR, talk comes first. Early face-to-face discussions between parties are encouraged and quite often offer the best results. The ADR process can also significantly reduce the cost of resolving outstanding conflicts and avoids costly discipline or grievance procedures, which are much more formal and labor intensive.

Finally, in focusing on the operationalization of the mission, vision, and values, and to ensure that the exercise does not become just another "notice on the wall," a department should consider the appointment of an ethics adviser. The principal role of this position would be to serve as an adviser to senior management and as an ambassador working with all employees to ensure that the core values are internalized and become part of one's everyday behavior. The ethics adviser would also be expected to articulate the relationship between the core values and discipline and grievance policies in effect in the department, and to bridge the values-based culture with compliance requirements.

The ethics adviser should be "a trusted and very senior officer who is respected all around for being of the highest integrity" (Change management 2000, 18). The ethics adviser also must have considerable experience in operational matters and professional standards. People must be able to consult with the ethics adviser on issues affecting both themselves and others, and much time is spent in traveling to various units advocating the inculcating of the mission, vision, and values into each and every activity and meeting employees face to face to explain and discuss the process undertaken. The ethics adviser could also assign the responsibility of championing the dissemination of best practices, the sharing of which is fundamental to the success of a continuous learning organization.

In the words of the Royal Canadian Mounted Police (RCMP) commissioner of the day, "Ethics is not a subject to be taught or a set of rules to be memorized, but rather a dimension of whom and what we are. We do not teach ethics as a module, rather, we follow a more holistic approach, integrating ethics with diversity, dignity and respect" (Change management 2000, 19). The RCMP core values of integrity, honesty, professionalism, compassion, respect, and accountability, as prescribed by the commitment of the RCMP to its employees and the communities they serve, are in fact the Code of Ethics for the RCMP. Further elaboration on the mission, vision, and values of the RCMP and of the organization itself can be obtained on the RCMP website (http://www.rcmp-grc.gc.ca).

Community-based policing is the very embodiment of the ethical behavior that police departments should implement. Community policing by principle-based leaders is about partnering with the communities an organization serves in open dialogue to identify policing problems and community-tailored solutions. It means putting the needs of the communities first and empowering all employees to make decisions on the front line. Acceptance of change is never easy. Only through valuing people and developing a truly ethical workplace can the diverse challenges of the coming years and the expectations of a department's many clients and stakeholders be met.

The process just described can be implemented by most departments to change culture and behavior. Initiatives such as policy reviews to streamline and eliminate redundancy, the use of in-house facilitators to lead discussion groups on organizational renewal, an alignment task force to permit the organization to be more flexible and adaptable, and the training of managers and supervisors in leadership and ADR are valuable tools in such a review process. An ethics adviser within a department could also be an integral player in supporting and promoting ethical behavior, integrity, and decision making and to shift the department from an emphasis on "rules-based" to a "values-based" form of leadership and to maintain the appropriate balance between the two. Recruiting and staffing procedures will also have to be reviewed to ensure that a department is employing individuals who emulate those ethics and values adopted by the department.

It is essential in today's environment to develop and maintain the trust of the community being served by a department. The constant monitoring of police activities by citizens, the media, and government agencies requires police departments to demonstrate that they are concerned with the ethical behavior of their employees. The implementation of an ethics and values program should provide a department with the tools required to inculcate expected behaviors throughout their organization and provide employees with a guide to handle their ethical dilemmas in service to their communities.

WILLIAM E. MAXWELL

See also **Accountability; Administration of Police Agencies, Theories of; Community-Oriented Policing: Practices**

References and Further Reading

Change management for community service—An interview with RCMP Commissioner Philip Murray. 2000. *Vanguard* 6 (3): 18.

EXCESSIVE FORCE

Malice Green, Rodney King, Amadou Diallo, Erroll Shaw, and Nathaniel Jones are all names that for many citizens have come to represent what is wrong with policing, that is, when officers appear to cross the line between what is a reasonable response to a perceived threat and move into the realm of excessive force. When officers have to use force in the line of duty, particularly deadly force, citizens often wonder: Could anything else have been done? Were other options available? How widespread is this problem?

The use of excessive force by police is not a new phenomenon. Few policing historians would argue that early law enforcement agencies in the United States were free from the use of excessive force. As Mark Haller (1992) points out, historically police felt justified in their use of excessive force. Many officers believed they had a duty and responsibility to punish criminals. Rather than making an arrest of a petty criminal, an officer in the 1880s in urban America would simply give the suspect a good beating to deter future lawbreaking. In addition to deterring crime, excessive force and violence were used to gain confessions during interrogations. Finally—and perhaps most relevant for sociology and criminal justice research— there was a subculture that supported this behavior, encouraging officers to use violence to maintain dignity (Kappeler et al. 1998).

The concept of a police subculture was first proposed by William Westley (1970) who studied the Gary, Indiana, police department in 1950 and found, among many things, a high degree of solidarity, secrecy, and violence. More recently, the issue of a subculture of violence resurfaced after the Christopher Commission examined the Los Angeles Police Department (LAPD) after the beating of Rodney King in 1991. After investigating the facts of the beating and culture of the LAPD, the commission found that a significant number of LAPD officers repeatedly misused force and ignored written department policies and guidelines on the use of force (Christopher 1991, 3–4). Officer Laurence Powell testified that before going on patrol the

evening of the King beating he was instructed to be more aggressive with baton blows in situations that called for the use of force (Alpert et al. 1992).

Law enforcement in the United States is decidedly different from nearly every other country in the world. Police in America work in a violent environment, and using force to end threats or to complete an arrest is a part of the job. Decisions about what amount of force should be applied are made by the individual officer even with restrictive guidelines given by the department; officers may find that they are in a unique situation that calls for drastic measures. Furthermore, because a disproportionate number of crimes and arrests occurs in minority neighborhoods, racial and ethnic relationships with the police may become further strained when officers must use force and there are allegations of excessive force.

Although considerable research and media attention is given to the police use of force, data from official police reports, citizen complaints, and victim surveys indicate that most police–citizen encounters rarely involve the use of force. A 1996 pretest of the Police Public Contact Survey estimated that nearly forty-five million people had contact with the police over a twelve-month period and that five hundred thousand people had force or the threat of force used against them (Greenfeld et al. 1997). As Adams (2002, 132) points out, these results must be taken with caution. As the definition of police contact changes, that is, calls for service versus contacts that result in arrest, the rates of use of force will vary considerable, with calls for service resulting in fewer use-of-force actions and arrest leading to higher rates.

Defining Excessive Force

Given the history and concern over police abuse of force, it may be surprising to learn that there is no standard definition of what excessive force is. Although it may seem clear-cut to determine if the use of force was excessive, many complexities are involved when trying to define what a reasonable use of force may be. In some circumstances where police must use force, the line between what is justifiable and excessive is fuzzy. Whenever individual discretion must be applied, misjudgments will occur—force may be used where none was warranted, for example. Force has been defined as the exertion of power to compel or restrain the behavior of others (Kania and Mackey 1977, 29).

Furthermore, force can be classified by how appropriate its use may be, for example, justifiable or excessive. Police departments use these definitions to determine if an officer's use of force was out of line and requires discipline or criminal prosecution. Legally, force becomes excessive when it is used for purposes that are unlawful or when it is out of proportion to what is needed to remove the threat or subdue the suspect (Cheh 1995). Kania and Mackey (1977) offer a more appropriate explanation for this discussion stating that excessive force is "violence of a degree that is more than necessary to effect a legitimate police function" (p. 29).

A closely related term that is often used in connection with excessive force is *brutality*. Few citizens can forget the shocking images of the Rodney King beating that was captured on videotape by George Halliday, or the equally disturbing photos from the emergency room of the injuries King sustained from the beating. Most recently, the case of Abner Louima has stood as an example of the wanton violence that citizens may suffer at the hands of the police. Louima testified that after he was arrested for allegedly assaulting a police officer he was savagely beaten and sodomized with a toilet plunger by Officer Justin Volpe.

Although researchers, police administrators, and citizens have a stake in eliminating police brutality, a standard definition is difficult to find. Kenneth Peak (2000) states that citizens may use the term *police brutality* to capture a wide array of behaviors and practices ranging from verbal abuse to violence. Peak further notes that there is a literal definition of brutality, in which there is physical abuse, but there may also be verbal abuse such as racial slurs. Also, some citizens feel brutalized by the mere presence of the police because they have come to represent the establishment and symbolize violence used to oppress minority groups.

There may be considerable overlap to many citizens between excessive force and police brutality, particularly as police brutality involves physical force. Nonetheless, there is a distinction between the two terms. Kenneth Adams (2002, 134) offers a clear definition of police brutality, stating that it is instances of serious physical injury or psychological harm to civilians with an emphasis on cruelty or savageness. Adams admits that the term does not have a standard meaning, and that some authors would prefer a less emotionally charged definition. However, the emphasis on "cruelty or savageness" is a clear delineation between force that is beyond what is necessary to effect a legitimate police function, which may be a judgment call, and actions such as the torture of Abner Louima.

The Research on Excessive Force

Determining the amount of force used and misused by police is difficult. Researchers have attempted to uncover these numbers through a variety of methodologies, from observational studies and official reports to officer surveys. Each method has its strength and is revealing; nonetheless, all have shortcomings. For example, observational studies try to place a trained observer with a police officer to document the officer's behavior. Worden (1995) performed a secondary data analysis of a

1977 Police Services Study on 5,700 police–citizen encounters and found that police used force in just over 1% of all the encounters, and in one-third of these encounters, the observer judged the force to be unnecessary or excessive. Once the data set was revised and included only suspects, instead of all citizens involved in the contact, improper force was observed in only 1% of the encounters.

Although revealing, observational research has limitations in that it is time consuming and expensive. Furthermore, there are issues with reactivity, because the officers are aware that they are the subject of observation and may alter their behavior. Even though the observer is being passive and nonjudgmental, they may simply not be seeing the officers behave as they normally would. Limitations also exist with the other methodologies. As Fridell and Pate (1997) point out, community surveys on excessive force measure *perceptions* of excessive force not *legally defined* excessive force. Surveys of police officers may reflect that officers have a narrower definition of excessive force than citizens do. Furthermore, official records may be incomplete and not capture use of force that officers chose not to report.

Notwithstanding these research issues, there is a base of information and knowledge about the police use of force and excessive force. In general, police use of force tends not to be related to age, race, and gender. Researchers such as Garner et al. (1996) and Crawford and Burns (1998) have found that officer and suspect characteristics are generally not good predictors of police use of force. More detailed analysis has revealed that officer use of force appears to be based on situational factors and what the suspect does. Police tend to respond to circumstances. Officer use of force is likely when they respond to a violent crime, deal with suspects who are under the influence of drugs or alcohol, or deal with suspects who use force against them.

As discussed earlier, definitions can vary and perceptions of excessive force may further complicate the issue, so finding a measure of excessive force that is agreeable to all interested parties may be equally difficult. Not unlike measuring the use of force in general, the methodologies involved in measuring excessive force are not without limitations. The most widely available measure of excessive force is civilian complaints and lawsuits. Civilian complaints alleging excessive force are infrequent and substantiated complaints are rare. Several studies that have calculated the average number of complaints received per year per officer show between 0.3 and 1 complaint per officer per year (Fridell and Pate 1997, 226). Wagner's (1980) findings support the claim that few complaints are substantiated by the police. In his study, only 2.1% of the excessive force complaints were substantiated.

Understanding how force in general is measured helps to understand the context of excessive force. Nonetheless, there is a major gap in knowledge about the extent of excessive force by police. There is simply a lack of precision in understanding whether the problem is systemic or merely tied to a handful of overzealous officers. Excessive force by officers is a critical problem facing many communities and law enforcement agencies across the country and there have been positive attempts across the nation to institute better controls and review systems.

Controlling Excessive Force

Internal policies and methods of controlling police deviance, whether manifested as corruption, brutality, or excessive force, must first be based on having qualified personnel. The 1991 Christopher Commission report on the LAPD after the Rodney King incident indicated that a relatively small number of officers were responsible for a large proportion of excessive force incidents. Researchers have attempted to draw correlations between officer personality and characteristics so that they might be able to predict misuse of force and develop better screening procedures. However, Grant and Grant (1995) state that there are *no* studies that effectively assess the link between screening and the use or misuse of force. Kappeler et al. (1998) offer that while there is no foolproof way to screen applicants for police work that will indicate how competent they will remain, officials should look beyond simple screening measures and at the larger issues of respect for human life and sensitivity to diversity. Background investigations may need to become especially demanding and check into violent histories and conflicts versus the typical concern about past drug use.

Selecting highly qualified candidates is important for having a professional police force and trying to reduce the likelihood of the misuse of force. Once these qualified people are in place, how they are trained is equally important. Proper training can have a tremendous impact on nearly all aspects of policing, most notably with the use of force. Police departments have recognized that if they wish to avoid or de-escalate violent encounters they must teach their officers proper skills in tactics and communication. For example, the Metro-Dade Violence Reduction Project used role-playing for police–citizen encounters to teach patrol officers how to enhance their skills in defusing potentially violent situations. Fyfe (1995) finds that this training has resulted in a 30% to 50% reduction in injuries to officers, complaints of abuse, and use of force by officers.

The emphasis in such training programs is to not view a potentially violent encounter with split-second syndrome, in which the officer suddenly has to make a choice to use force to respond to an attack, but rather to see the multiple steps involved in an escalating encounter and how they may be defused so force is avoided all together. As apart of this approach to training, it must be clear that excessive force will not be tolerated and that the department places a value on peaceful resolutions, not aggressive use of whatever force it takes to resolve a situation.

Having good people and training in place is essential, but clearly written policy is also important in controlling the use of force and curbing excessive force. One early study by Uelman (1973) that collected information from fifty police departments found that departments with the most restrictive use-of-force policies had half the shooting rates of departments with the least restrictive policies. Policy can shape how police operate in the field and it can be an effective tool of control. However, the best policy is useless if it is not enforced by the department. The content of policy must be clear, but the administrative commitment and posture must also be demanding and clear.

Undoubtedly most police departments would prefer to address excessive force through internal measures such as policy, recruit screening, and training. However, in some situations these remedies are too late or the actions of the officers are so egregious and the community reactions so strong that outside remedies become necessary to restrict the use of excessive force. Legal recourse is available to control excessive use of force by officers. The use of force by police departments falls under the Fourth Amendment, which governs the ability to search persons and places and to seize evidence and people. The seizure of people involves arrest and applies the standard of reasonableness to the use of force.

Therefore, any force that is excessive and by this definition unreasonable would violate the Fourth Amendment. Under federal law, Section 1983 of the Civil Rights Act of 1871 allows citizens to sue persons who, under color of state authority, deprive them of their constitutional rights. Most states also permit civil lawsuits against law enforcement agencies for the use of excessive or unreasonable force, and these state lawsuits are more common than federal suits. Lawsuits essentially put a high price on the improper actions of police officers and often gain national attention when the dollar amounts total into the millions. Depending on the officer's agency, the law can vary as to whether the individual officer, entire department, or even the city/state is liable for the misconduct.

Data on the number of lawsuits filed and judgments awarded are difficult to find on the national level. City-level data do provide some detail on the types of actions that are contested and the dollar amounts awarded. The following examples are particularly noteworthy:

- According to reports prepared by City Councilman Mel Ravitz, the city of Detroit spent $72 million on all police lawsuits between 1987 and 1994. Focusing on excessive force, between July 1, 1995, and April 1997, the city paid nearly $20 million in cases involving excessive force, wrongful death, vehicle pursuits, and minor accidents (Chesley 1997).
- The city of Los Angeles paid $11 million and $13 million in 1990 and 1991, respectively, for damage awards involving police misconduct (del Carmen 1993).
- The New York City Law Department (1996) reported that excessive force, false arrest, and shootings by police cost city taxpayers more than $44 million for fiscal years 1994–1995, averaging almost $2 million a month for police misconduct lawsuits alone.

As a result, those filing lawsuits receive compensation from the city, but little may be done to correct problems identified in the suits. Lawsuits over alleged police abuse have their place in controlling excessive force. They can be financially devastating to a city's budget; they are also more common than criminal prosecution of the officer. As the dollar amounts climb

into the tens of millions of dollars, the price tag for the failure to restrict officer's behavior also grows.

In addition to the use of the courts as an external control mechanism, civilian oversight committees have regained attention as a method of dealing with excessive force outside the department. Civilian oversight committees involve citizens receiving, reviewing, and analyzing complaints against the police. Many assumptions have been made about the nature and function of these committees, but very little research evaluation has been done to determine whether their goals are being accomplished. For example, it is assumed that civilian review is more effective than internal police investigations because they are more objective, they result in higher rates of sustained complaints, and there is greater deterrence and higher levels of satisfaction from the public (Walker and Kreisel 1997). As important as these assumed goals are, their effects have never been studied and no evaluations have been conducted concerning the best way to design a civilian review board.

Civilian oversight committees are typically set up as a cross section of the community, and their members are often appointed by political figures independent of the police department. This outsider position has been met with hostility in some departments. Officers may view committee members as being soft on crime, not understanding true police work, and out to "get" officers. Although civilian review boards may have an impact on controlling police actions, they are surprisingly lacking in power since they serve in a primarily advisory role. They do not have the ability to subpoena, cannot decide on punishments, and do not have an investigative body.

Nonetheless, civilian review boards have had some success in changing police departments. Even with the limitations and criticism, civilian review boards can create a structure in which citizens and police officers work together to deal with serious issues of misconduct. In addition, the review boards may help to resolve the question "Can the police police themselves?" For example, the Christopher Commission of the LADP (1991) found that investigations of complaints were severely lacking and there was no indication that the police investigators had made any attempt to locate witnesses or to seriously deal with the allegations.

Conclusion

The use of excessive force by police will continue to be a complex and troubling issue that faces many communities and police departments across the nation. Attempting to provide answers to questions of how to define excessive force, how widespread excessive force is, and how to control excessive force will remain difficult. The problem is costly as cities and departments face civil lawsuits that run into tens of millions of dollars and are forced to deal with solutions to the problem to satisfy both the courts and the public.

Research on police use of force and excessive force is important because it helps us to understand the nature of the encounters. For example, we have learned that very few police–citizen encounters involve the use of force and even fewer would be defined as involving excessive force. Furthermore, research has been able to provide answers to the questions of how and when police officers use force, which better enables us to define what is excessive and try to gain a working knowledge of the situations in which it is likely to occur. Research on this level can also guide the solutions to dealing with excessive force, illustrating whether it is a matter of training, selection policy, or even the culture of the department.

Although many questions remain to be answered about the police use of excessive force, there are promising signs across the nation of police departments willing to change and take allegations of misconduct

seriously. The number of citizen watch groups and review boards that have been created to assist departments in dealing with this problem is increasing. As community policing continues to grow as a concept and goal of police departments, attempts have also been made to improve police–citizen relationships, particularly in minority communities, so the involvement of citizens in controlling the use of excessive force and attempting to curb police misconduct in essential.

There will always be questions when officers have to use force, mainly when citizens and even police officers perceive that the fuzzy line between reasonable and excessive force has been crossed. As the research on this topic becomes more sophisticated, and as citizens become more aware of the subtleties in definition and demand solutions, there is optimism for change as the seeds of reform take root across the country.

CHARLES CRAWFORD

See also **Accountability; Arrest Powers of the Police; Attitudes toward the Police: Overview; Citizen Complaints in the New Police Order; Crowd/Riot Control; Deadly Force; Early Warning Systems; Independent Commission on the Los Angeles Police Department (The Christopher Commission); Liability and Use of Force**

References and Further Reading

Adams, K. 2002. What we know about police use of force. In *Crime and justice in America: Present realities and future prospects*, 2nd ed., ed. Palacios, Cromwell, and Dunham, 130–44. Upper Saddle River, NJ: Prentice-Hall.

Alpert, G. P., W. C. Smith, and D. Watters. 1992. Implications of the Rodney King beating. *Criminal Law Bulletin* 28 (5): 469–78.

Cheh, M. M. 1995. Are lawsuits the answer to police brutality? In *And justice for all: Understanding and controlling police abuse of force*, ed. Geller and Toch, 233–59. Washington, DC: Police Executive Research Forum.

Chesley, R. 1997. Police training program could cut lawsuits. *Detroit Journal*, April 20.

Christopher, W. 1991. *Summary: Report of the independent commission on the Los Angeles Police Department*. Los Angeles: City of Los Angeles.

Crawford, C., and R. Burns. 1998. Predictors of the police use of force: The application of a continuum perspective in Phoenix. *Police Quarterly* 1: 41–63.

Fridell, L., and A. M. Pate. 1997. Use of force: A matter of control. In *Contemporary policing: Personnel, issues and trends*, ed. Dantzker, 217–56. Newton, MA: Butterworth-Heinemann.

Fyfe, J. J. 1995. Training to reduce police–civilian violence. In *And justice for all: Understanding and controlling police abuse of force*, ed. Geller and Toch, 163–75. Washington, DC: Police Executive Research Forum.

Garner, J., J. Buchanan, T. Schade, and H. Hepburn. 1996. *Understanding the use of force by and against the police*. Research in Brief, NCJ 158614. Washington, DC: U.S. Department of Justice, National Institute of Justice.

Grant, J. D., and J. Grant. 1995. Officer selection and the prevention of abuse of force. In *And justice for all: Understanding and controlling police abuse of force*, ed. Geller and Toch, 151–61. Washington, DC: Police Executive Research Forum.

Greenfeld, L. A., P. A. Langan, and S. K. Smith. 1997. *Police use of force: Collection of national data*. NCJ 165040. Washington, DC: U.S. Department of Justice, Bureau of Justice Statistics and National Institute of Justice.

Haller, M. 1992. Historical roots of police behavior in Chicago, 1890–1925. In *Policing and crime control*, ed. E. H. Monkkonen. New York: K. G. Sauer.

Independent Commission of the Los Angeles Police Department. 1991. *Report of the independent commission of the Los Angeles Police Department*. Los Angeles.

Kania, R. R. E., and W. C. Mackey. 1997. Police violence as a function of community characteristics. *Criminology* 15 (1): 27–48.

Kappeler, V. E., R. D. Sluder, and G. P. Alpert. *Forces of deviance: Understanding the dark side of policing*. 2nd ed. Prospect Heights, IL: Waveland Press, 1998.

New York City Law Department. 1996. Letter to Human Rights Watch from the Law Department's corporation counsel Michael Sarner, November 8.

Peak, K. J. 2000. *Policing America: Methods, issues, challenges*. 3rd ed. Upper Saddle River, NJ: Prentice-Hall.

Walker, S., and B. Kreisel. 1997. Varieties of citizen review: The relationship of mission, structure and procedures to police accountability. In *Critical issues in policing: Contemporary*, 3rd ed., ed. Dunham and Alpert, 319–36. Prospect Heights, IL: Waveland Press.

Westley, W. A. 1970. *Violence and the police*. Cambridge, MA: The MIT Press.

Worden, R. E. 1995. The 'causes' of police brutality: Theory and evidence on police use of force. In *And justice for all: Understanding and controlling police abuse of force*, ed. Geller and Toch, 31–60. Washington, DC: Police Executive Research Forum.

EXCLUSIONARY RULE

Succinctly stated, the exclusionary rule stands for the principle of law that evidence seized in violation of the Constitution and attending Bill of Rights should be considered inadmissible in criminal proceedings. Although seemingly straightforward and well intentioned, the rule has met with some criticism—most notably the fact that it is a purely judge-made protection not specifically enumerated in the language of the Constitution. Initially conceived by the Supreme Court in the early 1900s, the exclusionary rule has since been applied, and in some instances retracted, to varying degrees over the intervening years. To better understand the rule's origin and intent, as well as the manner in which it is applied to contemporary legal questions, a review of the relevant case law is required. Following this review, a balanced summary of its relative contributions to American jurisprudence are contrasted with the most common criticisms regarding its application.

Origins of the Exclusionary Rule

Prior to the twentieth century, state and federal courts gave little if any attention at all to the method by which incriminating evidence was appropriated and subsequently presented for consideration at trial. Rather than focusing on how a particular piece of evidence had been obtained, the primary focus was on its probative value—did the evidence in question aid the court in determining guilt or innocence? This "don't ask, don't tell" approach to how evidence was obtained by law enforcement prevailed throughout the judiciary despite the Fourth Amendment's warrant requirement and prohibition against unreasonable search and seizure. This common law practice of giving greater consideration to probative value over the method of appropriation, at least with regard to federal proceedings, was struck down by the U.S. Supreme Court's decision in *Weeks v. U.S.* (1914) in response to a residential search undertaken by officers in the absence of a warrant. Specifically, the majority opinion stated "The tendency of those who excuse the criminal laws of the country to obtain conviction by means of unlawful seizures and enforced confessions . . . should find no sanction in the judgment of the courts which are charged at all times with the support of the Constitution and to which people of all conditions have a right to appeal for the maintenance of such fundamental rights" (*Weeks* at 392).

The decision in *Weeks*, however, only required the suppression of illegally acquired evidence in federal proceedings but did not apply to cases initiated against defendants at the state level. Consequently, the behavior of police at lower levels of government remained unchecked. It was during this period that state and local officers began the practice of turning illegally acquired evidence over to federal agents on a figurative "silver platter." Eventually, the Court closed this loophole in the case of *Elkins v. United States* (1960). The following year, the Supreme Court extended the rule's prophylactic measures via the Fourteenth Amendment to state criminal proceedings in the case of *Mapp v. Ohio* (1961).

Confusion Surrounding the Exclusionary Rule

These early cases served as watershed decisions for future proceedings, which, in turn, began to closely scrutinize the manner by which police had obtained evidence presented at trial. Over the years, several additional cases supporting the rule's principle that illegally obtained evidence should be suppressed at trial found their way to the Supreme Court's docket and today stand as reinforcing case law used to regulate police behavior. As with any newly adopted principle of law, however, questions regarding the rule's full protective scope began to emerge. Most notably, prosecutors and judges struggled with the issue of admissibility in instances where evidence had been obtained by all reasonable legal means only to find out later that some technical error had occurred, therefore, casting the entire case into question. In other words, lower courts needed to know if evidence was to be suppressed without exception in instances where a technical error or deficiency was found to have occurred.

Creation of the "Good Faith" Exception

The most commonly cited decision that ultimately addressed this issue is that rendered in *United States v. Leon* (1984). In this particular case, officers secured a search warrant that had been previously reviewed by several deputy district attorneys and ultimately approved by a judge. The warrant was used to seize a large quantity of drugs as evidence. Unfortunately, the federal district court refused to admit the evidence even though it had been obtained under warrant on grounds that the affidavit on which the order was based did not sufficiently establish the element of probable cause. On appeal, the

Supreme Court ruled that the exclusionary rule did not require the suppression of evidence obtained by officers who reasonably relied on a warrant that had been issued by a neutral magistrate but was later found to be deficient. The practical importance of this decision was the creation of what is now commonly referred to as the "good faith" exception to the exclusionary rule so that where officers are able to demonstrate that they were acting in such a manner, evidence that is found to be tainted by technical error remains admissible.

Criticisms of the Exclusionary Rule

Since the decision in *Leon*, the Supreme Court has at times expanded the good faith exception and at others has upheld the rule's prophylactic intent. Consequently, this area of the law is extremely complex. Because of this, law enforcement officials must remain constantly abreast of changes to the rule's relative status through participation in legal update training, generally at the agency level. Oftentimes, however, officers are reluctant consumers of such information based on the perception that the rule has the practical consequence of making their jobs more difficult.

Shortly after its initial application to federal proceedings, and most certainly upon its extension to state proceedings, the rule came under heavy criticism from crime control advocates for figuratively "handcuffing" the police and letting obviously guilty criminals go free on minor technicalities "because the constable has blundered" (*People v. Defore*, 242 N.Y. 13 at 21, 1926). This contention, combined with the Supreme Court's activism in other areas of criminal procedure, gave rise to the assertion that judges had gone too far in protecting the rights of criminals. Critics have also asserted over the years that the rule unnecessarily forces the police to work harder to obtain evidence and confessions while distracting their energies and attention from other matters—in essence claiming that the rule inadvertently impedes efficiency and effectiveness.

Whether or not this particular criticism holds true, other unintended consequences have surfaced. For example, the rule was clearly intended to deter police misconduct. Arguably, however, strict application of the rule could motivate the police to cut certain corners in the interest of obtaining evidence and convictions. Simply stated, the rule may have the latent effect of promoting questionable police practices rather than preventing them. Finally, it is important to note that the protective intent of the exclusionary rule is only triggered when the police and prosecutors plan to submit evidence at trial. However, in instances where police and prosecutors do not intend to bring a case against the defendant, no foul has occurred. This type of situation potentially leaves adversely affected individuals without remedy but for the ability to seek redress through civil action for deprivation of rights under Title 42, U.S.C. Section 1983.

Concluding Observations

In conclusion, the exclusionary rule is ideally intended to deter law enforcement and other government agents from obtaining evidence by means that contradict protections afforded by the Bill of Rights. Application of the rule has been extended over the years to not only physical evidence under the Fourth Amendment, but to improperly obtained confessions and admission under the Fifth Amendment as well. In limited instances, especially those where the police are acting in "good faith," exceptions have been created. Despite this acknowledgment by courts that the police do sometimes make honest mistakes, they should not generally assume that an exception will be granted, particularly where an important case is at stake.

Arguably, the rule has improved police professionalism by making police more conscientious abut their work and deterring them from cutting corners. On the other hand, the rule's prophylactic intent does not always sit well with officers, conservatives, and crime control advocates who see it as a mechanism that sometimes lets obviously guilty people go free. Whichever perspective one subscribes to—the due process rights of defendants or the crime control rights of the public—the rule has become such an integral component of American jurisprudence that it will most assuredly endure into the indefinite future.

R. ALAN THOMPSON

References and Further Reading

Arizona v. Evans, 514 U.S. 1 (1995).

del Carmen, Rolando V. 2004. *Criminal procedure: Law and practice*. 6th ed. Belmont, CA: Wadsworth/Thomson.

del Carmen, Rolando V., and J. T. Walker. 2004. *Briefs of leading cases in law enforcement*. 5th ed. Cincinnati, OH: Anderson.

Elkins v. U.S., 364 U.S. 206 (1960).

Hemmens, C., J. Worrall, and R. A. Thompson. 2004. *Criminal justice case briefs: Significant cases in criminal procedure*. Los Angeles, CA: Roxbury Publishing.

Illinois v. Krull, 480 U.S. 340 (1987).

Illinois v. Rodriguez, 497 U.S. 117 (1990).

Israel, Jerold H., Y. Kamisar, and W. LaFave. 2005. *Criminal procedure and the Constitution*. 5th ed. St. Paul, MN: West.

Mapp v. Ohio, 367 U.S. 643 (1961).

Maryland v. Garrison, 480 U.S. 79 (1987).

Massachusetts v. Sheppard, 468 U.S. 981 (1984).

Nix v. Williams, 467 U.S. 431 (1984).

People v. Defore, 242 N.Y. 13 (1926).

Rochin v. California, 342 U.S. 165 (1952).

U.S. v. Leon, 468 U.S. 897 (1984).

Weeks v. U.S., 232 U.S. 383 (1914).

Zalman, Marvin. 2006. *Essentials of criminal procedure*. Upper Saddle River, NJ: Pearson/Prentice-Hall.

EYEWITNESS EVIDENCE

Eyewitness testimony, particularly the identification of a suspect, is powerful evidence and can make the difference between a case solved and a case forever cold. However, because it is powerful and so compelling to juries, mistaken identifications are also the most frequent cause of *wrongful* convictions in the United States (Huff, Rattner, and Sagarin 1996). The problem is that it is difficult for jurors to distinguish between an eyewitness who has correctly identified the perpetrator of the crime and an eyewitness who has identified an innocent person. Both correct and incorrect eyewitnesses may testify at trial with great confidence, detail, and emotion.

Psychologists and legal scholars have, through empirical research, identified a number of factors that affect the accuracy of eyewitnesses. Some of the conditions that reduce the accuracy of memory are conditions over which the police have absolutely no control. Law enforcement cannot control a witness's opportunity to observe, cannot change the lighting of an event that has already occurred, and cannot encourage the witness to keep calm during the crime.

Here, we focus on factors within the criminal investigation over which the police have either some or complete control, specifically (1) the procedures for questioning and interviewing witnesses, (2) the way the lineup is composed, and (3) the way in which the lineup is presented to the witness. Much has been learned about these aspects of criminal investigations, some just in the last few years, and the research is leading to new insights and new procedures that have been shown to increase the identifications of perpetrators and decrease the misidentifications of innocent people.

This body of research has also led to several publications and training manuals that provide up-to-date guidelines for best practices in obtaining witness statements and eyewitness identification evidence. We note in particular an article published in *Law and Human Behavior* (Wells et al.

1998) and two reports by the U.S. Department of Justice that give very specific guidance and direction for interviewing witnesses and obtaining reliable identification evidence. We note also the *California Peace Officer's Legal Sourcebook* (Calandra and Carey 2004), which is published and updated every year by the California District Attorneys Association, as a guidebook for police officers. Although we do not endorse all of its recommendations, it is—with a few exceptions—consistent with research and with the U.S. Department of Justice guidelines.

Interviewing, Suggestive Questions, and Postevent Information

When interviewing witnesses, one must keep in mind two important properties of memory: Memory retrieval is cue dependent and dynamic.

Cue-Dependent Retrieval

By "cue dependent" we mean that the information retrieved from memory depends on the cues that are used to probe memory. In simpler terms, the witness report depends not only on the veracity of the witness's memory, but also on how the questions are asked.

Not only can a suggestive question influence how the witness answers that particular question, it can also influence how the witness answers questions asked later. Consider this example from Loftus and Palmer (1974): Participants were asked about the speed of the cars in a simulated car crash. They were asked one of two questions; either "About how fast were the cars going when they smashed into each other?" or "About how fast were the cars going when they hit each other?" Not surprisingly the "smashed" question produced higher speed estimates than the "hit" question. More surprising is how

these witnesses responded to subsequent questions. When asked if they had seen any broken glass (there was none), the "smashed" group was twice as likely as the "hit" group to erroneously state that they had.

From this example, an important lesson is illustrated. We typically think of interviewing as a one-way street in that the flow of information comes *from* the witness *to* the interviewer. However, as these experiments illustrate, the interview is actually a two-way street; witnesses can also obtain information from the interviewer.

Memory Is Dynamic

Memory changes over time; that is, it is dynamic. It would be extremely useful if memory were compartmentalized so that we would not confuse what we *saw* at Time A with what we *heard* at Time B. Unfortunately, memory does not work that way. When a witness is presented with information from outside sources, that information may find its way into the witness's subsequent statements and testimony (see Loftus 1992 for a review).

The two-way street of interviewing is one way in which information can be transmitted to, rather than from, the witness. Other sources of postevent information include other witnesses; television and print news media; the witness's friends, family, and acquaintances; and, of course, the police.

Lineup Composition

One of the major questions in constructing a lineup is how to pick the fillers. In two surveys (Wogalter et al. 1993, 2004), police officers indicated that they typically pick the fillers based on their similarity to the suspect. This certainly sounds, on the surface of it, appropriate.

However, as reasonable as it sounds, the strategy of selecting fillers based on their similarity to the suspect may lead to serious problems. When selecting fillers based on their similarity to the suspect, one question that arises is *How similar is similar enough?* A conscientious police officer, in trying to be careful to pick only "good" fillers, may select fillers that are unnecessarily similar to the suspect, making it more difficult to correctly identify the perpetrator (Wells, Rydell, and Seelau 1993).

A second problem of suspect-matched lineups may be more difficult to detect. Consider the case in which an innocent person is suspected of a crime, in part because he fits the description of the perpetrator given by the witness. This innocent suspect is placed in a lineup with five fillers who look similar to that innocent suspect. Given this scenario, one may ask *How many people are in the lineup because they fit the description of the perpetrator?* The answer is only one—the innocent suspect. *The other five people are in the lineup because they look similar to a person who fits the description of the perpetrator.* This situation suggests that the person in the lineup who will be the closest match to the witness's memory is the innocent suspect. It follows further that the innocent suspect is the person in the lineup who is the most likely to be identified. Indeed, laboratory research has confirmed this prediction as well (Clark and Tunnicliff 2001).

Because the biases in a lineup can be very subtle, they may not be immediately apparent. However, mistakes that initially seemed invisible may become glaring once someone else points them out. One such case involved a bank robbery in Chino, California, in 1997. A bank teller described the robber as "looking more like a college kid than a criminal." In the lineup shown to the bank tellers, the suspect wore a white t-shirt under a crisp-looking polo shirt, and was surrounded in the photo display by people who looked and dressed more in the style of the stereotypical criminal. This was pointed out to the jury, who quickly acquitted the defendant.

Either way one looks at this outcome, a serious mistake was made. If the defendant was guilty, then his "walking papers" came as the result of a poorly constructed lineup. If the defendant was innocent, then the criminal investigation went astray due to the poor lineup, an innocent person was forced to stand trial, and the real robber went free.

From the research on lineup composition comes two clear recommendations: (1) It is not necessary to pick fillers who are "gratuitously" similar in appearance to the suspect, but (2) it is necessary to make sure that the fillers are consistent with the description of the perpetrator given by the witness.

Lineup Presentation

Identification errors can also arise from the procedures used in presenting the lineup to the witness and recording the witness's response. Eyewitness identification research has pointed to two modifications to traditional identification procedures: that (1) the lineups be administered using a blind administration procedure and (2) lineups be presented sequentially, rather than simultaneously.

Blind Lineup Administration

One of the strongest, clearest recommendations that researchers have made about the presentation of lineups is the use of the blind testing procedure. Blind testing has a long history in the behavioral, social, and medical sciences, much too long to discuss here (see Rosenthal 1966). The main characteristic of the blind procedure, for present purposes, is that it is designed to minimize the influence of the lineup administrator.

The blind testing procedure requires that the police officer who administers the lineup not be involved in the investigation.

The lineup administrator should not know about other evidence in the case, should not know the identity of the suspect, and should not know the position of the suspect in the lineup.

It may seem odd to have the lineup administered by a person who knows *nothing* rather than a person who is deeply familiar with the case. However, a moment's reflection illustrates the usefulness of the blind-testing procedure. One way the defense can challenge the reliability of eyewitness evidence is to argue that the witness's identification was the product of the suggestive behavior of the police officer who administered the lineup (Nettles, Nettles, and Wells 1996). If the police officer becomes overinvolved in the identification with statements such as "I noticed you paused on number three," the court and the jury are left to wonder whether the identification was the product of the witness's memory or the police officer's comment. It is precisely because of this problem that the *California Peace Officer's Legal Sourcebook* states, "You must avoid any conduct during the identification which might be ruled suggestive. Never permit a witness's attention to be drawn to the suspect because of . . . remarks you make during the identification."

The leaking of information by the police officer need not be deliberate. Even the inadvertent leaking of information from the lineup administrator can taint the witness's identification. Thus, to minimize the possibility of inadvertently leaking cues, the *Sourcebook* continues, "Try not to say or do anything during the identification."

In considering the potential advantage of using the double-blind procedure, one need only to consider this: One cannot leak what one does not know.

Simultaneous and Sequential Lineups

In the standard identification procedure, a witness is presented with all of the individuals (or photos) in the lineup at the same time. This is called a simultaneous lineup. Research has provided strong evidence that witnesses, when presented with such a lineup, will often make *relative* decisions, identifying the person in the lineup who looks more like the perpetrator than anyone else in the lineup. It is not hard to see how such a decision strategy can lead to false identifications.

Researchers reasoned that these false identifications could be reduced if the witness's tendency to make such relative judgments could be minimized (Lindsay and Wells 1985). One way to do this is to present the lineup members sequentially, rather than simultaneously. In the sequential lineup, the witness must give a yes or no response to each lineup alternative as that person is presented. To see how the sequential lineup can reduce false identifications, consider the case in which an innocent person similar in appearance to the perpetrator is shown as the third person in the lineup. In the sequential lineup the witness may note the high level of similarity but decline to make an identification— waiting instead to see if an even better match might be yet to come. In contrast in the simultaneous lineup, the witness sees all the alternatives, and is more likely to make a positive identification of that very same person (because it is clear that no better alternative is available).

The research shows that the sequential presentation of the lineup results not only in fewer false identifications, but in fewer correct identifications as well. Those who advocate the use of the sequential lineup note that the decrease in false identifications is greater than the decrease in correct identifications.

Summary

Human memory has several properties that have been shown through research to lead to errors: Human memory is incomplete, error prone, cue dependent, and dynamic, allowing memory to be influenced by—and distorted by—outside sources. Moreover, human memory is not self-correcting. A memory stored incorrectly, or distorted by exposure to postevent information, cannot easily be "fixed," or undistorted. Finally, witnesses (at least some witnesses) make identification decisions using decision strategies that are error prone. Despite all of these inherent limitations, the likelihood of correct identifications can be increased and false identifications minimized by following procedures that have been developed in recent years.

STEVEN E. CLARK and ELIZABETH LOFTUS

See also **Arrest Powers of the Police; Constitutional Rights: In-Custody Interrogation; Constitutional Rights: Search and Seizure**

References and Further Reading

Calandra, D., and J. E. Carey. 2004. *2004 field guide for the California Peace Officers legal sourcebook*. Sacramento: California District Attorneys Association.

Clark, S. E., and J. L. Tunnicliff. 2001. Selecting lineup foils in eyewitness identification experiments: Experimental control and real-world simulation. *Law & Human Behavior* 25: 199–216.

Huff, C. R., A. Rattner, and E. Sagarin. 1996. *Convicted but innocent*. Thousand Oaks, CA: Sage.

Lindsay, R. C. L., and G. L. Wells. 1985. Improving eyewitness identifications from lineups: Simultaneous versus sequential lineup presentation. *Journal of Applied Psychology* 70: 556–64.

Loftus, E. F. 1992. When a lie becomes memory's truth. *Current Directions in Psychological Science* 1: 121–23.

Loftus, E. F., and J. C. Palmer. 1974. Reconstruction of automobile destruction: An example of the interaction between language and memory. *Journal of Verbal Learning and Verbal Behavior* 13: 585–89.

Nettles, W., Z. Nettles, and G. L. Wells. 1996. "I noticed you paused on number three": Biased testing in eyewitness identification. *Champion*, November, 10–12, 57–59.

Rosenthal, R. 1966. *Experimenter effects in behavioral research*. New York: Wiley.

U.S. Department of Justice. 1999. *Eyewitness evidence: A guide for law enforcement*. Washington, DC: U.S. Department of Justice.

———. 2003. *Eyewitness evidence: A training manual for law enforcement*. Washington, DC: U.S. Department of Justice.

Wells, G. L. 1993. What do we know about eyewitness identification? *American Psychologist* 48: 553–71.

Wells, G. L., S. M. Rydell, and E. P. Seelau. 1993. The selection of distractors for eyewitness lineups. *Journal of Applied Psychology* 78: 835–44.

Wells, G. L., M. Small, S. Penrod, R. S. Malpass, S. M. Fulero, and C. A. E. Brimacombe. 1998. Eyewitness identification procedures: Recommendations for lineups and photospreads. *Law and Human Behavior* 22: 603–43.

Wogalter, M. S., R. S. Malpass, and M. A. Burger. 1993. How police officers construct lineups: A national survey. In *Proceedings of the Human Factors and Ergonomics Society 37th Annual Meeting*, 640–44.

Wogalter, M. S., M. S. Maplass, and D. E. McQuiston. 2004. A national survey of U.S. police on preparation and conduct of identification lineups. *Psychology, Public Policy, & Law* 10: 69–82.

F

FEAR OF CRIME

Community policing and fear of crime have been inextricably linked since 1981, when the evaluation of a field experiment in Newark, New Jersey, found that the presence of a foot patrol made neighborhood residents feel safer. Soon after, a foot patrol study in Flint, Michigan, found the same thing. Since then, it has become widely accepted that fear reduction is a legitimate police objective and that community policing is perhaps the best fear reduction strategy in the police arsenal.

Except for a few studies in the early to middle 1980s, however, research attention has not stayed focused on the connection between policing and fear of crime. Similarly, police program and strategy development targeted at fear reduction seems to have waned. Police departments today have only a few dated studies and little in the way of practical information to rely upon if they want to implement fear reduction initiatives.

Background

Fear of crime is a significant issue for Americans. A 2002 Gallup Poll determined that 62% of adults believed there was more crime than in the previous year, and a 2000 ABC Poll found that 80% of adults rated the crime problem in the United States as bad or very bad (though only 23% gave the same rating to crime problems in their own community). A 2000 Pew Survey reported that fewer than half of adults nationwide felt very safe when walking in their neighborhoods after dark, at school, or when at a shopping mall at night. Only two-thirds felt very safe in their homes at night.

Fear of crime has a range of deleterious effects on citizens and communities. Fear can cause individual citizens to restrict their work and leisure activities. It is especially likely to constrain the lives of those who feel most vulnerable, including the elderly, children, and women. Fear can cause neighborhoods to lose businesses or residents, contributing to a downward cycle of deterioration, and it can generally interfere with the vibrancy and vitality of any community. Public life is damaged when fear of crime causes citizens to stay at home or to frequent only highly protected enclaves.

In contrast to the few studies about how police or others might reduce fear of crime, a tremendous amount of research attention has been focused on the social and psychological phenomenon of fear of crime. It is recognized that fear of crime is multidimensional, including (1) feelings of fear, concern, and/or worry for self versus others, such as children and spouses; (2) feelings of fear, concern, and/or worry in one's home, in one's neighborhood, and elsewhere; (3) perceived likelihood of becoming a crime victim; and (4) reported behavioral effects such as going out at night, going out during the daytime, going downtown, etc.

It has also been documented that fear often increases during periods when crime is decreasing, that the most fearful individuals are often not those at most risk of crime victimization, and that the most fearful communities are not always the ones with the highest levels of crime. Generally, elderly citizens and women report higher levels of fear than middle-aged people and men. When included in surveys, teenagers often report surprisingly high levels of fear. The most consistent finding, though, has been the inconsistent correlation between actual crime and fear of crime.

Broken Windows

Fear of crime played a crucial role in the development of the influential "broken-windows" theory. When James Q. Wilson and George Kelling sought to explain why a foot patrol reduced fear of crime even though it did not reduce actual crime, they noted that when neighborhood residents complain about crime, they typically cite graffiti, abandoned cars, panhandlers, loud kids, and other types of minor crime and incivility, rather than robberies and assaults. They then posited that foot patrol officers are more likely than motorized patrols to address these kinds of low-level crime and disorder that seem to be uppermost in people's minds. This explanation achieved face validity precisely because it built on the observed inconsistent correlation between levels of serious crime and fear of crime.

The broken-windows theory goes on to claim a second stage of effects—that when police address minor crime and disorder, residents are reassured and communities are strengthened, thus leading to reductions in serious crime as well. These second stage effects on the levels of serious crime are disputed by many researchers and social theorists. The underlying dynamic, though, that policing of minor crime and disorder can reduce fear of crime in a community, has become widely accepted.

COP and POP

For twenty years now, conventional wisdom has been that community policing and broken windows are the best approaches to reducing fear of crime. Because these conclusions were reached so quickly, however, few studies of specific techniques have been undertaken. Consequently, the evidence that specific community policing techniques, such as storefront offices, newsletters, door-to-door visits, citizen patrols, crime prevention programs, or bicycle patrol, are effective in reducing fear is largely missing. Similarly, how best to reduce fear of crime in settings where a foot patrol is not feasible, or in communities where the broken-windows approach is not applicable (such as upper-income neighborhoods without much disorder), has not received much concentrated attention.

A promising problem-oriented approach to fear reduction was implemented in Baltimore County, Maryland, in the early 1980s. That approach emphasized the necessity of analyzing the causes of elevated fear of crime in a neighborhood before designing and implementing responses. The Baltimore County experience revealed that a community's fear of crime might be caused by one or a few neighborhood kids, by rumors (true or not) about a series of crimes, by disputes between ethnic groups, by one hate crime, by aggressive panhandlers, or by a variety of other specific factors. The range of causes was broad enough to demonstrate that any one-size-fits-all solution to fear of crime, including foot patrol or broken-windows policing, would not always apply. This realization led Baltimore County to adopt a problem-oriented approach to reducing fear of crime, relying first on careful identification and analysis of neighborhood-level problems, followed by tailored responses.

Reassurance Policing

The British police have recently implemented a strategy that they call "reassurance policing." They noticed in the late 1990s that crime had declined for several years but the public's fear and concern about crime had not followed suit. They termed this situation the "reassurance gap" and set out to develop techniques for addressing the situation. In contrast to U.S. terminology, they elected not to emphasize fear of crime but rather risks, signals, neighborhood security, and community safety. The methodology is for locally assigned police officers to work jointly with local partners and the public to identify and target the specific problems that are of greatest concern to local people, using techniques such as environmental visual audits, tasking and coordinating groups, intelligence-oriented neighborhood security interviews, and key individual networks.

Reassurance policing seems to combine the best of broken-windows and problem-oriented policing. In particular, it relies on signal crimes theory, which holds that people's fears and concerns are determined more by specific events and conditions than by the mass of all crime and disorder. It naturally follows that if police and communities address the specific events and conditions that people are concerned about, their levels of fear will decrease and their feelings of security will improve.

Fear of Terrorism

The next frontier for police may be fear of terrorism. Three observations come to mind. (1) There would seem to be a qualitative difference between the generalized feelings of fear and helplessness experienced by Americans after the attacks of September 11, 2001, on the World Trade Center and the Pentagon and the more routine fear of crime caused by disorder and incivility in the local neighborhood. (2) If this is true, then the techniques developed by police during the past twenty years to deal with fear of crime may not be applicable to fear of terrorism. Nevertheless, (3) fear is the very objective of terrorism (the aim of terror), and therefore limiting the impact of terrorism would seem to require limiting the fear that it creates. Whether this will develop as an important role for local and state police, as opposed to national investigation agencies, intelligence services, the military, and/or politicians, remains to be seen.

GARY CORDNER

See also **Attitudes toward the Police: Measurement Issues; Broken-Windows Policing; Community-Oriented Policing: Practices; Community Watch Programs; Media Images of Policing; Order Maintenance; Police Reform in an Era of Community and**

Problem-Oriented Policing; Problem-Oriented Policing; Quality-of-Life Policing; Styles of Policing; Terrorism: Overview; Zero Tolerance Policing

References and Further Reading

Cordner, Gary. 1986. Fear of crime and the police: An evaluation of a fear-reduction strategy. *Journal of Police Science and Administration* 14: 223–33.

———. 1988, A problem-oriented approach to community-oriented policing. In *Community policing: Rhetoric or reality*, ed. Jack R. Greene and Stephen D. Mastrofski, 135–52. New York: Praeger.

Innes, Martin. 2005. What's your problem? Signal crimes and citizen-focused problem solving. *Criminology & Public Policy* 4 (2): 187–200.

Pate, Anthony, Mary Ann Wycoff, Wesley Skogan, and Lawrence W. Sherman. 1986. *Reducing fear of crime in Houston and Newark: A summary report*. Washington, DC: Police Foundation.

Police Foundation. 1981. *The Newark Foot Patrol experiment*. Washington, DC: Police Foundation.

Taft, Philip B., Jr. 1986. *Fighting fear: The Baltimore County COPE Project*. Washington, DC: Police Executive Research Forum.

Trojanowicz, Robert C. 1982. *An evaluation of the Neighborhood Foot Patrol Program in Flint, Michigan*. East Lansing: Michigan State University.

Wilson, James Q., and George Kelling. 1982, Broken windows: The police and neighborhood safety. *The Atlantic Monthly*, March, 29–38.

FEAR OF LITIGATION

In reviewing the existing literature and empirical research on the fear of litigation by police officers, it becomes quickly evident that this topic is still in its infancy. In fact, only one study prior to 1995 had examined how law enforcement officer candidates perceived the fear of litigation (Scogin and Brodsky 1991). In order to examine how fear of litigation impacts law enforcement, it is first necessary to gain an understanding of how this concept developed. The concern about litigation can be traced predominantly to the health professions, primarily physicians. As Brodsky (1988) noted, the fear of litigation has moved from a background issue of mild concern to a prominent topic of considerable concern in health professions. He concluded that it is not only the reality of a lawsuit but the possibility of malpractice or serious litigation that are sources of marked anxiety.

Brodsky (1983) utilized a case report on health professionals to describe the irrational and excessive fear of litigation, which he labeled "litigaphobia," defined as an excessive avoidance of legal actions prompted by irrational fear. Breslin, Taylor, and Brodsky (1986) went on to develop a psychometrically sound instrument that permitted measurement of the phenomenon of litigaphobia. They also suggested that the plethora of litigation is not restricted to physicians and that society as a whole is showing a rise in litigation as a means of solving interpersonal and societal difficulties.

Other studies have examined litigaphobia with other professionals, namely psychologists. Wilbert and Fulero (1988) surveyed practicing psychologists in Ohio and found two factors to be positively correlated with their degree of concern: the number of hours per week of clinical service and the number of hours per week of supervision. Overall, they concluded that there was no epidemic of litigaphobia. Brodsky and Schumacher (1990) estimated at least a 5% to 10% incidence of litigaphobia among practicing psychologists. Because labels such as "litigaphobia" suggest pathological responses, it was important to examine whether the fears are rational responses to genuine, immediate threats or whether they are irrational and excessive reactions to rare events. Since no research has been able to distinguish between the rationality and irrationality of these behaviors, the term "fear of litigation" is now used because it is free of psychopathological labeling (Brodsky 1988).

As has been noted, this fear of litigation is certainly not limited to health professionals. For instance, a commonality that is increasingly evident between policing and other professions is the threat of lawsuits. To examine the fear of litigation among law enforcement officers, Scogin and Brodsky (1991) assessed 101 trainees in a regional law enforcement academy, focusing on how much officers worry about being sued, what they do to prevent suits, and to what extent such concerns become excessive. They addressed such areas using a five-item questionnaire they developed.

Their results indicated that officers reported worrying moderately about work-related lawsuits. Sixty-nine percent reported taking specific actions to prevent lawsuits. The subjects reported moderate to severe distress when hearing of another officer being sued. The majority of officers indicated that they do *not* think their fears of litigation are irrational and excessive. In fact, only 9% indicated that they felt their fears of litigation were irrational and excessive. However, based on their responses to open-ended questions, the authors believe this rate to be higher. In response to open-ended questions such as asking which specific situations they fear might lead to lawsuits, subjects indicated several: shootings, auto accidents, improper arrest, and excessive force. When asked about the irrationality of their fear of litigation, most responses indicated that participants view lawsuits as an inevitable and practically unavoidable consequence of the job. Hence, their fears and concerns appear quite rational from this perspective.

However, in a study of the fear of litigation in college students and citizens in general, Brodsky and Gianesello (1992) found that almost 80% of the general public felt that too many lawsuits were being filed in the United States. They concluded that this feeling may be self-perpetuating; that is, the perception that increasing numbers of people are involved in litigation gives rise to the belief that lawsuits are an inevitable fact of life, which may result in feelings of vulnerability. This vulnerability may serve as a form of self-justification for suing others. Indeed, it seems that the law enforcement trainees exhibited such vulnerability since they felt that fear of litigation was an unavoidable consequence of their jobs (Brodsky and Gianesello 1992; Scogin and Brodsky 1991).

This idea that law enforcement officers' increased feelings of vulnerability may serve as a form of self-justification for suing others moves the fear of litigation from outside the department into it. The police department administration itself may have cause for a unique fear of litigation, which is intradepartmental. Indeed, Bale (1990) has examined stress litigation stemming from police work.

He looked at the connection among work, stress, and emotional distress and their role in extensive litigation in the workers' compensation system. Terry (1985) reported that police work has been viewed as either the most stressful or among the most stressful of all occupations and that perceived stresses and strains of police work are thought to cause certain physiological ailments among police officers, as well as the presence of high divorce and suicide rates. Likewise, Bale (1990, 413) stated:

> Police officers perform stressful and dangerous work that is highly visible to the public, both in the community and in its many media representations. Police officers are often covered by disability schemes that allow them generous presumptions of compensability for heart attacks. These provisions, reflecting a widely held view, expressed by some courts, that police work is inherently more stressful than most occupations, can directly aid police officers bringing claims that work stress helped induce other medical conditions, such as a peptic ulcer or a mental illness.

Bale (1990) goes on to state numerous cases in which police officers have been successful in workers' compensation claims that involved stress on the job. Some of the cited litigation addresses claims concerning harassment and abuse of authority; physical intimidation and other forms of threat; adverse personnel decisions; excessive demands; whistle-blowing; and internal investigations into alleged illegal activity. As Bale (1990) notes, a growing set of legal remedies is transforming distressing workplace situations into forms of money, medical care, and justice.

This growing area of stress litigation within law enforcement suggests that future studies on the fear of litigation in police officers need also to address the differences between the fears of officers who are in contact with the public and those of officers involved in administrative and organizational tasks. Furthermore, it may be useful to examine whether officers who feel that fear of litigation is an unavoidable consequence of their job indeed feel more vulnerable. If so, would they then feel more justified in bringing a stress-related lawsuit against their own department?

Although this concept of police fear of litigation is relatively abstract at present, numerous implications from the limited available research are relevant. First, Scogin and Brodsky (1991) suggested that preservice and in-service training on liability and the process of litigation is highly desirable. They also concluded that the impact of the concerns about litigation on work and personal functioning is not known. They proposed that fear of litigation may be adaptive in that it discourages questionable activities. On the other hand, it might be detrimental in that officers may become overly conservative and engage in avoidant law enforcement behavior. Their recommendation for further research was to contrast the litigation fears of veteran officers, as well as those who have undergone litigation preservice and in-service training, to recruits or those who have not received such training.

Scogin and Brodsky (1991) also commented that because law enforcement is inherently stressful, moderate levels of worry about lawsuits adds to the emotional wear and tear of the job. This point of view directly ties into the question about the self-perpetuating concept of the fear of litigation in police officers. Is there some point at which the stress induced by fear of litigation from outside the department becomes a contributor to increased stress litigation within the department? To better answer this question, future research should examine this issue to more fully understand the entire range of effects of fear of litigation in police officers.

JENNIFER F. GARDNER and
FORREST R. SCOGIN

See also **Police Legal Liabilities: Overview; Stress and Police Work**

References and Further Reading

Bale, A. 1990. Medicolegal stress at work. *Behavioral Sciences and the Law* 8: 399–20.

Breslin, F. A., K. R. Taylor, and S. L. Brodsky. 1986. Development of a litigaphobia scale: Measurement of excessive fear of litigation. *Psychological Reports* 58: 547–50.

Brodsky, S. L. 1983. Speaking out: A litigaphobic release from involuntary commitment. *Public Service Psychology* 2 (3): 11.

———. 1988. Fear of litigation in mental health professionals. *Criminal Justice and Behavior* 15: 492–500.

Brodsky, S. L., and W. F. Gianesello. 1992. Worrying about litigation: A normative study of college students and the general public. *Law and Psychology Review* 16: 1–12.

Brodsky, S. L., and J. E. Schumacher. 1990. The impact of litigation on psychotherapy practice: Litigation fears and litigaphobia. In *The Encyclopedic handbook of private practice*, ed. E. A. Margenau, 674–76. New York: Gardner Press.

Scogin, F., and S. L. Brodsky. 1991. Fear of litigation among law enforcement officers. *American Journal of Police* 10 (1): 41–45.

Terry, W. C. 1985. Police stress as a professional self-image. *Journal of Criminal Justice* 13: 501–12.

Wilbert, J. R., and S. M. Fulero. 1988. Impact of malpractice litigation on professional psychology: Survey of practitioners. *Professional Psychology: Research and Practice* 19: 379–82.

FEDERAL BUREAU OF INVESTIGATION

The Federal Bureau of Investigation (FBI) is the main investigative arm of the U.S. Justice Department. The FBI's mission encompasses both law enforcement and intelligence, including more than two hundred types of federal law violations. In the post-9/11 era, the FBI's top priorities are investigations of domestic and international terrorism and of foreign intelligence services operating within the United States. In addition, federal criminal law violations remain an important part of FBI responsibilities, including investigations of organized crime, white collar crime, cybercrimes, and certain major violent crimes. Approximately twenty-nine thousand employees, including more than eleven thousand special agents, carry out the work of the bureau throughout the United States, operating out of fifty-six field offices and four hundred smaller offices, known as resident agencies. There are also forty-five offices in foreign cities.

The FBI's role in law enforcement and domestic security has not always been so extensive. In fact, when the bureau was first established in 1908, its mandate was limited and uncertain. The original thirty-four agents were limited to investigating cases involving antitrust laws, interstate commerce laws, land frauds, and miscellaneous statutes not enforced by other federal agencies. It was not until 1910 that Congress assigned the Bureau of Investigation (renamed the Federal Bureau of Investigation in 1935) its first major investigative responsibility with the passage of the White Slave Traffic Act (or Mann Act). This legislation was aimed at curbing organized prostitution, specifically the interstate transportation of women for immoral purposes.

A central theme of the FBI story throughout the twentieth century is the expansion of its law enforcement authority. Although historically law enforcement has been (and is) a local and state function, the U.S. Constitution's Commerce Clause, which allows Congress to regulate interstate commerce, provided a basis for extending federal police powers. This clause was invoked in the passage of the Mann Act and later legislation involving auto theft (1919), kidnapping (1932), and bank robbery (1934). The administration of President Franklin D. Roosevelt (FDR) provided a major impetus for the expansion of the federal role in law enforcement. His attorney general, Homer Cummings, embarked on a "war on crime" as he and FBI Director J. Edgar Hoover pursued Depression-era gangsters, such as John Dillinger. The success of this anticrime crusade culminated in the 1934 passage of legislation that dramatically increased the FBI's role in crime control. It was during this period that the crime fighting G-man image of the bureau became embedded in American popular culture. In subsequent decades the FBI acquired additional law enforcement responsibilities: white collar and organized crime in the mid-1970s (made top priorities), drug enforcement in 1982, and violent crime in 1989 (became a high-priority program).

Paralleling the FBI's widening role in law enforcement was its development as an intelligence agency. In the bureau's early years, the "Palmer raids" of 1919 and 1920 marked a controversial foray into intelligence matters. U.S. Attorney General A. Mitchell Palmer formed a General Intelligence Division (GID) within the Justice Department as a response to the post–World War I threat of Reds (communists), alien anarchists, and radical workers, who it was feared were about to launch a revolution. The culmination of this Red Scare was the arrest and detention by bureau agents of several thousand aliens and radicals nationwide (the "Palmer raids") and the deportation of several hundred of the alien detainees.

The excesses of these raids along with other Justice Department scandals, such as Teapot Dome, led to major changes in both the Justice Department and the bureau. In 1924, the reform-minded attorney general, Harlan F. Stone, abolished the GID, limiting bureau investigations to federal criminal law violations, and at the same time appointed Hoover to head the FBI. FBI domestic intelligence authority was not restored until World War II—at first by a secret 1936 directive from FDR and then publicly in 1939 by an executive order at the outbreak of World War II. The 1939 order established the FBI as the national clearinghouse for all information pertaining to espionage, sabotage, and subversive activities.

In the postwar era (1950s), communists in the United States became the main target of FBI domestic intelligence activities, and in the 1960s, civil rights leaders and antiwar (Vietnam) activists were surveilled under various domestic security programs. During the early and mid-1970s, public disclosure of questionable FBI intelligence activities, such as COINTELPRO, culminated in congressional inquiries (the Church and Pike Committee hearings). The aftermath of this scandal led to reforms in FBI intelligence and a curtailing of such activities.

In 1982, during the administration of President Ronald Reagan, terrorism (which replaced the older term "domestic security") again became a national priority, but it was not until the 1990s (following the bombings of the World Trade Center and the federal building in Oklahoma City) that the FBI began to allocate significant resources to it. And it was not until after the 9/11 terrorist attacks that the FBI began to transform itself into an agency focused on the prevention of future terrorist attacks.

Key events in U.S. history (FDR's "war on crime," World War II, the Cold War, and the 9/11 terrorist attacks) have shaped the FBI's traditions and culture. All of these events left their mark on the bureau, but perhaps none was as noteworthy and long lasting as the forty-eight-year directorship of Hoover (1924–1972).

Hoover helped to professionalize the FBI and its agents by requiring higher training and education standards. He also attempted to bring an aura of science to crime investigation with the establishment of the FBI Crime Laboratory in 1932 and the extensive use of fingerprints in criminal identification. However, his long tenure as director gave him (and the FBI) power and autonomy unprecedented in the federal government. Major abuses of authority were publicly revealed only after his death in 1972, resulting in a major rethinking of FBI policies and investigative priorities in the mid-1970s.

The contemporary FBI faces many unresolved issues, some stemming from its controversial past, others from the circumstances of the historical moment. Among them are the federal role in law enforcement, the tension between law enforcement and intelligence functions, and the balance between national security and civil liberties. As fears and threats about law and order and national security wax and wane, each historical era has confronted these issues differently. Throughout FBI history, controversy has often centered on how to resolve these issues. The post-9/11 era is no different. The passage of the USA PATRIOT Act in 2001 and Attorney General John Ashcroft's revised guidelines on domestic intelligence gathering (May 2002) have once again expanded FBI powers in this historically controversial area of bureau operations—domestic security.

TONY G. POVEDA

See also **Abuse of Authority by Police; Academies, Police; American Policing: Early Years; Computer Crimes; Crime Laboratory; Criminal History Information; DNA Fingerprinting; Federal Bureau of Investigation Training Academy; Federal Police and Investigative Agencies; Fingerprinting; Fraud Investigation; Future of Policing in the United States; Hoover, J. Edgar; Informants, Use of; Offender Profiling; Organized Crime; PATRIOT Acts I and II; Professionalism;**

Role of the Police; Serial Murder; Terrorism: Domestic; Terrorism: International; Undercover Investigations; *Uniform Crime Reports*; White Collar Crime

References and Further Reading

Federal Bureau of Investigation. 2005. Home page, http://www.fbi.gov.

Gentry, Curt. 1991. *J. Edgar Hoover: The man and the secrets*. New York: W. W. Norton.

Lowenthal, Max. 1950. *The Federal Bureau of Investigation*. New York: Sloane.

9/11 Commission. 2004. *Final report of the National Commission on Terrorist Attacks upon the United States*. New York: W. W. Norton.

Powers, Richard Gid. 1983. *G-men: Hoover's FBI in American popular culture*. Carbondale: Southern Illinois University Press.

Sullivan, William, and Bill Brown. 1979. *The bureau: My thirty years in Hoover's FBI*. New York: Pinnacle.

Theoharis, A., T. Poveda, S. Rosenfeld, and R. Powers. 1999. *The FBI: A comprehensive reference guide*. Phoenix, AZ: Oryx.

U.S. Senate. 1976. *Final report of the Select Committee to Study Governmental Operations with Respect to Intelligence Activities*. Book III. Washington, DC: U.S. Government Printing Office.

Whitehead, Don. 1956. *The FBI story: A report to the people*. New York: Random House.

FEDERAL BUREAU OF INVESTIGATION TRAINING ACADEMY

The Federal Bureau of Investigation (FBI) is by far the most popularized federal law enforcement agency. The FBI originated from a special force of elite and specially trained law enforcement agents created in 1908 by then-Attorney General Charles Bonaparte under the presidency of Theodore Roosevelt. Today, the FBI is the major investigative arm of the U.S. Department of Justice, with its authority found in Title 28, Section 533 of the U.S. Code (Cole and Smith 2005).

J. Edgar Hoover was the director of the FBI from 1924 until his death in 1972. Under Hoover, the Bureau of Investigation was renamed the Federal Bureau of Investigation. Hoover established the *Uniform Crime Reports* (UCR) and institutionalized the FBI National Training Academy, an educational and training facility for law enforcement throughout the United States and the world (Cole and Smith 2005).

The FBI National Academy, established in 1935, provides a professional and academic course of study for U.S. and international law enforcement officers. It was created in response to the 1930s' Wickersham Commission that had recommended the standardization and professionalization of law enforcement across the country. Prior to the Commission, police training was on an ad hoc basis, with little uniformity existing in the training of law enforcement. When it was recognized that the performance of a police officer was not based solely on his personality but also his training, the FBI Academy became an accepted addition to law enforcement. With formal training needed to gain an understanding of the legal rules, weapon use, and the socialization of law enforcement officers, new agents and seasoned law enforcement officers in the field learn the various aspects of the job through other officers.

Included under the umbrella of the FBI Academy are various specialized units (to include the New Agents' Training Unit and the Investigative Computer Training Unit), the National Academy, and the International Academy. The academy's mission is "to support, promote, and enhance the personal and professional development of law enforcement leaders by preparing them for complex, dynamic, and contemporary challenges through innovative techniques, facilitating excellence in education and research, and forging partnerships throughout the world." Nowhere in the academy's mission are the themes of elitism or exclusion communicated. The academy works in partnership with all law enforcement in training.

The New Agents' Training Unit provides seventeen weeks of instruction in academics, firearms, operational skills, and integrated case scenarios. New Agents' Trainees (NATs) are also required to pass a physical training test and a defensive tactics test while attending the academy. In addition, NATs must conduct interviews, perform surveillance, and apply street survival techniques taught by the academy instructors. Instructors, for the most part, are agents in the field who volunteer to spend seventeen weeks at the academy to train future agents.

The Investigative Computer Training Unit (ICTU) provides computer instruction and curriculum development to FBI and other law enforcement personnel throughout the world. The training through ICTU includes how to use the computer (1) as an investigative tool, (2) as a communications device, and (3) to analyze digital evidence. ICTU has also developed partnerships with other federal law enforcement agencies to provide training to local and regional computer crime units (Evans 1991). Finally, ICTU provides investigative computer training internationally to law enforcement schools in Europe, Asia, and Africa.

The academy students, law enforcement leaders, attend the academy to gain the tools to improve their administration of justice within their home law enforcement agencies. Law enforcement officers, aware of the excellent quality of training within the FBI Academy, often wait years for their opportunity to attend it. For ten weeks, law enforcement officers, based throughout the country, attend undergraduate and/or graduate courses on the U.S. Marine Corps Base at Quantico, Virginia, in the areas of law, behavioral science, forensic science, leadership development, communications, and health/fitness. These selected officers dedicate themselves to the training at the academy as they place both their professional and personal lives on hold while attending their session.

The current facility, opened in 1972, is located on approximately four hundred acres of land and provides the private, safe, and secure environment necessary to carry out the training function required by the FBI. Within the facility is a firearms range as well as simulated communities for use in case scenarios. To date, the FBI National Academy has graduated approximately forty thousand law enforcement officers of all genders, races, and ethnicities. After graduation, each officer has the opportunity to join the National Academy Associates, an organization of more than fifteen thousand law enforcement professionals who continue to work together. This organization of associates is dedicated to the continued improvement of law enforcement through training and education.

In addition to the FBI National Academy, there is also the FBI International Training Program. After 9/11, the FBI and other federal law enforcement agencies began focusing their efforts on preventing terrorist threats against the United States. New laws, such as the PATRIOT Act, expanded the FBI's antiterrorism powers. In 2002, Congress created the Department of Homeland Security, which, in coordination with the CIA and the FBI, now coordinates the training efforts to combat terrorism. The FBI International Training Program is the FBI's part of that coordination. The mission of the International Training section is to administer and coordinate all international mission-oriented training for the FBI.

Because the director of the FBI is currently charged with the duty to detect and investigate crimes committed against the government, the establishment of the international training component was critical to carrying out this directive. The international training initiatives fall into the basic categories of (1) international country assessments, (2) international in-country training, (3) international training conducted in the United States, (4) FBI instructor development and cultural awareness, (5) international law enforcement academies, (6) Mexican/American Law Enforcement Training initiatives, and (7) the Pacific Rim Training Initiative (PTI). Through these initiatives, national and international efforts to protect the citizens of the United States and to train law enforcement are supported.

Finally, the FBI and its FBI Training Academy conduct three five-day seminars under its National Executive Institute. These seminars are for large local and state law enforcement agencies. In addition, they also conduct eighteen regional executive training mini-sessions each year for small law enforcement agencies.

The FBI is probably the most well-known federal law enforcement agency, although the facility is not open to the public. With more than ten thousand agents and an annual budget of more than $3 billion, the FBI and FBI Academy now place their greatest emphasis on investigations and training in the areas of white collar crime, organized crime, terrorism, foreign intelligence within the United States, and political corruption. Today the FBI Academy provides valuable assistance to state and local law enforcement through its programs. The FBI strives for excellence by adhering to the law and its duties as conferred by the U.S. Congress, through everyday ethical behavior, by demonstrating fairness, and through the training of law enforcement officers by the FBI Training Academy. The FBI's motto is "Fidelity, Bravery, and Integrity."

KIMBERLY A. MCCABE

See also **Federal Bureau of Investigation; Federal Law Enforcement Training Center (FLETC); Homeland Security and Law Enforcement; International Police Cooperation**

References and Further Readings

Casey, J. 2004. Managing joint terrorism task force resources. *FBI Law Enforcement Bulletin* 73: 1–6.

Cole, G., and C. Smith. 2005. *Criminal justice in America.* 4th ed. Belmont, CA: Wadsworth.

Crime Control Digest. 2005. 39 (45) (Nov. 11): 1.

Egan, N. 2005. Broken: The troubled past and uncertain future of the FBI. *Law Enforcement News* 31: S5.

Evans, P. 1991. Computer fraud—The situation, detection, and training. *Computer and Security* 10: 325–27.

Federal Bureau of Investigation. 2005. *Facts and figures.* http://www.fbi.gov/priorities/priorities.htm (accessed November 5, 2005).

Federal Bureau of Investigation Training Academy. 2005. http://www.fbi.gov/hq/td/academy/academy.htm (accessed December 14, 2005).

———. 2005. *The International Training Program.* http://www.fbi.gov/hq/td/academy/academy/itp/itp.htm (accessed December 14, 2005).

Hubbards, G., R. Cromwell, and T. Sgro. 2004. Mission possible: Creating a new face for the FBI. *The Police Chief* 71: 37.

King, L., and J. Ray. 2000. Developing transnational law enforcement cooperation. *Journal of Contemporary Criminal Justice* 52: 386–98.

Mueller, R. 2005. IACP speech. *FBI Law Enforcement Bulletin* 74: 16–20.

Oliver, W. 2002. 9-11, federal crime control policy and unintended consequences. *ACJS Today* 22: 1–6.

Siegel, L. 1998. *Criminology: Theories, patterns, and typologies.* 6th ed. Belmont, CA: Wadsworth.

FEDERAL COMMISSIONS AND ENACTMENTS

Federal commissions and enactments have had a significant impact on the police role in America. Commissions and laws have affected the function and funding of police at all levels of government. They have been instrumental in crafting an elastic police role that has stretched to include the police as "fun cops" (who raided speakeasies during Prohibition), riot participants (who triggered as well as controlled civil disturbances in the 1960s), gangbusters, narcotics officers, moral police (who strictly enforced pornography statutes and similar laws), intelligence gatherers and analysts, and homeland security agents.

Eighteenth Amendment of 1919

The Eighteenth Amendment prohibited the manufacture, sale, transportation, import, and export of intoxicating liquors. Its implementing legislation, the Volstead Act, gave the Bureau of Internal Revenue enforcement authority. Enforcement of Prohibition by Treasury agents was riddled with violence, dishonesty, and incompetence. In 1927, Prohibition agents were placed under civil service and in 1930 the Prohibition Bureau was transferred to the Justice Department. The Prohibition agents' overzealous, violent enforcement of the Volstead Act shocked the public and undermined Prohibition.

To make matters worse, Prohibition presented opportunities for gangs to take over the importation ("bootlegging"), manufacture, and distribution of alcoholic beverages. Al Capone, the king of the bootleggers, built his criminal empire on profits from illegal alcohol. In an effort to bust Capone, President Hoover launched the first federal attack on organized crime in 1929. It culminated in Capone's conviction for tax evasion in 1931.

1931 National Commission on Law Observance and Enforcement (Wickersham Commission)

Reacting to public fears about crime stemming from the gang wars in Chicago and to public concerns about Prohibition enforcement, President Hoover in 1929 established the National Commission on Law Observance and Enforcement, popularly known as the Wickersham Commission after its chairperson, a former U.S. attorney general. The Wickersham Commission performed the first federal assessment of law enforcement and published its findings in 1931. Its *Report on Lawlessness in Law Enforcement* indicted the police for their use of the "third degree" in interrogations (that is,

the use of physical brutality to obtain involuntary confessions). The report stirred public interest, mobilized reform efforts, and generated a new awareness of the need for legal controls over the police.

Although the commission documented the utter failure of Prohibition, the commissioners issued a politically safe final recommendation (which comported with President Hoover's own position on the issue): The commission opposed repealing the Eighteenth Amendment. Nonetheless, the Eighteenth Amendment was repealed in 1933.

1964 President's Commission on the Assassination of President Kennedy (Warren Commission)

The assassination of President John F. Kennedy on November 29, 1967, prompted the formation of the President's Commission on the Assassination of President Kennedy. The commission took its unofficial name—the Warren Commission—from its chairman, U.S. Supreme Court Chief Justice Earl Warren. In September 1964, after a ten-month investigation, the Warren Commission Report was published. The report concluded that Lee Harvey Oswald, acting alone, was responsible for the assassination of Kennedy. This conclusion has been challenged on many grounds. The final report also scored the Secret Service for failing to provide adequate security. This criticism caused the Secret Service to modify its security procedures.

1967 President's Commission on Law Enforcement and the Administration of Justice

This commission's report, *The Challenge of Crime in a Free Society,* bore the earmarks of Great Society thinking. The Great

Society was a set of liberal domestic programs enacted on the initiative of President Lyndon Johnson. Consistent with the Great Society's focus on ending poverty and racial injustice, the commission's goal was to reduce the fear of crime through criminal justice reforms aimed at attacking the "root causes" of crime.

Some of the commission's main contributions include (1) recognizing that criminal justice agencies and their processes should be viewed as a system, (2) stimulating criminal justice research and evaluation, (3) advocating higher education in the criminal justice professions, (4) introducing the victimization survey, and (5) emphasizing reintegration of offenders into the community. In the area of law enforcement, the commission suggested establishing citizen advisory boards and community relations units in minority neighborhoods, recruiting more minority police officers, and developing guidelines for the exercise of police discretion.

1968 National Advisory Commission on Civil Disorders (Kerner Commission)

The race riots of the summer of 1967 forced President Johnson to create yet another federal commission. This commission was known as the Kerner Commission after its chairperson, Illinois Governor Otto Kerner. The commission's famous conclusion was that "Our nation is moving toward two societies, one black, one white—separate and unequal."

Riot participants reported to researchers that abusive police practices were their number one grievance. The police had come to symbolize white power, white racism, and white repression. This symbolism was reinforced in the minds of African American citizens by a widespread belief within the African American community that police brutality against people of color was widespread and by a belief that the police used a double standard of justice and protection—one for African Americans and one for whites.

The commission called for establishing effective mechanisms for handling complaints against police, reviewing police operations in ghettos to ensure proper police conduct, improving protection for ghetto residents, recruiting more African Americans into policing, assigning well-trained police officers to patrol ghetto areas, and providing police training in riot prevention and control.

Omnibus Crime Control and Safe Streets Act of 1968

Title I established the Law Enforcement Assistance Administration (LEAA) to make grants to state and local governments for planning, recruiting, and training of law enforcement personnel; public education relating to crime prevention; building construction; education and training of special law enforcement units to combat organized crime; and the organization, education, and training of regular law enforcement officers, special units, and law enforcement reserve units for the prevention and detection of riots and other civil disorders. The grant programs significantly expanded federal involvement in local law enforcement. LEAA was eventually phased out after a twelve-year life and an expenditure of $7.5 billion.

Primarily because of Titles II and III, some critics charged that this law represented a move toward a police state. Title II attempted to overturn Supreme Court decisions by stating that all voluntary confessions and eyewitness identifications—regardless of whether a defendant had been informed of his or her rights—could be admitted in federal trials. Title III empowered state and local law enforcement agencies to tap telephones and engage in other forms of eavesdropping for brief periods without a court order.

1969 National Commission on the Causes and Prevention of Violence (Eisenhower Commission)

In June 1968, a few days after the assassination of Senator Robert F. Kennedy and two months after the assassination of the Reverend Martin Luther King, Jr., President Johnson issued an executive order authorizing another federal commission. The National Commission on the Causes and Prevention of Violence came to be known as the Eisenhower Commission after its chairperson, John Hopkins President Emeritus Milton S. Eisenhower. The commission advocated the licensing of handguns and the abandoning of television broadcasts of children's cartoons containing serious, noncomic violence.

Comprehensive Drug Abuse Prevention and Control Act of 1970 (Controlled Substances Act)

The Controlled Substances Act (CSA), Title II of the Comprehensive Drug Abuse Prevention Act of 1970, is the legal foundation of the federal government's fight against drug abuse. This law consolidates numerous laws regulating the manufacture and distribution of narcotics, stimulants, depressants, hallucinogens, anabolic steroids, and chemicals used in the illicit production of controlled substances. This statute is the legal basis by which the manufacture, importation, possession, and distribution of certain drugs can be regulated by the federal government of the United States. The Drug Enforcement Administration (DEA) is the lead agency in charge of federal drug law enforcement.

Organized Crime Control Act of 1970

Provisions of the Organized Crime Control Act of 1970 include stronger gambling laws, expansion of grand jury powers, and authorization for the attorney general to protect witnesses and their families. This last measure led to the creation of WITSEC, an acronym for witness security. Title IX of the act is the Racketeer Influenced and Corrupt Organizations (RICO) statute. During the latter part of the twentieth century, RICO was a major weapon in the federal government's drive to fight organized crime.

1970 President's Commission on Obscenity and Pornography (Lockhart Commission)

In 1968, the U.S. Supreme Court ruled in *Stanley v. Georgia* that people could read and look at whatever they wished in the privacy of their own homes. A "deeply concerned" U.S. Congress authorized $2 million to fund a federal commission to study pornography. President Johnson named as chairperson William B. Lockhart, Dean of the University of Minnesota Law School.

Because the commission did not finish its work until after Johnson had left office, the Nixon administration ultimately became the recipient of the Lockhart Commission's final report in 1970. In its final report, the commission recommended massive sex education and the legalization of pornography for adults. Vice President Spiro Agnew associated this commission with the Johnson administration, and said, "As long as Richard Nixon is president, Main Street is not going to turn into smut alley."

1972 National Commission on Marijuana and Drug Abuse (Shafer Commission)

In 1972, Chairperson Raymond Shafer presented the National Commission on Marijuana and Drug Abuse final report. It stated that "neither the marijuana user nor the drug itself can be said to constitute a danger to public safety." The commission recommended decriminalization of possession of marijuana for personal use on both the state and federal levels of government. President Nixon reportedly refused to even read the report.

1973 National Advisory Commission on Criminal Justice Standards and Goals

LEAA appointed the National Advisory Commission on Criminal Justice Standards and Goals in 1971 to formulate the first national standards and goals for crime control and prevention at both the state and local levels. In 1973, the commission issued six reports. The commission stressed the importance of police–community relations, neighborhood watch, SWAT and riot squads, and team policing.

1978 National Advisory Commission on Higher Education for Police Officers (Sherman Report)

The National Advisory Commission on Higher Education for Police Officers published *The Quality of Police Education* in 1978. Lawrence Sherman, the chairperson, and the other members criticized educational programs that emphasized the technical/vocational aspects of policing and those staffed by former police rather than academics. Colleges, the commission recommended, should employ full-time Ph.D. faculty and refuse to give college credit for completion of police academies.

Comprehensive Crime Control Act of 1984

The Comprehensive Crime Control Act of 1984 was part of President Ronald Reagan's crime fighting package for law enforcement. It allocated $69 million for programs that provided management training and technical assistance for police, created new laws for the seizure of evidence, broadened the scope of warrantless wiretaps, and expanded the list of crimes for which wiretaps could be used.

1986 Attorney General's Commission on Pornography (Meese Commission)

President Reagan set up this commission to obtain results more acceptable to his conservative supporters than those of the Lockhart Commission. Reagan appointed arch-conservative U.S. Attorney General Edwin Meese to chair the Attorney General's Commission on Pornography and stacked the panel with antipornography crusaders.

When the Meese Commission attempted to exert indirect pressure on magazine distributors to censor the books and magazines they sold or be publicly branded as pornographers, a federal district court ordered the commission to retract its threats. Predictably, the commission's final report highlighted harmful effects of pornography while minimizing evidence indicating that pornography is not dangerous.

1990 National Commission to Support Law Enforcement

The National Commission to Support Law Enforcement consisted of law enforcement officers as well as managers and academics specializing in law enforcement. This commission's report covered a variety of areas including the effectiveness of information-sharing systems, the adequacy of equipment, physical and human resources, and the quality of research, education, and training.

2001 U.S. Commission on National Security/21st Century (Hart-Rudman Commission)

The U.S. Commission on National Security/ 21st Century final report made perhaps the most accurate prediction ever made by a federal commission. The report warned in January 2001 that terrorists would attack America on U.S. soil. Yet, at the time the report was released, the administration of President George W. Bush did not implement any of its recommendations.

The bipartisan panel, known as the Hart-Rudman Commission because two former U.S. senators, Gary Hart and Warren Rudman, served as chair and cochair, respectively, also had the foresight to make a sound proposal: The panel recommended the establishment of a National Homeland Security Agency, an independent agency whose director would be a member of the president's cabinet.

2001 USA PATRIOT Act

Just forty-five days after the September 11, 2001, attacks on the World Trade Center and the Pentagon, with no debate, Congress passed the Uniting and Strengthening America by Providing Appropriate Tools Required to Intercept and Obstruct Terrorism Act (USA PATRIOT Act). This law expands law enforcement powers to fight terrorism. Many sections strip away checks and balances necessary to protect constitutional rights.

Critics claim that under this sweeping law the government can search your home and not even tell you; collect information about what books you read, what you study, your purchases, and your medical history; seize a wide variety of business and financial records; and read parts of your e-mails and monitor what you look at online. Some even allege that this law represents a step toward a police state.

Defenders claim that the threat of another terrorist attack justifies the PATRIOT Act's expansion of police powers.

2002 Homeland Security Act

In the aftermath of the 9/11 attacks, Congress enacted the Homeland Security Act (HSA) to protect America against terrorism. Following the recommendation of the Hart-Rudman Commission, Congress created the federal Department of Homeland Security (DHS) and assigned a number of government functions previously conducted in other departments to DHS.

The establishment of DHS is the most significant transformation of the U.S. government since 1947, when President Harry S. Truman merged the various branches of the armed forces into the Department of Defense in order to better coordinate the nation's defense against military threats.

2004 National Commission on Terrorist Attacks upon the United States (9/11 Commission)

President George W. Bush withheld support for the idea of creating an independent, bipartisan federal commission to investigate the 9/11 catastrophe until the media and the "Jersey Girls," a gutsy group of wives of 9/11 victims from New Jersey, pressured him into it. Bush finally signed legislation authorizing the so-called 9/11 Commission in late 2002. The commission was chartered to examine the causes of the 9/11 attacks, identify lessons learned, and provide recommendations to safeguard against future acts of terrorism.

The commission concluded that failures of the Central Intelligence Agency and the Federal Bureau of Investigation permitted the terrorist attacks to occur. It was the commission's view that if these agencies had acted more wisely and aggressively, the attacks might have been prevented. In addition, the commission outlined a global strategy for preventing Islamist terrorism and introduced a plan for reconfiguring U.S. national security institutions.

DENNIS E. HOFFMAN

See also **Crime Commissions; Department of Homeland Security; Law Enforcement Assistance Administration; National Advisory Commission on Civil Disorder; PATRIOT Acts I and II; Police Standards and Training Commissions; Terrorism: Overview; Wickersham, George W.**

References and Further Reading

Calder, James D. 1993. *The origins and development of federal crime control policy.* New York: Praeger Publishers.

Conley, John H., ed. 1994. *The 1967 President's Crime Commission Report: Its impact 25 years later.* Cincinnati, OH: Anderson.

National Advisory Commission on Civil Disorders. 1968. *Report of the National Advisory Commission on Civil Disorders.* New York: E. P. Dutton.

National Commission on Terrorist Attacks upon the United States. 2004. *9/11 Commission Report.* New York: W. W. Norton.

National Commission on the Causes and Prevention of Violence. 1969. *To establish justice, to insure domestic tranquility.* Washington, DC: U.S. Government Printing Office.

Walker, Samuel. 2005. *Records of the Wickersham Commission on Law Observance and Enforcement.* http://www.lexisnexis.com/academic/2upa/Allh/WickershamComm.asp.

FEDERAL LAW ENFORCEMENT TRAINING CENTER (FLETC)

The Federal Law Enforcement Training Center, also known as FLETC, is a law enforcement partnership funded by the federal government and operating under the auspices of the U.S. Treasury Department. FLETC's mission is to offer high-quality professional law enforcement training at cost efficient prices. This federal training center provides both federal law enforcement officers (excluding Federal Bureau of Investigation officers and agents) and state, local, and international police officers and agents with a multitude of training courses on a variety of different basic and specialty law enforcement topics.

History

FLETC officially took shape on March 2, 1970, and began its official operations in Washington, D.C. Later, in 1975, the center was relocated to its present headquarters near Brunswick, Georgia, in the small town of Glynco. The creation of FLETC was the result of a 1968 study conducted by an interagency task force comprised of various federal law enforcement agencies. The results of the study indicated that federal law enforcement officers reporting to the various federal agencies had no consistency in their formal law enforcement training. One of the major concerns with the study's findings centered on the fact that most federal law enforcement officers lacked the appropriate training, knowledge, and specific skill sets to do their job at even a minimum level of efficiency. In fact, most federal law enforcement training up to 1970 was conducted by part-time instructors, in dilapidated facilities, and with no consistent schedule of training courses or particular subject material.

To address this problem, the interagency task force proposed that a central Federal Law Enforcement Training Center be established. This proposed recommendation called for a centrally located state-of-the-art training facility that was to be operated and managed by a full-time staff that looked to offer high-quality programs ranging from basic law enforcement courses to highly specific investigative classes on a wide array of topics (for example, money laundering investigation, drug identification, fraud investigation).

Finally, in 1970, the federal interagency task force signed a federal Memorandum of Understanding for the Establishment of the Consolidated Federal Law Enforcement Training Center. It was further decided that the U.S. Treasury Department would provide both managerial and administrative support for the new facility since the department had already established a successful interbureau training organization known as the Treasury Law Enforcement Training School. At the conclusion of its first year of operation in 1970, FLETC had graduated 848 police officers from the center. By the end of 1975, the number of graduates had climbed to well above five thousand officers. Since 1970, more than 325,000 federal, state, local, and foreign law enforcement officers have successfully graduated from one of the many training courses and programs that FLETC has offered.

Organization

Today, FLETC falls under the auspices of the Department of Homeland Security (DHS), with the FLETC director answering to the under secretary for Border and Transportation Security. FLETC is governed by an eight-man interagency board of directors representing various federal law enforcement agencies throughout the country. Assisting the FLETC director is an executive staff comprised of one deputy director, six assistant directors, a team of legal counsel, and a chief of staff operations.

Today, FLETC offers training to a majority of federal officers and agents from more than eighty different federal agencies. Along with federal law enforcement training, the center also provides instruction to hundreds of state, local, and international police agencies. On average, FLETC graduates more than fifty thousand officers a year from its numerous training programs, with an annual budget

of more than $200 million. Currently, FLETC's fifteen-hundred-acre training center is the largest in the United States and is considered to be one of the elite training facilities in the world. Along with its main center in Glynco, Georgia, the center now has four satellite training campuses that offer a vast array of law enforcement courses, in Cheltenham, Maryland, Charleston, South Carolina, Artesia, New Mexico, and Gaborone, Botswana, Africa.

Mission and Operations

As previously stated, FLETC was created to serve as a high-quality training center for federal law enforcement officers. Since its inception, the mission has expanded to include law enforcement officers at various levels throughout the United States and abroad. Currently, FLETC offers more than two hundred training programs and courses ranging from basic to advanced policing and investigative techniques to international courses regarding global terrorism. All of these programs are continually evaluated and assessed through curriculum meetings and student evaluation reports to ensure that the quality of instruction remains extremely high, professional, and efficient. FLETC officials also offer a unique selection of technical, clerical, and managerial support services to enhance the overall training needs of a particular participating agency.

FLETC instructors are experienced and highly trained professionals who have at least five years of law enforcement or investigative experience. Instructors range from federal officers and investigators on assignment from their respective agencies to state and local police officers who have specialized skills in a particular area (such as fingerprint analysis or forensic investigation) to civil instructors who have particular training in a law enforcement–related field (such as hand-to-hand combat, behavioral profiling, or fraud investigation). Instructors include both full- and part-time faculty who are complemented by a full-time support staff.

It is also important to note that since both the Oklahoma City Federal building bombing and the terrorist attacks of 9/11, the Federal Training Center has seen a tremendous increase in issues involving terrorism. As a result, the need to create more specific courses centering on international and domestic terrorism has become one of the new operating goals of FLETC. With respect to international terrorism, FLETC has become an important venue for international officers and government officials to learn about the potential concerns regarding global terrorism.

PAUL M. KLENOWSKI

See also **Academies, Police; Bureau of Alcohol, Tobacco, Firearms and Explosives; Federal Bureau of Investigation; Federal Bureau of Investigation Training Academy; Federal Police and Investigative Agencies; U.S. Border Patrol; U.S. Marshals Service; U.S. Secret Service**

References and Further Reading

Bennett, Wayne, and Krden Hess. 2003. *Management and supervision in law enforcement.* Belmont, CA: Wadsworth Thomson.

Federal Law Enforcement Training Center. 2005. http://www.fletc.gov/ (accessed November 2005).

Olson, Steven P. 2005. *The Homeland Security Act of 2002: Legislation to protect America.* New York: Rosen Publishing Group.

Richards, James R. 1998. *Transnational criminal organizations, cybercrime, and money laundering.* Boca Raton, FL: CRC Press.

Warner, John W., Jr. 2001. *Federal jobs in law enforcement.* Lawrenceville, NJ: Thompson Peterson's.

FEDERAL POLICE AND INVESTIGATIVE AGENCIES

The policing and criminal law enforcement role of the federal government has always been constrained by two factors. The first of these is the limit on jurisdiction created by the U.S. Constitution. Article X reserves all powers not granted the federal government to the "States respectively, or to the people." Thus, the Constitution expressly delegated police power to the states. In addition, the political culture of the country has not accepted centralized power in general and centralized police power in particular. This is clearly evident in the distribution of state police power to local police and sheriffs.

The nation began with virtually no law enforcement structure at the federal level. When faced with the need for enforcing federal law, as in the Whiskey Rebellion of 1794, the president was forced to call up the state militia. The one exception to this was the creation of the U.S. Marshals for each federal judicial district in 1789. Although appointed by the president, marshals were neither police nor investigators in the modern sense. For the first century of their existence, they primarily functioned as court officers and were supported through fees charged for their services.

The functions of U.S. marshals expanded somewhat as the country expanded west and added territories, where they enforced federal law until a territory was admitted to the union as a state, yet they continued to lack any central management and lacked resources. Not until 1969 were the marshals placed in a centrally managed bureau within the Department of Justice, the U.S. Marshals Service (USMS). Today, deputy U.S. marshals protect judges, serve arrest warrants, transport federal prisoners, secure the courts, and oversee security of federal courthouses. The USMS possesses the broadest jurisdiction of any federal law enforcement agency, but it has a limited criminal investigative role in the current structure.

Federal law enforcement in the nineteenth century was primarily concerned with enforcing taxes on whiskey, collecting customs duties on imports, and protecting the mail. Though none of these functions produced a police or criminal investigative agency, revenue and customs officers were responsible for the collection of the taxes, and postal authorities enforced a variety of laws. Ironically, it was not in the Department of Justice but in the Department of Treasury that Congress established the first criminal investigative agency, the U.S. Secret Service (USSS).

Created to suppress counterfeiting, the USSS assumed responsibility for protecting presidents after the assassination of President McKinley in 1901. They have since assumed responsibility for protecting the vice president, the families of the president and vice president, former presidents, candidates for president and vice president, and foreign heads of state visiting the United States. Their investigative jurisdiction continues to include counterfeiting but now includes threats to those they protect, forgery of government documents, and certain fraud crimes. The Secret Service employs both special agents and uniformed officers, who guard the White House and protect foreign embassies. In 2002, the USSS was transferred from the Department of Treasury to the Department of Homeland Security.

Concurrent with the Treasury developing a law enforcement arm to protect the currency, the Post Office inspection function expanded from audit and inspection to include enforcing criminal laws against using the mails to defraud and theft from the mails. The current Postal Inspection Service continues to investigate crimes that use the mails for illegal purposes or attacks on the mails.

The twentieth century saw significant expansion in the federal criminal justice role. Much of this expansion was in the Department of Treasury, since the tax laws provided the justification for several federal moves into criminal enforcement. The Bureau of Internal Revenue, later the Internal Revenue Service (IRS), created the Intelligence Division, which conducted investigation of tax violations. These included violations of the first federal drug law, the Harrison Narcotics Act (1914). The Alcohol Tax Unit, created to suppress the distilling and sale of non–tax paid whiskey, became the Prohibition Bureau when the Eighteenth Amendment allowed Congress to outlaw production and sale of alcoholic beverages. The Federal Bureau of Narcotics (FBN) emerged from the Prohibition Bureau in 1930, creating yet another Treasury enforcement bureau.

Although the Intelligence Division of the IRS has remained stable in structure and mission, the other Treasury bureaus have experience significant change. The FBN was renamed the Bureau of Narcotics and Dangerous Drugs and moved to the Department of Justice in 1968, then again renamed the Drug Enforcement Administration in 1973. It has grown from an agency of a couple of hundred people to one employing more than five thousand special agents with offices throughout the United States and overseas.

Like the DEA, the Bureau of Alcohol, Tobacco, Firearms and Explosives has gone through a series of name changes and reorganizations. After returning to being a division of the Bureau of Internal Revenue at the end of Prohibition, the agency acquired jurisdiction over the newly passed National Firearms Act because Congress again used its taxing authority to pass a criminal statute. As the firearms laws were revised, the agency, now called Alcohol, Tobacco Tax Division, moved progressively away from liquor enforcement and toward investigating firearms violations.

After the passage of the Gun Control Act of 1968 and the Explosives Control Act of 1970 significantly expanded the agency's jurisdiction into bombing and explosives violations, the Nixon administration separated it from the IRS and established the Bureau of Alcohol, Tobacco and Firearms (ATF). ATF remained a Treasury bureau, acquiring added authority over arsons of businesses engaged in interstate commerce and interstate tobacco smuggling, until 2002, when it moved to the Justice Department. Now designated the

Bureau of Alcohol, Tobacco, Firearms and Explosives, it enforces firearms, arson, and explosives laws as well as regulating commerce in firearms and explosives. ATF, like the DEA, employs both special agents, who are criminal investigators, and inspectors, who enforce regulatory law.

The 2002 reorganization also moved the U.S. Customs Service and the Immigration and Naturalization Service from the Departments of Treasury and Justice to the Department of Homeland Security. Their functions were incorporated into two new agencies, Immigration and Customs Enforcement (ICE) and Customs and Border Protection. ICE special agents conduct investigations of violations of both the immigrations and customs laws, while Customs and Border Protection includes the Border Patrol as well as security and inspection functions. They employ inspectors, pilots, dog handlers, air marshals, and a variety of other specialized employees.

Although the Treasury role in federal law enforcement was significant during much of the twentieth century, the progressive use of interstate commerce authority by Congress to pass federal criminal legislation has moved much of the jurisdiction to the Justice Department. That trend has transformed the Federal Bureau of Investigation (FBI) from an obscure bureau within Justice to the largest criminal investigative agency in the federal government, with more than twenty-eight thousand employees. The FBI exercises jurisdiction over a wide variety of criminal and national security investigations and employs more than ten thousand special agents. Since 2001, the agency has shifted significant recourses to counterterrorism.

In addition to these large civilian law enforcement agencies, each of the military services has components charged with investigating criminal and security violations by its members. Only the Navy's Naval Criminal Investigative Service employs civilians exclusively as special agents. The other services use a combination of military and civilian investigators. The Department of Defense also maintains police agencies on many of its installations.

Numerous other federal entities including Congress, the Supreme Court, and the General Services Administration employ police forces to secure and enforce law on federal property. Natural resource agencies also employ police, rangers, and investigators for the enforcement of federal laws or for policing federal properties. The Park Service includes both the U.S. Park Police, primarily employed in Washington, D.C., as well as law enforcement rangers. Likewise, the Bureau of Land Management and Forest Service both employ law enforcement personnel to patrol large tracts of public land, and the U.S. Fish and Wildlife Service employs agents to enforce protection of endangered species and migratory fowl.

Virtually every department of government, from Agriculture to Education, employs investigators or agents to investigate fraud crimes. In most cases these investigators are housed in the Office of the Inspector General for the department in question.

All federal law enforcement agencies operate within jurisdictional constraints imposed by the Constitution, federal structure, and political traditions. Some, such as the FBI, DEA, and ATF, have attained broad mandates because Congress has used its power to regulate interstate commerce to criminalize a wide variety of behaviors, from car jacking to drug dealing, but even these agencies do not exercise the broad jurisdiction that police possess under state law. Federal law enforcement in the United States has largely retained its specialized focus and fragmented organizational structure.

WILLIAM J. VIZZARD

See also **American Policing: Early Years; Bureau of Alcohol, Tobacco, Firearms and Explosives; Drug Enforcement Administration (DEA); Federal Bureau of Investigation; Military Police; U.S. Border Patrol; U.S. Marshals Service; U.S. Secret Service**

References and Further Reading

Bureau of Alcohol, Tobacco, Firearms and Explosives. 2005. http://www.atf.treas.gov.

Drug Enforcement Administration. 2005. http://www.usdoj.gov/dea.

Federal Bureau of Investigation. 2005. http://www.fbi.gov.

McWilliams, J. C. 1990. *The protectors: Harry Anslinger and the Federal Bureau of Narcotics, 1930–1962*: Newark: University of Delaware Press.

Millsbaugh, A. C. 1937. *Crime control by the nation government.* Washington, DC: Brookings Institute.

U.S. Customs and Border Protection. 2005. http://www.cbp.gov.

U.S. Immigration and Customs Enforcement. 2005. http://www.ice.gov.

U.S. Marshals Service. 2005. http://www.usdoj.gov/marshals.

U.S. Postal Inspection Service. 2005. *Chronology.* http://www.usps.com/websites/depart/inspect/ischrono.htm.

U.S. Secret Service. 2005. http://www.ustreas.gov/usss/index.shtml.

Vizzard, W. J. 1997. *In the crossfire: A political history of the Bureau of Alcohol, Tobacco and Firearms.* Boulder, CO: Lynne Rienner.

FENCING STOLEN PROPERTY

"Fencing"—the crime of buying and reselling stolen merchandise—is one of the links that binds theft to the larger social system. Without someone to dispose of stolen property, thieves would have to rely on their own connections, and both the costs and the risks of crime would increase substantially. For the rest of society, the fence provides an opportunity for interested people to buy something at less than market price.

Fencing remains a rather poorly researched area in criminology, for several reasons. First, it often wears the cloak of legitimate business and is carried out in a rational, business-like manner, so that it has few of the qualities traditionally associated with crime. Second, because fencing is a crime with low visibility and is conducted in secrecy, researchers have directed their attention to more visible crimes such as theft or to violent crimes against persons, for which statistics are available. Third, the cloak of secrecy and the maintenance of a legitimate "front" make detailed investigation difficult.

The legal requirements for demonstrating that fencing has occurred are complex. In America, as in England, there are three elements to the crime: (1) The property must have been stolen; (2) the property must have been received or concealed (though the fence may not have actually seen or touched it); (3) the receiver must have accepted it with knowledge that it was stolen.

Case Studies of Fences

Much of what is known about fencing today comes from two in-depth studies of individual fences, one being Carl Klockars' work, *The Professional Fence* (1974), and the other being Darrell Steffensmeier's *The Fence: In the Shadow of Two Worlds* (1986). Klockars interviewed "Vincent Swaggi" (not his real name), a well-known fence in his city, while Steffensmeier interviewed "Sam Goodman" (also an alias), a well-known fence in an unnamed American city. Steffensmeier also interviewed thieves and customers who had contact with Sam, several other fences, and law enforcement officials to authenticate Sam's account of events. Subsequently, Steffensmeier and coauthor Jeffery Ulmer updated the criminal career and fencing operation of Sam in a recent work, *Confessions of a Dying Thief: Understanding Criminal Careers and Criminal Enterprise* (2005).

These works portray the fence as an "entrepreneur" and describe fencing as an enterprise requiring resourcefulness, charisma, ingenuity, and a good grasp of market practices and the rules of economic competition. Pricing norms and prevailing market conditions are used to determine what is "fair," and a sense of justice is developed based on the risks borne both by the thief and by the fence. Fences must pay a fair price so that thieves will come back to them again with stolen goods. However, because of their greater experience and knowledge, fences tend to dominate thieves in the pricing of stolen goods. The thieves often need money quickly, have few options other than to agree to the fence's offer, and are under pressure to get rid of the stolen merchandise.

Professional thieves who steal high-priced items are usually given the highest amounts—about 40% to 50% of the wholesale price. The amateur or drug addict thief who is not in a good bargaining position will receive the smallest amounts—often only ten to twenty cents on the dollar. Fences also often use chicanery to pad their profits by duping thieves (especially small-time thieves) about quality, quantity, and price.

These studies document that "wheelin' and dealin'" fences rely on extensive networking, developed through word of mouth, referrals, and sponsorship by underworld figures. Major fences also play an active role in coaching thieves on techniques of theft and product identification, and in developing long-term relationships with buyers. Rewards of fencing include money, reputation in the criminal community, excitement, a sense of mastery over one's life, and pride in being a "sharp businessman." Vincent and Sam justified their fencing involvement by claiming that the fence is not the same as a thief, does little harm to the victims of theft, does not differ much from legitimate business people, is able to operate only with the support of legitimate people (including the police), breaks no more rules than most people, and does a lot of good for others.

All fences are by definition businessmen: They are middlemen in commerce—albeit illegitimate commerce—providing goods and services to others, regardless of whether they operate from a legitimate business or rely solely on individual resources. Although a few operate independent of any business "front," most

fences are simultaneously proprietors or operators of a legitimate business, which provides a cover or front for the fencing. Businesses most often favored are those having a large cash flow (for example, a coin and gem shop, secondhand store, auction house, or restaurant) and the flexibility to set one's own hours (for example, a salvage yard or bail bonding). For some fences, the trade in stolen goods is their major source of income and the central activity of their business portfolio. For others, fencing is either a lucrative sideline to their legitimate entrepreneurship or just one of a number of illicit enterprises they are involved in.

Although some commentators (for example, Walsh 1974) have described the typical fence as essentially a "respectable businessman," the evidence that is available strongly suggests otherwise (see Steffensmeier and Ulmer 2005). The typical fence is characterized by one or more of the following: (1) prior criminal contact or background in criminal or quasi-legal activities, such as theft, hustling, or the rackets in general; (2) operation of a quasi-legitimate business such as a secondhand discount store, salvage yard, auction house, foundry, or bail-bonding business; (3) affinity with the underworld, such as ongoing business and leisure associations with its established members. It is hardly surprising that many organized crime members and associates are involved in the fencing of stolen property (Pennsylvania Crime Commission 1991). The significance of the fences having affinity with the underworld and not only within the realm of seemingly honest business is in terms of their acquiring the skills and contacts necessary to run a fencing business.

Types of Fences and Stolen Goods Handlers

Already by the late eighteenth and early nineteenth century, with the growth of fencing operations accompanying industrialization, it was commonplace for students of fencing to distinguish among receivers according to scale of operations and criminal intent (Colquhoun 1800; Crapsey 1872). Jerome Hall (1952) subsequently distinguished professional dealers from other criminal receivers (for example, "occasional" and "lay") by the intent to resell the stolen property and by the regularity or persistence with which they purchased stolen goods. Recently, Steffensmeier and Ulmer (2005) proposed that criminal receivers and other buyers of stolen goods may be differentiated by (1) whether they deal directly with thieves, (2) the frequency with which they purchase stolen property, (3) the scale or volume of purchases of stolen property, (4) the purpose of purchase (for personal consumption or resale), and (5) the level of commitment to purchasing stolen property.

They delineate four major groupings of criminal receivers or buyers of stolen goods, along with six more differentiated types of receivers (see Steffensmeier and Ulmer 2005, *Confessions of a Dying Thief*, pp. 90–96; see also Colquhoun 1800; Hall 1952; Henry 1977; Klockars 1974; Walsh 1977; Steffensmeier 1986; Cromwell, Olson, and Avary 1996; Sutton 1998). The four major groupings are as follows:

1. *Amateur or "Joe Citizen" buyers* refers mainly to someone who buys stolen goods once in a while to use himself or to peddle to a friend or close acquaintances. They tend to exhibit the lowest level of commitment and experience in buying stolen goods.

2. *Occasional or part-time dealers* are in-between dealers, the ones who buy off and on and then peddle the goods out of their business premises, on the street, or at an auction; fencing is a sideline activity within their primary occupation or business.

3. *Professional fences* refers to the "regular" or "bigger" dealers whose buying and selling of stolen goods is "a main part" of what they do. (Professional fences overlap so-called master fences, what *Confessions of a Dying Thief* characterizes as "referral" or "go-between" operators who do not deal directly with thieves but instead stay behind the scenes.)

4. *Online buyers and sellers* who fence stolen goods through websites have accompanied the rise in popularity of online auctions (such as eBay. com), a fast-growing distribution path that emerged in the late 1990s. The online trade in stolen goods overlaps the other forms of criminal receiving and is also a major avenue for "self-fencing" stolen goods today.

The other, more differentiated types include the following:

- *Referral or contact fences* are "background operators" who regularly buy stolen goods through another middleman and then resell them to other outlets, where the merchandise is then sold to the consuming public. These referral or contact fences thus do not deal directly with thieves. In a sense, referral fences are "the fence's fence," or "master fences." Referral fences tend to be all-around criminal entrepreneurs or "racketeers," with extensive criminal networks. For them, fencing stolen goods is usually part of a larger criminal portfolio. They tend to have a high commitment to crime and quasi-legitimate activities, but they may not necessarily be highly committed to fencing (it may depend on the significance of fencing for their overall criminal portfolio).

- *Associational fences* are those whose legitimate occupations place them in close contact and interaction with thieves. Examples might include police, bail bondsmen, bartenders, or defense attorneys.

- *Neighborhood hustlers* are those for whom fencing is one of several "hustles," or small-time criminal activities. They are often as apt to buy stolen goods for personal use as for resale.
- *Drug dealer fences* barter drugs for stolen goods. In addition, other suppliers of illegal goods and services are also known to sometimes fence stolen goods (for example, gambling operatives, pimps, or other providers of illicit sex).
- *Private buyers* are merchants or collectors who deal directly with thieves, but only with a small number of select or established thieves.
- *Merchant or business buyers* do not deal direct with thieves but buy stolen goods from other, perhaps more professional fences or referral/contact fences and then resell such goods to (probably unsuspecting) legitimate customers.

Fences can also be distinguished along other dimensions: first, by the kind of cover used to conceal their fencing trade—whether the trade in stolen goods is fully covered, partly covered, or uncovered by the fence's legitimate business identity—and second, by "product specialization"—the kinds of stolen goods they handle. At one pole is the generalist, a fence who will buy and sell virtually anything a thief offers. At the other pole is the specialist, who handles only certain kinds of goods, such as auto parts or jewelry.

Fence's Relationship to Theft Reconsidered

The fence does play a primary role in the marketing of stolen property, but that role is often hyped by commentators and law enforcement officials as bigger and more important than it actually is, and the involvement of other participants in the illegal trade is also ignored. The old saying "if no fences, no thieves" assumes that thieves are not autonomous or "free" in their stealing behaviors and that the police and the public have little or nothing to do with the maintenance of a criminal system.

While thieves are supposed to be dependent on fences, at the same time they are assumed to engage in their theft activities independently of the fences, so an inherent paradox exists. If they are independently motivated to theft, then they will steal irrespective of whether or not fences exist. Furthermore, emphasizing that they depend on and could not exist without fences ignores the fact that the fence is in precisely the same position as the thief: dependent on outlets or a market for stolen property.

Frequently, this problem is resolved by the involvement of merchants who are tempted to purchase stolen goods at cheap prices so that they may sell at a higher profit. Public demand for stolen goods also helps maintain the fences. Budget-conscious consumers are often willing to buy stolen goods, "no questions asked," and need little encouragement. In addition, when they are victims of theft, ordinary citizens are frequently willing to forgo prosecution once their stolen goods have been restored to them or they have received compensation. In a similar way, insurance companies and private detective agencies protect fences from public or legal reaction to a theft, either by diluting the rightful owner's desire to pursue those responsible by providing compensation or by cooperating with the owner for the return of stolen property.

Finally, the saying "if no fences, then no thieves" ignores that official complicity of some kind is often required if the prospective fence hopes to buy and sell stolen goods regularly and for a long time (Henry 1977; Klockars 1974; Steffensmeier and Ulmer 2005). Sometimes the official protection fences enjoy is an outgrowth of the corruption of law enforcement on a large scale. Present-day fences connected to Mafia or localized syndicates, for example, may benefit from the corruption of legal authorities achieved by way of general racketeering activities. Other times, the basis of police–fence complicity stems from the operating reality that both have access to resources desired by the other. In exchange for a muted investigation, for example, a fence is able to offer the police good deals on merchandise or to act as an informer who helps police recover particularly important merchandise and arrest thieves.

Thus, the sociolegal writings on the traffic in stolen property have addressed two complicated issues. One is the fence's role in the overall flow of stolen property from thieves to eventual consumers. The other is whether enforcement efforts should be more rationally directed at the fence than at other agents in the traffic in stolen property—thieves, occasional receivers, those to whom the fence sells, or complicitous authorities.

DARRELL STEFFENSMEIER

See also **Burglary and Police Response; Corruption; Crime Control Strategies; Criminology; Organized Crime**

References and Further Reading

Colquhoun, P. A. 1800. *A treatise on the commerce and police of the River Thames.* London: Printed for Joseph Mawman.
———. 1796. *A treatise on the police of the metropolis.* London: Printed by H. Fry for C. Dilly in the Poultry.
Crapsey, Edward. 1872. *The nether side of New York.* New York: Sheldon and Co.
Cromwell, Paul, James Olson, and D'Aunn Avary. 1996. *Breaking and entering: An ethnographic analysis of burglary.* Newbury Park, CA: Sage.
Hall, Jerome. 1952. *Theft, law, and society,* 2nd ed. Indianapolis, IN: Bobbs-Merrill Co.
Henry, Stuart. 1977. On the fence. *British Journal of Law and Society* 4: 124–33.
———. 1978. *The hidden economy.* London: Martin Robertson & Co.
Klockars, Carl. 1974. *The professional fence.* New York: Free Press.
McIntosh, Mary. 1976. Thieves, and fences: Markets and power in professional crime. *British Journal of Criminology* 16: 257–66.
Pennsylvania Crime Commission. 1991. *Organized crime in Pennsylvania—A decade of change: The 1990 report,* Darrell Steffensmeier, project director/principal writer.
Roselius, Ted, and Douglas Denton. 1973. Marketing theory and the fencing of stolen goods. *Denver Law Journal,* 50: 177–205.
Steffensmeier, Darrell. 1986. *The fence: In the shadow of two worlds.* Totowa, NJ: Rowman & Littlefield.
Steffensmeier, Darrell, and Jeffery Ulmer. 2005. *Confessions of a dying thief: Understanding criminal careers and criminal enterprise.* New Brunswick, NJ: Aldine Transaction.
Sutton, M. 1998. *Handling stolen goods and theft: A market reduction approach.* London: British Home Office Research Publications.

FIELD TRAINING AND EVALUATION PROGRAM

Program Overview

The San Jose (California) Police Department developed one of the first formal field training and evaluation programs (commonly referred to as the "San Jose model") in 1972. Department personnel realized that newly graduated academy trainees needed additional attention if they were going to become effective police officers.

The San Jose model was structured in accordance with a couple of important principles that have withstood the test of time. First, trainees must be provided sufficient time to learn how to apply their knowledge, skills, and attitudes (KSAs) in real-life settings. Second, field training personnel assess the performance and progress of a trainee's efforts using a standardized set of job-related skills and evaluation guidelines. Without these guidelines, the reliability and validity of the training would be jeopardized, leading to claims of bias and favoritism from trainees.

Field training programs (referred to as FTO programs) modeled after the San Jose model are typically administered for a period of eleven to sixteen weeks; the length varies in accordance with department resources and needs. Various job-related skills serve as benchmarks to which a trainee's performance is compared. To ensure program validity, these categories must be directly related to a detailed job task analysis of the position of a particular officer within that officer's respective agency. In other words, it is important to ensure that all trainees learn how to use their skills to perform the same job activities that veteran officers within their department are expected to perform.

Any number of job-related skills can be used within the program to measure a trainee's performance. A sample of these skills includes officer safety, field performance under stressful conditions, driving skills, control of conflict, report writing, use of the radio, self-initiated field activities, knowledge of policies, procedures, traffic laws, and the penal code, managing calls for service, and relationships with officers, supervisors, and citizens. These skills are critical because they represent primary tools trainees use to gain experience, maturation, and wisdom on the job.

It takes a special person to work with new trainees. The job requires each officer to perform multiple roles. First and foremost, each officer's primary duty is to deliver a multitude of diverse services to the public. Second, the officer either serves as an instructor (referred to as a field training instructor, or FTI) or as an evaluator (referred to as a field performance evaluator, or FPE). The degree of commitment made by instructors and evaluators significantly influences how well trainees perform within the program.

Program Format

Instruction Phases

Upon graduating from a recruit training program, a trainee will attend a brief orientation session for the purposes of being told how the FTO program is administered and what is expected of participants. Trainees will be assigned to an FTI and begin the process of completing a series of instructional phases (usually three phases, each phase lasting three weeks). Time spent in each instructional phase corresponds to a trainee's shift assignment. For example, a trainee could complete the first instructional phase on the day shift, the second instructional phase on the night shift, and the remaining phase on the evening shift. Continuity usually exists within departments relative to these assignments; however, each department may vary the sequence of the phase assignments.

As trainees progress through the instruction phases, they are expected to perform a number of predetermined activities. These tasks are administered in conjunction with a checklist contained in the trainee's training manual, which each FTO uses as a guide to document a trainee's exposure and accomplishments. The checklist also serves as a historical reference that communicates to the next FTI which activities a trainee has or has not performed. Concomitantly, as trainees complete each instructional phase and perform different tasks, they assume more and more responsibility for their own actions. Associated with this shift in responsibilities is a change in expectations by the FTI and the trainee.

Trainees must demonstrate the ability to perform the job of a police officer. Technically, by the end of the final instructional phase, trainees should be able to discharge their responsibilities in accordance with program standards (which is a direct reflection of what is expected of an officer working within the department the trainee is employed by). The FTIs determine whether trainees are capable of performing their job independently. As this becomes more evident, the FTIs begin to allow the trainees more flexibility in the performance of their duties throughout their tours of duty.

Part of each day is set aside for the FTI and the trainee to discuss daily performance. The FTI will provide detailed instructions designed to guide and improve a trainee's performance. At the end of each training day, detailed documentation of a trainee's performance is recorded by the FTI on a daily activity report. At the end of each week, the trainee, FTI, and a FTO program supervisor meet to discuss the trainee's weekly progress. Meetings are also held at the end of each instruction and evaluation phase. The purpose of these meetings is to provide the trainees with an opportunity to discuss any problems or strengths and/or weaknesses they may be experiencing. Meetings also provide an avenue to check the administrative performances of the FTI so as to ensure that program standards are being properly observed and followed.

Evaluation Phases

Once a trainee completes all instructional phases, the evaluation process begins. This phase usually lasts from two to three weeks. Trainees are expected to demonstrate a degree of independence in the performance of their duties. Again, a trainee's performance is assessed in accordance with how well the trainee performed job-related skills measured against standardized performance guidelines.

Remedial Training/Evaluation

If a trainee fails to successfully complete the evaluation phase, choices are available for management to consider. First, a trainee may be dismissed, as would happen during any other portion of the selection process if performance consistently fell below minimum standards. A second more viable option is to recycle a trainee through a "remedial training" phase. This phase can last up to three weeks. The trainee is placed with a new FTI, and they concentrate on the weaknesses shown by the trainee during the previous evaluation phase. Upon completion of the remedial training phase, the trainee enters a final evaluation phase, also lasting two to three weeks. If the trainee fails to successfully complete this second evaluation phase, the trainee is terminated. Successful completion allows the trainee to complete the remaining probationary period.

Program Considerations

Despite the similarities of the various FTO programs implemented within different agencies, a number of variations have enhanced program administration as well as improving validity and reliability.

Standardized Evaluation Guidelines

A valid program must require and accomplish compliance with the use of standardized evaluation guidelines. Those guidelines include a complete description of what constitutes unacceptable and various degrees of acceptable performance. Program administrators have generally chosen to use a "graphic scaling technique" to distinguish differences in performance. The San Jose model uses a sliding numeric scale, usually beginning with the number 1, designating unacceptable performance, and ending with the number 7, designating outstanding performance.

To ensure a reasonable degree of reliability, the San Jose model uses anchor points within the graphic rating scale. On a seven-point graphic rating scale, the numbers 1, 4, and 7 are designated as "behavioral anchor points." Since performance standards are specifically described for each of the anchor points, instructors and evaluators are more easily able to match observed performances with the other non–anchor scale points (that is, 2, 3, 5, and 6).

Additional documentation is required if performance is unacceptable or outstanding. Some departments require documentation for all observed performances, regardless of the scale designation awarded. Although program administration is perceived by management to be a fair and impartial way to screen prospective police officers, trainees will sometimes challenge recommendations for dismissal or termination. A chief of police or sheriff is usually the only person authorized to dismiss a trainee and will rely heavily on documentation generated by FTIs and FPEs to discount any allegations of favoritism, bias, or prejudice lodged against the department by a trainee.

Termination Review Committees

To assist a chief of police or sheriff in making a decision to keep or dismiss a trainee, termination review committees (TRCs) have been established in some departments. Committee members, designated by the department chief/sheriff, will assume responsibility for reviewing the trainee's file. The material reviewed consists of documentation associated with the trainee's performance while being trained or evaluated. The committee's review is specifically designed to determine whether inadequacies or unfair practices adversely affected the trainee's standing within the program.

The review process includes the ability to call FTIs, FPEs, supervisors, and/or program administrators before the committee to answer questions regarding the trainee's behavior or to address accusations of bias and favoritism. This procedure strengthens checks and balances

within the program and assures the trainee of a fair and impartial review to verify the validity of a recommendation for dismissal. The TRC ultimately makes a recommendation to the chief/sheriff regarding the trainee's continued employment.

Conclusion

The most recent modification to the FTO program occurred in 1999, when the Reno (Nevada) Police Department developed a different variation that has come to be known as the Police Training Officer (PTO) Program. This program relies heavily on a "problem-based" learning method in which the teaching method is "learner-centered," compared to the "teacher-centered" San Jose model. Core competencies (skills) are measured in terms of how well a trainee performs various activities associated with substantive topics (that is, nonemergency incident responses, emergency incident responses, patrol activities, and criminal investigation). Core competencies and substantive topics are commingled to form a "learning matrix" that serves as the heart of the PTO program. Problem solving is woven throughout the program and causes the trainees to become effective critical thinkers, which is a significant improvement over the focus of the more traditional San Jose model.

TIMOTHY N. OETTMEIER

See also **Academies, Police; Community-Oriented Policing: Overview; Discretion; Ethics and Values in the Context of Community Policing; Performance Measurement; Personnel Selection; Problem-Oriented Policing**

References and Further Reading

Eisenberg, Terry. 1981. Six potential hazards inherent in developing and implementing field training officer (FTO) programs. *Police Chief Magazine*, July, 50–51.

Fagan, M. Michael. 1985. How police officers perceive their field training officer. *Journal of Police Science and Administration* 13 (July): 138–52.

Houston Police Department. 1985. *Field Training and Performance Evaluation Program: Standard operating procedures manual.* Houston, TX: Field Training and Administration Office.

———. 1986. *Field Training and Performance Evaluation Program: Termination Review Committee standard operating procedures manual.* Houston, TX: Field Training and Administration Office.

Kaminsky, Glenn, and Michael Roberts. 1985. *A model manual for the training and development of field training and evaluation program concept.* Jacksonville: University of North Florida, Institute of Police Technology and Management.

Molden, Jack. 1987. Houston is new FTO resource. *Law and Order Magazine* 35 (3): 12.

Oettmeier, Timothy N. 1982. Justifying FTO terminations. *Journal of Police Science and Administration* 10 (March): 64–73.

Pogrebin, Mark R., Eric D. Poole, Robert M. Regole, and Jeanne D. Zimmerman. 1984. A look at police agency retention and resignation: An assessment of a field training officer program. *Police Science Abstracts* 12 (Jan.–Feb.): i–iv.

U.S. Department of Justice, Community Oriented Policing Services. 2005. PTO: An overview and introduction. Project supported by Grant No. 2001-CK-WX-KO38 in conjunction with the Police Executive Research Forum.

FINGERPRINTING

The gross patterns of fingerprints, namely arches, loops, and whorls, sometimes referred to as first-level detail, are primarily employed for classification or elimination purposes. The identification of individuals by fingerprints involves instead the minutiae of fingerprint patterns, such as ridge endings, bifurcations, and so forth, called second-level detail. The locations of pores on fingerprint ridges and the very structures of ridges, referred to as third-level detail, can, if the fingerprint is of good quality, be employed for identification as well.

A fingerprint obtained from an article of evidence is compared with an inked fingerprint if a suspect is on hand. Otherwise, it is entered into the Automated Fingerprint Identification System (AFIS) to be searched against the fingerprint database. This is referred to as cold searching. Similarly, a live fingerprint may be scanned (Livescan), mostly for security purposes, and compared with the fingerprint database. We do not in this entry belabor the AFIS and Livescan computer technology but focus instead on the methods for detecting fingerprints on articles of evidence to begin with, emphasizing milestones of fingerprint detection methodology.

Current State of the Art

The detection of fingerprints for criminal identification dates back to the late 1800s. At that time, it involved mainly dusting, iodine fuming, and silver nitrate processing. A number of additional techniques were devised over the years for specialized situations, but no truly major advance occurred until 1954, when Oden and von Hofsten reported the use of ninhydrin. This compound was discovered in 1910 by Ruhemann, who recognized it as an amino acid reagent. Soon thereafter, ninhydrin became a universal reagent for amino acid assay in the bioscience community.

It is unfortunate that it took so long for ninhydrin, which since the mid-1960s has become the workhorse of chemical fingerprint detection, to enter the fingerprint arena. From the mid-1960s to the early 1980s, a number of techniques were explored, mostly in England, including among others metal deposition in vacuo and fuming with radioactive sulfur dioxide. These techniques did not reach wide use, being applicable to special instances only. Physical developer, devised in England as well in the early 1980s, targets lipids in fingerprints. It is a photographic process reminiscent of the silver nitrate treatment. It is based on the formation of silver on fingerprints from a ferrous/ferric redox couple and metal salt mixture.

Physical developer reached wide use by the late 1980s.

Of these techniques, only dusting, ninhydrin, and physical developer remain in wide use. Fingerprint visualization with these techniques involves the basic phenomena of light absorption and reflection by substances, namely the principles of ordinary everyday color or black-and-white vision. This visualization is often referred to as "colorimetric."

The year 1976 marks the advent of fingerprint detection with lasers. The basic phenomenon involved is fluorescence, also referred to as luminescence or photoluminescence. Fluorescence detection differed markedly from the absorption/reflection-based, namely colorimetric, techniques then in use. Operationally, the article of evidence is illuminated with a high-intensity light source of the appropriate color and the article is visually inspected through a filter that blocks the illumination reflected from the article but transmits the fingerprint fluorescence produced via the illumination. The examination is conducted in a darkened room to eliminate interfering ambient light. The fingerprint is literally seen to glow in the dark, much like a firefly.

The rationale for attempting to detect fingerprints by photoluminescence techniques is that such techniques, regardless of the field of science, are quite generally characterized by very high sensitivity. Initially, the fluorescence detection of fingerprints by laser involved the inherent fluorescence of fingerprint material, dusting with fluorescent powder, and staining with fluorescent dye. When a finger touches an article, only very little material is deposited on the article in the form of a latent fingerprint. Nonetheless, this fingerprint must be made to fluoresce sufficiently intensely to be visible to the naked eye, hence the high-intensity requirement for the illumination source.

Initially, high-power argon-ion lasers (blue-green) were employed. Some agencies, notably in Israel, followed with adoption of copper vapor lasers, which have a green output and a yellow output. The latter is only of limited utility for fingerprint work. By the mid-1980s, frequency doubled Nd:YAG lasers, which operate in the green at 532 nm, began to see use as well. Their powers then were low, however. The technology has since matured, such that high-power 532-nm lasers that are easy to use are on the market today. A number of agencies have adopted them for fingerprint work.

The argon-ion laser and copper vapor laser are expensive and somewhat cumbersome to use. The 532-nm lasers are expensive as well. Ordinary lamps, such as xenon arc lamps, equipped with band-pass optical filters to extract the blue-green light used mostly for fingerprint fluorescence production, were examined from the very outset as well. Such lamps began to be commercialized by the mid-1980s and are often referred to as alternate light sources or forensic light sources. They do not provide nearly the sensitivity the large lasers are capable of, but they are cheaper and easy to use. One can equip them with a range of band-pass filters for a variety of forensic examinations that do not involve fingerprint detection.

In the early days of fingerprint detection with lasers, there was a need for a chemical fingerprint detection procedure that would lend itself to fluorescence visualization in order for the fluorescence approach to be a universal one, capable of detecting fingerprints, fresh or old, on porous items such as paper. Ruhemann's purple (RP), namely the product of the reaction of ninhydrin with amino acid, is not fluorescent, which is unfortunate given the wide use of ninhydrin for fingerprint work. The remedy came in 1982 with the discovery that a simple follow-on treatment with zinc chloride after ninhydrin would convert the nonfluorescent RP to a highly fluorescent complex, thus greatly increasing the sensitivity of ninhydrin.

In the early 1980s, efforts began, most notably in Israel, to synthesize ninhydrin analogs that would have the same chemical reactivity as ninhydrin but that would have superior colorimetric or fluorescence (in concert with zinc chloride) properties. Benzo(f)ninhydrin in particular, first synthesized by Almog and coworkers in Israel, was found, in concert with zinc chloride, to be very nicely tailored to the 532-nm laser, whereas ninhydrin/zinc chloride is not very effective with this illumination, being tailored, instead, to the argon-ion laser. In 1988, Pounds reported the use of 1,8-diazafluoren-9-one (DFO) for the fluorescence detection of fingerprints on paper. This reagent has since been adopted by many fingerprint examiners as an alternative to ninhydrin/zinc chloride. In 1998, 1,2-indanediones were reported for fluorescence detection of fingerprints. These compounds resemble ninhydrin but their reaction chemistry with amino acid differs from that of ninhydrin. There are claims that 1,2-indanedione is the most sensitive amino acid reagent yet devised for the fluorescence detection of fingerprints.

In the early days of laser fingerprint detection, old fingerprints on smooth surfaces, such as plastics, that might not be amenable to dusting, posed considerable problems. Development of such prints by staining with fluorescent dye proved tricky in that the dye solution tended to wash fingerprints away, as would solutions of chemical reagents. The situation changed for the better with the advent of cyanoacrylate ester fuming (Super Glue fuming). This material polymerizes on fingerprints to stabilize them. A white polymer is formed by which the fingerprint becomes visible. The technique was first devised in 1978 by the Japanese National Police Agency and was subsequently introduced to the United States by latent print examiners of the U.S. Army Criminal Investigation Laboratory in Japan and of the Bureau of Alcohol, Tobacco and Firearms.

From the fluorescence perspective, cyanoacrylate ester fuming is marvelously compatible with subsequent fluorescent dye staining and laser examination. The dye intercalates within voids of the polymer. Very high sensitivity gain over the Super Glue fuming alone is realized. A number of fuming procedures have been developed, including heat acceleration, chemical acceleration, and, most recently, fuming in a vacuum chamber. With the latter, the formed polymer tends to be colorless rather than white. Thus, the vacuum fuming is invariably followed by fluorescent dye staining.

In the late 1980s, fingerprint detection by reflective ultraviolet imaging systems (RUVIS) was developed, first in Japan. The light source typically is deep ultraviolet, namely a mercury lamp operating at 254 nm. When a fingerprint is located on a smooth surface, the ultraviolet light is specularly reflected from it but diffusely from the fingerprint. The article is inspected through a camera or night vision goggle that converts the UV light—invisible to the eye—to visible light via an image intensifier. The illumination is at a suitable angle such that the image intensifier only sees the diffuse reflectance (from the fingerprint). RUVIS is a variant of oblique lighting, long used for shoeprint examination, for instance. RUVIS is expensive, cumbersome, and useful only in special instances and thus is not widely employed.

Fluorescence represents the most sensitive approach to fingerprint detection currently available, and it is the approach of choice, especially in serious cases. Inherent fingerprint fluorescence, dusting with fluorescent powder, staining with fluorescent dye after Super Glue, and chemical development with ninhydrin/zinc chloride, DFO, or 1,2-indanedione are the bread-and-butter routine procedures. They have amply proved their mettle in worldwide use.

Meanwhile, fluorescence approaches have spilled over into other areas of forensic analysis, such as the detection of elusive fibers, body fluids (mostly semen), or bone and tooth fragments and the examination of documents for erasures, alterations, obliterations, or the like. Indeed, the labeling of DNA, which early on involved radioactive tags, now makes use of fluorescent tags as well. As a result of concern with terrorism, fluorescence is beginning to find its way into field methods for the detection of traces of explosives and nerve agents. It is safe to say that fluorescence methodology has become a new paradigm in forensic analysis.

Future Developments

Fluorescence techniques, though generally very sensitive, suffer from a major difficulty, namely that of background fluorescence. In the fingerprint context, that background would come from the article on which the fingerprint is located. Background fluorescences are ubiquitous and often so intense that they completely mask the fingerprint luminescence. Moreover, they frequently are spectrally very broad, such that there is a background component of the same luminescence color as that of the fingerprint. Thus, optical filtering is ineffective.

To make fingerprints detectable by fluorescence under these conditions, time-resolved techniques can be employed. Their details are left to the references. The feasibility of time-resolved fingerprint imaging was demonstrated by Menzel as early as 1979, but the technology to produce a practical instrument was not available then. Worse still, a range of fingerprint treatments that would produce luminescences with long lifetimes, as required in time-resolved imaging, did not exist either. With the advent of microchannel plate image intensifiers in the mid-1980s, it became possible to construct instruments that had practicality potential. By the early 1990s, the instrumentation issue was largely under control. The accompanying fingerprint treatment issue took longer to come to grips with. By the late 1980s, researchers began to gravitate toward europium-based fingerprint treatments because europium luminesces with an exceptionally long lifetime. By the mid-1990s, luminescent europium powders and staining dyes had materialized.

The chemical development of fingerprints, akin to ninhydrin, especially for old fingerprints, was more recalcitrant. That chemistry is now in hand as well, using SYPRO Rose Plus Protein Blot Stain, although, no doubt, improvements in europium-based chemical fingerprint processing remain desirable.

Although much progress has been made in the time-resolved methodology, several factors have so far mitigated against its adoption by law enforcement. The main one is the complexity of the instrumentation, which calls for a highly trained operator. Instrument cost is an issue as well. Furthermore, specialized fingerprint treatments pertain that otherwise would not be used.

An instrumentation design change reported in 2004 by Menzel and Menzel makes for a system that is much simpler and cheaper than the earlier ones, and even shows portability potential. The expensive computer controlled intensified and gateable CCD camera of earlier instruments is eliminated altogether and is replaced by the human eye for the observation of the time-resolved fingerprint. Most any garden variety photographic camera can then be employed for the recording of the fingerprint. The system still uses a laser, but one can foresee a further simplification and cost saving by replacing the laser with an electronically controlled array of light-emitting diodes (LEDs). The LED technology has matured greatly in recent years, such that such controlled arrays are now available. One can thus envision miniaturizing the instrument to where it may be worn at the crime scene, much like night vision goggles. It should be emphasized, though, that the instrumentation is still wedded to the europium-based fingerprint treatment strategy.

Even though the time-resolved fluorescence detection of fingerprints is not entirely mature yet, there is little doubt that in time it will become part of the fingerprint examiner's arsenal.

E. ROLAND MENZEL

See also **Forensic Evidence; Forensic Investigations; Forensic Science**

References and Further Reading

Bouldin, K. K., and E. R. Menzel. 2002. Latent fingerprint detection with SYPRO Rose Plus protein stain. *The Scientific World Journal* 2: 242–45. http://www.thescientific-world.com/SCIENTIFICWORLDJOUR-NAL/main/Home.asp.

Dalrymple, B. E., J. M. Duff, and E. R. Menzel. 1977. Inherent fingerprint luminescence: Detection by laser. *Journal of Forensic Sciences* 22: 106–15.

Hauze, D. B., O. G. Petrowskaia, B. Taylor, M. M. Joullie, R. Ramotowski, and A. A. Cantu. 1998. 1,2-indanediones: New reagents for visualizing the amino acid components of latent prints. *Journal of Forensic Sciences* 43: 744–54.

Herod, D. W., and E. R. Menzel. 1982. Laser detection of latent fingerprints: Ninhydrin followed by zinc chloride. *Journal of Forensic Sciences* 27: 513–18.

Lee, H. C., and R. D. Gaensslen, eds. 1991. *Advances in fingerprint technology*. New York: Elsevier; 2nd ed. Boca Raton, FL: CRC Press, 2001.

Lock, E. R. A., W. D. Mazella, and P. Margot. 1995. A new europium chelate as a fluorescent dye—cyanoacrylate pretreated fingerprints—EuTTAPhen: Europium thenoyltrifluoroacetone-ortho-phenanthroline. *Journal of Forensic Sciences* 40: 654–58.

Menzel, E. R. 1980. *Fingerprint detection with lasers*. New York: Marcel Dekker; 2nd ed., 1999.

Menzel, E. R., and J. Almog. 1985. Latent fingerprint development by frequency-doubled neodymium: yttrium aluminum garnet (Nd:YAG) laser: Benzo(f)ninhydrin. *Journal of Forensic Sciences* 30: 371–82.

Menzel, E. R., and L. W. Menzel. 2004. Ordinary and time-resolved photoluminescence field detection of traces of explosives and fingerprints. *Journal of Forensic Identification* 54: 560–71.

Menzel, E. R., and K. E. Mitchell. 1990. Intramolecular energy transfer in the europium–Ruhemann's purple complex: Application to latent fingerprint detection. *Journal of Forensic Sciences* 35: 35–45.

Menzel, E. R., J. A. Burt, T. W. Sinor, W. B. Tubach-Ley, and K. J. Jordan. 1983. Laser detection of latent fingerprints: Treatment with glue containing cyanoacrylate ester. *Journal of Forensic Sciences* 28: 307–17.

Menzel, E. R., L. W. Menzel, and J. R. Schwierking. 2004. A photoluminescence-based field method for detection of traces of explosives. *The Scientific World JOURNAL* 4: 725–35. http://www.thescientific-world.com/SCIENTIFICWORLDJOUR-NAL/main/Home.asp (open access article).

Oden, S., and B. von Hofsten. 1954. Detection of fingerprints by the ninhydrin reaction. *Nature* 173: 449–50.

Olsen, R. D., Sr. 1978. *Scott's fingerprint mechanics*. Springfield, IL: Charles C Thomas.

Pounds, C. A. 1988. Developments in fingerprint visualization. In *Forensic Science Progress*, ed. Maehly and Williams, 91–119. Berlin: Springer Verlag.

Ruhemann, S. 1910. Triketohydrindene hydrate. *Journal of the Chemical Society* 97: 2025–31.

Schwierking, J. R., L. W. Menzel, and E. R. Menzel. 2004. Organophosphate nerve agent detection with europium complexes. *The Scientific World Journal* 4: 948–55. http://www.thescientificworld.com/SCIEN-TIFICWORLDJOURNAL/main/Home. asp (open access article).

FIREARMS AVAILABILITY AND HOMICIDE RATES

The question of whether firearms availability helps cause homicides is important for two reasons. First, scholars want to understand why homicide rates differ over space and time, and access to guns may partly account for the patterns. Firearms are then one of many factors that might explain variations in the rates, making the relationship a matter of theoretical interest.

Second, and more controversially, the link between firearms and homicides has a bearing on gun control policies. If widespread gun ownership promotes lethal violence, stricter regulations may lead to fewer murders. If gun availability does not affect homicides, gun control laws will be of only symbolic value. Knowing that people have ready access to guns might even deter some potential killers, and tighter restrictions could endanger public safety.

No doubt exists that many murderers use firearms—usually handguns—to commit their crimes. Currently, guns are the instruments of death in about 65% of homicides in the United States. In 2002, firearms accounted for more than nine thousand killings in the nation, with seven thousand of these due to handguns (Federal Bureau of Investigation 2002a).

Homicides of police officers are even more likely to involve firearms than homicides of other citizens. Between 1993 and 2002, gunshot wounds claimed the lives of 93% of all law enforcement officers murdered in the line of duty (Federal Bureau of Investigation 2002b). Lester (1987) shows that the risk of firearm murder for a city police officer rises with the gun murder rate in the city at large.

Despite these figures, it does not necessarily follow that gun ownership levels influence homicidal violence. Homicide rates may depend mostly on the number of persons who wish to kill. If guns were not handy, murderers might simply switch to other weapons.

Two issues have received special attention in studying the impact of gun availability on murder. The first of these is a theory to explain how firearm ownership levels might affect homicide rates. The second is how much association exists between the two variables.

Weapon Choice Theory

The mechanism most often used to link firearm ownership to homicides is the weapon choice theory proposed by Zimring (1968; Zimring and Hawkins 1997). The theory rests on the idea that murderers often do not set out with a desire to kill. A robbery goes awry, for example, or an argument spirals into violence. The offender attacks the victim with whatever weapon is at hand, ending the assault after causing injury. The victim's fate then depends heavily on the weapon. If the weapon is highly lethal, it is more likely that the victim will die.

According to the weapon choice theory, shootings are more deadly than are other methods of attack. If fewer guns were available, the offender would not be as likely to have one and would use a less effective weapon instead, reducing the chances of death.

The theory assumes that people who are bent on killing can find guns if they make enough effort. Yet they must make more effort when firearms are less available, and fewer assailants will have a gun nearby if general levels of ownership are low.

The weapon choice theory suggests that lower rates of firearm ownership will not change the total amount of criminal violence. Violent persons can, and will, use other weapons. Still, if these weapons are not as dangerous as guns, assaults will not as often end as murders.

Evaluation of the Weapon Choice Theory

The weapon choice theory claims that guns are especially lethal instruments and that homicides are often unintentional. There is little question about the first point. In Zimring's (1968) study, the death rate for persons attacked with guns was five times higher than the death rate for persons attacked with knives.

It is not as easy to estimate how many murderers lack a firm wish to kill. This depends on motivations, and motivations can be elusive. Scattered evidence does suggest that criminal shootings are often a matter of chance. In one research project, Wright and Rossi (1986) surveyed a sample of felons about the weapons they used. Of the felons who had fired a gun during a crime, only 23% said that they had originally planned to do so.

These and other data measure motivations after the fact, and this part of the theory probably will remain arguable. The theory also does not consider the role that armed citizens might play in discouraging violent attacks. Due to issues such as these, the effect of firearm ownership on homicides must be found empirically.

Evidence on the Relationship between Firearm Availability and Homicides

Figure 1 plots homicides per hundred thousand residents of the United States and new firearms offered for sale per thousand residents. The data are annual, between 1950 and 1999. Both variables follow similar trends, with changes in the homicide rate roughly mirroring changes in the stock of new guns.

This comparison suggests that the relationship between firearm ownership and homicides deserves additional study. By itself, however, it is not enough to show that rising levels of gun availability lead to increases in murder. This is so for three reasons.

First, the number of firearms in private hands is difficult to measure. Estimates of available guns in the United States vary widely, and useful figures do not exist for areas smaller than the entire nation. Figure 1 uses new guns, and homicides may also involve firearms that people obtained in earlier years. Guns wear out over time, and no one knows how many older weapons remain in service.

Second, firearm ownership may depend partly on the same social conditions that generate homicide rates. To take only one example, attitudes favorable to violence may lead to higher levels of gun access and also to higher rates of murder. As far as this is so, the association between gun ownership and homicides exists only because of common causes.

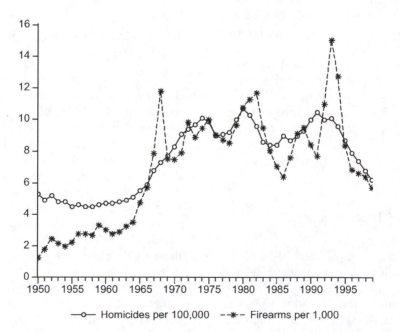

— o — Homicides per 100,000   - * - Firearms per 1,000

Figure 1   Homicides per hundred thousand and new firearm per thousand in the United States, 1950–1999.

Third, much firearm ownership may be a response to crime. That is, people may obtain guns to protect themselves as homicide rates rise. Then the two variables will be correlated because homicides help cause the demand for guns.

Many studies have considered the link between gun availability and homicides, and most have tried to deal with one or more of these problems. No study has satisfied all critics, and not all findings are in accord (Hemenway 2004; Kleck 1997). The bulk of this research nevertheless points in the same direction.

Studies of the Entire United States or of U.S. States

Several studies examine the stock of firearms and homicide rates in the entire United States or in individual states. As in Figure 1, they measure gun availability using data on firearm sales or production.

Examples are Kleck (1984), Magaddino and Medoff (1984), and Sorenson and Berk (2001). Each study included controls for common causes of gun availability and murders. Kleck and Magaddino and Medoff also considered whether homicide rates affected ownership levels. Except for Kleck, these researchers all found that increases in homicides accompanied increases in the supply of guns.

Studies that use production or sales figures must allow for the average lifetime of a firearm. Any estimate is no more than a guess, and errors here may affect the conclusions. In addition, murder rates are highest in large cities, but firearms are most common in rural areas. Findings for the nation or states may then rest on false correlations between crimes committed in urban areas and gun ownership in rural areas.

Studies of Cities and Counties in the United States

A second set of studies considers the association between firearms and homicides in U.S. cities or counties. These smaller areas avoid some of the problems with using the nation or states, but no accurate counts of gun owners exist for them. The city and county studies must therefore gauge firearm availability from indirect indicators. Common indicators include the fraction of robberies committed with guns, the fraction of suicides committed with guns, and sales of gun-oriented magazines. The values of these indicators presumably increase with levels of ownership.

Research that uses this approach includes Cook (1979), Duggan (2001), Kleck and Patterson (1993), and McDowall (1991). Each study controlled for common causes of firearm ownership and homicide, and Duggan, Kleck, and Patterson, and McDowall allowed for a mutual relationship between the two variables. Cook found that city robbery-murder rates rose with the volume of available guns. Duggan found that availability predicted homicide rates in a sample of counties, and McDowall found that availability influenced homicide rates in Detroit. In contrast, Kleck and Patterson concluded that gun ownership was unrelated to the murder rates of the cities that they examined.

These studies assume that firearm availability in a city or county depends on how often its residents use guns. Yet no indicator of use will be a completely satisfactory measure. One limitation is that most indicators focus on violent acts, and so they may have only a weak relationship to the number of responsible owners.

Employing a different strategy, a highly publicized study by Lott (2000) compared homicide rates before and after states relaxed their laws on carrying concealed weapons. Lott found that homicides fell after the laws began, and he argued that this was due to easier access to guns by honest citizens. Yet his study did not measure actual changes in available guns, and critics have serious doubts about its conclusions (Hemenway 2004).

International Studies

A third approach compares murder rates in nations that differ in their amount of access to firearms. In one study of this type, Killias (1993) used survey data to estimate gun ownership in fourteen nations. Ownership levels ranged from very high (the United States) to very low (the Netherlands), and homicides increased with ownership. Hemenway and Miller (2000) likewise correlated measures of firearm availability with homicide rates in twenty-six nations. As with Killias, they found that nations with higher gun availability had higher homicide rates.

Killias, von Kesteren, and Rindlisbacher (2001) used the same procedures as Killias, but they expanded the number of nations they examined to twenty-one. Unlike the original Killias study, their results showed little connection between gun ownership and homicide rates. This difference was mainly due to the presence of Estonia in the second study. Estonia had low levels of ownership, and its crime rates had surged after the breakup of the Soviet Union.

The fragile findings show a general problem with the international research: Only a few observations exist, and unusual cases can skew the results. Culture and history also complicate the comparisons, because both gun ownership and homicide are due in part to features unique to a nation. These features are hard to measure, and the small number of countries makes it difficult to control them.

Magnitude and Implications of the Relationship

Although the findings are not entirely consistent, studies using different methods largely agree that homicide rates rise as firearms become more available. Importantly, however, the sizes of the associations are often small. McDowall (1991) estimated that Detroit's 1986 homicide rate would have been 4% lower if access to guns had been at 1980 levels. Yet even then, the city's 1986 rate would have been a 45% increase above its 1980 value. Cook's (1979) results showed that a 10% decrease in gun availability would reduce a city's rate of robbery-murder by only 4%. This broadly agrees with Duggan (2001), who found that a 10% drop in county gun ownership would reduce total homicide rates by 2%.

Firearm availability may therefore have only a relatively modest impact on murder rates. The United States has many guns, and only a tiny fraction of owners use them in criminal violence. This makes it hard to find effective prevention policies, and it ensures that restrictive gun control laws will be controversial.

DAVID MCDOWALL

See also **Crime Control Strategies: Gun Control; Firearms: Guns and the Gun Culture; Firearms Regulation and Control**

References and Further Reading

Cook, Philip J. 1979. The effect of gun availability on robbery and robbery murder: A cross section study of fifty cities. In *Policy Studies Review Annual*, vol. 3, ed. Robert H. Haveman and B. Bruce Zellner, 743–81. Beverly Hills, CA: Sage.

Duggan, Mark. 2001. More guns, more crime. *Journal of Political Economy* 109:1086–1114.

Federal Bureau of Investigation. 2002a. *Crime in the United States*. Washington, DC: U.S. Government Printing Office.

———. 2002b. *Law enforcement officers killed and assaulted*. Washington, DC: U.S. Government Printing Office.

Hemenway, David. 2004. *Private guns, public health*. Ann Arbor: University of Michigan Press.

Hemenway, David, and Matthew Miller. 2000. Firearm availability and homicide rates across twenty-six high-income countries. *Journal of Trauma* 49: 985–88.

Killias, Martin. 1993. International correlations between gun ownership and rates of homicide and suicide. *Canadian Medical Association Journal* 148: 1721–25.

Killias, Martin, John van Kesteren, and Martin Rindlisbacher. 2001. Guns, violent crime, and suicide in 21 countries. *Canadian Journal of Criminology* 429–48.

Kleck, Gary. 1984. The relationship between gun ownership levels and rates of violence in the United States. In *Firearms and violence: Issues of public policy*, ed. Don B. Kates, 99–135. Cambridge, MA: Ballinger.

———. 1997. *Targeting guns: Firearms and their control*. New York: Aldine De Gruyter.

Kleck, Gary, and E. Britt Patterson. 1993. The impact of gun control and gun ownership levels on violence rates. *Journal of Quantitative Criminology* 9: 249–87.

Lester, David. 1987. The police as victims: The role of guns in the murder of police. *Psychological Reports* 60: 366.

Lott, John R., Jr. 2000. *More guns, less crime: Understanding crime and gun-control laws*, 2nd ed. Chicago: University of Chicago Press.

Magaddino, Joseph P., and Marshall H. Medoff. 1984. An empirical analysis of federal and state firearm control laws. In *Firearms and violence: Issues of public policy*, ed. Don B. Kates, 225–58. Cambridge, MA: Ballinger.

McDowall, David. 1991. Firearm availability and homicide rates in Detroit, 1951–1986. *Social Forces* 69: 1085–1101.

Sorenson, Susan B., and Richard A. Berk. 2001. Handgun sales, beer sales, and youth homicide, California, 1972–1993. *Journal of Public Health Policy* 22: 182–97.

Wright, James D., and Peter H. Rossi. 1986. *Armed and considered dangerous: A survey of felons and their firearms*. New York: Aldine de Gruyter.

Zimring, Franklin E. 1968. Is gun control likely to reduce violent killings? *University of Chicago Law Review* 35: 721–37.

Zimring, Franklin E., and Gordon Hawkins. 1997. *Crime is not the problem: Lethal violence in America*. New York: Oxford University Press.

FIREARMS: GUNS AND THE GUN CULTURE

Guns are versatile tools, useful in providing meat for the table, eliminating varmints and pests, providing entertainment for those who have learned to enjoy the sporting uses, and protecting life and property against criminal predators, so their broad appeal is not surprising (Cook, Moore, and Braga 2002). They are an especially common feature of rural life, where wild animals provide both a threat and an opportunity for sport. As America has become more urban and more violent, however, the demand for guns has become increasingly motivated by the need for protection against other people (Cook, Moore, and Braga 2002).

Gun enthusiasts are sometimes portrayed by the media as "nuts," "sexually-warped fetishists," "vigilantes," and "anti-citizens" (Kates 1997, 9). Research on gun owners, however, reveals that they are not more likely to be racist, sexist, or violence prone than non–gun owners (Kleck 1991). Only a small fraction of privately owned firearms are ever involved in crime or unlawful violence (Kleck 1991). For many Americans, guns are an integral and essential part of their identity. Guns are revered as a liberator and guarantor of freedom; guns symbolize independence and self-reliance (Slotkin 2003). For many young men, guns can be a symbol of masculinity, status, aggressiveness, danger, and arousal (Fagan and Wilkinson 1998). Not surprisingly, gun owners are more likely to approve of "defensive force" to defend victims when compared to their non–gun owning counterparts (Kates 1997).

The gun culture plays a central role in the contentious American debate on guns and gun control. Three key areas provide important insights on the role the gun culture plays in the larger gun debate: gun ownership patterns, the Second Amendment and the "rights and responsibilities" perspective, and the uses of guns for self-defense.

Patterns of Gun Ownership

The 1994 National Survey of the Private Ownership of Firearms (NSPOF) by the National Opinion Research Center found that 41% of American households included at least one firearm. Approximately 29% of adults say that they personally own a gun. These percentages reflect an apparent decline in the prevalence of gun ownership since the 1970s (Cook and Ludwig 1996). While the prevalence of gun ownership has declined, it appears that the number of guns in private hands has been increasing rapidly. Since 1970, total sales of new guns have accounted for more than half of all the guns sold during this century, and the total now in circulation is on the order of two hundred million (Cook and Ludwig 1996).

How can this volume of sales be reconciled with the decline in the prevalence of ownership? Part of the answer is in the growth in population (and the more rapid growth in the number of households) during this period; millions of new guns were required to arm the baby boom cohorts. Beyond that is the likelihood that the average gun owner has increased the size of his or her collection (Wright 1981). The NSPOF estimates that gun-owning households average 4.4 guns, up substantially from the 1970s (Cook and Ludwig 1996). Kleck (1991), however, suggests that the true prevalence trended upward during the past couple of decades and that survey respondents have become increasingly reluctant to admit to gun ownership during this period.

One addition for many gun-owning households has been a handgun. The significance of this trend toward increased handgun ownership lies in the fact that while rifles and shotguns are acquired primarily for sporting purposes, handguns are primarily intended for use against people, either in crime or self-defense. The increase in handgun prevalence corresponds to a large increase in the relative importance of handguns in retail sales: Since the early 1970s, the handgun fraction of new-gun sales has increased from one-third to near one-half (Cook 1993). The Bureau of Alcohol, Tobacco, Firearms and Explosives (ATF) estimated that one out of every two new guns sold in the United States in the early 1990s was a handgun. In the late 1990s, the handgun share of all new gun sales decreased to about 40% (ATF 2000).

Some of the increased handgun sales have been to urban residents who have no experience with guns but are convinced they need one for self-protection, as suggested by the surges in handgun sales after the Los Angeles riots and other such events (Kellerman and Cook 1999). But while the prevalence of handgun ownership has increased substantially during the past three decades, it remains true now as in 1959 that most who possess a handgun also own one or more rifles and shotguns. The 1994 National Survey of the Private Ownership of Firearms found that just 20.4% of gun-owning individuals have only handguns, while 35.6% have only long guns and 43.5% have both.

These statistics suggest that people who have acquired guns for self-protection are for the most part also hunters and target shooters. Indeed, only 46% of gun owners say that they own a gun *primarily* for self-protection against crime, and only 26% keep a gun loaded. Most (80%) grew up in a house with a gun. The demographic patterns of gun ownership are no surprise: Most owners are men, and the men who are most likely to own a gun reside in rural areas or small towns and were reared in such small places (Kleck 1991). The regional pattern gives the highest prevalence to the states of the Mountain Census Region, followed by the South and Midwest. Blacks are less likely to own guns than whites, in part because the black population is more urban. The likelihood of gun ownership increases with income and age.

The fact that guns fit much more comfortably into rural life than urban life raises a question. In 1940, 49% of teenagers were living in rural areas; by 1960, that had dropped to 34% and by 1990, to 27%. What will happen to gun ownership patterns as new generations with less connection to rural life come along? Hunting is already on the decline: The absolute number of hunting licenses issued in 1990 was about the same as in 1970 despite the growth in population, indicating a decline in the percentage of people who hunt (Cook, Moore, and Braga 2002). Confirming evidence comes from the National Survey of Wildlife-Associated Recreation, which found that 7.2% of adults age sixteen and above were hunters in 1990, compared with 8.9% in 1970. This trend may eventually erode the importance of the rural sporting culture that has dominated the gun "scene." In its place is an ever greater focus on the criminal and self-defense uses of guns (Cook, Moore, and Braga 2002).

The Second Amendment and the "Rights and Responsibilities" Perspective on Guns

Very much in the foreground of the debate on guns and gun control lies the Second Amendment, which states, "A well regulated Militia, being necessary to the security of a free State, the right of the people to keep and bear Arms, shall not be infringed." The proper interpretation of this statement has been contested in recent years. Scholars arguing the constitutionality of gun control measures focus on the militia clause and conclude that this is a right given to state governments (Vernick and Teret 1999). Others assert that the right is given to "the people" rather than to the states, just as are the rights conferred in the First Amendment, and that the Founding Fathers were very much committed to the notion of an armed citizenry as a defense against both tyranny and crime (Kates 1992; Halbrook 1986).

The Supreme Court has not chosen to clarify the matter, having ruled only once during this century on a Second Amendment issue, and that on a rather narrow technical basis. William Van Alstyne (1994) argues that the Second Amendment has generated almost no useful body of law to date, substantially because of the Supreme Court's inertia on the subject. In his view, Second Amendment law is currently as

undeveloped as First Amendment law was up until Holmes and Brandeis began taking it seriously in a series of opinions in the 1920s. Indeed, no federal court has ever overturned a gun control law on Second Amendment grounds.

Regardless of the concerns that motivated our founding fathers in crafting the Bill of Rights, the notion that private possession of pistols and rifles is a protection against tyranny may strike the modern reader as anachronistic—or perhaps all too contemporary when recent events with such groups as the Branch Davidians and the Aryan Nation are considered. Much more compelling for many people is the importance of protecting the capacity for self-defense against criminals. Some commentators go so far as to assert that there is a public duty for private individuals to defend against criminal predation, now just as there was in 1789 (when there were no police).

The idea that citizens have responsibility for their own self-defense is now widely embraced by police executives and is central to the "community policing" strategy, which seeks to establish a close working partnership between the police and the community. But the emphasis in this approach is on community-building activities such as the formation of block watch groups or neighborhood patrols, rather than on individual armaments. The argument is that if all reliable people were to equip themselves with guns both in the home and out, there would be far less predatory crime (Snyder 1993; Polsby 1993).

Other commentators, less sanguine about the possibility of creating a more civil society by force of arms, also stress the public duty of gun owners, but with an emphasis on responsible use: storing them safely away from children and burglars, learning how to operate them properly, exercising good judgment in deploying them when feeling threatened, and so forth (Karlson and Hartgarten 1997). In any event, the right to bear arms, like the right of free speech, is not absolute but is subject to reasonable restrictions and carries with it certain civic responsibilities. The appropriate extent of those restrictions and responsibilities, however, remains an unresolved issue.

Self-Defense Uses of Guns

While guns do enormous damage in crime, they also provide some crime victims with the means of escaping serious injury or property loss (Cook, Moore, and Braga 2002). The National Crime Victimization Survey (NCVS) is generally considered the most reliable source of information on predatory crime, since it has been in the field for more than two decades and incorporates the best thinking of survey methodologists. From this source it would appear that use of guns in self-defense against criminal predation is rather rare, occurring on the order of a hundred thousand times per year (Cook, Ludwig, and Hemenway 1997).

Of particular interest is the likelihood that a gun will be used in self-defense against an intruder. Cook (1991), using the NCVS data, found that only 3% of victims were able to deploy a gun against someone who broke in (or attempted to do so) while they were at home. Since 40% of all households have a gun, it is quite rare for victims to be able to deploy a gun against intruders even when they have one handy.

Gary Kleck and Marc Gertz (1995) have suggested a far higher estimate of 2.5 million self-defense uses each year and conclude that guns are used more commonly in self-defense than in crime. However, Cook, Ludwig, and Hemenway (1997) have demonstrated that Kleck and Gertz's high estimate may result from problems inherent in their research design. There is also no clear sense of how many homicides were justifiable in the sense of being committed in self-defense (Kleck 1991).

Of course, even if we had reliable estimates on the volume of such events, we would want to know more before reaching any conclusion. It is quite possible that most "self-defense" uses occur in circumstances that are normatively ambiguous: chronic violence within a marriage, gang fights, robberies of drug dealers, or encounters with groups of young men who simply *appear* threatening (Cook, Moore, and Braga 2002). In one survey of convicted felons in prison, the most common reason offered for carrying a gun was self-defense (Wright and Rossi 1986); a similar finding emerged from a study of juveniles incarcerated for serious criminal offenses (Smith 1996). Self-defense conjures up an image of the innocent victim using a gun to fend off an unprovoked criminal assault, but in fact many "self-defense" cases may not be so commendable (Cook, Moore, and Braga 2002).

The intimidating power of a gun may help explain the effectiveness of using one in self-defense. According to one study of NCVS data, in burglaries of occupied dwellings only 5% of victims who used guns in self-defense were injured, compared with 25% of those who resisted with other weapons (Cook 1991). Other studies have confirmed that victims of predatory crime who are able to resist with a gun are generally successful in thwarting the crime and avoiding injury (Kleck 1988; McDowall, Loftin, and Wiersema 1992). But the interpretation of this result is open to some question. Self-defense with a gun is a rare event in crimes such as burglary and robbery, and the cases where the victim does use a gun differ from others in ways that help account for the differential success of the gun defense. In particular, other means of defense usually are attempted after the assailant threatens or attacks the victim, whereas those who use guns in self-defense are relatively likely to be the first to threaten or use force (McDowall, Loftin, and Wiersema 1992). Given this difference in the sequence of events, and the implied difference in the competence or intentions of the perpetrator, the proper interpretation of the statistical evidence concerning weapon-specific success rates in self-defense is unclear (Cook 1991).

The ability of law-abiding citizens to be armed in public has been facilitated in recent years by changes in a number of state laws governing licensing to carry a concealed weapon, and by 1997 a majority of states had liberal provisions that enable most adults to obtain a license to carry firearms. A controversial study (Lott and Mustard 1997; Lott 2000) found evidence that states that liberalized their concealed-carry regulations enjoyed a reduction in violent crime rates as a result, presumably because some would-be assailants were deterred by the increased likelihood that their victim would be armed. However, other researchers, using the same data, conclude that there is no evidence of a deterrent effect (see Ludwig 2000 for a comprehensive review).

Many analysts are also skeptical of the deterrent effects of easing concealed-carry laws because the prevalence of carrying by likely victims is too small (less than 2% of adult residents) to generate the very large effects on homicide and rape suggested by the Lott studies (Cook, Moore, and Braga 2002). Given the available evidence, it is difficult to make firm conclusions about the effects of these laws on preventing crime.

ANTHONY A. BRAGA

See also **Crime Control Strategies: Gun Control; Firearms Availability and Homicide Rates; Firearms: History; Firearms Regulation and Control; Firearms Tracing**

References and Further Reading

Bureau of Alcohol, Tobacco, Firearms and Explosives (ATF). 2000. *Commerce Firearms in the United States.* Washington, DC: Bureau of Alcohol, Tobacco, Firearms and Explosives.

Cook, Philip J. 1991. The technology of personal violence. In *Crime and justice: A review of research,* vol. 14, ed. Michael Tonry, 1–72. Chicago: University of Chicago Press.

———. 1993. Notes on the availability and prevalence of firearms. *American Journal of Preventive Medicine* 9: 33–38.

Cook, Philip J., and Jens Ludwig. 1996. *Guns in America: Results of a comprehensive national survey on firearms ownership and use.* Washington, DC: Police Foundation.

Cook, Philip J., Jens Ludwig, and David Hemenway. 1997. The gun debate's new mythical number: How many defensive gun uses per year? *Journal of Policy Analysis and Management* 16: 463–69.

Cook, Philip J., Mark H. Moore, and Anthony A. Braga. 2002. Gun control. In *Crime: Public policies for crime control,* ed. James Q. Wilson and Joan Petersilia, 291–330. Oakland, CA: Institute for Contemporary Studies Press.

Fagan, Jeffrey, and Deanna Wilkinson. 1998. Guns, youth violence, and social identity in inner cities. In *Youth violence, crime and justice,* vol. 24, ed. Michael Tonry and Mark H. Moore. Chicago: University of Chicago Press.

Halbrook, Stephen P. 1986. What the framers intended: A linguistic analysis of the right to "bear arms." *Law and Contemporary Problems* 49: 151–62.

Karlson, Trudy A., and Stephen W. Hargarten. 1997. *Reducing firearms injury and death: A public health sourcebook on guns.* New Brunswick, NJ: Rutgers University Press.

Kates, Don B., Jr. 1992. The Second Amendment and the ideology of self-protection. *Constitutional Commentary* 9: 87–104.

———. 1997. Gun control and crime rates: Introduction. In *The great American gun debate,* ed. Don B. Kates and Gary Kleck. San Francisco: Pacific Research Institute for Public Policy.

Kellerman, Arthur, and Philip J. Cook. 1999. Armed and dangerous: Guns in American homes. In *Lethal imagination: Violence and brutality in American history,* ed. Michael Bellesiles, 425–40. New York: New York University Press.

Kleck, Gary. 1988. Crime control through the private use of armed force. *Social Problems* 35: 1–22.

———. 1991. *Point blank: Guns and violence in America.* New York: Aldine de Gruyter.

Kleck, Gary, and Marc Gertz. 1995. Armed resistance to crime: The prevalence and nature of self-defense with a gun. *Journal of Criminal Law and Criminology* 86: 150–87.

Lott, John. 2000. *More guns, less crime,* 2nd ed. Chicago: University of Chicago Press.

Lott, John, and David Mustard. 1997. Crime, deterrence, and the right-to-carry concealed handguns. *Journal of Legal Studies* 26: 1–68.

Ludwig, Jens. 2000. Gun self-defense and deterrence. In *Crime and justice: A review of research*, vol. 27, ed. Michael Tonry, 363–418. Chicago: University of Chicago Press.

McDowall, David, Colin Loftin, and Brian Wiersema. 1992. *The incidence of civilian defensive firearm use*. College Park: University of Maryland, Department of Criminology and Criminal Justice.

Polsby, Daniel D. 1993. Equal protection. *Reason* 10: 35–38.

Slotkin, Gary. 2003. Equalizers: The cult of the Colt in American culture. In *Guns, crime, and punishment in America*, ed. Bernard Harcourt. New York: New York University Press.

Smith, M. Dwayne. 1996. Sources of firearms acquisition among a sample of inner-city youths: Research results and policy implications. *Journal of Criminal Justice* 24: 361–67.

Snyder, Jeffrey R. 1993. A nation of cowards. *The Public Interest* 113: 40–55.

Van Alstyne, William. 1994. *The Second Amendment and the personal right to arms*. Durham, NC: Duke University School of Law.

Vernick, Jon S., and Stephen P. Teret. 1999. New courtroom strategies regarding firearms: Tort litigation against firearm manufacturers and constitutional challenges to gun laws. *Houston Law Review*, 36: 1713–54.

Wright, James D. 1981. Public opinion and gun control: A comparison of results from two recent national surveys. *Annals of the American Academy of Political and Social Science* 455: 24–39.

Wright, James D., and Peter H. Rossi. 1986. *Armed and considered dangerous: A survey of incarcerated felons and their firearms*. Hawthorne, NY: Aldine de Gruyter.

FIREARMS: HISTORY

Technological Developments

Firearm technology changed dramatically during the nineteenth century. The standard handgun in the early 1800s was a single-shot flintlock pistol loaded from the muzzle using black powder and a lead ball. These were available wrapped together in the form of a paper cartouche. The priming charge was poured into a small pan covered by a steel frizzen that sat in the arcing path of the spring-loaded cock. The cock grasped a piece of flint that, when the trigger was pressed, sprang forward to strike the steel frizzen to produce a shower of sparks. During the second quarter of the 1800s, the pressure-sensitive percussion cap containing fulminate of mercury came into use, and the flintlock gradually gave way to the new percussion lock. Importantly, this small explosive cap made it possible for Samuel Colt to design his multishot "revolver."

Colt's Paterson model revolver and other "cap-and-ball" style handguns of this general design had revolving cylinders typically featuring five or six chambers that could be loaded with powder and ball and left capped for immediate use. Prior to this development there was the major impediment to sustained and effective self-defense in that one had to have handy as many pistols as one might desire available shots. The revolver's half-dozen shots therefore was a tremendous leap forward in a person's capacity to counter an assault.

The next major development displaced the old technology of loose powder and lead ball, as well as the handier paper cartouche, through the introduction of the durable and far more reliable metallic cartridge. The self-contained metallic cartridge accomplishes several important ends; it confines the powder in its cavity and has its ignition source on one end in the form of a primer fitted into the base and at the other end, its bullet. Metallic cartridges are relatively impervious to moisture that always had plagued gunpowder.

The next major development was to bore the chambers of the revolver's cylinder straight through to accommodate metallic cartridges being inserted from the rear. Perhaps the most popular example is Colt's Firearms' Peacemaker.45 caliber introduced in 1873, which many consider to have been the standard of its day. For the military and police use, however, the "single-action" Peacemaker that was thumb-cocked prior to each shot would soon give way to double-action revolvers that had a second mechanism for simply pressing the trigger to cock and fire the revolver. These revolvers also would come to feature a swing-out cylinder to facilitate easier and quicker loading.

The metallic cartridge's final major development came around 1900, when "smokeless" propellants began to displace the black powder that discharged thick smoke that grew thicker with subsequent shots. This metallic cartridge was the catalyst for another technological leap around the turn of the century: the semiautomatic handgun. This type of handgun, also referred to as "self-loading," holds its ammunition not in a revolver cylinder but, rather, stacked inside a spring-loaded magazine that is then inserted into the frame of the pistol. During the span of the nineteenth century, the single-shot flintlock pistol that might be loaded and fired two to perhaps three times a minute gave way to semiautomatic handguns capable of continuous firing.

Arming of the U.S. Police

Nineteenth-century municipal patrolmen did not at first routinely carry handguns. The infrequent but sometimes calamitous riots in large urban areas gave some impetus to carrying handguns, but the uncertainties imbedded in routine police work provided the principal motivation. Precisely how officers and their departments approached the matter of carrying handguns during the late nineteenth century remains difficult to chronicle, but we gain some sense of this from among the larger urban departments. For example, in 1857, New York State quietly provided its "Metropolitan" police in New York City

with revolvers that were to be carried in a uniform pocket. Detroit patrolmen were not provided with revolvers through the mid-1860s, but they were allowed to carry personally owned handguns. In the mid-1880s, the Boston Police Commission armed its patrolmen with Smith & Wesson .38 caliber revolvers. Near the turn of the century, Commissioner Roosevelt in New York City (NYPD) settled on a .32 caliber Colt's Firearms revolver as the department's approved, though not issued, handgun. By the early 1900s, the official or unofficial norm was to carry handguns, and carrying them concealed gradually gave way to wearing them in a holster worn in plain view over their uniforms.

Colt's Firearms and Smith & Wesson dominated the U.S. police handgun market for roughly a century. The most popular cartridge was the Smith & Wesson .38 Special cartridge that the firm introduced in the early 1900s. Other revolver cartridges were developed during the middle of the twentieth century—such as the Smith & Wesson "magnums" in .357 caliber in 1935, .44 caliber in 1955, and .41 caliber in 1963—but were not widely adopted by U.S. police even though they offered far more power than available in a .38 S&W Special. This was due to practical drawbacks; the revolvers designed for these cartridges usually were more expensive as well as larger and heavier, ammunition was more expensive, and they produced far heavier recoil, louder muzzle blast, and brighter flash in the barrel lengths favored by police.

Semiautomatic pistols were introduced to the civilian market around the turn of the century, and the U.S. Army adopted Colt's Model of 1911 in .45 Automatic Colt Pistol (ACP) in the early 1900s. U.S. police remained faithful to various double-action, swing-out cylinder models by Colt's Firearms and Smith & Wesson chambered in .38 Special through the mid-1980s. Among the earliest departments to make the change were the El Monte,

California, Police Department, which adopted the Colt 1911 pistol in .45 ACP in 1966, and the Illinois State Police, which adopted Smith & Wesson's Model 39 double-action semiautomatic pistol in 1967. Revolvers gave up noticeable ground to semiautomatic pistols in the mid-1980s and today essentially have been replaced. Now it is rare to see anything other than a semiautomatic pistol in a police officer's holster. This also has had the effect of ushering in manufacturers that were relatively new to the U.S. police market, such as Beretta, Glock, and SigArms.

The Beretta and SigArms pistols usually are of the double-action variety in that the first shot is fired by way of a comparatively heavy, long pull on the trigger that both cocks and then releases the hammer. This is somewhat like the double-action revolver's trigger-cocking and helps explain this design's appeal. Subsequent shots with the double-action semiautomatic pistol, however, are fired using the second action that involves a shorter, lighter press on the trigger. This is because the hammer remains cocked after each shot. Some models are available in "double-action only," dispensing with the part of the mechanism that enables the shorter, lighter trigger press. The other major style of firing mechanism is the single-action venerable Colt Model of 1911 and the more recent Glock that features only one mechanism and thus a single manner for activating the firing mechanism.

Three pistol cartridges currently are popular among U.S. police. Two of these are the long-standing 9mm Parabellum and the .45 ACP, both of which trace their roots to the early 1900s, and the third is the .40 Smith & Wesson introduced in the 1990s. Glock added its .45 Glock Automatic Pistol (GAP) cartridge in 2004, which is a ballistic twin to the .45 ACP. The .45 GAP's shorter overall length, however, permits its use in Glock's already established line of smaller framed pistols designed for the 9mm and .40 S&W cartridges. This can be advantageous to

officers with smaller hands because of the reduced circumference of the frame.

Proficiency Training

Across the first half-century of U.S. policing (1840s–1890s), there essentially was no handgun instruction, and during the second half-century (1900s–1940s), it remained the exception to the rule. Handgun safety and proficiency instruction first appeared in New York City in 1895 when its police commissioner, Theodore Roosevelt, introduced semiannual bull's-eye target shooting through the School of Pistol Practice that he established. Although the approximately twenty shots fired by each patrolman seems very unlikely to have had much practical effect—contemporary entry-level training consumes two to three thousand cartridges per officer—this enlightened step nudged police practices toward meaningfully improving both officer and public safety.

In the 1920s, the National Rifle Association (NRA) (est. 1871) championed the introduction and improvement of handgun proficiency among the police from the editorial page to its national matches. NRA developed some practical shooting contests better suited to its practical-minded police contestants than the 25- and 50-yard bull's-eye target matches. These police matches featured such elements as humanoid silhouette instead of bull's-eye targets; simulated urban settings where targets appeared and disappeared from windows, doors, and corners or other concealed positions; and moving targets. NRA offered instructor development courses for police firearms instructors through it Small Arms Firing School, and it encouraged local affiliates to provide firing range access, instruction, and other assistance to state and local police.

During the 1930s and 1940s, the Federal Bureau of Investigation (FBI) was in its ascendancy as a law enforcement agency.

When its special agents were authorized by Congress in 1934 to be routinely armed, the FBI first looked to conventional military handgun training but then, around 1940, developed its well-known Practical Pistol Course (PPC), which became the basis for innumerable variants used widely by state and local police well into the 1980s. The generic elements of the PPC include a humanoid target; at least one close target distance of seven yards in better keeping with violent encounters; and greater emphasis upon gun handling such as drawing the handgun from its holster and reloading under time pressure.

Beginning in the 1980s, police slowly began to move toward more realistic firearms and deadly force training that reflects substantial change in the types and extents of marksmanship and gun handling skills, emphasis on tactics and judgment, and more comprehensive curriculum design and sophisticated instructional methods. Judgment and decision making are far more common today through live-fire tactics training, role-playing scenarios, and computer simulation exercises. Most recently, integrated training—for example, combining in one extended scenario such things as car stop procedures, approaching suspects, communication skills, applying one's knowledge of the law, cues that might warn of pending assault, and physical and weapon-based use of force to include firearms–has been advanced as a means for achieving more realism.

These approaches seem far more likely to enhance police potential for dealing with dangerous encounters than that previously offered by the static and seemingly irrelevant nature of bull's-eye target shooting or the rote nature of PPC courses that together formed the foundation for police firearms training during the twentieth century.

GREGORY B. MORRISON

See also **Academies, Police; Accidental Deaths/Assaults against Police and Murder of Police Officers; American Policing: Early Years; Deadly Force; Education and Training; Excessive Force; History of American Policing; Liability and Use of Force; Police in Urban America, 1860–1920; Police Reform: 1950–1970; Police Standards and Training Commissions; Post-Shooting Review; SWAT Units; Texas Rangers**

References and Further Reading

Berman, Jay. 1987. *Police administration and progressive reform: Theodore Roosevelt as police commissioner of New York*. Westport, CT: Greenwood Press.
Carte, Gene E., and Elanie H. Carte. 1975. *Police reform in the United States*. Berkeley, CA: University of California Press.
Gammage, A. Z. 1963. *Police training in the United States*. Springfield, IL: Charles C Thomas.
Geller, William A., and Michael Scott. 1992. *Deadly force: What we know*. Washington, DC: Police Executive Research Forum.
Hickman, Matthew. 2002. *State and local law enforcement training academies, 2002*. Washington, DC: U.S. Department of Justice, Bureau of Justice Statistics.
Jinks, Roy G. 1977. *History of Smith & Wesson*. North Hollywood, CA: Beinfeld Publishing Company.
Lane, R. 1967. *Policing the city: Boston, 1822–1885*. Cambridge, MA: Harvard University Press.
Morrison, Gregory. 2003. Police and correctional department firearm training frameworks in Washington State. *Police Quarterly* 6: 192–221.
Morrison, Gregory. Forthcoming. Deadly force programs among larger US police departments. *Police Quarterly*.
Morrison, Gregory, and Bryan Vila. 1998. Police handgun qualification: Practical Measure or aimless activity? *Policing: An International Journal of Strategies and Management* 21: 510–33.
Richardson, John. 1970. *The New York police: Colonial times to 1901*. New York City: Oxford University Press.
Sprogle, Howard. 1971. *The Philadelphia police, past and present*. New York City: Arno Press.
Vila, Bryan, and Gregory Morrison. 1994. Biological limits to police combat handgun shooting accuracy. *American Journal of Polices* 12: 1–30.
Wilson, R. L. 1979. *The Colt heritage: The official history of Colt firearms, from 1836 to the present*. New York: Simon & Schuster.

FIREARMS REGULATION AND CONTROL

The actual number of firearms in the United States is impossible to count with confidence, but Reiss and Roth (1993, 256) compiled a list of the best estimates of gun totals: "60–100 million in 1968 (Newton and Zimring 1969), 100–140 million in 1978 (Wright, Rossi, and Daly 1983), and 130–170 million in 1988 (Cook 1991)." In terms of the purchase and sale of firearms in the United States, recent data from the Annual Firearms Manufacturing and Exportation report from the Bureau of Alcohol, Tobacco, Firearms and Explosives (ATF) indicate that more than four million new firearms were added into commerce in 1999 (ATF 2002). Hahn et al. (2003) estimate that approximately 4.5 million new firearms are sold each year in the United States, including two million handguns, and Cook, Molliconi, and Cole (1995) and Cook and Ludwig (1996) estimate that secondhand firearms transactions (sales, trades, or gifts) range from 2 million to 4.5 million annually.

Most firearms policies in the United States focus on regulating the primary firearms market. The primary market encompasses the transfer of firearms by mainstream sources such as firearms manufacturers, retail gun dealers, and pawnbrokers (see Wintemute 2002 for a description of the character of legal and illegal firearms markets). A firearm enters the secondary market once it is in private hands and is transferred by an individual who is not a licensed firearms dealer to another individual (Cook, Molliconi, and Cole 1995). It is far easier in the primary market to identify and regulate who should and should not buy, own, or possess a firearm. Once a firearm has moved into the secondary market, it is difficult to identify and regulate who is eligible to purchase and own a gun. In addition to the regulation of the manufacture, transfer, and possession of guns, firearms policies in the United States attempt to control the illegal use and transfer of firearms.

Firearms policy frameworks are often organized in terms of the sequence of decisions associated with a firearm from its manufacturer through its ownership and on to its potential legal or illegal use. This type of policy framework can be characterized as a firearms life cycle approach to organizing firearms regulations and laws in the United States. Under this schema firearms laws and regulations are organized with respect to each stage in the life cycle of a firearm, from manufacture through its potential uses. From a policy analysis perspective this framework is useful for (1) identifying the particular point in the transfer, possession, or use of a firearm that is typically the focus of firearms laws and regulations and (2) highlighting the actors/agencies responsible for carrying out specific policies and regulations. Firearms regulations are examined in terms of the Firearms and Gun Violence Policy Life Cycle Framework:

1. Manufacture/import controls
2. Individual sale/purchase/ownership
3. Handling/carrying/storage/ accessibility
4. Use in a crime—penalty enhancements
5. Recovery—gun buybacks/exchange programs
6. Firearms tracing
7. Civil liability litigation

Manufacture/Import Controls

As articulated in the Gun Control Act of 1968 (GCA), the regulation of guns begins with either the manufacture or importation of a firearm. When this occurs, the firearm is considered a durable good and becomes subject to regulation. A manufacturer is defined as "any person engaged in the business of manufacturing firearms or ammunition for purposes of sale or distribution" [18 U.S.C. 44 Sec. 921 (a) (10)]. An importer is defined as "any person engaged in the business of importing or bringing firearms or ammunition into the United States for purposes of sale or distribution" [18 U.S.C. 44 Sec. 921 (a) (9)]. As required by the GCA of 1968, both manufacturers and importers need to be licensed in order to engage in business. An application must be submitted to the ATF. This license allows the licensee to transport, ship, and receive firearms and ammunition covered by such license in interstate or foreign commerce while the license is valid. Each applicant (licensee) must be at least twenty-one years of age and have a place of business that does not violate state or local laws. Once a license has been granted, the manufacturer or importer must keep records of "importation, production, shipment, receipt, sale or other disposition of firearms at his place of business" [18 U.S.C. 44 Sec. 923 (g) (1) (A)].

Individual Sale/Purchase/Ownership

After a firearm has been manufactured or imported, it is typically distributed either to a wholesaler or directly to a dealer, who ultimately transfers it to a private individual. A federally licensed firearms dealer (FFL) is defined as "any person engaged in the business of selling firearms at wholesale or retail and any person engaged in the business of repairing firearms or of making or fitting special barrels, stocks, or trigger mechanisms to firearms, or any person who is a pawnbroker" [18 U.S.C. 44 Sec. 921 (a) (11)]. Dealers, like manufactures and wholesalers, must be licensed by the ATF to engage in business [18 U.S.C. 44 Sec. 923 (g) (1) (A)].

Firearms policies that focus on the sale, purchase, and ownership of firearms can be divided into three broad categories: (1) the process of selling and owning a firearm, (2) the eligibility of who can sell, purchase, or own a firearm and/or those types of weapons that can be legally sold (that are eligible for sale), and (3) the taxation of firearms sales and purchases. There are generally two types of licensing systems: permissive and restrictive. Permissive systems, such as the federal regulations, exclude small groups, such as minors, the mentally ill, or convicted felons, from owning any firearms. Restrictive licensing systems, such as the Washington, D.C., gun ban, are more strategic in that they exclude large groups of people from owning a particular type of firearm, such as a handgun (Zimring and Hawkins 1987).

The minimum standards for buying a firearm, established by federal law, restrict individuals from buying a firearm if they have been convicted of a crime punishable by imprisonment for a term exceeding one year, are a fugitive from justice, are addicted to any controlled substance, are mentally defective, are an illegal alien, have been dishonorably discharged from the armed forces, have renounced U.S. citizenship, or have a court order related to domestic violence [18 U.S.C. 44 Sec. 922 (g) (1)–(9)].

The process for purchasing a firearm from a licensed dealer was significantly changed by the Brady Handgun Violence Prevention Act of 1993 (Brady Act), which became effective February 28, 1994. The central element of this law is the concept of background checks for firearms purchases from FFLs and the introduction of an initial waiting period. The intent behind waiting periods and background checks legislation is to decrease the purchases by ineligible people and to decrease crimes of passion or suicides by discouraging instant purchases. At the passing of the bill, only thirty-two states were affected. The remaining eighteen states and Washington, D.C., were exempt because they already had a comparable background check system in place (*Fact Sheet* n.d.).

Under the Brady Act, the National Criminal History Improvement Program (NCHIP) was established to help states to improve their criminal history information systems in order to enable more complete, accurate, and rapid background checks. Since its inception, NCHIP has made much advancement in connecting states to the federal government (Bureau of Justice Statistics 2004).

A major loophole of the Brady Act is that it only requires background checks to be performed when a firearm is purchased from a federally licensed dealer. As a result, the private sale of a firearm (from one private citizen to another) does not require a background check (Jacobs and Potter 1995). Another concern with the Brady Act is often referred to as the "gun show loophole." Here, unlicensed, private sellers are not compelled by federal law to conduct background checks (JoinTogether 2002), which makes it inapplicable to the secondary market and creates "anonymous" buyers (Jacobs and Potter 1995). Cook and Ludwig (2000, 12) propose that in order to regulate private sales, "law-enforcement authorities must be able to hold owners accountable for their firearms. Requiring that all transfers be channeled through federally licensed dealers, and holding owners responsible for misuse of their guns, would be a good start."

Handling/Carrying/Storage/Accessibility

Once the transaction from dealer to individual has occurred and that purchaser now legally owns that firearm, policies can be instituted and directed at how the owner handles, carries, or stores the firearm. Since the late 1990s, there has been a push to increase these types of laws, whether it is advocating for high-tech firearms, safety features, or storage requirements. Some of these laws are at the local level, such as when a firearm is purchased: A trigger lock needs to be purchased simultaneously. The intent behind carry laws, limiting where guns can be used, is to make them less immediately available and reduce firearms crime and accidental injury (Kleck 1997). Currently, there is no empirical data supporting their efficacy in stopping accidental deaths (Azrael et al. 2003).

Use in a Crime—Penalty Enhancements

Penalty enhancement refers to the policy of adding additional penalties for the use or possession of a firearm in the course of committing a crime. Penalty enhancement laws at the local, state, or federal levels are among the most popular of gun control measures. They fare well in opinion polls, which make them politically advantageous (Kleck 1991). Even firearms advocate groups agree that this type of policy is beneficial, because the target group is the people who misuse firearms and it places no restrictions on firearm ownership (Kleck 1991; Zimring 1991).

There are two types of penalty enhancement policies: mandatory and discretionary. Mandatory sentences represent minimum or additional prison terms that are automatically added to a convicted criminal's time for the use or possession of a firearm in crime regardless of the circumstances of that crime. Discretionary sentencing provides guidelines, to be used at a judge's discretion, for penalties that can be added for the use or possession of a firearm in a crime. On the federal level, the Comprehensive Crime Control Act of 1984, which overhauled the federal sentencing system, contains two sections that pertain to penalty enhancements: the Sentencing Reform Act of 1984 (SRA) and the Armed Career Criminal Act of 1984, which is often referred to as the "three-strikes" law. The Armed Career Criminal Act states that any person with three previous convictions (state or federal) must get an add-on, mandatory imprisonment of at least fifteen years if in possession of a firearm while committing a violent felony and/or serious drug offense [18 U.S.C. Sec. 924 (e) (1)]. These sentencing guidelines have periodically been updated and changed (Sentencing Guidelines Act of 1986, Sentencing Act of 1987, Crime Control Act of 1990).

Finally, the Violent Crime Control and Law Enforcement Act of 1994 added enhanced penalties (some to mandatory life imprisonment) for a multitude of crimes: smuggling firearms, theft of firearms, intentionally lying to an FFL, or using a firearm in the commission of counterfeiting or forgery, and it increased penalties for interstate trafficking. Research on the effectiveness of penalty enhancement laws is mixed. Research by Marvell and Moody (1995) concluded that these laws may have an impact in a few states, but generally they do not reduce crime or increase prison populations.

Recovery—Gun Buybacks/Exchange Programs

Gun buyback or gun exchange programs are intended to reduce the number of firearms in a community through a variety of programs, including exchange or trade-in programs, where goods such as concert tickets are given in exchange, amnesty programs, where the reward is no prosecution or possessor documentation for guns turned in, and buyback programs, which are voluntary and open to all firearms possessors and are either targeted specifically at handguns or give rewards for all types of guns.

The hypothesis behind these types of policies is that reducing gun availability will decrease gun-related crime since prior research has demonstrated a correlation between the availability of handguns and the frequency of fatal violence (Callahan, Rivara, and Koepsell 1994). These programs are generally implemented at the city or community level. A number of researchers (Kleck 1996; Romero, Wintemute, and Vernick 1998) argue that even though gun buyback programs may have removed thousands of firearms from circulation, they are largely ineffective.

Firearms Tracing

Firearms gun tracing is the systematic process of tracing a crime-related firearm recovered by a law enforcement agency from its manufacture or importation through the chain of distribution to first retail sale of the firearm to a private citizen. For an overview of firearms tracing, see Firearms Tracing.

Civil Liability Litigation

Relatively recently civil liability litigation has been introduced as a policy approach that is intended to reduce the damage inflicted by firearms and increase the responsibilities of gun manufacturers (Cook and Ludwig 2002). The use of litigation as a tool to influence the gun industry began with the high-profile lawsuits against asbestos and tobacco companies, which proved to be profitable and effective at influencing asbestos and tobacco companies (Butterfield 1998; Kairys 1998; Barrett 1999; Bogus 2000). The early lawsuits have central themes, based on grounds of traditional tort to attach liability through strict products liability, strict liability for abnormally dangerous activities, and negligence (Bonney 2000).

Partially in response to this type of litigation, the Protection of Lawful Commerce in Arms Act (Public Law No. 109-92) was enacted into law in October 2005 to limit the civil liability for gun manufacturers, distributors, dealers, and importers for damages resulting from the misuse of their products by others. At this time it is still unclear how this particular policy approach will proceed.

ROBERTA GRIFFITH and GLENN L. PIERCE

See also **Crime Control Strategies: Gun Control; Crime Prevention; Crime, Serious Violent; Firearms Availability and Homicide Rates; Firearms: Guns and the Gun Culture; Firearms: History; Firearms Tracing**

References and Further Reading

Armed Career Criminal Act of 1984. 18 U.S.C. § 924 (e) (1984).

Azrael, D., C. Barber, D. Hemenway, and M. Miller. 2003. Data on violent injury. In *Evaluating gun policy: Effects on crime and violence*, ed. J. Ludwig and P. J. Cook, 412–38. Washington, DC: Brookings Institution.

Barrett, P. M. 1999. Jumping the gun? Attacks on firearms echo earlier assaults on tobacco industry. *Wall Street Journal*, March 12, A1.

Blumstein, A., and D. Cook. 1996. Linking gun availability to youth gun violence. *Law and Contemporary Problems* 59: 5–24.

Bogus, C. T. 2000. Gun litigation and societal values. *Connecticut Law Review* 32, 1353–78.

Bonney, S. R. 2000. Using the courts to target firearms manufacturers: Comment. *Idaho Law Review* 37, 167. http://www.saf.org/lawreviews/bonneys1.htm (accessed August 25, 2004).

Brady Handgun Violence Prevention Act of 1993 (Brady Act). Pub. L. No. 103-159, 107 Stat. 1536 (1993), codified at 18 U.S.C. Sec. 922 (q)–(t) (1994).

Bureau of Alcohol, Tobacco and Firearms (ATF). 1992. *Protecting America: The effectiveness of the federal armed career criminal statute*. Washington, DC: U.S. Department of the Treasury.

Bureau of Justice Statistics (BJS). 2004. *National Criminal History Improvement Program fiscal year 2004 program announcement*. http://www.ojp.usdoj.gov/bjs/pub/html/nchip04.htm (accessed August 12, 2004).

Butterfield, F. 1998. Results in tobacco litigation spur cities to file gun suits. *New York Times*, December 24, A1.

Callahan, C. M., F. P. Rivara, and T. D. Koepsell. 1994. Money for guns: Evaluation of the Seattle gun buy-back program. *Public Health Reports* 109(4): 472–77.

Comprehensive Crime Control Act of 1984. Pub. L. No. 98–473 (1984).

Cook, P. J., and J. Ludwig. 1996. *Guns in America: Results of a comprehensive national survey on firearms ownership and use*. Washington, DC: U.S. Department of Justice.

———. 2000. *Gun violence: The real costs*. New York: Oxford University Press.

———. 2002. Litigation as regulation: The case of firearms. In *Regulation through litigation*, ed. W. K. Viscusi. Washington, DC: Brookings Institution Press.

Cook, P. J., S. Molliconi, and T. B. Cole. 1995. Regulating gun markets. *The Journal of Criminal Law and Criminology* 86: 59–92.

Crime Control Act of 1990. Pub. L. No. 101-647, 18 U.S.C. Sec. 922 (q) (1990).

Fact sheet: The Brady Handgun Violence Prevention Act, does it live up to its name? (n.d.) http://www.handguncontrol.net/Fact%20Sheet-The%20Brady%20Bill.htm (accessed August 5, 2004).

Gun Control Act of 1968 (GCA). Pub. L. No. 90-618, 82 Stat. 1213, 18 U.S.C. Sec. 921, et seq. (1968).

Hahn, R. A., O. O. Biluka, A. Crosby, M. T. Fullilove, A. Liberman, E. K. Mosicicki, et al. 2003. First reports evaluating the effectiveness of strategies for preventing violence: Early childhood home visitation and firearms laws. Findings from the task force on community preventive services. *Morbidity and Mortality Weekly Report* 52 (RR-14): 1–9.

Henderson, H. 2000. *Gun control*. New York: Facts on File.

Jacobs, J. B., and K. A. Potter. 1995. Keeping guns out of the "wrong" hands: The Brady law and the limits of regulation. *Journal of Criminal Law and Criminology* 86: 93–120.

JoinTogether. 2002. *Gun violence: Making connections with suicide, domestic violence and substance abuse*. Boston, MA: JoinTogether.

———. 1998. Legal claims of cities against the manufacturers of handguns [Electronic version]. *Temple Law Review* 71: 1–21.

———. 2000. The government handgun cases and the elements and underlying policies of public nuisance law. *Connecticut Law Review* 32 (4): 1175–87.

Kleck, G. 1991. *Point blank: Guns and violence in America*. Hawthorne, NY: Aldine de Gruyter.

———. 1996. Crime, culture conflict and sources of support for gun control: A multi-level application of the General Social Surveys. *American Behavioral Scientist* 39 (4): 387–404.

———. 1997. *Targeting guns: Firearms and their control*. Hawthorne, NY: Aldine de Gruyter.

Marvell, T. B., and C. Moody. 1995. The impact of enhanced prison terms to felonies committed with guns. *Criminology* 33: 247–81.

Newton, G. D., and F. Zimring. 1969. Firearms and violence in American life. A staff report to the National Commission on the Causes and Prevention of Violence. Washington, DC: U.S. Government Printing Office.

Protection of Lawful Commerce in Arms Act. Pub. L. No. 109–92 (2005).

Reiss, A. J., and J. Roth, eds. 1993. *Understanding and preventing violence*. Washington, DC: National Academy Press.

Romero, M. P., G. J. Wintemute, and J. S. Vernick. 1998. Characteristics of a gun exchange program, and an assessment of potential benefits. *Injury Prevention* 4: 206–10.

Sentencing Act of 1987. Pub. L. No. 100-182, § 24, 101 Stat. 1271 (1987).

Sentencing Guidelines Act of 1986. Pub. L. No. 99-363 (1986).

Sentencing Reform Act of 1984 (SRA). Pub. L. No. 98-473 (1984).

Vernick, J. S., and L. M. Hepburn. 2003. State and federal gun laws: Trends for 1970–1999. In *Evaluating gun policy: Effects on crime and violence*, ed. J. Ludwig and P. J. Cook. Washington, DC: The Brookings Institution.

Violent Crime Control and Law Enforcement Act of 1994. Pub. L. No. 103-322, 108 Stat. 1796 (1994).

Wintemute, G. J. 1996. The relationship between firearm design and firearm violence: Handguns in the 1990s. *Journal of the American Medical Association* 275 (22), 1749–53.

Wright, J. D., P. H. Rossi, and K. Daly. 1983. *Under the gun: Weapons, crime, and violence in America*. New York: Aldine de Gruyter.

Zimring, F. E., and G. Hawkins. 1987. *The citizen's guide to gun control*. New York: Macmillan.

FIREARMS TRACING

The Bureau of Alcohol, Tobacco, Firearms and Explosives (ATF) enforces federal firearms laws and regulations, as well as providing support to federal, state, and local law enforcement officials in their efforts to reduce violent crime and terrorist-related crimes involving firearms (ATF n.d.a). For example, the ATF's Strategic Plan for Fiscal Years 2004–2009 identifies firearms tracing as a key resource in the agency's program to reduce violent gun crime, stating that the ATF will "assist the law enforcement community in identifying firearms trafficking trends and resolving violent crimes by providing automated firearms ballistics technology, tracing crime guns, and developing advanced firearms trafficking investigative techniques" (ATF n.d.b, 4). Crime gun tracing is the systematic process of tracing a crime-related firearm recovered by a law enforcement agency from "its source (manufacturer/importer) through the chain of distribution (wholesaler/retailer) to the individual who first purchases the firearm" (ATF 2000, A-4).

The Legal Context of Firearms Tracing

The legislative mandate for ATF to trace crime-related firearms is the Gun Control Act of 1968 (GCA), which establishes a set of requirements that allows any given firearm to be traced from its manufacture or import to its first sale by a retail dealer. The GCA mandates that each new firearm, whether manufactured in the United States or imported, must be marked with a unique serial number. In addition, the GCA requires all federally licensed firearms dealers (FFLs), including manufacturers, importers, distributors, and retail dealers, to maintain records of all firearms transactions, including whole/retail sales and shipments received.

The GCA also requires FFLs, in response to a request for trace information, to provide details from transaction records to the ATF. The GCA also mandates that the ATF can perform an audit of an FFL's transaction records once during a twelve-month period to ensure compliance with record-keeping requirements of the law. Finally, when an FFL goes out of business, the GCA requires the FFL to transfer its transaction records to the ATF, which stores them for the purpose of tracing. In essence, the GCA established a set of record-keeping procedures that allows the ATF to trace firearms to first-time retail purchases (Pierce and Griffith 2005). In 1994, Congress further required firearms manufacturers and FFLs to respond to a firearms trace request within twenty-four hours (27 C.F.R. Part 178, Sec. 178.25a).

In addition to establishing requirements for the collection of firearms trace procedures, Congress also passed legislative mandates that regulate how the ATF manages firearms trace information. Specifically, Congress passed restrictions prohibiting the ATF from consolidating or centralizing records of receipt and disposition of firearms maintained by FFLs. For example, ATF's fiscal year 1979 appropriation provided (*Federal Register* 1978) that "no funds appropriated herein shall be available for administrative expenses in connection with consolidating or centralizing . . . the records of receipt and disposition of firearms maintained by federal firearms licensees."

The Firearms Tracing Process and the National Tracing Center

In order to provide investigative leads, the National Tracing Center (NTC), a division within the ATF, conducts crime traces (of firearms recovered at crime scenes and from youth or other persons prohibited from possessing firearms) from any federal, state, local, or international law enforcement agency (ATF, n.d.b). Requests for traces may be submitted by telephone (for high-priority/urgent requests), fax, mail, or electronically.

Figure 1 presents a flowchart of the basic firearms tracing process (from Pierce and Griffith 2005). The tracing process begins with a law enforcement agency's submission of a trace request to the NTC for a crime-related firearm recovered by their agency. The law enforcement requestor must submit one of two forms before a trace can be initiated: Form ATF F 3312.1 (http://www.atf.gov/forms/pdfs/f33121.pdf) for standard crime gun trace requests or form ATF F 3312.2 (http://www.atf.gov/forms/pdfs/f33122.pdf) for crime guns with an obliterated serial number or where there has been an attempt to obliterate the serial number. These forms require information regarding the firearm type (for example, pistol, revolver, shotgun, or rifle), manufacturer, caliber, serial number (unless obliterated), importer (if the gun is of foreign manufacture), the location where recovered, the criminal offense associated with the recovery, and the name and date of birth of the firearm possessor.

Each firearm trace request is assigned to an NTC firearms tracing program specialist. The information is first checked against an index of manufacturers and firearms serial numbers contained in the records of out-of-business FFLs that are stored by the ATF against the records of multiple handgun purchases reported on an ongoing basis by FFLs, as well as against records of weapons reported stolen by FFLs. If the firearm does not appear in these databases, the firearms tracing specialist contacts the manufacturer or importer and tracks the recovered crime gun through the distribution chain (the wholesaler and retailer) to the first retail sale dealer. If the dealer, wholesaler, or manufacturer is still in business, the dealer is asked to examine its records to determine the identity of the first retail purchaser. Data on traced firearms are entered into the Firearms Tracing System (FTS), a database system maintained by the NTC that manages the data on all

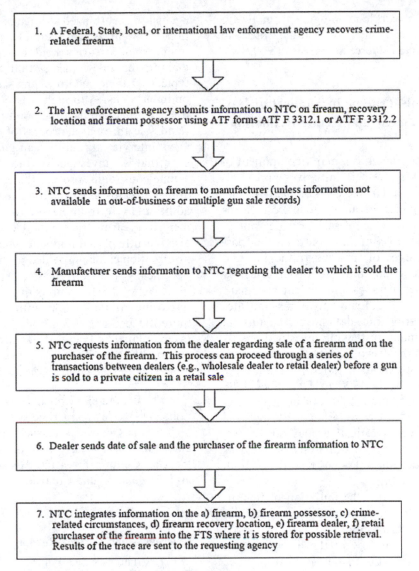

1. A Federal, State, local, or international law enforcement agency recovers crime-related firearm

2. The law enforcement agency submits information to NTC on firearm, recovery location and firearm possessor using ATF forms ATF F 3312.1 or ATF F 3312.2

3. NTC sends information on firearm to manufacturer (unless information not available in out-of-business or multiple gun sale records)

4. Manufacturer sends information to NTC regarding the dealer to which it sold the firearm

5. NTC requests information from the dealer regarding sale of a firearm and on the purchaser of the firearm. This process can proceed through a series of transactions between dealers (e.g., wholesale dealer to retail dealer) before a gun is sold to a private citizen in a retail sale

6. Dealer sends date of sale and the purchaser of the firearm information to NTC

7. NTC integrates information on the a) firearm, b) firearm possessor, c) crime-related circumstances, d) firearm recovery location, e) firearm dealer, f) retail purchaser of the firearm into the FTS where it is stored for possible retrieval. Results of the trace are sent to the requesting agency

Figure 1 Flowchart of the basic firearms tracing process.

prior firearms trace requests, multiple sales records, and reports of firearms stolen from FFLs that have been submitted to and processed by the NTC (Pierce and Griffith 2005).

The tracing process necessitates that the NTC communicate with many different organizations across the nation from both the private and public sectors and from the federal, state, and local levels of government. During fiscal year 2003, the NTC received more than 280,000 firearms trace requests from law enforcement agencies. In the course of conducting these firearms traces, the NTC communicated with approximately seven hundred different firearms manufacturers, 46,000 separate retail and wholesale firearms dealers, and 6,500 individual law enforcement agencies or units. In addition, information was collected on 203,933 crime gun possessors. The average time to complete a trace varies with this workload, ranging from twelve to seventeen days for routine traces in recent years (Pierce and Griffith 2005).

Firearms Tracing in Support of Law Enforcement and Crime Reduction

Firearms tracing is a major component of the ATF's strategic initiatives and goals (see ATF n.d.a, n.d.b). For many crime-related guns, the ability to trace firearms to a first-time retail sale provides potentially valuable information regarding possible sources of firearms trafficking and the possession and use of firearms by prohibited persons and violent criminals. Analysis of ATF investigations indicates that firearms trace data have been a useful tool in many trafficking investigations. A detailed analysis of 1,530 firearms trafficking investigations initiated during the period from July 1996 to December 1998 found that "almost 30% of investigations (448 of 1,530) were initiated through the innovative investigative methods of information analysis—analysis of firearms trace data, multiple sales records, or both (ATF 2000, x).

Further, after the initiation of investigations, tracing was used as an investigative tool to gain information on recovered crime guns in 60% of the investigations. Examples of the value of firearms trace information for strategic law enforcement planning are available in ATF's reports (for example, ATF 2002) and other analyses of firearms trace data (see Kennedy, Piehl, and Braga 1996; Pierce et al. 2003, 2004).

ATF's legal mandates place some restrictions on how firearms trace data can be used by law enforcement and the policy makers. ATF's legal mandates limiting what firearms-related data the agency can store in a central database repository (see *Federal Register* 1978) make it difficult to trace firearms beyond the first-time retail purchaser of a firearm. The restriction

against the centralized storage of information on firearms (for example, the serial numbers of firearms sold or the FFLs making the sales) means that the ATF typically has no record of the sale of secondhand guns. Although it is possible to trace a crime gun past the point of its first retail sale through a process of the ATF agent interviewing subsequent gun possessors (that is, "investigative traces"), this is a time-consuming process that cannot be applied to most firearms trace requests. In addition to restrictions on the management of firearms trace data, Congress has also recently placed limits on what type of information can be provided to the public. Specifically, the Consolidated Appropriations Act of 2004 prohibits the ATF from disclosing to the public information required to be kept as a record by an FFL (as mandated by law) or FFL information reported to the ATF.

GLENN L. PIERCE and ROBERTA GRIFFITH

See also **Bureau of Alcohol, Tobacco, Firearms and Explosives; Crime Control Strategies: Gun Control; Firearms Availability and Homicide Rates; Firearms: Guns and the Gun Culture; Firearms: History; Firearms Regulation and Control**

References and Further Reading

27 C.F.R. Part 178, Sec. 178.25a.
Brady Handgun Violence Prevention Act. Pub. L. No. 103-159, 18 U.S.C. Sec. 922 (1994).
Braga, A. A., P. J., Cook, D. M., Kennedy, and M. H. Moore. 2002. The illegal supply of firearms. *Crime and Justice*, 29: 319–52.
Bureau of Alcohol, Tobacco, Firearms and Explosives (ATF). n.d.a. *ATF 2003 performance and accountability report*, 7. Washington, DC: U.S. Department of Justice. http://www.atf.treas.gov/pub/gen_pub/strategicplan/2004-2009stratplan/2004-2009stratplan.pdf.
———. n.d.b. *Working for a safer and more secure America . . . Through innovation and partnerships: Strategic Plan for 2004 to 2009*, 4. Washington. DC: U.S. Department of Justice. http://www.atf.treas.gov/pub/gen_pub/2003annrpt/2003annrpt.pdf.

———. 2000. *Following the gun: Enforcing federal laws against firearms traffickers.* Washington, DC: U.S. Department of the Treasury.

———. 2002. *Crime gun trace reports (2000): National report.* Washington, DC: U.S. Department of the Treasury. http://www.atf.treas.gov/firearms/ycgii/2000/index.htm.

Consolidated Appropriations Act. Pub. L. No. 108-199 (January 23, 2004).

Federal Register. 1978. Firearms regulations. 43 (55), March 21.

Firearms Owners' Protection Act. Pub. L. No. 99-308, 100 Stat. 449, 458 (codified at 18 U.S.C. Sec. 924) (1986).

Gun Control Act. Pub. L. No. 90-351, 82 Stat. 225 (codified as 18 U.S.C. Chap. 44 §§ 921–929) (1968).

Kennedy, D. M., A. M. Piehl, and A. A. Braga. 1996. Youth violence in Boston: Gun markets, serious youth offenders, and a use-reduction strategy. *Law and Contemporary Problems* 59: 169–80.

Pierce, G., and R. Griffith. 2005. Comprehensive planning of criminal justice information and intelligence systems: ATF's experience in implementing firearms tracing in the United States. In *Information Technology and the Criminal Justice System*, ed. April Pattavina. Beverly Hills, CA: Sage.

Pierce, G., A. A. Braga, R. Hyatt, and C. Koper. 2004. The characteristics and dynamics of illegal firearms markets: Implications for a supply-side enforcement strategy. *Justice Quarterly* 20: 2.

Pierce, G., A. A. Braga, C. Koper, J. McDevitt, D. Carlson, J. Roth, et al. 2003. *The characteristics and dynamics of crime gun markets.* Final report to the National Institute of Justice and the Bureau of Alcohol, Tobacco, Firearms, and Explosives. Boston: Northeastern University, College of Criminal Justice.

FOOT PATROL

Definition

It has been said that patrol is the "backbone of policing, the central aspect of police operations, . . . the center of police activity" (Walker and Katz 2002, 87). There are three distinct functions of patrol: to deter crime, to make officers available for service, and to enhance the feelings of public safety. Foot patrol is but one method of patrol. It is characterized by officers making neighborhood rounds on foot. Like any other method of patrol, foot patrol has its drawbacks as well as its benefits: "While extremely expensive and able to cover only a limited ground, foot patrol allows for enhanced police–community relations" (Walker and Katz 2002, 492).

Significance

Police departments use foot patrols primarily to (1) increase visibility of officers, (2) make greater contact with the community, (3) increase rapport with community members, (4) increase community policing, and (5) improve police officer job attachment and satisfaction (Greene 1987; Walker and Katz 2002). Although motor vehicles have taken over much of modern life, many police departments across the country still rely on foot patrol officers to proactively reduce crime and improve relations with community members.

"While motorized patrol may have increased efficiency in terms of response time and area covered, several unintended and undesirable consequences also surfaced. With officers removed from the streets, informal contacts between officers and citizens were decreased" (Esbensen 1987, 45). However, with the increase of community policing and increased attention to the benefits of fostering informal contacts within a given community, some police departments have begun decreasing the number of officers assigned to mobile units and increasing the number of officers on foot patrol in select neighborhoods (Walker and Katz 2002). Certain departments employ officers whose primary function is foot patrol. Foot patrols allow officers to have a more approachable and welcoming presence within communities. In addition, foot patrol officers are often able to have better rapport with community members because they present a less threatening appearance than their mobile unit counterparts.

While a foot patrol officer can cover only a limited area, which in turn means that the cost of foot patrol is higher than vehicular patrol, such limitations can be offset by the gains in community relations. Moreover, depending on the area and the situation, sometimes foot patrol officers can respond more quickly to a scene than officers patrolling in vehicles.

Brief History

Between the 1920s and the 1950s, many departments converted from foot patrol to car patrol because car patrol was deemed more efficient. "A patrol car can cover more area, pass each point more often, return to particular spots in an unpredictable manner if necessary, and respond quickly to calls for service" (Walker and Katz 2002, 93). However, as noted above, direct contact with citizens was lost by officers patrolling an area and/or community within the confines of a patrol car. As a result, officers were starting to be viewed as an occupying army, or at least not very approachable, as had been those officers patrolling on foot. In response to crises of strained police–community/citizen relations during the 1960s, many departments started restoring foot patrols within select neighborhoods. In addition, many community policing programs implemented foot patrols to increase the officers' visibility and their approachability by citizens (Walker and Katz 2002).

In the 1980s, a number of evaluations examined foot patrols and found that though increased foot patrols did not reduce crime, they did increase feelings of safety (Walker and Katz 2002). In addition, these positive feelings were generalized to the whole department, not just assigned to the individual foot patrol officers in a community. Therefore, by increasing foot patrols and subsequently relationships between police and citizens, departments can increase knowledge about the specific roles of officers and possibly also reduce fear of crime.

Community Relations

The increase in the amount of motor patrols has lead to a decrease in interaction between citizens and police officers. "Decreased interaction between police and citizens has led not only to deterioration of relations but also to an inaccurate and unrealistic assessment of the police role" (Esbensen 1987, 46). This deterioration of relations not only may increase inaccurate views of police and their roles but may also increase fear of crime and/or victimization.

In the era of community policing, such trends may have begun to change: "In recent years there has been a resurgence of interest in programs that attempt to place the police and the community in greater harmony and interaction" (Greene 1987, 1). With the advent of community policing, many departments started increasing foot patrols to increase officer and citizen interactions and improve community relations. Although not ideal in every circumstance or community, foot patrols do appear to increase positive interaction between officers and citizens and improve community relations when compared to traditional motor patrols.

Even though motor patrols are often able to get to certain areas faster than foot patrols and are able to cover a larger area, officers on motor patrol often have less contact with community members and often do not have as good a relationship with the public as do foot patrol officers. Foot patrol officers, because of their heavy interaction with the public, are able to learn more about their community, their beat, and those who reside within it, thereby increasing public satisfaction with the police and encouraging community policing and better community–police relations.

An increased relationship between citizens and police may foster increased cooperation of citizens and increased crime reporting. Citizens who feel alienated or who have a negative image of police officers are less likely to report crimes to departments and less likely to offer tips when asked (Esbensen 1987). By increasing foot patrols and increasing a positive image of police and police–community relations, there is a higher likelihood that citizens will report crimes that occur and offer tips on unsolved crimes, thus helping police to make communities safer and solve crimes more often and/or more quickly.

Effectiveness

Another positive result of initiating foot patrol units, besides the increase in police–community relations, is that they may help to reduce crime. Although "this notion of high visibility being positively correlated with lower crime rates . . . remains suspect at best" (Esbensen 1987, 48), increased officer visibility may prevent certain crimes from occurring, reduce rates of crime, or, as noted in a study cited above, reduce fear of crime. Officers may be able to be more proactive in crime fighting because their knowledge of the community they serve allows them to better recognize when something is "not right." When a community and its members are better known by officers, it is clearer to officers when there is something suspicious occurring that demands their attention.

For example, if in a certain neighborhood a shopkeeper always turns out the lights and goes home at 7 P.M., an officer who knows the area will know that something is amiss if at 7:45 the officer walks by the shop and sees lights on. Whereas an officer who does not know the area or the shopkeeper may not think anything is wrong and potentially miss a crime that is in progress or just completed. Yet, "while previous evaluations of foot patrol programs have found support for improved community relations resulting from foot patrols, the findings have been inconsistent regarding any reduction in crime associated with foot patrols" (Esbensen 1987, 48).

Despite the fact that motor patrol officers can respond to calls for service more quickly than their foot patrol counterparts, the real effectiveness of foot patrols should not be measured in response time or area covered but in citizen perceptions of the police, police knowledge of the community and its residents, and citizen satisfaction with the police. "Foot patrol officers are involved with the public on a much more proactive basis than motor patrol officers" (Payne and Trojanowicz 1985, 24). Foot patrol officers, although they have many of the same duties as motor patrol officers and engage in traditional patrol activities, are generally more involved with and interact more frequently and positively with the public. Such information exchanges and nonadversarial situations make foot patrols ideal for community policing.

However, motor patrols still are faster than foot patrols in responding to serious situations, and the automobile has the ability to cover a larger area than a foot patrol. Therefore, foot patrols will never take over contemporary policing but can be of added value to departments by supplementing motor patrols with specialized foot patrol officers to increase community relations, improve officer job satisfaction and possibly effectiveness, decrease fear of crime, and perhaps also decrease victimization by allowing officers to more proactively fight crime.

JENEPHYR JAMES

See also **Accountability; Community-Oriented Policing: Effects and Impacts; Patrol, Types and Effectiveness of**

References and Further Reading

Esbensen, F. 1987. Foot patrols: Of what value? *American Journal of Police* 6 (1): 45–65.

Greene, J. R. 1987. Foot patrol and community policing: Past practices and future prospects. *American Journal of Police* 6 (1): 1–15.

Patterson, M. J. 1982. They're walking the beat again: In dozens of cities, foot patrol has returned. *Police Magazine* 5 (4): 53–59.

Payne, D. M., and R. C. Trojanowicz. 1985. *Performance profiles of foot versus motor officers.* East Lansing, MI: National Neighborhood Foot Patrol Center, Michigan State University.

Walker, S., and C. M. Katz. 2002. *The police in America: An introduction.* 4th ed. Boston: McGraw-Hill.

FORENSIC EVIDENCE

The adjective "forensic" is commonly used today to describe nearly every type of evidence related to a criminal case or in any way associated with a legal debate both in and out of a courtroom. Anything that has the potential to be evidence—aside from eyewitness evidence, hearsay, or speculation—can be considered forensic evidence. The word is typically associated with "forensic science" and is related to forensic evidence examined in crime laboratories, now commonly called forensic laboratories. "Material evidence" is synonymous with forensic evidence and is normally recovered from a crime scene. Physical items found at the crimes scene or on the victim are analyzed to determine what happened, who did it, how, and why.

Ideally, the thorough examination of the crime scene, the victim, and the associated items of evidence will result in clues for solving the case. However, no matter how thorough the investigation and the examination of the evidence, there is no guarantee a case will be solved. Some cases are solved immediately, while others may be solved years afterward when new techniques or new evidence develops; sadly, some are never solved.

A Criminal Act

The authority of forensic evidence is based on its probative value in court—that is, its ability to prove something. Forensic evidence may associate a person, place, or thing to another person, place, or thing or to a criminal act. However, sometimes valuable forensic evidence is destroyed or not located at all during the investigation. Legally, to have a crime there must be a person who commits an act, with a specific intent, and there must be a statute that makes the act illegal. For example, two people are killed in separate incidents as a result of being hit by an automobile; the first was deliberately run down by an enemy, while the second was a small boy whose parent accidentally ran over him while backing out of the driveway. Both deaths were the result of being hit by an automobile, but only the driver in the first case had criminal intent.

Intent is a key factor in determining whether or not a crime was committed, the severity of a crime, and whether a crime was a premeditated, first-degree crime or a lesser charge, such as first-degree murder as opposed to manslaughter. Intent is in the mind of the perpetrator. There is no forensic laboratory test for it—forensic scientists are not mind readers. However, the evidence may certainly give some indication of intent. A shotgun blast to the back of the head at the end of an abandoned road would likely lead an investigator to open a homicide case, because it appears that someone intended to kill the victim. An incident in which the victim was stabbed two hundred times and an incident in which the victim was stabbed once would each give a different impression of an accused killer to a jury, even though both victims died of stab wounds. Intent is determined by the jury, judge, or special panel only after hearing and studying all the facts and evidence associated with the case.

The Goal of Forensic Analysis

The goal of the analysis of forensic evidence is to find the truth. This is often accomplished by connecting the perpetrator to the criminal act itself through biological evidence (the exchange of blood and body fluids), physical evidence (such as chemicals, illegal substances, or tools or weapons used as implements of the act), and digital evidence (electronic evidence in a binary form found in computers, personal data assistants (PDAs), cell phones, digital answering machines, digital cameras, e-mails, etc.). Other biological evidence comes from identifying human features such as facial characteristics, scars, marks, and fingerprints, which may become forensic evidence if they can be used to connect the suspect to the act, the crime scene, or the victim. These same identifiers can also help identify the victim.

DNA-related forensic evidence is the most notable biological evidence. Prior to the use of DNA as evidence, blood types (O, A, B, and AB) were used to either include or exclude a suspect, but matching a blood type could not provide any individually identifying features.

The implements or tools used to commit an act, such as a car, a knife, a gun, or a pry bar, can also be associated to the crime scene and/or the victim through the development of forensic evidence. A car used to deliberately run down and kill a victim could have fibers or even large pieces of clothing attached to it that can be physically matched to the victim's clothing. Fragments of the car can be found on the victim's body as well. Additionally, the DNA in the blood on the car can be excellent forensic evidence to identify the victim hit by the car. A bullet removed from a shooting victim can be traced back to the gun used to fire the bullet. However, a bullet that fragments in the body may not have enough surface characteristics to trace the bullet fragments back to the weapon that fired it, even when investigators have the correct weapon for comparison. Tool marks from a pry bar used to forcibly enter a residence or business can be associated back to the tool. The association of the tool mark with a specific tool involves the comparison of the tool mark at the scene to a mark made in the laboratory by a tool taken as evidence from the suspect. Forensic science procedures and techniques make these associations possible. However, a forensic scientist may have the evidence from the scene, but it is not suitable for comparison to the known samples taken from the suspect due to degradation or destruction of the evidence or the known sample.

Characteristics of Evidence

Forensic evidence characteristics can be divided into two classifications: class characteristics and individual characteristics. For example, the largest percentage of the population has blood type O, whereas the smallest percentage of the population has blood type AB. Blood types are class characteristics. Suspects can be grouped by blood type and can either be set free or kept for further questioning. However, if the DNA of a suspect matched blood found under the victim's fingernails, the DNA profile would be an individualizing characteristic that would narrow it down to one individual suspect.

An example of physical evidence with the same class characteristics could include a group of athletic shoes that were the same brand, the same color, the same size, the same style, and the same tread pattern. If a footwear impression was left at a crime scene, a tread pattern in blood, soil, dust, or mud, all of the footwear in this class of shoes could be suspected of having made the impression at the scene. The impression at the scene would be preserved by photography or a lift or casting, depending on the circumstances, and a search for individual characteristics on the impression would begin.

Individual characteristics caused by wear and unique damage to a shoe sole are identified by the forensic scientist by shape and type. These features are mapped onto a photograph, much like the identifying features of a fingerprint are mapped onto an enlarged chart to show that they match the known fingerprint minutia of the suspect. Comparisons are made with impressions from the actual suspected footwear to see if the individual characteristics are unique and can be matched to the footwear impression found at the scene. The forensic scientist is able to match the shoe impression from the scene, which was submitted to the laboratory by the investigator, to the known shoe the investigator removed from a closet in the suspect's apartment during a legal search. On the witness stand the forensic scientist would testify only to the work performed personally, and the findings might read as in the following fictitious case:

> Footwear impressions and photographs, marked as exhibits Q1, Q2, and Q3 from the crime scene of case number 12346ABC, were hand carried in a sealed package to the forensic laboratory on June 2, 2005, by Investigator John Smith. We were requested to examine the footwear sole pattern for investigative leads, such as associating the tread pattern of the footwear impression to a particular brand and type of footwear.

On June 10, 2005, a pair of athletic-type footwear was submitted to the laboratory by Investigator Smith. The athletic footwear was described in the letter of submission as exhibits K1 and K2 and was taken from the closet of John Doe, on June 9, 2005, during the execution of a search warrant.

Visual examinations in the laboratory of K1 and K2 revealed that the sole and heel footwear patterns were consistent with the herringbone tread design of an athletic footwear impression at the crime scene. Extensive microscopic examination of the wear patterns to the sole and analysis of numerous individual characteristics revealed that exhibits K1 and K2 match the multiple individual characteristics on footwear impressions at the crime scene. Exhibit K2 was identified as having made the impression in photograph Q3.

The questioned exhibits Q1, Q2, and Q3 were returned to Investigator Smith by registered mail No. 345,876,213 on July 15, 2005. The known exhibits K1 and K2 were returned to Investigator Smith by registered mail No. 345,876,214 on July 15, 2005.

The official report would bear the signature of the forensic scientist who worked the case, and in the case file would be the initials of the case reviewer. This is a quality assurance measure. The reviewer would be able to testify to the findings if something happened to the original examiner.

Chain of Custody

Forensic evidence has no value in court unless it is accompanied by a rigorous legal "chain of custody" and is protected from degradation. Proper packaging is required to protect the evidence and documentation attached to the item or associated with the item. This documentation is critical and must describe the place from which it was seized and the date, time, and initials or notation of the person who collected the evidence (noted on an evidence tag attached to the evidence or its container).

Additionally, every time an item of evidence changes hands, the evidence must be signed for and properly documented by the person receiving the evidence. The person who had custody of it would have had to sign and date documentation when it was received, and the same process would occur when it was turned over to yet another person. It would not be accepted as evidence in the court without these procedures. The questioned and known exhibits should be packaged separately so that cross contamination does not occur. Forensic examiners must also "mark the evidence for identification" so that they can identify items on the witness stand as those examined in the laboratory. The "mark" is usually the initials of the forensic scientist and the date of examination, made in a manner not easily removed or destroyed.

Digital Evidence

One of the newer forms of forensic evidence is in binary format, found on computers, cell phones, digital voice recorders, and digital pictures and movies and referred to as digital evidence. Digital evidence was defined in 1998 by the Scientific Working Group on Digital Evidence (SWGDE) as "information of probative value that is stored or transmitted in a binary form."

In the past when a homicide of a woman in her bedroom was discovered, investigators secured the area so that they could look for physical evidence. Not just the bedroom but the entire house, garage, and yard are the crime scene. It was critical to photograph or videotape the scene as it was when the first responders arrived. The medical examiner would determine the official cause of death, but the investigators looked for a potential cause of death and evidence of a forced entry. This would help them decide if the perpetrator knew the victim. They would look for the object(s) that might have caused the victim's death. Was there anything unusual about the scene or how the victim was killed? Then they would look for items such as an address book, a diary, notes on the bedside table, numbers scribbled near the telephone, letters, bills, and other documents that might lead them to a suspect.

Today most of the addresses are not on paper but can be found in a PDA; letters, bills, and banking can be on a personal computer or the PDA. All of the same investigative information is now on computers or stored in a digital format on answering machines, faxes, cell phones, or the like.

Rules of Evidence

Related to giving testimony in court about forensic evidence, under the Federal Rules of Evidence, Rule 702 deals with the admissibility of expert testimony as follows:

> If scientific, technical, or other specialized knowledge will assist the trier of fact to understand the evidence or to determine a fact in issue, a witness qualified as an expert by knowledge, skill, experience, training, or education may testify hereto in the form of an opinion or otherwise, if (1) the testimony is based on sufficient facts or data, (2) the testimony is the product of reliable principles and methods, (3) the witness has applied the principles and methods reliably to the facts in the case.

Closing

Vital forensic evidence can be the smallest, most unlikely particle at the crime scene. It is only by the hard work and professionalism of crime scene processors that the potentially suspect items are collected, sealed and preserved in containers, labeled as to where they were located in the crime scene and with the evidence tags signed and dated by the collectors, and logged into the evidence log. It does not matter how large or small the crime scene; the same care and attention to detail must be maintained. The effort, professionalism, and dedication of forensic scientists give families of victims the rights afforded to them in a democracy and will continue to bring criminals to justice.

CARRIE MORGAN WHITCOMB

See also **Computer Crimes; Forensic Investigations; Forensic Medicine; Forensic Science; Information Security**

References and Further Reading

Eckert, William G. 1997. *Introduction to forensic science*. 2nd ed. Boca Raton, FL: CRC Press.

Fisher, Barry A. J. 2000. *Techniques of crime scene investigation*. 6th ed. Boca Raton, FL: CRC Press.

Saferstein, Richard. 2004. *Criminalistics: An introduction to forensic science*. 8th ed. Upper Saddle River, NJ: Pearson/Prentice-Hall.

FORENSIC INVESTIGATIONS

Introduction

Prior to the twentieth century, the traditional investigative techniques used by law enforcement were the obtaining of confessions by interrogation, the testimony of eyewitnesses, the utilization of informants, and undercover operations. There were very few uses of forensic evidence beyond basic identifications. Today physical evidence plays a vital role in many types of criminal investigation. Perhaps high-profile cases and what has been dubbed the "CSI effect" have generated enormous public interest in crime scene investigations and can partially explain this focus on forensic investigations. Advances in forensic sciences and the development of new crime scene techniques certainly offer new alternatives in finding the facts of a crime.

Utilization of Physical Evidence in Forensic Investigation

The following are some important uses of physical evidence in contributing to a forensic investigation:

1. *Establishing a corpus delecti.* Corpus delecti refers to those essential facts that show that a crime has taken place. It is the presence of elements of the law defining the occurrence of a criminal offense. Physical evidence and forensic testing results are often used to establish that a crime has, in fact, been committed. Establishing that a seized white powder substance is cocaine, that fire debris contains accelerant or gasoline residue, or that semen is present on a vaginal swab taken from a sexual assault complainant are all examples of utilizing physical evidence to establish corpus delecti.

2. *Determining the modus operandi.* Many criminals have a particular MO (modus operandi, or method of operation), which consists of their characteristic way of committing a crime. Physical evidence found at a crime scene often can help in establishing an MO. For example, in burglary cases, the means used to gain entry, tools that were used, types of items taken, and other telltale signs, such as urine left behind at the scene, are all important. In arson cases, the type of accelerant used and the way in which the fires are set constitute physical evidence that helps to establish the patterns, or "signature," of an arsonist.

3. *Identifying people.* The role of physical evidence in helping to identify a victim or a suspect is central to forensic investigation. Fingerprints have been used for more than a hundred years, but we have come to depend on DNA, bite marks, and a variety of other forensic techniques to identify a victim, a suspect, or a witness. Unambiguous identification is not restricted to homicide, or even to criminal cases. In accident or major disaster situations, victims have to be identified so that the remains can be returned to families.

In disputed parentage cases, the parent(s) of a particular child must be identified so that the law can assign proper responsibility for the child's care and support.

4. *Identifying substances.* The positive identification of an item of physical evidence is one of the most important functions of forensic laboratories. Substances that require chemical or instrumental analysis to be identified must be subjected to these tests to prove that an offense occurred. For example, analysis can show that white powder seized by a detective from a defendant contains a particular controlled substance—heroin. Similarly, the scientific determination that a sample of blood taken from a driver contains more alcohol than the law allows for someone to operate a motor vehicle is critical to a driving while intoxicated (DWI) case.

5. *Establishing linkages or exclusions.* The most important application of physical evidence is developing linkages between a suspect and a crime. Linkage of victims, suspects, witnesses, and physical evidence can apply at many levels, from a mere possibility that two items could have a common source to complete individualizations. For example, paint chips found at a hit-and-run scene match the suspect's vehicle, or DNA recovered from a vaginal swab of a sexual assault kit matches the suspect's DNA profile. Linking a victim or suspect to a crime scene in some cases can be as important as a connection between the victim and suspect. A simple illustration is the situation in which a victim's blood is found on a suspect's clothing. Another example might occur when a bloody fingerprint found at a victim's home matches a suspect's right thumb.

6. *Supporting or disproving statements.* Another useful application of physical evidence in a forensic investigation is corroborating or disproving statements or testimony of a witness or suspect. Corroboration can be critical in finding the facts of a case. For example, a suspect denies he has been at a homicide scene, but the investigator found bloody shoeprints at the scene that are matched to the suspect's shoes.

7. *Providing investigative leads.* Physical evidence can help investigators develop leads. For example, it can help in developing the perpetrator's MO. Perpetrators of criminal acts follow behavioral patterns. In many situations the ability to connect two or three seemingly unrelated incidents provides critical information to help the investigators to progress in their investigation. With recent advances in forensic technology, data mining and artificial intelligence have provided an additional dimension in forensic investigation. AFIS, CODIS, and NIBIN are the major causes of that change. Each of these three computerized databases allows cases to be connected even if the source of the evidence is still not known. This can energize an investigation and give it direction.

Forensic Investigation Process

As forensic-based investigations became more prevalent, the scope of potential evidence and methods for examining that evidence expanded. Evidence available from a crime scene consists of more than just physical objects. It also includes a wide variety of pattern evidence, such as blood stains, imprints, gunshot residue, or the like, conditional evidence, which is created by an action or event, transient evidence, which is temporary in nature, and trace/transfer or associative evidence, which provides a direct association between the victim and suspect.

The nature and mechanism of generation of such categories of physical evidence are critically important in forensic investigation. Identification and examination of physical evidence is only one part of forensic investigation. Knowing the mechanism that produced it in the precise location where it was found, observing changes at a crime scene, and determining the sequence of events are often the key in solving cases.

Utilization of forensic investigation in the justice system requires that a series of steps be taken in the proper sequence. This process may include any or all of the following major forensic activities:

1. *Recognition.* Recognition is the ability to separate important and potentially informative items in a case from the background and other unrelated materials. The evidence is selected on the basis of what is likely to help in distinguishing between the possibilities. The recognition process involves basic principles of forensic examination, pattern recognition, physical property observation, field testing, and information analysis.

2. *Documentation.* After recognition comes documentation. Proper and complete documentation is critical to fulfilling the requirements of chain of custody. Documentation of a scene is as important as documentation of individual items of physical evidence. Many types of pattern evidence and conditional evidence can be recorded only by proper documentation. The exact location where evidence was found can be very important in the reconstruction of an incident. A reconstruction requires the synthesis of all of the information available.

3. *Collection and preservation.* This is an important step to ensure that physical evidence was collected and preserved to meet the legal and scientific requirements. If a piece of physical evidence reaches the laboratory in a condition not suitable for laboratory analysis, it loses its legal and investigative value. Different types of physical evidence have somewhat different requirements in terms of packaging and marking. Investigators have to fellow the correct guidelines in handling physical evidence.

4. *Identification.* Identification is a process common to all of the sciences and, in fact, to everyday life. It may be regarded as a classification scheme, in which items are assigned to categories containing like items and given names. Different items within a given category all have the same generic name. In this way, botanists will identify plants by categorizing them and naming them. Likewise chemists identify chemical compounds. In forensic science, identification usually refers to the identification of items of physical evidence. Some types of physical evidence require that scientific tests be conducted to identify them. Drugs, arson accelerant, bloodstains, and seminal stains are examples. Objects are identified by comparing their class characteristics with those of known standards or previously established criteria.

5. *Classification.* Classification is done by comparing the class characteristics of the questioned evidence with those of known standards or control materials. If all of the measurable class characteristics are the same between the questioned sample and the known control, then these two samples could have come from the same source or origin. If there are significant differences in some of the class characteristic measurements, then the questioned sample can be absolutely excluded as having coming from the particular source. In other words, the exclusionary value of comparison in the forensic investigation is considered absolute.

6. *Individualization.* Individualization is unique to forensic investigation; it refers to the demonstration that a particular sample is unique, even among members of the same class. It may also refer to the demonstration that a questioned piece of physical evidence and a similar known sample have a common origin. Thus, in addition to class characteristics, objects and materials possess individual characteristics that can be used to distinguish members of the same class. The best examples are fingerprints and DNA matching.

7. *Reconstruction.* Reconstruction is based on the results of crime scene examination, laboratory analysis, and other independent sources of information to reconstruct case events. Reconstruction often involves the use of inductive and deductive logic, statistical data, information from the crime scene, pattern analysis, and laboratory analysis results on a variety of physical evidence. The developing fields of artificial intelligence and expert systems have opened up a new dimension in reconstruction. These systems allow the modeling and representation of laboratory analysis results, the reasoning and enacting of a crime scene, and the comparing and profiling of suspects.

8. *Interpretation and testifying.* Forensic scientists must be able not only to master analytical skills, but also to write clear and informative laboratory reports with proper interpretation of laboratory testing results. A final step in this multistep forensic investigation process is court testimony. Court testimony represents the capstone of a forensic scientist's work. It is essential to treat every item and every case as if it will go to a major trial. The most important aspect of court testimony is to maintain the scientific objectivity and neutrality. Although the majority of forensic scientists put forth every effort to maintain objectivity, there is no doubt that they may disagree about the meaning or interpretation of results.

Conclusion

Forensic science is the application of scientific principles and techniques to matters of law. Because of this unique application, a forensic scientist not only must master scientific methods but also must know the limitations of science. A forensic scientist not only has to be familiar with the law but also has to appreciate the rules of evidence. As scientists, we have to possess the ability of recognition, the skill of documentation, the knowledge of examination, and the power of reconstruction. Also, we have to faithfully testify regarding laboratory findings in court in an objective manner.

Perhaps the most important issue in forensic investigation is establishing professional standards. There is a need for standards of practice in the collection, examination, and analysis of physical evidence, the interpretation of results, and the giving of testimony in court. Both forensic and legal professions must carefully examine their role in examining and presenting scientific evidence in the court of law. The professionalism and ethical standards of both groups in criminal and civil investigations must continue to develop to ensure that justice can be served.

HENRY C. LEE and TIMOTHY M. PALMBACH

See also **Crime Laboratory; Crime Scene Search and Evidence Collection; Criminal Investigation; DNA Fingerprinting; Forensic Evidence; Forensic Science; Polygraphy**

References and Further Readings

Lee, Henry C., Timothy M. Palmbach, and Marilyn T. Miller. 2001. *Henry Lee's crime scene handbook*. San Diego: Academic Press.

Lee, Henry C., and Howard A. Harris. 2000. *Physical evidence in forensic science*. Tucson, AZ: Lawyers & Judges Publishing.

FORENSIC MEDICINE

Forensic medicine is the application of medicine to the legal arena. It is a very broad area of study integral to the entirety of forensic science. While many subdisciplines of forensics have had to struggle for acceptance from judges and attorneys, medical evidence has enjoyed a long history of courtroom acceptance. The historical record indicates that medical evidence was presented in courtrooms dating back to Ancient Greece and China. Since the 1960s and the due process revolution, medical and forensic evidence has become increasingly important to the resolution of cases within the criminal justice system, since fewer cases are resolved by confessions and more are resolved by the presentation of physical evidence to the judge and jury.

Forensic medicine is divided into three general subareas: forensic pathology, forensic psychiatry; and forensic toxicology and serology. There are also a number of fields closely related to forensic medicine, including forensic odontology and anthropology and forensic biology, chemistry, and biochemistry.

Forensic Pathology

Pathology is the study of disease and injury from the causative aspect, as distinct from those branches of medicine that are concerned with the diagnosis and treatment of disease. Within pathology are numerous subspecialties such as hematology (the study of blood), microbiology (the study of bacteria and other microorganisms), clinical biochemistry, and histopathology. Forensic pathology, a subdiscipline of pathology, is the study of how and why people die, concentrating on sudden, unexpected, and violent deaths. During a homicide investigation, either a forensic pathologist or the medical examiner will conduct the autopsy, which includes a thorough interior physical examination of the body and specialized laboratory tests.

The medical examiner is a physician appointed in a particular jurisdiction to oversee death investigation. It is the responsibility of the medical examiner to lead the investigation of all deaths that are sudden, unexpected, or violent, and make a determination as to the time, manner (natural, accident, suicide, homicide), and cause of death.

Initially, the colonies had a coroner system very much like the system that had been in place in Europe for 1,000 years. A coroner is an elected official who may or may not have medical training. Autopsies were carried out in Massachusetts prior to 1647. In 1666 coroners in Maryland were appointed by county. In the eighteenth century, Philadelphia became the major center of medical learning in colonial America with the first medical school being developed at the University of Pennsylvania. Prior to that time, physicians received training in Europe. In the late 1870s, growing dissatisfaction with the coroner system led jurisdictions to change to a medical examiner system. The first medical examiner, Frank W. Draper, was appointed in Boston. Draper also wrote a textbook on legal medicine in 1905. Currently about half of the U.S. population is served by a medical examiner. Those jurisdictions still using the coroner system are generally smaller, more rural areas. However, Pittsburgh, Pennsylvania, and its surrounding Allegheny County still use a coroner system. While Allegheny County's coroner is an elected official, individuals in this position have long since been medical doctors.

It is the primary duty of the medical examiner to establish the time, manner, and cause of death. Frequently, time of death is not in question, because most deaths are witnessed. It is only when a death is not witnessed that the question of time of death becomes important. Time of death can be established by looking at the interval between the time when the individual was last seen alive and the time when the body was found. The larger this interval, the more difficult it is to accurately pinpoint the time of death. The manner of death refers to whether the individual died of natural causes, accident, suicide, or homicide. Often, this is not a difficult question, but a suicide is not always clearly a suicide, and a perpetrator may attempt to disguise a homicide. The medical examiner will determine both the immediate and proximal causes of death. The immediate cause is the last event prior to a death, which may happen hours or days before death. The proximal cause of death is the first event leading up to a death, which may have been evident in the individual for years prior to death.

In a homicide investigation, the body is usually the single most important piece of evidence that will be processed. Also, the area surrounding the body will generally contain most of the forensic evidence in the case. The medical examiner may also be called upon to testify in a civil or criminal courtroom regarding the findings from the completed investigation.

Medical examiners have received a medical degree and frequently have received advanced training in pathology (the study of disease mechanisms and death) and forensic pathology (the study of how and why people die). They also generally acquire knowledge in a variety of fields related to forensic medicine, for example, ballistics, serology, and DNA analysis.

Forensic Psychiatry

Forensic psychiatrists combine knowledge and practical experience in medicine, mental health, the neurosciences, and the law. The vast majority of work that forensic psychiatrists (and psychologists) perform is on the civil side of the law and deals with product liability, custody issues, and competency to handle personal affairs.

In the criminal court, forensic psychiatrists may testify regarding issues of sanity and competency. Sanity refers to an individual's state of mind during the commission of a crime. Competency generally refers to competency to enter a plea, competency to stand trial, and competency to be executed.

A forensic psychiatrist may be called upon to construct an offender profile, or criminal personality profile. Offender profiling is a method of identifying the perpetrator of a crime based on an analysis of the nature of the offense, the victim, and the manner in which the crime was committed. It is typically used when there is little physical evidence that can be used to identify a suspect, when the crime is bizarre or appears to be serial in nature, or when murder with sexual overtones is committed.

A forensic psychiatrist may also be called upon to determine whether a sexual offender meets the statutory criteria to be deemed a violent sexual predator and subject to civil commitment. This evaluation takes into account the current offense and the statutory definition of "violent sexual predator."

Prior to any psychiatric evidence being presented in a courtroom, a forensic psychiatrist will conduct a thorough examination of the individual to evaluate mental status. The psychiatric testimony may also be supported by the results of psychological testing and neurological examination.

Forensic psychiatrists have received a medical degree and advanced training in psychiatry. Their knowledge of forensic psychiatry is acquired through working in a variety of forensic settings, including mental health facilities and prisons.

Forensic Toxicology and Serology

Forensic toxicology is concerned with chemicals (drugs and poisons) found in the human body. During a death investigation, forensic toxicologists may make a determination as to whether the victim was killed using a poison such as lead. Toxicology results can also determine whether a drug such as Rohypnol was used during a sexual assault.

Throughout history, poisons have been used to harm and kill. The Roman emperor Claudius may have been poisoned. During the fourteenth and fifteenth centuries, poisoning was quite common in Italy. There are numerous tales of poisoning involving the Borgia popes. Poisoning as a method of killing spread throughout Europe during the sixteenth, seventeenth, and eighteenth centuries. It was so common that it was universally feared by the nobility.

In the United States, the New York medical examiner's office established the first toxicology laboratory in 1918. This predates the inception of the first forensic science laboratory. The American Board of Forensic Toxicology was founded in 1975.

Serologists are involved with the identification and processing of blood, semen, saliva, and other bodily fluids; they may also be involved in bloodstain, bloodspatter, and DNA analysis. These types of evidence may be crucial in sexual assault cases or during a homicide investigation.

Related Fields

There are many fields that are related to forensic medicine. Professionals in the fields of forensic odontology and forensic anthropology assist in the identification of bodies. Professionals in the fields of forensic biology, forensic chemistry, and forensic biochemistry frequently work in laboratories.

Forensic Odontology and Anthropology

Generally, forensic odontologists (dentists) and anthropologists will assist in the

identification of a body that otherwise cannot be identified. It may be burned, in a significant state of decay, or even skeletonized. Forensic anthropologists are most frequently called upon when skeletonized remains are found. From these remains, the anthropologist will assist in identifying the victim and may also provide an approximate date and cause of death. Forensic anthropologists have a Ph.D. degree in anthropology.

Forensic odontologists compare antemortem dental records to present observations of dental characteristics in a body for the purpose of identifying the victim. They may also be called upon to link a suspect to bite marks left upon a living or dead victim. Forensic odontologists have completed dental school.

Forensic Biology, Chemistry, and Biochemistry

Individuals in the areas of forensic biology, forensic chemistry, and forensic biochemistry have received training in their primary disciplines, having received either a master's or a Ph.D. degree. These individuals often specialize in more narrow areas, such as optics, microbiology, molecular biology, or genetics. Forensic chemists may work in forensic laboratories, analyzing mostly drug samples, which makes up the bulk of the work of forensic laboratories. Forensic biologists may work with biological samples that are received in a laboratory.

AYN EMBAR-SEDDON and ALLAN D. PASS

See also **DNA Fingerprinting; Forensic Evidence; Forensic Investigations; Forensic Science**

References and Further Reading

Curran, William J., et al. 1980. *Modern legal medicine, psychiatry & forensic science*. Philadelphia: Davis.
DiMaio, V., and D. DiMaio. 1992. *Forensic pathology*. Boca Raton, FL: CRC Press.

Eckert, William G. 1997. *Introduction to forensic sciences*. New York: CRC Press.

Eckert, W. G., and R. J. Turco. 1997. Forensic psychiatry. In *Introduction to Forensic Sciences*, ed. William G. Eckert, 57–69. New York: CRC Press.

Gordon, Isidor, and H. A. Shapiro. 1982. *Forensic medicine: A guide to principles*. 2nd ed. New York: Churchill Livingstone.

Tedeschi, G. Cesare, et al. 1977. *Forensic medicine*. 3 vols. Philadelphia: Saunders.

Wecht, C. H. 1997. Legal medicine and jurisprudence. In *Introduction to forensic sciences*, ed. William G. Eckert, 81–92. New York: CRC Press.

FORENSIC SCIENCE

Definition

There have been many changes regarding the definition and common usage of the word "forensic." In college English departments, the term refers to a formalized debate. It is not uncommon for "forensic" mail, intended for the English department, to be delivered to the Forensic Science department in error. The addition of "science" to the word "forensic" implies a scientific debate. In the early 1900s, what we now refer to as forensic science was referred to as police science. Crime laboratories, as they were previously known, are now called forensic laboratories. Currently, the term is overused, and many jobs only remotely related to a legal activity or the courts have the adjective "forensic" attached to their job title. Television news coverage, reality and true crime programming, and prime-time crime dramas have had a great influence in perpetuating the overuse of the term.

Forensic science refers to the legal debate related to the scientific examination of evidence and its admissibility and value in a court of law. The debate is refereed by the judge, takes place in a courtroom, and involves the defense, the prosecution, and expert witnesses in a case. This debate is based on both legal issues and the valid application of the scientific method and technologies to the examination of the evidence.

History of Forensic Science

Historically, modern forensic science as we practice it today had its foundations in England and Europe in the 1800s, even though ancient history has many examples of forensic science being practiced. The practice that has evolved into the contemporary medical examiner system can be traced back to the British coroners, public officials who would pronounce a person dead and could describe the cause of death.

Physical evidence, prior to that time, was of much less importance than the testimony of an eyewitness. Behavioral studies since have shown that several people witnessing the same event will often have radically different accounts as to what occurred. For this reason alone, the importance of physical evidence became widely relied upon and required the associated development of a scientific basis for the analyses—hence the birth of the various forensic specialties.

In the 1800s, Hans Gross, a German, and Edmond Locard, a Frenchman, were responsible for developing the scientific principle for the exchange of trace evidence between two objects that come in contact with each other. This principle is the basis for seeking evidence that has been transferred to or from the people or things that come in contact with each other at a crime scene.

In 1923, Chief August Vollmer of the Los Angeles Police Department established a laboratory within the department where they practiced "police science" and used the scientific method in working their cases. Scientists were sought out by the police to help them solve problems. University professors served as some of the earliest forensic scientists. In the 1930s, Vollmer headed the first university program in the United States for criminology and criminalistics, at the University of California, Berkeley. It was not until 1948 that the university officially formed the School of Criminology, headed by criminalist Paul Kirk. Today in the United States there are more than forensic laboratories at the federal, state, and local levels and numerous private forensic laboratories. Many European forensic institutes were formed after World War II.

Forensic Science Specialties

There are many forensic science specialties, as exemplified by the various sections of the American Academy of Forensic Sciences (AAFS). AAFS was formed in 1950 and today has more than six thousand members internationally. The forensic specialty sections at AAFS are general, criminalistics, engineering sciences, jurisprudence, odontology, pathology/biology, physical anthropology, psychiatry/behavioral sciences, toxicology, and questioned documents.

Digital Evidence

The newest section under consideration by AAFS is a Digital and Multimedia Section. With the advent of personal computers, cellular telephones, and digital photographs and movies, information in a digital format has become a new category of forensic evidence. The Scientific Working Groups for Digital Evidence (SWGDE) and for Imaging Technologies (SWGIT) were developed and supported by the Federal Bureau of Investigation (FBI) so that forensic experts can work together to develop consensus guidelines for how digital evidence is to be identified, collected, preserved, and examined for evidence of a crime.

The development of the Internet has been a wonderful resource for forensic science while at the same time an international phenomenon for new forms of criminal activity. In past years, it was obvious when a bank was being robbed. Today, banks can be robbed electronically without it being immediately obvious to the customers or even the bankers themselves. E-mail and chat rooms can pose many dangers for children and adults alike. Luckily, forensic evidence exists on the Internet and on all electronic devices.

"Computer forensics" is a term that has been used to describe evidence on computers. It has almost become outdated, given the advent of cell phones with numerous computer-like capabilities and automobiles that operate almost completely by computer chips. "Digital forensics" is a more inclusive term that covers all technologies operating in a binary format. Universities are developing programs to meet these new challenges and to develop the scientific basis for these new digital forensic specialties.

Public Opinion

After the O. J. Simpson trial, "forensic" became a household word. This was later followed by numerous television shows, including the very popular *CSI* (*Crime Scene Investigation*) series. The public has been given both unreal expectations for forensic science laboratories and the false appearance that forensic scientists can be investigators in designer clothes at a crime scene as well as scientists in the laboratory. This has been referred to as the "*CSI* effect" by the *US News & World Report* (Roane 2005). Juries, based on their television knowledge, now second-guess the real forensic scientists during trials. It is important to remember that real-life forensic scientists work within a real-life legal system; sometimes justice prevails and sometimes it does not.

Professionalism

Forensic science is practiced by extremely dedicated professionals. Their opinions, while their own, are based on valid science. They must try not to be unduly influenced by the press or higher authorities. To that end, laboratory directors, with the assistance of the Federal Bureau of Investigation (FBI), formed the American Society of Crime Laboratory Directors in 1972. This professional organization supports the development of laboratory managers with high standards in both ethics and forensic science.

The Scientific Method

The basic process that a forensic scientist follows when looking at a crime scene or examining evidence in the laboratory is first to clearly understand the circumstances of the crime and the examinations requested by the law enforcement investigator. These observations along with the information that the evidence reveals allows the scientist to formulate what happened, how it happened, and when it happened. The initial assumption and rationale are considered a hypothesis. Further examination of the evidence and comparing the questioned exhibit to a known sample verify or discredit the original hypothesis. The examinations continue and comparisons are made until there is a clear association of the evidence with the crime, a clear exclusion of such an association, or a clear indication that the evidence is unsuitable for reaching a conclusion.

The implementation of the scientific method will extract the truth in a manner that can be duplicated by others who follow the same procedures. The scientific method as it applies to forensic science is as follows:

1. The forensic scientist makes an observation at a crime scene or about a particular item of evidence.
2. Based on the observations, the scientist develops a theory about what took place; this is referred to as "developing a hypothesis."
3. The scientist tests the hypothesis using logic and experimentation, including only those things in the experiment that are relevant and excluding those that cannot be proved relevant or whose source is unknown.
4. The scientist tests the hypothesis by examining the results of the experimentation, which lead to particular changes to the original hypothesis, the experimental design, and/or the way the experiment was conducted.
5. The testing and subsequent alterations of the hypothesis are repeated until all of the experimental data from the testing results in proving one solid and well-defined hypothesis.

The Role of the Forensic Scientist

The role of a forensic scientist is to use the logic of the scientific method when conducting the various observations and examinations of physical evidence. It is not the forensic scientist's role to determine guilt or innocence of the suspect, but rather through observation, experimentation, and interpretation of physical evidence, they determine what happened, how the crime took place, when and where it happened, and who could have been at the crime scene during the crime.

Because the U.S. legal system is based on the "presumption of innocence until proved guilty," it makes sense that the forensic scientist might assume that the evidence will support the innocence of the suspect. By developing a hypothesis of innocence, the forensic scientist tests the hypothesis by trying to prove that the physical evidence was not involved in the alleged crime and that the crime was not committed by the suspect. When all hypothetical theories, experiments, and data cannot uphold the suspect's innocence, but rather put the suspect at the crime scene holding the gun that killed the victim, then the "presumption of innocence" may not be upheld.

Evidence Examination

Typically, the "presumption of innocence" is the mind-set for all forensic scientists. The actual approach to evidence examination involves comparing a questioned exhibit from a crime scene to a known exhibit taken from a suspect by the investigator. Forensic laboratories and their scientists are given the legal responsibility to take possession of the physical evidence, to protect it from damage, contamination, or alteration, and to keep it under their care and control while they perform their scientific examinations. They make scientific observations that fall into three categories:

1. The evidence can be connected to the crime scene or victim.
2. The evidence can be eliminated as being related to the crime scene or victim.
3. The evidence is inconclusive.

In a criminal investigation, forensic scientists examine and analyze evidence using such tools as basic optical microscopes, which enhance visual observations. Evidence examination also utilizes advanced instrumentation such as infrared spectrometers, gas chromatographs, mass spectrometers, and scanning electron microscopes with energy dispersive X-ray analysis. Such instruments can be used to separate complex chemical and biological mixtures and to identify the molecular structure of each compound or elements of interest in the evidence related to the investigation of a crime. The scanning electron microscope is capable of doing elemental analysis of each layer of paint in a small paint chip that adheres to a pry bar for comparison to a known sample of paint from the door facing supposedly attacked by the pry bar. Computer databases allow for matching genetic material, deoxyribonucleic acid (DNA), from the biological stain at a crime scene to an individual whose DNA is in the national database.

Using science and technology allows the forensic scientist to draw conclusions about the evidence that is legally sound and scientifically valid. Information and physical evidence used in forming a valid conclusion must be attributed to a specific source. That source may be a class or group of items or connected to one specific item or person. If there is any question that the information or evidence is suspect or contaminated, it should not be analyzed or used as a basis for conclusions.

The science used to examine evidence must not only be valid but also provide a traceable chain of custody for each item of evidence, which must be maintained from the crime scene to the courtroom. In order for items of evidence that were examined by the forensic scientist to be admitted into court, the items must be handed to the expert on the witness stand for identification. The expert then describes from whom the evidence was received, how it was received, and how it was returned to the investigator. The expert will have made a mark in the evidence (usually initials and the date of examination or receipt), or if the evidence is very small and in a container, the expert will have initialed and dated the container, the seal, and the evidence tag. Without this secure chain of custody, the best scientific evidence will not be admitted into court as evidence.

The Forensic Scientist in Court

Forensic scientists must be qualified as an "expert" each time they go to court to testify in a particular case. Once qualified as experts, they are able to give their opinions on matters related to the evidence they have examined and analyzed. Nonexperts must testify to only the facts. After the expert is sworn in and on the witness stand, the individual must be "qualified" as an expert by a process called voir dire. The prosecuting attorney will ask his or her name, place of work, job title, length of time employed as a forensic scientist, education and training, number of publications, other experience relevant to expertise in the matter before the court, number of cases worked, reports written, testimonies given as an expert, so forth.

The defense attorney will then either accept the forensic scientist as an expert or ask additional questions that might discredit him or her, such as "Have you ever failed a course in college?" "Is the college you graduated from accredited?" "Have you ever made a mistake?" "Have you ever driven your car after drinking alcohol?" "Have you ever been arrested?" "Have charges of any kind been filed against you?" "Can you list three journals in forensic science that you have read in the past year?" If things are brought out that the jury might find questionable about the expert, then the prosecutor will redirect questions that will allow the expert to clarify any misleading impressions that the defense attorney's questions might have created. The defense can also have a redirect.

Once qualified, the expert is handed an item of evidence by the prosecutor and asked to identify it. Once the expert identifies the evidence item, questions begin as to the chain of custody and security of the evidence while in the expert's possession and, finally, the results of the examination. After this direct examination by the defense attorney, which may be minutes, hours, days, or weeks (depending on the circumstances), the defense attorney has the opportunity to cross-examine the expert. If the evidence is strong, the defense will attack the credibility of the expert.

Expert witnesses are called to render opinions as to the value of evidence they have examined or reviewed. The prosecution will have an expert testify to his or her findings. The defense will likewise have an opposing expert to refute the findings of the prosecutor's expert. For scientific evidence to be entered into court under the *Frye* standard, which dates back to 1923, the scientific specialty or technology has to be "generally accepted" by experts in the field.

In 1993, *Daubert v. Merrill Pharmaceutical* resulted in the judge being the "gatekeeper" for admitting scientific evidence into court. Both *Daubert* and later *Kumho* inquiries regarding scientific processes indicate that they should be flexible and suggest that the scientific theory or technique should be tested and its error rates known, should have relevant scientific articles published in peer-reviewed journals, should have standards related to the techniques applied, and should be accepted by the relevant scientific community.

The jury or judge (if the trial is before only a judge) has the responsibility to interpret all of the evidence, including physical evidence presented by the forensic scientists, and the testimony of witnesses, investigators, and the suspect to determine guilt or innocence. If the evidence is not strong enough to make a decision of neither guilt nor innocence, it is referred to as a "hung jury." The case will either be dismissed or scheduled for a retrial.

Forensic science specialties will continue to evolve as we move into new lifestyles and new technologies are developed. New issues and new evidence will always be facing our society and the forensic science community. The basic principles and ethics of forensic science, however, will remain the same.

Carrie Morgan Whitcomb

571

See also **Computer Crimes; Forensic Evidence; Forensic Investigations; Forensic Medicine**

References and Further Reading

Eckert, William G. 1997. *Introduction to forensic science.* 2nd ed. Boca Raton, FL: CRC Press.

Fisher, Barry A. J. 2000. *Techniques of crime scene investigation.* 6th ed. Boca Raton, FL: CRC Press.

Roane, Kit R. 2005. The CSI effect. *US News and World Report,* April, 48–54.

Saferstein, Richard. 2004. *Criminalistics: An introduction to forensic science,* 8th ed. Upper Saddle River, NJ: Pearson/Prentice-Hall.

FOSDICK, RAYMOND B.

Raymond Blaine Fosdick (1883–1972), lawyer, public servant, and author, was born in Buffalo, New York, the son of a high school principal. Of Puritan descent, Fosdick began his higher education at Colgate College but transferred to Princeton, where one of his intellectual idols, Woodrow Wilson, was president. Fosdick received his B.A. degree in 1905 and his M.A. in 1906 and was elected to Phi Beta Kappa. New York Law School granted him the LL.B. degree in 1908, after which he went to work for New York City Mayor George B. McClellan. At first assistant corporation counsel, Fosdick two years later became commissioner of accounts.

The next notable event in his life came when John D. Rockefeller, Jr., on behalf of the Rockefeller Bureau of Social Hygiene, asked him to make a broad study of police organizations in Europe. On the basis of a few previous meetings, two connected with an investigation of the white-slave traffic in prostitutes and one with a Bible class, Rockefeller had singled out Fosdick, a green attorney, for a demanding project. Fosdick immersed himself in the task and in 1915, *European Police Systems* was published. From his autobiography, *Chronicle of a Generation*:

> My itinerary took me to practically every large city in Europe except those in Russia . . . . In every city I visited I tried to see the police in actual operation . . . . The outstanding impression I received from my study in Europe was that police administration there was a distinct career which attracted the best brains obtainable . . . . Its elaborate training schools for recruits had no counterpart in the United States.

Fosdick's compliments continued to flow and American police appeared amateurish in comparison. Naturally, the book stirred immediate interest at home but gathered an even larger audience in Europe. An acute observer and fluent writer, Fosdick had proved his worth to such an extent that Rockefeller asked him to write a companion volume, *American Police Systems*, published in 1920. This time Fosdick visited seventy-two cities and, with what must have seemed a poison pen to the American police, indicted the whole system of law enforcement in this country:

> In America the student of police travels from one political squabble to another, too often from one scandal to another. He finds a shifting leadership of mediocre calibre . . . there is little conception of policing as a profession or as a science to be matured and developed.

Hardly finished yet, Fosdick continued:

> Every police department is a graveyard of projects and improvements which, had they been developed to maturity, would have reconstructed the police work of the city . . . . We have, indeed, little to be proud of.

He did explain, however, that in European cities the volume of crime was much lower and therefore more manageable. European populations were more homogeneous and less inclined to crime caused by assimilation barriers. With less crime to combat and people tied through kinship, European police could achieve a higher standard of professionalism. No matter, the word was out that, according to Fosdick, American police were decidedly inferior to European.

Criminal Justice in Cleveland, published in 1922, did not soften the blows dealt by the earlier books. Fosdick had joined ten other writers, such as Felix Frankfurter and Roscoe Pound, to conduct a "scientific study" of criminal justice in that city. Fosdick had, if anything, sharpened his criticism:

> Lack of intelligence and imagination in Cleveland's police work is shown in the ragged character of the internal arrangements of the department . . . . Inadequate equipment adds to this appearance of raggedness . . . . Official lethargy lies behind much that is distressing in this picture.

Cleveland and other American police departments (guilty in absentia) bristled at his denunciations, but the glaring public attention was impetus enough for most police departments to start on the uphill road to improvement.

Once again Rockefeller convinced Fosdick to take on a challenging project. He was to make a thorough study of how various countries of the world handled the sale of alcohol. In collaboration with Albert L. Scott, Fosdick wrote *Toward Liquor Control*, published in 1933. It presented the arguments for and against selling liquor through regulation by license or through a state authority system (preferred by Fosdick and Scott), though they admitted that no system was "final." Rockefeller's specific request for studies of the liquor business in Canada and certain European countries filled the appendices. The repeal of the Eighteenth Amendment in 1933, and this book written in anticipation of repeal, relieved much of the workload police had shouldered during the thirteen years of Prohibition.

Fosdick's substantial contributions to policing were only one side of his career. He lived a long life full of other accomplishments and honors. In 1916, he rode with "Black Jack" Pershing in Mexico against Pancho Villa. In 1917, he observed military training methods in Canada, England, and France. What he learned went into *Keeping Our Fighters Fit* (1918), written with E. F. Allen, a book made necessary because America had not fought in a full-scale conflict since the Civil War. After World War I, President Wilson chose him to represent the United States at the League of Nations; Fosdick resigned when the Senate failed to ratify the Covenant (1920). By 1930, he had been elected trustee of seven prestigious public service organizations: the Rockefeller Foundation, the Rockefeller Institute for Medical Research, the Rockefeller General Education Board, the International Education Board, the Spelman Fund, the Brookings Institution, and the National Institute of Public Administration. In 1936, he became president of the Rockefeller Foundation and the General Education Board. Entrusted with nearly $200 million dollars, he administered the money prudently, much of it going for educational grants and disease prevention research.

The author of fourteen books, Fosdick struck people as "a good conversationalist, genial, witty, and generous." Of course, his having been at the center of so much turbulent history enhanced his storytelling. Recipient of the Distinguished Service Medal and two doctorates, accorded the rank of commander of the French Legion of Honor, elected as a fellow of the American Academy of Arts and Sciences, and as a member of the American Philosophical Society, he had much to be proud of. Tragedy befell him in 1932 when his first wife shot and killed their two children before taking her own life. At the apogee of his public career in 1936 he married a second time, to Elizabeth Miner.

WILLIAM G. BAILEY

References and Further Reading

Current Biography. 1945. February, 18–20.

Fosdick, Raymond B. 1915/1969. *European police systems*. Montclair, NJ: Patterson Smith.

———. 1920/1969. *American police systems*. Montclair, NJ: Patterson Smith.

———. 1958. *Chronicle of a generation: An autobiography*. New York: Harper and Brothers.

Fosdick, Raymond B., and Albert L. Scott. 1933. *Toward liquor control*. New York: Harper and Brothers.

Fosdick, Raymond B., et al. 1968. *Criminal Justice in Cleveland*. Reprint of 1922 ed. Montclair, NJ: Patterson Smith.

New York Times. 1972. 41 (July 19): 3.

FRAUD INVESTIGATION

Throughout history some people have always cheated and tricked others. Since the fourteenth century, such dishonesty and deceit has been known generically as fraud, a word that has far older etymological roots. Yet, oddly to our eyes, English law failed for many centuries to grapple effectively with fraud. Not until 1677 did the Statute of Frauds become law, requiring wills to be written, signed, and witnessed and deeds to be provided for the creation and assignment of all trusts. Victims of fraud could in principle find relief in equity, provided their own unbusiness-like behavior had not been a contributory factor. The English judiciary was uneasy about laying down rules for the definition of various types of fraud. Lord Nottingham, the Lord Chancellor, said that such rules "would be perpetually eluded by new schemes which the fertility of men's invention would contrive."

There was a widespread feeling in the eighteenth century, and even into our own times, that a person defrauded deserved to lose. As an English jurist asked rhetorically in the eighteenth century, "Shall we indict a man for making a fool of another?" A legal maxim summed up the attitude of many jurists and of the public at large: caveat emptor, or "let the buyer beware."

Such hardheaded advice ignored the fact that many of the people defrauded were ignorant and gullible; that others, however prudent, had been cheated by master confidence tricksters; and that some offenses, such as the willful misrepresentation of goods or real estate, could be detected only by experts or after the fraudulent transaction had taken place. To be sure, many victims of fraudsters are trapped by their own greed, but to argue that they do not deserve redress is to shift the blame from where it really lies.

In the past decade or so, legal and popular attitudes in the United States have undergone a dynamic metamorphosis, with *caveat venditor* ("let the seller beware") replacing caveat emptor. There has also been a marked change in the attitude of police administrators. Until recently, many saw investigation of fraud as too time consuming and difficult, with a relatively low probability of successful prosecution and adequate sentencing. Fraud investigation therefore took a back seat to the more emotive crimes of violence, burglary, and automobile theft and drug-related offenses. Now there is growing recognition that the losses caused by fraud are often more traumatic, and have longer-term effects, than the quick and sudden violence of the average street offense or burglary.

Nature of Fraud

The "trilogy of fraud" describes the three basic forms of theft: false pretenses, trick and device, and embezzlement. All three are statutory offenses. Effective investigation requires fundamental knowledge of each type of fraud.

False Pretenses

The requisites are (1) *specific intent to defraud*, a frame of mind on the part of the thief, (2) *misrepresentations* by the thief of a material fact, which can be in any form of communication, expressed or implied, (3) *reliance* by the victim on the representation, inducing him or her to release property to the thief, and (4) *actual loss*, this being satisfied if the victim in fact did not receive what he or she bargained for.

The intent of the *victim* is also material. It has to be the victim's intent that title should accompany the transfer of property to the thief. The victim's intent is essential as it differentiates between the elements of false pretenses and theft by trick and device.

False pretenses thefts present an added requisite, *corroboration*. This is usually demonstrated by the "false token" or writing subscribed to by the accused, or the testimony of two witnesses and corroborating circumstances. This is a precaution against perjury by an ostensible victim. Frequently, allegations of false pretenses are based upon contractual arrangements. This brings into play the parole evidence rule, which precludes any evidence of prior or contemporaneous verbal agreements that would alter the provisions of a written contract. However, in a criminal action based upon the same facts, the parole evidence rule is generally held to be operative only between the original parties to the contract, and in a criminal prosecution the state may go outside the provisions of the contract to establish the accused's real intent and the truth of representations made during negotiations.

Trick and Device

In this form of theft the basic elements of specific intent, misrepresentation, and reliance and loss are the same as those required in prosecution of theft by false pretenses. However, trick and device is distinguished by the intent of the victim, who does not intend to relinquish title to the property, only its possession to the accused. The victim expects that it (money, or something of value) will be used only for a specific purpose, such as a loan, investment, or purchases. The accused, however, has no intention of putting it to such use, specifically intending from the outset to divert it to his or her

own use. There is no requirement here for the "corroboration" demanded in false pretenses prosecutions.

This form of theft is the basis for the prosaic street cons or bunco games. It is a fast-moving, high-mobility operation, usually with smaller losses involved (although this is relative to those victimized) and a higher frequency rate. The street con involves "the three G's" (greed, gullibility, and goodness). One or all can be present. Whether it is the victim's avarice, naiveté, stupidity, or misunderstanding, the con artist works to create a feeling of rapport and "confidence." The term "street-con" relates primarily to the "switch" scams, the "bank examiner," and similar approaches. However, this form of theft is not limited to the "short" or "street" buncos. The legal format (elements) has application to long-term, major frauds also, such as those in the securities investment field, fraudulent loans, and real estate scams.

Embezzlement

This form of theft is extremely difficult to prevent in spite of enforced basic accounting procedures and internal control methods utilized by the victim or his company. It is a crime of opportunity, frequently remains undiscovered for long periods, and is usually repetitive, not an isolated act. The embezzler, like the check writer, is the classic recidivist. The elements of the offense require that (1) there is a fiduciary relationship between the victim and the accused, a form of trust whereby the victim entrusts property to the accused (employee usually), (2) the property comes into the hand (dominion, control, possession) of the agent-servant-employee as the property of the victim, the title remaining with the victim at all times, (3) the employee-agent receives the property in the course of employment (some exceptions exist such as obtaining from a constructive trust) and it is lawfully in his or her hands, having received it properly in the scope of employment, (4) the agent-employee forms the intent to *take* the property for personal use or for some use not contemplated within the trust and deprives the owner of it, this intent forming *after* possession is acquired legally, (5) the agent-employee takes control-possession of the property, and (6) the victim never intends the agent-employee to use the property for any purpose other than that specified or agreed upon. The rule of corroboration as in theft by false pretenses is not required here.

Motive is important to establish in examining the embezzlement. The crucial question is, why does a certain suspect need the money? The need does not always have to be rooted in an antisocial behavior. It can represent perfectly legitimate problems, such as house payments, medical bills, or automobile expenses and costs.

Check Offenses

Although most jurisdictions have specific sections of the criminal codes that relate to the "paper" offenses—forgery, nonsufficient funds checks, fictitious checks, and so forth—the crimes are still essentially false pretenses. The technical areas involved include handwriting identification, document examination, paper typing, and check classification systems, but the fundamental principles still remain: deceit and trust. The act of forgery occurs when a person, with intent to defraud, signs the name of another person (or a fictitious person) without authority to do so, or falsely makes, alters, or forges an instrument (checks, notes, bills, contracts, and the like) and tenders, utters, or passes it.

Nonsufficient funds (NSF) checks probably are the most prevalent offenses. When a person with the intent to defraud makes a check, knowing *at the time* there are insufficient monies on hand or credit with the bank to pay in full the amount on the face of the check, and presents, utters,

or passes the instrument, he or she has committed the offense. The amounts required to differentiate between a felony and misdemeanor vary by jurisdiction. Because of the multiplicity of NSF check cases, many police agencies are forced to set an arbitrary minimum limit on the amounts involved. This administrative device does not satisfy the victim, but budgetary and personnel demands prevail.

The Investigative Process

With a few exceptions, most major frauds are legislatively mandated to federal and state agencies. That still leaves the police with more than enough offenses to consume the time and other resources they have available.

A police agency that investigates fraud must adhere to the basic rule applicable to any specialized area of inquiry: placing someone in control who has the needed training and knowledge. Just as efficient homicide investigators must have some understanding of physiology, biology, and psychology, so must fraud investigators be acquainted with the applicable law, business practices, accounting principles, modern data processing, and psychology. They must have this requisite array of knowledge, perhaps not to the level of the professional in these varied fields, but at least to the degree that enables them to recognize the significance of the information developed and the need for specialized help. Consequently, in this era of specialization, the general assignment investigator is losing ground in the larger and more progressive police agencies to specialized investigators.

Any investigation of a protracted nature requires the formulation of a plan that outlines definitively the areas of concern. One form that has proved its efficacy for countless years is a variation of the standard military operational order, or Five Paragraph Field Order: (1) the situation or assessment, (2) the mission, (3) the execution, (4) logistics, and (5) command.

1. *Situation assessment.* What allegedly occurred? Is the initial information received from a victim or informants, or the ensuing investigation? Victims, through embarrassment and confusion, frequently furnish erroneous facts. This requires a logical assessment of the victim's motivation, emotional and mental state, degree of reliance, and ability to relate accurately the representation being made, its falsity, and the actual property loss.

2. *Mission.* This segment relates the strategy to be used in a given case/situation. A case cannot be based solely upon the unsupported allegations of the victim. The legal requirements of the particular crimes have to be met. Investigative efforts will be directed to documentation, witness testimony, and instruments, all needed to prove or disprove that a crime in fact has been committed. This is the who, what, when, and where of an investigation.

3. *Execution.* What tactically is to be done to carry out the mission? To do this, consideration has to be given to the documentation to be developed, the witnesses to be identified and interviewed, the corroboration to be established, and the suspects to be identified and researched, including their net worth and the source and application of their funds, and the similar acts and transactions to be analyzed to establish the plan, scheme, design, and intent of the suspects and victim. Intent is a subjective thing, a frame of mind that is extremely difficult to establish and prove.

4. *Logistics (support).* Consideration is given here to the probable technical and expert assistance that will be needed to support the investigators. It may be available within the police agency or it may have to be obtained from outside. Examples of such outside experts range from accountants and security analysts to plumbers and tile setters and can include any type of help that is required to effectively carry out a successful inquiry. No approach is too ethereal or too prosaic.

5. *Command.* A fundamental principle applicable to all forms of police investigation concerns the director of operations. There can be *only one* person who has the responsibility, authority, and final overall accountability. These charges cannot be delegated or handled by a committee. A bifurcated approach, with its resulting duplication and conflicts of direction, hampers the effectiveness of any investigation, thereby reducing its chances of being successful.

ROBERT S. NEWSOM

See also **Identify Theft; White Collar Crime**

References and Further Reading

Bailey, F. Lee, and Henry B. Rothblatt. 1969. *Defending business and white collar crime.* Rochester, NY: Lawyers Cooperative Publishing.

Edelhertz, Herbert, et al. 1977. *Investigation of white collar crime.* Washington, DC: Department of Justice, Law Enforcement Assistance Administration.

Geis, Gilbert. 1968. *White collar criminal.* New York: Atherton Press.

Glick, Rush G., and Robert S. Newsom. 1974. *Fraud investigation: Fundamentals for police.* Springfield, IL: Charles C Thomas.

Soble, Ronald L., and Robert E. Dallos. 1975. *The impossible dream.* New York: New American Library.

Sutherland, Edwin H. 1967. *White collar crime.* New York: Holt, Rinehart and Winston.

FUTURE OF INTERNATIONAL POLICING

It is only recently that "international policing" has become a focus of scholarly concern, as evidenced by the previous two editions of the *Encyclopedia of Police*

Science. There was no entry on themes pertaining to "international policing" in the first edition (1989). In the second (1995), there was an entry on "international police cooperation," authored by Malcolm Anderson, which provides a thorough description and consideration of the implications of the many connections—in terms of formal legal-institutional connections and more informal practices—that link public police agencies in the international sphere. (Anderson has updated his entry for this current edition, and entries covering other issues of international policing have been added.)

This entry focuses on the broader issue of "the future of international policing." Its title speaks to changes in how scholars and practitioners think about and carry out policing at every level of collectivization, from the local level of municipal government to the national and inter-/supranational arenas. Criminologists and sociolegal scholars have come to understand policing as a process that involves a network of state (that is, "public") and private (that is, "nonstate") agencies (see especially Johnson and Shearing 2003; Kempa et al. 2004). These agencies include the public police, private security agencies, and other bodies that make a direct contribution to "collective security," such as citizens engaged in neighborhood watch programs and, in other less positive cases, vigilantes.

The activity of this network of bodies—which entails both cooperative and antagonistic relationships—entails the enforcement of a broader dominant normative order that is founded upon a particular "political-economic" context. Thus, it is possible to speak of the rise to dominance of "democratic policing" models that are founded upon the values of efficiency, efficacy, accountability, and community involvement that are deeply tied to the global spread of the neoliberal model of political economy that places much faith in the capacity of markets to distribute collective goods, such as security (see, for example, Kempa et al. 2004; O'Malley 1997; Rose 1996).

In keeping with these developments in policing scholarship, the issue of "the future of international policing" broadens to address not only what the public police are doing in the international realm but, further, to an analysis of the contributions made by private security and other agencies in the processes of the governance of international security. Further, the practical and normative quandary of what the future of international policing ought to be is directly connected to debates and contests between groups over what the future of global governance ought to look like. This entry canvasses these themes.

Context: The Changing Nature of International Space and Governance

It is widely acknowledged that we are living in globalizing times that entail profound shifts in how collective life is thought about, organized, and governed. Goods and (certain classes of) human beings are more globally mobile than they have been at any point in human history (Castells 2000). Further, the development of hypercommunications technology has given individuals around the planet the capacity for simultaneous contact, and, further, has rendered "information" itself a valuable commodity to be traded in the postindustrial economy (Castells 2000). Such massive transformations have tested the dominance of the "nation-state" as the primary envelope of collective life: Individuals currently conduct their personal and professional affairs across a wide range of local, national, and supranational/virtual collectivities, ranging from local community associations to transnational trade links and Internet chat groups.

In response to and partially driving these trends has been massive governmental restructuring at the local, national, international, and supranational levels. It is widely acknowledged that we have moved beyond the "modern" era of governance that was driven, in the first instance, by state governmental institutions. State-dominated governance has been usurped by a proliferation of other state and non-state "nodes" that participate in networked processes of governance.

These trends have wrought many benefits and posed major challenges to collective life, and to security more particularly: The global information economy has seen the rise of certain forms of crime and disorder—some new and some simply more advanced—ranging from Internet fraud and corporate espionage to human trafficking and violence directed against opposing cultures and ways of life (that is, terrorism).

Transformations in policing both reflect and drive these broader transformations in "governance": In the era of the neoliberal, networked, risk society, the public police have abandoned certain of their claims and aspirations for a "monopoly" over the business of governing security, while in other cases they have had their functions stripped from them against their will by nonstate actors of the corporate and civil varieties. State and nonstate policing agencies each behave in ways that reflect and shape the trends in governance described above.

Transformations in Public Policing in the International Domain

Cooperation between state policing agencies in the international domain has a long history, though these links have multiplied in number and form, and new types of "state-oriented" international policing bodies have proliferated in recent decades. Charting the formal and informal links between public policing agencies constitutes the focus of the "classic" sociolegal scholarship on international policing. To date, this work has been largely descriptive and empirical in nature: as Manning (2005) points out the driving forces and social implications of such trends have been undertheorized.

As Anderson (1995) outlined, information sharing and technology transfer between state police agencies were commonplace during the "high point" of the consolidation of the state project in the nineteenth century. Over the course of the twentieth century, these initiatives became more formalized and widespread and can be categorized into three general types: formalized liaison between state police agencies, "supranational" coordination institutions, and probate or unofficial investigation forms.

A noteworthy aspect of formalized liaison entails the exchange of "police liaison officers" between police bodies: These agents participate in policing initiatives of mutual concern through providing advice on investigative approaches and technical support in foreign jurisdictions. One of the objectives of recent rounds of pan-European legislation has been to extend and render increasingly uniform and efficient the liaison officer system. With respect to supranational coordination, INTERPOL plays the most direct role in having the explicit mandate of acting as the institutional hub for police information; it does not, however, have any executive police powers in any of the member states to carry out the business of law enforcement. Probate or unofficial investigation forms are essentially "one off" exchanges or lending of officers in foreign jurisdictions.

International public police cooperation of these forms is furthest developed in the European region, though significant institutional efforts have developed in the Australasia region in recent years. The cornerstone of European police cooperation has been the TREVI group: the regular meeting of the ministers of justice and the interior of the European community countries originally set up in 1975 to coordinate measures against terrorism. Within the TREVI system, four committees were established: TREVI 1 manages the secure communications link for passing sensitive terrorist-related intelligence along to the twelve member countries; TREVI 2 exchanges information about police techniques, training, and equipment between member states; TREVI 3 is a forum for discussing serious crime other than terrorism, such as illegal drugs, migration, and human trafficking; and TREVI 4 is the special committee minted in 1992 concerned with coordinating the measures made necessary by the proposed abolition of frontier controls.

The plurality of the international state-backed policing initiatives described above are most concerned with combating organized crime and global terrorism. For some commentators, this raises concerns about "rings of steel" being thrown up around Europe and other Western regions, with policing agencies acting as the essential bulwarks controlling ingress to and egress from the privileged spaces of the First World (Weber and Bowling 2004).

In the classic sociolegal international policing scholarship, the main thematic issues raised are centered around practical concerns over the efficacy of international policing collaborations and normative concerns over accountability of international policing practices. Critically, both of these issues are reducible to the common theme of the inadequacy of the flow of information between policing agencies themselves and between the policing agencies and governmental and/or community agencies (Sheptycki 2002). A long history of poor information sharing and antagonistic relationships between state nodes in networks for international policing has limited the efficacy of their efforts to combat organized networks of international crime and terrorism. Accountability concerns also arise on the difficult legal issue of what nation's jurisdictional rules ought to apply where foreign police services

undertake operations on soil other than their own (Sheptycki 2002). In this connection, national governments have proved very reluctant over time to cede aspects of their sovereign authority upward to regional policing bodies and laterally to foreign policing agencies (Sheptycki 2002; Deflem 2002; Marx 1997).

The increasing "paramilitarization" of state-backed international policing is a further significant trend in this domain. On the one hand, national armies are increasingly engaged in what are essentially crime control functions at home and in foreign jurisdictions. Such military policing functions were concentrated first upon the Western (principally American) "war on drugs," which since the late 1990s has been surpassed by the same nations' "war on terror" (see, generally, Sheptycki 2002).

The role of the military in the policing of international crime raises important practical and normative concerns. Most obviously, there are concerns about the ability of soldiers who have been trained for mortal combat and view opposition as "the enemy" to adhere to "democratic policing" standards, which characterize suspects as citizens who are innocent until proved guilty (Dunlap 2001). Conversely, there is legitimate concern that immersing soldiers in relatively nuanced "policing" functions may inappropriately "soften" those who may later be called upon to engage in mortal combat in high-intensity conflicts (Dunlap 2001).

In addition to the increased involvement of conventional armies in international policing issues, recent decades have seen the resurgence of specialist forces—gendarmeries—that engage in "national security" policing functions within their own borders and across borders in collaboration with parallel agencies abroad (Lutterbeck 2004). These bodies are typically modeled along the lines of the French Gendarmerie (Gendarmerie nationale), which was created in the late eighteenth century. Similar to the French model, the preponderance of gendarmeries is connected to both their ministries of defense (which are responsible for the conventional military) and ministries of the interior/justice (which traditionally hold jurisdiction over the public police). Gendarmeries play a central role in securing national borders.

Further, in the event of war, gendarmeries would perform more combat-related tasks, such as protecting sensitive infrastructure and gathering intelligence toward maintaining national security. Also significantly, gendarmeries play a critical and increasingly intrusive role in multilateral peacekeeping missions: The missions that national gendarmeries have engaged in from the early 1990s have included such "frontline" duties as crowd control, combating organized crime, protecting returning refugees, and the reorganization of local police forces (Lutterbeck 2004, 60). The blurring of military organizations and public police organizations that conduct their operations within and external to the borders of nation-states indicates the convergence of internal and external security concerns.

An important subissue that arises in the area of public agency involvement in international policing concerns the active role taken by Western states in supporting "democratic" policing reform abroad. A massive industry has blossomed in this domain, with the United States of America and Britain spearheading such efforts (Bayley 2005). David Bayley estimates that the government of the United States, as the dominant bilateral provider, currently spends about $750 million USD on programs that contribute to developing public police forces abroad (Bayley 2005, 206).

Additionally, international programs of police reform are carried out by other multilateral institutions, including the European Union, the World Bank, the International Monetary Fund, and the Inter-American Development Bank. Many of these reforms are driven by the recognition that economic development can be undermined by disorder, crime, and instability: Thus, policing reform and the development of local security is seen by the major players in global development as underpinning so-called second-generation social reforms. Significantly, therefore, the successful implementation of Western-orientated programs for policing reform serves as a precondition for loans and other forms of foreign assistance from the major global development agencies. Thus, the connection of policing reform to broader questions of the "political economy of human security" are rendered stark in the case of foreign assistance programs.

International policing reform assistance has for the most part amounted to the transplantation of technocratic methods of policing and policing governance that years of evidence suggest are of dubious benefit in the West itself (Bayley 2005; Kempa and Johnston 2005). In terms of accounting for this peculiar practice, attention can be paid to both "challenges of intention" and "challenges of imagination," which both relate to "challenges of implementation." On the one hand, many police reform agencies act in their own partisan interests: It has literally become an "industry" that follows the same profit-making imperative of conventional industry. Yet, there are very many policing reformers who harbor the very best of intentions. Nevertheless, their programs for policing reform reflect in many cases outdated, state-dominated "habits of mind" as to what "good governance" and, by extension, "good policing" can and should look like, which are maladaptive in the current network society (Kempa and Johnston 2005).

In addition to being ineffective, the transplantation of Western policing models throughout the developing world has in many cases produced "malignant" outcomes (Cohen 1988). In a very important sense, technocratic policing reforms often simply increase the efficiency and efficacy of a policing system in maintaining a broader unjust social system and tenuous global political-economic order. In other cases, Western policing models undermine indigenous ordering practices and create a culture of dependency. Such deleterious impacts are so pervasive that some authors have wondered whether such processes are deliberate, in the sense that international policing assistance models that are aligned with Western worldviews and interests function as "one mechanism for a country to gain political control over another state" (Huggins 1998, 19).

Here, therefore, there is a clear need to look at alternate conceptualizations of what local and international "human security" can and ought to look like and, by extension, what alternate forms the institutions for effecting these standards and institutional visions might take (see especially Agozino 2004; Dixon 2004; Finlay and Zvekic 1993).

Corporate Policing in the International Domain

It has become well known that there are no functions performed by the public police that are not also, somewhere and sometimes, performed by paid private security agencies (Johnston 2002; Stenning 2000). Thus, corporate entities engage in all manner of policing functions in the international domain, just as they do at the local level. Paid private security engages in such functions at the behest of both corporate and state authorities.

Under corporate direction, private security agencies principally guard against espionage and data theft. Further, private security agencies are often "linked up" with state agencies in undertaking "national security" functions: typically, they perform a data gathering and analysis function. This is convenient, in the sense that nonstate bodies are not subject to the same constitutional controls as are public authorities in undertaking surveillance of the public.

Nonstate agencies also act as "armies for hire" under both corporate and state direction (Johnston 2002). On the one hand, they act to secure corporate interests and property/natural resources in disorderly political contexts. Further, they act sometimes to secure the interests of armies that have invaded states, even where such invasions have been against international law and counter to the consensus of the United Nations. For example, the current occupation of Iraq by the forces of the United States of America and its "coalition of the willing" has been supported by a massive contingent of nonstate policing agencies in the so-called green zone (that is, the administrative "nerve center" of the American invasion) in Central Baghdad.

These practices raise serious concerns over accountability. Operating, as they do, at "arms length" from state authorities, the involvement of corporate security agencies in exercising coercion to secure state interests creates opportunities for "plausible deniability" on the part of government ministers for policing operations gone wrong (Toombs and Whyte 2003). While it is generally acknowledged that accountability mechanisms for private security agencies are inadequate at all levels of collectivization (see especially Stenning 2000)—they are nearly nonexistent in the international realm (Toombs and Whyte 2003). Indeed, the bodies that do exist for the regulation of private security are so limited in their authorities that some commentators have questioned the motivations of state governments in establishing them at all. Toombs and Whyte (2003), for example, wonder whether such agencies have been created to provide a "scintilla of legitimacy" to the impure actions of elite members of state government and corporations in steering networks for security in their partisan interests.

The Future of International Policing: Research and Policy Agenda

What therefore is the future of international policing, in terms of the interrelated issues of a research agenda and practical ways forward? One critical set of issues concerns the need to develop institutions and mechanisms to ensure the efficacy and accountability of networks for international security. Technically speaking, there is a need for the development of information sharing mechanisms between state *and* nonstate nodes involved in international policing.

In a deeper sense, there is a need for institutions that will bring together groups with competing visions for the future of planetary security and justice to deliberate on the form and nature of future international policing arrangements. The critical question here will be at what level these agencies ought to be situated: regional; continental; hemispheric; completely global? Further, there are the questions of what powers these coordinating agencies ought to have and how they might be linked up with existing bodies toward ensuring legal, political, and fiscal accountability on the part of all agencies that engage in international policing processes. Examples of questions that must be addressed include (1) What might the role of the International Court be in bringing to heel inappropriate state and nonstate policing action in the international domain? (2) Who might initiate proceedings against a pariah corporation that deploys corporate security agents in brutalizing policing practices? (3) What are the prospects for actually achieving these reforms, in the absence of support on the part of the United States of America for the International Court?

MICHAEL KEMPA

See also **Accountability; Autonomy and the Police; Continental Europe, Policing in; Environmental Crime; Future of Policing in the United States; International Police Cooperation; International Police Missions; INTERPOL and International Police Intelligence; Role of the Police; Terrorism: International**

References and Further Reading

Agozino, Biko. 2004. Imperialism, crime and criminology: Towards the decolonization of criminology. *Crime, Law and Social Change* 41: 343–58.

Bayley, David. 2005. Police reform is foreign-policy. *The Australian and New Zealand Journal of Criminology* 38 (2): 206–15.

Castells, Manuel. 2000. *The rise of the network society: The information age, economy, society and culture*. 2nd ed. Oxford, UK; Blackwell.

Cohen, Stanley. 1988. *Against criminology*. Oxford: Transaction Books.

Deflem, Mathieu. 2002. *Policing world society. Historical foundations of international police cooperation*. Oxford: Oxford University Press.

Dixon, Bill. 2004. In search of interactive globalization: Critical criminology in South Africa's transition. *Crime, Law and Social Change* 41: 359–84.

Dunlop, Charles J., Jr. 2001. The thick green line: The growing involvement of military forces in domestic law enforcement. In *Militarizing the American criminal justice system*, ed. P. B. Kraska, 29–42. Boston, MA: Northeastern University Press.

Findlay, Mark, and Ugljese Zvekic, eds. 1993. *Alternative policing styles: Cross cultural perspectives*. Cambridge, MA: Kluwer Law and Taxation Publishers.

Huggins, Martha. 1998. *Political policing: The United States and Latin America*. Durham, NC: Duke University Press.

Johnston, Les. 2002. Transnational private policing: The impact of global commercial security. In *Issues in Transnational Policing*, ed. James Sheptycki, 21–42. New York: Routledge.

Johnston, Les, and Clifford Shearing. 2003. *Governing security: Explorations in policing and justice*. New York: Routledge.

Kempa, Michael, and Les Johnston. 2005. Challenges and prospects for the development of inclusive plural policing in Britain: Overcoming political and conceptual obstacles. *Australian and New Zealand Journal of Criminology* 38 (2): 181–91.

Kempa, Michael, Phillip Stenning, and Jennifer Wood. 2004. Policing communal spaces: A reconfiguration of the "mass private property" hypothesis. *British Journal of Criminology* 44 (4): 562–81.

Lutterbeck, Derek. 2004. Between police and military: The new security agenda and the rise of gendarmeries. *Cooperation and Conflict: Journal of the Nordic International Studies Association* 39 (1): 45–68.

Manning, Peter. 2005. The study of policing. *Police Quarterly*, 8 (1): 23–43.

Marx, Gary. 1997. Social control across borders. In *Crime and Law Enforcement in the Global Village*, ed. W. F. McDonald, 23–38. Cincinnati, OH: Anderson Publishing.

O'Malley, Pat. 1997. Policing, politics, postmodernity. *Social and Legal Studies* 6 (3): 363–81.

Rose, Nikolas. 1996. The death of the social? Refiguring the territory of government. *Economy and Society* 25 (3): 327–56.

Sheptycki, James. 2002. *In search of transnational policing: Towards a sociology of global policing*. Aldershot, UK: Ashgate.

Stenning, Philip. 2000. Powers and accountability of the private police. *European Journal on Criminal Policy and Research* 8: 325–52.

Toombs, Steve, and Dave Whyte. 2003. Unmasking the crimes of the powerful. *Critical Criminology* 11: 217–36.

Weber, Leanne, and Benjamin Bowling. 2004. Policing migration: A framework for investigating the regulation of global mobility. *Policing and Society* 14 (3) 195–212.

FUTURE OF POLICING IN THE UNITED STATES

Though some believe there is nothing new under the sun in the field of law enforcement, the question of what the future holds for U.S. policing really is an interesting one. The answers lie in studying the past and applying those tried-and-true tactics using the technology of the present and appreciating their potential impact on the future. The terrorist attacks on the World Trade Center and the Pentagon of September 11, 2001, and the hurricanes of 2005 have heightened the public's awareness of their communities' and their own personal vulnerability. In light of this, they look to their local, state, and federal governments for prevention, protection, and mediation of these events. This entry looks at some key points that provide both opportunities and barriers to providing essential services for the future.

Philosophy of Policing

A tactic that has proved to be successful in meeting these demands from the public with a high level of customer satisfaction is community policing. Reciprocally, police officers—in essence, community service practitioners—seem to be highly satisfied as well. For law enforcement and political executives it is a win–win situation. Direct community involvement in the police decision-making process is the key.

For the process to be most effective, the police agency and community leaders must be immersed in it from top to bottom and across all functions. The success of the problem solving, prevention, and mitigation of negative impacts of crime or social unrest on the community are dependent upon the immersion levels. The lack of success, efficiency, and effectiveness in providing essential and problem-solving services in times of crisis, often the result of poor police or government communication with the community, results in community frustration and the judging of police and government agencies. However, raising the level of a community's expectation by providing token "community policing" efforts is a recipe for failure and deepening mistrust between the public and its police. Every officer, support person, supervisor, and commander must be directly involved and accountable.

With the integration of services, there exist opportunities for customized services and timely solutions to current and emerging problems. These services allow for greater success at a reduced cost to the citizen in both economic and social terms. There is no substitute for success. Trust and knowledge among service providers can break down the barriers associated with "turf" issues and allow them to work across agency lines more efficiently and effectively—in other words, more successfully.

"Turf" issues are among the many challenges facing chiefs of police and other leaders trying to facilitate interagency cooperation. Whose turf is it anyway? The taxpaying citizens demand and deserve their combined and focused attention in solving problems and preserving the peace. As demands for service and the costs of adding additional officers increase, it will be imperative that alternative resources—both physical and financial—be identified. Police chiefs and other agency leaders will need to know what other resources are available within their community and how to bring them together to better serve the community.

Government Structure

The government structure itself is one of the greatest barriers to providing effective and efficient services. This is especially true in the eastern region of the United States, with its archaic form of government. Boroughs, townships, and counties have long outlived their usefulness in providing services to their constituents. Add the state and federal levels, and is it any wonder why things are not accomplished faster and more effectively?

There are many examples of agencies working at cross-purposes to one another, to the detriment of the public. Systems of information sharing (or the lack thereof) between intelligence operations, emergency disaster response agencies, and other government and law enforcement agencies have proved problematic. Duplication and wasteful services compound problems. In many instances various agencies even within the same branch of government have no idea what the other segments are doing or toward what goal. Attempts at

regionalization have been made with varying degrees of success, but no one wants to give up the "palace guard."

Communications

Communications between fragmented and disproportionately assigned service providers present a communications nightmare. Distribution and assignment based on political subdivisions rather than need or risk analysis sets the stage for a potential disaster. Even where there are regional communications centers, fire fighters, police, and emergency medical services often cannot talk to one another despite standing side by side at the scene using their radio equipment to communicate with their respective headquarters and commanders. Even if they could agree upon using a unified command approach to providing emergency services, they would be thwarted by the lack of communication interoperability. In such situations, sadly, it is the taxpaying citizen who suffers most.

Leadership

Preparations for working under a unified command in a majority of circumstances are not practiced. Turf battles are constantly interfering with the basic ability and affinity of emergency and law enforcement agencies to cooperate. Egos play a major role where volunteer, sworn and non-sworn services overlap. However, when personalities are put aside, great gains in the service delivery systems are attainable with little or no added cost. Minimizing egos in the interest of providing the best service is the responsibility of those in command or leadership positions in both the public and private sectors. When the citizenry gain, all will prosper and get their share of the credit.

Ironically, the key element in this dynamic is each individual's confidence level. Exposure to various command schools and practitioners from other disciplines must become an essential step toward the development of leaders within the law enforcement profession. Providers of such exposure and training include the Federal Bureau of Investigation Training Academy and the Police Executive Research Forum's Senior Management Institute. Membership and participation in professional organizations such as the International Association of Chiefs of Police, Police Futurist International, American Management Association, and local Chambers of Commerce provide avenues of discussion and experimentation with relatively low risk. These associations are essential resources when a leader is reaching out to the community to form multidisciplinary teams capable of responding to various crises and events within the community. Examples of these multidisciplinary units include police service areas, youth aid panels, and Drug Abuse Resistance Education programs. Volunteers can be drawn from all segments of a community, including but not limited to churches, schools, social services, the criminal justice system, businesses, and the general citizenry.

Technology

The use of technology in solving recurring problems is a function that citizens have come to expect. For example, programs that examine and analyze calls for service have proved to be very effective in reducing the incidence of repeat calls. In the coming years, as the development and use of various forms of technology continue to grow increasingly more sophisticated, so too will technology's applications in law enforcement.

The timely dissemination of information to officers at the point of service delivery allows them to customize the service as needed by the individual citizen. People have to be in the know and have their opinions, ideas, and concerns addressed. Technology will permit the few to inform and empower the many. Personal contact plays an important role in providing essential services, and interactive technology is an effective tool for augmenting personal contact as a part of the service delivery system. The use of interactive Internet-based communications can be done in real time. Distance learning regimens make information and training available and accessible when the officer or citizen is available. Through the use of analytical computer-based tools, the analysis of problems will take on a more reasoned approach to solvability.

The crunching of volumes of information into usable products will hasten intervention so as to keep small problems small and to allow for various service teams to become directly involved in a situation as quickly as possible. This is a precursor to the advent of multidisciplinary teams being deployed from within the existing community structure.

Education and Training

Education and training are the keys to success in any organization. The process of team and trust building, the ability to develop and stick to an effective plan, and coordination of timing and sensibility all have their roots in the shared experience of training. In a high-risk (and high-failure) environment, it is training that provides the skills necessary for risk reduction and the high probability of success. Integrated training provides a platform for trust building among multidisciplinary team members.

The selection and recruitment of persons to fill these essential roles takes on even greater importance in a world facing a staggering increase in speed and volume of communications and information. These persons must come to law enforcement training with an already solid foundation of learning. It is the community that bears the responsibility for providing qualified and dedicated individuals as service candidates.

It is education and training that allow for the customization of security and safety services delivery. Training provides for the increased proficiency of and the retention of key law enforcement personnel at all levels. Investing in personal development pays big dividends by reducing costs associated with recruitment and pre-assignment training. Training permits the introduction of new ideas and practices while reducing the probability of mistakes and negative influences associated with defending the status quo. The introduction of technology has added another tool to the educator's arsenal. Distance learning, utilizing PC-based technology, has changed the concept of place regarding the delivery of training. Training will now be available on demand, by an officer in the car, on a beat, in the station house, or while off duty at home.

As the demand for services continues to increase, the need for interdisciplinary teams will become the norm. Shared knowledge deployed at the point of service will increase effectiveness and decrease costs of more complicated interventions. Nanotechnology will enable the portability and instant recall of knowledge and information on an as-needed basis at the point of service delivery. Successful operations will breed further experiments with the use of teams. Unique training opportunities will break down stereotypical concepts that have blocked cooperative efforts among departments.

A true training academy, based on the military model, with two career tracks (noncommissioned and commissioned) will be essential to meet the new demands.

The present K-to-12 education system does not adequately prepare an individual to take on the responsibilities and rigors associated with law enforcement practices. It now takes someone who has finished at least two years of college education to equal the level attained by a high school graduate in former times. In a similar fashion, present military training academies are in the same situation. In a previous era, many candidates served in the military prior to entering law enforcement. Today, that tends to be the exception, not the rule. Self-discipline is not learned in a few weeks. Twelve to twenty weeks of training does not produce a police officer.

Society is changing so rapidly that it will take an individual of ever increasing skill and knowledge to provide police services to America's communities. The growth of elderly and minority populations, increased demand for personalized services and common opportunities, concerns about threats to security, and the new awareness of how much help is needed in the aftermath of natural and human-made tragedies are but a few of the ongoing changes that will have an impact on the practice of law enforcement. There is both an increased need for and increased competition for qualified candidates for law enforcement positions at all levels.

As law enforcement training academies look to the future, they would also benefit greatly by looking to the past. Heretofore, law enforcement leaders have unwittingly permitted highly trained and experienced officers to merely disappear from the scene via the retirement route. They have not fully utilized this tool to the benefit of the profession. Just as there is no such thing as an ex-marine, police officers remain officers at heart. Veteran officers represent an underutilized resource that could assist in the ongoing training and mentoring of new officers, supervisors, and commanders.

CLIFFORD BARCLIFF

See also **Accountability; Autonomy and the Police; Community Attitudes toward the Police; Community-Oriented Policing: Rationale; Education and Training; Homeland Security and Law Enforcement; Public Image of the Police; Technology and the Police**

References and Further Reading

Berger, Lance. 2005. *Management wisdom from the New York Yankees.* New York: Wiley.

Bostrom, Matthew D. 2005. Higher education and police work habits. *The Police Chief,* October.

Bradley, Patrick L. 2005. 21st century issues. *The Police Chief,* October.

Cosner, Thurston. 2005. Law enforcement driven action research. *The Police Chief,* October.

Falk, Kay. 2005. Nothing new under the sun. *Law Enforcement Technology,* September.

Koper, Christopher S. 2005. *Hiring and keeping police officers.* Washington, DC: National Institute of Justice.

Marks, Gary. 2005. *Sixteen trends: Their profound impact on our future.* Arlington, VA: Educational Research Service.

————. 2006. *Future focused leadership.* Alexandria, VA: Association for Supervision and Curriculum Development.

Maxwell, John C. 2005. *Winning with people.* Nashville, TN: Nelson Books.

Rotondo, Rick. 2005. Improve efficiency with integrated information. *Law Enforcement Technology,* October.

Scott, Elsie. 2005. Managing police training. *The Police Chief,* October.

Scrivner, Ellen. 2005. Lessons learned from community policing. *The Police Chief,* October.

Shyman, Rose. 2005. Making a place for ethics. *Chief Security Officer,* November.

Simpson, Carl. 2005. *COPS interoperable communications.* Washington, DC: U.S. Department of Justice, September.

Sirota, David. 2005. *The enthusiastic employee.* Philadelphia, PA: Wharton School Publishing.

Sumner, Dave. 2002. Implementing community-oriented policing. *College Planning & Management,* April.

Trojanowicz, Robert. 1985. *Perceptions of safety.* April. East Lansing: Michigan State University.

Whitman, Mark. 2005. The culture of safety. *The Police Chief,* November.

G

GANG RESISTANCE EDUCATION AND TRAINING (G.R.E.A.T.)

Program History and Current Structure

The Gang Resistance Education and Training (G.R.E.A.T.) program can be described as an accident of history. In a detailed history of the program, Winfree and colleagues (1999) describe what can be summarized as a haphazard and uncoordinated effort that accidentally produced a widely popular, school-based gang prevention program. G.R.E.A.T. was certainly not the product of a well-orchestrated and planned effort to develop a national, let alone international, program.

During the late 1980s, gang-related crime had increased substantially throughout much of the United States (part of what has been described as a "youth crime epidemic") and the situation in Phoenix, Arizona, was no different. While visiting constituents in Phoenix, Senator Dennis DeConcini was struck by the volume of gang violence in his state's largest city and called for efforts to confront this crime problem. The Phoenix Police Department, in conjunction with several other area police agencies, was charged with developing a program to provide "students with real tools to resist the lure and trap of gangs" (Humphrey and Baker 1994, 2). The police officers assigned the task of creating a gang prevention program relied on their knowledge of and experience with D.A.R.E. as they developed what became known as the G.R.E.A.T. program. Considerable effort, however, was made to develop an antigang program that was distinct from a drug prevention program. Early versions of the curriculum were reviewed by educators and pretested by several classrooms of students and their teachers. By the end of 1991, G.R.E.A.T. had been born.

This school-based gang prevention program taught by uniformed police officers that was "never intended to go beyond the Valley of the Sun, went national almost before the ink was dry on the lesson

589

plans and workbooks" (Winfree et al. 1999, 164). From its inception, G.R.E.A.T. experienced rapid acceptance by both law enforcement and school personnel; as of 2004, more than seven thousand law enforcement officers had been certified as G.R.E.A.T. instructors and nearly four million students had graduated from the G.R.E.A.T. program (http://www.great-online.org). Coinciding with this program development was creation of an organizational structure to facilitate national-level coordination and training. From 1992 to 2004 the Bureau of Alcohol, Tobacco, Firearms and Explosives (ATF), the Federal Law Enforcement Training Center (FLETC), and representatives from what eventually grew to be five local law enforcement agencies (Phoenix, Arizona; Portland, Oregon; Philadelphia, Pennsylvania; La Crosse, Wisconsin; and Orange County, Florida) shared responsibility for and oversight of the program. In 2004, Congress transferred administrative responsibility for the G.R.E.A.T. program from ATF to the Bureau of Justice Assistance (BJA) in the U.S. Department of Justice.

Program Description

The stated objectives of the G.R.E.A.T. program are (1) "to reduce gang activity" and (2) "to educate a population of young people as to the consequences of gang involvement" (Esbensen et al. 2001, 109). The original curriculum consisted of nine weekly lesson plans offered once a week to middle school students, primarily seventh graders. Officers were provided with detailed lesson plans containing clearly stated purposes and objectives. The G.R.E.A.T. program is illustrative of a general prevention approach to the gang problem. As such, uniformed law enforcement officers introduced students to conflict resolution skills, cultural sensitivity, and the negative aspects of gang life. Discussion about

gangs and their effects on the quality of people's lives were also included. The original eight lessons were as follows:

1. *Introduction:* Acquaint students with the G.R.E.A.T. program and presenting officer.
2. *Crime/Victims and Your Rights:* Students learn about crimes, their victims, and their impact on school and neighborhood.
3. *Cultural Sensitivity/Prejudice:* Students learn how cultural differences impact their school and neighborhood.
4. *Conflict Resolution* (two sessions): Students learn how to create an atmosphere of understanding that would enable all parties to better address problems and work on solutions together.
5. *Meeting Basic Needs:* Students learn how to meet their basic needs without joining a gang.
6. *Drugs/Neighborhoods:* Students learn how drugs affect their school and neighborhood.
7. *Responsibility:* Students learn about the diverse responsibilities of people in their school and neighborhood.
8. *Goal Setting:* Students learn the need for goal setting and how to establish short- and long-term goals.

As evidenced by the curriculum, the G.R.E.A.T. program was intended to provide life skills that would empower adolescents with the ability to resist peer pressure to join gangs. The strategy is a cognitive approach that seeks to produce attitudinal and behavioral change through instruction, discussion, and role-playing.

Evaluation Results

The national evaluation of the G.R.E.A.T. program sought to answer the following question: Can a cognitive-based prevention program produce a measurable treatment effect? A second issue of considerable policy interest concerns the role of law enforcement in such programs; that is, are officers suitable deliverers of prevention programs in schools? Previous evaluations of law enforcement prevention efforts similar to G.R.E.A.T. have provided mixed results. However, contrary to the mixed reviews of DARE (e.g., Lynam et al. 1999; Rosenbaum and Hanson 1998), the national evaluation of G.R.E.A.T. produced modestly positive results (Esbensen and Osgood 1997, 1999; Esbensen et al. 2001).

The first component of the National Evaluation consisted of a cross-sectional study of almost six thousand students enrolled in public schools in eleven U.S. cities. Esbensen and Osgood (1997, 1999) found that students who had completed the G.R.E.A.T. program reported committing fewer delinquent acts and expressed more prosocial attitudes, including more favorable attitudes toward the police, higher levels of attachment to parents and self-esteem, and greater commitment to school. The second component, conducted in twenty-two schools in six American cities, consisted of a longitudinal, quasi-experimental design with pretests and post-tests plus four years of annual follow-up surveys. Once again, modest program effects were reported: Students participating in the G.R.E.A.T. program expressed more prosocial attitudes after program completion than did those students who had not been exposed to the G.R.E.A.T. curriculum (Esbensen et al. 2001).

In spite of these consistent yet modest program effects of the G.R.E.A.T. program, two issues need to be addressed. First, the program's primary stated objective is to reduce gang activity. While the cross-sectional evaluation did find slightly lower rates of gang membership and self-reported delinquency, this was not the case in the longitudinal study. Second, while the cross-sectional findings reflected a difference between groups *one year* after

program completion, the longitudinal design did not produce any significant group differences until *three to four years* after program exposure. Had the evaluation been concluded after a one- or two-year follow-up period, the conclusions would have been different.

The finding that the benefit of G.R.E.A.T. became evident only gradually over many years can be considered curious and unexpected. For a program such as G.R.E.A.T., one might expect the impact to be strongest immediately after program delivery and to be subject to decay over time. However, a number of relatively recent evaluations have reported similar lagged or long-term effects (see Esbensen et al. 2001 for discussion).

The Current G.R.E.A.T. Program

In 1999, following reports from the national evaluation that there were no significant programmatic effects two years after program exposure (Esbensen et al. 2001), the G.R.E.A.T. National Policy Board (NPB) requested that the national evaluation team conduct a rigorous assessment of the curriculum. Concerned about the lack of effect, the NPB wanted to improve their product. Following a critical assessment, the review team recommended a major curriculum revision: Retool the current curriculum to be more skill based with a focus on interactive and cooperative learning strategies. The revised program was unveiled in 2002 and consists of the following thirteen lessons (http://www.great-online.org/corecurriculum.htm):

1. *Welcome to G.R.E.A.T.:* Introduction and relationship between gangs, violence, drugs, and crime.
2. *What's the Real Deal?:* Message analysis and facts and fictions about gangs and violence.
3. *It's About Us:* Community, roles and responsibilities, and what you can do about gangs.

4. *Where Do We Go From Here?:* Setting realistic and achievable goals.

5. *Decisions, Decisions, Decisions:* G.R.E.A.T. decision-making model impact of decisions on goals, and decision-making practice.

6. *Do You Hear What I Am Saying?:* Effective communication, verbal and nonverbal communication.

7. *Walk in Someone Else's Shoes:* Active listening, identification of different emotions, and empathy for others.

8. *Say It Like You Mean It:* Body language, tone of voice, and refusal-skills practice.

9. *Getting Along Without Going Along:* Influences and peer pressure, refusal-skills practice.

10. *Keeping Your Cool:* Anger management tips, practice cooling off.

11. *Keeping It Together:* Recognizing anger in others, tips for calming down.

12. *Working It Out:* Consequences for fighting, tips for conflict resolution, conflict resolution practice, where to go for help.

13. *Looking Back:* Program review, "making my school a G.R.E.A.T. place" project review.

Thus, the length of the program was increased, the delivery mode was changed to a focus on interactive learning, and rather than a cognitive emphasis, the new curriculum was skill based. The new program has slowly replaced the original, although no evaluation of the new program has yet been implemented. As of school year 2004–2005, G.R.E.A.T. was offered in schools throughout the United States, at military bases around the globe, and in a number of other countries. In addition to the middle school program, the G.R.E.A.T. program has also developed a family component; an elementary school program for third- and fourth-grade students; and a summer component. To date, G.R.E.A.T. remains the best-known gang prevention program, although its impact remains questionable.

FINN-AAGE ESBENSEN

See also **Drug Abuse Resistance Education (D.A.R.E.); Juvenile Crime and Criminalization; Juvenile Delinquency; Youth Gangs: Interventions and Results**

References and Further Reading

Esbensen, Finn-Aage, Adrienne Freng, Terrance J. Taylor, Dana Peterson, and D. Wayne Osgood. 2002. National evaluation of the Gang Resistance Education and Training (G.R.E.A.T.) program. In *Responding to gangs: Evaluation and research*, ed. Winifred L. Reed and Scott H. Decker, 139–67. Washington, DC: U.S. Department of Justice, Office of Justice Programs.

Esbensen, Finn-Aage, and D. Wayne Osgood. 1997. *Research in brief: National evaluation of G.R.E.A.T.* Washington, DC: U.S. Department of Justice.

———. 1999. Gang Resistance Education and Training (GREAT): Results from the national evaluation. *Crime and Delinquency* 36: 194–225.

Esbensen, Finn-Aage, D. Wayne Osgood, Terrance J. Taylor, Dana Peterson, and Adrienne Freng. 2001. How great is GREAT? Results from a longitudinal quasi-experimental design. *Criminology and Public Policy* 1: 87–118.

Humphrey, Kim, and Peter R. Baker. 1994. The G.R.E.A.T. program: Gang resistance education and training. *FBI Law Enforcement Bulletin* 63: 1–4.

Lynam, Donald R., Richard Milich, Rick Zimmerman, Scott P. Novak, T. H. K. Logan, Catherine Martin, Carl Leukefeld, and Richard Clayton. 1999. Project DARE: No effects at 19-year follow-up. *Journal of Counseling and Clinical Psychology* 67: 1–4.

Rosenbaum, Dennis P., and Gordon S. Hanson. 1998. Assessing the effects of school-based drug education: A six-year multi-level analysis of Project D.A.R.E. *Journal of Research in Crime and Delinquency* 3: 381–412.

Winfree, L. Thomas, Jr., Dana Peterson Lynskey, and James R. Maupin. 1999. Developing local police and federal law enforcement partnerships: G.R.E.A.T. as a case study of policy implementation. *Criminal Justice Review* 24: 145–68.

GENDER AND CRIME

One of the most widely accepted conclusions in criminology is that females are less likely than males to commit crime. The gender difference in crime is universal: Throughout history, for all societies, all groups, and nearly every crime category, males offend more than females. The correlation between gender and the likelihood of criminal involvement is quite remarkable, though many take it for granted.

Since the prototypical offender is a young male, most efforts to understand crime have been directed toward male crime. However, examining female crime and the ways in which female offending is similar to and different from male crime can contribute greatly to our understanding of the underlying causes of criminality and how it might better be controlled.

Similarities and Differences in Male and Female Offending

There are important similarities between male and female offending (Daly 1994; Steffensmeier and Allan 1996; Steffensmeier and Schwartz 2004). First, females and males have similar patterns of offending with higher arrest rates for minor compared to serious offenses. Both males and females have much lower rates of arrest for serious crimes such as homicide or robbery and higher rates of arrest for minor property crimes such as larceny-theft, or public order offenses such as alcohol and drug offenses or disorderly conduct.

Second, female and male arrest patterns are similar over time and across groups and geographic regions. For example, in the second half of the twentieth century, both women's and men's rates of arrest increased dramatically for larceny-theft and fraud and declined even more dramatically in the category of public drunkenness. Similarly, states, cities, or countries that have higher than average arrest rates for men also have higher arrest rates for women (Steffensmeier and Allan 2000). This symmetry implies that there are similar social and legal forces underlying offending for both sexes.

Third, as is the case with male offenders, female offenders tend to come from backgrounds marked by poverty, discrimination, poor schooling, and other disadvantages. However, women who commit crime are somewhat more likely than men to have been abused physically, psychologically, or sexually, both in childhood and as adults.

While substantial similarities between female and male offending exist, any gender comparison of criminality must acknowledge significant differences as well.

First, females have lower arrest rates than males for virtually all crime categories except prostitution. This is true in all countries for which data are available. It is true for all racial and ethnic groups, and for every historical period.

Second, the biggest gender difference is the proportionately greater *female* involvement in minor property crimes, and the relatively greater involvement of *males* in more serious personal or property crimes. Relative to males, women's representation in serious crime categories is consistently low. For example, since the 1960s in the United States, the female percent of arrests has generally been less than 15% for homicide, robbery, and burglary. Aside from prostitution, female representation has been greatest in the realm of minor property crimes such as larceny-theft, fraud, forgery, and embezzlement with female involvement as high as 30% to 45%, especially since the mid-1970s. The thefts and frauds committed by women typically involve shoplifting (larceny-theft), "bad checks" (forgery or fraud), low-level employee theft or fraud, and welfare and credit fraud—all compatible with traditional female consumer/domestic roles.

Third, when women *do* engage in serious offenses, they perpetrate less harm. Women's acts of violence, compared to those of men, result in fewer and less serious injuries. Their property crimes usually involve less monetary loss or property damage.

Fourth, women are less likely than men to become repeat offenders, and long-term careers in crime are very rare among women. Some pursue relatively brief careers (in relation to male criminal careers) in prostitution, drug offenses, or minor property crimes like shoplifting or check forging.

Fifth, female offenders operate solo or in two- or three-person partnerships more often than male offenders do. Girls' involvement in gangs remains relatively low, accounting for about 10% to 15% of gang members. When women do become involved with others in offenses, the group is likely to be small and relatively nonpermanent. Males are overwhelmingly dominant in the more organized and highly lucrative crimes and women's roles in these operations are generally as accomplices to males or in other low-level positions (Steffensmeier 1983).

Sixth, the context of female offending differs from that of males. Even when the same offense is charged, there are often differences in the setting; victim–offender relationship; offender's culpability, level of damage, modus operandi, and/or purpose; presence of co-offenders; and other contextual features. For example, whereas males tend to perpetrate violence in street or commercial settings against acquaintances or strangers, women are more likely to offend within or near the home against family or other primary group members. Female robbers typically are unarmed and victimize mainly other females, whereas male robbers are more likely to target other males by directly confronting them with physical violence and guns (Miller 1998).

Explaining Female Offending

Causal factors identified by traditional gender-neutral theories of crime such as anomie, social control, and differential association-social learning appear equally applicable to female and male offending (Steffensmeier and Allan 1996). For both males and females, the likelihood of criminal behavior is increased by weak social bonds and parental controls, low perceptions of risk, delinquent associations, chances to learn criminal motives and techniques, and access to criminal opportunities. In this sense, traditional criminological theories are as useful in understanding overall female crime as they are in understanding overall male crime. They can also help explain why female crime rates are so much lower than male rates. For example, females develop stronger bonds, are subject to stricter parental control, and have less access to deviant type-scripts and criminal opportunity.

On the other hand, a *gendered approach* may offer insight into the subtle and profound differences between female and male offending patterns. Recent "middle range" approaches, which typically draw from the expanding literatures on gender roles and feminism, typically link some aspect of female criminality to the "organization of gender" (that is, identities, roles, commitments, and other areas of social life that differ markedly by gender). These approaches delineate structural and subjective constraints placed on females that limit the *form* and *frequency* of female deviance (see, for example, Broidy and Agnew 1997; Cloward and Piven 1979; Harris 1977; Daly 1994; Chesney-Lind 1997; Gilfus 1992; Miller 1998; Richie 1996).

Steffensmeier and Allan (1996) draw on these approaches to identify at least five aspects of the organization of gender that tend not only to inhibit female crime and encourage male crime, but also to shape the patterns of female offending that do occur:

- *Gender norms.* Female criminality is both constrained and molded by gender norms. The constraints posed by child-rearing and other relational obligations are obvious. Femininity stereotypes (for example, nurturing, submissive) are the antithesis of those qualities valued in the criminal subculture (Steffensmeier 1983, 1986) and a criminal label is almost always more destructive of life chances for females than for males. In contrast, stereotypical ideas about masculinity and valued criminal traits share considerable overlap. Risk-taking behavior is rewarded among boys and men but censured among girls and women.

- *Moral development and affiliative concerns.* Women are more likely than men to subscribe to an "ethic of care," whether via socialization or differences in moral development or both (Gilligan 1982), that restrains them from violence and other behavior that may injure others or cause emotional hurt to those they love. Men, on the other hand, are more socialized toward status-seeking behavior and may therefore develop an amoral ethic when they feel those efforts are blocked.
- *Social control.* The ability and willingness of women to commit crime is powerfully constrained by social control. Particularly during their formative years, females are more closely supervised and discouraged from misbehavior. Careful monitoring of girls' associates reduces the potential for influence by delinquent peers (Giordano, Cernkovich, and Pugh 1986). Even as adults, women find their freedom to explore worldly temptations constricted by social control.
- *Physical strength and aggression.* Gender differences in strength—whether actual or perceived—put females at a disadvantage in a criminal underworld where physical violence and power are functional not only

for committing crimes, but also for protection, contract enforcement, and recruitment and management of reliable associates.
- *Sexuality.* Stereotypes of female sexuality both create and hinder certain criminal opportunities for women. The demand for illicit sex generates the opportunity for women to profit from prostitution, which may reduce the need for women to seek financial gain through serious property crimes. However, it is a criminal enterprise still largely controlled by men: pimps, clients, police, and businessmen. The extent and nature of involvement in other criminal groups, also predominantly controlled by men, are often limited to sexual service roles or other secondary positions.

These five aspects of the organization of gender overlap and mutually reinforce one another. In turn, they condition gender differences in criminal motives and opportunities and also shape contexts of offending. Offenders, male or female, tend to be drawn to criminal activities that are easy and within their skill repertoire, and that have a good payoff with low risk. The organization of gender limits the subjective willingness of women to engage in crime, but inclinations are further constrained by a lower level of criminal motivation and limited access to criminal opportunity.

Criminal motivation is suppressed in women by their greater ability to foresee threats to life chances, their predisposition to an ethic of care, and by the relative unavailability of female criminal typescripts that could channel their behavior. Women's risk-taking preferences differ from those of men (Steffensmeier 1983; Steffensmeier and Allan 1996). Consistent with gendered relational obligations and norms of nurturance, women tend to take greater risks to protect loved ones or to sustain relationships. Men will take risks to build status or gain competitive advantage.

Limits on female access to legitimate opportunities also put constraints on their criminal opportunities, since women are less likely to hold jobs such as truck driver, dockworker, or carpenter, which would provide opportunities for theft, drug dealing, fencing, and other illegal activities. The scarcity of women in the top ranks of business and politics limits their chance for involvement in price-fixing conspiracies, financial fraud, and corruption. In contrast, abundant opportunities exist for women to commit petty forms of theft and fraud, low-level drug dealing, and sex-for-sale offenses.

Like the legitimate business world, the underworld has its glass ceiling. If anything, women face even greater occupational segregation in underworld crime groups, at every stage from selection and recruitment to opportunities for mentoring, skill development, and, especially, rewards (Commonwealth of Pennsylvania 1991; Steffensmeier 1983; Steffensmeier and Ulmer 2005).

Recent Trends in Female-to-Male Offending

The perception that females are gaining equality has caused both the media and criminologists to question whether female crime is increasingly emulating more masculine forms and levels of offending and, if so, what explains this convergence in the gender gap.

Researchers have found that, for the most part, *there has been neither a significant widening nor a significant narrowing of the gender gap in criminal offending during the past several decades* (Steffensmeier 1993; Steffensmeier and Schwartz 2004). The main exceptions to this general pattern of stability in female-to-male offending (that is, much smaller female rates) involve (1) substantial increases in the female share of arrests for the minor property crimes of larceny-theft, forgery, and fraud where the female percent of arrests doubled between 1960 and 1975 (from around 15% to 30% or more), with slight additional increases since then; and (2) recent increases in the female share of arrests for criminal assault where simple assault increased from about 20% in 1980 to about 33% in 2004 and aggravated assault grew from 15% to 24%.

Some criminologists, as well as the media, have attributed the female increases in minor property crimes to gains in gender equality (for example, increased female labor force participation)—dubbing this phenomenon the "dark side" of gender equality. However, other criminologists have pointed to the peculiarity of the view that improving girls' and women's economic conditions would lead to disproportionate increases in female crime when almost all the existing criminological literature stresses the role played by poverty, joblessness and marginal employment, and discrimination in the creation of crime (Miller 1986; Steffensmeier 1993; Steffensmeier and Allan 2000). In addition, it is generally not the "liberated woman" who is offending; traditional rather than nontraditional gender views are associated with greater criminality (Pollock-Byrne 1990; Steffensmeier and Allan 2000). In this same vein, female property crimes continue to be mainly minor, low yield, and perpetrated within the context of stereotypical female roles (for example, consumer/domestic roles, pink-collar employment).

Instead, most students of female crime propose that a combination of factors explains the increases in female-to-male offending during the past several decades (Steffensmeier and Schwartz 2004). Besides possible changes in gender roles allowing girls and women greater independence from traditional constraints, these factors include the increasing economic marginalization of large segments of women; increased opportunities for traditionally female crime (for example, shoplifting, check fraud, welfare fraud); rising levels of drug use, which may increase motivational pressures and initiate females into the underworld; and the social and institutional transformation of the inner city toward greater detachment from mainstream social institutions. This body of explanations collectively asserts the possibility that girls' and women's lives and experiences are changing in ways that lead to profound shifts in their propensities or opportunities to commit crimes.

Another possibility is that female arrest gains are *artifactual*, a product of changes in public sentiment and enforcement policies that elevate the visibility, reporting, and sanctioning of female offenders. The rather large increase in female arrests for violence during the past two decades may be explained, in large part, by such changes. A recent study by Steffensmeier and colleagues (2005) finds that the rise in girls' violence *as counted* in police *arrest* data from the *Uniform Crime Reports* is *not* borne out by other longitudinal sources that include unreported offenses independent of criminal justice selection biases. Victim reports of offender characteristics from the National Crime Victimization Survey along with the self-reported violent behavior of the Monitoring the Future and National Youth Risk Behavior Survey show *little overall change* in girls' levels of violence during the past one or two decades and constancy in the gender gap in youth violence. Rather than girls and women becoming more violent, several *net-widening* policy shifts have apparently escalated their *arrest-proneness*: (1) the stretching of definitions of violence to include more minor incidents that girls and women in relative terms are more likely to commit, (2) the increased policing of violence between intimates and in private settings (for example, home, school) where female violence is more widespread, and (3) less tolerant family and societal attitudes toward female violence. This study provides strong evidence supporting the position that it is policy rather than behavioral change that is driving violent arrest trends.

Conclusion

The various aspects of the organization of gender discussed here help explain why women are far less likely than men to be involved in serious crime, regardless of data source, level of involvement, or measure of participation. Recent theory and research on female offending have added greatly to our understanding of how the lives of delinquent girls and women continue to be powerfully influenced by gender-related conditions of life. Profound sensitivity to these conditions is essential for understanding gender differences in type and frequency of crime, for explaining differences in the context or *gestalt* of offending, and for developing preventive and remedial programs aimed at female offenders.

DARRELL STEFFENSMEIER and
JENNIFER SCHWARTZ

See also **Age and Crime; Crime, Serious; Crime, Serious Violent; Criminology; Domestic (or Intimate Partner) Violence and the Police; Juvenile Delinquency; National Crime Victimization Survey (NCVS);** *Uniform Crime Reports;* **Victim Rights Movement in the United States**

References and Further Reading

Arnold, R. 1995. The processes of criminalization of black women. In *The criminal justice system and women*, ed. B. Price and N. Sokoloff, 136–46. New York: McGraw-Hill.

Bonger, William. 1916. *Criminality and economic conditions*. Boston: Little, Brown. This book was first published, in French, in 1905.

Broidy, L., and R. Agnew. 1997. Gender and crime: A general strain theory perspective. *Journal of Research in Crime and Delinquency* 34: 275–306.

Campbell, A., 1984. *The girls in the gang*. Oxford: Basil Blackwell.

Chesney-Lind, M. 1986. Women and crime: The female offender. *Signs* 12: 78–96.

———. 1997. *The female offender*. Thousand Oaks, CA: Sage.

Cloward, R., and F. Piven. 1979. Hidden protest: The channeling of female protest and resistance. *Signs* 4: 651–69.

Commonwealth of Pennsylvania, 1991. *Organized crime in Pennsylvania: The 1990 report*. Conshohocken: Pennsylvania Crime Commission.

Daly, K. 1994. *Gender, crime, and punishment*. New Haven, CT: Yale University Press.

Gilfus, M. 1992. From victims to survivors to offenders: Women's routes to entry and immersion into street crime. *Women and Criminal Justice* 4: 63–89.

Gilligan, C. 1982. *In a different voice: Psychological theory and women's development*. Cambridge, MA: Harvard University Press.

Giordano, P., S. Cernkovich, and M. Pugh. 1986. Friendships and delinquency. *American Journal of Sociology* 91: 1170–1203.

Harris, A. 1977. Sex and theories of deviance: Toward a functional theory of deviant typescripts. *American Sociological Review* 42: 3–16.

Miller, E. 1986. *Street women*. Philadelphia, PA: Temple University Press.

Miller, J. 1998. Up it up: Gender and the accomplishment of street robbery. *Criminology* 36: 37–65.

Richie, B. 1996. *The gendered entrapment of battered, black women*. London: Routledge.

Steffensmeier, D. 1983. Sex-segregation in the underworld: building a sociological explanation of sex differences in crime. *Social Forces* 61: 1080–1108.

———. 1993. National trends in female arrests, 1960–1990: Assessment and recommendations for research. *Journal of Quantitative Criminology* 9: 413–41.

Steffensmeier, D., and E. A. Allan. 2000. Looking for patterns: Gender, age, and crime. In *Criminology: A Contemporary Handbook*, ed. J. F. Sheley, 3rd ed. New York: Wadsworth.

———. 1996. Gender and crime: Toward a gendered theory of female offending. *Annual Review of Sociology* 22: 459–87.

Steffensmeier, D., and R. Terry. 1986. Institutional sexism in the underworld: A view from the inside. *Sociological Inquiry* 56: 304–23.

Steffensmeier, D., J. Schwartz, H. Zhong, and J. Ackerman. 2005. An assessment of recent trends in girls' violence using diverse longitudinal sources: Is the gender gap closing? *Criminology* 43: 355–405.

Steffensmeier, D., and J. Ulmer. 2005. *Confessions of a dying thief: Understanding criminal careers and criminal enterprise*. New Brunswick, NJ: Aldine Transaction.

"GOOD" POLICING

The question of what makes for good policing overlaps many of the topics covered in this encyclopedia, such as accountability, community-oriented policing, and integrity. Many aspects of "bad" policing are also covered, such as corruption, deviant subcultures, and excessive force. What counts as good policing is as debatable as what counts as bad policing. Some citizens will want a tolerant, highly discretionary, form of policing, tending in the direction of social work. Others will want a hardline approach, with police being quick to prosecute offenses, especially public nuisance misdemeanors and juvenile disorder. A challenging task for police managers, therefore, is to negotiate these conflicting demands and keep as many citizens as possible satisfied with police crime prevention and law enforcement services.

Modern concepts of good policing remain strongly influenced by a model adopted with the formation, in 1829, of the "New Police" in London. At the time, there was widespread opposition to the idea of an organized police force on the assumption that it would be militaristic and oppressive. Partly in response to this concern, the London bobby walked the beat without a firearm, equipped only with a strengthened hat, a truncheon, and a rattle (Critchley 1967, 51). Police were to be courteous, helpful, and use force as an absolute last resort; and they were meant to focus on prevention rather than prosecution. From this beginning came the idea of the local police officer as a reassuring presence, who makes personal contact with residents and visitors, and responds quickly to calls for assistance.

However, although the foot patrol officer is still in existence, policing functions have developed well beyond this simple picture, and the idea of good policing has become a much more measurable product.

Legitimacy

Modern ideas of good policing are also firmly rooted in the social contract theory of government that developed during the Enlightenment period in European history (Pollock 2004). Police derive their authority from government, with legitimacy dependent on the consent of the people. Governments that operate police departments and set the general direction for policing need to be fairly elected and consultative, so that the policy framework is representative and balances community concerns wherever possible. Police who operate in nondemocratic regimes need to acquire as much legitimacy as they can from indirect sources of democratic authority, such as sensitivity to local concerns about crime and equity in the application of criminal law (Bayley 2001).

Although policing needs to be part of the democratic process, it also needs to be above "politics." Policing is highly susceptible to "politicization," where a party or faction has undue influence over police strategies or receives biased support from police (Guyot 1991, cf. chap. 10). Good policing requires a higher degree of operational independence from elected officials. But this higher level of freedom needs to be matched with a policy of "triage"—focusing police resources through objective criteria based on the greatest criminal threats to human welfare. And accountability requires genuine freedom of information and transparency so citizens can know how decisions about policing are being made and by whom.

Responsiveness and Community Policing

Even in a strong democracy the principles of police public service and legitimacy are challenged by social inequality. Left-wing critics argue that crime reduction strategies involving arrest, force, and deterrence are misdirected away from the social origins of crime (Rock 1997). In this critique, policing methods are dismissed as largely ineffective and repressive, with negative implications for ideas of "good" policing. It is certainly the case that crime is often rooted in low social capital and in disadvantaged communities (Sherman 1997a), and the history of policing also shows that police have often served as guardians of ruling class property and power. The term *police state* refers to a regime where terror, arbitrary arrest, torture, and murder are carried out in the interests of the state and the ruling class by police. However, even in prosperous, relatively egalitarian, welfare states, opportunity is often a critical element in crime (Gabor 1994), and many motivating factors in crime—such as envy, passion, or peer pressure—operate at a tangent to inequality. This means that the types of incapacitative and deterrence-oriented crime fighting techniques typically adopted by police retain relevance. And in places where crime is deeply rooted in inequality, police can provide a front-line protection service for the poor and defenseless.

In relation to the issue of policing and social equality, Michael Buerger has argued for the variability of police legitimacy. Drawing on the social contract theory, he states that "police authority is weakest when officers act on their own initiative, and strongest when they act on behalf of citizens requesting assistance" (Buerger 1998, 93). Police responsiveness is therefore a cornerstone of good policing when it is focused on serving "the people" rather than prioritizing elites. Police, however, also need to be responsive to the victims of crimes who may be intimidated into silence: the victims of sexual assault, for example, or child abuse, fraud, extortion, coerced prostitution, or the illicit drug trade.

Responsiveness also entails communication well beyond simply reacting to calls for assistance or preempting unreported crime (Bayley 2001; Guyot 1991). Good police will regularly inform their local constituency of crime risks—through newsletters or local newspapers and radio. They will also need to seek advice about residents' concerns through regular meetings—such as "community consultative committees"—or different types of surveys. Advocates of community policing also argue that police should extend their crime prevention capability by enlisting residents in copolicing arrangements such as Neighborhood Watch or Crimestoppers. Even where such programs have little impact on overall crime rates, they can be useful in reducing fear of crime and assist in solving specific offenses. Personal contact in fact remains a major criterion for citizen satisfaction with police (Reisig and Parks 2002). Again, however, it must be emphasized that in working closely with communities police need to guard against undue influence from particularly vocal or powerful residents whose preferences for police action may not match the needs or preferences of all groups.

Ethical Standards

One way of analyzing good policing is to break it into two primary areas: ethical conduct and performance. One can imagine a police department that is considered effective in terms of catching offenders, but officers might do this in part by beating up suspects, forcing confessions, and generally riding roughshod over suspects' rights. On the other hand, one could imagine a police department that is free of corruption but is unable to effectively penetrate the crime problem. While ethical conduct entails being conscientious and therefore as competent as possible, the theoretical example illustrates the importance of getting both of these aspects of policing into alignment.

The best guide to ethical policing is found in codes of conduct, such as that of the International Association of Chiefs of Police (IACP). IACP's Law Enforcement Code of Conduct adopts specific positions on ethical issues, including protection of confidential information and rejection of bribes and gratuities. In terms of the use of force, the code emphasizes that threats and physical force should be used "only after discussion, negotiation and persuasion have been found to be inappropriate or ineffective" (IACP 2005, 2). The most important general principle is that of equal treatment:

> A police officer shall perform all duties impartially, without favor or affection or ill will and without regard to status, sex, race, religion, political belief or aspiration. All citizens will be treated equally with courtesy, consideration and dignity. (IACP 2005, 1)

Few people would dispute such ideals, but police managers need to ensure that behavior is consistent with principles. For example, if officers are regularly dining at restaurants that provide discount meals to them, then a double standard applies between commitment to the code and police practice. With issues of discretion, where the ethical course of action may be less clear, the guiding principles should be public interest and impartiality. If police decisions are motivated by racism, self-interest, or personal biases, then these decisions are unethical.

The principle of minimum force also obliges police to carefully match the level of force they use to the level of threat. The principle has diverse implications for police action, including the management of public protests. Police need to allow people to exercise freedom of speech and assembly, but cannot stand back if people are being hurt, property damaged, or legitimate activities disrupted. At the same time, police need to avoid unnecessary force and physical harm in dispersing demonstrators. Here the concept of *negotiated management* is useful in reducing the likelihood of violence by involving protest leaders in planning for order maintenance (Waddington 2003).

Observance of due process is also a key element of good policing (Guyot 1991). The "Dirty Harry syndrome" (named after a film character) or "noble cause corruption" occurs when police are tempted to use illegal means to obtain justice, such as coercing a suspect into confessing. In some situations, breaches of due process might be considered justified in terms of a higher goal such as saving a life. Generally though, police ethicists and lawmakers hold that any gains that might be achieved by illegal means are not worth the miscarriages of justice and negative precedents that might result (Kleinig 1996; Pollock 2004). Consequently, maintaining ethical standards may mean that offenders escape justice, or harms are committed, in some instances.

Efficiency, Effectiveness, and Performance Indicators

Police services are funded by taxpayers, and police are engaged in the realization of fundamental human values of protection of life and property and bringing offenders to justice. Efficient use of resources is therefore crucial to good policing. From the earliest days of the formation of organized police services, some degree of accountability was usually required via reporting to parliament or local assemblies. But the old image of the local bobby involved a great deal of trust in regard to fulfillment of delegated tasks. The 1980s and 1990s saw a growing emphasis on accountability through quantitative measures, and police were obliged to adopt an increasing range of performance indicators.

The traditional culture of policing has tended to be averse to research and evaluation, focusing instead on working through cases with a view to solving as many as possible. However, this is not necessarily the most efficient way to reduce crime, and police must be able to show they are producing the best possible outcomes from the inputs they receive. In a paper, "It's Accountability, Stupid," police studies scholar David Bayley (1994) sums up many of the issues involved in police performance management. He begins by cautioning against expecting too much of police—given the many factors involved in crime that are beyond police control—while at the same time examining ways of enlarging the police contribution to crime minimization. Governments now frequently require that police set goals and report the extent to which they reach these goals. Average response times, for example, are frequently reported, but these need to be set at a realistic standard. Similarly, reported crimes need to be set against numbers of prosecutions and convictions (the clearance rate) while the limited capacity of police to solve crimes is also understood. Police are expected to initiate innovative crime reduction programs and measure their impacts—targeting stolen goods outlets, for example, or confiscating the proceeds of organized crime. They are also now expected to make use of surveys in areas such as public confidence and victim satisfaction (Mawby 1999). These areas often overlap with ethical conduct issues. Some jurisdictions survey "arrestees" for their views on how police managed the arrest process. "Ethical climate" surveys are being adopted to obtain rank-and-file police views on ethical issues, willingness to report misconduct, and perceptions of colleagues' compliance with ethical standards. Complaints against police and the outcomes of investigations of complaints are additional indicators of police compliance with conduct standards (Klockars et al. 2000).

The danger with a measurement approach to policing is that it becomes fixed on activity rather than real achievements (Bayley 1994). *Problem-oriented policing* (POP) is a term used for the more sophisticated application of statistics and research. POP is a strategy in which police systematically analyze crime-related problems, develop targeted intervention strategies, evaluate the impact, and make modifications where necessary. Some of the most promising research in this area concerns intervening in repeat victimization. This stems from the finding that police often attend to the same victims or visit the same localities on numerous occasions. In a review of successful crime reduction programs, Sherman (1997b, 1) concluded:

> Hiring more police to provide rapid 911 responses, unfocused random patrol, and reactive arrests do[es] not prevent serious crime. Community policing without a clear focus on crime risk factors generally shows no effect on crime. But directed patrols, proactive arrests and problem-solving at high-crime "hot spots" has shown substantial evidence of crime prevention. Police can prevent robbery, disorder, gun violence, drunk driving and domestic violence, but only using certain methods and under certain conditions.

Random breath testing (RBT) to reduce drunk driving is a good example of this systematic approach to prevention. Dramatic reductions have been achieved in crashes, injuries, fatalities, and noncompliance with traffic laws from strict application of randomization and testing of all drivers (in combination with widespread advertising) to ensure the maximum deterrent effect. The success of RBT depends on police refraining from traditional and preferred practices of nonsystematic, discretionary testing of drivers who police think might be drunk (Homel 1994).

Problem-oriented policing is also useful to identify counterproductive policing strategies. High-speed vehicle pursuits are an example of this. Police often believe that they must engage in vehicle pursuits, even for minor offenses, in order to remove offenders and maintain respect for the rule of law. However, research shows that the risks to public safety and police safety considerably outweigh the crime reduction effects of pursuits. Few offenders are caught in pursuits and offenders are usually not deterred by fear of imprisonment. Pursuits also result in numerous accidents and injuries, and some deaths, and many offenders are attracted to committing traffic offenses by the thrill of a police chase (Homel 1994). From the perspective of "good" policing, the natural tendency of many officers to want to engage in hot pursuits needs to be curtailed and carefully managed.

Policies of maximum efficiency and effectiveness need to be kept in the foreground but also moderated by other policies, such as responsiveness (Bayley 1994). An example involves how to deal with "volume crimes" such as burglary. Burglaries generate a large number of calls for police attendance at the scene, but by the time police arrive the thief has usually left without leaving any evidence behind. As a result, typically less than 10% of burglaries are solved. Police attendance is largely a waste of money. Nonetheless, members of the public expect this service. It provides reassurance and may be necessary for an insurance claim. Managers concerned exclusively with efficiency would put a stop to police callouts to burglaries. However, this would likely be highly unpopular and conflict with the democratic principle of responsiveness.

Cooperation between Policing Agencies

One feature of modern policing with important implications for good policing practices is the proliferation of agencies involved in different aspects of law enforcement. This phenomenon has occurred partly in response to the lack of expertise in conventional police forces, for example, in fighting sophisticated economic crimes. But the existence of multiple agencies can exacerbate jealousies and conflicts over who has jurisdiction or who is in command in different crime cases, or it can produce "buck-passing" where no agency wants to take responsibility. Lack of cooperation can mean crimes remain unsolved and criminals remain free to commit further offenses. Hence, the IACP code of conduct (2005, 2) states that "Police officers will cooperate with all legally authorized agencies and their representatives in the pursuit of justice. . . . It is imperative that a police officer assist colleagues fully and completely with respect and consideration at all times." The diversification of policing agencies has also involved large growth in "private police." Private security services operate on fundamentally different bases to public police, with the private sector focused on selective services to owners and clients. Nonetheless, the traditional enmity between public and private police needs to be overcome in the public interest. Cooperation can occur in areas such as intelligence sharing, but, again, police need to guard against favoring one private security firm and its clients over others.

External Monitoring and Instituting Good Policing

Another feature of modern policing is the growth of civilian oversight through external "watchdog" agencies concerned primarily with corruption prevention. These agencies have variable names, including *police ombudsman* or *Police Integrity Commission*. They provide a vital independent means of investigating complaints and of evaluating how police handle complaints internally and integrity management strategies. Nongovernment agencies are an important part of this process, including human rights groups, such as Amnesty International, and civil liberties groups. The 1998 Human Rights Watch report *Shielded from Justice: Police Brutality and Accountability in the United States* is an example of a major exposé of problems of police misconduct by a community sector organization. Good policing is reliant on scrutiny by outside agencies and police need to cooperate as much as possible with providing information and access to these groups to counter the natural tendency toward coverups, secrecy, and dependence on self-validating internal planning and evaluation processes.

Human Resource Management

Many of the problems of corruption, brutality, racism, and lack of innovation associated with traditional police departments relate directly to a military model of recruitment of young men through narrow selection procedures focused on physical criteria. In Western countries policing was dominated by poorly educated "white" or "Anglo-Saxon" males with little interest in a scientific approach to policing, multiculturalism, or principles of community policing. Women and people from ethnic minorities, considered "outsiders," were frequently subject to intense discrimination, and male police officers, even those with a family at home, were expected to be on call twenty-four hours a day.

Fair employment practices have been largely imposed on police from the outside, through antidiscrimination legislation and court orders. Many police departments in the last thirty years have been subject to recruitment targets, and even quotas, for women and minorities. The influx of women and a "family-friendly" agenda meant that management has had to consider flexible rostering practices and improved leave arrangements. The growth of police studies and the police reform agenda also emphasized the value of higher education in making police more socially tolerant, with a more educated, critical approach to the job. Good policing now requires a well-educated, demographically diverse workforce. There is an argument that in principle the police profile should approximate the composition of the communities police serve. There are likely to be beneficial operational outcomes from this approach if it is properly managed. For example, there is a growing body of research that shows that women police attract far fewer complaints than men and are less likely to engage in corruption. They also are generally better able to manage conflict with citizens without resorting to force (Waugh, Ede, and Alley 1998). Good human resource management policies will also involve the deployment and promotion of police on the basis of merit, as opposed to seniority or "cronyism," with civilian staff placed on an equal footing with sworn officers.

Conclusion: Does One Size Fit All?

Can we set down principles of good policing that apply everywhere in the world? Some proponents of cultural relativity would suggest we cannot assume that general requirements—scientific measurement of performance, for example, or prohibition of gratuities—can simply be applied anywhere in the world without problems of cultural fit. Nonetheless, in a report commissioned by the U.S. Department of Justice, *Democratizing the Police Abroad: What to Do and How to Do It*, David Bayley (2001) identifies four basic norms that need to be pursued in order for police anywhere to be genuinely accountable and "democratic":

1. Police must give top operational priority to servicing the needs of individual citizens and private groups.

2. Police must be accountable to the law rather than to the government.
3. Police must protect human rights, especially those that are required for the sort of unfettered political activity that is the hallmark of democracy.
4. Police must be transparent in their activities (pp. 13–14).

Bayley argues, however, that accountable policing entails responsiveness to local needs and conditions. Police need to be sensitive to local customs, while actively educating their constituency in principles such as the avoidance of favoritism. It is also hard to imagine a good modern policing service that is not subject to some form of civilian oversight in disciplinary matters and that is not engaged in some form of measurement of inputs and outputs and of public satisfaction. There can be little doubt over the need for these norms and standards. The challenge lies in putting them into practice.

TIM PRENZLER

See also **Accountability; Attitudes toward the Police: Measurement Issues; Attitudes toward the Police: Overview; Autonomy and the Police; Civil Restraint in Policing; Codes of Ethics; Ethics and Values in the Context of Community Policing; Integrity in Policing; Performance Measurement; Police Misconduct: After the Rodney King Incident; Role of the Police**

References and Further Reading

Bayley, D. 1994. It's Accountability, Stupid! In *Un-peeling tradition: Contemporary policing*, ed. Bryett and Lewis. Melbourne: Macmillan.
———. 2001. *Democratizing the police abroad: What to do and how to do it*. Washington, DC: National Institute of Justice.
Critchley, T. 1967. *A history of police in England and Wales 900–1966*. London: Constable and Company.
Gabor, T. 1994. *Everybody does it!: Crime by the public*. Toronto: University of Toronto Press.

Guyot, D. 1991. *Policing as though people matter.* Philadelphia, PA: Temple University Press.

Homel, R. 1994. Can police prevent crime? In *Un-peeling tradition: Contemporary policing,* ed. Bryett and Lewis. Melbourne: Macmillan.

Human Rights Watch. 1998. *Shielded from justice: Police brutality and accountability in the United States.* New York: Human Rights Watch.

International Association of Chiefs of Police. 1995. *Law enforcement code of conduct.* http://www.theiacp.org (accessed November 2005).

Kleinig, J. 1996. *The ethics of policing.* New York: Cambridge University Press.

Klockars, C., S. Ivkovich, W. Harver, and M. Haberfeld. 2000. *The measurement of police integrity.* Washington, DC: National Institute of Justice.

Mawby, R. 1999. Police services for crime victims. In *Policing across the world,* ed. R. Mawby. London: UCL Press.

Pollock, J. 2004. *Ethics in crime and justice: Dilemmas and decisions.* Belmont, CA: West/Wadsworth.

Reisig, M., and R. Parks. 2002. *Satisfaction with police—What matters?* Washington, DC: National Institute of Justice.

Rock, P. 1997. Sociological theories of crime. In *The Oxford handbook of criminology,* ed. Maguire, Morgan, and Reiner. Oxford: Clarendon Press.

Sherman, L. 1997a. Communities and crime prevention. In *Preventing crime: What works, what doesn't, what's promising?,* ed. Sherman et al. Washington, DC: National Institute of Justice. http://www.ncjrs.org/works/index. htm (accessed November 2005).

———. 1997b. Policing for crime prevention. In *Preventing crime: What works, what doesn't, what's promising?,* ed. Sherman et al. Washington, DC: National Institute of Justice. http://www.ncjrs.org/works/index. htm (accessed November 2005).

Waddington, P. 2003. Policing public order and political contention. In *Handbook of policing,* ed. Newburn. Uffculme, Devon: Willan.

Waugh, L., A. Ede, and A. Alley. 1998. Police culture, women police and attitudes towards misconduct. *International Journal of Police Science and Management* 1: 288–300.

H

HATE CRIME

What Is Hate Crime?

"Hate crime" and "bias crime" are terms that were coined during the 1980s to describe criminal behavior motivated by bigotry. They represent the most recent development toward understanding and eradicating offenses committed out of animosity for members of a particular group. "Bias" more accurately reflects the notion that an offense is committed out of animus for a group with certain attributes, whereas the connotation of "hate" suggests anger at a particular person for reasons particular to that individual. However, given that "hate crime" has become more popularly associated with the phenomenon, that term will be used herein.

Definitions of hate crime can vary widely. The Anti-Defamation League (2005) defines a hate crime as "a criminal act against a person or property in which the perpetrator chooses the victim because of the victim's real or perceived race, religion, national origin, ethnicity, sexual orientation, disability or gender." The Prejudice Institute (2005) includes a broader set of behaviors in what they label "ethnoviolence." This "is an act or an attempted act which is motivated by group prejudice and intended to cause physical or psychological injury. These violent acts include intimidation, harassment, group insults, property defacement or destruction, and physical attacks. The targets of these acts involve persons identified because of their race or skin color, gender, nationality or national origin, religion, or other physical or social characteristic of groups such as sexual orientation."

Hate crime statutes differ from these behaviorally based definitions since they need to cover specific legal situations. They also differ significantly by state, although most statutes share a few broad commonalities. As Jenness (2001) describes, the "canon" of hate crime laws addresses three issues. It provides for state action, contains a subjective standard to interpret the intent of the offender, and specifies a list of protected status characteristics (race, sexual orientation, disability, and so forth) (Jenness 2001).

The Federal Bureau of Investigation (FBI), which is responsible for collecting data on hate crimes reported to law enforcement agencies in the United States, defines hate crimes as "criminal offenses that are motivated, in whole or in part, by the offender's bias against a race, religion, sexual orientation, ethnicity/national origin, or disability, and committed against persons, property, or society" (1999). Some other definitions expressly state that the characteristics motivating the offenders may be falsely perceived and that the victims may be targeted for reasons other than their own characteristics (for example, their association with members of a particular group). However, the FBI's definition makes this unnecessary by focusing specifically on the *offender's bias* against a particular protected group—not the victim's status. Definitions of hate crime have not typically addressed the goals of the perpetrators (Boeckmann and Turpin-Petrosino 2002), attending only broadly to their motivation.

The two defining elements of hate crime are the interchangeability of victims and the potential for secondary victimization (McDevitt et al. 2001). Victims of hate crime are singled out because of characteristics shared with a particular group; it is these shared (or perceived) characteristics rather than something unique to the individual that make someone a target. Hate crimes are often committed with the purpose of "sending a message" to other members of that group. Part of what makes hate crime particularly egregious is that, because one's immutable characteristics make one a target, victims cannot protect themselves from future victimization as readily as victims of non–bias crimes sometimes can.

It is important to recognize that hate crime statutes do not criminalize thoughts, beliefs, or legal forms of expression. Rather, depending on the statute, they (1) establish an additional category of offense specifying that an existing criminal act was committed out of bias or (2) permit a sentencing enhancement for existing criminal offenses that can be shown to have been committed based in part on bias against a particular group. Although crimes motivated by such bias, bigotry, or prejudice pervade human history, only during the past three decades has this behavior been defined and constructed as a social problem that may be combated through public policy and legislation.

Who Are the Victims of Hate Crime?

In *Hate Crime Statistics, 2003,* the FBI reports that 9,100 individuals were victimized in 7,489 incidents of reported hate crimes. Approximately half of the offenses were motivated by racial bias. Of this group, two-thirds (66%) were motivated by an anti-black bias. Of the other third, more than 21% were motivated by anti-white bias, 6% were motivated by anti-Asian/Pacific Islander bias, 2% were motivated by anti-American Indian/Alaskan Native bias, and almost 5% were committed against targeted groups of individuals with more than one race represented.

Religious and sexual orientation bias each motivated more than 16% of hate crimes committed. Of the religiously motivated crimes, 69% were anti-Jewish, 11% were anti-Islamic, 8% targeted individuals perceived to be from other religious groups not specified by the reporting agency, almost 6% were anti-Catholic, almost 4% were anti-Protestant, 2% were against groups of varying religions, and 1% were antiatheist/agnostic. Of those victimized because of their sexual orientation, 62% were targets of anti–male homosexual bias, 21% were targets of antihomosexual bias, both male and female, 16% were targets of anti–female homosexual bias, 1% were targets of antiheterosexual bias, and almost 1% were targets of antibisexual bias.

Of the 1,326 victims of hate crimes committed because of people's ethnicity or national origin, 45% were targets of anti-Hispanic bias, and 55% were victims of other biases.

Who Are the Perpetrators of Hate Crime?

There were 6,934 "known offenders" in 2003. According to *Hate Crime Statistics, 2003*, "the term *known offender* does not imply that the suspect's identity is known but that an attribute of the suspect is identified which distinguishes him or her from an unknown offender." Race is the only offender attribute collected. Of these known offenders, 62% were white, 19% were black, groups of individuals of varying races accounted for 6%, more than 1% were Asian/Pacific Islander, and almost 1% was American Indian/Alaskan Native.

What Types of Crime Are Reported as Hate Crimes?

In 2003, agencies reported a total of 5,517 victims of crimes against persons and 3,524 victims of crimes against property. Of the crimes against persons, 50% of victims were targets of intimidation, 33% were targets of simple assault, 17% were targets of aggravated assault, and less than 1% targets of murder or rape. Of property crime victims, 83% were targets of acts of destruction, damage, or vandalism, more than 5% of burglary, more than 5% of larceny-theft, more than 4% of robbery, and more than 1% of arson.

Where Does Hate Crime Occur?

The 2003 report states that approximately one-third (32%) of reported hate crimes occurred in or near residences or homes, 18% took place on highways, roads, alleys, or streets, 12% were committed at schools or colleges, 6% occurred in a parking lot or garage, and 4% took place at a church, synagogue, or temple.

What Are the Effects of Hate Crimes?

While there is a substantial body of research showing the negative psychological effects of chronic discrimination (Dunbar 2001), little systematic research has been conducted on the effects of hate crime on its victims as compared to individuals similarly victimized but without experiencing an element of bias. Critics of hate crime legislation claim that the motivation of the offender does not cause additional injury, while victim advocates have long argued that the consequences of hate crimes can be considerably more detrimental than those of the same offense without the bias element. What research does exist appears to lend support to the contention that hate crimes are more destructive than offenses lacking a bias motivation.

Comparison studies in which victims of hate and non–hate crimes are surveyed show that hate crime victims indicate a greater number of symptoms and behavior change (Ehrlich et al. 1994; Barnes and Ephross 1994; and Herek et al. 1999, as discussed in McDevitt et al. 2001). In McDevitt et al. (2001), a mail survey was sent to all victims of bias-motivated aggravated assault in Boston over five years and a random sample of non–bias assault victims over the same time period. Results showed significantly greater consequences for hate crime victims in the aftermath of the victimization. There was little difference between groups in terms of behavior change following incidents, which the authors suggested reflects the notion that victims are chosen because of their immutable characteristics and cannot avoid future victimization through changes in their own actions. However, the study showed differential psychological impact, with hate crime victims showing a greater tendency to feel angry, nervous, and depressed, have greater trouble concentrating, and feel like not wanting to live any longer when compared to the sample of non–bias assault victims.

Why Do People Commit Hate Crimes?

Although many theories have been offered, it is not yet clear why people commit crimes based on hatred of a particular group. Unresolved methodological issues have prevented widespread and rigorous study of the causes of hate crime. These relate to the inclusiveness of hate crime legislation, the etiology of hate crime, and data collection limitations.

Issues of Definition

There is no agreement as to how inclusive a definition of hate crime should be. Some state laws are written very broadly to include a victim targeted for membership in any group whatsoever; others are very limited in their scope, such as those of Indiana and South Carolina, which apply only to acts of institutional vandalism (Anti-Defamation League 2005).

All-inclusive statutes can be problematic for research purposes if the specific circumstances and group affiliations are not recorded. Since offender motivations and tactics (as well as hate crime prevention and response strategies) will differ for a white-on-black attack as opposed to a black-on-white attack, this information is extremely important.

Whether to include gender as a protected group is also controversial. If any attack against a woman is considered a hate crime if the crime was motivated primarily because of gender, should all sexual assaults against women be counted as hate crimes? If so, should acquaintance rapes and domestic violence be excluded, since the victim is not interchangeable? Some of the more than twenty-five states that include gender in their hate crime laws have tried to answer these questions with limited success. For example, the Massachusetts attorney general requires at least two previous restraining orders issued to protect two different domestic partners for an individual to be prosecuted under the hate crime statute. During the policy's first ten years, fewer than ten cases met these criteria. California law requires an articulated threat by the offender against women in general. It is unrealistic to expect such an utterance during most offenses (Levin and McDevitt 2002, 21–22).

Issues of Etiology

As a result, it is not surprising that little systematic study has been done on the causes of hate crime. To date, more research has concentrated on descriptive elements of hate crime rather than investigations into its causes. This research lacks an explanatory or predictive theory, and there is little or no evaluation research to guide its development. Such a theoretical base would be valuable to provide a useful framework for criminal justice practitioners, social service organizations, and other government agencies (Shively 2005).

In their critique of the state of hate crime research, Green, McFalls, and Smith (2001) argue that theories attempting to explain the etiology of hate crime "must distinguish between two broad levels of analysis: individual and societal" (Green, McFalls, and Smith 2001). Factors at the individual level include psychological orientations, while causes at the societal level attend to social forces such as integration and changes in the economy. The authors note that these categories are blended to some degree and that there are six general types of explanations for hate crime in the literature: psychological, social-psychological, historical-cultural, sociological, economic, and political.

Thus far, there is little support for theories speculating that economic downturns and unemployment rates are responsible for increased levels of hate crime. However, several studies have found in-migration to be positively correlated with hate crime incidence (Green, McFalls, and Smith 2001), and particular events such as the terrorist attacks of September 11, 2001, are likely motivators for bias crime. According to Shively (2005), there was a seventeen-fold increase from 2000 to 2001 for crimes motivated by anti-Islamic bias.

Issues of Data Collection

Although the U.S. government is required to collect data on hate crimes, state participation in the collection effort is voluntary, which has resulted in several thousand agencies electing not to participate. Additionally, McDevitt et al. (2000) have shown that of the nearly twelve thousand law enforcement agencies participating in the Uniform Crime Reporting (UCR) Hate Crime Reporting Program, nearly 83% reported zero hate crimes in 1996 (McDevitt et al. 2000). Complicating matters further, 37% of agencies that didn't participate or that reported zero incidents in 1997 believed their departments had investigated at least one hate crime incident. To understand the reasons for these phenomena, McDevitt et al. examined the hate crime reporting process and the barriers to obtaining accurate data. These barriers are broken down into two groups: individual (victim) inhibitors and police disincentives. The former refers to such obstacles as not recognizing that a hate crime has been committed, feeling the incident was not serious enough to report, and

mistrust of the police. Police disincentives include failing to recognize the commission of a hate crime, putting a low agency priority on taking hate crime reports, and lacking formal policies on the reporting of hate crimes.

The authors state (p. 134) that improving the national documentation of hate crimes "requires a broad-based strategy that addresses four overarching areas: (1) building trust between members of the minority community and their local police, (2) improving law enforcement's ability to respond to victims who do come forward to report bias crimes, (3) making the national data more 'user friendly' for local law enforcement purposes, and (4) using supplemental data to both shed light on the level of unreported hate crime and promote community collaboration."

A few studies have systematically investigated the motivations of hate crime offenders. Levin and McDevitt (2002) and Levin, McDevitt, and Bennett (2002) have offered a typology of perpetrators based on their motivations. The support for this framework comes from data on hate crimes reported to the Boston Police Department during an eighteen-month period in the early 1990s. The typology includes the following motivations for offenders:

1. Thrill seekers, who constitute about two-thirds of offenders, have little commitment to bias per se. Although the underlying factor is bigotry, thrill seeking offenders appear to be motivated by the desire for excitement or for peer acceptance.
2. Defensive offenders view members of a group as unfairly using up the offender's groups resources, such as when a minority member moves into a previously all-white neighborhood.
3. Retaliatory incidents are carried out when the offender reacts to a real or perceived hate crime on his or her group by attacking someone from the group of the first perpetrator.

4. Offenders on a mission have often joined hate groups and make it their mission in life to rid the world of groups they consider evil or inferior.

The typology also provides useful investigative information. For example, while nine out of ten thrill seeking offenders in the study reportedly left their own neighborhood in search of a victim, defensive offenders tend to attack victims within the offenders' own neighborhoods. The typology is currently being used by the FBI and in other national training curricula.

How Is Hate Crime Addressed in the Law?

In 1979, Massachusetts became the first state to enact modern legislation targeting hate crime. The Massachusetts Civil Rights Act did not include particular protected status groups but was aggressively enforced with the interpretation that it covered crimes based on religious or racial characteristics. By 1985, another seven states (Rhode Island, Connecticut, New York, Illinois, Pennsylvania, Oregon, and Washington) had passed laws punishing individuals who committed offenses because of race, ethnicity/national origin, and religion (Levin 2002). By 1991, twenty-eight states had passed hate crime laws; by 2000, forty-one had.

In the past decade, hate crime laws have been institutionalized federally and in more than 80% of the states. During the 1990s, the federal government introduced four pieces of hate crime legislation. The Hate Crime Statistics Act (HCSA) was passed in 1990 and requires the attorney general to collect data on crimes motivated by race, religion, sexual orientation, and ethnicity for five years. Responsibility for collecting hate crime data was given to the director of the FBI, who assigned the task to the UCR program. HCSA did not criminalize any behavior, and it neither provided funding for localities to collect data nor required them to submit data. However, training provided to local law enforcement by the FBI in order to increase reporting did much to sensitize many agencies to the importance of hate crimes.

The Violent Crime Control and Law Enforcement Act of 1994 added disability, both physical and mental, to the list of protected constituencies. Also passed in 1994, the Hate Crime Sentencing Act increases by about 30% the sentence for underlying violations of federally protected activities in which the victim is intentionally chosen because of his or her race, color, religion, national origin, ethnicity, gender, disability, or sexual orientation. The Church Arson Prevention Act of 1996 expands the list of federally protected activities to cover religious worship and increased penalties for the arson of churches. It also makes the collection of hate crime data, originally mandated for five years following passage of the HCSA, a permanent feature of the UCR.

Originally introduced in 1998, the Hate Crime Prevention Act would extend federal protection on the basis of gender, disability, and sexual orientation, but in cases of interstate commerce only, and would broaden the current protected circumstances that require a victim to have been attacked both because of his or her status and in the exercise of a specific activity protected by the list of federally protected activities. Despite support in the Senate, the bill has not successfully made it to the floor of the House for a vote.

Hate crime legislation is criticized by some for what they view as criminalizing thoughts and beliefs in violation of the First Amendment. Indeed, in *R.A.V. v. St. Paul* (1992), the Supreme Court "invalidated those hate crime laws in which the criminality of a particular act hinged solely on the idea expressed through the use of a particular symbol" (Levin 2002) (in this case, cross burning). The Court has, however, upheld hate crime legislation that takes into account an offender's biased intent during sentencing for an underlying offense. In *Wisconsin v. Mitchell* in 1993, the Court determined that the penalty enhancement for choosing an assault victim because of his race was constitutional because the state law did not prevent anyone's free expression, that motivation has traditionally been one of the factors used in determining sentences and the Constitution does not bar admitting the offender's beliefs at sentencing, and that the severity of the effect of hate crimes warrants its use as an aggravating factor in making sentencing decisions. Legislation often specifies that this extra penalty can be served only after the original sentence, guaranteeing its function as a true enhancement.

What Is the Main Critique of Hate Crime Law?

As mentioned above, some critics have argued that federal hate crime legislation is a step toward criminalizing unpopular beliefs. This is not, however, the only criticism of the concept of hate crime. In *Hate Crimes: Criminal Law and Identity Politics*, James B. Jacobs and Kimberly Potter (1998) offer a critique of the major justifications for hate crime legislation. In addition to this analysis, which is discussed below, critics have also addressed several issues concerning hate crime legislation that deal with the feasibility of enforcing hate crime laws, poorly written laws, and laws that ultimately function as unfunded mandates (Jacobs and Potter 1998; Shively 2005). We do not discuss these concerns here because, while they may reflect important considerations, they address implementation rather than substantive issues relating to the concept of hate crime legislation per se.

To begin with, Jacobs and Potter (1998) argue that although they do not object in principle to correlating punishment and motive, they question whether prejudice is any worse a motive than, for example, "greed, power, lust, spite, desire to dominate, and pure sadism" (p. 80). They also ask whether there is not an argument to be made that hate criminals are *less* culpable due to early indoctrination by parents and peers. The evidence, they state, does not support the notion that bias-motivated assaults tend to be excessively brutal or somehow worse than non–bias assaults, which already are governed by a severity continuum when it comes to sentencing. In terms of psychological injury, the authors point to a lack of comparison groups of non–hate crime victims in studies of the deleterious effects of hate crimes on victims. They note the existence of one study that found less severe injury in victims of hate crimes versus non–hate crimes.

In response to claims that hate crimes impact innocent third parties in addition to the primary victim, Jacobs and Potter argue that other non–bias crimes, such as murder, rape, child abduction, carjacking, and subway crime, similarly can elicit fear in the broader community. On the other hand, they say, hate crimes that include such low-level offenses as vandalism do not spread terror.

In response to the critique of Jacobs and Potter, many researchers and advocates have pointed out that historically we have always considered the status of the victim (for example, children or elderly) and the impact on the community in assessing punishment for a crime. Hate crime legislation follows this standard but expands the values being safeguarded from age and potential vulnerability to the increasing diversity of our society.

Hate Groups

Hate groups have been defined as "any organized group whose beliefs and actions are rooted in enmity toward an entire class of people based on ethnicity, perceived race, sexual orientations, religion, or other inherent characteristic" (Woolf and Hulsizer 2004). According to the Southern Poverty Law Center, there were 762 active hate groups in the United States during

2004, including black separatists, Christian identity, Ku Klux Klan, neo-Confederacy, neo-Nazi, and racist skinhead groups in addition to other groups representing other biased doctrines. "Active" refers to criminal acts, marches, rallies, speeches, meetings, leafleting, or publishing (Southern Poverty Law Center 2006).

Interestingly, there is evidence showing that most hate crimes committed in the United States are not committed by individuals who are part of hate groups. This is not to say that hate groups aren't harmful. For one thing, they help perpetuate prejudice, stereotyping, and discrimination and prompt other members of society to violent acts. Teenagers and young adults, predominately males, are particularly susceptible to hate groups' messages regardless of whether they are actual members (Woolf and Hulsizer 2004). Additionally, acts of domestic terrorism are typically perpetrated by individuals associated with hate groups (for example, Timothy McVeigh and Terry McNichols were connected with right-wing militia and Christian identity groups).

The members of organized hate groups have broadened the meaning of the term "defense" to include aggressive behavior attacking innocent victims. For example, in a recent issue of the White Aryan Resistance (WAR) newsletter, the group's leader asserts "We have every right to use force in self-defense, in retaliation, and in preemptive strikes against those who openly threaten our freedom." Thus, no pretext of a precipitating event is necessary; the very presence of members of a particular group may be considered sufficient to call for a group response (Levin and McDevitt 2002, 101).

The advent of the Internet has, unfortunately, widely broadened the reach of hate groups. There are hundreds of websites operated by various hate groups. This enables hate groups to communicate with a potentially enormous audience, including children, and makes it possible to sell wares (for example, "white power" music) that would not be permitted in mainstream stores.

In the little research that has been done to systematically measure the impact of the organized hate groups, it appears that their effect is greater through their messaging than their individual actions. In those jurisdictions that measure hate group involvement by the offenders in hate crimes, they find that generally less than 10% of the hate crimes committed in a jurisdiction are committed by members of a hate or bias group. It does appear to be the case, though, that a much larger number of hate crime offenders have seen hate group literature or logged on to a hate group website.

Hate Crime Prevention

There are two options for addressing the commission of hate crimes: prevention and rehabilitation. The former seeks to increase awareness of the consequences and to stop hate crime before it occurs, while the latter strives to deter an offender from committing future hate crimes. There are several strong prevention programs offered in the United States, some of which are directed at schoolteachers. Some examples follow:

- *World of Difference program.* Sponsored by the Anti-Defamation League, it has trained more than three hundred thousand teachers in the skills necessary to identify and combat acts motivated by hate in their schools.
- *Teaching Tolerance program.* Offered by the Southern Poverty Law Center, it has trained thousands of teachers to foster equity, respect, and understanding inside and outside the classroom.
- *Facing History and Ourselves.* Aimed at middle and high school history and social studies teachers, this

curriculum uses the Holocaust to teach about the dangers of bigotry and emphasizes the positive and negative roles bystanders can play in hate crimes.

Hate crime rehabilitation programs for offenders face many obstacles. However, Levin and McDevitt (2002) argue that model programs should include the following elements:

- Assessment of the offenders
- Discussion of impact on victims
- Cultural awareness
- Restitution/community service
- Delineation of legal consequences
- Participation in a major cultural event
- Aftercare

Conclusion

While much debate involves the exact role the law and the criminal justice system should play in violence motivated by bias or hatred, there is little debate that a number of crimes are committed annually on the basis of victims' races, ethnicities, or other group characteristics. In a society that is becoming increasingly diverse, history informs us that as diversity increases, interpersonal tensions and all too often violence follow. Hate crime laws and the response to these crimes by the police, courts, and, most important, members of our communities will be increasingly important in helping our society to grow and to respect the contributions and dignity of all its members.

JACK MCDEVITT and RUSSELL WOLFF

See also **Accountability; Crime, Serious; Criminology; Minorities and the Police**

References and Further Reading

Anti-Defamation League. 2006. http://www.adl.org/ctboh/Responding1.asp (accessed January 11, 2006).

———. 2006. http://www.adl.org/education/ (accessed January 11, 2006).

Boeckmann, Robert J., and Carolyn Turpin-Petrosino. 2002. Understanding the harm of hate crime. *Journal of Social Issues* 58 (2): 207–25.

Dunbar, Edward. 2001. Counseling practices to ameliorate the effects of discrimination and hate events: Toward a systematic approach to assessment and intervention. *The Counseling Psychologist* 29 (2): 281–307.

Federal Bureau of Investigation. 1999. *Hate crime data collection guidelines, 1999*. Washington, DC: U.S. Department of Justice.

———. 2003. *Hate crime statistics, 2003*. Washington, DC: U.S. Department of Justice.

Green, Donald P., Laurence H. McFalls, and Jennifer K. Smith. 2001. Hate crime: An emergent research agenda. *Annual Review of Sociology* 27: 479–504.

Jacobs, James B., and Kimberly Potter. 1998. *Hate crimes: Criminal law and identity politics*. New York: Oxford University Press.

Jenness, Valerie. 2001. The hate crime canon and beyond: A critical assessment. *Law and Critique* 12: 279–308.

Jenness, Valerie, and Ryken Grattet. 2001. *Making hate a crime: From social movement to law enforcement*. New York: Russell Sage Foundation.

Levin, Brian. 2002. From slavery to hate crime laws: The emergence of race and status-based protection in American criminal law. *Journal of Social Issues* 58: (2), 227–45.

Levin, Jack, and Jack McDevitt. 2002. *Hate crime revisited: America's war against those who are different*. Cambridge, MA: Westview Press.

McDevitt, Jack, Jennifer M. Balboni, Susan Bennett, Joan Weiss, Stan Orchowsky, and Lisa Walbolt. 2000. *Improving the quality and accuracy of bias crime statistics nationally: An assessment of the first ten years of bias crime data collection*. Washington, DC: U.S. Department of Justice, Bureau of Justice Statistics.

McDevitt, Jack, Jennifer Balboni, Luis Garcia, and Joann Gu. 2001. Consequences for victims: A comparison of bias- and non–bias-motivated assaults. *American Behavioral Scientist* 45 (4): 697–713.

McDevitt, Jack, Shea Cronin, Jennifer Balboni, Amy Farrell, James Nolan, and Joan Weiss. 2003. *Bridging the information disconnect in national bias crime reporting*. Washington, DC: U.S. Department of Justice, Bureau of Justice Statistics.

McDevitt, Jack, Jack Levin, and Susan Bennett. 2002. Hate crime offenders: An expanded typology. *Journal of Social Issues* 58, (2): 303–17.

Office for Victims of Crime. 2000. *Responding to hate crime: A multidisciplinary curriculum for law enforcement and victim assistance professionals.* Washington, DC: U.S. Department of Justice.

Prejudice Institute, The. 2006. http://www.prejudiceinstitute.org/ethnoviolenceFS.html (accessed January 11, 2006).

Shively, Michael. 2005. *Study of literature and legislation on hate crime in America.* June. Washington, DC: U.S. Department of Justice, National Institute of Justice.

Southern Poverty Law Center. 2006. http://www.splcenter.org/intel/map/hate.jsp (accessed January 11, 2006).

———. 2006. http://www.splcenter.org/center/tt/teach.jsp (accessed January 11, 2006).

Woolf, Linda M., and Michael R. Hulsizer. 2004. Hate groups for dummies: How to build a successful hate group. *Humanity and Society* 28 (1), February.

HISTORY OF AMERICAN POLICING

This article examines the history of American policing, from its English heritage to the community policing movement of the latter part of the twentieth century.

The English System

The origins of modern policing in the United States are linked directly to its English heritage. Ideas about police and the community, crime prevention, the posse, constables, and sheriffs developed from English law enforcement. Beginning at about 900 C.E., the role of law enforcement was placed in the hands of the common, everyday citizen. Each citizen was held responsible for aiding neighbors who might be victims of outlaws and thieves. Because no police officers existed, individuals used state-sanctioned force to maintain social control. This model of law enforcement is known as "kin police"—individuals were considered responsible for their "kin" (relatives) and followed the adage, "I am my brother's keeper." Slowly this model developed into a more formalized "communitarian," or community-based, police system.

After the Norman Conquest of 1066, a community model was established, which was called frankpledge; this system required that every male above the age of twelve form a group with nine of his neighbors, called a tything (a group of ten). Each tything was sworn to apprehend and deliver to court any of its members who committed a crime. Each person was pledged to help protect fellow citizens and, in turn, would be protected. This system was "obligatory" in nature, in that tythingmen were not paid salaries for their work but were required by law to carry out certain duties (Klockars 1985, 21). Tythingmen were required to hold suspects in custody while they were awaiting trial and to make regular appearances in court to present information on wrong doing by members of their own or other tythings. If any member of the tything failed to perform his required duties, all members of the group would be levied severe fines.

Ten tythings were grouped into a hundred, directed by a constable (appointed by the local nobleman), who in effect became the first policeman. That is, the constable was the first official with law enforcement responsibility greater than simply helping one's neighbor. Just as the tythings were grouped into hundreds, the hundreds were grouped into shires, which are similar to counties today. The supervisor of each shire was the shire reeve (or sheriff), who was appointed by the king.

Frankpledge began to disintegrate by the thirteenth century. Inadequate supervision by the king and his appointees led to its downfall. As frankpledge slowly declined, the parish constable system emerged to take its place. The Statute of Winchester of 1285 placed more authority in the hands of the constable for law enforcement. One man from each parish served a one-year term as constable on a rotating basis. Though not paid for his work, the constable was responsible for organizing a group of watchmen who would guard the gates of the town at night. These watchmen were also unpaid and selected from the parish population. If a serious disturbance took place, the parish constable had the authority to raise the "hue and cry." This call to arms meant that all males in the parish were to drop what they were doing and come to the aid of the constable.

In the mid-1300s, the office of justice of the peace was created to assist the shire reeve in controlling his territory. The local constable and the shire reeve became assistants to the justice of the peace and supervised the night watchmen, served warrants, and took prisoners into custody for appearance before justice of the peace courts.

The English system continued with relative success well into the 1700s. By the end of the eighteenth century, however, the growth of large cities, civil disorders, and increased criminal activity led to changes and eventually a new system. In 1829 Parliament passed the London Metropolitan Police Act, which established a paid, full-time, uniformed police force with the primary purpose of patrolling the city. Sir Robert Peel, Britain's home secretary, is credited with the formation of the police. Peel synthesized the ideas of his predecessors, convinced Parliament of the need for police, and guided the early development of the force.

American Policing in the Colonial Period

In colonial America, policing followed the English systems. The sheriff, constable, and watch were easily adapted to the colonies. The county sheriff, appointed by the governor, became the most important law enforcement agent, particularly when the colonies remained small and primarily rural. The sheriff's duties included apprehending criminals, serving subpoenas, appearing in court, and collecting taxes. The sheriff was paid a fixed amount for each task he performed. Since sheriffs received higher fees based on the taxes they collected, apprehending criminals was not a primary concern. In fact, law enforcement was a low priority.

In the larger cities, such as New York, Boston, and Philadelphia, constables and the night watch conducted a wide variety of tasks. They reported fires, raised the hue and cry, maintained street lamps, arrested or detained suspicious persons, and walked the rounds. For the most part, the activities of the constables and the night watch were "reactive" in nature. That is, these men responded to criminal behavior only when requested by victims or witnesses (Monkkonen 1981). Rather than preventing crime, discovering criminal behavior, or acting in a "proactive" fashion, these individuals relied on others to define their work.

Nineteenth-Century American Policing

In the nineteenth century, American cities and towns encountered serious problems—urban areas grew at phenomenal rates, civil disorders swept the nation, and crime was perceived to be increasing. New York, for example, sprouted from a population of 33,000 in 1790 to 150,000 in 1830. Between the 1830s and 1860s, numerous conflicts and riots occurred because of ethnic and racial differences, economic failures, and moral questions and during elections of public officials. At the same time, citizens perceived that crime was increasing. Homicides, robberies, and thefts were thought to be on the rise. In addition, vagrancy, prostitution, gambling, and other vices were more observable on the streets. These types of criminal activities and the general deterioration of the city led to a sense of a loss of social control.

The first American police departments modeled themselves after the London Metropolitan Police. The most notable carryover was the adoption of the preventive patrol idea—the notion that police presence could alter the behavior of individuals and could be available to maintain order in an efficient manner.

American police systems followed the style of local and municipal governments. City governments, created in the era of the "common man" and democratic participation, were highly decentralized. City councilmen or aldermen ran the government and used political patronage freely. The police departments shared this style of participation and decentralization. The police were an extension of different political factions, rather than an extension of city government. Police officers were recruited and selected by political leaders in a particular ward or precinct.

Cities began to form police departments from 1845 to 1890. Once large cities such as New York (1845) had adopted the English model, the new version of policing spread from larger to smaller cities rather quickly. Where New York had debated for almost ten years before formally adopting the London style, Cleveland, Buffalo, Detroit, and other cities readily accepted the innovation.

Across these departments, differences flourished. Police activity varied depending upon the local government and political factions in power. Standards for officer selection (if any), training procedures, rules and regulations, levels of enforcement of laws, and police–citizen relationships differed across the United States. New officers were sent out on patrol with no training and few instructions beyond their rulebooks. Proper arrest procedures, rules of law, and so on were unknown to the officers. Left to themselves, they developed their own strategies for coping with life in the streets.

Police officers walked a beat in all types of weather for two to six hours of a twelve-hour day. The remaining time was spent at the station house on reserve. During actual patrol duty, police officers were required to maintain order and make arrests, but they often circumvented their responsibilities. Supervision was extremely limited once an officer was beyond the stationhouse. Sergeants and captains had no way of contacting their men while they were on the beat since communications technology was limited.

One of the major themes in the study of nineteenth-century policing is the large-scale corruption that occurred in numerous departments across the country. The lawlessness of the police—their systematic corruption and nonenforcement of the laws—was one of the paramount issues in municipal politics during the late 1800s. Officers who did not go along with the nonenforcement of laws or did not approve of the graft and corruption of others found themselves transferred to less than desirable areas. Promotions were also denied; they were reserved for the politically astute and wealthy officer (promotions could cost $10,000 to $15,000). These types of problems were endemic to most urban police agencies throughout the country. They led to inefficiency and inequality of police services.

A broad reform effort began to emerge toward the end of the nineteenth century. Stimulated mainly by a group known as the Progressives, attempts were made to create a truly professional police force. These reformers found that the police were without discipline, strong leadership, and qualified personnel. To improve conditions, the progressives recommended three changes: (1) The departments should be centralized, (2) personnel should be upgraded, and (3) the police function should be narrowed (Fogelson 1977). Centralization of the police meant that more power and authority should be placed in the hands of the chief. Autonomy from politicians was crucial to centralization.

Upgrading the rank-and-file meant better training, discipline, and selection. Finally, the reformers urged that police give up all activities unrelated to crime. Police had run the ambulances, handled licensing of businesses, and sheltered the poor. By concentrating on fighting crime, the police would be removed from their service orientation and their ties to political parties would be severed.

From 1890 to 1920, the Progressive reformers struggled to implement their reform ideology in cities across the country. Some inroads were made during this period, including the establishment of police commissions, the use of civil service exams, and legislative reforms.

A second reform effort emerged in the wake of the failure of the Progressives. Within police circles, a small cadre of chiefs sought and implemented a variety of innovations that would improve policing generally. From about 1910 to 1960, police chiefs carried on another reform movement, advocating that police adopt the professional model. This model embodied a number of characteristics. First, the officers were experts; they applied knowledge to their tasks and were the only ones qualified to do the job. Second, the department was autonomous from external influences, such as political parties. Third, the department was administratively efficient, in that it carried out its mandate to enforce the law through modern technology and businesslike practices. These reforms were similar to those of the Progressives, but because they came from within the police organizations themselves, they met with more success.

Overall, the professional movement met with more success than the Progressive attempt. The quality of police officers greatly improved during this period. In terms of autonomy, police reformers and others were able to reduce the influence of political parties in departmental affairs. Chiefs obtained more power and authority in their management abilities, but continued to receive input from political leaders.

In terms of efficiency, the police moved forward in serving the public more quickly and competently. Technological innovations clearly assisted the police in this area, as did streamlining the organizations themselves. However, the innovations also created problems. Citizens came to expect more from the police—faster response times, more arrests, and less overall crime. These expectations, as well as other difficulties, led to trying times for the police in the 1960s.

Crisis of the 1960s

Policing in America encountered its most serious crisis in the 1960s. The rise in crime, the civil rights movement, antiwar sentiment, and riots in the cities brought the police into the center of a maelstrom. During the decade of the 1960s, crime increased at a phenomenal rate. Between 1960 and 1970, the crime rate per hundred thousand persons doubled. Most troubling was the increase in violent crime—the robbery rate almost tripled during these ten years.

The civil rights movement and antiwar sentiments created additional demands for the police. The police became the symbol of a society that denied blacks equal justice under the law. Eventually, the frustrations of black Americans erupted into violence in Northern and Southern cities. Riots engulfed almost every major city between 1964 and 1968. Most of the disorders were initiated by an incident involving the police. In Los Angeles and Newark, the riots were set off by routine traffic stops. In Detroit, a police raid on an after-hours bar touched off the disorders. In Chicago, the brutality of the police toward antiwar demonstrators during the Democratic National Convention highlighted the difficulties of the police and the community.

The events of the 1960s forced the police, politicians, and policy makers to reassess the state of law enforcement in the United States. For the first time, academics rushed to study the police in an effort to explain their problems and crises. With federal funding, researchers began to study the police from a number of perspectives. Sociologists, criminologists, political scientists, psychologists, and historians began to scrutinize different aspects of policing. Traditional methods of patrol development, officer selection, and training were questioned. Racial discrimination in employment practices, in arrests, and in the use of deadly force were among the issues closely examined.

In addition, the professional movement itself came into question. The professional movement had unintended consequences— a police subculture developed, police– community relations suffered, modern technology separated the officer from routine contact with citizens, and the impersonal style of professionalism often exacerbated police–community problems. Tactics such as aggressive patrol in black neighborhoods, designed to suppress crime efficiently, created more racial tensions.

As a result of the problems of the 1960s and 1970s, a third wave of reform of police operations and strategies began to emerge— community-oriented policing. Community policing came to light as an idea and philosophy in response to the communication gap between police and community and because of research studies that questioned police tactics and strategies. A new paradigm that incorporated the "broken-windows" theory, proactive policing, and problem-oriented policing shaped the community policing reform era.

Police strategists recognized that simply reacting to calls for service limits the ability of law enforcement to control crime and maintain order. Police on patrol cannot see enough to control crime effectively— they do not know how to intervene to improve the quality of life in the community. The reactive strategy used during the professional era no longer was effective in dealing with complex problems in the 1980s

and 1990s. Instead, Herman Goldstein (1979, 1990) and James Q. Wilson and George Kelling (1982) called for police to engage in proactive work and problem-oriented policing. Like other reform movements, community policing took time, resources, and strong leadership before it was adopted by law enforcement agencies. By the end of the twentieth century, however, many agencies had adopted the community policing philosophy, and all of the largest agencies in the country had community policing officers working on the street.

CRAIG D. UCHIDA

See also **Accountability; Administration of Police Agencies, Theories of; Authority within Police Organizations; Autonomy and the Police; Community-Oriented Policing: History; Continental Europe, Policing in; Crime Commissions; Police in Urban America, 1860–1920; Police Reform in an Era of Community and Problem-Oriented Policing; Police Reform: 1950–1970; Professionalism**

References and Further Reading

Fogelson, Robert. 1977. *Big-city police.* Cambridge, MA: Harvard University Press.

Goldstein, Herman. 1979. Improving policing: A problem-oriented approach. *Crime and Delinquency* 25: 236–58.

———. 1990. *Problem-oriented policing.* New York: McGraw-Hill.

Klockars, Carl. 1985. *The idea of police.* Beverly Hills, CA: Sage.

Monkkonen, Eric H. 1981. *Police in urban America, 1860–1920.* Cambridge: Cambridge University Press.

Wilson, James Q., and George Kelling. 1982. Broken windows: The police and neighborhood safety." *Atlantic Monthly* 249: 29–38.

HOMELAND SECURITY AND LAW ENFORCEMENT

Homeland security has been defined (Dobbs 2001) as

The prevention, deterrence, and preemption of, and defense against, aggression targeted at U.S. territory, sovereignty, population,

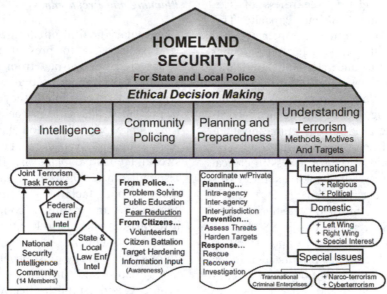

Figure 1 Homeland Security responsibilities for state, local, and tribal police.

and infrastructure as well as the management of the consequences of such aggression and other domestic emergencies.

As the idea of homeland security has been embraced (often reluctantly) by state, local, and tribal law enforcement agencies, a pattern has emerged with respect to the programmatic, training, and policy implications for law enforcement agencies. There are four broad pillars of responsibility that have been embraced by policing as the strategic components of homeland security: intelligence, community policing/ partnerships, planning and preparedness, and understanding terrorism.

There are significant implications of these responsibilities with respect to re-socialization of the police work force, resource development and reallocation, and organizational development that go beyond any change experienced in modern American policing. Each law enforcement agency and community will respond in a different way, depending on the level and nature of the threat inherent in the community characteristics, the political and community mandate with respect to homeland security, the ideology of police leadership on these issues, and the resource

capacity of the jurisdiction. Since every community is different, every community must make a self-assessment of how the pillars of homeland security will apply to its law enforcement agency.

Because of the changes brought to contemporary society by the threat of terrorism, new aggressive actions by the law enforcement and intelligence communities have been undertaken. Yet, an essential element of maintaining a secure homeland is to protect the constitutional principles that the United States is founded on. Hence, an ethical (and ideological) dilemma has emerged. Because of this dilemma, the overriding capstone to the four pillars of homeland security is to ensure adherence to our founding principles via ethical and judicious decision making by law enforcement personnel. If these principles are lost, so is our homeland.

The Pillars

Law Enforcement Intelligence

The National Criminal Intelligence Sharing Plan (NCISP) states that every law

621

enforcement agency, regardless of size, should have an intelligence capacity. This means that law enforcement agencies need to have, at the least, a person who has been trained to understand the guidelines for collecting raw information for the intelligence process, proper means of storing and reviewing data in intelligence records systems, and rules for disseminating intelligence and sensitive information. That person should also have access to critical information systems, such as the FBI's Law Enforcement Online (LEO) and/or the Regional Information Sharing System's (RISS) secure system RISS.net.

Intelligence is critical to understanding the nature of terrorists' threats, identifying local suspects and local targets, and determining intervention and prevention strategies. Intelligence is the currency by which homeland security is managed within a jurisdiction. The need to develop and share intelligence is unequivocal for the success of the homeland security initiative.

Community Policing

Inherent to the success of identifying threats within a jurisdiction is to have an effective, trusted line of communication between citizens and the law enforcement agency. Hence, the strong foundation that has been laid in America's law enforcement agencies with community policing as a tool to reduce disorder and prevent crime can be translated to counterterrorism and homeland security. Law enforcement agencies must educate citizens about the signs and symbols of terrorism as well as provide direction on what to do when suspicious activity is observed. Lessons learned in Israel, Turkey, and the United Kingdom have found that good community partnerships can be critical in preventing terrorism. Indeed, each of these countries has policing programs with the community designed specifically for counterterrorism.

Planning and Preparedness

The primary goal of intelligence in homeland security is to prevent a terrorist attack. Lessons learned from crime prevention have shown us that while many crimes can be prevented, they cannot *all* be prevented. The same is true with terrorism. Hence, part of the homeland security responsibility is to ensure that comprehensive and effective plans are in place to respond to a terrorist attack in a manner that will both facilitate the safety of the community and permit a comprehensive investigation in order to identify and prosecute the offenders. As a result, the law enforcement agency must develop coordinated plans and incident management protocols and establish effective working relationships with neighboring law enforcement agencies as well as the first responder community (Bea 2005).

Understanding Terrorism

Terrorist threats emerge from both ends of the political spectrum and can be domestic or international in nature. History has shown criminally extremist acts committed by such diverse groups as al-Qaeda, the Earth Liberation Front, and religious extremists. Regardless of their cause, there is a foundation of information that is consistent among all groups— each has motives, methods, and targets. For a law enforcement agency to be most effective in identifying the signs and symbols of terrorism, personnel must understand the motives, methods, and targets of the group(s) that threaten the community. This permits officers—and citizens—to focus their attention and more readily identify behaviors and circumstances that are truly suspicious. Understanding terrorism plays critical roles for successful intelligence and community policing.

Translating Responsibilities to Police Policy

Overarching the four pillars of responsibility for homeland security are critical organizational functions that must be addressed.

Information Management

There is a great deal of information associated with all policing tasks; homeland security is no different. Information management includes a broad array of responsibilities ranging from public education—which can contribute to fear reduction or aid in identifying threats—conducting threat assessments, establishing effective communications between agencies, and managing complaints or tips. This last element has significant implications and can be a labor-intensive investment for the organization.

For example, during the anthrax scare occurring shortly after the 9/11 attacks, police agencies across the United States received a large number of calls about potential anthrax. Fortunately, almost all of those calls were unfounded; nonetheless, they required some type of response from the police. Important questions emerged:

- How should an agency respond when the probability of a problem is extraordinarily low?
- Can the police agency afford to simply dismiss the call?
- If the agency responds, is there a mechanism for filtering which calls will receive a response?
- How would such a determination be made?
- What are the implications of not responding to a complaint that turns out to be valid?
- What will be the cost of responding and what, if any, other police responsibilities would have to be reduced in order to manage such calls, particularly in a time of crisis?

Although tempting, one has to be careful about dismissing a call. As an example, during the course of the sniper shootings occurring in Maryland, Virginia, and the District of Columbia during October 2002, a tip line was created that generated tens of thousands of calls. It was later learned that one of the suspects, John Muhammad, had actually called the tip line twice and the call was dismissed by an overwhelmed staff member. If contact had been established sooner, would lives have been saved? The answer is unknown; however, the point remains: A mechanism must be established to manage information.

Physical Responsibilities

When potential targets are identified within a community, there are inherent obligations to harden and protect those targets. In some cases, such as an electrical power generating plant, the target will typically have private security with whom the police must work to ensure that protection of the target is maximized. In other cases, such as a municipal water treatment plant, the only security available may have to be provided by the police. Moreover, if the threat to those targets should be heightened, the police agency must then become more vigilant in physical protection, often even supplementing private security forces.

When the wide range of potential critical infrastructure targets within a community are considered, then the impact of potential security responsibilities becomes even more profound. Not only are security responsibilities inherently labor intensive (and hence costly), but when personnel are at a security assignment, there are typically no other policing duties they can fulfill. As such, the options include the following:

- Minimize other police activities (for example, not respond to every call for service, decrease investigative follow-ups, reassign officers working in the schools, and so on).
- Pay overtime to officers to work security assignments.
- Contract with a private security firm to work the security assignments.
- Develop a volunteer force of citizens to supplement police security responsibilities.
- Employ a combination of these methods, depending on the nature or seriousness of the threat and the duration of the threat period.

Regardless of the option, there are significant resource implications for the police response. Law enforcement leaders must ask the question "How will we fund this?"

Procedural Responsibilities

Homeland security requires that there simply be "a number of things which must be done" to accomplish the responsibilities discussed so far. These include the following:

- Developing and implementing a terrorism investigative capability
- Developing, teaching, and implementing prevention strategies
- Developing, continually reviewing, and practicing response plans
- Developing interagency planning responsibilities and agreements, with constant monitoring of changes that need to be made in such agreements as a result of fluctuations in the budget and agency staffing and the changing characteristics of the jurisdictions involved

As in the previous cases, the resource implications are significant, particularly for staff time.

Two factors cannot be stressed enough: (1) Each of these responsibilities has significant resource implications. (2) These are new responsibilities not previously bestowed on state, local, and tribal law enforcement. Thoughtful planning is essential for success to be achieved without undue sacrifice to other policing obligations.

The Impact on State, Local, and Tribal Governments

This is an uncharted journey that requires research, careful thought, and effective planning. As noted previously, homeland security is an added police responsibility with two broad concerns: *policy* and *resources*. An example will illustrate the issues:

- Police departments need to make policies on how to respond when the Homeland Security Advisory System (HSAS) alert status increases. If, for example, the alert status moves from yellow to orange, what does this mean to a police agency? Are police and emergency services placed on a standby status? If so, are there overtime costs associated with this? Are duty hours extended? If so, there are further salary implications.
- As a result of the higher alert level, will personnel be reassigned for contingency purposes? If so, what are the implications for managing calls for service? For example, during a high alert status will "priority three" calls be ignored because of staffing implications?
- What equipment—vehicles, radios, hazardous materials (hazmat) tools, and so forth—is needed and how will it be deployed? How will operational priorities change? For example, will officers be directed to be more proactive in stopping vehicles of people thought to be involved in terrorism? If so, the obvious concern is allegations of racial profiling and deprivation of civil rights.

This simple, yet realistic, example illustrates that the impact of homeland security on local police policy and resources can be dramatic. Expanding this line of thought, the National Preparedness Goal has significant implications for training, staffing, deployment, and resource allocation. Importantly, police administrators should fully analyze the expectations and role of their agencies in homeland security. This is a laborious, and somewhat subjective, process, yet it is essential.

Second, the department must conduct an operations analysis to understand its capacity to fulfill the homeland security mission. Were plans executed as anticipated? Were responses effective? Was intelligence accurate? Self-directed evaluations provide important insight for refining plans and responses.

Third, methods must be explored to determine how these homeland security needs may be met (for example, exploring grants and creative funding, partnering with agencies on a regional basis, public–private partnerships, working with community service groups, and developing a volunteer program). Of course, these must also consider the balance between homeland security with other police responsibilities.

Fourth, once methods are determined, they must be operationalized. This includes establishing a command structure, identifying responsibilities, developing operating policies and procedures, and implementing plans.

Fifth, implementation begins with training and education. Not only must skills be developed (that is, training), but there must also be an understanding of the broader issues. This includes ensuring that reasonable, consistent decision-making skills have been inculcated in personnel (that is, education). Finally, the homeland security initiative must be implemented and evaluated. Fundamentally, the question to be answered is, "Did it work?"

In determining if the plan "worked," it must be recognized that homeland security has implications for changing all aspects of the police organization. Any type of change has implications for resources, management, the development of new expertise, defining accountability, and evaluating activities/initiatives to ensure that new plans and initiatives are meeting expectations. Examples of changes include the following:

Line level officers—greater awareness of the potential for terrorism, including scanning the community for "signs" or indicators of threats, establishing relations and communications with segments of the community that may have some relationship with extremist groups, and creating a new public dialogue for public education and fear reduction associated with terrorism.

Investigations—new knowledge and responsibilities for detectives who must develop expertise for investigating the different types of extremist groups that may pose a threat to the community. This includes developing confidential informants, understanding local dynamics of criminal extremism, and developing the ability to infiltrate group(s) in an undercover capacity.

Intelligence—a more proactive intelligence capability within the police department to address homeland security issues, including more frequent and more substantive relationships with multiple agencies at all levels of government, including the FBI Field Intelligence Groups (FIG), Joint Terrorism Task Forces (JTTF), and intelligence fusion centers.

Public/private partnerships—required to maximize the protection of critical infrastructure as well as to coordinate resources and capabilities for a response to a terror attack.

Multiagency cooperation—both within the jurisdiction and between neighboring jurisdictions. The police agency must revisit formal relationships—such as mutual aid pacts or memoranda of understanding—to have a clear understanding of relationships, authority, responsibility, resource sharing, and types of aid that will be provided in prevention, planning, and response to terrorism.

First responders—ensuring that those who would respond first to a terror attack have the equipment, knowledge, and expertise to effectively manage virtually any type of terror scenario that could be anticipated. This requires a significant investment in training and equipment and cannot be strictly limited to a unique team since the first responders will frequently be patrol officers who, at the minimum, will need to render aid and manage the scene until specialists arrive. Hence, first responder training will need to include varied levels of expertise, ranging from those who are truly the first to arrive at a scene and need to manage the immediate emergency to the incident commander who will ensure stability of the scene, rescue, recovery, and investigative/evidence gathering responsibilities.

Prevention/target hardening—developing greater attention, knowledge about, and expertise in prevention and the hardening of potential terrorist targets. This requires broadened expertise and time, which translates into a greater number of dedicated staff hours to meet these responsibilities.

Training—new training must be provided at virtually all levels of the organization to meet several purposes. These include providing baseline information about threats, issues, plans, and responsibilities, providing more detailed/intensive training to develop new expertise in a wide range of areas from intelligence to investigations, and managing a response to weapons of mass destruction (WMD).

Planning—both long-range and short-range plans must add a new dimension not previously included in the police planning equation: having a greater sense of urgency when considering growing and changing terrorism threats to a community and how the law enforcement agency will respond to those threats.

Questions include the following:

- Are new businesses on the horizon that may be targets of any type of terrorist group?
- Is the demography of the community or region changing in a way that may suggest new targets or attract people who may be involved in terrorism?
- Are there changes occurring within the design of the community that will change a response plan?
- Are new resources—such as a hospital—emerging within the community that need to be included within the critical incident plan?

The implications of these activities can be dramatic. They all require two things that are inherently in short supply: *money* and *people*. There will be some financial support available from the federal government for the purchase of equipment and training personnel; however, these represent only a fraction of the costs. The personnel costs of learning to use the new equipment and to attend the training can be significant. Moreover, addressing these new homeland security responsibilities is more than a simple "add on" to the police department. Decisions have to be made about how the department will balance homeland security with other responsibilities:

- Will there be fewer burglary follow-up investigations in order to devote more time to investigating extremist threats?
- Will less emphasis be devoted to gangs or drug enforcement in order to develop an intelligence expertise related to terrorism?
- Will less emphasis be placed on traffic enforcement and more emphasis on developing a comprehensive expertise in first response?
- Will less public education be devoted to fear of crime and more public education be devoted to fear of terrorism?
- Will citizen volunteers spend less time in assisting parking enforcement and more time observing critical infrastructure facilities looking for security lapses?

The answers to these questions, and others, must be unique to a community, as will be the method of paying for the added homeland security activities.

A Local Police Response to Federal and Public Demands

The impact of the added homeland security responsibility on police departments since 9/11 is substantial. A number of agencies—such as the police departments in New Orleans and Austin as well as sheriffs' departments, such as in Orange County, Florida, and Harris County, Texas— have created homeland security units. Many other agencies have reassigned personnel to new homeland security–related areas as well as purchased equipment and increased training. (For the most part, the threat of terrorism has not translated into the hiring of more officers.) While efforts vary according to each community's

resources and perceived vulnerability, among the steps local law enforcement agencies have taken are the following:

- Strengthened liaisons with federal, state, local, and tribal law enforcement agencies, fire departments, emergency planners, emergency responders, and private businesses representing critical infrastructure or unique targets
- Refined their training and emergency response plans to address terrorist threats, including attacks with chemical, biological, radiological, and nuclear (CBRN) weapons
- Increased patrols and strengthened barriers around landmarks, places of worship, ports of entry, transit systems, nuclear power plants, and other "hard" targets that include utilities, telecommunications, key transportation facilities, and government buildings
- Ensured that public speeches, parades, and other public events have greater police involvement in planning and, as appropriate, greater police presence
- Created new counterterrorism initiatives and reassigned officers to counterterrorism and/or intelligence from other assignments such as drug enforcement or gangs
- Employed new technologies such as devices that can test for and sense chemical and biological substances

The benefit of these initiatives is that police agencies are taking positive steps to deal with terrorism threats and make their communities safer. The problem, however, is that all too often these steps have been taken based upon assumptions of threats, not careful threat assessments related to the types of groups that pose threats, the character of those groups' targets, the character of attack from those groups, and the probability of attack. In other words, most of these initiatives have been reactive and based on assumptions, rather than being the product of planning based on intelligence.

Federal, State, and Local Cooperation: The Joint Terrorism Task Forces

One aspect of law enforcement that has evolved significantly is local police involvement in the Joint Terrorism Task Forces (JTTF). The concept for these joint task forces, combining federal, state, local, and tribal law enforcement capabilities, was first used by the FBI in New York City in 1979, due to an overwhelming number of bank robberies. Because this approach proved to be a valuable investigative tool, it was applied to the counterterrorism program in 1980 when the first JTTF was established in New York. This was the direct result of the increasing number of terrorist bombings in the late 1970s and early 1980s, which mandated an immediate and coordinated response. The JTTF's have a wide variety of law enforcement agencies at all levels of government—FBI, ATF, Secret Service, immigration and customs enforcement, U.S. Marshals, and other federal organizations as well as state, county, municipal, and tribal police organizations within a defined geographic area. There are currently more than a hundred JTTFs operating out of all FBI field offices and many FBI resident agency offices.

The unfunded mandate of homeland security has broad implications that reach beyond protecting our communities from terrorist attacks. How will it affect yours?

DAVID L. CARTER

See also **Authority within Police Organizations; Autonomy and the Police; Community-Oriented Policing: Practices; Department of Homeland Security; Intelligence Gathering and Analysis: Impacts on Terrorism; Intelligence-Led Policing and Organizational Learning; INTERPOL and International Police Intelligence; PATRIOT Acts I and II; Technology and the Police; Terrorism: Domestic; Transnational Organized Crime**

References and Further Reading

Carter, David L. 2004. *Law enforcement intelligence: A guide for state, local and tribal law enforcement*. Washington, DC: Office of Community Oriented Policing Services.

Department of Homeland Security. 2005. http://www.dhs.gov/.

Dobbs, M. 2001. Homeland security: New challenges for an old responsibility. *Journal of Homeland Security*, http://www.homelandsecurity.org.

Federal Bureau of Investigation. 2005. Law enforcement online (LEO). http://www.fbi.gov/hq/cjisd/leo.htm.

International Association of Chiefs of Police. 2002. Criminal intelligence sharing: A national plan for intelligence-led policing at the federal, state, and local levels. A summit report. Alexandria, VA: International Association of Chiefs of Police.

National Criminal Intelligence Sharing Plan (NCISP). 2005. http://it.ojp.gov/documents/NCISP_Plan.pdf.

National Preparedness Goal. 2005. https://www.llis.dhs.gov/member/secure/dynamicpage.cfm?pagetitle=Preparedness.

Regional Information Sharing System (RISS). 2005. http://www.rissinfo.com/services.htm.

White, Jonathan. 2005. *Terrorism and homeland security*. Bridgeport, CT: Wadsworth Publishing Company.

HOMICIDE AND ITS INVESTIGATION

Counterposed with many other aspects of policing there is a comparative lack of research on homicide investigation. This is somewhat surprising given its predominance in both fictional and factual mass media representations of police work. Whereas media accounts of homicide investigation often portray detectives as able to solve cases through flashes of brilliant insight, the reality is often significantly different. The majority of homicide investigations typically involve and owe their success to meticulous, painstaking, and detailed work, following fairly standard organizational operating procedures. This routinization of investigative practice is structured by several problems that are regularly encountered and have to be resolved by detectives if they are to successfully investigate a homicide case.

Problem one for homicide investigators is that when confronted with a death under suspicious circumstances, how, in the early stages of enquiries, do they decide whether it is an accidental death, suicide, a death from natural causes, or the result of the (possibly criminal) actions performed by some other person? As such, the classification of a death is one of the key tasks and will be informed by medical opinion and information collected through a postmortem examination. Overall, though, early decisions taken in terms of establishing whether this is a homicide or not do much to structure subsequent investigative actions. Of course, any such classifications are provisional and may be revised in light of further information. Nevertheless, there is a widespread belief among murder squad detectives that if one gets the initial classification wrong, the rest of the investigation will be more difficult.

A second, related problem regularly encountered by homicide detectives concerns how homicide as a legal classification actually provides an appearance of homogeneity that masks the diverse ways in which people kill and are killed. The reality of homicide investigation is that cases are not easily comparable units—they differ in terms of their circumstances and their respective "solvability." The circumstances of some incidents simply make them more difficult to successfully investigate than others. But it can be hard at the outset of an investigation to predict how difficult it is going to be to identify a suspect and, consequently, what level of resources should be made available to an investigation.

Resourcing represents the third problem in the structuring of homicide investigation work. Given the public and legal scrutiny that homicide investigations are often subject to, effective and efficient investigation of major crimes is a resource intensive activity. As such, the capacity of police to investigate either large numbers of homicides or a small number of very high profile cases needs to be understood as interrelated to their ability to deliver other policing services demanded by the public.

The resourcing issue remains an important one despite the increasing use of a variety of sophisticated technologies to assist in the conduct of investigations. There is little doubt that the development of increasingly sophisticated investigative technologies has enabled police to successfully investigate cases that would previously have been intractable. However, such technologies have also required of the police increasing levels of technical expertise and greater care in terms of the identification, collection, processing, and interpretation of many kinds of physical evidence.

All of these problems are routinely encountered by homicide investigators and serve to structure to some degree the tasks that they perform. However, by far the most important problem in the structuring of homicide investigation work is that of information management. The essential dynamic of a homicide investigation is that when starting at a new crime scene, by undertaking a number of lines of enquiry the police start to acquire a lot of information about the circumstances of the death, the identity of the victim, and so forth in a comparatively short space of time. In essence then, the information problem for an investigator is to distinguish between the relevant and irrelevant data.

Given the volume of the information being captured and processed by murder squads, computers are increasingly being used to assist in handling the large data flows. However, while computers do assist the information management task, one of the unintended consequences of their introduction into homicide investigations has been that in some cases it actually amplifies the problem. This is due to investigators thinking that just because the computers can process large amounts of data, they need to be given lots of data.

Often this results in an investigation losing focus and direction.

Investigative Systems

Different policing jurisdictions employ different approaches in responding to criminal homicides, although as a general trend, major crime investigations have become increasingly specialized and rely upon a diverse range of technical expertise. Thus, working alongside the police detectives investigating the homicide will be a number of other different specialist responsible for particular aspects of the investigation, possibly including crime scene search officers, a pathologist, experts in different branches of forensic science, fingerprint specialists, offender profilers, legal advisers, police intelligence officers, police surveillance teams, and so forth. Consequently, a key skill for the police detectives leading a homicide investigation is the ability to coordinate, respond to, and synthesize the intelligence and evidence derived from these separate roles. It is a different division of labor than that which routinely occurs in "volume" crime investigations.

In many ways the technological advances discussed above have changed and are changing the investigative practices relating to major crimes. Rapid advances in areas such as DNA processing technologies and other branches of the forensic sciences are fundamentally altering how suspects can be identified and how legal cases against them can be constructed.

Investigative Process

Research on homicide has repeatedly demonstrated that the majority of victims are killed by someone known to them. This is important in defining the contours of the standard police investigative process for homicides. In many homicide investigations, the early lines of enquiry will focus upon the family, friends, and acquaintances of the victim as possible suspects for the crime, and it is only if these individuals are eliminated from suspicion that police attention tends to consider the possibility of a stranger assault.

When a victim is thought to have been killed by someone known to them, the focus of police activity is frequently less upon "whodunit," since this is comparatively easy to establish. Rather, police lines of enquiry are typically directed to the issues of how and why. So while there are differences evident in terms of the investigative process employed, most homicide investigations tend to follow a basic trajectory of three key phases of activity: initial response, suspect development, and case construction. It is important to note that these phases may not occur in a strictly linear sequence, since there is frequently a degree of overlap between them.

In the initial response phase, the focus is upon assembling the investigative team, classifying the incident, identifying the victim, and establishing initial lines of enquiry into the circumstances of the death. As implied previously, the conduct of this work in the initial response phase is subject to time pressure. There is a widespread recognition that there are limited opportunities for collecting both physical and other sorts of evidence from the crime scene in the hours and days after a death in suspicious circumstances is discovered. With the passing of time any contact trace materials that were present may well degrade in quality, as may witnesses' memories. Therefore, if opportunities are missed or mistakes made at this early point in an investigation, the evidence is unlikely to be recovered at all. More than this though, research in the United Kingdom has identified that in a significant proportion of successful homicide investigations, police identify a prime suspect in the first forty-eight hours of their response (Innes 2003).

Following on from the initial response where the basic facets of the investigation will have been defined, the suspect development phase involves a variety of lines of enquiry being conducted in order to develop a more detailed understanding of how death occurred and, on the basis of this knowledge, who might be considered as potential suspects for it. It is not uncommon in homicide investigations for a number of individuals to be identified as potential suspects, only for them to be eliminated from further suspicion upon investigation by police. At some stage though, the police will hope to identify a "prime suspect" (or suspects). When this occurs, the tenor of the investigation shifts from trying to develop knowledge about the incident to a more focused collection of intelligence about the involvement of this individual.

If sufficient intelligence and evidence can be developed by the police against a particular suspect (or suspects), the investigation enters the case construction phase. This is where all of the information that the police have collated, through their varied lines of enquiry, is brought together and organized in such a fashion to support the charging and prosecution of the suspect. This is often complex, lengthy, and detailed work. In the contemporary legal environment a significant aspect of case construction work often concerns anticipating potential lines of attack that might be adopted by the defendant's legal team and attempting to neutralize them.

MARTIN INNES

See also **Crime Control Strategies; Crime Scene Search and Evidence Collection; Criminal Investigation; Detective Work/ Culture; Detectives; DNA Fingerprinting; Firearms Availability and Homicide Rates; Forensic Evidence; Forensic Investigations; Homicide: Unsolved; Managing Criminal Investigations; Serial Murder; Technology and the Police**

References and Further Reading

Geberth, Vernon. 1983. *Practical homicide investigation: Tactics, procedures and forensic techniques.* New York: Elsevier.
Innes, Martin. 2003. *Investigating murder: Detective work and the police response to criminal homicide.* Oxford: Clarendon Press.

HOMICIDE: UNSOLVED

Arresting a suspect of any crime is critical because without an arrest, there is little that the courts or correctional systems can do. Court-ordered sanctions or treatments depend on the apprehension and arrest of a suspect. Crimes that go unsolved reflect poorly on the criminal justice system and indicate an inability of the system to achieve the goal of reducing future crime. When the murders of citizens cannot be solved, the problem of uncleared crimes becomes particularly revealing of the criminal justice system's inability to reduce violent crimes (Wellford and Cronin 1999). Researchers have attempted to explain the difficulties of solving homicides by comparing incident variables of cleared and unsolved homicides. Police administrators have implemented cold case units in their efforts to increase clearance rates.

Clearance Rates

The national clearance rate for homicide, according to the *Uniform Crime Reports* (UCR), has declined from 94% in 1961 to 64% in 2002 (U.S. Department of Justice 2002). Although UCR rates are not always considered the most dependable measure of crime, they are probably the most dependable for the crime of murder. It is important to recognize that UCR clearance rates are established by dividing the number of homicides by the number of arrests, but also included are murder-suicides and self-defense cases. Including suicides and self-defense cases, in which the offender can be easily identified, lowers the actual clearance rates of homicides.

Variables Affecting Clearance of Homicides

There was little research on the solvability factors of homicide investigations until the early 1990s. Previously, Greenwood, Chaiken, and Petersilia (1977, as cited in Wellford and Cronin 1999) studied outcomes of detectives and questioned their usefulness, but did not study investigative strategies. Keppel and Weis (1994, as cited in Mouzos and Muller 2001) examined the distances between important areas of the crime itself, for example, the point of contact and disposal site, and clearance rate. They concluded that information about the time and location issues increases the crime solvability. Reidel and Rinehart (1996) found that the single most important factor was whether the homicide was related to another crime. If it was committed in connection with such crimes as robbery or rape, it was less likely to be solved than if involving a dispute. It is reasonable to assume that most of these unsolved homicides were committed by strangers or others who had not been directly known by the victims or their associates.

Wellford and Cronin (1999) examined fifty-one characteristics and constructed eight regression models from the significant variables. The offender–victim models disclosed that if the offender was African American and/or the victim had a history of drug use, the solvability increased over the base rate. The computer-check model that included computer checks of the victim, suspect, witnesses, and guns resulted in all four of these variables adding to the increase in solvability. The witness model increased the solvability to 95%, with three of its predictors being significant: witness provided valuable information, friends or acquaintances

interviewed, and neighbors interviewed. Crime scene variables that were significant included the notification of the homicide unit, medic, and crime lab by the first officer, the attempt to locate witnesses, and proper crime scene sketch and measurement.

The model that examined detective variables was particularly impressive. Four variables—three or more detectives working the case, arrival by detectives to the crime scene within thirty minutes of being notified, detailed description of the crime scene in detectives' notes, and following up on all witness information—rated a 96% chance of solving the case. Circumstances such as occurring in a private residence, having an eyewitness to the crime, and not being drug related improved the base rate from 74% to 98%. Of the original fifty-one variables identified as associated with clearance, thirty-seven were associated with police practices rather than the event itself. Wellford and Cronin (1999) found that these variables remained significant across different sizes of cities. These researchers concluded that the practices and policies of law enforcement agencies can impact the clearance rates of homicides.

Although there are differences among homicides and their level of solvability, there is support for the conclusion that the necessary allocation of resources for homicide investigations does increase the probability that cases will be cleared. Mouzos and Muller's Australian study (2001) supports many of Wellford and Cronin's findings. They found a few more incident and victim characteristics that made cases less likely to be solved, such as older victims (thirty years or older), working at the time of the incident, lack of alcohol consumption, and occurrence between 6 P.M. and 6 A.M.. They also included the importance of forensic evidence and specialists and modern technology, emphasizing the growing importance of DNA evidence and national databases such as AFIS (Automated Fingerprint

Identification Systems) and CODIS (Combined DNA Index System).

The Implementation of Homicide Cold Case Units

With advanced technology to analyze physical evidence and DNA and fingerprint national databases, there has been an increased interest in old homicide cases that have never been solved. Many police agencies began adding cold case homicide investigators around the year 2000 as advancements in DNA and other forensic technology progressed. A few departments such as the Metropolitan Police Department in Washington, DC, implemented a unit as early as 1992. Utilizing six homicide detectives and eight FBI agents full time, the Metropolitan Police Department closed 157 cold cases within the first five years (Regini 1997).

Making use of other resources, several agencies are teaming with their prosecutors' offices. Harris County Police in Texas formed a homicide cold case unit that works in conjunction with the division chief of their major offender unit of the district attorney's office, who prosecutes cold cases exclusively. In Fairfax County, Virginia, the state's attorney works along with the local police agency's cold case unit. Other agencies such as Charlotte-Mecklenburg Police Department in North Carolina have included volunteers with previous law enforcement backgrounds. These individuals review case files and meet with designated cold case investigators to help them establish investigative leads (Lord 2005).

Selecting cold cases that have solvability possibilities is critical. Agencies have found that the availability of physical evidence that is conducive to modern technology, of witnesses, and of an identifiable and living suspect are important criteria. The following are two examples of solved cold cases.

After several decades, a skeleton was found, then identified and publicized. After seeing the broadcast of the discovery on *America's Most Wanted,* the defendant's ex-wife came forward to report the murder of a young girl by her then-husband. There was no physical evidence or weapon to link the defendant to the crime; the case revolved around the ex-wife's testimony. She described how she drove while he attempted sex with and then killed the girl. The defendant was convicted (Lord 2005).

An example of one of many cases in which samples for DNA analysis are submitted to CODIS for comparison was in Iowa, where a suspect was tried in 2003 for the sexual assault and murder of a woman in 1981. The decision to prosecute was first made in 1996 when DNA analysis was conducted on swabs taken at the victim's autopsy. At that time, the ratio was one in ten thousand chances that the DNA could be from a different individual than the defendant. In 2003, the DNA was reanalyzed, and the chance was increased to one in 100 billion chances of wrong identity. The defendant was convicted (Lord 2005).

There are still several problems in solving cold cases. In the past, technicians and detectives collected evidence based on the analysis that could be conducted at that time. Therefore, evidence that could be analyzed today and would have been helpful in connecting the suspect to the crime scene or the victim may not have been collected. Second, old technologies, such as ABO or enzyme typing, used up a great deal of the evidence in analysis, so often there is little evidence left to analyze with new technologies. Also, the packaging of the evidence in some cases is deteriorating, so the evidence might have become contaminated. In addition, the memory of living witnesses and the admission of previous statements from witnesses who have died can be an issue (Lord 2005).

A large volume of unsolved homicides is a stain on any law enforcement agency's credibility. Cold case homicide units have caught the imagination of the public, and families of the victims have renewed faith that the murderers of their loved ones will still come to trial.

VIVIAN B. LORD

See also **Accountability; Criminal Investigation; DNA Fingerprinting; Forensic Investigations; Homicide and its Investigation**

References and Further Reading

Lord, V. 2005. Implementing a cold case homicide unit: A challenging task. *FBI Law Enforcement Bulletin*, 1–6.

Mouzos, J., and D. Muller. 2001. Solvability factors of homicide in Australia: An exploratory analysis. In *Trends and issues in crime and criminal justice*, Graycar (director). No. 216. Canberra: Australian Institute of Criminology.

Regini, C. L. 1997. Cold case concept. *FBI Law Enforcement Bulletin* 66 (8): 1–6.

Reidel, M., and T. Rinehart. 1996. Murder clearances and missing data. *Journal of Crime and Justice* 19 (2), 83–102.

U.S. Department of Justice. 2002. *Crime in the United States*. Washington, DC: Federal Bureau of Investigation.

Wellford, C., and J. Cronin. 1999. *Analysis of variables affecting the clearance of homicides: A multi-site study*. National Institute of Justice, Award 96-IJ-CX-0047, document number 181356. Washington, DC: National Institute of Justice.

HOOVER, J. EDGAR

J. Edgar Hoover (1895–1972), director of the Federal Bureau of Investigation, was born in Washington, DC, son of a career government employee who rose to become superintendent of engraving and printing in the Coast and Geodetic Survey. Young Hoover's mother taught her children the tenets of Calvinism and would not let them forget the sinfulness of human ways. Because of her and the example of a Presbyterian preacher whom he admired excessively, J. Edgar wanted to be a minister. He graduated from high school as valedictorian of the class of 1913 and began law school at night, working days in the Library of Congress as a messenger.

Exactly why he turned from the ministry to law is not known, but during this time he still continued to participate in Bible classes and to preach moral values to anyone within earshot. Those who knew him in youth remembered that he loved sports, was a loner, and was humorless. In 1916, George Washington University awarded him the LL.B. degree and the following year the LL.M. degree.

His first law job was with the Department of Justice as a file reviewer. He enjoyed the detail work that others disliked and pleased his superiors with his diligence and organizational skills. In 1919, Attorney General A. Mitchell Palmer choose Hoover to help with prosecution of alien agitators, deportation of every "red" being the goal. Hoover wrote a report on the "communist conspiracy" and prepared numerous legal briefs sanctioning government raids of suspected "red" hideouts. The raids terrorized hundreds of innocent aliens, though in a major legal action Hoover and other Department of Justice lawyers won the deportation of anarchists Emma Goldman and Alexander Berkman. Hoover was later to regret his role in the mostly unwarranted persecution.

Favorable political winds blew his way on August 22, 1921. President Warren G. Harding's attorney general, Harry Daugherty, had fired William J. Flynn, chief of the Bureau of Investigation, and replaced him with William J. Burns, the celebrated detective. On that date the highly visible Hoover was named assistant director. The bureau's sphere of activity before World War I had encompassed investigating violations of neutrality, bankruptcy, antitrust laws, and white-slave trafficking. During the war it had focused on sabotage, espionage, and other subversive activities. Vice President Calvin Coolidge fired Harry Daugherty and gave the job of attorney general to Harlan Fiske Stone. When Burns announced that he planned to retire soon, Stone and Secretary of Commerce

Herbert Hoover (no relation) jointly recommended promotion of the assistant director. So on May 10, 1924, J. Edgar Hoover took control of the Bureau of Investigation (at first as acting director; full confirmation came seven months later). Hoover would not relinquish that control for the next forty-eight years.

Hoover's early changes in the bureau's functioning included the hiring of lawyers and public accountants as special agents, expansion of the central fingerprint bureau, and introduction of the latest scientific methods of detection. On June 11, 1930, a congressional act authorized the compiling of crime statistics gathered from police agencies throughout the nation. Hoover, the premier detail man, delighted in this task. To this day, the FBI *Uniform Crime Reports* is the standard work by which the incidence of American crime is measured.

Federal legislation such as the National Kidnapping Act, the National Extortion Act, and the Bank Robbery Act gave FBI agents more leverage in the fight against crime and also more crime to contend with. "Public enemies" fled from state to state, posing a difficult problem for local authorities, who could not easily cross jurisdictional lines. But FBI agents could, and because they were Hoover's men, bent on subduing gangsterism, they often conducted their business ruthlessly. Hoover wanted quick results once he had committed his "G-men"—so called by the press and popularized in the movies—to running down a public enemy. His methods of ensuring capture garnered criticism, since at times he appeared to flaunt the law. However, faultfinding by the legal and law enforcement establishments did not diminish the fact that the FBI was very effective in apprehending the foremost criminals of the day.

In 1935, the Bureau of Investigation officially became the Federal Bureau of Investigation, and in that same year the FBI Training Academy at Quantico, Virginia, opened. The academy's purpose was to train "selected police officers from every State in the Union and many foreign countries" in state-of-the-art law enforcement techniques. Inception of the academy may have been the single most important event in Hoover's tenure in office. But no matter what the event, he was swift to publicize it. Hoover knew that the press created public opinion, and he wanted the best press possible for his FBI. So while G-men risked their lives in volatile confrontations, he spoke at public gatherings of their exploits, and before long the FBI assumed a legendary status. To acquaint America further with the bureau, he wrote *Persons in Hiding* (1938), which was filled with thrilling accounts of criminal cases. The book added considerable luster to the federal arm of the law and told Americans who had not yet heard of J. Edgar Hoover just who he was.

As World War II dawned, President Franklin Roosevelt directed Hoover to engage in the same activities as he had in World War I, namely, stamping out subversion at home. Hoover already had a list of enemy aliens, so within twenty-four hours of the attack on Pearl Harbor 1,771 of them were in custody. The usual number of FBI agents, six hundred, was increased to a wartime peak of five thousand. This buildup successfully prevented any major instance of "foreign-directed sabotage." Hoover was rewarded with the Medal for Merit, the U.S. Selective Service Medal, and the Order of Honor and Merit of the Cuban Red Cross for his domestic peacekeeping efforts.

When the war was over, the FBI undertook a prodigious assignment: to test the loyalty of more than 2.8 million federal employees. In addition, it was to investigate all violations of the Atomic Energy Act of 1946. Hoover made the transition from war to peace easily and with his customary zeal for any assignment soon asserted publicly that the FBI had matters in hand.

On May 10, 1949, the twenty-fifth anniversary of his appointment as director,

Hoover could justifiably take pride in his accomplishments. Due to his leadership, about four thousand agents enforced some 120 major federal laws with a conviction rate of 97.2%—the envy of the law enforcement world. That was surely his high point. By the late 1950s, he was talked about in a much different way. Prolific wiretapping and McCarthyism fueled the debate over his unchecked power. He listened in on private conversations of whomever he desired, and not necessarily of those who threatened the country. He assisted Senator Joseph McCarthy's purge of communists, even though the memory of his earlier red-baiting still haunted him. Yet he continued to direct his men to ferret out communists and in 1958 promulgated his fear in *Masters of Deceit: The Story of Communism in America and How to Fight It*, a book that sold 2.5 million copies.

Sharp criticism of Hoover did not prevent President John F. Kennedy from reappointing him as director in 1960. Attorney General Robert Kennedy, though, did not get along with the feisty director and broke with him completely after his brother's assassination. Hoover disliked taking orders from the attorney general when before he had always gone straight to the head man. Besides, Robert Kennedy demanded that he assign more agents to civil rights and organized crime cases, which he had neglected to do. Networking the country with wiretaps and hunting communists had been Hoover's priorities for too long.

Presidents Lyndon B. Johnson and Richard M. Nixon also reappointed the indomitable Hoover, waiving the mandatory retirement age of seventy. Hoover was at his imperial best in the latter stage of his career. He told off the Warren Commission, investigating President Kennedy's assassination, when he was accused of not sharing FBI intelligence with it, and he called the Reverend Dr. Martin Luther King, Jr., "the most notorious liar in the country" when the civil rights leader had said that the FBI cared little or nothing about protecting blacks.

In his final years and particularly after his death, Hoover attracted many written appraisals of his character and influence. The tendency has been to expose the roots of his power. The jurist, the politician, the psychiatrist, and the law enforcement officer can all find much to ponder in his life, but none should forget that J. Edgar Hoover turned a politically subservient bureau into a globally recognized force, suppressed kidnapping and gangsterism during the 1930s, stopped the infiltration of spies during World War II, and muffled the voice of communism in the postwar period.

His honorary academic degrees filled a wall, as did his awards for good citizenship. Never married, he died alone in his bedroom after having worked a full day in his office. High blood pressure had overtaxed his heart.

WILLIAM G. BAILEY

See also **Federal Bureau of Investigation; Surveillance**

References and Further Reading

Messick, Hank. 1972. *J. Edgar Hoover: A critical examination of the director and of the continuing alliance between crime, business, and politics*. New York: David McKay.

Nash, Jay Robert. 1972. *Citizen Hoover: A critical study of the life and times of J. Edgar Hoover and his FBI*. Chicago: Nelson-Hall.

New York Times. 1972. 52 (May 3): 1.

O'Reilly, Kenneth. 1983. *Hoover and the un-Americans: The FBI, HUAC and the red menace*. Philadelphia: Temple University Press.

Powers, Richard G. 1986. *Secrecy and power: The life of J. Edgar Hoover*. New York: Free Press.

Welch, Neil J., and David W. Marston. 1984. *Inside Hoover's FBI: The top field chief reports*. New York: Doubleday.

HOSTAGE NEGOTIATIONS

In the mid-1970s, police administrators nationwide began to realize that there was really no mystique to dealing with hostage, barricade, or suicide attempt situations—all that was really needed was in-depth training of qualified officers, an interdisciplinary team that included individuals trained in mental health, an overall department policy, and a list of guidelines that would fit various types of incidents. Police negotiation teams were formed, trained, and became operational throughout the country. Not surprisingly, many high-anxiety situations were defused, lives were saved, and the accepted policy of talking people out of their dramatic intentions rather than relying on firepower became part of police method and policy.

There are two primary goals to hostage negotiations. The first goal is that no one gets hurt, either outside or inside the scene. The apprehension of a perpetrator who uses a hostage to further escape is secondary to the life and safety of the hostage. The second goal is for the situation to be resolved without assault. Assault should be a last resort, used only after there is clear and convincing evidence that the perpetrator is about to kill or has killed the victims. The situation can easily be escalated when and if necessary, but seldom can it be deescalated easily. Under no circumstances should the perpetrator be allowed to become mobile with the victims.

Types of Hostage Situations

A hostage situation can arise in a variety of ways, and the police approach to a situation often depends on the type of subject being dealt with and on the type of incident. Four common types of hostage takers are criminals, mentally ill individuals, unorganized groups, and terrorist groups.

The criminal hostage taker is typified by the armed offender who is caught in the act by quick police response and takes a hostage in order to facilitate escape. The hostage taker can predict with some accuracy how far the police can go and knows what to expect from them during the incident and after capture. Usually the negotiating team can convince the hostage taker that the best course of action is to give up.

The hostage taker suffering from mental health or mental retardation issues can be the most challenging for negotiators and law enforcement. It is very important for the negotiators to receive as much information as possible regarding the hostage taker's diagnosis, propensity to violence, and whether the individual is taking medication. If an accurate psychiatric history can be obtained, it can assist the negotiators tremendously.

The unorganized group that takes hostages is usually the result of a spontaneous riot or jail break. This situation requires a rapid response because once the group gains cohesion and a leader or leaders are chosen, the response becomes increasingly difficult. Negotiations with prisoners differ from negotiations in the outside world. Prisoners rarely are seeking to escape but generally are asking for improvements in living conditions.

Hostages may be taken by terrorist organizations. In general, local police agencies would not deal with this sort of a group without outside assistance. Many of the concessions demanded would not fall within the scope of police responsibilities, and the terrorists know it. Also, the terrorists may be willing to die to further their cause and take any and all hostages with them. Whenever the hostage taker is willing to die, negotiations will be more difficult and the situation less likely to result in a successful outcome. For the most part the terrorist does not want to deal with police and would want higher-level government officials and/or the media involved in the negotiation sessions.

Negotiations may also be used to deal with individuals who are threatening suicide. Even though many suicidal individuals pose a danger only to themselves, some will not hesitate to risk the lives of others in their suicide attempts. Any suicidal individual with a weapon should be regarded as posing a definite threat and must be handled accordingly.

The strategy for each situation will depend upon the factors involved. If the perpetrator is armed, there is a greater risk involved. If the perpetrator has a bomb, there will be a large-area evacuation plan and the possibility for greater collateral damage. In this case, establishment of perimeter security is more difficult due to the range of destruction, and a higher level of medical response is necessary. Guns pose less of a threat than bombs because they have a much shorter range. In this type of a situation, the evacuation plan covers a smaller area, and there will be less collateral damage. The hostage taker who is unarmed, of course, presents the least amount of risk to everyone involved.

Resolution

The successful resolution of any hostage situation requires that the negotiation team contains, controls, and diffuses the situation.

Containment

The first step is containment. When the team arrives at the scene, very little is known about the situation. Because of this lack of knowledge, this is the most dangerous time during a negotiation. At this point, anything could happen; for this reason, the scene must be approached with extreme caution. It should not be approached by a single officer; a team response is necessary because many things will be occurring simultaneously. The scene should be quarantined immediately using multiple perimeters. The primary perimeter comprises the negotiators and a small tactical group with advisers and communications specialists. The secondary perimeter comprises the sniper squad, bomb squad, and a police backup force with heavy arms. The tertiary perimeter comprises medical airlift if needed, technical advisers, media, and in some cases family members of the perpetrator and hostages.

Contact with the perpetrator should be initiated by trained primary and secondary negotiators; the primary conducts all communication with the perpetrator, and the secondary acts as an on-site adviser to the primary. The secondary is also responsible for collating the intelligence data on the perpetrator as provided by the technical staff. Face-to-face negotiations are to be avoided; negotiations should be conducted only over the phone.

While the primary and secondary negotiators make contact with the perpetrator, other members of the negotiation team are assisting them in a variety of ways. The media should be controlled, and only selected information should be released. All utilities should be shut off (this provides something that the primary negotiator can "give back" to the perpetrator during the course of negotiations). There should be a show of force as soon as possible, with large numbers of police all dressed in the same military assault gear and heavy weaponry and special equipment. The sniper squad should be positioned as close to the scene as possible. Data should be collected on the perpetrator and victims. Medical issues that are at risk should be identified, and backup agencies should be notified for medical coverage and treatment.

The key to the successful resolution of many hostage situations is the availability of information for the negotiator. It is extremely difficult to negotiate in the blind; the more known about the perpetrator, victims, and logistics of the area, the greater the chance for successful resolution. Data should be collected on the perpetrator and victims. This includes the stressor that caused the current incident, the perpetrator's criminal record, mental health data, strong points, weak points, family relationships, probability ratings for extreme violence, familiarity with weapons, and motivation in normal settings. Data on the victims should include personality constructs, medical conditions, and mental health information regarding the ability to sustain stress and to lead rather than follow other victims.

Control

The second step in the negotiation process is control. This is accomplished through talking. A negotiator should talk as much as possible with the perpetrator. This talking will accomplish several goals. First, the negotiator can determine the level of stability of the perpetrator and the intent to harm self or others. Second, the negotiator can establish what the needs of the perpetrator are. These needs should be met at the lowest level possible in incremental levels to create the perception that the perpetrators are in control by giving them what they think they want via negotiation. Third, negotiators are required to slow down the sense of pressure created by the uncertainty of the situation and to build trust between themselves and the perpetrators. The longer the crisis drags out, the greater the potential for peaceful resolution.

This is the number one rule applying to all high-anxiety situations. Stalling for time is beneficial for everyone involved. It provides time to contain and isolate the scene. The initial state of high emotion is given time to subside and rational thinking to return. As time passes, the lives of hostages become more secure as the perpetrator realizes the value of their continued safety and is subjected to increasing awareness of them as persons and not pawns. A long-range benefit is that fatigue will set in and alertness will fade.

Diffusion

The final step in the negotiation process is diffusion. Through give-and-take between the negotiator and the perpetrator, terms can be agreed upon under which the perpetrator will surrender hostages, weapons, and self to law enforcement. The vast majority of perpetrators do not want to die; this alone makes diffusion likely.

Regardless of whether the resolution was successful or unsuccessful, each incident should be objectively critiqued by the entire team and their responses refined. This debriefing will increase the success and value of the team over time.

AYN EMBAR-SEDDON and ALLAN D. PASS

See also **Arrest Powers of the Police; Conflict Management; Psychology and the Police; SWAT Units; Terrorism: Overview**

References and Further Reading

Feldman, T. B., and P. W. Johnson. 1999. Aircraft hijacking in the United States. In *Lethal violence: A sourcebook on fatal domestic, acquaintance, and stranger violence*, ed. H. V. Hall, 403–40. Boca Raton, FL: CRC Press.

Jacobs, J. 1986. *SWAT tactics: The tactical handling of barricaded suspects, snipers and hostage-takers.* New York: Gordon Press.

Maher, George F. 1977. *Hostage: A police approach to a contemporary crisis.* Springfield, IL: Charles C Thomas.

McMains, M. J., and W. C. Mullins. 1996. *Crisis negotiations: Managing critical incidents and hostage situations in law enforcement and corrections.* Cincinnati, OH: Anderson.

Miller, Abraham H. 1980. *Terrorism and hostage negotiations.* Boulder, CO: Westview Press.

Miron, Murray S., and Arnold P. Goldstein. 1979. *Hostage.* New York: Pergamon.

Noesner, G. W., and J. T. Dolan. 1992. First responder negotiation training. *FBI Law Enforcement Bulletin* 61: 101–4.

Rogan, Randall G., Mitchell R. Hammer, and Clinton R. Van Zandt. 1997. *Dynamic process of hostage negotiation: Theory, research, and practice.* Westport, CT: Praeger.

HOT SPOTS

Introduction

"Hot spots" of crime are defined as "small places in which the occurrence of crime is so frequent that it is highly predictable, at least over a one-year period" (Sherman 1995, 36). Hot spots are places such as street corners, malls, apartment blocks, subway stations, and public parks that generate a large number of complaints to police. Research shows that about 3% of all places generate more than half of all citizen complaints about crime and disorder to the police.

Policing these hot spots of crime is generally regarded as an effective use of scarce police resources. By targeting hot spots, research shows that the police can directly contribute to an overall reduction in crime problems in a city.

Identifying Hot Spots

Crime analysts in police departments are generally responsible for identifying hot spots of crime. Crime analysts employ sophisticated spatial analysis techniques using geographic information systems (GISs) to understand the distribution of crime and pinpoint the locations of crime hot spots. Many techniques have been used to empirically and conceptually describe the clustering of crime into hot spots, and new, innovative techniques often developed in the physical sciences are used to understand the nonrandom distributions of crime.

One recent line of inquiry in the crime and place tradition is the application of trajectory research—traditionally used to describe individual offending patterns over the life course (see Weisburd et al. 2004). The use of trajectory analysis enables researchers and crime analysts to view crime trends at places over long periods of time and to use group-based statistical techniques to uncover distinctive developmental trends and identify long-term patterns of offending in crime hot spots.

Researchers from a number of disciplines including geography, architecture, environmental planning, sociology, social psychology, political science, and criminology have helped advance the theories and methods used by crime analysts to identify hot spots of crime. The "crime and place" perspective that informs today's hot spots of crime research has a long history dating back to late nineteenth-century researchers in France (for example, Andre-Michel Guerry and Adolphe Quetelet) and early twentieth-century researchers in Chicago (for example, Clifford Shaw and Henry McKay). Recent research on hot spots of crime straddles a number of theoretical perspectives such as ecology of crime, environmental criminology, routine activities theory, crime pattern theory, defensible space, crime prevention through environmental design, and situational crime prevention.

Routine activities theory is particularly relevant for understanding both the reasons why crime becomes clustered in hot spots as well as for thinking through ways that the police can be effective in controlling crime problems in these places. Most recently, routine activities theory has been extended to explicitly delineate the importance of "amenable places" (that is, hot spots) and those who discourage crimes and criminogenic places (that is, the police). John Eck refers to these people as "place managers." Routine activities theory crime event equation is now understood as follows: Crime occurs when there is the convergence in time of a desirable target without an effective guardian, a motivated offender without an effective handler, at a facilitating place without an attentive manager.

Places are seen as being amenable when certain place attributes influence the likelihood that a crime event will occur. For example, places located near bars or main throughways and places that have multiple access points, weak place management, or indicators of decay all correlate highly with places that become crime hot spots.

Routine activities theory as well as other crime and place theories all contribute to our understanding of why crime clusters into hot spots. Research using these theoretical perspectives consistently demonstrates that crime is not a random event but rather the result of environmental factors. These environmental (and situational) factors create opportunities for crime in some places and prevent crime from occurring in others.

Sherman (1995) draws from these (and other) theories to propose six primary dimensions that help to define and distinguish one hot spot of crime from another:

1. *Onset.* This dimension examines the factors that cause a place to become a hot spot. Such factors that might cause the onset of a crime hot spot include change in the management of a local bar, the construction of a parking lot that has poor environmental design, some type of change in the routine activities of a neighborhood, or mere chance.

2. *Recurrence.* This dimension deals with the point in time when a crime analyst labels a place as a hot spot. For example, we know that when a place experiences three robberies during a one-year period, that place has a 58% chance of recurrence. Recurrence encourages us to ask whether there is a threshold of activity that would define a place as a hot spot.

3. *Frequency.* This dimension deals with the number of times per year crime occurs in a defined hot spot of crime.

4. *Intermittency.* This dimension deals with two issues. The first is the amount of time *between* criminal events. The second is what explains intermittency. Such factors as the criminal habits of the occupants, the economic difficulties of place owners, and changes in traffic flow that impacts the flow of targets and offenders have been considered.

5. *Career length and desistence.* The fifth dimension is concerned with the desistence of crime problems in a particular hot spot. Places desist from having crime problems for five reasons: death (for example, a hot spot bar is torn down), vigilante behavior (for example, omnipresence patrol by police or patrol by citizens), incapacitation (for example, civil remedies or boarding up buildings), blocking opportunities (for example, rerouting a bus route), or building insulators (for example, community cohesion and problem solving).

6. *Crime types.* The final dimension describes the fact that some places tend to have crime specialization because the place characteristics limit the types of crimes possible (for example, drug dealing).

Policing Hot Spots

The work of crime analysts is crucial for frontline officers to obtain a comprehensive understanding of the concentration of crime in hot spots. Results generated by crime analysts are used by operational law enforcement officers in their efforts to target police resources at hot spots involving street-level drug markets, burglary, violent crimes, traffic, gun markets, and motor vehicle theft and at other places where crime problems cluster together.

Research into hot spots of crime highlights the importance for frontline officers to use both formal as well as informal crime control efforts that specifically target hot places and seek to alter their attributes. These crime control efforts fall into two distinct categories: those that increase formal surveillance of a place (for example, increased levels of preventive patrol, or directed patrol) and those that change the environmental and situational characteristics of a place (for example, civil remedies or problem-oriented policing).

Evaluations of police efforts to target a variety of different types of hot spots suggest significant crime control potential for policing the hot spots of crime. Anthony Braga's systematic review of five randomized experiments and four nonequivalent control group quasi-experiments reveals that focused police actions (for example, crackdowns, problem-oriented policing, directed patrols, aggressive patrols, raids, or civil remedies) can prevent crime and disorder in crime hot spots. His review also showed that focused police actions do not necessarily result in crime displacement, but rather crime prevention benefits were observed as a result of these focused law enforcement efforts in crime hot spots.

Generally speaking, we know that policing hot spots of crime is an effective approach for controlling street crime problems. But there are two important dimensions to understand in order to maximize the effectiveness of policing in crime hot spots. First, we need a comprehensive understanding of the policing strategies that work best in responding to crime in hot spots, and second, we need to understand whether or not different types of crime hot spots respond differently to different types of interventions. The research evidence is limited, yet instructive, on these matters.

Types of Policing Strategies Conducive to Hot Spots Policing

The types of policing strategies that are typically used to target crime hot spots include problem-oriented policing, increased presence of uniformed police patrols (directed patrols), crackdowns, court authorized raids, civil remedies, and zero tolerance policing.

Problem-oriented policing is an approach to policing in which problems are subject to in-depth examination (drawing on the specially honed skills of crime analysts and the accumulated experience of operating field personnel) in the hope that what is learned about the problem will lead police to implement new and innovative ways for dealing with it.

Crackdowns are defined as abrupt escalations in proactive enforcement activities that are intended to increase the perceived or actual threat of apprehension for certain offenses occurring in certain situations or locations. During crackdowns police operations are typically highly visible and involve uniformed and/or undercover officers.

Raids are localized search and secure–type operations that generally target residential and commercial (that is, clubs, motels, and the like) properties that are the source of numerous drug, crime, and disorder problems (that is, calls for service, arrests, or citizen complaints). Raids generally involve arrests and seizures and are typically highly visible, with the intention of acting as a deterrent to others.

Civil remedies are procedures and sanctions, specified by civil statutes and regulations, used to prevent or reduce criminal problems and incivilities. In third-party policing, the police partner with other regulators and use civil remedies to persuade or coerce nonoffending third parties to take responsibility and action to prevent or end criminal or nuisance behavior. Civil remedy approaches often target nonoffending third parties (for example, landlords or property owners) and use nuisance and drug abatement statutes to control problems.

Zero tolerance involves the strict enforcement of minor offenses.

More detailed descriptions of each of these strategies can be found elsewhere in this encyclopedia. What is important about each of these police tactics is that they have been consistently used by the police in dealing with problems in crime hot spots. Of these, problem-oriented policing and civil remedies used in third-party policing efforts show the most promise for controlling problems in crime hot spots.

Types of Crime in Hot Spots

People generally think of crime hot spots as having some level of crime specificity. Indeed, a hot spot is often thought of in terms of being a drug market hot spot or a car theft hot spot or a violent crime hot spot or that of other categories of crime. However, research suggests that some crime hot spots do experience a plethora of specific types of crime problems. For example, examining the distribution of crime problems in Minneapolis, Weisburd and his colleagues found that theft problems and domestic disturbances are two types of crime problems that showed signs of crime specificity in a hot spot. Data from the five cities (Jersey City, Kansas City, San Diego, Pittsburgh, and Hartford) involved in the Drug Markets Analysis Program funded by the National Institute of Justice reveal consistent and similar types of crime specificity for street drug market activity.

Crime-specific perspectives on crime and crime prevention, notably situational crime prevention, are useful for understanding the factors that cause specific crime problems. Analysis of the environmental causes in the crime hot spots that experience some degree of crime specialization are then used to develop highly tailored types of policing responses.

While some categories of crime tend to dominate some hot spots (such as drug-dealing places), many hot spots of crime experience a range of different types of problems, such as domestic violence, burglary, assaults, and robberies. These "potpourri" hot spots are places that experience a clustering of different crime problems. They are likely to have environmental and situational features that operate similarly to cause a variety of problem outcomes. For example, a nightclub that has weak management and poor alcohol serving practices might be situated in an area with low levels of informal social control. This type of hot spot is likely to have a variety of problem outcomes, such as assaults, robberies, drunk and disorderly behavior, as well as domestic disputes. Policing these potpourri hot spots is usually more difficult than policing those hot spots that exhibit a high degree of crime specialization.

Conclusion

Research shows that focused police activities—such as directed patrols, raids, civil remedies, crackdowns, and problem-oriented policing—that target crime hot spots can reduce crime problems. Further, research shows that focused policing in street-level drug markets, violent crime places, and gun markets can markedly reduce crime and disorder problems in these places. Police resources for dealing with street crime problems are thus best utilized when crime prevention resources are focused at micro places with large numbers of crime events.

Recent research agrees with this "hot spots policing" approach but adds that police need to distinguish between short-lived concentrations of crime in hot spots versus those hot spots that have long histories (see Weisburd et al. 2004). Indeed, Weisburd and his colleagues (2004) suggest that if hot spots of crime shift rapidly from place to place, it makes little sense to focus crime control resources at such locations. By contrast, the police would be most effective by identifying and targeting resources at those hot spots with long histories of crime.

LORRAINE MAZEROLLE

See also **Crime Analysis; Crime and Place, Theories of; Crime Control Strategies; Drug Markets; Intelligence-Led Policing and Organizational Learning; Problem-Oriented Policing; Situational Crime Prevention**

References and Further Reading

Braga, A. A. 2001. The effects of hot spots policing on crime. *The Annals of the American Academy of Political and Social Science* 578: 104–25.

Eck, J. and D. Weisburd. 1995. Crime places in crime theory. In *Crime and place: Crime prevention studies*, ed. J. Eck and D. Weisburd, Vol. 4, 1–33. Monsey, NY: Criminal Justice Press and Police Executive Research Forum.

Sherman, L. 1995. Hot spots of crime and criminal careers of places. In *Crime and place: Crime prevention studies*, ed. J. Eck and D. Weisburd, Vol. 4, 35–52. Monsey, NY: Criminal Justice Press and Police Executive Research Forum.

Sherman, L. W., and D. Weisburd. 1995. General deterrent effects of police patrol in crime hot spots: A randomized controlled trial. *Justice Quarterly* 12 (3): 625–48.

Sherman, L. W., P. Gartin, and M. E. Buerger. 1989. Hot spots of predatory crime: Routine activities and the criminology of place. *Criminology* 27: 27–55.

Taylor, R. (1998). Crime and small-scale places: What we know, what we can prevent and what else we need to know. In *Crime and place: Plenary papers of the 1997 Conference on Criminal Justice Research and Evaluation*. Washington, DC: National Institute of Justice.

Weisburd, D., and J. Eck. 2004. What can the police do to reduce crime, disorder and fear? *The Annals of the American Academy of Political and Social Science* 593 (May): 42–65.

Weisburd, D., S. Bushway, C. Lum, and S. Yang. 2004. Trajectories of crime at places: A longitudinal study of street segments in the city of Seattle. *Criminology* 42 (2): 283–322.

I

IDENTITY THEFT

Knowingly using another person's identity without authority for a criminal or illicit purpose has become, according to the U.S. Federal Trade Commission (FTC), the Federal Bureau of Investigation (FBI), and the U.S. Secret Service, an increasingly common offense, victimizing nearly ten million Americans in the year ending in mid-2003, and more than twenty-seven million in the previous five years. The term *identity theft* is used to describe several types of criminal activity, including theft and illegal use of identity documents (driver's license, passport, birth certificate), checks, credit cards, account information, or identifying data, usually to obtain goods or cash fraudulently in the name of another person. Offenses include opening new accounts in another's name, taking over someone's existing accounts, and claiming to be another person when arrested. Identity theft is often involved in bank fraud, Social Security, mail, wire, and Internet frauds, bankruptcy fraud, money laundering, terrorism, espionage, and fugitive crimes.

Examples

Internet auction frauds occur when the buyer pays, but receives no goods from a seller using a false identity, or the seller is paid with a worthless or stolen check or credit card. Customers' credit card information, obtained by scanning at a gas station or restaurant, is used to manufacture credit cards for fraudulent purchases of high-priced items. Gangs steal purses and mail to take or make fake identification documents (IDs), checks, and credit cards for frauds.

Computer hackers, often operating abroad, break into a firm's computer system, copy customers' account data, and demand payment from the firm, threatening to post the data on the Internet and/or commit multiple frauds. Victims of "phishing" receive e-mail apparently from a bank or e-commerce firm asking for account information, which when entered into a realistic but fake website is used for frauds.

Motivation

Identity theft occurs for a wide variety of reasons, but most often to hide the true identity of the perpetrator and to gain access to credit, currency, or privileges in the name of the person whose identity is stolen. Examples include people who pick pockets for cash and credit cards; impersonate a legal U.S. resident to work or avoid deportation; or assume another's identity to avoid detection or apprehension (as a fugitive, terrorist, spy), to obtain goods (for example, phone or utility services) or cash using another's credit, to flee bill collectors or an abusive spouse, to live "underground," undetected (for example, a terrorist), to enable a fraudulent business enterprise (for example, drug dealing, fraud schemes such as medical insurance fraud, education loan fraud, mortgage fraud, stock fraud), to avoid arrest in one's own name, or to impersonate a privileged person (for example, club member) to enjoy benefits. Fraudulent claims of identity theft have increased, as consumers attempt to avoid paying just debts. Teenagers often use "fake IDs" to buy alcohol or cigarettes. A student who assumes a friend's identity to take an examination as a favor may graduate to filing false income tax returns with the Internal Revenue Service to obtain fraudulent refunds. The frauds described are federal U.S. Code Title 18 and/or state crimes.

Causes

Identity theft has increased markedly due to many factors, among which are automation, Internet and telephone transactions for which the physical credit cards are not present, thefts of unsecured databases of customer credit information, vulnerable technologies (for example, devices that allow cloning of credit cards by copying the magnetic stripe data), and merchant policies of accepting risk in relatively low-value transactions. Computers, scanners, and printers can produce low-cost, high-quality counterfeit documents, and available commercial equipment allows for the manufacture of cloned credit cards. Privacy protections in law and practice are overcome by security breaches by insiders and intruders. Like many crimes, identity frauds often are perpetrated by drug abusers to obtain cash quickly.

Impacts

The FTC's September 2003 Identity Theft Survey Report estimated that U.S. businesses lost $48 billion in 2002–2003, and consumers spent about $5 billion to reconstitute their identity documents and credit. The FTC's and other studies indicate a rapid growth in identity crimes, during a period of generally lower or steady property crime rates. Led by the financial services industry, business has increased security spending in response.

Law enforcement, criminal justice, and private security practices have been heavily impacted by the rise in identity crimes. Many agencies find it difficult to investigate and prosecute multijurisdictional crimes (for example, involving a New Mexico resident's credit card stolen in Seattle, and used in New York City to buy a laptop computer). Internet fraud further complicates the issue of venue. Most financial institutions will not hold victims responsible when their identity is misused, even for the advertised "$50 maximum." Often, the merchant who took a credit card or check in a fraudulent transaction will be charged with the loss, while the issuing bank is protected by contract. Many state and local police agencies, acting under instructions from district attorneys who declined to prosecute individually small extraterritorial frauds, did not investigate ID crimes or even take a report until the Fair and Accurate Credit Transaction Act

(P.L. 108-159) passed in 2004. Extraterritoriality includes the county next door and interstate and international venues.

Rapid increases in identity crimes prompted the U.S. Congress to pass the 1998 Identity Theft and Assumption Deterrence Act (18 USC § 1028) and the 2004 Fair Credit Reporting Act amendments, among others, to establish federal criminal jurisdiction and enhance punishments for identity theft crimes.

Jurisdictional issues and increased fraud have led to enforcement changes at federal, state, and local levels. The FTC, federal law enforcement, and many states collect identity fraud case data, provide it to agencies with local jurisdiction, and collate and analyze patterns of multiple and large-scale offenders. The FBI uses the Internet Crime Complaint Center (IC3) website, run by the National White Collar Crime Center, to take reports of frauds and many types of crimes. Unfortunately, FTC figures show that only 36% of identity crimes are reported to law enforcement. Of those reported, an even smaller number of cases are investigated, due to volume, priorities, unavailable local resources, and multijurisdictional issues.

Studies, best practices, and training materials on identity crimes are proliferating, created by the FTC, Justice Department, International Association of Chiefs of Police, Secret Service, states, financial services firms, and others, to help consumers to reconstitute stolen identity documents and credit, assist law enforcement in responding to identity crimes, and make it harder to obtain false identity documents. Resources include http://www.consumer.gov/idtheft/ (FTC) and http://www.usdoj.gov/criminal/fraud/idtheft.html (Justice Department).

American Identity

Unlike other countries, the United States has rejected national identity credentials. Privacy protection, anonymous transactions, and the Fourth Amendment are guiding public values. Accepted types of identification are Social Security cards/numbers, birth certificates, driver's licenses, state and employer identification cards, credit cards, and passports. Some can be used as "breeder documents" for others, such as a birth certificate presented to a motor vehicle bureau to obtain a driver's license. Exploitation of some states' vital records systems has allowed impersonators to obtain and use birth certificates of dead persons to get driver's licenses and U.S. passports. To prevent this practice, many states (and counties, where they hold vital statistics repositories) are automating systems and cross-checking. U.S. motor vehicle administrators are standardizing driver's license security features, and vital statistics administrators are improving security of vital records. These efforts are spurred by the realization that terrorists and criminals have used false identities for activities in the United States and that driver's licenses and their breeder documents are being counterfeited widely for illicit purposes.

Besides the national security need for federal confidence in the identity of individuals (for example, for employment, investigations, air transportation, and government business), there are social issues, including medical care, insurance, and Social Security. Due in part to a high rate of Medicare fraud, states and the federal government have taken steps to improve antifraud efforts, including increased staff, technologies, and interagency cooperation.

Biometrics, digital signatures, and other innovative technologies are being applied to the problem of identity verification. In the absence of a national identity standard, many employers, financial institutions, universities, military and government agencies, and others are using or experimenting with more positive authentication. By using three types of identity verification—something you are (for example, fingerprint), something you know (for example, personal identification number), and something you have (for example, identity card)—more positive identification could facilitate credit and bank transactions, air transportation, secure Internet business, substitute for cash on campus, and so forth. Among the problems being addressed are flaws in developmental technologies, privacy issues, and the added risk of fraud, if databases of customer personal data and biometrics were stolen.

Trends

Increased consumer response and public agencies' and private companies' intensified efforts have made reduction of identity theft a prime goal. The ease of identity falsification for illegal and illicit purposes, and the limited enforcement response, help explain the rapid increase in identity crimes. Investigators employed by large financial institutions, credit card companies, and transaction processors have begun sharing much of their expertise and automated tools and resources to enable investigation and prosecution by law enforcement. Public–private partnerships are emerging that should facilitate the prevention and response efforts already under way. Nevertheless, identity crimes promise to remain serious in scope, incidence, and impact for the foreseeable future.

EDWARD J. APPEL

See also **Computer Crimes; Computer Forensics; Computer Technology; Constitutional Rights: Privacy; Constitutional Rights: Search and Seizure; Criminal Investigation; Forensic Evidence; Forensic Investigations; Fraud Investigation; Information Security; White Collar Crime**

References and Further Reading

Anti-Phishing Working Group. 2004. *Phishing attack trends report*. http://www.antiphishing.org (accessed January 2004).

Australasian Center for Policing Research. 2004. *Standardisation of definitions of identity crime terms*. Discussion paper. http://www.austrac.gov.au/policy/DEFINITIONSjoint.pdf (accessed May 2004).

BBBOnLine/Better Business Bureau. 2004. Identity theft. http://www.bbbonline.org/idtheft/.

Carroll, Randall, and Edward Appel. 2003–2004. *Identity falsification project*. Ongoing study by the Subcommittee on Information Age Crime, Private Sector Liaison Committee, International Association of Chiefs of Police, in conjunction with the Defense Personnel Security Research Center. Contact: appel@jciac.org.

Cramer, Robert J. 2003. *Security: Counterfeit identification and identification fraud raise security concerns*. Testimony to the U.S. Senate Finance Committee on behalf of the Government Accountability Office, September.

Federal Trade Commission. 2003. *Identity theft survey report*. Prepared by Synovate, September.

Hoar, Sean B. 2001. *Identity theft, the crime of the new millennium*. United States Attorneys Bulletin. http://www.usdoj.gov/criminal/cybercrime/usamarch2001_3.htm (accessed March 2001).

House of Representatives. 1998. Identity Theft and Assumption Deterrence Act of 1998. H.R. 4151. http://thomas.loc.gov/home/thomas.html; http://www.ftc.gov/os/statutes/itada/itadact.htm.

———. 2003. Fair and Accurate Credit Transactions Act. H.R. 2622.

———. 2004. Identity Theft Penalty Enhancement Act. H.R. 1731.

Identity Theft Resource Center. 2004. http://www.idtheftcenter.org/index.shtml.

IdentityTheft.org. 2004. http://www.identitytheft.org.

Legard, David. 2003. Internet fraud and attacks rise in tandem. *Computer World*. http://www.computerworld.com/securitytopics/security/story/0,10801,86025,00.html (accessed October 2003).

Lewis, Linda R. 2003. *Driver's license security issues*. Testimony to the U.S. Senate Finance Committee on behalf of the American Association of Motor Vehicle Administrators, September.

National Conference of State Legislatures. 2004. *Driver's license integrity*. http://www.ncsl.org (accessed June 2004).

National White Collar Crime Center. 2002. *Identity theft*. http://www.nw3c.org (accessed September 2002).

Newman, Graeme R. 2004. *Identity theft.* Washington, DC: Center for Problem-Oriented Policing, Community Oriented Policing Services, U.S. Department of Justice. http://www.cops.usdoj.gov/mime/open.pdf?Item=1271 (accessed June 2004).

Office of the Inspector General, U.S. Department of Education. 2004. *Identity theft.* http://www.ed.gov/about/offices/list/oig/misused/idtheft.html.

Pistole, John F. 2003. *Homeland security and terrorism threat from document fraud, identity theft and Social Security number misuse.* Testimony to the U.S. Senate Finance Committee on behalf of the Federal Bureau of Investigation, September.

Rusch, Jonathan J. 2001. *Making a federal case of identity theft: The Department of Justice's role in identity theft enforcement and prevention.* http://www.usdoj.gov/criminal/fraud/fedcase_idtheft.html.

Social Security Administration. 2004. *Identity theft and your Social Security number.* http://www.ssa.gov/pubs/10064.html (accessed February 2004).

U.S. Department of Homeland Security, U.S. Secret Service. 2003. *Identity crime resource project—CD ROM and video.* http://www.secretservice.gov/press/pub2103_fact2.pdf (accessed July 2003).

IMMIGRANT COMMUNITIES AND THE POLICE

The fabric of the United States is woven of an extremely complex patchwork of minority groups—based on race, ethnicity, or national origin. Some minorities have been part of American society for a long time (for example, African Americans and Native Americans), others are foreign-born, recent legal immigrants, or undocumented aliens; some come from Europe, others from Asia, South America, or Africa. They are political refugees, migrant workers, economically driven immigrants, members of international organized crime groups, or highly educated professionals. Immigrants have always been very important in the United States, but never before has the immigrant population been so large and diverse as it is today.

More than 11% of the population (thirty-one million people) were born in another country, according to the 2000 U.S. Census, which represents an increase of more than eleven million people compared to a decade earlier (Khashu, Busch, and Latif 2005, 1). Approximately half of the foreign-born immigrants entered the United States after 1990. The national origins of the recent immigrants are considerably different than earlier groups of immigrants, most of whom were born in Europe. In 2000, Europe accounted for about 14% of the new immigrants, with 53% coming from Latin America and 25% originating in Asia. In New York City, more than one-third of the population was foreign born according to the 2000 U.S. Census, coming from some two hundred countries.

Although large cities such as New York, Los Angeles, and Chicago remain important destination cities for immigrants, many immigrants now move to regions that have not been traditional immigrant destinations. In the one hundred largest U.S. cities, the Hispanic population grew by 43% and the Asian population increased by 38% during the 1990s; the increase was even larger in midsize cities. The Census Bureau projects that the foreign-born population will continue to grow during the next few decades, and so will the importance of improving police relations with immigrant communities. The focus of this article is on immigrant communities, permanent ethnic communities that have been formed as part of the process of integration in the new country (for example, Chinatown in San Francisco).

Immigrants and Crime

America is a nation of immigrants; it is thus only natural that the crime of foreign-born and recent immigrants has always been an issue, although at times overshadowed by interest in crime by blacks (Hawkins 1995). Immigrants have always played an important role in organized crime in the United

States. Organized crime in the United States has long been thought of as an underworld enterprise composed almost exclusively of traditional white ethnic (immigrant) groups such as Italians, Irish, and Jews. Recent evidence suggests that new ethnic groups have been "waiting their turn" in the ethnic queue for getting involved in organized crime activities: blacks (African and Caribbean), Hispanics (Cuban, Mexican, Puerto Rican, Colombian, Venezuelan), Asians (Chinese, Japanese, Vietnamese, Filipino, and Korean), Soviet Jews, Nigerians, and Ghanians (O'Kane 1992, 89).

The line between "organized crime" and "youth gangs" is becoming increasingly blurred now that more youth gangs are getting involved in organized criminal activity and criminal networks operate more frequently through youth gangs (Marshall 1997, 25). With the influx of new immigrants, the American youth gang picture is no longer dominated by urban black and Hispanic gangs. At the beginning of the twenty-first century, the U.S. urban landscape provides an increasingly complex amalgamation of gangs. For instance, Chicago has black and Hispanic gangs, but there are also Chinese, Cambodian, Vietnamese, Filipino, and Greek gangs; in Los Angeles, Samoan, Tongan, Guamanian, and Hawaiian gangs have emerged, as well as Filipino, Salvadorian, Mexican, Korean, and Vietnamese. The presence of these gangs reinforces the belief that certain non-native ethnic communities are dangerous and crime ridden.

Still, contrary to public belief, there is no evidence that immigrants or noncitizens commit more crimes than American citizens. Most research in this area indicates that—overall—immigrants have lower crime rates than natives. (For an excellent study of crime rates of immigrants in Chicago, see Sampson, Morenoff, and Raudenbush [2005].) Three factors play a role in the lower crime rates of first-generation immigrants: the availability of support groups of earlier and now settled immigrants from the same areas of emigration, the desire to succeed, and the fear of deportation. Undocumented immigrants, in particular, are typically believed to be more law abiding than their legal counterparts—they have much to lose by police detection.

This situation seems to be changing, however, with respect to the most recent (first-generation) immigrants, in particular the undocumented newcomers. The widespread trafficking in undocumented aliens sometimes results in criminal involvement of these new arrivals. There is a growing body of evidence that undocumented immigrants are frequently exploited by those who imported them in violation of the law. To pay back the debts incurred for their illegal transportation into the country, they are forced to work as prostitutes or to get involved in drug dealing. They are reluctant to go to the police, even though they are victims of criminal exploitation (Marshall 1997, 237).

Starting in the late 1990s, there has been renewed interest in the link between immigrants and criminality. Concepts such as "country of origin," "nationality," and "citizenship" have made a comeback in American scholarly and public debate about crime. It is not difficult to see why that is happening. There is a growing number of foreigners in U.S. prisons, although it must be noted that a large proportion of the noncitizens are in prison because of immigration offenses. Highly publicized violent terrorist acts committed by foreigners on U.S. territory, or against U.S. citizens or property, have shaped the public image of "the foreigner" as dangerous. The terrorist events of September 11, 2001, solidified the belief that international organized crime groups represent a major threat to U.S. national security interests and to the democratic world order. With the spotlight on the international character of crime comes a renewed interest in the foreign-born as criminal. After 9/11, law enforcement used racial profiling based on Muslim or Arabic background in several ethnic communities with a high population of Muslims.

Immigrant Communities and the Police

The American police have a long history of mistrust and strained relations with minorities, in particular African Americans. Minority communities feel both over-policed and underprotected; minorities have a lower trust in the police and often feel they are being unfairly treated. Community policing models have been introduced to improve police relations with minority communities; yet, black citizens who encounter police (whether as a victim or as a suspect) continue to have less chance of receiving civil and fair treatment than whites (Donziger 1996).

The problems related to policing racial minorities are likely to be exacerbated when communities contain large numbers of foreign-born minorities (Davis and Henderson 2003, 565). Just as there are some well-known examples of police abuse of American-born blacks (for example, Rodney King), there also have been several well-publicized incidents of abuse by the police of immigrants. Two notorious allegations of police misconduct in New York City threw a national spotlight on police dealings with immigrants. In the 1997 Abner Louima case, New York police officers were accused (and convicted) of brutalizing a Haitian immigrant held at a Brooklyn precinct house. In the 1999 case of Amadou Diallo, four special unit New York police officers faced grand jury charges of second-degree murder in the shooting of an unarmed West African immigrant. The two incidents tapped into deep-seated frustrations that immigrants and established minorities have harbored concerning their treatment at the hands of the police (Davis and Henderson 2003, 565).

The growing importance of large and diverse numbers of immigrants, combined with the threat of terrorism, and the perceived growing problems of ethnic gangs has forced law enforcement agencies to reexamine their relationships with hard-to-reach immigrant communities (Khashu, Busch, and Latif 2005). There is no doubt that many new immigrants have been reluctant to work with the police as witnesses to a crime, to report their own victimization, or to apply as new recruits. A number of barriers exist between immigrant communities and police to explain this:

- *Imported negative perceptions of police, crime, and justice systems.* Many immigrants come from corrupt, violent, and undemocratic countries, where they have had bad experiences with the police. They fear and mistrust the police. Immigrants who have experienced the police in their country of origin as ineffective or dishonest are unlikely to have confidence in the effectiveness of the police when they migrate to the United States (Davis and Henderson 2003, 565–566). These perceptions are often reinforced after they enter the United States where the police—whose actions are often seen at a distance and can appear arbitrary and bewildering—are made into an object of "mystery and local urban legend" (Ibarra 2003, 147).
- *Fear of deportation.* The 2005 Report of the Vera Institute of Justice (Khashu, Busch, and Latif 2005) states that immigrant groups often cite fear of deportation (their own or that of family members or friends) as a major barrier to building trust and partnerships with the police. Even legal immigrants from regions that produce many undocumented immigrants avoid police contact for fear of endangering their undocumented associates. As local and

state law officials have begun to work more closely with federal immigration authorities in the aftermath of September 11, 2001, immigrants have had even more difficulty distinguishing among these agencies (Khashu, Busch, and Latif 2005, 3). Because they assume the police will inquire about immigration status (although many cities prohibit these practices), they are reluctant to contact the police.

- *Linguistic isolation and cultural differences.* Limited or no English language skills are an everyday reality for many new immigrants. In many cities, 911 operators do not speak or understand other languages. Immigrants may have negative contacts with the police because of misunderstandings arising from language differences. The language barrier prevents immigrants from receiving information about policing from mass media or officers themselves to the same extent as English speakers (Henderson and Davis 2003, 655). A nationwide study found that cultural misunderstandings and language barriers lead immigrants to access public safety and justice services less often than native-born citizens do (Davis and Erez 1998). Although language is very important, cultural differences represent an even more challenging obstacle to smooth relations between police and immigrants.

- *Community norms against seeking help from outsiders.* Immigrants often come from countries that are accustomed to resolving disputes informally; there is a sense of interdependence and reliance on one's own rather than a state-run police system. Immigrants may also have "relatively thick skin regarding what is truly dangerous or police relevant" (Ibarra 2003, 140). Making direct contact with the police is often viewed as a last resort to deal with trouble. Some new immigrants have little experience with modern technology, such as using the phone to call the police.

- *Fear of retaliation.* Because of their relative isolation from mainstream society in the host country, and their reluctance to rely on the police, new immigrants are favored targets of criminals. Often, immigrants are victimized by members of their own nationality (including those involved in the illegal trafficking of immigrants). Many immigrants are victimized by organized groups involved in prostitution, extortion, and fraud. These criminals are likely to know the victim and where he or she lives and are often ruthless in retaliating against victims who seek redress through the criminal justice system (Davis and Henderson 2003, 567).

A number of additional factors explain why immigrants regard the police with suspicion, or why they are reluctant to call on the police for assistance. Many immigrants have suffered some form of trauma, in war or as a result of persecution or economic collapse; for many, relocation to a new country is itself a deep trauma. Traumatic experience breeds distrust that not only affects immigrants' relations with the authorities (especially the police) in their new country of residence, but also alienates members of an immigrant community from one another (Khashu, Busch, and Latif 2005, 3). Also, many immigrants tend to settle in impoverished, high-crime urban neighborhoods— exactly the kinds of communities likely to promote apathy, a lack of social cohesion, and a sense of helplessness (Davis and Henderson 2003, 567). And last but not least, many immigrants have encountered discrimination and prejudice since they entered the United States: from stores, landlords, potential employers, and the police. Ibarra (2003, 150) summarizes the predicament of immigrants very well: "[I]nteractions with the police have a very unpredictable quality to them in their neighborhood. If you call the police, you cannot be sure that the police will respond; if they do respond, you cannot be sure that they will treat you courteously; and, even if you are treated courteously, you cannot be sure that you will not be considered a 'rat' by neighbors. . . ."

Police–immigrant community relations are not a one-way street, of course. The police themselves—with its preconceptions, its policies, its practices—also play a crucial role in how immigrant communities interact with law enforcement. Individual police officers are not exempt from the more general prejudice and hostility that permeates American society's attitude towards immigrants. Aside from the possibility that explicit prejudice influences officers' behavior, the police may also have very different interpretations of "problems" in immigrant communities. The police often act on misconceived ideas about what represents a sign of crime and disorder in need of being "nipped in the bud, ideas which are not shared by the residents themselves" (Ibarra 2003, 157). For example, police may view young men hanging in an immigrant neighborhood as "gang bangers, taggers, drug dealers, or people who are on their way to becoming the same" (Ibarra 2003, 139), ideas that are not shared by the immigrant community members themselves, who view the police treatment of their youth as unduly harsh.

Community Policing and Immigrant Communities

Law enforcement agencies across the country are having unprecedented levels of contact with immigrants—as victims, witnesses, suspects, and potential recruits. Immigrant communities are becoming more prevalent and diverse; because of

association with terrorism and crime, they are becoming very important to the police. At the same time, immigrant communities typically are very averse to contact with the police, who have a bad record in their dealings with immigrant communities.

A very popular approach used to improve police–community relations is community policing because of its mandate to build bridges between the police and the many different types of neighborhoods. "The importance of building such bridges represents recognition that effective and productive police work is contingent on the 'input' of residents concerning both the needs of the community and the best way in which the police can meet these needs" (Skogan and Hartnett 1997, as cited in Ibarra 2003, 155). Through consulting with residents on their beats, police departments gain insights into neighborhood problems, and they can adjust their policing strategies street by street and thus be viewed as "responsive to local concerns and worthy of the community's confidence and trust" (Ibarra 2003, 155).

However, when residents are mistrustful of the police, as tends to be the case in immigrant communities, it is very difficult for the police to establish a working relationship with the people in the neighborhood. The police cannot function effectively in communities where tensions are prevalent; community outreach is essential for gaining trust. Gaining trust is especially challenging in light of the long history of strained and often volatile relationships between the police and minorities (Fridell et al. 2001, 99). Community policing relies on an ingredient that is in very low supply in many immigrant communities: trust in the police. Immigrants' strained relationship with the police is evidenced by low levels of contacting the police in order to report a crime, reluctance to serve as a crime witness, and little eagerness to join the police force. However, a number of recent promising community policing efforts have attempted to rebuild this trust (Khashu, Busch, and Latif 2005; Fridell et al. 2001).

Those who design programs to try to improve police–community relations must realize that a particular neighborhood context not only influences the way the residents perceive the police, but also how the police interact with the residents. The "locality" provides the police with cues on how to act appropriately, given the neighborhood they are in. Police must realize that immigrant communities are made up of ethnically, culturally, socioeconomically, and often linguistically diverse subgroups (Khashu, Busch, and Latif 2005). When police work with immigrant communities, they must realize that immigrant communities differ not only in size, but also in how recently they have arrived in the United States, and the degree of integration in the larger society. Some immigrant communities are quite homogeneous (that is, they consist of one particular ethnic group, with one shared language, strong interdependence, and mutual reliance); others are very heterogeneous (that is, there are several different immigrant groups with different native languages and religions, with high degrees of internal conflict). Effective, efficient, and humane policing of non-native communities requires a genuine understanding of the dynamics, culture, and composition of a particular immigrant community or neighborhood. There is no such thing as a "one-size-fits-all" community policing model for immigrant communities.

INEKE HAEN MARSHALL

See also **Accountability; Attitudes toward the Police: Overview; Minorities and the Police; Multiethnic Communities: Interactive Model**

References and Further Reading

Davis, Robert C., and Edna Erez. 1998. *Immigrant populations as victims: Toward a multicultural criminal justice system*. Research in Brief. Washington, DC: U.S. Department of Justice, National Institute of Justice.

Davis, Robert C., and Nicole J. Henderson. 2003. Willingness to report crimes: The role of ethnic group membership and community efficacy. *Crime and Delinquency* 49 (4): 564–80.

Donziger, S. R., ed. 1996. *The real war on crime: The report of the National Criminal Justice Commission*. New York: Harper Collins.

Fridell, Lorie, Robert Lunney, Drew Diamond, and Bruce Kubu. 2001. Minority community outreach. In *Racially biased policing: A principled response*, ed. L. Fridell et al. Washington, DC: Police Executive Research Forum.

Hawkins, D. F., ed. 1995. *Ethnicity, race and crime: Perspectives across time and place*. Albany: State University of New York Press.

Ibarra, Peter R. 2003. Contacts with the police: Patterns and meanings in a multicultural realm. *Police and Society* 7: 133–64.

Khashu, Anita, Robin Busch, and Zainab Latif. 2005. *Building strong police-immigrant community relations: Lessons from a New York City project*. August. New York: Vera Institute of Justice. http://www.vera.org.

Marshall, Ineke Haen, ed. 1997. *Minorities, migrants, and crime: Diversity and similarity across Europe and the United States*. Thousand Oaks, CA: Sage.

O'Kane, J. M. 1992. *The crooked ladder: Gangsters, ethnicity, and the American dream*. New Brunswick, NJ: Transaction.

Sampson, Robert, Jeffrey D. Morenoff, and Stephen Raudenbush. 2005. Social anatomy of racial and ethnic disparities in violence. *American Journal of Public Health*, February.

INDEPENDENT COMMISSION OF THE LOS ANGELES POLICE DEPARTMENT (THE CHRISTOPHER COMMISSION)

Introduction: The Rodney King Incident

On March 3, 1991, members of the Los Angeles Police Department (LAPD) pursued Rodney King shortly after midnight after he was clocked driving at more than one hundred miles per hour according to officer reports (Independent Commission on the Los Angeles Police Department [Independent Commission] 1991). During the pursuit, officers assumed that King was under the influence of PCP due to his sporadic, reckless driving. However, King was later found to only be under the influence of marijuana (Independent Commission 1991). In total, there were more than eleven squad cars, as well as one police helicopter that heard the announcement of the pursuit (known as a code 4) and proceeded to join in on the chase of King and the two passengers who accompanied him in the car (Independent Commission 1991). The officers eventually ended the pursuit with King and, upon forcefully removing him from his vehicle, proceeded to hit him with more than fifty strikes of a baton. The strikes were in response to the officers' belief that King was resisting arrest, but whether that justified fifty swipes of a baton is quite subjective.

The police report filed on the incident mentioned the aggressive nature of King resisting arrest in order to justify the excessive force that was implemented. However, the accuracy of this report received considerable attention because Holliday, a citizen who witnessed the event, videotaped the incident from a distance (Independent Commission 1991). Not only did this tape provide visible proof of the beating, but it also captured some derogatory and unnecessary racist remarks made by one of the arresting officers: "Nigger, hands behind your back" (Independent Commission 1991). Holliday and King's brother immediately filed complaints to the department, but both were ignored. At that point, it appeared as though the LAPD would take no further action, and the department was going to let this overly excessive display of force go unnoticed. However, the videotape was released to the public, which allowed the entire nation to see the event and form their own judgments, and the Christopher Commission

was created in response to investigate the department and determine how this act could take place.

The Christopher Commission

After viewing the videotapes and thoroughly analyzing the LAPD's policies and procedures in the time period leading up to the King incident, the Christopher Commission identified numerous issues within the LAPD (Independent Commission 1991). First, the presence of a sergeant who did not attempt to stop the onslaught led the commission to question the ability of senior officers and upper management to control and discipline their subordinate officers. The commission concluded that there was no professional model for management to follow in supervising, which led to flawed recruiting, training, and promotional processes, causing several officers with histories of use of excessive force to be promoted to high ranks (Independent Commission 1991). It also discovered that unqualified candidates were being promoted to high-ranking positions. For example, many of the field training officers believed that they had been promoted to the position much too quickly or without the training to properly evaluate possible candidates (Independent Commission 1991).

Additionally, the obscene transmissions over the police computer systems also raised concerns about the LAPD's racially biased policies and attitudes toward blacks and other minorities (Independent Commission 1991). The commission concluded that the LAPD failed as an organization because it was not concerned with serving everyone in the community in a humane and civil manner, and failed to deal with the overwhelmingly strong presence of racism, sexism, and other types of biases that had developed over the years within its department. Many officers who were interviewed by the commission indicated that they were instructed each day at roll call to use extreme caution when dealing with minority communities because they usually were more likely to be aggressive and carry guns, unlike people in white neighborhoods.

Furthermore, the commission uncovered an overwhelming number of complaints by residents of Los Angeles concerning the LAPD's inability to successfully and effectively handle complaints made about officers who used excessive force (Independent Commission 1991). For example, the commission discovered the manner in which police reports and citizen complaints were handled to be complicated and unreliable with the majority of complaints never being filed, and reports being totally inaccurate. The commission asserted that this was due in part to the LAPD's Internal Affairs division's incompetence because it lacked valuable resources. For example, of eighty-three civil litigations examined from 1987 to 1991, only 29% resulted in a sustained complaint against an officer.

The Christopher Commission also found the use of excessive force to be the central problem associated with every pitfall within the department. Nearly 25% of all complaints filed by citizens were for cases involving an excessive amount of force (Independent Commission 1991). After examining these cases of excessive force, the commission concluded that the department's policy on the use of force allows officers to use whatever force necessary in order to prevent bodily harm to themselves, which allows room for discretion in determining a reasonable situation to apply force. Additionally, the Christopher Commission also places the blame on the officers for their abuse of the California policy and guidelines on the proper situations to use excessive force, which also gives officers too much discretion when deciding the level of force necessary.

Finally, after examining almost every aspect of the LAPD, the commission expressed the department's desperate need for a system in which accountability is clearly stated, as well as a flowing process in which the recommendations and suitable punishments stemming from the complaints of excessive force can be administered properly (Independent Commission 1991). The commission describes a successful professional model of policing as a department that is well trained, disciplined, and humane, and one that is prepared to adapt to situations that vary in terms of the amount of necessary force required.

In 1996, a follow-up commission was created to assess the implementation of the suggestions made by the Christopher Commission, and it found that many of the same problems still existed within the LAPD (Bobb 1996). Many people questioned whether the department was amenable to change or doomed to continue its unlawful practices. Despite the abundance of problems and inefficiencies documented by both commissions that investigated the LAPD, the department continues its operation and receives its share of funding from the city of Los Angeles.

Conclusion

Fayol's (1949) elements of an organization serve as guidelines that organizations should follow in order to be efficient and effective. Organizations should clearly define accountability and responsibility for tasks throughout the chain of command. Without clearly defined tasks, employees tend to adopt status consciousness and claim that things are not their problems (Fayol 1949). Additionally, it is essential that communication be open up and down the scalar chain in order to ensure that accidents do not become normalized. Proper training and task specialization is the best way to prevent accidents from becoming normalized, but the LAPD failed to properly train its officers. Finally, it is essential for management to take proper disciplinary action against its officers when they do adopt deviant means of policing. The LAPD's inability to properly manage these aspects of the department enabled an incident like the Rodney King beating to occur.

After assessing all of the issues within the LAPD, the Christopher Commission found the organization to be inefficient and flawed. Sergeants did not closely supervise their subordinate officers, and they failed to take disciplinary action against them despite the numerous citizen complaints (Independent Commission 1991). The department's division for handling and filing complaints was not "customer friendly," and most people interviewed by the commission agreed on the difficulty of officially filing a claim within the department. The department's training and recruitment programs had deteriorated over the years because it lacked the necessary resources to properly evaluate officers for any psychological deficiencies. Promotions were given to undeserving officers who had an extended history of complaints (Independent Commission 1991). The burden caused by each of these departmental downfalls is shared by every member of the organization.

According to Charles (2000), no organization is completely free or resistant to encountering risk factors that could potentially lead to a crisis. Problems are bound to occur, but successful organizations are able to work through them because they have managers who work diligently to find the root of the risk (Charles 2000). Every officer on the chain of command, including the LAPD chief of police, shared in the responsibility for the department's failures outlined by the Christopher Commission. The Rodney King beating was the result of the normalization of deviance at the workplace, which Hall (2003) refers to as the inability of organizations to make note or take action of problems in their infrastructure over a long period of time. The King beating was not an accident or a coincidence, for the department continued to operate according to flawed policies and procedures for a number of years with no attempts to amend them. The overall inability of the LAPD to follow correct policies and the poor supervision and administration of sergeants and other members of management allowed for a crisis like the King incident to occur.

DOUGLAS R. HAEGI and TYLER S. KRUEGER

See also **Accountability; Attitudes toward the Police: Overview; Excessive Force; Los Angeles Police Department (LAPD); Police Misconduct: After the Rodney King Incident**

References and Further Reading

Bobb, Merrick. 1996. *Five years later: A report to the Los Angeles Police Commission on the Los Angeles Police Department's implementation of independent commission recommendations*. Los Angeles: Los Angeles Police Commission.

Charles, Michael T. 2000. Agency report: Accidental shooting: An analysis. *Journal of Contingencies and Crisis Management* 8: 151–60.

Fayol, Henri. 1949. *General and industrial management*. London: Pitman.

Hall, Joseph L. 2003. *Columbia* and *Challenger:* Organizational failure at NASA. *Space Policy* 19: 239–47.

Independent Commission on the Los Angeles Police Department. 1991. *Report of the Independent Commission on the Los Angeles Police Department (The Christopher Commission)*. Los Angeles: Independent Commission on the Los Angeles Police Department.

INDIA, POLICING IN

History

The Indian police force has a long and impressive past going back to recorded history. A famous work on statecraft and public administration, *Arthasahtra*, traceable to 300 B.C.E. and written by Kautilya, a minister in the Maurya Dynasty, confirms the use of spies to keep track of criminal elements. The Laws of Manu (200 B.C.E. to A.D. 200) speak of the king's duty to maintain fixed police posts, run spies to help in criminal justice administration, and punish those indulging in violence by imposing penalties on them. There follows a dark period of several centuries, during which only sketchy information is available. Reliable material starts appearing only about the fifteenth century, when a mixed race of Persian, Turkish, and Mughal elements stabilized in the Indian subcontinent to establish a formal Mughal Empire. Chronicles of this period speak of various officials looking after public administration, of whom the *Kotwal* was an urban police officer. *Ain-I-Akbari*, a treatise written by Abul Fazl Allami, one of Emperor Akbar's advisers, also gives glimpses of police management.

The British, who followed the Mughals in the early seventeenth century, tried out several experiments before introducing the Royal Irish Constabulary system, first in Sind (now part of Pakistan) in 1843, and extending it later to other parts of the country. The report of the Police Commission (1860) was a landmark, since it saw the abolition of the military police and the launching of a homogenous civil police. It also resulted in the coming into being of the Police Act of 1861, which remains to this day as the fundamental enactment outlining the police charter for the whole country. Several police reforms followed, until India obtained independence from the British in 1947.

Present Structure

India is a quasi-federation with a clear demarcation of authority between the federal government (officially known as the Union Government) based in New Delhi and the twenty-eight states. There are also seven union territories (UTs) directly administered by the Ministry of Home Affairs (MHA) of the federal government.

Under the constitution of India promulgated in 1950, the subjects of "police" and "public order" are within the legislative competence of the state legislature. Policing is, therefore, the specific responsibility of state governments. The federal government has only an advisory role, except in UTs where the MHA has control over the police. However, with the help of its own paramilitary and specialist forces such as the Border Security Force (BSF), Central Reserve Police Force (CRPF), Central Industrial Security Force (CISF), and the Railway Protection Force (RPF), the federal government assists state governments in crisis situations, such as widespread rioting or a natural calamity. Interestingly, however, those who belong to the Indian Police Service (IPS), the elite corps of police officers who occupy the senior ranks in the force, are recruited and appointed by the federal government, although they spend a major part of their career with state governments.

Every state police force is headed by a director-general (DGP) to whom several additional directors-general (ADGP) and inspectors-general (IGP) report. There are at least seven ranks below them, going down to the police constable (PC), who is at the bottom of the pyramid.

The authorized strength of the Indian police (federal and state police forces together) is about two million. About 10% of positions at any point in time remain unfilled for a variety of reasons, such as dismissals, resignations, or deaths. (Police casualties in action are about one thousand personnel every year.) There are 41 policemen per one hundred square kilometers and 1.2 policemen per one thousand of the population.

Composition

Affirmative action is known to India. Nearly 22% of policemen are from the Scheduled Castes and Tribes (two disadvantaged groups in society that had been traditionally neglected) and 8% are Muslims. Women police (thirty thousand nationally) are a well-established wing, and have proved quite useful in a variety of positions, such as guarding and escorting women prisoners, handling women demonstrators in the streets, and settling marital disputes.

The sizes of the state police forces vary enormously. In a large state, such as Uttar Pradesh in north India, there are more than 150,000 policemen. A small state, Mizroam in the northeast, has less than 4,000. The country has about 12,900 police stations. Of these, more than 230 are staffed wholly by women, which cater mainly to women with complaints of various forms of sexual harassment and domestic disputes.

Division of Work

State police personnel are normally distributed among three functional groups: law and order (equivalent to what patrol officers do in the United States), crime (analogous to the work of detectives), and road traffic enforcement. This division of work is more common to urban police stations. In the rural stations, all three functions are performed by the same group. There is a fourth group, known as the Armed Police, which is basically the riot police available at state headquarters as well as in districts, which are administrative divisions of a state headed by a district collector (generalist) and a district superintendent of police. Except under grave circumstances, the average patrolman in the country seldom carries firearms on beats. He uses the firearms (normally .303 rifles) kept in custody at police stations for handling any major situation.

Police Response

Police stations and supervisory staff are connected by VHF radio. Polnet is a major federal government project that is under way. It is designed to connect online all police stations in the country for the quick exchange of crime information. The public have telephone access to the police for an emergency response through control rooms in cities that are manned on a 24/7 basis and have a limited number of mobile patrol vehicles. While police response is reasonably fast in major cities, it is slower elsewhere.

Use of Science

Each state has a forensic science laboratory and a chain of regional laboratories. DNA testing as part of crime investigation is now common, but is available only in a few laboratories that are shared by two or more states.

Major Operational Problems

Terrorism

The issues that occupy police attention are mostly on the law and order front. These take the form of terrorism (especially in Kashmir and a few northeastern states such as Manipur and Assam) and interreligious riots (as witnessed in the western state of Gujarat in 2002). The Indian police force has tackled terrorism imaginatively and with great courage. The success it achieved in the Punjab by breaking the back of Sikh terrorism in the late 1980s and early 1990s is a testimony to its professional competence. Terrorism is still a problem that keeps the police on their toes in some parts of the country.

Religious Riots

Hindu–Muslim clashes test the neutrality of a heavily Hindu-dominated force, and several post-riot commissions of inquiry have indicted the police for partisanship. The situation has been changing with better training methods and through judicial monitoring. A rapid action force (RAF) under the CRPF of the federal government is available to states to provide impartial and prompt handling of interreligious riots.

Handling of Crime

The serious crime rate (that is, offenses per one hundred thousand population) holds steady at around 170. The trend is one of a marginal increase or decline over the years. Police investigation time is taken up mostly by homicides (about thirty-five thousand to forty thousand annually), burglaries (one hundred thousand), riots (seventy thousand), and auto thefts (sixty thousand). The use of firearms in violent crime has been increasing, despite a restrictive gun license policy. About one-third of homicides in 2002 were committed with the help of firearms, many of which were unlicensed.

Crimes against Women

Crime in India, an annual publication of the National Crime Records Bureau (NCRB) of the federal government, recognizes twelve categories of offenses with respect to women. It reports an annual figure of about 140,000 cases. Rapes alone account for about 16,000 cases, nearly 90% of which are committed by persons known to the victims. Success rate in court prosecutions of offenders is low.

Public Image

Under the British rule, the Indian police force was considered a tool in the hands of an alien power to suppress the freedom movement led by Mahatma Gandhi. The present perception of the common man is one of an insensitive and corrupt force that will not hesitate to use torture to extract information from crime suspects. (Eighty-four deaths in police custody were reported in 2002.) Integrity levels, even among senior ranks, have dipped, inviting public ire and ridicule.

Lack of Autonomy

Perhaps the most trenchant criticism is that the Indian police force does not enjoy sufficient operational autonomy, as a result of which it acts as the handmaiden of whichever political party runs the government in a state. Several reform bodies, including the National Police Commission (1977), have suggested measures on how the police could be insulated from misuse by political leaders. These have mostly been ignored because of a lack of political will.

R. K. RAGHAVAN

References and Further Reading

Bayley, David H. 1969. *The police and political development in India*. Princeton, NJ: Princeton University Press.
Ghosh, S. K., and K. F. Rustamji. 1993. *Encyclopedia of police in India*. New Delhi: Ashish Publishing.
Griffith, Sir Percival. 1971. *To guard my people: The history of the Indian police*. London: Ernest Benn.
Gupta, A. S. 1979. *The police in British India, 1861–1947*. New Delhi: Concept Publishing.
Karan, Vijay. 1996. *War by stealth: Terrorism in India*. New Delhi: Viking Penguin.
Marwah, Ved. 1995. *The uncivil wars*. New Delhi: Harper Collins.
Ministry of Home Affairs. 1979–1981. *Reports of the National Police Commission*. Vols. I–VII. New Delhi: Ministry of Home Affairs.
Natarajan, Mangai. 1996. Women police units in India: A new direction. *Police Studies* 19 (2).
National Crime Records Bureau. 2004. *Crime in India 2002*. New Delhi: National Crime Records Bureau.

Raghavan, R. K. 1989. *Indian police: Problems, planning and perspectives.* New Delhi: Manohar.

———. 1999. *Policing a democracy.* New Delhi: Manohar.

———. 2000. Indian police: Expectations of a democratic polity. In *Transforming democracy,* ed. Francine Frankel. New Delhi: Oxford University Press.

———. 2002. On police reforms. *Frontline (Hindu),* August 17–30. http://www.flonnet.com.

———. 2003. The Indian police: Problems and prospects. *Publius: The Journal of Federalism* 33 (4).

———. 2004. Understanding crime. *Frontline (Hindu),* September 25–October 8.

Rajgopal, P. R. 1987. *Communal violence in India.* New Delhi: Uppal Publishing.

INFORMANTS, USE OF

Although police informants have been around for centuries—longer than professional police forces—we know little about them. Not only is their work a well-guarded secret, but their identity is almost always protected by the courts and can only be divulged in common law countries as a last resort to save an innocent from wrongful condemnation. The main source of knowledge with respect to informants is press clippings.

The field of informants is evolving rapidly and there have been important developments from the 1960s until the turn of the new millennium. This article on informants is divided into three parts: history, typology, and trends in the use of informants. We conclude with a discussion of changes that have occurred with respect to informants.

History

Informants were known in Greek and Roman antiquity. They were called *sycophants* by the ancient Greek. Sycophants originally denounced thieves who stole figs. In Rome, an informant was known as a *delator*. This word derives from a verb (*deferre*) meaning "to give notice" or "to refer to" the proper authorities those guilty of fiscal evasion. The term later came to apply to all public accusers.

Informants began to cast a wide shadow with the establishment of the French police by King Louis XIV in 1667. The French king created an organization with a new magistrate, the general police lieutenant, who was responsible for developing a police agency. In so doing, the lieutenant recruited police inspectors and they created a vast network of informants, known as *mouches,* which translates as "flies." (The word is said to have come from the name of a notorious police informant, *Mouchy.*) There were so many of these informants that a French lieutenant of police could boast to King Louis XV that whenever three Frenchmen would come together, one of them would be a police informant. Prostitutes were tolerated insofar as they were police informants.

The French police were created to protect the political regime and kept this mission after the 1789 revolution and during the first empire. Hence, the extensive reliance on police informants came to be associated with political or "high" policing and, during the twentieth century, with totalitarian states. Informants have also exercised an important influence on knowledge. Our common representations of organized crime have been to a significant extent shaped by informants who, like Joseph Valachi, Tommaso Buscetta, Antonino Calderone, and Salvatore Contorno and Marino Mannoia, have decided to go public.

Typology of Informants

The political use of informants is far from being their only use. Although they were used in this capacity in democracies, albeit in a limited way, they mainly serve as a tool against organized crime (for example, drug trafficking). However, their political usage is being rediscovered in the face of the new terrorist threat that has emerged after the September 11, 2001, terrorists attacks against the United States. It is impossible to be efficient against deviant groups that rely on networks without succeeding in infiltrating them with police informants.

The police make a distinction between human and technical sources, the former being live informants and the latter various types of technological devices (for example, wiretaps). The acronyms HUMINT (human intelligence) and SIGINT (signals intelligence) refer, respectively, to human and technical sources. The different types of human sources, which should not be confused, are discussed next.

Occasional Sources

The police refer to anyone giving information to them as a source or an informant. Most of these people are simply crime victims or witnesses to a crime. Others are trying to help the police solve a crime by giving them clues as to who the perpetrator may be. Many are answering calls for information that are aired during TV programs. The distinctive character of these informants is that they are not repeat informants—they are connected to a particular crime—and that they are generally acting out of goodwill.

Informers

This is a wide category encompassing various kinds of police informants. Despite their differences, they have three things in common: (1) They inform the police on a regular basis, (2) they have a personal stake in informing the police, and (3) they generally do not testify in court, their value being as mid- or long-term infiltrators. Each of these statements needs to be further qualified.

First, informers do not provide only intelligence to the police; in many cases, they take a more active part, for instance, as a party in a sting operation. Their personal stakes vary greatly, ranging from a grant of partial immunity from prosecution or the promise of a reduced charge and sentence (for example, "working a beef" for narcotics agents), substantial sums of money, and protection of family and friends against retaliation from the state in political cases. When taking a more active part than merely providing intelligence, informers may become *agents provocateurs*. Such agents are party to the entrapment of persons who had no intention of committing a crime, or they perpetrate crimes themselves for the purpose of falsely accusing innocent people (for example, inciting people to riot). Finally, many informers are double agents, in the sense that they are informers for a particular police unit (for example, drugs), while covering up their crimes in another criminal field (for example, car theft). Being a double agent is the rule rather than the exception in a walk where loyalty has little or no meaning at all.

Special Witnesses

There is no accurate word in English for these informers who agree to testify in court. These trials are not only public but highly publicized by the media. These witnesses for the prosecution are called *supergrass* in Northern Ireland, *pentiti* (repentants) in Italy, and *delateurs* in France and in Canada. Special or protected witnesses are a new development in the field of informants. It goes against police wisdom to assert that blowing the cover of an informant to obtain convictions in court does not balance the loss of the intelligence that the informant could have provided if he had not testified in court and been kept active as an infiltrator. In Italy, however, *pentiti* such as Tommaso Buschetta and Antonio Calderone have been highly instrumental in defeating organized crime. The Italian police force maintains a network of some five thousand informants against organized crime and the Mafia,

Whistle-Blowers

In most languages, dictionaries define informers as persons informing the police for "contemptible" reasons. This definition would not apply to the latest kind of public accusers, called *whistle-blowers.* Whistle-blowers share with informers the characteristic of being insiders. However, they are generally motivated by the public good, although some private companies give whistle-blowers a share of the money they will save the company by denouncing deviant business practices. Three such whistle-blowers were named "persons of the year" in 2003 by the U.S. magazine *Time* for their role in bringing to light the Enron scandal. Following business scandals such as the 2002 bankruptcy of the Texas company Enron, an increasing number of private enterprises are establishing mechanisms through which their employees are incited to denounce wrongdoing. This is a momentous development, because private enterprise may eventually supersede the state as the facilitator of denunciations.

Undercover Police

Police who are working undercover are not considered informants of a police force. However, their field work as infiltrators is little different from that of professional informers.

Trends

Important trends can be noted with respect to informants. However, it does seem that each trend is paired with its own counter-trend.

Formalization

Relationships between informants and special witnesses and their handlers are increasingly formalized through contracts spelling out their mutual obligations. These contracts are administered by agencies independent of the police such as the U.S. Marshall's office. However, research conducted in police files shows that despite the multiplication of regulations with respect to the management of informants and special witnesses, the case officers still retain a great amount of discretionary power. In Canada, special police witnesses have formed a pressure group denouncing the fact that their contracts were not respected by the police.

Legalization

The biggest problem in dealing with informants is that they are granted a license to commit crimes in order to infiltrate criminal organizations at a deeper level and also to protect their cover. In Canada, there is even a law that explicitly allows undercover police and their agents to commit crimes (for example, to buy drugs in "buy-and-bust" operations). These attempts to regulate what crimes are permissible for police informants often end up in failures. In Canada, a professional assassin who testified against accomplices was authorized to plead guilty to forty-two reduced charges of manslaughter and ended up serving only four years in prison, before being released into the community.

HUMINT

The failure of the very powerful U.S. agencies collecting SIGINT to prevent the 9/11 attacks has resulted in the rediscovery of the necessity of HUMINT and of infiltrating terrorist and other criminal organizations. However, infiltration is now much more difficult to practice in the context of global immigration, multiethnicity, and multilinguisticity. The language obstacle is particularly formidable

Conclusion

In the past, the state and its various agencies (for example, the police or the Department of Revenue) were the main recipients of the intelligence provided by informants. In the wake of the Enron scandal, pressure is growing on private enterprise employees to blow the whistle on extralegal business practices; the state may not be the prime recipient of denunciations anymore. Whistle-blowing is facilitated by the legal protection given to the whistle-blowers and by the establishment of efficient channels (for example, special telephone lines) to proffer denunciations.

On a more fundamental level, we should ask whether the information society will not foster the advent of a society of informants. Phenomena such as the exponential growth of Internet blogs may increase the scope and frequency of denunciation to levels that were not imaginable even in the most totalitarian of societies.

JEAN-PAUL BRODEUR

References and Further Reading

Arlacchi, Pino. 1992. *Men of dishonor. Inside the Sicilian mafia*. New York: William Morrow and Company.

Brodeur, Jean-Paul. 1983. High policing and low policing: Remarks about the policing of political activities. *Social Problems* 30: 507–20.

———. 1992. Undercover policing in Canada: Wanting what is wrong. *Crime, Law and Social Change* 18: 105–36.

———. 2000. Cops and spooks, the uneasy partnership. *Police Practice and Research* 1: 299–322.

Harney, M., and L. Cross. 1960. *The informer in law enforcement*. Springfield, IL: Charles C Thomas.

Maas, Peter. 1969. *The Valachi papers*. Toronto: Bantam Books.

Manning, Peter K. 2004. *The narcs' game*. 2nd ed. Prospect Heights, IL: Waveland Press.

Manning, Peter, and L. Redlinger. 1977. Invitational edges of corruption. In *Politics and drugs*, ed. P. E. Rock. New Brunswick, NJ: Transaction.

Marx, Gary. 1974. Thoughts on a neglected category of social movement participant: The agent provocateur and the informant. *American Journal of Sociology* 80 (1): 402–42.

Williams, Jay, Lawrence Redlinger, and Peter Manning. *Police narcotics control: Patterns and strategies*. Washington, DC: U.S. Department of Justice.

INFORMATION SECURITY

Police thrive on information. Without information it would be impossible for them to perform their jobs, much less perform them efficiently and effectively. Nogala (1995, 193, as cited in Chan 2003) characterizes police work as primarily "information work," and the police as knowledge workers (Ericson and Haggerty 1997, 19, as cited in Chan 2003). The need for information in the police organization has been affected by crime control and police internal administrative demands and is now affected by police risk management needs (Chan 2003). Without timely accurate information, the police would simply be the primary agents of social control minimally able to enforce laws, but certainly not able to investigate violations of laws.

It is imperative that police have access to information. Police must also be able to transmit accurate information without concern that the information will be intercepted and completely lost, or intercepted and modified. Therefore, information security for police operations must be considered an important and necessary practice for contemporary organizations trying to meet the challenges of the twenty-first century.

Information security (infosec) is "the protection of information and its critical elements, including the systems and hardware that use, store, and transmit that information" (Whitman and Mattord 2004, 4). Physical security, personal security, operational security, communications security, and network security all contribute to the information security program as a whole (Whitman and Mattord 2004, 4).

The C.I.A. triangle—confidentiality, integrity, and availability—are three desirable characteristics of information and have historically formed the cornerstone of information security and security policies and practices. These concepts in and of themselves have now become somewhat dated and inadequate because of their limited scope and the dynamic environment of information technology (IT). As a result of the dynamic nature of the IT environment, threats to confidentiality, integrity, and availability have increased with subsequent additional measures to combat threats being absolutely necessary. The C.I.A. triangle, therefore, has been updated to include more necessary critical characteristics (for example, authenticity, privacy) (Whitman and Mattord 2004).

Confidentiality ensures that only those with a demonstrated need for the information and sufficient privileges can access the information in question. Measures that protect the confidentiality of information include but are not limited to information classification, secure document storage, application of general security policies, education of end users who are responsible for the information, and cryptography (Whitman and Mattord 2004). Confidentiality of information concerning people is extremely important, regardless of the type of organization, but is even a greater concern within law enforcement where a breach could result in the loss of life or serious physical injury. Confidentiality may be breached by either insiders (for example, officers, employees) or outsiders to the organization (for example, hackers).

Integrity is the "quality or state of being whole, complete and uncorrupted" (Whitman and Mattord 2004, 6). Integrity is threatened when information is corrupted, damaged, destroyed, or altered from its authentic state. This can occur accidentally or be the result of more purposeful behavior. Corruption can happen when the information is in various states of storage, entry, or transmission. Specific threats include viruses, Trojan horses, worms, faulty programming, application errors, or noise in the transmission channel. Like confidentiality, integrity can be threatened both internally and externally. Measures to combat threats to integrity include redundancy bits, check bits, algorithms, hash values, and error-correcting codes.

Availability, the third component of the C.I.A. triangle, means that authorized users have timely access to information in a usable form without interference or obstruction. The distributed denial-of-service attacks that occurred in early 2001 demonstrated the importance of access to information and how costly this threat could really be.

In addition to the C.I.A. triangle, other essential characteristics of information are privacy, identification, authentication, authorization, and accountability. Privacy, while more of a policy issue, is closely related to confidentiality. Privacy is concerned with the rights and obligations of individuals and organizations with respect to the collection, use, retention, and disclosure of personal information. In other words, the information that is collected from its owner is to be used only for purposes stated by the collector and is not to be disclosed without the permission of the individual. If a collector of information uses it for purposes other than those that were stated, or discloses information without the proper authorization, the collector is violating the owner's privacy, and in some jurisdictions, the law. Typical security controls related to privacy include detailed policies, procedures, and guidelines.

Identification is the first step for a user to gain access to a system and is essential for authentication and authorization. Identification deals with the ability to distinguish among various users. Typical security controls here include user IDs and more recently biometrics (for example, fingerprints, iris scans).

Authentication is the act of proving or validating that the user is whom he or she claims to be. Controls such as passwords are weak methods of authentication and are being replaced by stronger authentication controls such as two-factor authentication (for example, password plus a security token) and biometrics.

Once a user has been identified and authenticated, the privileges that these users or programs have on a system(s) need to be established. This is referred to as authorization. Authorization allows users to perform certain functions with information, such as reading, writing, modifying, updating, and deleting the information. An example of an authorization control is an access control list (ACL).

Accountability provides an audit trail of all access and activities related to the information (Whitman and Mattord 2004). Typical controls include log files or other related files (for example, event logs).

Nunn (2005) identifies the following as significant information systems for police: communications, database and record keeping, and decision support systems. Communications systems include analog and digital radio systems, digital wireless systems such as local-area networks (LANs) and wide-area networks (WANs). Database and record-keeping systems used by the police include but are not limited to National Crime Information Center (NCIC), Automated Fingerprint Identification System (AFIS), National Auto Theft Bureau (NATB), criminal histories, and warrants. The NCIC includes information on guns, securities, vehicles and license plates, and missing persons. The other databases are self-explanatory.

Manning (2005) characterizes modern policing information technology systems in the following ways:

- Many nonlinked databases that are locally sourced
- Other databases that are nominally national
- Storage capacity and use that are not calibrated
- Numerous software systems
- Websites with descriptive materials, some data on calls for service or crime patterns, and hyperlinks to other websites
- Secrecy and nonlinked access points
- Multiple and incompatible channels of communication between the public and the police within the police department
- Inconsistent user and backside technology interfaces
- A tendency to use mapping information for short-term tactical interventions absent "problem solving" (pp. 230–31)

Consequently, certain problems arise from these characteristics. The two biggest challenges for police are interoperability and security between the information systems. Interoperability is the ability for various systems to communicate with one another and pertains to both voice and data communications. If agencies do not have the same type of resources (or databases), they cannot access or share information. With the variation in resources between police organizations, this is a common problem. Typically, one agency does not have the most advanced technology, and so is unable to maximize the use of their resources.

A lack of proper database security is problematic and also quite common. Breaches of a database are always a possibility given the inherent vulnerabilities of these systems. The risk is compounded further if proper security controls have not been implemented (for example, encryption, access controls). Unfortunately, law enforcement has been inadequately trained in information security, risk management, and security controls, resulting in a situation in which many of the attacks on the information systems could have been easily prevented, or at least more easily identified.

Most of the risks associated with information technology include violations of privacy and confidentiality. These may come in the form of unrestrained official use of information, unauthorized access of information, and certain types of cyber-crime such as identity theft. If certain controls are not put on the official use of information, potentially confidential information can be easily transmitted after which control of the information is lost. Both insiders and outsiders could gain access to information, thereby jeopardizing privacy. It should come as no surprise that criminals are developing innovative ways to access vital information and the police are challenged to keep up with them (Dunworth 2005).

Major threats to information systems include but are not limited to unauthorized access to information, unauthorized use of information, unauthorized disclosure of information, unauthorized diversion of information, unauthorized modification of information, unauthorized destruction of information, unauthorized duplication of information, and unavailability of information (Wood 2002). When considering the police organization it is readily apparent that any one of these threats to information systems could be extremely problematic, whether done by an insider (police personnel) or outsider to the police organization. For example, if information from police records was destroyed without authorization, this could hinder investigative activity. Additionally, if information that was to be evidence in a trial was modified, the evidence might not be admissible.

Risk management is a necessary process for information technology in an organization. Risk management is the process of identifying the threats, vulnerabilities, and likelihood of attacks to information systems and then creating a plan to mitigate or reduce the risk to these systems, thus managing the risk. The process includes conducting a risk analysis and then identifying and implementing security controls. Risk management is more common in the private business sector, but with the increase in federal regulations it is now starting to become part of the public-sector (police organizations) approach to information security as well. While the process might have to be modified somewhat for organizations in the public sector, it is good practice to follow recommended risk management practices regardless of the organization type and size. Police administrators must decide on certain strategies to manage and/or control risk in their organizations.

With risk management there are four strategies to choose from: avoidance, transference, mitigation, and acceptance. Avoidance is the strategy that attempts to prevent the exploitation of a vulnerability by a threat or threat agent (for example, hacker, virus). The goal of transference is to shift the risk to another organization such as an Internet service provider, insurance company, or other third party. Mitigation focuses on reducing the potential damage caused by exploitation of a vulnerability through planning and preparation—this is the most common strategy used given the fact that risk is inherent with today's networks and technology. Finally, acceptance is to do nothing about the vulnerability and simply accept the outcome of the exploitation (Whitman and Mattord 2004).

The use of protection mechanisms or controls is an important part of ensuring that information is secure. The most commonly used protection mechanisms for information systems are access controls, firewalls, virtual private networks (VPNs), antivirus system intrusion detection systems (IDS), scanning and analysis tools, and cryptography. In many cases these controls are implemented in a layered manner, providing what is commonly termed *defense in-depth,* the logic being that no one control is 100% effective so by layering these defenses, the controls as a whole are stronger. Unfortunately, these security controls are not without cost. These costs are in terms of resources as well as capital. Administrators must perform cost–benefit analyses when determining what is best and reasonable for their information systems.

A firewall is "any device that prevents a specific type of information from moving between the outside world, known as the untrusted network (e.g., the Internet), and the inside world, known as the trusted network" (Whittman and Mattord 2004, 375). Firewalls include separate computer systems, separate networks, or specific services running on existing routers or servers. VPNs are temporary encrypted and authenticated connections that allow someone on the outside (remotely) to access resources and information on the inside network. Antivirus systems attempt to detect and block malicious code (for example, worms, viruses, Trojan horses) from successfully entering a system, device, or network. Intrusion detection systems work like burglar alarms and produce an alert or notification if an attack against any of the protected systems or network occurs. Scanning and analysis tools are used to conduct vulnerability analyses in order to identify areas of concern within the IT environment. Cryptography involves the coding and decoding of messages, so that anyone who does not have the key cannot make sense of the information (Whittman and Mattord 2004).

Physical or environmental security is one of the most fundamental domains of information security, yet for some reason it seems to be the most neglected. The physical security of information technology (IT), network technology, and telecommunications is paramount. If physical access to a system or device containing critical information is possible (either by an insider or outsider), then most of the technical controls described thus far are moot (for example, firewalls, access control lists). Despite the importance of physical

security, most of today's modern IT facilities are not designed with this concept in mind (Erbschloe 2005).

Physical security is important for numerous reasons. First, information technology equipment is expensive to integrate into an information system within an organization. Second, when the information system goes down, work oftentimes must stop. Disruptions can be not only costly, but also potentially dangerous if a law enforcement organization were not able to access its information. Finally, laws require the protection of most data, so when the data are not adequately protected there is the potential for violations of these laws (Erbschloe 2005).

Access to mobile computing devices such as laptops and personal digital assistants (PDAs) is also problematic and, like physical security, these have been inadequately addressed. Therefore, when taking physical security into account, it is wise to include mobile computing in any assessment and planning for improvement. Physical security measures should be taken into account for each of the following types of technologies: wiring and cabling, laptops, remote computers, desktops, department servers, telecommunications equipment, and data communications equipment (Erbschloe 2005).

Cowper (2005) describes today's police organization as a "Net-Centric" organization. This organization is one in which "real-time information is delivered to all the right people in an entire networked organization . . . [with] an organizational structure and policies, both administrative and operational, [that is] fully adapted to our technology" (p. 121). Cowper also says that "policing could see a dramatic increase in overall efficiency and effectiveness" (p. 121). If police follow proper risk management processes (that is, appropriately assess threats and vulnerabilities and identify proper security controls to mitigate the risk), and take into account operational, technical, and physical security, the benefits of IT to policing will far outweigh any of the risks and will allow policing to evolve into the twenty-first century.

KATHRYN E. SCARBOROUGH and MARCUS K. ROGERS

See also **Computer Crimes; Computer Technology; Technology and the Police**

References and Further Reading

Chan, J. B. L. 2003. Policing new technologies. In *Handbook of policing*, ed. T. Newburn. Portland, OR: Willan Publishing.

Chu, J. 2001. *Law enforcement information technology: A managerial, operational, and practitioner guide*. Boca Raton, FL: CRC Press.

Cowper, T. J. 2005. Emerging technology. In *Issues in IT: A reader for the busy police chief executive*. Washington, DC: Police Executive Research Forum.

Dunworth, T. 2005. IT and the criminal justice system. In *Information technology and the criminal justice system*, ed. A. Pattavina. Thousand Oaks, CA: Sage.

Erbschloe, M. 2005. *Physical security for IT*. Boston, MA: Elsevier Digital Press.

Ericson, R. V., and K. D. Haggerty. 1997. The militarization of policing in the information age. *Journal of Political and Military Sociology* 27: 233–55.

Foster, R. E. 2005. *Police technology*. Upper Saddle River, NJ: Pearson/Prentice-Hall.

Manning, P. K. 2005. Environment, technology, and organizational change: Notes from the police world. In *Information technology and the criminal justice system*, ed. A. Pattavina. Thousand Oaks, CA: Sage.

Nogala, D. 1995. The future role of technology in policing. In *Comparisons in policing: An international perspective*, ed. J. P. Brodeur. Aldershot: Avebury.

Nunn, S. 2005. The technology infrastructure of criminal justice. In *Criminal justice technology in the 21st century*, ed. L. Moriarity. Springfield, IL: Charles C Thomas.

Osterberg, J. W., and R. H. Ward. 2004. *Criminal investigation: A method for reconstructing the past*. 4th ed. Cincinnati, OH: LexisNexis.

Whitman, M. E., and H. J. Mattord. 2004. *Management of information security*. Canada: Thomson Learning.

Wood, C. C. 2002. *Information security roles and responsibilities made easy*. Houston, TX: Pentasafe.

INFORMATION WITHIN POLICE AGENCIES

The police have a great many facts stored and information in abundance, all of which can be used diversely. Unfortunately, the ways in which such facts and information are coordinated, analyzed, and used are determined by factors other than their raw availability. The primary determinant of information distribution is the structure and strategies of Anglo-American policing based on the premise that one distributes randomly (in theory, but based largely on workload or past levels of calls) a large percentage of the available personnel ecologically around a city, keeps them in radio contact, and assigns investigators to later investigate some of the reported incidents. The raw data, the facts, that are taken in via the 911 number (and 311 and seven- to ten-digit numbers) and written by patrol officers are a vast, diverse, and selective, stylistically shaped (written and reported by officers) bundle. These "bundles" are a selective, abstracted, formatted, and strikingly partial reflection of what might be called the "natural incident"—that which is seen, reported, and told that stimulates the police action to investigate. Thus, what is seen and reported is a partial version of the event, and that which is of concern to the police is even more stylized and fitted to the contours of police work.

If one considers the natural event (a fight, a dispute, lost property, bodily harm) as a kind of stimulus, it must be socially constructed or defined as police work, not a job for sanitation workers, electricians, a coroner, or a physician. The conversion of the stimulus-of-natural-incidents-as-reported into facts to be further considered is a version metaphorically of how the organization "sees and gives" meaning to the complex, environment. This is what Weick (2001) calls the "enacted environment," those facts that the organization identifies and processes. The police as an organization is like the person who hears the tree fall in the forest. If he or she does not hear it, it cannot be acted upon. These facts as known are of passing utility, not systematically analyzed, disposed of, or stored for very long. Until recently, it would be safe to say that police departments operated on a loosely coupled model in which specialized units, divisions, and ranks above the patrol officer shared information largely on a "need to know" basis except when exchanges were required by functional connections such as those between patrol and the investigative units and by ad hoc staff functions (IAD, research and development, the chief's staff) that serve the chief's office directly.

Facts, Information, and Knowledge

It is necessary to distinguish *fact* from *information,* and information from *knowledge.* A fact is a free-standing piece of data. Examples of facts might be the score of a Boston Red Sox game; the square miles of France in 1940; the present population of Gervais, Oregon; the number of people named Sean born in 1962; and the average height of Mexican Americans in Texas. Absent a context in which these facts are considered, they are mere clutter. Context is what is brought to facts, usually more than an isolated one; context tells us how they are framed and connected. One result of a visible shared context is that intersubjectivity and shared meanings are possible. In one respect the occupational culture of policing is a framework for knowing what a fact is and why it is such. This embedded matter is information, or a difference that makes a difference. Knowledge is that which can be transmitted broadly across contexts, so that it is a kind of information about information.

It has been argued that the police are "information dependent" (Willmer 1970; Manning 1988, 1997, 2003). This means in effect that the police rely on information from the public, other agencies, and their own records and databases to direct their strategies and tactics. This is a proposition or hypothesis to be tested, because the facts the police gather must be processed to become information. Information is not a physically identifiable, clearly established empirical matter that can be defined absent context. Think, for example, of calls to the police: Some considerable number of them are about dreams, vague memories, requests for information (When do the Red Sox play? How can I reach city hall? What time is it?), reports of fires or matters that cannot be entered into the menus offered. The number of calls processed by a police department does not index in a sensitive fashion what the police know, nor are the calls easily classified in binary, mutually exclusive Aristotelian fashion (either this or that, logically discrete, and with essential features).The content is also highly stylized and selectively entered. Workable or actionable facts are those the police define as such.

Making Facts into Information

The police are located in a world of complex communications and are the first-line receptors of information about anything that might get worse, to paraphrase Bittner (1970). They process facts and buffer demand (Manning 1988):

> The world is constituted of a flow or stream from which "strips" are extracted or framed. Some of these strips concern natural events which may be reported or witnessed and communicated to the police. As such they become police-relevant or workable *facts.*

Facts are ordered. Once processed in the police organization, they result in a *message*—an ordered selection of signs from an agreed source (for example, a code, alphabet, or dictionary) intended to convey information beyond the communications center.

The police receive messages from four different message sources: the general public, alarm calls, operating units (vehicles, walking officers, special squad detectives, and so on), and cell phone calls (which require special treatment because their location is not given when the call is received as with other landlines).

These *sources* are differentially organized. The response of police varies by the degree of organization of the source. The more organized the source, the more ritualized or predictable the response. Response to alarms is highly ritualized, whereas citizens' calls, because they are the least organized as a source, are more pragmatic and less predictable. This is why officers are almost always sent to "have a look" at calls made by citizens.

These messages come into the police organization on four different channels. Three are disembodied, calls from 911, 311, and seven-digit numbers, and one is embodied, face-to-face reporting, made at police stations or to officers.

The messages are *screened* (ranked, some eliminated, some dealt with summarily at source) and given priority. This is done at three positions in the police communications system (PCS): at the operators' position, at the dispatchers' position, and at the officers' position. The final meaning of an incident is determined by the officer.

Once the messages are in the system, they are converted from facts into information (facts-in-context), but the contexts are different for each of the positions just listed. The flow of information in a police department is highly context bound. The ability to define and redefine the meaning of the message is very great, and the emphasis in the organization is that facts on the ground have to be assessed directly by an office if they are to be given credibility.

Once information is lodged in the organization, it can be classified in accord with the degree to which it has been processed and refined. Facts from the social world that are incident relevant have a kind of quasi-independence in that they can be measured by data other than reports to the police (for example, victim surveys, public opinion polls, elections, data from other agencies such as emergency rooms and hospitals, accident and insurance reports, fires, and observations by the media and scholars). But within the organization, there is no independent measure of the salience or meaning of the messages-as-information that exist in files. In the organization, there are four levels or kinds of information:

- *Primary*—data gathered by officers, lodged in reports, arrest records, field stops, and calls for service data (CAD)
- *Secondary*—data processed further by investigators (detectives, special task forces, and so on)
- *Tertiary*—data processed by internal affairs, special units such as hate crimes or domestic violence units, and research and development units within the department
- *Policy-like information*—data organized into abstract categories that are not incident or crime driven (for example, CAD data), but the result of problem-solving activities such as crime analysis meetings (Boston Police Department) or the New York Police Department's COMPSTAT

These kinds of information are roughly aligned by their degree of abstraction. The further the data from primary information, the greater the energy of interpretation required to act on it.

Facts that are originally gathered by officers in the course of patrol, investigation, or records analysis are the result of police *proactive work*. Facts to which officers respond, originating with citizens, alarms, or the media, are the result of police *reactive work*. Policing originated as a mechanism for scanning the environment is still largely reactive and responsive, and is little concerned with victims, crime prevention, intelligence (knowledge gathered in advance of an incident), or policy analysis.

Influences That Shape Information

The term *influences* as used here refers to five social structural features of police organizations. These are contexts, much as the three positions in the PCS are contexts. Police organizations are (1) vertically (by rank) and (2) horizontally differentiated (by ecology or the spatial distribution of functions and personnel), and these both shape information. (3) Police tasks are clustered into routines that make some kinds of facts more relevant than others. (4) Police information is formatted or placed in standardized bureaucratic, numbered forms that sustain its meaning. (5) This information is also encoded and decoded or put into organized functional units or ensembles (such as the codes used to classify computer-assisted dispatches; criminal categories provided by NIBRS or the former UCR; rules and regulations of the organization that outline internal violations and their investigation). Let us discuss these five sources of shaping information.

Police organizations are divided by ranks, a mode of vertical differentiation in police departments that varies from six to twelve or more. To these distinctions are tied prestige, salary, perks of the office, and duties and tasks. It also gives authority to request documents as well as the power to create and demand them. The top command in effect has information about information and where it is located, and can sequester information and refuse to divulge it. This is bureaucratic power. Because the top command can rule on exceptions that arise, it can alter the paper reality.

Police organizations are ecologically disbursed, and in effect the patrol officer is a semi-independent nodule of information processing. Traditionally, the patrol officer is expected to act as a buffer, translator, information channel, and receptacle of information and fact, all the while scanning the environment for information that should be either processed at that time, or processed and passed on subsequently to investigators, internal affairs, juvenile departments, or vice officers. Much remains in the memories of officers and is unwritten. The decisions faced are complex, fateful, and persistent. The patrol role has *decision-making features* displayed repeatedly. These include the centrality of autonomy and discretion with respect to a set of limited functions—those involving encounters with the public (this is in effect an index of organizational power) that are either initiated or occur as a result of a response to a call. The autonomy of the officer, although constrained by tacit standards within the department and organizational reward systems, is manifested in decisions made to intervene, and how to intervene, and with what intended consequence. Because the decisions made are typically "low visibility," and most are unreviewed, the net effect is to empower the officer as a gatekeeper who accesses and sets in motion the criminal law.

Officers' decisions are very consequential in the lives of citizens and in the quality of life of neighborhoods and communities. The initial decision to stop and arrest sets in motion fateful mechanisms producing expense, stress, economic loss, and possible punishment. They are binary: intervene or not; arrest or not; ticket or not; and so forth. Furthermore, when compared with other legal decision making, police decision making is marked by complexity. The less serious the offense, the wider the choice of actions. The conduct subject to policing control varies widely from untoward behavior of great triviality to major violations of the criminal law of the utmost gravity. The perceived gravity or triviality of an act or event will almost certainly have implications for judgments made about whether to enforce or not. This decision, however, is not entirely a binary choice—action or inaction—because the question of how to act is equally important. Police can choose to do nothing, refer to other agencies, give advice, warn, threaten, formally caution, or arrest.

The contingencies, risk, and uncertainty confronted daily must be reduced to manageable proportions, fit standing patterns of behavior in the force, fit the expectations of immediate supervisors, and be carried out with some style. Recall that police work is learned apprentice-like; it is a craft with uncertain contours; styles and tactics vary widely and are accepted as such; and one's personal style, if any, emerges in a dialectic between past experiences such as the services, one's field training officer, and one's current and past partners. This description of the patrol officers' role is a microcosm of the police communication problem more generally. Patrol officers look "up," hoping to avoid trouble and not have things come back to them, while command staff look "down" as well as up and across, hoping to produce compliance and have it reciprocated, and to connect performance expectations, technology, and supervision within organizational context with interorganizational relationships in a chaotic, turbulent external environment. Both of these segments, mediated by the supervisors' role, are concerned with how to create and manage compliance from the public and the external environment and how to sustain the morale and autonomy necessary to mobilize work effort.

The roles and tasks of police, seen as routines, place them somewhere in the information flow stream. As noted earlier, the primary information flow is to and from patrol officers who are at the face or boundary of the organization. The levels of abstraction are critically based on a decision that cannot be made with impunity by any other segment or rank: whether to enter a fact or set of facts into the organization's database.

The last two influences are more syntactical than the others, because they bear on the ways the facts are formatted and interpreted. The first is the *formatting effect,* the forms and requirements for assembling facts. These are the many forms, the paperwork, the electronic and paper files, and their vertical and horizontal ordering. Consider as examples the format of a traffic ticket, with its several fields; the categories used in communications centers to classify messages; the several menus used in the mobile digital terminal in a car; and the highly standardized police report form for reporting an incident. These forms reduce and elevate some types of facts over others; they omit some facts that are not requested; and they enable the incident to be transmitted, filed, recovered, coupled with others, and aggregated and disaggregated statistically. These are the data much favored by criminologists.

The second effect is the *coding effect.* Facts must be sorted in some systematic fashion within an organization to produce lasting organizational memory, guide decisions, reveal contradictions and errors, and otherwise stabilize social relations. Organizations encode facts to make information that is relevant to operations. Thus, the police use a variety of formal and semiformal codes such as the legal code (misdemeanors, felonies, civil violations, violations of housing and other codes), the rules and regulations of the organization, a product of years of responding to threatening errors and omissions in practice, and the union contracts where unions are present.

There are at least three problems with this formulation of the information question in police departments. The first is that the officer is viewed as the fundamental trustworthy source, and "you had to be there" is the cardinal rule of the job (in other words, don't second guess). If the officer does not report it, because the alternative sources of information, citizens, are distrusted, as are police investigators of citizen complaints, then the facticity of what are considered "facts" according to official reporting may be in serious doubt. This is a powerful filter upon what the organization knows and knows that it knows.

The second problem has to do with the influences as described. The fact of different contexts of determining facts means it is very difficult to exercise control via formal information sources alone. The flow of knowledge is asymmetrical (more goes up than down), but the power to determine meaning, reverse decisions, and redefine them lies at the top.

The third problem is that the police are the front end of the criminal justice system and, as such, are a screening and boundary maintaining agency for other agencies. While they receive a wide range of information, they tend not to share it with other organizations; they prize secrecy and primarily communicate with citizens as individuals, insurance companies, the courts, and prosecuting and defense attorneys.

PETER K. MANNING

See also **Administration of Police Agencies, Theories of; Authority within Police Organizations; Discretion; Performance Measurement; Technology and Police Decision Making; Technology and the Police;** *Uniform Crime Reports*

References and Further Reading

Bittner, Egon. 1970. *Functions of the police in modern society*. Washington, DC: National Institute of Mental Health.

Manning, Peter K. 1988. *Symbolic communication*. Cambridge, MA: The MIT Press.

———. 1997. *Police work*. 2nd ed. Prospect Heights, IL: Waveland Press.

———. 2003. *Policing contingencies*. Chicago: University of Chicago Press.

Weick, Karl. 2001. *Making sense of the organization*. Malden, MA: Blackwell.

Willmer, M. A. P. 1970. *Crime and information theory*. Edinburgh: Edinburgh University Press.

INSPECTION

Police departments serve several purposes. These are to protect life and property, prevent crime, detect and arrest offenders, preserve the peace, and enforce the laws. Every function of the agency should be aimed at one or another of these objectives. Deviations are dysfunctional. To achieve these objectives, the agency must compartmentalize itself into the box and function model that typifies the organizational structure. These organizational boxes are created to achieve the prioritized goals.

Functions

Most municipal police agencies basically approach their tasks from a three-pronged perspective:

1. *Attack street crime.* This means organizing the agency to detect and arrest criminals, and to make it more difficult to commit crimes.
2. *Better service.* The great majority of police work involves responding to emergencies, accidents, illnesses, and mishaps. The response mechanism involves 911, single-person patrols, prioritization of calls, and other factors that focus on improving the speed and efficiency of the response.
3. *Traffic safety.* Promoting the safe, speedy flow of traffic requires concentration on engineering, education, and enforcement—the three E's of traffic policy.

A well-organized police department has recognized its mission, prioritized its approach, and organized itself in the most relevant and cost-effective manner. The result should be an organization that understands its objectives and is moving effectively toward their realization. With the mission defined and the objectives established, the question for the chief must be "How well are we doing?" This is where inspection comes in.

Management

Despite the complaints of many executives, there seems little doubt that the true problem in government is not money but management. Under the widening pressures of budgetary constraints, police managers have learned how to get more bang for the taxpayer's buck through inventive cutback management techniques. In a very real sense, the budget crises that attended much of municipal life in the 1970s and 1980s proved a boon to executives who were forced to manage, as opposed to being mere caretakers of, police enterprises.

Management implies making maximum use of the resources available to achieve the organizational aims. The final responsibility for the results lies with the chief. Removed as he or she is from the daily functionings of the agency, how can he or she establish that subordinates adhere to policy faithfully? Tools have to be devised to enable verification that the operating levels are conforming to the program. The size and complexity of the models used to inspect the processes will, of course, depend on the size and complexity of the organization being examined.

Information becomes central to effective functioning. The accuracy of the information is critical to the outcome. Subordinates will be inventive in finding ways to report faithful conformity with procedures.

Control is central to the chief executive's direction of his or her agency, and it will not be effective without essential pieces of information about the actual performance of the organization's members.

Inspection can serve as the helm that steers the vessel through uncharted seas. It enables the captain to make the necessary adjustments.

Inspection will not only establish whether there is compliance and conformity but will also reveal needs and deficiencies that need to be addressed, as well as whether programs that are being faithfully implemented actually work. Thus, it is a very broad management strategy that goes beyond mere verification and assessment of stewardship, important as these factors are.

Control

One of the constants of police administration is nasty surprises. How many chiefs and mayors have awakened to such scandals as narcotics evidence missing from police custody, some egregious brutality complaint that clearly reflects loss of control, collections or other corrupt practices that indicate a climate of wide-open practices, or any of a hundred other problems that communicate a sense of total loss of control over a police agency? Inspections will serve to restrict acts of non-, mal-, and misfeasance to the occasional, specific, and individual—as opposed to the tolerated, systemic, and clearly widespread.

Inspection

Inspection is an examination of persons, places, or things intended to establish whether they are contributing to the achievement of organizational objectives. Performance is evaluated, deficiencies discovered, needs are identified, and corrections suggested. It is a method for monitoring and controlling organizational behavior. It may be defined as an auditor verification.

Procedures

Inspection procedures can be reactive or proactive. The former involves after-the-fact inquiries, examinations, or investigations to establish the when, where, why, how, what, and who of an event, action, program, incident, or procedure. The latter involves cover testing of the process, frequently through replicating situations to establish whether abuses really are occurring.

Inspection is primarily aimed at determining the quality of a commander's stewardship, as opposed to specific inquiries into individual wrongdoing that characterizes the work of internal affairs units (IAUs). It is important that the distinction be understood if organizational confusion is to be avoided. A police officer is accused of police brutality and an investigation is launched. This is typically the work of internal affairs. A command is accused of widespread and systemic use of brutality as an instrument of policy, which is at least tolerated—and perhaps even encouraged—by the commander. This requires an inspection. An officer is charged with a dishonest act and is investigated by internal affairs. Citizens complain of shakedowns, thefts, or extortions by the police, with the commander doing nothing. This falls within the province of inspections.

A precinct commander is accused of falsifying crime statistics to make his or her unit look good. This would fall within the purview of the IAU, but charges that the data are being fudged widely would be examined by inspections. The distinction centers on whether we are examining a specific, individual act or assessing the pervasiveness of a negative condition.

Inspection then becomes the verifying, auditing, and examining arm of the chief executive. It establishes the degree of compliance, detects deviations from policies, and informs the chief as to the operational realities, as opposed to the upbeat reports he or she is certain to be receiving from those charged with the responsibility for carrying out the chief's program.

An inspections unit will determine what the agency's priorities and policies are and then undertake examinations to establish how faithfully they are kept. It will do so through examination of records, the monitoring of performance, the observation of managerial competence, and the verification of findings through such independent

means as polling, replications, and the use of undercover operatives.

Stewardship

Since the function centers on the commander's stewardship, and since modern theories emphasize the importance of managerial autonomy, in order to allow the development of the individual's talent, it becomes more important than ever that a chief executive officer have the tools necessary for the evaluation of progress made by his or her subordinates toward organizational goals. This, of course, makes the clear and explicit enunciation of those goals essential.

A police chief, for example, will typically require that any citizen, appearing at a police installation to report an act of police wrongdoing, be treated courteously and that the complaint be recorded and forwarded for investigation. This is the policy. If the chief asks for a report on the degree of compliance, he or she will inevitably receive a glowing account of how faithfully the requirement is observed. Executives who rely on such indices are in for rude surprises.

A proactive approach will involve the chief executive's replication of the situations he or she wants to verify. Are the troops complying with requirements? Send an agent, posing as an irate citizen, into a police station to ask how to report an incident of police brutality. The treatment of that agent will establish, more accurately than the report, the reality that complaining citizens encounter.

Integrity tests might involve turning valuable property over to a cop on the street to see how he or she handles it. An errant motorist might explore a cop's honesty by hinting at a payoff. The law cannot be broken by those seeking to enforce it. The point is to replicate the circumstances pinpointed as possible sources of problems to establish the true state of things.

Overt and Covert

A solid inspection will operate on two levels, overt and covert. The overt function involves interviews, examination of records, physical inventories, random sampling, polling, and related techniques intended to elicit facts. Covert operations will involve the use of police informers within the ranks to report on actual conditions, as well as self-initiated and proactive integrity tests or checking on adherence to procedures. It might involve as simple a process as making a number of phone calls to establish a commander's accessibility to the public, or willingness to be the target of police shakedowns in order to test a suspicion, which under such controlled conditions would enable the inspectors to verify and record the activities.

A sound organization understands its mission and develops strong programs and sound policies to achieve its goals. It cannot then rest on its laurels and hope all will be faithfully performed. Systems of verification have to be established to ensure adherence to policy, at the street level.

Goals of Inspection

A sound inspection program will identify the effective leaders as well as those who must be weeded out. It will promote the organization's progress by identifying the high performers and pointing them toward higher responsibilities. It will also enable the agency to pinpoint those paying little more than lip service to organizational policies and goals. The importance of this latter point is frequently ignored, because of the desire to avoid negative connotations. The fact is that identifying the losers and winners becomes one of the key features of any system attempting to enhance organizational effectiveness.

A comprehensive inspection program will provide the chief executive with a report that completely describes the operations of the unit examined, thereby enabling the chief to make informed judgments on the levels of performance and to take corrective action or otherwise respond to positive findings. Such an inspection program will also promote organizational introspection—forcing commanders to focus on policy and then to verify how faithfully it is carried out. No commander would want to risk the chief's discovering the problems first.

Conclusion

An organization exists for a purpose. To achieve that purpose, it must organize itself into boxes, assign tasks, and prioritize functions. Once it sets out to produce results, the administration needs to verify how well it is doing. Inspection is the key to this process. The key ingredient of any such process of monitoring and control is the commitment of the chief to the task; the chief executive must believe in the process or it will fail.

ANTHONY V. BOUZA

INTEGRITY IN POLICING

The public expects its police to enforce the law while obeying the law. To be more precise, the police are expected to enforce the criminal code while adhering to certain procedural constraints. But this represents only our minimum threshold requirement. We further expect our police to comport themselves with honesty, fairness, and impartiality; in short, we expect the police to embody our collective notion of justice. We extend this expectation beyond their uniformed life, to include off-duty activity as well. To summarize using a commonly expressed sentiment, we hold police officers to a "higher standard" than we might hold ourselves.

Integrity in policing thus includes not only adherence to procedural law, but in a broader sense, adherence to a set of morals that guide officer decision making. The public presumes that officers have been subjected to a rigorous screening, selection, and training process, and that police agencies are vigilant in monitoring and responding to officer behavior. But because policing is such a visible occupation, involving direct personal contacts with citizens, the presumption of integrity can quickly be destroyed by incidents involving poor officer behavior. The public cannot see integrity within the officer; they see integrity as it manifests in officer behavior—how officers carry out their official duties, including their decision making and subsequent actions. The public experiences officer behavior through direct police–citizen contact, and indirectly through exposure to the experiences of family, friends, and acquaintances, as well as media reports of police misbehavior and portrayals in the entertainment industry.

Police integrity is partly perceptual, and officer behavior has direct consequences for public perceptions. Although police administrators, reformers, and others have long recognized this perceptual component of policing, it wasn't until the United States reached a national crisis of race relations and police legitimacy during the 1960s that public opinion data motivated large-scale change efforts to improve the relationship between the police and the communities served. For example, national surveys cited by the President's Commission on Law Enforcement and the Administration of Justice (1967) provided evidence that while the public as a whole exhibited favorable attitudes toward the police, African Americans consistently gave lower ratings on police effectiveness and conduct. One survey found that while only 9% of the public believed police brutality existed in their community, this overall figure included 35% of African American males. The same survey found that two-thirds of whites believed the police were "almost all honest," but only one-third of African Americans felt so. Ten percent of nonwhites believed the police were "almost all corrupt," compared to less than 2% of whites. Another survey found that 15% of African Americans believed that the police in their communities took bribes, compared to less than 4% of whites. In summarizing these findings, the commission wrote that attitudes toward the police are influenced most by the actions of officers, and that community programs will be ineffective to the extent that citizens—particularly minority citizens—are mistreated during contacts with the police.

The National Advisory Commission on Criminal Justice Standards and Goals (1973) considered these findings in writing Standard 1.2: "Every police chief executive immediately should establish and disseminate to the public and to every agency employee written policy acknowledging that police effectiveness depends upon public approval and acceptance of police authority." Further, police departments should periodically survey the public ". . . to elicit evaluations of police service and to determine the law enforcement needs and expectations of the community." Today, many agencies conduct surveys of the public. In 2000, about one-quarter of the roughly thirteen thousand local police departments in the United States, including more than 60% of those serving populations of one hundred thousand or more residents, surveyed citizens during the prior year (Hickman and Reaves 2003). Eighteen percent of all departments, and more than half of the larger departments, inquired about citizen satisfaction with police services. About two-thirds of agencies provided this information to their officers.

The linkage between officer behavior and public perceptions is demonstrated by recent research showing that incidents of police misconduct substantially influence public opinion about the police. For example, Weitzer (2002) examined public opinion trends in Los Angeles and New York prior to and following several negative incidents. In Los Angeles, these included the 1979 killing of an African American woman, the 1991 Rodney King incident, a 1996 videotaped beating, and the unfolding scandals involving the LAPD's Rampart Division in the late 1990s. A substantial drop in favorable ratings of the police followed each incident. For example, prior to the King incident, the percentage approving of the LAPD's job performance was 80% among Hispanics, 74% among whites, and 64% among blacks. These figures fell to 31%, 41%, and 14%, respectively, following the King incident and eventually returned to preincident levels, although recovery took longer among Hispanics and blacks as compared to whites.

Integrity in policing is thus best conceptualized in terms of two components: police behavior and the public perception of that behavior. Police behavior within a particular neighborhood, throughout cities, and across the states is interpreted and reacted to by the citizens served. The public can view police behavior as being respectful of the awesome and necessary power entrusted to them, or as a violation of that trust. Integrity in policing at any time and place, whether speaking of a specific officer or an entire agency, is strong when actual police behavior is trustworthy and the public perceives police behavior as trustworthy, and weak when either actual police behavior is untrustworthy or the public perceives police behavior as untrustworthy.

Evidence suggests that how the police treat citizens and procedural justice (that is, the extent to which the process police use to arrive at decisions is viewed as fair) are the most important factors influencing public judgments of police legitimacy, which includes elements of trust and confidence in the police (Tyler 1990; Tyler and Huo 2002). Tyler and Huo argue that citizens are in general more likely to cooperate and defer to police authority when the

police are viewed as legitimate, and that citizens will be more likely to accept negative outcomes because they are more focused on fairness in decision making. Their research suggests that the police may be able to influence long-term public perceptions of the police by ensuring fair treatment in citizen contacts.

Citizen allegations of wrongdoing will occur, however, and these events give rise to the timeless question of "Who will police the police?" Integrity in policing depends on the extent and effectiveness with which officer behavior is monitored, and the adequacy of agency responses to integrity lapses. The monitoring of and responses to integrity lapses are tied to the notion of police accountability; simply stated, integrity in policing is diminished where accountability is weak. Here, accountability can be defined in terms of two aspects: (1) whether the behavior that the public views as a violation of trust is acknowledged by the agency and other governing bodies as a violation of public trust; and (2) whether something is being done to correct the problem (that is, to compensate or restore the damage, punish the wrongdoer, and/or punish the agency to ensure the behavior does not continue to occur). Police accountability at any time and place, whether speaking of a specific officer or an entire agency, is strong when the answers to these two questions are in the affirmative and weak when they are not. Here, too, the issues of treatment and procedural justice are important—allegations of wrongdoing must be taken seriously, and processed fairly.

The monitoring of officer behavior can be described in terms of both internal and external processes, with the traditional internal process being an internal affairs unit or its equivalent. Most large agencies have an internal affairs unit, while smaller agencies have designated personnel to handle the internal affairs function on an as-needed basis. External processes include those of other government agencies (for example, city agencies and, more recently, the federal government) as well as citizen-based entities such as civilian complaint review boards (CCRBs) or similar agencies (see Walker 2001).

A growing trend in police monitoring is the development and use of early warning systems (EWSs) to identify negative officer behavior patterns before they develop into more serious problems. EWSs are essentially data management tools in which information about officers is continuously compiled and analyzed, with the goal of averting potential problems. Some EWSs are fairly simple and operate on a "three-strikes" approach; for example, the generation of three citizen complaints in a short period of time triggers a "flag" suggesting that an officer may be having some problems and is in need of assistance. Other EWSs are more sophisticated and take into consideration officer background histories, academy performance, work context, and other factors. EWSs have been around since the late 1970s, when the idea of early warning was focused largely on the use of force, and has expanded into other areas of officer behavior. Recently, EWSs have been recast as early intervention (EI) systems having four key components: performance indicators, a process for identifying officers in need of formal intervention, formal intervention (for example, retraining, counseling), and post-intervention follow-up (Walker 2003).

In sum, integrity in policing is rooted in both police behavior and the public perception of police behavior as trustworthy. Integrity in policing also depends on effective monitoring of officer behavior and the adequacy of responses to integrity lapses. Available evidence suggests that the treatment of citizens, procedural fairness, and attention to public opinion are key issues for agencies committed to the maintenance of integrity in policing.

MATTHEW J. HICKMAN

See also **Abuse of Authority by Police; Accountability; Attitudes toward the Police: Overview; Civilian Review Boards;** **Complaints against Police; Corruption; Early Warning Systems; Ethics and Values in the Context of Community Policing; Risk Management**

References and Further Reading

Hickman, Matthew, and Brian Reaves. 2003. *Local police departments, 2000.* Washington, DC: Bureau of Justice Statistics.

National Advisory Commission on Criminal Justice Standards and Goals. 1973. *Police.* Washington, DC: U.S. Government Printing Office.

President's Commission on Law Enforcement and the Administration of Justice. *Task force report: The police.* Washington, DC: U.S. Government Printing Office.

Tyler, Tom. 1990. *Why people obey the law.* New Haven, CT: Yale University Press.

Tyler, Tom, and Yuen Huo. 2002. *Trust in the law.* New York: Russell Sage Foundation.

Walker, Samuel. 2001. *Police accountability: The role of citizen oversight.* Belmont, CA: Wadsworth.

———. 2003. *Early intervention systems for law enforcement agencies: A planning and management guide.* Washington, DC: Office of Community Oriented Policing Services.

Weitzer, Ronald. 2002. Incidents of police misconduct and public opinion. *Journal of Criminal Justice* 30: 397–408.

INTELLIGENCE GATHERING AND ANALYSIS: IMPACTS ON TERRORISM

In the wake of the September 11, 2001, terrorist attacks, the United States expanded law enforcement and policing powers to fight against international terrorism. The main areas of expansion were in the pursuit of domestic terrorists, drug traffickers, and organized crime. The expanded powers made it easier for police and intelligence agencies to share information that could be used for the possible prosecution of suspected terrorists. Changed policies and laws promoted efforts to collect personal information, religious and political affiliations, and records of finances and travel. Revisions of investigative rules expanded surveillance of oral and electronic communications and legalized a wide variety of undercover operations against suspected terrorist targets. The most controversial innovations allowed law enforcement agencies to arrest suspected terrorists and detain them indefinitely without providing access to counsel or opportunities to seek judicial review. New criminal laws relaxed the definition of terrorism sufficiently enough to potentially reclassify drug trafficking and organized crime as threats to national security. Expansions of criminal involvement also made it possible to pursue fringe members of terrorist organizations without requiring individualized information about whether and how particular defendants promoted the aims of the organization with which they associated.

These expansions of law enforcement powers were not simply a reaction to the 9/11 attacks. They were built on initiatives under way well before 9/11 that targeted organized crime. Starting in the late 1980s and accelerating through the 1990s, many European nations established laws that, for the first time, tried to better control law enforcement powers. These controversial powers included covert policing methods, such as wiretaps, electronic bugs, and the strategic deployment of informants and undercover agents. Like the post-9/11 initiatives against terrorism, these developments arose from a perception that the targeted problem of organized crime transcended national borders, threatened the survival of the democratic state, and resisted more conventional modes of police inquiry. And like the post-9/11 antiterrorism campaigns, Europe's revamping of its covert policing apparatus was designed to facilitate international cooperation, particularly with U.S. law enforcement agencies.

The Bush administration, in reaction to the large-scale 9/11 terrorist attacks, made national security one of the priorities of the government. Securing the United States from additional terrorist attacks had become part of the administration's policy of combating terrorism. The administration's first response was to establish the USA PATRIOT Act, which was modeled after the Foreign Intelligence Surveillance Act (1978). The USA PATRIOT Act stands for "Uniting and Strengthening America by Providing Appropriate Tools Required to Intercept and Obstruct Terrorism." Congress enacted it virtually without significant debate, without detailed committee reports, without a conference committee, and with little floor commentary. Submitted just days after the 9/11 attacks, it was rushed through Congress at lightning speed for a statute of its size and complexity. It passed the House on October 24, 2001, by a vote of 357 to 66, and passed the Senate the next day, October 25, 2002, by a vote of 98 to 1. It was signed into law by President Bush the following day, October 26.

The PATRIOT Act contains more than 150 sections. It is divided into ten separate titles and is hundreds of pages long. The powers it grants to federal investigative agencies and law enforcement agencies are unprecedented and reach everything from voice mail to consumer reports to banking records. The act is among the most wide-ranging laws passed in recent memory, bringing new federal offices into being, creating new crimes, amending at least twelve federal statutes, mandating dozens of new reports, and directly appropriating $2.6 billion, with more funding to come from approval of various "authorizations" of unnamed amounts, scattered throughout the statute.

In the Justice Department, the attorney general issued information-sharing protocols authorized by the PATRIOT Act. These protocols make it clear that the Justice Department will use to the fullest extent the authorities granted to it by the act. Among this information sharing is communication by Justice Department personnel to intelligence personnel within thirty days on whether a criminal investigation will be launched based on a given crime report, if the crime report indicates that foreign intelligence may be involved. Federal investigative task forces have been created under the Justice Department, including identification by the U.S. attorney for each judicial district of members of a terrorist task force, which can be quickly assembled from local federal agency personnel when the need arises. Also, there are several ongoing cross-agency task forces to investigate terrorism or terrorist financing.

The PATRIOT Act has given not only new authorities but also a new hubris to federal investigative agencies. Its emphases on information collection, information sharing, expanded definitions, new regulations, cross-agency cooperation, wider authorities, enhanced surveillance techniques, swifter prosecutions, and more severe sentences have brought law enforcement and terrorism investigation in America to new levels.

The entire PATRIOT Act is designed for increased surveillance, information gathering, and investigation of terrorism with a minimum of judicial review. Under the PATRIOT Act, mostly under Title II, investigators can obtain information ranging from consumer reports, certain telephone data, certain details from Internet service providers, educational records, and banking transactions, all without a court order. All that is required is a certification by a federal investigator that the information is necessary or required for a particular investigation, which does not even reach the standard of probable cause that is required with ordinary search and seizure warrants. There is no opportunity for judicial review of these information-gathering activities because, in general, the information obtained is obtained in secret and the act provides that the person or entity providing the information is immune from civil liability. The act's establishment of single-jurisdiction search warrants and national service of search warrants effectively means that federal investigators only have to stop by one federal district court to obtain a search warrant for a particular investigation. Investigators will not be required to further justify their information request and continue to meet search warrant standards in any other federal court even if the investigation goes into other jurisdictions. This is "one-stop shopping" for federal search warrants and essentially takes the federal courts out of the loop.

The information sharing mandated chiefly by Titles II and IX is conducted by and large without any judicial review. In those limited instances where judicial review might be involved, such review is limited to specific challenges and those challenges can be delayed at the request of the government.

"Special measures," which under Title III can be imposed by federal investigators on domestic banks and other financial institutions, are completely unprecedented in the history of federal banking regulation and represent a total rewrite of banking law. Yet these "special measures" can be submitted to banks by investigators once various required "certifications" are made by the Treasury Department, without any condition for a court order or court review.

Title IV of the PATRIOT Act identifies three types of terrorist organizations: "Section 219" designations of terrorist groups borrowed from existing immigration law, terrorist groups identified by the government under a similar procedure but with fewer requirements and no express judicial review, and a wide-ranging category of any group of two persons or more "whether organized or not" that engages in any of the broadly defined list of "terrorist activities." The act therefore gives federal investigators or agencies tremendously wide latitude in designating terrorist groups. It must be noted that the definitions of "terrorism" and "domestic terrorism" and "foreign intelligence" do not exclude the potential involvement of American citizens, so investigations, surveillance, and prosecution are not restricted to aliens.

The mandatory detention of aliens under Title IV allows for habeas corpus review. The only review allowed by an alien in indefinite detention is a request for administrative review of the detention every six months. This provision does not rely on judicial oversight to review the detention. There is limited judicial oversight of many other act provisions such as forfeiture provisions, long-arm jurisdiction, and reduced or eliminated statutes of limitations. Although these provisions may be seen as giving federal courts more power, in actuality the power is being given to federal prosecutors and investigators, who continue to drive federal criminal investigations and prosecutions.

The PATRIOT Act provisions for information sharing, grants and funding, and cross-agency training and cooperation, as well as the "fellow PATRIOT Acts" passed by state legislatures, have given state and local governmental law enforcement units a new emphasis and a new influence. Now, the county sheriff or local municipal law enforcement unit may be involved in a terrorism investigation, can search for "foreign intelligence," and can watch out for "domestic terrorism." The professionalism of these organizations can sometimes be called into question, not to mention their lack of experience in these types of investigations.

No one can argue that the PATRIOT Act has not given federal agencies and law enforcement agencies new powers, which can be used to gather and analyze information on a potential terrorist threat. But the real question is this: Have the provisions of the USA PATRIOT Act helped analysts and law enforcement agencies uncover and prosecute that threat?

In the first two years after 9/11, federal investigators and law enforcement agencies recommended the prosecution of more than 6,400 individuals who the government believed committed terrorist acts or who became targets on the grounds that charging them with some crime would "prevent or disrupt potential or actual terrorist threats." Based on these recommendations, as of September 30, 2003, the government had in one way or another processed 2,681 individuals who had been the subject of the recommended prosecutions. Analysis of the case-by-case data obtained by the Transactional Records Access Clearinghouse (TRAC), revealed the following data. Of the 6,400 individuals recommended for prosecution, 1,802 individual cases were closed without conviction; 879 were convicted of a terrorist-related offense. Of the 879 convictions, only 5 individuals were sentenced for more than twenty years; 23 were sentenced to five to twenty years; and 373 were sentenced to one day up to five years in prison. There were still 642 cases pending trial at the time of the report on December 8, 2003. Unfortunately, the Bush administration began withholding information that the government had previously released to TRAC. As a result it is no longer possible to determine exact numbers of individuals who the investigative agencies recommended be prosecuted.

However, TRAC's analysis of Justice Department data estimates that from September 11, 2001, to September 30, 2003, the total number of such "referrals" involved more than 6,400 individuals. However, the two years' worth of collected data are more than sufficient to show an overwhelming increase in the number of arrests and convictions by the federal agencies and law enforcement agencies.

Whatever the case, the absolute number of terrorism and antiterrorism situations that have been recorded by assistant U.S. attorneys around the country in the two years after the 9/11 attacks is sobering. As a result of the 9/11 attacks, the Justice Department added a number of new crime categories to its internal record-keeping system, tracking actions that in its view are in some way related to terrorism. Most prominent among the new groupings is what it now calls "Anti-Terrorism." This area, according to the department's data manual, covers immigration, identity theft, drugs, and other such cases brought by prosecutors that were intended to prevent or disrupt potential or actual terrorist threats. Even if we were to set aside the antiterrorism matters referred to prosecutors by investigative agencies during the two-year period, more than half, approximately 3,500, were cases that were classified as involving actual acts of terrorism from one of the following categories: financial terrorism (added after 9/11), international terrorism, or domestic terrorism.

Without question, the events of 9/11 resulted in a dramatic escalation in the government's enforcement activities in the terrorism area. Justice Department referrals for prosecution received during the two years prior to September 30, 2001, when compared to two years after 9/11, show the following: Both terrorism and antiterrorism experienced a sixfold increase in cases that were referred to prosecutors, from 594 such actions before to 3,555 after. There was an eightfold jump in convictions, 110 to 879. Some of this growth is naturally the result of the addition of "Anti-Terrorism" as a new category to be tracked under terrorism after the terrorist attacks of 9/11. When antiterrorism was put aside, the increase in the terrorism cases that were prosecuted or declined was less dramatic, from 544 to 1,778. Convictions grew by three and a half times: from 96 prior to 9/11 to 341 after. Surprisingly, despite the three-and-a-half-fold increase in terrorism convictions, the numbers who were sentenced to five years or more in prison has not grown at all from pre-9/11 levels. In fact, the number actually declined, dropping from 24 individuals whose cases began before the attacks to 16 after. What has jumped are the numbers of individuals convicted but sentenced to little or no prison time.

When looking at international terrorism, only investigative referrals that were either prosecuted or declined increased five times, jumping from 142 individuals before the 9/11 attacks to 748 after. The climb in convictions was even sharper, jumping over seven and a half times, from 24 to 184. Once again, despite the *increase* in convictions, the number who received sentences of five or more years declined from 6 individuals in the two years before 9/11 to only 3 in the two years after. Out of the 184 convictions under international terrorism, 80 received no prison time, and 91 received sentences of less than a year. Although not all cases following the two years after 9/11 have been completed, current data suggest that terrorism investigations, prosecutions, and convictions all were sharply higher after 9/11, but the actual number of individuals who were sentenced to five or more years in prison has fallen.

The intelligence community in the United States has a very disorganized and often questionable history. The entities that make up this community still bicker among themselves as to who has the authority to perform what action and who should share information with whom. Unfortunately, unless all intelligence-gathering and analysis functions were to be moved under one agency and all of the subagencies disbanded, true cooperation and communication across the entire community will never be achieved. One can only hope that with the events of 9/11 the intelligence community as a whole has realized that the status quo is not working and something needs to change. Local law enforcement should never be asked to take over the functions of the intelligence community. Most of the day-to-day operations of the intelligence community can and should remain classified to law enforcement personnel, but, by allowing this massive group of officers to develop some working knowledge of intelligence gathering prior to the next terrorist event, a resource will be ready and willing to assist the intelligence community in any way that it can.

KATHLEEN M. SWEET

See also **Accountability; PATRIOT Acts I and II; Terrorism: Overview**

References and Further Reading

Criminal terrorism enforcement since the 9/11/01 attacks. 2003. TRAC Special Report, December 8. 2003. http://trac.syr.edu/tracreports/terrorism/report031208.html (accessed October 11, 2005).

FBI and law enforcement. 2004. http://www.cfrterrorism.org/security/law.html (accessed October 10, 2005).

Foreign intelligence surveillance act of 1978. 2005. http://en.wikipedia.org/wiki/Foreign_Intelligence_Surveillance_Act (accessed October 10).

Impact of terrorism on state law enforcement. 2005. http://www.law.uiuc.edu/conferences/policing/ (accessed October 9).

USA PATRIOT act. 2005. http://en.wikipedia.org/wiki/USA_PATRIOT_Act (accessed October 10).

INTELLIGENCE-LED POLICING AND ORGANIZATIONAL LEARNING

Intelligence-led policing (ILP) has become a top priority among policy makers and police officials. Law enforcement agencies have always been engaged to some extent in using intelligence to identify and respond to criminal threats. However, recent changes in the political, technological, and cultural contexts in which policing organizations must operate have presented some major challenges as agencies attempt to adapt to the growing demand for intelligence gathering, analysis, and dissemination. The purpose of this article is to describe the issues police organizations face as they attempt to respond to changes in their working environment brought on by the increasing focus on intelligence.

A discussion of the political context surrounding the increasing emphasis on ILP begins with the aftermath of the terrorist attacks of September 11, 2001. The legislation enacted shortly after the attacks is significant because it called for rapid changes in the way police work was to be carried out, especially with regard to the collection and management of intelligence.

The USA PATRIOT Act of 2001 was the first major piece of legislation passed by Congress after 9/11. The legislation mandated that the war on terrorism be fought at all levels of government, meaning that all police organizations at the federal, state, and local levels now had a role in combating terrorism. Section 218 of the act is significant because it called for the removal of the barrier between law enforcement and intelligence investigations.

The "tearing down of the wall" between law enforcement and intelligence was designed to promote greater cooperation and information sharing among governmental entities. Further clarification about the nature of information to be used in support of antiterrorist intelligence was necessary, and it was provided by the Homeland Security Act of 2002. This legislation established the Office of Homeland Security to oversee the new mandate of collecting and sharing law enforcement intelligence for the purposes of preventing future domestic attacks. The Office of Homeland Security is interested in any information possessed by a federal, state, or local agency that (1) relates to the threat of terrorist activity; (2) relates to the ability to prevent, interdict, or disrupt terrorist activity; and (3) improves the identification or investigation of a suspected terrorist organization.

The Intelligence Reform and Terrorism Prevention Act (2004) established a national intelligence program that creates and prioritizes the tasks of collection, analysis, production, and dissemination of intelligence information. Section 1016 explains how this goal will be attained through an *information sharing environment* (ISE). The ISE is designed to (1) create an information sharing environment in a manner consistent with national security and applicable legal standards relating to privacy and civil liberties; (2) designate the operational and management structures that will be used to operate and manage the ISE; and (3) determine and enforce the policies, directives, and rules that will govern the content and usage of the ISE (The Intelligence Reform and Terrorism Prevention Act 2004).

As of 2006 the intelligence community (IC) included fifteen executive branch agencies and organizations that conduct intelligence activities for purposes related to foreign relations and national security (http://www.intelligence.com). Those agencies include the intelligence elements of the Army, Navy, Marine Corps, and Air Force; the Central Intelligence Agency; the Defense Intelligence Agency; the Department of Homeland Security; the Department of Energy; the Federal Bureau of Investigation; the National Geospatial-Intelligence Agency; the National Reconnaissance Office; the National Security Agency; the Department of Treasury; the Department of State; and the Coast Guard. Indeed, the list of old agencies and the creation of new federal agencies enlisted to fight the war on terrorism is expansive. These agencies, which historically had separate missions and lacked the capacity for coordination and collaboration, are now being mandated to work with each other. Moreover, they are now required to work with state and local law enforcement agencies in the pursuit of criminal enterprises that support terrorists.

The legislation following 9/11 advanced three important law enforcement priorities that have implications for ILP and organizational learning. The first priority is that prevention should be a primary goal. The second is that information sharing should become a standard practice. The third is that the intelligence cycle should be more clearly defined. In the sections that follow, we describe each priority and discuss how each impacts the relationship between ILP and organizational learning.

The Philosophical Shift to Crime Prevention

One of the most important changes in law enforcement since 9/11 is that the FBI has shifted focus and procedure from prosecution to prevention—from collecting information after a crime has been committed to preventing terrorist attacks from taking place (Etzioni 2004). Further, although the IC website does not specifically include local law enforcement agencies in its partner list, it is apparent that since local police will be first responders to a domestic terrorist act, and given the link between terrorist activity and local crime (for instance, organizations engaged in drug trafficking to sponsor international crimes), local police agencies are considered to be instrumental in the development of intelligence (Loyka et al. 2005). Major efforts have been under way to link the intelligence efforts of federal and local law enforcement agencies (see reports by Loyka et al. 2005; Carter 2004).

Local law enforcement agencies were already dealing with a shift from a reactive to a proactive community-based approach to dealing with crime that was dependent on intelligence. This is evident in Maguire's observation of police rhetoric that emerged in the United Kingdom during the 1990s, but can also be said of U.S. law enforcement. Maguire (2000) observed that many agencies claim to be ". . . implementing a 'community safety strategy'; to be practicing 'proactive', 'intelligence-led', 'targeted' or 'problem oriented' policing; and to be committed to 'partnership' and 'information sharing'" (p. 316). He further claims that what is common to these policing efforts is "a strategic, future oriented and targeted approach to crime control that focuses on the identification, analysis and management of persistent and developing problems or risks (which may be people, activities or areas) rather than on the reactive investigation and detection of individual crimes" (p. 316).

In these policing environments, homeland security threats become an additional problem for the police to manage. In fact, Carter (2004) argues that community policing has already infused important skills, such as problem solving, environmental scanning, public communication and mobilization, and fear reduction, that are directly transferable to the intelligence-led approach. The challenge is to apply these skills to focus on the identification and disruption of criminal enterprises and organizations that support terrorist activities.

Information Sharing as a Standard Practice

The expansion of formal practices governing the sharing of information among criminal justice agencies has become a priority since 9/11. Large-scale information sharing has required a major paradigm shift in criminal justice organizations. Information sharing is inseparable from an organization's formal and informal structures and its culture (Stojkovic, Kalinich, and Klofas 2003). Outdated security procedures and traditions that evolved during the Cold War have become detrimental to security concerns in the post–Cold War world. Law and tradition previously required a "need to know" before reluctant investigators could share information (9/11 Commission 2004). "Although there was some capacity to share information, the law was complex and as a result, agents often erred on the side of caution [and] refrained from sharing the information" (Baginski 2005, 3). This labyrinth of complex rules and laws created a wall that discouraged investigators from sharing information about cases (9/11 Commission 2004).

The 9/11 terrorist attacks changed the belief that withholding information enhanced security. An organizational social environment is now being established that encourages the sharing of information. Laws are being promulgated and passed that enable, encourage, or mandate the proper movement of relevant information, and give a level of comfort to individuals in organizations who were reluctant to share information. The post-9/11 world requires that the old paradigm be replaced by an information sharing environment that emphasizes a decentralized network model that protects information through an "information rights management" approach and controls access to data, not access to the whole network (Intelligence Reform and Terrorism Prevention Act 2004).

Sections 203 and 218 of the USA PATRIOT Act specifically concern the authority to share criminal investigative information and foreign intelligence information, respectively. Sections 203(b) and 203(d) allow law enforcement officials to disclose electronic, wire, oral, and/or foreign intelligence information to federal officials when the information involves knowledge concerning the national defense or security of the United States. The USA PATRIOT Act explicitly authorizes intelligence sharing in this circumstance. It is likely that this was done to counter any reluctance to share such information based on past vagaries of the law or organizational culture.

Defining the Intelligence Process

The anticipated value of intelligence is that it helps to identify a threat, determines how likely it is to occur, and recommends a response. Efforts are currently under way to develop a shared understanding of definitions and procedures involving the development and use of intelligence in law enforcement. In a recent report, intelligence is defined "as the analysis, evaluation, interpretation and sharing of information" (Loyka, Faggiani, and Karchmer 2005, 1). In this same report intelligence is distinguished from information. Information is translated into intelligence through organization, analysis, and interpretation. Issues to be considered in this process involve identifying the information to be collected, deciding how it will be analyzed and by whom, determining what information must be shared and what must remain confidential, and managing how information on individuals is to be collected and shared without violating their rights.

While establishing standards to guide the intelligence process is a useful endeavor, there appears to be much more attention given to describing how the process should work than understanding how it actually does work. Sheptycki (2004) identifies the "organizational pathologies" agencies must strive to overcome in order to realize the potential benefits of ILP. In general, these pathologies represent the conflicts associated with requiring and incorporating new ways of working into agencies with long-standing traditions that are often resistant to change. In particular, they reflect attempts to create new priorities for information management and analysis, redefining the value of information in a way that promotes sharing, and the introduction of new intelligence-focused occupational roles into existing bureaucracies.

Information Management and Analysis

The goal of intelligence analysis is to create timely and useful information in an efficient and effective manner. Sheptycki (2004) identifies several issues that complicate this effort. The first involves the impact of new computer technology. During the past few decades, significant and rapid advances in information technologies have been made available to police departments for information management and analysis. In the United States this effort was spearheaded by the Crime Bill of 1994, which allocated a significant amount of money to improve information technology in law enforcement agencies.

The effort to improve technology, however, took place with little guidance about how systems should be designed and used. Because of the lack of technology planning, many software and hardware vendors developed and marketed crime reporting systems without an understanding of the nature of police work and with little input from police organizations. As a result, many police officers were reluctant to embrace new technology and, compounded with a pronounced lack of training and support, merely viewed it as a burdensome administrative tool rather than an opportunity to develop new ways of managing information that would serve a community-based or ILP approach.

As agencies are increasingly presented with a variety of information technologies for information management and analysis, the need for planning and coordination becomes paramount. Without it, agencies may be inefficient where using multiple databases for tracking information results in entering the same data into more than one system, and ineffective where systems are unable to electronically communicate both within and across agencies.

A lack of analytic capacity in the area of administrative support is also evident across police agencies. Often the result is what Sheptycki (2004) refers to as "intelligence overload." He argues that capacity is often taken up in data input and investigative analysis. This is exacerbated not only by the multiple recordings of data on multiple systems at multiple levels, but also by the increasing demand for more surveillance and more data rather than better data or better data analysis when problems are identified. Moreover, given that agencies focus data collection and analysis on issues that are already a priority, lesser known problems may go undetected.

Redefining the Value of Information

As agencies attempt to develop intelligence-led environments, they must deal with shifts in the value of information in ways that promote knowledge management and sharing in this context. A move in this direction directly challenges traditional ways of collecting, using, and sharing information often embedded in police culture. First, Sheptycki (2004) argues that the value of information is directly related to decisions about recording and dissemination. Analysts are often removed from decisions about recording information from police field work. The larger this gap, the greater the capacity for "noise" in the intelligence process because of inefficiency in the collection of data relevant to the analysts tasks.

The second relates to intelligence hoarding. The 9/11 attacks graphically highlighted the need to quickly and efficiently exchange information between law enforcement agencies and emergency personnel. Unfortunately, deeply imbedded bureaucratic tendencies and informal policies do not change easily. Often, the organizational knee-jerk reaction to share information is reluctance. This reaction often serves the needs of individuals within a given organization as well as the needs of the organization itself.

In ILP, the value of information lies in its capacity to identify a threat for the purpose of prevention and sharing. This is in contrast to the information hoarding that has traditionally characterized the enforcement-oriented police subculture (Sheptycki 2004). In this traditional subculture, having information that leads to an arrest is a measure of professional success and can advance a career. This is a major incentive to hold onto information.

In many law enforcement agencies, information has historically tended to flow in a vertical direction, moving through the levels of command in the policing hierarchy. Agencies are much less equipped to share information horizontally across agencies, which is essential to the intelligence sharing function. The result is what Sheptycki (2004) refers to as "linkage blindness." This is particularly problematic when crime series span across territorial boundaries. Duplication of effort is a similarly situated issue and arises when criminal activity is of interest to more than one agency. Duplication fosters the development of information silos with the resulting intelligence sharing process resembling the spokes of a wheel rather than a complex web of interagency and intra-agency connections that promote information sharing horizontally as well as vertically.

Introduction of New Occupational Roles

To accommodate the growing demands of the intelligence-based model, new occupational roles have been introduced to police agencies. Typical job titles include "intelligence analyst" or "crime analyst." According to Carter (2004, 110), "the intelligence analyst is a professional who collects various facts and documents circumstances, evidence and interviews, and other material related to a crime and places them in a logical related framework to develop criminal cases, explain a criminal phenomenon, or describe crime and crime trends." Very often these positions are filled with civilians or even former clerical staff.

Long-serving police personnel may have difficulties adapting traditional ways of thinking to the new intelligence-based approach and/or the associated occupational roles. Sheptycki (2004) argues that conflicts emerge because of the imbalance in status and prestige of occupational roles. He claims that since the detective role is embedded in police culture and is much more prestigious, crime analysts often get usurped of basic investigative tasks. The result is that crime and intelligence analysts are often underutilized and undervalued (Cope 2004). Chan (2001) further suggests that the increase in funding and staffing of technology-related functions can lead to bitterness and envy among officers.

Not only must agencies deal with the changes in work processes and meanings brought on by the shift to ILP, they must do so in a rapidly changing technological environment. Advances in computer technology will undoubtedly play a major role in the success of ILP to identify and prevent crime and terrorist threats. An example of a local law enforcement model that uses computer technology is the COMPSTAT model. COMPSTAT is a comprehensive system for managing police operations, a model where patrol commanders are held accountable for all problems and issues in their reporting areas. Carter (2004) argues that the COMPSTAT model is in many ways comparable to the ILP model. They are both prevention oriented, data driven, and stress accountability.

A brief discussion of the use of COMPSTAT in promoting accountability and problem solving can inform the challenges ILP models will likely face. Crime analysis supports COMPSTAT and involves a data-driven approach to identify and study crime problems that relies on advanced information technologies such as geographic information systems. Policing scholars, while recognizing the capacity of information technologies to disrupt and realign power in police organizations, find that advances have not resulted in greater police effectiveness (Manning 2001, 2005).

Chan (2001, 145) describes three technological frames for understanding IT and organizations: (1) the nature of technology, which involves an understanding of the potential of IT; (2) technology strategy, which is individuals' views of why technology was introduced to their organization; and (3) technology in use, which is an understanding of how technology is to be routinely used. Conflict is likely when inconsistent frames exist within an organization.

Evidence suggests that conflict exists in law enforcement agencies with regard to technology and crime analysis because (1) training for crime analysts is lacking, which limits the understanding of the potential of IT; (2) crime analysis is not commonly used to examine crime problems in depth, which is why crime analytic IT was introduced into the organization; and (3) traditional enforcement responses are often used, such as increased surveillance,

when problems are identified (National Academy of Sciences 2004).

Although many law enforcement agencies were already moving in directions compatible with ILP at the time of 9/11 and subsequent legislation, there are additional aspects of the legislation that are in contrast with a community-based approach to policing. As agencies continue to shift from a reactive approach to crime, collecting information after a crime has been committed, to preventing terrorist acts from taking place, the net may widen concerning persons of interest. What this means is that there will be many people interrogated, including those not suspected of anything, in efforts to thwart terrorist plots that authorities believe might involve members of that group (Etzioni 2004). Moreover, to the extent that information on these persons and groups is gathered and entered into intelligence databases, questions of privacy and civil rights violations come into focus. These problems may lead to a backlash against community policing as many residents of minority communities claim to be victims of racial profiling.

There is a hopeful expectation that "more" and "better" intelligence generated by police agencies will aid in the identification of criminal threats that threaten the safety of citizens. Considerable federal, state, and local resources are being devoted to a large-scale shift toward the ILP paradigm in the form of training, information technology improvements, and administrative support and oversight. Before we can determine the success with which ILP has met expectations, there must first be an understanding of how police organizations have adjusted to the growing demand for intelligence gathering, analysis, and dissemination. As organizations face political, cultural, and technical challenges to the traditional models of police work, change and learning in the ILP environment will be visible, but how it will be reflected in the rationalization of policing will likely evolve at a slow and discontinuous pace.

APRIL PATTAVINA and ERIC BELLONE

See also **Accountability; Administration of Police Agencies, Theories of; Community-Oriented Policing: Practices; COMPSTAT; Future of Policing in the United States; Homeland Security and Law Enforcement; Intelligence Gathering and Analysis: Impacts on Terrorism; Problem-Oriented Policing; Terrorism: Police Functions Associated with**

References and Further Reading

Baginski, Maureen A. 2005. *Statement of Maureen A. Baginski executive assistant director-intelligence Federal Bureau of Investigation before the Subcommittee on Crime, Terrorism, and Homeland Security House Committee on the Judiciary*. 108th Congress 2005. Testimony of Maureen A. Baginski. http://www.fbi.gov/congress/congress05/baginski041905.htm.

Carter, David. 2004. *Law enforcement intelligence: A guide for state, local, and tribal law enforcement agencies*. Washington, DC: U.S. Department of Justice.

Chan, J. B. L. 2001. The technology game: How information technology is transforming police practice. *Criminal Justice* 1 (2): 139–59.

Cope, Nina. 2004. Intelligence-led policing or policing-led intelligence? *British Journal of Criminology* 44: 188–203.

Etzioni, Amitai. 2004. *How patriotic is the Patriot Act?* New York: Routledge.

Homeland Security Act of 2002 (H. Res. 5005 107th Congress). http://www.dhs.gov/interweb/assetlibrary/hr_5005_enr.pdf.

Intelligence Community Website. http://www.intelligence.com

Intelligence Reform and Terrorism Prevention Act of 2004 (S. Res. 2845 108th Congress). http://thomas.loc.gov/cgi-bin/query/F?c108:2:./temp/~c108wCpO42:e0:2004.

Loyka, S. A., D. A. Faggiani, and C. Karchmer. 2005. Protecting your community from terrorism: Strategies for local law enforcement. In *The production and sharing of intelligence*. Vol 4. Washington, DC: Police Executive Research Forum.

Maguire, Mike. 2000. Policing by risks and targets: Some dimensions and implications of intelligence-led crime control. *Policing and Society* 9: 315–36.

Manning, P. K. 2001. Technology's ways: Information technology, crime analysis and the rationalization of policing. *Criminal Justice* 1: 83–103.

———. 2005. Environment, technology and organizational change: Notes from the police world. In *Information technology and the criminal justice system*, ed. April Pattavina, 221–35. Thousand Oaks, CA: Sage.

National Academy of Sciences. 2004. Fairness and effectiveness in policing: The evidence. Washington, DC: National Academy of Sciences.

9/11 Commission. 2004. *Final report of the National Commission on the Terrorist Attacks upon the United States*. New York: W. W. Norton.

Sheptycki, J. 2004. Organizational pathologies in police intelligence systems: Some contributions to the lexicon of intelligence-led policing. *European Journal of Criminology* 1 (3): 307–32.

Stojkovic, S., D. Kalinich, and J. Klofas. 2003. *Criminal justice organizations: administration and management*. 3rd ed. Belmont, CA: Wadsworth-Thomson.

USA PATRIOT Act of 2001 (H. Res. 3162 107th Congress). http://thomas.loc.gov/cgi-bin/bdquery/z?d107:H.R.3162:2001.

Violent Crime Control and Law Enforcement Act of 1994 (H. Res. 3355 103rd Congress). http://thomas.loc.gov/cgi-bin/query/z?c103:H.R.3355.ENR:.

INTERNATIONAL ASSOCIATION OF CHIEFS OF POLICE (IACP)

The International Association of Chiefs of Police (IACP) was founded in 1893. Headquartered in Alexandria, Virginia, as of 2006 the organization had more than 20,000 members and 130 staff members. The IACP has more than thirty-five standing committees. The committees cover the wide array of issues and topics local law enforcement executives face, including terrorism, crime prevention, organized crime, and environmental crimes. The association is also represented by three divisions—the State and Provincial Police Division, the International Policing Division, and the State Associations of Chiefs of Police—and sixteen sections, including

Police Psychological Services and Public Transit Policing sections.

The association's goals are to advance the science and art of police services; to develop and disseminate improved administrative, technical, and operational practices and promote their use in police work; to foster police cooperation and the exchange of information and experience among police administrators throughout the world; to bring about recruitment and training in the police profession of qualified persons; and to encourage adherence of all police officers to high professional standards of performance and conduct.

Since 1893, the International Association of Chiefs of Police has been serving the needs of the law enforcement community in a variety of capacities. Throughout those past one-hundred-plus years, the IACP has launched historically acclaimed programs, conducted groundbreaking research, and provided innovative and exemplary programs and services to the policing community across the globe.

The IACP has been instrumental in advancing the policing profession and serving as a voice for law enforcement leadership over the course of its history. Professionally recognized programs such as the FBI Identification Division and the *Uniform Crime Reports* (UCR) system trace their origins back to the IACP. In addition, the IACP and the FBI in 1934 established the FBI National Academy for state and local police, and the association began publication of the *Police Chiefs Newsletter,* the forerunner of *Police Chief* magazine. In the 1940s, the IACP's wartime mobilization plans provided guidelines for police executives for handling planned disorders, sabotage, and the movement of troops and material in truck convoys. In the 1950s and 1960s, the association developed minimum training standards for all law enforcement officers—a major development at the time—and urged them on state governments. In the 1970s, the IACP established a national bomb data center. In the 1980s, the IACP

opened its first world regional division in Europe. Subsequently, the IACP has established world regional offices in North America, South America, Europe, Africa, and Asia. Today, the IACP conducts international policing executive seminars across the globe. During this time, the IACP and the Bureau of Justice Assistance established a National Law Enforcement Policy Center. The IACP also helped establish the Commission on Accreditation for Law Enforcement Agencies (CALEA).

In the 1990s, IACP efforts focused attention on international narcotics trafficking, drunk driving, police use of force, civil disorder, and criminal aliens. A priority for the association during this period was assisting departments in implementing community policing in their jurisdictions. The IACP also expanded its legislative agenda as its influence on legislation at the federal, state, and local levels grew. More recently, since the terrorist attacks of September 11, 2001, the IACP has worked with its members to develop a series of initiatives, including reports and publications, on the role of local law enforcement in the nation's efforts to address homeland security and domestic preparedness demands.

JERRY NEEDLE and ANDREW MORABITO

See also **Professionalism; Research and Development**

Reference and Further Reading

International Association of Chiefs of Police website. http://www.theiacp.org.

INTERNATIONAL POLICE COOPERATION

The intensity of international law enforcement cooperation has greatly accelerated in recent years, although some forms of police cooperation among independent states are as old as professional police forces. Throughout modern European history, there have been contacts and networks among police authorities across international borders. Before 1914, these were essentially concerned with "high policing"—in other words, state security. They also dealt with "low policing," mainly fugitives, itinerant criminals, pirates, bandits, and smugglers.

The need for police cooperation has greatly increased with economic and social change. Indeed, virtually all the factors that, in the nineteenth and twentieth centuries, were associated with the growing prosperity of the highly developed countries—urbanization, rapid transport, improved communications, the development and integration of international markets—contributed to the growth of international criminality, both petty and sophisticated. These factors assisted the mobility of criminals, the transportation of illegal substances, and the organization of complex conspiracies, and also provided new opportunities for theft, fraud, and the disposal of the profits of crime. Certain conditions also allow the growth of international criminality, such as the lack of stable political authority and social dislocation.

The types of cooperation introduced to combat the increasing problems posed by transborder or international criminality can be classified as bilateral, global, and regional. The modes of cooperation are formalized liaison, coordination institutions, and probate or unofficial investigation. The obstacles to cooperation are the diversity of police systems and of legal systems, the doctrine of sovereignty, deeply held beliefs about political independence and the sacredness of state territory, and the divergence of national interests.

Bilateral Cooperation

This is the oldest and remains, in some respects, the most important type of police cooperation. Although often based on informal understandings, bilateral police treaties first appeared in the nineteenth century and have become increasingly common in the last twenty-five years. These seldom give an accurate impression of the significance and the value of this cooperation. The scope of the agreements, as the model agreement prepared by INTERPOL in 1975 illustrates, is potentially very wide. They can cover the exchange of general police information concerning matters such as traffic accidents, missing or stolen property, the exchange of crime prevention information about the operating methods of criminals, people in need of protection, the surveillance of suspects, and the reporting of the transport of dangerous substances.

Cooperation in criminal investigations can consist of the exchange of information or evidence, exchange of police investigation records, police officers on mission, and hot pursuit of offenders across international borders. Agreements can also include the naming of police authorities competent to engage in transborder cooperation, the location and frequency of international meetings, methods of communication between the cooperating police forces, the role of the National Central Bureaus of INTERPOL, requests to enter the territory of another state, regulations concerning the use of vehicles and the carrying of firearms, and civil liabilities of police in foreign countries. In practice, police treaties or agreements never include all of these items. Agreements may also take the form of semiconfidential protocols or the exchange of letters of understanding. One type of agreement is virtually universal among neighboring friendly countries—the arrangements for policing land frontiers. Recently in Europe, these have been developed to include joint police stations, which can be important points of contact and coordination.

Another form of police cooperation is the exchange or the posting of police liaison officers in foreign countries. After World War II, the United States pioneered the practice of having law enforcement officers as embassy attachés. The large number of federal law enforcement agencies led to a proliferation of police officers on overseas postings: Members of the FBI, the DEA (Drug Enforcement Administration), U.S. Customs, the Internal Revenue Service, the Secret Service, and the Immigration and Naturalization Service can be found in some key embassies. This law enforcement presence is sometimes a sensitive political matter in host countries; the entrepreneurial style of activities of some U.S. law enforcement officials can be viewed as constituting an infringement of sovereignty.

The FBI, under J. Edgar Hoover, was the first to establish overseas representation in the aftermath of World War II through *legats* (legal attachés) in major embassies for the purposes of counterintelligence and in the fight against international organized crime, including terrorism. The DEA, which has maintained up to sixty permanent offices in forty-three countries, has more personnel overseas than does the FBI. The DEA and its supporters believe that intelligence gathering, in source and transit countries, reduces the importation of drugs into the United States. The more flamboyant Latin American operations of the DEA have included the arrest of drug traffickers in foreign jurisdictions and bringing them to the United States for trial, and joint operations with police and military in Latin American countries to destroy drug crops. The other two federal agencies, U.S. Customs and the Secret Service, prominently involved in international affairs have much less extensive overseas presence.

The practice of police liaison officers in foreign postings has spread from the United States to countries as far apart as Canada, Japan, and Israel. In Europe, the French Technical Service for International Police Cooperation (the SCTIP) has, since the 1960s, developed an impressive international network for advising on police techniques, equipment, and training. In 1971 the Franco-American agreement on arrangements to combat the "French connection" (the flow of Turkish opium, which is refined into heroin in the Marseilles area for onward shipment to the United States) included the exchange of liaison officers, and in 1986 it was extended to include Canada and Italy. In the 1980s drug liaison officers were also sent out from various European countries to drug producing and transit countries. Since the mid-1980s, liaison officers specializing in terrorism have been exchanged among France, Italy, and Germany. The number of liaison officers has subsequently grown, and increasingly they have become generalists rather than specialists.

The liaison officer system has advantages because it allows direct personal contact among law enforcement officers in different countries. This can expedite investigations, particularly by putting investigating officers in touch with the right authorities in the cooperating country. The good liaison officer can be a valuable resource in helping to clear up misunderstandings, and provide information about a foreign jurisdiction and its criminal investigation policies. Sending police officers on a temporary mission for particular inquiries or missions is not usually regarded as an adequate substitute for liaison officers, because often the former cannot acquire sufficient information about the country in a short time.

Global Cooperation

INTERPOL is the key agency for global law enforcement cooperation, but the United Nations, the Customs Cooperation Council, the G8 (Group of the world's most highly industrialized nations), and the Organization for Economic Co-operation and Development also play important, if intermittent, roles in promoting cooperation. INTERPOL provides a system of multilateral communication of police information; it helps coordinate inquiries and its secretary general can initiate them.

The origins of INTERPOL are curious and its international status uncertain—some observers feel that the lack of a treaty basis for the organization detracts from its authority and legitimacy. But the organization is now almost universally accepted as an intergovernmental organization and has received important support from the United States. It has radically upgraded its computer and communications equipment, become more open with the media, dropped its practice of noninvolvement in terrorist cases, and has generally become more adaptable in the face of changing patterns of international crime. Although its reputation varies in the law enforcement community over time and according to region of the world, it is an indispensable communications system and an important link between national police forces.

The United Nations plays an essential supportive role in international law enforcement—as a forum in which international treaties can be negotiated (on subjects such as trafficking in people, crime prevention, and human rights), a repository for statistical and legal information about criminal matters, and provider of aid to improve the capacity for criminal law enforcement in less developed countries. Its biggest influence on practical law enforcement has been in the field of drug trafficking. The work of the United Nations' Division of Narcotic Drugs (UNDND), established shortly after the founding of the UN, has since January 1992 amalgamated with other antidrug activities of the UN International Drug Control Program (UNIDCP) and promoted four basic conventions: the 1961 *Convention on Narcotic Drugs*, the 1971 *Convention on Psychotropic Drugs*, the 1988 *Vienna Convention* (mainly concerned with law enforcement measures), and the 1999 *Convention on Organized Crime*.

The harmonization of efforts in drug law enforcement and the repression of financial crime has been supported by the action of the Group of Eight (now known as G8, an organization of the most highly developed countries that holds periodic meetings), through measures against money laundering, including the setting up of a Financial Action Task Force (FATF) in the Organization for Economic Co-Operation and Development (OECD) and encouraging the setting up of national financial intelligence units. These latter members of an international network known as the Egmont Group, act as clearinghouses for information and are national points of contact.

Regional Cooperation

In the Americas there is much law enforcement interaction on a multilateral basis through the regional meetings of INTERPOL, the International Drug Enforcement Conference, the Organization of American States, and the International Association of Chiefs of Police, but very little of this directly involves police operations. Operational cooperation is almost entirely on a bilateral basis, and most of it is initiated by the United States. Apart from interesting developments within the Association of South East Asian Nations, this applies also to other continents. The exception is Western Europe, where there have been moves toward institutionalized forms of law enforcement cooperation during the last two decades.

The most intensive regional cooperation is now taking place in the European Union. This started with the Trevi Group—the regular meeting of the Ministries of Justice and the Interior of the EC countries set up in 1975 to coordinate measures against terrorism but whose remit was widened to include other forms of serious crime, and exchanges about police techniques, training, and equipment. The 1991 Maastricht Treaty gave a legal basis to Europol, specifically to developments in the fields of coordination of investigation and search procedures; the creation of databases; the analysis of criminal intelligence on a Europe-wide basis; joint crime prevention strategies; and measures relating to further training, research, forensic matters, and criminal records departments. Europol, based in The Hague, became fully operational in 1996.

The two Schengen Agreements (1985 and 1990) "compensate" for the abolition of border checks on goods and persons between EU member states, and contain measures for operational police cooperation. All members of the European Union are members of Schengen, although Britain, Ireland, and Denmark have partial opt-outs. The Schengen system provides the instruments that are needed for policing the external frontiers (that is, frontiers with non-EU countries) and for quick responses to any law enforcement problem between member countries. The first objective is to be achieved mainly by means of an online database, the Schengen Information System (SIS now SIS II), containing information such as wanted persons or persons in need of protection, prohibited immigrants, and stolen or suspected vehicles. The second objective is sought through an emergency operations system called the SIRENE. In SIRENE, national offices review requests for immediate operational action, which a check on the legality of the action requested and forward it to the appropriate police authority.

The EU law enforcement agenda moved on decisively under the influence of two developments. First, in 1999 the EU adopted the Tampere program, which envisaged development of more integrated operational police cooperation in order to confront shared law enforcement problems. Second, the terrorist events of September 11, 2001, in the United States gave a political impetus to this program and resulted in the European Arrest Warrant (which replaces the cumbersome extradition proceedings), cross-border freezing of assets, rapid procedures for the transfer of evidence, joint investigation teams, better cooperation between prosecution services, upgrading of Europol's anti-terrorist unit, and enhanced cooperation with U.S. law enforcement agencies.

Problems and Prospects of Cooperation

Formal arrangements, such as the bilateral exchange of liaison officers, INTERPOL and Europol, are indispensable instruments, but their effectiveness depends on political willingness to cooperate and to release information. They usually have a modest operational role. INTERPOL has such a role through its communications network and its work in criminal intelligence analysis. Europol has an enhanced role in these fields as well as coordinating transborder inquiries involving two or more EU member states. But there remains a reluctance to hand over executive police powers to international institutions. Informal cooperation has often gone further than cooperation through formal channels. The methods of the private investigator—going into foreign jurisdictions without legal authority, but often with the cooperation of the foreign authorities to investigate suspects and criminal acts—are occasionally an essential element of the investigation of complex cases. These activities risk crossing the boundary into illegality and creating political tensions among states.

In general, the obstacles to international cooperation are legal, organizational, and operational. The classic, long-standing legal difficulty is the delay, expense, and technicalities involved in extraditing persons and evidence from one jurisdiction to another. In principle, this should no longer happen between the countries of the EU with the adoption of the European Arrest Warrant. Other formidable obstacles to close cooperation, however, do exist. Joint or coordinated operations performed by police forces of different countries are often made very difficult by different police powers, different police–judiciary relations, and different criminal procedures. What are called joint operations are often national inquiries with the advice and support of police officers from another jurisdiction.

Difficulties also occur because police forces are organized in very different ways in different countries. This makes it difficult for police officials to understand the professional ethos of foreign forces and their modus operandi when they come into contact. When direct relations are established in frontier regions, for example, it is frequently difficult to find equivalent officials in the respective police forces who can efficiently liaise with one another. The different relationship between police and political authorities also creates difficulties. When police officers know or suspect that their opposing counterparts are controlled too tightly by politicians or too inclined to take instruction from them, cooperation is likely to be withheld. Practical reasons for operational difficulties in cooperation include lack of efficient communications' equipment or a mutually comprehensible language, less commitment in pursuing an enquiry on the one side rather than the other, and the absence of a common policy in investigating particular forms of crime. None of these legal, organizational, and operational difficulties is insuperable. They are well known and taken into account throughout the developed world.

MALCOLM ANDERSON

See also **International Association of Chiefs of Police (IACP); International Police Missions; INTERPOL and International Police Intelligence; Terrorism: International**

References and Further Reading

Anderson, Malcolm. 1989. *Policing the world: Interpol and the politics of international police co-operation.* Oxford: Clarendon Press.

Anderson, Malcolm, and Joanna Apap, eds. 2002. *Police and justice co-operation and the new European borders.* The Hague: Kluwer Law International.

Bayley, David H. 1985. *Patterns of policing: A comparative international analysis.* New Brunswick, NJ: Rutgers University Press.

Deflem, Mathieu. 2002. *Policing world society: Historical foundations of international police.* Oxford: Oxford University Press.

McDonald, William F., ed. *Crime and law enforcement in the global village.* Cincinnati, OH: Academy of Criminal Justice Sciences, Anderson Publishing Company.

Nadelmann, Ethan A. 1993. *Cops across borders: The internationalization of U.S. criminal law enforcement.* University Park: Pennsylvania State University Press.

Santiago, Michael. 2000. *Europol and police co-operation in Europe.* Lampeter: Edwin Mellon Press.

INTERNATIONAL POLICE MISSIONS

International police missions (IPMs) can be defined broadly as involving any situation in which the police of one or more countries are sent to another country or region to perform police duties; or more narrowly as transnational police operations, which are conducted under the mandate of a regional (such as the Organization for Security and Cooperation in Europe [OSCE]) or international organization (for example, the League of Nations or the United Nations).

The practice of police from one country working in another has a long history and has occurred in various forms and for various reasons. The first documented international missions are probably the European police contingents sent to establish law and order in Crete from 1897 to 1908, and the Dutch police sent to the new nation of Albania, just liberated from Ottoman rule, in 1913–1914 to help establish a police force. During the 1920s and 1930s, the United States dispatched Marines and military police to help establish constabulary forces (armed police units) in Central American and Caribbean countries. After the cessation of fighting in World War II, the United States sought to establish new policing systems based on American models in Japan and in the American occupation zone in Germany. (The French, British, and Russians did the same in their respective occupation zones—rebuilding the German police after their own practices.) More recently, the United States has been quite active—as have most European and developed countries—seeking to influence reforms of policing systems in developing and transitional (former socialist) countries by sending training teams and advisers across the world, in the 1960s and 1970s under the auspices of the Office of Public Safety (OPS), and after the late 1980s under the organizational umbrella of the International Criminal Investigative Training and Assistance Program (ICITAP).

More recently, regional organizations have conducted IPMs in states wracked by conflicts, political instability, or civil wars or in response to massive humanitarian crises. For example, in recent years, the OSCE police mission to Serbia has been the lead agency in helping reform the former communist policing system; the European Union has taken over police mission activities from the UN in Bosnia, and, as part of preparation for new member states to the EU (ten new members joined in 2005), has sent assessment and assistance teams and police advisers to potential accession countries to bring their policing (and criminal justice) systems up to European standards. ECOWAS, the Economic Community of West African States, has taken the lead role in sending military and police to control the violence that has subverted the political stability of Liberia and Sierra Leone. The Australian government in 2004 sent its police (with a sprinkling of police from other countries) to the Solomon Islands to control disorder and crime and familiarize the local police with democratic norms and practices.

The most important and frequent IPMs, though, have taken place under the authority and mandate of international organizations. The League of Nations, during its brief existence after World War I, authorized a number of missions that included police components, such as the mission to Saarland, then disputed territory between France and Germany.

Since 1948, the United Nations has authorized fifty-nine peacekeeping missions, some of which have lasted (as in Cypress) for more than forty years. Peacekeeping missions have increased in frequency over the years as violent hot spots—ranging from the complete breakdown of states and their ability to provide any domestic security, to civil strife, insurrections, rebellions and civil wars, to genocide—have erupted across the globe. Since the late 1980s, peacekeeping missions have typically incorporated a civilian police (CIVPOL) component. The first UN mission to do so was the UN operation in the Congo from 1960 to 1965, during which Ghanaian and Nigerian police contingents assisted the Congolese police. In October 2005, thirteen IPMs involving about six thousand police officers were operating under a UN mandate.

The doctrine of how to conduct and end peacekeeping missions has evolved over time. The first goal, still, is to stop the fighting and bloodshed that led to the initial peacekeeping intervention by the global community and then, as order is imposed, begin a transition to civilian rule. Institutionally, that implies a shift from military forces, to semimilitary ones (*gendarmes*) to regular police; and ideologically the mission shifts from peacekeeping to peacebuilding, a process in which the police must play a crucial role. As the need for military forces declines, formal social control will increasingly shift to the police and a supporting criminal justice system. The sequencing and speed of the transition from peacekeeping to peacebuilding has no clear answer as yet. It has become conventional wisdom, though, that policing systems cannot be established or transformed while massive insecurity, violence, and chaos continue, which can only be suppressed by military force or community self-help.

The UN has sought to create a more effective capacity for deploying CIVPOL, which, starting in 2006, were called UN police. A small seconded police force has been established that is prepositioned and is under UN command. Programs to help countries prepare their police, as part of their formal training, for international missions have gained a foothold among many European nations; discussions are under way, in the United States and the United Nations, on how to create a police "stability force" ready to be deployed if called on by the UN. The mandate of CIVPOL has expanded over time, from establishing, monitoring, advising, and training local police to, beginning with Kosovo and East Timor in the late 1990s, doing actual law enforcement, or executive policing. That trend is likely to continue.

Issues

A number of issues have plagued UN efforts to conduct peacebuilding. The most obvious is that the UN has no police officers, but depends on member countries to be willing to contribute their police to a police mission. The unit in the UN, the Civilian Police Unit in the Department of Peace-Keeping Operations (DPKO), which supervises and organizes the police component once a mission has been authorized by the Security Council, goes hat in hand to different countries and begs for police officers. CIVPOL officers are well paid, about $100,000 annually, including incentives. It has not been difficult to attract police officers from developing countries since their pay as CIVPOL is many times their annual salaries back home.

The most difficult to deal with has been the United States—the hegemonic security actor on the global scene—since it does not have a national police force. The UN approaches the U.S. delegation to the UN, which sends the request to the Department of State, which, if the White House signs off, forwards it to the Department of Justice, which delegates recruiting international police to one of its subunits (ICITAP), which then hires a private contractor (almost always the Dyne Corporation) to find, select, train briefly, deploy, and supervise the required number of police officers. The United States is the only country in which the police who are sent on UN policing missions are not employed by the government but by a private company, a practice that raises important questions about the quality of officers recruited and their training, and the accountability of "private" police (though labeled "American" police) to the U.S. government, local communities, and the UN.

A second issue is the varying quality of police received by the UN. The minimum qualifications stated by the UN are five years of service as a police officer, twenty-five to fifty years of age, and ability to speak English and drive a four-wheel-drive vehicle. Many officers from some countries do not even meet these minimum qualifications and often work in policing systems in which respect for the rule of law and protection of human rights has not been integrated into police thinking and work.

In addition, police come imbued with the knowledge and practices of their own countries but are expected to follow common UN guidelines when they work. Generally police contingents include police from many countries, and in each mission they are commanded by a high-ranking police officer from one country. For example, the police mission in Cambodia (UNTAC) from early 1992 to late 1993 deployed 3,359 police officers from thirty-two countries, and was commanded by a police officer from the Netherlands, with the second in command being from Bangladesh. This causes some obvious problems of communication, coordination, and consistency of style of policing. The result is that UN policing has no specific quality to it but depends on the leadership abilities of the head of the police mission and the creativity of police who do the work in completely unfamiliar cultural and political environments. Because UN police typically work unarmed, concerns for their own safety add to the difficulties of how to work together and with their communities.

A third issue relates to accountability, or the lack thereof. A few UN police have been implicated in criminal activities (rapes, participation in prostitution rings, robberies and thefts, and cooperating with organized crime groups to smuggle goods and people). In general, UN police are not subject to the laws of the location in which they work. The punishment, if found to be corrupt, abusive, or criminal, is to be sent home; it is up to the home police organization to impose such sanctions as it sees fit. Because accountability is one of the main characteristics of a democratic policing force, the creation of which is the nominal goal of intervention and assistance, the perceived impunity of UN police for their conduct does not reinforce the message promoted by the rhetoric of reform.

CIVPOL have been stopgap measures to bridge the gap between civil strife and democratic stability. They are deployed only as long as their international mandate lasts and do not leave until local police are capable of policing on their own. Because international mandates tend to be short and it is well known that establishing effective and humane police forces takes time, the general assessment of CIVPOL and their performance and impact is that, at best, they will buy some time, but probably not enough, to help a country move from disorder to stability and democratic governance.

OTWIN MARENIN

See also **Accountability; International Police Cooperation**

References and Further Reading

Chappell, Duncan, and John Evans. 1997. *The role, preparation and performance of civilian police in United Nations peacekeeping operations.* Vancouver, Canada: The International Centre for Criminal Law Reform and Criminal Justice Policy, University of British Columbia.

Doyle, Michael W. 1995. *UN peacekeeping in Cambodia: UNTAC's civil mandate.* International Peace Academy Occasional Paper Series. Boulder, CO: Lynne Rienner Publishers.

Dwan, Renata, ed. 2002. *Executive policing. Enforcing the law in peace operations.* SIPRI Research Report No. 16. Oxford: Oxford University Press.

Hansen, Annika. 2002. *From Congo to Kosovo: Civilian police in peace operations.* Adelphi Paper No. 343. London: International Institute for Strategic Studies.

Holm, Tor Tanke, and Espen Barth Eide, eds. 2000. *Peacebuilding and police reform.* London: Frank Cass.

Marenin, Otwin. 2005. *Restoring policing systems in conflict torn nations: Process, problems, prospects.* Occasional Paper No. 7. Geneva: Geneva Centre for the Democratic Control of Armed Forces. http://www.dcaf.ch.

Mobekk, Eirin. 2003. *Law-enforcement; creating and maintaining a police service in a post-conflict society: Problems and pitfalls.* Occasional Paper. Geneva: Geneva Centre for the Democratic Control of Armed Forces. http://www.dcaf.ch.

Oakley, Robert B., Michael J. Dziedzic, and E. M. Goldberg, eds. *Policing the new world disorder: Peace operations and public security.* Washington, DC: National Defense University Press.

Peake, Gordon. 2004. *Policing the peace: Police reform experiences in Kosovo, Southern Serbia and Macedonia.* London: Saferworld.

Perito, Robert. 2004. *Where is the Lone Ranger when we need him? America's search for a post-conflict stability force.* Washington, DC: U.S. Institute of Peace Press.

Schmidl, Erwin R. 1998. *Police in peace operations.* Informationen zur Sicherheitspolitik, Nummer 10. September. Vienna: Landesverteidigungsakademie.

Tschirgi, Neclâ. 2004. *Post-conflict peacebuilding revisited: Achievements, limitations, challenges.* New York: International Peace Academy.

United Nations general note: There are numerous UN publications on each UN-mandated peacekeeping mission, as well as summations of past missions, such as the series *The blue helmets. A review of United Nations peace-keeping*. (The last, the third edition was issued in 1996); or training manuals, such as United Nations, 2000, *Principles and guidelines for United Nations civilian police*, August 11, New York: United Nations, Department of Peacekeeping Operations, Civilian Police Unit; or United Nations, 1994, *United Nations criminal justice standards for peace-keeping police*, Handbook prepared by the Crime Prevention and Criminal Justice Branch. Vienna: United Nations Office at Vienna.

Washington Office on Latin America. 1995. *Demilitarizing public order. The international community, police reform and human rights in Central America and Haiti*. Washington, DC: Washington Office on Latin America.

INTERNATIONAL POLICING

International policing refers to police practices that involve citizens or jurisdictions of more than one nation. *Police* is hereby defined as the institution associated with crime control and order maintenance as it has been legitimated in the context of nation-states. Justified by an increasing internationalization of criminal activities, international police operations have gradually expanded, with historical roots tracing back to at least the nineteenth-century formation of national states. In the contemporary era, concerns over illegal immigration, the international drug trade, and international terrorism have greatly impacted the scope of international policing.

At least three forms of international policing can be distinguished. First, certain societal developments that extend beyond the boundaries of individual nation-states affect police organizations and practices across nations supranationally. The influences of political and economic modernization, most notably, bring about important reorganizations of policing, for instance, in the context of the spread of capitalism and the development of democratization. Second, police institutions cross the boundaries of their respective nations by means of transnational operations. Transnational policing involves police actions oriented at foreign citizens within the police organization's own jurisdiction or investigative and intelligence work initiated against nationals and foreigners located abroad. Third, international police cooperation involves various types of collaboration among the police institutions of different countries to form bilateral or multilateral unions and cooperative agreements of temporary or more permanent duration. The functions of such cooperative measures can include investigative enforcement tasks, such as joint operations to track down international fugitives from justice, as well as international assistance in the methods and organization of police work, such as the importation and exportation of police technique.

In the context of industrialized nations, important historical changes can be observed in the forms of international policing as they began to develop from the nineteenth century onward. First of all, the goals of international policing transformed from political objectives to distinctly criminal enforcement tasks. The earliest nineteenth-century efforts to organize international police work, especially on the European continent, involved distinctly political objectives to counteract the popular opposition against conservative governments. In 1851, for example, the Police Union of German States was formed among the police of seven sovereign states, including Prussia and Austria, to gather intelligence on social democrats, anarchists, and other politically suspect groups and individuals. The Police Union organized regular meetings among the heads of participating police and instituted systems of international information exchange. Because of the union's political objectives, however, cooperation was limited in international scope to several German-language states, and the union eventually dissolved in 1866 when war broke out between Prussia and Austria.

During the latter half of the nineteenth century, police institutions gradually underwent a process of bureaucratization whereby police began to develop expertise in terms of the proper means of police investigation as well as with respect to the enforcement tasks that were conceived on the basis of expert systems of knowledge concerning crime and its internationalization. International police work therefore gradually moved away from the political dictates of the governments of national states toward the adoption of enforcement tasks of a distinctly criminal nature. Under conditions of increased police bureaucratization across industrialized nations, criminal enforcement tasks could be shared among the police of various national states to become the basis of expanded international cooperation. Toward the latter half of the nineteenth century, police institutions thus moved away from the policing of politics toward the policing of international crimes such as the international organization of prostitution and the rendition of international fugitives from justice.

A second important historical development in international policing involved a move from transnational police measures and limited international cooperation plans instigated for a specific purpose toward the establishment of international cooperation on a permanent and multilateral basis. Throughout much of the nineteenth century, most international police activities were either transnational in kind, originating from one country to another, or involved cooperation that was limited in international scope to the participation of the police of only a few nations, initiated only for a specific purpose, and ended after completion of the operation. Toward the turn of the century, however, more and more attempts were made to establish an international police organization as a permanent structure and with wide multilateral participation. At first, most of these efforts failed because they did not take into account achieved levels of police bureaucratization. In 1898, for instance, the government of Italy tried to foster international police cooperation to fight international anarchism, a political type of violation police organizations across different nations no longer agreed on to collaborate. In 1914, the government of Monaco initiated the First International Criminal Police Congress, which was restricted to the fight against criminal violations, but which was attended only by legal and political officials and failed to attract any participation from police officials.

The first efforts to organize international police cooperation on the basis of achieved levels of police bureaucratization took place in the 1920s. In 1922, the New York City Police Department established the International Police Conference with the express purpose of fostering police cooperation on a wide international scale. Yet, this effort remained largely ineffective because systems of technology in the areas of communication and transportation were at the time insufficiently developed for there to be any truly international criminal concerns that involved the United States. The geographical proximity of a multitude of nations in Europe, conversely, led to the formation of a successful international police cooperation effort when the International Criminal Police Commission was formed in Vienna in 1923. The commission established a central headquarters and various systems of international information exchange, such as printed bulletins, a radio communications network, and regularly held meetings. The commission gradually expanded its international membership and even survived the turmoil of the Second World War, during which period its headquarters were taken over by the Nazi regime. Reformed in 1946 as the International Criminal Police Organization, the organization still exists today, better known as INTERPOL, and now counts member agencies from 184 countries.

Throughout the history of international policing until today, a persistence of nationality can be observed in at least three ways. First, police organizations prefer to work unilaterally without cooperation from a foreign police force. As such, transnational police operations remain the most preferred form of international policing activities, especially among those police organizations that have sufficient means to undertake international activities alone. Second, most police cooperation efforts are limited in international scope and initiated on the basis of a specific need. Rather than relying on formal membership in a broad multilateral organization, police prefer to work out arrangements pragmatically with one another on the basis of specific needs. Third, whenever police engage in international cooperation through an organization with relatively extensive international membership, the form under which cooperation takes place is collaborative and does not involve the formation of a supranational police force. Instead, exchange and communications among the police organizations of different nations take place through a central headquarters, personal meetings, technologically advanced systems of information exchange, and other agreed-on efficient methods of collaboration.

The conditions that facilitate international policing activities include societal developments in the internationalization of crime as well as organizational and technical changes in policing. With respect to the internationalization of crime, an expansion of the opportunities to engage in criminal activities is often the explicit basis on which international police actions take place. Thus, the international organization of the political opposition in the nineteenth century and the international dimensions of various types of criminal conduct from the latter half of the nineteenth century onward influenced police organizations to adopt strategies that likewise were international in nature. In more recent times, international crimes propelling international policing include such diverse activities as international fugitives from justice, the international drug trade, international trafficking in illegal goods, smuggling, illegal immigration, and cyber crimes. Most important in the present era has been the proliferation of security concerns surrounding international terrorism.

Certain aspects in the development and organization of policing are also responsible for the internationalization of the police function. Especially relevant in this context are technological changes in the areas of communication and transportation as well as criminal identification methods. Among the relevant communications technologies that have historically increased international police work are telegraph, telephone, radio, and the Internet, whereas relevant transportation technologies include railways, automobiles, and aircraft. Ironically, these very same technologies also contributed to the internationalization of crime to which police organizations respond. Additionally, police can rely on advances in criminal identification technologies, ranging from fingerprinting in the late nineteenth century to DNA analysis today. These techniques are shared among police in different nations and thus facilitate international police cooperation through the exchange of information.

In the modern context, it is important to observe that police agencies from the United States are disproportionately more involved in international policing activities than police from any other nation. U.S. participation in international policing is primarily dictated by concerns over the international drug trade, illegal immigration and border control, and international terrorism. Unlike the insularity that marked U.S. police work until the earlier half of the twentieth century, police organizations from the United States, especially those at the federal level, have a very significant international presence. The most preferred method of international policing among U.S. agencies is unilaterally instigated transnational police work. The Federal Bureau of Investigation (FBI) and the Drug Enforcement Administration (DEA), most notably, each oversee hundreds of agents who are permanently stationed abroad through a system of so-called legal attachés. FBI agents, for instance, are stationed in more than fifty countries in all continents of the world. The FBI also oversees international police training programs at the FBI National Academy in Quantico, Virginia, and the International Law Enforcement Academy in Budapest, Hungary. Similarly, the Operations Division of the DEA organizes international activities through its Office of International Operations, involving an extensive system of legal attachés, border-related activities, and international training programs. U.S. police assistance programs organized by the Department of State have also been implemented during peacekeeping missions and in postwar situations, such as in Haiti, Kosovo, and Iraq.

The extent to which U.S. law enforcement has been involved in international police actions has led to an Americanization of police practices in foreign nations. At the same time, however, other nations have also been developing relatively autonomous systems of international policing in terms of the specific needs of their local and regional concerns. Most clearly, the member nations of the European Union have established a new European Police Office (Europol) with headquarters in The Hague, The Netherlands. The establishment of Europol was first specified in 1992 in the Treaty on the European Union. In 1995, a Europol convention was drawn up that went into force in 1998, and a year later Europol's headquarters opened. Europol's range of activities includes the fight against all serious forms of international crime, such as drug trafficking and terrorism, that affect two or more member states of the European Union. Like other similar international police organizations, Europol is not a supranational police force, but a coordinating mechanism among designated police organizations in the various member states of the European Union.

Since the terrorist events of September 11, 2001, in the United States, international terrorism has become the central catalyst of international policing activities. The events of 9/11 have in the first instance brought about an expansion and strengthening of police powers within nations as well as on an international scale. In the United States, the PATRIOT (Providing Appropriate Tools Required to Intercept and Obstruct Terrorism) Act of 2001 has broadened police powers especially toward foreign suspects and terrorist organizations. The police attention toward international terrorism amplifies the centrality of U.S. agencies in international policing activities, but U.S. law enforcement is not alone in its counterterrorism investigations. In many nations across the world, police powers oriented at suppressing terrorist groups have also expanded greatly. At the level of international police organizations, likewise, counterterrorism has become a key concern. INTERPOL and Europol, in particular, have expanded their respective programs and strategies against international terrorism.

Interestingly, many of the current counterterrorist police strategies have been developed irrespective of legal and political concerns, but have been based on professional expert conceptions of the policing of terrorism. Police organizations typically depoliticize international terrorism to conceive of it as a crime that has repercussions beyond the borders of national states. Since 9/11, many governments have again attempted to exert control over their respective nation's police and intelligence forces to bring counterterrorism measures in line with national security issues, but long-standing developments in the bureaucratization of a global police culture can often withstand these political pressures so that international policing operations, even in the ideologically sensitive area of terrorism, remain planned and executed on the basis of the professional standards of police expertise.

MATHIEU DEFLEM

See also **Drug Enforcement Administration (DEA); Federal Bureau of Investigation; Future of International Policing; International Police Cooperation; International Police Missions; INTERPOL and International Police Intelligence; Terrorism: International**

References and Further Reading

Anderson, Malcolm, and Monica den Boer, eds. 1994. *Policing across national boundaries*. London; New York: Pinter Publishers.

Deflem, Mathieu. 2001. International police cooperation in Northern America: A review of practices, strategies, and goals in the United States, Mexico, and Canada. In *International police cooperation: A world perspective*, ed. Daniel J. Koenig and Dilip K. Das, 71–98. Lanham, MD: Lexington Books.

———. 2002. *Policing world society: Historical foundations of international police cooperation*. New York: Oxford University Press.

———. 2004a. The boundaries of international cooperation: Problems and prospects of U.S.–Mexican police relations. In *Police corruption: Challenges for developed countries—comparative issues and commissions of inquiry*, ed. Menachem Amir and Stanley Einstein, 93–122. Huntsville, TX: Office of International Criminal Justice.

———. 2004b. Social control and the policing of terrorism: Foundations for a sociology of counter-terrorism. *The American Sociologist* 35: 75–92.

Deflem, Mathieu, and Lindsay C. Maybin. 2005. Interpol and the policing of international terrorism: Developments and dynamics since September 11. In *Terrorism: Research, readings, & realities*, ed. Lynne L. Snowden and Bradley C. Whitsel, 175–91. Upper Saddle River, NJ: Pearson/Prentice-Hall.

Liang, Hsi-Heuy. 1992. *The rise of the modern police and the European state system*. New York: Cambridge University Press.

Marenin, Otwin, ed. 1996. *Policing change, changing police: International perspectives*. New York: Garland Press.

McDonald, William F., ed. 1997. *Crime and law enforcement in the global village*. Cincinnati, OH: Anderson Publishing Company.

Nadelmann, Ethan A. 1993. *Cops across borders: The internationalization of U.S. criminal law enforcement*. University Park: Pennsylvania State University Press.

INTERPOL AND INTERNATIONAL POLICE INTELLIGENCE

Competition: The Historical Conflict within Police Work

Cooperation among the police has not always been as straightforward as might be thought. In policing, cooperation appears to be a learned behavior conditioned by many factors, among which are the historical traditions and rivalries of police agencies and their officers. The history of cooperation between police agencies, either within or across countries, has been complicated by many factors as well. For example, when the Stadtguardia and the Military Police had to work together in Vienna in the beginning of the fifteenth century, overt conflict often existed between the two forces, which hindered the development of cooperative arrangements. It seemed that the only way to gain cooperation was to eliminate one of the protagonists. Ultimately the emperor of Austria had to abolish the Stadtguardia altogether, favoring the Military Police as the preferred state institution for providing security in cities and towns throughout Austria. Such historical examples of police agency conflict can be found in practically every modern country in the world, and they persist to this day.

Competition among police agencies continues to be a regular part of police work, in part because agencies are evaluated on the strength of their own and not others' accomplishments. Such competition highlights the need for continued development of these agencies within their own countries, as well as highlighting the necessity of an expanded framework in order for there to be international police cooperation.

This expanded framework of cooperation is becoming increasingly more important today as the new age of crime becomes more and more international, especially in regard to the phenomena of international terrorism, organized crime, and drug trafficking. The internationalization of crime and of the consequences of crime focus the question of how police agencies worldwide will cooperate, not compete. This is the subject of this article.

INTERPOL

In April 1914, Prince Albert I of Monaco convened an international conference of police and other criminal justice officials. At this meeting, the members formulated the preliminary design for an international police organization and resolved to meet again in two years to implement this design. Two months later, on June 28, 1914, a twenty-one-year-old Serbian, Gavrilo Prinzip, who was watching a military procession in Sarajevo, fired three shots from a Browning pistol, killing Archduke Franz Ferdinand of Austria and his wife (Fooner 1989, 8). This event ignited World War I. Five years after the end of World War I, in September 1923, INTERPOL, or the International Criminal Police Commission (the name of which was changed later to International Criminal Police Organization), came into existence.

Dr. Johann Schober, the head, or police president, of Vienna's police service, played a key role in assembling the conference that culminated in the establishment of INTERPOL. Schober not only served as police president but also acted as Austria's chancellor from 1921 to 1922. Schober and his colleagues performed what has to be rated as an astonishing feat: Within five days, they put together a functional international organization, a permanent body with a constitution, officers, a headquarters, and operational procedures. Police chiefs from twenty countries met in Vienna, without authority or instructions from their governments, and formed the organization that today bears the name INTERPOL. Article 2 of INTERPOL's Constitution establishes the organization's aims as follows:

> To ensure and promote the widest possible mutual assistance between all criminal police authorities within the limits of the laws existing in the different countries and in the spirit of the "Universal Declaration of Human Rights"; and To establish and develop all institutions likely to contribute effectively To the prevention and suppression of ordinary law crimes. (INTERPOL Constitution and General Regulations, http://www.interpol.int)

In the 1920s and 1930s, INTERPOL refined its multinational police cooperation system at a time when counterfeiting was a major international crime problem. During the mid-1980s, INTERPOL adapted its multinational cooperation system to address international terrorism. In recent decades, international terrorists have taken in the whole world as their field of operation, whereas police and law enforcement systems belong to particular nations and thus are confined within the borders of their respective countries.

INTERPOL was founded and developed for the pragmatic purposes of stopping international criminals and preventing international crimes. To accomplish these tasks, INTERPOL seeks to improve international police cooperation. This requires INTERPOL to remain politically neutral; in fact, its constitution requires that before INTERPOL can become involved in an investigation or provide information there must be overlapping interest in the crime(s) among member countries. INTERPOL also does not focus on "political crime" so as to maintain its respect for member state sovereignty. Today its work is focused on terrorism, organized crime, trafficking in humans, drugs, or weapons, money laundering, and high-tech crime.

With its 184 member countries, INTERPOL is now the world's second largest international organization, following the United Nations. It is financed by annual contributions from its member countries and is headquartered in Lyon, France.

International Police Intelligence

Police work has changed from reactive to proactive measures. However, as a German prosecutor once said, "Criminals are using jets, the police use cars, and the Justice [System] uses horses." Such rapid change in the nature of crime and the resulting worldwide response require not only international police and justice system cooperation, but also improvements in the methods of crime analysis and other police techniques to illuminate and address the problem of international crime. Several recommendations have been issued by governments to act on the basis of this strategy, which emphasizes using intelligence and crime analysis to achieve international criminal investigative aims. Specialized police arrangements as well as investigation and prosecutorial structures have now been created and charged with improving the level and consequences of international crime analysis and the apprehension of international criminals and terrorists. INTERPOL has become a primary vehicle for the police community worldwide to engage in cooperative and more sophisticated approaches to international crime prevention.

Max Edelbacher

See also **Future of International Policing; International Police Cooperation; International Police Missions; International Policing; Terrorism: International; Transnational Organized Crime**

References and Further Reading

Council of Europe Octobus Programme. 2004. *Combating organised crime: Best practice surveys of the Council of Europe*. Strasbourg: Council of Europe Publishing.

Deflem, Mathieu. 2002. *Policing world society: Historical foundation of international police cooperation*. New York: Oxford University Press.

Fooner, Michael. 1989. *INTERPOL: Issues in world crime and international criminal justice*. New York: Plenum Press.

Koenig, Daniel J. 2001. *International police cooperation: A world perspective*. Boulder, CO: Lexington Books.

9/11 Commission. 2004. *Final report of the National Commission on the Terrorist Attacks upon the United States*. New York: W. W. Norton.

INTERROGATIONS, CRIMINAL

A criminal interrogation is an exercise in persuasion, the goal of which is to obtain truthful information. An interview may evolve into an interrogation if the interviewee is perceived as being unwilling to offer the truth. During an interview a person is questioned about his or her knowledge of a crime that has been committed. The purpose is to gather information. The interviewee may be a victim, a witness, or someone who can provide details regarding the incident. The subject questioned during an interview is assessed by the interviewer for credibility through objective nonaccusatory conversion. An interview typically is conducted during the early stages of an investigation in a variety of environments.

An interrogation is different from an interview in many ways. Often the primary difference is in the perception of the interviewer. A change from interviewing to interrogation is evidenced by a change from the nonaccusatory approach to one that is accusatory. Often occurring in a controlled environment, an interrogation involves eliciting information from a suspect who is perceived as unwilling to admit his or her role in a crime or it may involve an individual with reason to hide the truth. Statements are sometimes asserted by the interrogator rather than posed in the form of questions.

Sought by the interrogator is a confession or admission regarding participation in or knowledge of the crime. A confession is a statement made by a suspect disclosing guilt of the crime and excluding the possibility of a reasonable inference to the contrary. A confession is not limited to words, but may also include the demeanor, conduct, and acts of the person charged with a crime. For example, in *People v. Balidi* (1974) the defendant showed the interrogators how he had committed the murder of a young girl by acting out the manner in which he stabbed her.

An admission is an acknowledgment of conduct, containing only facts from which guilt may or may not be inferred. The statement of admission may be a word, act, conduct, or any other type of information that infers guilt. Information about the suspect and his or her role or relationship to the crime, the victim, or the place of the offense may be part of the admission. Because the courts do not differentiate between degrees of incrimination, no distinction is drawn between confessions and admissions for purposes of their use as evidence against the individual in criminal court.

The law governing interrogation methods is not specified in any one place; criminal interrogations are guided by evolving standards of acceptable practices. Constitutional law, federal and state statutes, and Anglo-American tradition blend together with a current emphasis on the Fifth Amendment against self-incrimination, the Sixth Amendment guarantee of the right to counsel, and the Fourteenth Amendment guarantee of due process.

Interrogation Controversy

The controversy surrounding interrogation involves the methods that are used to extract a confession from the suspect. Early common law allowed an admission or confession as evidence of guilt regardless of it being the product of force or duress. Rather than conducting an investigation to establish guilt, enforcement officers resorted to torture to extract a confession from the accused during an interrogation. Isolated attempts to prohibit torture as an interrogation method are documented in English jurisprudence as early as 1628 according to the U.S. Supreme Court in *Bram v. United States* (1897).

Practices of torture as an interrogation method eventually led to the development of rules on the admissibility of confessions in the late eighteenth century. The common law rule excluded coerced confessions from being admitted at trial due the unreliability of evidence that was the product of torture. In *Bram* (1897) the Court incorporated the common law rule with the requirement in the Fifth Amendment, which prohibited compelling an individual to give witness against himself, as the standard for judging the admissibility of confessions.

The common law rule was abandoned for the free and voluntary rule stated in American jurisprudence during the early twentieth century. It required that statements must be freely and voluntarily made, without duress, fear, or compulsion, and with knowledge of the consequences of the confession. Articulated in *People v. Fox* (1926), the rule required that confessions of the accused would be voluntary only when they were made of free will without any threat or harm or by promise or inducement or reward. Torture as a means to extract confessions was expressly denounced in *Brown v. Mississippi* (1937). Using a totality of the circumstances test, the Court in *Brown* concluded that repeated whippings of the suspect produced a coerced statement that could not be used against him in court.

The U.S. Supreme Court through its decision in *Miranda v. Arizona* (1966) has defined interrogation as the questioning initiated by law enforcement officers after a person has been taken into custody or otherwise deprived of his freedom of action in any significant way.

False confessions fuel the debate over criminal interrogation practices. A false confession is a written or oral statement acknowledging guilt, made by someone who did not commit the crime. False confessions are known to occur in rare circumstances, although there is no existing estimate on the numbers of persons who have provided false confessions. In cases of proven false confessions, a common factor was a lengthy interrogation of the suspect.

People may voluntarily give a false confession due to a pathological desire for notoriety; a conscious or unconscious need to relieve guilt over prior wrongdoings; an inability to distinguish fact from fantasy; and a desire to aid and protect the real criminal. Individuals may offer false confessions without any external pressure from the police. These people simply turn themselves in to the authorities claiming they have committed a crime.

False confessions may occur when the suspect tries to escape a tough situation, avoid an explicit or implied threat, or to gain a promised or implied reward. False confessions may also result from the physical or psychological pressures of the interrogation process. Because the suspect perceives immediate gains that outweigh the long-term consequences, this person will confess despite knowing that he did not commit the crime. Persons who are particularly vulnerable are those who are young, tired, confused, or suggestible and those exposed to false information.

Critics denounce police procedures involving the observation of the behavior of suspects as a way to select someone for more intensive interrogation tactics. Excessive focus on an individual because of a hunch or a lack of eye contact narrows the police vision. The problem may be overcome by following the facts of the case, investigating all leads possible, and interviewing all suspects. One of the best times to read suspect behavior is during the establishment of rapport. After that point behavioral indicators should be carefully interpreted within the entire context of the interrogation and not as specific indicators of guilt. This is particularly true when interrogating persons with mental illness, retardation, or personality disorders.

Some individuals are particularly susceptible to police interrogation techniques that may lead to a false confession. Examples are youthfulness, low or borderline IQ, mental handicap, psychological inadequacy, recent bereavement, language barrier, alcohol or other drug withdrawal, illiteracy, fatigue, or inexperience with the criminal justice system. A method to overcome the charge of advantage over a suspect is achieved through a background investigation on questionable suspects prior to the interrogation. Placing the vulnerability in context at the beginning of the interrogation provides an opportunity to understand the limitations of the suspect.

Police officers themselves may inadvertently cause false compliant confessions by contamination. Contamination of confessions may occur when police officers use questions that provide crime scene information about which the suspect would not otherwise have knowledge. Using crime scene photos may amplify this flaw and educate the suspect about the crime. The use of open-ended questions and obtaining narrative responses from the suspect are helpful for reducing the chance of contamination.

To avoid the controversies surrounding police interrogations, there is a trend to require that interrogations be electronically recorded. Illinois, Maine, and the District of Columbia became the first states to require by statute that electronic recording be used in custodial interrogations in homicide investigations. State courts are beginning to express a preference that interrogations be recorded whenever practicable in custodial interrogations or interviews at a place of detention. Serious or major felony cases in addition to DUI, child abuse, and domestic violence investigations are the common crimes that would be recorded. The manner in which the recordings take place vary among states; many allow covert recording with the suspects unaware that they are being videotaped. Massachusetts and Washington are among the few two-party consent states that do not make an exception for police custodial interviews.

Lawful Interrogation Practices

The importance of interrogation as part of the investigatory process is a well-established fact. The Supreme Court in *Bruton v. U.S.* (1968) recognized that the suspect's own confession lawfully obtained may be the most damaging evidence that can be admitted against him.

In order for an interrogation to be conducted lawfully, the opportunity to interrogate a suspect must be legally obtained. Additionally, there must be compliance with requirements for warnings of constitutional rights to a custodial suspect. Finally, there must be an absence of force or threat of force during the interrogation. The U.S. Constitution and the Bill of Rights protect citizens from actions of government officials and their agents, but not from other citizens. Evidence that is obtained from the interrogation of one citizen by another citizen is not held to the same standard as an interrogation by a police officer.

An absence of police misconduct is necessary to obtain the opportunity to interrogate lawfully. An example of police misconduct within this context would be the entering of a home without consent or a valid warrant for the purpose of extracting a suspect for interrogation.

The second requirement for a lawful interrogation is that police must be in compliance with the requirements for the warnings of constitutional rights to a custodial suspect. Conformity requires an understanding of the conditions that indicate a custodial versus a noncustodial interrogation.

A noncustodial interrogation takes place when the suspect being questioned is not in police custody or under arrest. The suspect must be fully aware that he or she is free to leave at any time. This awareness may be based in part on the location of the interrogation, the attitude of the interrogator, and follow-through by not arresting the suspect at the time of the interrogation. *Miranda* warnings are not required if the suspect is not in custody, but must be provided if the situation changes to custodial. A noncustodial interrogation is not an option after the individual has been arraigned in court on the crimes under investigation or asks to speak to an attorney.

The custodial interrogation occurs when the suspect is under arrest or is not free to leave because arrest is impending. The *Miranda* warnings are necessary prior to questioning the suspect in custody. The offender must understand his or her rights and voluntarily waive them. A knowing waiver of rights is compromised if the individual has a mental disability, cannot read or write, or is under the influence of alcohol or drugs. It is the responsibility of the interrogator to assess the ability of the suspect to understand his or her rights and make a voluntary waiver. An individual may not be coerced or forced to give up his or her rights. There is no requirement that *Miranda* rights be given verbatim or that a waiver be made in writing. Typically police department policy dictates the manner in which these rights are given to the suspect and the method of documenting that waiver. The waiver of rights can be revoked by the suspect at any time. Four out of five suspects who are given rights per *Miranda* will waive them and submit to questioning (Leo and White 1999). Neither the subsequent charging nor the severity of punishment is affected by a waiver, although case resolution through plea bargaining is increased (Leo 1996).

The third requirement for a lawful interrogation is that there must be an absence of force or threat of force after the initial waiver of rights and during the interrogation. Factors surrounding the interrogation, or the totality of the circumstances, will determine whether physical or psychological pressures unduly influenced the accused to make a statement. A promise of leniency will typically nullify a confession. Small deceptions may be used by the police during interrogations according to the ruling in *United States v. Guerrero* (1988). In the more recent decision of *United States v. Mendoza-Cecelia* (1992), the U.S. Court of Appeals ruled that isolated incidents of deception usually do not invalidate the free waiver of the suspect and that police may use some psychological tactics in interrogating a suspect. Threats to arrest members of a suspect's family may cause an involuntary confession. The individual factors that the court will look at in determining if the process was coercive are similar to those considered coercive in obtaining a waiver. The federal courts have stated a preference that a person under arrest be brought to court for arraignment without unnecessary delay in order for a confession to be admissible against him. This requirement aimed at addressing incommunicado interrogation and coerced confessions is known as the McNabb-Mallory doctrine. The Court has never imposed the rule on the states nor did it set a specific time after which a confession would be invalid. Congress in 1968 legislated to set a six-hour period for interrogation following arrest before the suspect must be presented to court as part of the Omnibus Crime Control and Safe Streets Act (82 Stat. 210, 18 U.S.C. Sec. 3501(c)). Some states have adopted the rule voluntarily.

Interrogation Methods

Police officers are successful in obtaining a confession or admission in the vast majority of interrogations attempted (50% to 75%). Prior to conducting an interrogation the investigator prepares by interviewing the victim and witnesses and reviewing the evidence collected in the case. The collection of background information on the suspect including his or her criminal history is an essential aspect of preparation. The investigator makes the determination on the location of the interrogation and the person best suited to conduct the questioning.

Experts themselves do not agree on the best method for conducting criminal interrogations. A common approach involves forceful claims by the interrogator that the suspect is guilty without giving him or her opportunity to deny the assertion. Other methods are based on the level of guilt that the suspect experiences. A third approach involves the establishment of a relationship between the suspect and interrogator that would facilitate the flow of information to the interrogator. The top four interrogation tactics that were most frequently observed in a study of 182 police interrogations (Leo 1996) are (1) an appeal to the suspect's self-interest (88%), (2) confronting the suspect with existing evidence of guilt (85%), (3) undermining the suspect's confidence in his or her denials (43%), and (4) identifying contradictions in the suspect's alibi or story (42%).

DENISE KINDSCHI GOSSELIN

See also **Constitutional Rights: In-Custody Interrogation; Exclusionary Rule; Eyewitness Evidence**

References and Further Reading

Gosselin, D. 2006. *Smart talk: Contemporary interviewing and interrogation.* Upper Saddle River, NJ: Prentice Hall.
Inbau, F. E., J. Reid, J. Buckley, and B. Jayne. 2001. *Criminal interrogation and confessions.*

4th ed. Gaithersburg, MD: Aspen Publishers.

Leo, R. 1996. Inside the interrogation room. *Journal of Criminal Law and Criminology* 86: 266–303.

Leo, R. A., and W. White. 1999. Adapting to *Miranda:* Modern interrogators' strategies for dealing with the obstacles posed. *Minnesota Law Review* 84: 397–472.

Stephen, J., and E. Sweeney. 2004. *Officer's interrogation handbook*. Charlottesville, VA: LexisNexis.

INVESTIGATION OUTCOMES

The process of a law enforcement–based investigation often begins with the allegation of a criminal act and is resolved through several classifications. However, not all policing investigations concern criminal allegations and not all investigations result in arrest and prosecution. Successful investigative outcomes are almost always portrayed in television as those involving a street toughened suspect being interrogated "in the box" by the seasoned detective who eventually obtains a full confession. In the world of television policing, the inability to obtain a confession would imply that the suspect will not be convicted resulting in the investigation being classified as failed and unsuccessful. Contrary to popular media renditions of criminal investigations, few investigative operations end with a suspect confessing to his or her role in the crime under investigation. In many cases suspects are arrested and criminal charges are filed with little interaction from the suspect. The findings of all investigations, even those not resulting in an arrest, often provide valuable information to law enforcement sometimes assisting in closing other investigations.

Criminal Cases

Criminal cases are generally classified as cleared or not cleared, with definitive guidelines as to the proper closure classification. A review of the Federal Bureau of Investigation's *Uniform Crime Reports* (UCR) revealed that over a five-year period criminal investigations have generally cleared at a consistent rate, 46% for violent crimes ("crimes against person") and 16% for property crimes. A closer review reveals that specific crimes of violence are cleared at higher rates than others; that is, murder has a 62% clearance rate, aggravated assault has a 56% clearance rate, forcible rape has a clearance rate of 42%, and robbery has a clearance rate of 26%. The higher clearance rate is assumed to be associated with the enhanced investigative efforts afforded certain crime types, as well as by the fact that in many crimes of personal violence the victim may know the identity of the perpetrator.

Law enforcement agencies that report their jurisdiction's criminal incidents to the FBI's UCR are subject to a strict guideline by which to classify investigative outcomes. However, an important caveat is that the standards by which an individual policing agency considers an investigation to be cleared do not always mirror the UCR guidelines. According to the UCR guidelines, in order for an investigation to be classified as cleared, one of two situations must be present. An investigation may be cleared by arrest meaning that three criteria have been met: someone was arrested; that person(s) was charged with the commission of an offense; and the case was accepted for prosecution, that is, referred to the court of proper jurisdiction. The number of persons arrested does not impact the determination of cleared by arrest because the arrest of one person may concern several criminal incidents (serial rapist, repeat armed robber), while the arrest of multiple persons may involve the same single criminal act (coconspirators involved in a simple burglary). In clearing multiple investigations with the arrest of one suspect, some police departments have been accused of clearing the books, a procedure in which an offender admits guilt in criminal cases they did not commit in exchange for a promise of a reduced sentence (with the investigator "putting in a good word with the prosecutor") by the case detective. In such a situation a suspect receives a lesser sentence (often in terms of length of incarceration) for pleading guilty to multiple cases than they might have received if convicted of the one offense they had committed and the investigator can close multiple investigations from his caseload (Territo, Halsted, and Bromley 2004).

Additionally, the recovery of goods in a property crime does not impact the classification of cleared by arrest. The successful recovery of a stolen car without the arrest of a suspect does not result in an investigation being labeled as cleared by arrest, while the arrest of a suspect without recovery of the property does not negate the cleared by arrest classification. However, some police agencies will allow investigations to be considered closed (and successful) when the victim decides to defer prosecution in lieu of return of the stolen money or property, often due to interaction between the investigator and the parties involved. This outcome is usually noted in internal theft cases involving monetary funds (that is, embezzlement, misappropriation of funds, and theft). The investigation produced positive results for the victim without criminal charges being brought against the suspect.

A second classification of a cleared investigation is *cleared by exception/exceptional means.* According to UCR guidelines, this classification concerns investigations that involve circumstances beyond the law enforcement agency's control that prevent formal charges from being issued. For an investigation to be considered cleared by exception/exceptional means, four criteria must be met: the investigation identified the offender; the investigation resulted in enough evidence to support an arrest, justify formal charges being filed, and for the case to be referred for prosecution; the investigation identified the offender's location so an arrest could be effected; and the law enforcement agency encountered circumstances beyond its control that precluded the physical arrest and subsequent charging of the offender. Examples of qualifying circumstances would include the death of the offender (whether by natural causes, a criminal act, or justifiable homicide, that is, offender fatally shot by law enforcement during the commission of a crime), refusal of the victim to cooperate, and denial of extradition by another jurisdiction. Other circumstances could include an expired statute of limitations; the criminal act falls outside prosecution guidelines (refusal to accept case by prosecutor), that is, first-time offender, low dollar loss, local standards; or when a case is referred to another agency such as a juvenile justice authority or federal authority due to lack of jurisdiction. The failure of an investigative agency to obtain enough probable cause to justify an arrest does not meet the standard of being a circumstance beyond the control of the agency.

While not a classification within the UCR guidelines, some law enforcement agencies utilize a cleared by warrant classification that is generally understood to mean that the investigation has produced enough evidence to effect an arrest and refer the case for prosecution but the suspect has not been physically placed in custody because his or her whereabouts are not currently known. An arrest warrant is issued and the agency considers the investigation to be closed and cleared by the issuance of the warrant.

As noted by the historical review of annual clearance rates, a number of investigations do not result in clearance by either arrest or exception. This nonclearance, "unsolved" classification does not necessarily mean that the investigation did not disclose valuable information to law enforcement. In some cases the original investigation was not cleared but as a result of information developed during the investigative process the suspect (in the original investigation) was identified as being the perpetrator in another open criminal case, resulting in that case now being cleared by arrest. In other situations a suspect, during the course of an investigation, may disclose information (either accidentally or in order to gain an advantage in his or her case) leading to the arrest of a perpetrator in a separate nonrelated pending criminal manner resulting in the clearance of that case. Some investigative interviews have led the police to learn of planned but not yet executed criminal acts leading to investigations being opened on that newly developed information. Information obtained from investigations, both cleared and not cleared, will sometimes produce leads in "cold cases," a phrase often used in referring to homicide cases that have been opened for an extended time without new investigative leads being forthcoming and with investigators hampered in their efforts by the lack of quality evidence. On average, only one-third of all homicides are cleared in the year they were committed (Johns, Downes, and Bibles 2005). The newly obtained information may lead directly to an arrest or produce additional viable investigative leads that may subsequently lead to an arrest.

In multijurisdictional (both in terms of geographic locations and types of agencies involved) investigations, such as those involving organized crime or homeland security, the investigative outcome at the local level may not produce a definite closed-case status by UCR guidelines in that no arrest is made because the design and purpose of that investigation was information gathering, not prosecution. However, the outcome of the localized investigation is important to the larger scale operation, possibly producing evidence that will assist in obtaining warrants in the primary jurisdiction or by determining that this specific aspect of the investigation is not worth pursuing further. In some cases the local investigation will produce information contrary to what had been alleged in the primary investigation, leading to possible further inquiry about the original source, who may then have his or her reliability as a credible witness impugned.

Oftentimes the outcome of an investigation results in no criminal charges being brought forward and with a travesty of justice being prevented. Evidence in some criminal investigations when accepted at face value may lead casual observers to believe that a crime has been committed and the identity of the suspect is obvious. However, subsequent proper investigation may reveal that a criminal act did not occur and there is no need for arrest or prosecution. Examples of this case type include sudden infant death syndrome (SIDS), a suicide or accidental death originally presumed to be a homicide, an assault that was actually justified self-defense, a fraudulent claim of sexual battery, and a possession of illegal narcotics charges filed against an unknowing/uninvolved party. In all these cases, suspects could easily be arrested: a young mother previously arrested for drugs calls the paramedic when her baby won't wake up, an acquaintance found inside a residence with his deceased roommate, a "Good Samaritan" charged with assault after rescuing a person who was being attacked but no witnesses remained at the scene to confirm his version of events, a college student with a history of excessive drinking and lewd behavior found in a compromising position with another student, and a young man stopped while driving a friend's car and narcotics are located during a search. The outcome of these investigations, rather than generating clearance findings, prevented persons from being wrongfully charged and being entered into the criminal justice system.

Juvenile Cases

Although allegations of juvenile criminal activity are investigated in the same manner as adult (persons over the age of majority) criminal activity, the outcomes are classified differently. Juveniles can be investigated for acts that are age-related status offenses (activities for which adults could not be charged), including curfew violation, possession of cigarettes/alcohol, runaway, truancy, and incorrigibility. Juveniles can also be investigated for a *delinquent act,* the commission of an act that if committed by a person over the age of eighteen would be considered a crime. The outcomes of these investigations do not result in prosecution, therefore, precluding a finding of guilty or not guilty. They instead result in a finding of *adjudication* (similar to a conviction in adult court), a ruling by a juvenile judge that a juvenile has committed the acts in questions and is in need of services (Champion 2004). Depending on the jurisdiction and the seriousness of the crime, some juvenile offenders are waived (also known as transfers or certifications) to criminal courts where investigative outcomes result in convictions.

Noncriminal Cases

Investigative outcomes can also concern noncriminal cases such as internal administrative investigations. Investigations of this type will involve violations of police agency administrative rules that on face value are not violations of applicable criminal codes. Examples of this type of violation include conduct unbecoming an officer, failure to file reports in a timely manner, disregard of uniform policies, discourteous behavior toward citizens, violations of traffic codes, failure to report mileage on a patrol vehicle when beginning the transport of a prisoner, violations of residency requirements, and failure to report to an assigned post as scheduled. Inciardi (2005) reported that the New York Police Department police officer rules and regulations handbook is almost one foot thick. The outcomes of this type of investigation could result in administrative sanctions, including but not limited to reduction in rank, loss of acquired leave, suspension without pay, mandatory education or counseling, and termination. Outcome classifications in this type of investigation are generally classified as substantiated or not substantiated.

In some instances the outcomes of administrative investigations may lead to subsequent criminal investigations, or concurrent criminal investigations may already be in progress. Internal police investigations that involve or progress to the level of violations of criminal codes would be treated as criminal investigations and their outcomes would be as indicated under a standard such as the UCR. Investigations of this type would include allegations of malfeasance in office, bribery, theft, sexual misconduct, battery, and sale or release of confidential police data, that is, National Crime Information Center (NCIC) records, advance warning of raids or surveillances, and copies of nonpublic investigative records.

Another type of noncriminal police investigation concerns the security of the police operation itself. Investigators may be asked to determine if police computers, confidential records, sensitive areas, or tactical operations are subject to assault by outsiders. The focus of the investigation is not to obtain criminal prosecution, but to ascertain if weaknesses exist in established protocols. While this is often commonly associated with computer security, the investigative process is used in determining if either design failure or improper adherence to established policies would subject the physical police operation to unwanted access by nonlegitimate parties. The outcome of such an investigation could result in tighter internal controls as well as a reemphasis of current policies.

PATRICK D. WALSH

See also **Clearance Rates and Criminal Investigations; Criminal Investigation;**

Juvenile Delinquency: Status Crimes;
Uniform Crime Reports

References and Further Reading

Champion, D. 2004. *The juvenile justice system.* Upper Saddle River, NJ: Prentice-Hall.

Federal Bureau of Investigation. 2004. *Crime in the United States, FBI uniform crime reports.* Washington, DC: U.S. Government Printing Office.

Inciardi, J. 2005. *Criminal justice.* 7th ed. New York: McGraw-Hill.

Johns, L., G. Downes, and C. Bibles. 2005. Resurrecting cold case serial homicide investigations. *FBI Law Enforcement Bulletin* 74 (8).

Territo, L., J. Halsted, and M. Bromley. 2004. *Crime and justice in America.* Upper Saddle River, NJ: Prentice-Hall.

INDEX

INDEX

Alcohol (*cont.*)
  server interventions, 455
  status crimes and, 729–730
  trafficking, 123
  violent crime and, 45
Alcohol, drugs, and crime, 42–46
  among adults, 45
  crime and, 45–46
  crime types, 43
  illicit substances and, 46
  among juveniles, 45
  overview of, 42–43
  among prison inmates, 45
  traffic fatalities and, 46
Alcohol Misuse Prevention Study, 437
Alcohol Rehabilitation Act (1968), 306
Alcohol Tax Unit, 516
"Alco-test," 862
Aldermen, 50
Alexander II, Tsar, 1276
Alfred P. Murrah Federal Building, 1265, 1279
Algeria, 1277
Alibi, 359
Alien(s)
  CLEAR act for, 1013
  detaining, 893, 896, 897
  U.S. admission, 893
Alien conspiracy theory, 1293
Alien smuggling, 1298
Alignment task force, 481
Allan, E. A., 594
Allen, E. F., 573
Allen, S., 1010
Allred, James V., 1285
Alpert, Geoffrey, 76, 90, 461, 754, 818, 977
Altercations, violent, 855–856
  close-contact, 855
  immediate-response, 855, 856
  stand-off, 855, 856
Alternative dispute resolution (ADR), 480
Alternatives, 409, 410
  to drugs, 438
  to incarceration, 1052
  responses, 1058, 1060
  to U.S. Military, 790
  to youth violence, 98
Altruism, 370
Alvarez, Carlos, 789
AMBER alerts, 330
Ambivalent Force, The: Perspectives on the Police
  (Niederhoffer, Blumberg), 850–851
Ambush, 378
"Amenable places," 640
Amendola, Karen L., 1068, 1180, 1213, 1255
American Academy of Arts and Sciences, 573
American Academy of Forensic Sciences (AAFS),
  235, 321
  members of, 568
  specialty sections of, 568

American Association of Retired Persons
  (AARP), 467
American Bar Association (ABA), 1, 217
  abatement study by, 2–3
  discretion research by, 405
American Board of Forensic Toxicology, 566
American cities
  disadvantaged assistance agencies in, 947
  economic/population shifts in, 943
  growth of, 942–943
  intense political atmosphere of, 946
  police brutality/corruption in, 946
  service demands for, 943
  social/political turmoil in, 943
  uniformed police for, 943
  WASP *v.* ethnic immigrants in, 945
American Civil Liberties Union, 1007, 1099
American Communist Party, 861
American Constitutional Law (Tribe), 254
American Correctional Association, 795
American criminal justice system, 142
American Dilemma, An: The Negro Problem and
  Modern Democracy (Mrydal), 802
American Express Philanthropic Program, 440
American Federation of Labor (AFL), 100,
  102, 103
American Federation of State, County and
  Municipal Employees (AFSCME, AFL-CIO),
  1315
American Federation Reform Society, 426
American Heritage Dictionary, 1085
American Indian Movement, 1319
American Indians. *See also* Native Americans
  bias against, 608
  in Charlotte, North Carolina, 157
  Plains, 1283
  Southern Ute tribe, 1299
American Institute for Research (AIR), 847
American Journal of Sociology, 1110
American Jury, The (Kalven/Zeisel), 278
American Management Association, 586
American Philosophical Society, 573
American Police Systems (Fosdick), 299, 572
American policing: early years, 46–52
  1600–1860, 46–47
  English example for, 48–50
  rise of urban police departments in, 50–52
  urban growth/need for police in, 47–48
American Political Science Association (APSA),
  1358
American Polygraph Association (APA), 918, 1030
American Protestants, 47
American Psychiatric Association, 364
American Psychological Association (APA), 1076
American Red Cross (ARC), 387, 472
American Revolution, 48, 1034, 1322
American society, 424
American Society for Industrial Security (ASIS),
  1050

I4

Arson and its investigation, 33, **58–61,** 60, 182, 338
  arrests for, 58
  crime scene handling, 58–59
  defined, 58
  desired outcome of, 58
  evidence handling, 59
  explosive investigations and, 60
  magnitude of problem, 58
  motives for, 59–60
  as Part I offense, 1306, 1307, 1308
  purpose of, 58
  as secondary crime, 60
  training for, 60
Arsonists, 60
Arthrasahtra, 657
Arthur Andersen company, 1351
Arthur Niederhoffer Memorial Fellowship, 852
Articles of War, 1629, 811
Artificial intelligence, 561, 1250
Aryan Nation, 537, 1264
Asbestos abatement companies, 477
ASC. *See* American Society of Criminology
ASCLD. *See* American Society of Crime Laboratory
  Directors
ASCLD/LAB. *See* American Society of Crime
  Laboratory Directors/Laboratory Accreditation
  Board
Ashcroft, John, 504, 1013
Asian gangs, 861
Asian policing systems, 61–66, 206
  in China, 62–63
  in Japan, 63
  in Korea, 63–64
  in Malaysia, 64–65
  overview of, 61–62
  in Singapore, 65
Asians
  in Charlotte, North Carolina, 157
  number of immigrants, 649
ASIS. *See* American Society for Industrial Security
Assassinations
  of Kennedy, John F., 301, 508
  of McKinley, William, 1321
  political, 1272, 1276
  as terrorism, 1276
Assassins
  medieval, 1275
  professional, 663
Assault and battery, 8
  defense of, 952
  defined, 951
  as improper use of force, 951
  by LAPD, 964
  by Morse, 966
  reasonable force and, 951–952
  self/others-defense, 952
  spousal exemption in, 1039
Assaults, 338, 423, 430. *See also* Accidental deaths/
  assaults against/murders of police officers;

Aggravated assault; Assault and battery; Jail
  assaults; Sexual assault; Spouse Assault
  Replication Program
  groups, 1236
  lethal, 377
  life-threatening, 364
  line-of-duty, 15
  nonlethal, 377
  against police, 377
  simple, 1306
  street, 199
  threat of, 378
Assessment, 1155. *See also* Comprehensive Personnel
  Assessment System; Homicide Assessment and
  Lead Tracking System; Organizational
  assessment; Preliminary damage assessment;
  Scanning, Analysis, Response, and Assessment;
  Workload assessment plan
  for accountability, 1058
  biopsychosocial/lethality, 991
  for effective performance, 1058
  focus on results, 1059
  in fraud investigation, 577
  by helicopter unit, 973
  independent researchers for, 1059
  measuring inputs/activities/outputs/outcomes, 1059
  of militarization of police, 789–790
  of police role, 554
  of POP, 982, 1021, 1060, 1154
  in preemployment applicant screening, 1075
  of recidivism, 1043–1044
  of response times, 907
  of results of efforts, 1058
  of school shooters, 1124–1125
  in strategic planning, 1204, 1205, 1206–1207
  of threats, 469
  for traditional supervision, 1167
Assessment centers (AC), personnel, 66–69
  assessors for, 68
  dimensions for, 68
  exercises in, 66–67
  implementation of, 68
  roles of, 66
  testing in, 66–67
  validity of, 67–68
Assistance requests, 230
Association of Black Law Enforcers in Canada, 831
Association of Caribbean Commissioners of
  Police, 148
Association of Certified Fraud Examiners, 1354
Association of Chief Police Officers (Britain), 111
Association of Firearm and Toolmark
  Examiners, 321
Association of South East Asian Nations, 695
Associative evidence, 561
ATAC. *See* Anti-Terrorism Advisory Council
Aten, Ira, 1285
ATF. *See* Bureau of Alcohol, Tobacco, Firearms and
  Explosives

INDEX